EDITION 5

Learning Mathematics in Elementary and Middle Schools

A Learner-Centered Approach

W. George Cathcart
University of Alberta

Yvonne M. Pothier
Mount Saint Vincent University

James H. Vance
University of Victoria

Nadine S. Bezuk
San Diego State University

Boston Columbus Indianapolis New York San Francisco Upper Saddle River
Amsterdam Cape Town Dubai London Madrid Milan Munich Paris Montreal Toronto
Delhi Mexico City Sao Paulo Sydney Hong Kong Seoul Singapore Taipei Tokyo

Series Editor: *Kelly Villella Canton*
Editorial Assistant: *Annalea Manalili*
Vice President, Director of Marketing: *Quinn Perkson*
Senior Development Editor: *Mary Kriener*
Senior Marketing Manager: *Darcy Betts*
Production Editor: *Gregory Erb*
Editorial Production Service: *Nesbitt Graphics, Inc.*
Manufacturing Buyer: *Megan Cochran*
Electronic Composition: *Nesbitt Graphics, Inc.*
Interior Design: *Nesbitt Graphics, Inc.*
Cover Designer: *Linda Knowles*

Library of Congress Cataloging-in-Publication information was unavailable at press time.

10 9 8 7 6 5 4 3 2 1 WEB 14 13 12 11 10

www.pearsonhighered.com

ISBN-10: 0-13-242099-6
ISBN-13: 978-0-13-242099-0

This edition is dedicated to my husband, Steve, and my son, Peter, whose encouragement and support made this work possible.

—N.S.B.

Brief Contents

Contents

CHAPTER 5 Developing Number Concepts 76

CHAPTER 6 Developing Understanding of Numeration 99

Preface

Teaching mathematics today is an exciting prospect, but it can be an overwhelming idea, as well. As a teacher, you need to be comfortable enough with your own mathematical understanding to teach these concepts to elementary and middle school students. You need to recognize what students learn about each math concept, how they think about solving problems, and how you can modify your teaching to adapt to your students' cognitive needs. You also need to be familiar with effective teaching methods, with how and when to use manipulatives, and with the best uses of technology in the classroom. Finally, when you have all of this down, you must know how to align your teaching with the NCTM *Principles and Standards* and the *Curriculum Focal Points*.

Daunting? That is why we have written *Learning Mathematics in Elementary and Middle Schools: A Learner-Centered Approach*— to ease your mind by giving you a sound background in basic math concepts and the tools for helping all of your students grasp these concepts. By focusing on *how* students think and work through problem solving, the fifth edition of the book prepares you to teach mathematics effectively so that *all* of your students are successful. This learner-centered approach places children squarely at the center of their own learning. To help your growth as an effective teacher of mathematics, this edition emphasizes four important themes throughout:

1. A focus on children's thinking, including artifacts of student work and activities built around videos that explore student problem solving;
2. Elements of assessment that are interwoven throughout each chapter, including conducting preassessments, analyzing assessments, and using the results of assessments to plan instruction, in order to help you further understand children's thinking as they work through mathematical processes;
3. A focus on classroom practice, including examining classroom practice through videos and vignettes and strategies to reach all learners, and developing effective lesson plans;
4. Alignment with NCTM's *Principles and Standards* and *Curriculum Focal Points.*

New to This Edition

Users of earlier editions of *Learning Mathematics in Elementary and Middle Schools* will notice important revisions that reflect constant changes in mathematics education. Changes include:

- A strong focus on assessing children's understanding, including preassessments of mathematics understanding, for use with children or while studying each chapter;
- Examination of how to interpret assessment results, focusing on what the assessment results tell us about children's mathematics understanding;
- Strategies for using assessment results to plan instruction and consideration of how to apply knowledge about children's understanding of a mathematics concept to plan a lesson centered on improving and remediating learner understanding;
- Integration of Curriculum Focal Points, applying NCTM's recommendations to instructional planning;
- Sample lessons in the instructional chapters (5–17) that model how to connect chapter topics to classroom practice;
- Strategies to Reach All Students are integrated into the activities to meet the needs of English Language Learners and students with special needs.
- Close integration with MyEducationLab offers opportunities to extend and connect learning. MyEducationLab callouts in every chapter offer students the opportunity to assess their understanding of chapter content, explore their mathematics content knowledge, examine real student thinking, evaluate real classroom practices, and much more through this rich online resource.

Book Organization and Features

Learning Mathematics in Elementary and Middle Schools is organized around one guiding principle: understanding how children process math concepts. This fifth edition extends this principle a step further by also providing clear guidance on recognizing how this affects children's ability to learn those concepts and what you can do to intercept and remediate any problems.

Chapters 1–4 provide base knowledge in understanding the theory behind math instruction and the NCTM national standards that guide that instruction. Chapters 1–4 provide you with the understanding you will need to create a learner-centered environment that draws children and adolescents into mathematics problems and guides them as they construct mathematic principles. Chapters 5–17 break down the key instructional concepts in mathematics, following a common structure and feature set:

- **A strong NCTM Standards focus** runs through all chapters. In addition to the opening *Connecting with the Standards* feature that discusses key NCTM Principles and Standards and Curriculum Focal Points related to the chapter, a standards matrix near the beginning of chapters clearly outlines the developmentally appropriate content standards covered, and *Principles and Standards Links* boxes throughout identify specific NCTM Curriculum and Evaluation Standards for 2000 and align them with mathematical concepts addressed in the text.
- The **Assessing Mathematics Understanding** feature follows the Connecting with the Standards section. This feature introduces a preassessment of mathematics understanding discussed in the chapter, followed by vignettes that take you to explore students' problem solving or examine classroom practices by using authentic video examples that illustrate teaching and student solutions and discussion of common children's errors and misunderstandings to help you learn to assess children's development of math knowledge and skills and provide remediation when necessary. Additionally, this feature helps you analyze results of the opening exercise and to build upon the findings of the assessment to inform your instructional planning.
- **Examining Children's Reasoning** sections examine real student work, explore what their work says about their reasoning skills and math development, and identify remediation strategies.
- A **wealth of problem-based activities** throughout each chapter helps you understand and practice chapter content and implement effective classroom applications into your own instruction. **Strategies that Reach All Students** (denoted by a special icon) are integrated into the activities to meet the needs of English Language Learners and students with special needs.
- **Children's Literature Links** throughout the book serve as extension activities that connect mathematics and literacy and illustrate how to use trade books to develop mathematical ideas and concepts.
- A **Sample Lesson Plan** at the end of each chapter models how to use preassessment results to plan NCTM standards-based instruction to meet children's needs.
- **In Practice activities** at the end of each chapter provide activities or assignments that apply the chapter's key concepts to classroom practice.
- **MyEducationLab boxes integrated** throughout each chapter bring teaching to life and encourage the development of the skills and dispositions necessary for success in the elementary math classroom by linking you with classroom videos and activities directly correlated to the text.

MyEducationLab

PEARSON myeducationlab
The Power of Classroom Practice

The power of classroom practice.

"Teacher educators who are developing pedagogies for the analysis of teaching and learning contend that analyzing teaching artifacts has three advantages: it enables new teachers time for reflection while still using the real materials of practice; it provides new teachers with experience thinking about and approaching the complexity of the classroom; and in some cases, it can help new teachers and teacher educators develop a shared understanding and common language about teaching. . . ."[1]

As Linda Darling-Hammond and her colleagues point out, grounding teacher education in real classrooms—among real teachers and students and among actual examples of students' and teachers' work—is an important, and perhaps even an essential, part of training teachers for the complexities of teaching in today's classrooms. For this reason, we have created a valuable, time-saving website—MyEducationLab—that provides you with the context of real classrooms and artifacts that research on teacher education tells us is so important. The authentic in-class video footage, interactive skill-building exercises

[1]Darling-Hammond, l., & Bransford, J., Eds.(2005). *Preparing Teachers for a Changing World.* San Francisco: John Wiley & Sons

and other resources available on MyEducationLab offer you a uniquely valuable teacher education tool.

MyEducationLab is easy to use and integrate into both your assignments and your courses. Wherever you see the MyEducationLab logo in the margins or elsewhere in the text, follow the simple instructions to access the videos, strategies, cases, and artifacts associated with these assignments, activities, and learning units on MyEducationLab. MyEducationLab is organized topically to enhance the coverage of the core concepts discussed in the chapters of your book. For each topic you will find most or all of the following resources:

Connection to National Standards

Now it is easier than ever to see how your coursework is connected to national standards. In each topic of MyEducationLab you will find intended learning outcomes connected to the NCTM national standards. All of the Assignments and Activities and all of the Building Teaching Skills and Dispositions in MyEducationLab are mapped to the appropriate national standards and learning outcomes as well.

Assignments and Activities

Designed to save instructors preparation time, these assignable exercises show concepts in action (through video, cases, or student and teacher artifacts) and then offer thought-provoking questions that probe your understanding of theses concepts or strategies. (Feedback for these assignments is available to the instructor.)

- **Video** Authentic classroom videos show how real teachers handle actual classroom situations and one-on-one instructional moments. Video includes clips from **Integrating Mathematics and Pedagogy to Illustrate Children's Reasoning (IMAP)** project previously offered on CD for past editions of *Learning Mathematics in Elementary and Middle Schools*. this well-known and highly-lauded IMAP footage allows you to explore children's mathematical reasoning and problem solving strategies more closely.

enVision MATH

These assignments allow you to examine and work with chapters from across the grade levels of *enVisionMATH*, a widely adopted K-6 mathematics program.

Building Teaching Skills and Dispositions

These learning units help you practice and strengthen skills that are essential to quality teaching. First you are presented with the core skill or concept and then given an opportunity to practice your understanding of this concept multiple times by watching video footage (or interacting with other media) and then critically analyzing the strategy or skill presented.

General Resources on Your MyEducationLab Course

The *Resources* section on your MyEducationLab course is designed to help you pass your licensure exam, put together an effective portfolio and lesson plan, prepare for and navigate the first year of your teaching career, and understand key educational standards, policies, and laws. This section includes:

- *Licensure Exams*: Access guidelines for passing the Praxis exam. The *Practice Test Exam* includes practice questions, *Case Histories*, and *Video Case Studies*.
- *Portfolio Builder and Lesson Plan Builder*: Create, update, and share portfolios and lesson plans.
- *Preparing a Portfolio*: Access guidelines for creating a high-quality teaching portfolio that will allow you to practice effective lesson planning.
- *Licensure and Standards*: Link to state licensure standards and national standards.
- *Beginning Your Career*: Educate yourself—access tips, advice, and valuable information on:
    - Resume Writing and Interviewing: Expert advice on how to write impressive resumes and prepare for job interviews.
    - Your First Year of Teaching: Practical tips to set up your classroom, manage student behavior, and learn to more easily organize for instruction and assessment.
    - Law and Public Policies: Specific directives and requirements you need to understand under the No Child Left Behind Act and the Individuals with Disabilities Education Improvement Act of 2004.
- *Special Education Interactive Timeline*: Build your own detailed timelines based on different facets of the history and evolution of special education.

Book-Specific Resources

Study Plan

A MyEducationLab Study Plan is a multiple choice assessment tied to chapter objectives, supported by study material. A well-designed Study Plan offers multiple opportunities to fully master required course content as identified by the objectives in each chapter:

- *Chapter Objectives* identify the learning outcomes for the chapter and give you targets to shoot for as you read and study.

- *Multiple Choice Assessments* assess mastery of the content (tied to each chapter objective) by taking the multiple choice quiz as many times as needed. Not only do these quizzes provide overall scores for each objective, but they also explain why responses to particular items are correct or incorrect.
- *Study Material: Review, Practice and Enrichment* gives you a deeper understanding of what you do and do not know related to chapter content. This can be accessed through the Multiple Choice Assessment (after you take a quiz you receive information regarding the chapter content on which you still need practice and review) or through a self-directed method of study. This material includes text excerpts, activities that include hints and feedback, and media assets (video, simulations, cases, etc.).

Activities

This section under most chapters allows you to explore mathematical reasoning related to chapter content by completing additional problem Activities from the book.

Blackline Masters

Book-specific Blackline Masters, previously listed at the back of the text, appear under each chapter and provide templates for creating cardboard manipulatives and more.

Visit www.myeducationlab.com for a demonstration of this exciting new online teaching resource.

Instructor Resources

The text has the following ancillary materials to assist instructors. These instructor supplements are available for download from the Instructor Resource Center at www.pearsonhighered.com/irc.

Instructors Manual/Test Bank

The Instructors Manual/ Test Bank provides concrete suggestions to promote interactive teaching and actively involve students in learning. Each chapter contains chapter objectives, a discussion of key concepts, helpful instructional tips, and additional activities for using assets available on MyEducationLab.

Computerized Test Bank

Pearson MyTest is a powerful assessment generation program that helps instructors easily create and print quizzes and exams. Questions and tests are authored online, allowing ultimate flexibility and the ability to efficiently create and print assessments anytime, anywhere! Instructors can access Pearson MyTest and their test bank files by going to www.pearsonmytest.com to log in, register, or request access. Features of Pearson MyTest include:

Premium assessment content

- Draw from a rich library of assessments that complement your Pearson textbook and your course's learning objectives.
- Edit questions or tests to fit your specific teaching needs.

Instructor-friendly resources

- Easily create and store your own questions, including images, diagrams, and charts using simple drag-and-drop and Word-like controls.
- Use additional information provided by Pearson, such as the question's difficulty level or learning objective, to help you quickly build your test.

Time-saving enhancements

- Add headers or footers and easily scramble questions and answer choices—all from one simple toolbar.
- Quickly create multiple versions of your test or answer key, and when ready, simply save to MS-Word or PDF format and print!
- Export your exams for import to Blackboard 6.0, CE (WebCT), or Vista (WebCT)!

PowerPoint™ Presentations

Ideal for lecture presentations or student handouts, the PowerPoint" Presentation for each chapter includes key concept summaries.

Acknowledgments

As in any project, realizing this point would not have been possible without the assistance of numerous individuals who helped sharpen the focus of this edition. We appreciate the thoughtful comments and suggestions made by the reviewers for this edition: Elsie Babcock, Wayne State University; Caroline Burleigh, Baptist Bible College; Michael T. Charles, Pacific University; Yolanda De La Cruz, Arizona State University; Greg Gierhart, Murray State University; Heidi Higgins, University of North Carolina at Wilmington; Thomasina Lott Adams, University of Florida; Amy McBride Martin, University of Evansville; Michael Mikusa, Kent State University; Todd

Sundeen, University of Northern Colorado; Robin Ward, University of Arizona; and Melvin Wilson, Virginia Tech.

We would like to thank Dr. Patricia Moyer-Packenham of Utah State University for her contribution in developing the Children's Literature Links, and Dr. Sally Robison for her assistance in revising Chapters 14 and 17. We are also grateful to several colleagues at San Diego State University, including Dr. Lisa Clement Lamb for her help in developing the section on integrating standards that appears in Chapter 1; Gail Moriarty and Dr. Susan Nickerson for their help in revising Chapter 9; Sharon Moore for her help in developing the vignette in chapter 15; Judy Bippert for her help in revising Chapter 17, and Steve Klass for his help in developing the vignette in chapter 17 and the preassessment feature. A special thank you to each of the professionals involved in the development of the wonderful MyEducationLab activities integrated throughout this book: Mary Baker, University of North Dakota; Maria Droujkova, University of California, Berkley; Jackie Ennis, Barton College; Vickie Harry, Clarion University; Jackie Sack, University of Houston; and Carolann Wade, Peace College.

In addition, the suggestions and encouragement received from colleagues and students at San Diego State University, numerous teachers in the San Diego Unified School District, and the children, teachers, and administrators at Rosa Parks Elementary School were invaluable. Thank you all.

Finally, we want to thank the staff at Pearson for their wonderful guidance and thoughtful suggestions: Acquisitions Editor, Kelly Villella Canton; Sr. Development Editor, Mary Kriener; Editorial Assistant, Annalea Manalili, and Sr. Marketing Manager, Darcy Betts.

N. Bezuk
C. Cathcart
Y. Pothier
J. Vance

About the Lead Author

Nadine Bezuk is a Professor of Mathematics Education in the School of Teacher Education at San Diego State University. As a former elementary, middle and high school mathematics teacher prior to teaching at the university level, Nadine brings a strong understanding of the needs of teachers to her writing. She is one of the founders of the Professional Development Collaborative, which works with teachers in the San Diego area to develop a deeper understanding of math and science ideas and concepts that can be incorporated into their classrooms, and helped to design the Mathematical Specialist Certificate Program at SDSU. Nadine currently serves as the Executive Director of the Association of Mathematic Teacher Educators (AMTE) and is a regular speaker at NCTM conferences.

CHAPTER

1

Teaching Mathematics: Influences and Directions

How should mathematics be taught? What should children know about mathematics and be able to do? Think about these questions as you go to MyEducationLab to view a clip of Gretchen, a second grader who has been asked to solve the problem 70–23. In the clip Gretchen solves the problem in three different ways and discusses her answers and solution strategies.

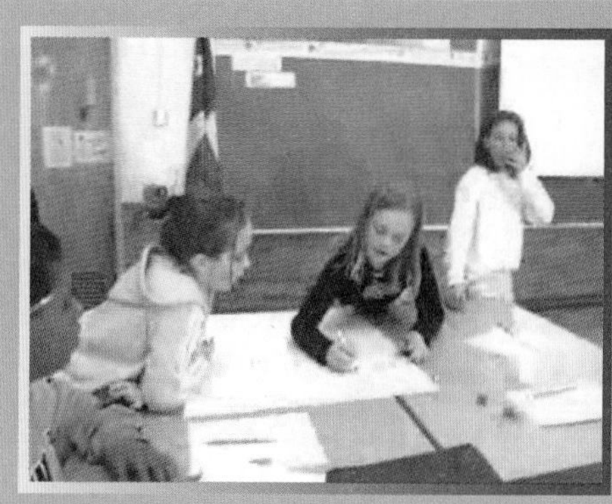

> **myeducationlab** The Power of Classroom Practice — Go to the Assignments and Activities section of Topic 2: "Children's Mathematical Thinking" in the MyEducationLab for your course. Complete the activity entitled "IMAP—Student Reasoning" and note how one student solves problems.

Gretchen begins by using the standard subtraction algorithm, getting 53 as the answer. When first presented with the problem, she comments, "That's easy." Then the interviewer asks her to use base-ten blocks, representing ones and tens, to solve the same problem. This time Gretchen gets 47 as the answer. She seems to notice that this is a different answer than the one she got with the algorithm, so she retraces her steps, both with the blocks and with the algorithm. When rechecking the algorithm, she says, "Zero take-away three, we know that's three." When asked by the interviewer which answer she thinks is right, Gretchen points to her first method, using the algorithm.

The interviewer then asks Gretchen if there is another way to solve the problem, asking her if she ever used a hundreds chart. Gretchen uses a hundreds chart to solve the problem for a third time, once again getting an answer of 47. As soon as she realizes that she got 47 again, she says, "But I don't get it." The interviewer then asks her what she got this time (47), what she got with the base-ten blocks (47), and what she thinks the answer should be, to which Gretchen responds, "Fifty-three."

Gretchen justifies her answer of 53 by going back and repeating the steps she used originally. Then she says, "Forty-seven, umm, like couldn't be right. Because . . . like it has to be fifty-three."

What is the "bug" in Gretchen's subtraction algorithm? (In other words, what does she do wrong when using the subtraction algorithm?)

Developing Your Math Teaching Skills

When you have finished studying this chapter, you should be able to do the following:

- Describe some of the factors that influence the teaching of mathematics.
- Discuss some of the current directions in teaching mathematics.
- Explain how national, state, and local mathematics curriculum standards influence classroom teaching.

Why might she make this mistake? She consistently subtracts 3 from 0 and gets the result of 3, rather than recognizing that one way to solve this would be to regroup so that she has 10 ones. Then she can subtract 3, resulting in 7. This is a very common error children make.

Gretchen seems to put more faith in the procedures she tries to use than in her own understanding of the concept. Where or how might she have gotten the message that learning the procedure was more important than understanding the underlying concept? Why do you think Gretchen trusts the symbolic algorithm more than the other two methods she used? If you were Gretchen's teacher, what might you do next to help her?

Let's revisit our first questions: how should mathematics be taught, and what should children know about mathematics and be able to do? Keep these questions in mind as you read this chapter. We will come back to these issues later in the chapter.

According to the Mathematical Sciences Education Board and National Research Council (1990), "More than ever before, Americans need to think for a living; more than ever before, they need to think mathematically" (p. 3). Mathematics permeates all facets of our lives. Jennifer organizes her collection of baseball cards into a 5-by-8 array and wonders how many cards she has. Marco counts his change to be sure he has received the correct amount after buying his brother a birthday present. Mom asks daughter Jasmine to mentally calculate 15% of the family's restaurant bill and figure out how much money they should leave to pay the bill. Elementary school children decide how much money they need to earn at a fund-raiser in order to purchase new playground equipment for their school.

Often the mathematics in real-life situations is not recognized until after one stops and reflects. Children need help in recognizing that mathematics is all around them. They need the right kinds of experiences to appreciate the fact that mathematics is a common human activity and that it is important to their present and future well-being.

Teaching mathematics is both challenging and stimulating because significant changes are taking place in mathematics education. New insights, new materials, and, of course, children who are growing up in an ever-changing society dictate a different approach to the teaching of mathematics. This chapter is about the various factors that influence the principles, practices, and future direction of mathematics and mathematics instruction.

Influences on Mathematics Education

Many factors and movements have influenced what and how mathematics is taught. It is helpful for you to be aware of these influences to better understand the current state of the art and to put future directions in mathematics instruction into perspective. The following sections address some of the major influences.

Science, Mathematics, and Technology

Today's world relies on information. To process and make decisions based on the vast quantities of information available today, average citizens must be able to think mathematically and to access information provided in a variety of new and visual ways, including graphs, tables, grids, and charts. Those without the ability to think mathematically have limited career possibilities; this also limits the pool of scientists, mathematicians, and engineers for our nation.

According to the American Association for the Advancement of Science (AAAS, 1989), "Because mathematics plays such a central role in modern culture, some basic understanding of the nature of mathematics is requisite for scientific literacy. To achieve this, students need to perceive mathematics as part of the scientific endeavor, comprehend the nature of mathematical thinking, and become familiar with key mathematical ideas and skills" (p. 33).

Mathematics is the chief language of science and comprises the rules for analyzing scientific ideas and data. To be successful today and in the future, children need to develop and be able to use problem-solving, reasoning, communication, connection, and representation skills.

In addition, mathematics has two diverse personalities, if you will. It is at the same time logical and practical, creative and productive. Scientists and engineers use mathematics to solve real-world problems, while mathematicians and others appreciate and enjoy mathematics for its beauty and intellectual challenge. A challenge for you, however, is to help children understand and appreciate the dual uses of mathematics—to go beyond seeing mathematics as a tool and to find a way to appreciate its variety of uses.

The Diversity of Our World: Learner Influences

Children, regardless of their gender, race, ethnicity, language ability, or other factors, are capable of understanding mathematics and deserve full access to high-quality mathematics teaching. The *Principles and Standards for School Mathematics* recommends that "all students should have access to an excellent and equitable mathematics program that provides solid support for their learning and is responsive to their prior knowledge, intellectual strengths, and personal interests" (National Council of Teachers of Mathematics, 2000, p. 13).

Mathematics instruction is the great equalizer. Children who are successful in mathematics have access to a wide range of careers, while those who are not successful have only limited opportunities. The key factor in the achievement of all children is the quality of the teaching. All children can succeed in mathematics if their teachers are aware of how to modify instructional experiences to best meet their needs.

Gender considerations. How can we develop girls and boys who are confident in their mathematics abilities? Some evidence suggests that, beginning in late elementary school, some differences in the mathematics performances of boys and girls are noticeable. For example, fourth- and eighth-grade boys performed significantly better than girls in the most recent National Assessment of Educational Progress (NAEP) (McGraw & Lubienski, 2007). Looking more closely at students' performance in each content strand on the NAEP, boys performed better than girls on tasks in the measurement, number and operations, and algebra and functions strands.

Two other findings from the NAEP are perhaps of more concern: At all grade levels, more boys than girls believe that they are good at mathematics, and more girls tend to drop out of higher-level mathematics courses. According to Casey, Nuttall, and Pezaris (2001), their poorer spatial abilities contribute to girls' lower math achievement in middle school. Therefore, the authors recommend that teachers throughout the elementary grades systematically teach spatial skills and encourage students to use spatial as well as numeric reasoning to solve problems.

Teachers should carefully consider the following facts:

- Girls tend to have less confidence in their mathematical competence, even when they have equal ability. Girls (and their parents) are more likely to attribute their struggles to lack of ability, whereas boys attribute their struggles to a lack of work.
- Girls have lower enrollment rates in advanced Grade 12 and postsecondary mathematics and science courses. This results in limited career choices for women.

Possible causes for this type of thinking include the following:

- Although boys tend to score higher on spatial visualization tasks, there is no conclusive evidence that genetic factors cause the observed differences.
- The above point notwithstanding, some internal factors, such as affective considerations (motivation, interest, etc.) could be at work.
- Expectations and perceptions of society and families (i.e., mathematics is a male domain) are thought to be major factors. External factors may also include boys' increased access to or use of technology.
- Different treatment of boys and girls in the classroom has been documented and may contribute to differences in performance. Teachers tend to interact more with boys than girls (calling on them more often and giving them more criticism and praise) and have higher achievement expectations for boys.

What can teachers do? Perhaps more than anyone else, teachers can help girls achieve equity in mathematics. You can take these steps:

- Interact more with girls on high-cognitive-level mathematics activities, encourage them to engage in independent learning, ensure that they attend to their tasks, and expect them to be successful.
- Make relevant connections between math and girls' lives.
- Place more emphasis on cooperative mathematics activities (which increase girls' achievement) and less emphasis on competitive activities. Include team-building activities.
- Provide girls with opportunities to learn about and interact with female role models in math-based careers.
- Provide girls with opportunities to work in same-gender groups of children rather than always using mixed-gender groups.

Students with special needs. All students need to understand mathematics, including students with special needs. "Special needs learners" include students with learning difficulties as well as gifted students. In the past, some educators believed that students with learning difficulties could be successful only in rote memorization of mathematics facts and procedures, and that, with lots of practice, students would eventually become competent in performing low-level tasks. But the federal No Child Left Behind Act mandates that all children complete a more rigorous mathematics curriculum in order to receive a high school diploma, including passing Algebra I.

Similarly, gifted students need to be challenged but also supported in developing higher-order thinking skills and understanding the meaning and applications of mathematics. Current thinking centers on providing learners with special needs with high-quality mathematics instruction that is differentiated to meet their needs and focuses on developing understanding and building on their unique strengths.

Most students with learning problems share some common characteristics (Lovin, Kyger, & Allsopp, 2004). Learners with special needs tend to

- Be passive learners;
- Attribute their successes and failures to external, uncontrollable factors;
- Have little motivation to be actively involved in learning;
- Have attention problems;
- Focus on irrelevant details;
- Have difficulty controlling impulses; and
- Have memory and vocabulary difficulties.

What can teachers do? To support the learning of special needs children, good instruction should support children's needs while building on their strengths. Teachers can modify instruction to make learning mathematics more accessible to special needs students by

- Creating a structured, consistent learning environment in which they communicate clear expectations;
- Actively engaging children in relevant, exciting learning experiences that focus on both concept development and skill development;
- Involving children in a variety of activities in which they move and are physically engaged in learning;
- Carefully connecting prior knowledge to new learning activities;
- Reviewing important vocabulary and symbols;
- Posing meaningful problems set in familiar situations; and
- Creating a classroom environment where children are comfortable sharing, discussing, and comparing solution strategies.

English language learners. Students who are learning English while they are learning mathematics have special challenges but can be successful if involved in high-quality instruction. English language learners (ELLs) need support and patience because learning mathematics while learning English takes time, and communicating in a second language can seem risky (Meyer, 2000).

ELLs often make good progress in computational skills but have difficulty with word problems. Even though ELLs may have developed conversational fluency in English, they may still need additional support in developing proficiency in the more specialized language of mathematics. Teachers should carefully vary sentence complexity, problem context, and response complexity in word problems to help ELLs be successful (Garrison, Ponce, and Amaral, 2007).

Other strategies that are effective in supporting ELLs include visual scaffolding, realia strategies, manipulative strategies, cooperative learning, advance organizers, preview/review, modeled talk, attribute charting, and word walls (Herrell and Jordan, 2008). We will revisit these strategies throughout this book as we focus on helping children learn specific mathematics topics.

What can teachers do? Teachers can modify instruction to make learning mathematics more accessible to English language learners by

- Using demonstrations and modeling;
- Using manipulative materials;
- Using technology;
- Using graphic organizers and pictures;
- Connecting symbols with words;
- Using cooperative group work and peer tutoring;
- Simplifying, clarifying, and paraphrasing instructional language;
- Directly teaching instructional vocabulary and using vocabulary in meaningful contexts;
- Encouraging students to "retell";
- Building on children's prior experiences and knowledge and posting problems in familiar situations;
- Using dramatization or acting out problem situations;
- Creating mathematics language banks, such as a "Math Word Wall," where mathematics terms are posted on a bulletin board or wall;
- Focusing on meaning and developing understanding rather than memorization.

Curriculum Guided by Standards

Toward the end of the 1980s, the National Council of Teachers of Mathematics (NCTM) acknowledged that much criticism had been leveled at school mathematics during the 1980s. International studies showed that children in the United States did not fare very well on tests of mathematics proficiency compared with children in some other countries (Lapointe, Mead, & Phillips, 1989; Travers & McKnight, 1984).

TIMSS. The Trends in International Mathematics and Science Study (TIMSS) examined the mathematics and science achievement of children at five grade levels in more than 40 countries in 1995, 1999, 2003, and 2007. The 2003 TIMSS results showed that U.S. fourth graders scored above the international average but were outperformed by students in 11 of the 25 participating countries. Similarly, U.S. eighth graders scored above the international average but below students in 9 of the 45 participating countries. U.S. students have shown gains in comparison with students from other countries, but there is still room for improvement (Plisko, 2004).

NAEP. The National Assessment of Educational Progress (NAEP), often referred to as "The Nation's Report Card," periodically examines the achievement of U.S. children in nine content areas—including mathematics—at grades 4,

8, and 12. The mathematics assessment includes five mathematics content areas: (1) number properties and operations, (2) measurement, (3) geometry, (4) data analysis and probability, and (5) algebra. NAEP results are useful in identifying mathematics topics in which students are doing well and those "in which students could do better" (Kloosterman & Lester, 2007). We include NAEP results throughout this book.

Curriculum and Evaluation Standards. In an effort to improve this situation, NCTM developed a set of standards for school mathematics, published in 1989, entitled *Curriculum and Evaluation Standards for School Mathematics* (hereafter referred to as the Curriculum Standards). The Curriculum Standards described criteria for a quality mathematics curriculum from kindergarten through the 12th grade, including what children should learn at each level and strategies for teaching the recommended material. Principles and Standards Link 1-1 highlights the challenge of the vision of this document.

Teaching Standards. The NCTM recognized that teaching was another important influence on children's learning, but teaching was not addressed in the Curriculum Standards. The NCTM subsequently produced a companion document, *Professional Standards for Teaching Mathematics* (hereafter referred to as the Teaching Standards) (NCTM, 1991). This document outlined six standards for teaching mathematics, eight standards for the evaluation of the teaching of mathematics, six standards for the professional development of teachers of mathematics, and four standards for the support and development of mathematics teachers and teaching.

Assessment Standards. A belief that "new assessment strategies and practices need to be developed that will enable teachers and others to assess students' performance in a manner that reflects the NCTM's reform vision for school mathematics" (NCTM, 1995, p. 1) prompted the NCTM to develop and publish in 1995 a third set of standards, *Assessment Standards for School Mathematics* (hereafter referred to as the "Assessment Standards"). This document outlines six mathematics assessment standards and then discusses their use for purposes such as monitoring children's progress, making instructional decisions, evaluating children's achievement, and assessing programs. It is discussed in detail in Chapter 4.

NCTM Principles and Standards Link 1-1

Vision for mathematics education described in *Principles and Standards for School Mathematics* is highly ambitious. Achieving it requires solid mathematics curricula, competent and knowledgeable teachers who can integrate instruction with assessment, education policies that enhance and support learning, classrooms with ready access to technology, and a commitment to both equity and excellence. The challenge is enormous, and meeting it is essential. Our students deserve and need the best mathematics education possible—one that enables them to fulfill personal ambitions and career goals in an ever-changing world. (NCTM, 2000, p. 3)

Principles and Standards. In the late 1990s, NCTM reviewed and revised the 1989 Curriculum Standards, producing the *Principles and Standards for School Mathematics* (NCTM, 2000), which was released in April 2000. (Hereafter, this document will be referred to as the Principles and Standards.) This section highlights the contents and vision of the Principles and Standards and emphasizes the implications of the Principles and Standards for classroom teaching.

The Principles and Standards document contains a set of principles as well as content and process standards for prekindergarten through Grade 12. According to the NCTM (2000):

> The Principles describe particular features of high-quality mathematics education. The Standards describe the mathematical content and processes that children should learn. Together, the Principles and Standards constitute a vision to guide educators as they strive for the continual improvement of mathematics education in classrooms, schools, and educational systems. (p. 11)

The principles. "The Principles are statements reflecting basic precepts that are fundamental to a high-quality mathematics education" (NCTM, 2000, p. 6). These principles, listed next, guide educators in making decisions about teaching and learning and in creating a classroom environment conducive to learning.

- *Equity.* Excellence in mathematics education requires equity—high expectations and strong support for all students.
- *Curriculum.* A curriculum is more than a collection of activities: It must be coherent, focused on important mathematics, and well articulated across the grades.
- *Teaching.* Effective mathematics teaching requires understanding what students know and need to learn and then challenging and supporting them to learn it well.
- *Learning.* Students must learn mathematics with understanding, actively building new knowledge from experience and prior knowledge.
- *Assessment.* Assessment should support the learning of important mathematics and furnish useful information to both teachers and students.

- *Technology.* Technology is essential in teaching and learning mathematics; it influences the mathematics that is taught and enhances students' learning (NCTM, 2000, p. 11).

These six principles describe important issues that are related to all aspects of school mathematics programs. It is important that you consider these principles when planning mathematics instruction and designing mathematics learning environments. In addition to these principles related to teaching and learning, the NCTM Principles and Standards document identifies 10 standards and describes the mathematical content and processes that children should know and be able to use.

The standards. The Principles and Standards includes five *content standards,* which describe the mathematics content children should know, and five *process standards,* which describe the mathematical processes children should be able to use in prekindergarten through Grade 12. These standards are listed in Tables 1-1 and 1-2 and include the following:

CONTENT STANDARDS	PROCESS STANDARDS
• Number and operations	• Problem solving
• Algebra	• Reasoning and proof
• Geometry	• Communication
• Measurement	• Connections
• Data analysis and probability	• Representation

The grade bands. Although each of the content and process standards applies across all grade levels from prekindergarten through grade 12, the Principles and Standards also describes in greater detail what children should know and be able to do at different points across the grade continuum. The Principles and Standards discusses four grade-level ranges, called *grade bands,* which cluster the grade levels into four grade bands: Prekindergarten through grade 2, grades 3 through 5, grades 6 through 8, and grades 9 through 12.

According to the Principles and Standards, "even though each of these ten Standards applies to all grades, emphases will vary both within and between the grade bands. For instance, the emphasis on number is greatest in prekindergarten through grade 2, and by grades 9–12, number receives less instructional attention" (NCTM, 2000, p. 30).

Learner expectations. Within each grade band, the Principles and Standards describes more specifically what children should know in relation to each content standard. This is referred to as *expectations.* The expectations for each grade band help teachers understand what children are expected to understand within each content standard. Table 1-3 gives an example of content standards and expectations for number and operations for grades 3 through 5.

Integrating the content and process standards. The content and process standards should not be viewed as discrete elements but rather should be integrated throughout mathematics instruction. Consider how you can link

TABLE 1-1 Content Standards for School Mathematics

Number and Operations	Algebra	Geometry	Measurement	Data Analysis and Probability
Instructional programs from prekindergarten through Grade 12 should enable all students to—				
• Understand numbers, ways of representing numbers, relationships among numbers, and number systems. • Understand meanings of operations and how they relate to one another. • Compute fluently and make reasonable estimates.	• Understand patterns, relations, and functions. • Represent and analyze mathematical situations and structures using algebraic symbols. • Use mathematical models to represent and understand quantitative relationships.	• Analyze characteristics and properties of two- and three-dimensional geometric shapes and develop mathematical arguments about geometric relationships. • Specify locations and describe spatial relationships using coordinate geometry and other representational systems. • Apply transformations and use symmetry to analyze mathematical situations. • Use visualization, spatial reasoning, and geometric modeling to solve problems.	• Understand measurable attributes of objects and the units, systems, and processes of measurement. • Apply appropriate techniques, tools, and formulas to determine measurements.	• Formulate questions that can be addressed with data and collect, organize, and display relevant data to answer them. • Select and use appropriate statistical methods to analyze data. • Develop and evaluate inferences and predictions that are based on data. • Understand and apply basic concepts of probability.

Source: From *Principles and Standards for School Mathematics,* 2000, pp. 392–400.

TABLE 1-2 Process Standards for School Mathematics

Problem Solving	Reasoning and Proof	Communication	Connections	Representation
Instructional programs from prekindergarten through Grade 12 should enable all students to—				
• Build new mathematical knowledge through problem solving. • Solve problems that arise in mathematics and in other contexts. • Apply and adapt a variety of appropriate strategies to solve problems. • Monitor and reflect on the process of mathematical problem solving.	• Recognize reasoning and proof as fundamental aspects of mathematics. • Make and investigate mathematical conjectures. • Develop and evaluate mathematical arguments and proofs. • Select and use various types of reasoning and methods of proof.	• Organize and consolidate mathematical thinking through communication. • Communicate mathematical thinking coherently and clearly to peers, teachers, and others. • Analyze and evaluate the mathematical thinking and strategies of others. • Use the language of mathematics to express mathematical ideas precisely.	• Recognize and use connections among mathematical ideas. • Understand how mathematical ideas interconnect and build on one another to produce a coherent whole. • Recognize and apply mathematics in contexts outside of mathematics.	• Create and use representations to organize, record, and communicate mathematical ideas. • Select, apply, and translate among mathematical representations to solve problems. • Use representations to model and interpret physical, social, and mathematical phenomena.

Source: From *Principles and Standards for School Mathematics,* 2000, p. 402.

TABLE 1-3 Sample Content Standards and Expectations

Content Standard	Student Expectations
Instructional programs from preK–12 should enable all students to— • Understand numbers, ways of representing numbers, relationships among numbers, and number systems.	*In Grades 3–5 all students should—* • understand the place-value structure of the base-ten number system and be able to represent and compare whole numbers and decimals; • recognize equivalent representations for the same number and generate them by decomposing and composing numbers; • develop understanding of fractions as parts of unit wholes, as parts of a collection, as locations on number lines, and as divisions of whole numbers; • use models, benchmarks, and equivalent forms to judge the size of fractions; • recognize and generate equivalent forms of commonly used fractions, decimals, and percents; • explore numbers less than 0 by extending the number line and through familiar applications; • describe classes of numbers (e.g., odds, primes, squares, and multiples) according to characteristics such as the nature of their factors.

Source: From *Principles and Standards for School Mathematics,* 2000, p. 148.

mathematics content and processes by integrating these standards into mathematics lessons and activities.

Integrating state and local standards with national math standards. In addition to helping children meet the national standards for mathematics, you need to think about helping children meet state and local standards for mathematics learning. The following section shows how national, state, and local mathematics standards could be linked in two different mathematics activities—one on multiplication facts for grades 3 through 5 and another on geometry for grade 2.

Curriculum Focal Points. In 2006, NCTM released the *Curriculum Focal Points for Prekindergarten through Grade 8 Mathematics* (NCTM, 2006) to highlight critical topics that should be the focus of instruction in certain grades. (Hereafter, this document will be referred to as the Curriculum Focal Points.) These focal points are the most important topics in each grade level, topics that lay the foundation for further mathematics learning. These focal points provide "targets" for each grade level to help teachers recognize the key topics that are critically important for students to understand and that provide a strong foundation for future mathematics learning.

For example, this document lists three focal points for grade 3:

- Number and Operations and Algebra: Developing understandings of multiplication and division and strategies for basic multiplication facts and related division facts.
- Number and Operations: Developing an understanding of fractions and fraction equivalence.
- Geometry: Describing and analyzing properties of two-dimensional shapes. (NCTM, 2006, p. 15)

We will highlight the related Curriculum Focal Points for each topic throughout this book.

Teacher Influences

How can we help all children succeed in mathematics? Perhaps the most important influence on what mathematics children learn and on how that knowledge is constructed is an enthusiastic, understanding, and knowledgeable teacher. What does a teacher need to know and be able to do in order for all children to succeed?

The federal No Child Left Behind Act of 2001 mandates that every teacher must be "highly qualified" in each subject he or she teaches. This legislation recognizes the importance of teachers' knowledge. To help children, teachers need to have a deep understanding of the mathematics they are teaching, as well as an understanding of how to help children construct mathematical understandings.

The view that children should construct their own mathematical knowledge does not imply that you should sit back and wait for it to happen. Rather, you must actively observe and listen to children as they engage in and talk about their mathematical explorations. You must be skilled in detecting seeds of mathematical concepts and in providing experiences that will enable those seeds to grow into mature understandings. You must develop lessons that align with standards but also build on children's thinking.

A key feature of this textbook is its link to children's thinking, as you saw at the beginning of this chapter when you viewed the video clip of Gretchen solving a subtraction problem. There is much to learn about how children think about and come to understand different mathematics concepts. As you read through this book, pay particular attention to how children are thinking about mathematics and how teachers can help children extend their understandings.

Directions in Mathematics Education

Although many changes have occurred as a result of the preceding influences, looking into the future is difficult. It seems reasonable, however, to predict that problem solving, communication, reasoning and proof, connections within mathematics and between mathematics and other curricular areas, and the use of multiple representations will continue to be emphasized. Further, equity with regard to achievement, the use of technology, an appropriate role for computation and estimation, and authentic assessment will be implemented. In addition, the issue of parent involvement to enhance children's learning must be considered. The most notable direction in mathematics instruction is problem solving.

Problem Solving

Problem solving has always been an important part of a mathematics program. In recent years, however, the importance of problem solving has been reemphasized, with its inclusion as one of the process standards of NCTM's (2000) *Principles and Standards for School Mathematics.* This increased emphasis on problem solving is evident in textbook series and government curriculum guides, which now include many good problem-solving activities. This focus on problem solving will continue but will take on a different form as mathematics programs move toward developing mathematics from real-world settings. For example, children may be working on a collection of baseball or Yu-gi-oh! cards. The problem setting may focus on how to display the collection, which will probably lead children to explore an array. Multiplication problems arise when the children want to know how many stamps they have displayed in a particular arrangement of stamps. The NCTM Principles and Standards Link 1-2 describes the problem-solving process strand.

Researchers have been actively trying to document the characteristics of good problem solvers. Likewise, teachers have been experimenting with strategies (often called *heuristics*) that develop problem-solving skills in children. Because problem solving is at the heart of school mathematics, it is discussed in great detail in Chapter 3.

Communication

Communication is another important direction in mathematics education. A major factor in shaping mathematics

NCTM Principles and Standards Link 1-2

Process Strand: Problem Solving

Instructional programs from prekindergarten through grade 12 should enable all students to—

- build new mathematical knowledge through problem solving;
- solve problems that arise in mathematics and in other contexts;
- apply and adapt a variety of appropriate strategies to solve problems;
- monitor and reflect on the process of mathematical problem solving. (NCTM, 2000, p. 52)

Literature Link 1-1

Imagine a World Full of "Math Curses"!

Scieszka, J., & Smith, L. (1995). ***Math Curse.*** New York: Penguin Books.

Children's literature provides a context through which mathematical concepts, patterns, problem solving, and real-world contexts may be explored. Many of us take the mathematics in the world around us for granted. In *Math Curse,* the main character thinks of everything in life as a math problem. How can you engage your students in a similar manner?

- Keep a math journal for one day, recording all of the mathematical problems you encounter. Be as creative as the narrator in the book and think about ways mathematics may be hidden in typical activities. Create a class book of children's "math curse" experiences.
- Record or bring cut-out examples from magazines, the newspaper, or the Internet of numbers and symbols used in everyday life. Examples might include (1) graphs or other statistics presented in a newspaper, (2) the dollar sign and decimal used in our monetary system, or (3) pictures of repeating or tessellating patterns in various designs. Design a class bulletin board called "Mathematics in the World Around Us."
- Communicate using the vocabulary of mathematical terms and symbols in the book. For example, investigate the Mayan numeral system of counting presented in the story. Discuss why the mathematics teacher in the book is named "Mrs. Fibonacci."
- Model and solve some of the mathematical puzzles in the book and determine which ones are simply nonsense.
- Investigate the mathematical conversions, tables, measures, and terms illustrated on the endpapers of the book.
- Books such as ***Math in the Bath (and Other Fun Places, Too!)*** (Atherlay, 1995) for younger children and ***Counting on Frank*** (Clement, 1991), whose witty narrator will amuse older children, show children how mathematics is a part of their everyday experiences.

Source: Dr. Patricia Moyer-Packenham, Utah State University.

programs and teaching in the next decade concerns mathematics as communication. Children need an opportunity to reflect on and explain or justify their ideas and solutions both orally and in writing. There are two aspects to mathematical communication. First, mathematics is a language. Like English, Spanish, or any other language, mathematics has words (symbols) and semantic and syntactical rules; meaning is conveyed through mathematical symbols and their associated rules. A second aspect of mathematical communication involves the use of language within mathematics. This can be a powerful determinant of what is learned and how it is learned. Principles and Standards Link 1-3 describes the communication process strand.

NCTM Principles and Standards Link 1-3

Process Strand: Communication

Instructional programs from prekindergarten through grade 12 should enable all students to—

- organize and consolidate their mathematical thinking through communication;
- communicate their mathematical thinking coherently and clearly to peers, teachers, and others;
- analyze and evaluate the mathematical thinking and strategies of others;
- use the language of mathematics to express mathematical ideas precisely. (NCTM, 2000, p. 60)

McKenzie (1990) draws a parallel (and highlights some differences) between reading for meaning and solving a mathematics problem with meaning. Both processes require the use of prior knowledge. Indeed, in both processes, children are continually predicting, sampling, confirming, self-correcting, and reprocessing—further evidence that reading is not an isolated subject to be taught at a particular time of day. Rather, reading for meaning is a process that must permeate all subject areas. Literature Link 1-1 is an example of how children's literature may be used in the mathematics classroom.

Talking, reading, writing, listening, and representing are important components of communication in mathematics. Children need to engage in all of them. Figure 1-1 suggests a variety of activities for each component that serves to reinforce each component's role in mathematical communication. In addition, asking thought-provoking questions will encourage quality communication.

Reasoning and Proof

Mathematics programs often have been criticized for their emphasis on memorization of basic facts, rules, and principles. Today, however, more emphasis is being placed on mathematical reasoning and other higher-order thinking skills such as application, analysis, synthesis, and evaluation. These skills often are included in problem-solving

FIGURE 1-1 Components of Mathematics as Communication

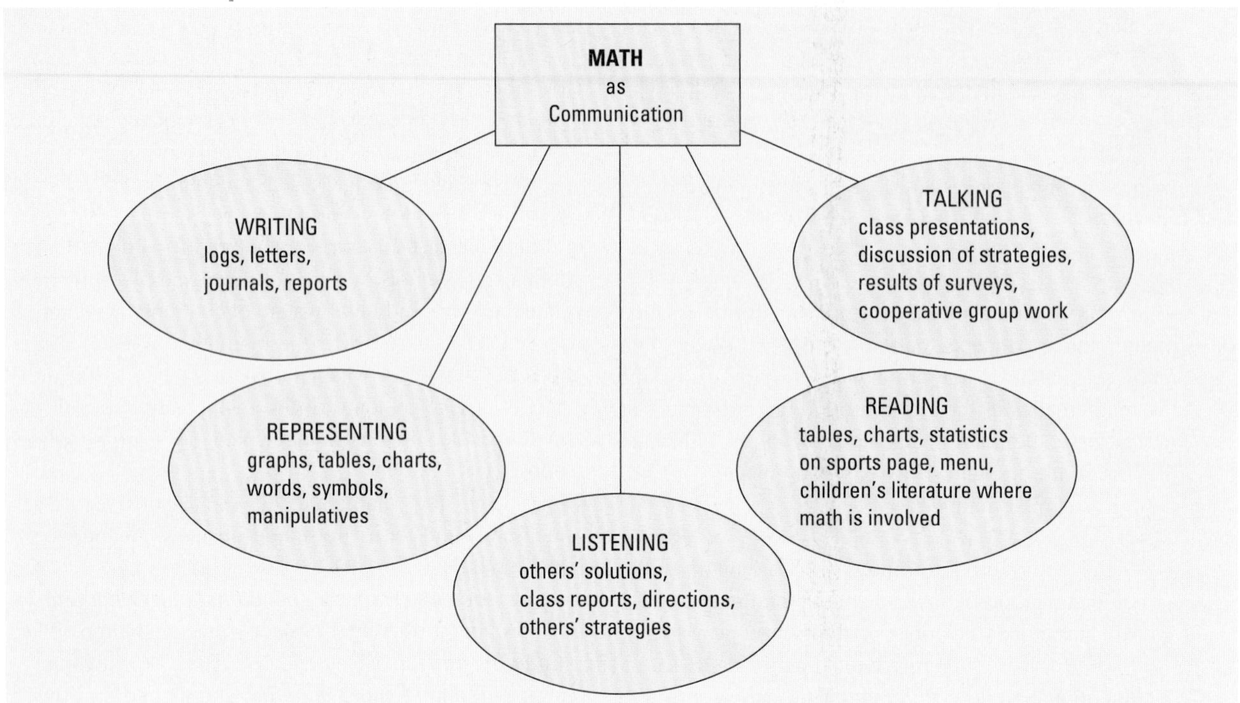

Source: M. Cappo & G. Osterman (1991). Teach students to communicate mathematically. *The Computing Teacher* (now *Learning & Leading with Technology*), *18*(5), 34–39 © 1991. International Society for Technology in Education, (800) 336-5191, cust_svc@iste.org, www.iste.org. Reprinted with permission.

activities. Problems such as the following help children develop reasoning skills:

> *Sarah is younger than Alyssa. She is also older and shorter than Patrick. Alyssa is taller and younger than Juan. Juan is taller than Patrick.*

1. Arrange the four people by age.
2. Arrange the four people by height.

Encourage children to solve this problem using whatever strategy makes sense to them. After they have solved the problem, ask children to share their solution processes. Follow this with a discussion about the problem and the solution strategies children used. Having children share their solution strategies helps them learn from each other and models different types of reasoning. Principles and Standards Link 1-4 describes the reasoning and proof process strand.

Connections

In the past, mathematics was often considered a subject unto itself. Frequently, it was broken down internally into many unrelated parts. In the future, however, you can integrate mathematics throughout the curriculum and punctuate it with real-world applications. Principles and Standards Link 1-5 describes the connections process strand.

Integration with other school subjects. When children recognize that mathematics can be used in other subject areas, it becomes more relevant to them. For example, graphing is a skill that children can apply to problems in

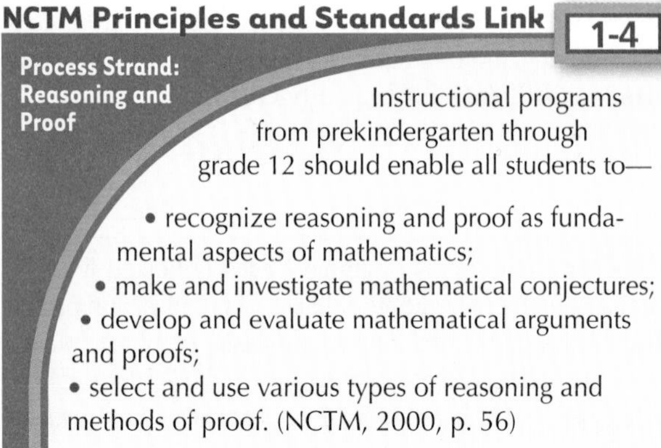

NCTM Principles and Standards Link 1-4

Process Strand: Reasoning and Proof

Instructional programs from prekindergarten through grade 12 should enable all students to—

- recognize reasoning and proof as fundamental aspects of mathematics;
- make and investigate mathematical conjectures;
- develop and evaluate mathematical arguments and proofs;
- select and use various types of reasoning and methods of proof. (NCTM, 2000, p. 56)

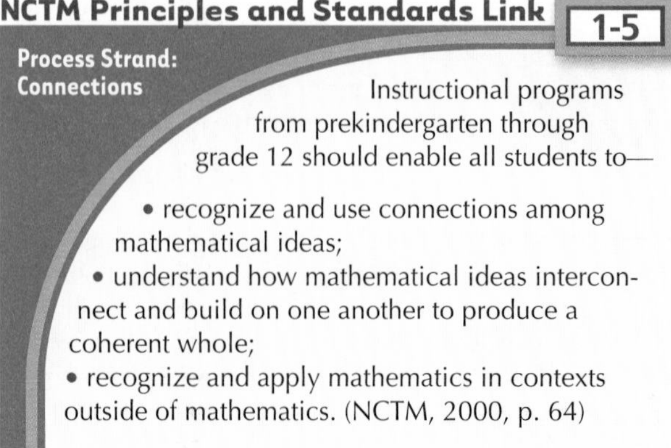

NCTM Principles and Standards Link 1-5

Process Strand: Connections

Instructional programs from prekindergarten through grade 12 should enable all students to—

- recognize and use connections among mathematical ideas;
- understand how mathematical ideas interconnect and build on one another to produce a coherent whole;
- recognize and apply mathematics in contexts outside of mathematics. (NCTM, 2000, p. 64)

social studies and science. In art class, geometric concepts such as slides, flips, and turns can be applied to create a variety of interesting designs. And finally, as a language-learning assignment, children can write about the way they solved a problem, how they feel about the mathematics they are doing, or what successes or difficulties they experience in understanding mathematics.

Consider the following example: Ms. Jacobs's kindergarten class discussed how they got to school each day. As part of their discussion, they made a graph showing how they arrived that morning. Some children walked, some rode the bus, some rode their bikes, and others came in a car, as illustrated here:

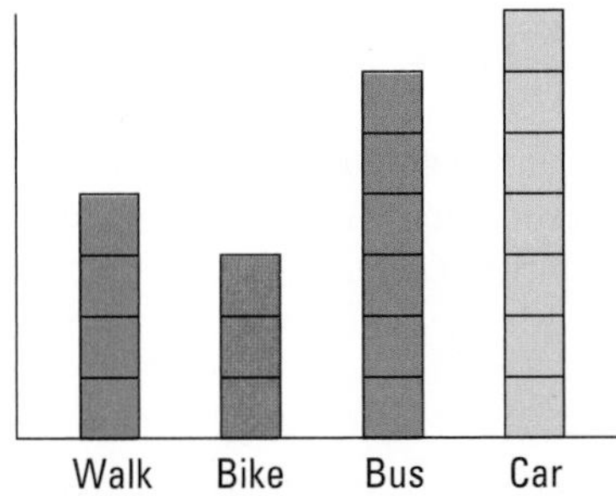

The class used this graph to notice that most of the children arrived by car, and fewer walked or rode their bikes.

Integration with real-world settings. In the real world, people solve mathematics problems that arise from a particular setting. Pilots use mathematics for navigational problem solving, firefighters apply measurement concepts and processes when they fight fires, interior designers employ mathematics when they order carpeting and wallpaper, and so on. The 1995 NCTM yearbook, *Connecting Mathematics Across the Curriculum,* focuses on mathematics in the real world. Mathematics is holistic in the sense that integrative threads that connect other content areas in the curriculum will be explicitly identified so that children can "see" the connections. Some connections are mentioned in subsequent chapters of this book. One example, a connection between elementary and secondary levels, is illustrated here. A simple number, 7425, familiar to elementary school-aged children, is written in expanded form and, through a series of generalizations, transformed into a polynomial, familiar to secondary school students.

$$7425$$
$$7 \times 1000 + 4 \times 100 + 2 \times 10 + 5$$
$$7 \times x^3 + 4 \times x^2 + 2 \times x + 5$$
$$7x^3 + 4x^2 + 2x + 5$$
$$ax^3 + bx^2 + cx + d$$

Representation of Mathematical Ideas

Much in mathematics is abstract, and making it meaningful to children has been a continuing challenge for teachers. In the past, mathematics was taught at an abstract level, even in elementary school, where children are not yet fully able to make the kinds of abstractions expected for understanding. Because we know now that children learn in different ways, it makes sense for teachers and children to represent mathematical concepts in different ways as well.

Considerable emphasis is placed on representing mathematical ideas with concrete materials: Blocks, counters, and many other physical apparatuses that children can manipulate have been used to embody mathematical ideas. This emphasis will continue, but, currently, there is a shift to a more multirepresentational approach that includes spoken language, concrete objects, pictures, real-life situations, and written symbols. Observing and making relationships within and among these representations helps children develop understanding (Behr, Lesh, Post, & Silver, 1983; Cuoco, 2001; Hiebert, 1990). Principles and Standards Link 1-6 discusses how children should be able to use representations. This topic is discussed in more detail in Chapter 2.

Equity

An achievement gap in mathematics has existed for far too long. In the past, achievement gaps based on gender, race, ethnicity, culture, native language, and socioeconomic status have been noted. The gender gap has begun to narrow in recent years, but other gaps continue to exist. To develop equity in a mathematics program, the NCTM Curriculum Standards include five NCTM goals to apply to all children:

1. They learn to VALUE mathematics.
2. They become CONFIDENT in their ability to do mathematics.
3. They become mathematical PROBLEM SOLVERS.
4. They learn to COMMUNICATE mathematically.
5. They learn to REASON mathematically.

It is important that you have high expectations for each child and work toward ensuring the learning of every child.

NCTM Principles and Standards Link 1-6

Process Strand: Representation

Instructional programs from prekindergarten through grade 12 should enable all students to—

- create and use representations to organize, record, and communicate mathematical ideas;
- select, apply, and translate among mathematical representations to solve problems;
- use representations to model and interpret physical, social, and mathematical phenomena. (NCTM, 2000, p. 67)

Technology

We believe that the use of calculators and other technologies will continue to increase. This prediction stems from the following reasons:

- Calculators and other forms of technology continue to be used extensively in the home and office.
- The cost of calculators and other forms of technology continues to decrease, while their power and functions continue to increase.
- Curriculum documents increasingly encourage the use of calculators and other forms of technology.
- Some tests currently available allow and even encourage calculator use.

Computation and Estimation

In the past, a heavy emphasis was placed on computation and computational procedures in elementary schools. But according to the Mathematical Sciences Education Board and National Research Council (1989), "Mathematics today involves far more than calculation; clarification of the problem, deduction of consequences, formulation of alternatives, and development of appropriate tools are as much a part of the modern mathematician's craft as are solving equations or providing answers" (p. 5).

The Principles and Standards emphasizes the importance of interrelated skills and concepts: Children need not only to be able to compute fluently but also to understand the meanings of operations and to make reasonable estimates. The recommendations regarding these skills are listed in Principles and Standards Link 1-7.

Currently, although the need for children to learn how to perform paper-and-pencil computations is recognized, the focus is on less complex calculations. More complex computations (for example, multiplying two three-digit numbers) are more realistically done on a calculator than with paper and pencil. Furthermore, the current emphasis is on solving real problems that may require the use of a calculator, rather than computation for computation's sake. The focus will continue to be on supporting children in choosing the appropriate computational tool in solving a problem. That is, is an estimate sufficient? If not, is mental computation feasible? Can this be done easily with pencil and paper, or should a calculator be used? Figure 1-2, adapted from the Curriculum Standards, reflects this philosophy.

In addition, emphasis is placed on estimation (approximating the answer) and mental computation (performing an exact computation mentally). Estimation and mental computation are useful in helping children develop number and operation sense. The renewed emphasis on estimation and mental computation can be traced, at least in part, to the advent of the calculator. The calculator will display a result when keys are pressed, but were the correct keys pressed? Were they pressed in the right sequence? An estimate will tell you whether your answer is reasonable. (Estimation and mental computation are discussed more fully in Chapter 9.)

NCTM Principles and Standards Link 1-7

Content Strand: Number and Operations

Instructional programs from prekindergarten through grade 12 should enable all students to—

- understand numbers, ways of representing numbers, relationships among numbers, and number systems;
- understand meanings of operations and how they relate to one another;
- compute fluently and make reasonable estimates.

(NCTM, 2000, p. 32)

Assessment

According to the Principles and Standards, "Assessment should support the learning of important mathematics and furnish useful information to both teachers and students" (NCTM, 2000, p. 22). The nature of assessment and strategies for assessing student learning are changing markedly. This topic is discussed in depth in Chapter 4. We mention it here, however, because it is another important area in which significant change is occurring. Assessment must be more than just a score on a test and should be an ongoing part of instruction that guides you in making instructional decisions.

Parent Involvement

Collaboration between teachers and parents is an effective strategy for increasing children's success in mathematics. According to Bezuk, Whitehurst-Payne, and Aydelotte (2000), "collaboration between teachers and parents is critically important to increase student achievement in order to achieve the goal of all students succeeding in mathematics" (p. 148).

There are many ways you can involve parents to enhance a child's learning. Some of these strategies include the following:

- Help parents learn more about *what* their child is learning about mathematics and *how* their child is learning mathematics.
- Provide activities parents can do with their children at home to reinforce and extend their children's learning.
- Discuss why mathematics is important for future success, including noting careers that involve using mathematics.

FIGURE 1-2 Computational Decision-Making Process

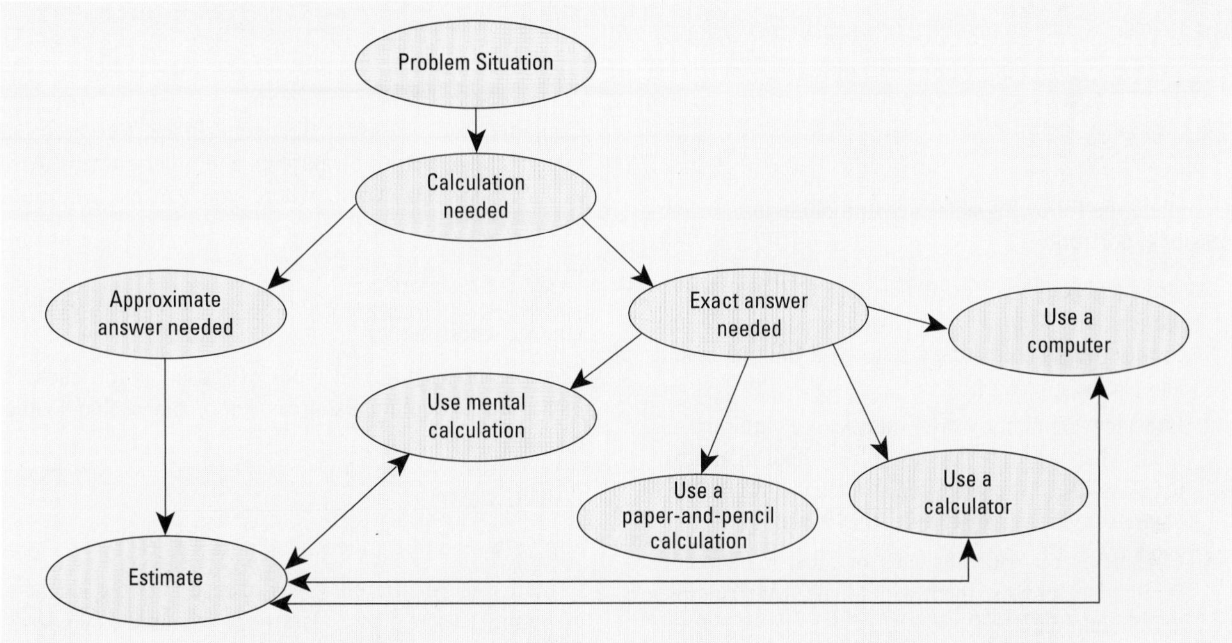

Source: From *Curriculum and Evaluation Standards for School Mathematics,* NCTM, 1989, Reston, VA: NCTM. © 1989 by NCTM. Used with permission.

Suggestions and ideas for activities that can be sent home with children to do with their parents are included throughout this book.

Conclusion

This chapter has described a number of factors that have influenced the course of mathematics education in schools. These factors have changed and will continue to change both the mathematics curriculum and how mathematical ideas are taught.

Think back to Gretchen, the second grader in the opening video, and the questions posed there:

- How should mathematics be taught?
- What should children know about mathematics and be able to do?

Now that you've read this chapter, has your thinking about these questions changed? What do you want to know more about related to the teaching and learning of mathematics? As a teacher of mathematics, how will these influences affect your teaching?

Sometimes influences pull in opposite directions, making it difficult to maintain a balance. Educators often describe a need for a balance in school mathematics among three needs: the needs of the child, the needs of society, and the needs of the subject. If we overemphasize any one area, such as the computation component of mathematics, we may tend to neglect its application in society and also the needs of the child, resulting in an imbalance.

The suggestions and activities in subsequent chapters of this book will enable you to devise a mathematics program for the children in your classroom that develops mathematical ideas in a nontrivial way, makes applications to everyday situations apparent, and carefully considers the needs of the child, making allowances for differences in background, learning style, and motivation to learn mathematics. Throughout the instructional process, the teacher is the most important factor in determining the strength of the mathematics program. Your challenge as a future teacher is to learn as much as you can about how to help children learn mathematics.

IN PRACTICE

Complete the following activities to include in your professional portfolio.

1. Browse through issues of *Teaching Children Mathematics* and *Mathematics Teaching in the Middle School.* Begin collecting articles you find interesting and useful.
2. Interview elementary or middle school children. Ask them what they like and don't like about mathematics class. Describe what you as a teacher might do to change any negative attitudes they have.
3. Consult a copy of your state or local mathematics standards. Compare them with the NCTM Principles and Standards.

LINKS TO THE INTERNET

National Council of Teachers of Mathematics

http://www.nctm.org

Contains information about the NCTM Standards and other publications as well as news releases related to mathematics teaching and learning.

Math Forum

http://mathforum.org/

Contains Student Center, Teachers' Place, Research Division, and a section for parents and other citizens. Also includes Ask Dr. Math, where you can ask questions about K–12 mathematics.

Teachers' Net

http://teachers.net

Contains many different types of resources for teachers, including curriculum resources, lesson plans, chat boards, and mailrings.

Math.com

http://www.math.com/teachers.html

Contains many different types of resources for teachers, including lesson plans, classroom resources, standards, and free stuff.

RESOURCES FOR TEACHERS

Reference Books: Increasing Equity in Learning Mathematics

Edwards, C. A. (Ed.). (1999). *Changing the Faces of Mathematics: Perspectives on Asian Americans and Pacific Islanders.* Reston, VA: National Council of Teachers of Mathematics.

Hankes, J. E., & Fast, G. R. (Eds.). (2002). *Changing the Faces of Mathematics: Perspectives on Indigenous People of North America.* Reston, VA: National Council of Teachers of Mathematics.

Jacobs, J. E., & Rossi Becker, J. (Eds.). (2000). *Changing the Faces of Mathematics: Perspectives on Gender Equity.* Reston, VA: National Council of Teachers of Mathematics.

National Council of Teachers of Mathematics (2006). *Curriculum Focal Points for Prekindergarten Through Grade 8 Mathematics: A Quest for Coherence.* Reston, VA: Author.

Ortiz-Franco, L., Hernandez, N. G., & De la Cruz, Y. (Eds.). (1999). *Changing the Faces of Mathematics: Perspectives on Latinos.* Reston, VA: National Council of Teachers of Mathematics.

Secada, W. G. (Ed.). (2000). *Changing the Faces of Mathematics: Perspectives on Multiculturalism and Gender Equity.* Reston, VA: National Council of Teachers of Mathematics.

Strutchens, M. E., Johnson, M. L., & Tate, W. F. (Eds.). (2000). *Changing the Faces of Mathematics: Perspectives on African Americans.* Reston, VA: National Council of Teachers of Mathematics.

Children's Literature

Atherlay, S. (1995). *Math in the Bath (and other Fun Places, Too!).* New York: Simon & Schuster Books for Young Readers.

Clement, R. (1991). *Counting on Frank.* Milwaukee, WI: Gareth Stevens Publishing.

CHAPTER

Learning and Teaching Mathematics

NCTM CONNECTING WITH THE STANDARDS

The National Council of Teachers of Mathematics (NCTM) *Professional Standards for Teaching Mathematics* (1991), also known as the Teaching Standards, stresses the importance of helping students develop mathematical power. Mathematical power involves being able to reason logically, communicate about mathematics, solve nonroutine problems, and develop personal self-confidence in one's ability to solve math problems. The Teaching Standards emphasizes the critical importance of high-quality teaching in order to help children achieve:

> *WHAT students learn is fundamentally connected with HOW they learn it. Students' opportunities to learn mathematics are a function of the setting and the kinds of tasks and discourse in which they participate. What students learn—about particular concepts and procedures as well as about thinking mathematically—depends on the ways in which they engage in mathematical activity in their classrooms. Their dispositions toward mathematics are also shaped by such experiences. Consequently, the goal of developing students' mathematical power requires careful attention to pedagogy as well as to curriculum.* (NCTM, 1991, p. 21)

The NCTM document goes on to note that "by learning problem solving in mathematics, students should acquire ways of thinking, habits of persistence and curiosity, and confidence in unfamiliar situations that will serve them well outside the mathematics classroom" (p. 21).

One of the most important tasks elementary teachers can accomplish is that of helping children develop a deep understanding of mathematics. This chapter focuses on providing teachers with strategies and suggestions to help children learn mathematics.

What should children know about mathematics and be able to do? How do children best learn mathematics? Think about these questions as you go to MyEducationLab to view a clip of June, an exemplary teacher who engages her students in reasoning mathematically. For this video, June was asked to teach her students a lesson from a

Developing Your Math Teaching Skills

When you have finished studying this chapter, you should be able to do the following:

- Describe how the behaviorist approach to teaching differs from the constructivist approach to teaching.
- List and give examples of the five different modes in which a mathematics concept may be represented.
- Discuss the importance of communication in the mathematics classroom.
- Compare and contrast conceptual knowledge with procedural knowledge, and give an example of each of these types of knowledge.

state-adopted textbook in which the focus is on learning a procedure for converting mixed numbers to improper fractions. Her students were then assessed, and several of them were videotaped solving problems. Five weeks later, June taught another lesson focusing on the same topic, only this time she focused on developing understanding of the concept. Again, her students, including Rachel, were assessed and videotaped.

> PEARSON **myeducationlab** The Power of Classroom Practice Go to the Assignments and Activities section of Topic 1: "Planning and Teaching Mathematics" in the MyEducationLab for your course. Complete the activity entitled "IMAP—Learning Mathematics" to watch how one teacher helps her students use mathematical reasoning.

What do you think Rachel learned from the first lesson focusing on learning the rule? After this lesson, Rachel wasn't able to convert $3\frac{3}{8}$ to an improper fraction. She commented, "We did this before. But I don't really remember it as well, because I didn't figure it out for myself." When asked by the interviewer what she meant by that, Rachel said, "Well, when she (the teacher) tells us the answer to something, then I try and find out how she got it. And so when I figure that out, it's easier. And once I figure it out, it stays there, because I was the one who brought it there."

When asked if that's how the teacher usually does it, Rachel responded affirmatively, saying, "And then this little time, it was different. And it was harder."

Then June taught a lesson on the same topic conceptually, focusing on developing children's understanding. She commented that "when students create their own algorithms, it is something that they keep forever."

In the fourth video segment, Rachel was asked to solve the same problem, converting $3\frac{3}{8}$ to an improper fraction. She began by applying a rule incorrectly, multiplying the whole number 3 by the numerator 3 and adding 8, then putting that over 8, for a result of $\frac{17}{8}$, which is incorrect. Rachel's work is shown here.

$$3 \times \frac{3}{8} \qquad \begin{array}{r} 9 \\ +8 \\ \hline 17 \end{array} \qquad \frac{17}{8}$$

Then Rachel offered another way to solve this problem, drawing one circle cut into eight parts, then drawing two more circles and then three-eighths, as shown below, but she had difficulty finishing the problem.

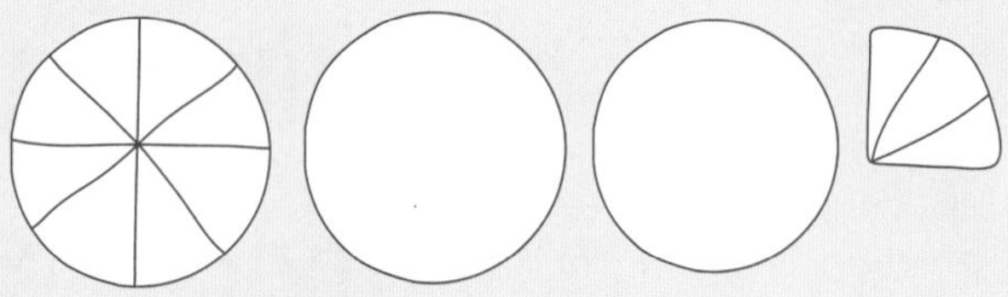

The interviewer asked her how many parts she had in each circle (8), and Rachel was able to correctly determine that there are 27 pieces, which is $\frac{27}{8}$. The interviewer noted that Rachel got two different answers and asked her which one she thought was correct. Rachel thought her second answer, $\frac{27}{8}$, was correct. With some questioning from the interviewer, Rachel developed a correct rule for converting $3\frac{3}{8}$ to an improper fraction.

After solving this problem, the interviewer asked Rachel why she began solving this problem with a correct procedure even though she had recently been taught how to solve such problems conceptually. Rachel attributed that to the fact that she was taught the rule first. She said that she'd prefer learning the second lesson, the conceptual lesson, first, because she felt that she "would have remembered how to do it the right way, and the correct way."

What do you think children need to know about the concept of the lesson: converting between mixed numbers and improper fractions? It seemed that Rachel learned best when she was expected to know more than the rule and when she was expected to understand the concepts behind the process.

Based on this video clip, it seems that Rachel knows that she learns best when she is able to make sense of what she's doing. What does June think is important in helping children learn mathematics? Did this video clip confirm or challenge any of your beliefs about what's important in mathematics teaching or learning?

Learning Theories

Theories about how children learn have been classified in various ways (Pa, 1986). These theories have a significant bearing on how mathematics is taught. For example, a predominant theory in the late 19th century, *mental discipline,* viewed the mind as a kind of muscle that required a reasonable amount of exercise to keep it properly tuned. In mathematics, lengthy or complex computations were used as a major form of exercise. Instruction stressed ways to perform these computations accurately. More recent theories fall into two general camps: the behaviorist approach and cognitive or constructivist approaches.

The Behaviorist Approach

During the early part of the 20th century, curricula and instruction were influenced by behavioral psychology. E. L. Thorndike's stimulus–response (S–R) theory gradually replaced the mental discipline theory. The S–R theory stated that learning occurred when a "bond" was established between some stimulus and a person's response to it. Drill became a major component in the instructional process because the more often a correct response was made to a stimulus, the more established the bond became. Programmed instruction, often attributed to B. F. Skinner, was one educational outcome of this theory.

In the 1960s, Robert Gagné, a *neo-behaviorist,* began to publish some of his research results on intelligence and conditions of learning. One of Gagné's major contributions to curriculum development was an emphasis on analyzing the structure of a task or concept to be learned. Gagné focused on identifying the knowledge that is necessary or prerequisite to completing a task. A question frequently asked in a Gagné-type approach is "What must the child already know or be able to do to learn this new concept or perform this new skill?"

Consider this example: In order for children to learn the addition facts to 18, they must understand the concepts of addition and place value, understand the commutative property, and be able to decompose numbers. For example, to solve $9 + 3$, one could decompose 3 into $1 + 2$, and then add $9 + 1$ first, then add 2, as follows: $9 + 3 = 9 + 1 + 2 = 10 + 2 = 12$. Considering what children need to understand and be able to do in order to be successful in solving a problem is helpful to you when planning instruction.

The Cognitive/Constructivist Approach

More recently, mathematics teaching and learning has been influenced by cognitive or constructivist approaches to education. Because we have opted for very broad categories of learning theories in this section, cognitive and constructive theories are discussed together. For the purposes of this text, it is adequate to consider constructivism as an extension of the cognitive approach.

Constructivism is based on the premise that knowledge is actively constructed by the individual, not passively received from an outside source (Goldin, 1990). Constructivists believe that children must be actively involved in constructing their own understandings of a concept. In other words, according to constructivists, children must play an active role in developing their own understandings rather than passively receive knowledge.

The role of the teacher. One way to think of the difference between the behaviorist and constructivist views of learning is with respect to *where* knowledge comes from and *how* knowledge is acquired. The behaviorist view is that the teacher or curriculum designer is the source of knowledge and that person's main task is to transmit this knowledge to the child, who is a passive recipient. A constructivist, on the other hand, believes that the child constructs her or his own knowledge.

The constructivist point of view suggests at least two significant implications for teaching mathematics (Kamii, 1990). To support children's learning, you can

- Focus on children's thinking rather than on their writing correct answers, and
- Encourage children to discuss, even disagree, among themselves rather than concentrate on getting right answers and correcting wrong ones.

The teacher's role is to structure appropriate experiences so that the child can actively construct meaning.

It is difficult to describe a classroom or lesson that would reflect a constructivist approach because there would be considerable variation, based on children's needs. The following elements are often included in constructivist lessons:

- A high level of interaction,
- An emphasis on student autonomy or responsibility,
- Interaction of children with materials, and
- Frequent group work.

In constructivist classrooms, children frequently interact with the teacher, who encourages, nurtures, and provides help, but often in the form of higher level questions to encourage children to reflect on what they have done in order to construct meaning. Questions would require children to explain and justify: "Why?" "What does that tell you?" "What can you tell me?" "Why not?" "What do you mean 'it doesn't work'?" (Confrey, 1990). Questions involving classifying, giving examples, generalizing, applying, and other higher-level questions would also be asked frequently. Table 2-1 provides examples of different types of questions.

TABLE 2-1 Questions to Stimulate Communication

Category	Example
Classifying	How are these shapes alike? How are they different?
Hypothesizing	What if . . . ? What could be true here?
Specializing	Can you give a specific example of how this works?
Generalizing	Can you see a pattern? Describe it.
Convincing	How do you know you are right?
Analyzing	Is this diagram correct? What is this all about?

In a constructivist setting, the teacher is responsible for establishing a learning environment that will spark children's interest and open up areas (topics) of study. You can do this by providing appropriate materials, activities, and reinforcement. Some children may need supplemental or different materials and activities from other children in order to help them move forward in understanding the concept.

Learner-centered instruction. Good instruction meets the needs of *all* children in the classroom. It's a teacher's responsibility to determine the learning needs of his or her children and design instruction that helps each child progress. When designing learner-centered instruction, consider the ability, achievement, and special needs of all the children. Throughout this textbook, you will learn more about how to assess the abilities and needs of children and how to use those abilities and needs to make instructional decisions.

Cooperative learning. Group work, although not essential, is very likely a feature of a constructivist learning environment. Small-group *cooperative learning* has been much discussed in current professional literature (Artzt & Newman, 1990a, 1990b; Davidson, 1990a, 1990b; Good, Reys, Grouws, & Mulryan, 1989–90). What is cooperative learning? (Some prefer to use the term *collaborative* rather than *cooperative.*) It is both an organization and a process in which a small group of children (usually three to five in number, heterogeneous in both ability and some personal characteristics) work together to complete a task or project or solve a problem. There are many ways to incorporate cooperative learning into the classroom, but they seem to have four elements in common (Artzt & Newman, 1990a):

> First, the members of a group must perceive that they are part of a team and that they all have a common goal. Second, group members must realize that the problem they are to solve is a group problem and that the success or failure of the group will be shared by all of the members of the group. Third, to accomplish the group's goal, all students must talk with one another—to engage in discussion of all problems. Finally, it must be clear that each member's individual work has a direct effect on the group's success. Teamwork is of utmost importance. (pp. 2–3)

The Principles and Standards supports the use of small-group learning in mathematics. "Working in pairs or small groups enables students to hear different ways of thinking and refine the ways in which they explain their own ideas. Having students share the results of their small-group findings gives teachers opportunities to ask questions for clarification and to model mathematical language" (NCTM, 2000, p. 128). Representing, talking, listening, writing, and reading can all be addressed in a cooperative learning setting. It is also an excellent forum for cooperatively and actively exploring a concept with concrete materials.

Davidson (1990b) concludes from research that small-group cooperative learning has a positive effect on "academic achievement, self-esteem or self-confidence as a learner, intergroup relations including cross-race friendships, social acceptance of mainstreamed children, and ability to use social skills (if these are taught)" (p. 54).

Many educators and psychologists have influenced the development of constructivism. We will emphasize the work of one: Jean Piaget.

Jean Piaget. The work of Jean Piaget, a Swiss philosopher-epistemologist, has influenced our thinking about how mathematics is learned. Key concepts in Piaget's theory of learning include *schema, adaptation,* and *operations.* A schema is a cognitive structure that one constructs by putting pieces of knowledge together. For example, children might develop a "matching" schema and later an "intuitive qualitative correspondence" schema in order to determine whether two sets are numerically equivalent. For example, a "matching" schema refers to children's being able to line up two sets of objects to show the one-to-one correspondence between the elements in each set. If the elements match exactly, the sets are numerically equivalent. In Figure 2-1, each item in set A is in a one-to-one correspondence with an item in set B, with no items left over, so sets A and B are the same size.

An "intuitive qualitative correspondence" schema is less procedural and more holistic. It involves children's making an intuitive decision about the relative size of two sets. In diagram B in Figure 2-1, a child using the "intuitive qualitative correspondence" schema would determine that set A seems to have more elements than set B, without counting or making a one-to-one correspondence.

Schemas are developed by a process of *adaptation,* which can take two forms: *assimilation* and *accommodation.* Assimilation of a schema occurs when one's existing cognitive structure requires little modification to include the new idea, and the new idea can be added to the existing structure. On the other hand, if no relevant schemas exist, new behavior sequences are built up through experimentation, instruction, or both. Piaget calls this process

FIGURE 2-1 Schemas for Determining If Sets Are Numerically Equivalent

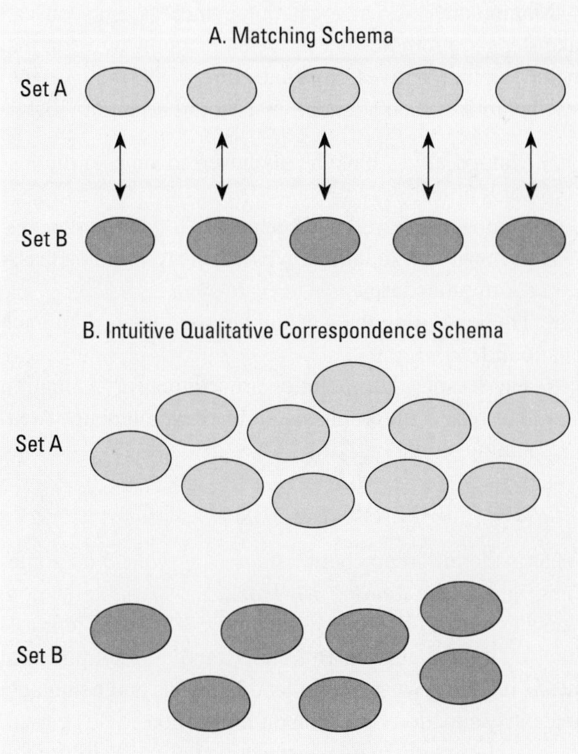

accommodation. The mechanism by which a schema is assimilated or accommodated into one's cognitive structure is an *operation,* an internalized action that can modify knowledge. Putting things into a series (for example, arranging sticks from shortest to longest) and constructing a classification (for example, sorting laundry by putting the whites in one pile and the colors in another pile) are examples of operations that help modify children's mathematical understandings.

The changed mental structures resulting from operations help move an individual through the developmental stages for which Piaget is so well known:

- Sensorimotor,
- Preoperational,
- Concrete operational, and
- Formal operational.

Research suggests that there is considerable variation in the age at which an individual enters a particular stage. The age is affected by many factors, including cultural considerations.

Piaget identified four factors that affect how rapidly an individual moves through these stages.

1. *Maturation:* the process of organic growth, a necessary but not a sufficient condition for certain behavior patterns to develop.
2. *Experience:* the physical and psychological experiences an individual has.
3. *Social transmission:* another name for teaching or the imparting of knowledge.
4. *Equilibration:* a process of bringing conflicting "ideas" into balance. It involves the notion of "self-regulation." For example, after a child acknowledges that two pieces of clay are the same size, the child is asked to flatten one and is then asked whether there is the same amount of clay in both pieces or if one has more than the other. Because some children are not yet ready to grasp the notion of the conservation of matter, flattening the clay may cause some disequilibrium in the child's thinking. To convince herself or himself, the child may restore the ball to its original shape and announce that both balls have the same amount of clay. This ability to reverse a transformation leads to a state of equilibrium in which the child knows that the transformation did not change the amount of clay.

Teachers do not have much control over maturation, but they can play a significant role in experience and social transmission and, to some extent, in producing equilibration through the quantity and quality of experiences they provide children.

Educational implications. Most children in the elementary grades are in what Piaget called the *concrete operations stage*. This means that elementary school children will learn mathematical concepts by manipulating materials and observing what happens. You must provide the kind of concrete experiences that will facilitate learning. Even for the middle school level, experience and research suggest that children are not yet able to think about many concepts at an abstract level and, in fact, still need concrete representations. Visual learners may continue to find such models helpful throughout their educational careers.

Piaget's *conservation* tasks provide us with methods for assessing readiness for certain concepts. Conservation involves recognizing that a change or transformation does not change the property in question. For example, a row of 10 counters still contains 10 counters when spread out or pushed together. "Spreading out" and "pushing together" are transformations that don't change the quantity of counters, but children who are non-conservers don't realize this. A number conservation task is described in Chapter 5, and several measurement conservation tasks are described in Chapter 15.

Piaget's work also has implications for sequencing the curriculum. For example, children seem to conserve numbers early in the concrete operational stage, while mass and volume are not conserved until the end of this stage. These findings suggest that formal measurement of area and volume should be delayed until intermediate grades.

Piaget's observations on knowledge development suggest that the ideal learning environment is one that allows the elementary and middle school child to explore ideas.

In mathematics learning, this is most effectively done with the aid of concrete manipulative materials.

Basic Principles Reviewed

Several basic principles can be derived from the work of Piaget and many others. The following six guidelines, based on this work, are essential to making mathematics instruction meaningful for all children.

Begin with Concrete Representation

Children seem to learn best when learning begins with a concrete representation of a mathematical concept. In fact, it is best to provide children with *multiple embodiments* of the concept. To provide multiple embodiments, the use of *manipulative materials* is essential in all mathematics classrooms. This does not mean that concrete manipulatives should be used exclusively. Other forms of representation are also important, including mental images and computer images (Clements & McMillen, 1996).

When building an understanding of the addition algorithm, have children set out bundles of popsicle sticks (or equivalent objects) and manipulate them to represent the process of addition (Figure 2-2). The use of different manipulatives at different times helps children to abstract the essence of the concept and lends variety to the mathematics program.

FIGURE 2-2 Using Manipulatives to Represent Addition

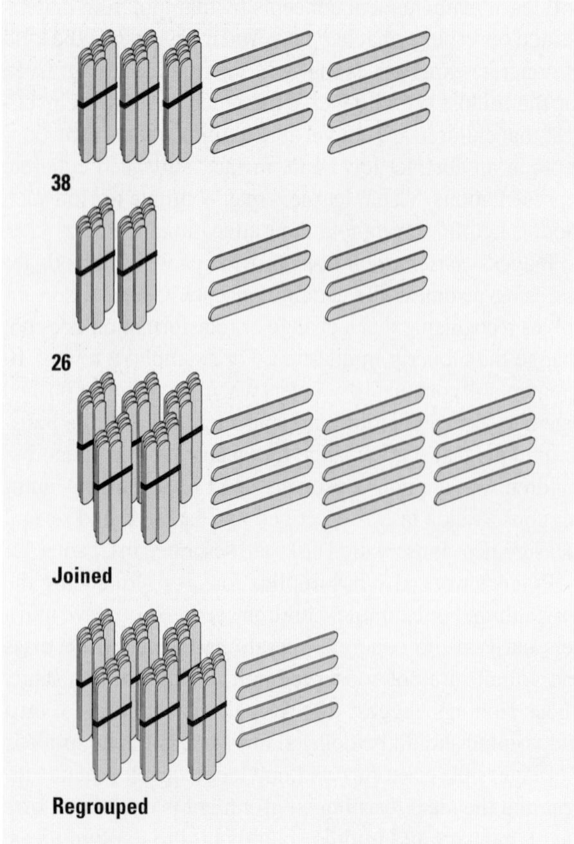

Manipulatives do not guarantee success, but you can take steps to promote success when planning a lesson that includes manipulatives. Ross and Kurtz (1993) suggest that when planning such a lesson, you should be certain that

- Manipulatives have been chosen to support the lesson's objectives.
- Significant plans have been made to familiarize children with the manipulatives and corresponding classroom procedures.
- The lesson involves the active participation of each child.
- The lesson plan includes procedures for evaluation that reflect an emphasis on the development of reasoning skills. (p. 256)

Develop Understanding

What is the difference between *knowing how to do* something and *understanding* it? Think about multiplication. Knowing how to multiply usually means knowing a procedure to find the answer. But understanding multiplication means realizing what multiplication means and being able to identify situations in which multiplication could be used.

A goal of mathematics instruction is for all children to develop a deep understanding of mathematics concepts. Structuring activities and experiences that enable children to build understanding is the essence of teaching.

Modes of representation. One way to help children develop understanding is for you to carefully select the *modes of representation* they use in instruction, or the way in which mathematics concepts are represented (Behr, Lesh, Post, & Silver, 1983). The five modes of representation include real-world situations, manipulative models, pictures, oral language, and written symbols (see Figure 2-3). For example,

FIGURE 2-3 Modes of Representation

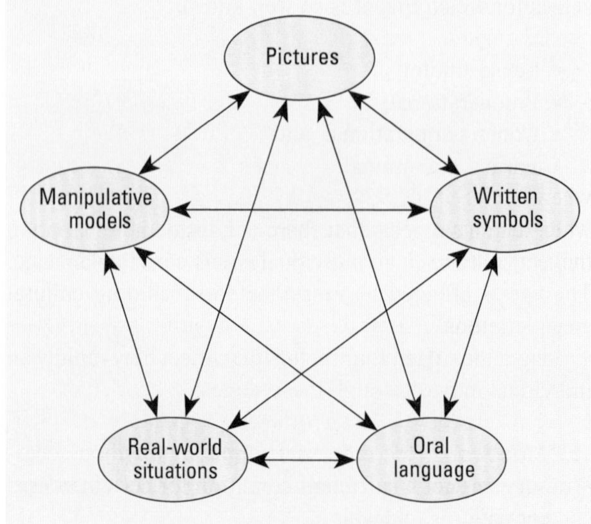

the concept of five might be represented with five fingers (real-world situation), with five Unifix cubes (manipulative model), with a picture of five flowers (pictures), by saying the word *five* (oral language), and by writing the word *five* or the symbol *5* (written symbols).

Using the preceding example of the concept of five, you might ask a child who has displayed five fingers whether she or he could show the same number in another way, such as by drawing a picture of five objects or picking up a group of five blocks. This is called *translation.* Translation refers to asking children to represent a concept in more than one mode and is indicated by the arrows in Figure 2-3.

Why is this concept important? Research shows that instruction in which children are encouraged to make translations between modes of representation enhances children's understanding. Thus, good teachers ensure that their lessons include a variety of modes of representation and opportunities for children to make translations between modes.

Hiebert (1990) states, "Meaning or understanding in mathematics comes from building or recognizing relationships either *between* representations or *within* representations" (p. 32).

Building relationships *between* representations occurs, for example, when a child listens (spoken language) to a problem, represents and manipulates it with blocks (concrete objects), and then writes a response on paper (written symbols).

Building relationships *within* representations often involves recognizing patterns within the representation. Hiebert (1990) uses the base-ten blocks in a decimal context as an example. In this setting, children can recognize the "pattern of *repeated* partitioning by 10 and the corresponding decrease in the size of the blocks" (p. 33), which could go on forever if the blocks could be cut finely enough.

Reflection enhances children's understanding of a concept. Reflection is often needed to observe patterns within a representational system. Teachers or children can encourage reflection by asking appropriate questions or by challenging each other's observations. Note again the importance of communication. For example, you might ask a child to compare his or her solution strategy with that of another child and to describe the differences.

Understanding of new concepts is more likely to occur when children understand prerequisite concepts than when they have only a superficial understanding or when they have learned previous skills and concepts by rote. Just as we would not consider building a house without proper footings, so children cannot build mathematical structures without meaningful prerequisite learning. For example, children who do not have a good understanding of the place-value concept often have considerable difficulty ordering decimal fractions. Rather, they sometimes arrange the decimals based on the number of digits (see Chapter 12).

NCTM Principles and Standards Link 2-1

Process Strand: Representation

Representations can help students organize their thinking. Students' use of representations can help make mathematical ideas more concrete and available for reflection. In the lower grades, for example, children can use representations to provide a record for their teachers and their peers of their efforts to understand mathematics. In the middle grades, they should use representations more to solve problems or to portray, clarify, or extend a mathematical idea. (NCTM, 2000, p. 68)

Making connections. Van de Walle (2004) points out that understanding is demonstrated when connections are formed between procedural knowledge and conceptual knowledge. *Procedural knowledge* is the knowledge of the symbolism used to represent mathematical ideas and the rules and procedures used to perform a mathematical task. *Conceptual knowledge* consists of relationships that connect a number of mathematical ideas or concepts. For example, the concepts of addition and subtraction are related: that is, knowing that $6 + 5 = 11$ helps one think about $11 - 5 = 6$. This conceptual knowledge greatly helps children acquire the procedural knowledge of addition and subtraction computation. An example that nicely illustrates the difference between knowing *how* and knowing *why* involves division of common fractions. Recalling and applying the rule "invert and multiply" is procedural knowledge; being able to explain or justify why it works is conceptual knowledge. Being able to see or make connections between conceptual knowledge and procedural knowledge is what Skemp (1989) calls *relational understanding* (Figure 2-4), an important goal to help children think mathematically.

Encourage Communication

Communication plays an important role in children's mathematics learning. It "forces" children to think through a concept, often resulting in more refined understanding. Highlighted in the NCTM standards, communicating in

FIGURE 2-4 Connections Leading to Relational Understanding

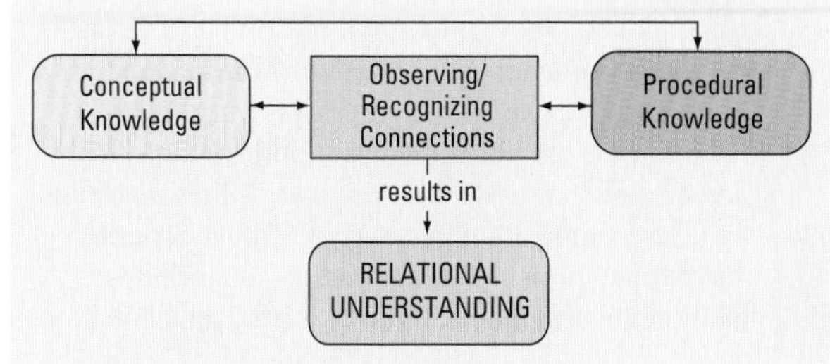

Literature Link 2-1

Why Do We Count?

Schmandt-Besserat, Denise. (1999). ***The History of Counting.*** New York: Morrow Junior Books.

Children use their own representations as a part of their mathematical development. Yet it is also important that they learn common representations, such as the numerals and number words used in counting and calculating in the base-ten system. In the historically accurate and beautifully illustrated ***The History of Counting,*** children can investigate the development of this precise and efficient system.

- Encourage children to create their own system of symbols for 1–30 and beyond. Have children describe how they will write very large numbers in their system.
- Demonstrate for children how to count using the ancient system of body counting presented in the text. How might ancient people recall which number is represented by a part of the body?
- Many objects have been used for counting throughout recorded history. Model interesting and efficient record-keeping systems, such as the *quipus* used by people of the Inca empire in Peru. Quipus were made from colored strings made of dyed cotton or wool. Using 10 as the base, the knots in the cords appeared in the 100s, 10s, and units positions. Children can easily represent these cords with colored string or yarn while reinforcing their understanding of our own system of place value.
- Use paint and Styrofoam cutouts of numerals in different numbers systems (such as Egyptian, Mayan, Babylonian, or Roman) to stamp numbers on cloth.
- Investigate the different ways that time has been recorded using ancient clocks (sundials, water clocks, sand clocks) and calendars (Aztec calendar). Have children collect and analyze information and draw illustrations to accompany their text information. Create a class book on the way time was recorded throughout history and call it ***The History of Time.***
- ***Mathematics,*** by Irving Adler, teaches children about angles, square numbers, Fibonacci numbers, the golden ratio, prime numbers, triangles, polygons, and square roots.

Source: Dr. Patricia Moyer-Packenham, Utah State University.

mathematics means encouraging children to engage in interactive conversations as they work through mathematical processes. Interactions with other children can help children clarify what they do or do not understand about mathematical concepts or processes. According to Stigler (1988), Japanese teachers spend more time than do most American teachers encouraging students to communicate verbally about mathematics concepts and procedures. It is time for American teachers to capitalize on opportunities to get students talking about mathematics.

Problems and models provide many opportunities for communicating about mathematics. In addition, talking and writing about mathematics helps children solidify their understanding of mathematics.

NCTM Principles and Standards Link 2-2

Process Strand: Communication

Students gain insights into their thinking when they present their methods for solving problems, when they justify their reasoning to a classmate or teacher, or when they formulate a question about something that is puzzling to them. Communication can support students' learning of new mathematical concepts as they act out a situation, draw, use objects, give verbal accounts and explanations, use diagrams, write, and use mathematical symbols. (NCTM, 2000, pp. 60–61)

Communication in the mathematics classroom can take many forms. It can be oral or written. It can be from child to child or between a child and the teacher. It can be a report, a story, a word problem for other children to solve, a description of how a child solved a problem, or an entry in a math journal. Keeping a journal is generally associated with the language arts discipline, but a math journal can be used to reinforce a child's understanding of mathematical concepts.

Math journals. A math journal serves many purposes. It offers an opportunity for children to think about and write about the mathematics concepts they are learning. Further, it provides teachers with an excellent assessment tool. Journals should be a regular part of mathematics class activities and can be included routinely as part of homework assignments.

Math journal prompts might include the following:

I think the answer is . . .

I solved the problem by . . .

Another way to solve the problem would be . . .

I still have a question about . . .

The thing I liked most was . . .

Literature Link 2-2

Learning to Talk Mathematically!

Schwartz, David. (1998). ***G is for Googol.*** Berkeley: Tricycle Press.

A critical mode of representation for children is oral language. Children learn to represent and defend their mathematical ideas through the use of language. ***G is for Googol: A Math Alphabet Book*** is filled with interesting mathematics vocabulary. The definitions are child friendly while maintaining mathematical accuracy. Mathematics words are given with their meanings, and the diagrams and illustrations support the explanations presented in the text.

- In addition to the mathematical terms given for each letter, other words on each page are presented for children to investigate. For example, on the "P is for probability" page, P is also for palindrome parabola, parallel, percent, pi, point, polygon, prime number, and Pythagorean theorem. Have the children investigate and make connections to find the mathematical significance of these additional words.
- Design your own mathematics alphabet book. Select one of the additional words listed in the book and create a child-friendly mathematical definition. Along with the definitions, use drawings, diagrams, and examples that would help children to understand the meaning of the mathematical terms.
- Copy and assemble the children's definition pages into one large alphabet book so that each child has his or her own copy for reference.

Source: Dr. Patricia Moyer-Packenham, Utah State University.

Communication in the mathematics classroom provides you with valuable insights into children's understanding, which helps you plan further instructions.

Make Connections

When children build connections between mathematical ideas and other content areas, mathematics becomes more meaningful and understanding is enhanced. Using a thematic approach is one way to build an integrated curriculum because it can address not only basic skills but also more open-ended and higher level objectives. Individual interests and other individual differences may be more easily accommodated in a thematic unit. The cooperative learning approach lends itself to thematic units.

Thematic units also provide opportunity to connect mathematics to real life through field trips and related activities. For example, as part of a theme about products and consumers, children might visit a nearby shopping mall (with permission from the administration) to conduct discussions with retail shop owners to see how mathematics knowledge is useful in their jobs. They could also calculate the total cost for each member of their small group to purchase a particular snack at one of the food outlets or observe and describe geometric shapes in the mall decor, observe slides, flips, and turns in shop logos, and so on.

Even without a thematic approach, however, many opportunities to integrate mathematics with other subjects are encountered daily. For example, an art teacher might reinforce one-to-one correspondence by having a child distribute one paint brush to every child in class. In physical education, children might measure distance and time, count when skipping, and keep track of scores and other statistics in games. Social studies and science lessons offer many opportunities for creating and interpreting graphs. Make sure to seize and discuss serendipitous opportunities so that children "see" the connection of mathematics to their in-school and out-of-school experiences.

Connections are not automatic. You must provide experiences in which the connections are "obvious" or at least where they can be made explicit, as described in the previous paragraph. This will encourage children to look for other connections and eventually to recognize the pervasive nature of mathematics in the world around them.

Take Time to Motivate Children

> Motivation fuels mathematical learning. If children are motivated, they attend to instruction, strive for meaning, and persevere when difficulties arise. Competent teachers, effective instructional models, and thought-provoking activities guide the process, but children must first be motivated to learn mathematics. (Holmes, 1990, p. 101)

NCTM Principles and Standards Link 2-3

Process Strand: Communication

Clarifying understanding. Through communication, ideas become objects of reflection, refinement, discussion, and amendment. Students who have opportunities, encouragement, and support for speaking, writing, reading, and listening in mathematics classes reap dual benefits: they communicate to learn mathematics, and they learn to communicate mathematically. (NCTM, 2000, p. 60)

NCTM Principles and Standards Link 2-4

Process Strand: Communication

Writing in mathematics can also help students consolidate their thinking because it requires them to reflect on their work and clarify their thoughts about the ideas developed in the lesson. Later, they may find it helpful to reread the record of their own thoughts. (NCTM, 2000, p. 61)

Motivating a child encourages the child to give attention, time, energy, and perseverance to learning. It is the willingness to accept the challenge to understand a concept or solve a problem. Motivation also is associated with the belief that one can succeed. Almost all children begin kindergarten with this belief. As the years pass, some lose faith in their ability, especially in mathematics. Thus, the level of motivation is one of many ways in which children within the classroom differ.

Although motivation is largely internal to each child, there are strategies you can employ to increase motivation. On a general level, individuals become motivated when the concepts they are learning are meaningful and when they experience satisfaction, success, and recognition. Communication and meaningful opportunities for students to engage in mathematics conversations about real-world problems can be very motivating, in addition to enhancing children's understanding of mathematics concepts. Give children meaningful tasks and assignments at which they can be successful, and then recognize their achievements.

More specifically, there are differences in what motivates children. So-called academically inclined children are motivated by achievement. Special challenges such as puzzles, nonroutine problems, and strategy games will capture their attention and increase motivation. Other children experience increased motivation when they can see the utilitarian value of what they are learning. Application or real-world types of activities should be designed for these children. This does not imply that certain children are given one type of experience exclusively. All children should experience different types of activities, although some may simply opt for a larger dose of one type than another. Variety in activities helps to enhance motivation.

In the literature, motivation has often been categorized as *extrinsic* (grades, stars, etc.) or *intrinsic* (internal interest and desire to learn). The goal of teachers is to engage children in motivating activities that offer extrinsic experiences and "light an intrinsic fire" related to mathematics in children.

Attitudes. Attitudes are an important part of motivation. Children who feel good about mathematics and their ability to do mathematics are often motivated to learn. On the other hand, children who have negative attitudes about

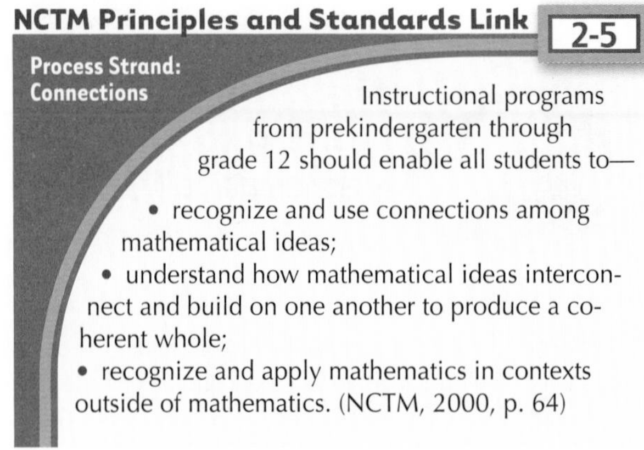
NCTM Principles and Standards Link 2-5

Process Strand: Connections

Instructional programs from prekindergarten through grade 12 should enable all students to—

- recognize and use connections among mathematical ideas;
- understand how mathematical ideas interconnect and build on one another to produce a coherent whole;
- recognize and apply mathematics in contexts outside of mathematics. (NCTM, 2000, p. 64)

mathematics or their ability in mathematics often exhibit disinterest. Given that there is a positive correlation between attitude and achievement in mathematics, it is important for you to provide experiences and the kind of environment that will foster positive attitudes. Minimal stress, emphasis on meaning and understanding rather than memorization, successful experiences, meaningful use of manipulatives, relating mathematics to the real world, and meaningful cooperative group work are some generalized guidelines for fostering the development of positive attitudes regarding mathematics.

It is essential to add that your attitude toward mathematics also is influential in forming children's attitudes. Being positive and enthusiastic while engaging in mathematics can make a difference in children's success. Your interest in mathematics and its connections to everyday life can affect your children's motivation to learn mathematics.

Provide Opportunities for Practice

The belief that mathematics needs to be meaningful and the idea that children construct their own mathematical knowledge do not rule out the need for practice. Practice contributes significantly to making routine procedures automatic. This results in more efficient execution of a procedure and, thus, to the expenditure of less mental effort (Hiebert, 1990). Expending as little mental effort as possible on a routine procedure is important because it allows one to give more effort to a more complex task of which the routine is only a part. If a person has to devote too much effort to the routine task, attention to the major task may be lost.

Practice does not have to be dull and boring, though. Games, puzzles, riddles, little surprises, and calculators all are useful ways of providing practice. Of course, this is not to say that worksheets, flash cards, and other traditional means of providing practice should not be used. The difference is in the purpose: thinking versus rote memorization. The following guidelines may be helpful in selecting activities for practice purposes. As a teacher, though, you will want to recognize that any one activity may not meet all of the guidelines.

To be effective, practice activities should

- Be based on a well-defined cognitive objective; they should not be "busy work."
- Be self-motivating and fun.
- Make use of the concept or procedure being reinforced in a new and interesting form.
- Be self-checking; that is, children should know when they have done it correctly.
- Be adaptable for use with the whole class, a small group, or an individual child.
- Provide for extension of knowledge; further exploration of an idea should be stimulated.

Games. Children enjoy playing games. Games certainly are self-motivating and fun and, in fact, meet most of the preceding guidelines for practice activities. Many games that meet specific mathematics objectives are available at educational and general merchandise stores, and are available for computers and hand-held digital games. More important, you can create or adapt games that are appropriate for the curricular objectives. For example, you might create a template (Figure 2-5) for a bingo-like game. By changing what goes in the cells and the nature of the calling cards, bingo-type games can be created to reinforce many different mathematical ideas and procedures. (If templates are created with a word processor, changes can be made quickly and easily.) Note the use of "I can" in the conventional "Free" space in Figure 2-5. Messages such as this can help to enhance a child's self-concept with respect to mathematics.

Puzzles and riddles. Various forms of puzzles and riddles can be used to provide interesting, often self-checking practice. Puzzles can range from simple join-the-dot pictures to complex pattern recognition. Magic squares could also be included in this category. The sample puzzle in Figure 2-6 involves placing numbers from 1 through 14, 3 in each box, so that the sum in each circle is 21. No number may be used more than once. Note that 3, 6, 7, 10, and 12 have been placed as starters.

FIGURE 2-5 Bingo Template

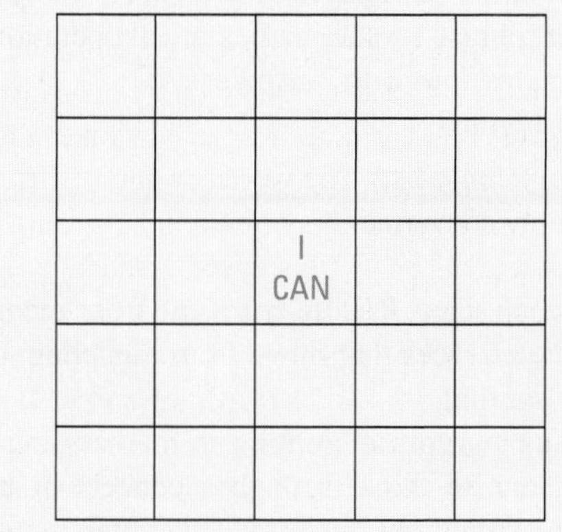

FIGURE 2-6 Sample Puzzle

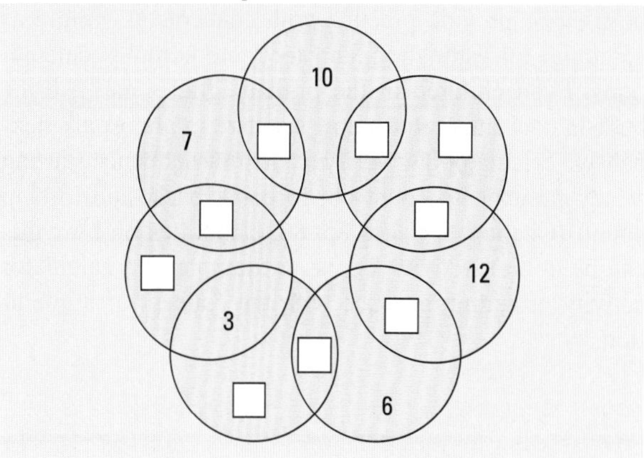

Riddles are closely related to puzzles. Many school libraries contain books with riddles of the type "What fish do you see at night?" It takes only a few minutes to turn these into interesting and useful practice exercises. Children can solve these types of riddles by completing a set of practice problems and then using a decoder provided to convert each answer to a letter. In our fish riddle for example, a solution of 19 might be replaced with the letter "A," spelling out the answer to the riddle, STARFISH.

Surprises. There are many little "surprises" in mathematics that can be used as warm-up activities at the beginning of a class. For example, you might give the following instructions:

1. Write a three-digit number in which the first and third digits are different by at least 2.
2. Reverse the digits to create a second number. Subtract the smaller number from the larger.
3. Reverse the digits in the difference and add to the difference.
4. Did you get 1089?

$$\begin{array}{r} 591 \\ \underline{195} \\ 369 \\ \underline{693} \\ 1089 \end{array}$$

A challenge such as "Do you think this will work for all three-digit numbers" will motivate children to do more of these problems. In the process, they will get a great deal of practice with addition and subtraction—and you don't have to photocopy a worksheet. This could also be turned into a problem-solving activity by asking children to explain why this process works.

The calculator as a practice tool. The calculator can be used to provide practice with concepts as simple as counting, for estimation, and for more complex calculations. Even children in the primary grades can use the built-in constant feature (now standard in almost all inexpensive calculators) to verify a counting sequence starting at any number, to count on, to count back, and to skip count. (Chapter 5, pages 85–86, elaborates on how this can be done.) Activity 2-1 is an example of a calculator activity providing practice with the concept of numeration.

ACTIVITY 2-1 Place Value on the Calculator

Materials Calculators

Procedure

1. Player A announces a number that all other participants enter into their calculators. (For example, Player A selects the number 972.)
2. Player A then announces which digit in the chosen number is to be changed to zero without changing any of the other digits. (For example, Player A wants the 7 in 972 to be changed to a zero—so the calculators would display the number 902.)
3. All remaining players attempt to change the given digit to zero by doing only one subtraction. (The correct answer in this example would be to subtract 70, because 972 – 70 = 902.)

Thinking About Teaching

Teaching mathematics requires thinking about three things: how children learn, the teaching process, and what to teach. The first has already been discussed; the latter two are the focus of this section, but first we start with a discussion of understanding the needs of each child.

Understanding Individual Needs

When thinking about teaching, we must consider factors related to meeting the needs of all learners. What is the role of communication in teaching and learning mathematics? How does the language of math affect children's understanding of math? How can we help English language learners succeed in mathematics? How can we prevent math anxiety? What are some myths about gender-related issues in learning mathematics?

Role of communication revisited. Earlier in this chapter, we stated that communication about mathematics significantly influences the mathematics curriculum and the learning of mathematics.

Communication also is an important factor in daily teaching activities and deserves additional comment here. The Principles and Standards states:

> When students are challenged to think and reason about mathematics and to communicate the results of their thinking to others orally or in writing, they learn to be clear and convincing. Listening to others' explanations gives students opportunities to develop their own understandings. (NCTM, 2000, p. 60)

Why are communication skills important in mathematics? Primarily because they help children clarify their thinking and sharpen their understanding of concepts and procedures. Representing an idea or problem in a different form, talking about a concept or algorithm, listening to explanations by others, writing a definition in our own words, and reading textual material all contribute to an individual's building mathematical understandings. Reuille-Irons and Irons (1989) state:

> Children's knowledge and excitement about mathematics grow if situations are provided to encourage discussion about their learning. This allows children to extend their own strategies and build new ones. It is important to plan learning experiences that will foster exploration and investigation. These activities will promote the use of language that can be gradually extended to more sophisticated ideas that might be associated with the important mathematical concepts. (p. 86)

Reuille-Irons and Irons go on to identify four sequential stages in which the development of language in mathematics can occur:

1. *Child's language.* This is the natural language of the child.
2. *Material language.* This is language that might be associated naturally with a specific representation of a mathematical idea. "Cover up" might be an example of a material-specific expression if pictures are being used to represent a subtractive situation.
3. *Mathematical language.* This involves using a word or short phrase for the mathematical operation.
   8 apples "put with" 2 apples
   Start with 3, "add" 5
4. *Symbolic language.* The words or phrases from stage 3 are now converted to symbols.

Within each stage, Reuille-Irons and Irons recommend language experiences that move from modeling aloud to creating to sharing.

The major purpose of writing in mathematics is that it "forces" one to think through a concept or process, resulting in a honing of one's understanding.

McIntosh (1991) suggests four useful forms of writing:

1. In *learning logs*, children can reflect on what they are doing and learning. For example, children may keep track of what problems they solved and how they solved them.
2. *Journals* are similar but often less formal and may, therefore, be more communicative than logs. They may also provide more insight into a child's feelings about mathematics than logs. For example, a child might describe his or her feelings about learning a concept or being involved in a mathematics activity.
3. In *expository writing*, children explain an idea or process. For example, a child may explain to a new student how she or he does multiplication.
4. *Creative writing* gives children a chance to use abilities not often a part of school mathematics. Children may write poems about mathematical ideas or stories about concepts, mathematicians, etc. Here are some examples:
   - Write a story about 6.
   - Write a story about shapes.
   - Write a poem about addition.

Writing about mathematics leads to enhanced understanding and increased achievement. Evans (1984) asked her Grade 5 children to engage in three kinds of writing: explanations, definitions, and troubleshooting (e.g., describe an error and tell why it was made). The children made much larger gains in achievement than a control class in which no writing was done other than what was required to answer questions, exercises, and problems.

Language influences. Admittedly, the language of mathematics is precise, and mathematical terms often have very specialized meanings. For example, the expression *fairly small* may be adequate in some settings, but if you were telling mission control how much rocket fuel was stored in and present for launching the shuttle, it is a totally inadequate expression of quantity.

However, even in mathematics, there is room for children's own informal language. Allowing children to use their own language when first learning about concepts enables them to focus more on the concepts. Their expressions will develop into more precise language as their understanding progresses.

The language used to convey a mathematical idea has a bearing on the child's understanding of the concept. For example, some children do not understand the term *perimeter.* If you talked about the "distance around" a shape, or if you drew a diagram and asked how much fencing would be needed to enclose the shape, many more children would understand and be able to successfully respond to the question. Likewise, the introduction of terms such as *commutative, associative,* and *distributive* serves no useful purpose if children have not already formed generalizations about these properties from repeated experiences examining them.

Another language-related factor of which you should be aware is children's ability to use mathematics vocabulary without really understanding the concepts. For example, most children can talk about a triangle, but there are many who think that a figure is not a triangle unless it is equilateral, or they might say that the figure on the left (see below) is a triangle. Others might argue that the figure at the right is not a triangle because one side is not horizontal or parallel to the bottom of the page. Children's misconceptions may be due to the visual images presented to them. Are the triangles you draw always equilateral in appearance? You must be aware of your own teaching behaviors.

Supporting English language learners (ELL). Currently many children in elementary and middle schools are English language learners whose first language is a language other than English. You must be careful not to confuse limited ability to communicate in English with limited potential for learning mathematics. Many teaching strategies are available, such as sheltered instruction, ESL (English as a Second Language), and SDAIE (Specially Designed Academic Instruction in English), to help children learn English as they learn mathematics. Strategies that many good teachers use to help all children learn mathematics, such as cooperative groups, manipulative materials, and visuals, are especially helpful for English language learners as well, as discussed in Chapter 1.

Herrell and Jordan (2008) discuss strategies for teaching English language learners. The following list contains several strategies that are particularly helpful in supporting mathematics learning.

- Visual Scaffolding: Providing language support through visual images
- Realia Strategies: Connecting language acquisition to the real world
- Manipulative Strategies: Using objects to connect concepts
- Cooperative Learning: Having groups interact to accomplish a goal
- Advance Organizers: Getting the mind in gear for instruction
- Preview/Review: Building vocabulary and concepts to support understanding
- Modeled Talk: Showing while you talk
- Attribute Charting: Organizing information to support understanding
- Word Walls: Displaying and organizing words for easy access

These strategies are discussed in more detail, with examples, in Chapters 5 through 17.

Mathematics anxiety. Mathematics anxiety, also known as math phobia, is a fear of mathematics. There is evidence that mathematics anxiety often starts in elementary school, although the symptoms often are not evident until years later. According to Burns (1998), "the way we've traditionally been taught mathematics has created a recurring cycle of math phobia, generation to generation, that has been difficult to break" (p. x).

Kennedy and Tipps (1999) list five teacher practices that contribute to mathematics anxiety: an emphasis on memorization, an emphasis on speed, an emphasis on doing one's own work, authoritarian teaching, and lack of variety in the teaching–learning process.

So what can you do to reduce or prevent math anxiety in children? Martinez and Martinez (1996) suggest that teachers use the following instructional strategies to prevent math anxiety:

- Create an anxiety-free math class, which could include seating children in circles and small groups, with the teacher taking on the role of facilitator of learning.
- Match instruction to children's cognitive levels.
- Plan instruction that connects mathematics to familiar situations in children's everyday lives.
- Incorporate math games and puzzles into instruction.
- Teach math through reading and writing.
- Empower children by using technology and collaborative learning.

Social factors can contribute to an individual's attitude and motivation to learn mathematics. Placing children in nonthreatening cooperative groups can improve their self-concept, raise achievement, and increase motivation for learning. Group work is as important in mathematics as it is in social studies, science, or any other school subject.

Social considerations may also include factors such as the child's home situation and the amount of sleep the previous night. A tense home situation can reduce a child's attentiveness and desire to learn. Furthermore, if an elementary school child was awake until midnight the night before a test, the child's performance will likely be below expectation.

The teacher significantly influences the social situation within the classroom. However, you cannot control factors such as a child's home situation or sleep patterns. Thus, parents, the child, and you share accountability for learning.

Myths about learning mathematics According to Ginsburg and Baron (1993), there are five myths about learning mathematics. It is important that all teachers be aware of the fallacy of these myths so that they can plan appropriate instruction.

Myth 1: Some children cannot learn math. There is no reason all children cannot learn math, provided that they have good mathematics instruction. It is a challenge to every teacher to expect that all children will succeed in mathematics and to use a variety of instructional strategies to help them do so.

Myth 2: Boys learn math better than girls. There is a persistent belief in our society that boys are better at mathematics than girls are. In fact, in recent years girls have actually closed the gap, particularly at the middle school and high school levels. Differences that do occur seem to be due more to cultural influences than ability differences. It is important to provide opportunities for all children, girls as well as boys, to fully experience a variety of mathematics experiences, and to have opportunities both to talk and listen in mathematics class.

Myth 3: Poor children and children from underrepresented groups cannot learn math. Many success stories point to the fallacy of this myth. The key components of programs that are successful for poor children and children from underrepresented groups include motivation, high expectations, role models, appropriate teaching, and real-world applications.

Myth 4: American children have less mathematical ability than Asian children. Differences in mathematics achievement emerge between American and Asian children after a year or two of schooling. However, these differences seem to be related not to ability but to differences in teaching and in expectations. For example, a common American notion is that "you're either good at math or you're not, and if you're not good at math, there's nothing you can do about it." We must change our expectations to believe that *all* children, given good teaching, can learn mathematics.

Myth 5: Mathematics learning disabilities are common. There are many cases in which children do not seem to learn mathematics. However, as illustrated by the previous myths about learning mathematics, usually this lack of achievement is due not to learning disabilities but to a lack of motivation and appropriate teaching.

Clearly, good math teaching is critical. A teacher who is motivated and knowledgeable can help any child to understand and achieve success in mathematics.

The Teaching Act

The teaching act is a three-phase process: what the teacher does *before* the lesson, what the teacher does *during* the lesson, and what the teacher does *after* the lesson. This is not a totally linear process. Each phase provides input or feedback or both for the others.

Preteaching Activities

Before teaching a lesson, you must understand the nature of your students, diagnose what they already know, decide on an appropriate approach that will make the content meaningful, and then plan the instructional sequence and activities in more detail.

Identifying children's learning needs. The first preteaching activity requires you to consider each individual child, who has unique learning needs, interests, attitudes, background, and motivation for learning. Identifying the needs of learners, including their prerequisite knowledge, should help make planning more individualized and thus more effective.

To make instructional decisions about current and future mathematical concepts children might be ready to learn, you must first determine what mathematics understandings children have already built. Only when you know what children understand and are still working on can you plan appropriate learning activities that will expand children's knowledge.

You can diagnose children's understanding in several ways: by administering a pretest, by conducting individual interviews of a few children in the class, or by carefully observing children involved in mathematics activities. Each of these types of assessment is described in Chapter 4. The key factor here is that rather than automatically teaching the next lesson in the textbook, a good teacher decides what lesson to plan next based on what the children understand and what they need to continue working on.

Lessons should involve learners in active engagement, with experiences that meet the needs of and yet challenge some students. Planned activities might take many forms: physical as well as mental, verbal as well as written. Activity choices should foster different opportunities for involvement. Note, however, that not all mathematical ideas will be learned as the result of one lesson. Individual mathematical abilities and skills develop over time, some more slowly than others, which will require greater patience and more careful planning on your part.

Children's active involvement, like the planned activities, needs to take many forms: physical as well as mental, verbal as well as written. You should plan for activities that foster, perhaps at different times, all of these forms of involvement. Because success is a powerful motivator, make sure you plan learning activities in which children will be successful. This does not necessarily mean that the activity is to be easy, however. If work is too easy, children lose motivation. Plan activities to be challenging but within the range of a child's ability to complete.

Using mathematics textbooks. Consider what mathematics textbook resources are available to you. Become familiar with the wealth of resources accompanying the textbook, including suggestions for modifying lessons to enhance the concept development through the use of manipulative materials, adaptations for special needs students, and lessons for enrichment or reteaching. Keep in mind that a textbook is meant to be a resource for a thoughtful teacher, rather than a prescription that you must follow.

Considering state and local standards. Another important consideration when planning lessons is the expectations of your local school district or state board of education. Think about what children are expected to learn, according to your state or local standards. How might you help them meet those standards?

> PEARSON myeducationlab The Power of Classroom Practice To enhance your understanding of planning with content standards go to IRIS Center Resources section of Topic 1: Planning and Teaching Mathematics in the MyEducationLab for your course and complete the module entitled "Content Standards."

Planning. There are two types of planning: unit planning and lesson planning. Unit planning focuses on planning a sequence of lessons on a particular concept, while lesson planning deals with daily lessons.

Planning mathematics units. Decisions and observations described above lead naturally into unit planning. The unit plan generally expands on one curriculum topic and includes lesson plans and teaching strategies for several days or several weeks. The unit plan might consist of a series of headings such as goals, standards, prerequisites, sequence of new skills to be introduced, developmental activities, practice activities, application of new skills, problem solving, enrichment activities, and assessing children's learning.

Another strategy for developing a unit plan is to use a *graphic organizer*. A graphic organizer is a pictorial organization of information about a particular topic, helping a student compress a lot of seemingly disjointed information into a structured, simple-to-read, graphic display. A graphic organizer for a unit on multiplication of a two-digit number by a one-digit number has been *started* in Figure 2-7. As you read more about specific instructional strategies for teaching multiplication, you could add to this graphic organizer. You must decide what type of format to use for unit planning. The process, rather than the form, is what is important.

Lesson plan formats. Lesson plans translate unit plans into daily activities and experiences for the children. As with unit plans, many special formats can be used. Some consist of as few as four components—objective, materials, procedures, and evaluation—some have much more complex outlines. The format will, in part, be determined by such considerations as your preferred teaching style, the nature of the activities, and the topic. Again, it is the process, rather than the format, that is important.

FIGURE 2-7 Two-Digit by One-Digit Multiplication

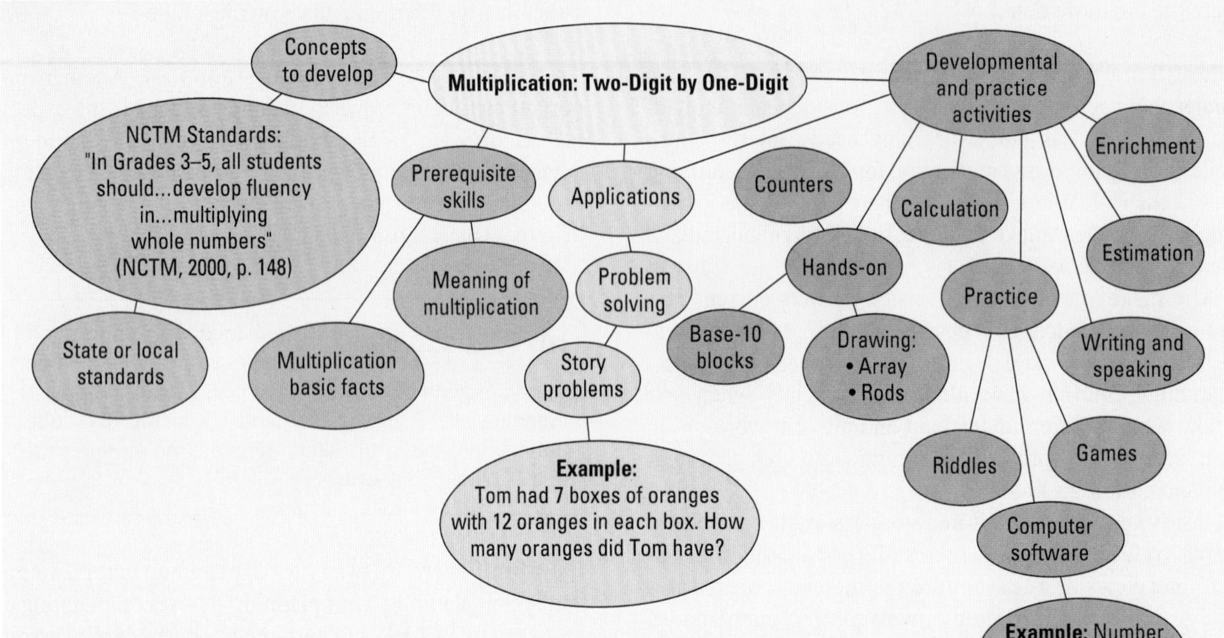

One format that is widely used is a three-part model. The names of the three parts vary. The following are some examples:

- Before—during—after
- Launch—explore—summarize

Whatever terminology is used, the critical elements of a three-part format are the same:

- In the first part you introduce the task, connect with prior knowledge, and motivate the children.
- The second part is the heart of the lesson, where the children are actively involved in exploring and describing mathematics concepts.
- The final part involves children's sharing and reflecting on what they learned, while you assess their understanding.

Each of these parts is important in supporting children's learning.

Planning mathematics lessons. Lesson planning involves several steps. Each step requires your careful consideration in determining what best meets children's needs.

1. Think about the mathematics. What should children learn about mathematics in this lesson? What is your long-term goal? What do the standards say children should understand about this topic?
2. Think about the learners. What do your children already know about this topic? What special needs should you keep in mind?
3. Choose the task. What should the children do to learn this concept?
   a. Review available resources, such as the mathematics textbook and other teacher resources, for tasks that will help children meet the objective.
4. Plan the three parts of the lesson, and write your lesson plan.
   a. Write the lesson objectives. What will children know and be able to do as a result of this lesson?
   b. What materials will you need?
   c. How will you launch the lesson? On what prior knowledge will you build? How will you motivate children and get them excited about the upcoming learning activity?
   d. What will children be doing in the "explore" part of the lesson? How will they construct their understanding of the topic? What do you expect that children will do? What might they have difficulty with? How will you provide guidance without "telling"? How will children communicate, reason, make connections, and solve problems? What representations will children use?
   e. Think extra carefully about the "summarize" portion of the lesson; it must be more than just having children put away their papers. How will you help children reflect back on what they learned? How will you use this part of the lesson to assess what the children have learned and what they may need more practice with?
5. Plan how you will assess children's learning. Lesson planning is time consuming but is crucial in providing

TABLE 2-2 Content Standards and Expectations: Number and Operations, Pre-K–2

Content Standards	Student Expectations
Instructional programs from pre-K–12 should enable all students to—	**In prekindergarten through Grade 2 all students should—**
• Understand numbers, ways of representing numbers, relationships among numbers, and number systems.	• count with understanding and recognize "how many" in sets of objects; • use multiple models to develop initial understandings of place value and the base-ten number system; • develop understanding of the relative position and magnitude of whole numbers and of ordinal and cardinal numbers and their connections; • develop a sense of whole numbers and represent and use them in flexible ways, including relating, composing, and decomposing numbers; • connect number words and numerals to the quantities they represent, using various physical models and representations; • understand and represent commonly used fractions, such as $\frac{1}{4}$, $\frac{1}{3}$, and $\frac{1}{2}$.
• Understand meanings of operations and how they relate to one another.	• understand various meanings of addition and subtraction of whole numbers and the relationship between the two operations; • understand the effects of adding and subtracting whole numbers; • understand situations that entail multiplication and division, such as equal groupings of objects and sharing equally.
• Compute fluently and make reasonable estimates.	• develop and use strategies for whole-number computations, with a focus on addition and subtraction; • develop fluency with basic number combinations for addition and subtraction; • use a variety of methods and tools to compute, including objects, mental computation, estimation, paper and pencil, and calculators.

Source: From *Principles and Standards for School Mathematics,* 2000, p. 78.

high-quality instruction that helps all children make sense of mathematics.

A sample lesson integrating content standards and process standards in grades pre-K–2. The following section contains a sample lesson within the number and operations content standard, appropriate for grade 2 children. Before describing the lesson, we list the goals of the lesson, using the appropriate expectations from the Content Standards and Expectations: Number and Operations, Pre-K–2 (NCTM, 2000, p. 78) and Curriculum Focal Points, which are listed in Tables 2-2 and 2-3. After a brief summary of the lesson, examples of the children's work are provided. Then you will find a brief description of how each process standard (problem solving, reasoning and proof, communication, connections, and representation) is woven into this particular lesson. Although every process standard comes into play in some way during the lesson, not every aspect of each process standard is addressed in this lesson.

TABLE 2-3 Selected Curriculum Focal Points, Grade 2

Strand and Focal Points	Description
Number and Operations: Developing an understanding of the base-ten numeration system and place-value concepts	Children develop an understanding of the base-ten numeration system and place-value concepts (at least to 1000). Their understanding of base-ten numeration includes ideas of counting in units and multiples of hundreds, tens, and ones, as well as a grasp of number relationships, which they demonstrate in a variety of ways, including comparing and ordering numbers. They understand multidigit numbers in terms of place value, recognizing that place-value notation is a shorthand for the sums of multiples of powers of 10 (e.g., 853 as 8 hundreds + 5 tens + 3 ones).
Number and Operations and *Algebra:* Developing quick recall of addition facts and related subtraction facts and fluency with multidigit addition and subtraction	Children use their understanding of addition to develop quick recall of basic addition facts and related subtraction facts. They solve arithmetic problems by applying their understanding of models of addition and subtraction (such as combining or separating sets or using number lines), relationships and properties of number (such as place value), and properties of addition (commutativity and associativity). Children develop, discuss, and use efficient, accurate, and generalizable methods to add and subtract multidigit whole numbers. They select and apply appropriate methods to estimate sums and differences or calculate them mentally, depending on the context and numbers involved. They develop fluency with efficient procedures, including standard algorithms, for adding and subtracting whole numbers, understand why the procedures work (on the basis of place value and properties of operations), and use them to solve problems.

Source: Curriculum Focal Points, 2006, p. 14.

Sample Lesson

Solving Problems Involving Multidigit Addition

Grade Level: Second

Materials: Make a variety of tools available to children such as

- Base-ten blocks
- Paper and pencil
- Counting frames (that have 10 metal rods with 10 beads on each rod).

Lesson Objectives: The learner will

1. Use multiple models to develop initial understandings of place value and the base-ten number system.
2. Develop a sense of whole numbers and represent and use them in flexible ways, including relating, composing, and decomposing numbers.
3. Develop and use strategies for whole-number computations, with a focus on addition and subtraction.
4. Develop fluency with multidigit addition and subtraction.
5. Use a variety of methods and tools to compute.

Launch: Ask children if they collect anything. Have children share their responses. Pose the problem below, noting that Ian collects shells. Ask children to work together in pairs to solve the following problem in two different ways:

Ian had 186 shells in his collection. Over the summer he went to the beach and collected 149 more shells. How many shells does Ian have now?

Explore: Children may select the tool that they are most comfortable working with to solve this problem. As the children solve the problem, move around the room, observing the children as they work, listening to children's strategies, and asking questions to help children clarify their thinking.

Summarize: After children solve the problem in two ways, bring the class back together and ask children to share their solution strategies. Carefully select children to share, based on what you observed during the group work. Here are a few of the children's solution processes.

Chris wrote:

$$\begin{array}{r} 186 \\ +\ 149 \\ \hline 200 \\ 120 \\ +\ 15 \\ \hline 335 \end{array}$$

He explained:

"I added 100 and 100 to get 200; then 80 and 40 is 120, and 6 and 9 is 15. I added 200, 120, and 15 to get 335."

The teacher asked Chris, "Why did you decide to start by adding the hundreds?"

Sarah said:

"149 is only 1 away from 150, so 150 and 100 from the 186 is 250, and 80 more is 330, and 6 more is 336. Then I have to subtract the 1, so it is 335."

The teacher recorded on her clipboard that Sarah used estimation to solve this problem.

Pat used base-ten blocks to solve the problem. Pat said:

> *"I took one flat for the 100 in 186 and 1 flat for the 100 in 149. I took 12 longs—8 for the 80 in 186 and 4 for the 40 in 149. I took 15 singles for the 6 in 186 and the 9 in 149. Then I counted like this, '100, 200,' then the longs: '210, 220, 230, 240, 250, 260, 270, 280, 290, 300, 310, 320'; then the singles: '321, 322, 323, 324, 325, 326, 327, 328, 329, 330, 331, 332, 333, 334, 335.' So the answer is 335."*

The teacher recorded on her clipboard that Pat used base-ten blocks to solve this problem.

A. J. wrote:

$$\begin{array}{r} {\scriptstyle 11} \\ 186 \\ +\ 149 \\ \hline 335 \end{array}$$

She explained:

> *"First I added 6 and 9 to get 15. I wrote down the 5 and carried the 1. Then I added 8 and 4 to get 12, plus 1 is 13; I wrote down the 3 and carried the 1 to get 1 and 1 and 1 is 3. So my answer is 335."*

The teacher asked A. J., "What do the ones that you wrote above the 186 mean?"

After several children share their solution strategies, and the class asks questions to make sure they understood each others' methods, ask follow-up questions such as the following:

- Which approach was easiest for you to use?
- Which approach was fastest for you to use?
- What if the numbers in the problem had been 200 and 350? Which approach would you prefer to use then?
- Could you pick an approach that you did not use this time and use it next time to solve the next problem? How are the approaches similar? How are they different?

When the students in the class finish their task of solving the problem in two different ways, ask the students to share. One student complains that Sarah did the problem wrong, since she started with 149 and not 186. Sarah claimed that it did not matter which number she started with. She would still get the same answer. The teacher asks the students if, when they add two numbers together, they will always get the same answer, no matter which number they begin with. Some agree, and others disagree. The teacher asks a student to restate the conjecture while the teacher writes it on the board. The teacher decides that they will discuss and test the conjecture the following day and that this conjecture is something for the students to continue to think about.

If some students have difficulty explaining their thinking, prompt them by asking follow-up questions such as the following:

- Did you start by adding the hundreds or the ones?
- You have some interesting writing on your paper. Can you show that to us?
- Has someone already shared an approach that was the same as yours? No? Can you explain what parts are different?

After several students have shared their approaches, ask about the relationships among and between the strategies:

- Who had strategies that were the same? What made them the same?
- Who had strategies that were different? How were they different?

Notice that the students in this class used a variety of representations to solve this problem. Chris and A. J. both represented the problem vertically on paper but used different approaches, and thus recorded their thinking in different ways. Pat represented the problem using base-ten blocks, whereas Sarah represented her thinking orally. The teacher encouraged the students to solve the problem in two ways to allow the children to think flexibly about the problem and also to encourage the students to use and make connections among different representations of the problem. For example, Pat's second approach was to write down with symbols what she had done with the base-ten blocks. She wrote 100 + 100, 200 + 10, 210 + 10, 220 + 10, 230 + 10, etc. She was thus making a connection between her work with the base-ten blocks and her work with the symbols.

Teacher's postlesson reflections. After school ended that day, the teacher reflected on the lesson. She recalled that four children shared very different strategies to solve this problem, including modeling with manipulatives (Pat), estimation (Sarah), the standard algorithm (A. J.), and an informal algorithm (Chris). She recalled that all the other children in the class successfully solved the problem as well. She considered what the next lesson should focus on. Since this lesson was centered on solving a three-digit addition problem and all children were successful, the next lesson might focus on a similar subtraction problem. The teacher made a note to continue to watch a few children closely: Pat, to help him gradually move toward using symbols to solve the problem, and Chris, to keep an eye on his strategy of adding from left to right.

Use of the process standards in this lesson. Each process standard was woven into the lesson within the content standard of number and operations. Although every process standard comes into play in some way during the lesson, not every aspect of each process standard is addressed. Table 2-4 describes how this was done in this lesson.

The Process of Teaching

There are many different models or styles of teaching. At a very simplistic level these have sometimes been described as being along a continuum from "pure telling" to "pure discovery" (Riedesel, 1990). No teacher operates at only one location along this continuum. Teachers normally have a region or range along the continuum in which they feel most "comfortable." Many of the decisions made in the preplanning stage will influence the teaching style for a particular lesson.

Models for teaching mathematics. Several models are available for teaching mathematics, including the developmental model, the diagnostic model, the translation model, and the investigative model.

Developmental model. A teacher with a constructivist theory of learning is likely to employ a *developmental model* of teaching in which children are actively engaged

TABLE 2-4 How the NCTM Process Standards Were Implemented in the Lesson

Process Standard	Standard Addressed	How Implemented in Lesson
Problem Solving What kinds of problem solving might children be engaged in?	By solving this problem in two different ways, students will • solve problems that arise in mathematics and in other contexts. • apply and adapt a variety of strategies to solve problems. • monitor and reflect on the process of problem solving. (p. 116)	By asking the students to solve a problem in two different ways, the teacher challenges the students to consider the variety of strategies that can be used to solve this problem. The teacher can then follow up with questions about the approaches so that the children can reflect on the process of problem solving.
Reasoning and Proof How could children demonstrate their arguments for reasoning and proof?	While discussing this problem, students will • make and investigate mathematical conjectures. (p. 122)	By asking the students to describe their solution processes, the teacher encourages the students to describe and justify their thinking.
Communication How might children communicate what they are thinking?	While discussing the various approaches classmates used to solve this problem, students will • communicate their mathematical thinking coherently and clearly to peers, teachers, and others. • analyze and evaluate the mathematical thinking and strategies of others. (p. 128)	By asking the students to share their solution strategies and by prompting students who have difficulty explaining their thinking by asking follow-up questions, the teacher assists students in communicating their thinking.
Connections What kinds of connections might children make?	In reflecting on their problem-solving processes, students will • recognize and use connections among mathematical ideas. • recognize and apply mathematics in contexts outside of mathematics. (p. 132)	By asking students to discuss the similarities and differences to solving the problem, the teacher is helping students to recognize similarities and differences among mathematical ideas.
Representation How would children represent what they are thinking?	While creating solutions to this problem, students will • create and use representations to organize, record, and communicate mathematical ideas. • select, apply, and translate among mathematical representations to solve problems. (p. 136)	By encouraging students to solve the problem in two ways, the teacher encourages students to think flexibly about the problem and to make connections among different representations of the problem.

Source: From Principles and Standards for School Mathematics, 2000.

in making sense of mathematics. Even then, there are times when an explanatory approach with the whole class is appropriate.

Riedesel (1990) identifies four aspects in which the "developmental" approach is different from the "telling" approach:

1. The developmental approach emphasizes *active* learning as opposed to waiting for the teacher to explain.
2. The developmental approach builds new knowledge on experience; therefore, it is socially relevant. The explanatory approach tends to build dependence on the teacher or a textbook.
3. Developmental approaches stress children's thinking; therefore, the classroom is learner centered. In an explanatory environment, children tend to wait to see what the teacher thinks.
4. The developmental approach emphasizes a "search for relationships and patterns and leads to an understanding of mathematical structure." (p. 12)

Diagnostic model. A *diagnostic model* places assessing children's current level of mathematical understanding at the core of the teaching process. That knowledge is then used to structure learning activities that will help the child build onto existing mathematical knowledge. A diagnostic model developed by Ashlock, Johnson, Wilson, and Jones (1983) suggested a sequence of five types of lessons arising from a diagnostic core:

1. *Initiating:* Provides experiences with the new concept to be learned.
2. *Abstracting:* Focuses on the attributes of the new concept to develop understanding.
3. *Schematizing:* Focuses on interrelationships between the new concept and previously learned concepts.
4. *Consolidating:* Provides practice to sharpen and clarify the new concept.
5. *Transferring:* Includes problem-solving activities that show application of the new concept to new settings.

Translation model. Earlier we referred to the claim of Behr. et al. (1983) that meaning in mathematics results from building or recognizing relationships *between* or *within* representations. Building relationships between representations leads to a type of *translation* model for teaching. You might state a problem (spoken language) and ask the children to represent (translate) it using concrete materials. At other times pictures may be used to represent the idea. Later, translations or connections will be made between verbal, concrete, pictorial, and symbolic representations (Sawada, 1985). The translation model may be observed most often in lessons involving the operations.

Investigative model. Children build mathematical knowledge when they explore and experiment with ideas, processes, or data. The *investigative model* focuses on experimentation as well as inquiry. A possible sequence of steps in such a lesson might be as follows:

- Structure a problem or make a statement that stimulates investigation.
- Then children do something—experiment, collect data.
- Record or summarize data. Discuss and decide on appropriate form (table, graph, chart, etc.) for the data.
- Analyze or interpret the data. Look for patterns, relationships, etc., and describe the pattern (oral, written, or both).
- Make a generalization or hypothesis and test with other data.
- Respond to the initial problem or statement, and then write a report on the experiment/project.
- Extend generalization to other problems, settings, or applications.

The preceding steps are not to be interpreted rigidly. They are fluid and flexible and will need to be adapted or modified for different problems and experiments. The emphasis is on exploration, experimentation, interpretation, hypothesizing, and generalizing. The investigative model fits well into a cooperative learning approach.

These models of teaching mathematics are not exclusive. Good teachers adapt a model based on their physical classroom setting, the nature of their children's needs, the children's individual differences, the mathematical topic, and their own philosophy of teaching and concepts that need to be covered.

Postteaching Activities

Your primary responsibilities in the postteaching phase include the ongoing activities of evaluation and reflection. Evaluation is the process of gathering information and using it to make judgments that in turn are used to make decisions. You should evaluate the lesson and your teaching, reflect on the teaching strategies used, and assess learning. (Assessment of children's learning is discussed in Chapter 4.)

Evaluation of teaching. According to NCTM (1991), the goal of evaluating mathematics teaching is to "improve teaching and enhance professional growth" (p. 72). Evaluation should be ongoing and linked to professional development. You should have opportunities to analyze your own teaching and discuss your teaching with colleagues and supervisors. Evaluation should be based on your goals and expectations for children, your plans, and evidence of children's learning and understanding.

The NCTM (1991) Teaching Standards lists many components of the evaluation of teaching. In general,

FIGURE 2-8 The Learner-Centered Classroom

When developing activities, lessons, or unit plans, consider if the learning environment fosters the development of all children s mathematical power.

Teaching Mathematical Concepts, Procedures, and Connections

- Do you have a sound knowledge of the mathematical concepts?
- Have children been given tasks that promote their understanding of those concepts?
- Have you engaged children in tasks and discussions that will enable them to see and use connections within mathematics and with other disciplines?

Teaching Mathematics as Problem Solving, Reasoning, and Communication

- Did you model different aspects of problem solving and engage children in activities and discussions related to a variety of aspects of problem solving?
- Did you model mathematics as communication, monitor children's mathematical language, and provide opportunities for children to engage in a variety of communication forms?
- Did you emphasize reasoning processes and provide opportunities for children to reason mathematically?

Promoting Mathematical Disposition

- Did you model a disposition to do mathematics?
- Did you demonstrate the value of mathematics as a way of thinking and its application in other disciplines and in society?
- Did you promote children's confidence, flexibility, perseverance, curiosity, and inventiveness in doing mathematics through the use of appropriate tasks and by engaging children in mathematical discourse?

Assessing Children s Understanding of Mathematics

- Did you use a variety of appropriate assessment methods?
- Did these methods match the level and background of the children and the way in which the concepts were taught?
- Did you analyze the results for reporting purposes and to modify future instruction?

the evaluation of teaching should focus on the teacher's ability to (1) teach concepts, procedures, and connections; (2) promote mathematical problem solving, reasoning, and connections; (3) foster children's mathematical dispositions; (4) assess children's understanding of mathematics; and (5) create a learning environment that promotes the development of each child's mathematical power.

Reflection on teaching. It is critical that you spend time reflecting on your instruction (Hart, Schultz, Najee-Ullah, & Nash, 1992), including the general approach to teaching and the type of learning activities developed for the children as well as the more overt teaching strategies. Such reflection results in professional growth. Self-evaluation of teaching practices and effectiveness is strongly encouraged in the Teaching Standards. Specific standards directly related to evaluation of teaching are presented in Figure 2-8.

Thinking About the Curriculum

The mathematics curriculum can be thought about at two levels: first, as the mathematics concepts, procedures, and processes to which the child is exposed; second, especially as it is experienced by the child, as all the activities and tasks the child engages in that are designed to help the child build some mathematical understanding. The beginning teacher is initially more concerned about what to teach; the more experienced teacher is probably more interested in the kinds of activities that help develop the concepts. However, every teacher needs to be concerned with both aspects.

The Mathematics

You need to know what mathematics knowledge the children have at the start of the school year, what concepts they are expected to learn during the year, and where these concepts will lead. Consider what the standards expect children to understand about mathematics at this grade level. Assess children's understanding to see what they already know about these topics. Examine the textbook series and curriculum guide used in the school district, as well as the end-of-year assessment that children are required to complete.

You must assess what mathematical understandings the children actually possess and then adapt the stated curriculum so that children understand prerequisite skills and concepts before attempting to build new ones.

The Activities

The real curriculum consists of much more than the concepts listed in a mathematics curriculum guide or state or district standards. It is the total of all the mathematics-related experiences a child has, both in and out of school. These experiences include playing counting games at recess, going to the store to purchase something after school, and engaging in the activities designed by the teacher. All such experiences contribute to a child's construction of mathematics knowledge.

When selecting or developing mathematics activities for children, it is important that you keep in mind the standards that the children are expected to meet so that you can clearly write objectives for each lesson and goals for each unit.

Conclusion

The importance of meaning or understanding in learning mathematics cannot be overemphasized. The model shown in Figure 2-9 may help focus the picture. It shows meaning as a function of the child's exploration, often, but not exclusively, with concrete models, construction, and communication—all active, not passive, processes.

Teaching mathematics requires hard work. A teacher's task is to create and help children create for themselves representations of mathematical ideas that will enable the child to build a significant mathematical knowledge structure. To do this effectively, you must be

- Cognizant of how children learn mathematics;
- Familiar with the mathematics included in the curriculum;
- Able to design strategies and activities that will help children learn the concepts meaningfully; and
- Able to assess the level of development of the concept in children.

FIGURE 2-9 The Process of Making Meaning

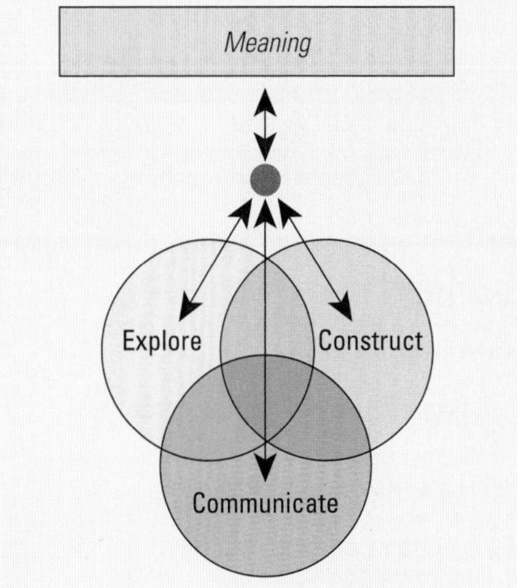

A child's attitude toward mathematics must also be assessed and that information should be used to plan activities that will generate a positive attitude.

IN PRACTICE

Complete the following activities to include in your professional portfolio.

1. Explain the five different modes in which a mathematics concept may be represented, and give an example of each for a concept of your choice.
2. Write a lesson plan for a concept of your choice. Include at least two different modes of representation in this lesson, and describe the translations that take place during the lesson.
3. Write a lesson plan that develops conceptual knowledge for a concept of your choice.
4. Write a lesson plan that includes several forms of communication to teach a mathematics concept of your choice.

PEARSON myeducationlab The Power of Classroom Practice Now go to Topic 2: "Children's Mathematical Thinking" in MyEducationLab (www.myeducationlab.com) for your course where you can:

- Find learning objectives for "Children's Mathematical Thinking" along with the national standards that connect to these objectives.
- Complete Assignments and Activities that can help you more deeply understand the chapter content.
- Apply and practice your understanding of the core teaching skills identified in the chapter with a Building Teaching Skills and Dispositions learning unit.
- Check your comprehension on the content covered in the chapter by going to the Study Plan in the Book-Specific Resources for your text. Here, you will be able to take a chapter quiz, receive feedback on your answers, and then access Review, Practice, and Enrichment activities to enhance your understanding of chapter content.

LINKS TO THE INTERNET

The Educator's Reference Desk

http://www.eduref.org/cgi-bin/lessons.cgi/Mathematics

Contains many resources for teachers, including more than 2,000 lesson plans.

ProTeacher

http://www.proteacher.com

Contains lesson plans and education news.

Education World

http://www.educationworld.com/math/

Contains lesson plans and other resources for teachers.

RESOURCES FOR TEACHERS

Reference Books: Preventing Math Anxiety

Aren, C. (2002). *Conquering math anxiety.* Florence, KY: Brooks Cole.

Burns, M. (1998). *Math: Facing an American phobia.* Sausalito, CA: Math Solutions.

Martinez, J., & Martinez, N. (1996). *Math without fear.* Needham Heights, MA: Allyn & Bacon.

Tobias, S. (1995). *Overcoming math anxiety.* New York: W.W. Norton & Company.

Children's Literature

Bay-Williams, J. & Martinie, S. (2004). *Math and literature, Grades 6–8.* Sausalito, CA: Math Solutions.

Bay-Williams, J. & Martinie, S. (2004). *Math and nonfiction, Grades 6–8.* Sausalito, CA: Math Solutions.

Bresser, R. (2004). *Math and literature, Grades 4–6* (2nd edition). Sausalito, CA: Math Solutions.

Burns, M. & Sheffield, S. (2004). *Math and literature, Grades K–1.* Sausalito, CA: Math Solutions.

Burns, M. & Sheffield, S. (2004). *Math and literature, Grades 2–3.* Sausalito, CA: Math Solutions.

Petersen, J. (2004). *Math and nonfiction: Grades K–2.* Sausalito, CA: Math Solutions.

Sheffield, S. & Gallagher, K. (2004). *Math and nonfiction: Grades 3–5.* Sausalito, CA: Math Solutions.

Thiessen, D., Matthias, M., & Smith, J. (1998). *The wonderful world of mathematics.* Reston, VA: National Council of Teachers of Mathematics.

Ward, Robin A. (2008). *Literature-Based Activities for Integrating Mathematics with Other Content Areas,* (editions for K–2, 3–5, and 6–8) Boston, MA: Pearson Education.

CHAPTER

Developing Mathematical Thinking and Problem-Solving Ability

NCTM CONNECTING WITH THE STANDARDS

The National Council of Teachers of Mathematics (NCTM) Principles and Standards stresses the importance of problem-solving experiences, stating that children "should have frequent opportunities to formulate, grapple with, and solve complex problems that require a significant amount of effort and should then be encouraged to reflect on their thinking" (NCTM, 2000, p. 51). The NCTM document goes on to note that "by learning problem solving in mathematics, students should acquire ways of thinking, habits of persistence and curiosity, and confidence in unfamiliar situations that will serve them well outside the mathematics classroom" (p. 51).

myeducationlab The Power of Classroom Practice — Go to the Video Examples section of Topic 3: Problem Solving in the MyEducationLab for your course to view the Annenberg clip "This Small House."

Teacher Bobbi Bateson uses problem solving to engage her second- and third-grade children in solving interesting problems based on real-world situations. In "This Small House," Ms. Bateson's children decorated "homes" they had constructed out of milk cartons. The children had only $1 each to cover and decorate the interior and exterior of their homes, including furniture, carpet, and wall coverings.

Children worked in pairs, with one child serving as the homeowner and the other child serving as the decorating consultant. The children were given a list of items they could use to create floors, curtains, wall coverings, furniture, and so on. The unit cost of each material was provided to help children develop their decorating plans. The chart on the next page identifies the materials children could use, suggestions for using the materials, and the cost of each item.

After completing their decorating plan, each pair of children went to the classroom store, selected and purchased their materials, and paid for them, with the child serving as the decorating consultant responsible for making change and completing the transaction. Then the children went back to their tables and used the purchased materials to compete the renovations to their milk-carton homes.

Developing Your Math Teaching Skills

When you have finished studying this chapter, you should be able to do the following:

- Describe what constitutes a true problem.
- Describe four different types of problems and discuss how they differ from each other.
- List and describe the four steps involved in the problem-solving process.
- Discuss why problem solving is integral to mathematics instruction.
- Discuss several problem-solving strategies and give an example of each.

While the children were working, Ms. Bateson circulated around the classroom, observing them and asking clarifying questions. Children sometimes had difficulties planning correct measurements, organizing their work, or finding their errors, but a question or two from Ms. Bateson usually helped them move forward in solving the problems.

This lesson illustrates how children who work together can solve a problem. According to Ms. Bateson, "The children, by working together, are able to do a lot of problem solving that they might not be able to do on their own. One child might say something that would spark another child's idea, and they could go on to solve a problem in that direction. By the same token, it's teaching them that they can be coming to the same answer from different directions, and that that's okay."

One important role elementary teachers play is to help children develop an ability to use mathematics to solve problems. This chapter focuses on helping you develop those abilities in children.

Items Available for Decorating Milk-Carton "Homes"

Item	Possible Uses	Cost
Contact paper	Flooring	8¢ per square
Felt squares	Rugs	11¢ per square
Fabric	Curtains	11¢ each
Yarn	Trimming	5¢ per yard
Poster board	Shutters, stairs, flooring, decks	7¢ per small square, 12¢ per large square
Gift wrap and wallpaper	Wall coverings	5¢ each
White paper squares	Paintings, pictures	2¢ each
Bottle caps, lids, and boxes	Furniture	8¢ each

Problem Solving: An Integral Part of Mathematics Instruction

> A teacher of mathematics has a great opportunity. If he fills his allotted time with drilling his students in routine operations, he kills their interest, hampers their intellectual development, and misuses his opportunity. But if he challenges the curiosity of his students by setting them problems proportionate to their knowledge, and helps them to solve their problems with stimulating questions, he may give them a taste for, and some means of independent thinking. (Polya, 1957, p. v)

Problem solving is a daily activity for most people. A college student considers the most efficient route to the campus from a number of alternatives. A parent examines the contents of the cupboard, wondering what to prepare for dinner. A 10-year-old wants to buy an ice cream bar at the local store. She knows that she has several coins in her pocket and recalls that she has at least two quarters. Before approaching the cashier, she wonders whether she has enough money to buy a 75-cent ice cream bar.

There has been a resurgence during the past three decades of interest in problem solving as an integral part of the mathematics curriculum. Although problem solving has always been a part of mathematics programs, during the 1980s, the NCTM and other influential groups promoted problem solving as a significant component of mathematics programs. More recently, the NCTM has reiterated the importance of problem solving in mathematics learning by designating it as one of the five process standards for Grades pre-K–12 in the *Principles and Standards* (NCTM, 2000). The council notes that "problem solving is an integral part of all mathematics learning, and so it should not be an isolated part of the mathematics program" (NCTM, 2000, p. 52). This focus on problem solving may be interpreted as a shift from a concern with algorithms or fixed content toward an emphasis on mathematical thinking and inquiry.

This chapter is about teaching and learning considerations that involve children in solving problems so that they will develop mathematical thinking abilities and learn mathematics via problem solving. It is also about teaching children how to solve problems. Different strategies that

NCTM Principles and Standards Link 3-1

Process Strand: Problem Solving

Instructional programs from prekindergarten through grade 12 should enable all students to:

- build new mathematical knowledge through problem solving;
- solve problems that arise in mathematics and in other contexts;
- apply and adapt a variety of appropriate strategies to solve problems;
- monitor and reflect on the process of mathematical problem solving. (NCTM, 2000, p. 52)

children should learn to enable them to devise solution plans are discussed. Problem examples with some solution processes also are provided.

Mathematical Considerations

The science of mathematics was born from people's efforts to understand their environment. The process of solving environmental problems led to the discovery of mathematical facts, which in turn enabled people to solve other problems. Children can experience the power and usefulness of mathematics through the process of problem solving. When children are asked to solve problems that are meaningful and interesting, they will wholeheartedly engage in problem-solving activities.

What Is a Problem?

Charles and Lester (1982) define a mathematical problem as a task for which

1. The person confronting it *wants* or *needs* to find a solution;
2. The person has *no readily available procedure* for finding the solution; and
3. The person must *make an attempt* to find a solution. (p. 5)

From this definition, it would seem that the traditional story problems found at the end of textbook chapters do not qualify as problems. Generally, there is no evidence that children want to work at this type of problem. Usually, children quickly glance at the problem to note word clues (*altogether, left, times*), then immediately apply some operation to the data to arrive at an answer. Solving this type of problem hardly serves to develop one's mathematical thinking. Thus, other kinds of problems must be included in mathematics programs if children are to develop their thinking processes. This chapter will focus on non-routine problems; story problems or word problems will be discussed in Chapter 7.

Children must be presented with some interesting and challenging problems so that they will gain experience in analyzing information and in proposing and testing hypotheses. It is essential that they be given the opportunity to develop their problem-solving and reasoning abilities.

Types of Problems

We will discuss four different types of problems: process problems, translation problems, application problems, and puzzles.

Process problems. Process problems are a type of mathematics problem that requires solution processes other than computational procedures. Such problems are important because of the processes used in solving them. Two examples of process problems follow.

NCTM Principles and Standards Link 3-2

Process Strand: Problem Solving

By learning problem solving in mathematics, students should acquire ways of thinking, habits of persistence and curiosity, and confidence in unfamiliar situations that will serve them well outside the mathematics classroom. In everyday life and in the workplace, being a good problem solver can lead to great advantages. (NCTM, 2000, p. 52)

PROBLEM 3-1: Air Show

At an air show, 8 skydivers were released from a plane. Each skydiver was connected to each of the other skydivers with a separate piece of ribbon. How many pieces of ribbon were used in the skydiving act?

According to Polya (1949), "to solve a problem is to find a way where no way is known off-hand, to find a way out of a difficulty, to find a way around an obstacle, to attain a desired end that is not immediately attainable, by appropriate means" (p. 1). From this definition, it is clear that problem solving involves higher-order thinking, forcing children to think creatively and innovatively to find a new way to solve a problem. In solving a process problem, one uses available knowledge and employs certain strategies to devise a solution. Have you tried solving the air show problem? If not, try it, and then review the following solution.

A SOLUTION TO THE AIR SHOW PROBLEM

Skydiver 1 (S1) is connected to 7 skydivers. Each skydiver is connected to 7 other skydivers.

But it takes one ribbon to connect S1 to S2 and S2 to S1. Therefore, the total number of ribbons used is $56 \div 2 = 28$. Twenty-eight ribbons are needed.

Other strategies that could be used to solve this problem are construct a diagram, model the situation, and solve a simpler problem. These strategies are discussed in a later section. Try them.

Prior to the 1980s, process problems were not usually found in mathematics textbooks for the elementary grades. Currently, process problems are an important part of most mathematics programs, and one can expect that their importance will increase.

 Go to the Assignments and Activities section of Topic 3: "Problem Solving" in the MyEducationLab for your course. Complete the activity "Finding Area" to see how one teacher incorporates problem solving into instruction.

NCTM Principles and Standards Link 3-3

Process Strand: Problem Solving

Problem solving means engaging in a task for which the solution method is not known in advance. In order to find a solution, students must draw on their knowledge, and through this process, they will often develop new mathematical understandings. (NCTM 2000, p. 52)

Although process problems are an important component of a mathematics program, other types of problems should also be included. These are the kinds of problems that have traditionally been a part of programs, namely, translation and application problems.

Translation problems. Translation problems include the one- and two-step story problems typically found in textbooks. These problems can be a vehicle to help children develop understanding of the basic operations or to construct their own computational algorithms. Approached in this way, story problems can enhance children's knowledge of mathematics and their mathematical thinking. Review the following two examples of translation problems. Note that if story problems are presented to children after they have learned how to compute, then the problems are mere practice exercises, and they do not help to develop problem-solving ability.

PROBLEM 3-2: Seating Capacity
A school auditorium can seat 648 people in 18 equal rows. How many seats are there in each row?

PROBLEM 3-3: Jogging Rate
Ryan jogged 2 miles in 15 minutes. At this rate, how long would it take him to jog 26 miles?

Application problems. Solve the following application problem to see how this type of problem differs from process and translation problems.

PROBLEM 3-4: Electricity Costs
How much does the school board pay for the electricity used in your school in a school year? What is the average monthly cost?

Children generally solve application problems using computation. Once the required data have been gathered and a decision has been made about a solution process, a calculator can reduce the time needed to arrive at an answer. Solving applied problems that are of interest to children can enhance their appreciation of mathematics. Recall Ms. Bateson's lesson. How did the children utilize calculators in this lesson?

Puzzles. Children love to solve puzzles. Puzzles are the fourth type of mathematical problems.

PROBLEM 3-5: Nine-Dot Puzzle
Can you join all nine dots using four straight lines without lifting your pencil from the paper?

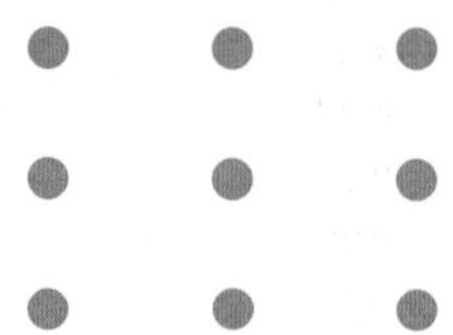

PROBLEM 3-6: Four Congruent Parts
Can you partition the figure into four congruent parts?

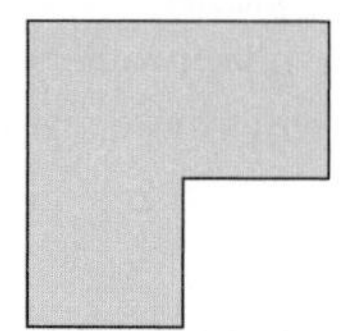

It is sometimes difficult to identify what strategy to use to solve a given puzzle. Usually, mathematical processes such as visualization, analysis, conjecturing, and testing are involved. Did you use any of the skills to solve the puzzles? The solutions follow.

SOLUTIONS TO PROBLEMS 3-5 AND 3-6

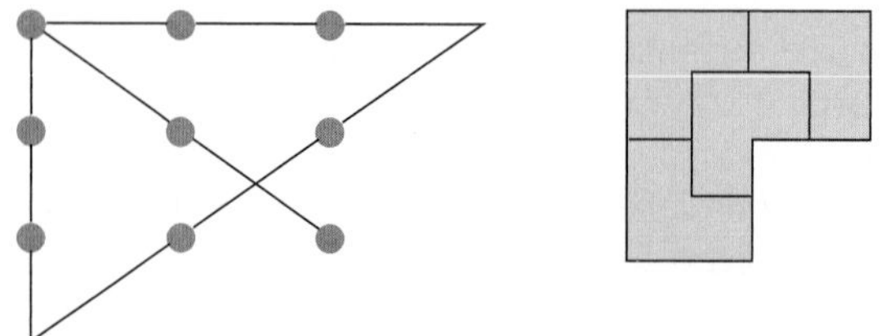

The Problem-Solving Process

You can help children become successful problem solvers by helping them understand and use the four phases of the problem-solving process. Polya's (1957) four phases of problem solving have become the framework often recommended for teaching problem solving. Help children

1. Understand the problem;
2. Devise a plan to solve the problem;
3. Implement a solution plan; and
4. Reflect on the problem.

Understanding the Problem

This first phase of the problem-solving process is important, although some children do not see it as such. Children who do not try to understand the problem look for word clues, or they quickly decide on an operation to apply to the data. Instead, this first phase of problem solving should be stressed so that children will come to see the need for understanding a problem.

Understanding a problem is more than a matter of reading comprehension. It consists of identifying the goal being sought, differentiating between required information and extraneous information, and detecting missing information. It also involves checking for assumptions regarding the given conditions.

Provide time for children to familiarize themselves with a problem. Familiarization can happen by rereading the problem in an effort to visualize the situation. Children can be encouraged to "see in their mind the problem situation" and "tell the problem story to themselves." Children can also be asked to tell the problem story to the class in their own words. The intent here is to have children verbalize the problem clearly and succinctly, giving all necessary information to solve the problem. Questions to ask children include the following:

- How would you tell the problem story?
- Can someone describe the problem another way?
- Did __________ give all the important information?
- Is there something that needs to be added to what was said?
- Could some information that __________ gave have been left out?
- What will you know when you have solved the problem?

When children understand a problem, they are more likely to accept the problem and devote themselves to finding a solution.

Devising a Plan to Solve the Problem

Allow time for children to reflect on possible solution processes. You might invite children to share possible solution strategies with one or two classmates. A group of children working together may discuss possible solution strategies. A child would tell the group why she or he thinks a particular strategy is an appropriate one for a given problem. The group may then decide to try a common strategy or have each member try a different strategy.

For a potentially difficult problem, you might invite the class as a whole to discuss solution strategies. This sharing can provide ideas for children who are stumped as to how to begin, without removing the challenge to develop a solution process.

Whenever appropriate, encourage children to make an estimate about the quantity, measure, or magnitude of the solution before proceeding to implement a solution plan. The estimate can be revised as they progress through the solution process and recorded as a first estimate, second estimate, and so on. Making estimates requires that children reflect on what is happening and "think ahead," which can assist them in "seeing" a solution pattern without having to work through all the cases of the problem.

Implementing a Solution Plan

When children have personally decided on a plan, they begin to implement it to find a solution. Children should be allowed and encouraged to use their own ingenuity to develop a solution plan. Figure 3-1 depicts three different tables that fifth-grade children constructed to solve the same problem. Children enjoy the freedom to select and develop solution processes rather than being forced to follow uniform procedures.

Children should be encouraged to solve problems in different ways and to discuss the different solution processes. For example, elementary school children could solve the Barnyard problem in Figure 3-2 by drawing a picture, through trial and error, or by constructing a table and considering all possibilities. Middle school children could possibly solve the problem algebraically by writing an equation, as shown in part d of Figure 3-2.

In addition, suggest that children develop their solution process in detail, without erasing "mistakes" or partial solutions. By commenting on the different approaches, you can help children realize that processes that don't work can be informative in subsequent problem-solving activities. The analogy can be made to a scientist's performing numerous experiments in an effort to discover, for example, a cure for a disease. A scientist does not destroy unsuccessful experimental results but keeps the data to inform further research efforts. Likewise, when children are trying to solve a problem, comparisons can be made with previous attempts to solve a somewhat similar problem. Recorded problem-solving attempts can also provide insights into children's thinking and assist you in assessing their understanding.

When engaging in problem-solving activities, children should not expect to find a solution to every problem they attempt to solve. The activity of problem solving, that is, the attempt, often is as important as finding the solution.

Reflecting on the Problem

You should encourage children to reflect on their solution process after an answer has been reached or while working through a solution strategy. For example, pausing to reflect on one's approach to solving a problem may lead one to abort a plan and seek another solution strategy.

After finding a solution, ask children to *look back* to the problem to see whether the conditions of the problem have been met. Did they make the correct assumptions? Did they answer the problem question? Is the answer unique, or are there other answers?

At this stage, also invite children to reflect on the solution process and to think of other appropriate solution strategies. They might note that the problem could have been solved not only by a different approach but also through a more efficient process.

Also encourage children to *look forward* for ways to extend a problem. Asking the question "What if . . . ?" is a good approach to modifying a problem. Changing one aspect of a problem, such as the setting, the conditions, or the data, and then attempting to solve the new problem can lead to insightful learning. It is also worthwhile to ask how the

FIGURE 3-1 Solutions for a Problem

Problem:
Josh has 3 pairs of pants, 4 sweaters, and 2 pairs of shoes. How many different pant-sweater-shoes combinations can Josh choose from to wear to school on Monday?

Solution 1 (Paula, Grade 5)

Sweaters				Pants			Shoes		Sweaters				Pants			Shoes	
O	Y	B	W	B	B	A	B	G	O	Y	B	W	B	B	A	B	G
X				X			X		X				X				X
X					X		X		X					X			X
X						X	X		X						X		X
	X			X			X			X			X				X
	X				X		X			X				X			X
	X					X	X			X					X		X
		X		X			X				X		X				X
		X			X		X				X			X			X
		X				X	X				X				X		X
			X	X			X					X	X				X
			X		X		X					X		X			X
			X			X	X					X			X		X

24 Combinations

Solution 2 (Mark, Grade 5)

P	S	SH	
Jeans	Fluorescent	Reeboks	Vision Streetwear
Joggers	Rockshirt	Reeboks	Vision Streetwear
Acid Washed	White	Vision Streetwear	Reeboks
Jeans	Trappers	Vision Streetwear	Reeboks
Jeans	Rockshirt	Reeboks	Vision Streetwear
Jeans	White	Vision Streetwear	Reeboks
Joggers	Trappers	Reeboks	Vision Streetwear
Joggers	Fluorescent	Vision Streetwear	Reeboks
Joggers	White	Reeboks	Vision Streetwear
Acid Washed	Trappers	Vision Streetwear	Reeboks
Acid Washed	Rockshirt	Reeboks	Vision Streetwear
Acid Washed	Fluorescent	Vision Streetwear	Reeboks

24 combinations

Solution 3 (Carl, Grade 5)

Pants	Sweaters	Shoes	No. of Ways
1	1	1	1
1	2	1	2
1	3	1	3
1	4	1	4
1	1	2	5
1	2	2	6
1	3	2	7
1	4	2	8

Think: Since there were 3 pants and each had 8 different ways, you get 24 different ways to dress.

Source: "Writing to Communicate Mathematics," by Y. Pothier, 1992, in Daiyo Sawada (Ed.), *Communication in the mathematics classroom.* Edmonton, AB: Mathematics Council of the Alberta Teacher's Association. Used with permission.

FIGURE 3-2 The Barnyard Problem

Jill counted 20 pigs and chickens in the barnyard. Jack counted a total of 54 legs for the 20 animals. How many pigs and chickens were there?

a) Draw a diagram

2 legs each. This is 40 legs. Need 14 more. I'll add 2 to 7 animals.
Answer: There are 7 pigs and 13 chickens.

b) Trial and error

10 pigs and 10 chickens	$40 + 20 = 60$	Too many legs.
8 pigs and 12 chickens	$32 + 24 = 56$	Still too many.
6 pigs and 14 chickens	$24 + 28 = 52$	Not enough.
7 pigs and 13 chickens	$28 + 26 = 54$	That's it!

Answer: There are 7 pigs and 13 chickens.

c) Consider all possibilities

Pigs	Chickens	Legs	Total
1	19	4 + 38	42
2	18	8 + 36	44
3	17	12 + 34	46
4	16	16 + 32	48
5	15	20 + 30	50
6	14	24 + 28	52
7	13	28 + 26	54
8	12	32 + 24	56
9	11	36 + 22	58

Answer: There are 7 pigs and 13 chickens.

d) Solve algebraically

Let $x =$ the chickens
Let $y =$ the pigs

$$x + y = 20$$
$$2x + 4y = 54$$

Solve for y

$$2x + 4y = 54$$
$$\underline{2x + 2y = 40}$$
$$2y = 14$$
$$y = 7$$

Solve for x

$$x + y = 20$$
$$x + 7 = 20$$
$$x = 20 - 7$$
$$x = 13$$

Check

$$x + y = 20$$
$$13 + 7 = 20$$

$$2x + 4y = 54$$
$$2(13) + 4\ (7) = 54$$
$$26 + 28 = 54$$

Answer: There are 7 pigs and 13 chickens.

problem is similar to or different from other familiar problems.

Children should "feel right" about their solutions before declaring that they have solved the problem. Therefore, this final step in the problem-solving process should not be quickly dismissed but should lead children to be ready to explain and justify their solutions when asked.

Problem-Solving Strategies

Learning a number of problem-solving strategies is an asset for problem solving. However, children first should be encouraged to develop their own problem-solving strategies and to become facile at using those strategies. This helps them gain confidence in their mathematics ability and enhances their reasoning skills.

After children have developed and refined their own problem-solving strategies, you can, at a given time, highlight a particular strategy and lead the children in a class discussion and application of the strategy. In time, children will acquire a repertoire of different strategies from which to choose when faced with a problem. A number of problem-solving strategies are described in this section. Two examples of a problem that can be solved using each strategy are included. Some possible solutions are also provided.

Dramatizing or Modeling the Situation and Solution Process

PROBLEM 3-7: The Class Reunion

Twelve people came to celebrate their 10-year high school reunion. Each person shook hands once with all the other people. How many handshakes were exchanged at the reunion?

PROBLEM 3-8: Karla's Farewell Party

Karla is moving to another state, and her best friend has planned a farewell party for her. The people arrive at the house in the following manner: The first time the doorbell rings, Karla, as the first guest, enters. On each

NCTM Principles and Standards Link 3-4

Process Strand: Problem Solving

As with any other component of the mathematical tool kit, strategies must receive instructional attention if students are expected to learn them. In the lower grades, teachers can help children express, categorize, and compare their strategies. Opportunities to use strategies must be embedded naturally in the curriculum across the content areas. By the time students reach the middle grades, they should be skilled at recognizing when various strategies are appropriate to use and should be capable of deciding when and how to use them. (NCTM, 2000, p. 54)

successive ring, a group enters that has two more people than the group that entered on the previous ring. How many guests will have arrived after the twelfth ring?

Dramatization is a powerful medium to demonstrate understanding of a problem situation and can also lead one to "see" a solution. The Class Reunion and Karla's Farewell Party are examples of problems that children enjoy acting out.

Rather than participate in a dramatization, children may prefer to model the problem situation. For example, children could use objects to represent guests at Karla's party and to keep track of the separate groups arriving at the party.

SOLUTION TO THE CLASS REUNION PROBLEM

In acting out this problem, groups of 12 children could be formed. (The problem could be solved for a smaller group of people to accommodate all the children.)

In a dramatization, each child would shake hands with each of the other people in the group. The realization that there is only one handshake when, for example, Sue shakes hands with Tom and Tom shakes hands with Sue, will assist children in arriving at a solution. The discussion could be as follows:

There are 12 of us. Each one has shaken hands with 11 other people. That means 12 × 11 or 132 handshakes have taken place. But, there were really only half that number because when two people shake hands, there is only one handshake and not two. Therefore, when 12 people shake hands with each other, there are 66 handshakes.

Drawing a Picture or Diagram

Drawing a picture is a favorite strategy of many problem solvers. Some people draw a picture to help them visualize the situation, and, when they understand the problem, they use another strategy to solve it.

Young children like to draw and usually enjoy developing a solution process to problems by using pictures. This strategy can be time consuming, because children may want to draw objects in great detail. In time, they will realize that representational diagrams are all that are required in problem solving.

PROBLEM 3-9: The Cycle Problem

Kyle and Jason watched the children's bicycle and tricycle parade during the summer festival. They agreed to keep count of the number of cycles and the number of wheels as the children's parade passed by. At the end of the parade, Kyle declared he had counted 17 cycles, and Jason said he had counted 43 wheels. How many bicycles and tricycles were in the parade?

PROBLEM 3-10: The Barnyard Problem

Jill counted 20 pigs and chickens in the farmyard. Jack counted a total of 54 legs for the 20 animals. How many pigs and chickens were there? (See Figure 3-2.)

SOLUTION TO THE CYCLE PROBLEM

There were 17 cycles in the parade.

Altogether there were 43 wheels.

Begin by drawing all the cycles with two wheels each.

Seventeen cycles with two wheels each make 34 wheels.

Nine wheels are missing. Draw them on the cycles.

There were 8 bicycles and 9 tricycles in the parade.

If children have solved the Barnyard problem (see Figure 3-2), they should notice the similarity between Problems 3-9 and 3-10.

Constructing a Table or Chart

Constructing a table involves identifying and using appropriate labels to keep track of pertinent data as one works through a solution process. Some children may be able to set up a table with proper headings but may not be able to systematically list the data to assist them in arriving at a solution. Therefore, provide time for children to practice making organized lists of data. The three solutions in Figure 3-1 show how differently each child organized the data regarding clothing combinations.

PROBLEM 3-11: Clear Pond

Today one blade of grass took root in Clear Pond. Every day the amount of grass doubles; that is, tomorrow there will be two blades of grass, the next day, four blades, and so on. On the 10th day, how many blades of grass will be in the pond? If the capacity of the pond is 1 million blades of grass, on what day will it be filled? Estimate first, and then figure it out.

PROBLEM 3-12: The Garden Fence

A gardener has 60 feet of fence to keep animals out of the garden. What is the largest area of garden that this fence will enclose?

SOLUTION TO THE CLEAR POND PROBLEM

On Day 1, there is one blade of grass.

Each day the number doubles.

Setting up a table will help to keep the data organized. The table headings will be "Days" and "Blades of Grass." I'll use my calculator to find the products.

DAYS	BLADES OF GRASS
1	1
2	2
3	4
—	—
10	512
—	—
—	—
20	524,288
21	1,048,576

Using a calculator, I find that there will be 524,288 blades of grass on day 20. Doubling this amount gives more than a million.

Clear Pond will be filled to capacity on day 21.

Finding a Pattern

An efficient way to solve some problems is to record data in a table and then look for a pattern. When children analyze data in a table, encourage them to look for a pattern that will enable them to make a prediction about unknown data. Finding a pattern can make it easier and faster to solve the problem.

The Streamer Problem that follows was presented to one combined class of fifth- and sixth-graders. The children first suggested that acting it out would be a good way to begin. Children were provided with streamers, and they formed groups of six so that they could model a five-sided and then a six-sided room. The children then returned to their desks to record what they had observed and continued to solve the problem.

One sixth-grader's work is presented in Figure 3-3. Although Jennifer began by drawing diagrams, she decided that organizing the data in a table would help her find a pattern.

PROBLEM 3-13: The Streamer Problem

Imagine that you have been hired to decorate a room with streamers. The streamers are to be attached at the ceiling so that all opposite corners of the room are connected. How many streamers are needed to decorate a 10-sided room?

PROBLEM 3-14: The Patio Walk Problem

Suppose you have concrete tiles that measure 2 feet by 1 foot and you wish to use them to construct a patio walk that is 2 feet wide. Three sample patio walks that could be constructed with six blocks are pictured here.

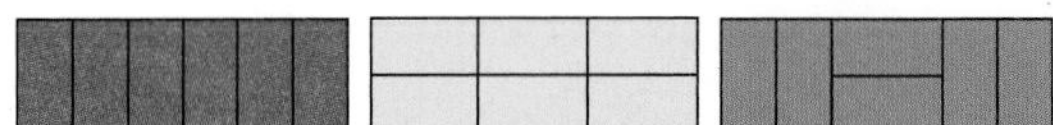

But there are other possibilities. How many different patio walks can be built using eight blocks?

Solving a Simpler Problem

Changing a given problem to a simpler problem can be helpful in visualizing the situation and in determining what procedure to use. Sometimes, beginning with the simplest case and progressing systematically to more difficult cases can yield a pattern that quickly leads to a solution.

PROBLEM 3-15: The Checkerboard Problem

How many squares (of different sizes) are there on an 8-by-8 checkerboard?

PROBLEM 3-16: Connecting Points

A circle has 25 points marked on it. How many straight lines will there be when each of the points is connected to each of the other points on the circle?

A SOLUTION TO THE CHECKERBOARD PROBLEM

I'll probably get confused as I count the squares on an 8-by-8 checkerboard, so I'll begin with a smaller board. This should help me find all the squares on an 8-by-8 checkerboard.

Literature Link 3-1

Problem Solving

Birch, David. (1988). ***The King's Chessboard.*** New York: Puffin.

Children need many opportunities to problem solve in meaningful contexts and to practice strategies that make sense of the mathematics in these problem situations. ***The King's Chessboard*** demonstrates the number pattern of exponential growth. In the story, the king wishes to reward a wise old man who desires no reward from the king. To make a point, the wise old man requests grains of rice according to the number of squares (64) on the king's chessboard. For the first square, 1 grain of rice; the second square, 2 grains of rice; the third square, 4 grains of rice; the fourth square, 8 grains of rice; the fifth square, 16 grains of rice, and so on. With each successive square on the chessboard, the number of grains of rice doubles. Translating the problem in the story into a mathematical sentence is an interesting challenge for children.

- Before children solve the problem posed in the story, have a class discussion eliciting various predictions on how much rice the king will need to give to the wise man.
- Use a representation to record the very large numbers in the story. As children are working, ask them questions, such as "Is it possible to use tally marks to keep track of the rice the king gave in the book?" and "Can you think of a way to determine the total number of grains of rice?"
- Write several mathematical sentences to analyze and visualize the problem presented in the story. Share and discuss these mathematical expressions. Encourage the use of calculators.
- While children are working, use questions to help them focus on successful and unsuccessful solution routes. Promote their use of charts, drawings, number tallying, mathematical sentences, and other problem-solving methods that will support their attempts.
- When children are finished, encourage them to share their solution routes and attempts. What methods worked, and what did children do when a method did not work? How did they know they were headed in the wrong direction?
- Create a large chessboard bulletin board display and have children write the number of grains of rice on each square of the chessboard.

Source: Dr. Patricia Moyer-Packenham, Utah State University.

FIGURE 3-3 The Streamer Problem

(Jennifer, Grade 6)

Situation: Decorating a room with streamers. Streamers are needed to connect all opposite corners.

Question: How many streamers are needed to decorate a 10-sided room?

1. -5 streamers
   -walls form a pentagon
   -we made a pentagon

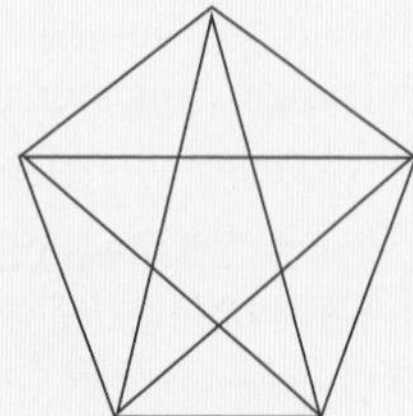

2. -9 streamers
   -walls form a hexagon
   -we made a hexagon with the streamers

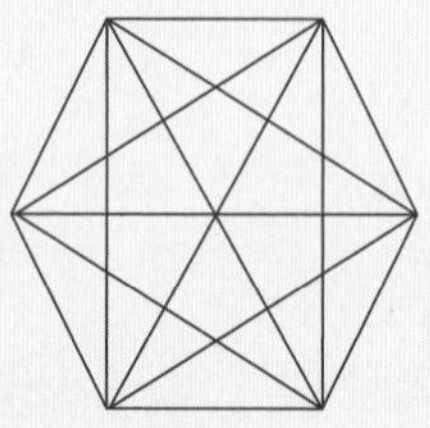

Table:

Walls	4	5	6	7	8	9	10	
		3	4	5	6	7	8	9
Streamers	2	5	9	14	20	27	35	

I felt proud of myself for having discovered the pattern.

Source: "Writing to Communicate Mathematics," by Y. Pothier, 1992, in Daiyo Sawada (Ed.), *Communication in the mathematics classroom.* Edmonton, AB: Mathematics Council of the Alberta Teachers' Association. Used with permission.

Number of Squares per Size

	1 × 1	2 × 2	3 × 3	4 × 4	. . .	Total
1 × 1	1					1
2 × 2	4	1				5
3 × 3	9	4	1			14
4 × 4	16	9	4	1		30
5 × 5	25	16	9	. . .	. . .	. . .
. . .						

I notice that the number of squares on each different-sized checkerboard is the sum of the square number that is the area of the board and the other smaller square numbers. For example, a 4-by-4 checkerboard has 16 + 9 + 4 + 1 total squares. A 5-by-5 checkerboard has 25 + 16 + 9 + 4 + 1 squares. So an 8-by-8 checkerboard will have 64 + 49 + 36 + 25 + 16 + 9 + 4 + 1 squares or 204 squares.

Beginning with a simpler case helped me notice a pattern in the table. This enabled me to find the answer.

Guessing and Checking

For some problems, one sometimes first makes a guess and then checks its accuracy. If the guess is not correct, one uses the knowledge obtained from the guessing-and-checking process to make another more educated guess or to change to a different strategy to solve the problem. A disadvantage of this method is that it is usually not efficient, often taking longer than other methods. Use this strategy to solve Problems 3-17 and 3-18.

PROBLEM 3-17: Balanced Triangle

Arrange the digits 1, 2, 3, 4, 5, and 6 to form a triangle, using each digit only once, so that the 3 numbers on each side of the triangle add up to 12.

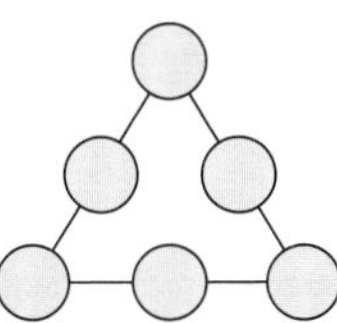

PROBLEM 3-18: Multiples of Five

Find 6 consecutive multiples of 5 that when added make a sum of 345.

A SOLUTION TO THE BALANCED TRIANGLE

I've made several guesses without any luck.

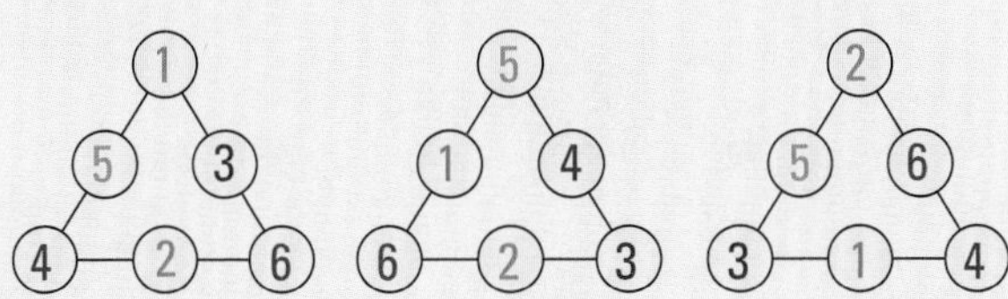

I'll try putting the smallest numbers in the vertices. This doesn't work either. But they all equal 9! I've found one solution!

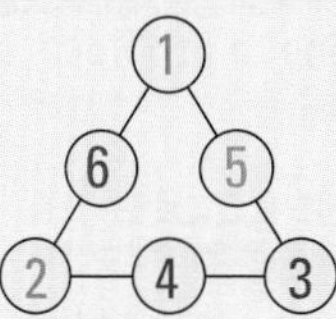

I'll try the largest numbers in the vertices. Yes, I've found a solution for 12.

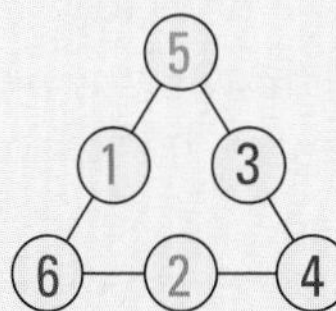

An organized list of all the possibilities of sums of 12 is another strategy one could use to solve the problem. The numbers that are used twice go in the vertices.

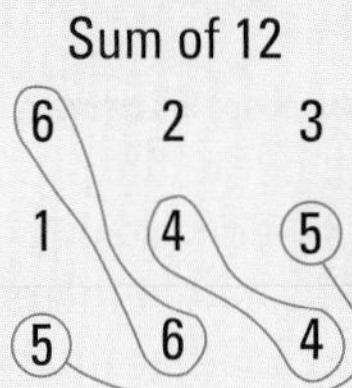

Working Backward

Notice that the Rock Star Pictures and Apple Orchard problems that follow describe a series of actions or events. Problems of this type are often best solved by starting at the final situation and working backward to find the solution.

PROBLEM 3-19: Rock Star Pictures

Shane gave one-half of his rock star pictures to Samantha, then gave 6 pictures to Darryl, and had 12 left. How many rock star pictures did Shane have before he gave any away?

Elementary school children sometimes find this type of problem difficult to understand and solve. They have to learn that working backward means not only beginning at the end and working one's way through the steps backward but also that the operations in the problem must be reversed. One way to have children practice reverse operations is to describe a route from place A to place B and then have them tell how to get from B to A. They will realize that all the right turns become left turns and vice versa.

PEARSON **myeducationlab** The Power of Classroom Practice Go to the Assignments and Activities section of Topic 3: "Problem Solving" in the MyEducationLab for your course. Complete the activity "Math Strategies for Problem Solving" and consider what teachers say about incorporating problem-based teaching methods.

In arithmetic situations, one can ask, what is the opposite of giving away $10? (receiving $10); the opposite of halving 6 (doubling 6); the opposite of 3 times 6 ($\frac{1}{3}$ of 6). When children understand reverse operations, they can be asked to find solutions to problems that can be solved by working them backward.

A SOLUTION TO THE ROCK STAR PICTURES PROBLEM

Shane gave half his pictures to Samantha and 6 to Darryl.

Then he had 12 pictures left.

I have to find out how many pictures he had to start with, so I'll work backward.

12 pictures. Add the 6 given to Darryl. 18 pictures. Double 18 because half were given to Samantha. 36 pictures.

Shane originally had 36 pictures.

Considering All Possibilities

PROBLEM 3-20: Buying Stamps

Megan's mother sent her to the post office to purchase some 20-cent and 37-cent stamps. When Megan arrived at the post office, she remembered that she was to buy 18 stamps, which her mother had figured out would cost $4.96. Can you help Megan find out how many 20-cent and 37-cent stamps her mother wants?

PROBLEM 3-21: Police Vehicles

A city's police department has 15 cars and motorcycles. The total number of wheels on the cars and motorcycles is 42. How many police cars does the police department have?

Some problems involve the consideration of data in different combinations to find a right combination. A strategy used in such instances is to consider all possibilities so that the right combination(s) is (are) found. Making a table and systematically considering all possibilities is an efficient way to resolve such problems.

A SOLUTION TO THE POLICE VEHICLES PROBLEM

Information: 15 vehicles. 42 wheels in all.

I'll set up a table and list all the combinations of 15 until I find one that gives 42 wheels.

MOTORCYCLES	CARS	VEHICLES	WHEELS
15	0	15	$30 + 0 = 30$
14	1	15	$28 + 4 = 32$
13	2	15	$26 + 8 = 34$
12	3	15	$24 + 12 = 36$

I see that the total goes up by 2.

MOTORCYCLES	CARS	VEHICLES	WHEELS
9	6	15	$18 + 24 = 42$

There are 9 motorcycles and 6 cars in the police fleet.

Logical Reasoning

PROBLEM 3-22: Partners

Mona, Rita, and Sandra are married to Allan, Fred, and John, but (a) Sandra does not like John, (b) Rita is married to John's brother, and (c) Allan is married to Rita's sister. Who is married to whom?

PROBLEM 3-23: Ranking by Age

Peter is twice as old as Ann will be when Sarah is as old as Peter is now. Can you tell who is the youngest, next youngest, and oldest?

The development of logical reasoning is often stated as a requirement for the successful learning of mathematics. When children state that they solved a problem by thinking it through, encourage them to reflect on how they did it and to discuss the thinking steps they followed. This can help other children to develop logical thought processes. Problems encountered in everyday life often require logical thinking to arrive at a suitable decision.

A SOLUTION TO THE PARTNERS PROBLEM

Setting up a grid will help me organize the information.

	Mona	Rita	Sandra
Alan		X	
John		X	X
Fred			

Because of the information given in the problem, I can mark several X's on the chart. By studying the chart, I see that John must be married to Mona, and Rita must be married to Fred. That leaves Sandra and Allan as partners.

Changing Your Point of View

PROBLEM 3-24: Planting Tomatoes

Mrs. Andrews planted 10 tomato plants in 5 rows of 4 plants each. How did she do this?

PROBLEM 3-25: Looking for Squares

Find a square with an area of five square units on the grid.

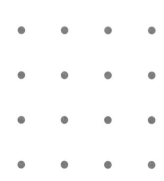

Have you ever not been able to solve a problem because of the perspective you took in attempting a solution? Often, by taking a certain perspective, we set limits to the considerations of possible solutions. For example, in the nine-dot puzzle (Problem 3-5), many people think of the perimeter of the square formed by the dots as the boundary for constructing lines. However, to solve the problem, three lines must be extended beyond the dots.

A SOLUTION TO THE PLANTING PROBLEM

Trial and error is the only way that I can see to solve this problem.

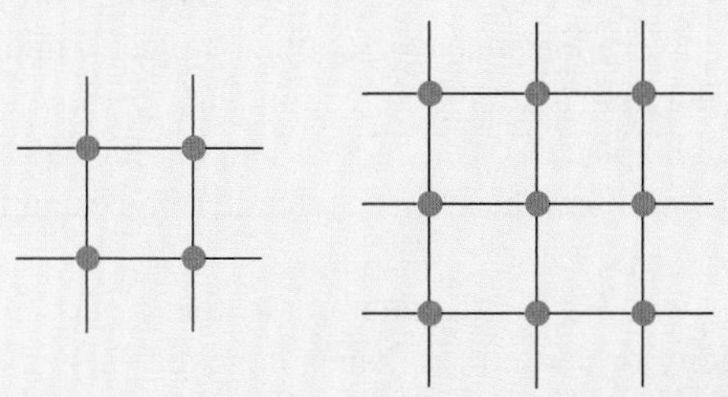

I tried parallel lines without success.

Oh, what about lines intersecting at vertices?

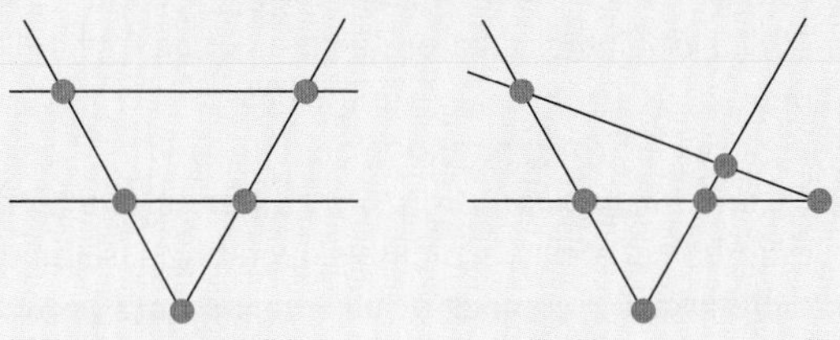

I'm getting only 3 plants per row. But I need another row.

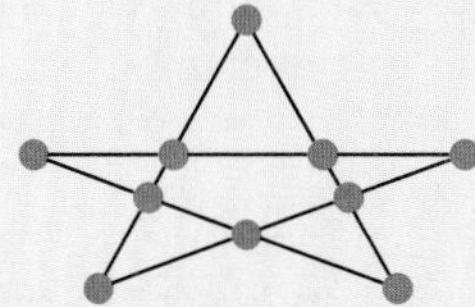

That's it. It looks like a five-pointed star.

I can see how 12 plants could be planted in 6 rows of 4 plants each. Can you? What about 19 plants in 9 straight rows with 5 plants in each row?

Writing an Open Sentence

PROBLEM 3-26: Fruit Problem

Elaine bought 5 peaches and 3 apples. She figures out that she would have to pay 8 cents more if she bought 3 peaches and 5 apples. What is the difference between the price of one peach and one apple?

PROBLEM 3-27: Rectangle Size

Find the dimensions of a rectangle whose perimeter is 26 cm and whose area is 36 cm^2.

Some problems presented to elementary school children can be solved by writing an open sentence and then solving it. For example, the Barnyard problem (see Figure 3-2) can be solved by writing equations and solving first for one variable and then the other. Middle school children will learn how to write mathematical sentences for word expressions such as "twice as old" ($2x$), "3 times as many plus 6" ($3x + 6$), and then use algebraic skills to solve problems.

A SOLUTION TO THE FRUIT PROBLEM

p = peaches a = apples

$5p + 3a = 3p + 5a + 8$

$2p - 2a = 8$

$p - a = 4$

The difference between the price of a peach and the price of an apple is 4 cents.

Planning for Instruction on Problem Solving

The problem-solving instructional process has several important components (Charles & Lester, 1982):

- Selecting appropriate tasks and materials;
- Identifying sources of problems;
- Clarifying the teacher's role;
- Organizing and implementing instruction; and
- Changing the difficulty of problems.

The following section describes the essential elements that make up these components of instruction.

Selecting Appropriate Tasks and Materials

Good instruction on problem solving not only uses a variety of problems (Kroll & Miller, 1993), but also considers that problems should

- Be motivating and culturally relevant;
- Sometimes contain missing, extraneous, or contradictory information;
- Invite the use of calculators, computers, and other technology;
- Engage children in activities that use a variety of problem-solving strategies; and
- Involve children in activities that promote communication about mathematical thinking.

Problems that are motivating and culturally relevant. Children are interested in solving problems about things they are interested in; problems that are based in realistic, familiar settings; problems that are relevant to their culture; and problems that they or other students have written. It is important to revise problems as necessary to make sure they are motivating and culturally relevant for children.

Problems with missing, extraneous, or contradictory information. Motivating, realistic problems often contain irrelevant or incomplete information and are not well structured. Because children need practice in solving such problems, instruction should include discussions on organizing the information provided and eliminating or ignoring extraneous information.

Problems that encourage the use of calculators, computers, and other technology. Calculator use stimulates children to think more about their approaches to problem solving and permits them to solve more realistic problems.

Activities that require the use of a variety of problem-solving strategies. Children who can use a variety of problem-solving strategies are better able to deal with unfamiliar problem situations. Also, children who use strategies such as making a diagram or solving a simpler problem are able to more flexibly select another strategy if their first strategy does not work.

Activities that promote communication about mathematical thinking. Children need to be able to explain how they solved a problem. Such explanations are important in refining their own understanding and communicating their understanding to others. Asking children to write word problems, to solve problems written by other children, and to look for errors in the problems or explanations of other children helps to develop their mathematical communication skills.

Identifying Sources of Problems

Problems arising from mathematics itself can be about the following:

- *Number theory:* Are there more prime numbers from 100 to 200 than there are from 1 to 100? How can I find the greatest common factor of three numbers? Sixty-four is both a square number and a cube. What is the next number greater than 64 that has this property?
- *Properties of number systems:* Is there a multiplicative identity element for fractions? Does the commutative property hold true for integers? If so, for which operations?
- *Arithmetic:* Is there another algorithm for subtracting whole numbers? How can I subtract 4 from 6?

NCTM Principles and Standards Link 3-5

Process Strand: Problem Solving

When technological tools are available, students can focus on decision making, reflection, reasoning, and problem solving. (NCTM, 2000, p. 24)

Projects about the school environment can be related to the school store, a school fund-raising project, a paper-conservation endeavor, or other project. Children can gather data from a number of community service organizations, public places, or businesses and use the data to pose and solve problem questions. Here are some examples:

- *Airport:* Gather data about air traffic, passenger capacity of certain airplanes, baggage capacity, flight schedules, or ticket prices.
- *City park:* Obtain data on the number of trees, area for flower beds, types of flowers, or maintenance costs.
- *Bridge:* Obtain data about daily traffic, income from bridge tolls, or maintenance costs.
- *Orchard:* Gather data on the area of an orchard, the number of fruit trees, average harvest per tree, selling price of fruit, or anticipated profits.
- *Public transportation system:* Obtain information on a city's fleet of buses, monthly operating costs, and the daily average number of passengers on a particular route.

Some mathematical problems can be found in math journals or other publications and on the Internet. The "Resources for Teachers" and "Links to the Internet" sections at the end of the chapter offer some specific examples.

Ask children to write problems. Another source of problems but more importantly an excellent way to help children become comfortable and familiar with problems and the problem-solving process is to have children write problems. Through such experiences, children develop critical thinking skills, learn to collect and organize data (Fennell & Ammon, 1985), and learn how to express ideas clearly.

To get children started in problem writing, you might ask them to write a problem from a given mathematical sentence. Some examples follow:

1. Write a problem that fits the number sentence $46 + 17 = 63$.
2. Write a problem that fits the number sentence $35 - 28 = 7$ and that asks the question "How many more . . .?"

3. Write a multiplication story problem for the array shown here:

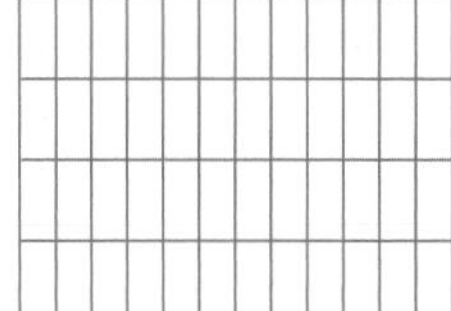

4. Write a division story problem that asks one to solve 138 divided by 6.
5. Write a word problem in which one has to first add, then subtract, to answer the question.

The writing process. When asking children to write problems, direct them through a process similar to that of writing stories: that is, a prewriting stage is followed by the writing, conferencing, and revising stages. Final stages can include publication and follow-up (Ford, 1990).

The prewriting stage is a time to create or examine a set of data and to think of a story to add interest to the data. When a problem has been written, share it with other children. Conferencing about the problem can help children clarify their ideas. When other children cannot understand a problem, the writer must revise it until ideas are clearly expressed. Children may find that some problems may be missing data or have extraneous information or that the question does not fit the data. Such feedback helps children to revise the problem so that it is comprehensible and acceptable (Ford, 1990).

To help children create meaningful problems, collect newspaper clippings, restaurant menus, sale flyers from local businesses, statistics from government departments, concert schedules, bus or subway schedules, etc., and make them available to children to use when writing problems. Ask children to work in small groups and share the following guidelines with them. Then have children practice writing problems and sharing them with other children:

1. Choose a scenario for creating a problem setting, either from the resource materials previously listed or based on a familiar situation, such as a home or classroom event.
2. Think about what might be happening in this problem setting and describe it.
3. Now add numeric details to the situation, such as the number of people involved, etc.
4. Then think about questions that might be asked in this problem setting, such as who, what, when, how many, or how much. Choose a question or two for problem solvers to answer.

Children can "publish" their problems on paper to place in a binder or on cards for easy access. Follow-up activities include having the class discuss some problems in order to highlight particular types or having children solve each other's problems. The successful experience of reading and solving a problem written by a classmate may augment a child's interest in learning mathematics.

Posing problems. It is much different for children to pose problems than to write problems as previously described. Problem posing usually refers to the process of *changing* an existing problem into a new one by modifying the *knowns,* the *unknowns,* or the *restrictions* placed on the answer (Moses, Bjork, & Goldenberg, 1990).

A trusting and supportive relationship between you and your students sets the stage for both you and them to pose interesting problems and helps classrooms "come alive." As children actively participate in problem solving by questioning, conjecturing, and testing possibilities for solutions, you can easily encourage them to modify problems to create new and possibly more interesting and challenging ones. In this way, children become comfortable as problem posers and, with practice, masterful at generating new problems.

Initiate problem-posing activities with children by

> . . . modeling the process personally by wondering openly *with* the students, fostering the free exchange of ideas and actively encouraging collaboration among students, honoring students' spontaneous what-ifs and conjectures, and being as interested in *how* students thought about a problem as in *what* they came up with. (Moses et al., 1990, p. 86)

Moses et al. (1990) offer the following principles for guiding children to engage in posing problems:

1. Begin with a comfortable mathematics topic.
2. Have children learn to focus their attention on *knowns, unknowns,* and *restrictions.* Then consider the following questions: What if different things were known and unknown? What if the restrictions were changed?

The process of problem posing can enrich mathematics classes by actively engaging children in constructing mathematics for themselves, and it can assist in intrinsically motivating children to embrace mathematics as an interesting, relevant, and essential dimension of their lives.

Clarifying the Teacher's Role

You play an important role in problem-solving instruction. Rigelman (2007) notes that "when teachers carefully choose tasks that require students to engage in mathematical thinking and problem solving, then draw out students' thinking through their questioning, and finally encourage reflection and sense-making, their students make significant gains in mathematical understanding and attain higher levels of achievement (p. 314). Rigelman makes several recommendations for teachers' roles in problem-solving instruction:

Instead of:	The teacher:
Focusing on helping students "find an answer,"	Is prepared to see where the students' observations and questions may take them.
Providing solution strategies,	Encourages multiple approaches and allows time for communication and reflection about those strategies.
Expecting specific responses,	Is ready to ask questions that uncover students' thinking and press for the students' reasoning behind the process (p. 312).

All children can become problem-solvers. Buschman (2003) discusses how he helped his students, who didn't like to solve problems and thought they weren't good at solving problems, to enjoy and be good at solving problems. He found that "children's enjoyment of problem solving increases when they

- Solve problems in ways that make sense to them;
- Learn to appreciate mistakes as a necessary and valuable part of the problem-solving process;
- Experience the satisfaction of overcoming a challenge;
- Share and discuss their solutions with peers; and
- Receive support and encouragement when their development slows or appears to regress (2003, p. 544).

How can teachers create a problem-solving climate in their classrooms? Buschman (2002) recommends that teachers give all children "broad and rich experiences . . ., pose challenging problems, ask children to share their solutions orally or in writing, and give them feedback in the form of questions or comments about their solutions" (p. 103).

The teacher's role in problem-solving instruction includes what you do *before* children begin to solve a problem, *while* children are solving a problem, and *after* children solve the problem.

Before children begin to solve the problem. Begin the lesson by posing a problem to children. Problems can be presented to children orally or in written form. When presented orally, you can use a story format such as "Suppose you were asked to . . ." or "There once was. . . . How would you have solved the problem?" or "What would happen if . . .?" In another format, you can read the problem orally and write key information on the board. A third way is to have children read the problem. Then, the problem can be written on the board, on an overhead transparency, or on paper with a copy provided for each child. In the latter case, children can glue the piece of paper on a notebook page or in their math journal and develop a solution plan there. In this way, a record of the problem is kept with the children's work.

Before asking children to solve the problem, make sure that children understand it. This means asking children to identify what is being asked in the problem, discussing any terms that might be unclear, brainstorming possible solution strategies, and clarifying the task at hand. Finally, you should ask children to devise a plan or select a strategy for solving the problem.

While children are solving the problem. While children are working on the problem, you should circulate among them, observing and questioning individuals or groups working together about the strategies they are using, what they are finding, and what it means. Further, you should ask children questions to help them clarify the direction in which their solution process is taking them. You should provide hints to children who are stuck and encourage children who are finished to solve the problem in a different way or to solve an extension of the problem. The critical factor is to make sure that children are answering the question the problem asks.

After children solve the problem. After children are finished working on a problem, encourage them to reflect on their solutions and the problem-solving processes they used. Usually this can be done through a whole-class discussion. Most valuable is to emphasize the process as well as the answer and to encourage all children to participate in this discussion. Getting children to communicate their ideas through words and diagrams and with manipulative materials strengthens their understanding.

Examining children's work. Throughout instruction, you should pay close attention to how students are solving problems in order to assess their understanding and decide on the next instructional steps. You will be able to practice this by examining samples of children's work in this textbook and on MyEducationLab. The idea of looking carefully at children's work is often new to beginning teachers, who often think that a teacher's role when examining work is merely to determine if it is correct or incorrect, and that children's errors are usually

NCTM Principles and Standards Link 3-6

Process Strand: Problem Solving

The teacher's role in choosing worthwhile problems and mathematical tasks is crucial. By analyzing and adapting a problem, anticipating the mathematical ideas that can be brought out by working on the problem, and anticipating students' questions, teachers can decide if particular problems will help to further their mathematical goals for the class. . . . Choosing problems wisely, and using and adapting problems from instructional materials, is a difficult part of teaching mathematics. (NCTM, 2000, p. 53)

random. But this is not the case. Children's errors in problem solving are rarely random. These errors reflect children's understanding of math concepts and their ability to use solution strategies. Experienced teachers know what errors and misunderstandings are most common. You will have an opportunity to learn more about common errors and misunderstandings throughout this book. Each chapter will contact examples of children's work, which you will examine and reflect on, and then consider how to help expand these children's understandings.

Organizing and Implementing Instruction

Establishing an effective problem-solving program involves thinking about factors related to organization and implementation. These factors include providing children with a classroom climate that is conducive to learning, grouping children to facilitate interactive learning, allocating appropriate instructional time, and planning for children's assessments.

Classroom climate. A classroom that promotes problem solving is open and supportive, encouraging children to try different solution strategies and endorsing children's efforts. Such a supportive environment encourages children to take risks and to defend their solutions. Make sure you encourage children to persevere in their problem solving and to respect each other's efforts.

Grouping children. A classroom that promotes problem solving includes individual, small-group, and whole-class problem-solving experiences. Each of these formats helps children develop distinct and important types of problem-solving skills. Small-group work is particularly useful in that it provides opportunities for all children to interact, discuss, and share solution strategies.

Allocating time. A classroom that promotes an adequate allocation of instructional time for problem solving on a regular basis supports children's learning. Problem solving should be an integral part of mathematics instruction, not an add-on, "Fridays only" topic.

Assessing children's understanding. A classroom that promotes problem solving includes ongoing assessment of children's understanding, problem-solving skills, and strategy usage. Chapter 4 discusses assessment in greater detail.

Changing the Difficulty of Problems

Remember the discussion at the beginning of this chapter on types of problems? We know much about which problems are easier than others to solve and ways to construct problems to make them easier or harder. For example, the wording of a problem can affect the difficulty level of a problem. Because teachers can control how easy or difficult problems can be and thus meet individual needs, it is important to be aware of the factors involved in adapting problems. These factors include problem context and problem mechanics or structure.

Problem context. The context of a problem is the nonmathematical setting in which it is placed. For example, because of the setting or context of the problem, a problem about two children sharing six cookies is different from a problem about two aliens sharing six megablasters. As shown in Figure 3-4, different contexts can

FIGURE 3-4 Types of Problem Contexts

Abstract Setting
A certain number is 5 more than 7. What is the number?

Concrete Setting
Matt has 7 baseball cards. Peter has 5 more baseball cards than Matt has. How many baseball cards does Peter have?

In Ms. Garcia s class, there are 7 boys and some girls. There are 5 more girls than boys in the class. How many girls are in Ms. Garcia's class?

Hypothetical Setting
Peter has some baseball cards. If Peter has 5 more baseball cards than Matt has, and Matt has 7 baseball cards, how many baseball cards does Peter have?

Personalized Setting
{Insert Child A's name here} has 7 {insert relevant item here}. {Insert Child B's name here} has 5 more {insert relevant item here} than {Insert Child A's name here} has. How many {insert relevant item here} does {insert Child B's name here} have?

Literature Link 3-2

Problem Solving

Anno, Mitsumasa. (1995). ***Anno's Magic Seeds.*** New York: Philomel Books.

A good story often places mathematical problems in the context of familiar situations. The problem-solving context is much more convincing when the development of mathematical topics occurs naturally as part of the story, rather than as a context in which mathematics is overlaid on a story where it does not normally arise or is just not appropriate. ***Anno's Magic Seeds*** demonstrates how an interesting story and an interesting mathematics problem can create a wonderful mathematical situation.

- Provide a variety of experiences in which children apply several different problem-solving strategies to make mathematical discoveries. Have children recognize and select different strategies and reason which strategies might work better for certain kinds of problems and why.
- Develop a chart to record the way the number of golden seeds in the story changes. Help children to identify key elements of the mathematical situation, such as what year it is (year 1, 2, 3, etc.) and the number of seeds either eaten or planted.
- Note how this problem is set in a real-world context. The number of seeds follows a mathematical pattern only until some event changes it (for example, Jack gets married and has a child, changing the number of seeds eaten each year, and there is a hurricane that wipes out most of the golden seeds). These real-world occurrences make the mathematics in the story realistic, showing that real-world problems are sometimes "messy."
- For another example of an interesting problem situation, read ***How the Second Grade Got $8,205.50 to Visit the Statue of Liberty*** by Nathan Zimelman.

Source: Dr. Patricia Moyer-Packenham, Utah State University.

include abstract (using symbolic or intangible elements), concrete (involving a real situation or objects), factual (describing an actual situation), hypothetical (describing possible situations), and personalized (using the solver's own interests and characteristics in the problem) (Hembree & Marsh, 1993).

Problems involving concrete, factual, or personalized settings are easier for children to solve than are hypothetical or abstract problems.

Problem structure. A problem's structure consists of several aspects related to how problem data are presented. These aspects include problem length, readability, whether the problem includes action (e.g., "Tom *gave* Maria 2 more cookies"), the order in which data are presented, the inclusion of extraneous data, and the use of familiar versus unfamiliar terms. The difficulty of each of these aspects is as might be expected. More difficult problems might include any of these factors: longer, more difficult readability, lack of action, presence of extraneous data or information, and unfamiliar terms.

NCTM Principles and Standards Link 3-7

Process Strand: Problem Solving

Problem solving is an integral part of all mathematics learning, and so it should not be an isolated part of the mathematics program. . . . The contexts of the problems can vary from familiar experiences involving students' lives or the school day to applications involving the sciences or the world of work. Good problems will integrate multiple topics and will involve significant mathematics. (NCTM, 2000, p. 52)

Classroom implications. You must be aware of factors that affect problem difficulty, and systematically vary those factors to help children become better problem solvers. A common way to sequence problem-solving instruction is to begin with problems involving action and reasonably sized numbers in concrete or personalized settings, later progressing to more complicated problems by varying the factors previously described.

This is not to say, however, that you must always pose easy problems. Realistic, real-world problems encountered in everyday situations usually are not clean, tidy, or clearly stated. Children need to learn how to solve such problems. When planning instruction, you must find a balance between supporting children's learning and challenging children to solve realistic problems. Make sure you systematically vary problem structure and format to help children learn strategies and develop confidence that will help them solve more complicated problems.

Other Factors Contributing to Children's Difficulties in Problem Solving

From their review of the literature, Kroll and Miller (1993) have identified major factors that contribute to middle school children's difficulties in problem solving: knowledge, beliefs and affective factors, control, and sociocultural factors. All teachers should address each of these areas during instruction. In particular, the elementary grades should be viewed as a time of "preparation for good problem solving" (Hembree & Marsh, 1993, p. 166).

Knowledge factors. Beginning in the elementary grades and throughout the middle school grades, children should have ample experience in problem solving so that they can come to recognize structurally similar problems (schema knowledge) and learn varied strategies to solve process problems (strategic knowledge) (Kroll & Miller, 1993). Thus, building prior knowledge required for successful problem solving includes making teachers accountable for developing algorithmic, linguistic, conceptual, and schema and strategic knowledge. As a teacher, you must not only enable children to read problems and compute accurately but also help children come to understand problems so that they can make a wise choice on what operation or strategy to use to develop a solution. Choosing a solution process should emerge from a clear understanding of a problem, rather than be dependent on word clues or other unreliable strategies.

Beliefs and affective factors. Success in problem solving is negatively affected by a lack of confidence in one's own ability to create solutions to problems. Teachers who have a narrow view that there is only one right way to solve a problem can prevent children from experiencing the joy of truly "doing" mathematics. Instead, encourage children to try different ways to solve a problem.

Control factors. Kroll and Miller (1993) mention the need for children to be able to monitor their own thinking when engaged in problem solving. Research shows that children do not spend sufficient time reflecting on their thinking process or on their approaches to problem solving. It is important for you to engage children in reflecting on their own thinking processes.

Sociocultural factors. Children's out-of-school experiences are varied; therefore, children develop various problem-solving strategies. However, children sometimes are unable to use their "natural" problem-solving abilities in school mathematics, although such abilities serve them well in out-of-school situations (Kroll & Miller, 1993). As stated earlier in this chapter, the classroom atmosphere is important in mathematics learning because it can positively or negatively affect children's achievement. Keep in mind that you control the environment and context of children's experiences. This is an awesome responsibility but one that separates good instruction from poor student experiences.

Consider Children's Preferences

A problem-solving teaching project with fourth-, fifth-, and sixth-grade children revealed that children valued certain instructional practices when engaged in problem solving (Pothier & Sawada, 1990). Some of the favored characteristics of the teaching–learning situation expressed by the children include time to complete a problem, freedom to choose a solution strategy, receipt of personal attention, and an understanding teacher.

- Children need *time* to work through a problem; they do not want to be rushed to complete a set of problems. When relieved of the pressure to complete work, children feel free to explore solution possibilities.
- Children appreciate the *freedom* to personally select and develop a solution strategy, rather than follow a uniform procedure. This provides them with the opportunity to transform a problem into something personal, and it becomes an enjoyable task.
- Children appreciate receiving personal *attention* when engaged in problem solving. This attention can be in the form of a teacher's asking questions to direct their thinking, offering hints regarding solution procedures, or merely listening to fellow students talk about what they are doing.
- Children value an *understanding* teacher. When a trusting relationship is established, children will readily request assistance knowing that, as one child expressed it, "It's all right if you don't know how to do it." Students will take risks in tackling problems that they might not otherwise attempt, an important component in a mathematics classroom.

A nonthreatening and supportive classroom atmosphere is effective in promoting children's progress as they develop their problem-solving abilities.

Benefits of Using a Problem-Solving Approach to Mathematics Instruction

A teacher who decides to approach all mathematics work from a problem-solving point of view has children solve computation problems, work at geometry and measurement activities, and approach number theory investigations from a problem-solving perspective. Process problems that relate to the different mathematics topics are an important part of this kind of program. Children learn problem-solving strategies that enable them to gain insights into mathematical connections and understand that problems are the context for learning concepts and skills, that is, children learn mathematics via problem solving. Such a program promotes children's mathematics understanding and achievement.

Another benefit of a problem-solving approach to mathematics teaching is that it supports children with different learning styles. According to Moser (1992), "an orientation toward problem solving can accommodate individual differences, especially if the philosophy is adopted that there is more than one way to solve most problems" (p. 131). A classroom in which problem solving is the central feature of the mathematics instruction and in which more than one way to solve a problem is not merely tolerated but is valued is an environment that promotes the learning of all children.

Conclusion

This chapter discussed current thinking about problem solving, including its integral role in mathematics programs. This vision centers on children learning mathematics through problem solving and teachers teaching in a way that allows children to learn how to solve problems. Mathematics programs should include different types of problems, with more emphasis placed on process problems.

It is not only appropriate but also imperative for you to provide instruction in problem-solving strategies to help children develop many processes to use when solving problems. The instructional goal is to ensure that children will develop confidence and flexibility in using different problem-solving strategies.

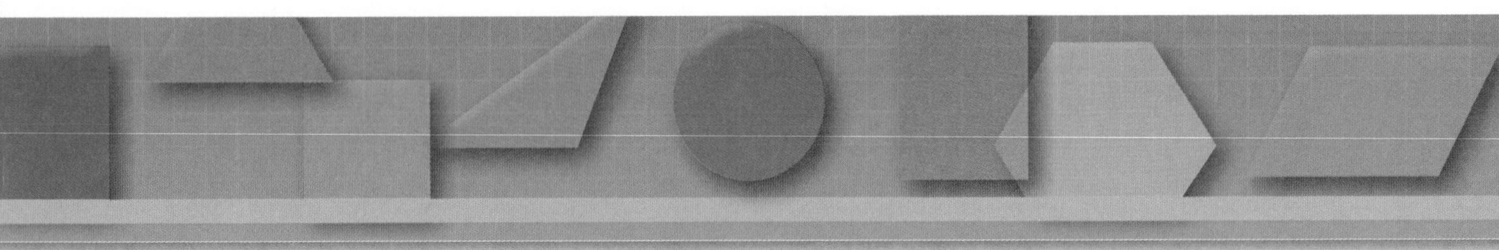

IN PRACTICE

Complete the following activities to include in your professional portfolio.

1. Describe how you would establish a classroom environment conducive to problem solving.
2. Begin a collection of process problems.
3. Write a lesson plan for a problem-solving lesson focusing on teaching children to use a solution strategy of your choice. Include the questions you would ask.
4. Visit a classroom and observe the solution strategies used by children. Describe these strategies and the follow-up lessons you might plan if you were the teacher in that classroom.

PEARSON myeducationlab The Power of Classroom Practice Now go to Topic 3: "Problem Solving" in the MyEducationLab (www.myeducationlab.com) for your course, where you can:

- Find learning objectives for "Problem Solving" along with the national standards that connect to these objectives.
- Apply and practice your understanding of the core teaching skills identified in the chapter with a Building Teaching Skills and Dispositions learning unit.
- Complete Assignments and Activities that can help you more deeply understand the chapter content.
- Check your comprehension on the content covered in the chapter by going to the Study Plan in the Book-Specific Resources for your text. Here you will be able to take a chapter quiz, receive feedback on your answers, and then access Review, Practice, and Enrichment activities to enhance your understanding of chapter content.
- Go to the Book-Specific Resources for Chapter 3 to explore mathematical reasoning related to chapter content in the Activities section.

LINKS TO THE INTERNET

Problems of the Week

http://www.mathforum.org/pow/

Contains several weekly "Problems of the Week" as well as a mechanism to submit solutions electronically. Past "Problems of the Week" and solutions are also available.

Open-ended Math Problems

http://www.fi.edu/school/math2/

Contains open-ended math problems at several different levels of difficulty for middle school students.

Education Place's BrainTeasers

http://www.eduplace.com/math/brain/

Contains math puzzles for Grades 3–8 as well as solution hints.

RESOURCES FOR TEACHERS

Reference Books: Problem Solving

Baroody, A. (1993). *Problem Solving, Reasoning, and Communicating: Helping Children Think Mathematically.* New York: Macmillan.

Charles, R., Lester, F., & O'Daffer, P. (1987). *How to Evaluate Progress in Problem Solving.* Reston, VA: National Council of Teachers of Mathematics.

O'Daffer, P. G. (1988). *Problem Solving: Tips for Teachers.* Reston, VA: National Council of Teachers of Mathematics.

Reys, B. (1982). *Elementary School Mathematics: What Parents Should Know about Problem Solving.* Reston, VA: National Council of Teachers of Mathematics.

CHAPTER

Assessing Mathematics Understanding

NCTM CONNECTING WITH THE STANDARDS

The National Council of Teachers of Mathematics (NCTM) Principles and Standards emphasizes the importance of assessment, stating that "assessment should support the learning of important mathematics and furnish useful information to both teachers and students" (NCTM, 2000, p. 11). The NCTM document goes on to state the following:

> *Assessment should be more than merely a test at the end of instruction to see how students perform under special conditions; rather, it should be an integral part of instruction that informs and guides teachers as they make instructional decisions. Assessment should not merely be done to students; rather, it should also be done for students, to guide and enhance their learning. (p. 21)*

Assessment in mathematics no longer refers only to a child's score on a test. Instead, assessment involves a more holistic view of each child's understanding, skill, and attitude about mathematics. Assessment communicates to children what we believe is important for them to know and to be able to do. It is essential that assessment be aligned with the mathematics curriculum and the instructional strategies in use. This chapter discusses recommendations and methods for assessing children's understanding of mathematics.

One important task for you is to assess your children's understanding of mathematics concepts and procedures. In the video clip, "IMAP—Using Mathematical Reasoning" located on MyEducationLab, Nicole, a second-grader, is asked to solve the following problem:

Matalie has 14 marbles. She gives 5 marbles to Nicole. How many marbles does Matalie have left?

PEARSON myeducationlab The Power of Classroom Practice Go to the Assignments and Activities section of Topic 4: "Assessment" in the MyEducationLab for your course. Complete the activity "IMAP—Using Mathematical Reasoning" to see how one teacher helps her students use mathematic reasoning.

Developing Your Math Teaching Skills

When you have finished studying this chapter, you should be able to do the following:

- Explain the purposes of assessment.
- Describe the different types of assessment and communicate the benefits of each type.
- Understand the advantages of using performance assessment and of using portfolio assessment.

Watch the clip and think about what Nicole understands about subtraction. Notice that Nicole quickly states that the answer is "three," which is incorrect. Rather than telling Nicole that her answer is incorrect, the interviewer asks Nicole how she got that answer, to which Nicole replies, "I guessed!" The interviewer repeats the problem, getting the same response from Nicole. Then the interviewer asks Nicole if using blocks would help her; he adds that her using blocks would help him to see how she is thinking. The interviewer helps Nicole organize the blocks by separating the blocks she has counted out from the rest of the blocks. Nicole counts out 5 from the initial set, counts the remaining blocks, and gives an answer of 10. The interviewer responds, "Ten? Okay, I see just how you solved that."

Based on what you observed by watching this vignette, what does Nicole understand about subtraction? Why did she get an incorrect answer even after she modeled the problem with blocks? (You may need to watch the end of the video again to catch the mistake!) Are there other questions you'd like to ask her? What does she need more practice with? If you were Nicole's teacher, what would you do next to help her understanding grow?

The Assessment Standards

In 1995, the NCTM published the *Assessment Standards for School Mathematics*. Completing the trilogy of standards developed by NCTM, these Assessment Standards describe new assessment strategies and practices that "enable teachers and others to assess students' performance in a manner that reflects the NCTM's reform vision for school mathematics" (NCTM, 1995, p. 1). For the purpose of this text, we will refer to the *NCTM Assessment Standards for School Mathematics* as the Assessment Standards.

The NCTM Principles and Standards lists *assessment* as one of its six principles for school mathematics. As mentioned in the previous section, the Standards note the important role of assessment in supporting learning and providing useful information to teachers and students. The Principles and Standards reinforces the importance of assessment as stated in the Assessment Standards.

The Assessment Standards describe five shifts that are needed to attain the vision of the Curriculum Standards (see Table 4-1). These shifts clearly characterize the recommended changes in mathematics teaching, learning, and assessment.

What Is Assessment?

Assessment is " the process of gathering evidence about a student's knowledge of, ability to use, and disposition toward mathematics and of making inferences from that evidence for a variety of purposes" (NCTM, 1995, p. 3).

The Assessment Standards include six standards to guide mathematics assessment and focus on six important areas: mathematics, learning, equity, openness, inferences, and coherence. These six standards set the criteria for determining the quality of mathematics assessments and ultimately the quality of instruction.

The *mathematics standard* states that "assessment should reflect the mathematics that all students need to know and be able to do" (NCTM, 1995, p. 11). This means that you must make sure you assess children's understanding of the mathematics concepts and procedures that current recommendations, such as the NCTM Curriculum Standards, say that children should know.

The *learning standard* states that "assessment should enhance mathematics learning" (NCTM, 1995, p. 13); that is, good assessments are those that not only assess children's understanding but also encourage and support further growth in that understanding.

TABLE 4-1 Recommended Shifts in Mathematics Instruction

A Shift in	Toward	Away from
• Content	• A rich variety of mathematical topics and problem situations	• Just arithmetic
• Learning	• Investigating problems	• Memorizing and repeating
• Teaching	• Questioning and listening	• Telling
• Evaluation	• Evidence from several sources	• A single test judged externally
• Expectation	• Using concepts and procedures to solve problems	• Just mastering isolated concepts and procedures

Source: Adapted from Assessment Standards for School Mathematics (pp. 2–3) by National Council of Teachers of Mathematics, 1995, Reston, VA: National Council of Teachers of Mathematics. Copyright 1995 by the National Council of Teachers of Mathematics. Used with permission.

The *equity standard* states that "assessment should promote equity" (NCTM, 1995, p. 15). Equity in this context means that all children should be successful in math. Thus, assessments should take into account differences among children to support the learning of all children. This can be done, for example, by permitting different modes of responses to an assessment.

The *openness standard* states that "assessment should be an open process" (NCTM, 1995, p. 17). An open process includes informing the public about the process, involving teaching professionals, and being accepting of review and change.

The *inferences standard* states that "assessment should promote valid inferences about mathematics learning" (NCTM, 1995, p. 19). Valid inferences are those based on relevant evidence, which could include evidence from multiple sources, such as tests, teacher observations, and portfolios.

The *coherence standard* states that "assessment should be a coherent process" (NCTM, 1995, p. 21). Specifically, the assessment process must (1) be complete and sensible, (2) match the purposes for which it is being conducted, and (3) be consistent with curriculum and instruction that have been implemented.

Clearly these standards show that the purposes of assessment are moving toward a broader view focused not on merely assigning grades but on developing children's understanding.

Purposes of Assessment

According to the NCTM Principles and Standards, assessment may be used for several purposes, including diagnosis, instructional feedback, grading, generalized mathematical achievement, and program evaluation. When done well, assessment helps children and parents realize what children have learned and what they still need to learn. It also allows you to understand what the children know so you can plan appropriate instruction.

Similarly, the Assessment Standards identify four purposes for assessment:

1. *Monitoring children's progress* toward learning goals is a continuous process that includes setting high expectations and collecting evidence about children's understanding and progress.
2. *Making instructional decisions* refers to teachers using evidence of children's understanding to modify instruction to better meet children's needs and to lead to increased learning.
3. *Evaluating children's achievement* must be done at regular intervals and includes collecting evidence, summarizing it, and reporting it. This serves both to inform parents and to ensure that important milestones are attained.

NCTM Principles and Standards Link 4-1

Instead of assuming that the purpose of assessment is to rank students on a particular trait, the new approach assumes that high public expectations can be set that every student can strive for and achieve, that different performances can and will meet agreed-on expectations, and that teachers can be fair and consistent judges of diverse student performances. (NCTM, 1995, p. 1)

4. *Evaluating programs* must be done by collecting evidence about children's learning to ensure that all children are making progress.

Each of these four purposes of assessment is an important component in improving teaching and learning. For example, in monitoring a child's progress, you can recognize increased growth or a lack of growth on the part of the child. This assessment data can be used to guide instructional decision making and improve instruction. Also, because evaluating a child's achievement is a part of effective instruction, assessment records are accumulated to reflect a child's accomplishments or underscore a need for an evaluation to determine the appropriateness of giving special learning support services to the child. Further, evaluating the mathematics program itself can lead to a decision to make program modifications. Each of these assessment purposes provides you with information to benefit children's learning. The use of any one of them, however, requires several phases of planning.

Phases of Assessment

Assessment generally has four parts or phases: planning what kind of assessment tool to use, gathering evidence, interpreting that evidence, and applying the results to measure growth or determine the need for change. These phases are interconnected, although not necessarily sequential. It often is helpful, however, to keep these phases in mind to aid decision making related to assessment choices.

When *planning assessment*, think about the purpose of the assessment, the methods you will use to collect and interpret evidence, the criteria you will use to judge performance, and the format you will use to summarize findings. For example, do you intend to use the results of the assessment primarily to decide how to plan tomorrow's math lesson? Or will the results be used to help parents understand their child's strengths and the areas that need growth?

When *gathering evidence*, consider the activities, tasks, and procedures you will use to involve children. For example, might the children choose to respond in different ways—such as by using manipulative materials, drawing a

> **myeducationlab** The Power of Classroom Practice — Go to the Assignments and Activities section of Topic 4: "Assessment" in the MyEducationLab for your course. Complete the activity "IMAP—Authentic Assessment in Math" to see how one teacher helps her students use mathematical reasoning.

picture, or writing a description—to convey their understanding of a concept?

When *interpreting evidence*, think about how you will determine comprehension and the criteria you will use to analyze the evidence. For example, how do you hope the children will respond to a question? What other responses are acceptable to demonstrate understanding?

When *applying results* from assessment, consider how the results will be reported, and decide how the results will affect future instructional decisions. For example, will you share the results with parents on written report cards or orally during parent–teacher conferences? How will you use student comprehension to plan instruction for the next lesson or the next unit or to reteach particular concepts?

Assessment Choices

The purpose of the information you gather from assessment determines how it should be used. For example, generalized mathematics achievement can best be assessed with standardized testing instruments. Standardized testing also is useful to indicate how well the class is doing as a whole and the effectiveness of instruction or instructional programs. Individual diagnosis, however, is better done through a variety of other means, including observation, interviews and oral questioning, performance tasks, and a collection of children's work over time (such as in the maintaining of portfolios). Through the use of any of these means, you can assess the children's understanding of mathematical concepts, as well as their computational ability, problem-solving ability, thinking processes and solution strategies, attitudes, and oral and written communication skills. Recall the video clip of Nicole mentioned earlier in this chapter. What were you able to observe about Nicole's mathematics understanding, strategies, and other skills from this short clip?

Achievement Tests

Tests are probably the first measurement tools that come to mind when considering the evaluation of a child's progress. An achievement test generally falls into one of two categories: standardized or teacher-made.

Standardized tests. Most standardized achievement tests are norm-referenced tests because their purpose is to compare a child's level of performance to the performance of a large number of similar children. The norming population usually represents a cross section of children in a school system, a state, or even a nation. Other standardized tests are criterion-referenced, measuring student achievement as compared to a set of state or national standards. Standardized tests usually are administered on the mandate of a school district or state department of education and sometimes are given at incremental levels, such as second grade, fourth grade, and so on. Some states and local school districts have expended considerable time, effort, and money to design tests that would be valid for the state or local objectives at different levels. Widely used standardized tests include the Stanford Achievement Test and the Iowa Test of Basic Skills.

Teacher-made tests. Teacher-made tests are criterion-referenced tests because they measure knowledge of specific objectives. A chapter test in a textbook often does not reflect all of the objectives you have covered, so you may decide to devise a test to assess children's progress in understanding material in the chapter. Teacher-made tests often are given as pretests as well as post-tests. Pretests are important to help you plan instruction based on class needs. Here are some steps to follow when you design a test:

- List all the objectives to be measured.
- List the thought processes children may need to answer test questions.
- Design test items that will match both the objectives to be measured and the critical thinking processes involved.

Further, it is necessary to edit all items carefully to eliminate ambiguity. The teacher should prepare the test in an attractive and clear format. The final step is to analyze the results, examining how children responded to each item, as discussed in the following section.

Using tests to determine children's learning needs. Teacher-made tests as well as chapter tests from a textbook can be used to diagnose or determine children's learning needs. These tests may be used as pretests, given before beginning instruction on a concept, or as post-tests, used after a unit of instruction has been completed. The key element in diagnosing children's learning needs is *how* these tests are used.

Teachers need to go beyond simply calculating a child's score on a test and assigning a grade to each child. The main point is not merely to get a score to record in your gradebook, but to figure out what children have learned and on what concepts they need more practice. Carefully examine each child's response to each item and also look for overall patterns in children's responses and errors. You may want to tally or make a table showing the number of children who answered each item incorrectly.

Then use these results to determine instructional needs by analyzing the class's performance on each item. Which items did most or all of the children answer correctly? Next, look for patterns in the errors. For example, if many children made errors on a certain set of items measuring understanding of a particular concept, you may choose to provide more learning experiences on those concepts. Observation and interviews, as described in the next section, are other ways to gather diagnostic data. The key is to use assessment information to fine-tune your instruction to help all children meet the standards.

Individualizing Assessment

Individual diagnosis of children's understanding of mathematical concepts, computational ability, problem-solving ability, thinking processes and solution strategies, attitudes, and oral and written communication skills is best made through a variety of means. These means include observation, conferences and interviews, performance tasks, collecting children's work over time in portfolios, and self-assessment.

Observation. Observation involves systematically examining children's behavior. It is a powerful way to learn more about what children know and are able to do.

Observation is most effective when you concentrate on a few children each day and systematically observe specific aspects, such as solution strategies used, types of problems solved, and level of skill of concept development.

Using Preassessments to Inform Instruction

To decide where to focus their instructional time, teachers can use teacher-made tests as well as chapter tests from a textbook to determine what children know about topics BEFORE beginning instruction. There may be some topics that children already know. Sometimes teachers ask, "How can children know anything about this topic if I haven't taught it yet this year?" Children learn about math concepts in many ways and in many places. They may have learned something about a topic in the previous school year. They may have learned something outside of school. If children already understand a topic, there's no need to spend time on that topic, freeing up valuable instructional time for other topics that children have not yet mastered.

Preassessments don't have to be complicated. Teachers can have their children complete a short pretest of the key concepts in the upcoming unit of instruction, and then analyze the children's performance, looking for patterns in the errors, similar to what they may do when analyzing posttests. This analysis will indicate which concepts most children in the class understand, which concepts they are struggling with. The teacher can use this information to decide which, if any, topics can be omitted, and which may need more time and a variety of approaches to help children develop understanding.

Each of the following chapters in this textbook will include sample preassessments for the concepts in the chapter, and sample student work for you to analyze and consider the next instructional steps. The practice of using preassessment to determine how to focus upcoming lessons to best meet children's needs is very effective in helping children be successful in mathematics and is a very useful strategy for all teachers to use.

Examining Children's Reasoning

"'To me as a teacher, there's a lot of value in looking at students' explanations. We get a more complete picture of what our students have learned and how they are thinking about a particular math concept. I feel that I'm better able to make instructional decisions based on this information'" (Parke, Lane, Silver, & Magone (2003), p. 1).

Think back to the opening video clip of Nicole. What did you observe about Nicole's understanding of subtraction? Describe what she was able to do and what errors she made. For example, after prompting by the interviewer, Nicole was able to use blocks to model the problem situation, starting with a certain number of blocks and removing 5 blocks, then counting to find the answer. However, she made a mistake and counted out 15 blocks to start with, rather than 14 as stated in the problem, so her answer was off by one. She got the wrong answer—does this mean she is not able to do this type of problem? We don't have evidence from this short clip that she is able to solve subtraction word problems, but since the error she makes is a counting error seemingly not connected with subtraction, we could expect that she would usually be able to correctly solve problems such as these. It would be important, however, to pose a similar problem as a follow-up to test this hypothesis.

You can record observation data by keeping anecdotal records that include written notes describing children's behaviors. Checklists are another good way to organize data collected via observation. For example, to plan instruction, you might be interested in assessing the counting strategies children use to solve addition problems. You could use a checklist to keep track of which children are using the "counting on from the first addend" strategy and which children are using the "counting on from the larger addend" strategy. The checklist should contain the names of all the children in the class, with columns listing the date on which you observed each child using each strategy and the particular problem on which the strategy was used. Table 4-2 shows part of a sample observation checklist a teacher used to organize these data. Notice that the teacher completed this table over a period of several months. This checklist shows children's progress over time in using the two counting strategies observed.

TABLE 4-2 Part of a Sample Observation Checklist for First Graders' Use of Counting Strategies

	Date/Problem Application	
Child's Name	Counting on from FIRST Addend	Counting on from LARGER Addend
Andrew	*10/23* 2 + 5 =	*1/15* 3 + 9 =
Anton	*9/22* 3 + 4 =	*12/2* 2 + 9 =
Crystal	*10/23* 6 + 3 =	*11/15* 4 + 7 =
Gabriella	*1/22* 3 + 6 =	
Heather	*9/22* 3 + 4 =	*10/23* 3 + 8 =
Juan	*9/22* 3 + 4 =	*11/15* 4 + 7 =

Conferences. At times you may want to schedule a conference with a child. A planned conference would be more likely to occur when a child does one of the following:

- Reveals a special interest or expertise in a particular topic (you may help the student plan some additional work, culminating with a report or demonstration to the class).
- Demonstrates unusual insight or an unusual algorithm.
- Transfers into the class from another school.
- Demonstrates a particularly negative attitude.

Conferences with parents often reveal information and background that are helpful in understanding their children. For example, learning about previous attitude-forming experiences (positive and negative), experiences that contribute to the child's mathematical knowledge, experiences with computers, and parental attitudes toward mathematics often is useful in helping assess a child's progress or lack of progress. Some schools encourage conferences in which both the child and the parents are present.

Interviews. Interviews also may be planned when you want to assess the level of development of a concept. This could involve asking children to solve an addition word problem or to show three different representations of 3 times 6, for example. You can learn much about children's mathematical thinking through such interviews.

Spontaneous interviews usually occur as you watch children work. "Tell me how you did that" and "Here is another problem—think aloud as you work it out" are the kinds of questions or statements you might make in these more unstructured interviews. Giving a few words of encouragement may also be classified as a spontaneous interview.

Learning how to interview children. How can you learn how to interview children in order to assess their mathematics understanding? In the video clip "IMAP—Assessing Student Understanding 1" on MyEducationLab, a prospective elementary school teacher who has little interviewing experience begins an interview with Stephanie, a girl in first grade. The interviewer tries to set Stephanie at ease by explaining that the interview will not be graded and that the child is not expected to answer all the questions correctly. The interviewer tries to prepare Stephanie for probing questions by telling her that the interviewer may ask her how she thought about a problem. The interviewer also explains to Stephanie that she may use any materials available, including her fingers, to answer a question. This video clip provides an example of an introduction to an interview. Notice that a main purpose of this introduction is to put the child at ease.

PEARSON myeducationlab The Power of Classroom Practice Go to the Assignments and Activities section of Topic 4: "Assessment" in the MyEducationLab for your course. Complete the activity "IMAP—Assessing Student Understanding 1" to see how one teacher interviews a child to assess her math understanding.

Next view video clip "IMAP—Assessing Student Understanding 2" on MyEducationLab, to see Nicole, a second-grade girl, who is interviewed by an experienced interviewer. This interview takes place in a class of prospective elementary school teachers. Again, the start of the interview emphasizes making the child comfortable. Then the interviewer begins asking Nicole questions. Notice that the interviewer tries to avoid commenting on whether Nicole's answers are correct or incorrect; he focuses instead on the effort Nicole exerts. The interviewer does not lie to the child by telling her that her answer is correct when it is not; instead he generally avoids commenting on correctness and instead makes comments such as "I see just how you thought about that" or "Wow, that is a big number!" Occasionally the interviewer gently cuts the child off during counting, after he has learned what he set out to learn. The interviewer takes notes designed to help him remember specifics of the interview and usually explains to the child that he is taking notes because he wants to remember how she thought about the problems.

PEARSON myeducationlab The Power of Classroom Practice Go to the Assignments and Activities section of Topic 4: "Assessment" in the MyEducationLab for your course and complete the activity "IMAP—Assessing Student Understanding 2." How do these interviewing techniques differ?

Later in this book you will view other interviews of children. Each time, notice the interaction between the interviewer and the child, and try to assess what the child understands about the concepts being addressed in each interview.

Record keeping. You can keep records describing children's understanding of the content standards and their use of the process standards. One effective method to do this is to use an assessment checklist such as that shown in Table 4-3. This checklist specifies some of the number strand expectations stated in the NCTM Principles and Standards for Grades 3 through 5, linking these expectations with the five process standards: problem solving, reasoning and proof, communication, connections, and representation. You could make one copy of this checklist for each child in the class to track children's progress toward using each process while developing their understanding of each concept within that strand.

Performance assessment. Performance assessment in mathematics involves "presenting students with a mathematical task, project, or investigation, then observing, interviewing, and looking at their products to assess what they actually know and can do" (Stenmark, 1991, p. 13). Performance assessment can include evaluation of children's daily work, observations, conferences, and interviews.

When involved in a performance assessment, children demonstrate "their ability to use the skills they have learned and the conceptual understanding they have developed in the context of a real-life application or complex problem" (Collison, 1992). Collison uses the analogy of a driving test to describe processes involved in and characteristics of a mathematical performance assessment.

Performance assessment presents children with an opportunity to demonstrate their understanding rather than just their speed and accuracy. It provides you with more detailed information about children's thinking, solution processes, misconceptions, and errors. For example, a performance assessment can tell you if children are able to use chips to represent fractions as parts of a set as well as parts of a region, such as parts of a circle. Performance assessment can show if children are able to construct a graph from a set of data.

TABLE 4-3 Assessment Checklist Linking Content and Process Standards

	Problem Solving: Can the Child Solve Problems Related to This Concept?		Reasoning and Proof: How Does the Child Reason About This Concept?	
Child Expectation: Number Strand	Developing as expected	Needs development	Developing as expected	Needs development
Understand the place-value structure of the base-ten number system and be able to represent and compare whole numbers and decimals.				
Recognize equivalent representations for the same number and generate them by decomposing and composing numbers.				
Develop understanding of fractions as parts of unit wholes, as parts of a collection, as locations on number lines, and as divisions of whole numbers.				
Use models, benchmarks, and equivalent forms to judge the size of fractions.				
Recognize and generate equivalent forms of commonly used fractions, decimals, and percentages.				
Explore numbers less than 0 by extending the number line and through familiar applications.				
Describe classes of numbers (e.g., odds, primes, squares, multiples) according to characteristics such as the nature of their factors.				

NCTM Principles and Standards Link 4-2

To demonstrate real growth in mathematical power, students need to demonstrate their ability to do major pieces of work that are more elaborate and time consuming than just short exercises, sets of word problems, and chapter tests. Performance tasks, projects, and portfolios are some examples of more complex instructional and assessment activities. (NCTM, 1995, p. 36)

Performance assessment can also be a part of daily lessons. For example, at the start of a lesson, you can ask the children to do a "quick-write" of everything they know about the topic of the lesson. During a lesson on fractions, for instance, you could ask children to quickly write everything they know about the fraction $\frac{1}{2}$. At the end of the lesson, you ask the children to add anything they'd like to their quick-write. These performance assessments provide feedback to you and the child about what the child knows at the beginning of the lesson and what the child has learned from the lesson.

Examples of performance tasks. Performance tasks include an elaborate problem-solving activity or an activity as simple as asking a child to set out counters in an array to illustrate a particular multiplication problem. Indeed, concrete materials often are part of the assessment. Performance assessment frequently is done with individuals or small groups. Figures 4-1, 4-2, and 4-3 include examples of performance assessment tasks.

Figure 4-2 contains tasks designed to assess students' understanding of the concept of division (discussed in Chapter 7). Notice the several different types of questions. One question asks students to show how they would use blocks to solve the problem $35 \div 5$. Another question asks students to explain how two different division problems are alike and different. Other questions ask students to solve story problems involving division. Each question assesses another aspect of students' understanding of the concept of division and provides you with a detailed picture of students' thinking about all aspects of this concept.

Communication: Can the Child Communicate Effectively About This Concept?		Connections: Can the Child Make Connections Related to This Concept?		Representation: How Does The Child Represent the Thinking Related to This Concept?	
Developing as expected	Needs development	Developing as expected	Needs development	Developing as expected	Needs development

FIGURE 4-1 Sample Performance Assessment Tasks

Fractions: Ask third-grade students who are learning about fractions to show you with manipulatives how they would divide different items, such as 5 candy bars, 10 pencils, or 11 comic books, among 4 students.

Place Value: Have students explain how they would teach a younger sibling to understand the meaning of tens and ones in place value.

Long Division: Give each group of students a different division problem. Ask each group to make a poster to share with the class that explains the methods they used in solving their problem.

Organizing and Displaying Data: Ask a group of students to find and demonstrate the value of *pi* by measuring the diameter and circumference of different circles, expressing the ratios, and finding decimal equivalents on a calculator. Allow the students to choose a way to explain and display their findings.

Data Collection: Your group s task is (1) to identify an interesting question that may be answered by collecting data, (2) to develop a plan for investigating this question, and (3) to prepare an oral report, with overheads or other displays, for the class. Here is a sample question: "How many bicycles are there within two miles of this school?" Your group's planning report is due in three days. Please keep a daily log of your work. Final reports will be due two weeks from today.

Source: *Mathematics assessment: Myths, models, good questions, and practical suggestions* (pp. 14–15), by J. K. Stenmark (Ed.), 1991, Reston, VA: National Council of Teachers of Mathematics. Copyright 1991 by NCTM. Used with permission.

FIGURE 4-2 Understanding the Concept of Division

Do the students understand what division means?

Can the students interpret different representations of division?

For example:

- Partitioning, or sharing—If there are 6 cookies and 2 people, how many will each person get?
- Measuring, or repeated subtraction—If you have 6 cookies and want each person to get 3 cookies, how many people will get cookies?

Take 35 blocks. Use the blocks to show how to do this problem: $35 \div 7 =$.

Solve these two problems and explain how they are alike or different:

- If you divide 35 blocks into 7 groups, how many will be in each group?
- If you put 35 blocks into groups of 7, how many groups will there be?

Solve these two problems and explain how they are alike or different:

- José had 6 children at his party. How would he divide 25 cookies among them?
- Jamie wanted each child in the game to have 6 marbles. She had 25 marbles. How many children could be in the game?

Assessment questions:

- Did students distinguish between the two forms of division?
- Were their block arrangements or explanations accurate and explanatory?
- Do they understand how division by grouping and by distributing are alike and different?

Source: *Mathematics assessment: A practical handbook for grades 3–5* (p. 9), by J. K. Stenmark and W. S. Bush, 2001, Reston, VA: National Council of Teachers of Mathematics. Copyright 2000 by NCTM. Used with permission.

Another example is presented in Figure 4-3, this time about the concept of fractions (discussed in Chapter 10). As in the previous example, these tasks ask students to use models, explain their thinking, and solve story problems centered around important concepts of fractions, including equivalence and comparison.

Materials designed for instruction can be quickly modified for use as a performance assessment by modifying the final question and changing the way it is administered.

The key to an effective performance task is to require children to provide *explanations* rather than *products*. For example, consider a basic activity in which children are asked to use a manipulative material, such as base-ten blocks, to represent a list of numbers. Figure 4-4, which shows possible responses, is an example. This task can easily be modified to focus on children's thinking by asking them to represent one number, say 37, in as many different ways as possible and to explain *why* they are the same. Children who understand that 37 is the same as $27 + 10$, for example, show that they understand equivalent representations and are able to think flexibly about the concept of place value.

What makes a good performance assessment task? According to Stenmark (1991), quality performance assessment tasks include several characteristics: They are *essential* (consistent with the core curriculum), *authentic* (use appropriate mathematics processes), *rich* (have many possibilities), *engaging* (thought-provoking), *active* (children interact with other children), *feasible* (can be done in time available), *equitable* (accessible to children with different learning styles), and *open* (can be solved with more than one solution strategy).

Using rubrics to score performance tasks. Performance tasks give you a great deal of information to use in evaluating children's mathematics understanding. Sometimes you may choose to quantify children's performance on a performance task. One way of doing this is by using a structure or scoring system known as a *rubric*. A rubric is a scale, often ranging between two and six points, used to holistically score a child's work.

You might begin by using a two-point rubric, sorting children's work into two piles based on whether or not the children's work demonstrates understanding. This

FIGURE 4-3 Understanding the Concept of Fractions

Can the students show that the size of the fractional part depends on the size of the "whole"?

Your friend states that the fractions $\frac{2}{3}$ and $\frac{5}{6}$ are the same size because both have one "piece" fewer than the whole unit.

Is your friend correct? Use words, numbers, and pictures to explain your answer.

What is the same about the two fractional parts and what is different? What fraction is shaded in each of the shapes below?

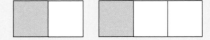

Assessment questions:
- Can the students explain the relationship of the various fractional parts to the whole unit?
- Can they distinguish between shapes that are identical in size and shape but that represent different parts of the whole?

Can they show an understanding of the relative value of a variety of fractions?

On the number line below, put these fractions in order from the smallest to the largest: $\frac{1}{4}, \frac{2}{3}, \frac{3}{6}, \frac{1}{5}, \frac{3}{4}$.

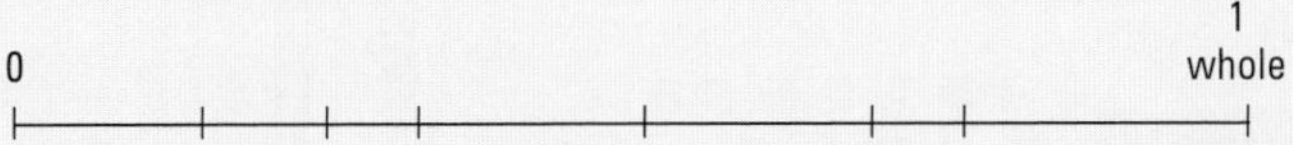

Explain how you decided where to put each fraction.

Assessment questions:
- Are the fractions placed fairly close to where they should be?
- Do the explanations make sense?
- What suggestions would you make to improve or modify the responses?

Source: Mathematics assessment: A practical handbook for grades 3–5 (p. 12), by J. K. Stenmark and W. S. Bush, 2001, Reston, VA: National Council of Teachers of Mathematics. Copyright 2000 by NCTM. Used with permission.

somewhat crude analysis provides some information about children's performance, but if you need more detailed information, you may choose to move to a three-point scale.

A three-point rubric includes three levels, which might be differentiated as follows:

3 points	Demonstrates good understanding of the concept
2 points	Demonstrates some understanding of the concept
1 point	Demonstrates no understanding of the concept

A four-point rubric allows for more differences to be noted among the children's work. The following is an example of a four-point rubric (California Mathematics Council, 1996):

4 points	Fully accomplishes the purpose of the task
3 points	Substantially accomplishes the purpose of the task
2 points	Partially accomplishes the purpose of the task
1 point	Little or no progress toward accomplishing the purpose of the task

Table 4-4 shows a six-point rubric developed by the California Department of Education (Pandey, 1991). This rubric can be used to evaluate a variety of performance tasks with much detail.

Consider the following performance task: Four children want to share three cookies. Show how to share the cookies and explain how you know each person has the same amount. Figure 4-5 shows the work of three children who performed this task.

Notice that Andy does not complete the task. He does not seem to realize that each child could get part of a cookie. Using a four-point rubric, the score for his solution would be a "1." He makes little or no progress toward accomplishing the task.

In contrast, Becky makes a good start at solving the problem. She understands that each child will get part of a cookie and cuts each cookie into fourths. But she does not explain how much of a cookie each child gets in all. Using a four-point rubric, the score for her solution would be a "3." She substantially accomplishes the purpose of the task.

Chantal solves the problem completely. She cuts the cookie so that each child gets the same amount, and she uses fraction language to identify the total amount each child receives. Using a four-point rubric, the score for her solution would be a "4." In other words, she fully accomplishes the purpose of the task.

FIGURE 4-4 Changing a Learning Activity to a Performance Assessment Task

Learning Activity	Performance Assessment
Use base-ten blocks to show each number below:	Use base-ten blocks to show the number 37 as many different ways as you can:
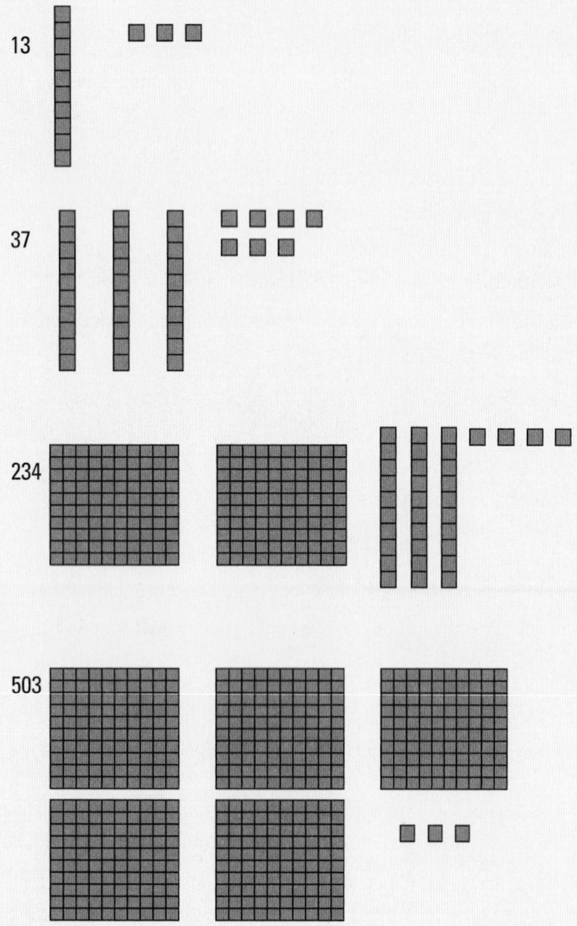 13	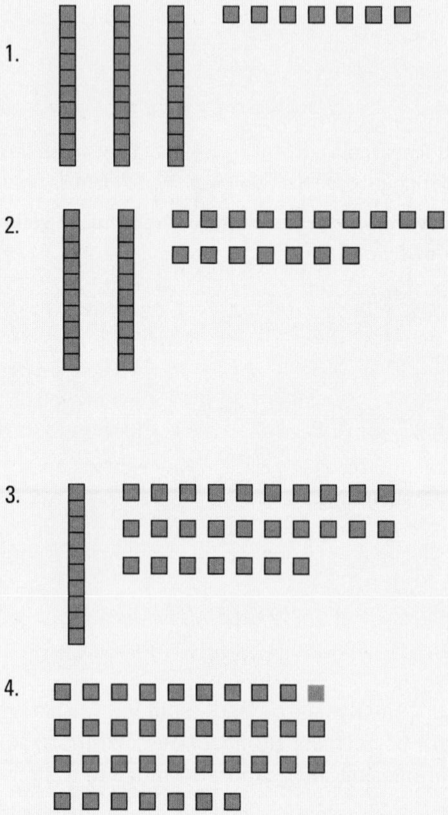 1.
37	2.
234	3.
503	4.

Children can use rubrics to assess their own work and that of other children. One benefit is that children come to understand why their work received the score that it did. But more important, using rubrics helps children recognize that developing an understanding of a concept occurs on different levels. Thus, the children's goal is to try to continue to enhance their understanding of mathematical tasks.

As with all forms of assessment, you should keep track of children's rubric scores on performance assessment tasks. Table 4-5 shows a sample record sheet for performance assessment tasks. Note that this record sheet includes children's names, the names of each performance task, and each child's score using a four-point rubric. You also may want to include a space for notes or comments on each child's understanding.

Portfolio assessment. A portfolio is a collection of selected children's work (Crowley, 1993). It provides an opportunity for children to showcase their work and growth in mathematics over a period of time, such as a school year. The use of portfolios promotes children's self-assessment, "encourages students to communicate their understandings of mathematics with a high level of proficiency, and emphasizes the role of the student as the active mathematician and the teacher as the guide" (Lambdin & Walker, 1994, p. 318).

Portfolios can provide children, teachers, and parents with much more detail about a child's performance in and understanding of mathematics than a letter grade offers. Further, portfolios are useful for supporting points of discussion in parent–teacher conferences.

What should be included? Portfolios may include a child's daily work, written descriptions of investigations, solved and unsolved problems, excerpts from the child's math journal, group reports, problems that the child wrote,

TABLE 4-4 Performance Standards for Children's Work

Level	Standard to Be Achieved for Performance at Specified Level
6	Fully achieves the purpose of the task while insightfully interpreting, extending beyond the task, or raising provocative questions.
	Demonstrates an in-depth understanding of concepts and content.
	Communicates effectively and clearly to various audiences, using dynamic and diverse means.
5	Accomplishes the purposes of the task.
	Shows clear understanding of concepts.
	Communicates effectively.
4	Substantially completes purposes of the task.
	Displays understanding of major concepts, even though some less important ideas may be missing.
	Communicates successfully.
3	Purpose of the task not fully achieved; needs elaboration; some strategies may be ineffectual or not appropriate; assumptions about the purposes may be flawed.
	Gaps in conceptual understanding are evident.
	Limits communication to some important ideas; results may be incomplete or not clearly presented.
2	Important purposes of the task not achieved; work may need redirection; approach to task may lead away from its completion.
	Presents fragmented understanding of concepts; results may be incomplete or arguments may be weak.
	Attempts communication.
1	Purposes of the task not accomplished.
	Shows little evidence of appropriate reasoning.
	Does not successfully communicate relevant ideas; presents extraneous information.

Source: A sampler of mathematics assessment (p. 30), by T. Pandey, 1991, Sacramento, CA: California Department of Education. Copyright 1991 by the California Department of Education. Reprinted by permission of the California Department of Education.

illustrations, photographs of the child's mathematics projects, and videotapes of the child's mathematics presentations or projects.

One method is to have two portfolios: a working portfolio and a permanent portfolio. Children can use the working portfolio over time to collect materials they might want to keep in their permanent portfolios. At the end of a designated period of time, or as the grading period nears its end, children can reevaluate their work in their working portfolios and decide which entries to move to their permanent portfolios. A child may ask for help in selecting items to move to the permanent portfolio. To ensure that the portfolio reflects a range of work assignments, you may decide to specify that children include at least one example of a variety of types of activities, such as journal entries, investigations, nonroutine problems, projects, application problems, and group work.

It can be helpful if the children write a brief description for each portfolio entry, explaining their selections and what they demonstrate about their understanding, attaching the description to the appropriate entry. Some teachers also ask that each child select another child to conduct a written review or peer evaluation of his or her portfolio, as well as complete a personal review for self-assessment.

Evaluating portfolios. Several criteria can be used for evaluating portfolios. One is to evaluate children's characteristics such as problem-solving skills, ability to make mathematical connections, ability to communicate mathematically, and attitudes toward mathematics and self (Crowley, 1993).

TABLE 4-5 Sample Teacher's Record Sheet for Performance Assessment Tasks

	Rubric Score on Performance Tasks (Using 4-Point Scale)			
Students	Cookie Sharing Task	Ways to Make 37		
Andy	1			
Becky	2			
Chantal	4			
Jeff	2			
Juan	3			

FIGURE 4-5 A Cookie-Sharing Performance Task

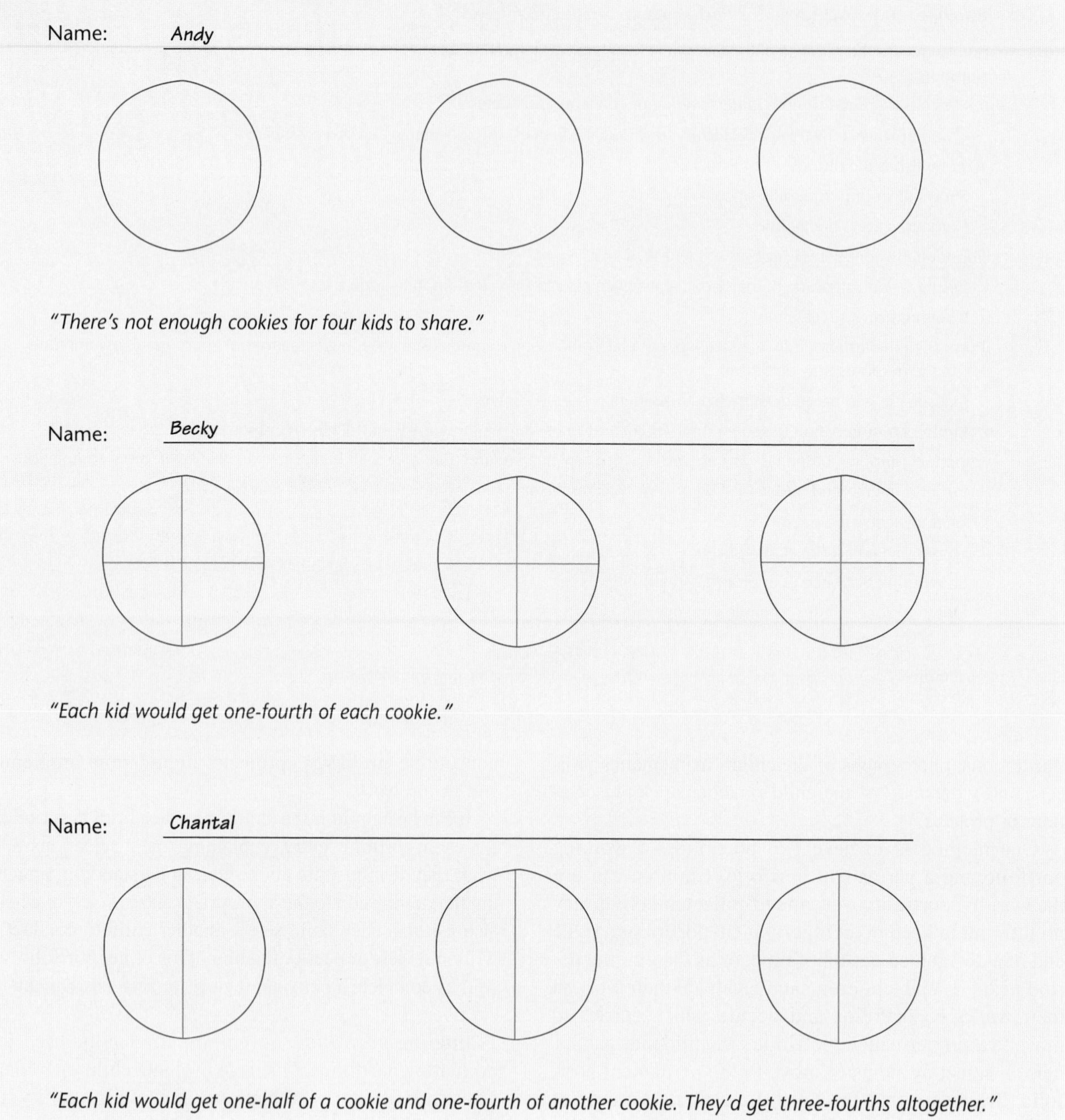

Name: Andy
"There's not enough cookies for four kids to share."
Name: Becky
"Each kid would get one-fourth of each cookie."
Name: Chantal
"Each kid would get one-half of a cookie and one-fourth of another cookie. They'd get three-fourths altogether."

Another set of portfolio evaluation criteria (Stenmark, 1991) includes the following:

- Understands the problem or task.
- Uses a variety of strategies.
- Uses models, technology, and other resources.
- Interprets results.
- Solves problems in a cooperative group.
- Relates mathematics to other subjects and the real world.
- Uses appropriate mathematics language and symbols.
- Shows evidence of self-assessment and self-correction of work.

Before starting to use portfolios in your classroom, think about which criteria are most important, and make sure your portfolio evaluation plan measures them.

Self-assessment. Self-assessment helps children to reflect critically on their own work and reasoning while also encouraging them to take responsibility for their learning and to think independently. One way to include self-assessment

> **myeducationlab** The Power of Classroom Practice Go to the Assignments and Activities section of Topic 4: "Assessment" in the MyEducationLab for your course. Complete the activity "Using a Rubric" and consider the importance of self-assessment for students.

in the classroom is to have children keep math journals. Have children write in their math journals regularly, reflecting on what they know about a certain concept and what parts of it may be unclear.

The following sample prompts are related to multiplication:

- Tell me everything you know about multiplication.
- How do you like to solve multiplication problems? Is there another way to solve multiplication problems that you'd like to learn?
- Is there anything about multiplication that's still a little unclear or confusing?
- What else would you like to know about multiplication?
- Are you good at doing multiplication? Why or why not?
- Is there anything about multiplication you'd like to do better?

Writing prompts also may focus on more general issues:

- How are you doing in math class?
- What in math class comes easily to you? Why do you think so?
- What do you have to work harder to understand?

Helping children develop self-assessment skills empowers them to become more independent math learners.

Assessing Attitudes Toward Mathematics

Success in mathematics often is positively correlated with favorable attitudes toward mathematics. It is important that you assess children's attitudes toward mathematics at the beginning of and throughout the school year. A number of ways are available for assessing children's feelings toward mathematics. A Likert-type attitude scale is the most common. In this type of scale, the child responds to statements such as "I am happier in mathematics class than in any other class" on a five-point scale ranging from strongly disagree to strongly agree. For children in the primary grades, the statements can be simplified and the choices reduced to three faces, as in Figure 4-6. The happy face is a positive response, the sad face is negative, and the middle face is neutral.

Literature Link 4-1

Assessment

Lankford, Mary D. (1998). ***Dominoes Around the World.*** New York: Morrow Junior Books. Ledwon, Peter, & Mets, Marilyn. (2000). ***Midnight Math.*** New York: Holiday House. Maisner, Heather. (1996). ***Planet Monster.*** Cambridge, MA: Candlewick Press.

Various children's books assess children's mathematical thinking through games, puzzles, and brief investigations. Children can read and solve the problems posed in the stories individually or with a partner. These books challenge children and provide individualized activities and assessments that do not need teacher guidance.

- ***Dominoes Around the World*** is a collection of domino games and puzzles from around the world. These games are challenging and can be initiated by children with little assistance from the teacher. Children apply mathematics skills and problem-solving strategies during the games.
- ***Midnight Math*** is a collection of 12 brief mathematics games for young children. Children practice basic skills, such as sorting, addition, subtraction, multiplication, and probability. Many of the games require the use of regular playing cards. Observe children as they work in small groups, and record your observations for individual conferences with children or parents.
- ***Planet Monster*** is a self-directed book in which children work through a number puzzle adventure. Basic skills that children use in the book include classifying, sorting, counting, telling time, and discriminating shapes. Children can work independently and record their answers, and then do a self-assessment by using the answers that appear at the end of the book.

Source: Dr. Patricia Moyer-Packenham, Utah State University.

FIGURE 4-6 Faces to Assess Attitudes About Mathematics

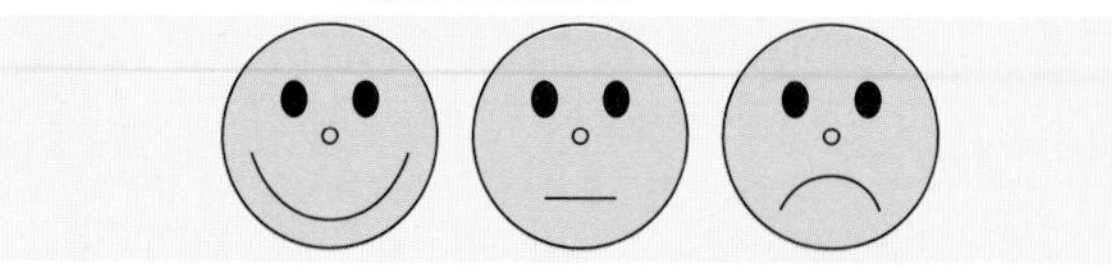

The semantic-differential approach to assessing attitudes consists of devising pairs of opposites, for example, "Easy" and "Hard" (or "Difficult," depending on the level of the children). Children mark a point on a five-point scale to indicate which word most closely represents their feelings. A typical presentation format is shown here:

A mark on the left above "Easy" usually is assigned a value of 1, whereas a mark on the right above "Hard" usually is assigned a value of 5, with corresponding values falling in between. The greater the total score, the more positive the attitude toward mathematics.

Sentence completion also can be used to assess attitudes. Give children the beginning of a sentence and ask them to complete it. For example,

Mathematics is important because __________.

Compared with other subjects, mathematics is __________.

Results are not easily quantifiable but often reveal very important insights into how children feel about mathematics.

Finally, daily routine observations yield important clues about children's attitudes toward mathematics. Children's half-muttered statements, level of enthusiasm, degree of perseverance, and other behaviors are indications of their feelings toward mathematics. You can collect these data and use them to improve your teaching.

Conclusion

Assessment is an integral part of mathematics teaching and learning, providing information about children's growth and development in conceptual understanding. Many types of assessment are available to you; each type plays an important role in evaluating and maximizing children's learning. The type of assessment you choose to use is dependent on the purpose for the assessment.

IN PRACTICE

Complete the following activities.

1. Visit an elementary or middle school classroom and interview a teacher. How does the teacher assess children's mathematics understanding and achievement? Characterize the assessment according to the types discussed in this chapter.
2. Visit a classroom and ask for samples of the written mathematics work of at least two children. How would you assess the children's understanding based on that written work?
3. Interview a teacher who uses either performance tasks or portfolios as part of a mathematics assessment plan. How does the teacher employ performance tasks or portfolios in assessing the children?

PEARSON myeducationlab The Power of Classroom Practice Now go to Topic 4: "Assessment" in the MyEducationLab (www.myeducationlab.com) for your course, where you can:

- Find learning objectives for "Problem Solving" along with the national standards that connect to these objectives.
- Apply and practice your understanding of the core teaching skills identified in the chapter with a Building Teaching Skills and Dispositions learning unit.
- Complete Assignments and Activities that can help you more deeply understand the chapter content.
- Check your comprehension of the content covered in the chapter by going to the Study Plan in the Book-Specific Resources for your text. Here you will be able to take a chapter quiz, receive feedback on your answer, and then access Review, Practice, and Enrichment activities to enhance your understanding of chapter content.

LINKS TO THE INTERNET

Assessment in Mathematics Teaching

http://mathforum.org/mathed/assessment.html

Contains links to publications and presentations about mathematics assessment.

Assessment Resources

http://score.kings.k12.ca.us/assess.html

Contains links to mathematics assessment resources.

Balanced Assessment in Mathematics

http://balancedassessment.concord.org/

Contains sample mathematics assessment tasks for elementary and secondary grades.

RESOURCES FOR TEACHERS

Reference Books: Assessment

Bryant, D., & Driscoll, M. (1998). *Exploring classroom assessment in mathematics*. Reston, VA: National Council of Teachers of Mathematics.

Burrill, J. (Ed.) (2005). *Grades 6–8 mathematics assessment sampler*. Reston, VA: National Council of Teachers of Mathematics.

Bush, W. S. (Ed.). (2001). *Mathematics assessment: Cases and discussion questions for grades K–5*. Reston, VA: National Council of Teachers of Mathematics.

Bush, W. S., & Leinwand, S. (Eds.). (2000). *Mathematics assessment: A practice handbook for grades 6–8*. Reston, VA: National Council of Teachers of Mathematics.

Gawronski, J. D. (Ed.) (2005). *Grades 3–5 mathematics assessment sampler*. Reston, VA: National Council of Teachers of Mathematics.

Glanfield, F., Bush, W. S., & Stenmark, J. K. (Eds.). (2003). *Mathematics assessment: A practice handbook for grades K–2*. Reston, VA: National Council of Teachers of Mathematics.

Huinker, D. (Ed.) (2006). *Prekindergarten – grade 2 mathematics assessment sampler*. Reston, VA: National Council of Teachers of Mathematics.

Stenmark, J. K., & Bush, W. S. (Eds.). (2001). *Mathematics assessment: A practice handbook for grades 3–5*. Reston, VA: National Council of Teachers of Mathematics.

CHAPTER

Developing Number Concepts

Developing Your Math Teaching Skills

When you have finished studying this chapter, you should be able to do the following:

- Describe the types of prenumber activities that support the development of children's understanding of number concepts.
- Describe the types of counting abilities that are important for children to develop.
- Describe several ways in which children must be able to represent numbers.
- Describe the types of number relationships that are essential for children to understand.

NCTM CONNECTING WITH THE STANDARDS

The National Council of Teachers of Mathematics (NCTM) Principles and Standards stresses the importance of early experiences to help young children develop a positive disposition about mathematics, stating that "opportunities for learning should be positive and supportive. Children must learn to trust their own abilities to make sense of mathematics" (NCTM, 2000, p. 74). The NCTM document goes on to list everyday activities through which children learn mathematical concepts:

- Sorting (putting toys or groceries away);
- Reasoning (comparing and building with blocks);
- Representing (drawing to record ideas);
- Recognizing patterns (talking about daily routines, repeating nursery rhymes, and reading predictable books);
- Following directions (singing motion songs such as "Hokey Pokey"); and
- Using spatial visualization (working puzzles). (p. 74)

The NCTM (2006) *Curriculum Focal Points* discusses the development of number concepts in prekindergarten and kindergarten. It states that prekindergarten students should:

- Understand that number words refer to quantity;
- Use one-to-one correspondence to solve problems by matching sets and comparing number amounts and in counting objects to 10 and beyond;
- Understand that the last word that they state in counting tells "how many";
- Count to determine number amounts and compare quantities (using language such as "more than" and "less than"); and
- Order sets by the number of objects in them (NCTM, 2006, p. 11).

Similarly, they state that kindergarten students should:

- Use numbers, including written numerals, to represent quantities and to solve quantitative problems, such as counting objects in a set, creating a set with a given number of objects, comparing and ordering sets or numerals by using both cardinal and ordinal meanings, and modeling simple joining and separating situations with objects; and

- Choose, combine, and apply effective strategies for answering quantitative questions, including quickly recognizing the number in a small set, counting and producing sets of given sizes, counting the number in combined sets, and counting backward (NCTM, 2006, p. 12).

One important role elementary teachers play is to help children develop an awareness of how mathematics exists in the world around them and how numbers can be used to help communicate about real-world situations.

ASSESSING MATHEMATICS UNDERSTANDING

In order to become familiar with the mathematics concepts and procedures discussed in this chapter, take a few minutes and complete the *Chapter 5 Preassessment,* following this paragraph. First, answer each question on your own and think about how you got the answer. Then think about the possible misunderstandings some elementary-school children might have about each topic. If you're able to, administer this assessment to a child, and analyze the child's understanding of these topics.

1. How high can you count? Show me. (Place 6 Unifix cubes or other counters on the table.) How many cubes are there? (Note how the child counts.) When the child finishes counting, ask again "How many cubes are there?" (Note his/her response.)
2. What number comes after 8? After 19? After 27? After 73? After 100? Before 16? Before 30? Before 58? Before 100?
3. Can you count by 2s? 3s? 5s? 10s? 100s? Show me (for each).
4. (Place Unifix cubes on the table; have 4 ten sticks and about 30 loose cubes.) Can you show me 24 with the cubes? (Note how the child counts out 24—by ones, tens?)
5. (Place an additional ten stick down.) How many do I have now? (Note how the child counts. If the child counts by tens (*10, 20, 30*), use the numbers in parentheses in the following problems. If the child counts by ones, use the numbers given in the problem.)

Examining Classroom Practice

Janice Sette-Lund's kindergarten classroom, featured in the video "Cubes and Containers" (Annenberg Video Series), includes a rich collection of materials that children enjoy using in mathematics tasks, including materials she has collected over the years, such as keys, bread tags, and erasers. Every day she begins with transition time, in which children can choose what they do. Ms. Sette-Lund's room is structured into many areas to support children's learning styles and preferences.

PEARSON myeducationlab The Power of Classroom Practice Go to the Video Examples section of Topic 5: "Number Concepts and Numeration" in the MyEducationLab for your course to view the Annenberg clip "Cubes and Containers."

In a small-group activity, Ms. Sette-Lund assigns two children the tasks of "manager" and "materials person." The materials person's responsibilities include getting a bucket of Unifix cubes for the group. She begins by asking the children to explore the materials. Several of the children decide to make trains of Unifix cubes, many of them in different patterns. After a few minutes, Ms. Sette-Lund asks the children to share what they did during their exploration time.

Next, Ms. Sette-Lund poses a challenge to the children: "What are some of the ways you can sort the Unifix cubes?" Children suggest several ways, including color and "feel" (texture). She asks if they could sort the cubes by shape, to which the children respond "no," explaining that they're all the same shape. One child suggests they might be able to sort them by size, and Ms. Sette-Lund asks how they would do that. The child replies that some of them might be different sizes, to which Ms. Sette-Lund responds, "Well, take a look. What do you think?" The child compares two cubes, verifies that they are the same size, and decides that the cubes cannot be sorted by size.

Ms. Sette-Lund then asks the children to sort the Unifix cubes by color. She asks the materials person to get tins for the group to use for sorting, but first asks each group to determine how many tins they need.

The children then begin sorting the cubes by color. During the task, children solve many smaller problems, such as how they should work together to do the sorting and what to do when their tins get too full.

Partway through the task, one group decides that they needed more than 10 containers to complete the sorting, because they feel that there are two shades of maroon, light and dark, and each shade should have a separate container. Ms. Sette-Lund honors their thinking and supports their decision to have an additional container, even asking follow-up questions about how many containers they needed (11), and *how many more* that was than what they started with (1).

This lesson shows children working together in cooperative groups to complete tasks that involved free exploration, patterning, and sorting.

Analyzing Assessment Results

Now let's look at the assessment results. These problems involve number concepts, including counting and place value. What was your general reaction to solving the problems? What in general do you think a teacher's goals should be regarding developing understanding of number concepts? If you had a chance to give the *Chapter 5 Preassessment* to a child, take a few minutes and analyze the results. How did the child answer these questions?

Analyze each question. How did you (and the student you administered the assessment to) solve each of the following problems? Let's look at questions 1 and 2 first.

1. How high can you count? Show me.
2. (Place 6 Unifix cubes or other counter on the table.) How many cubes are there? (Note how the child counts.) When the child finishes counting, ask again "How many cubes are there?" (Note his/her response.)

Comments: Questions 1 and 2 are basic counting questions. Does the child know the number-word sequence for counting? Does s/he make a one-to-one correspondence between the number words and the objects being counted? Does s/he understand that the last word said when counting tells how many there are in all?

3. What number comes after 8? After 19? After 27? After 73? After 100? Before 16? Before 30? Before 58? Before 100?
4. Can you count by 2s? 3s? 5s? 10s? 100s? Show me (for each).

Comments: Question 3 assesses whether a child understands numbers that come before or after other numbers. Is it harder to find the numbers that come *before* rather than the numbers that come *after*? Question 4 focuses on skip counting, which is helpful when learning multiplication facts. Is the child more successful in skip counting by some numbers? Which ones? Why do you think that is?

5. (Place Unifix cubes on the table; have 4 ten sticks and about 30 loose cubes.) Can you show me 24 with the cubes? (Note how the child counts out 24—by ones, tens?)
6. (Place an additional ten stick down.) How many do I have now? (Note how the child counts. If the child counts by tens [*10, 20, 30*], use the numbers in parentheses in the following problems. If the child counts by ones, use the numbers given in the problem.)

Comments: Questions 5 and 6 assess some basic notions of grouping by tens, which lay the foundation for place value understanding (which will be discussed in Chapter 6). Does the child use tens or does s/he work only with ones (or units)?

Take a minute and reflect on this assessment. Did your child have more difficulty with some of the questions? What do you want to learn more about in order to help children understand number concepts?

Building on Assessment Results

Think about what we can do to help strengthen children's understandings and minimize (and hopefully eradicate) their misunderstandings and misconceptions.

Children need lots of experiences to develop understanding of number concepts. Quite often, children's errors related to these concepts are due to limited experiences. Teaching about number concepts must begin by assessing children's understanding and then provide experiences for children to develop new understandings and skills. The table below lists several common misunderstandings and errors children make regarding number concepts and what a teacher can do to help children who have these misunderstandings or make these errors.

IF students . . .	THEN . . .
make mistakes in the number-word counting sequence	*give them more opportunities* to count objects, and *model* the number-word sequence.
make mistakes with one-to-one correspondence while counting	*give them more opportunities* to count objects, and *model* the process of making a one-to-one correspondence between each object and the number describing that object.
don't understand that the last word they say when counting a group of objects tells how many objects there are in all	*model* the process of counting and then stating the total number of objects in the group.
do not use groups of ten in counting large sets of objects	*model* the process of making and using groups of ten, and *discuss* the benefits.

NCTM NUMBER AND OPERATIONS STANDARDS AND EXPECTATIONS ADDRESSED IN THIS CHAPTER		
Instructional programs from Pre-K–12 should enable all students to—	**In Prekindergarten through grade 2 all students should—** (NCTM, 2000, p. 78)	**In grades 3–5 all students should—** (NCTM, 2000, p. 148)
• understand numbers, ways of representing numbers, relationships among numbers, and number systems.	• count with understanding and recognize "how many" in sets of objects. • develop understanding of the relative position and magnitude of whole numbers and of ordinal and cardinal numbers and their connections. • develop a sense of whole numbers and represent and use them in flexible ways, including relating, composing, and decomposing numbers. • connect number words and numerals to the quantities they represent, using various physical models and representations.	• understand the place-value structure of the base-ten number system and be able to represent and compare whole numbers and decimals. • recognize equivalent representations for the same number and generate them by decomposing and composing numbers. • describe classes of numbers (e.g., odds, primes, squares, and multiples) according to characteristics such as the nature of their factors.

The Foundations of Numbers

Counting activities, comparing sets, and learning the sequence of number names and the numerals to represent one-digit numbers have traditionally formed an important part of kindergarten and first-grade mathematics programs because it is believed that such activities help a child develop an understanding of number concepts.

Other activities that support the development of number concepts are classifying, seriating, and patterning (Piaget, 1965). As with counting, by the time children enter kindergarten, they will have had experiences in these processes, whether through play or through interactions with adults. At school, you should plan activities for children so that these processes will eventually extend to number classification, ordering, and patterning.

Understanding numbers resides in the recognition and knowledge of number relationships (Van de Walle, 1994). Knowing the number 5 means more than being able to rationally count a set of 5. It involves knowing about this number in relationship to other numbers. For example, 5 is 1 less than 6, 5 is 1 more than 4, and 5 is 3 plus 2. Developing number relationships is at the heart of kindergarten and first-grade mathematics learning.

Prenumber Activities

Classification. The process of classifying or sorting a collection of objects involves focusing on an attribute or characteristic of the objects and grouping the objects based on that characteristic. For example, children could sort a collection of books according to the characteristic "stories about animals."

Connecting with science and social studies. Classification is a topic that lends itself nicely to integrating mathematics with other subject areas such as science and social studies. For science and social studies projects, teachers often take children on outings—trips to the zoo, nature walks, or visits to local establishments such as a grocery store, a department store, a bank, a factory, or a post office. During an outdoor excursion, you can ask children to gather a small collection of objects. On return to the classroom, you might focus a science lesson on the characteristic "growing," and the objects collected can be classified in sets of "things that grow" (e.g., leaves, moss, mushrooms, twigs) and "things that do not grow" (e.g., stones, metal, paper). While at a grocery store, children might be asked to observe how food displays are organized (fruits in one section, vegetables in another, meats in another, etc.); at a department store, they could observe the furniture area (bedroom furniture displayed together, living room furniture together in another area, etc.) or how shoes are displayed (children's shoes in one area, women's and men's in other separate areas).

If it is not feasible to go on class field trips, children could be encouraged to notice how objects are classified during family outings or in their home. For example, children can examine kitchen cabinets, clothes drawers or closets, etc., to see how objects are organized. Provide time for the children to report their findings to the class. Encourage children to describe what things were grouped together and why.

Other classification activities. In class, the children themselves can be the objects for classification activities. Attributes that can be considered for classification include wearing shoes with laces or without laces, wearing something red or wearing something green, wearing a buttoned blouse or shirt or wearing a t-shirt or other shirt without buttons. Depending on the classification category, some children in a class may not be able to participate in a particular activity. The class should discuss this so that children will know why they "do not belong" in either category being classified. Sometimes, all children can participate if two categories are specified as, for example, children wearing shoes with laces or without laces. It is also possible to select more than two classification categories, such as people wearing red, people wearing green, and people wearing neither red nor green. This sort of classification, however, is more complex for children.

Commercial classification sets. A commercial set of Attribute Logic Blocks lends itself to numerous classification activities of varying sophistication. The set consists of plastic blocks in five shapes (triangle, square, rectangle, hexagon, and circle), two different sizes (large and small), two thicknesses (thin, thick), and three colors (yellow, red, and blue), for a total of 60 pieces. The set is structured; that is, there is only one block for every possible combination of values for the attributes. For example, there is only one large, thin, red circle. If purchasing a set of Attribute Logic Blocks is problematic, try making a set from felt or foam. The shapes can be placed on flannel- or felt-covered boards for display.

In a lesson observing attributes, children may first focus on color. Through maturation and experience, children are able to concentrate on other perceptual characteristics and eventually can classify sets according to abstract attributes such as number.

Class conversation. When all the children have had an opportunity to sort a particular set of materials, you could gather the children on a mat for a class conversation. Your opening remark might be "Did you notice many differences in the things you've been sorting? Let's see what differences you noticed. Who would like to share one difference?" As children voice their observations, you could note their comments on cards to attach to the bulletin board. Sometime during the day or week, each child can post objects on the bulletin board or gather them into a group under their proper characteristic.

Class conversations can take place following any mathematical activity to provide an opportunity for children to talk about the mathematics they are doing. Such dialogue enhances the development of mathematical understanding (Baker & Baker, 1990).

Examining Children's Reasoning

Think back to Ms. Sette-Lund's classroom. What did her children understand, and what were they able to do related to classification? How did Ms. Sette-Lund structure the classroom environment and the lesson to support the development of children's reasoning and communication skills?

The following six activities describe classification experiences using unstructured materials. An additional activity using commercial attribute blocks is described in Activity 5-1.

1. Classifying

- Ask a small group of children to stand side-by-side in front of the others.
- Ask the class, "Can you tell why these girls and boys belong together?" (You decide on an attribute.)

2. Classifying

- Choose three children who are wearing something blue and one who is not.
- Ask the class, "Who doesn't belong in this group? Why not?"
- Choose someone to replace the child who does belong in this group, based on the chosen attribute.

3. Classifying

- Provide children with a collection of buttons, seeds, or other objects that have easily distinguishable attributes.
- Ask them to group the objects in ways they are the same.
- Have them tell or write about the groupings they made.
- Over a period of class days, provide children with lots of opportunities to classify objects, beginning with concrete items and moving to semi-concrete objects such as pictures of objects.

4. Describing Properties

- Have all children stand beside their chairs, and ask one child to volunteer to stand where all the children can see her or him.
- Have children, in turn, tell something about the volunteer. Example: "Jeremy has brown hair."
- As you write "brown hair" on the board, all children who have a different hair color should sit down. Other statements could refer to clothing and jewelry worn or other known facts about the person (e.g., Jeremy takes music lessons).
- Children continue to name properties of the volunteer until the volunteer is the only student left standing.

5. What Can We Sort?

- Ask the class to think of some collections they could classify.
- When a list has been generated, have children, on different days, select one of the collections named and think of ways to classify the collection.
- Children should record their ideas to be used at another time.

6. How Can We Sort This Collection?

- Using one of the collections identified by the children (previous activity), have them present their ideas about possible ways to sort the objects. If it is feasible to gather a set of the objects, do so for only one day, because some children may need to have the objects visible to think of characteristics.
- The particular set of objects gathered should then be classified.

Seriation. *Seriation* is the process of focusing on an attribute and then arranging or ordering a set of objects according to that attribute. For example, given a set of pencils or crayons, children could arrange them according to length. Cuisenaire Rods are a commercial set consisting of 10 rods—each of a different color and length—that can be ordered by length.

Before asking children to order a set of three or more objects, you should have them compare two objects so as to recognize different attributes and learn comparative terms. For example, children should be able to examine two objects and make such statements as the following:

This pencil is longer than that pencil.

This tower is shorter than that tower.

The red paper is larger than the green paper.

The tub of beans is heavier than the tub of macaroni.

When children are able to make these kinds of comparisons, ask them to order larger sets with more than two items according to various attributes.

In seriating or ordering activities, make sure you vary the number of objects to be ordered, because some children are successful in seriating 7 or fewer items but not with sets of 10 or more. Objects can be ordered, for example, according to mass, shade of color, length, size, height, or thickness.

Objects that can be seriated include the following:

Attribute	Objects to Be Ordered
Length	Sets of pencils, nails, pieces of rope or yarn
Size	Mittens, socks, containers, jars
Capacity	Measuring spoons, jars, boxes
Mass	Small containers of sugar, flour, rice, beans, etc.
Height	Children, potted plant seedlings, towers of cubes

You can construct sets of objects that vary in length, height, or size according to a fixed ratio such as strips of cardboard, cylinders cut from paper towel rolls, rectangles and other regular shapes, and outlines of houses or other objects. Pairs of objects of different lengths, such as vases and flowers, dolls and hats, or bats and balls, can be constructed and used for double seriation activities, as in Activity 5-2.

ACTIVITY 5-1 Guess Which Block I Have?

Materials

A set of attribute blocks for each child and the teacher

Procedure

1. Have the children select one block from their sets. The teacher does the same without showing the block to the children.
2. A child asks the teacher a question about the chosen block. Example: "Is your block red?" If the teacher's block is not red, the teacher answers, "No, my block is not red." The children who had chosen a red block must change their blocks for a nonred block.
3. The questioning continues until the teacher's block has been identified. By this time, every child should be holding a block that is the same as that of the teacher.
4. Have a child identify the block by naming attributes. Example: "The block is a large, thin, blue triangle."
5. Repeat procedures with another block. Children could guess the block selected by a child rather than by the teacher.

ACTIVITY 5-2 Double Seriation

Realia Strategies

Materials

A set of 8 to 12 similar paper balls and bats; each bat differs in length by 1 cm and each ball is proportionally larger

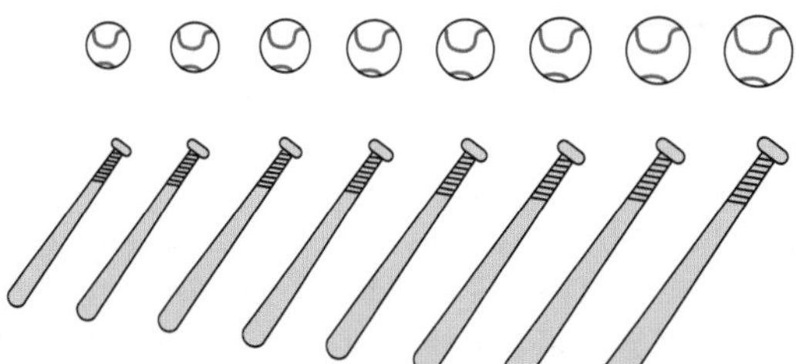

Procedure

1. First, ask children to order the balls from smallest to largest. You may place the smallest and the largest ball in place.
2. Next, ask children to match each bat with the ball to which it belongs. Again, match the first and the last bat.

Variation

After children have ordered the balls only, point to one bat from the set and ask children to find the ball to which it belongs.

During classification and seriation activities, you can observe and assess how children's observation skills, logical reasoning abilities, and problem-solving strategies are developing, and use these findings to guide their instructional decisions.

Patterns. The recognition of patterns is a basic skill that enhances the development of mathematics concepts. Prior to recognizing number patterns, children should become familiar with concrete patterns. Varied kinds of patterns such as A B A B A B . . . and A B B A B B . . . can be clapped, tapped, danced, walked, jumped, or otherwise acted out. Patterns can also be sung, read, or recited.

Patterns can be constructed, for example, with colored beads on a string or made by gluing shapes onto paper. Other materials include a pegboard and colored pegs, Unifix cubes and multilink cubes of various colors, and pattern blocks. The following two activities serve as examples.

1. **Creating Patterns**
   - Provide children with buttons in two colors and a piece of 2-cm grid paper.
   - Invite children to create patterns by placing the buttons on the grid paper.
   - Have children describe the pattern they made.
2. **Creating Patterns**
   - Provide children with Unifix cubes in two colors.
   - Ask children to construct a pattern by interlocking the cubes a certain way.
   - Have children describe their patterns.

Eventually, children will recognize simple number patterns such as "counting by one," "adding one," or "counting by twos" to generate number series. Upper elementary children will learn that *looking for a number pattern* is a useful problem-solving strategy.

Classification, seriation, and patterning skills can be learned from storybooks. Examples of good storybooks to read to or with a class include *I Was Walking Down the Road* (Barchas, 1975), *Nancy No-Size* (Hoffman, 1990), *Have You Seen Birds?* (Oppenheim & Reid, 1986), *I Love Spiders* (Parker, 1988), *Who Said Red?* (Serfoza, 1988), and *Red Is Best* (Stinson, 1982).

The next step with patterning is to encourage children to translate patterns from one medium to another. For example, an extension or follow-up task to "Creating Patterns" (Activity 2 above) is as follows: Ask children to represent the pattern they showed with the Unifix cubes in another way—for example, by using another manipulative, such as buttons, or by using letters, such as A and B. Activities of this sort *help children abstract the key features of patterns.*

One-to-one correspondence. Prior to developing counting capabilities, children can compare sets by using a one-to-one correspondence strategy. This involves children's learning to pair up objects, for example, putting one cookie on each plate. According to Baroody and Benson (2001), instruction on one-to-one correspondence should begin by asking children to match one or two items, then three, and later four and more. For example, children can be asked to find out whether there are enough books or pencils for each child in a group. Children can be given a set of miniature dolls, a set of cars, small raisin boxes, or other small objects and asked to record in some way (tallies or circles, for example) "how many" objects they have. There should be one tally or mark per object. Children should be aware that the diagram (tallies) shows how many objects there are in the set.

Children need to learn the meaning of comparative terms such as "more than," "fewer than," "the same number as," and "as many as." These terms should be used when comparing sets. As children learn to count objects in sets, they will compare and order sets according to the number of objects in each set. The following activities describe comparison and one-to-one correspondence experiences for children.

1. **Comparing Groups**
   - Direct children to stand in groups of two, three, and four.

- Ask children to make a statement to compare one group with another. ("This group has one more than that one. This group has one fewer than that one.")

2. **Comparing Collections**
   - Show children collections of small objects on three plates, each plate with a different number of objects.
   - Ask them to compare the collections.
   - Change the size of the collections and have children compare the sets again.

3. **Comparing Collections**
   - Place six small objects, all the same, on each of three paper plates and seven objects on another plate.
   - Ask the children, "Which set does not belong?" and "Can you make it belong?"

4. **One-to-One Correspondence**
   - Provide a child with a set of Valentine's Day cards and envelopes.
   - Ask the child to find out whether there are enough envelopes for the cards.
   - Have the child make a statement about the situation. ("There are more cards than envelopes.")

Other objects to use for one-to-one correspondence include cups and saucers, pencils and paper, books and children, paint jars and brushes.

5. **Comparing Picture Sets**
   - Prepare a set of six cards with stickers on them. Each card except one has the same number of stickers on it. One card has one more or one fewer.
   - Ask a child, "Which card is different?" and "How is it different?"

Example

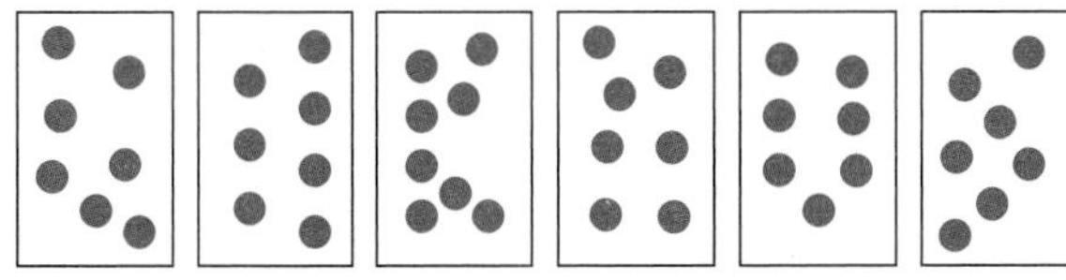

6. **Comparing Picture Sets**
   - Show the children a set of six cards with 2, 3, 3, 4, 4, and 5 dots on them.
   - Ask the children, in turn, to select two cards and make a comparative statement: "This card has as many dots as this one"; "This card has more dots than this one"; "This card has one fewer dot than this one."

Classifying according to number. In one-to-one correspondence activities, pay close attention to the language children use when describing comparisons. When children use expressions such as "as many books as children," the expression "as many as" can be used to classify sets. Such sets have the same number. *Number is a property of sets that is independent of attributes such as color, shape, size, and arrangement.* Also, the objects within a set do not have to be the same; for example, there could be a group of different objects, such as a ball, sock, shoe, and doll, but it still is a set of four things.

Conservation of number. The ability to conserve number quantities arranged in different ways marks a certain mental maturity. Piaget has identified the age of 6 to 7 years as the time when many children are successful at number conservation tasks, but not all children attain the capability at that age. It is important for you to be aware of children's conservation abilities in order to pose problem situations that are appropriate for children's cognitive development (Marchand, Bye, Harrison, & Schroeder, 1985). For example, a child who cannot yet conserve large numbers will have difficulty making sense of number groupings.

Conservation of large numbers can be assessed by having a child count two sets of the same objects, such as Unifix cubes. One set of, say, 32 cubes is left spread out on the table, while the other set is placed in small transparent plastic glasses in groups of 10. The child is then asked to compare the sets. Children who realize that both sets have the same number, regardless of their arrangement, are said to be able to conserve number.

Number Meanings

As children use numbers in their daily lives, they will come to differentiate between three uses of numbers: cardinal, ordinal, and nominal.

Cardinal Use of Numbers

"Cardinal" numbers are used to designate the quantity of a set. The *cardinal* aspect of number is the idea that whenever a set is counted, the last number named is the total number of objects in the set. For example, a child who is asked to count the pieces of chalk on the board ledge and states, after counting to seven, that *there are seven pieces of chalk on the ledge,* is using the cardinal aspect of number. This is the most common use of numbers.

Ordinal Use of Numbers

Ordinal means "order"; ordinal numbers are used to denote the order of an object. In their play, children will often make statements such as the following: "Michelle finished *first*" or "Marc came in *third.*" Other times, children will hear expressions such as "This is the *fifth* time

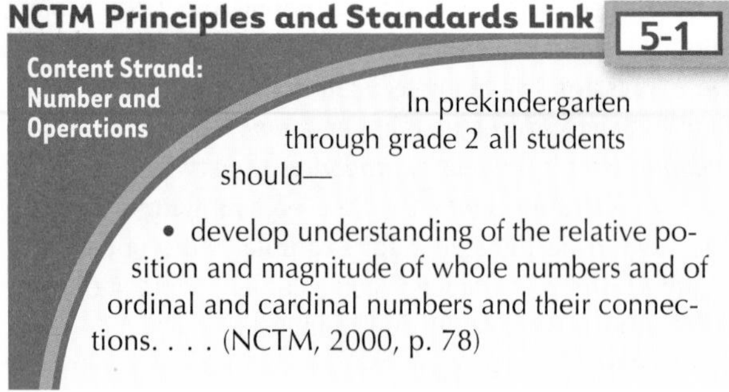

the phone has rung since dinner" or "Christmas is on the 25th day of December." The use of numbers such as *first*, *second*, *third*, etc., is an *ordinal* use of numbers.

NCTM Principles and Standards Link
5-1
Content Strand: Number and Operations
In prekindergarten through grade 2 all students should—
• develop understanding of the relative position and magnitude of whole numbers and of ordinal and cardinal numbers and their connections. . . . (NCTM, 2000, p. 78)

Nominal Use of Numbers

"Nominal" means *name*; nominal numbers are used to name objects. A third use of number is for a *nominal* purpose; that is, numbers are used to identify objects. Numbers are used in a nominal sense, for example, to identify a house on a street, a postal code, a license plate, floors and rooms in large buildings, or a player on a team.

1. **Number Walk**
   - Take children on a "number walk" along a city block.
   - Have children look for numerals. Jot them down and also record where the children saw them.
   - Back in class, discuss what "numbers" they saw. Ask, "What did the number tell?" (How many; it identified something.) "Did you notice a pattern?"

2. **Different Uses of Numbers**
   - Have children bring to class newspaper or magazine clippings that depict numbers used in a cardinal, an ordinal, and a nominal sense.
   - Discuss the different uses of numbers.
   - The clippings can subsequently be posted on a bulletin board under appropriate headings.

Counting

Discrete and Continuous Quantities

As children engage in counting objects in their environment, they will come to realize that counting is not appropriate for some objects. For example, one does not count the amount of water in the bathtub or the amount of cake on a plate. In time, children will be able to discriminate between discrete and continuous quantities.

Discrete objects are those that can be counted to find out "how many" are in the group. For example, one can ask, "How many people are in your family?" "How many books do you own?" *Continuous quantities,* on the other hand, measure "how much." Examples are "How much milk did you drink?" "How long did it take you to clean your room?" Measurements can be of length, area, volume, temperature, mass, or time. Note the use of the phrases "how many" and "how much"; "how many" is used for discrete quantities, whereas "how much" is used for continuous quantities. Most adults use these phrases correctly without much thought, but for many children correct usage is not automatic. Help children see the differences in when to use "how much" versus "how many."

Rote Counting

Rote counting is simply the reciting of the number name sequence in proper order. Some children learn the number sequence to 20 and beyond, even up to 100, without being able to count a set of objects less than 20. Some children who know the number name sequence sometimes make counting errors by counting objects in a set more than once or not counting others; that is, they do not establish a one-to-one correspondence between number names and objects. Rote counters sound as if they know how to count, but, because they do not make the one-to-one correspondence described earlier, they often incorrectly count the number of items in a set.

Rational Counting

Rational counting is the goal of instruction on counting. According to Gelman and Gallistel (1978), children who are rational counters possess the following capabilities:

- They are able to *recite the number–word sequence* (i.e., "one, two, three").
- They make a *one-to-one correspondence* between the items being counted and saying the number (i.e., they say "one" as they touch the first item, say "two" as they touch the second item, etc.).
- They realize that the *last number they say represents the total number* of objects in the set.

To test the last capability, after a child has counted a set of eight objects, for example, blocks, ask the child to show you eight blocks. Does the child point to the last block counted or to the set of eight blocks?

Children should have ample opportunities to count objects. Sets arranged in linear fashion, such as beads on a string or a row of blocks, are easier to count than a set of objects in scatter formation. Some children may need to be shown how to organize objects when counting to avoid making errors. They can be told to move the objects to the side as each one is counted.

For sets of 20 or more, children can be asked to count the objects twice to see whether they arrive at the same number. If not, a third count should match one of the first two totals.

1. **Oral Counting**
   - Say to a child, "Count for me."
   - Allow the child to continue counting until several errors are made in the number sequence.

2. **Counting Objects**
   - Place some Unifix cubes before a child seated at a table.
   - Say, "Count the cubes."
   - Allow the child to continue counting until you notice several errors.

You may want to record the types of errors the child made: Were they number sequence errors? Did the child skip cubes? Did the child count a cube more than once?

3. **How Many Do You See?**
   - If there is a window in the classroom that faces a street, have a child count vehicles as they pass by over a period of several minutes.
   - As they look out the window, have children count how many buildings they see; how many trees they see.
   - Ask some children to walk down the hallway and count the doors they see. Then, have children walk down the stairs and count the steps.
   - During recess, ask children to count the windows on one side of the school; count how many cars they see in the parking lot.

4. **Counting Objects**
   - Place several objects on plates or in boxes, plastic tubs, or jars.
   - Have children count to find out how many objects are in each container.

Children can record their work. ("I counted 12 buttons." "I counted 15 sticks.")

When children know the number-name sequence to at least 20 and can count objects, they can be engaged in more sophisticated counting activities.

Counting All, Counting On

Children use different counting procedures when quantifying sets. For example, suppose a child counts 6 apples in a basket and then 5 apples are placed beside the basket and the child is asked to find how many apples there are in all. A child might say "six" then continue to count "seven, eight, nine, ten, eleven" and state that there are 11 apples in all. This is a *counting-on* strategy.

Another possibility is to begin counting at one and recount the 6 apples in the basket and continue counting until 11 has been reached. This latter strategy is called *counting all.*

Make sure you observe how children count sets. For those who always count all the objects, a teacher should demonstrate a counting-on method. See Activity 5-3 for a sample task. Children could use a counting-on and then a counting-all strategy to prove that they produce the same count. Children will eventually see that the counting-on strategy is the quicker way to count. To facilitate this, you might say, "I have six pennies in my hand and these (seven on the table) are left. Count to find how many pennies in all."

ACTIVITY 5-3 Counting On

Realia Strategies

Materials

Purse or similar container and approximately 20 pennies or other counters

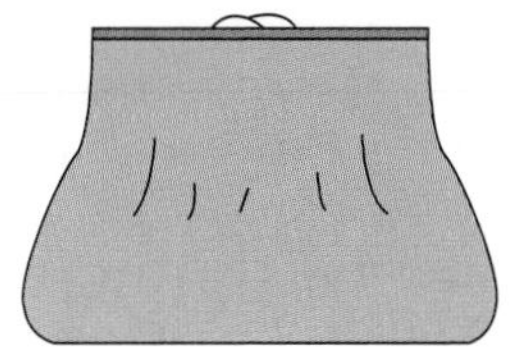

Procedure

1. Put 7 pennies inside the purse and 5 beside the purse.
2. Say, "There are seven pennies in the purse and five pennies beside the purse. Count to find out how many pennies there are altogether."
3. If the child wants to count the pennies in the purse, allow the child to do so. When the child has counted the 12 pennies, tell the child that another way to count the pennies is to begin at seven and continue to count on.
4. Have the child count several collections as above by first counting all, then counting on.

When children are able to count on to find the number of objects in given sets, you can then ask them to count on from a given number as shown on the cards in Figure 5-1 to

FIGURE 5-1 Practicing Counting On

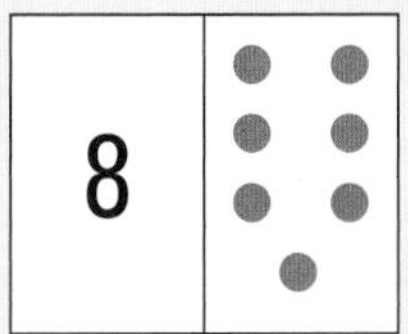

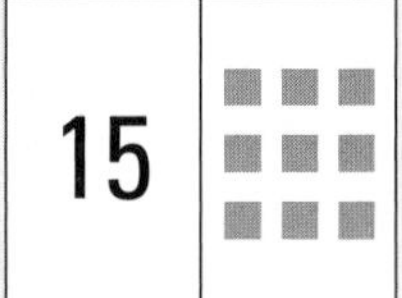

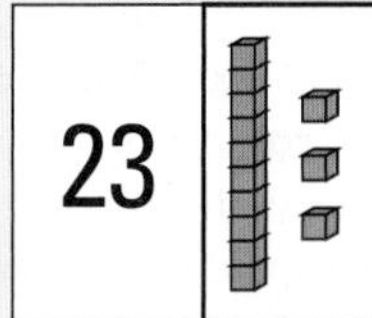

find how many in all. For example, in the first card in Figure 5-1, a child would start at 8 and count on 7 times, saying "nine, ten, eleven, twelve, thirteen, fourteen, fifteen." Note that counting on can be done for any number but is easier when the number being counted on (the second number) is small, such as 3 or less.

Counting Back

Some children who are proficient counters are unable to *count backward.* An introduction to counting backward can be to ask, "What number is 1 less than 9?" When the child responds, say, "Tell what number is 1 less than 8." Continue in this manner for several more numbers. Then ask the child to write or recite the numbers, counting backward from 9 to 0, thinking of "one less than" the last number named. Another resource is to look at a number line while counting, moving from right to left. In time, counting-back activities should include bridging decades (32, 31, 30, 29, . . .) and eventually centuries (202, 201, 200, 199, . . .).

myeducationlab The Power of Classroom Practice — To explore your own understanding of counting back, go to Chapter 5 in the Book-Specific Resources section in the MyEducationLab for your course and complete the Counting Back activities. Go to the Assignments and Activities section of Topic 5 to complete the activity "Skip Counting" to see how one teacher introduces this concept.

Skip Counting

Skip counting refers to counting by multiples of a certain number. For example, "skip counting by 5" means to count "5, 10, 15, 20," and so on. Skip counting lays the foundation for understanding the concept of multiplication. It usually is introduced in first grade, with children first learning to skip count by 2, 5, and 10.

Skip counting can be taught conceptually by counting groups of objects. For example, skip counting by 2 can be introduced by counting all the feet in the class. All the children stand in a line. As you move along the line, you point to each set of two feet and encourage the class to skip count together by 2.

Later work on skip counting can also be based on patterns. A first-grade child was asked what he could say about the number series 2, 4, 6, 8, . . . He quickly responded, "They're even numbers, and it's counting by twos." And what about the numbers 1, 3, 5, 7, . . . ? "They're odd," he responded. The teacher asked, "This is counting by what?" "By threes. No. I don't know." The latter example is also counting by twos, but in this case starting with 1.

In later grades, when children do some skip-counting activities, they should begin counting with different numbers. For example, when counting by 10, have children begin with any single-digit number (e.g., 2, 12, 22, 32, . . . ; 6, 16, 26, 36, 46, . . .). Activities 5-4 and 5-5 provide sample activities for skip counting.

A calculator can assist a child in skip-counting sequences. Calculators that have an automatic constant for addition or multiplication are particularly useful for this. For calculators with an automatic constant for addition, a keystroke sequence to count by 5 beginning at 4 would be 4 + 5 = = = =.

ACTIVITY 5-4 Counting by Tens

Procedure

Count by tens. Begin with

10 ___ ___ ___ ___
___ ___ ___ ___

3 ___ ___ ___ ___
___ ___ ___ ___

8 ___ ___ ___ ___
___ ___ ___ ___

12 ___ ___ ___ ___
___ ___ ___ ___

ACTIVITY 5-5 Counting Backward by Tens and Fives

Materials

Pencil and paper

Procedure

1. Write the numbers, counting by tens
   - from 60 to 10
   - from 120 to 50
2. Write the numbers, counting by fives
   - from 45 to 20
   - from 110 to 75

Counting backward can also be done on a calculator with the following keystroke sequence for counting by threes beginning with 30: 30 − 3 = = = = . Some calculators have the constant number registered before the operation sign in the keystroke sequence rather than the number following it. When using a calculator to develop number sequences, children should be encouraged to say the number first, then press the equal key and check the display to see whether they said the right number. This procedure provides instant feedback, and children can practice by themselves.

Simple computer programs can be written to "make the computer count." Computer or calculator printouts of number sequences can be helpful to children when studying number patterns.

Representing Numbers

How can the abstract idea of number be modeled so that children will come to know numbers and their properties? An approach has been to use concrete materials and pictures quite extensively in the early grades.

While children are engaged in counting activities, you should give attention to developing number-related ideas of equality, more than, less than; to combining groups; and to separating groups. The symbolic form of these operations or relations should be used only to record some meaningful action. The mathematical symbols =, +, and − are usually introduced in the latter part of Grade 1, and the symbols < and > in grade 2 or grade 3.

Concrete Models

Readily available concrete materials are invaluable in number development activities. Most primary classrooms are well equipped with boxes or buckets of small discrete objects for the children to use in counting activities and may include collections of acorns, small pine cones, ceramic tiles, and buttons. Besides using such materials at their desks, children may be asked to find out how many crayons are in a box, how many books are on a shelf, how many children have brought a lunch, how many rooms are on one floor of the school, etc. Activities 5-6 through 5-8 present sample activities using concrete materials for number development activities.

ACTIVITY 5-6 Making Sets

Materials
Nine paper plates and small objects for each child

Procedure
Make sets of all the counting numbers to nine.

ACTIVITY 5-7 Showing Numbers One to Nine

Materials
Toothpicks, glue stick, and a piece of cardboard

Procedure
Glue toothpicks on the cardboard to show the numbers from one to nine.

ACTIVITY 5-8 Counting Objects and Writing Numerals

Materials
A collection of buttons or other small objects (the size of the collection can be 20 to 50 objects).

Procedure
1. Count the number of objects you have, and record the amount in a statement. ("I counted 26 buttons." "There are 32 blocks in the box.")
2. Now recount the amount, checking for accuracy.
3. If the count number is not the same, the collection should be counted a third time.

Variation
One child could count a collection and then another child could count the collection. The children then check their count numbers with each other.

In another counting activity, square tiles can be used to model numbers in geometric patterns. For example, children can be asked to make "number rectangles," as pictured in Activity 5-9. From this activity, the ideas of even and odd numbers can be discussed as well as what happens when one combines two even numbers, two odd numbers, or an even and an odd number.

ACTIVITY 5-9 Number Rectangles

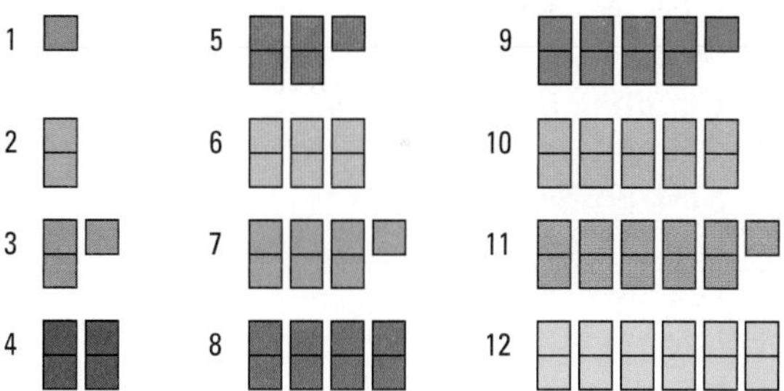

Materials
Square tiles

Procedure
1. Show numbers with the tiles in the manner above
2. Which numbers form rectangles? What can you say about them?
3. Try joining pairs of even and odd numbers. What do you notice?
4. Join two odd numbers. What do you notice?
5. Join two even numbers. What do you notice?

NCTM Principles and Standards Link 5-2

Content Strand: Number and Operations

Concrete models can help students represent numbers and develop number sense; they can also help bring meaning to students' use of written symbols and can be useful in building place-value concepts. (NCTM, 2000, p. 80)

Literature Link 5-1

Developing Counting

Anderson, Lena. (2000). ***Tea for Ten.*** New York: R & S Books.
Anno, M. (1977). ***Anno's Counting Book.*** New York: HarperCollins.
Anno, M. (1982). ***Anno's Counting House.*** New York: Philomel Books.
Bang, Molly. (1983). ***Ten, Nine, Eight.*** New York: Mulberry Books.
Carle, Eric. (1968). ***1, 2, 3 to the Zoo.*** New York: Trumpet Club.
Charles, Faustin, & Arenson, Roberta. (1996). ***A Caribbean Counting Book.*** Boston: Houghton Mifflin.
Crews, Donald. (1968, 1986). ***Ten Black Dots.*** New York: Mulberry Books.
Ernst, Lisa C. (1986). ***Up to Ten and Down Again.*** New York: Mulberry Books.
Falwell, Cathryn. (1993). ***Feast for 10.*** New York: Scholastic Press.
Feelings, M. (1971). ***Moja Means One: Swahili Counting Book.*** New York: Dial Press.
Geisert, Arthur. (1996). ***Roman Numerals I to MM.*** Boston: Houghton Mifflin.
Hutchins, P. (1982). ***1 Hunter.*** New York: Greenwillow Books.
Lesser, Carolyn. (1999). ***Spots: Counting Creatures from Sky to Sea.*** San Diego, CA: Harcourt Brace & Co.
McGrath, Barbara B. (1998). ***The Cheerios Counting Book.*** New York: Scholastic.
Mora, Pat. (1996). ***Uno, Dos, Tres: One, Two, Three.*** New York: Clarion Books.
Pallotta, Jerry. (1992). ***The Icky Bug Counting Book.*** New York: Trumpet Club.
Sierra, Judy. (2001). ***Counting Crocodiles.*** New York: Gulliver Books.
Walsh, E. S. (1991). ***Mouse Count.*** Orlando, FL: Voyager Books.

Counting is a complex process that requires various and multiple experiences. There are many counting books that illustrate such concepts as number, order, and classification. Using a variety of approaches and books with different features helps children to abstract the essential features of number.

- The most interesting counting books are those that embed counting in a clever story or interesting information. In ***Counting Crocodiles,*** a resourceful monkey counts crocodiles and in the process is able to walk on the crocodiles' backs to get to the bananas he wants on an island across the sea. In the story ***Mouse Count,*** mice are counted into a jar by a hungry snake. A sock puppet can be used to model the snake in the story, and children can practice counting plastic or felt mice into a large jar to reinforce the concept of one-to-one correspondence.
- Children can practice counting by writing and illustrating their own counting books. Books such as ***1 Hunter; Ten, Nine, Eight;*** and ***Ten Black Dots*** provide a model for creating and illustrating simple counting books. Other books that explore the numbers from 1 to 10 include ***Feast for 10; Up to Ten and Down Again*** (beautiful illustrations); ***Tea for Ten;*** and ***1, 2, 3 to the Zoo.*** Write large numerals on paper plates, which can be ordered in a line on the floor. As children step on each plate, they can practice counting aloud.
- Some books embed counting in informative science content. For example, ***Spots: Counting Creatures from Sky to Sea*** counts from 1 to 10 using animals that live in different biomes. ***The Icky Bug Counting Book*** counts bugs from 0 to 26 (one bug for each letter of the alphabet) and provides information about an interesting variety of bugs.
- ***Anno's Counting House*** relies on illustrations alone to communicate the basic addition fact combinations for the number 10. Classify the children by sex, clothes, or their possessions. Discuss how the number of children in the houses remains the same even though the children move from house to house. Write number sentences that represent the mathematics in the text.
- Manipulate concrete objects and match these objects with the items on the page of a book to support the development of one-to-one correspondence and conservation of number. Sort and manipulate objects such as Cheerios® using ***The Cheerios Counting Book*** or linking cubes using ***Anno's Counting Book.***
- Many counting books provide children with information about counting in different cultures. In ***Roman Numerals I to MM,*** children learn to count using Roman numerals; ***Uno, Dos, Tres: One, Two, Three*** counts from 1 to 10 in English and Spanish, with drawings set in Mexican culture; ***A Caribbean Counting Book*** contains counting rhymes from the Caribbean; and ***Moja Means One*** introduces children to the counting numbers from 1 to 10 in Swahili, with beautiful drawings in the text that present information about East African culture.

Source: Dr. Patricia Moyer-Packenham, Utah State University

FIGURE 5-2 Using Concrete Models to Represent Numbers

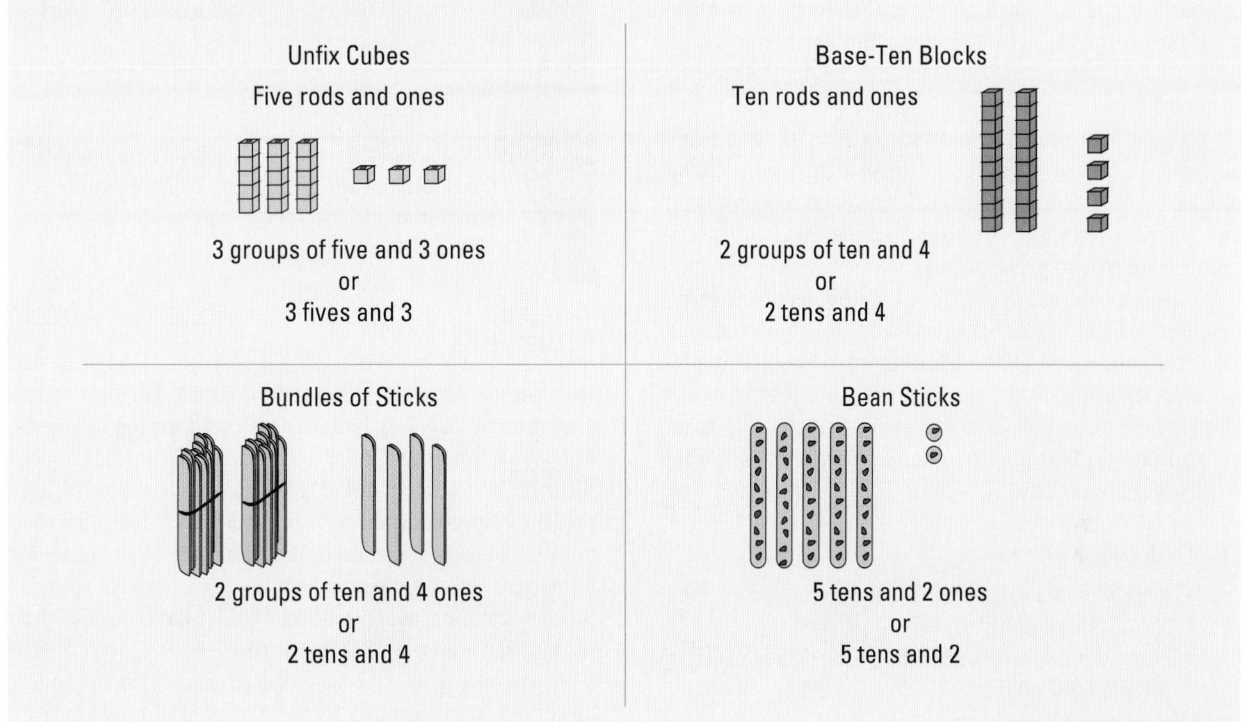

Square tiles also can be used to model square numbers such as 1, 4, 9, and 16 by constructing squares and the triangular numbers such as 1, 3, 6, and 10 by making staircases.

The base-ten blocks may be used by children when they understand grouping, particularly a group of 10. See Figure 5-2 and Blackline Master 1 on MyEducationLab.

> myeducationlab The Power of Classroom Practice — Go to Chapter 5 in the Book-Specific Resources section in the MyEducationLab for your course and select Blackline Masters to obtain "Blackline Master 1."

Pictorial and Graphic Representation of Numbers

Many children enjoy drawing. You can use this interest to record the results of their number-related explorations. Children can be asked to draw pairs of sets with different numbers of objects and to indicate which set has more objects or which set has the greater number. Provided with graph paper, children can draw the "number rectangles" they constructed with tiles, as shown in Activity 5-10.

Children can sketch base-ten blocks or use rubber stamps of the blocks. Later, they can more informally represent base-ten blocks using a dot for ones, a line for tens, and a square for hundreds, as shown in Figure 5-3.

Symbolic Representation of Numbers

Kindergarten number activities have children counting sets, constructing sets concretely and pictorially, and matching sets with number names and numerals. What is important for children to internalize are number relationships, not how to write numerals or recognize number

FIGURE 5-3 Pictorial and Graphic Representations of Numbers

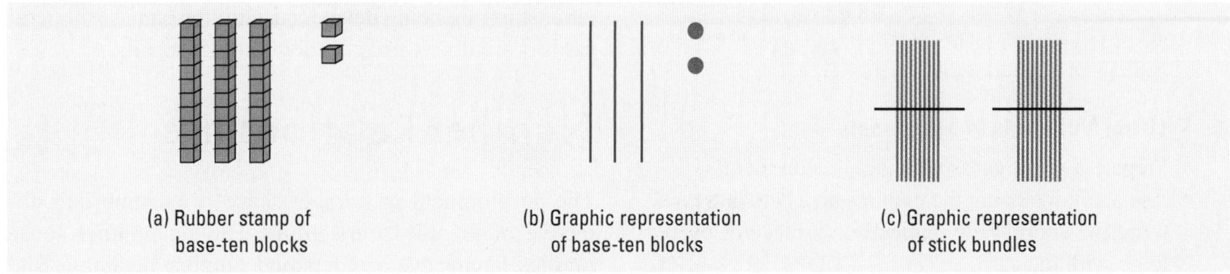

(a) Rubber stamp of base-ten blocks (b) Graphic representation of base-ten blocks (c) Graphic representation of stick bundles

symbols. Thus, children should be encouraged to talk about their number work and to record in their own way what they do. Work with number symbols should not appear to be of prime importance and can be delayed for some time.

You can introduce an activity in one of four ways: concretely, pictorially, symbolically, or orally, using number words. You can also ask children to respond in any of the four ways. An effective teaching or assessment strategy is to present a task in one mode and to have the children respond in a different mode, as discussed in Chapter 2 (Figure 5-3). Children's flexibility in transferring from one mode to another demonstrates their degree of understanding. Some materials for number work are shown in Figure 5-4. The following four activities are appropriate for learning to match numerals with number words and quantities.

1. **Ordering Numerals**
    - Cut out some magazine or newspaper pictures that show a large numeral.
    - Have the children order the pictures according to the numeral on them.

2. **Matching Sets with Numerals**
    - Prepare a set of numbered boxes representing garages and a set of cars with dots on them (e.g., one dot on one car, two dots on another).
    - Direct a child to match the cars with the garages.

3. **Matching Numerals, Number Names, and Picture Cards**
    - Prepare three sets of cards: one with number names, one with numerals, and one with pictures.
    - Have a child match the picture card with its number name and numeral.

Sample Cards

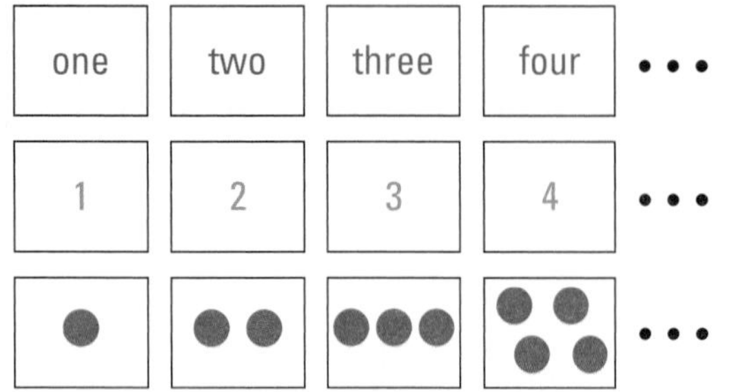

4. **Writing Numerals to Match Sets**
    - Prepare a set of cards with pictures on them.
    - Ask a child to count the pictures on a card and then write the appropriate numeral on a piece of paper to go with the card.

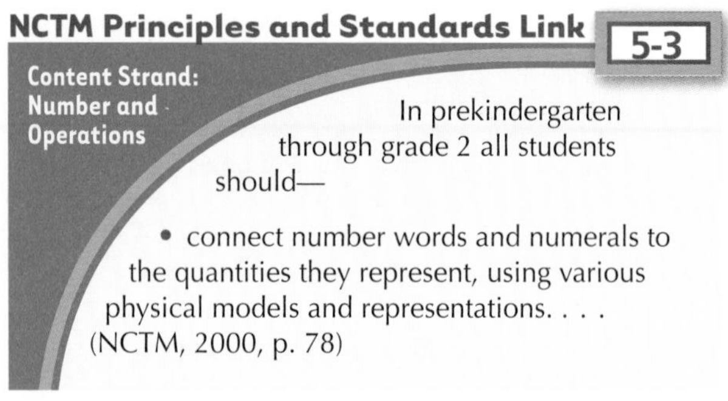
NCTM Principles and Standards Link 5-3

Content Strand: Number and Operations

In prekindergarten through grade 2 all students should—

- connect number words and numerals to the quantities they represent, using various physical models and representations. . . . (NCTM, 2000, p. 78)

Numerals

Just as individuals develop their own handwriting styles, children also develop their own ways of forming numerals. For some numerals there is more than one acceptable form (e.g., 4 and 4, 2 and 2, 9 and 9). Teachers usually present young children with one numerical form for each number. However, children will likely see other forms for numerals, such as those shown on a calculator display. A poster depicting acceptable numerals may help children recognize and write different forms.

Make sure you observe children as they form numerals, either when copying them or when writing them from memory. Devote some time to having children practice forming numerals so that they can internalize an efficient way of writing each numeral. A recommended stroke sequence is presented here (Baratta-Lorton, 1987).

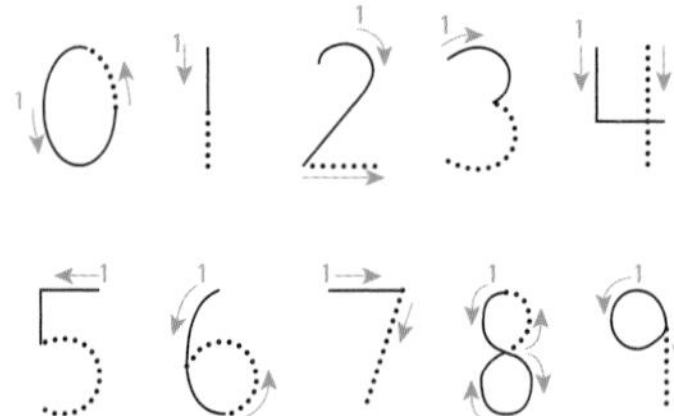

The first stroke (solid line) for each numeral is made in a downward (straight or curved) or horizontal motion. Only the second stroke (dotted line) in the zero, the six, and the eight has an upward motion. Children can practice forming the numerals with their fingers on their desks, in the air, in the sandbox, or in shaving cream; they can write numerals on the board, on individual slates or blackboards, with crayons, and in their notebooks with pencils.

Although children must learn how to form numerals, this activity must not interfere with or take precedence over the development of number sense. When number relationships are being developed, children can use numeral cards or number words to show activity results.

Number Relationships

The development of number sense is an important objective of the K–4 curriculum. Having number sense implies having well-understood number meanings and

FIGURE 5-4 Materials That Can Be Used to Practice Ordering

Number cards

one	two	three	four	five	six	seven	eight	nine

Numeral cards

1	2	3	4	5	6	7	8	9

Sets

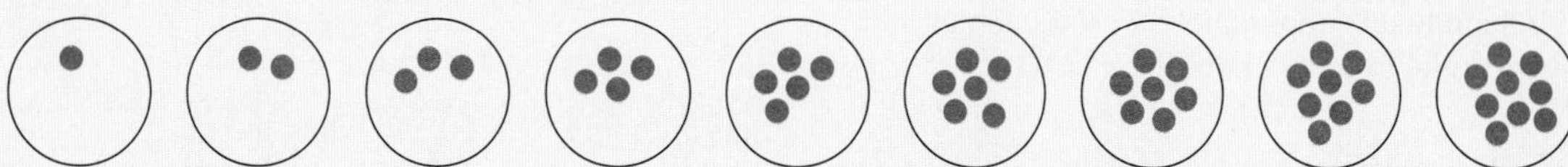

Bundles of sticks

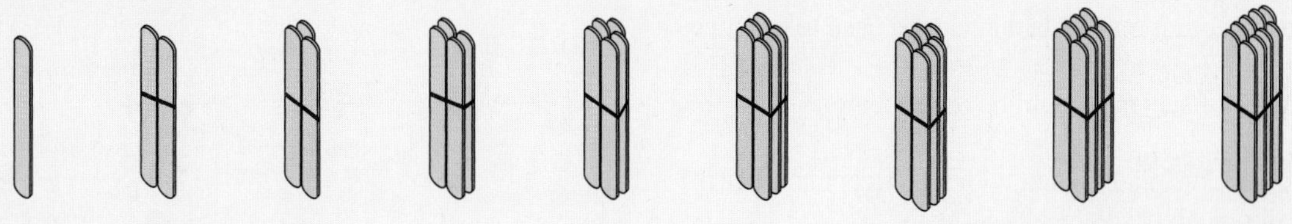

Marbles in bags

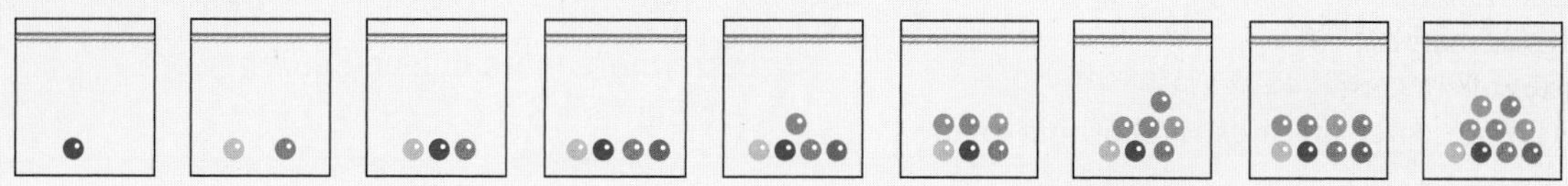

Pictures of sets

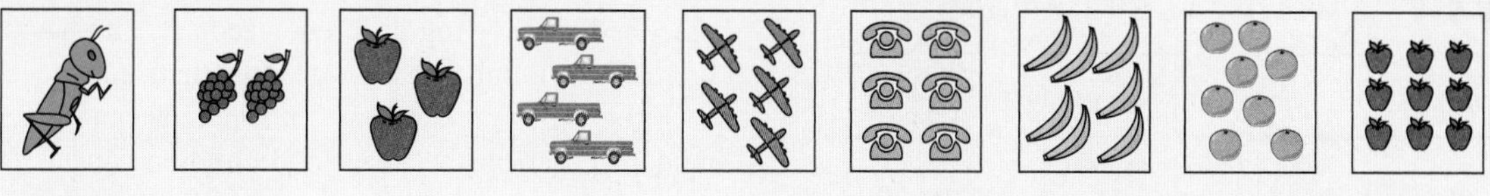

Pattern dot cards

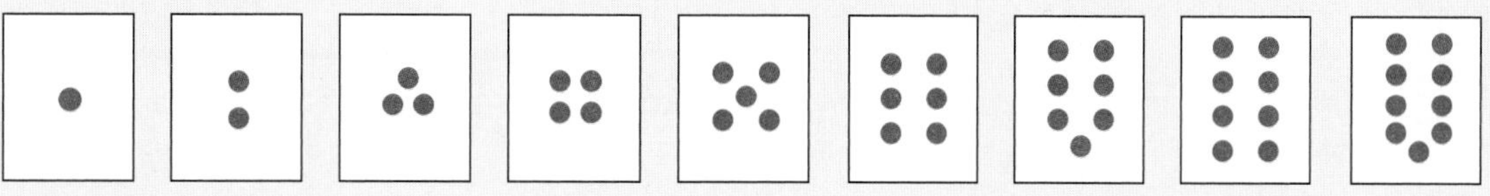

Dot cards

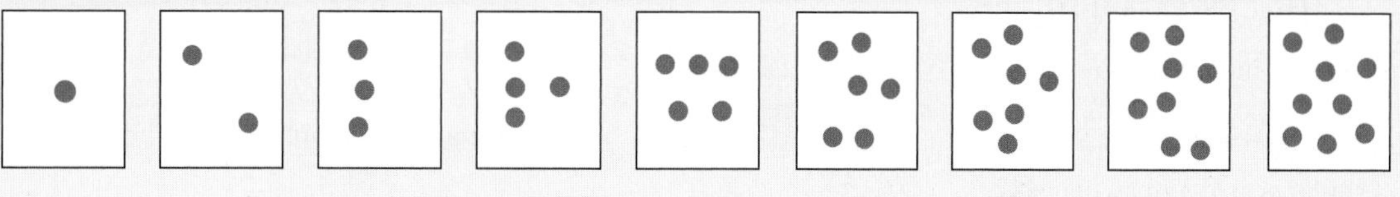

having developed multiple relationships among numbers (NCTM, 1989, p. 38). Number sense develops as children "understand the size of numbers, develop multiple ways of thinking about and representing numbers, use numbers as referents, and develop accurate perceptions about the effects of operations on numbers" (Sowder, 1992, as cited in NCTM, 2000, p. 79). Number relationships cannot be taught directly; instead, children must construct these understandings through their own mental activity (Hughes, 1986; Kamii & Joseph, 1988; Van de Walle, 1994). Children need to engage in number explorations so that number relationships can be discovered. Invite them to talk about number relationships and, when they are able, to write about them.

Order Relations

Children should be able to order sets with different number of elements from smallest to largest. Figure 5-4 presents many different materials that can be used to practice ordering.

Examples of sets that could be ordered are:

- A set of five plates, each with a different number of small objects;
- Vases (paper cups), each with a different number of paper flowers;
- Bags of marbles;
- Boxes of crayons;
- Sets represented on cards, as shown in Figure 5-5; and
- Discs on vertical rods, as shown in Figure 5-6.

FIGURE 5-5 Cards of Sets for Ordering

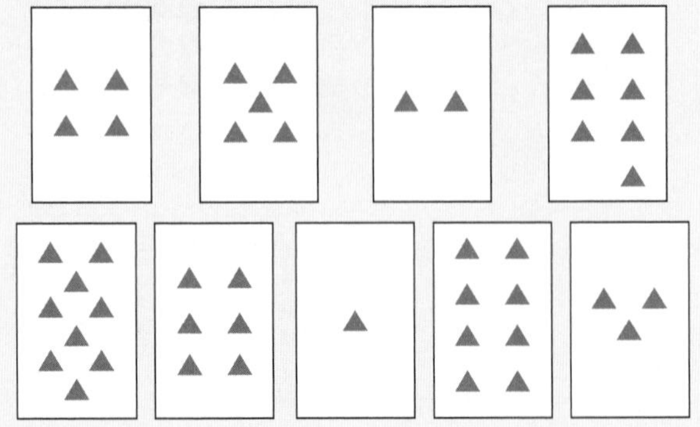

More Than, Fewer Than

When children compare sets by counting, you might ask such number relation questions as: Which set has more? How many more? Which set has fewer? How many fewer? Does this set have as many as that set?

Sets with a small number of objects are easily identified as "more than" or "fewer than" another set. However, the comparative task becomes more challenging when the sets are more than 10 and when the objects are arranged in scatter formation (see Figure 5-7). Children may use a variety of strategies to make this determination, including one-to-one matching, pattern identification, or counting.

FIGURE 5-6 Disks on Rods for Ordering

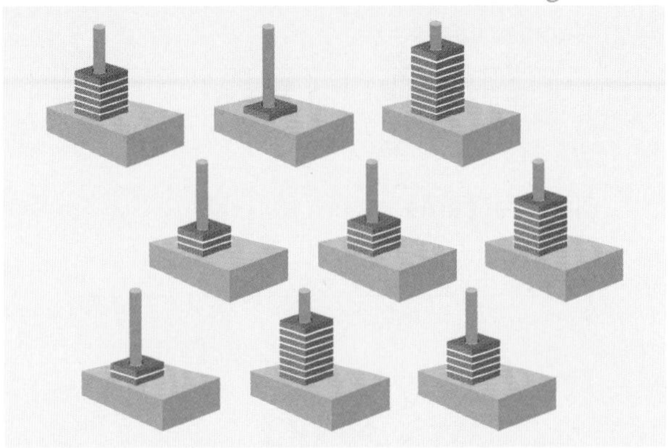

FIGURE 5-7 Comparing Sets

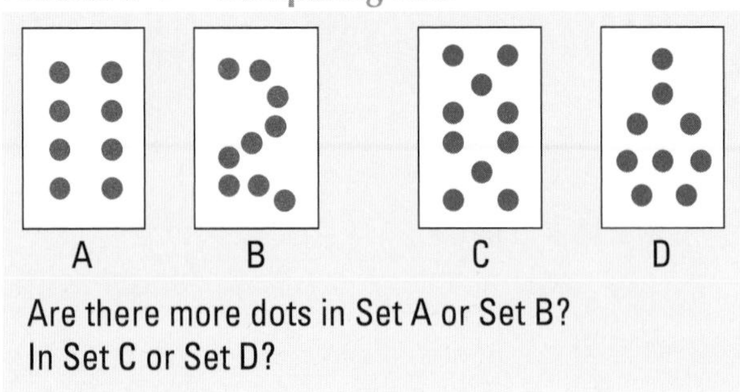

A
B
C
D
Are there more dots in Set A or Set B?
In Set C or Set D?

One Greater Than, One Less Than

"One greater than" and "one less than" relationships can be practiced by showing different sized sets and having children tell the number that is one more than and one less than each set. When numerals are known, they can be written in random order on the board and children can be asked to name the number that is one greater (also, one less) than the numeral they see (Activity 5-10). Children may use a number line or construct sets of objects to assist them.

ACTIVITY 5-10 One Greater Than and One Less Than Relationships

Procedure

1. Write numbers on the board. For example:

   6 3 9 5 2 8 4 1 7

2. Have a child read the numbers.
3. Then have the child say the number that is one greater than each number on the board

   (7, 4, 10, . . .).

4. Have the child say the number that is one less than each number on the board (5, 2, 8, . . .).

FIGURE 5-8 Number Patterns on Pegboards

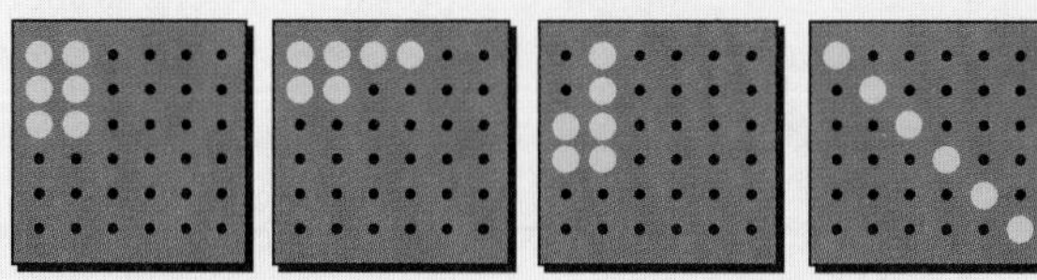

What can you say about six? *(Six is two and two and two. Six is four and two. Six is two and four. Six is six ones.)*

Part-Part-Whole Relationships

Children should have experiences in showing numbers concretely in different ways. For example, children could be asked to arrange six blocks in different ways. The patterns could be reproduced on a large chart to form the focus of a class discussion. Number patterns can also be shown with pegs on a pegboard (see Figure 5-8).

Splitting numbers on a "two-part mat" is another good activity for developing number relationships (see MyEducationLab).

The "family" of combinations for a given number can be easily constructed with Unifix cubes in two colors (Activity 5-11). When children are constructing two parts of numbers, the idea of the combination of zero and another number may arise. If it has not been done earlier, a discussion on the meaning of the number zero should take place, including the fact that zero is a number.

ACTIVITY 5-11 Two Parts of Six with Unifix Cubes

Visual Scaffolding

Materials

15 Unifix cubes in each of two colors

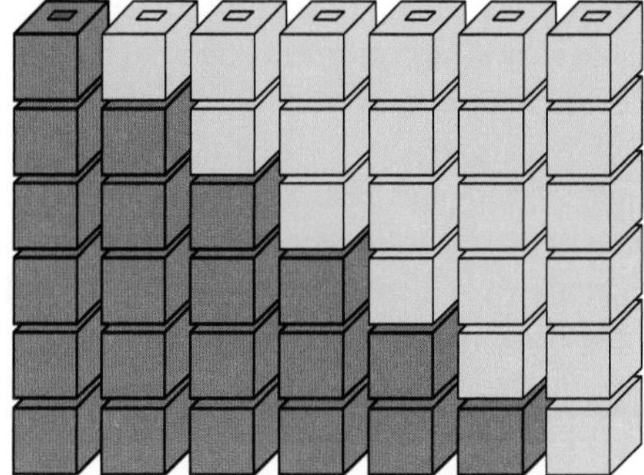

Procedure

1. Ask children to make rods to show two parts of six using cubes in two colors.
2. If children suggest "six and zero" as two parts of six, provide 6 additional cubes for each color so that a rod of each color can be made.
3. Direct children to arrange their rods in a pattern as pictured.
4. Say: "Look at your rods and read the two parts of six in order" (zero and six, one and five, two and four, etc.).
5. Invite children to close their eyes and try to say to themselves the two parts of six. If they get mixed up, tell them to open their eyes to look and to begin again.

Tell children that the number zero tells "how many" when a group or set has no members. For example, ask them "How many live horses are in the room?" (zero). You and the class may decide that when making two parts of numbers, say 6, the combinations "0 and 6" and "6 and 0" are entirely appropriate, as exemplified in Activity 5-11.

As children make concrete representations of numbers, they will begin to use the language of addition and subtraction. Statements to be encouraged include "Six blocks is four blocks and two blocks." "Seven robots is the same as five robots and two robots." "Three keys and four keys are seven keys altogether." Some children have difficulty understanding questions such as "How many are four and five?" Changing the question to "How many pencils are four pencils and five pencils?" is easier for children to understand (Hughes, 1986). Thus, it is recommended that early work with part-part-whole number relationships should be with and about physical objects. Part-part-whole addition and subtraction situations will be discussed in more detail in Chapter 7.

As children work at constructing parts of numbers (Seven is four and three.), comparing the whole to its parts (Is eight the same as three and five?), or finding a missing part (Four is one part of six. What is the other part?), observe them to find out whether they have developed the logic of considering the whole and its parts simultaneously. The logic of number addition requires that the parts be considered in relation to each other and that both parts be considered in relation to the whole (the sum). In the absence of these logical ideas, a child solves part-part-whole problems perceptually (Labinowicz, 1980).

Research has shown that children can complete addition statements such as $1 + 7 =$ ______ symbolically and not be successful at similar problems logically (Labinowicz, 1980). Therefore, it is important that children, particularly in the primary grades, explore concrete representations of numbers so as to construct logical number relationships.

Relationship to 5 and 10. One part-part-whole relationship that is particularly important is the relationship of numbers to 5 and 10. This relationship will be especially useful when children begin learning number facts. For example, if a child knows that 6 is 1 more than 5, that will help the child reason that 6 + 3 must be 1 more than 5 + 3. Thus, if 5 + 3 = 8, then 6 + 3 must be 1 more than 8, or 9.

One way to help children understand the relationship of numbers to 5 and 10 is to use the ten-frame. The ten-frame consists of a 2-by-5 array of squares in which dots are placed to represent numbers (see Blackline Master 2 on MyEducationLab). One convention generally followed when working with the ten-frame is that the top row of squares should be filled with dots before any dots are placed in the second row. When the top row is filled, there are 5 dots in the ten-frame. When both rows are filled, there are 10 dots.

PEARSON myeducationlab The Power of Classroom Practice Go to the Strategies section of Topic 5: "Number Concepts and Numeration" in the MyEducationLab for your course to obtain "Blackline Master 2."

Ten-frames can be made on plain white paper or construction paper. Dots to represent the numbers can be bingo chips, buttons, or stick-on dots, which can easily be removed from paper that has been laminated.

It is important to discuss the relationships children observe in a ten-frame. For example, when the number 7 is represented in the ten-frame, as in Figure 5-9, the top row is filled, and there are two dots in the bottom row. This shows that 7 is 2 more than 5.

FIGURE 5-9 Representing Numbers on a Ten-Frame

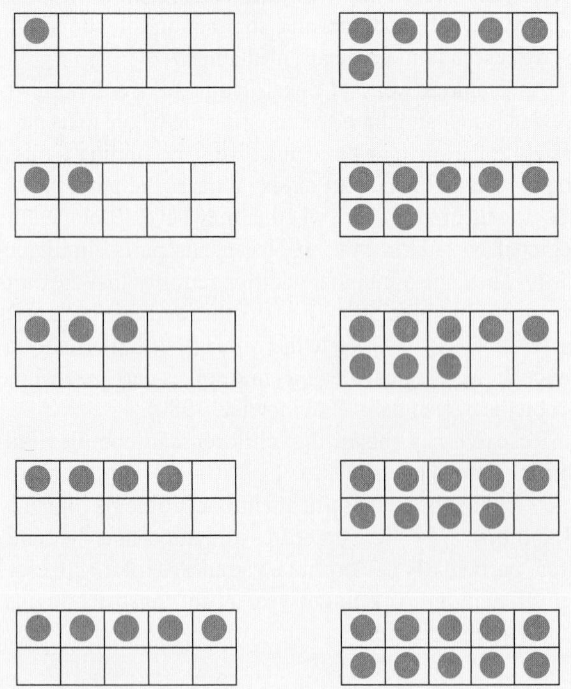

Using action language. The formal language of addition and subtraction should be delayed until children are able to perform mental actions on numbers. For example, children may not understand the meaning of "five plus three" or "eight minus five." While working with concrete materials, the language expressing actions is more appropriately used (Skemp, 1989). For example, after an addend has been identified, one could say about the second addend, "I am giving you three more . . . ," "If you put three more . . . ," or "three more arrived . . .". For subtraction, the expressions "take away four . . . ," "gave away four . . . ," or "four were removed . . ." could be used. In time, children will be able to, for example, partition a set of nine objects and state, "Nine is six and three." or "Five add four is nine." Addition and subtraction will be discussed in detail in Chapter 7.

Number relationships can also be developed through the use of patterned cards. Activities with patterned cards, as described in the following list, help children learn the combinations of numbers.

1. **Two Parts of a Number**
   - Prepare patterned cards for a selected number, say, six. Sets of cards as pictured in Figures 5-10(a)–(d) can be used.
   - Children are told that a set of cards shows two parts of six.
   - Each card is shown, in turn, for a brief moment.
   - Ask: What two parts of six did you see?

2. **Two Parts of a Number**
   - Prepare a set of patterned number cards for two or three consecutive numbers (e.g., 4, 5, and 6).
   - Show each card, in turn, for a brief moment.
   - Ask: How many objects did you see? What two parts of the number did you see?

Finding the "missing part" of a number helps children learn subtraction facts.

3. **Finding the Missing Part**
   - Prepare number cards showing a number and one part of the number, (as in Figure 5-10(e)).
   - Show a card for a moment and ask children to give the *missing part.*

The number activities just described can be used for a few minutes of mental arithmetic at the beginning of a mathematics period two or three times a week. By the end of first grade, children should have learned the basic addition facts for single-digit numbers. Basic facts are discussed in more detail in Chapter 8.

Bidirectional Relationship of an Equation

Research has shown that children in third grade do not accept as correct equations in the following forms: 6 = 4 + 2, 4 + 5 = 5 + 4, 3 + 6 = 6 + 3, and 5 = 5

FIGURE 5-10 Types of Patterned Number Cards

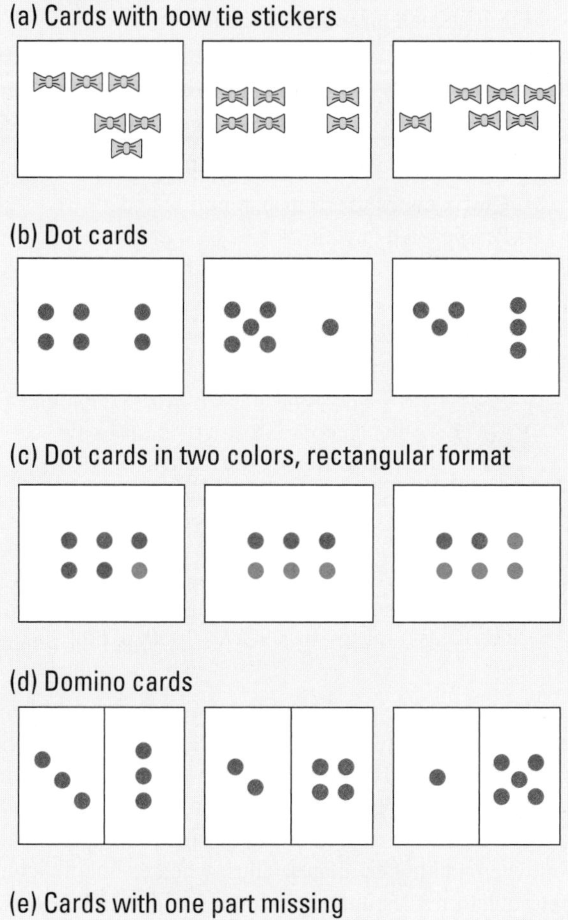

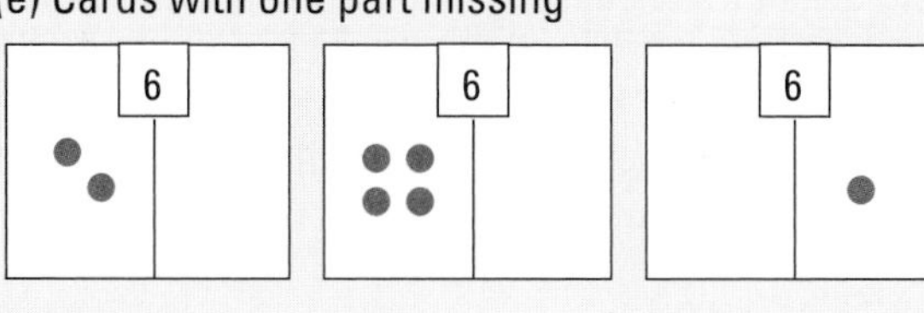

(Labinowicz, 1985). This explains their narrow understanding of the equal sign. To some, the equal sign means that you "put the answer after it" and operation signs do not belong on the right side of an equal sign.

Before the equality or operation symbols are introduced, the language of equality statements should be developed. Thus, when developing the part-part-whole relationships, the children should verbalize and write statements such as the following:

9 is 4 and 5

4 and 5 is the same number as 5 and 4

6 and 3 is the same number as 4 and 5

9 is the same number as 9 and 0

9 is the same number as 9

As children eventually replace the operation and relation words with symbols, it will be easier for them to accept varied forms of equations if they have developed an understanding of the language of equality statements through a variety of meaningful experiences. Thus, "9 is 4 and 5" can be stated as "9 equals 4 plus 5" and is symbolized as $9 = 4 + 5$. The number sentence "4 and 5 is the same as 5 and 4" can be stated as "4 plus 5 equals 5 plus 4" and is written symbolically as $4 + 5 = 5 + 4$. The focus should be on the correctness of the relationship expressed rather than on the form of the equation. This is different from asking children to "find the answer" to a question such as "What is 4 and 5?" or "4 plus 5 equals what?" Such questions cause children to focus on "the answer," which they record after the "equal sign." There is no opportunity for children to develop an understanding of the meaning of the equality symbol.

A math balance is a good instrument to use in exploring equality statements (Activities 5-12 to 5-13). Children can be asked what they notice on the balance when the numbers are not equal (the *greater* number is *lower*, not higher, on the balance).

ACTIVITY 5-12 Working with a Math Balance

Materials
Math balance

Procedure

1. Place some weight on either side of the math balance to make it balance.
2. Record your work.

Examples
4 and 2 balance with 1 and 5; 8 balances with 4 and 4; 10 balances with 2 and 2 and 6.

ACTIVITY 5-13 Finding the Sum of "Doubles"

Materials
Math balance

Procedure

1. Put two weights on hook 4 on the left-hand side.
2. Balance the load by placing a weight on one hook on the other side.
3. Write the number sentence that is represented on the balance.
4. Put two weights on another hook and make a balancing load as before.
5. Do this three more times.
6. Write the number sentences that are represented on the balance.

Estimation

The meaning of the term *estimate* can be developed by referring to the word *about.* Questions such as "About how many apples are in the box?" and "About how many books are on the shelf?" can be used to develop children's understanding of estimation.

Estimates are approximations rather than exact quantities. Referring to the question "About how many apples are in the box?" explain to children that, for example, "twelve" is the exact number of apples in the box but that "ten" is a good estimate.

When giving estimates, it is important that "good estimates" be identified. Children should be told that within the range of acceptable estimates, the exact answer is no better than any of the other amounts (NCTM, 1989).

During the primary grades, children should be asked to estimate small quantities and progress to larger amounts as they demonstrate success. Also, ask children to tell how they arrived at their estimates. Estimating strategies should be discussed so that children can learn from each other. Estimation activities with numbers less than 20 are described next:

1. **Estimating Quantities**
   - Place a collection of 12 objects on a table.
   - With the objects covered, gather the children around the table.
   - Uncover the objects for a moment, and then have the children make an estimate of the number of objects displayed.

2. **Estimating Quantities**
   - Place 12 or 15 objects on an overhead projector.
   - Turn on the projector briefly; then have the children estimate the number of objects that are shown on the projector screen.

3. **Estimating Quantities**
   - Find a large picture with 15 to 20 objects pictured. These could be animals, fruit, cars, or other appropriate objects.
   - Show the picture to the children, and have them estimate the quantity.

4. **How Many Jelly Beans?**
   - Fill a small jar with jelly beans.
   - Ask children to estimate how many jelly beans are in the jar.

   Other materials for estimating "large" quantities include

   - Unshelled walnuts or peanuts in a clear plastic bag;
   - Unifix cubes in a transparent tub; and
   - Pennies in a jar.

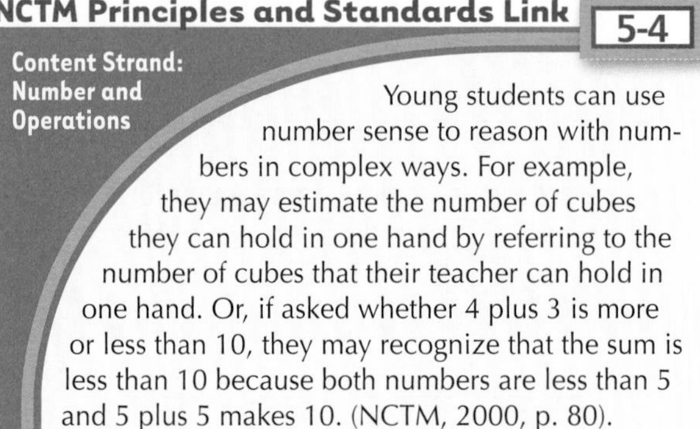

NCTM Principles and Standards Link 5-4

Content Strand: Number and Operations

Young students can use number sense to reason with numbers in complex ways. For example, they may estimate the number of cubes they can hold in one hand by referring to the number of cubes that their teacher can hold in one hand. Or, if asked whether 4 plus 3 is more or less than 10, they may recognize that the sum is less than 10 because both numbers are less than 5 and 5 plus 5 makes 10. (NCTM, 2000, p. 80).

Children can be taught to look for groups of 5 to help them make estimates of quantities over 10. As the quantities are increased, 10 and 20 should be given as important benchmarks in making estimates.

The size of the objects must be taken into consideration when making estimates. Thus, when estimating concrete quantities, estimation interacts with number sense and spatial sense to help children develop an awareness of reasonable results (NCTM, 1989). Specific estimation strategies will be developed when children begin to compute with large numbers.

Conclusion

This chapter described basic concepts related to the development of number. The principal idea to bear in mind when planning number activities for children is the importance of developing number relationships. This is a significant change from the traditional count, read, and write number program. The activities described are useful in helping children construct number relationships to facilitate mental operations with numbers.

CHAPTER

Sample Lesson

A Lesson on What Is More?

Grade level: Kindergarten

Materials: At least one manipulative, such as Unifix cubes, or assorted objects to count

Lesson objective: Students will use objects to correctly represent and compare whole numbers.

Standards link: Students solve problems that involve representing, comparing, and ordering whole numbers (NCTM *Curriculum Focal Points,* kindergarten).

Launch: Display two groups of objects, for example, one group of 5 cubes and another group of 7 cubes. Ask students, "how could we figure out which group has more?" Solicit recommendations about how to determine this, including making a one-to-one correspondence between objects in both sets; the larger set will have objects that don't have a partner with objects in the other set. Then state what they've observed regarding the size of the groups, such as "7 is more than 5". Next, make a drawing of the two sets, write the numeral representing the number in each group, and either write a sentence stating which number is more than the other, or circle the larger set.

Next ask two students to come to the front of the room. Each student should pick up a few cubes and hold them up. Then ask the class, "who has more and how do you know?" Discuss ways to determine which is more. Then sketch the two sets, state which is larger, and circle the larger set.

Explore: In pairs, have students repeat this process twice: (1) each student selects a set of cubes, (2) both students determine which set is larger, (3) using the same sheet of paper, each student sketches their set and together they circle the larger set and explain how they know.

Summarize: Coming together as a whole class, select one pair of students to come to the front of their room and explain their sketch. Focus on their explanations of how they determined which set was larger.

FOLLOW-UP

Complete the following questions.

1. Consider any cautions regarding selecting the manipulatives to use in this lesson. Would other manipulatives work well? Might you want to avoid using certain manipulatives or objects? Why? What would be the advantages and/or disadvantages of each manipulative?
2. Consider difficulties students might have with this concept and this lesson. What modification could you make to avoid or minimize these issues? What modifications could you make for students with special needs?
3. What might the *next* lesson focus on, and why?

IN PRACTICE

Complete the following activities to include in your professional portfolio.

1. Write a lesson plan to help children who are rote counters become rational counters.
2. Write a lesson plan to introduce the relationship of numbers to 5 and 10.
3. Write a lesson plan in which students are asked to represent numbers in more than one way.

myeducationlab The Power of Classroom Practice Now go to Topic 5: "Number Concepts and Numeration" in the MyEducationLab (www.myeducationlab.com) for your course, where you can:

- Find learning outcomes for "Number Concepts and Numeration" along with the national standards that connect to these outcomes.
- Apply and practice your understanding of the core teaching skills identified in the chapter with a Building Teaching Skills and Dispositions learning unit.
- Complete Assignments and Activities that can help you understand the chapter content more deeply.
- Complete *enVision MATH* Sample Curricula assignments that allow you to examine and work with chapters from *enVision MATH,* a K-6 mathematics program.
- Check your comprehension on the content covered in the chapter by going to the Study Plan in the Book-Specific Resources for your text. Here you will be able to take a chapter quiz, receive feedback on your answers, and then access Review, Practice, and Enrichment activities to enhance your understanding of chapter content.
- Go to the Book-Specific Resources for Chapter 5 to explore mathematical reasoning related to chapter content in the Activities section.

LINKS TO THE INTERNET

Teach Me 1, 2, 3's

http://funschool.kaboose.com/formula-fusion/games/game_teach_me_1-2-3s.html

A fun game to practice counting objects in a picture.

Number Matching

http://funschool.kaboose.com/preschool/games/game_number_matching.html?trnstl=1

A fun game to practice matching numerals to sets of objects.

RESOURCES FOR TEACHERS

Reference Books: Number Concepts and Number Sense

Baratta-Lorton, M. (1976). *Mathematics Their Way.* Menlo Park, CA: Addison-Wesley.

Burton, G. M. (1993). *Number Sense and Operations: Curriculum Evaluation Standards for School Mathematics Addenda*

National Council of Teachers of Mathematics (2006). Curriculum Focal Points for Prekindergarten Through Grade 8 Mathematics: A Quest for Coherence. Reston, VA: Author.

Children's Literature

Anno, M. (1997). *Anno's Math Games*. New York: Paper Star.

Baker, A. (1998). *Little Rabbits' First Number Book*. New York: Scholastic.

Bartch, M. (1999). *Math & Stories*. Palo Alto, CA: Celebration.

Brisson, P. (1995). *Benny's Pennies*. New York: Yearling.

Carle, E. (1996). *The Grouchy Ladybug*. New York: HarperCollins.

Dee, R. (1990). *Two Ways to Count to Ten: A Liberian Folktale*. New York: Holt.

Fleming, D. (1992). *Count!* New York: Scholastic.

Giganti, P. (1988). *How Many Snails? A Counting Book*. New York: Greenwillow Books.

Hoffman, M. (1990). *Nancy No-size*. London: Little Mannoth.

Jernigan, G. (1988). *One Green Mesquite Tree*. Tucson, AZ: Harbinger House.

Lottridge, C. B. (1986). *One Watermelon Seed*. Toronto: Oxford University Press.

Morozumi, A. (1993). *One Gorilla*. Pleasantville, NY: Sunburst.

Oppenhiem, J., & Reid, B. (1986). *Have You Seen Birds?* Richmond Hill, ON: Scholastic-TAB.

Sloat, T. (1991). *From One to One Hundred*. New York: Dutton Children's Books.

Tildes, P. L. (1995). *Counting on Calico*. New York: Scholastic.

Trinca, R., & Argent, K. (1982). *One Woolly Wombat*. New York: Puffin.

Turner, P. (1999). *Among the Odds & Evens*. New York: Farrar Straus Giroux.

Walton, R. (1993). *How Many, How Many, How Many?* Cambridge, MA: Candlewick Press.

Wells, R. (2000). *Emily's First 100 Days of School*. New York: Hyperion.

Wise, W. (1993). *Ten Sly Piranhas: A Counting Story in Reverse. (A Tale of Wickedness—and Worse!)* New York: Dial.

CHAPTER 6

Developing Understanding of Numeration

NCTM CONNECTING WITH THE STANDARDS

The National Council of Teachers of Mathematics (NCTM) Principles and Standards stresses the importance of helping young children develop a strong understanding of place value, stating that "during the early years teachers must help students strengthen their sense of number, moving from the initial development of basic counting techniques to more sophisticated understandings of the size of numbers, number relationships, patterns, operations, and place value" (NCTM, 2000, p. 77). The NCTM document goes on to recommend that teachers "emphasize place value by asking appropriate questions and choosing problems such as finding ten more than or ten less than a number and helping them contrast the answers with the initial number" (p. 77).

Children should develop a rich understanding of numbers as they progress through elementary and middle school grades. This rich understanding of numbers should include "what they are; how they are represented with objects, numerals, or on number lines; how they are related to one another; how numbers are embedded in systems that have structures and properties; and how to use numbers and operations to solve problems" (NCTM, 2000, p. 32). The NCTM (2006) *Curriculum Focal Points* mentions developing understanding of the place value at several grade levels. They state that first-grade students should:

- compare and order whole numbers (at least to 100) to develop an understanding of and solve problems involving the relative sizes of these numbers;
- think of whole numbers between 10 and 100 in terms of groups of tens and ones (especially recognizing the numbers 11 to 19 as 1 group of ten and particular numbers of ones); and
- use mathematical reasoning, including . . . beginning ideas of tens and ones, to solve two-digit addition and subtraction problems with strategies that they understand and can explain (NCTM, 2006, p. 13).

Similarly, they state that second-grade students should:

- develop an understanding of the base-ten numeration system and place-value concepts (at least to 1000), . . . (including) ideas of

Developing Your Math Teaching Skills

When you have finished studying this chapter, you should be able to do the following:

- Discuss why our number system is called a "place-value" system.
- Give an example of a proportional base-ten model and a nonproportional base-ten model. Discuss how these models differ.
- Describe equivalent representations and why they are important.

counting in units and multiples of hundreds, tens, and ones, as well as a grasp of number relationships, which they demonstrate in a variety of ways, including comparing and ordering numbers;

- understand multidigit numbers in terms of place value, recognizing that place-value notation is a shorthand for the sums of multiples of powers of 10 (e.g., 853 as 8 hundreds + 5 tens + 3 ones); and
- use place value and properties of operations to create equivalent representations of given numbers (such as 35 represented by 35 ones, 3 tens and 5 ones, or 2 tens and 15 ones) and to write, compare, and order multidigit numbers. They use these ideas to compose and decompose multidigit numbers (NCTM, 2006, p. 14).

Moving on to third grade, students should "extend their understanding of place value to numbers up to 10,000 in various contexts," and "apply this understanding to the task of representing numbers in different equivalent forms (e.g., expanded notation)" (NCTM, 2006, p. 15).

Regarding the upper elementary grades, *Curriculum Focal Points* states that fourth-grade students should "extend their understanding of place value and ways of representing numbers to 100,000 in various contexts," (NCTM, 2006, p. 16), while fifth-grade students should "extend their understanding of place value to numbers through millions and millionths in various contexts" (NCTM, 2006, p. 17).

This chapter highlights ways you can help children develop a rich understanding of numbers, focusing on developing number sense and an understanding of our system of numeration.

ASSESSING MATHEMATICS UNDERSTANDING

In order to become familiar with the mathematics concepts and procedures discussed in this chapter, take a few minutes and complete the *Chapter 6 Pre-Assessment* following this paragraph. First answer each question on your own, and think about how you got the answer. Then think about the possible misunderstandings some elementary-school children might have about each topic. If you are able, administer this assessment to a child, and analyze the child's understanding of these topics.

1. There are 25 children at the beach. Each child has 10 sand toys. How many sand toys do they have at the beach?
2. Jaime has $180. He wants to buy some Pokémon® cards. Each pack of Pokémon cards costs $10. How many packs of Pokémon cards can Jaime buy?
3. There are 10 candies in a roll. How many candies are in 4 rolls?
4. Add 638 + 476.
5. How can you write "10 hundred"?
6. How many tens are in 32?
7. How many tens are in 120?
8. How many ones are in 316?
9. How many tens are in 192,000?
10. How many hundreds are in 192,000?
11. Use the digits 0, 1, 2, 3, 4, and 5 to solve the problems below. Don't use any digits more than once in any problem.
    - **a.** Make the largest 2-digit number possible.
    - **b.** Make the largest 3-digit number possible.
    - **c.** Make the largest number possible.

Examining Classroom Practice

Cinzia Fisher, a second-grade teacher, holds high expectations of her students. She expects them to listen to the problem, to think clearly about how to solve it, and to explain their reasoning. She often follows up students' first responses with questions designed to help her students draw additional distinctions and clarifications.

Video clip "IMAP—Problem Solving in Grade 2" on MyEducationLab shows a lesson in which Ms. Fisher is working with a group of her students who are solving problems. She poses the following problem; the students work independently to solve the problem in several ways.

There are 25 children at the beach. Each child has 10 sand toys. How many sand toys do they have at the beach?

PEARSON myeducationlab The Power of Classroom Practice — Go to the Assignments and Activities section of Topic 5: "Number Concepts and Numeration" in the MyEducationLab for your course. Complete the activity "IMAP—Problem Solving in Grade 2" to see how one teacher helps a group of students work through a problem.

NCTM NUMBER AND OPERATIONS STANDARD AND EXPECTATIONS ADDRESSED IN THIS CHAPTER

Instructional programs from Pre-K–12 should enable all students to—	In Prekindergarten through grade 2 all students should— (NCTM, 2000, p. 78)	In grades 3–5 all students should— (NCTM, 2000, p. 148)	In grades 6–8 all students should— (NCTM, 2000, p. 214)
• understand numbers, ways of representing numbers, relationships among numbers, and number systems.	• use multiple models to develop initial understandings of place value and the base-ten number system.	• understand the place-value structure of the base-ten number system and be able to represent and compare whole numbers and decimals. • recognize equivalent representations for the same number and generate them by decomposing and composing numbers.	• develop an understanding of large numbers and recognize and appropriately use exponential, scientific, and calculator notation.

As they finish, children share their thinking with a neighbor while the last children are completing their work. One child, Maryann, solves the problem by taking 25 base-ten blocks and counting by tens to get 250, while another child uses base-ten blocks a little differently by using a flat to represent 10 groups of 10 children's toys. A third child, Jenny, uses base-ten blocks in another way; a ten and five ones to help keep track of her skip-counting by tens to solve the problem.

Next, Ms. Fisher poses another problem for the children to solve:

> *Jaime has $180. He wants to buy some Pokémon® cards. Each pack of Pokémon cards costs $10. How many packs of Pokémon cards can Jaime buy with his money?*

As they did for the first problem, the children solve this problem in various ways and then share their strategies with the group. For example, Amber uses different pictorial representations, including boxes, squares, and lines, to represent the packs of cards. Then a boy named Dylan explains his solution to the teacher. When the teacher asks him clarifying questions, Dylan gets a different answer and then seems unsure as to which answer is correct.

Ms. Fisher's questioning of Dylan is an excellent example of a teacher's probing a child's reasoning and, in the process, helping the child notice any flaws in his reasoning and make appropriate revisions. Ms. Fisher helps Dylan clarify the difference between the cost of a pack of cards ($10) and the number of packs each base-ten block represents (1 pack).

Throughout this lesson, Ms. Fisher interacts with the children, questioning them about their thinking in order to help them make sense of the mathematics. Note that the number 10 appears as one quantity in each of the two problems above. Also notice the different ways that the children represent the 10 in these two problems.

Analyzing Assessment Results

If you had a chance to give the *Chapter 6 Preassessment* to a child, take a few minutes and analyze the results. How did the child solve these problems? How did the child think about these problems?

Analyze each problem. How did you (and the student you administered the assessment to) solve each of the following problems? Let's look at problems 1–3 first.

1. There are 25 children at the beach. Each child has 10 sand toys. How many sand toys do they have at the beach?
2. Jaime has $180. He wants to buy some Pokémon® cards. Each pack of Pokémon cards costs $10. How many packs of Pokémon cards can Jaime buy?
3. There are 10 candies in a roll. How many candies are in 4 rolls?

Comments: How are these problems alike, and how are they different? Which were more difficult, or were they equally difficult? Did you use counters or draw a picture, or solve it in another way? All three problems involve groups of 10. Did you think about place value when solving these problems?

4. Add 638 + 476.
5. How can you write "10 hundred"?

Comments: These problems are related, because when adding "6 hundred" and "4 hundred" you get

"10 hundred." Children sometimes have difficulty writing "10 hundred" not realizing that "10 hundred" is the same as 1 thousand.

6. How many tens are in 32?

7. How many tens are in 120?

8. How many ones are in 316?

9. How many tens are in 192,000?

10. How many hundreds are in 192,000?

Comments: These problems are fairly common place-value problems. Were any of these problems easier than others? Problem 6 is the easiest problem. Sometimes problems 7 and 8 seem tricky. A common incorrect answer to problem 7, for example, is 2, since there is a 2 in the tens place of 120. But there are also 10 tens in the 100 part of 120, so there are 12 tens in 120. Similar reasoning is useful in problems 8, 9, and 10.

11. Use the digits 0, 1, 2, 3, 4, and 5 to solve the problems below. Don't use any digits more than once in any problem.
    a. Make the largest 2-digit number possible.
    b. Make the largest 3-digit number possible.
    c. Make the largest number possible.

Comments: These problems give children an opportunity to think more flexibly about place value. Some children may think that 45 and 54 have the same value. Can the child you worked with explain why the number he or she made was the largest? What place value concepts did he or she use?

Take a minute and reflect on this assessment. Were some problems easier than others? What factors made them easier? What do you want to learn more about in order to help children understand place value?

Common Student Misconceptions or Misunderstandings about Place Value:

- Numbers with the same digits have the same value (for example 23 and 32).
- Confusion about the value of each place.
- Lack of understanding of the relationships between different place values.

Are there any other misunderstandings that children may have about place value? It's important to assess what children understand, and are still working on understanding, in order to plan instruction that meets their needs.

Building on Assessment Results

Think about what we can do to help strengthen children's place value understandings and minimize (and hopefully eradicate) their misunderstandings and misconceptions.

Sometimes teaching about place value focuses on memorizing the names of the places. While we want students to learn the names of the places, they also need to understand relationships between places, which will enable them to make sense of place value. So what might we do next to help students develop this understanding?

A key element of all instruction is to make sure that students understand the concept. Students need to visualize concepts and relationships. This usually is best done with some sort of manipulative material, asking students to solve problems set in familiar, meaningful situations and to examine the reasonableness of their solutions. The table below lists several common misunderstandings about place value and what a teacher can do to help children overcome these misunderstandings.

IF students think that . . .	THEN have students . . .
numbers with the same digits have the same value (for example, 23 and 32, or 15 and 150)	*model* two such numbers with a manipulative material, ask students to compare their values, and discuss why these numbers have the same digits but different values.
numbers that look different must have different values (for example, 23 and 1 ten and 13 ones)	*model* two such numbers with a manipulative material, ask students to compare their values, and discuss why these numbers have the same value but look different.
there is no relationship between the values of each place	*describe* the values of adjacent places; for example, 1 ten is the same as 10 ones, and tens are 10 times the value of ones. Modeling with a manipulative can help.

Numeration

A numeration system is a system that enables one to record numbers. To understand why the numerals 10 and 100 represent the numbers ten and one hundred, respectively, and why the two symbols 2 and 5 can be combined to represent twenty-five, one needs to understand the structure of our numeration system.

Historically, people developed the idea of number before a structured system of numeration. As symbols were assigned to quantities of one and successive increments of one, people likely became concerned over the potentially large number of different symbols that would need to be created. To limit the number of symbols, rules for using a basic set of symbols were devised. In the case of the Hindu-Arabic numeration system, rules were refined over centuries, until the system we know today was in place. Once a numeration system for recording whole numbers was established, other number systems such as fractions, decimals, and integers were developed to solve particular problems.

Number Systems

A *number system* is characterized by a set (infinite) of elements called *numbers,* basic operations to perform on those numbers, and some generalizations or principles that hold true for a particular number system. Understanding basic principles about numbers in our numeration system is the focus of this chapter. The operations on whole numbers, fractions, decimals, and integers are the focus of subsequent chapters.

Numeration Systems

A *numeration system* includes a set of symbols for certain numbers together with a set of rules governing the use of those symbols. The set of numbers represented by particular symbols is known as the *digits* of the system. The digits of four different numeration systems are presented in Figure 6-1. Within each system, combinations of the digits represent larger numbers and are interpreted according to established rules, which can vary across numeration systems.

Different civilizations developed numeration systems to meet their needs. Each system was characterized by its own particular set of symbols and rules. In time, the Western world adapted aspects of a numeration system used by the Hindus and one developed by the Arabs, thus the name *Hindu-Arabic numeration system.*

The Hindu-Arabic Numeration System

An understanding of the Hindu-Arabic numeration system is a prime goal of elementary mathematics programs. Children begin to learn the particular characteristics of the system by constructing numbers concretely in groups of tens and ones and describing what they have done. For example, a child who says that with 26 buttons she was able to make two groups of 10 and had 6 left will later be able to describe 26 as two tens and six. The Hindu-Arabic numeration system can be described by five characteristics, which are described in the following sections: base-ten, positional or place value, multiplicative principle, additive principle, and zero as a placeholder.

Base Ten

The *base* of a system is the number of objects used in the grouping process. Our system is a base-ten system; that is, whenever we have 10 or more objects, they may be regrouped to make one group of the next larger place value. There is no one numeral for ten, rather, the number 10 is expressed as 1 ten and 0 ones, or 10. There are ten digits in the base-ten system: 0 through 9.

Positional or Place Value

If the number of digits in a numeration system is limited, it follows that digits will need to be repeated in order to represent larger numbers. In a place-value system, a digit takes on a value determined by the place it occupies in a number. The unit digits occupy the place farthest to the right in a multidigit numeral. Ten is the value of the place to the immediate left of the "ones" place. Thus, we can say that the second place (to the left) in a numeral is the "tens" place. The numeral 10, therefore, designates "one group of ten and zero ones." One more than nine groups

FIGURE 6-1 Digits in Four Different Numeration Systems

System	Digits of the System
Hindu-Arabic	0, 1, 2, 3, 4, 5, 6, 7, 8, 9
Roman	I, V, X, L, C, D, M
Mayan	•, —
Egyptian	𓏺, 𓎆, 𓍢, 𓆼, 𓂭, 𓆐, 𓁨

FIGURE 6-2 Base-Ten Place Value

Places	$base^5$	$base^4$	$base^3$	$base^2$	$base^1$	$base^0$
Base Power	10^5	10^4	10^3	10^2	10^1	10^0
Place Names	hundred thousand	ten thousand	one thousand	hundred	ten	one
Place Value (base-ten)	100,000	10,000	1,000	100	10	1

of ten and nine (99) requires a regrouping to show "one group of ten groups of ten" and is represented by the numeral 100. The third place in a numeral, therefore, has the value of "ten groups of ten" or "ten times ten" and is named "hundred." The symbolization system is extended to the left by designating place values for successively larger groups of ten. Figure 6-2 depicts place values for base-ten.

To summarize, the *place-value principle* enables one to distinguish between the face value of a digit (e.g., 5 as five) and its value because of its particular position in a numeral. For example, the digit 5 has the value of fifty in 52 and five hundred in 534.

Multiplicative Principle

Multiplication is used to determine the value of each digit in a numeral. For example, in the base-ten numeral 333, each 3 has a different quantitative value: The 3 on the left has the value of 3 times one hundred, the 3 in the center has the value of 3 times ten, and the 3 on the right has the value of 3 times one. When children first decode numbers, they are not likely to use the multiplicative term *times;* rather, they talk about "groups." For example, the 2 in 28 is explained as "two groups of ten" or "two tens."

Additive Principle

In the Hindu-Arabic system, the additive principle means that numbers are the sum of the products of each digit and its place value in a numeral. For example,

$$\begin{aligned}765 &= (7 \times 100) + (6 \times 10) + (5 \times 1)\\ &= 700 + 60 + 5\\ &= 765\end{aligned}$$

In numeration systems without a multiplicative principle, the value of a number is determined by the sum of the digits in a numeral. For example, in Roman numeration the number represented by XXVII is determined by adding 10 + 10 + 5 + 1 + 1 to make 27.

When they have learned the multiplication operation, children can describe numbers as, for example, 36 means "3 times 10 plus 6" or write them in symbolic form as "$(3 \times 10) + 6$."

Zero as a Placeholder

The genius of our numeration system lies in the combined characteristics of place value and a placeholder numeral, that is, a symbol for the number zero.

Although zero is first introduced as a number, children can be asked to do numeration activities that have them specifically think of zero as a placeholder. For example, you might ask:

1. "I have eight hundreds and three tens. What's my number?" (Children write the number on paper; then one child writes the number on the board. Children check their work.)
2. "I have three hundreds and six ones. What's my number?"
3. "I have one thousand, four tens, and nine ones. What's my number?"
4. "I have five ones and nine hundreds. What's my number?"

Some children will make errors when answering these questions. For example, a common incorrect response to the first question is "80030," and "3006" is often given for the second question. Encourage children to think back to the meaning of each place. Ask follow-up questions such as "How can we write eight hundred? Eight hundred ten? Eight hundred twenty? Eight hundred thirty?" Connecting a question with something that they already understand helps children link their existing understandings to new concepts.

Each of the characteristics described above must be used when interpreting a multidigit numeral.

Understanding Place Value

What Research Says about Place-Value Learning

There is evidence that elementary school children do not understand our numeration system, specifically place value (Kamii & Joseph, 1988; Ross, 1986, 1989; Smith, 1973). One may be surprised at Kamii and Joseph's findings that third- and fourth-graders were unable to respond

FIGURE 6-3 Place-Value Task

Place-Value Task

Show the numeral 16 on a card.

16

Ask: What does this part (circle the 6 in 16) mean? Could you show me with the chips what this part means?

Have the child show (count out) the appropriate number of chips.

Ask: What about this part (circle the one in 16)? Show me with the chips what this part means.

Source: Adapted from "Teaching Place Value and Double-Column Addition," by C. Kamii and L. Joseph, 1988, *Arthimetic Teacher,* 33, p. 48.

correctly to a tens place-value question. Kamii and Joseph report that, generally, no first-grader gives the expected response that in the numeral 16, "one means ten," and that only about 33% of third-graders and 50% of fourth-graders are able to respond appropriately (Figure 6-3). Kamii and Joseph concluded that first-grade children are unlikely to understand place value; rather, they understand 16 as 16 ones, not as 1 ten and 6 ones. These findings corroborate those of Ross (1986, 1989).

Others, however, believe that with carefully planned experiences of counting and grouping by tens and ones, first graders can learn place value to some significant level of performance (Payne, 1988). You should engage first-graders in grouping activities as foundational experiences for place-value development. Generally, second-graders are expected to develop understanding of two-digit numbers, and third graders work with numbers greater than 99.

Stages in Place-Value Development

Ross (1989) proposed a five-stage development of place value understanding. At **Stage 1,** children associate two-digit numerals with the quantity they represent. For example, 28 means the whole amount. At **Stage 2,** children can identify the positional names but do not necessarily know what each digit represents. For example, in 54, a child may state that there are 4 ones and 5 tens. This is mere verbal knowledge based on positional labels. At **Stage 3,** children can identify the face value of digits in a numeral as, for example, in 34, the 3 means "3 tens" and the 4 means "4 ones." The value of each digit is not necessarily known, that is, "3 tens" meaning 30. Success in representing numerals with base-ten blocks could merely signify a Stage 3 performance. Ross describes **Stage 4** as a transitional stage during which children construct true understanding of place value. Children progress from unreliable performance on tasks to the point at which they know that the tens digit represents quantities of 10 units and they can coordinate the part-whole relationships within two-digit numbers. **Stage 5** is the stage at which children understand the structure of our numeration system. Children know that digits in a two-digit numeral represent a partitioning of the whole quantity into tens and ones and that the number represented is the sum of the parts (Ross, 1989).

NCTM Principles and Standards Link 6-1

Content Strand: Number and Operations

It is absolutely essential that students develop a solid understanding of the base-ten numeration system and place-value concepts by the end of grade 2. (NCTM, 2000, p. 81)

Knowledge of place value has a major impact on children's success in computational tasks as will be seen, in part, in Chapter 9. Therefore, helping children develop a rich understanding of place value should be a priority in the primary grades.

Grouping

The foundation for developing place-value concepts lies in *grouping activities.* Thus, first-graders should engage in grouping activities and counting activities with sets of objects greater than 9.

When children know the numbers 0 through 9 and can identify and write the respective numerals, they can participate in grouping activities. Grouping activities can vary by

- the materials used;
- the size of the groups;
- the number of groups formed; and
- the manner of recording.

Activities 6-1 through 6-4 help children learn more about grouping.

ACTIVITY 6-1 Making Groups of Buttons

Realia Strategies

Materials

Each child will need a set of 36 buttons and 10 small plates.

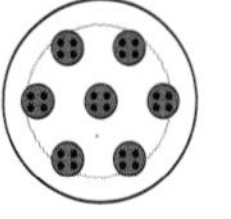
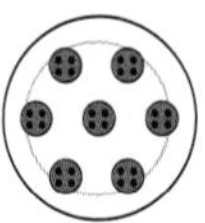
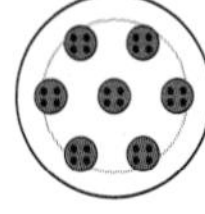
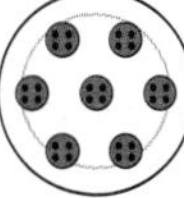
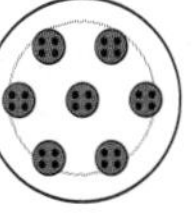

Procedure

1. Direct the children to choose a number and to make groups of that size on each plate.
2. Have the children verbalize what they have done. For example, "I made five groups of seven and have one button left."

ACTIVITY 6-2 Making Groups of Unifix Cubes

Materials
Each child will need 50 Unifix cubes.

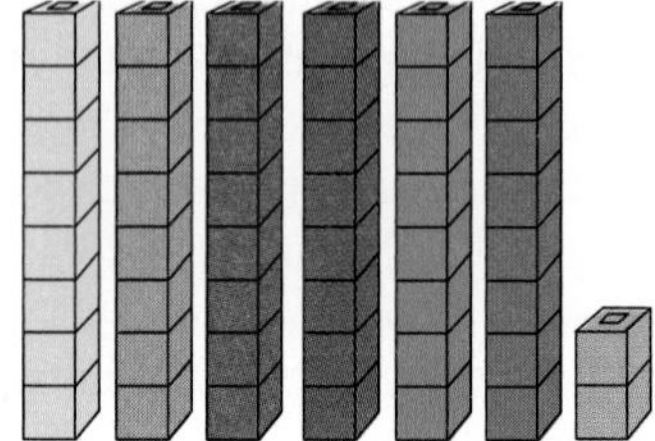

Procedure

1. Direct the children to choose a number and to make towers of that size with the cubes.
2. Have the children verbalize what they have done. For example, "I made six towers that are eight blocks high. I have two blocks left."

ACTIVITY 6-3 Counting in Groups of Six

Materials
Numerous Popsicle sticks and elastic bands

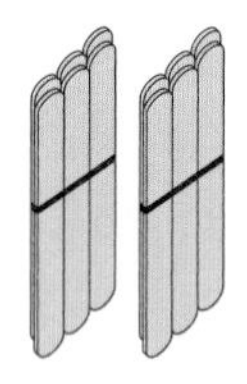

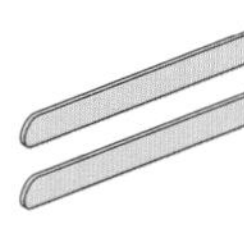

Procedure

1. Provide each child with 29 sticks and direct them to put the sticks in bundles of 6. After the bundles have been made, have the children count as follows:

   One bundle of six,

   One bundle of six and one,

   One bundle of six and two, . . .

   Two bundles of six,

   Two bundles of six and one, . . .
2. Repeat the above procedure with different-sized bundles.

In grouping activities, the group sizes usually are numbers between 2 and 9, but larger sized groups can be formed. A first-grade class was given 28 Unifix cubes to place in groups as described in Activity 6-4. Although most children chose to make groups of sizes 2 to 9, several made groups of 10, 15, and 25. Melissa, after having made groups of 6, 2, and 5, decided to make groups of 1 and was surprised to discover—upon counting all the groups she had made—that she had 28 groups of 1. (She knew she had 28 cubes, but she had to recount them to find out how many groups of 1 there were!) In the same class, Jonathan decided to make groups of zero using the eight plates he had on his desk. His written record of this activity was: "I made 8 groups of 0 and 28 (left)." From this experience, one learns not to be too prescriptive when assigning tasks to children. Left to their own decisions, children will conduct experiments that are meaningful to them.

NCTM Principles and Standards Link 6-2

Content Strand: Number and Operations

Using concrete materials can help students learn to group and ungroup by tens. For example, such materials can help students express "23" as 23 ones (units), 1 ten and 13 ones, or 2 tens and 3 ones. (NCTM, 2000, p. 81)

ACTIVITY 6-4 Making Groups and Recording

Realia Strategies

Materials
Each child will need a set of small objects (between 30 and 50), pencils and paper, and several small plastic or paper plates. Children need not have the same number of counters.

Procedure

1. Have children first count how many objects they have and then record the number on their papers. A second counting can serve to verify the first count.
2. Tell the children to decide on a group size and to make as many groups of that size as they can with their materials. Children then record what they have done.
3. The children then select another number as a group size and, using the same materials, make as many groups as they can. Recording follows.
4. Children could then select a different number of counters and repeat the above steps.

Communicating Mathematics

In early grouping activities, children can be requested to "tell what you have done." Statements such as "I made four groups of three airplanes" and "I made five groups of four buttons and had two left" should be encouraged.

When first recording on paper, you can use a form such as the one shown in Figure 6-4. In time, the recording can be in the form of a table as depicted in Figure 6-5. A sample of a child's work is presented in Figure 6-6. In these discussions, be sure to emphasize that the children made a certain number of groups and had some left over. This will help them make the connection later that the number 23, for example, is 2 groups of 10 and 3 left over.

Grouping by Tens

When making groups of 10, the grouping and recording can progress from "5 groups of ten and 3" to "1 group of ten and 0." Recording the latter statement in a table similar to that shown in Figure 6-5 will be an easy link to the numeral 10. Thereafter, when children hear that "when writing numbers, we show groups of ten and ones" they should understand that in 25 there are "2 groups of ten and 5 ones" or "2 tens and 5." Your role as a teacher is to help children realize that it is the 1 in 10 that indicates ten and the 0 that indicates it is an even group of ten, whereas the numeral 11 indicates 1 group of ten and 1 more.

FIGURE 6-4 Grouping Activities Form

Name: ______________________

I had ______________ buttons.

I made ______ groups of ______ buttons and ______ .

I made ______ groups of ______ buttons and ______ .

I made ______ groups of ______ buttons and ______ .

FIGURE 6-5 Grouping Activities Table

a)

Groups of Five	Number Left
4	2

b)

Number in Group	Ones
EIGHT	
5	2

FIGURE 6-6 Sample of a Child's Description of a Grouping Activity

I counted 38 squares.
I made seven groups of 5 and had 3 left.
I made nine groups of 4 and had two left.
I made three groups of 10 and had 8 left.
I made five groups of 7 and had 3 left.
I made six groups of 6 and had 2 left.

Margie, Grade One

An unhurried introduction to grouping experiences enhances the development of place-value understanding. When children are involved in grouping activities, it is important that they not only construct groups but also use their own language to describe what they have done before they are given an explanation of two-digit numerals.

Equivalent representations. One important component of developing place-value understanding is the notion of equivalent representations. The term *equivalent* means "equal value." *Equivalent representations* refers to the fact that a number can be represented in many different ways, *all of which have the same value but may look different.* For example, the number 32 can be represented in a variety of ways using groups of 10: as 3 groups of 10 and 2 singles, as 2 groups of 10 and 12 singles, as 1 group of 10 and 22 singles, and as 0 groups of 10 and 32 singles (see Figure 6-7). You need to help children understand that each of these representations is equivalent because each represents the number 32. Children who are able to think flexibly and recognize these equivalent groupings will be better able to regroup and rename two-digit numbers. Knowing how to regroup and rename will assist them later in computation work, such as when they need to regroup to solve a subtraction problem.

Types of Place-Value Materials

As making groups of 10 becomes the most common type of grouping activity, children will work with proportional and nonproportional materials to represent numbers. *Proportional materials* should be used first because the representative piece for 10 is actually 10 times larger than the piece that represents 1 (see Figure 6-8). Examples of proportional materials are:

- Prebundled sticks in singles, groups of 10, and groups of 100;
- Base-ten blocks in which a "rod" is constructed of 10 "units" and a "square" is made up of 10 rods or 100 units; and
- Meter, decimeter, and centimeter sticks.

Within the category of proportional models there are variations in the level of abstraction of different models. Counters such as beans or buttons are the most concrete. Ten counters can be put into a cup to represent the number 10. A one-to-one correspondence exists between the material and the number being represented. Craft sticks or connecting cubes such as Unifix cubes are only slightly more abstract in that groups of 10 can be easily formed to create a one-to-ten relationship. The bundles or rods, however, can be taken apart easily for verification. Bean sticks, made by gluing beans onto craft sticks, or base-ten blocks represent one more step toward abstraction. Here the groupings are permanent, but verification still is

FIGURE 6-7 Equivalent Representations of 32 Objects

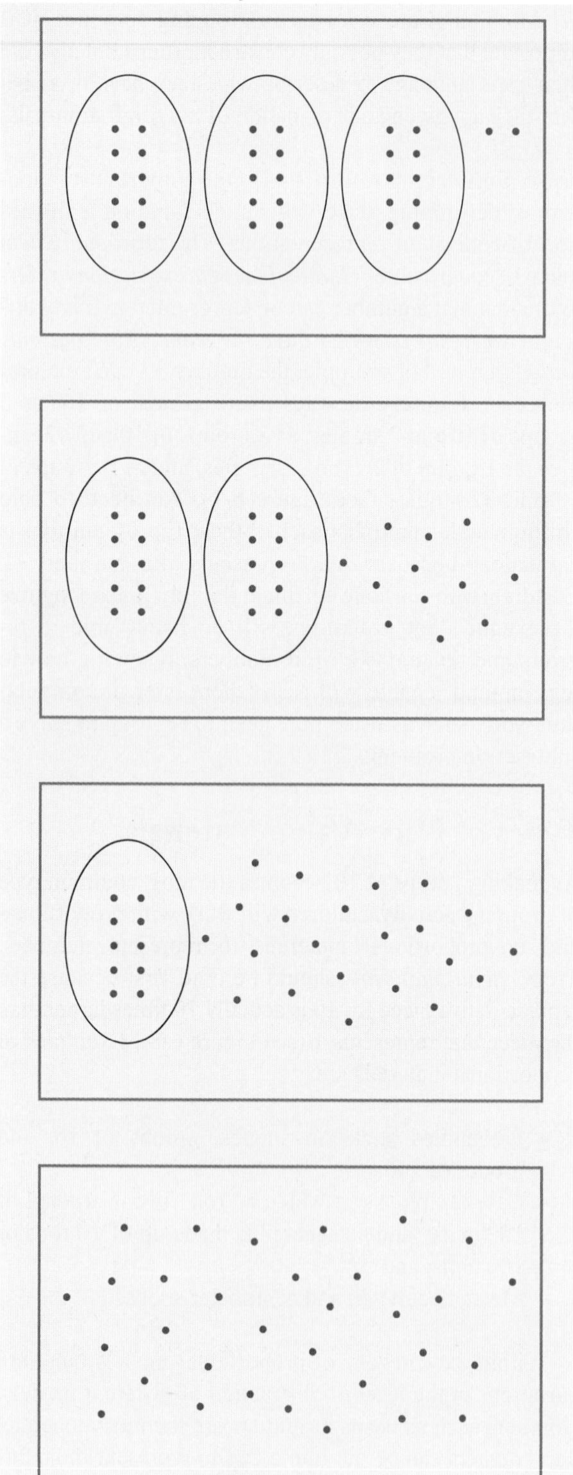

possible through matching or counting because one-to-one correspondence still exists. Unscored base-ten blocks require more abstraction on the part of the child and could serve as a transition to nonproportional materials. The unscored blocks maintain the one-to-ten proportion, but there is no longer a visual one-to-one correspondence.

In *nonproportional materials,* the same object is sometimes used to represent ones, tens, and hundreds (see Figure 6-9). Some nonproportional materials are challenging because they necessitate a focus on the position, color, size, or value of objects. For example, consider a place-value mat. A place-value mat includes two (or three) columns labeled "ones" and "tens" (and "hundreds" if it is three columns). It is used with manipulative materials to represent numbers (see Figure 6-12 later in this chapter). When using centimeter cubes on a place-value mat, one must pay careful attention to the position of a cube to determine its value rather than on a visible "group of 10" or "group of 100."

Chip Trading Materials, shown in Figure 6-9, contain at least four different colors of chips, along with a place-value mat with colors indicating the value of each chip. For example, in Figure 6-9, the red chips have a value of one, yellow chips are 10, blue chips are 100, and green chips are 1,000. When using Chip Trading Materials, position and color must be considered. Size may have to be considered depending on the materials selected to represent different amounts. When coins (dollars, dimes, and pennies) are used, one must take into consideration the value of each coin. Examples of nonproportional materials are place-value mats and chips, an abacus, pocket charts, and money.

Examining Children's Reasoning: Using Models to Represent Place-Value Concepts

Think back to Ms. Fisher's third- and fourth-grade class described at the beginning of the chapter. What models for place-value concepts did Ms. Fisher's children use to solve problems? Recall that some children used base-ten blocks while other children used other representations, including drawings of base-ten blocks. What types of place-value models did these children use? What models might Ms. Fisher next make available to her children, and why?

Developing Understanding of Two-Digit Numbers

When you are beginning to help children understand the meaning of two-digit numbers, you should use unstructured materials such as loose craft sticks or interlocking blocks and have the children construct the groupings themselves. At some time in the primary grades, children should have the experience of constructing numbers in this manner even beyond 100. Bundling 10 bundles of 10 sticks or constructing a square with 10 rods of interlocking Unifix cubes will aid children in developing understanding of 100 as 10 tens. The following representative experiences could be used for this purpose:

- Have children use Unifix cubes to show two-digit numbers, for example, 36, by constructing three rods of 10 cubes and six singles.

FIGURE 6-8 Examples of Proportional Base-Ten Materials

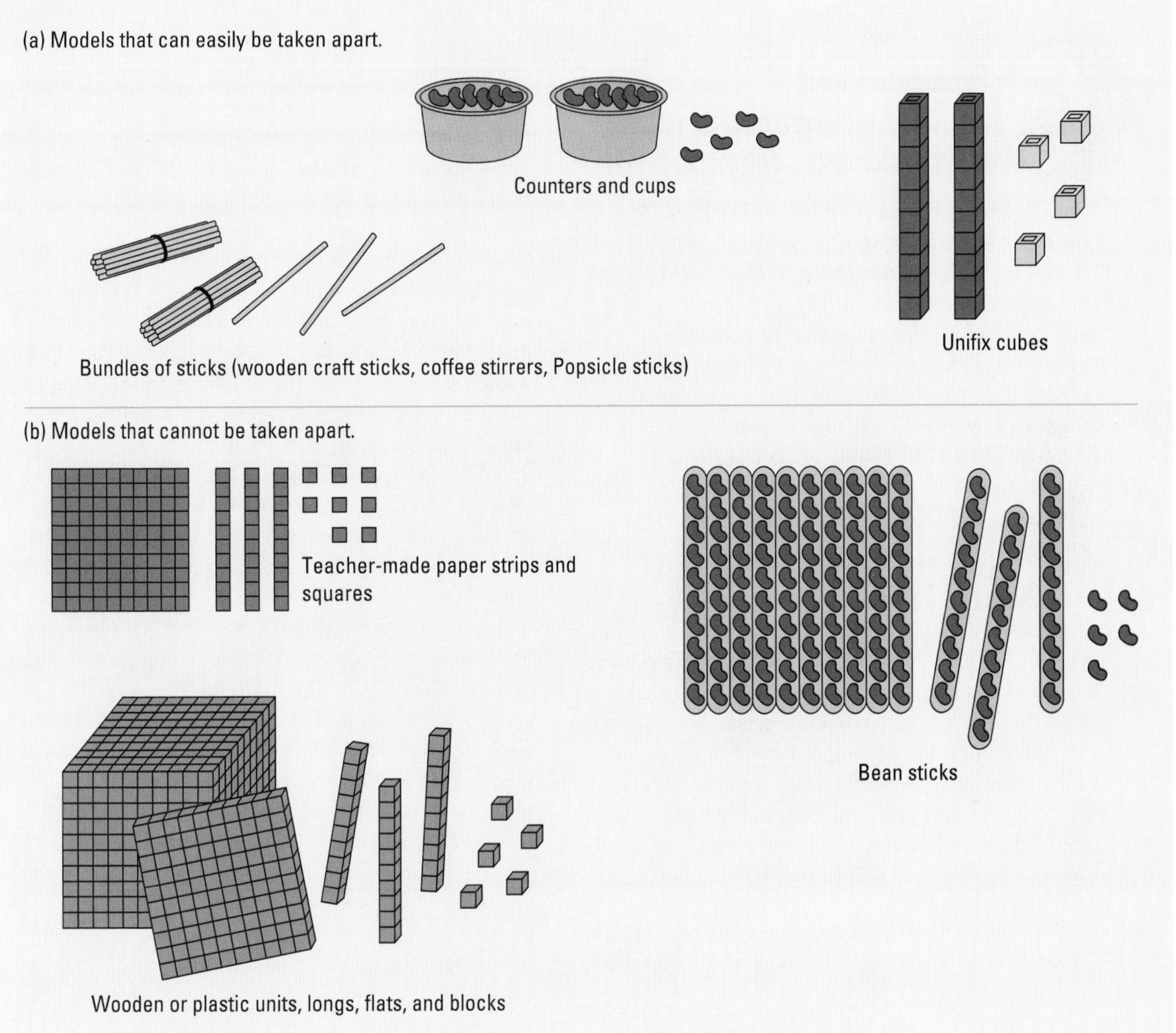

- Children can use multilink cubes in the same manner as Unifix cubes to make groups of 10. For 100, 10 rods are interlocked to make a square.
- Children can place elastic bands around groups of 10 craft sticks and use the bundles and single sticks to show two-digit numbers. For three-digit numbers, 10 bundles of 10 are grouped together.
- Using interlocking Unifix cubes, each child in a class can have the experience of constructing a hundred square to use with rods of 10 and singles to show three-digit numbers. (Unifix cubes are readily available in large quantities.)

Although the main focus of these activities is the development of the meaning of two-digit numbers, some children

FIGURE 6-9 Examples of Nonproportional Base-Ten Materials

Money

Chip Trading Materials

Green	Blue	Yellow	Red

Abacus Model

Literature Link 6-1

Equivalent Representations and Grouping Relationships

Dodds, Dayle Ann. (1999). ***The Great Divide.*** Cambridge, MA: Candlewick Press.
Giganti, P. (1992). ***Each Orange Had Eight Slices.*** New York: Greenwillow Books.
Long, Lynette. (1996). ***Domino Addition.*** Watertown, MA: Charlesbridge Publishing.
Murphy, Stuart J. (1996). ***Too Many Kangaroo Things to Do!*** New York: HarperCollins.
Schwartz, David M. (1989). ***If You Made a Million.*** New York: Mulberry Books.
Tang, Greg. (2001). ***The Grapes of Math.*** New York: Scholastic.

The foundations for place value and the whole-number operations rely heavily on children's facility with grouping relationships. Being able to group numbers to make 10 (such as 6 and 4, 7 and 3, or 5 and 5) and group tens to make hundreds develops number sense. Activities that focus children on the decomposition of numbers using various equivalent representations support later work with computational procedures and estimation skills. Using both pictorial and symbolic representations of various groupings helps to solidify these understandings.

- In ***The Grapes of Math*** children are encouraged to use grouping relationships to make counting more efficient. Give children groups of objects (i.e., 24, 50, or 100) in small bags. Ask them to find different ways to group the objects and to represent these groupings. For example, 50 can be represented as 2 groups of 25 or as 5 groups of 10. Record these various representations (using symbols or drawings) on chart paper.
- Systems of money (both coins and dollar bills) represent different ways of grouping monetary amounts. For example there are many different ways to use coins to make 10¢, 25¢, 50¢ and $1. Use the book ***If You Made a Million*** to explore the use of different coins to equal sums of money ranging from $1 to $1 million. What could children buy with $1 million?
- ***Too Many Kangaroo Things to Do*** examines grouping relationships using 10, 20, 30, 40, and 100. Challenge children to write their own "Too Many Things to Do" stories using different grouping relationships that equal 100.
- Other books that explore the ways numbers are grouped for addition, subtraction, multiplication, and division include ***Domino Addition*** (shows fact family combinations that add to get numbers from 1 to 12), ***Each Orange Had Eight Slices*** (shows objects in groups of groups and reinforces the concept of multiplication as repeated addition), and ***The Great Divide*** (where 80 participants in a race divide themselves repeatedly until there is only one participant at the finish line). Children can model the operations in these books as they investigate various number combinations and grouping relationships.

will be interested in knowing how to represent hundreds with the materials. It can be explained that another grouping is made and that this grouping consists of "10 groups of 10."

As children model numbers with bundles or groups of 10 they have constructed, ask them to describe the numbers. One second-grader's work is presented in Figure 6-10.

When you observe that children know the meaning of two-digit numbers—that is, when they can show, for example, that 48 means 4 tens and 8 ones—you can give them word problems with two-digit numbers to solve using proportional materials.

Introducing Base-Ten Blocks

A natural progressive step in helping children further their understanding of two-digit numbers is to present word problems and ask children to solve them using the rods of 10 and singles they have constructed with Unifix cubes. When children use the materials to solve addition and subtraction problems with two-digit numbers with regrouping, the rods and units from the

FIGURE 6-10 Sample of a Second-Grader's Work

Meaning of Numbers

Task: Use the Popsicle sticks to represent numbers. Write how you modeled each number.

Wendy s work:

52 5 bundles of ten and 2 singles
47 4 tens and 7 singles
29 2 groups of ten and 9 ones
40 4 groups of ten
7 7 singles and 0 bundles

Note: Wendy used varied expressions in this exercise. It is wise to encourage students to describe events in different ways.

base-ten block set can be introduced in the following manner:

1. You might say, "Someone thought it would be good to make rods that do not come apart, like these (show rods), to use with singles (show units). Let's see how we can represent numbers with these blocks."
2. Provide the children with some rods and units of base-ten blocks and ask them to represent 37 (three rods and seven units).
3. Ask the children if they can represent the number another way. When someone suggests exchanging a rod for 10 units, direct children to do this. Have the children determine that 2 rods and 17 units are also 37.
4. Direct the children to exchange another rod to determine that 1 rod and 27 units also represent 37. The next move would be to exchange the last rod to obtain all singles. Note that these are all equivalent representations.

After the children have completed an activity similar to Activity 6-5, stimulate discussion by asking, "What is the simplest way to represent 42 with the blocks?" or, in other words, "How can we represent 42 using the fewest blocks?" (Figure 6-11).

ACTIVITY 6-5 Modeling Two-Digit Numbers

Manipulative Strategies

Materials

Base-ten blocks (rods and units)

Procedure

1. Represent the number 42 with the blocks.
2. Show 42 another way.
3. How many different ways can you show 42 with the blocks?
4. Draw a picture or write about what you did.

To solve addition and subtraction problems using the base-ten blocks, children *exchange* or *trade* a rod for 10 units rather than "take apart" a rod, as they did with rods made from Unifix cubes. (Solving addition and subtraction problems with base-ten blocks is discussed in detail in Chapter 9).

Using Place-Value Mats

A caution is offered when using proportional materials to model numbers on a place-value mat. For example, when using base-ten blocks, if 10 unit blocks are replaced on a place-value mat with a "rod" (10 units) in a column labeled "tens," then a misleading notion about place value can develop because the value of a rod in the tens column is 100. Whenever the expectation is that children will replace 10 unit blocks with a "rod" to represent a two-digit number, an organizational mat (without column headings) should be used rather than a place-value mat (with headings) (Figure 6-12).

To be consistent with numeral representation, do not place more than nine units in any of the columns on a place-value mat. When there are 10 or more units in any column, a trade must be made.

Using a tens rod, or 10 sticks for a bundle of 10 sticks, is a concrete representation of numbers. Representing the number 10 on a place-value mat with one chip or a unit cube in the tens column is a more abstract representation of numbers. The introduction of a place-value mat signifies a move from the concrete type of modeling to the semiabstract type.

Introducing Nonproportional Materials

Recall that there are two main types of base-ten manipulative materials: *proportional*, such as base-ten blocks, and *nonproportional*, such as chips. With proportional materials, the size of the piece is proportional to its value, so the larger the piece, the larger its value. But for nonproportional materials, the size is not proportional to its value. For example, a red chip is the same size as a yellow chip, but might be worth 10 times the value of a yellow chip.

The fact that two objects that are the same size may have different values is often difficult for children to understand. For example, sometimes young children are

FIGURE 6-11 Modeling 42 with Base-Ten Blocks

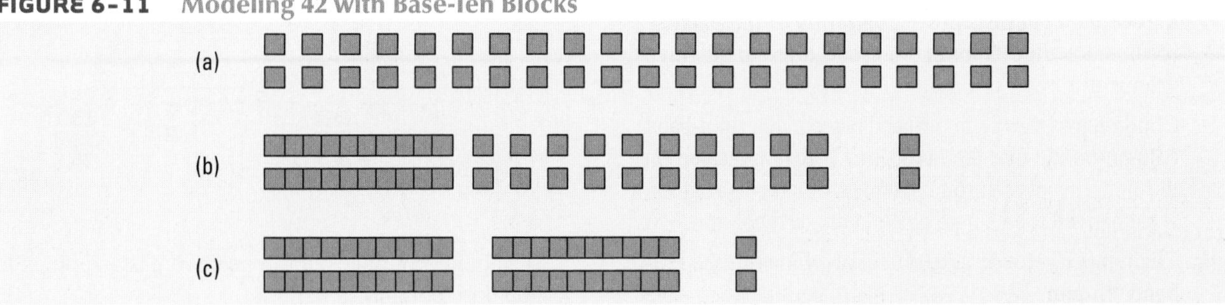

FIGURE 6-12 An Organizational Mat Versus a Place-Value Mat

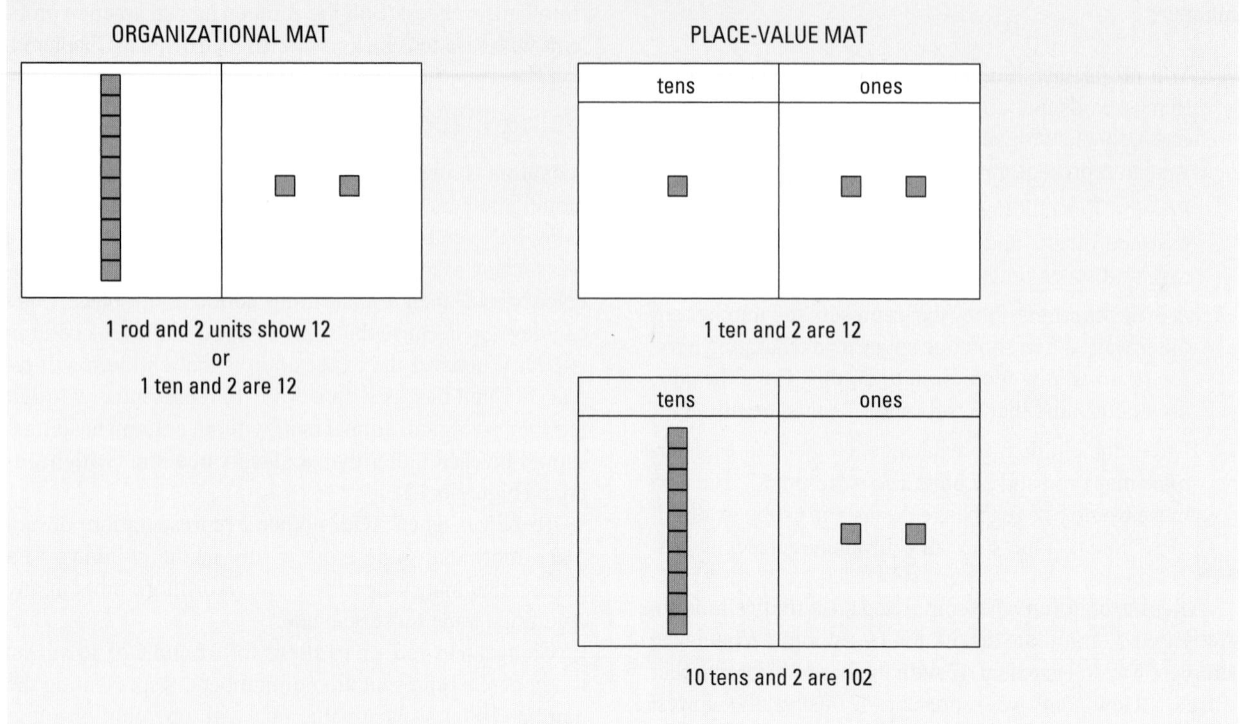

willing to trade away a dime for a penny because the penny is physically larger, so they think it's worth more. But an older child, who understands the value of the coins, would be happy to make this trade, because he knows that the value of a dime is greater than the value of a penny, even though its size is smaller. Coins are another example of a nonproportional material. It is important that children have experiences with both proportional and nonproportional manipulatives.

One way to introduce nonproportional place-value materials to children is to have them play trading games. These can be played with unit blocks from the base-ten set, a die, and mats. The procedures for using a place-value mat and unit blocks to play with bases other than base-ten are as follows:

1. Children in groups of three or four decide on a number to be the maximum number of blocks allowed in one column, say, two if the group uses base three.
2. Columns are used from right to left. One block in the column farthest to the right represents one, a block in the second column represents a group of three, and a block in the third column represents a group of "three groups of three," or nine.
3. Children toss the die in turn and place in the right-hand column on the mat the number of blocks indicated on the die. Whenever a group of three is obtained, the group is exchanged for a single block in the next column.
4. The winner is the first to obtain one block in the left-hand column.

A sample game with two as the maximum number of blocks per column might proceed as follows:

1. Jan tosses the die and gets a five. She counts five blocks, puts them in the ones column, and notices that she needs to make a trade, because she cannot have more than two blocks in any column. She takes three of the blocks in the ones column and trades them in for one block in the middle column (the threes column). When finished with this turn, Jan has one block in the middle column and two blocks in the ones column.
2. Timmy tosses the die and gets a six. He counts out six blocks, puts them in the ones column, and notices that he needs to make a trade. He trades in six blocks in the ones column for two blocks in the middle (threes) column, since he had two groups of three. When finished with this turn, Timmy has two blocks in the middle column and no blocks in the ones column.

GAME

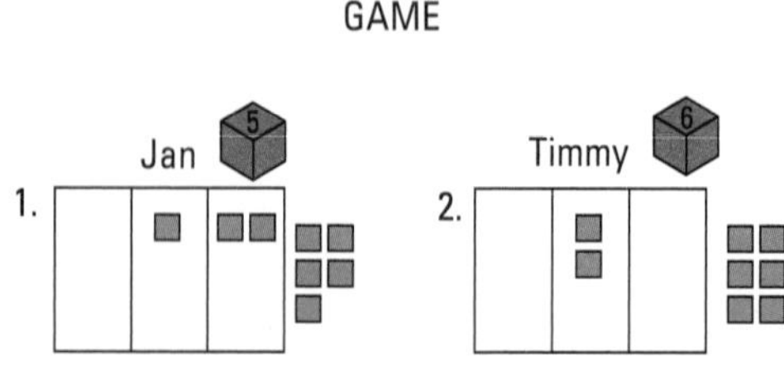

3. The game continues until one child has one block in the third column.

FIGURE 6-13 Backward Trading Game

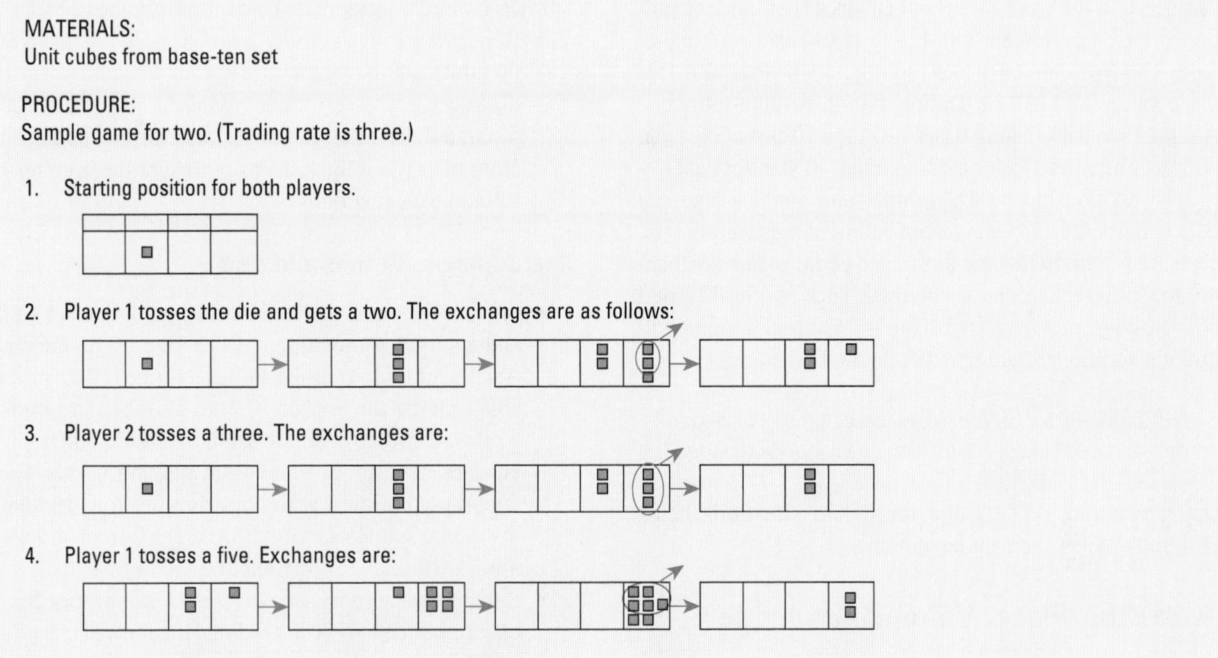

MATERIALS:
Unit cubes from base-ten set
PROCEDURE:
Sample game for two. (Trading rate is three.)
1. Starting position for both players.
2. Player 1 tosses the die and gets a two. The exchanges are as follows:
3. Player 2 tosses a three. The exchanges are:
4. Player 1 tosses a five. Exchanges are:

Materials from the Chip Trading Materials, shown earlier in Figure 6-9, could also be used. The game procedures are similar to those described above except that color is a factor: Yellow chips have a value of one, blue chips represent the group size, green chips represent "groups of groups" or square numbers, and red chips represent the next place value in the particular system chosen. A sample game with two players using four (for base-five) as the maximum number of chips allowed per column might proceed as outlined next. The goal is to accumulate two red chips.

1. Jamal tosses the die and gets a four. He counts four yellow chips and places them on the first column (headed yellow) on his mat.
2. Tanya tosses the die and gets a six. She counts six yellow chips, notices a group of five, and exchanges them for a blue chip. She completes her move by placing the blue chip in the second column (headed blue) and the remaining yellow chip in the first column.
3. Jamal tosses again and gets a six. He counts out six yellow chips, notices a group of five, and exchanges them for a blue chip. Then he notices that he has another group of five with the one chip remaining and the four yellow chips on his mat from the first play. He exchanges this set of five for another blue chip, which he places in the second column.
4. Tanya tosses and gets. . . .

The trading games can be played in a backward manner, that is, beginning with blocks or chips on the mat. When a die is tossed, exchanges are made to "subtract" an amount from that shown on the mat. Figure 6-13 illustrates the beginning of a sample game in which the trading rate is three. Games can be lengthened by changing the starting position, for example, a game starting with one chip in the left-most column will usually take more time than one starting with a chip in the column second from the left. Also, the game can begin with players having one cube in each column on the mat.

Trading games can be extended to include experiences such as the following:

1. Provide children with 38 counters and a place-value mat with four columns.
2. Have the children make groups of five, model the number on a place-value mat, and then write the numeral in base-five (123). The procedure should be to count groups of 5, then see if there are *at least* 5 groups of 5, and represent them with one counter in the third column on a mat, then count the remaining groups of 5 and represent them with two counters in the appropriate column on the mat, and lastly the 3.

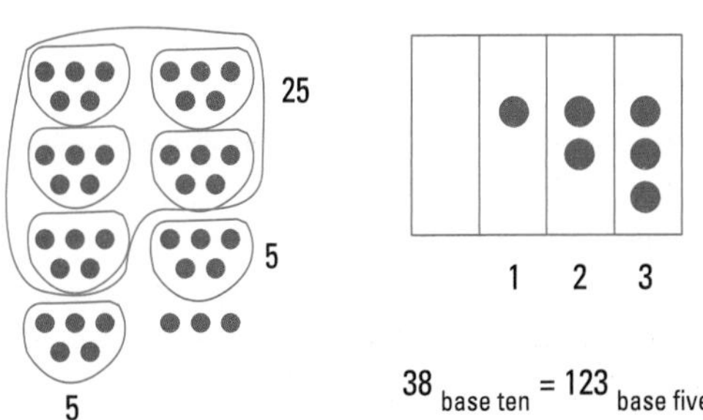

3. Repeat the procedure for other bases.

Children's ability to represent quantities on a place-value mat in different bases will enhance their understanding of base-ten numeration. Using base-five or a smaller base, children can carry out regroupings to four and five place values and still be dealing with three-digit numbers. Another benefit of using bases less than 10 is that children will get more practice in making trades in smaller bases.

The relationship between dimes and pennies also can help children develop an understanding of numeration concepts. Give children some dimes and pennies and ask them to show different amounts with them, such as 46¢, 72¢, and 36¢. Solving problems involving money transactions will provide additional trading experiences. For example:

> *Jack paid 68¢ for his lunch at school one day, and gave the cashier $1. What coins should Jack get in change?*

Using concrete models and real-world situations helps children deepen their understandings.

Assessing Place-Value Knowledge

When assessing children's place-value understanding, focus on observing children's understanding and use of groups of 10. The following tasks are just a few examples of ways to assess children's place-value understanding. Each task includes a description of how a child might respond and a general interpretation of what the child's understanding may be. You, as the teacher, will be better able to interpret children's responses to such tasks.

Using manipulatives to represent numbers

- Provide the child with a numeral, for example, 36, written on a card, and ask the child to read the number. Then ask the child to count that many of some sort of counter, say, toy cars. Observe the child as he or she counts the cars. Does the child move the cars? Does the child group the cars in twos, fives, or tens? After the child has counted out 36 cars, point to the "6" in the 36 on the card and ask the child, "Does this part of the 36 have anything to do with how many cars you have?" Repeat the question, this time pointing to the "3" in 36. A child who understands the meaning of 36 will match 6 cars with the "6" and 30 with the "3." A child who does not see the connection between the "3" and 30 cars needs more practice in making and using groups of 10 and observing the connections between the groups of 10 and two-digit numerals.

Understanding tens and ones

- Provide the child with a collection of Unifix cubes, including some singles and some stacked together in tens. Ask the child to show you 24 cubes. Notice if the child uses the tens sticks of cubes, or, instead, uses 24 ones. Children who use only ones to represent 24 need more work in making and using groups of 10 counters to represent two-digit numbers.
- Repeat the above activity with base-ten blocks. Note that this task may be a little harder, because base-ten blocks are a pregrouped material and cannot be separated. The key factor to look for is whether the child uses the longsticks to represent the number or instead uses just ones.

Regrouping with tens and ones

- Provide the child with a collection of base-ten blocks and an organizational mat. Place one ten on the mat. Ask the child to remove 4 ones. Notice if the child is able to trade the ten for 10 ones and then to remove 4 ones. Children who are unable to trade one ten for 10 ones need more practice in making trades. Provide these children with opportunities to participate in trading games in which they get lots of practice trading 10 ones for one ten and vice versa.
- Repeat the activity above with a nonproportional material, such as a Chip Trading Kit, and a place-value mat. Children who are unable to correctly trade with nonproportional materials may need more practice with this type of material. As above, trading games played with nonproportional materials will be helpful.
- Follow-up task: Ask the child to *show 24* on the mat, and then to *add 8*. Observe how she uses the materials.

Three-Digit Numbers

After children understand two-digit numbers, the transition to three-digit numbers may be fairly smooth. Three-digit numbers can be introduced by an activity such as Activity 6-6. Significant learning will occur as you question the children during and after the activity. Ask the children about the meaning of each digit in the numeral produced. Explain that when representing numbers, 10 items make a new group. Ten ones are grouped to make a 10 and 10 groups of 10 are grouped to make 100.

ACTIVITY 6-6 Three-Digit Numbers

Realia Strategies

Materials

At least 125 craft sticks for each child

Procedure

1. Make as many groups of 10 as you can.
2. If you have 10 groups of 10, put them together in one pile.
3. Write a numeral to show how many piles of 10 tens, how many groups of 10, and how many ones you have.

Children should be told that 100 also can be represented with a group of 100 singles but that groups of tens make it easier to solve problems using the materials. The language corresponding to groupings of hundreds, tens, and ones should ensue. For example, you could write on the chalkboard (or say) a numeral such as 134 and ask the children to model it with bundles of 10 sticks and singles. Have them identify the "hundred," the "thirty," and the "four." Tell them that the 10 groups of 10 for 100 can be bundled together for easy counting.

Focus discussion after completing the modeling through questions such as the following:

- What is the value of the third place in a numeral?
- How can we describe the value when using bundles of sticks?

(The third place value in a numeral is 10 bundles of 10. Thus, 100 is "1 bundle of 10 bundles of 10," 200 is "2 bundles of 10 bundles of 10," etc.)

The same activity can be done with base-ten blocks. These usually are available in large quantities so that each child in a class can have the experience of putting together 10 rods of 10 to make a 100 square. Three-digit numbers can be modeled using squares, rods of 10, and units. Discussion questions similar to the preceding two could be used for number work with base-ten blocks.

If children have been constructing different-sized groups, they can be asked to construct, for example, three rods of three, four rods of four, and five rods of five. They will notice that each set can be put together to form a square. Thus, the pattern is, regardless of the group size, singles, rods, and squares. The following game helps children develop mental pictures for numbers and also the language for number relationships. The procedure is described for base-three in Activity 6-7. It is easily adapted for other groupings.

ACTIVITY 6-7 Working in Base-Three (an Activity for 3 or 4 Players)

Materials

- 25 interlocking cubes for each child
- 2 dice (red and white) for each group of children
- Game card as pictured

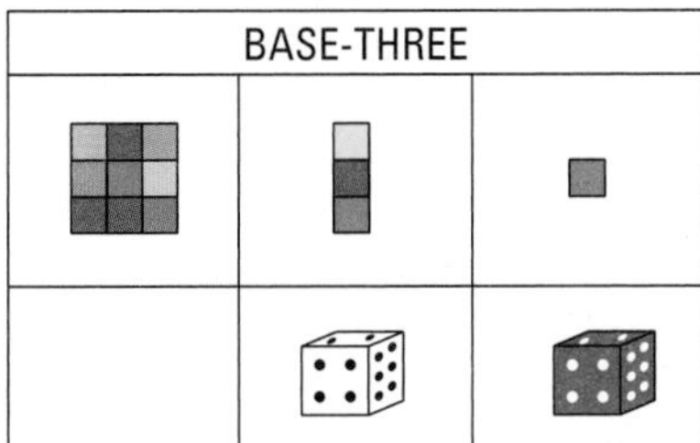

Procedure

1. One child throws the dice and places the red one in the first column and the white one in the second column.
2. Each child makes sets according to the numbers on the dice. When appropriate, they construct rods and squares. Children check their work to see whether they all agree.
3. Procedures are repeated, with children taking turns tossing the dice.

NCTM Principles and Standards Link 6-3

Content Strand: Number and Operations

As a result of regular experiences with problems that develop place-value concepts, second-grade students should be counting into the hundreds, discovering patterns in the numeration system related to place value, and composing (creating through different combinations) and decomposing (breaking apart in different ways) two- and three-digit numbers. (NCTM, 2000, p. 82)

Have children tell what they did. Listen for expressions such as "three rods," "three squares," "three groups of three," "three threes," and "one three." A class of second graders played the base-ten game. Afterward, children made the following statements about the values:

Ten rods have one hundred ones.

One square is one hundred.

One square has ten rods.

Ten squares make one cube.

One cube is one thousand.

One cube has one hundred rods.

Number Meanings: Oral Expressions

Children should learn to describe three-digit numbers in several ways. For example, 125 can be described as:

- 125 items is 1 group of 10 groups of 10 plus 2 groups of 10 plus 5.
- 125 is 10 tens plus 2 tens plus 5.
- 125 is 12 tens and 5.
- 125 means 100 plus 20 plus 5.

Note that 125 should be read "one hundred twenty-five," not "one hundred *AND* twenty-five." The term *and* is reserved for indicating a decimal point, which will be discussed in Chapter 12.

When focusing on place-value notation, the numeral 100 represents one group of hundred, zero tens, and zero ones. However, children should think of 100 as 10 groups of 10 and as 100 ones.

Developing Number Relationships

Building on their understanding of single-digit numbers, encourage children to develop mental computation strategies with two-digit numbers. Activities 6-8 and 6-9 help children develop an understanding of number relationships. Instructions for these activities should be given orally and repeated several times using different series of numbers.

ACTIVITY 6-8 Counting On—Base-Ten Blocks

Materials
Base-ten blocks

Procedure

1. Show 64 with the blocks (6 tens and 4 units).
2. Now show 74.
3. Tell your partner what you did. (*Added another 10*)
4. Now show 86.
5. Tell your partner what you did. (*Added a 10 and 2 units*)

ACTIVITY 6-9 Counting On—Craft Sticks

Materials
Craft sticks in bundles of tens and singles

Procedure

1. Show 35 with the sticks.
2. Now add sticks to count up to 67.
3. Record what you did. (*35 + 10 + 10 + 10 + 2 = 67*)
4. Show 28. Count up to 64. Record. (*28 + 10 + 10 + 10 + 2 + 4*)

Note that in the last exercise in Activity 6-9, the child counts from 28 to 60, then to 64. A worksheet could be prepared as presented in Figure 6-14.

FIGURE 6-14 Activity Worksheet

Worksheet for Activity 6-9

Name: ____________________

Begin with	Count up to
35	67
28	64
61	85
72	91
44	70

Mathematics sentence

35 + 10 + 10 + 10 + 2 = 67

28 + 10 + 10 + 10 + 2 + 4 = 64

____

____

Using Hundreds Charts

An activity similar to Activity 6-9 could be done using a hundreds chart. Hundreds charts are 10 × 10 charts with numbers written in order. Some hundreds charts contain the numbers 0 through 99; others contain the numbers 1 through 100 (see Figure 6-15 and Blackline Masters 3 and 4 located on MyEducationLab). You could use a large hundreds chart that all children in the classroom can see from their desks. You can create such a chart by enlarging a hundreds chart or making an overhead transparency of a hundreds chart. Also, each child or pair of children should have an individual hundreds chart and instructions such as the following:

1. Begin with 16 and count up to 38: (16, 26, 36, 37, 38).
2. Record what you did: (16 + 10 + 10 + 2 = 38).
3. Repeat with other numbers.

Children may use the base-ten blocks when they understand grouping, particularly a group of 10. See Figure 6-2 and Blackline Master 1 on MyEducationLab.

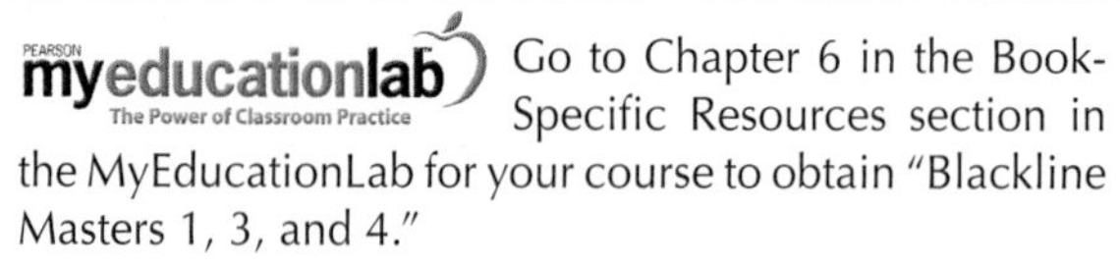

Go to Chapter 6 in the Book-Specific Resources section in the MyEducationLab for your course to obtain "Blackline Masters 1, 3, and 4."

Hundreds charts help children understand place value and patterns. For example, consider the following activities:

- Put a marker on 37. Put another marker on the number that is 10 more than 37. Now put another marker on the number that is 10 less than 37. What patterns do you notice about those three numbers?
- Put a marker on 43. Put another marker on a number that is 15 more than 43. You could count 5 spaces to the right, which is 5 more than 43, and count down 1 row, which is 10 more, ending up on 58.
- Put a marker on 21. How would you use the hundreds chart to find a number that is 35 more than 21? (You could, for example, count 5 spaces to the right, which is 5 more than 21, and count down 3 rows, which is 30 more.)

FIGURE 6-15 Hundreds Charts

0	1	2	3	4	5	6	7	8	9
10	11	12	13	14	15	16	17	18	19
20	21	22	23	24	25	26	27	28	29
30	31	32	33	34	35	36	37	38	39
40	41	42	43	44	45	46	47	48	49
50	51	52	53	54	55	56	57	58	59
60	61	62	63	64	65	66	67	68	69
70	71	72	73	74	75	76	77	78	79
80	81	82	83	84	85	86	87	88	89
90	91	92	93	94	95	96	97	98	99

1	2	3	4	5	6	7	8	9	10
11	12	13	14	15	16	17	18	19	20
21	22	23	24	25	26	27	28	29	30
31	32	33	34	35	36	37	38	39	40
41	42	43	44	45	46	47	48	49	50
51	52	53	54	55	56	57	58	59	60
61	62	63	64	65	66	67	68	69	70
71	72	73	74	75	76	77	78	79	80
81	82	83	84	85	86	87	88	89	90
91	92	93	94	95	96	97	98	99	100

Activities and questions such as these help children think about numbers as groups of tens and ones.

Children enjoy counting beyond 100. Give each child an egg carton and 350 to 550 small objects (e.g., buttons, cubes, pieces of straws, match sticks). Have children count the objects by making groups of 10 in each cup (using 10 cups). Instruct children to write about the counting procedures they followed. Two children's sample work is presented in Figure 6-16.

Thinking and Writing about Numbers

One way to find out how children think about numbers is to ask them to respond to number questions in writing.

FIGURE 6-16 Children's Samples of Counting Beyond a Hundred

I am counting blocks.
I have ten sets of ten so I have 100.
I have another ten sets of ten so I have 200.
I have 240.
I have another ten sets of ten so I have 300 blocks.
I have another ten sets of ten so I have 400.
I have 460!

Michael, Grade 2

I am counting blocks. Now I have 100.
I got 100 from grouping tens.
Now I have 200. I got 200 from grouping more tens.
I now have 300. I got 300 from still grouping tens.
I have ended at 350. I have grouped all these numbers and got 350.

Jenny, Grade 2

The following are sample questions that are appropriate for second-graders.

- What can you say about the number 25? 45? 90? 100? Write statements about each number.
- Write the following numerals on the board:

2, 3, 4, 5, 6, 10, 12, 15, 30

How many different number sentences can you make?

- How are these numbers different?

86 and 806   45 and 450

- Is the answer more than 100? Write about how you found out.

$25 + 55 + 25 \qquad 67 + 45 \qquad 22 + 33 + 44$

Some second-graders' responses to similar problems are presented next:

$88 + 15$

I knew that 90 + 10 = 100, so I took 2 of the 15 and that made 90 on one hand and 13 on the other, so now I just added 13 and it made 103. —*Jill, Grade 2*

$35 + 35 + 35$

First I remembered that 3 threes equaled 9. So I knew that three 30s equaled 90, so I added 15, and it left me with 105! —*Annie, Grade 2*

$73 + 37$

73 + 37 = 110 *because 70 from the 73 and 30 from the* 37 = 100 *plus 7 and the 3 left over* = 110.
—*Danny, Grade 2*

Examining Children's Reasoning: Understanding Place Value

How does children's understanding of place value develop? What aspects of the concept of place value are more difficult for children to understand? Reflect on these questions for just a moment before you read on. What have you understood from this chapter about teaching place value and children's understanding of it?

As children's understanding of place value evolves, children are able to think more flexibly about quantities. For example, consider the following questions:

How many tens are in 120? How many ones are in 316?

How might children answer the first question—2 tens or 12 tens? You hope they give the correct response of 12 tens. For the second question, the correct response is 316, but often children will say there are only 6 ones in 316, along with 3 hundreds and 1 ten.

To see how children think about problems such as these, view the video clip "IMAP—Understanding Place Value." In this clip Zenaida, a third-grade girl, solves the problems listed above, along with a few others. When asked, "How many tens are in 32? In 120?" Zenaida responds that there are 3 and 12 tens, respectively. She explains her first response by writing $10 \times 3 = 30$ and justifies her second response by saying that there are 10 tens in 100 and 2 tens in 20. Next she is asked, "How many ones are in 316?" to which she responds by saying 316, and she justifies her response by writing 316×1. Finally, the interviewer asks Zenaida, "How many ones are in 32?" Zenaida responds, "Thirty-two."

> PEARSON **myeducationlab** The Power of Classroom Practice Go to the Assignments and Activities section of Topic 5: "Number Concepts and Numeration" in the MyEducationLab for your course and complete the activity "IMAP—Understanding Place Value" to see how students think about problems. Complete the activity that follows.

The reasoning used by Zenaida in this clip is rare among elementary school children because Zenaida understands the quantities within the number. For example, the common response to "How many tens are in the number 120?" is "Two." This response is the correct answer to a different question: "What digit is in the tens place?" To many children, these two questions are the same, but to people who have a deeper understanding of place value and of the quantities associated with numbers, these questions are not the same. Children need to develop a flexible understanding of number, and that is your challenging role as a teacher. For example, you want children to come to understand that 120 is simultaneously 1 hundred, 2 tens, and 0 ones; 0 hundreds, 12 tens, and 0 ones; 1 hundred, 1 ten, and 10 ones; 120 ones; and so on. Such understanding is also needed in order to make sense of the standard subtraction algorithm taught in the United States.

But it takes time to develop the sort of reasoning displayed by Zenaida. To observe another child who thinks differently about place value, go to MyEducationLab to view video clip "IMAP—Complexities of Place Value." In this clip Talecia, a third-grade girl, has some difficulty with place value in solving the problem $638 + 476$. In solving the problem, she correctly states that the sum of $600 + 400$ is 10 hundred, but she incorrectly records that number as 110. Talecia realizes that her answer of 224 to the problem $638 + 476$ is much too small. The two prospective elementary school teachers who are interviewing Talecia find base-ten blocks useful to help Talecia draw connections, though she continues to have difficulty making connections between the symbolic and verbal representations of the numbers. The interviewers' discussion with Talecia shows that her misunderstanding is robust and has no "easy fix."

> PEARSON **myeducationlab** The Power of Classroom Practice Go to the Assignments and Activities section of Topic 5: "Number Concepts and Numeration" in the MyEducationLab for your course and complete the activity "IMAP—Complexities of Place Value." Complete the activity that follows.

After viewing this clip, take a moment to reflect on the decisions the prospective elementary school teachers made during the interview. The interviewer on the right side had more experience than the one on the left in considering children's mathematical thinking and is able to devise questions and tasks first to induce disequilibrium for Talecia and then to help her through it. What are some other questions the interviewers might have used to help Talecia? This video clip provides an example of the complexity of the concept of place value and the importance of helping children develop a rich understanding.

For more practice, go to MyEducationLab to view video clip "IMAP—Grades 3-4 Reasoning." This clip shows a portion of a discussion in a grade 3-4 classroom in which children were thinking about whether it was correct to express 192,000 as 19,200 tens and as 1,920 hundreds. Pay particular attention to the children's reasoning in this clip and to the teacher's comments as she responds to one child's description of his solution.

> PEARSON **myeducationlab** The Power of Classroom Practice Go to the Assignments and Activities section of Topic 5: "Number Concepts and Numeration" in the MyEducationLab for your course and complete the activity "IMAP—Grades 3-4 Reasoning."

FIGURE 6-17 Japanese Number Names

1—ichi	11—juichi	100—hyaku
2—ni	12—juni	101—hyakuichi
3—san	13—jusan	111—hyakujuichi
4—shi	14—jushi	200—nihyaku
5—go	15—jugo	201—nihyakuichi
6—roku	16—juroku	211—nihyakujuichi
7—shichi	17—jushichi	
8—hachi	18—juhachi	1000—sen
9—kyu	19—jukyu	1997—senkyuhyakukyujushichi
10—ju	20—niju	
	21—nijuichi	

NCTM Principles and Standards Link 6-4

Content Strand: Number and Operations

Place-value concepts can be developed and reinforced using calculators. For example, students can observe values displayed on a calculator and focus on which digits are changing. If students add 1 repeatedly on a calculator, they can observe that the units digit changes every time, but the tens digit changes less frequently. Through classroom conversations about such activities and patterns, teachers can help focus students' attention on important place-value ideas. (NCTM, 2000, p. 81)

Understanding Large Numbers

Number Names

Although children learn the number name sequence fairly early, it is recognized that the words for 11, 12, 13, etc., to 19 are more difficult than the decade names because they do not exhibit a 10 grouping in their names. For the decades, a child can understand the "ty" in each number name to be a derivation from the name ten. Japanese children, for example, have a head start on English-speaking children when it comes to number names. The Japanese system of number names follows a logical development, employing only the names of the digits plus a name for 10 and each successive power of 10. Examine the number names in Figure 6-17; notice how relatively easy it is to progress in naming successive numbers.

Writing Consecutive Numbers

It is a common practice in school programs to have children write numbers in sequence from 1 to 100. These numbers are often pictured on wall charts or on a hundreds board. Usually, the numbers are recorded in 10 rows of 10. The task can be made somewhat more challenging by providing children with blank charts featuring fewer or more than 10 spaces per row (Figure 6-18).

Elementary school children should have the experience of writing numbers in sequence beyond 100, because counting by tens or hundreds to 1,000 does not give them a sense of the size of 1,000. Also, when asked to complete a number sequence, children frequently make errors in bridging decades and centuries. A teacher could watch for these difficulties by organizing a group project such as the following:

- Prepare charts for children to write numbers in some organized way. The charts could be strips of poster board with spaces for 50 numbers, or they could be 12 by 12 squares for 144 numbers per chart.
- Children can share the work of writing numbers to 1,000 by each filling in a part of a chart or charts.
- The charts could be displayed on a bulletin board and used in number activities.

Magnitude of Numbers

Asking children to compare numbers is one way to assess their understanding of numbers. One task is to write a set of six numbers on individual cards and have children order the numbers from least to greatest.

Example

a. 146 116 106 164 104 140

b. 2105 2015 1520 2520 1250 2555

FIGURE 6-18 Different Ways to Write Consecutive Numbers

1	2	3
4	5	6
7	8	9
10	11	12
13	14	15
16	17	..

1	2	3	4	5	6
7	8	9	10	11	12
13	14	15	16	17	18
19	20	21	22	23	24
25	26	27	28	29	30
31	32	33	..	..	..

1	2	3	4	5	6	7
8	9	10	11	12	13	14
15	16	17	18	19	20	21
22	23	24	25	26	27	28
29	30	31	32	33	34	35
36	37	..	..	..	..	..

Ask the child: How can you tell which is larger? A child's response for **set a** could be:

> *I first look at the digit in the hundred's place. If they are all the same, then I examine the digit in the ten's place; if these are different, I know that the one with the most tens is the greatest number. When two numbers have the same hundreds and tens, then I compare the ones.*

It is possible that children could be learning to list sets of names or other words in alphabetical order at the same time as they are learning to order multidigit numbers. Certainly, the similarity should be discussed.

Counting to a Thousand and Beyond

Children should engage in at least a few activities that require them to count objects in the hundreds, thousands, ten thousands, and beyond. This is necessary if they are to develop a sense of the magnitude of large numbers. Activities 6-10 and 6-11 are helpful in developing the relative size of numbers.

ACTIVITY 6-10 Showing a Thousand

- Provide children with several cards (2 in. by 4 in.) and some toothpicks.
- Have them count out 10 toothpicks and glue them close together and centered on the card. (You may wish to place a piece of cellophane tape across the toothpicks to secure them in place.) The class should prepare enough cards to demonstrate at least a thousand.
- Take 10 cards and attach them to a sufficiently long piece of poster board. Repeat this for each set of 10 cards. Ten strips of poster board can be mounted to a bulletin board or wall with additional strips mounted alongside but separate from the set of a thousand. This is for easy identification of a thousand toothpicks.
- The toothpicks can be the focus of counting activities.

ACTIVITY 6-11 Counting Toothpicks

- Ask children to count different numbers of toothpicks.

  Example: Count 156 toothpicks.
  Possible response: A child might begin counting at one hundred (while pointing to the first strip of 100 toothpicks), then continue on with "one hundred ten" (pointing to the next group of 10 toothpicks), "one hundred twenty, one hundred thirty, one hundred forty, one hundred fifty, one hundred fifty-one, . . . , one hundred fifty-six."

Today, numbers in the millions and billions often are heard in media reports; therefore, children must develop some understanding of large numbers. It seems a reasonable expectation to have children at least once in their elementary grades devise a way to represent a million of something. A visual representation of a million dollar signs or other keyboard character can be obtained from a computer printout, although this is not deemed economical to do in terms of computer storage space and time. What may be preferred is to type a page full of dots and photocopy sufficient copies to total a million or part of a million, such as one-quarter or one-half a million. The pages could be mounted on poster board and, following some estimation activity, displayed for some time in the classroom. A teacher may want to organize the "million things" (or part of a million things) by typing 100 characters per piece of paper in a 10-by-10 array. Ten papers of 100 each could then be mounted on a sheet of paper. Thus, the organization of 10, 100, 1,000, or 10,000, and so on, would be easily recognized.

Another model of one million is to suspend a centimeter cube in a meter cube or skeleton model of a meter cube. It would take a million of the smaller cubes to fill the larger cube.

Children should be asked to use large numbers in reporting distances, weights, or other scientific information obtained from an encyclopedia or other source. An example is the mass of the earth expressed in kilograms (600, 000,000,000,000,000,000,000). For interest's sake, children may want to learn number period names beyond the familiar billion and trillion. The first 12 number period names are presented in Figure 6-19.

Expanded Notation

As children progress in developing an understanding of numbers and numeration they will learn how to write numbers in expanded notation in several ways. In the primary grades, children are expected to write numbers as the sum of two or more parts.

Example

$$63 = 60 + 3 = 6 \text{ tens} + 3$$

In upper elementary grades, numbers will be written in expanded form using the multiplicative property.

FIGURE 6-19 Number Period Names

ones	billions	quintillions	octillions
thousands	trillions	sextillions	nonillions
millions	quadrillions	septillions	decillions

Example

$$785 = (7 \times 100) + (8 \times 10) + 5$$

$$4692 = (4 \times 1000) + (6 \times 100) + (9 \times 10) + 2$$

By grade 6 or 7, children should be able to use exponential notation.

Example

$$4692 = (4 \times 10 \times 10 \times 10) + (6 \times 10 \times 10) + (9 \times 10) + 2$$
$$= (4 \times 10^3) + (6 \times 10^2) + (9 \times 10^1) + 2$$

Rounding Numbers

There are occasions when it is practical to use number approximations. For example, when asking what the population of the United States is, you would expect not an exact number but a response such as 305 million, that is, a number rounded to the nearest million. When completing income tax returns, taxpayers are allowed to round off all amounts reported to the nearest dollar, because it is believed that dollar rounding makes for fewer errors. Rounding skills are used frequently in determining estimates for computation questions.

Rounding Rules

In elementary schools, rules taught for rounding numbers are as follows: When rounding a number to a specified place value, locate the place value and examine the digit to its immediate right (the key digit). If the key digit has a value of 5 or greater, replace all digits to the right of the place value by zeros and increase the place value digit by one; if the key digit has a value less than 5, replace the digits to the right of the place value by zeros. Table 6-1 shows some examples of rounding off.

Children can learn these rules by modeling numbers to be rounded with base-ten blocks or by drawing number lines to compare numbers between decades, hundreds, etc.

The model children will construct for Activity 6-12 is shown below. A number line model can be found on MyEducationLab in the Strategies section.

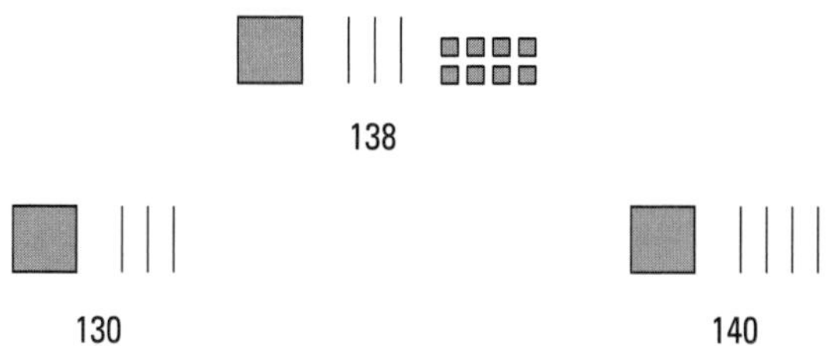

TABLE 6-1 Rounding Numbers

Place Value	Number	Rounded Off
Nearest ten	543	540
Nearest hundred	629	600
Nearest hundred	748	750
Nearest ten	748*	700
Nearest hundred	5,496	5,500

*Note that one does not first round off to tens.

ACTIVITY 6-12 Rounding to Nearest Ten—Concrete Model

Materials
Base-ten blocks

Task
Round 138 to the nearest ten.

Procedure
1. Show the number with base-ten blocks.
2. What are the two multiples of 10 that are closest to 138?
3. Show these two multiples with the blocks.
4. Examine the three numbers shown. Is 138 closer to 130 or 140?

The Computer Rule for Rounding

Note that in the activities described, numbers with a 5 in the determining place value have been omitted. This case merits special attention. When children are successful in rounding off numbers according to the rules previously described, they should be informed that there are instances when another rule governs the process—a computer rule governed by the key digit 5. Children could be asked to gather a set of data and then compute the average (see Activity 6-13). In Set B of Activity 6-13 the numbers ending in 5 in Set A have all been rounded up, whereas in Set C the numbers ending in 5 in set A preceded by an even number have been rounded down, those preceded by an odd number have been rounded up. This rule, known as the computer's rule, avoids the possibility of cumulative errors in rounding off and is employed by scientists, statisticians, and actuaries, among others. Children may notice that when following the computer's rule in rounding off numbers, the retained terminal digit will always be an even number. Children could be asked to determine which rounding-off rule their calculator is programmed to use.

ACTIVITY 6-13 Effects of Rounding

Materials

Data collected

Procedure

1. Study the following sets of numbers for which the average has been calculated:

	Set A	*Set B*	*Set C*
	243	240	240
	247	250	250
	245	250	240
	235	240	240
	236	240	240
	231	230	230
	225	230	220
	255	260	260
Average:	239.63	242.5	240

2. Which average is closer to the exact average of Set A? Why?

Estimating

Good number sense enables one to estimate quantities. Rounding numbers is one way to estimate totals or products. (Additional estimating strategies are discussed in Chapter 9.)

There are times when one needs to estimate a quantity "at a glance." For example, an approximation of the number of people in attendance at a rally or sports event may be required. Children who have developed good number sense both in physical representations and in understanding number compositions (additive and multiplicative) will feel competent in providing a sensible estimate of the group size.

What strategies could be employed in making such estimates? In a large gathering, one could note a "group of ten" or a "group of twenty" and quickly determine ten or five such groups for the physical size of a "group of hundred." From this number, a look around the arena or other area will enable one to determine "at a glance" an approximate number for the gathering. Whole student body or multiple class gatherings can be occasions when children can practice estimating quantities in the tens and hundreds. You can use different occasions to have children make estimates. Examples include the following:

- *Holiday concert:* About how many parents attended the concert?
- *Class visit to a museum:* About how many samples are in the rock collection? About how many butterflies are in the display?
- *Class visit to the public library:* About how many science fiction books are there in the children's section? About how many adventure books?

Children can be asked to estimate the number of small objects in a jar or clear plastic bag. A child estimating the number of jelly beans in a cylindrical jar might think the following:

> *There are about 20 jelly beans in 1 layer and 12 layers altogether. Twenty times 10 is 200 and 2 times 20 is 40, so I estimate that there are about 240 jelly beans in the jar.*

Another estimation activity is to scatter a number of centimeter cubes (25 to 35) on an overhead projector and then turn on the projector for a brief moment. Have children tell about how many blocks they saw pictured on the screen. Other small objects could be placed on a table, and children could be directed to look at the objects for a few seconds and then to make an estimate about the number. Children should be encouraged to see "groups of five" or "groups of ten" to help them make quick approximations about the number of objects there are in all. To discourage random guessing, be sure to allow students a reasonable time to estimate the number and then, after an estimate has been made, ask, "How did you figure out the amount?" Other children can learn estimating strategies from hearing classmates' descriptions.

Consolidating Number Skills

Children who have experienced the kinds of activities described in this chapter, along with talking and writing about their work, should eventually develop an understanding of our numeration system together with number sense. To consolidate these ideas, additional experiences may be necessary. The following are examples of consolidating activities.

1. **Numeral Cards**
   - Write each of the digits 1 to 9 on three cards (27 cards in all).
   - Shuffle the cards.
   - Have a child draw six cards and write the numbers drawn in any order on a chart (Figure 6-20). Zeros are then written in the empty places.
   - Have the child read the number.
   - Fewer or more number cards can be drawn, and the chart can be extended to other number periods (groups of three places, such as ones, tens, and hundreds).

FIGURE 6-20 Numeral Cards Chart

Billions			Millions			Thousands			Ones		
hundred	ten	one	hundred	ten	one	hundred	ten	one	hundred	ten	one
				9	1	0	0	4	6	3	4
			4	5	0	2	1	9	0	3	0
	1	4	0	0	2	0	0	0	2	1	8

2. **Pocket Chart**
   - Place a place-value pocket chart showing three or more number periods (groups of three places, such as ones, tens, and hundreds) on the board ledge.

Thousands			Ones		
2	0	1	1	1	2

   - Have children take turns putting digits on the chart and ask classmates to read the numbers aloud. The aim should be to represent "tricky" numbers to challenge their classmates.
3. **Colored Chips**
   - Ask children to represent the number 111 on a four-column mat with colored chips (1 yellow, 1 red, and 1 blue).
   - Ask them to show the number using only two colors.
   - Have them record the two parts of 111 (see diagram).

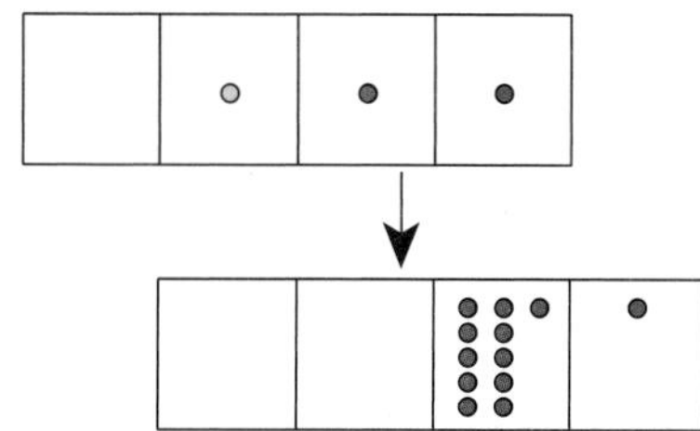

   - Repeat the task with different three-digit numbers.
   - With four-digit numbers, have the children represent a number using two or three different colors.
4. **Calculator Activity**
   - Direct children to enter a six-digit number on their calculators and ask them to "wipe out" a specified digit.

Example: Enter 345 876. Wipe out the digit 8.

   - Children can keep a record of their work as shown below (Reys, Suydam, & Lindquist, 1984, p. 79).

Enter	Wipe Out	Keys Pressed	Display
345876	8	–800	345076

5. **Die or Number Cards 0 to 9**
   - Ask players to create the largest possible multi-digit number using the digits generated by repeatedly tossing a die or drawing a card from a set of cards 0 to 9.
   - As each digit is revealed, players must write it in one of the place-value positions and cannot later change a position.

Example: 5 4 3 6 2

   - The player making the greatest number is the winner.

Conclusion

This chapter has discussed the structure of our numeration system together with suggestions of ways to help children develop understanding of number meanings and relationships. A good understanding of numeration is a prerequisite for mental computation and computational estimation with whole numbers. Place-value tasks of renaming and regrouping numbers underlie algorithmic procedures for computation. Therefore, children's understanding of numbers and numeration should be assessed before proceeding to the development of computational procedures.

CHAPTER 6

Sample Lesson

A Lesson on Place Value: Making Groups of Ten

1. There are 25 children at the beach. Each child has 10 sand toys. How many sand toys do they have at the beach?

2. Jaime has $180. He wants to buy some Pokémon® cards. Each pack of Pokémon cards costs $10. How many packs of Pokémon cards can Jaime buy?

This lesson is designed to help students who had difficulty with problems 1 or 2 on the Chapter 6 Pre-assessment. Students who have difficulty with these problems may need more help in making groups of ten.

Grade level: First

Materials: At least one place-value manipulative, such as Unifix cubes

Lesson objective: Students will use objects to make groups of 10 to represent numbers between 10 and 100.

Standards link: Students think of whole numbers between 10 and 100 in terms of groups of tens and ones (especially recognizing the numbers 11 to 19 as 1 group of ten and particular numbers of ones) (NCTM *Curriculum Focal Points*, grade one).

Launch: Display a pile of approximately 40–50 Unifix cubes. Ask students, "how could we figure out how many cubes are in this pile?" Solicit recommendations about how to determine this; many students will suggest that we count them. Ask, "how should we count them?" A common suggestion will be to count by ones. Model counting the pile by ones but losing track partway through and needing to count again. Ask if there's another way to count the cubes. Suggest making groups of tens.

Model counting 10 cubes and making a ten-stick with those cubes, repeating until no more tens can be made. Then determine the total number of cubes by counting by tens and then by ones. For example, "10, 20, 30, 40, 41, 42, 43, 44, 45, 46, 47." There are 47 cubes in that pile.

Then ask, "how many tens and ones do we have?" Point out that in 47 there are 4 tens sticks, meaning there are 4 tens, and there one 7 individual cubes, so we can say that there are 7 ones. In 47 there are 4 tens and 7 ones.

Explore: In pairs, have students repeat this process twice: (1) one student creates a pile of Unifix cubes, (2) both students work together to create groups of tens and ones to determine the number of cubes in the pile, (3) one student records the number of cubes in the pile, both as a numeral (e.g., 53) and as the number of tens and the number of ones (e.g., 5 tens and 3 ones).

Summarize: Coming together as a whole class, select one pair of students to come to the front of the room and show their cubes, with ten-sticks and ones, and state the total number of cubes (e.g., 53) and the number of tens and ones (e.g., 5 tens and 3 ones). Ask students how making groups of tens helped them count the cubes in their piles. Answers should focus on the ease of counting by tens.

FOLLOW-UP

Complete the following questions.

1. Consider any cautions regarding selecting the manipulatives to use in this lesson. Would other manipulatives work well? Might you want to avoid using certain manipulatives or objects? Why? What would be the advantages and/or disadvantages of each manipulative?

2. Consider difficulties students might have with this concept and this lesson. What modification could you make to avoid or minimize these issues? What modifications could you make for students with special needs?

3. What might the *next* lesson focus on, and why?

IN PRACTICE

Complete the following activities to include in your professional portfolio.

1. Write a lesson plan to help children understand the concept of grouping tens. Make sure you describe the type of base-ten model you would use.
2. Write a lesson plan to help children understand the concept of equivalent representations.

myeducationlab The Power of Classroom Practice Now go to Topic 5: "Number Concepts and Numeration" in the MyEducationLab (www.myeducationlab.com) for your course, where you can:

- Find learning outcomes for "Numbers Concepts and Numeration" along with the national standards that connect to these outcomes.
- Apply and practice your understanding of the core teaching skills identified in the chapter with a Building Teaching Skills and Dispositions learning unit.
- Complete Assignments and Activities that can help you understand the chapter content more deeply.
- Complete *enVision MATH* Sample Curricula assignments that allow you to examine and work with chapters from *enVisionMATH*, a K-6 mathematics program.
- Check your comprehension on the content covered in the chapter by going to the Study Plan in the Book-Specific Resources for your text. Here you will be able to take a chapter quiz, receive feedback on your answers, and then access Review, Practice, and Enrichment activities to enhance your understanding of chapter content.
- Go to the Book-Specific Resources for Chapter 6 to explore mathematical reasoning related to chapter content in the Activities section.

LINKS TO THE INTERNET

Ask Dr. Math (place value)

http://www.mathforum.org/library/drmath/sets/select/dm_place_value.html

Contains a list of interesting questions about place value and answers given by Dr. Math.

RESOURCES FOR TEACHERS

Reference Books: Numeration

Brodie, J. (1995). *Constructing Ideas about Large Numbers.* Mountain View, CA: Creative.

Burns, M. (1994). *Math By All Means: Place Value, Grade 2.* Sausalito, CA: Math Solutions.

National Council of Teachers of Mathematics (2006). *Curriculum Focal Points for Prekindergarten through Grade 8 Mathematics*. Reston, VA: Author.

Reak, C., Stewart, K., & Walker, K. (1995). *20 Thinking Questions for Base-10 Blocks, Grades 3–6.* Mountain View, CA: Creative.

Reak, C., Stewart, K., & Walker, K. (1995). *20 Thinking Questions for Base-10 Blocks, Grades 6-8.* Mountain View, CA: Creative.

Richardson, K. (1999). *Developing Number Concepts: Place Value, Multiplication, and Division.* White Plains, NY: Seymour.

Children's Literature

Books on Place Value

Anno, M., & Anno, M. (1983). *Anno's Mysterious Multiplying Jar*. New York: Philomel. (p. 117)

Friedman, A. (1995). *The King's Commissioners*. New York: Scholastic.

Fisher, Leonard Everett (1984). *Number Art: Thirteen 123s from Around the World*. New York: Simon & Schuster.

Gag, W. (2006). *Millions of Cats!* New York: Penguin.

Lopresti, A. S. (2003). *A Place for Zero.* Watertown, MA: Charlesbridge Publishing.

McKissack, P. (1996). *A Million Fish . . . . More or Less*. New York: Dragonfly.

Murphy, S. J. (2004). *Earth Day—Hooray!* New York: HarperCollins.

Murphy, S. J. (1997). *Betcha*. New York: Harper Trophy. (p. 117)

Schwartz, D. M. (1985). *How Much Is a Million?* New York: HarperCollins.

Schwartz, D. M. (1999). *On Beyond a Million*. New York: Random House.

Seuss, Dr. (1989). *The 500 Hats of Bartholomew Cubbins*. New York: Random House.

Zimelman, N. (1992). *How the Second Grade Got $8,205.50 to Visit the Statue of Liberty*. Morton Grove, IL: Whitman.

CHAPTER 7

Developing Whole-Number Operations: Meaning of Operations

NCTM CONNECTING WITH THE STANDARDS

The National Council of Teachers of Mathematics (NCTM) emphasizes how important it is for children to understand the meaning of operations, stating that "understanding the fundamental operations of addition, subtraction, multiplication, and division is central to knowing mathematics" (NCTM, 1989, p. 41). There are four key aspects of "developing operation sense," or understanding operations, that include

- recognizing real-world settings for each operation;
- developing an awareness of models and properties of each operation;
- recognizing relationships among the operations; and
- understanding the effects of an operation.

The NCTM (2006) *Curriculum Focal Points* mentions developing understanding of the meaning of operations in two different grade levels. They state that first-grade students should:

- develop strategies for adding and subtracting whole numbers on the basis of their earlier work with small numbers; and
- use a variety of models, including discrete objects, length-based models (e.g., lengths of connecting cubes), and number lines, to model "part-whole," "adding to," "taking away from," and "comparing" situations to develop an understanding of the meanings of addition and subtraction and strategies to solve such arithmetic problems (NCTM, 2006, p. 13).

Similarly, they state that third-grade students should "understand the meanings of multiplication and division of whole numbers through the use of representations (e.g., equal-sized groups, arrays, area models, and equal 'jumps' on number lines for multiplication, and successive subtraction, partitioning, and sharing for division)" (NCTM, 2006, p. 15).

Understanding mathematical operations and their related computational procedures requires that children grasp the concepts of each of the operations, learn the basic facts, and develop computational procedures. This chapter discusses understanding the concepts of addition,

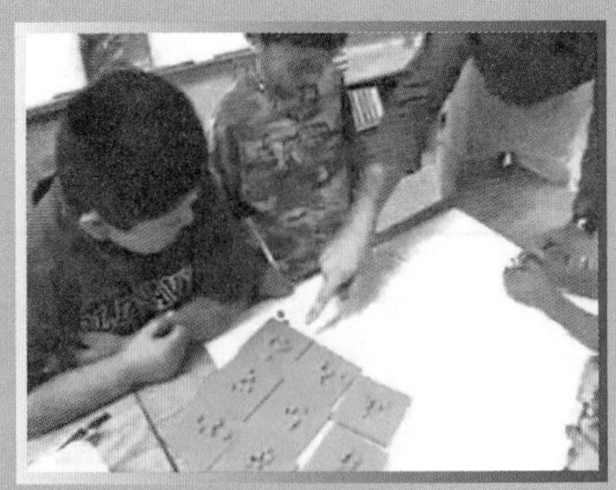

Developing Your Math Teaching Skills

When you have finished studying this chapter, you should be able to do the following:

- Write a word problem for each type of addition, subtraction, multiplication, and division problem.
- Explain how each of these word problems can be modeled with objects. Create a model that illustrates each type.
- Explain the difference between partitive and measurement division. How might a child use counters to show $6 \div 2$ for each interpretation of division?

subtraction, multiplication, and division. (Learning facts and developing computational procedures are examined in subsequent chapters.)

Carefully examine the story problems written by the children in Ms. Pearson's class and consider these children's understanding of operations. How are the problems different? How are they the same? How can teachers help children make sense of operations? One important role elementary teachers play is to help children understand the meaning of the four operations of addition, subtraction, multiplication, and division of whole numbers.

ASSESSING MATHEMATICS UNDERSTANDING

In order to become familiar with the mathematics concepts and procedures discussed in this chapter, take a few minutes and complete the following *Chapter 7 Pre-Assessment.* Answer each question on your own and think about how you got the answer. Then think about how elementary-school children might use counters or draw pictures to solve these problems, and any possible misunderstandings some children might have about each problem. If you are able, administer this assessment to a child and analyze his or her understanding of these topics.

1. Eric has 5 apples. His mom gives him 7 more apples. How many does he have altogether?
2. Jake has six marbles. How many more marbles does he need to buy to have 13 altogether?
3. Nicole has 14 colored marbles. Eight are blue, and the rest are red. How many red marbles does Nicole have?
4. Sharon has 9 marbles, and Tom has 4 marbles. How many more marbles does Sharon have than Tom does?
5. Maria has 14 toy cars. She gives 5 toy cars to Jennifer. How many toy cars does Maria have left?
6. Andre has 3 packages of gum. There are 5 sticks of gum in each package. How many pieces of gum does Andre have altogether?
7. At a party there were 18 M&Ms left to be shared fairly among 3 children. How many M&Ms would each child get?
8. Tom's mother had 20 cookies. She packed 4 cookies in each bag. How many bags of cookies could she pack?

Examining Classroom Practice

One of the daily activities for teacher Flo Pearson's first- and second-graders is to gather at the classroom calendar and write "Amazing Equations" [Annenberg Video Series]. These are story problems that have answers equal to the day's date. On the morning of April 20, for example, children write problems that have an answer of 20.

> PEARSON **myeducationlab** The Power of Classroom Practice — Go to the Video Examples section of Topic 6: "Whole Number Operations" in the MyEducationLab for your course, select Video Examples and then the video "Amazing Equations."

At the beginning of the lesson, Ms. Pearson has the children sit together on the rug in front of an easel. She asks children to think of and share Amazing Equations that equal 20. As the children state their problems, Ms. Pearson records the problems, modeling the appropriate use of mathematical symbols on a large sheet of blank paper clipped to the easel.

Ms. Pearson wraps up the whole-group part of the lesson by reviewing how to write the equations with symbols and then asking, "Is there more than one way to get to twenty? (*Children:* "Yes!") All right, let's see how many more ways we can find today."

Working in groups of three, children write story problems with 20 as the answer. Some children use manipulatives to model the story as they write it. Ms. Pearson circulates around the room, asking questions and providing assistance as needed. She encourages students to develop an oral story first and then write down what happened in that story.

At the end of the class time, Ms. Pearson reconvenes the class as a whole group on the rug to share their Amazing Equations. She asks one child from each group to read its story and another to read the corresponding equation.

Erin and Vi's Amazing Equation:

Erin: "Ten candles on a cake for my little brother's birthday plus ten more candles equals twenty."

Vi: "Ten plus ten more equals twenty."

Colanthia and Cam's Amazing Equation:

Colanthia: "I am on the tot lot playing with my friends, and we had fun. We is swinging and sliding."

Cam: "Nineteen plus one more is twenty."

Matt, Pat, and Rommel's Amazing Equation:

Matt: "Me and Pat and Rommel and Ms. Pearson we each found five bikes and when we—I didn't get to finish the rest."

Ms. Pearson: "So we each had five bikes and how many did we end up with? (Twenty). Did you write the equation?"

Matt: "Five plus five plus five plus five equals twenty."

Nate and Shea's Amazing Equation:

Nate: "We had nineteen books and Chris gave us one at the library and then we had twenty books."

Shea: "Nineteen plus one equals twenty."

Analyzing Assessment Results

Analyze each problem. How did you (and the student you administered the assessment to) solve each of the problems? Let's look at problems 1–5 first.

1. Eric has 5 apples. His mom gives him 7 more apples. How many does he have altogether?
2. Jake has six marbles. How many more marbles does he need to buy to have 13 altogether?
3. Nicole has 14 colored marbles. Eight are blue, and the rest are red. How many red marbles does Nicole have?
4. Sharon has 9 marbles, and Tom has 4 marbles. How many more marbles does Sharon have than Tom does?
5. Maria has 14 toy cars. She gives 5 toy cars to Jennifer. How many toy cars does Maria have left?

Comments: How are these problems alike, and how are they different? Which were more difficult, or were they equally difficult? Did you use counters or draw a picture, or solve it in another way? Problems 1 and 5 are usually the easiest of these five problems; they are the most common forms of addition and subtraction problems. What kinds of problems are problems 2, 3, and 4? We will talk about those problems later in this chapter.

6. Andre has 3 packages of gum. There are 5 sticks of gum in each package. How many pieces of gum does Andre have altogether?

Comments: This is a typical multiplication problem. If you asked students to solve this, did they use counters, or skip counting (for example, 5, 10, 15)? This problem is one of the easiest multiplication problems to solve by skip counting, since counting by fives is one of the first types of skip counting children learn.

7. At a party there were 18 M&Ms left to be shared fairly among 3 children. How many M&Ms would each child get?
8. Tom's mother had 20 cookies. She packed 4 cookies in each bag. How many bags of cookies could she pack?

Comments: Look at problems 7 and 8 together. These are both division problems, but how are they different? In problem 7, M&Ms are being shared among several students, so we know how many groups are being made. But in problem 8, we know how many are in each group, but do not know how many groups we are making.

Take a minute and reflect on this assessment. Were some problems easier than others? What factors made them easier? What do you want to learn more about in order to help children understand these operations?

Common Student Misunderstandings about Operations on Whole Numbers:

- Inability to distinguish between different operations.
- Lack of familiarity with different problem situations.

Are there any other difficulties that children may have about whole number operations? It is important to assess what children understand, and what they are still working on understanding, in order to plan instruction that meets their needs.

Building on Assessment Results

Think about what can be done to help strengthen children's understandings and minimize (and hopefully eradicate) their misunderstandings and misconceptions.

Sometimes teaching about operations focuses on memorizing facts and producing answers quickly. While we want students to accomplish those things, they also need to understand the meaning of operations, which will enable them to make sense of problem situations.

A key element of all instruction is to make sure that students understand the concept. Students need to visualize concepts and relationships. This usually is best done with some sort of manipulative material, asking students to solve problems set in familiar, meaningful situations and to examine the reasonableness of their solutions. The table below lists common misunderstandings and what you can do to help children with these misunderstandings.

IF students think that. . .	THEN have students . . .
solving problems means just pulling out the numbers and doing something to them	*model* the problem with a manipulative material.
solving problems means looking for *key words,* such as "of" meaning "times"	*ask* them to solve problems that include key words but aren't solved in the way that using traditional key words would imply.

Introduce Operations with Word Problems

Learning about operations should be based on developing meaning and understanding, which begins with an exploration of real-world settings or story problems. As you read at the beginning of the chapter, even young children are able to write many story problems based on real-life experiences. Children begin to construct meaning for mathematical operations before they enter school through informal, real-life experiences such as sharing cookies or combining collections of cards or action figures. Because these experiences can be translated into word problems and because word problems in familiar contexts are more meaningful to children than symbolic expressions, early instruction on operations should introduce children to addition, subtraction, multiplication, and division by having children solve word problems.

NCTM Principles and Standards Link 7-1

Content Strand: Number and Operations

During the primary grades, students should encounter a variety of meanings for addition and subtraction of whole numbers. . . . Multiplication and division can begin to have meaning for students in prekindergarten through grade 2 as they solve problems that arise in their environment, such as how to share a bag of raisins fairly among four people. In grades 3–5, helping students develop meaning for whole-number multiplication and division should become a central focus. (NCTM, 2000, p. 34)

A Model for Beginning with Word Problems

Young children develop an understanding of operations by solving a variety of word problems. If those problems come from familiar real-world experiences, children can see more personal relevance, which enables them to more easily analyze the problem and its component parts. Real-world problems can come from everyday classroom opportunities, such as routine opening activities like Ms. Pearson's daily calendar exercise, classroom events, or even examples from children's literature. In addition, children can help make decisions about sharing and distributing classroom supplies, especially when many-to-one groupings need to be made—which are meaningful contexts for multiplication and division (Kouba & Franklin, 1993). For example, if 10 children get 5 minutes each to use the computer, how much time will be needed? Teachers can take advantage of these familiar experiences to pose problems and discuss operations. Such rich, familiar contexts in which mathematical operations are introduced naturally not only help children recognize personal relevance and math connections but also help them judge the reasonableness of their answers.

After introducing a real-world problem, a good teacher encourages children to represent or translate it into some model (see Figure 7-1). Initially, this model should be a

FIGURE 7-1 A Model for Introducing Operations with Word Problems

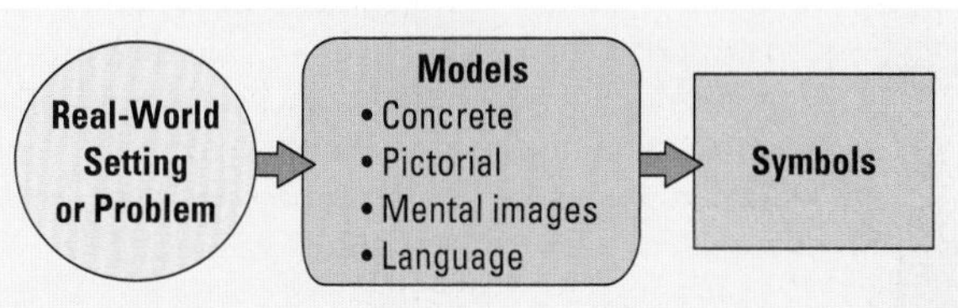

concrete representation of the setting, for example, using actual objects mentioned in the problem, such as cookies, or blocks or counters to represent the objects in the problem. Later the teacher can introduce pictorial representations. Mental images and children's natural language skills also play key roles in developing conceptual understanding.

As a teacher, you can make different materials available to children to use in modeling problems. You can also encourage children to be creative in their representations of problem situations, whether concretely or pictorially, and provide ample opportunities for children to discuss and interpret situations presented concretely and pictorially. For example, a daily classroom routine could include children's sharing how they modeled a problem. Once children are able to interpret different types of problems and identify and model the operation needed to solve each one, they can write number sentences to represent solution processes. It is important to remember, however, that children must have an extensive number of experiences with meaningful problem solving before they are introduced to symbolic expressions, and symbolic expressions are best introduced as a way to record concrete representations.

Meanings develop over time and, while they are being developed, children should not be pressured to memorize basic facts. In fact, understanding the meaning of the operations is a critical component of mastering the basic facts. Likewise, working with word problems should be the basis of children's early experiences with operations and must not be delayed until children "know their facts." The most important consideration is for children to connect their real-life experiences and language with the mathematical language and symbolism associated with each operation (Trafton & Zawojewski, 1990).

It also is important to mention that the "key word" strategy of replacing certain words with others, such as "*is* means *equal*" and "*of* means *times*," is not helpful to children. In fact, teaching children to look for "key words" to solve word problems is ineffective and detrimental (Sowder, 1988). Instructional time is better used helping children develop an understanding of the meaning of operations through solving real-world story problems with concrete objects.

NCTM Principles and Standards Link 7-2

Content Strand: Number and Operations

As students in the early grades work with complex tasks in a variety of contexts, they also build an understanding of operations on numbers. Appropriate contexts can arise through student-initiated activities, [through] teacher-created stories, and in many other ways. . . . In developing the meaning of operations, teachers should ensure that students repeatedly encounter situations in which the same numbers appear in different contexts. (NCTM, 2000, p. 83)

Encoding and Decoding Word Problems

Once children understand the meaning of a variety of problem situations, provide them with opportunities to both *encode* and *decode* their number sentences. In other words, not only should children translate a real-life setting into a model or mathematics sentence (encoding), but they should also, given a model or mathematics sentence, be able to write a word problem that illustrates that situation. Encourage children to describe and justify their translation. For example, you might give children the following problem to solve:

> *Tom had 7 cookies and gave 3 to Matt. How many cookies does Tom have left?*

You might ask the children to solve the problem using counters or by drawing a picture and to write a number sentence that matches the problem situation. On another occasion, you might give children a number sentence and ask them to write a word problem that illustrates that number sentence. As a follow-up to the "Amazing Equations" lesson you read about at the beginning of the chapter, Ms. Pearson may choose to give children story problems and ask them to model them with manipulatives, or to give children number sentences and ask them to write corresponding story problems.

Different parts of this generalized conceptual model, depicted in Figure 7-1, are emphasized at different stages in the three-part process just described. When developing the concept or meaning of operations, it is most effective for children to focus on the real-world setting, the model for the setting, and the translation of one to the other. Mathematical symbols are not ignored but are used only as a tool.

In summary, research suggests that exposure to a wide range of word problems from the beginning of the school experience significantly improves children's mathematics performance (Stigler, Fuson, Ham, & Kim, 1986). Engaging children in solving word problems before they learn the basic facts enables them to focus on the nature of the problem and to model it to find an unknown answer (Burns, 1991).

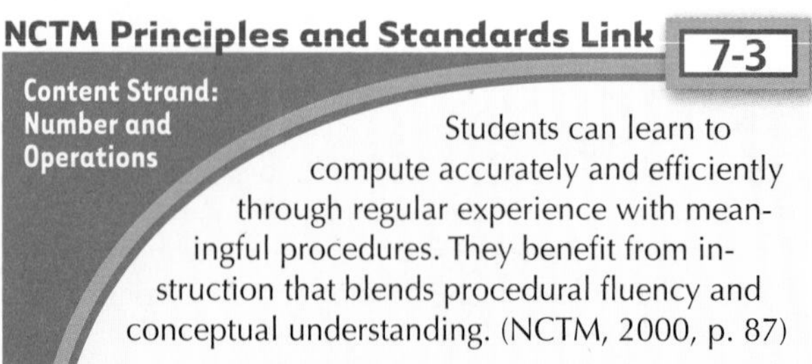

NCTM Principles and Standards Link 7-3

Content Strand: Number and Operations

Students can learn to compute accurately and efficiently through regular experience with meaningful procedures. They benefit from instruction that blends procedural fluency and conceptual understanding. (NCTM, 2000, p. 87)

NCTM NUMBER AND OPERATIONS STANDARDS AND EXPECTATIONS ADDRESSED IN THIS CHAPTER

Instructional programs from Pre-K–12 should enable all students to—	In Prekindergarten through grade 2 all students should— (NCTM, 2000, p. 78)	In grades 3–5 all students should— (NCTM, 2000, p. 148)
• understand meanings of operations and how they relate to one another.	• understand various meanings of addition and subtraction of whole numbers and the relationship between the two operations. • understand the effects of adding and subtracting whole numbers. • understand situations that entail multiplication and division, such as equal groupings of objects and sharing equally.	• understand various meanings of multiplication and division. • understand the effects of multiplying and dividing whole numbers. • identify and use relationships between operations, such as division as the inverse of multiplication, to solve problems.

Understanding Addition and Subtraction

Researchers have identified four types of addition and subtraction problems: Join, Separate, Part-Part-Whole, and Compare (Carpenter & Moser, 1982). Join and Separate problems involve action. Part-Part-Whole and Compare problems do not involve action but are identified by the relationships of the quantities in the problems. Research shows that this classification system matches the way children think about these problems (Fennema, Carpenter, Levi, Franke, & Empson, 1997).

Types of Addition and Subtraction Word Problems

The four addition and subtraction problem types—Join, Separate, Part-Part-Whole, and Compare—are distinguished by the presence or absence of action and the types of relationships involved. The basic structure of each of these problem types is illustrated in Figure 7-2.

Let's take a look at examples of each problem type. In each of the addition and subtraction problem types, two quantities are given, and one is unknown. The examples in Figure 7-2 use the fact family 4, 7, and 11 to illustrate each problem type.

Join problems. In a *Join problem,* elements are being added or joined to a set. The three quantities involved are the starting amount, the change amount, and the resulting amount.

Separate problems. In a *Separate problem,* elements are being removed from a set. As in Join problems, the three quantities involved are the starting amount, the change amount, and the resulting amount. In Figure 7-3 (see p. 133) Amy, a second grader, wrote and illustrated a Separate problem and wrote a corresponding number sentence. Notice that she showed that one fish swam away by crossing it out in the picture.

Part-Part-Whole problems. In *Part-Part-Whole problems* there is no action. Instead, these problems focus on the relationship between a set and its two subsets. The three quantities involved are the two parts and the whole. Unlike Join and Separate problems, there is no change over time. Figure 7-4 shows a sample of a Part-Part-Whole problem (see p. 133). Notice that Amy's use of two different colors of snails clearly shows the two parts of the problem.

Compare problems. There is no action in *Compare problems*. Instead, they involve comparisons between two different sets. The three quantities involved are the two wholes and the difference.

These 4 types of addition and subtraction word problem result in 11 different kinds of addition and subtraction problems. Figure 7-2 provides a comprehensive look at these types of problems so you can better examine their similarities and differences.

Examining Children's Reasoning: Linking to "Amazing Equations"

Relate these problem types to the story problems the children wrote for their "Amazing Equations," discussed at the beginning of this chapter. Use the terminology described in the previous section and in the samples given in Figure 7-5 to identify the problem type for each problem.

What do you notice about the problems the children wrote? Most of these problems are Join-Result-Unknown, with one Part-Part-Whole, Whole Unknown. No one wrote a Separate problem or a Compare problem. What might account for this? It may be that children are more familiar with Join situations as compared to other problem types.

How might Ms. Pearson use this information? In future lessons, she might decide to expose the children to Separate, Part-Part-Whole, and Compare problems in order

(continued on page 134)

FIGURE 7-2 Structure of the Four Types of Addition and Subtraction Problems

PROBLEMS WITH ACTION

Problem Type	Example Problem	Model of Problem Type	Number Sentence
Join	***Result Unknown:*** Peter had 4 cookies. Amy gave him 7 more cookies. How many cookies does Peter have now?	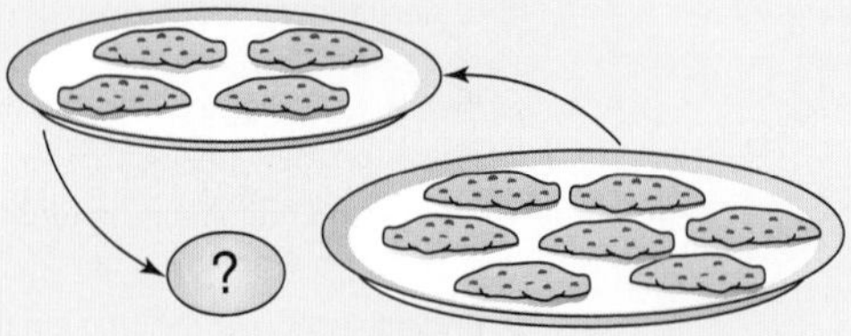 ?	4 + 7 = ___
	Change Unknown: Peter had 4 cookies. Amy gave him some more cookies. Now Peter has 11 cookies. How many cookies did Amy give Peter?	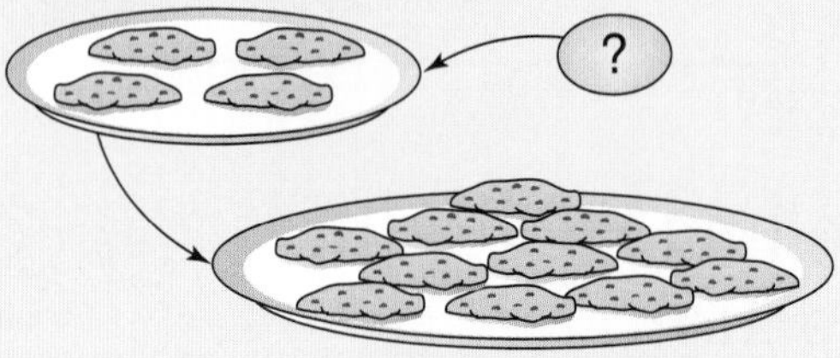 ?	4 + ___ = 11
	Start Unknown: Peter had some cookies. Amy gave him 7 more cookies. Now Peter has 11 cookies. How many cookies did Peter have to start with?	 ?	___ + 7 = 11
Separate	***Result Unknown:*** Peter had 11 cookies. He gave 7 cookies to Amy. How many cookies does Peter have now?	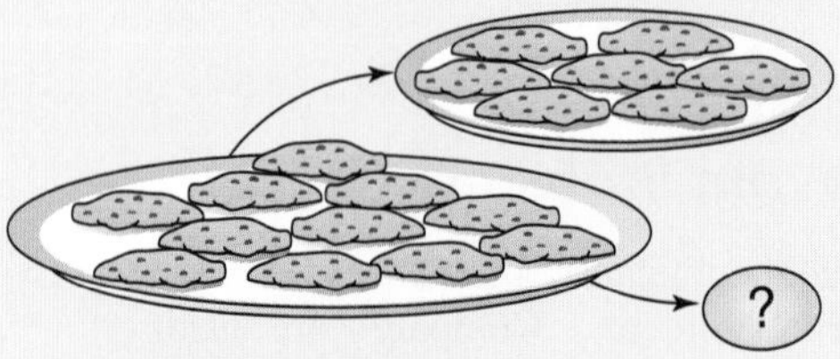 ?	11 − 7 = ___
	Change Unknown: Peter had 11 cookies. He gave some cookies to Amy. Now Peter has 4 cookies. How many cookies did Peter give to Amy?	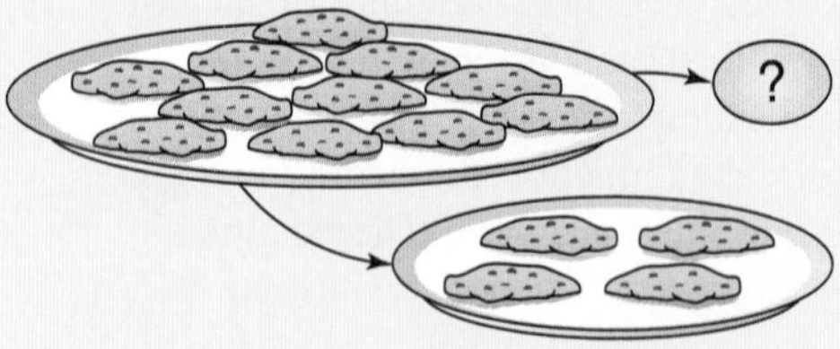 ?	11 − ___ = 4
	Start Unknown: Peter had some cookies. He gave 7 cookies to Amy. Now Peter has 4 cookies. How many cookies did Peter have to start with?	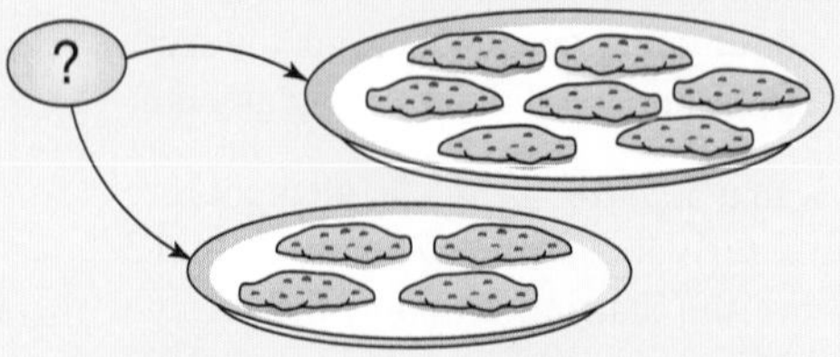 ?	___ − 7 = 4

(*continued*)

FIGURE 7-2 Continued

PROBLEMS WITH NO ACTION

Problem Type	Example Problem	Model of Problem Type	Number Sentence
Part-Part-Whole	***Whole Unknown:*** Peter has some cookies. Four are chocolate cookies and 7 are oatmeal raisin cookies. How many cookies does Peter have?	?	4 + 7 = ___
	Part Unknown: Peter has 11 cookies. Four are chocolate cookies and the rest are oatmeal raisin cookies. How many oatmeal raisin cookies does Peter have?	? 11	4 + ___ = 11
Compare	***Difference Unknown:*** Peter has 11 cookies and Amy has 7 cookies. How many more cookies does Peter have than Amy?	?	7 + ___ = 11
	Larger Unknown: Amy has 7 cookies. Peter has 4 more cookies than Amy. How many cookies does Peter have?	?	7 + 4 = ___
	Smaller Unknown: Peter has 11 cookies. Peter has 4 more cookies than Amy. How many cookies does Amy have?	?	4 + ___ = 11

FIGURE 7-3 A Separate Problem Written by a Second Grader

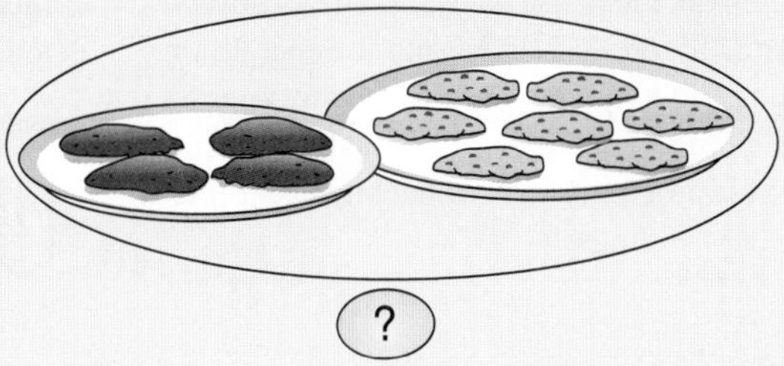

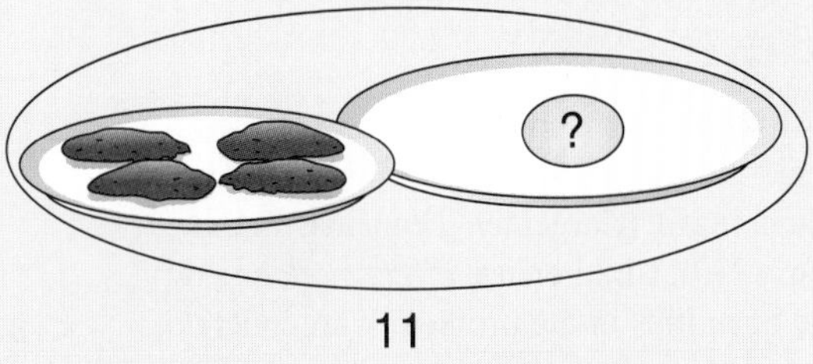

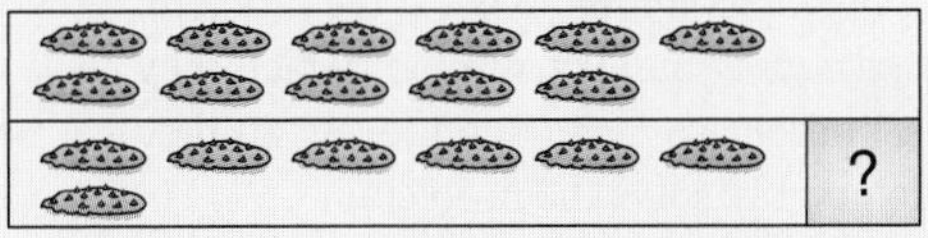

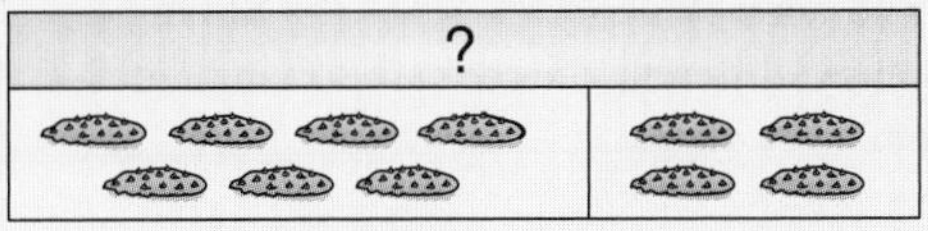

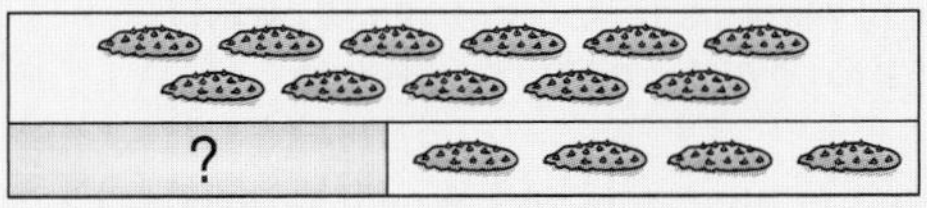

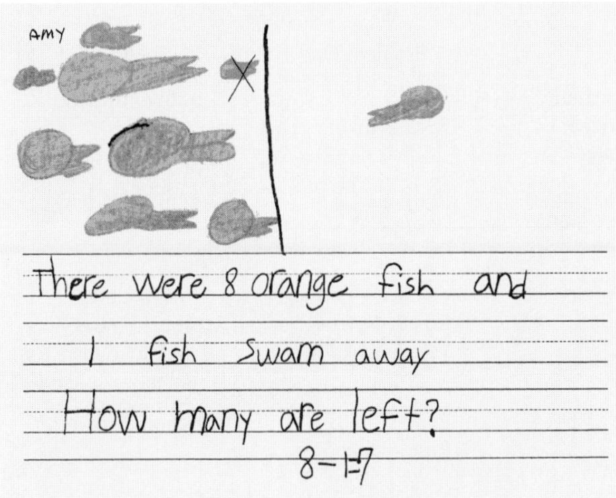
AMY
There were 8 orange fish and
1 fish Swam away
How many are left?
8-1=7

FIGURE 7-4 A Part-Part-Whole Problem Written by a Second Grader

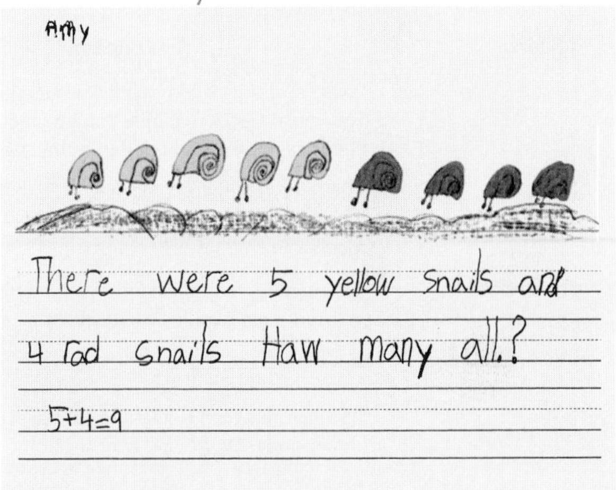
Amy
There were 5 yellow Snails and
4 red Snails Haw many all?
5+4=9

to expand their experiences with these problem types. Ms. Pearson might decide to share a problem of her own during an "Amazing Equations" lesson, perhaps writing a Separate, Part-Part-Whole, or Compare problem and asking the children to write a number sentence for it. For example, she might decide to use Nate and Shea's library book context from Figure 7-5 and write a Separate or Compare problem. Providing children with new types of problems set in familiar contexts and situations helps them make sense of problems and connect new learning with existing understandings.

Examining Children's Reasoning: Strategies for Solving Story Problems

Children solve story problems in several different ways, including strategies that utilize direct modeling, counting, derived facts, and recall (Carpenter, Fennema, Franke, Levi, & Empson, 1999). Children use *direct modeling* by representing the quantities in the problem with concrete objects. Children use *counting strategies* such as counting on, counting back, or skip counting to solve the problem. Children use *derived facts* to build on or modify facts they have memorized. Children use *recall* to retrieve facts they have memorized to quickly solve the problem.

To see how children use these strategies, go to MyEducationLab to view video clip "IMAP—Strategies." In this clip, three different children are solving the same basic problem.

Nicole (or some other child) had 6 stones (or some other object). How many more stones (or other object) does she/he need to collect to have 13 altogether?

What problem type is this problem? Which problem-solving strategy is each child using? Figure 7-6 summarizes the strategy each child used.

Note that a child who uses the recall strategy has memorized the needed fact and needs only to retrieve it from memory. This is the most sophisticated strategy—and a long-term goal of instruction—but one that is developed over time. (Chapter 8 focuses on helping children memorize the basic facts *after* they have developed an understanding of the meaning of the operations.)

myeducationlab The Power of Classroom Practice Go to the Assignments and Activities section of Topic 6: "Whole Number Operations" in the MyEducationLab for your course and complete the activity "IMAP—Story-Solving Strategies." Also look at the activity "IMAP—Identifying Solution Strategies" to see how a second-grade boy solves different problems.

Using Models to Solve Addition and Subtraction Problems

Direct modeling. Addition and subtraction problems can be modeled with many different types of materials, including real-world objects (such as pencils) and manipulative materials (such as poker chips). The term *direct modeling* refers to the process in which children use concrete materials to exactly represent the problem as it is written. For example, consider the following Join problem:

Joyce had 3 pencils. Scott gave her 5 more pencils. How many pencils does Joyce have now?

This problem can be solved by having two children (representing Joyce and Scott) directly model or act out the problem. Have one child display three pencils and another child give her five more pencils. The children can

FIGURE 7-5 Sample Problems Written by Children in "Amazing Equations" Lesson

Children	Amazing Equation	Problem Type	Notes
Matt	I wa s at a store and bought seventeen pieces of candy. Two more pieces of candy that my uncle gave to me. I need one more and I got it from my big sister Katy."	Join Result Unknown	Action involved
Darnell	"There were nineteen roaches in Dee's house then one more came from Jennifer's house. Then there was twenty roaches in Dee's house."	Join Result Unknown	Action involved
Erin and Vi	"Ten candles on a cake for my little brother's birthday plus ten more candles equals twenty."	Unclear—perhaps Part-Part-Whole, Whole Unknown	Unclear, but the problem does not seem to involve action
Nate and Shea	"We had nineteen books and Chris gave us one at the library and then we had twenty books."	Join Result Unknown	Action involved

FIGURE 7-6 Strategies Used by Different Students to Solve the Same Problem

Child	Problem	How Solved	Solution Strategy	Notes
Nicole	Nicole had 6 stones. How many more stones does she need to collect to have 13 altogether? 6 + ___ = 13	Counts out 6 cubes. Counts more cubes till she has 13 cubes altogether. Separates out original 6 cubes and counts remaining cubes.	Direct Modeling	She *models* all the quantities in the problem with cubes.
Michaela	Your sister has 6 marbles. How many more marbles does she need to have 13 marbles altogether? 6 + ___ = 13	Counted on from 6, saying "seven, eight, nine, ten, eleven, twelve, thirteen." She uses her fingers to keep track of how many times she's counted.	Counting	She does not need to count 6, but instead starts at 6 and *counts on* to 13.
Miguel	Ramona has 6 goldfish. But she wants 13. How many more does she need to buy? 6 + ___ = 13	"Six plus six is twelve, and one plus is seven is thirteen." Since 6 plus 6 is 12, and 13 is one more than 12, the answer must be one more than 6, or 7.	Derived Facts	He uses a fact he has memorized, 6 + 6, to find the result to a problem he has not memorized.

NCTM Principles and Standards Link 7-4

Content Strand: Number and Operations

As students explain their written work, solutions, and mental processes, teachers gain insight into their students' thinking. (NCTM, 2000, p. 83)

then count the number of pencils in the joined sets of pencils now held by Joyce.

It usually is easier for children to solve a problem by modeling it with the actual objects referred to in the problem, as done in the previous example. Ask the children to solve the problem and discuss its solution. Then, after solving a number of problems using the actual objects in the problem for direct modeling, begin to use counters. You should be aware, however, that using a manipulative material such as poker chips to model a problem about pencils is somewhat more abstract and will be a bit more difficult for young children to successfully solve.

NCTM Principles and Standards Link 7-5

Content Strand: Number and Operations

An understanding of addition and subtraction can be generated when young students solve "joining" and take-away problems by directly modeling the situation or by using counting strategies, such as counting on or counting back (Carpenter & Moser, 1984). Students develop further understandings of addition when they solve missing-addend problems that arise from stories or real situations. Further understandings of subtraction are conveyed by situations in which two collections need to be made equal or one collection needs to be made a desired size. (NCTM, 2000, p. 83)

Problems involving action, such as Join and Separate, are easiest for children to solve by direct modeling. Part-Part-Whole and Compare problems are more difficult to model. Delay introducing these types of problems until children can successfully use direct modeling to solve Join and Separate problems.

Note that diagrams such as that shown in Figure 7-7 are sometimes confusing. For example, when asked how many trucks are in set C, a young child may respond that there are none. Some young children do not understand class inclusion, that is, that set A and set B are both part of set C. These children may say that all the trucks are in sets A and B, so there are none in set C. This is one reason why concrete objects should be used first in developing problem-solving skills. When children physically join two sets, the initial sets are no longer apparent but the children can remember that they started with two sets, and the difficulty sometimes associated with a diagram like the one that appears in Figure 7-7 does not occur.

Modeling separate problems. Separate problems are fairly easy for children to model. To do so, remove an amount from the starting amount and observe the difference. Consider the following problem:

> *Megan had 6 cookies* (the starting amount). *She gave 2 to her brother. How many cookies does Megan have left?*

FIGURE 7-7 Diagram Showing One Set with Two Subsets

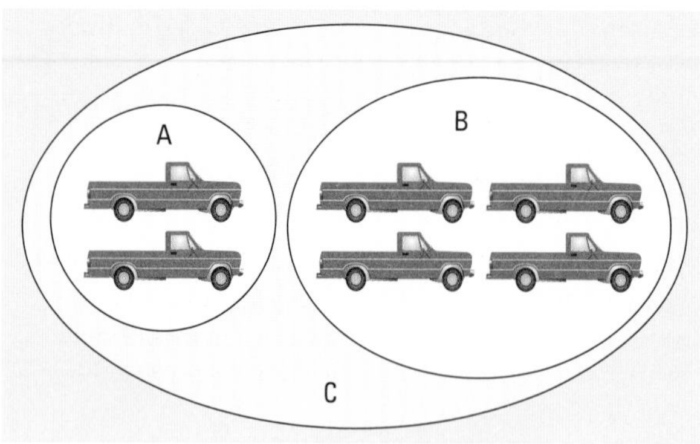

Using counters, children could set out six, physically remove two, then count the four remaining counters. Using a pictorial model, children might place an X through the two cookies given away.

It is usually more difficult for children to use pictorial models for subtraction, and these models can be confusing at times. A typical textbook picture to illustrate 3 − 1 would show three objects, with one of the objects crossed out. Some children write 2 − 1 because they see groups of two and one in the picture.

A better approach would be to show or have children draw a "before" and "after" picture as in Figure 7-8. The pictures show that there were three flowers at the beginning, that one flower was "taken away" (as shown in the "after" picture with one flower crossed out), and there are two flowers left, which is the difference.

Another way to show an amount being taken away is to circle that set and use an arrow to show it being removed. Children can easily learn to identify the starting amount, the amount being taken away, and the difference in such diagrams.

Modeling Part-Part-Whole and Compare problems. Modeling Part-Part-Whole and Compare problems involves matching two sets by using one-to-one correspondence and then observing the number of objects in one set that are unmatched. The real-life setting for this approach to subtraction usually focuses on "how many more" or "how many fewer" there are in one group than another. Figure 7-9 uses a pictorial model to represent the following problem:

FIGURE 7-8 Diagram Showing "Before" and "After"

FIGURE 7-9 Pictorial Model for Candy Problem

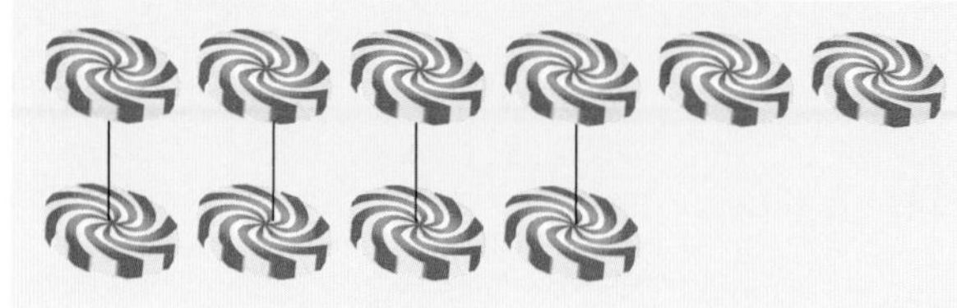

> *Manuel had 6 candies and Keisha had 4 candies. How many more candies did Manuel have than Keisha?*

Children could solve this problem by creating one group of six candies or counters to represent Manuel's candies and another group of four candies or counters to represent Keisha's candies. To find how many more candies Manuel had, children can arrange the candies to show a one-to-one correspondence between Manuel's and Keisha's candies, placing one candy from Manuel's set beside or on top of another from the other set and observing the number of candies that do not have a match, showing how many more candies Manuel had than Keisha.

Using measurement models to model problems. Another way to model addition and subtraction problems is by using measurement models. In this approach, lengths, rather than discrete, countable objects, are used to represent the quantities in the problem. Towers of Unifix cubes, trains of Cuisenaire rods, and a number line are appropriate and effective ways to represent different quantities.

Unifix cubes can be broken apart and used as individual cubes, but, because they interlock, they also can be used as "towers" or "trains" to indicate length. To represent addition, two towers can be constructed separately and then joined. Figure 7-10 illustrates using towers of Unifix cubes to solve 3 + 6 = 9.

FIGURE 7-10 Unifix Cubes Showing 3 + 6 = 9

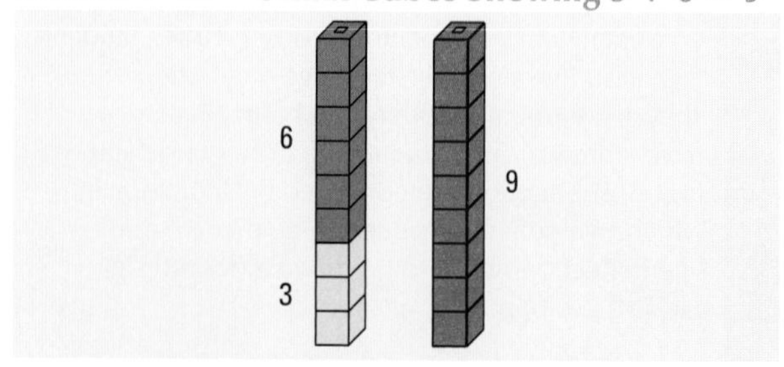

FIGURE 7-11 Number Line Model for $2 + 7 = 9$

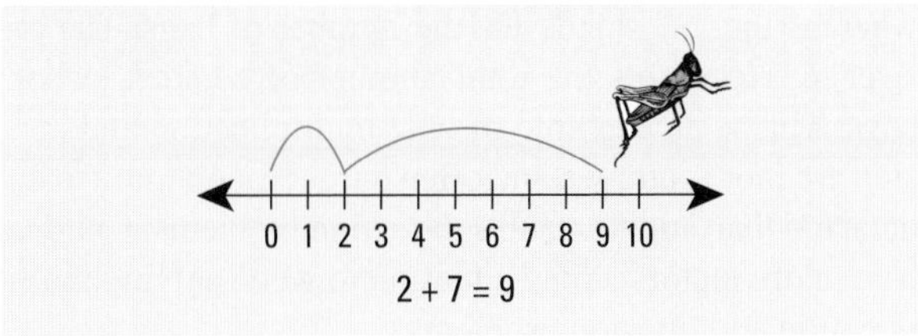

Cuisenaire rods are color-coded wooden rods. The unit rod is white, and each of rods 2 through 10 is a different color. The red rod (2) and the light green rod (3) are joined in the illustration below to solve the problem $2 + 3 = 5$. The combined length is five unit rods, which is equivalent to the yellow rod. A measurement model such as this one is useful for representing a real-world problem.

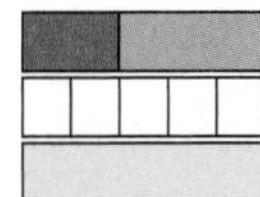

Addition and subtraction also can be represented on a number line, which is a semiconcrete model. Children can use toy grasshoppers or kangaroos to hop along the number line, making it more concrete. The addition sentence $2 + 7 = 9$ may be modeled by starting at 0, then a hop of 2 units followed by a hop of 7 units along the number line, as shown in Figure 7-11.

Similarly, Separate problems also can be solved using the number line model. For example, to solve the problem $6 - 2 =$ __, a child could begin at 6, take a hop backward of 2 units, and observe the resulting position on the line, which will be at the number 4.

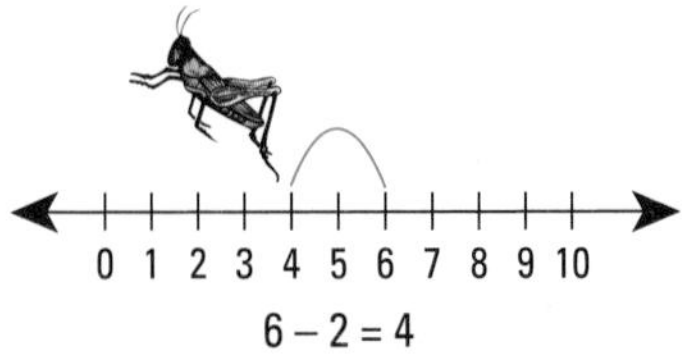

The number line is often a difficult model for children to understand and should not be the first model used to represent an operation. For example, children sometimes want to start at "1" instead of "0" and confuse spaces with points on the line. However, after children have had experiences with other models, introduce the number line, which is handy and concise and a common model for representing integers and the operations with integers—concepts that help develop algebraic thinking. These concepts will be discussed in Chapter 17. Also, you may want to use a more abstract model, such as a number line, to assess children's ability to transfer from a concrete model to a more symbolic representation.

Writing Number Sentences for Addition and Subtraction

After children have had many experiences modeling and talking about real-life problems, encourage them to use mathematical symbols to represent problems. Figure 7-12 illustrates the three-step process of modeling a problem situation with a concrete model, with a semiabstract model, and with symbols. Activity 7-1 presents a way for the process to go in the opposite direction: that is, from pictorial models to real-world problem situations. This activity can be modified to provide children with additional opportunities to write story problems that match situations. The key here is to provide children with meaningful real-world situations in which mathematics problems occur.

Although it is important that children explore addition and subtraction word problems of each type, there is often more than one correct way to write a number sentence for a problem. For example, consider the problem below:

Steve wants to buy a book that costs $11. He has $7. How much more money does he need to buy the book?

One child might represent this problem as $7 +$ __ $= 11$, whereas another child might represent it as $11 - 7 =$ __. Either way is acceptable. What is most important is

FIGURE 7-12 Representing $2 + 4 =$ ____ in Three Ways

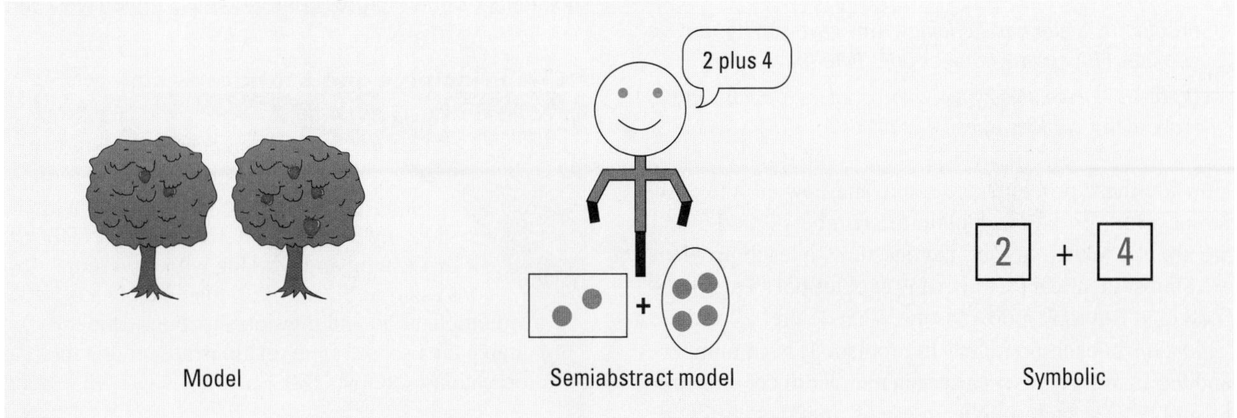

encouraging children to make sense of problem situations and to represent those situations with symbols in meaningful ways.

ACTIVITY 7-1 **Writing a Problem**
Visual Scaffolding

Materials
The diagram below

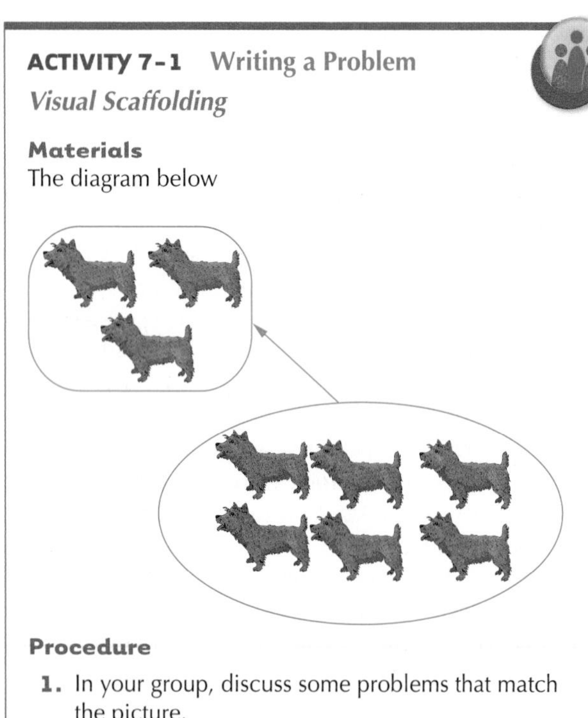

Procedure

1. In your group, discuss some problems that match the picture.
2. Decide on two problems. Write them in your notebook.

Understanding Multiplication and Division

Multiplication and division problems are fundamentally different from addition and subtraction problems because of the different types of quantities represented in multiplication and division problems. For example, consider the differences between these problems:

> *Problem 1: Peter has 2 cookies. Amy gave him 3 more cookies. How many cookies does Peter have now?*
>
> *Problem 2: Peter has 2 bags with 3 cookies in each bag. How many cookies does Peter have?*

How are these problems the same, and how are they different? Both problems contain the numbers 2 and 3 and are about cookies. In fact, the questions in each problem are almost identical ("How many cookies does Peter have [now]?"). But look more closely: What do the "2" and the "3" *mean* in each problem? In problem 1, both numbers and the answer represent a certain number of cookies. But in problem 2, each number means something different: The "3" represents the number of cookies in each bag, whereas the "2" stands for the number of bags. The answer, 6, represents the total number of cookies in both bags. This is an example of why multiplication and division are more complex and often harder for children to understand than addition and subtraction problems: Children have more factors to pay attention to when solving multiplication and division problems.

Another difference between multiplication and division as compared to addition and subtraction is the type of counting children are asked to do. In addition and subtraction, children use counting by ones to find the result. But in multiplication and division, children are counting by groups, sometimes called *skip counting,* to find the result. The transition to counting by groups is significant and often more difficult for children.

Making the Transition from Adding to Multiplying

How can teachers help children understand multiplication and division? The basics are the same as for addition and subtraction: Good instruction helps children connect multiplication and division to representations that make sense to them (Kouba & Franklin, 1993). Just as you have children use their own words to describe relationships and problem situations, you help children link their own less formal language with the more formal mathematical language.

Language is very important in helping children understand multiplication. Many of the difficulties children have with multiplication relate to the clarity and familiarity of the language used. For example, a child might understand "give each child four cookies" but not understand "give four cookies per child." The following are important tips to help children understand the language associated with multiplication.

Encourage children to use the phrase "groups of" to indicate creating a number of equal groups. Children can learn to use language, such as "I have three groups of five—that's fifteen." Note, however, that the meanings of other expressions, such as "three fives" and

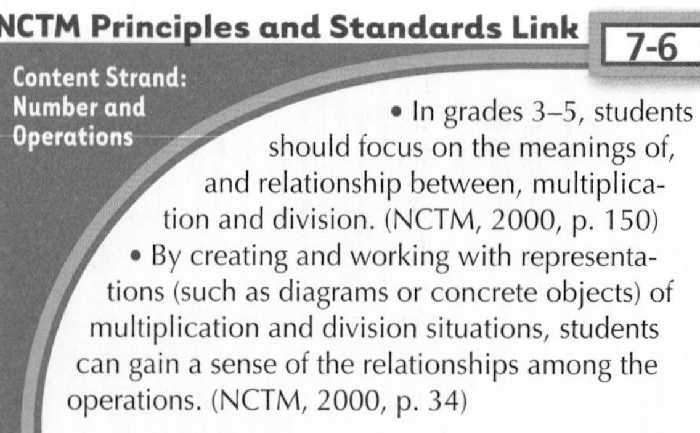

NCTM Principles and Standards Link 7-6

Content Strand: Number and Operations

• In grades 3–5, students should focus on the meanings of, and relationship between, multiplication and division. (NCTM, 2000, p. 150)

• By creating and working with representations (such as diagrams or concrete objects) of multiplication and division situations, students can gain a sense of the relationships among the operations. (NCTM, 2000, p. 34)

"three times five," should be developed before the symbolic expression "3 × 5 = 15" is expected to be used.

Help children understand the meaning of each quantity. Notice that the multiplication problem 2 × 3 = 6 can be interpreted as "2 groups of 3 objects" or 3 + 3 = 6. This is different from 3 × 2 = 6, which means "3 groups of 2 objects" or 2 + 2 + 2 = 6. Even though the total number of objects is the same in both problems, the problems have different meanings. Until children understand the commutative property, saying that "2 × 3 is the *same as* 3 × 2" will confuse many children. For young children, three groups of two objects is fundamentally different from two groups of three objects. Children think in concrete terms: Two children who each get three pieces of candy are luckier than three children who each get two pieces of candy (Anghileri & Johnson, 1992). The fact that the total amount of candy is the same may not be important to the child who is thinking about the lucky children who each got three pieces of candy!

The following sections discuss different types of multiplication and division problems and describe ways to support children in developing understanding of these operations.

Types of Multiplication Word Problems

Researchers have identified several different types of multiplication and division problems (Greer, 1992). These include Equal Groups, Area and Array, Multiplicative Comparison, and Combination problems. Examples of each of the four types of multiplication problems are shown in Figure 7-13.

Equal Groups problems. Equal Groups problems are based on making a certain number of equal-sized groups. The three numbers in the problem represent the number of groups, the size of the groups, and the total number of objects. Equal Groups problems generally are the most familiar type of multiplication problems. In Equal Groups problems, the multiplication sign can be interpreted as "groups of." For example, the problem 2 × 3 means "2 groups of 3" or "2 copies of 3" using the equal groups interpretation of multiplication.

Area and Array problems. Area and Array problems involve finding the area of a rectangular region or finding the total number of objects in a rectangular array (or arrangement). The area of a rectangle can be found by covering the region with unit squares and counting them or by multiplying the length by the width. In contrast, arrays are rectangular arrangements of discrete, countable objects, such as desks arranged in rows in a classroom.

Multiplicative Comparison problems. Multiplicative Comparison problems involve comparing two quantities multiplicatively. In other words, these problems describe *how many times as much* one quantity is compared to another quantity. These situations also can be thought of as *stretching* the original quantity by a certain factor. These problems are more difficult to model with concrete objects.

Combination problems. Combination problems, also known as Cartesian products, involve different combinations that can be made from sets of objects, such as the number of outfits that can be made from two blouses and three pairs of slacks. This type of problem is the most difficult type of multiplication or division problem to model.

NCTM Principles and Standards Link 7-7

Content Strand: Number and Operations

In grades 3–5, students should focus on the meanings of, and relationship between, multiplication and division. It is important that students understand what each number in a multiplication or division expression represents. For example, in multiplication, unlike addition, the factors in the problem can refer to different units. If students are solving the problem 29 × 4 to find out how many legs there are on 29 cats, 29 is the number of cats (or number of groups), 4 is the number of legs on each cat (or number of items in each group), and 116 is the total number of legs on all the cats. Modeling multiplication problems with pictures, diagrams, or concrete materials helps students learn what the factors and their product represent in various contexts. (NCTM, 2000, p. 150).

Introducing Children to Division

As in multiplication, the clarity and familiarity of the language used in division problems is very important. Children experience division situations throughout their everyday lives—but they may not recognize that when they're sharing food with other family members, they're doing division.

One way to help children make everyday connections to division problems is to *use familiar language* when first modeling division situations, and then build on these understandings when introducing more formal language. The terms "shared by" and "equal groups" make sense to children and should be used in early experiences. Similarly, the phrase "divided by" is more formal and it should not be used until children are successful at solving problems using less formal language. Then you can help children understand the connections between this informal and formal terminology.

Division with remainders. If children are solving division problems set in meaningful real-world settings, they will encounter some problems that don't have a whole number as the solution. For example, when sharing 5 cookies among 2 people, each person will get 2 cookies

FIGURE 7-13 Structure of the Four Types of Multiplication and Division Problems

Problem Type	Example Problem	Model of Problem Type	Number Sentence
Equal Groups	**Multiplication:** Maria has 2 bags of oranges. There are 3 oranges in each bag. How many oranges does Maria have altogether?	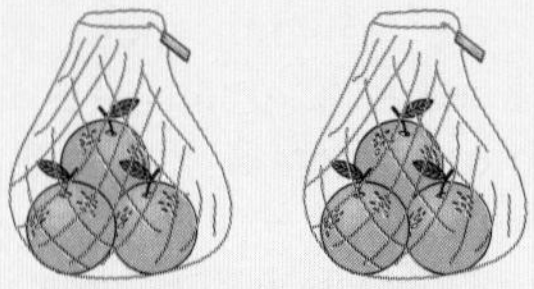	2 × 3 = 6
	Partitive Division: Maria has 6 oranges. She put the oranges into 2 bags with the same number of oranges in each bag. How many oranges are in each bag?	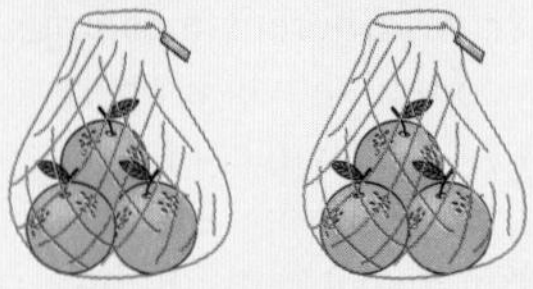	6 ÷ 2 = 3
	Measurement Division: Maria has 6 oranges. She put 2 oranges into each bag. How many bags of oranges did she make?		6 ÷ 2 = 3
Area and Array	**Multiplication:** Maria's parents have some orange trees planted behind their house. There are 2 rows of orange trees with 3 trees in each row. How many orange trees are planted behind Maria's house?		2 × 3 = 6
	Division: Maria's parents are going to plant 6 orange trees behind their house. They want to plant the trees in 2 equal rows. How many orange trees should they plant in each row?		6 ÷ 2 = 3
Multiplicative Comparison	**Multiplication:** Maria has 3 oranges. Tony has 2 times as many oranges as Maria does. How many oranges does Tony have?		2 × 3 = 6
	Division: Tony has 6 oranges, which is 2 times as many oranges as Maria has. How many oranges does Maria have?		6 ÷ 2 = 3
Combination	**Multiplication:** How many different outfits can be made with 2 blouses and 3 pairs of slacks?	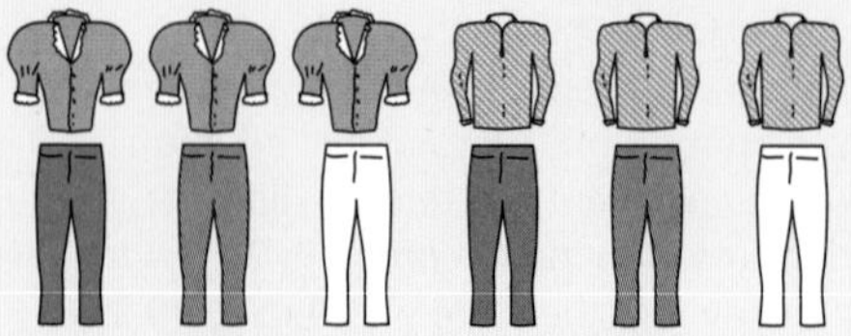	2 × 3 = 6
	Division: How many pairs of slacks are needed to make 6 different outfits by using 2 blouses?	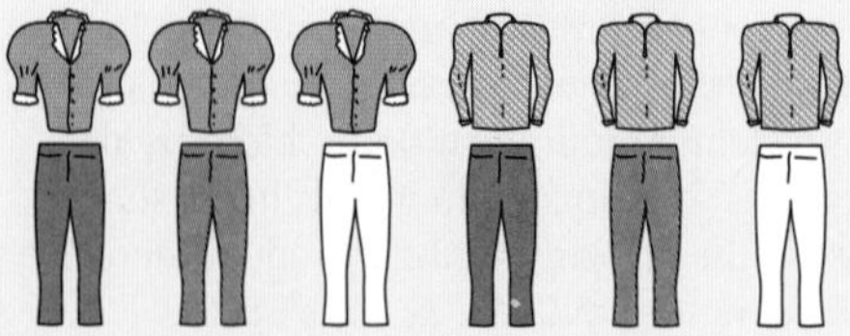	6 ÷ 2 = 3

Literature Link 7-1

Meaning of Multiplication

Friedman, Aileen. (1994). ***The King's Commissioners.*** New York: Scholastic.

Neuschwander, Cindy. (1998). ***Amanda Bean's Amazing Dream.*** New York: Scholastic.

By using different representations of mathematics concepts, we provide children with many opportunities to develop intuitive, computational, and conceptual knowledge. Although children can solve mathematical exercises, they may have difficulty expressing their work using mathematical symbols. Many children's books provide a contextualized problem that children can translate into a symbolic equation.

- ***The King's Commissioners*** shows children several ways of skip counting (by twos, fives, and tens), a foundational skill for learning multiplication, division, and place value. Investigate and make a list of things that are counted by twos, fives, and tens. Practice skip counting by other numbers (such as threes or fours) using a hundreds board. Select a number between 50 and 100 and represent the number in groups of twos, fives, and tens just like the characters in the story do.
- ***Amanda Bean's Amazing Dream*** encourages children's transition from counting to skip counting to multiplication as Amanda learns how important it can be to know her multiplication facts. Model arrays of the groups of objects in the story by using graph paper or concrete objects. Write multiplication sentences that will help Amanda solve the mathematical problems she encounters in the story.
- Use other books that count things in groups, such as ***Reese's Pieces Count by Fives*** (Pallotta, 2000), which uses candy to count by fives to 100, and ***"M&M's"® Brand Chocolate Candies Counting Book*** (McGrath, 1994), which uses candy to count 1 to 12 and explores factors of 12.

Source: Dr. Patricia Moyer-Packenham, Utah State University

and there will be one left over. Take advantage of this opportunity for a rich discussion about what to do with the cookie that's left over. Frequently, even young children will suggest that they split the remaining cookie into smaller parts.

This type of problem is an excellent introduction to other types of division problems (those whose solution is not a whole number) and to a discussion about what to do with "leftovers" when dividing. Such discussions about realistic problems can be extended to include situations in which it may be appropriate to continue to divide what's left into fractional parts, when the leftovers might just be set aside, and when it may be appropriate to make unequal groups. (For example, when 9 children need to ride in 2 cars, it would not be appropriate to cut a child in half or to leave one home, but rather to put 4 children in one car and 5 in the other.) This topic will be discussed in more detail in Chapter 9. Begin introducing division problems to children by helping them understand two basic types—Equal Groups and Area and Array problems. As children mature cognitively, they will need to be exposed to the other two types of division problems—Multiplicative Comparison problems and Combination problems. All four types are described in the following section.

NCTM Principles and Standards Link 7-8

Content Strand: Number and Operations

Students should consider and discuss different types of problems that can be solved using multiplication and division. . . . They should learn the meaning of a remainder by modeling division problems and exploring the size of remainders given a particular divisor. (NCTM, 2000, p. 151)

Types of Division Word Problems

Each of the four types of multiplication problems can be expressed as a division problem. In addition, there are two types of Equal Groups division problems. The following sections discuss each interpretation and describe ways to support children in developing an understanding of these operations. The four types of division problems were shown earlier in Figure 7-13.

Equal Groups problems. Equal Groups problems involve splitting a larger group into several smaller groups. The three numbers in the problem represent the number of groups, the size of the groups, and the total number of objects. There are two different types of Equal Groups division problems: Partitive and Measurement division.

In Partitive division problems, the total number of objects is *partitioned* into a specified number of groups.

In the Partitive division example of Figure 7-13, 6 oranges are split, or partitioned, into 2 *equal groups*. Partitive division is also referred to as *"fair sharing."*

In contrast, in Measurement division problems, the total number of objects is *measured out* into groups of a certain size. In the Measurement division example of Figure 7-13, 6 oranges are split into *groups of 2 oranges*. Measurement division is also referred to as "repeated subtraction."

Here's another way to look at the distinction between these two types of division: When you know the number of groups (or *parts*) to make, the problem is known as a *Partitive* division problem. And when you know the size of the groups *to be measured out,* the problem is known as a *Measurement* division problem. These distinctions should help you remember the names.

Area and Array problems. Area and Array problems for division involve finding one of the dimensions of a rectangular region or of a rectangular array (or arrangement) when the total area or total number of objects in the arrangement is given.

The following interpretations of division appear much less often, but are included here for the sake of completeness. These problems rarely occur in elementary school mathematics curricula.

Multiplicative Comparison problems. Multiplicative Comparison problems for division involve comparing two quantities multiplicatively, i.e., expressing one quantity in terms of *how many times* it is when compared to another, such as "Eric ate twice as many cookies as Patrick did." But in the case of division, the multiplicative relationship, i.e., *how many times as much* one quantity is compared to another quantity, is known, as is one of the quantities being compared. The task is to find the second quantity being compared. For example, consider this problem: "Eric ate twice as many cookies as Patrick did. If Eric ate eighteen cookies, how many cookies did Patrick eat?" These situations also can be thought of as shrinking the original quantity by a certain factor. Figure 7-13 provides an example problem.

Combination problems. Combination problems, also known as Cartesian products, involve different combinations that can be made from sets of objects, such as the number of outfits that can be made from 2 blouses and 3 pairs of slacks. In the case of Combination division problems, the total number of combinations is known, as is the number of one of the elements being combined. The task is to find the number of the second element being combined. Figure 7-13 provides an example problem.

Avoiding misconceptions and dead ends. There are two common misconceptions about multiplication and division: that "multiplication makes bigger" and "division makes smaller." For example, students will sometimes *incorrectly* generalize that when you multiply, the answer is *bigger than* the two factors, whereas when you divide, the answer is *smaller than* the starting amount (the dividend). These generalizations *are correct for whole-number multiplication and division.* However, they *are incorrect when considering multiplication and division of fractions and decimals.* It is important for you to be aware of these misconceptions in order to address them and not to reinforce or accept them when they come up in class discussions.

In addition, there is an instructional "dead end" to avoid: that division means only fair shares (or partitive division). You will make many instructional decisions. These decisions sometimes are even harder to make when faced with the large amount of content to be covered in what never seems to be enough class time. It may be tempting for you to consider omitting some of the interpretations of operations discussed in this chapter. In particular, you may sometimes want to teach only one interpretation of division, partitive division, which often is the meaning of division that is most familiar to children. But if you do not help your students understand both meanings of equal-groups division (partitive and measurement division), you will be leading your students into an instructional dead end. This dead end may not show up until students are introduced to division of fractions, but students who see division only as fair sharing will have more difficulty understanding division of fractions. Consider the following problems:

Problem 1 *Peter has 6 cookies. He wants to give 2 cookies to each of his friends. How many friends will get cookies?* (Measurement division problem—whole-number divisor)

Problem 2 *Peter has 6 cookies. He wants to give $\frac{1}{2}$ of a cookie to each of his friends. How many friends will get cookies?* (Measurement division problem—fraction divisor)

Problem 3 *Peter has 6 cookies. He wants to put the cookies into 2 bags with the same number of cookies in each bag. How many cookies will be in each bag?* (Partitive division problem—whole-number divisor)

Problem 4 *Peter has 6 cookies. These cookies fill $\frac{1}{2}$ of a bag. How many cookies does he need to fill a whole bag?* (Partitive division problem—fraction divisor)

Problems 1 and 2 are both measurement division—and both are reasonable problems, as is problem 3, which is partitive division. But what about problem 4? It presents a situation that is harder to visualize.

Problem 4 illustrates the dead end—partitive division situations with fraction divisors are harder to understand; measurement division situations with fractions make more sense to most children. But what if you have decided not to cover the measurement division interpretation? Your students will be at a disadvantage when learning division of fractions. Division of fractions will be discussed in more detail in Chapter 11; it is mentioned here only to encourage you to make sure that students understand both partitive and measurement division in order to avoid a dead end in future learning.

Examining Children's Reasoning: Strategies for Solving Story Problems

The strategies for solving addition and subtraction story problems discussed earlier in this chapter also are used to solve multiplication and division problems. To see how one child uses these strategies, go to MyEducationLab to see how Nicole, a second-grade girl, solves the following problem:

At a party there were 18 M&M's to be shared fairly among 3 children. How many M&M's would each child get?

How did Nicole solve the problem? She *directly modeled* the problem with cubes, separating 18 cubes into 3 equal piles (after a slight adjustment to correct the number of M&Ms that were shared).

> **myeducationlab** The Power of Classroom Practice — Go to the Assignments and Activities section of Topic 6: "Whole Number Operations" in the MyEducationLab for your course and complete the activity "IMAP—Modeling as a Strategy."

How might a child use a *counting* strategy to solve this problem? This is not an easy problem for which to use skip counting, but a child might skip count as follows: "six, twelve, eighteen, so the answer is three, since I counted by six three times." Skip counting may be best used in this problem to check an estimate. For example, a child might think "three groups of five is fifteen, but I have eighteen M&M's, so the answer might be six" and then proceed to check that estimate by skip counting by sixes.

How might a child use a *derived facts* strategy to solve this problem? She would build on a fact she already knows, such as $15 \div 3 = 5$. She might think "I know fifteen divided by three equals five, but I have eighteen M&M's, which is three more, which means each child will get one more M&M, so they each get six M&M's."

How might a child use the *recall* strategy to solve this problem? He would say that the answer is 6, because $18 \div 3 = 6$. Children using the recall strategy have memorized the needed fact and need only to retrieve it from memory. More will be said about helping children memorize basic facts in Chapter 8.

More about Nicole: Think back to Clip #23 that you just viewed, or view it again. Nicole initially got the wrong answer to the problem, saying the answer was 5. What did she do wrong? What does this clip show about Nicole's understanding of the concept of division?

Nicole seemed to be solving a different problem: $15 \div 3$. When the interviewer reread the problem, what did Nicole do? She quickly took 3 more cubes and put 1 in each pile, saying then that each child gets 6 M&M's. Nicole initially got the problem wrong not because she did not understand division, but because she was solving a different problem.

This video shows that sometimes children who understand a concept get an incorrect answer for a trivial reason, such as solving a different problem or making a counting mistake. It is important when assessing children's understanding to carefully examine the way children solve problems to identify those who may understand the concept but get an incorrect answer because of a small or careless error. You can use these observations to guide further instruction and discussions with children.

Using Models to Solve Multiplication and Division Problems

As in addition and subtraction, many different models can be used to illustrate relationships posed in multiplication and division problems. The following section describes some of these models.

Modeling Equal Groups and Multiplicative Comparison problems. Equal Groups problems, such as in the following example, can be modeled using a set model.

Maisha and Peter decided to sell cookies in packages of 3 at their school's bake sale. Mrs. Walsh bought 6 packages. How many cookies did Mrs. Walsh buy?

A set model is illustrated in Figure 7-14, in which six groups of three are assembled. Activities could include the children placing an equal number of cookies or counters on a specified number of plates or putting an equal number of marbles in bags. The mathematics sentence for the representation is $6 \times 3 = 18$.

FIGURE 7-14 Equal Groups Problem for 6×3

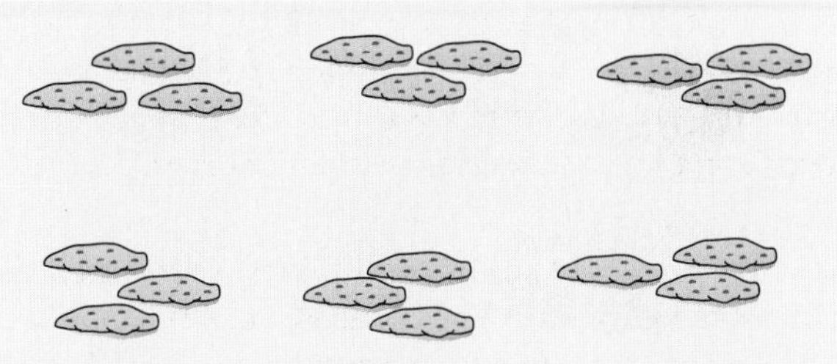

FIGURE 7-15 Repeated Subtraction for 12 ÷ 3

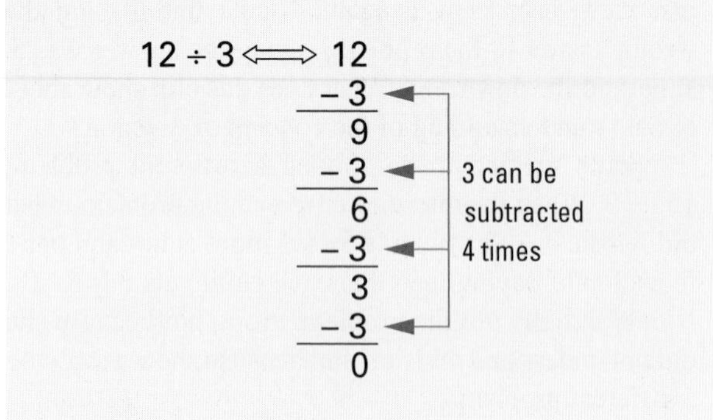

Similarly, Measurement division and Partitive division problems can be modeled using a set model. Generally, children are introduced to division using a subtractive, or measurement, setting. They are to find the number of groups. The repeated subtraction process for the following problem is symbolically represented in Figure 7-15.

Janice has 12 cookies. She wants to put 3 cookies into each bag. How many bags does she need?

In a partitioning setting, the total number and the number of equal groups are known. The child is to determine the number in each group. For example:

Three children want to share 12 cookies equally. How many cookies will each child get?

Children can find the solution by acting out a sharing or "dealing out" process (Figure 7-16). At its most basic level, a child might say "one for me, one for Tom, one for Margaret, one for me, one for Tom, one for Margaret...". Later, children will realize that they can share two or more at a time, thereby making the process more efficient.

Modeling Area and Array problems. Area and Array problems can be modeled by making a rectangle with the given number of rows of a certain length. Consider the following problem:

FIGURE 7-16 Sharing Cookies to Solve 12 ÷ 3

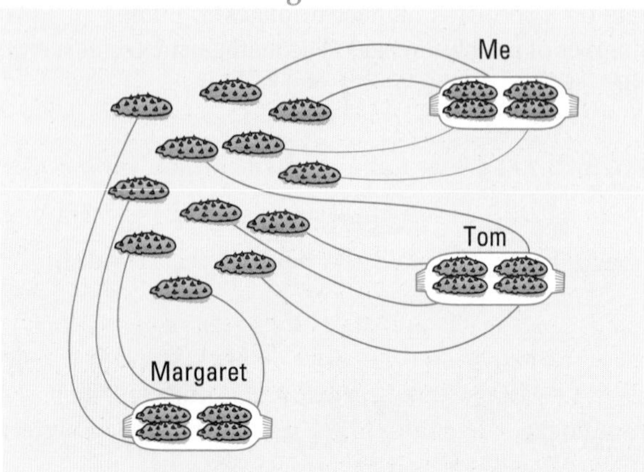

Maisha and Peter decided to sell cookies at their school's bake sale. They arranged the cookies on trays. They put 6 rows of cookies with 3 cookies in each row on one tray. How many cookies were on the tray?

This problem could be represented by the array shown below. By convention the rows represent the number of groups and the columns represent the number in each group. The array pictured here is a 6-by-3 array, or 6 rows of 3.

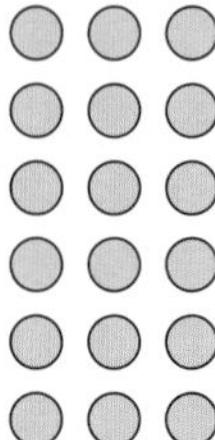

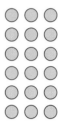

A teaching aid that helps children model Area and Array problems is the 10-by-10 multiplication array (Blackline Master 5 on MyEducationLab). This array consists of 10 rows of circles with 10 circles in each row. Children use pieces of paper or index cards to frame the circles corresponding to the problem they are solving (and to cover the extra circles not needed for that problem). For example, for the bake sale problem above, with 6 rows of cookies and 3 cookies in each row, children would lay their index cards on the 10-by-10 array so that only a 6-by-3 array of circles was visible, covering the rest of the circles in the 10-by-10 array with their index cards. They could then count the number of circles in the visible 6-by-3 array to find the answer to the problem. The multiplication array saves time by eliminating the need to actually arrange the counters into 6 rows of 3. Note, however, that the multiplication array should be introduced only *after* children are able to construct arrays of counters themselves.

> PEARSON **myeducationlab** The Power of Classroom Practice — Go to the Strategies section of Topic 6: "Whole Number Operations" in the MyEducationLab for your course to obtain "Blackline Master 5."

Modeling Combination problems. Although Combination problems are the least used of the four approaches, they can be very helpful in building the concept of multiplication—particularly multiplication with zero. Consider the following example:

Lindsay has a choice of 6 flavors of ice cream and 3 different toppings. How many different kinds of ice cream sundaes could Lindsay have?

Some children have difficulty matching each topping to one flavor and then repeating that for each of the flavors. The use of a 6-by-3 chart (similar to an array) facilitates understanding this approach (Kouba & Franklin, 1993).

Literature Link 7–2

Meaning of Division

Hutchins, Pat. (1986). ***The Doorbell Rang.*** New York: Morrow.

A challenging mathematical investigation set in the context of an interesting story provides the perfect setting for using a children's book to investigate mathematics. ***The Doorbell Rang*** engages children in the common situation of fair sharing, which is a foundational concept for learning division. The story shows that real-world problems sometimes have multiple solutions and are not typically static, such as those problems children frequently see in their textbooks.

- Connect the story with mathematics by writing addition number sentences that show the number of people arriving at the house each time the doorbell rings. Write division number sentences that show the sharing of the cookies throughout the story.
- Manipulate counters to represent the cookies in the story and investigate various ways to group the 12 cookies. Explore ways to group other numbers of cookies, such as 16 cookies, 24 cookies, or 60 cookies.
- Partition a large piece of construction paper into eight sections and use it as a storyboard. Show number sentences and pictorial representations of the mathematics in the book. This is an important exercise because children often have difficulty translating problems into number sentences and other representations.
- Make a reasonable estimate of the number of cookies on Grandma's tray at the end of the story. Write a number sentence and an illustration to show various ways to divide these cookies. Discuss what to do if the number of cookies does not divide evenly.

Source: Dr. Patricia Moyer-Pockenham, Utah State University.

Consider how the preceding problem about ice cream sundaes would change if there were *zero* flavors of ice cream and 3 toppings. In this situation, no sundaes could be made, illustrating that $0 \times 3 = 0$.

An instructional sequence for modeling multiplication and division. Kouba and Franklin (1993) use the problem "If 8 plates hold 4 cookies each, how many cookies are on all the plates?" to illustrate a sequential development in understanding multiplication:

> *Developmental Level 1:* A child sets out 8 plates, puts 4 cookies (or objects) on each plate, and counts the total number.
>
> *Developmental Level 2:* A child makes 8 groups of 4 without using separate objects for plates.
>
> *Developmental Level 3:* A child makes one group of 4 and recounts it 8 times, keeping track of how many groups have been counted by using fingers or another memory device.

"More advanced levels of representation include counting by fours; counting on when they cannot recall the next multiple, for instance, 4, 8, ..., 9, 10, 11, 12, and so on; adding fours; and using such derived facts as 'Four groups of 4 are 16 and 16 plus 16 is 32'" (Kouba & Franklin, 1993, pp. 575–576). Understanding the developmental sequence of children's understanding of multiplication helps you assess and plan instruction.

Another Word about Notation and Children's Language

Children have a natural way of talking about the action involved in the operations. Capturing this natural language and using it in the classroom can help children better understand whole-number operations. Do not rush into using symbolic notation. Instead, make a slow, gradual transition from natural language to symbolic language.

Listen to the language children use as they talk about problems. They will use phrases such as "ran away" and "joined in" as they describe real-life actions. You also will hear language such as "and three more," "start with seven and cross out four," "three bags with two each," and "twelve to be shared by four." Encourage children to write statements about the problems they are solving and to write number sentences using words rather than mathematics symbols.

To capture this natural language, write key terms or phrases on cards such as those shown in Figure 7-17. The cards created for a specific class will vary with the language used by the children in the class. Also prepare numeral cards with the numbers encountered in the basic facts. Encourage the children to create sentences for problems and for concrete or pictorial models of the operations by using the cards as in Figure 7-18.

FIGURE 7-17 Phrases Used in Word Problems

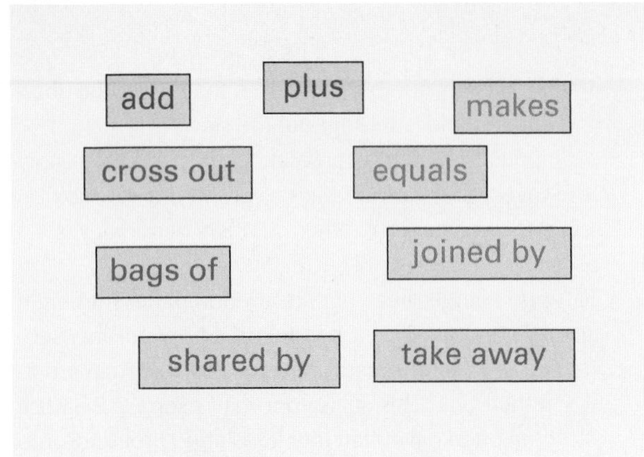

FIGURE 7-18 Sentences Representing Word Problems

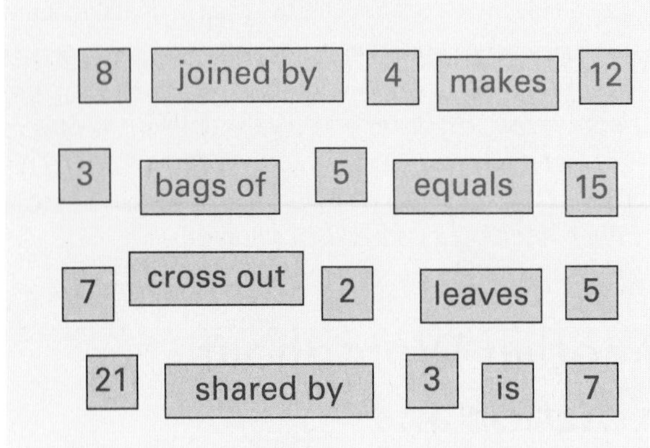

FIGURE 7-19 A Vertical Sentence for a Word Problem

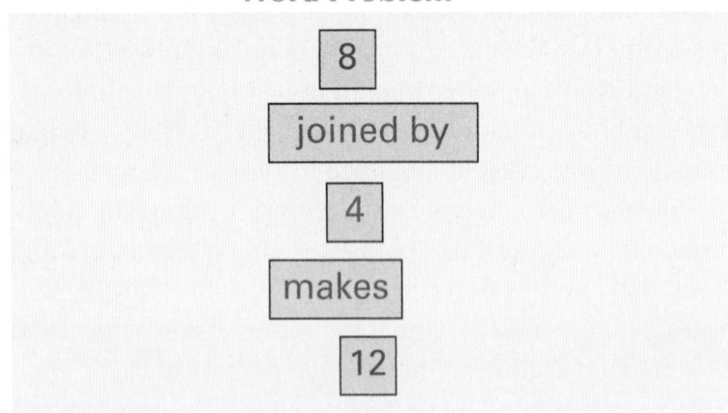

Using number and language cards in the classroom can help make the transition from horizontal to vertical notation more natural. Sentences such as those shown in Figure 7-18 can be arranged in vertical format. Initially, the sentences might be formed as a simple 90-degree rotation of the horizontal sentence (Figure 7-19). Later, the format can be altered to conform more closely to conventional notation. See Figure 7-20.

FIGURE 7-20 Sentence in Conventional Position

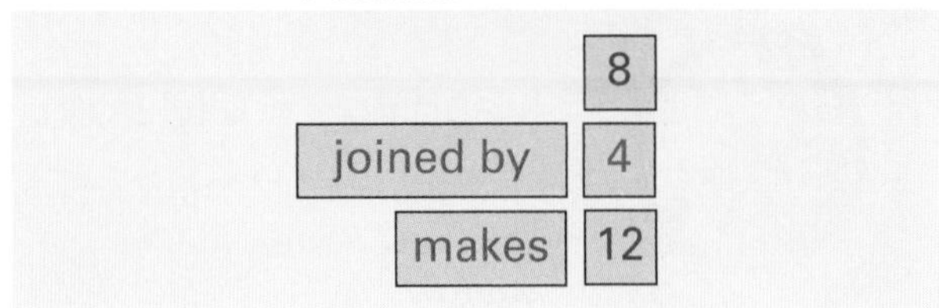

Over a period of time, introduce the conventional symbols for the different action words. Also introduce the "=" symbol for words such as "makes" and "leaves." Write these conventional symbols on cards as well and have children use them to generate sentences for problems and models in the same way they did with the natural language cards.

Children should understand that the "=" sign means "is the same number as" or "is another name for." Having children write several expressions equivalent to a given expression should facilitate this understanding. For example, give children $5 + 7 =$ ___ and ask them to write at least three true expressions (not just one number) in the blank. They may respond with:

$5 + 7 = 6 + 6$ $\qquad$ $5 + 7 = 10 + 2$

$5 + 7 = 24 \div 2$ $\qquad$ $5 + 7 = 15 - 3$

Note that the notation for division is particularly confusing to children. Three symbolic representations are commonly used for division: $6 \div 2$, $2\overline{)6}$ and 6/2 or $\frac{6}{2}$. The latter format usually is delayed until children are studying fractions. The first usually is read as "six divided by two" and the second as "two goes into six," although it should also be read as "six divided by two." The second representation is the most common, but also it is the only symbolic representation that *should not be read from left to right,* as "two goes into six." It is important to help children connect the phrase "six divided by two" to each of the common symbolic forms.

Conclusion

It is critical that children build a sound understanding of whole-number operations. Therefore, children should be allowed time to manipulate and solidify their ideas. Solving word problems of many different types is necessary for children to develop this "operation sense." To rush on to "more advanced" work is a mistake that often comes back to haunt children and teachers.

CHAPTER

Sample Lesson

A Lesson on Solving Comparison Problems

Grade level: First

Materials:

- At least one manipulative, such as Unifix cubes, or assorted counters or objects

Lesson objective: Students will use objects to correctly represent and compare whole numbers.

Standards link: Students use a variety of models to model "part-whole," "adding to," "taking away from," and "comparing" situations to develop an understanding of the meanings of addition and subtraction and strategies to solve such arithmetic problems (NCTM (2006) *Curriculum Focal Points,* Grade One).

Launch: Pose the following problem:

Sharon has 9 marbles, and Tom has 4 marbles. How many more marbles does Sharon have than Tom does?

Ask the students how they might solve the problem. Solicit recommendations about how to solve the problem, including modeling each quantity with counters, making a one-to-one correspondence between objects in both sets, and counting how many more are in the larger (Sharon's) set.

Explore: In pairs or small groups, have students solve a similar problem and draw a picture of their solution.

Summarize: Coming together as a whole class, select one pair of students to come to the front of the room and explain how they solved the problem and to show the picture of their solution. Focus on their explanations of how they determined how much larger one set was than the other.

FOLLOW-UP

Complete the following questions.

1. Consider any cautions regarding selecting the manipulatives to use in this lesson. Would other manipulatives work well? Might you want to avoid using certain manipulatives or objects? Why? What would be the advantages and/or disadvantages of each manipulative?
2. Two types of number sentences are appropriate for comparison problems: $4 + \_\_ = 9$ and $9 - 4 = \_\_$. How might you help children learn how to write a number sentence for comparison problems?
3. What might the <u>next</u> lesson focus on, and why?

IN PRACTICE

Complete the following activities to include in your professional portfolio.

1. Interview a child to assess his or her understanding of operations. (You may choose to use problems from the Early Number or Place-Value Interviews on the IMAP clips or problems that you write.) Describe the problems you asked the child to solve and the strategies he or she used to solve problems. Describe what the child seemed to understand and what understanding the child still needs to develop.
2. Write a lesson plan to help introduce children to the Join type of addition problems.

3. Write a lesson plan to help introduce children to the Equal Groups type of multiplication and division problems.

myeducationlab — The Power of Classroom Practice. Now go to Topic 6: "Whole Number Operations" in the MyEducationLab (www.myeducationlab.com) for your course, where you can:

- Find learning outcomes for "Whole Number Operations" along with the national standards that connect to these outcomes.
- Apply and practice your understanding of the core teaching skills identified in the chapter with a Building Teaching Skills and Dispositions learning unit.
- Complete Assignments and Activities that can help you understand the chapter content more deeply.
- Complete *enVision MATH* Sample Curricula assignments that allow you to examine and work with chapters from *enVision MATH*, a K-6 mathematics program.
- Check your comprehension on the content covered in the chapter by going to the Study Plan in the Book-Specific Resources for your text. Here you will be able to take a chapter quiz, receive feedback on your answers, and then access Review, Practice, and Enrichment activities to enhance your understanding of chapter content.
- Go to the Book-Specific Resources for Chapter 7 to explore mathematical reasoning related to chapter content in the Activities section.

LINKS TO THE INTERNET

ProTeacher

http://www.proteacher.com/100000.shtml

Contains links to lessons to help children understand and practice addition, subtraction, multiplication and division.

RESOURCES FOR TEACHERS

Reference Books: Whole-Number Operations

Brodie, J. (1995). *Constructing Ideas about Multiplication and Division, Grades 3–6.* Mountain View, CA: Creative.

Burns, M. (1991). *Math by All Means: Multiplication, Grade 3.* Sausalito, CA: Math Solutions.

Creative Publications. (1994). *The Maharajas' Tasks: Investigating Division.* Mountain View, CA: Creative.

National Council of Teachers of Mathematics (2006). *Curriculum Focal Points for Prekindergarten through Grade 8 Mathematics*. Reston, VA: Author.

Ohanian, S., & Burns, M. (1995). *Math by All Means: Division, Grades 3–4.* Sausalito, CA: Math Solutions.

Richardson, K. (1999). *Developing Number Concepts, Book 2: Addition and Subtraction.* White Plains, NY: Seymour.

Richardson, K. (1999). *Developing Number Concepts, Book 3: Place Value, Multiplication, and Division.* White Plains, NY: Seymour.

Ward, S. (1995). *Constructing Ideas about Number Combinations.* Mountain View, CA: Creative.

Children's Literature

Addition and Subtraction

Becker, John (2007). *Seven Little Rabbits*. New York: Walker Books for Young Readers.

Derubertis, Barbara (2005). *Count On Pablo*. New York: The Kane Press.

Jonas, Ann. (1997). *Splash*. New York: HarperTrophy.

Merriam, Eve (1996). *Twelve Ways to Get to 11*. New York: Aladdin.

Murphy, S. (1996). *Too Many Kangaroo Things to Do!* New York: Harper Trophy.

Multiplication and Division

Giganti, Paul (1999). *Each Orange Had 8 Slices*. New York: HarperTrophy.

Hulme, Joy N. (1999). *Sea Squares*. New York: Hyperion.

Mahy, Margaret (1993). *17 Kings and 42 Elephants*. New York: Puffin.

Neushwander, Cindy (1999). *Amanda Bean's Amazing Dream, a Mathematical Story.* New York: Scholastic Press.

Pinczes, Elinor J. (1995). *A Remainder of One*. Boston: Houghton Mifflin.

Pinczes, Elinor J. (1999). *100 Hungry Ants*. Boston: Houghton Mifflin.

CHAPTER

Developing Whole-Number Operations: Mastering the Basic Facts

NCTM CONNECTING WITH THE STANDARDS

The National Council of Teachers of Mathematics (NCTM) Principles and Standards (2000) affirms the importance of children's developing proficiency with basic facts and algorithms but cautions against overemphasizing the memorization of facts before understanding is developed, or to the exclusion of other important topics.

The NCTM (2006) *Curriculum Focal Points* discusses learning basic facts in grades one through four. They state that first-grade students "use properties of addition (commutativity and associativity) to add whole numbers, and they create and use increasingly sophisticated strategies based on these properties (e.g., "making tens") to solve addition and subtraction problems involving basic facts" (NCTM, 2006, p. 13), while second graders "use their understanding of addition to develop quick recall of basic addition facts and related subtraction facts" (p. 14). Similarly, third-grade students "use properties of addition and multiplication (e.g., commutativity, associativity, and the distributive property) to multiply whole numbers and apply increasingly sophisticated strategies based on these properties to solve multiplication and division problems involving basic facts" (p. 15), while fourth-grade students "use understandings of multiplication to develop quick recall of the basic multiplication facts and related division facts" (p. 16).

In learning the basic facts, children focus less on real-life problems and more on the relationship between models and the symbolic representation of the facts. Children need many opportunities to discuss this change in emphasis and to translate from physical model to symbol and vice versa before they can be expected to operate solely at the symbolic level.

Developing Your Math Teaching Skills

When you have finished studying this chapter, you should be able to do the following:

- Name the three components of instruction on basic facts.
- For each whole-number operation, describe some thinking strategies that children can use. Describe several thinking strategies for each operation.
- Explain the role of consolidating activities for drill and practice. Describe several of these activities.
- Discuss how games are useful in promoting the immediate recall of basic facts.

ASSESSING MATHEMATICS UNDERSTANDING

In order to become familiar with the mathematics concepts and procedures discussed in this chapter, take a few minutes and complete the following *Chapter 8 Preassessment.* Answer each question on your own and think about how you got the answer. Then think about how elementary-school children think about each problem

and any possible misunderstandings some children might have about each problem. If you are able, administer this assessment to a child, and analyze his or her understanding of these topics.

Part 1: Addition Facts

1. $8 + 0 =$ ___ **2.** $7 + 1 =$ ___

3. $4 + 2 =$ ___ **4.** $3 + 5 =$ ___

5. $5 + 5 =$ ___ **6.** $9 + 2 =$ ___

7. $6 + 4 =$ ___ **8.** $8 + 6 =$ ___

Part 2: Multiplication Facts

9. $6 \times 0 =$ ___ **10.** $8 \times 1 =$ ___

11. $4 \times 2 =$ ___ **12.** $3 \times 5 =$ ___

13. $7 \times 4 =$ ___ **14.** $8 \times 6 =$ ___

15. $7 \times 6 =$ ___ **16.** $8 \times 7 =$ ___

Examining Classroom Practice

Teacher Alma Wright uses dominoes to help her first- and second-graders identify different combinations of numbers for a given sum (Annenberg Video Series). The children gather in a circle around a large set of dominoes arranged on the floor. Ms. Wright asks the children to find dominoes that show 4. One child chooses a domino with 4 dots on one end and 0 dots on the other. Another child chooses a domino with 1 dot on one end and 3 dots on the other end. Ms. Wright helps the students verbalize the number sentence this domino represents by saying, "One plus three equals four."

> PEARSON myeducationlab The Power of Classroom Practice Go to the Video Examples section of Topic 6: "Whole Number Operations" in the MyEducationLab for your course to view the Annenberg clip "Domino Math."

After children identify other dominoes that show 4 and state the corresponding number sentence, Ms. Wright uses stick-on dots to create a pictorial representation of the first domino selected, showing $0 + 4 = 4$.

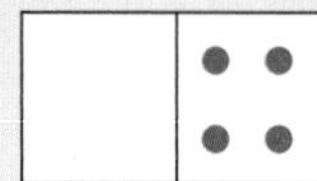

As children watch, she moves 1 dot from one end of the domino picture to the other, creating the number sentence $1 + 3 = 4$.

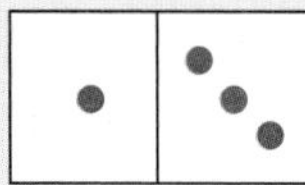

She then rotates the paper 180 degrees, asking students what number sentence it now represents ($3 + 1 = 4$).

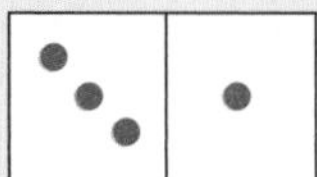

Ms. Wright then encourages children to work in small groups to find dominoes that have a sum of five: first locating the dominoes, then using stick-on dots to create a picture of each domino, and finally writing number sentences to represent each domino they choose. For groups that finish quickly, Ms. Wright poses the task of finding three dominoes that add to a total of eight.

As the children solve problems, Ms. Wright circulates around the room, asking clarifying questions and posing follow-up tasks as needed. Most students count the dots to determine the total, while other students seem to have memorized a few of the number sentences.

Analyzing Assessment Results

Analyze each problem in the *Chapter 8 Preassessment.* How did you (and/or the student you administered the assessment to) solve each of the problems? Which facts were harder? Why do you think that was?

1. $8 + 0 =$ ___

2. $7 + 1 =$ ___

Discussion: These problems are two of the easiest addition facts. Both involve adding 0 or 1. These are often some of the first addition facts that children memorize.

3. $4 + 2 =$ ___

4. $3 + 5 =$ ___

Discussion: These problems are a bit harder, but still fairly easy. Both involve adding 2 or 3. Counting on still works easily for these facts. Children memorize these facts fairly easily.

5. $5 + 5 =$ ___

Discussion: This problem is a "double," meaning that both addends are the same. Doubles are often some of the first addition facts that children memorize.

6. $9 + 2 =$ ___

Discussion: This addition fact involves 9. Children can reason that adding 9 is the same as adding 10 and then subtracting one. This makes problems with 9 fairly easy.

7. $6 + 4 =$ ___

Discussion: This addition fact is called a "sum to 10." This means that it is one of the pairs of numbers that equals 10. Sums to 10 also are fairly easy.

8. $8 + 6 =$ ___

Discussion: This is one of the harder addition facts. Students can use a compensation strategy, discussed later in this chapter, to solve this fact. For example, they could think of it as $6 + 6 + 2 = 14$.

Now let's analyze the multiplication facts. How did you (and/or the student you administered the assessment to) solve each of the following problems?

9. $6 \times 0 =$ ___

10. $8 \times 1 =$ ___

Discussion: These problems are two of the easiest multiplication facts. Both involve multiplying by 0 or 1. These are often some of the first multiplication facts that children memorize.

11. $4 \times 2 =$ ___

12. $3 \times 5 =$ ___

Discussion: These problems are still fairly easy. Both involve multiplying by 2 or 5. Skip counting works easily for multiplying by 2 and 5; for example, you can solve 3×5 by counting by fives 3 times: 5, 10, 15. These are also some of the first multiplication facts that children memorize.

13. $7 \times 4 =$ ___

14. $8 \times 6 =$ ___

15. $7 \times 6 =$ ___

16. $8 \times 7 =$ ___

Discussion: These are some of the harder multiplication facts. Students can use thinking strategies, discussed later in this chapter, to solve these facts.

Take a minute and reflect on this assessment. What aspects of basic facts are particularly difficult for you and/or for the student you assessed? What do you want to learn more about in order to teach these concepts effectively?

Common Student Misunderstandings about or Difficulties with Basic Facts:

- "I either know it, or I don't." This misunderstanding leads some students to give up quickly, rather than to use thinking strategies to help derive a fact.
- "I have to be fast" or "If I can't get it fast, I should stop trying." This misunderstanding makes some students anxious and prevents them from reasoning to solve the problem.
- Lack of the knowledge of thinking strategies to use facts they know to find other facts.

Are there any other difficulties that children may have about basic facts? It is important to assess what children understand, and are still working on understanding, in order to plan instruction that meets their needs.

Building on Assessment Results

Now that we have analyzed assessment results, think about what can be done to strengthen children's understandings and minimize (and hopefully eradicate) their misunderstandings and difficulties with basic facts. What might lead students to develop these misconceptions? Their learning experiences may focus on a set of procedures to be memorized rather than a set of concepts to be understood. So what might you do to help students understand these concepts?

You will learn later in this chapter that there are three components of instruction on basic facts: understanding the meaning of the operation, using thinking strategies to retrieve facts, and using consolidating activities for drill and practice. To help children be successful with basic facts, you need to consider all of these components when planning instruction. The table below lists several common misunderstandings or difficulties and what you can do to help children overcome these misunderstandings.

Think back to Ms. Wright's lesson. In what ways did children represent number sentences? In this lesson children made connections among concrete materials (dominoes), pictures, and symbols (number sentences), in the process of learning combinations for certain sums. This chapter will focus on ways to help children learn basic facts.

IF students think that . . .	THEN help students . . .
"I either know it, or I don't"	see that they can build on what they know to get answers to facts they don't know. For example, if they know that $6 \times 6 = 36$, then they can figure out what 7×6 is: 7×6 is 1 group of 6 more than 6×6. $36 + 6 = 42$.
"I have to be fast" or "If I can't get it fast, I should stop trying."	see that they can solve problems faster if they understand what the operations mean, know some thinking strategies, and practice.

NCTM NUMBER AND OPERATIONS STANDARDS AND EXPECTATIONS ADDRESSED IN THIS CHAPTER

Instructional programs from Pre-K–12 should enable all students to—	In Prekindergarten through grade 2 all students should— (NCTM, 2000, P. 78)	In grades 3–5 all students should— (NCTM, 2000, P. 148)	In grades 6–8 all students should— (NCTM, 2000, P. 214)
• meanings of operations and how they relate to one another. • compute fluently and make reasonable estimates.	• develop fluency with basic number combinations for addition and subtraction.	• identify and use relationships between operations, such as division as the inverse of multiplication, to solve problems. • understand and use properties of operations, such as the distributivity of multiplication over addition. • develop fluency with basic number combinations for multiplication and division and use these combinations to mentally compute related problems, such as 30 × 50.	• understand and use the inverse relationships of addition and subtraction, multiplication and division, and squaring and finding square roots to simplify computations and solve problems.

What Are Basic Facts?

The basic facts for addition and multiplication involve all combinations of single-digit addends and factors. For example, $7+9=16$ is an addition basic fact, because the two addends, 7 and 9, are each single-digit numbers. Because there are 10 digits, there are 100 combinations for both addition and multiplication.

10 possibilities for the first addend (0 through 9)
× 10 possibilities for the second addend (0 through 9)
= 100 different basic facts for addition (and similarly for multiplication)

The addition facts are listed later in Figure 8-1, and the multiplication facts are listed in Figure 8-8.

We should note here that some states and curriculum materials take a broader view of basic facts and include addends from 0 through 10 or even from 0 through 12. In this textbook, we will take the most constrained view of basic facts and only include those with addends from 0 through 9.

The basic facts for subtraction are the inverses of the addition facts. Using the previous example, the addition problem $7+9=16$ may be transformed into two subtraction basic facts: $16-7=9$ and $16-9=7$. So there are 100 basic facts for subtraction.

Similarly, the basic facts for division are the inverses of the multiplication facts. For example, the multiplication fact $3\times 8=24$ may be transformed into two division basic facts: $24\div 3=8$ and $24\div 8=3$. There are 90 basic facts for division because there are no facts with zero as a divisor. Therefore, there are a total of 390 basic facts.

THESE ARE BASIC FACTS:	THESE ARE *NOT* BASIC FACTS:
$3+9=12$	$4+11=15$
$14-8=6$	$19-9=10$
$7\times 4=28$	$5\times 10=50$
$6\times 0=0$	$46\div 9=5$ r 1
$48\div 6=8$	$15\div 0$ is undefined
$0\div 5=0$	$20\div 10=2$

Can you decide why each of the number sentences in the second column above is not a basic fact? Remember that basic facts consist of addends or factors that are between 0 and 9, inclusive, and the corresponding subtraction and division facts.

Some children will memorize some of the basic facts while developing number relationships and the meaning of the operations. In fact, many children come to school knowing a few basic facts. For example, many kindergarteners know that "one and one is two." But for children to learn all 390 basic facts, teachers must do more than have them endlessly repeat basic facts with the hope that children will memorize them.

A Three-Step Approach to Fact Mastery

Many beginning teachers believe that children will automatically memorize basic facts if they just get enough practice. Practice is important, but it is not effective if other understandings and skills are not already in place.

One very effective method for helping children learn basic facts is the three-step approach (Rathmell, 1978). The three-step approach includes (1) understanding the meaning of the operations, (2) using thinking strategies to retrieve facts, and (3) using consolidating activities for drill and practice. This approach is the best way to help children recall the basic math facts.

NCTM Principles and Standards Link 8-1

Content Strand: Number and Operations

Students should develop strategies for knowing basic number combinations . . . that build on their thinking about, and understanding of, numbers. Fluency with basic addition and subtraction number combinations is a goal for the pre-K–2 years. By fluency we mean that students are able to compute efficiently and accurately with single-digit numbers. (NCTM, 2000, p. 84)

Step 1: Understanding the Meaning of the Operations

As discussed in Chapter 7, children must understand the meaning of each operation. This understanding lays the foundation for children's further use of these operations and the development of operation sense. Children who understand the meaning of operations are then able to use thinking strategies to relate the facts they've already learned to new facts.

Step 2: Using Thinking Strategies to Retrieve Facts

Thinking strategies are mental strategies that can be used to relate known facts to unknown facts. For example, if children know that $2 + 2 = 4$, the "one more than" thinking strategy would help them determine that the sum of $2 + 3$ must be one more than the sum of $2 + 2$, or 5.

Thinking strategies help children find the answer to basic facts problems without using concrete materials by "providing structure for organizing facts so that recall is easier" (Rathmell, 1978, p. 18). Although many children will "invent" one or more of these thinking strategies on their own (Thornton, 1978), explicit teaching on the use and selection of thinking strategies is necessary. Buchholz (2004) describes how she helped her students learn their basic facts and enhance their mathematical reasoning by focusing on strategies for learning basic facts.

Other helpful thinking strategies include counting on, counting back, skip counting, one more or less than a known fact, and compensation, to name a few. A list of thinking strategies for each operation is given later in this chapter, along with detailed descriptions of how to help children learn to use these strategies.

Step 3: Using Consolidating Activities for Drill and Practice

Consolidating activities include games, worksheets, and other activities that give children opportunities to practice facts they are learning in order to memorize them. Drill and practice are most effective after children have learned efficient thinking strategies for recalling those basic facts.

NCTM Principles and Standards Link 8-2

Content Strand: Number and Operations

Fluency with whole-number computation depends, in large part, on fluency with basic number combinations—the single-digit addition and multiplication pairs and their counterparts for subtraction and division. Fluency with the basic number combinations develops from well-understood meanings for the four operations and from a focus on thinking strategies (Thornton, 1990; Isaacs & Carroll, 1999). (NCTM, 2000, p. 152)

NCTM Principles and Standards Link 8-3

Content Strand: Number and Operations

Young children often initially compute by using objects and counting; however, prekindergarten through grade 2 teachers need to encourage them to shift, over time, to solving many computation problems mentally or with paper and pencil to record their thinking. (NCTM, 2000, p. 152)

FIGURE 8-1 Addition Facts

+	0	1	2	3	4	5	6	7	8	9
0	0	1	2	3	4	5	6	7	8	9
1	1	2	3	4	5	6	7	8	9	10
2	2	3	4	5	6	7	8	9	10	11
3	3	4	5	6	7	8	9	10	11	12
4	4	5	6	7	8	9	10	11	12	13
5	5	6	7	8	9	10	11	12	13	14
6	6	7	8	9	10	11	12	13	14	15
7	7	8	9	10	11	12	13	14	15	16
8	8	9	10	11	12	13	14	15	16	17
9	9	10	11	12	13	14	15	16	17	18

Addition and Subtraction Facts

The 100 addition facts often are organized in an addition table as shown in Figure 8-1. To find the sum of 4 and 6, find the first addend, 4, in the left-hand column, and the other addend, 6, along the top row, or vice versa. Then find the intersection of this row and column, which is the sum, 10.

The 100 subtraction facts can also be found by using this addition table. To find the result for $10 - 4$, begin by finding the minuend (10) in the row with the number being subtracted (4), also known as the subtrahend, in the left-hand column. Find the difference (6) by reading the number in the top index row.

Usually children are given part of the addition table rather than the whole table at once, because the table contains facts children may not have had an opportunity to learn.

All of the joining, separating, and comparing activities described in Chapter 7 can be used to help children learn the basic facts by developing an understanding of the meaning of the operations. These activities should now be extended to include more symbolic representation of the facts. Using Cuisenaire rods, activities such as those in Activity 8-1 emphasize the model–symbol interaction. Interlocking Unifix cubes could be used equally as well for this activity.

ACTIVITY 8-1 Number Sentences for Trains

Manipulative Strategies

Materials

Cuisenaire rods

Procedure

1. Write number sentences for these trains. Write the sum.

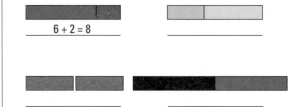

   6 + 2 = 8

2. Make a train for each of the sentences below. Write the sum.

   8 + 5 = ☐ 4 + 0 = ☐
   9 + 1 = ☐ 5 + 7 = ☐

Thinking Strategies for Addition and Subtraction

Rathmell (1978) described several important thinking strategies that children use when learning addition and subtraction basic facts: counting on, counting back, one more or one less than a known fact, and compensation. You need to provide children with many opportunities to use such strategies so that they may learn to use thinking strategies flexibly.

An effective sequence for helping children learn thinking strategies is to begin by focusing on teaching one of the strategies. Then provide daily opportunities for children to use, and talk about the strategy for several days before introducing another strategy.

Counting on. The counting-on strategy involves beginning with one addend and counting on the number of the second addend. For example, to solve the problem $6 + 3$, a child could start with 6 and count forward three times, saying "seven, eight, nine."

Another, more sophisticated version of counting on, called *counting on from larger,* requires a child to identify the larger addend and count on from it the number of the second addend, making note of the ending result. For the problem $2 + 5$, a child would note that 5 is the larger addend. He or she would then start with 5 and count forward two times, saying "six, seven." Although counting on is a somewhat "natural" strategy for children, they need specific guidance in learning to count on from the larger addend. Children have a tendency to start with the first number, in this case 2, and count on a number of times corresponding to the second number, in this case 5. But it is more difficult to count on by 5 than by 2. You should encourage children to pick the larger addend and count on from there. In this way, the counting-on strategy will be more useful to children. When counting on from

FIGURE 8-2 A Calendar to Use to Practice Counting On

Sun	Mon	Tue	Wed	Thur	Fri	Sat
			1	2	3	4
5	6	7	8	9	10	11

either addend, note that counting on is most effective when one of the addends is relatively small.

> myeducationlab The Power of Classroom Practice — To explore your own understanding of "counting on," go to Chapter 8 in the Book-Specific Resouces section in the MyEducationLab for your course. Select the Activities section and complete the activity "Counting On."

Counting on in subtraction. Counting on also is a useful strategy for solving subtraction problems. It is best used in situations in which the difference is small, for example, in problems such as 10 − 7. Children could begin with the subtrahend and count on to the minuend, keeping track of the number of times they counted. In using counting on to find the answer to 10 − 7, a child would start at 7 and count forward to 10, saying "eight, nine, ten." The answer is the total number of counts forward—in this example, three.

A number line and a calendar are helpful devices for counting on in subtraction. For example, a child might wonder on Thursday how many days it has been since Monday (9 − 6 on the calendar in Figure 8-2). Counting on from 6 would give the answer, 3.

Working with children who have learning disabilities. Weill's (1978) "Hill" strategy is an example of a counting-on strategy that is effective with children with learning disabilities (see Figure 8-3). It works with minuends greater than 10. For example, consider the problem 16 − 7. Have the children draw a curve to represent the hill, and underneath the curve place the minuend (16) near the top, the subtrahend (7) near the bottom and the number 10 between them. The children should determine how many steps (by counting on) from the subtrahend to 10, then write that number above the hill as shown in Figure 8-3, and then do the same using 10 and the minuend. Then add the two numbers above the curve to get the difference of 9.

FIGURE 8-3 The "Hill" Subtraction Strategy

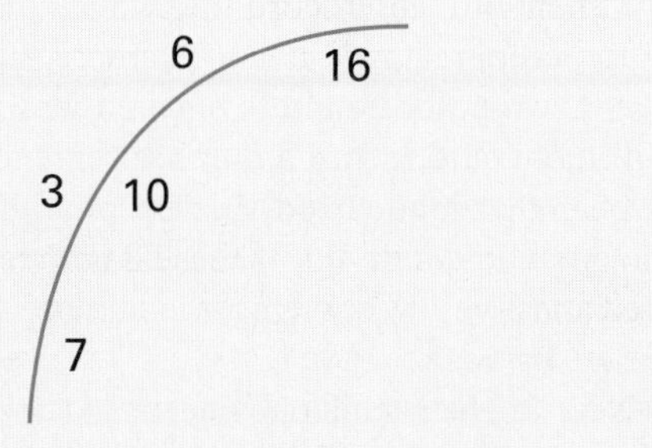

NCTM Principles and Standards Link 8-4

Content Strand: Number and Operations

Teachers should also encourage students to share the strategies they develop in class discussions. Students can develop and refine strategies as they hear other students' descriptions of their thinking about number combinations. For example, a student might compute 8 + 7 by counting on from 8: ". . ., 9, 10, 11, 12, 13, 14, 15." But during a class discussion of solutions for this problem, she might hear another student's strategy, in which he uses knowledge about 10; namely, 8 and 2 make 10, and 5 more is 15. She may then be able to adapt and apply this strategy later when she computes 28 + 7 by saying, "28 and 2 make 30, and 5 more is 35." (NCTM, 2000, p. 84)

Counting back. Counting back is a particularly useful strategy for learning the subtraction facts. This strategy involves counting backward from the minuend by an amount equal to the subtrahend. For example, to find the answer to 10 − 2, a child would start at 10 and count backward two times, saying "nine, eight."

It is not as easy for children to count backward as it is to count forward. To use the counting-back strategy, children need to be able to count backward. Providing children with experiences with counting backward outside of the context of subtraction can help them develop this skill. Counting backward on a hundreds chart, a calendar, orally, or by writing the numbers in order from some starting point, such as from 11 to 8, can be helpful.

Once children are able to count backward, they can then apply this skill to subtraction. Show the children a set of objects and ask them to count backward to tell how many are left when, for example, 2 are subtracted. Figure 8-4 presents a sample interaction. This strategy is useful when the subtrahend is small.

FIGURE 8-4 Counting-Back Strategy

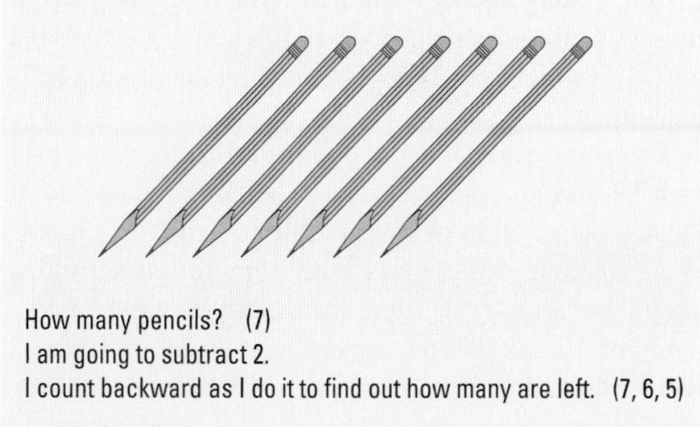

How many pencils? (7)
I am going to subtract 2.
I count backward as I do it to find out how many are left. (7, 6, 5)

Another difficulty children sometimes have with the counting-back strategy is that they also have to keep track of the number of steps, which can become confusing. Baroody (1984) found that both the number line and a classroom clock are effective aids to help children count backward in subtraction. For example, the problem 8 − 5 could be solved by counting back starting at 8 on a number line or a clock, as shown below, and counting to 5, then counting the number of times they counted, or the "hops" on the number line.

One more or one less than a known fact. Recognizing if an unknown fact is one more or one less than a known fact is helpful, especially with the harder facts. For example, if children know a "doubles fact" such as 4 + 4 = 8, they can use this knowledge to find the sum of 5 + 4, that is, they might think "4 plus 4 is 8, and 5 plus 4 is one more, which is 9."

Similarly, if children know that 4 + 4 = 8, they can use this strategy to reason that 4 + 3 must be one less than 8, or 7.

The one-more or one-less strategy can be demonstrated through activities such as the following:

1. Show two groups of 6 objects.
2. Ask, "How much is 6 plus 6?"
3. Add one more to one of the groups.
4. "Now we have 6 plus 7. How many altogether?"
5. If necessary, say, "One more than 12."
6. Verify that there are 13 objects.
7. "6 + 6 is 12, so 6 + 7 is one more, or 13."

Compensation. The compensation strategy involves increasing one addend while decreasing the other by the same amount. This can be used for any combination but is especially useful where the sum is greater than 10. For example, 8 + 5 has the same sum as 10 + 3. Children can imagine taking 2 away from the 5 (which becomes 3) and giving it to the 8 (which becomes 10), so 8 + 5 is the same as 10 + 3, which is 13. These two changes compensate for each other.

The compensation strategy is most useful when used with 10, because it is very easy to add a number to 10. Most young children will be able to relate to this because of their experiences with numeration activities. They have already learned, for example, that 17 is one group of 10 and 7 and, conversely, a group of 10 and 7 is 17. In small groups, have the children work on exercises such as the one in Activity 8-2. Encourage the children to talk about the process (that is, what they do in this activity). Later, pencil-and-paper exercises such as the one shown below can help children practice the compensation strategy. It is important to also ask children to describe *why* one problem is easier than another.

> **myeducationlab** The Power of Classroom Practice — To explore your own understanding of compensation, go to Chapter 8 in the Book-Specific Resources section in the MyEducationLab for your course and complete the activity "Practicing the Compensation Strategy."

ACTIVITY 8-2 Compensation

Manipulative Strategies

Materials
Counters

Procedure

With your counters, show these groups:	Change it into a problem with 10. Draw your new groups.
8 and **4**	

10 + □ = □
So: 8 + 4 = □

Draw a ring around the easier problem in each pair:

10 + 5 = ______	or	9 + 6 = ______
9 + 5 = ______	or	10 + 4 = ______
8 + 6 = ______	or	7 + 7 = ______

Another type of activity that helps children learn the basic facts involves making all possible combinations of a sum, as the children in Ms. Wright's class did with dominoes in the lesson described at the beginning of this chapter. Another manipulative that can be used is two-color counters, which are chips with a different color on each side. Using this material, or beans that have been spray painted on one side only, children take a given number of chips (18 or fewer), shake them, spill them out, and record the two addends determined by the colors showing. For example, have each child take 8 two-color counters, shake them in their hands, spill them, and record a number sentence showing the number that landed red-side-up plus the number that landed yellow-side-up. If these 8 counters landed with 3 red and 5 yellow showing, the number sentence would be 3 + 5 = 8.

Next, to help children understand the compensation strategy, ask them to flip over some of the chips and record the new number sentence. The total should still be 8, but they might now have 4 red and 4 yellow chips showing. Continue this several times with the 8 chips. Discuss how these number sentences are the same (e.g., all total 8) and different (different addends). Then repeat with another number of chips. Activities such as this help children think flexibly about number combinations.

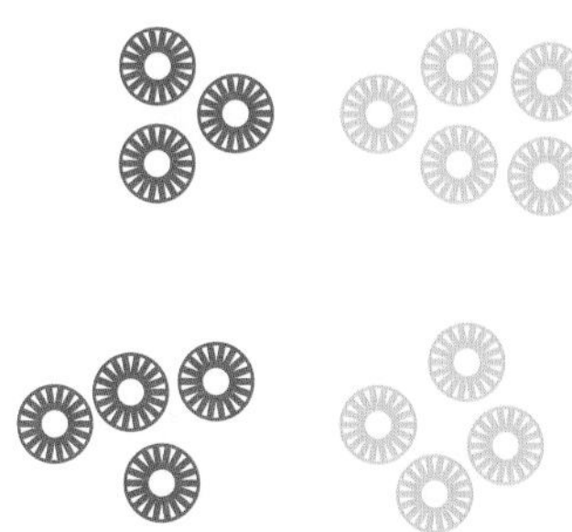

Using thinking strategies to organize instruction. Instruction on mastering the basic facts often is organized around the size of the number combinations. Instruction frequently begins with facts with sums up to 5 (e.g., $1+2=3$; $2+3=5$). However, research has shown that the size of the numbers is not the only issue to be considered in planning instruction (Baroody, 1984; Moser, 1992).

Basic facts instruction organized around thinking strategies has been shown to be very effective in promoting mastery of basic facts. For example, doubles facts and their corresponding subtraction facts, such as $6+6=12$ and $12-6=6$, are the easiest to learn, as are the facts with 0 (e.g., $6+0=6$ and $8-0=8$) and the facts with 1 (e.g., $6+1=7$ and $8-1=7$). Combinations to make 10 (e.g., $3+7=10$ and $10-3=7$) and "one more than doubles" facts (e.g., $6+7=13$ and $13-7=6$) also are among the easier facts for children to learn. These types of basic facts are a good place to begin instruction on basic facts and to introduce children to manipulation of number combinations. Teaching children how to use thinking strategies will prepare them to understand mathematical properties of addition, subtraction, multiplication, and division, which are discussed later in this chapter.

Mathematical Properties of Addition and Subtraction

Understanding the commutative and associative properties of whole numbers and the zero property of addition significantly helps children understand the operations and master the basic facts. The distributive property is discussed in the multiplication section of this chapter. As children model problems, you can help them develop understanding of these properties by asking questions that help children notice patterns. Memorizing the actual words or names of the properties is not most important; what is more important is that children recognize the properties and be able to use them when working with the operations.

Commutative property. The commutative property is also known as the *order property.* Informally, it states that numbers may be added (or multiplied) in any order without changing the result. More formally, the commutative property states that for all whole numbers a and b, $a+b=b+a$ and $a\times b=b\times a$. The child might say, "I know that seven and eight is fifteen, so eight plus seven must also be fifteen," or "Since three times seven is twenty-one, seven times three must be twenty-one," or more generally, "I can add or multiply the numbers in any order."

It is important to note that children do not just automatically "know" the commutative property but must be helped to learn this property. For example, a child may have memorized that $3+4=7$ but may have not memorized $4+3$. Only after working through a number of problems and activities, as described in the next section, will a child recognize that both sums are the same.

Understanding the commutative property is a great help in learning basic facts. Children who understand the commutative property in effect have fewer facts to memorize. For every fact a child memorizes, he or she can use the commutative property to get the corresponding fact, thus cutting the 100 number of facts that need to be memorized in half!

Helping children learn the commutative property. Many activities can be used to help children build an understanding of the commutative property. One activity that works well is to clip clothespins on a hanger and arrange the clothespins in two distinct sets (Figure 8-5). Ask the children to write the number sentence $3+5=8$ for the problem shown. Then rotate the hanger 180° horizontally. Ask the children to write the sentence for the new problem shown: $5+3=8$. After several examples of this type, ask the children what they notice in each of the pairs of problems. Guide them to describe the commutative property for addition of whole numbers.

When learning a concept, children should also encounter nonexamples of the concept. Examples of commutativity outside of mathematics and operations in which commutativity does not hold true should be discussed.

FIGURE 8-5 Demonstrating the Commutative Property

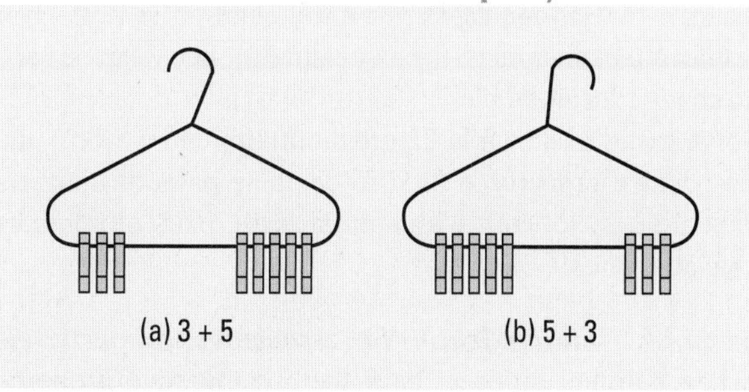

Activity 8-3 suggests one approach to doing this. Through activities, you should help children to understand that the commutative property does not hold for either subtraction or division, that is, $6 - 2$ is not equal to $2 - 6$, nor is $24 \div 6$ equal to $6 \div 24$. A clear understanding of where the commutative property can be applied (in other words, to addition and multiplication but not to subtraction or division) may help reduce the tendency of some children to always subtract the smaller number from the larger and to make other common computational errors.

ACTIVITY 8-3 Commutative and Noncommutative Examples

Procedure

1. Discuss the truthfulness of these statements. Is the result the same?
   - Put on right shoe *followed by* left shoe = put on left shoe *followed by* right shoe
   - Put on socks *followed by* shoes = put on shoes *followed by* socks
2. Write other examples of commutativity and noncommutativity.

Associative property.

Addition and multiplication are binary operations, meaning that only two numbers can be joined at a time. The associative property makes it possible to combine more than two sets in sequence.

The associative property is also known as the *grouping property.* Informally, it states that addends or factors may be grouped in different ways without changing the result. More formally, the associative property states that for all whole numbers a, b, and c, $(a + b) + c = a + (b + c)$ and $(a \times b) \times c = a \times (b \times c)$. A child may informally say, "When I add (or multiply) three (or more) numbers, I can group them any way I like." Children will often accurately combine the commutative and associative properties and simply say, "It doesn't matter in what order I add or multiply numbers." This is an informal but completely correct statement.

The associative property is useful in allowing the combination of "easy numbers" first. Figure 8-6 shows two ways in which this can be done. Because the "doubles" basic facts (such as $6 + 6$) are easier for many children to learn than some of the other facts, the associative property can be used to change "near doubles" (such as $7 + 6$) into "doubles" plus some extra, as shown in Figure 8-6(a). In Figure 8-6(b), the associative property is used to combine pairs of numbers that are easy to work with—in this case, pairs of numbers that add to ten.

FIGURE 8-6 Associative Property Examples

(a)
$$\begin{aligned} 6 + 7 &= 6 + (6 + 1) \\ &= (6 + 6) + 1 \\ &= 12 + 1 \\ &= 13 \end{aligned}$$

(b)

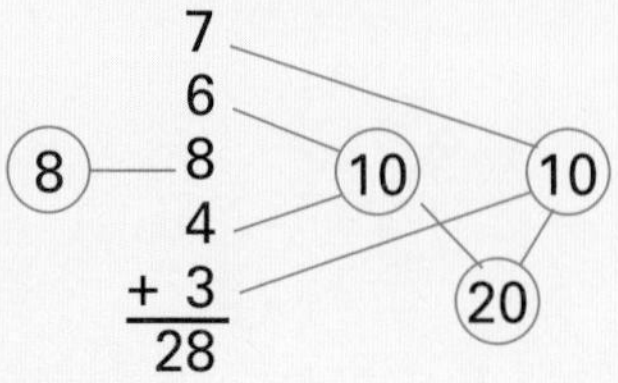

Helping children learn the associative property. As when helping children learn the commutative property, activities in which children notice patterns related to the property are helpful. For example, present children with pairs of problems such as the following to solve: $2 + (8 + 6)$ and $(2 + 8) + 6$. Ask children to solve each pair of problems and then notice any similarities in the problems. Encourage children to notice that some problems are easier to solve (such as the second problem in the example above) but both problems in each pair have the same answer, thus helping them to see the usefulness of the associative property.

Addition property of zero.

The addition property of zero is also known as the *identity element for addition.* Formally, the addition property of zero states that for any whole number a, $a + 0 = a$. Children might use less formal language, such as "when you add zero to any number, the answer doesn't change" or "you get the same number." An understanding of the addition property of zero helps children learn the 19 addition facts involving zero.

Helping children learn the addition property of zero. Provide children with a set of problems in which zero is being added to other numbers, and ask them to solve them and then describe the patterns they observed. For example, consider the following problem:

> *Juan had 0 cookies and his mother gave him 4 cookies. How many cookies did he have then?*

This is a very simple situation that children can quickly solve. Teachers can use problems such as this to help children make the generalization that zero added to any number or any number added to zero results in that number. This is what the addition property of zero means.

Fact Families for Addition and Subtraction

The relationship between addition and subtraction allows the basic facts to be organized into "families." Except for the

FIGURE 8-7 Illustration of an Addition and Subtraction Fact Family

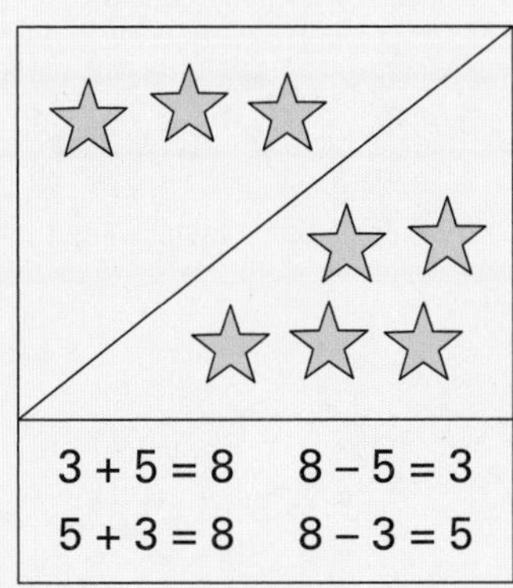

"doubles" (e.g., $4 + 4$), each family consists of four related facts as illustrated for 3, 5, and 8 in Figure 8-7. Organizing facts into families helps children learn them. More particularly, when they know the addition facts, children can more easily recall the related subtraction facts. The 10 family (sums that equal 10) is particularly important because of its usefulness with several thinking strategies, such as compensation. It is also one of the easiest fact families for most children to learn.

Helping children learn fact families. One way to help children learn fact families is to construct a set of cards with a variety of pictorial models similar to the stars in Figure 8-7. Have the children form small groups, draw a card, then discuss and write the family of related facts. This activity could easily be converted into a game format.

In curricula that incorporate the fact families, addition and subtraction are taught together. The addition facts for a family (for example, $2 + 3 = 5$ and $3 + 2 = 5$) normally are learned first, followed by the subtraction facts (for example, $5 - 2 = 3$ and $5 - 3 = 2$). Children should work with addition facts from several fact families together before focusing on the corresponding subtraction facts.

Multiplication and Division Facts

The multiplication facts can be organized in a multiplication table, as shown in Figure 8-8. For example, to find the product of 4×6, find the first factor, 4, in the left-hand column, and the other factor, 6, along the top row, or vice versa. Then find the intersection of this row and column, shown by the arrows, which is the product, 24.

The two related division facts, $24 \div 4 = 6$ and $24 \div 6 = 4$, also are shown in this figure, with the divisor and quotient (4 and 6) found on the outside of the table and the dividend (24) found in the cell that is the intersection of those two numbers. As for addition and subtraction, this table illustrates the interrelationship between multiplication and division.

FIGURE 8-8 Multiplication Table

X	0	1	2	3	4	5	6	7	8	9
0	0	0	0	0	0	0	0	0	0	0
1	0	1	2	3	4	5	6	7	8	9
2	0	2	4	6	8	10	12	14	16	18
3	0	3	6	9	12	15	18	21	24	27
4	0	4	8	12	16	20	24	28	32	36
5	0	5	10	15	20	25	30	35	40	45
6	0	6	12	18	24	30	36	42	48	54
7	0	7	14	21	28	35	42	49	56	63
8	0	8	16	24	32	40	48	56	64	72
9	0	9	18	27	36	45	54	63	72	81

Figure 8-8 summarizes in one table all multiplication and division basic facts, but this table is not intended for children to use in its entirety—at least not until all of the facts have been introduced. Rather, children could be asked to complete such a table as they work on learning different facts.

Thinking Strategies for Multiplication and Division

Rathmell (1978) described several thinking strategies that children use when learning multiplication and division basic facts. They are:

- Repeated addition,
- Skip counting,
- Splitting the product into known parts,
- Facts of five, and
- Patterns.

The following section discusses these important strategies.

Repeated addition. Using repeated addition, children might say that three groups of five is "five plus five plus five." In this example, a child would "repeatedly add" 5 three times.

Skip counting. Skip counting involves counting by the second factor the number of times indicated by the first factor. For example, 3×5 could be found by skip counting by 5 three times, saying: "5, 10, 15." This strategy builds on the meaning of multiplication, because counting by five three times corresponds with counting three groups of five. Children can use counting by five to generate the entire "fives" multiplication table.

Skip counting also may be done with a calculator. To skip count by five on most inexpensive nonscientific calculators, the child would enter the following keystrokes: 5 + = = ... The display would show the multiples of 5: 5, 10, 15, 20, and so on.

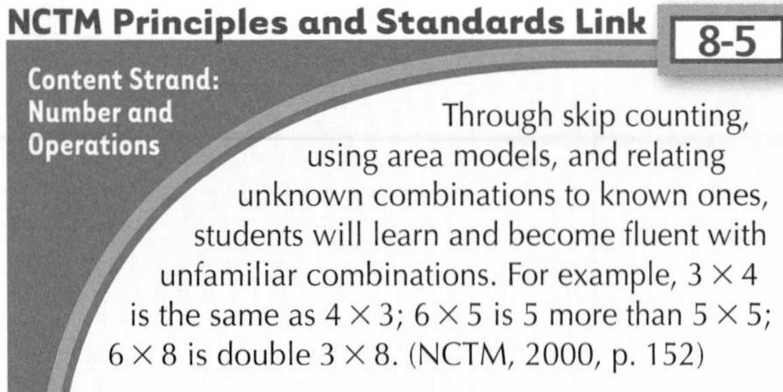

NCTM Principles and Standards Link 8-5

Content Strand: Number and Operations

Through skip counting, using area models, and relating unknown combinations to known ones, students will learn and become fluent with unfamiliar combinations. For example, 3 × 4 is the same as 4 × 3; 6 × 5 is 5 more than 5 × 5; 6 × 8 is double 3 × 8. (NCTM, 2000, p. 152)

Splitting the product into known parts. This strategy actually includes two strategies: *one-more-set* and *twice-as-much as a known fact.*

One-more-set strategy. The one-more-set (or group) strategy is very useful, especially for learning the facts in sequence. Each fact, in turn, can be used to help learn the next fact for either factor. Given the model in Figure 8-9 showing 6 groups of 3 strawberries separated into 5 groups of 3 and 1 group of 3, the child would verbalize along these lines: "I know that 5 threes is 15, and 1 more group of 3 is 18, so 6 groups of 3 is 18 and 6 × 3 is 18."

To help children learn this strategy, show them 3 groups of 7 objects and ask them to tell (write) a number sentence for the display. Then show one more group of 7 and ask, "If 3 sevens is 21, what will one more group, or 4 sevens be?" This type of activity should take just a few minutes each day. It can be efficiently executed if you prepare a series of folded cards similar to the one shown in Figure 8-10. Some of these cards also could be used for the next strategy (twice-as-much) as well, and a few may be used with the facts-of-five strategy. Create folded card sets to illustrate at least 9 or 10 different multiplication facts to allow children lots of experiences with this strategy. Review the twice-as-much strategy and the facts-of-five strategy to determine which folded card sets can be utilized to demonstrate all three thinking strategies.

FIGURE 8-9 The One-More-Set Strategy

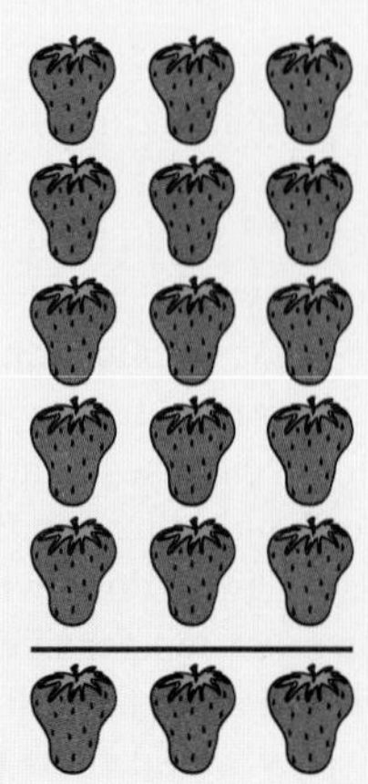

FIGURE 8-10 Folded Card for Use with Multiplication Strategies

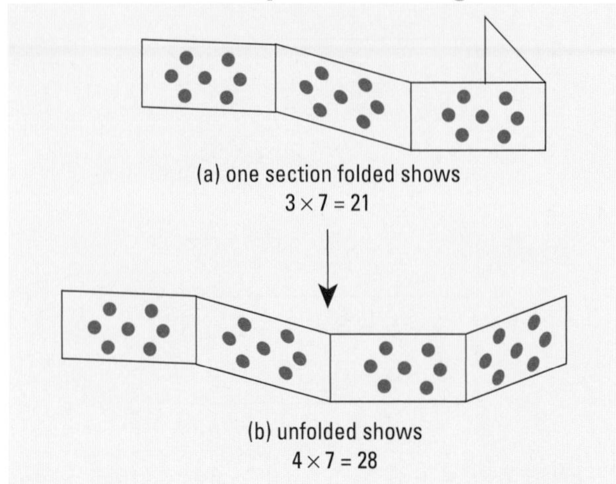

Twice-as-much strategy. When at least one of the factors is even, the product may be split into two equal parts. This is referred to as the twice-as-much strategy. The model in Figure 8-11 suggests a thought process such as "since 2 sixes is 12, 4 sixes is *twice as much,* which is 24."

Show the children arrays that already are split in half and have them write (or orally state) a number sentence for each half and then for the total. Also give the children arrays of 4, 6, and 8, and ask them to split each array in half and write number sentences for each part and the total.

Facts of five. Another strategy, the facts-of-five strategy, is useful for the "larger" facts. One of the factors must be greater than 5, because this strategy involves breaking one of the factors into a group of 5 and another group. It is assumed that the children already know the facts with 5. Figure 8-12 illustrates this strategy for the problem 7 × 6.

Using this strategy, a child would reason, "I know that 5 sixes is 30 and 2 sixes is 12, so 7 sixes must be 30 + 12, or 42." This strategy is easier to use when the factor that's not being split is 6 or 8, because the answers to 5 × 6 and 5 × 8 are multiples of 10, which are easy to add to other

FIGURE 8-11 The Twice-as-Much Strategy

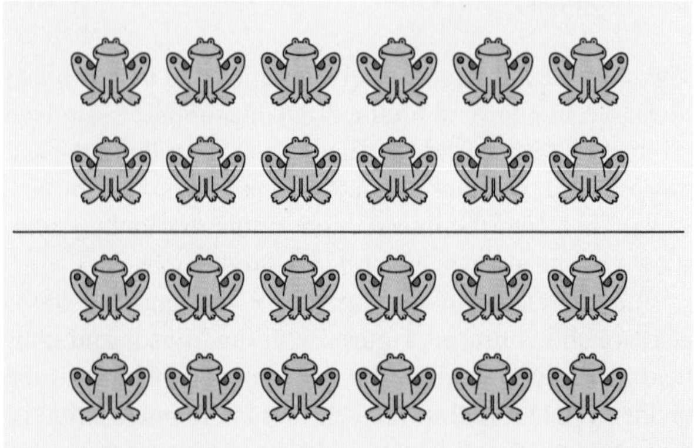

FIGURE 8-12 The Facts-of-Five Strategy

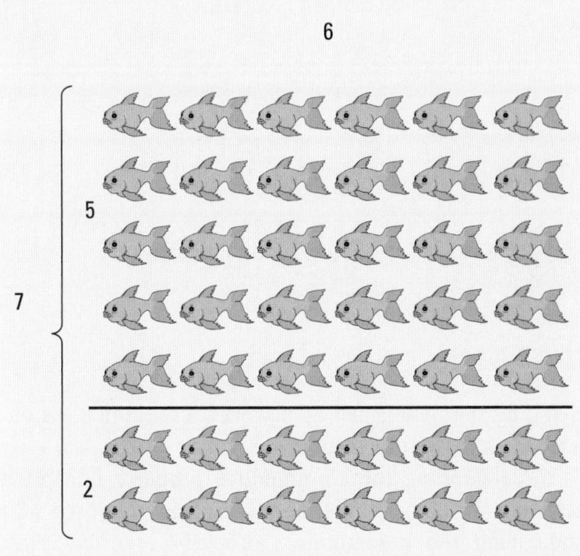

numbers. Otherwise, the first product has a 5 in the ones position, which makes the addition in the second step a little harder. If one of the factors is less than 6, the child would probably use another strategy.

Activities to teach the facts-of-five strategy are similar to the ideas suggested for the twice-as-much strategy. In this case, the children would break the array into two smaller arrays, one that has 5 rows and another whose number of rows is the difference between the factor and 5. For example, the array for 7 × 8 would be broken into two smaller arrays: 5 rows of 8 and 2 rows of 8, so the product would be the sum of 40 + 16 or 56. To make this activity useful to children and give them opportunities to exercise their thinking skills, encourage them to orally share how they solved a problem by breaking one factor into 5 groups or rows plus whatever number of groups or rows are left.

Patterns. A pattern strategy can be used for many of the facts, but it is most helpful and most often used with the facts involving 9. Encouraging children to solve multiplication problems by looking for patterns in the multiplication table is one situation in which the multiplication table could be used prior to the introduction of all the facts. Children shade all the multiples for each fact in a multiplication table and then look for patterns. For example, by lightly shading in all the multiples of 5, children will observe that all the multiples of 5 end in either a 0 or a 5 and appear in only one row and one column in the multiplication table.

To help children look for patterns, give them several copies of the multiplication table and ask them to use different colors to shade in multiples of different factors. Multiples of 3 and 9 are shaded in Figure 8-13. Focus on one set of multiples and ask the children to describe the patterns they observe. Then ask them to find and describe another pattern in the table.

FIGURE 8-13 Multiplication Table Highlighting Multiples of Three and Nine

X	0	1	2	3	4	5	6	7	8	9
0	0	0	0	0	0	0	0	0	0	0
1	0	1	2	3	4	5	6	7	8	9
2	0	2	4	6	8	10	12	14	16	18
3	0	3	6	9	12	15	18	21	24	27
4	0	4	8	12	16	20	24	28	32	36
5	0	5	10	15	20	25	30	35	40	45
6	0	6	12	18	24	30	36	42	48	54
7	0	7	14	21	28	35	42	49	56	63
8	0	8	16	24	32	40	48	56	64	72
9	0	9	18	27	36	45	54	63	72	81

Exploring patterns on the multiplication table for the factor 9 shown in Figure 8-14, children will make all or some of the following observations:

- The sum of the digits for each product, other than zero, always is 9.
- The tens digit increases sequentially from 1 to 8.
- Except for the zero fact, the units digits decrease by one from 9 to 1.
- The tens digit is always one less than the non-nine factor (for example, for 7×9, the tens digit will be one less than the 7 [that is, 6], and since the sum of the digits equals 9, the ones digit must be 3, so the answer is 63).

Finger multiplication is another interesting strategy for working with facts of 9. This strategy is illustrated in Activity 8-4.

ACTIVITY 8-4 Finger Multiplication with Nines

Manipulative Strategies

Procedure

1. Hold both hands in front of you with the palms facing away from you.
2. To show 2 × 9, begin counting at the left. Bend the second finger. The finger to the left represents the tens and the fingers to the right of the bent finger represent the ones.

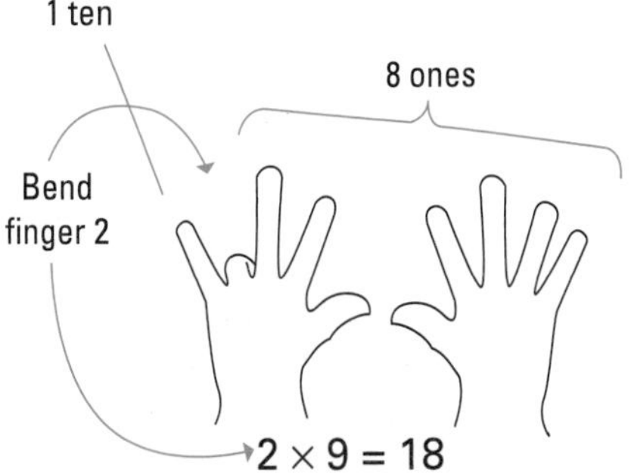

3. Use the finger method to show other multiplication facts of 9.

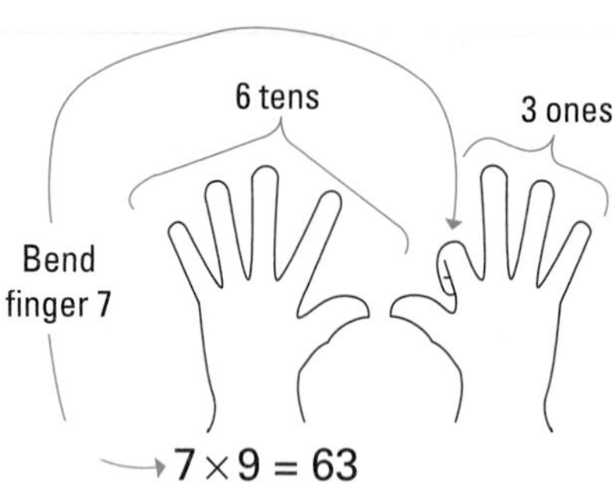

FIGURE 8-14 Exploring Patterns in Multiples of Nine

$0 \times 9 = 0$
$1 \times 9 = 9$
$2 \times 9 = 18$
$3 \times 9 = 27$
$4 \times 9 = 36$
$5 \times 9 = 45$
$6 \times 9 = 54$
$7 \times 9 = 63$
$8 \times 9 = 72$
$9 \times 9 = 81$

Several children's books include thinking strategies for learning basic facts. Literature Link 8-1 describes how to use *The Best of Times* (Tang, 2002) to help children learn multiplication thinking strategies.

Mathematical Properties of Multiplication

Children who understand mathematical properties develop a strong understanding of mathematical operations. Understanding properties helps children use mathematical reasoning and think flexibly about numbers and problem situations. The addition and subtraction section of this chapter included descriptions of the commutative and associative properties and the identity element for addition. This section illustrates these concepts for multiplication and discusses the multiplication properties of one and zero and the distributive property of multiplication over addition.

Commutative property. The commutative property of multiplication, also known as the *order property,* states that numbers may be multiplied in any order without changing the result, just as it works for addition, as described earlier in this chapter.

Understanding the commutative property is a great help in learning multiplication basic facts. Children who understand the commutative property in effect have fewer facts to memorize. For every fact a child memorizes, such as $3 \times 6 = 18$, he or she can use the commutative property to get the corresponding fact, $6 \times 3 = 18$, thus cutting the number of facts that need to be memorized in half! Recognizing how the commutative property makes this possible will require many instructional experiences, such as those described in the following section, before children can use this property to help them memorize multiplication facts.

Helping children learn the commutative property. This important property can be modeled by building an array or gluing or drawing an array of objects on a card, as in Figure 8-15(a). Ask the children to write the mathematics sentence for the array $4 \times 6 = 24$. Now rotate the array 90° as shown in Figure 8-15(b). Have the children write a sentence for the new arrangement: $6 \times 4 = 24$. Repeat the procedure with several other arrays. Ask the children to talk about the different situations, discussing how they are different and what is common to each. Rotating an array of

Literature Link 8-1

Multiplication Thinking Strategies

Tang, Greg (2002). ***The Best of Times: Math Strategies That Multiply.*** New York: Scholastic.

As discussed in this chapter, thinking strategies are effective mental techniques and reasoning processes that help children find the answers to basic facts. ***The Best of Times*** helps children learn their multiplication basic facts by using a variety of thinking strategies. It helps children strengthen their understanding of multiplication and memorize the basic facts. Organized by strategy type, this book creatively describes the zero property of multiplication, the identity element for multiplication, doubling, and the patterns with nines in fun settings. For example, in "Absolute Zero," penguins go ice fishing while learning about the multiplication property of zero. Through interesting situations and eye-catching illustrations, children experience and apply multiplication thinking strategies in many situations. After reading the book, have children practice thinking strategies as described in the activities in this section.

FIGURE 8-15 Illustration of the Commutative Property of Multiplication

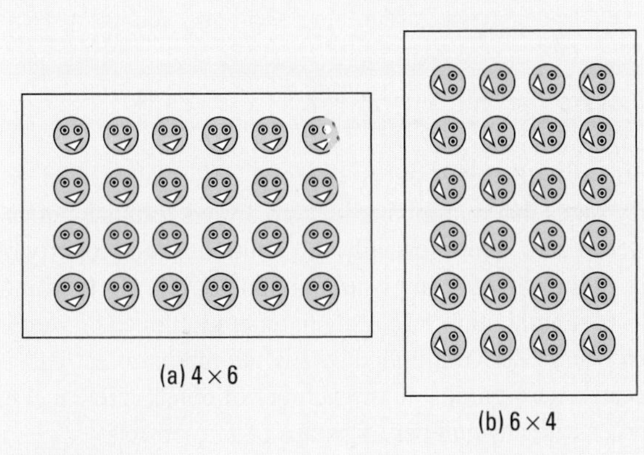

squares cut from graph paper, an array on a pegboard, or a rectangular region marked off on a geoboard would provide additional illustrations of the same concept.

Associative property. As with the associative property of addition, the associative property of multiplication is also known as the *grouping property.* Informally, it states that factors may be grouped in different ways without changing the result. More formally, the associative property states that for all whole numbers *a, b,* and *c,* $(a \times b) \times c = a \times (b \times c)$. A child may informally say, "When I multiply three (or more) numbers, I can group them any way I like."

Children will find the associative property useful in situations that involve fairly large computations such as $26 \times 5 \times 2$. They will recognize that if they multiply 5×2 first, the problem becomes very easy compared with trying to multiply 26×5 first.

Helping children learn the associative property. A concrete model helps children visualize the associative property. Consider the following example: $3 \times 2 \times 4$. Ask the children, "Will it make a difference if we multiply 3×2 first or 2×4 first? How might we see if it makes a difference?" Using interlocking cubes to build models for each problem, have half of the class solve the problem by first multiplying 3×2, while the other half of the class solves the problem by starting with 2×4.

The first group will use interlocking cubes to build a 3-by-2 array, which shows 3×2, and then will build 3 more arrays to show 4 times (3×2) (using the commutative property). Have the children count the total number of cubes used. The product is 24 [see Figure 8-16(a)].

Similarly, the second group of children will construct a 2-by-4 array and then will build 2 more arrays to show 3 times (2×4). The product still is 24 [see Figure 8-16(b)]. Ask the children to compare the final models and answer the original question posed, "Will it make a difference if we multiply 3×2 first or 2×4 first?"

Distributive property of multiplication over addition. The distributive property of multiplication over addition, often just referred to as the *distributive property,* is also known as the *break-apart property.* Informally, it states that a product may be separated (or broken apart) into two separate products without changing the result. More formally, the distributive property states that for any whole numbers *a, b,* and *c,* $a \times (b + c) = (a \times b) + (a \times c)$ or $a\,(b + c) = ab + ac$. A child might say, "Six times seven is the same as six times five plus two, which is the same as six times five plus six times two." This example may be represented using a number sentence as follows: $6 \times 7 = 6 \times (5 + 2) = (6 \times 5) + (6 \times 2)$.

Using the distributive property makes learning some of the more difficult basic facts easier. Consider the following, for example: 8×7 can be thought of as $8 \times (5 + 2)$. Note that 8×5 and 8×2 are easier facts to learn. The products, 40 and 16, can now be added to obtain the product.

Helping children learn the distributive property. Children can use an array of counters, as in Activity 8-5, to develop

FIGURE 8-16 Illustration of the Associative Property of Multiplication

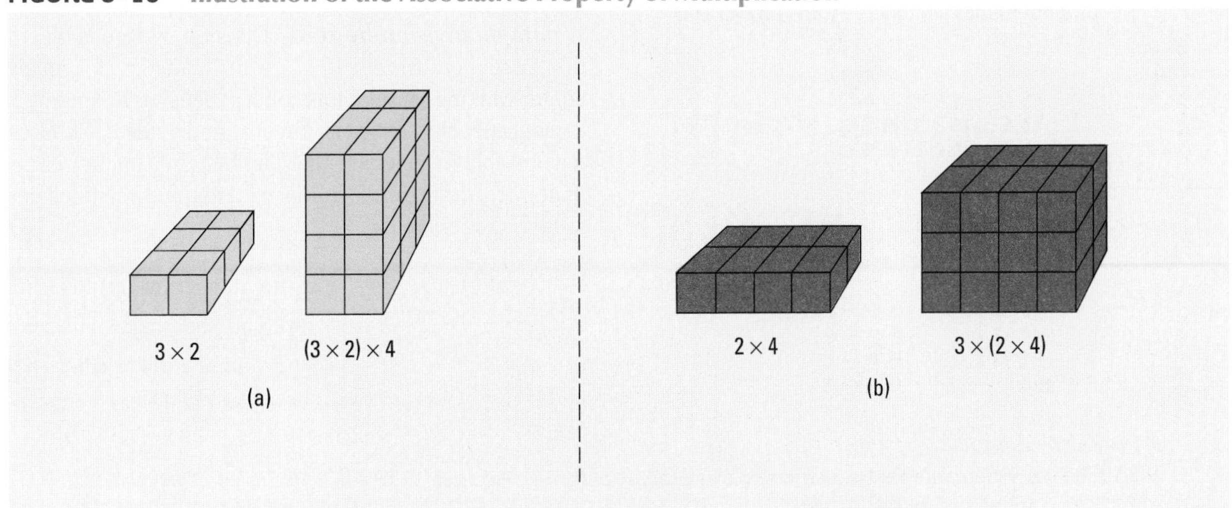

understanding of the distributive property. Notice that in this activity the original product is broken into two parts, which may also be referred to as *partial products,* because they are *parts of the product*. This property can be used when multiplying larger numbers. For example, to multiply 4×13, children could break apart this problem into two simpler problems as follows: $4 \times 13 = (4 \times 10) + (4 \times 3)$. In this example, 40, which is the product of 4×10, and 12, the product of 4×3, are the *partial products.* Repeat Activity 8-5 with other multiplication facts to practice using the distributive property. The distributive property will be an important tool in understanding the multiplication algorithm, which is discussed in Chapter 9.

Multiplication property of one. The multiplication property of one is also known as the *identity element for multiplication.* Informally, it states that multiplying by one does not change a number. More formally, the multiplication property of one states that for any whole number a, $a \times 1 = a$. A child might say, "Any number multiplied by one gives you the same number." The multiplication property of one helps children learn the 19 multiplication facts that have 1 as one of the factors.

Helping children learn the multiplication property of one. Children can model problems that have 1 as one of the factors by making one set of the given size, making one jump of the given length along a number line, or forming an array with one row or one column. Such modeling helps children understand the multiplication property of one.

ACTIVITY 8-5 Distributive Property from Arrays

Visual Scaffolding

Materials

Counters

Procedures

1. Write a mathematics sentence for this array.

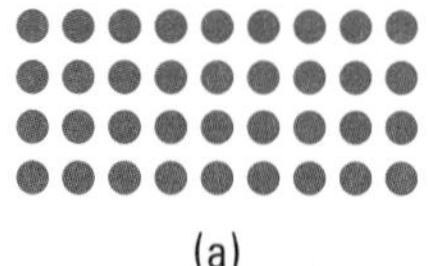

(a)

2. Write two mathematics sentences, one for each array.

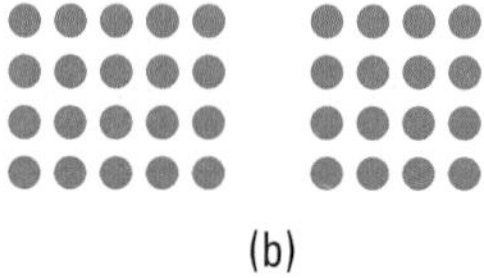

(b)

3. What do you notice about the sentence for array (a) and the two sentences for (b)?
4. Use counters and set out a 4-by-9 array. How many different ways can you separate it into two parts?
5. For each way, complete a sentence, such as $4 \times 9 = (4 \times \_) + (4 \times \_)$.

Multiplication property of zero. Informally, this property states that multiplying by zero always results in an answer of zero. More formally, the multiplication property of zero states that for any whole number a, $0 \times a = 0$, or $a \times 0 = 0$. A child might say, "Any number multiplied by zero is zero" and "Zero multiplied by any number is zero." This is because zero groups of any number of objects are equal to zero, as are any number of groups of zero objects.

Helping children learn the multiplication property of zero. Building on the meaning of multiplication as equal groups or arrays, pose real-world situations to children in which any number of groups with zero elements are created. For example, "Jason put zero marbles in each of four bags. How many marbles did he use?" Even though word problems involving multiplication of zero may seem a bit contrived or funny to children, they will help children understand that zero sets of anything or any number of zero sets still is nothing.

When problems are posed in familiar situations, it is easy for children to see that zero groups or zero rows of any size are equal to zero. Similarly, problems can be shared with children that involve any number of rows with a length of zero or zero rows of a certain length.

In addition, children can be asked to find the pattern in the following examples and then deduce that $0 \times 3 = 0$.

4 rows of 3 are 12.
3 rows of 3 are 9.
2 rows of 3 are 6.
1 row of 3 is 3.
0 rows of 3 are 0.

A note on division by zero. Division by zero is one of the more confusing issues in mathematics for many adults. Making sense of this concept depends on linking it to concepts that learners already understand. Children may be able to generalize the fact that division by zero is undefined through observing patterns and relationships such as the following:

$3 \div 0 = n$	$3 = 0 \times n$ (no number makes this true)
$2 \div 0 = n$	$2 = 0 \times n$ (no number makes this true)
$0 \div 0 = n$	$0 = 0 \times n$ (any number makes this true)
$6 \div 2 = n$	$6 - 2 - 2 - 2 = 0$ (subtract 3 twos to get 0)
$6 \div 0 = n$	$6 - 0 - 0 - 0 \ldots$ (never get to 0 by subtracting zeros)

Mathematicians say that division by zero is undefined. The generalizations above may be visualized through somewhat contrived problems such as this measurement situation (Watson, 1991):

The ballpark is 10 blocks from your home. If you walked 2 blocks each minute, how many minutes would it take to get to the park? If you walked one block per minute, how long would it take? If you walked zero blocks each minute, how long would it take? (You'd never get there!)

Another measurement division situation that can help children understand why division by zero is undefined is the following:

6 cookies distributed by putting 6 in each bag ⟶ 1 bag of cookies

6 cookies distributed by putting 3 in each bag ⟶ 2 bags of cookies

6 cookies distributed by putting 2 in each bag ⟶ 3 bags of cookies

6 cookies distributed by putting 1 in each bag ⟶ 6 bags of cookies

6 cookies distributed by putting 0 in each bag ⟶ an infinite number of empty bags of cookies

In the measurement division context, the problem is complete when all items are distributed. In the two examples above, involving walking and cookies, this condition never occurs—that is, the person walking never arrives at the ballpark, and all the cookies are never distributed. These situations show that there is something unusual about dividing by zero, which is the most important part of this concept for children to understand.

Fact Families for Multiplication and Division

As with addition and subtraction, the multiplication and division basic facts can be organized into number sentence families. Organizing facts into families helps children learn them. With the exceptions noted below, fact families have four members. An array can be used to find the four facts listed below the diagram in Figure 8-17.

For the "square" facts, there are only two facts in the family. For example, the family of facts relating 4, 4, and 16 consists of $4 \times 4 = 16$ and $16 \div 4 = 4$. When one of the factors is 0, there are only 3 facts in the family. For example, the fact family for 0, 3, 0 includes only three facts: $0 \times 3 = 0$, $3 \times 0 = 0$, and $0 \div 3 = 0$. Notice that because division by zero is undefined, fact families containing zero have three rather than four members.

Children need time and many rich experiences to make the concept of fact families a part of their thinking.

FIGURE 8-17 An Array for Finding Fact Families

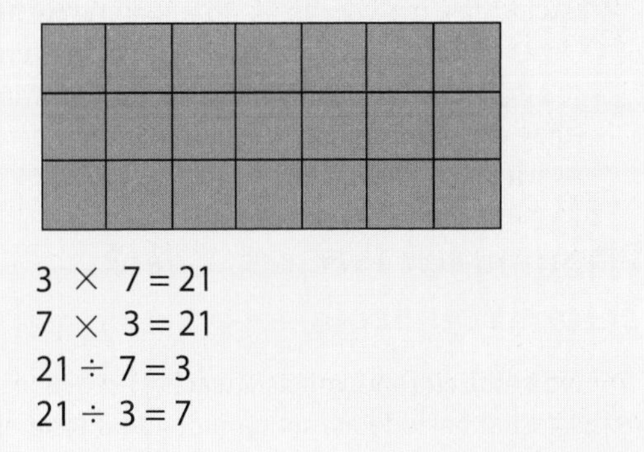

Activities such as Activity 8-6 may facilitate the process. For the first part of the activity, you may elect to construct arrays or groups on the overhead projector and have the children write sentences on paper, before children move on to working independently.

ACTIVITY 8-6 Fact Families

Procedure

1. For each picture below, write all the multiplication and division sentences that you can.

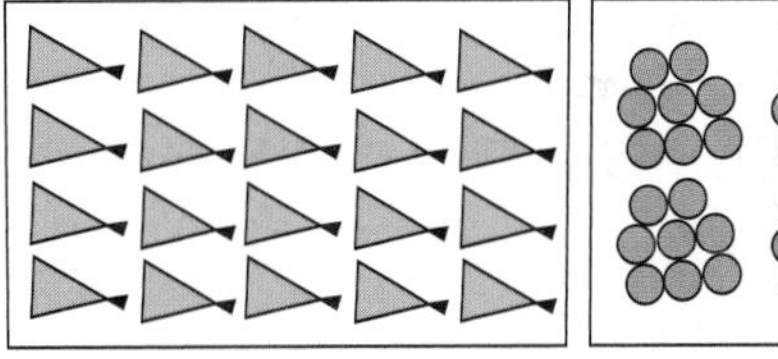
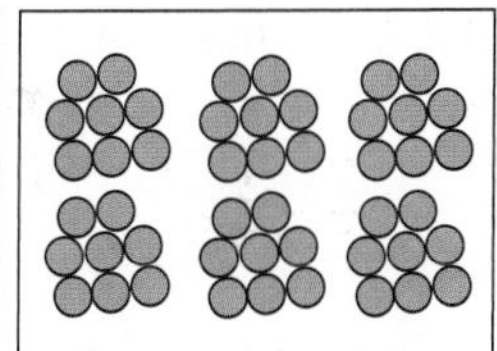

2. For each sentence, write 7 more related sentences (use the same numbers).

   $3 \times 6 = 18$ $35 = 5 \times 7$

3. Draw a picture to show each family in part 2.

Consolidating Activities for Drill and Practice

During the process of helping children develop meanings for the operations and learn basic facts, you should take time periodically to provide consolidation activities. These are intended primarily to improve speed and accuracy, but they also can sharpen understanding and provide another means of assessment for the teacher.

Effective consolidating activities have the following features:

- Activities are short and interesting.
- Activities are organized around sets of facts based on thinking strategies and fact families.

- Activities are self-checking.
- Activities include an approximately equal mix of facts children have and have not yet mastered.
- Children should understand the goals toward which they are working and visually see their progress toward those goals.

Planning for Progress Checks Before You Begin

To help children (and you as a teacher) see their progress in mastering basic facts, set up individual progress charts that children get to see at least once a week. Create a chart that includes a list of facts to be learned and provides spaces for children to record the number they got correct and the date. Children will need several columns for each fact family. Figure 8-18 shows a sample progress chart for addition facts. Tracking children's progress on fact learning assumes two things: (1) You have already spent considerable time developing concepts before engaging in timed tests, and (2) children are ready to be assessed with timed tests on number fact knowledge and retention.

Children should have individual charts showing their goals and progress. You should not use a class chart showing individual children's progress or lack thereof. Such charts cause great anxiety to many children, which reduces, rather than enhances, their progress.

Setting up Consolidating Activities

Effective consolidation of concepts and facts can occur through a variety of brief activities at the beginning of class. Some examples include the following:

- Write a set of single-digit numbers on the chalkboard in random order. Beside them write a rule such as "add 4."

  ADD 4: 3 6 4 9 2 7

  Ask specific children to use the rule on each number. Listen for cases in which a child hesitates.
- Prepare a set of cards with a single-digit number on each. Say, "Let's think about the number fifteen." Show a card and have children tell the other part of 15. For example, if you showed the card with 6 on it, children should respond with 9.
- Display an expression such as $7 + 8$ on the overhead projector. Have the children give you the sum and then tell how they know. For example, a child might respond, "Fifteen, because I know seven plus seven is fourteen, so seven plus eight is one more." (This type of exercise enables you and the children to focus on strategies, reasoning, and patterns rather than only on the answer.)

In Chapter 2, several categories of activities were suggested for consolidating or practice activities. Sample activities from some of the categories are described below

FIGURE 8-18 Addition Basic Facts Progress Chart for (insert name of child)

Facts with	Date	Number Correct	Date	Number Correct	Date	Number Correct
0						
1						
2						
3						
4						
5						
6						
7						
8						
9						

to illustrate that these activities do not have to be boring or routine but instead can be enjoyable and motivating for children.

Using Games

Games are a motivational and fun way for children to both develop and maintain mastery of basic facts. To play a bingo-type game, give the children a copy of the template from Figure 8-19 and ask them to randomly fill in the cells with numbers. For addition and subtraction facts, they should use only the numbers 0 through 18. Five of these numbers can be repeated to complete the 24 cells. The teacher or a child calls out basic addition and subtraction facts that can be generated from flash cards or slips of paper, or randomly selected by a computer. Otherwise, the

FIGURE 8-19 Bingo-Type Game for Mastering Basic Facts

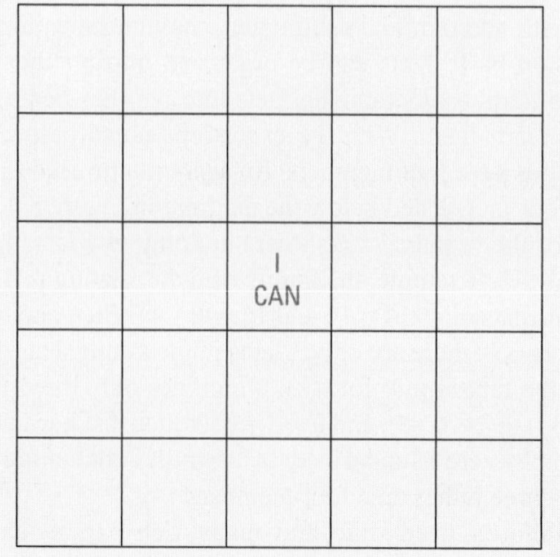

game is played similarly to bingo, and the winner is the first person to get five in a row, column, or diagonal.

The same strategy works for multiplication, except that the numbers on the cards should be randomly chosen from the set of possible products. There are 37 acceptable numbers from which to choose. This time there need be no repeats.

Another popular game for practicing basic facts is the *24 Game* (Suntex International). The object of the game is to make 24 using all four numbers on a card by adding, subtracting, multiplying, or dividing. For example, one card contains the numbers 1, 5, 7, and 8. One possible solution for this card is the following number sentence: $(8-5)\times(1+7)=24$. Several versions of the game are available as well that include addition and subtraction only, factors and multiples, fractions, and exponents. Kamii and Anderson (2003) describe how to make and use several different multiplication games.

Puzzles and Riddles

The sample riddle from Chapter 2 (What fish do you see at night?) can be made into a practice exercise. Because the teacher knows the answer (starfish) the teacher can assign numerical values to each of the letters in the answer, then make up a question that has that answer. Figure 8-20 is a sample riddle sheet that could be given to children for consolidating division facts. Note that a few extra questions are inserted so that children will be less likely to try to simply rearrange the letters into a sensible word. Some children might prefer to create their own riddle practice activities.

Using Novel Formats/Novel Ideas

Using formats different from what children have seen is another way to provide interesting consolidation activities. Create an array of numbers. Figure 8-21 is one example. Ask the children to circle as many pairs as they can of adjacent numbers that have a specified difference in a column, row, or diagonal. Two pairs of numbers with a difference of four have been circled in Figure 8-21. Create arrangements of numbers to help children practice different basic facts.

FIGURE 8-20 Sample Riddle Sheet

WHAT FISH DO YOU SEE AT NIGHT?

__ __ __ __ __ __ __ __
9 2 5 8 7 4 9 6

48 ÷ 8 = □ ⟶ H
7 ÷ 7 = □ ⟶ B
18 ÷ □ = 9 ⟶ T
15 ÷ 5 = □ ⟶ E
27 ÷ 3 = □ ⟶ S
35 ÷ 7 = □ ⟶ A
63 ÷ □ = 9 ⟶ F
16 ÷ 4 = □ ⟶ I
32 ÷ □ = 4 ⟶ R

FIGURE 8-21 Finding Pairs of Numbers with a Difference of Four

12	(15	11)	16
8	4	(3	7)
9	7	13	10
3	5	9	6

Another example of a novel idea is to set up a Math Fact Club, in which children who need practice with different groups of basic facts work together for extra practice. Set aside 10 to 15 minutes daily for practice, and make the practice fun, including games and puzzles. Such a club provides extra practice in a motivating setting.

Using Computer Software

Computer software is an engaging form of practice for many children, but it needs to be carefully evaluated by the teacher to ensure it provides the kind of practice children need and that it does so in a pedagogically sound way. *Math Blaster* (Knowledge Adventure) is a popular, fast-moving, arcade type of game that provides practice with the basic facts for all four operations. The teacher can control the level of difficulty and the teacher or children can generate their own problem sets. The objective is to launch a rocket corresponding to the correct answer to a problem that appears at the top of the screen. The game can be played at different speeds to encourage both accuracy and quick recall.

Millie's Math House (Riverdeep) has some interesting activities at the conceptual level that younger children would enjoy. Likewise, *KidsMath* (Freeware Palm) and *Treasure MathStorm* (The Learning Company) could be used with older children. Parts of these programs provide practice with basic facts in a game setting. Many other programs also contain good practice activities. See "Links to the Internet" at the end of this chapter for websites for practicing basic facts.

Conclusion

This chapter described a three-step approach to mastery of basic facts. This approach includes understanding the meaning of the operations, using thinking strategies to retrieve facts, and using consolidating activities for drill and practice. It is critical that children memorize the basic facts but this memorization must be based on an understanding of the operations and thinking strategies. Rushing memorization before this understanding is developed is a mistake that often comes back to haunt children and teachers.

CHAPTER

Sample Lesson

A Lesson on Understanding the Commutative Property

Grade level: First

Materials:
At least one manipulative, such as Unifix cubes, or assorted objects to count

Lesson objective: Students will use the commutative property of addition to add whole numbers and help them memorize the addition basic facts.

Standards link: Students use properties of addition (commutativity and associativity) to add whole numbers, and they create and use increasingly sophisticated strategies based on these properties (e.g., "making tens") to solve addition and subtraction problems involving basic facts. (NCTM *Curriculum Focal Points*, Grade One).

Launch: Display an addition basic facts number sentence, such as "5 + 3 = __." Ask students what the answer is, and how they know. Then model this problem with counters. Adjacent to this problem, write its commutative version: "3 + 5 = __." Ask students what the answer is, and how they know. Then model this problem with counters.

Ask students, "how are these problems alike?" Discuss the fact that both problems involve adding the same two numbers in a different order, and that the answers are the same. Ask, "Do you think that will be true when adding any two numbers? How might we investigate that?"

Explore: In pairs or individually, have students solve a set of problems consisting of the commutative pairs, such as 6 + 2 and 2 + 6. You may want to create a worksheet of problems for them to solve, or have students create their own problems and their commutative pairs. Students may use manipulatives if needed to solve the problems.

Summarize: Coming together as a whole class, select students to share the number sentences they solved and what they discovered. The goal is for students to make the generalization that the order in which numbers are added doesn't matter; the sum is still the same. Tell them that this relationship they discovered is very special in math. It's called the order property of addition, or the commutative property of addition, and says that the sum is the same regardless of the order in which the numbers (addends) were added.

FOLLOW-UP

Complete the following questions.

1. Consider difficulties students might have with this concept and this lesson. What modification could you make to avoid or minimize these issues? What modifications could you make for students with special needs?
2. How might a lesson on the commutative property of multiplication be similar to and different from this lesson, and why?

IN PRACTICE

Complete the following activities to include in your professional portfolio.

1. Design a nonbingo type of game that could be used to practice some of the basic facts.
2. Create two sets of folded cards as in Figure 8-10 to help children practice two different thinking strategies, and describe how you would use them.
3. Using (a) manipulative activities, (b) calculator explorations, or (c) both, write a lesson plan to help children understand the concept that division by zero is undefined.
4. Write a lesson plan to help children master one of the thinking strategies discussed in this chapter.

PEARSON myeducationlab The Power of Classroom Practice Now go to Topic 6: "Whole Number Operations" in the MyEducationLab (www.myeducationlab.com) for your course, where you can:

- Find learning outcomes for "Whole Number Operations" along with the national standards that connect to these outcomes.
- Apply and practice your understanding of the core teaching skills identified in the chapter with a Building Teaching Skills and Dispositions learning unit.
- Complete Assignments and Activities that can help you understand the chapter content more deeply.
- Complete *enVision MATH* Sample Curricula assignments that allow you to examine and work with chapters from *enVision MATH*, a K-6 mathematics program.
- Check your comprehension on the content covered in the chapter by going to the Study Plan in the Book-Specific Resources for your text. Here you will be able to take a chapter quiz, receive feedback on your answers, and then access Review, Practice, and Enrichment activities to enhance your understanding of chapter content.
- Go to the Book-Specific Resources for Chapter 6 to explore mathematical reasoning related to the chapter content in the Activities section.

LINKS TO THE INTERNET

A1 Math

http://www.aplusmath.com

Contains many different practice activities for operations, including games and electronic flash cards.

FunBrain

http://www.funbrain.com/kidscenter.html

The Math Brain Center contains several games for practicing operations.

RESOURCES FOR TEACHERS

Children's Literature

Tang, Greg (2002). *The Best of Times: Math Strategies That Multiply*. New York: Scholastic.

Tang, Greg (2004). *The Grapes of Math*. New York: Scholastic.

Tang, Greg (2003). *Math Appeal*. New York: Scholastic.

Tang, Greg (2005). *Math for All Seasons*. New York: Scholastic.

CHAPTER

9

Estimation and Computational Procedures for Whole Numbers

NCTM CONNECTING WITH THE STANDARDS

The National Council of Teachers of Mathematics (NCTM) emphasizes the importance of *computational fluency*, that is, "having efficient and accurate methods for computing" (NCTM, 2000, p. 152). Computational fluency includes children being able to choose computational methods flexibly, understand these methods, explain these methods, and produce answers accurately and efficiently. According to the NCTM, by the end of fifth grade, children should be computing fluently with whole numbers.

The NCTM Principles and Standards recommends that children should come to view algorithms as "tools for solving problems rather than as the goal of mathematics study" (NCTM, 2000, p. 144). Other tools that support computational fluency include being able to make reasonable estimates, perform mental computations, and connect mathematics to real-world situations—all of which help children judge the reasonableness of solutions.

The NCTM (2006) *Curriculum Focal Points* discusses learning multidigit computation in grades two through five. It states that second-grade students should "develop fluency with efficient procedures, including standard algorithms, for adding and subtracting whole numbers, understand why the procedures work (on the basis of place value and properties of operations), and use them to solve problems" as well as "select and apply appropriate methods to estimate sums and differences or calculate them mentally, depending on the context and numbers involved" (NCTM, 2006, p. 14). Similarly, fourth graders should "develop fluency with efficient procedures, including the standard algorithm, for multiplying whole numbers, understand why the procedures work (on the basis of place value and properties of operations), and use them to solve problems" (p. 16), while fifth graders should accomplish the same for dividing whole numbers. In addition, both fourth- and fifth-grade students should "select appropriate methods and apply them accurately to estimate products" (for grade 4) and "quotients" (for grade 5) "or calculate them mentally, depending on the context and numbers involved" (pp. 16–17).

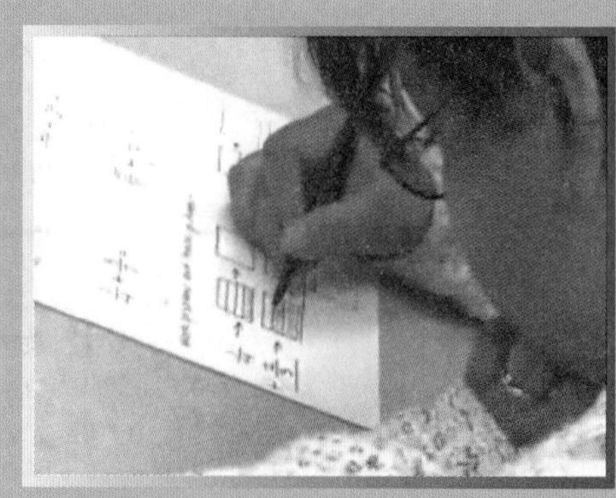

Developing Your Math Teaching Skills

When you have finished studying this chapter, you should be able to do the following:

- Explain how to use models to help children understand algorithms for each operation. Give an example of how to use a model for each operation.
- Describe a bridging algorithm for each operation and explain why bridging algorithms are important.
- Describe the importance of linking mental computation and computational estimation with paper-and-pencil computation and the use of calculators.

ASSESSING MATH UNDERSTANDING

In order to become familiar with the mathematics concepts and procedures discussed in this chapter, take a few minutes and complete the following *Chapter 9 Preassessment.* Solve each problem on your own. As you solve the problems, think about how you came up with your answer. After you solve the problems, think about how you can tell if your answers are reasonable. Then think about the possible misunderstandings or difficulties some elementary-school children might have when solving each problem. If you are able, administer this assessment to a child, and analyze his or her ability to solve these problems.

Solve each problem. Think about how you get your answer.

Part 1: Addition and Subtraction Problems

1. $\begin{array}{r} 28 \\ +34 \\ \hline \end{array}$ **2.** $\begin{array}{r} 63 \\ -24 \\ \hline \end{array}$

Part 2: Multiplication Problems

3. $\begin{array}{r} 24 \\ \times 3 \\ \hline \end{array}$ **4.** $\begin{array}{r} 67 \\ \times 25 \\ \hline \end{array}$

Part 3: Division Problems

5. $5\overline{)67}$ **6.** $6\overline{)739}$

Examining Classroom Practice

Not unlike when she teaches reading, Mary Holden often divides her fourth- and fifth-grade math classes into three groups. While one group independently solves problems on computers, another works on math games and puzzles. That allows Ms. Holden a chance to work with a third small group and talk about real-world applications of problem solving. She asks children to "choose a method," or several different methods, to solve the same problems.

> PEARSON myeducationlab The Power of Classroom Practice Go to the Video Examples section of Topic 7: "Estimation and Computation with Whole Numbers" in the MyEducationLab for your course to view the Annenberg clip "Choose a Method."

Ms. Holden begins by having children build structures using base-ten blocks. They then estimate each structure's value, based on price values assigned to each type of block, and determine the three children's structures that they think are worth the most. Ms. Holden records children's estimates in a chart (see below) on the chalkboard and asks children to explain the reasons for their estimates. For example, one boy notes that another child's building contains two blocks worth one dollar and several blocks that are worth a dime. A girl thinks that another building is worth the most since it includes a lot of blocks worth one dollar each. Next Ms. Holden has children determine the exact value of each building, which she also records in the chart. Finally, the children compare their estimates with the actual value of each building.

Child's Name	Estimated Value of Their Building	Actual Value of Their Building
Nataya	\$2.73	\$3.58
Aubrey	\$3.47	\$4.20
Andy	\$3.48	\$4.01

The group decides that their estimates are close enough to the actual values to be reasonable. Then Ms. Holden asks, "As a group, would you say that we are underestimators or overestimators?" The children overwhelmingly agree that they are underestimators. Ms. Holden recommends, "Sometimes you need to know that about yourself so the next time you estimate you know to aim a slight bit higher."

Ms. Holden asks one child to model 23¢ with base-ten blocks. Then she asks, "What if you had five times that much? How would you show that?" She asks the group to tell the child who is working with the base-ten blocks what to do. The group instructs the child to make 5 different piles with 23¢ in each pile, as shown below, getting an answer of \$1.15.

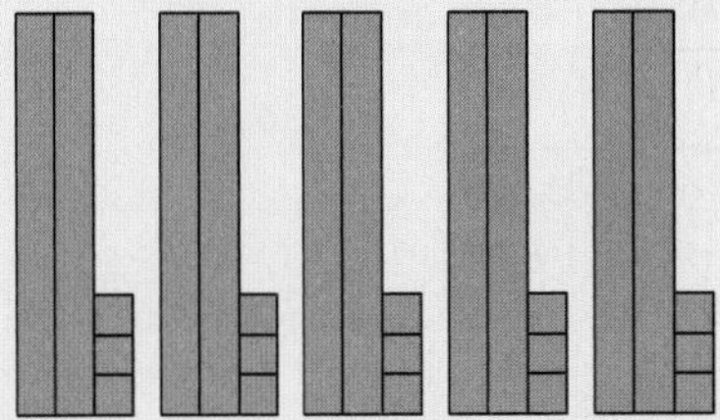

Ms. Holden then asks the children how to solve the problem using mental math. She asks the children, "What coin is 23¢ close to?" (a quarter), and then asks them to mentally calculate what 5 quarters are worth (\$1.25), and they determine that the answer they got with base-ten blocks for the problem 5 × 23¢ is probably correct. Ms. Holden realizes that asking children to consider how likely their answers are is a valuable mathematics skill. Judging the reasonableness of answers helps children decide if they are confident in their answers or if their answers need to be reexamined more closely.

To provide children with more practice, Ms. Holden poses another problem for the children to solve:

Slushies are on sale today for 29¢. You're going to buy one for everyone who sits at your table (4 children sit at each table). How much did you spend?

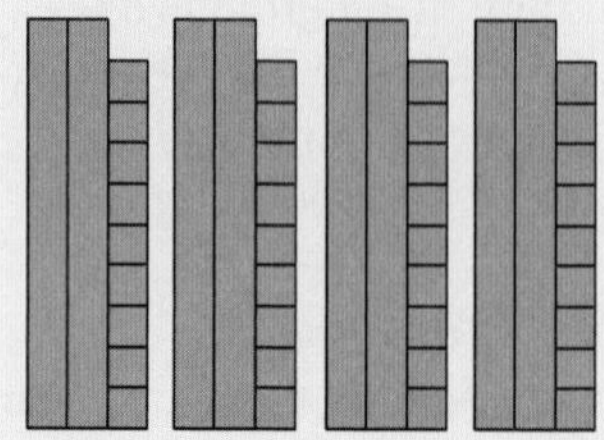

Ms. Holden encourages children to think about how to solve the problem in various ways, with some using base-ten blocks, some using mental math, some using calculators, and others using paper and pencil.

At the end of the lesson, Ms. Holden reflects on her view of teaching mathematics: "I think the best kind of math communication and the best kind of math writing come from feeling safe to express 'math thinking' in front of other people even if we express 'wrong turns.' Feeling safe to make a 'wrong turn' aloud in children's mathematical thinking is essential in classroom practice. Feeling safe to think out loud—safe from teacher or peer criticism—not only allows teachers to hear what children process as they think but also creates a natural setting for teachers to model out loud the logical steps one might take to work through a potential solution. Some children may not realize that all people do not arrive at a correct answer in the same way and that not all people always come up with correct answers."

Analyzing Assessment Results

Analyze these problems, starting first with the addition and subtraction problems. How did you (and/or the student you administered the assessment to) solve each of the following problems?

1. $\begin{array}{r} 28 \\ +34 \\ \hline \end{array}$ **2.** $\begin{array}{r} 63 \\ -24 \\ \hline \end{array}$

Discussion: These problems are fairly straightforward. Common errors with these problems tend to involve difficulties with regrouping. How did you think of the regrouping?

3. $\begin{array}{r} 24 \\ \times 3 \\ \hline \end{array}$ **4.** $\begin{array}{r} 67 \\ \times 25 \\ \hline \end{array}$

Discussion: These multiplication problems get more complicated, particularly problem 4. Common errors with these problems also tend to relate to regrouping. In other words, where do you write the answers? And these problems also tend to be a bit more difficult to determine the reasonableness of answers. Estimation becomes important here. For example, we could use rounding to estimate the answer to problem 4, rounding 67 to 70 and 25 to 30, and finding the product of 70 and 30, which is 2100. Note that the exact answer will be less than 2100, since we rounded both factors up.

5. $5\overline{)67}$ **6.** $6\overline{)739}$

Discussion: These division problems are even more complicated, particularly problem 6. Common errors again tend to relate to where to record the answers. This indicates that problem solvers often don't stop to think about whether their answers were reasonable. For example, we could use estimation to help us solve problem 6: 600 divided by 6 is 100, so 739 divided by 6 is going to be a little more than 100.

Take a minute and reflect on this assessment. What aspects of computation are particularly difficult for you and/or for the student you assessed? What do you want to learn more about in order to teach these concepts effectively?

Common Student Misunderstandings about or Difficulties with Computation:

- Difficulty in remembering the sequence of steps necessary to solve the problem.
- "This isn't supposed to make sense. Just follow the rules."
- Not using estimation to decide if their answer is reasonable.

Are there any other difficulties that children may have with computation? It is important to assess what children understand, and are still working on understanding, in order to plan instruction that meets their needs.

Building on Assessment Results

Think about what can be done to help strengthen children's understandings and minimize (and hopefully eradicate) their misunderstandings and difficulties with computation. Why do students have these difficulties? It's possible that students' previous learning experiences may have focused on memorizing a set of procedures rather than making sense of what they're doing (see comments in second bullet above).

To help children be successful with computation, you need to help them see that computation is just an extension of what they already know about adding, subtracting, multiplying, and dividing. The table below lists several common misunderstandings or difficulties and what you can do to help children with these misunderstandings.

IF students think that . . .	THEN help students . . .
it's hard to remember the sequence of steps necessary to solve the problem	see that the steps make sense. Make sure to build on what they already understand about the meaning of operations and place value.
this isn't supposed to make sense—just follow the rules	see that computation does make sense and that they'll get more correct answers if they can make sense of it.
once they get an answer, they're finished (not using estimation to decide if their answer is reasonable)	realize that it's easy to get a quick estimate to the problem and that estimating will help them know if their answer is correct.

What Is Computation?

A common but somewhat narrow view of *computation* is that it is a sequence of steps for producing an answer in standard form. These step-by-step procedures are commonly referred to as *algorithms*. This chapter discusses how to help children learn the standard algorithms, but first, three points need to be emphasized.

First, computation is much broader than using just the standard paper-and-pencil algorithms. It also includes estimation, mental computation, and the use of a calculator. Many times all that is needed is an estimate. Strategies for estimating an answer to a problem can be quite different from the standard paper-and-pencil procedures. Sometimes an exact answer may be more efficiently calculated using mental procedures than by using either a calculator or paper and pencil. Estimation and mental computation often make better use of good number sense and place-value concepts than are explicitly employed when using a paper-and-pencil algorithm.

The second point to emphasize is that children can and should be allowed to create and use their own algorithms. The following shows a child's procedure for subtracting:

$$\begin{array}{r} 63 \\ \underline{-24} \\ -\ 1 \\ \underline{+40} \\ 39 \end{array}$$

What is this child thinking? This child could be thinking as follows: "3 minus 4 is −1. 60 minus 20 is 40. −1 plus 40 is 39. Other interesting child-created computational procedures have been described in the professional literature (c.f., Harel & Behr, 1991; Madell, 1985). The important point to note here is that *there is no one best way to solve a problem*. Many different solution strategies can be used to solve the same problem. Rather than stressing that all children learn the same way to solve a problem, encourage children to use whatever method makes sense to them, sometimes creating their own ways to solve problems. The child's method above might not make sense to all (or most) children, but it made sense to that child, which makes it a powerful and effective method for him to use.

Third, *there is no* one *correct algorithm*. Just as we can alter our normal routine for getting ready for work in the morning, we can alter computational procedures depending on the situation. There are many algorithms that are efficient and meaningful. In fact, different computational algorithms are used in different parts of the world, even by different cultures within the same country. For this reason, and because of the mobile nature of our society, teachers should be familiar with some of the more common alternative algorithms. Some of the bridging algorithms described later in this chapter, such as the equal additions algorithm, are used in other countries.

Children should explore different algorithms for several reasons:

- Alternative algorithms may help children develop more flexible mathematical thinking and "number sense."
- Alternative algorithms may serve reinforcement, enrichment, and remedial objectives.
- Alternative algorithms provide variety in the mathematics class.
- Awareness of different algorithms demonstrates the fact that algorithms are inventions and can change.

NCTM Principles and Standards Link 9-1

Content Strand: Number and Operations

• Developing fluency requires a balance and connection between conceptual understanding and computational proficiency. On the one hand, computational methods that are over-practiced without understanding are often forgotten or remembered incorrectly. On the other hand, understanding without fluency can inhibit the problem-solving process. (NCTM, 2000, p. 35)

• Part of being able to compute fluently means making smart choices about which tools to use and when. Students should have experiences that help them learn to choose among mental computation, paper-and-pencil strategies, estimation, and calculator use. (NCTM, 2000, p. 36)

This needs to be communicated to children so that they will not develop a belief that there is only one way to perform a mathematical computation.

Helping children develop computational procedures does not center on helping them memorize a series of steps. Instead, it involves helping children understand and choose among computational methods and judge the reasonableness of their results, with a goal of having all children develop computational fluency. This chapter explains how you can help children attain this goal.

Estimation and Mental Computation

Estimation and mental computation play such a pervasive role in out-of-school settings that children must have a wide variety of experiences with these skills. More than 80% of out-of-school problem-solving situations involve mental computation and estimation (Reys & Reys, 1986). These processes are often used together but involve quite different ideas. Mental computation involves finding an *exact answer* without the aid of paper and pencil, calculators, or any other device. Estimation involves finding an *approximate answer*. Estimation may also employ mental computation, but the end result is an approximate answer rather than an exact answer.

In practice, estimation and mental computation should not be taught in isolation but should be incorporated into the teaching of paper-and-pencil computation and other topics. For example, if children are solving the following problem, the first question you might ask them is "*About* how many more children are enrolled at Rosa Parks Elementary than Kennedy Elementary?"

There are 826 children enrolled at Rosa Parks Elementary School and 589 children enrolled at Kennedy Elementary School. How many more children are enrolled at Rosa Parks than at Kennedy?

You can help children understand the importance of estimation and mental computation by not only asking for exact answers but by also asking for estimates, as in the example above.

Estimation and mental computation skills should be developed along with paper-and-pencil computation because they help children spot unreasonable results. They also contribute to an understanding of the paper-and-pencil procedures and provide a fertile source for computational creativity on the part of children.

Mental Computation

Mental computation has had a turbulent history with respect to curricular emphasis. Around the turn of the 20th century, mental computation was advocated as a form of mental discipline. As this theory fell into disfavor, the emphasis on mental computation decreased. The recent renewal of interest is based on the way in which mental computation can enhance an understanding of numeration, number properties, and operations and promote problem solving and flexible thinking (Reys, 1985; Reys & Reys, 1990).

If children are encouraged to compute mentally, they will develop their own strategies and, in the process, develop good number sense. Good number sense helps students use strategies effectively. Children should be asked, on occasion, to explain to you or to the class how they did the computation.

It is important for children to learn to solve problems such as $80 + 60$ through mental computation. Children can talk about this as 6 *tens* joined to 8 *tens*, which makes 14 *tens*. From their numeration experiences, they will recognize this as 140.

In addition, mental computation is often employed even when a calculator is used. For example, when adding 350, 785, 256, and 150, individuals with good number sense will mentally combine 350 and 150 and enter 500 into the calculator before entering the other numbers (Sowder, 1990).

Estimation

Researchers have investigated a variety of factors related to computational estimation. Reys (1986) describes five strategies for computational estimation: front-end, rounding, clustering, compatible numbers, and special numbers. Each of these can be used to some extent by children in the elementary grades, whereas older children can apply them with greater sophistication. Each strategy will be described in greater detail later in this chapter.

NCTM NUMBER AND OPERATIONS STANDARDS AND EXPECTATIONS ADDRESSED IN THIS CHAPTER		
Instructional programs from Pre-K–12 should enable all students to—	**In Prekindergarten through grade 2 all students should—** (NCTM, 2000, p. 78)	**In grades 3–5 all students should—** (NCTM, 2000, p. 148)
• compute fluently and make reasonable estimates.	• develop and use strategies for whole-number computations, with a focus on addition and subtraction. • use a variety of methods and tools to compute, including objects, mental computation, estimation, paper and pencil, and calculators.	• develop fluency with basic number combinations for multiplication and division and use these combinations to mentally compute related problems, such as 30×50. • develop fluency in adding, subtracting, multiplying, and dividing whole numbers. • develop and use strategies to estimate the results of whole-number computations and to judge the reasonableness of such results. • select appropriate methods and tools for computing with whole numbers from among mental computation, estimation, calculators, and paper and pencil according to the context and nature of the computation and use the selected method or tools.

Front-end strategy. The *front-end strategy* focuses on the left-most or highest place-value digits. For example, children using this strategy would estimate the sum of $267 + 521$ by adding the front-end digits, 2 and 5, and estimating 700 for the sum.

Rounding strategy. Rounding is a familiar strategy to most adults. Children using the rounding strategy to estimate the problem above would round 267 to 300 and 521 to 500 and find the sum of 800.

Clustering strategy. The clustering strategy is used when a set of numbers is close to each other in value. For example, to estimate the sum of $17 + 29 + 23$, one could note that $17 + 23$ is 40, so the sum is close to $40 + 29$, so it's about 70.

Compatible numbers strategy. When using the compatible numbers strategy, children adjust the numbers so that they are easier to work with. For example, using compatible numbers in division involves altering the divisor, the dividend, or both so that they are easy to work with mentally. For example, to estimate the answer to $32 \div 3$ one could note that 33 is close to 32 and is divisible by 3, so then would solve $33 \div 3$, which is 11.

Special numbers strategy. The special numbers strategy involves looking for numbers that are close to "special" values that are easy to work with, such as one-half or powers of ten. For example, to estimate the answer to 53% of 125, one could note that 53% is close to $\frac{1}{2}$, and $\frac{1}{2}$ of 125 is about 60.

Paper-and-Pencil Computation

How are U.S. children doing on paper-and-pencil computation? The most recent National Assessment of Educational Progress (NAEP) assessment, conducted in 2007 noted fairly strong performance of fourth and eighth graders on simple numeric whole-number problems and one-step word problems, but they do not do as well on computation problems involving more complex reasoning. According to Warfield & Meier (2007), "The inability of students to deal successfully with items requiring complex reasoning is a concern" (p. 65). Children did best on one-step problems. For example, on a problem that involved adding two three-digit numbers with regrouping, at least 89% of the fourth- and eighth-graders were able to choose the correct sum. However, only 34% of the fourth-graders were able to subtract a six-digit number from a seven-digit number with regrouping. Similar trends were noted for multiplication and division.

Results on the NAEP show children have difficulties with regrouping in subtraction, with interpreting the meaning of remainders in division, with multistep multiplication and division problems, as well as with justifying and explaining their work. These findings point to the need for a continued emphasis in the mathematics classroom on teaching for meaning and on reasoning.

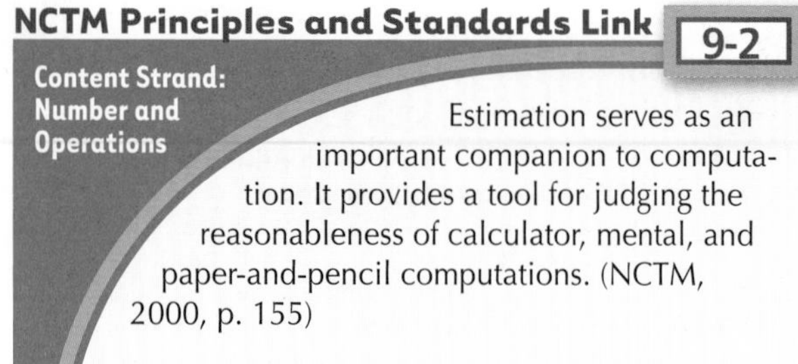
NCTM Principles and Standards Link 9-2

Content Strand: Number and Operations

Estimation serves as an important companion to computation. It provides a tool for judging the reasonableness of calculator, mental, and paper-and-pencil computations. (NCTM, 2000, p. 155)

An Instructional Philosophy

It is important for children to know how to compute using paper and pencil. However, once children can complete with understanding and reasonable skill exercises such as those shown later in this section, they will not learn anything new by working with larger numbers or by doing many exercises.

Computational procedures will continue to be an essential component of the elementary school program, but the many hours children currently spend doing long, complex calculations are essentially wasted. Some of the time saved by not having children do tedious paper-and-pencil computation should be added to the time spent developing an understanding of the operations and computational procedures through concrete manipulations and simple examples such as those given earlier. Time also needs to be allocated for children to explain and write about the procedures they use.

Usiskin (1998) lists several reasons for having and using algorithms as well as the dangers that are inherent in all algorithms. Reasons for having and using algorithms include (1) power, (2) reliability, (3) accuracy, and (4) speed. Dangers include (1) blind acceptance of results, (2) overzealous application of algorithms, (3) a belief that algorithms train the mind, and (4) helplessness if the technology for the algorithm is not available. Usiskin notes that both paper-and-pencil algorithms and calculator or computer algorithms require access to some piece of equipment or technology.

The instructional model for developing mathematics understanding described in Chapter 7 (see page 129 emphasized connecting the real world and the world of mathematical symbols when learning computational procedures. That is, computation should emerge from the need to solve some problem.

If children have had adequate experiences with concrete and pictorial models when solving simple computational problems, they will understand the concept of the operations and can focus on meaningful procedures to find answers to problems with larger numbers. Our recommended approach is to allow children ample time and opportunity to develop computational procedures for themselves. Initially, problems should be solved with manipulatives. Children should then be encouraged to record, *in their own way*, the processes they used. Children's *verbal descriptions* of the processes provide them with a connection between concrete and symbolic procedures (Sawada, 1985; Stanic & McKillip, 1989). Children can then begin to translate their recording into a more symbolic form, but still in their own way. Over time, the symbolic recording can become more concise, eventually resulting for most children in the standard algorithm. As we emphasized earlier, this process may differ in different countries or regions of a country.

Prerequisites

Before children can be expected to develop paper-and-pencil computational procedures, they should demonstrate a conceptual understanding of the operations of addition, subtraction, multiplication, and division by recognizing different contexts that require the operations to resolve a problem (NCTM, 1989).

Knowledge of *some* basic facts is required before children begin computation with larger numbers. Strategies for knowing the basic facts continue to be developed and practiced as children work at solving problems with larger numbers. Second-graders, for example, usually do not know all the basic facts for addition and subtraction, but they can still solve some two-digit problems. The final objective, however, for learning paper-and-pencil procedures is for children to be able to use them efficiently without the use of models. Achievement of this objective does require a mastery of the basic facts.

Children need to have a good understanding of the place-value numeration system because each algorithm is based on principles of the numeration system. In particular, children need to be able to group ones into tens, tens into hundreds, and so on; and they need to be able to break hundreds into tens, tens into ones, and so on.

An understanding of some mathematical properties of whole numbers learned during the concepts and basic facts stages of instruction, described in Chapters 7 and 8, can help children with computational procedures. In particular, the *commutative law* and the *distributive property* of multiplication over addition can facilitate computation. For example, the exercise shown in Figure 9-1(a) would be easier to work if the commutative law was applied, as in Figure 9-1(b).

Understanding the distributive property also is a prerequisite to efficient algorithm development. An exercise such as 8×37 can be reorganized mentally or on paper to $(8 \times 30) + (8 \times 7)$ or $8\,(30 + 7)$. The extension fact, 8×30,

FIGURE 9-1 Using the Commutative Property to Make a Problem Easier to Solve

(a) $\begin{array}{r} 40 \\ \times\ 27 \\ \hline \end{array}$ (b) $\begin{array}{r} 27 \\ \times\ 40 \\ \hline \end{array}$

is relatively easy to determine mentally and 8×7 is a known basic fact. The product, then, is the sum of 240 and 56. Notice that expanded notation is included in the use of the distributive property $(37 = 30 + 7)$.

Estimation may also be considered a prerequisite to engaging children in computation. Rather, what is even more essential is an *attitude* of estimation. Children should approach computation with an attitude that estimation is a legitimate mathematical tool.

Important Considerations When Teaching Computational Procedures

When teaching computational procedures to children, focusing on each of the four number operations is natural. When engaging children in each operation, the following components are important to keep in mind:

- Pose story problems set in real-world contexts. Problems are more meaningful, and children are better able to determine the reasonableness of their solutions, when instruction begins with problems that are based in familiar, real-world contexts.
- Use models for computation. Concrete models, such as base-ten blocks, help children visualize problems.
- Use estimation and mental computation. These processes help children determine the reasonableness of their solutions.
- Develop bridging algorithms to connect problems, models, estimation, and symbols. Bridging algorithms help children connect manipulative materials with symbols in order to make sense of the symbolic representation. Several bridging algorithms are available to help children connect their existing understandings.
- Develop the traditional algorithm. The traditional algorithm can be developed meaningfully through the use of language and models.
- Examine children's work. You can learn a great deal about children's understandings by examining their work. This analysis will help you assess students' learning and plan instruction.
- Determine the reasonableness of solutions. Many approaches, including estimation and checking answers, are important final steps in solving computation problems.

Each of these considerations is an important component of instruction aimed at helping all students develop computational fluency. It is also important to consider children's language and their understanding of place value and help them connect these understandings to their computational work.

A note about models for computation. The first work with computation should be with *proportional* materials, such as the base-ten blocks. *Nonproportional* materials should be used only when children can easily solve problems with proportional materials. (Refer to Chapter 6 for a discussion of proportional and nonproportional place-value materials.) If children can transfer the execution of a computation from proportional to nonproportional materials, then they probably have a good understanding of the process. Once children have explored both types of materials, they will freely move back and forth from proportional to nonproportional materials.

A note about language. As indicated in Chapter 7, children should continue to use their own, less formal language to describe computational processes. During work with computation, the teacher should use mathematical language associated with each operation so that children will develop more technical language. Children should be allowed to use informal language for some time while they are learning precise mathematical terminology.

In addition, place-value language can help children make sense of computation. For example, in the problem 38 + 59, when adding the digits in the tens column, it is preferable to say "30 + 50 equals 80" rather than "3 + 5 equals 8," which ignores the place value of the 3 and the 5.

A note about the role of calculators in computation. Checking computation can be done on the calculator. However, this is a *poor* use of time and of the calculator. The calculator should be used in a more substantive way to help children think about the algorithms, develop estimation skills, and solve computational problems. Activity 9-1 involves finding patterns related to multiplication. Activity 9-2 can be used to help children think about the multiplication and division algorithms, and Activity 9-3 suggests one way the calculator can be used to enhance estimation skills.

ACTIVITY 9-1 Patterns

Materials
Calculator

Procedure

1. Choose some two-digit numbers. Use your calculator to multiply each by 99. Record and compare the results. When you think you see a pattern or a relationship, use it to predict some other results. Write a statement describing your pattern.
2. Choose only 2 three-digit numbers. Multiply each by 999. Record and examine the results. Predict the results of multiplying 2 other three-digit numbers by 999.

Write statements that tell how this pattern is

- The same as the one for two-digit numbers $\times$ 99.
- Different from the two-digit $\times$ 99 pattern.

ACTIVITY 9-2 Missing Numbers

Materials
Calculator

Procedure

1. Estimate first, then use your calculator to help you find the missing numbers.

65 R2 over 6)□□□   □□ over 7)2□3   109 R4 over □□)3819

2. Use only 5, 7, 8, and 9 to make
   - The largest possible product.

     □□□
     × □

   - The smallest possible product.

     □□□
     × □

3. Find the missing numbers. All four partial products are shown.

```
    □ 5
 ×  3 □
 ------
    □□
  1 0 0
  1 □ 0
□□□□
□□□□
```

ACTIVITY 9-3 Estimation

Materials
Calculator

Procedure
Play with a partner. Each player needs a calculator.

1. Agree on a target number. Circle it.

   76   1111   410   309
   107   2345   731
   96   296

2. Enter any number into your calculator.
3. Press the × key.
4. Within 5 seconds enter another number that you think will give you a product close to the target number. Then press the = key.

   Example: Target = 107
   Entered: 38 ×
   then 3 =
   Display shows 114
5. The person closest to the target number wins the round.
6. Play 10 rounds. Repeat the procedure using the ÷ key.

A note about childrens thinking. In the process of doing paper-and-pencil computation, children will sometimes make errors. Many errors children make are systematic and may reveal children's misunderstandings or limited understandings of computational algorithms. Discovering error patterns or children's lack of understanding is why examining children's work is one of the important roles you will play in the math classroom.

Ashlock (2010) notes that errors can be helpful in the process of learning if they are used to analyze patterns of errors. Error-pattern analysis gives you information that can be used to modify instruction to meet children's needs.

According to Ashlock (2010), "We need to examine each student's paper diagnostically—looking for patterns, hypothesizing possible causes, and verifying our ideas. As we learn about each student we will find that a student's paper is sometimes a problem or puzzle to be solved" (p. 15). Children's errors often are a result of overgeneralizing or making generalizations based on limited data. Children's thinking and examples of children's common error patterns are discussed throughout this chapter for each operation, along with suggestions for helping children who make such errors.

Addition

Posing Story Problems Set in Real-World Contexts

You should begin your addition instruction by asking children to solve problems situated in real-world settings. This will help children make sense of their work and be better able to judge the reasonableness of their answers. When solving addition problems that are placed in real-world settings, terms such as *joined to* are meaningful to children. (See Chapter 7 for more on realistic problems for addition.) For example, you could begin instruction by posing a problem such as the following:

On the last grade 3 field trip, there were 28 children on one bus and 34 children on the other bus. How many children went on the field trip?

Note that in the past it was common to introduce the addition algorithm with computation that did not require children to regroup. However, if one begins instruction using realistic problems, some solutions will require renaming, others will not. If children have been doing computation in which no regrouping is involved and then encounter a problem for which regrouping is needed (or vice versa), they will notice the difference,

FIGURE 9-2 Regrouping Base-Ten Blocks When Solving a Problem

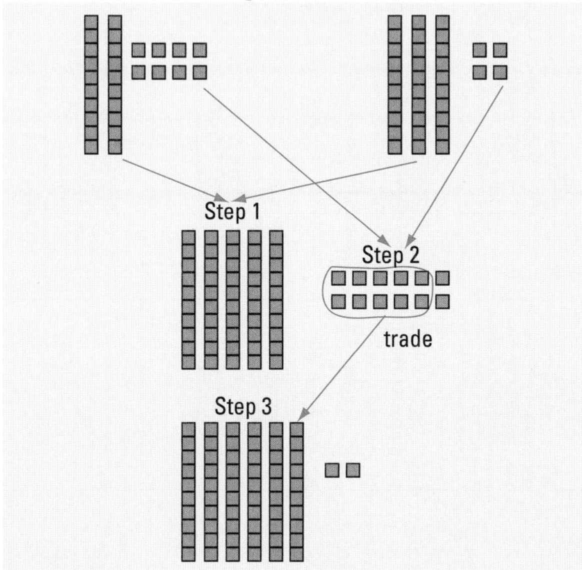

grapple with it, and resolve it with proper guidance from the teacher.

The following section describes how to guide children in the use of models to solve an addition problem.

> myeducationlab The Power of Classroom Practice — Go to the Assignments and Activities section of Topic 7: "Estimation and Computation with Whole Numbers" in the MyEducationLab for your course and complete the activity "Equations" to see the strategies students use to solve equations.

Using Models for Computation

If necessary, suggest that children use the base-ten blocks to solve the problem described in the previous section. They will likely first group the tens as shown in Figure 9-2, then combine the ones. Finally, they will trade 10 ones for 1 ten to get 6 tens and 2 ones; that is, children naturally want to group the larger pieces first (Lee, 1991). This left-to-right process is discussed later in this chapter.

Using the blocks (without recording), children can easily extend this process to include numbers in the hundreds, provided they have had relevant numeration experiences. In fact, children gain satisfaction from working with larger numbers. They should be exposed to working with larger numbers because of a need to solve relevant real-life problems that typically involve larger quantities. This is also a good setting in which to encourage estimation. Children could use their previous experience with extension facts and say, "There are at least 20 plus 30, or 50, children on the field trip."

A transition to the recording phase could be made by giving children an organizational mat, as described in Chapter 6 on page 108, on which they could do their manipulations. Children may need some initial guidance in how to use each space. The second column in Figure 9-3 illustrates how this mat might be used for the field trip problem. At this stage, children would do only the steps illustrated in the second column.

Place-value language. Encourage children to use place-value language as they describe their manipulations. For example, "2 tens and 3 tens make 5 tens" and "8 ones plus 4 ones is 12 ones." This will help them to focus on the value of the digits and prepare them for multiplication and division computation in which the use of place-value language is more critical.

Using Estimation and Mental Computation

As children are solving problems, you should ask questions that will help them connect the meaning of the problem with the solutions they are obtaining. For example, in the field trip problem, a teacher could ask questions such as "Will the answer be more than or less than 100? Why?" and "What will the answer be *close to* (60)?"

Strategies for mental computation. Mental computation often is done by looking for *compatible* (or "friendly") *numbers*. The following examples indicate two ways in which children might mentally add 16 + 11 + 24 + 35.

16 + 11 + 24 + 35	16 + 11 + 24 + 35
40 + 35 = 75	35 + 35 = 70
75 + 11 = 86	70 + 16 = 86

Strategies for computational estimation

Using the front-end strategy for addition. The front-end strategy is probably the easiest for younger children to use. This strategy can be introduced when children know some basic facts and the meaning of larger numbers. This strategy focuses on the left-most or highest place-value digits. At the most basic level, children would estimate the sum of 267 + 521 by adding the front-end digits, 2 and 5, and estimating 700 for the sum. Later, children will look at the remaining digits and adjust their estimate by thinking "67 and 21 is nearly one more hundred so I'll estimate 800."

For elementary and middle school children, the front-end estimation strategy has one of its most relevant applications in money settings.

Brad wants to buy some school supplies. The items he has picked out cost $1.29, $3.59, and $1.99. About how much will Brad spend?

Because children naturally want to group the dollars first, the front-end strategy is a natural one to use in this

FIGURE 9-3 Concrete and Symbolic Representations for Solving the Field Trip Problem

Problem/Steps	Concrete Representation	Symbolic Representation
28 on first bus. 34 on second bus. How many in all?	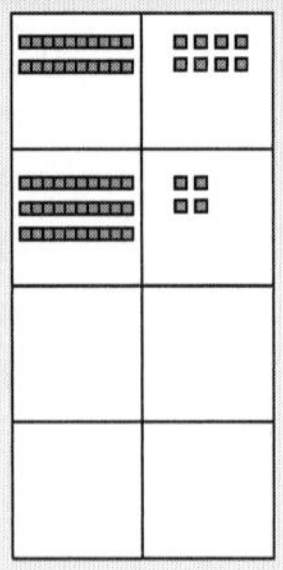	2 8 + 3 4
Join the tens and record.	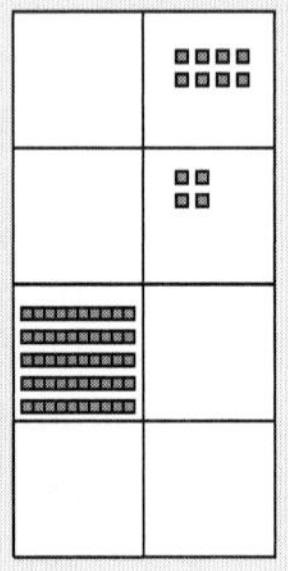	2 8 + 3 4 5 0
Join the ones, trade, and record.	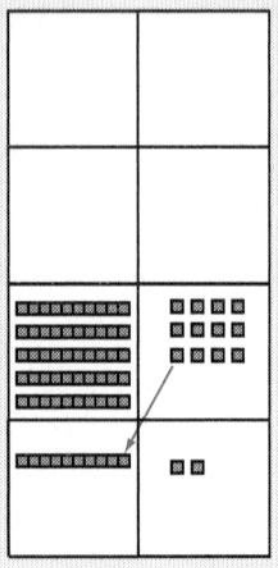	2 8 + 3 4 5 0 1 2
Join the tens, join the ones, and record.	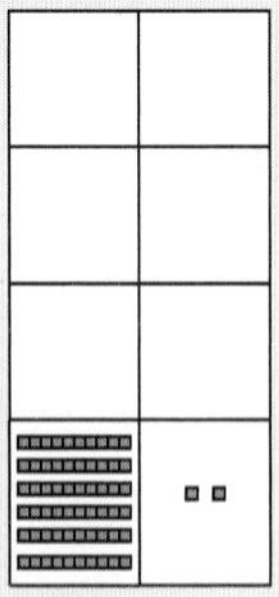	2 8 + 3 4 5 0 1 2 6 2

setting. Some children will look only at the dollar amounts and estimate about \$5. Others will adjust this step because they recognize that \$0.99 is almost another dollar and \$0.29 + \$0.59 is also close to another dollar. They would estimate \$5 + \$1 + \$1 or \$7.

Children will soon recognize that the front-end strategy with whole numbers always results in an estimate that is *less than or equal to* the actual product. This level of estimation is adequate for most purposes for most elementary school children. Older children will be able to add a second-level front-end adjustment to their original estimate.

Using the rounding strategy for addition. Rounding is a skill that is often introduced in the third or fourth grade, usually in the context of numeration. Computing mentally or using paper and pencil with rounded numbers is another frequently used estimation strategy. In the previous example of 267 + 521, children might round to the nearest hundred. Their estimate of the sum, then, would be 300 + 500, or 800. In the money problem, children could round to the nearest whole dollar. Their estimate would then be \$1 + \$4 + \$2 or \$7. Older children, recognizing whether rounding results in an overestimate or an underestimate, may make an adjustment similar to that used in the front-end approach.

Rounding can be made concrete by using a number line; marking multiples of 10, 100, or whatever place-value position one wants to round to; and having children note which of two adjacent multiples a given number is closest to. Bohan and Shawaker (1994) also suggest using stacks of chips for the same purpose.

Is 53 closer to 50 or 60? How do you know?

30 40 50 60 70 80

Using the clustering strategy for addition. The clustering strategy is used when the numbers in a set are close to each other in value.

Juan surveyed each room in his school. He prepared this table for his group. About how many children are in Juan's school?

Room 1	*29*	*Room 5*	*28*
Room 2	*32*	*Room 6*	*29*
Room 3	*30*	*Room 7*	*31*
Room 4	*34*	*Room 8*	*27*

With guidance, children can observe that all the numbers are close to 30, so a good estimate would be 8 × 30, or 240. Children who have worked with the concept of "average" will recognize that 30 is an estimate of the average number of children in each room.

Using the compatible numbers strategy for addition. When using the compatible numbers strategy, children adjust the numbers so that they are easier to work with. A form of the compatible numbers strategy can be used in addition when there are multiple addends, as in the following example.

Six children kept a record of how many minutes of television they watched on Monday. Altogether, about how many minutes did the children watch television?

Heather	*25*	*Trevor*	*60*
Roberta	*44*	*Gwen*	*57*
Sam	*35*	*Ernesto*	*80*

Given the preceding addition exercise, children could use the compatible numbers strategy to look for groups of 100. They would estimate that together the children watched about 300 minutes of television.

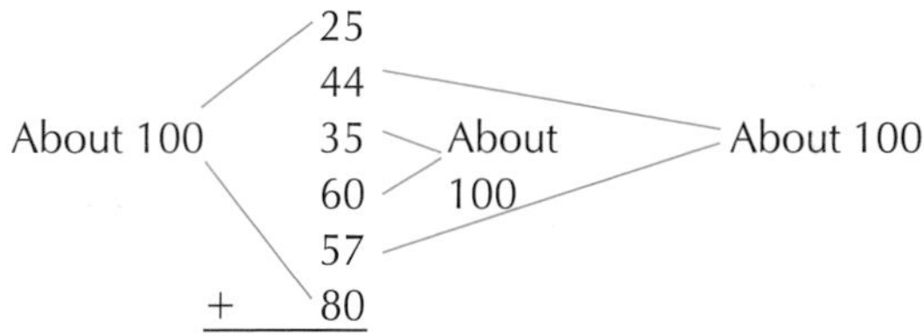

Developing Bridging Algorithms to Connect Problems, Models, Estimation, and Symbols

Once children feel confident using the base-ten blocks to add two numbers and can estimate sums, the next step is to begin keeping a record of what was done. This recording will go through a series of refinements and culminate in a concise and efficient symbolic procedure.

Children might begin by using an organizational mat for doing the manipulations with the blocks and a sheet of paper for recording. To avoid skipping steps in the recording, children could work in pairs: one recording, the other manipulating. Figure 9-4 illustrates each step in the process and the corresponding record. Note that the series is based on the assumption that children naturally work from left to right (Lee, 1991). This method is referred to as the *partial sums algorithm* because children record each partial sum individually before combining the partial sums to find the sum. Figure 9-4 shows two addition problems solved using this algorithm.

FIGURE 9-4 Symbolic Representation When Solving Problems from Left to Right

```
  28       367
 +34      + 85
 ---      ----
  50       300
  12       140
 ---        12
  62      ----
           452
```

Some educators recommend that once recording begins, children should be told to work right to left. However, this adds an additional component to an already big and important step. It makes more sense to allow children to be as natural as possible and match paper-and-pencil work as closely as possible to the steps used in the concrete mode: Besides, working right to left may not alter the notation used in the last row of Figure 9-4, only some of the intermediate steps.

Other activities, such as working with money—where people almost always group the largest denomination first and proceed to the smallest denomination (Lee, 1991)—reinforce left-to-right procedures. In fact, the only reason to add right to left is when several multidigit numbers need to be added. Even then the left-to-right procedure works well, but the recording can become a little "messy." Keep in mind that these computations should be done on a calculator.

Developing the Traditional Algorithm

You can help children connect the partial sums algorithm to the traditional (or compact) algorithm for addition. For example, consider the partial sums algorithm as shown in the previous section. Refer back to the third-grade field trip problem posed on page 172. Using the partial sums algorithm shown below, you could discuss with children the meaning of the 12, which is the total of the digits in the ones place, and ask if they can think of any other way to record the 12. If no children suggest the idea of recording the 1 ten above the first addend (28), you could demonstrate and explain (see the following figure). It is very important to discuss with the children the meaning of the one ten that was regrouped and written above the first addend, so that this method becomes a meaningful procedure.

	2	8
	3	4
	1	2
	5	0
	6	2

	$\overset{1}{2}$	8
	3	4
	5	2

Expanded notation is another type of transitional step. Children might compute the answer to the field trip problem like this:

2 tens and 8 ones
+ 3 tens and 4 ones
5 tens and 12 ones or
6 tens and 2 ones or
62

Whatever approach is encouraged, it is important to remember that children will shorten the steps on their own. Some children need more transitional steps than others, and some need to spend a longer time at some steps than other children. You should allow children to discover their own shortcuts. Do not rush them into using the standard algorithm.

When children feel competent in working through computations using two-digit numbers, they should be invited to solve problems with larger numbers. The organizational mat, described in Chapter 6, could be extended to four columns (thousands through units).

It is the number and type of regroupings more than the magnitude of the numbers that the teacher needs to consider when planning instruction. The following three problems are about the same level of difficulty and could be worked on at the same time. In practice, however, we would not normally expect second graders to do the last two problems, despite the fact that they have learned all the skills they need to know to solve them.

$$\begin{array}{r} 32 \\ +\ 147 \\ \hline \end{array} \qquad \begin{array}{r} 564 \\ +\ 1{,}231 \\ \hline \end{array} \qquad \begin{array}{r} 8{,}704 \\ +\ 11{,}263 \\ \hline \end{array}$$

Problems with two and three regroupings are more difficult for children. Again, we stress the importance of adequate preparation in the form of concrete numeration experiences and addition in a concrete mode. Such experiences will minimize the difficulty children will have with multiple regroupings.

Activity 9-4 will stimulate discussion and provide experience with estimation, addition computation, and the calculator. Children should work in a group or with a partner.

ACTIVITY 9-4 Calculator Game (Addition)

Materials

Calculator for each student

Procedure

1. One person writes four numbers on paper for all others to see.
2. Without the others seeing, add three of the numbers on your calculator.
3. Write the sum on paper for the others to see.
4. The others decide, by estimation, which one of the four numbers was not used and then check their guesses on their calculators.
5. Take turns doing the activity several more times.

Examining Student Work

Figures 9-5 and 9-6 contain samples of children's work in practicing adding whole numbers: Look closely at the work and try to determine the errors the children are making. Why might they be making these errors? If you were their teacher, what might you do to help them?

FIGURE 9-5 Addition Error Pattern 1

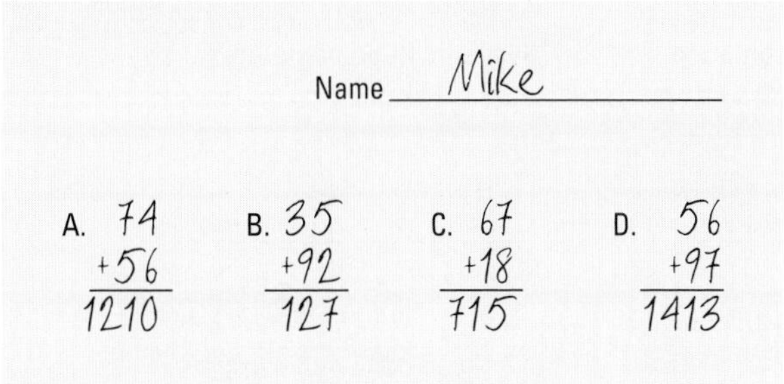

Name Mike

A.	B.	C.	D.
74	35	67	56
+56	+92	+18	+97
1210	127	715	1413

Source: Error Patterns in Computation 8/e by Ashlock, © 2010, p. 19. Reprinted by permission of Pearson Education, Inc., Upper Saddle River, NJ.

FIGURE 9-6 Addition Error Pattern 2

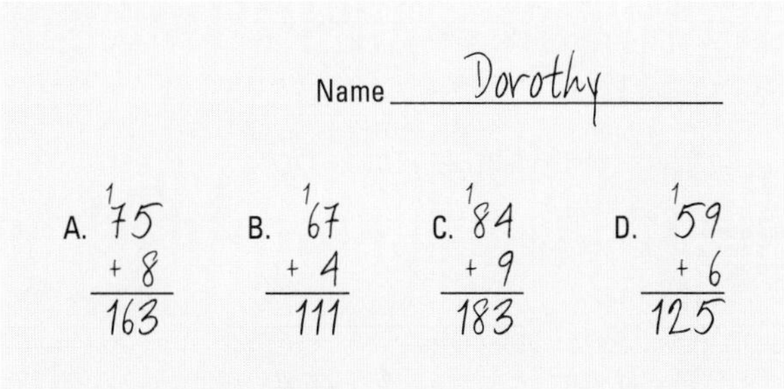

Name Dorothy

A.	B.	C.	D.
1	1	1	1
75	67	84	59
+ 8	+ 4	+ 9	+ 6
163	111	183	125

Source: Error Patterns in Computation 8/e by Ashlock, © 2010, p. 21. Reprinted by permission of Pearson Education, Inc., Upper Saddle River, NJ.

Description of addition error pattern 1. In Figure 9-5, Mike is not regrouping. When he gets a sum greater than 9, he simply records it in the answer rather than regrouping.

How a teacher might help. You could strengthen Mike's understanding of place value by using a manipulative material for place value, such as base-ten blocks or bundles of 10 sticks and individual sticks. Emphasize the process of regrouping when there are more than 9 ones. The grouping activities discussed in Chapter 6 could help Mike understand the process of regrouping.

Description of addition error pattern 2. In Figure 9-6, Dorothy is adding the second addend to both the digit in the ones column and the digit in the tens column of the first addend. This error commonly appears after children have learned multiplication with one-digit multipliers, such as 23 × 4.

How a teacher might help. You could encourage Dorothy to estimate the result of each problem. For example, in problems A through D, the number being added is less than 10, so the sum should be about 10 more than the first addend. Her answers are much larger.

Determining the Reasonableness of Solutions

After children finish solving problems, ask questions to help them evaluate the reasonableness of the solutions they found. For example, in the field trip problem, ask questions such as "Does it make sense that the answer is less than 100? Why?" and "What would you say to another child who said the answer was 512? Is that right or wrong? How do you know?" Such questioning is very important to help children understand the importance of judging the reasonableness of their solutions after solving any problem.

Subtraction

Posing Story Problems Set in Real-World Contexts

As with addition, it has been common practice to introduce the subtraction algorithm with computation that did not require children to regroup. But beginning with realistic problems exposes children to subtraction with regrouping in a realistic context, which will help them make sense of the situations. For example, teachers could begin instruction by posing a problem such as the following:

> *The clerk in the doughnut shop counted 63 doughnuts on the shelf. A family bought 24 doughnuts. How many doughnuts were left?*

Encourage children to use terms for regrouping and renaming such as *trade, group, break apart, break a ten*, and *make a group*. Avoid using the term *borrow*. "Borrowing" does not match what is actually happening in the problem situation. Encourage children to use the terms *subtract, subtraction*, and *difference* meaningfully in a sentence. (See Chapter 7, page 126, for more on realistic problems for subtraction.)

Using Models for Computation

Start all subtraction instruction with concrete models and an organizational mat, which helps connect the concrete representation to the symbolic. For subtraction, the organizational mat should be modified as shown in Figure 9-7. In the unstructured activities phase, children would simply manipulate the blocks in the spaces provided on the mat, as illustrated in the second column in Figure 9-7.

Children should begin with 63 displayed in the first row, then separate 24 and put them in the second row (regrouping as necessary), resulting in 39 blocks remaining to be moved to the bottom row. These 39 blocks represent the number of doughnuts left.

As children become successful with this process, you can ask them to be more systematic, beginning by first taking away the 4 ones and moving the remaining ones to the bottom row, before working with the tens place. This procedure more closely mirrors the symbolic algorithm.

FIGURE 9-7 Concrete and Symbolic Representations for Solving the Doughnut Problem

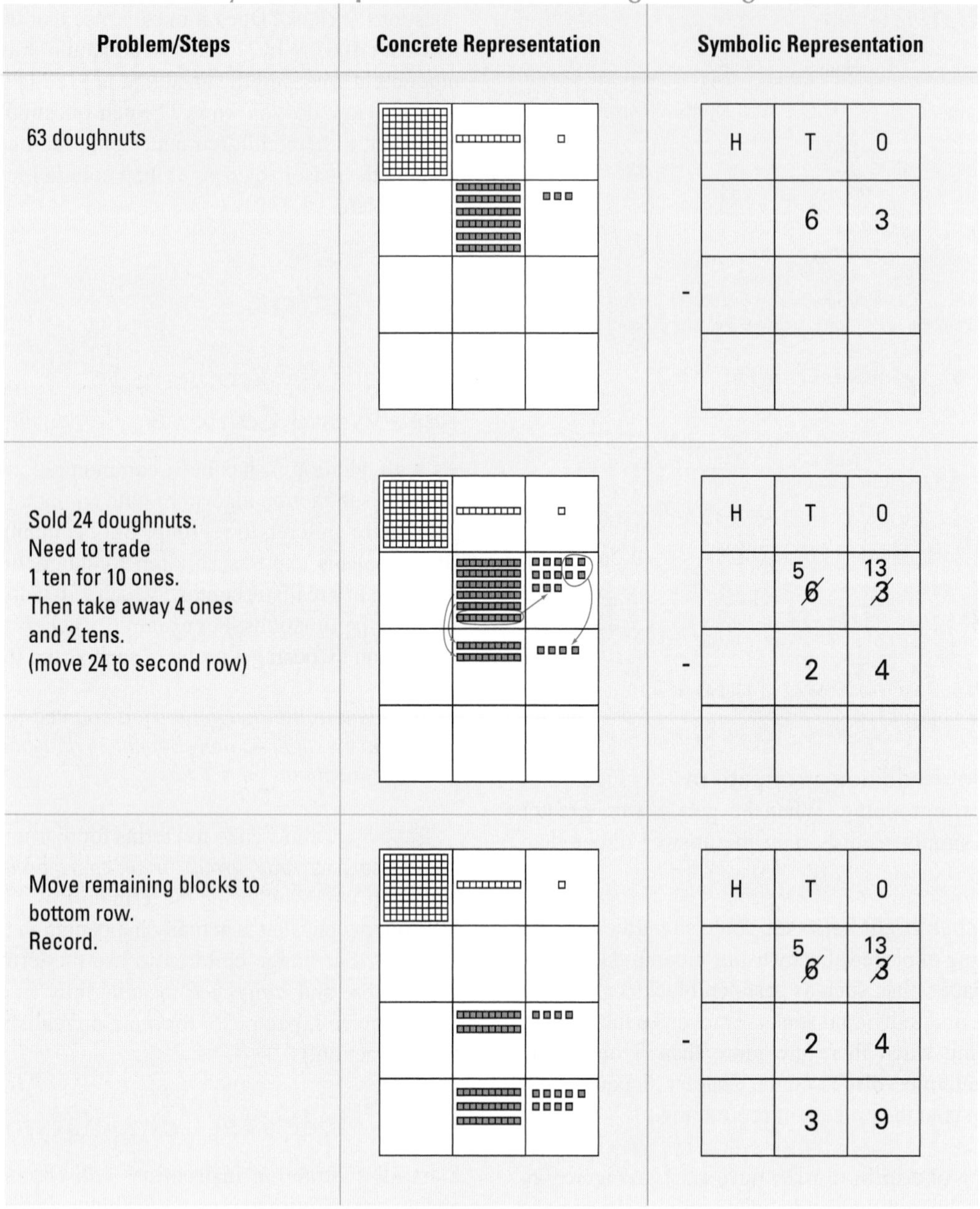

Problem/Steps	Concrete Representation	Symbolic Representation
63 doughnuts		H T O 6 3 −
Sold 24 doughnuts. Need to trade 1 ten for 10 ones. Then take away 4 ones and 2 tens. (move 24 to second row)		H T O 5 13 ~~6~~ ~~3~~ − 2 4
Move remaining blocks to bottom row. Record.		H T O 5 13 ~~6~~ ~~3~~ − 2 4 3 9

When children use only the base-ten blocks without recording, they are able to extend the above process to three-digit numbers if they have had trading experiences involving hundreds. As with other problems, it is helpful if these larger numbers come from some real-life problem that must be solved.

Using Estimation and Mental Computation

Encouraging children to estimate an answer will help them verify and feel confident about their concrete solution. Children might say, "My answer should be about 40 because I know that 60 minus 20 is 40." (This is an extension fact, discussed in Chapter 8.)

Using the front-end strategy. Given a real-life setting that involved subtracting 254 from 725, younger children could estimate the result by subtracting the front-end digits (7 hundreds minus 2 hundreds) to get 500. Middle school children can make adjustments to get a closer estimate. They might reason that another 54 to be subtracted means that the answer is closer to 450. Others with good number sense might also consider the additional 25 and decide that 475 is a closer estimate.

Additional problems such as those done in Activity 9-5 could be structured to provide experience with estimation and mental computation.

ACTIVITY 9-5 Difference of 50

Procedure

In 1 minute, find as many pairs of numbers as you can from this list whose difference is 50.

32 9 97 36 62 37 76 58
64 81 14 39
82 69 93 71 19 85 22
86 25 121 24 47

Developing Bridging Algorithms to Connect Problems, Models, Estimation, and Symbols

The development of a paper-and-pencil subtraction algorithm should follow as closely as possible the method used by children when they subtract with base-ten blocks. As with addition, two children could work together using an organizational mat and a sheet of paper, with one child manipulating the blocks and the other child recording the results on paper. Children then change roles. Figure 9-7 illustrates steps a child might use to solve the doughnut problem with base-ten blocks and the corresponding symbolic representation for each step.

Let's look more closely at the process of regrouping shown in Figure 9-7. Notice that, after regrouping, the 10 ones were joined to the 3 ones in the first row rather than in a regrouping space, as was done in addition. Why? In the concrete mode, the 10 ones were joined to the group of 3 ones, making 13 ones. Putting all 13 ones in the same cell on the mat better illustrates an intermediate step of the regrouping process. Also notice that in the symbolic representation, this regrouping is shown as 13 ones and the original 3 ones are crossed out, rather than inserting a smaller 1 above the 3 to indicate 13 ones as is traditionally done. Recording the number of ones in this way better matches the concrete representation and, therefore, makes more sense to children.

After regrouping 6 tens and 3 ones into 5 tens and 13 ones, children can then take away 4 ones to solve the problem. This process links the concrete representation to the symbolic representation as shown in Figure 9-7.

Developing the Traditional Algorithm

After children have had some experiences with connecting concrete and symbolic representations as shown in Figure 9-7 and can explain the steps in the subtraction procedure, they will begin to make refinements, which

FIGURE 9-8 Moving from a Place-Value Chart to Conventional Notation

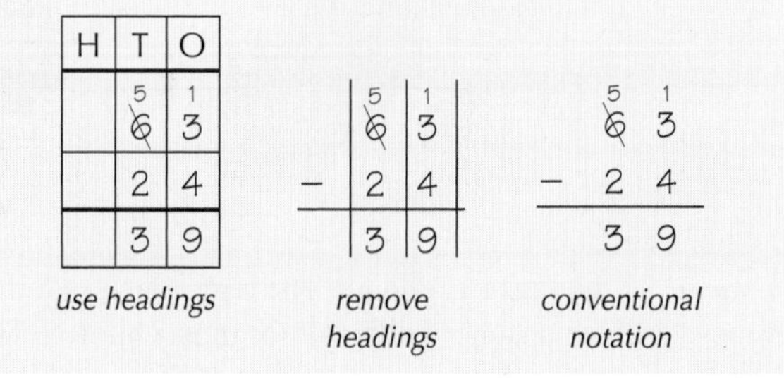

become more symbolic, shorter, and more efficient. The sequence of refinements illustrated in Figure 9-8 is one possibility. Many variations on these may be developed. For example, some teachers encourage the use of expanded notation as a transitional step. The notation shown here illustrates one way the doughnut problem might be recorded and solved using expanded notation.

$$\begin{array}{r} 6 \text{ tens} + 3 \text{ ones} \\ -2 \text{ tens} + 4 \text{ ones} \end{array} \quad \rightarrow \quad \begin{array}{r} 5 \text{ tens} + 13 \text{ ones} \\ -2 \text{ tens} + 4 \text{ ones} \\ \hline \end{array}$$

$$\rightarrow \quad \begin{array}{r} 5 \text{ tens} + 13 \text{ ones} \\ -2 \text{ tens} + 4 \text{ ones} \\ \hline 3 \text{ tens} + 9 \text{ ones} \end{array} \quad \rightarrow \quad 39$$

Because the need to do a particular computation is based on the need to solve some real-life problem, the size of numbers that children need to deal with will vary based on the real-life situations. As the number of required regroupings increases, so does the difficulty level. You may want to structure or filter problems so that children can experience success and not become frustrated with problems that they are unable to solve.

The number of regroupings needed provides a guideline to the difficulty of a problem. When subtracting up to a three-digit number from a three-digit number, there are several possibilities in terms of the number of regroupings involved: no regrouping, tens to ones, hundreds to tens, hundreds to ones, and tens to ones and hundreds to tens, as shown in Figure 9-9.

Special cases: zeros in the minuend. Sometimes children need to solve problems with one or more zeros in the

FIGURE 9-9 Different Regrouping Situations in Subtraction Problems

376 − 51	246 − 29	325 − 172	305 − 109	355 − 186
no regroupings	*tens to ones*	*hundreds to tens (via tens)*	*hundreds to ones*	*tens to ones and hundreds to tens*

FIGURE 9-10 Showing Regrouping with Base-Ten Blocks and with Symbols

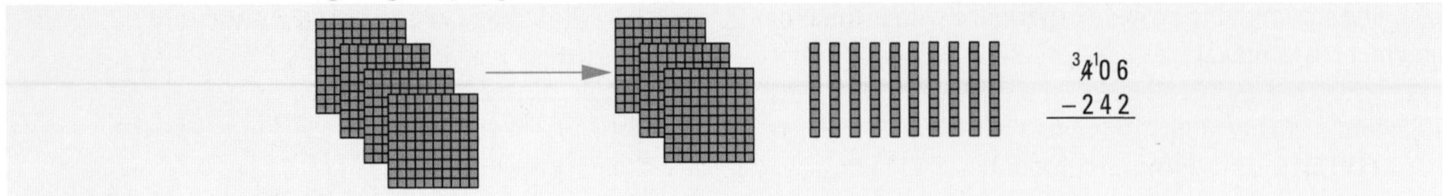

minuend, or the starting amount. The regrouping required in these problems is more difficult for most children. The following sections describe three cases of these problems and how to help children solve them successfully.

CASE 1: Zero in the ones place

Sometimes children want to begin reading the following problem as "5 minus 0." Help them connect their previous experiences with grouping and regrouping to rename 60 as 5 tens and 10 ones.

760 → 7 ~~6~~ [5] [1]0
− 345 → − 345

CASE 2: Zero in the tens place

One example involves only one regrouping, from hundreds to tens, as required, for example, in 406 − 242 as shown in Figure 9-10. Using the base-ten blocks, children will quickly see that 4 hundreds can be renamed as 3 hundreds plus 10 tens. Children can show this regrouping with symbols as shown on the right side of Figure 9-10.

A second example in which regrouping also is needed in the ones position is more difficult. Consider the problem 403 − 246 shown below. There are two approaches children might take. Most children will regroup the 4 hundreds as 3 hundreds and 10 tens (first example) and then rename the 10 tens as 9 tens and 13 ones as shown below. This parallels what would be done using base-ten blocks.

403   ~~4~~ ~~0~~ 3 (3, 9, 1 written above)
− 246   − 246

In a second approach, children with more experience with regrouping might recognize that the 40 tens can be renamed as 39 tens and 10 ones. This could be noted in one step as shown below.

~~40~~3 (39 and 1 written above)
− 246

CASE 3: Zeros in both the tens and ones places

This is the most difficult case. Children should have many experiences using concrete simulations with these problems before they move to paper-and-pencil recording. Figure 9-11 shows how to use base-ten blocks to solve the problem 400 − 245.

The same steps are shown symbolically below. Children may include some transitional steps if they need them. As indicated earlier, some children may combine the two renaming steps, that is, they will think of the 40 tens as 39 tens and 10 ones and record it as the second example in case 2 (zero in the tens place). Children with good number sense sometimes mentally compute the answer to this type of problem by saying, "From 245 to 250 is 5, 50 more to 300 is 55, another hundred to 400 is 155."

FIGURE 9-11 Using Base-Ten Blocks to Solve 400 − 245

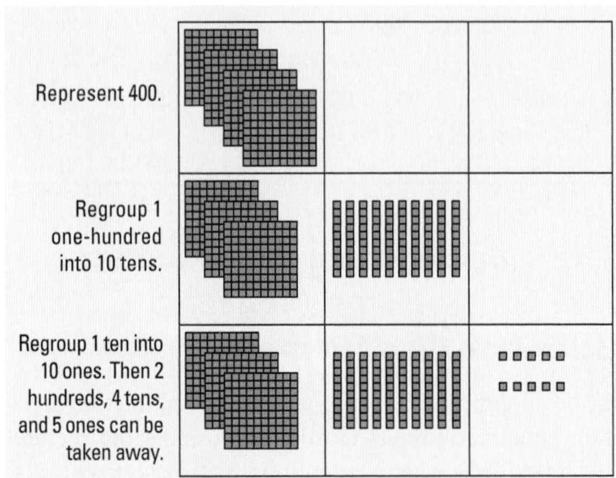

~~4~~00 (3, 1 written above)   ~~4~~ ~~0~~ 0 (3, 9, 1 written above)
− 245   − 245

Examining Children's Reasoning

What are some different ways that children solve subtraction problems? View the clip "IMAP—Multiple Strategies to Solve Problems" on MyEducationLab. In this clip Gretchen, a second-grade girl, is asked to solve the problem 70 − 23. (Notice that this problem has a zero in the ones place of the minuend, as discussed earlier in case 1.) Gretchen first solves the problem by using the standard algorithm, getting an answer of 53, then solves it by using base-ten blocks, and finally by using a hundreds chart, getting a result of 47 for the last two methods. Gretchen is puzzled by the different results, but asserts that the solution she got by using the standard algorithm "has to be right."

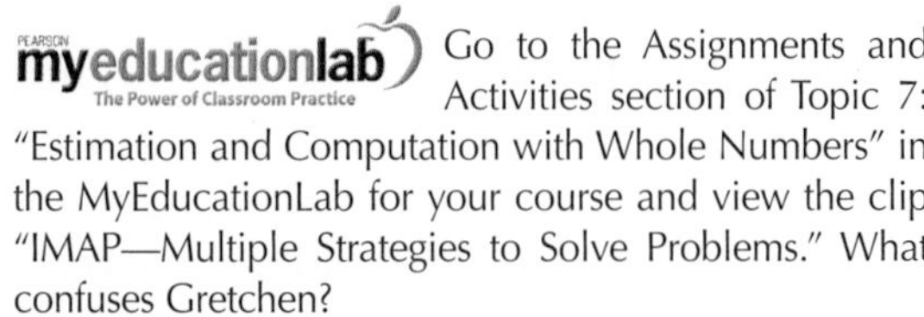

Go to the Assignments and Activities section of Topic 7: "Estimation and Computation with Whole Numbers" in the MyEducationLab for your course and view the clip "IMAP—Multiple Strategies to Solve Problems." What confuses Gretchen?

View the clip to see each of the ways Gretchen solved the problem. What mistake did she make to get the incorrect answer using the standard algorithm? In the first step of the algorithm, when subtracting in the ones place, she decided that 0 minus 3 was 3, and in the tens place, 7 minus 2 was 5, so the answer was 53. Next, consider the following questions:

- Is this a common error?
- Why might Gretchen have made this error?
- Why do you think Gretchen felt so strongly that the answer she got by using the standard algorithm was correct?
- If you were Gretchen's teacher, how might you have responded? What additional instructional experiences might you design for her to experience to strengthen her understanding?

Developing Other Algorithms

Algorithms based on the comparison interpretation of subtraction. So far in this chapter, we've focused on the separate or "take-away" interpretation of subtraction. But the comparison interpretation of subtraction, discussed in Chapter 7, must be modeled differently than the "take-away" interpretation. Comparison problems can be modeled using matching techniques. Figure 9-12 illustrates the comparison suggested by the following problem.

There are 364 children in Roseville Elementary School and 198 in Brooklyn Park Elementary School. How many more children go to Roseville than Brooklyn Park?

The difference, 166, is the number represented by the blocks in the upper row that are not matched to a block in the lower row. The symbolic algorithm is identical to the separate interpretation.

Activity 9-6 parallels Activity 9-4 but involves subtraction. Children should work in a group or with a partner and discuss reasons for their choice of number.

ACTIVITY 9-6 Calculator Game (Subtraction)

Materials

Calculator for each student

Procedure

1. One person writes three numbers on paper for all others to see.
2. Without the others seeing, find the difference between two of the numbers on your calculator.
3. Write the difference on paper for the others to see.
4. The others decide, by estimation, which two numbers were subtracted and then check their guesses on their calculator.
5. Take turns doing the activity several more times.

Equal additions algorithm. This algorithm was taught in North America until the mid-1900s (Brownell, 1947; Brownell & Moser, 1949). Thereafter its use declined, and the decomposition (or regrouping) method prevailed. The equal additions algorithm, also known as the "same change" algorithm, is taught in some new curricula and in some other countries, so teachers should be aware of it and understand how it works. When taught meaningfully, both the equal additions and the decomposition algorithms are effective. The two methods are compared in Figure 9-13.

Using the equal additions method, a child might reason: "I can't subtract 8 from 6, so I will add 10 ones. Since I added 10 to the top number (346), I must add 10 to the bottom number (178). I will increase the 7 tens to 8 tens. Eight from 16 is 8. Now I can't subtract 8 tens from 4 tens so I'll add 10 tens to the top number (346) and 10 tens in the form of one hundred to the bottom number (178).

FIGURE 9-12 Using Base-Ten Blocks to Model a Comparison Subtraction Problem

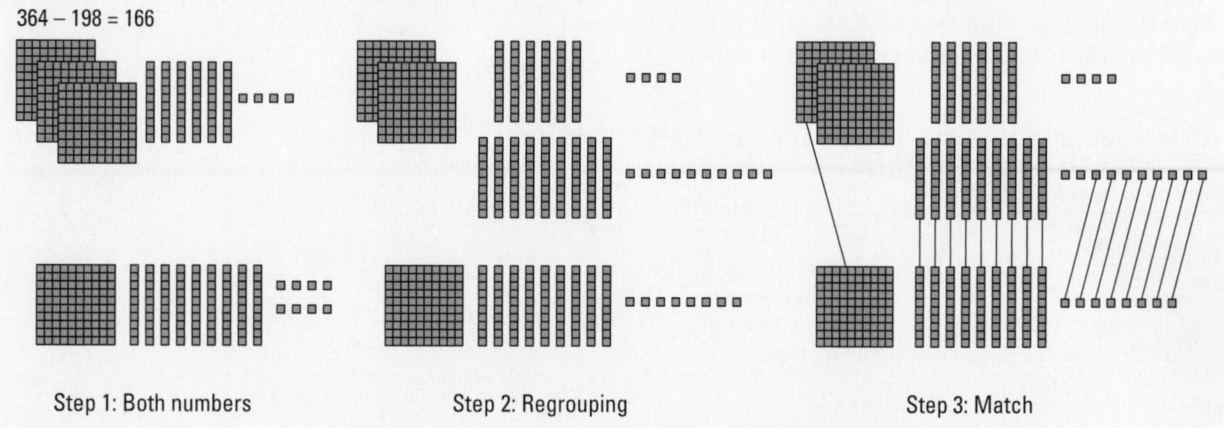

FIGURE 9-13 Comparing the Decomposition Algorithm with the Equal Additions Algorithm for Subtraction

Decomposition	*Equal additions*
$\begin{array}{r} {}^{2}\not{3}\ {}^{3}\not{4}\ {}^{1}6 \\ -\ 1\ \ 7\ \ 8 \\ \hline 1\ \ 6\ \ 8 \end{array}$	$\begin{array}{r} 3\ \ {}^{1}4\ \ {}^{1}6 \\ -{}^{2}\not{1}\ {}^{8}\not{7}\ \ 8 \\ \hline 1\ \ 6\ \ 8 \end{array}$

Eight tens from 14 tens is 6 tens and 2 hundreds from 3 hundreds leaves 1 hundred."

Note that this method is based on compensation. In other words, to keep the difference the same, whatever is added to the top number (the minuend) must be added to the bottom number (the subtrahend) to keep the difference the same.

Children can easily be convinced of the truth of compensation through an exercise such as the one in Activity 9-7. The purpose of this activity is to help children generalize that the difference stays the same when the same amount is added to the minuend and the subtrahend. This is a powerful generalization that will be useful in more advanced mathematics.

ACTIVITY 9-7 Compensation Investigation

Procedure

1. Find the difference.

8	9	10	8	18	28	18	19	20
−3	−4	−5	−3	−13	−23	−13	−14	−15

2. Write a sentence about what you notice.

Mental computation in subtraction. A form of the equal additions algorithm is sometimes used to subtract mentally. Given the problem $725 - 294$, if 6 is added to each number, the subtraction becomes easy: $731 - 300 = 431$. Instead of adding 10, as in the equal additions algorithm, any convenient number can be used. Children could be taught this strategy, which then could be reinforced occasionally with brief mental practice exercises or warm-ups.

NCTM Principles and Standards Link 9-3

Content Strand: Number and Operations

Regardless of the particular algorithm used, students should be able to explain their method and should understand that many methods exist. They should also recognize the need to develop efficient and accurate methods. (NCTM, 2000, p. 154)

Examining Student Work

Figures 9-14 and 9-15 contain samples of children's work in practicing subtraction of whole numbers. Look closely at the work and try to determine the errors the children are making. Why might they be making these errors? If you were their teacher, what might you do to help them?

Description of subtraction error pattern 1. In Figure 9-14, Cheryl is subtracting the smaller number from the larger number instead of subtracting the subtrahend (bottom number) from the minuend (top number). Note that problem A ($32 - 16$) is correct, perhaps because it is a double and Cheryl knows that answer. Cheryl may be applying a rule she has heard that you "always subtract the little number from the big one" (Ashlock, 2006, p. 114). She may not understand place value and regrouping.

How a teacher might help. You could strengthen Cheryl's understanding of place value and regrouping by using a manipulative material for place value, such as base-ten blocks or bundles of sticks. Emphasize the process of regrouping when the digit in the subtrahend is greater than the digit in the minuend. Be sure to stress that it is possible to take a larger number away from a smaller number if the number can be regrouped.

Description of subtraction error pattern 2. In Figure 9-15, George always regroups, even when not needed, such as in problem B, where George regroups to change $6 - 3$ to $16 - 3$ and records the answer of 13

FIGURE 9-14 Subtraction Error Pattern 1

Name Cheryl

A.	B.	C.	D.
32	245	524	135
−16	−137	−298	−67
16	112	374	132

Source: Error Patterns in Computation 8/e by Ashlock, © 2010, p. 22. Reprinted by permission of Pearson Education, Inc., Upper Saddle River, NJ.

FIGURE 9-15 Subtraction Error Pattern 2

Name George

A.	B.	C.
${}^{8}\not{9}\,{}^{1}7$ with 1 crossed: $1\not{9}7$	$1\not{7}{}^{1}6$ (7 → 6)	$3\not{8}{}^{1}4$ (8 → 7)
−43	−23	−59
1414	1413	325

Source: Error Patterns in Computation 8/e by Ashlock, © 2010, p. 23. Reprinted by permission of Pearson Education, Inc., Upper Saddle River, NJ.

below. He needs help in determining when regrouping is needed.

How a teacher might help. You could reinforce George's understanding of regrouping by modeling these problems with manipulative materials and discussing whether regrouping is needed. Encourage George to verbalize the rule he uses for determining when to regroup.

Determining the Reasonableness of Solutions

It is often more difficult for children to determine the reasonableness of their solutions to subtraction problems than to addition problems. This makes it even more important for teachers to help children by asking questions; for example, for the doughnut problem, you could ask "Why is your answer less than (or greater than) 100? Why does this make sense?"

Multiplication

Posing Story Problems Set in Real-World Contexts

Think back to the different interpretations of multiplication discussed in Chapter 7, including equal groups and area and arrays. To help children make sense of bigger multiplication problems, help them build on their understanding of simple multiplication problems. These connections will help children make sense of problems with larger numbers, which may seem more complicated to them but actually just take a little longer to solve.

While all of the interpretations of multiplication can help children understand the concept of multiplication, when developing a multiplication algorithm, the equal groups and array interpretations are the most helpful. In fact, the array interpretation may be the most powerful because it enables one to easily represent large numbers, which will be described later.

Remember, just as for other operations, children's first multiplication computations should arise from real-life problems. A problem involving one-digit multipliers, such as the following, could serve as a context for exploring multiplication:

> *The principal bought 3 cases of sodas for the second-grade party. Each case had 24 cans. How many cans were purchased?*

Using Models for Computation

To solve the preceding problem, children can set out a rectangular array using as few base-ten blocks as possible, as shown in Figure 9-16(a), and note that the answer is 60 (3 rows of 20) plus 12 (3 rows of 4) or 72. They will recognize from previous experiences that 3×20 is 3 groups of 2 tens and the result is 6 tens. To this end, encourage children to verbalize in different ways what they have done and encourage them to use *place-value language*. The following sequence of activities suggests a possible approach:

1. Ask children to construct a 2-by-6 rectangle using as few base-ten blocks as possible (see Figure 9-16[b]). They can to do this by using only unit cubes. Encourage children to use place-value language, such as "2 ones times 6 ones equals 12 ones."
2. Have the children construct a 2-by-60 rectangle using as few pieces as possible (see Figure 9-16[c]). They should be able to say "2 ones times 6 tens equals 12 tens." From these kinds of experiences, children will be able to generalize the following:
   - 3×10 is 3 tens, or 30.
   - 3×20 is 3×2 tens, which makes 6 tens, or 60.

It is important to allow children ample time to solve numerous problems concretely while recording, *in their own way*, what they did. In the process, encourage them to describe their work using place-value language.

Once children feel comfortable with place-value language, they can then record products and regroup them in a place-value chart as shown here:

H	T	O
		6
	×	2
		12
	1	2

H	T	O
	6	0
×		2
	12	0
1	2	0

A note about language for multiplication. In the case of multiplication computation, children *may* eventually learn lots of terms. In a problem requiring the computation $27 \times 42 = n$, the *multiplicand* (42) is the number in each group and the *multiplier* (27) is the number of groups. These are often referred to simply as *factors*. In typical classroom interaction, the terms *multiplicand* and *multiplier* are not used extensively. Children should be

FIGURE 9-16 Constructing Arrays with Base-Ten Blocks

allowed to use informal language for some time, rather than be expected to memorize "proper" terminology. It is important, however, for you to know this terminology so that you can communicate with other professionals.

Using Estimation and Mental Computation

Encouraging children to estimate an answer will help them verify their concrete solutions. For example, for the preceding problem, children might say, "My answer should be about 60, because I know that 3 times 20 is 60." You can also ask questions such as "What if another child said that the answer was 600? Is that correct? Why or why not?"

Strategies for mental computation in multiplication. Before children can become proficient with mental computation, they must master multiplication by powers of 10; that is, they need to be able to mentally compute products such as 6×10, 6×100, $6 \times 1{,}000$, and 36×100.

Next, children should be able to use multiples of powers of 10; that is, they should be able to mentally compute exercises such as 6×30, 6×400, and $14 \times 2{,}000$. In the last two examples, children might think as follows: $6 \times 4 = 24$, so $6 \times 400 = 2{,}400$; $14 \times 2 = 28$, so $14 \times 2{,}000 = 28{,}000$.

The *front-end strategy* for multiplication involves multiplying the left-most digit in each factor and using zeros in all other positions. A front-end estimate of the product of 6 and 43 would be 6×40, or 240. When both numbers have two or more digits, the number of zeros in the estimate becomes more critical. Children need a solid understanding of place-value understanding and a good facility with place-value language to become good estimators. For example, the front-end estimate of 76×93 is 7×9 or 63, but 63 what? Because we are multiplying tens by tens, the result is hundreds, so the estimate will be 6,300. Writing (or thinking) 70×90 will help children make the association between "hundreds" and the two zeros in the factors.

Using *front-end estimation*, children can solve problems such as 50×70. The ability to mentally compute exercises such as this facilitates estimation. A good grasp of place-value language will help children recognize that 50×70 is 35 hundreds because tens multiplied by tens are hundreds.

Upper elementary and middle school children working with larger numbers will encounter a small problem with computations such as 7000×30, or 21 ten thousands, which normally is thought of as 210,000. Children will need some experiences with this dual form to become proficient at mental computation. These experiences should be included in the development of computational procedures.

Rounding is a useful strategy in multiplication. On occasion, rounding actually becomes front-end estimation. For example, in 6×43, 43 is rounded to 40, which gives the same factors used with the front-end method.

One of the most useful strategies for computing a multiplication exercise mentally is to employ the *distributive property*. For example, 5×76 can be computed as $(5 \times 70) + (5 \times 6)$. Note that it is best to multiply the tens first to get 350, and then add the 30 ones to get 380. Can you see how this property is very useful?

Also, a type of *substitution* is particularly useful in mental computation when one factor ends in 7, 8, or 9. For example, 6×48 can be thought of as $(6 \times 50) - (6 \times 2)$, or $300 - 12$.

Developing Bridging Algorithms to Connect Problems, Models, Estimation, and Symbols

After children have solved the cases of soda problem by making a rectangular array of base-ten blocks as in Figure 9-16 and noting that the solution is 72, encourage them to examine the array and look for patterns. Notice that the array is made up of two parts: a 3-by-4 array of unit cubes, and a 3-by-20 array of tens. These two parts of the array are parts of the product, or *partial products*. Children should record each of the partial products, as shown in Figure 9-17. Also note that the language shown in Figure 9-17 uses place-value language to help children make sense of their results. For example, 3 ones times 4 ones is 12 ones, and 3 ones times 2 tens is 6 tens. Making these connections among concrete representation, place-value language, and symbols helps children make sense of computation. Children should have many experiences making these three-way connections before moving to the traditional algorithm.

Activity 9-8 helps children with the connections suggested in Figure 9-17. You will need to prepare in advance a set of problem cards with problems similar to the earlier problem about the principal buying the soft drinks for a class party.

ACTIVITY 9-8 Problem Cards

Manipulative Strategies

Materials

A set of problem cards; base-ten blocks

Procedure

Work in groups of three.

1. Choose a problem card.
2. One person uses the blocks to show the problem.
3. Another describes the partial products shown by the blocks. Use language such as "4 ones times 2 tens equals 8 tens."
4. The third person records the problem and its solution in written form.
5. Change roles and do another problem.

FIGURE 9-17 Connecting an Array of Base-Ten Blocks with a Bridging Algorithm

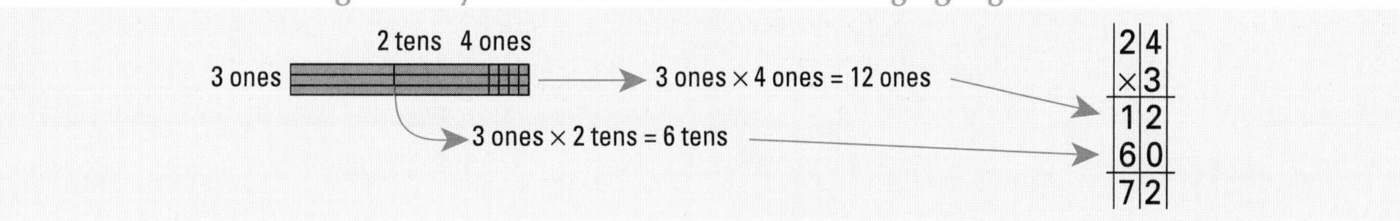

Two-digit multiplier. Problems with two-digit multipliers, such as 25 × 67, are more complicated. For example, consider the following problem:

> *There were 25 rows of cars in the parking lot at the shopping mall. There were 67 cars in each row. How many cars were there in all?*

It is important that teachers do not rush to present these problems. Be sure children can solve problems with one-digit multipliers and can explain the meaning and the procedure before introducing problems with two-digit multipliers. Problems such as these require two extensions to children's place-value language, as described and illustrated below.

1. "2 tens times 7 ones equals 14 tens." This is the commutative form of the "ones × tens = tens" concept learned with one-digit multipliers.

   67
   ↑
   ×25

2. "2 tens times 6 tens equals 12 hundreds."

   67
   ↑
   ×25

Helping children make sense of this. Children should have many opportunities to use this sort of place-value language in the context of building arrays with base-ten blocks before doing any symbolic recording. To help children with the "tens × tens = hundreds" concept, have them set out several arrays with the blocks showing multiplication with multiples of 10, as shown. When children are encouraged to talk about their array, they will develop meaningful expressions such as "2 tens times 6 tens makes 12 hundreds."

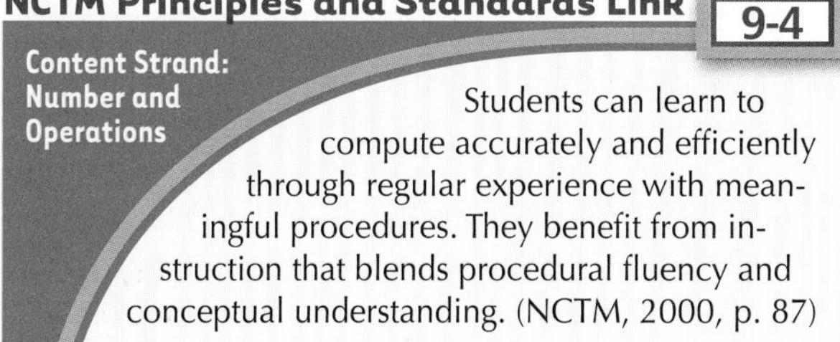

NCTM Principles and Standards Link 9-4

Content Strand: Number and Operations

Students can learn to compute accurately and efficiently through regular experience with meaningful procedures. They benefit from instruction that blends procedural fluency and conceptual understanding. (NCTM, 2000, p. 87)

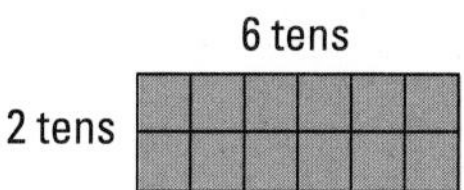

This type of array can now be extended to represent a problem such as 25 × 67, as illustrated in Figure 9-18. Children should have many experiences representing this type of problem with base-ten blocks, recording their work in their own way. Children could then transfer their individual method of recording to a place-value chart much like the one suggested for one-digit multipliers. The arrows in Figure 9-19 show the two new partial products from 25 × 67.

Again, children need to see the connections between the concrete representations, place-value language, and the paper-and-pencil algorithm. These connections are shown in Figure 9-20, which is best interpreted by considering the dimensions of the base-ten pieces rather than the area. For example, the rod consists of 10 units (area) and has dimensions 1 × 10. One dimension (for example, the width) of an array composed of a rod and a flat would be 11 (10 from the flat plus 1 from the rod), or 1 ten and 1 unit.

FIGURE 9-18 Array of Base-Ten Blocks for a Larger Problem

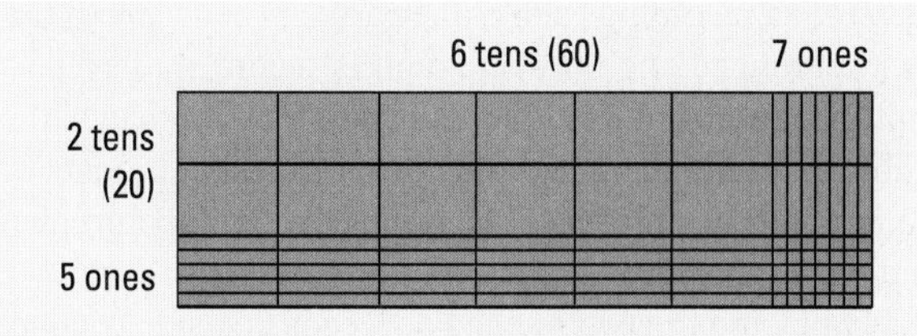

FIGURE 9-19 Two Partial Products for 25 × 67

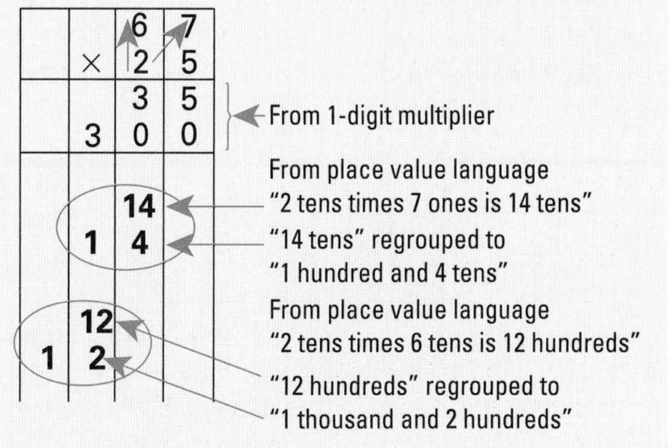

FIGURE 9-20 Connecting an Array with the Partial Products Algorithm

6 tens (60)
7 ones
2 tens (20)
5 ones

2 tens × 6 tens = 12 hundreds
2 tens × 7 ones = 14 tens
5 ones × 6 tens = 30 tens
5 ones × 7 ones = 35 ones

		6	7
	×	2	5
		3	5
	3	0	0
	1	4	0
1	2	0	0
1	6	7	5

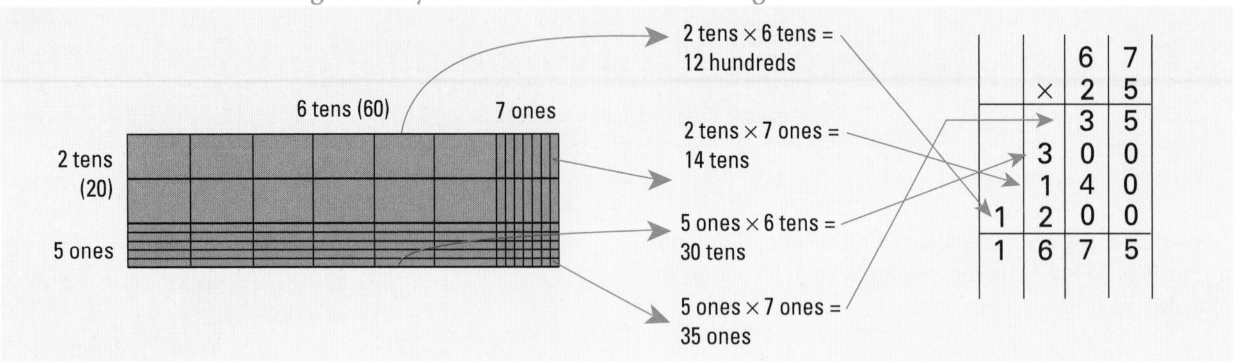

Note that the written record can be recorded left to right or right to left, the only difference being the order of the partial products. Some children might record their work in horizontal form prior to the vertical format: $(5 \times 7) + (5 \times 60) + (20 \times 7) + (20 \times 60)$.

Developing the Traditional Algorithm

After children have had lots of experiences solving multiplication problems using the base-ten blocks and writing a corresponding algorithm for the representation, they should be encouraged to think about how to shorten the algorithm. In the more common form, the traditional algorithm, only one partial product is recorded for each digit in the multiplier. Encourage children to "compress" the partial products by asking questions such as "Try to find a shorter way to record a multiplication with two partial products."

For the problem in Figure 9-17, 3 × 24, the final step in the progression toward the traditional algorithm is to record the final product in one line. The difference is that rather than recording each of the partial products, they are first regrouped and only one digit is recorded after each multiplication. For example, in Figure 9-21, notice on the right that rather than recording the first partial product of 12, it could be regrouped, recording the 2 in the product and the 1 ten above the factors.

By placing the two methods of recording side by side, as illustrated in Figure 9-21, children will be able to compare and connect the two and notice that the 1 ten is present in both versions, just recorded in a different location.

FIGURE 9-21 Comparing the Partial Products Algorithm with the Traditional Algorithm

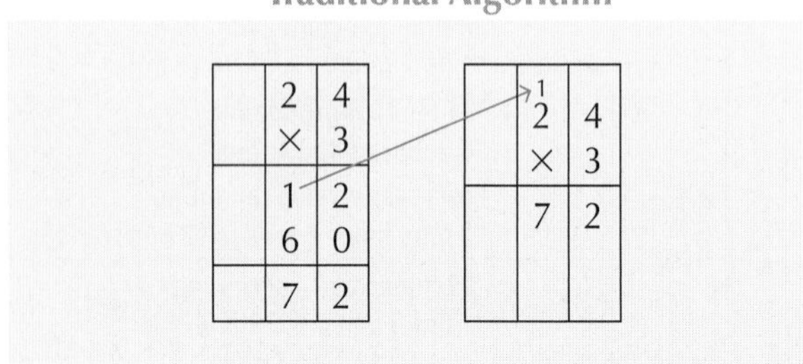

FIGURE 9-22 Comparing the Partial Products Algorithm with the Traditional Algorithm: One-Digit Multiplier

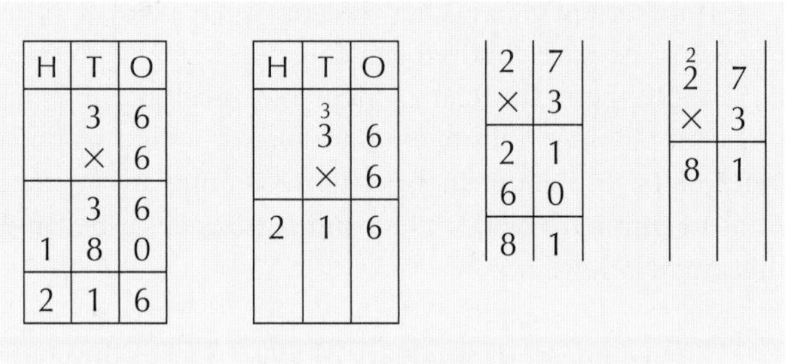

H	T	O
	3	6
	×	6
	3	6
1	8	0
2	1	6

H	T	O
	3 (small 3 above)	6
	×	6
2	1	6

2	7
×	3
2	1
6	0
8	1

2 (small 2 above)	7
×	3
8	1

Allowing the children to use either format will make the transition to the traditional algorithm easier. Use examples similar to those shown in Figure 9-22 for a class discussion. Ask the children to describe how the two procedures are the same and how they are different. Also ask the children to explain the meaning of the "little" 3 and "little" 2 in Figure 9-22 and to identify the corresponding numbers in the algorithm on the left.

For two-digit multipliers, using the 25 × 67 example in Figure 9-20, children could begin the transition by focusing only on the 5 and treating the problem as 5 × 67. They could then focus on the 2 tens as the multiplier. Because tens × ones = tens, the first digit in the second partial product will be placed in the tens position. There are 14 tens (2 tens × 7 ones), so the 4 tens will be recorded and the remaining 10 tens will be regrouped and recorded as 1 hundred in the hundreds column, as shown in Figure 9-19.

The connection between the long form (four partial products) and the condensed form (two partial products) should be apparent to children. To ensure this, you might present both forms side by side, as shown in Figure 9-23, and ask children to explain the similarities and differences. Children may draw arrows as in Figure 9-23 to show the connection between the two forms.

Three-and-more-digit multipliers. Children who are confident solving problems with two-digit multipliers should be able to move to three-digit multipliers on their own. The main extension is in the use of the place-value

FIGURE 9-23 Comparing the Partial Products Algorithm with the Traditional Algorithm: Two-Digit Multiplier

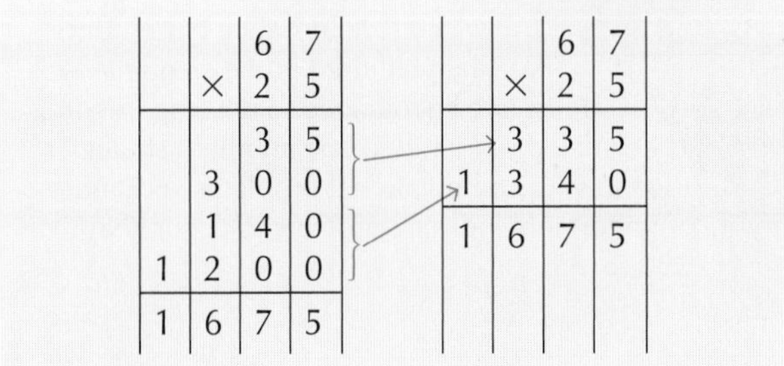

language developed for one- and two-digit multipliers. Although calculators will normally be used to solve multiplication problems with large numbers, children could be invited to "prove" that they know how to multiply large numbers by writing a few examples in horizontal form using the distributive property and in vertical form.

Connections. Many concepts run like threads through the mathematics curriculum from early elementary school through high school and beyond. For example, when high school students expand $(a + b)(c + d)$ as $ac + ad + bc + bd$, they are actually doing the same thing they did in elementary school when they identified and listed the four partial products in an exercise such as 27×35. In fact, they may well use a diagram similar to the representation with base-ten blocks (Figure 9-24). The expansion of $(a + b)^2 = a^2 + 2ab + b^2$ is just a special case of multiplication.

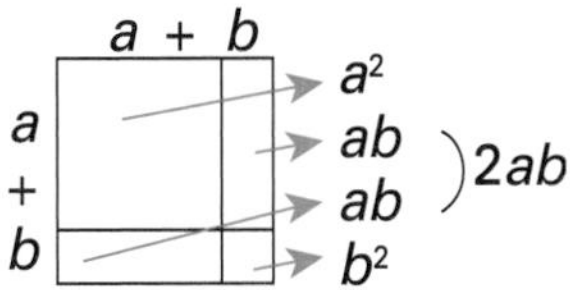

Examining Children's Reasoning

Focus on an individual student. How can children think flexibly in solving multiplication problems? View the clip "IMAP—Solving Multiplication" on MyEducationLab, in which Javier, a fifth-grade boy, is asked to solve several problems involving multiplying by 12. He begins solving

FIGURE 9-24 Connecting Multiplying Two Binomials with the Partial Products Algorithm

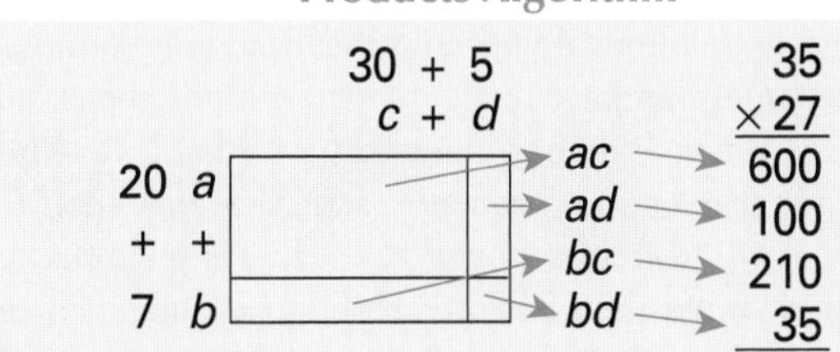

the problem 6×12 by thinking about it as two partial products. He finds 5×12 and 1×12 and then adds their products, $60 + 12$, to get the result of 72. Javier seemed to know that 5×12 was 60; when asked by the interviewer how he knew that answer, he noted that he knew that 10×12 was 120, so 5×12 was half as much, or 60.

Next, Javier solves 12×12. He starts by noting that 10×12 is 120, and 2×12 is 24, so the answer is 120 plus 24, which is 144.

PEARSON myeducationlab The Power of Classroom Practice — Go to the Assignments and Activities section of Topic 7: "Estimation and Computation with Whole Numbers" in the MyEducationLab for your course. Complete the activity "IMAP—Solving Multiplication" to see how one student uses mathematical reasoning.

View the clip to see how Javier flexibly uses number sense to solve these problems. It is interesting to note that Javier is a second language English speaker. Just a year before this clip was made he did not speak much English, yet his explanations are clear, and his thinking is solid. Consider the following tasks:

- Explain Javier's way of thinking. What is the logic behind his strategy? Why does his strategy work?
- Write another problem on which Javier might use the same reasoning. Explain how he would reason on the new problem.
- What might you do in your class to help other children think the way Javier thinks?

Focus on a whole class. How can you structure a lesson to encourage children to make sense of solving multiplication problems? View the clip "IMAP—Making Sense of Solutions" on MyEducationLab, in which Mrs. Kick, a first-grade teacher, asks her class to solve the following problem:

Mrs. Kick bought 4 seed packets. Each packet contains 11 seeds. How many seeds did she buy in all?

The children work independently or together to solve the problem. The teacher helps students make sense of the situation. Four children share their solutions. The rest of the class is encouraged to ask those who share solutions questions about their methods or to compliment them on their thinking.

PEARSON myeducationlab The Power of Classroom Practice — Go to the Assignments and Activities section of Topic 7: "Estimation and Computation with Whole Numbers" in the MyEducationLab for your course and complete the activity "Making Sense of Solutions."

View the clip to see how the children work together to solve the problem and how the teacher structures the class discussion to support children's making sense of multiplication. Consider the following tasks:

- Explain how Mrs. Kick engaged the children in mathematical problem solving. How did she encourage the children to communicate their mathematical thinking?
- Describe some ways Mrs. Kick organized the classroom environment and the class discussion to support children's making sense of multiplication. How did this support children's understanding?
- Mrs. Kick selected 11 for the number of seeds in the problem, thinking that some of her children might reason using place-value knowledge: Four elevens is 4 tens plus 4 ones. When none of her children thought in this way, she chose not to raise this issue on this day. If you wanted to raise this issue with your children, describe how you might do so.

Examining Student Work

Figures 9-25 and 9-26 contain samples of children's practice in multiplying whole numbers. Look closely at their work and try to understand children's thinking and understand any errors the children are making. Why might they be making these errors? If you were their teacher, what might you do to help them?

FIGURE 9-25 Multiplication Error Pattern 1

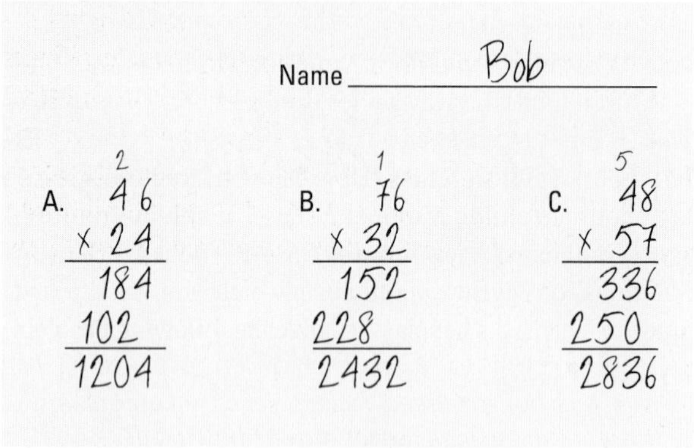

Name Bob

A. 46 × 24 (carry 2): 184, 102, 1204

B. 76 × 32 (carry 1): 152, 228, 2432

C. 48 × 57 (carry 5): 336, 250, 2836

Source: Error Patterns in Computation 8/e by Ashlock, ©2010, p. 40. Reprinted by permission of Pearson Education, Inc., Upper Saddle River, NJ.

FIGURE 9-26 Multiplication Error Pattern 2

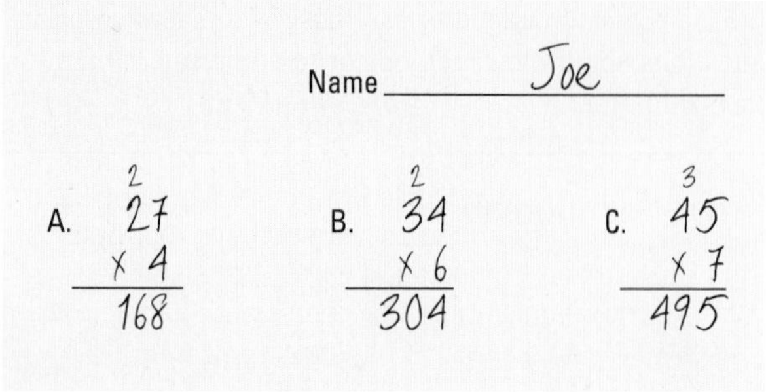

Name Joe

A. 27 × 4 (carry 2): 168

B. 34 × 6 (carry 2): 304

C. 45 × 7 (carry 3): 495

Source: Error Patterns in Computation 8/e by Ashlock, ©2010, p. 40. Reprinted by permission of Pearson Education, Inc., Upper Saddle River, NJ.

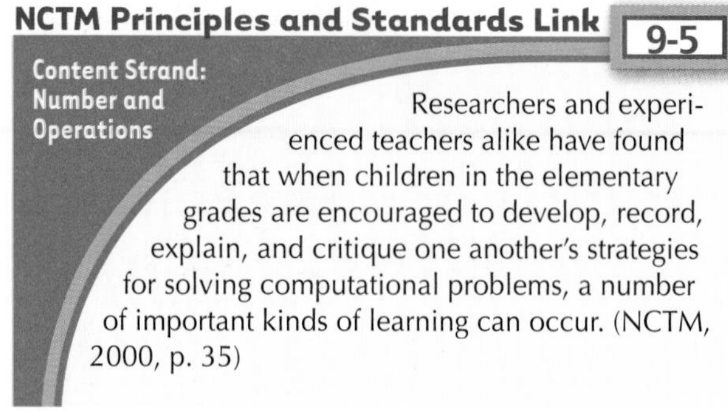
NCTM Principles and Standards Link 9-5

Content Strand: Number and Operations

Researchers and experienced teachers alike have found that when children in the elementary grades are encouraged to develop, record, explain, and critique one another's strategies for solving computational problems, a number of important kinds of learning can occur. (NCTM, 2000, p. 35)

Description of multiplication error pattern 1. In Figure 9-25, when multiplying by tens, Bob reuses the number regrouped (recorded above the tens column) when multiplying by ones.

How a teacher might help. Use the partial product algorithm and compare the answer Bob gets when using that algorithm with his original answer. Relate the partial products algorithm to the compact algorithm that Bob uses. Assist Bob in describing the differences and generalizing how to correct his errors.

Description of multiplication error pattern 2. In Figure 9-26, Joe adds the number regrouped (recorded above the tens column) before multiplying the digit in the tens column, rather than multiplying first and then adding on the number regrouped. This error could be carried over from how Joe was taught to add; perhaps Joe was taught that "the first thing you do is to add the number you carry" (Ashlock, 2006, p. 129).

How a teacher might help. Use the partial product algorithm or build an array with base-ten blocks to solve the problem. Compare the answers obtained in each way. Assist Joe in describing the correct sequence for dealing with the number regrouped.

Determining the Reasonableness of Solutions

It is often more difficult for children to determine the reasonableness of their solutions to multiplication problems than to addition or subtraction problems. This difficulty is typically a result of children not fully understanding place value and its relationship to multiplication. For example, children sometimes have difficulty determining the result to 3×70, even though they know that 3×7 is 21. It is important for teachers to frequently ask questions such as "How is 3×70 different from 3×7? How is it similar to 3×7?" Other questions that are helpful to ask include (for the problem 3×74) "What will the answer be *close to*?"

and "Another child said the answer was 2112. Is this reasonable? Why or why not?"

Division

Although the process of division is a natural part of children's experiences, computational procedures for division have proved to be difficult for children to learn for several reasons. Probably the most significant is that not only do children need to know the division basic facts, but they also need to be able to multiply and subtract efficiently.

A great deal of time is spent in elementary and middle school trying to help children master the division algorithm. This is unjustifiable given that adults will reach for a calculator when a long-division computation is needed.

Instruction on division computation should emphasize division with one-digit divisors so that children can develop an understanding of the steps involved. Some experience with two-digit divisors also is necessary, particularly to help children develop skill in estimating partial quotients. Extending this to a four-digit dividend can provide all the experience needed to become proficient with paper-and-pencil division computation. Beyond that, virtually all adults reach for a calculator, so why shouldn't children? There are times when division with larger numbers is required to solve a problem and a calculator may not be available. These large computations, however, should not be the focus of instruction.

Posing Story Problems Set in Real-World Contexts

Instruction should begin with a real-life problem, either an equal-groups or array situation, as in the following examples.

> *Five children agreed to share equally all the apples they collected on Halloween. They collected 67 apples. How many apples did each child get?*

Notice that this problem results in a remainder. Sharing situations in which there is no remainder are rare, and they can be treated as a special case of the general algorithm.

The problem with the same numbers can be posed using an area and array interpretation, as follows:

> *A teacher wanted to arrange 67 chairs into 5 equal rows. How many chairs will be in each row?*

Using Models for Computation

Children can use base-ten blocks to find the solution to the preceding apples problem, as shown in Figure 9-27 on p. 198. Notice that the blocks are split evenly among the five groups.

The chair problem from the preceding section also can be solved using base-ten blocks. For problems involving the array interpretation, however, it makes more sense to model the problem as an array, as shown in Figure 9-28. Notice that in division problems using the area and array interpretation, the area (67) is known and the number of rows (5) is known, and the task is to find the length of the rows.

In both interpretations, make sure children understand the meaning of each of the numbers in the problem and how those numbers connect with the base-ten blocks. For example, ask the children what the 5 means in the apples problem (the number of equal groups they're making). What does it mean in the chairs problem (the number of equal rows they're making)? As with the other operations, making the connections shown in Figure 9-27, on p. 198, among concrete representation, place-value language, and symbols helps children make sense of computation. Children should have many experiences making these three-way connections before moving to the traditional algorithm.

A note about language for division. As with multiplication, there are many terms related to division that children *may* eventually learn. In a division setting, the total number to be "divided up" (shared) is the *dividend*, the number in each group is the *divisor*, and the resulting number of groups is the *quotient*. (Some problems require the divisor and quotient to exchange meanings.) The number of objects, if any, that cannot be shared equally is referred to as the *remainder*. Children often call these the "leftovers" as they become familiar and comfortable with division language, which is perfectly acceptable.

FIGURE 9-28 Using an Array to Solve a Division Problem

Problem/Steps	Concrete Representation
67 chairs arranged into 5 rows. How many in each row?	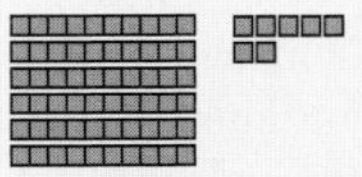
Arrange tens into 5 rows.	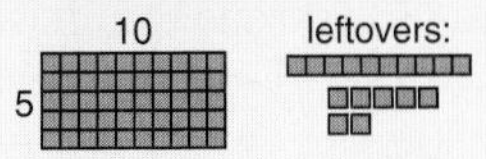 10; 5; leftovers:
Regroup ten to ones. Arrange ones into 5 rows.	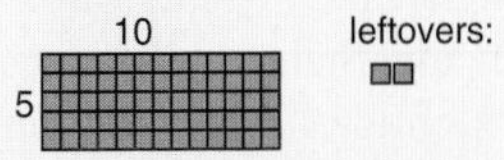 10; 5; leftovers:
Result: There are 13 chairs in each row, with 2 chairs left over.	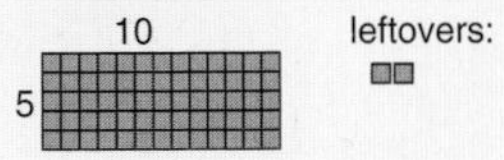 10; 5; leftovers:

FIGURE 9-27 Solving a Division Problem by Using Base-Ten Blocks, Bridging Algorithms, and the Traditional Algorithm

Problem/Steps	Concrete Representation	Symbolic Representation		
		Ladder Algorithm	Pyramid Algorithm	Traditional Algorithm
67 apples shared among 5 children. How many does each child get?		5)67	5)67	5)67
Distribute tens.		5)67 −50 | 10 17	10 5)67 −50 17	1 5)67 −50 17
Regroup tens to ones. Distribute ones.		5)67 −50 | 10 17 −15 | 3 2	3 10 5)67 −50 17 −15 2	13 5)67 −50 17 −15 2
Result: Each child gets 13 apples. There are 2 apples left over.		13r2 5)67 −50 | 10 17 −15 | 3 2 | 13	13r2 3 10 5)67 −50 17 −15 2	13r2 5)67 −50 17 −15 2

Using Estimation and Mental Computation

Mental computation with division problems is probably best achieved by thinking of division as the inverse of multiplication; that is, using a basic fact example, 48 ÷ 6, children can think, "What number times 6 is 48?" This works particularly well when the dividend is a number such as 18,000 and the divisor is a single digit. For example, 18,000 ÷ 6 is 3000 because 6 × 3 is 18, so 6 × 3,000 is 18,000.

Where the divisor is also a multiple of 10, there are two main approaches children could use to compute mentally. First, children are commonly taught to mentally divide each number by 10. In this case, 240 ÷ 40 becomes 24 ÷ 4, 2,400 ÷ 40 is 240 ÷ 4, and so on. These examples are now equivalent to the examples in the preceding paragraph. The second way is to consider only the nonzero digits and then determine the place value of the quotient afterward. For 18,000 ÷ 60, think: "6 × what is 18? 6 × 3 = 18. The 3 must be hundreds because tens (60) × hundreds (300) is thousands (18,000). The quotient is 300." For the most part, computations more complex than these should be done by elementary and middle school children using paper-and-pencil algorithms or calculators rather than mentally.

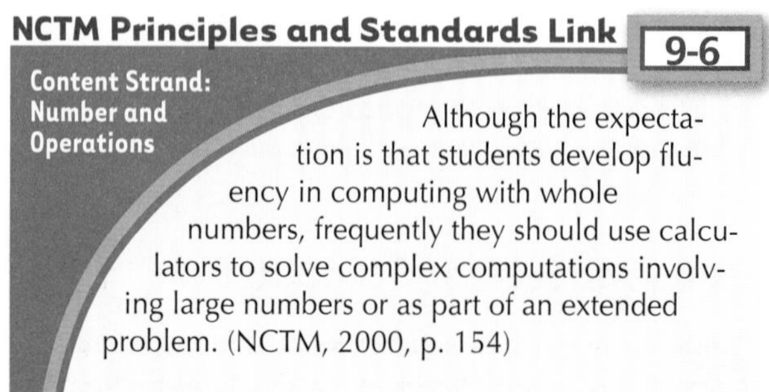
NCTM Principles and Standards Link 9-6

Content Strand: Number and Operations

Although the expectation is that students develop fluency in computing with whole numbers, frequently they should use calculators to solve complex computations involving large numbers or as part of an extended problem. (NCTM, 2000, p. 154)

Developing Bridging Algorithms to Connect Problems, Models, Estimation, and Symbols

Learning the paper-and-pencil algorithm is essentially learning a means of recording what is done concretely. Using place-value language and the base-ten blocks is a natural and efficient way to do this.

The first step is to introduce children to another way of writing 67 ÷ 5, using the traditional division box, as shown here:

$$5\overline{)67}$$

When solving division questions such as 67 divided by 5, the phrase "5 goes into 67" should *not* be used because it has no mathematical meaning. Rather, language that is appropriate for the context should be used such as "67 apples to be shared among 5 people" or "5 groups to share 67 apples." In a measurement context, expressions such as "67 apples to be separated into groups of 5" might be used. In an area or array context, a phrase such as "67 chairs arranged into 5 rows" could be used.

Figure 9-27 illustrated two different ways the sharing and place-value language could be translated into a paper-and-pencil recording process. These algorithms are known as the *ladder* (or *repeated subtraction*) algorithm, and the *pyramid* (or *partial quotients*) algorithm. Notice that in the ladder method, the number in each group is recorded *down the right side* of the problem like a ladder, and then added and transferred above the dividend. Similarly, in the pyramid method, the number in each group is recorded *above* the divisor, stacked in a way roughly resembling a pyramid, then added to form the quotient. The usefulness of these algorithms will become more apparent in the following section, where we consider three-digit dividends. It is important, however, to begin using these algorithms with two-digit divisors for consistency.

Three-digit dividend. Problems with three-digit dividends are a bit more complicated than those with two-digit dividends. Consider the following problem:

Three children agreed to share 449 baseball cards. How many baseball cards did each child get?

You should try it. Set out the base-ten blocks and manipulate them in step with the sequence in Figure 9-29, in which 449 objects shared among 3 children is illustrated.

After solving the problem using base-ten blocks, start again, this time recording the result of each step by using the ladder algorithm and the pyramid algorithms. Think about what each number means in each algorithm.

For example, what does the 100 mean in the ladder algorithm? It means that we put 100 into each group or, using the context of the problem, that each child got 100 baseball cards. Now consider the 100 in the pyramid algorithm—it means the same thing but is written in a different location. Finally, consider the 100 (or the 1 in the hundreds place) in the traditional algorithm. Its meaning is the same, but it appears a little more abstract because, rather than being written as 100, it is written as 1 in the hundreds place. This distinction is often overlooked or misunderstood by children, so it is important for you to call attention to it through discussion.

Children need to solve many problems involving one-digit divisors and two- and three-digit dividends. Teachers should not rush into introducing division with two-digit divisors until children can clearly verbalize and model what they are doing as they solve one-digit divisor problems using base-ten blocks and then paper and pencil.

Developing the Traditional Algorithm

After children have had adequate experiences solving division problems using base-ten blocks and using either the ladder algorithm or the pyramid algorithm for the representation, they will begin to shorten the algorithm. In the traditional algorithm, only a one-digit partial quotient is recorded for each digit in the dividend. You can encourage children to "condense" the partial quotients by suggesting tasks such as "Try to find a shorter way to record a division problem." The following section describes how to do this in greater detail.

For the sample problem in Figure 9-27, 67 ÷ 5, the final step in the progression toward the traditional algorithm is to record the quotient on one line above the dividend, as shown in the far right column in Figure 9-27. Making sense of the traditional algorithm depends on children's having a strong understanding of place value as well as the teacher's using language and asking questions that emphasize place value.

The difference between the traditional algorithm for division and the ladder and pyramid algorithms is the emphasis on place value. For example, rather than recording the 10 obtained when 67 is split into 5 groups, in the traditional algorithm this would be recorded as 1 group of ten by writing a 1 above the 6 tens in the divisor. By placing the three algorithms side by side, as illustrated in Figure 9-27, children will be able to connect the algorithms and see that the 1 ten in each case is the same. The connection and transition will be facilitated if children are allowed to use either format.

Similarly, for problems with three-digit divisors, such as 449 ÷ 3, as shown in Figure 9-29, rather than recording the 100 obtained when 449 is split into 3 groups, in the traditional algorithm this would be recorded as 1 group of one hundred by writing a 1 above the 4 hundreds in the divisor. By placing the three algorithms side by side, as illustrated in Figure 9-29, children will be able to connect the algorithms and see that the 1 ten in each case is the

FIGURE 9-29 Solving a Larger Division Problem by Using Base-Ten Blocks, Bridging Algorithms, and the Traditional Algorithm

Problem/Steps	Concrete Representation	Symbolic Representation: Ladder Algorithm	Symbolic Representation: Pyramid Algorithm	Symbolic Representation: Traditional Algorithm
449 baseball cards shared among 3 children. How many cards does each child get?	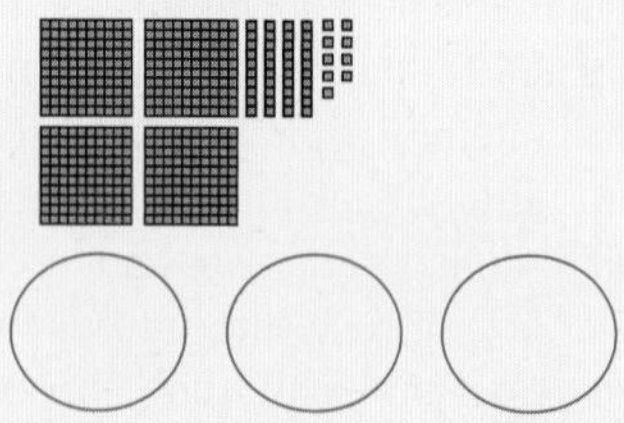	3)449	3)449	3)449
Distribute hundreds into 3 groups.	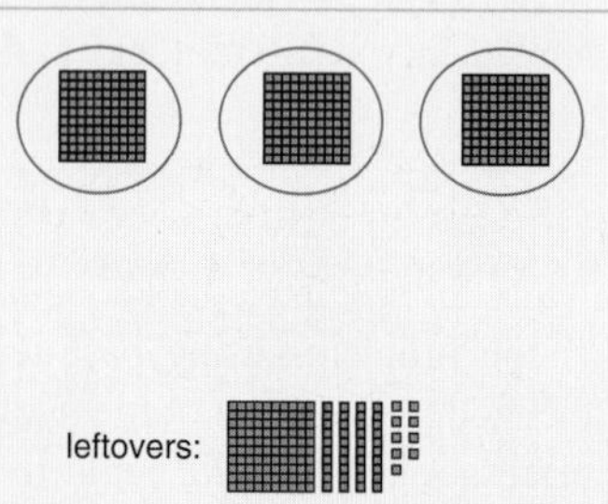 leftovers:	3)449 −300 │ 100 149	100 3)449 −300 149	1 3)449 −3 149
Regroup hundred into tens. Distribute tens into 3 groups.	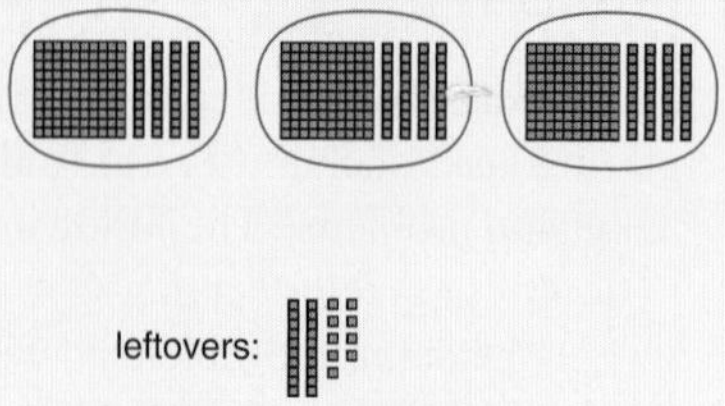 leftovers:	3)449 −300 │ 100 149 −120 │ 40 29	40 100 3)449 −300 149 −120 29	14 3)449 −3 149 −12 29
Regroup tens into ones. Distribute ones into 3 groups.	 leftovers:	3)449 −300 │ 100 149 −120 │ 40 29 −27 │ 9 2	9 40 100 3)449 −300 149 −120 29 −27 2	149 3)449 −3 149 −12 29 −27 2
Result: Each child gets 149 baseball cards. There are 2 cards left.	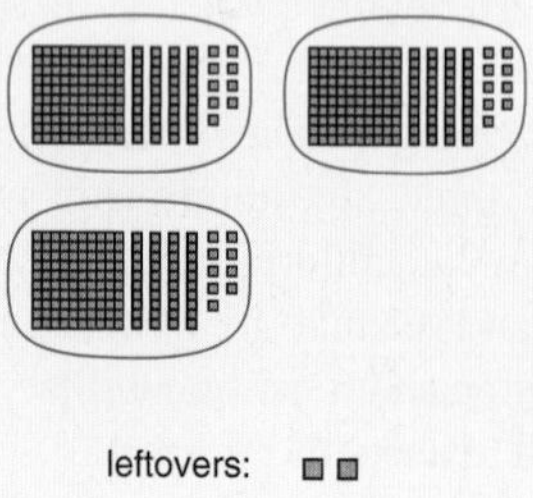 leftovers:	3)449 −300 │ 100 149 −120 │ 40 29 −27 │ 9 2 │ 149	149r2 9 40 100 3)449 −300 149 −120 29 −27 2	149r2 3)449 −3 149 −12 29 −27 2

Literature Link 9-1

Addition, Subtraction, Multiplication, Division, Estimation, and Computational Procedures

Pinczes, Elinor. (1995). ***A Remainder of One.*** New York: Houghton Mifflin.

Developing the language of mathematics, including both the words that children use to communicate orally and the written symbol system, is essential for mathematical understanding yet it lags behind the performance of mathematical computations. Using children's books with authentic problem situations helps children see that learning computation solves a real-life purpose. ***A Remainder of One*** is the story of a squadron of 25 bugs who try unsuccessfully to divide evenly for a parade. After several attempts, the squadron finds that five rows of five is the solution to their mathematical dilemma.

- Create groups or arrays using snap cubes or centimeter cubes to model the formations of the 25th squadron in the story.
- Represent numbers other than 25. Determine which of those numbers divide evenly and which of them have remainders.
- Have children select a number between 26 and 50 and divide their number by 2, 3, 4, and 5. Write number sentences showing each of these division sentences and illustrate the division of their own bug squadron on large sheets of construction paper. Look for patterns, such as those numbers that always have a remainder or those that never have a remainder.
- Determine the different factors of numbers by using color tiles or graph paper to group different numbers into arrays. Identify numbers that have several factors and those that have only two factors. Make a chart of these numbers and identify them as "prime" and "composite" numbers.

Source: Dr. Patricia Moyer-Packenham, Utah State University.

same. The connection and transition will be easier if children are allowed to use either format.

Making sense of remainders. All of the examples in this section involved remainders. It is customary to record remainders in one of two ways, as shown next. In the first case, the remainder is simply reported as a remainder. In the second example, the remainder is reported as a fraction of the divisor and is an integral part of the quotient. The children's book *A Remainder of One* provides an interesting context for the discussion of remainders (see Literature Link 9-1).

$$6\overline{)625} = 104 \text{ R}1 \qquad 6\overline{)625} = 104\tfrac{1}{6}$$

Either of the above is an acceptable response if the computation is strictly a symbolic process. When the computation arises from a real-life context, the remainder must be interpreted in the context of the problem and handled in a way that is appropriate to that context. Consider the following four cases.

CASE 1: Part of the answer

I have a 19-inch length of ribbon from which I want to make two award ribbons of equal length. How long will each ribbon be?

Here the answer, 9 with 1 inch left over, or 9 R1, does not make sense because there is no need to have wasted material if they made two 9-inch ribbons and discarded the one-inch piece that was left over. In this case, it makes more sense to cut two pieces each 9.5 inches long, using all the ribbon. The "remainder" becomes part of the answer.

CASE 2: Include remainders

Seven parents have volunteered to drive Mrs. Clemenson's class on their field trip to the zoo. There are 31 people going on the trip, including the parents. How many people will be in each car?

Neither 4 R3 nor 4 makes any sense in this case. What would actually happen is that 4 cars would take 4 people and 3 cars would have 5 people. No one will be left behind. Again, there really is no remainder. The "remainder" has to be included by evenly distributing it among as many groups as necessary.

CASE 3: Round up

A grocery store sells spaghetti sauce at 2 jars for $1.39. How much would a customer pay for one jar?

Again, neither 69 R1 nor 69 makes any sense. The quotient would be rounded up, and the customer would pay 70¢ if he bought only one jar.

FIGURE 9-30 Connecting Place-Value Language with Symbols for Two-Digit Divisors

Language	Record
I can t share 4 hundreds among 62 groups. I can't share 49 tens among 62 groups, but I can share 493 ones among 62 groups.	62)493
I will estimate how many ones I can share by rounding the 62 groups to 70.	Think 70 → 62)493
What number is compatible with 70 that I can use for the dividend? 490	Think 70 → 62)493 ← Think 490 70)490
7 × 70 is 490 so I can distribute 7 ones to each group. Record the 7 in the ones position since I am distributing ones.	7 62)493
How many ones were distributed to the 62 groups? 7 × 62 = 434	7 62)493 434
How many ones are left? 59. Can I distribute any more ones? No. There is a remainder of 59.	7 62)493 434 59

CASE 4: Ignore remainder

Thirty-seven children try out for three teams. If 11 players are allowed on each team, how many teams can be formed?

Clearly, neither 3 R4 nor 3 is an appropriate answer. Four children cannot be included on a team. To follow the rules exactly, they can be scorekeepers, timers, or equipment managers but have to be "ignored" or go uncounted as team members.

Two-digit divisors. The role of estimation becomes much more significant when children need to solve problems with a divisor of two or more digits. Consider a problem such as 493 ÷ 62. Children can take several approaches to estimating the quotient.

1. *Rounding.* By rounding the divisor to the nearest 10, a logical estimate is 8 because 8 × 60 is 480. However, 8 × 62 = 496, which is larger than the dividend.
2. *Ignore the last digit in both the divisor and the dividend.* This results in the exercise, 49 ÷ 6. Again, 8 is a reasonable, but too high, estimate.
3. *Round the divisor up to the nearest 10.* The above example would be thought of as 493 ÷ 70. Because 7 × 70 is 490, a reasonable estimate is 7, which works well. However, if the problem had been 503 ÷ 62, the estimate would still be 7 because 7 × 70 = 490 and 8 × 70 = 560, which exceeds the dividend. However, 7 is too small in this second case.
4. *Change both the divisor and the dividend to the nearest pair of compatible numbers.* Compatible numbers are numbers that work together easily. For division, compatible numbers are a pair of numbers that evenly divide. So for the problem 493 ÷ 62, think of a pair of numbers close to 493 and 62 that are divisible. One such pair is 480 and 60, since 480 ÷ 60 = 8.

The language corresponding to the steps in the algorithm is essentially the same as for the one-digit divisor. Samples of the language associated with each step in computing 493 ÷ 62 is described in Figures 9-30 and 9-31. The final result of the algorithm must be recorded in either form (a) or form (b) in Figure 9-32.

Examining Student Work

Figures 9-33 and 9-34 contain samples of children's work in practicing dividing whole numbers. Look closely at the work and try to determine what the children understand about division and analyze the errors the children are making. Why might they be making these errors? If you were their teacher, what might you do to help them?

Description of division error pattern 1. In Figure 9-33, Gail records the quotient (answer) from right to left. She may be overgeneralizing procedures that she uses in addition, subtraction, and multiplication, where the ones digit of the answer is usually recorded first.

FIGURE 9-31 Connecting Meaningful Language with Symbols in Division

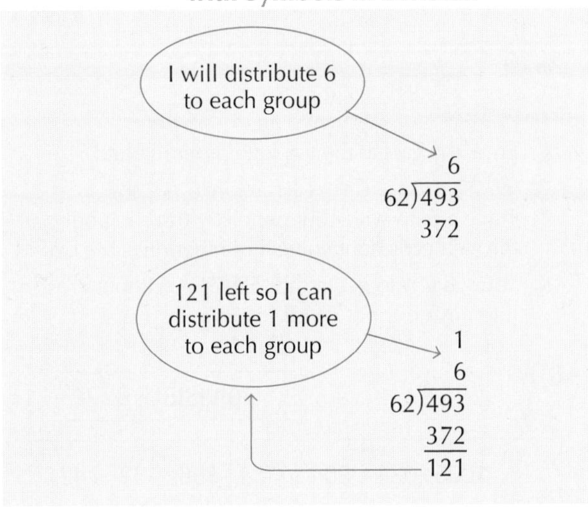

FIGURE 9-32 Two Ways to Record the Final Answer in the Division Algorithm When Using Estimates

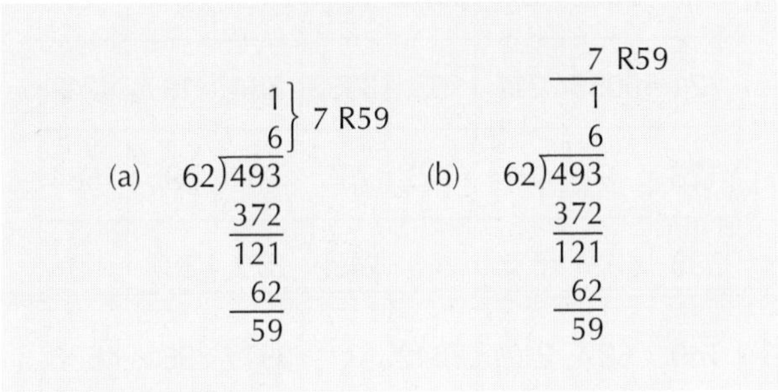

```
      1 }                        7 R59
      6 } 7 R59                  1
(a) 62)493                       6
      372               (b) 62)493
      121                     372
       62                     121
       59                      62
                               59
```

FIGURE 9-33 Division Error Pattern 1

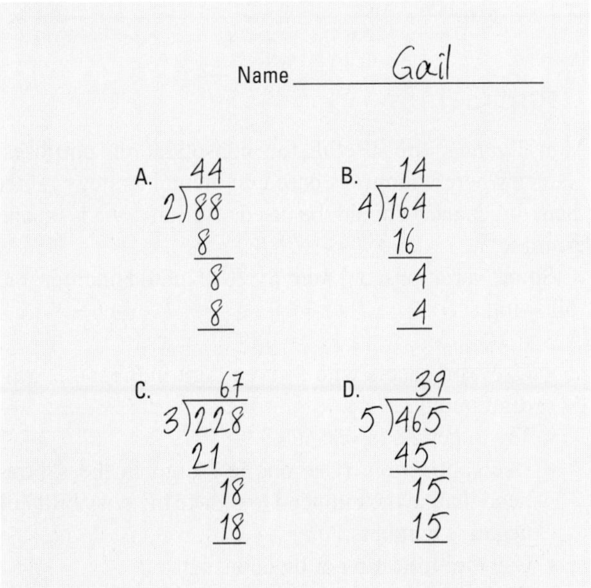

Name Gail

```
A.  44        B.  14
  2)88          4)164
    8             16
     8              4
     8              4

C.  67        D.  39
  3)228         5)465
    21            45
     18            15
     18            15
```

Source: Error Patterns in Computation 8/e by Ashlock, ©2010, p. 43. Reprinted by permission of Pearson Education, Inc., Upper Saddle River, NJ.

FIGURE 9-34 Division Error Pattern 2

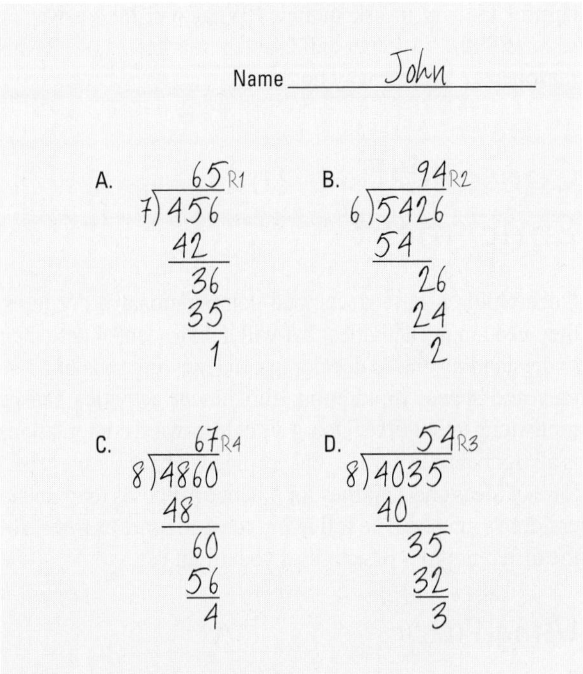

Name John

```
A.   65 R1     B.   94 R2
   7)456          6)5426
     42             54
      36             26
      35             24
       1              2

C.   67 R4     D.   54 R3
   8)4860         8)4035
     48             40
      60             35
      56             32
       4              3
```

Source: Error Patterns in Computation 8/e by Ashlock, ©2010, p. 44. Reprinted by permission of Pearson Education, Inc., Upper Saddle River, NJ.

How a teacher might help. You could emphasize estimating the quotient for each problem. For example, in problem B, 164 ÷ 4 should be about 40, and in problem D, 465 ÷ 5 should be about 90. Encourage Gail to compare these estimates with her answers. Discuss with Gail the correct placement of digits in the quotient.

Description of division error pattern 2. In Figure 9-34, John does not record a zero in the quotient. He may be bringing down one digit at a time and not recording a zero when he cannot divide, or he may be bringing down groups of two digits at a time from the dividend.

How a teacher might help. Use the pyramid algorithm to help John understand the role of place value in the answer to a division problem. Also, encourage John to estimate each result before beginning a division problem.

Determining the Reasonableness of Solutions

It is critically important for children to think about the reasonableness of their solutions to division problems. With division, as with other operations, teachers' questioning can help children focus on reasonableness. For example, consider the problem 804 ÷ 2. The 0 in the dividend will often cause difficulties for children; a common incorrect answer to this problem is 42. It is important for teachers to frequently ask questions such as "If 804 candies are shared by 2 children, *about how many* will each child get?" Each child should get about 400 candies. Other questions that are helpful for you to ask include "What will the answer *be close to*?" and "Another child said the answer was 42. Is this reasonable? Why or why not?"

Consolidation and Enrichment

Once children have developed computational procedures, they need many activities that will help to consolidate their understanding and to develop proficiency in terms of accuracy and speed. In addition, enrichment activities can be motivating to children. Doing straightforward computations is all right once in a while, but you need to have a large repertoire of ideas and activities for practice purposes to maintain children's interest. The following categories are examples of the different types of activities you might use.

Using Puzzles

Puzzles provide an interesting and novel way for children to practice computation (Neufeld, 1991). Children will get a great deal of practice with addition and subtraction as they attempt to complete the puzzle in Activity 9-9. In this activity, children are to arrange the numbers from 1 through 19 in each of the vertical "columns" in the honeycomb so that the sum of each "column" is 38. How could you use this activity to give children practice with subtraction?

ACTIVITY 9-9 Honeycomb Sum

Materials

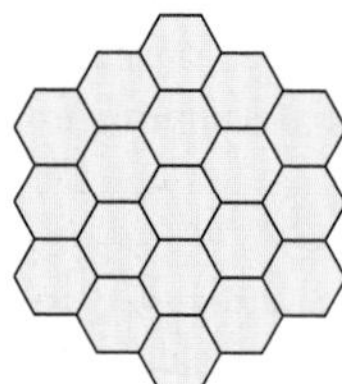

Procedure

1. Make each column sum to 38. You can use only the numbers 1 through 19. Use each number only once.
2. Can you do it a different way?

In the puzzle in Activity 9-10, the task is to trace a path from the upper left cell to the lower right cell by joining cells that contain a number divisible by 7. Cells may be joined vertically, horizontally, or diagonally. You can change this activity to provide children with practice for other multiples.

ACTIVITY 9-10 Divisibility Path

Materials

Pencil

Procedure

1. Enter the grid at the top left corner marked "START."
2. Trace a path with your pencil by traveling only through cells containing a number divisible by 7.
3. Your goal is to get to the "FINISH" without crossing into any cells not divisible by 7.

START ↓

DIVISIBLE BY 7

7	1005	634	904	1111	156	63	427
238	268	928	56	1215	297	5123	5
494	84	1015	96	140	307	77	7963
47	2047	82	5326	217	3131	9876	357
721	6055	214	63	3333	384	197	4242
128	9	4014	546	753	2114	595	1584
539	4021	535	246	2499	872	287	59
749	587	2121	8642	37	3977	861	4536

↑ FINISH

Using Games

Many games are useful for consolidation purposes. Games where winning is based on mental strategy rather than on chance should be used. Activity 9-11 is one example.

Some variations on Activity 9-11 could include the following:

- Use worksheets with 3 three-digit numbers, 3 two-digit numbers, etc.
- Try to get the lowest sum.
- Use subtraction. (Use one less digit in the subtrahend than in the minuend to reduce the possibility of negative numbers.)
- Use multiplication or division.
- Will your strategy be different if balls are *not* replaced?

ACTIVITY 9-11 Greatest Sum

Materials

- A spinner with digits 0 through 9
- Worksheet as below. (Several grids can be placed on one page to facilitate multiple games.)

Procedure

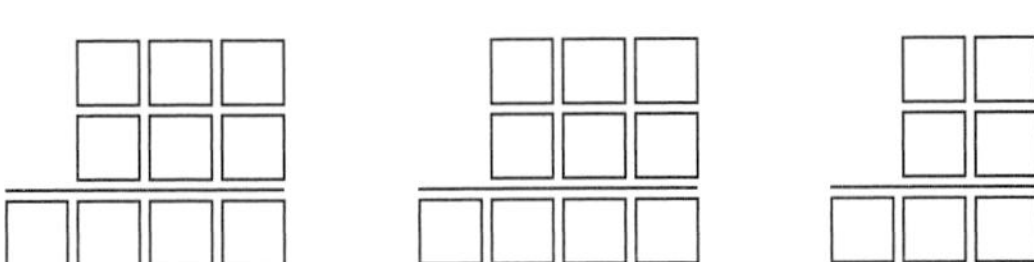

1. Select a leader to spin the spinner. (If this is a whole-class activity, the teacher may act as leader.)
2. The leader spins and announces the number on it. All players write this number in one of the addend boxes on the worksheet. Once a number has been placed, it cannot be moved or changed.
3. Spin again.
4. Repeat steps 2 and 3 until all addend boxes are filled.
5. Compute the sum.
6. The winners are all those with the greatest sum.

Activity 9-12 encourages children to use number sense about possible combinations while providing some practice with the algorithms involving small numbers. Many of the combinations will not involve division because division will not produce a whole number. Nevertheless, children will need to consider division and make a mental decision as to whether the number will divide evenly.

Two of the dice must be specially prepared, as will a variety of game boards. See Blackline Master 6 for a pattern to make dice to use with this activity. Numbers from 1 to 1,296 can be used randomly to create the game boards. How can you make a 1 with the possible numbers on the dice? How can you make 1,296?

Like all bingo-type cards, the sample game board in Activity 9-12 will not contain responses for some rolls of the dice. If a combination cannot be found in a reasonable time, play goes to the next player. Does the sample game board in Activity 9-12 have a response for a roll of 5, 9, or 17?

Using Riddles

Riddles are another motivating way for children to practice computation. The solution to a riddle similar to the one suggested in Chapter 8, page 167, could be developed with larger numbers to provide addition and subtraction computation practice. Once you have found or created a riddle, it is not difficult to construct exercises such as those shown in Activities 9-13 and 9-14. Knowing the answer to a riddle, the teacher can simply create the kinds of questions the class or small group of children needs practice with and then associate each letter with the answer to a computation. The difficulty level can be changed to suit the level of the class. The exercises could also be altered to include decimals or common fractions.

Using Computer Software

Research suggests that the use of the computer enhances computational performance (Cathcart, 1990, 1991). Computer software is one more ingredient in your repertoire of ideas that you can use to provide variety in practice activities. Many excellent software programs are available to practice computation. You can search on the Internet, using the phrase "math software" to find helpful programs.

ACTIVITY 9-12 All-Ops

Materials

- 3 dice:
  - 1 regular (numbers 1–6)
  - 1 with numbers 7–12
  - 1 with numbers 13–18
- Game board (see sample below)

ALL-OPS

4	88	19	38	89
1024	55	76	106	8
60	3	I Can	111	635
149	91	384	9	63
904	210	788	500	1296

Object

To be the first to place 5 markers in a row, column, or diagonal.

Procedure

1. One player shakes all 3 dice.
2. All players then use the 3 numbers showing and any combination of the 4 operations to try to produce a number on their card.
3. Each player must have one other player verify his or her work.
4. Players take turns rolling the dice.

ACTIVITY 9-13 Why Does a Hummingbird Hum?

Procedure

Do each computation, then use the code to find the matching letter. The first one is done as an example.

Code

37 – W	122 – C	232 – H
54 – N	123 – O	241 – K
73 – M	154 – R	259 – E
78 – T	162 – D	287 – S
83 – I	163 – L	341 – A

36 + 47 =	83	I
143 − 65 =	____	____
64 + 98 =	____	____
12 + 69 + 42 =	____	____
345 − 86 =	____	____
402 − 115 =	____	____
92 − 38 =	____	____
97 + 26 =	____	____
212 − 134 =	____	____
386 − 145 =	____	____
618 − 564 =	____	____
66 + 9 + 48 =	____	____
100 − 63 =	____	____
155 − 77 =	____	____
155 + 77 =	____	____
167 + 92 =	____	____
108 − 71 =	____	____
254 − 131 =	____	____
88 + 66 =	____	____
115 + 47 =	____	____
136 + 295 − 144 =	____	____

Valuing Other Algorithms

Philipp (1996) describes the benefits of teachers talking with children and their families about the algorithms they use to solve problems. Many people, especially those who learned mathematics in another country, use different algorithms from those customarily taught in this country. According to Philipp, this "legitimizes the mathematics learning of either the child or a member of the child's family but also presents an opportunity to honor this learning in both the child's eyes and, depending on what is done with the information, in the eyes of all the students in the class" (p. 129).

Conclusion

Solving a problem involving computation can be done in a number of ways, and children should be encouraged to develop their own computational procedures. This takes some time, but it is time well spent.

In developing computational procedures, try to capture as many serendipitous events as possible to provide a meaningful context. Choose events that are current, involve the children, and have some bearing on their lives.

In general, children will proceed through several phases as they learn computational procedures. They should begin by finding the answer to a real-world problem through the manipulation of base-ten blocks or other concrete material. Children should then be encouraged to record in their own way the process they used to find the answer. Over time, this recording will become more symbolic and concise, but still it is done in the child's own way. Later, children can be guided into recording in the most concise form (standard algorithm). Even here variations may result because algorithms are not universally common.

Throughout the process of developing computational procedures, children should be encouraged to use estimation and mental computation. This helps children learn computational strategies and develop number sense. Estimation and mental computation can also provide a check on the accuracy of paper-and-pencil or calculator computations. As such they become a part of the looking-back phase of problem solving. Calculators should be available to help children solve problems, particularly with larger numbers.

Children also need practice to become proficient with computational procedures. The key is to employ a *variety* of interesting activities for practice.

Sample Lesson

A Lesson on Estimating Quotients

Grade level: Fifth

Materials: Base-ten blocks

Lesson objective: Students will estimate quotients by using base ten blocks.

Standards link: Students select appropriate methods and apply them accurately to estimate quotients or calculate them mentally, depending on the context and numbers involved (NCTM *Curriculum Focal Points*, grade 5).

Launch: Pose the following problem:

Three children shared 439 baseball cards. How many baseball cards did each child get?

Ask students, "How could we estimate the size of the quotient?" Review the meaning of the term "quotient," which is the answer in a division problem. Solicit recommendations about how to determine this. Then display base-ten blocks representing 439, and ask, "How would three children share these fairly?" Demonstrate, following students' suggestions, separating the hundreds blocks into three equal-sized groups, resulting in 1 hundred for each child. After distributing the hundreds blocks, ask students, "How many does each child have so far (100)? So is the answer going to be 100 something (no)? Can it be 200 (no)? Or less than 100? (no)"

Next, write the problem symbolically: $3\overline{)439}$ Ask, "How would we enter what we know about the quotient so far?" Record the 100 in each group above the 439. State "So this means that each child will get at least 100 of the baseball cards."

Next pose another problem, such as the following:

Four children shared 943 M&Ms. How many M&Ms did each child get?

Ask, "About how many M&Ms will each child get?" As in the previous problem, solicit estimates, then model distributing 9 hundreds blocks into 4 groups. Then write the problem symbolically: $3\overline{)943}$ and record the 200 in each group above the 943. State "So this means that each child will get at least 200 M&Ms."

Explore: In pairs, have students estimate the quotient in several division problems by using base-ten blocks. Then have them write the estimate and an explanation of how they determined it.

Summarize: Coming together as a whole class, ask for volunteers to describe how they estimate the quotient in a division problem. Focus on their explanations of how they used the largest place value in the answer to estimate the quotient.

FOLLOW-UP

Complete the following questions.

1. Consider the number sentences to use in this lesson. Why start with a dividend in the hundreds? Under what conditions might you use a dividend in the tens? How would a dividend in the thousands change the lesson? Why?
2. Consider difficulties students might have with this concept and this lesson. What modification could you make to avoid or minimize these issues? What modifications could you make for students with special needs?
3. How would a lesson on estimation in multiplication be similar to this lesson? Describe that lesson.

IN PRACTICE

Complete the following activities to include in your professional portfolio.

1. Estimate each sum and describe the thinking processes you use.

258	4,921
819	2,121
234	866
560	7,295
602	

2. For each list of exercises below, describe the error pattern, complete the remaining problems using the error pattern, and describe a remediation plan for each type of error.

I.

347	468	516	739	604
− 189	− 342	− 209	− 485	− 368
242	126	313		

II.

28	394	476	366	37
36	+ 242	+ 708	+ 547	21
+ 21	5136	11714		+ 55
715				

3. Visit elementary classrooms and, with the teacher's permission, make copies of children's written work using algorithms to solve problems. Identify the errors made and any patterns in those errors. Discuss what you might do if you were their teacher to enhance the children's understanding.

4. Write a lesson to help children connect meaning to symbols for an algorithm of your choice.

LINKS TO THE INTERNET

Ask Dr. Math

http://mathforum.org/library/drmath/drmath.elem.html

Contains numerous resources for computation, including alternate algorithms such as lattice multiplication.

 Now go to Topic 7: "Estimation and Computation with Whole Numbers" in the MyEducationLab (www.myeducationlab.com) for your course, where you can:

- Find learning outcomes along with the national standards that connect to these outcomes.
- Apply and practice your understanding of the core teaching skills identified in the chapter with a Building Teaching Skills and Dispositions learning unit.
- Complete Assignments and Activities that can help you understand the chapter content more deeply.
- Complete *enVision MATH* Sample Curricula assignments that allow you to examine and work with chapters from *enVision MATH*, a K-6 mathematics program.
- Check your comprehension on the content covered in the chapter by going to the Study Plan in the Book-Specific Resources for your text. Here you will be able to take a chapter quiz, receive feedback on your answers, and then access Review, Practice, and Enrichment activities to enhance your understanding of chapter content.
- Go to the Book-Specific Resources for Chapter 9 to explore mathematical reasoning related to chapter content in the Activities section.

RESOURCES FOR TEACHERS

Reference Books

National Council of Teachers of Mathematics (2006). Cirriculum Focal Points for Prekindergarten through Grade 8 Mathematics. Reston, VA: Author.

Warfield, Janet, & Sherry L. Meier (2007). Whole number properties and operations. In Peter Kloosterman & Frank K. Lester, Jr. (Eds.), Results and interpretations of the 2003 mathematics assessment of the National Assessmet of Educational Progress. Reston, VA: National Council of Teachers of Mathematics.

Children's Literature

Chinn, Karen (1995). *Sam and the Lucky Money*. New York: Scholastic.

Pinczes, E. (1995). *A Remainder of One*. New York: Houghton Mifflin. (p. 193).

CHAPTER 10

Developing Fraction Concepts

NCTM CONNECTING WITH THE STANDARDS

The National Council of Teachers of Mathematics (NCTM) *Principles and Standards for School Mathematics* recommends that a significant amount of instructional time be devoted to rational numbers in Grades 3–5, stating that "the focus should be on developing students' conceptual understanding of fractions and decimals—what they are, how they are represented, and how they are related to whole numbers—rather than on developing computational fluency with rational numbers" (NCTM, 2000, p. 151). The document goes on to list several concepts related to fractions that children should experience and come to understand:

- Build their understanding of fractions as parts of a whole and as division;
- See and explore a variety of models of fractions, focusing primarily on familiar fractions such as halves, thirds, fourths, fifths, sixths, eighths, and tenths;
- See how fractions are related to a unit whole, compare fractional parts of a whole, and find equivalent fractions by using an area model in which part of a region is shaded;
- Develop strategies for ordering and comparing fractions, often using benchmarks such as $\frac{1}{2}$ and 1;
- See fractions as numbers, note their relationship to 1, and see relationships among fractions, including equivalence; and
- Understand that between any two fractions, there is always another fraction. (NCTM, 2000, p. 150)

The NCTM (2006) *Curriculum Focal Points* mentions fraction understanding as one of the three focal points for grade 3. It states that students should:

- develop an understanding of the meanings and uses of fractions to represent parts of a whole, parts of a set, or points or distances on a number line;
- understand that the size of a fractional part is relative to the size of the whole;

Developing Your Math Teaching Skills

When you have finished studying this chapter, you should be able to do the following:

- Discuss what children should understand about fractions.
- Describe three models that can be used in teaching the part-whole interpretation of fractions, discuss the teaching considerations involved in using each model, and give an example of each.
- List and describe strategies teachers can use to help children understand how to compare fractions.
- Explain the importance of helping children understand the equivalence of fractions.

- use fractions to represent numbers that are equal to, less than, or greater than 1;
- solve problems that involve comparing and ordering fractions by using models, benchmark fractions, or common numerators or denominators; and
- understand and use models, including the number line, to identify equivalent fractions (NCTM, 2006, p. 15).

Teachers need to understand what fractions are and what children should come to understand about them. As with many other mathematics topics, traditionally there has been a rush to introduce abstract symbols before children understand the underlying concepts. This chapter discusses how to help children develop a strong understanding of fraction concepts.

ASSESSING MATHEMATICS UNDERSTANDING

In order to become familiar with the mathematics concepts and procedures discussed in this chapter, take a few minutes and complete the following *Chapter 10 Preassessment.* Answer each question on your own. Then think about the possible misunderstandings some elementary-school children might have about each topic. If you are able, administer this assessment to a child, and analyze his or her understanding of these topics.

1. Circle the figures that have $\frac{1}{4}$ shaded. Explain why each shaded region does or does not represent $\frac{1}{4}$.

a. 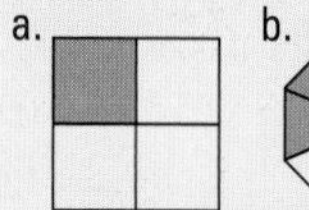 b.  c. 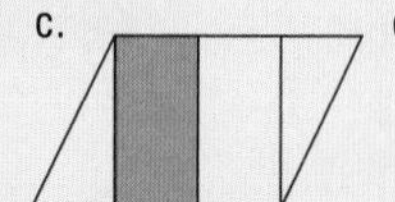 d. 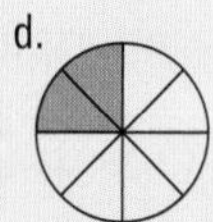

2. When 5 children shared 2 cookies equally, how much of the cookies does each child get?
3. Explain what $\frac{4}{3}$ means.
4. For each of the following, circle the larger number or write "=" if they are equal.

a. $\frac{1}{6}$ $\frac{1}{3}$ **b.** 1 $\frac{4}{3}$ **c.** $\frac{3}{6}$ $\frac{1}{2}$
d. $\frac{1}{7}$ $\frac{2}{7}$ **e.** $\frac{3}{10}$ $\frac{1}{2}$ **f.** $\frac{1}{2}$ $\frac{4}{6}$

5. For each of the following, fill in the blank to make the number sentence true.

a. $\frac{1}{2}$ = __/6 **b.** $\frac{2}{3}$ = 6/__

6. Change $4\frac{1}{3}$ into an improper fraction.

Let's see how a fifth-grader answered some of these questions. Go to MyEducationLab to view a clip that shows Ally, an average fifth-grade child at a high-performing school, solving several problems. The first six problems she solves are the same as Item 4 above. While viewing the clip, pay particular attention to Ally's explanations of how she compared these 6 pairs of fractions.

PEARSON **myeducationlab** The Power of Classroom Practice — Go to the Assignments and Activities section of Topic 8: "Fraction Concepts and Computation" in the MyEducationLab for your course and complete the activity "IMAP—Fraction Misconceptions."

Let's analyze Ally's reasoning. How does she solve each of the following problems?

a. Compare $\frac{1}{6}$ and $\frac{1}{3}$

Ally's answer: She initially says $\frac{1}{6}$ is larger, but changes her answer to $\frac{1}{3}$.

Ally's explanation: "Because if you changed the digit down more 3, and then if it was 1 one, then it would have to be ... it would equal to 1. And 1 is a whole number, so it's bigger."

An interpretation of Ally's explanation: The difference between 1 and 3 (in $\frac{1}{3}$) is less than the difference between 1 and 6 (in $\frac{1}{6}$), so $\frac{1}{3}$ is closer to 1, and 1 is larger than any fraction. (Think about the mathematics in Ally's reasoning. Is she correct? Is she sometimes correct, never correct, or always correct?)

b. Compare 1 and $\frac{4}{3}$

Ally's answer: 1 is larger.

Ally's explanation: "I thought 1 was bigger because it's a whole number, and it's just one group of just a one number."

c. Compare $\frac{3}{6}$ and $\frac{1}{2}$

Ally's answer: She indicates they're equal, but in her explanation changes her answer to $\frac{1}{2}$ is larger.

Ally's explanation: "If you changed the denominator to 1, just one digit lower, then it would equal to 1. And 1 is a whole number, so ...."

d. Compare $\frac{1}{7}$ and $\frac{2}{7}$

Ally's answer: $\frac{1}{7}$ is larger.

Ally's explanation: "I thought it was just the smallest number. And usually, you go down to the smallest number to get to the biggest number."

e. Compare $\frac{3}{10}$ and $\frac{1}{2}$

Ally's answer: $\frac{1}{2}$

Ally's explanation: "I could just change the bottom number one more digit, then—and it would be 1."

f. Compare $\frac{1}{2}$ and $\frac{4}{6}$

Ally's answer: $\frac{1}{2}$

Ally's explanation: (none given)

Analyzing Assessment Results

What do these responses tell us about Ally's understanding of fractions? What does she understand? Ally knows how to read fraction symbols correctly, for example, by reading $\frac{1}{7}$ as "one-seventh," and she knows that $\frac{1}{1}$ is equal to the whole number one. What does your child understand?

What does Ally not understand? Most of Ally's answers are incorrect, though she appears to have logical reasons for each of her incorrect answers. But her strategies also are incorrect and in fact are misconceptions that many children hold. Think back to the video clip (or watch it again). What are three misconceptions that Ally holds about fractions?

Common Misunderstandings about Fractions

- Whole numbers are always larger than fractions (even improper fractions). For example, she states that 1 is greater than $\frac{4}{3}$, noting that "One is bigger because it's a whole number."
- "Smaller is bigger with fractions." For example, she believes that $\frac{1}{7}$ is greater than $\frac{2}{7}$ because "you go down to the smallest number to get the biggest number (in fractions)."
- The difference between the denominator and numerator indicates how close the fraction is to 1.

Does this work? Well, it works sometimes. For example, consider the fractions $\frac{6}{7}$ and $\frac{1}{2}$. The difference between 7 and 6 is 1 and $\frac{6}{7}$ is close to 1. But what about $\frac{1}{2}$? The difference between 2 and 1 is also 1. Does that mean that $\frac{1}{2}$ is as close to one whole as $\frac{6}{7}$ is? No, but Ally seems to think that it does. Notice that she also thinks that $\frac{1}{2}$ is greater than $\frac{4}{6}$, presumably for this same reason.

Are there any other misunderstandings that children may have about comparing fractions? It is important to assess what children understand and are still working on understanding, in order to plan instruction that meets their needs.

Building on Assessment Results

Think about what can be done to help strengthen children's understandings and minimize (and hopefully eradicate) their misunderstandings and misconceptions.

The video clip shows that Ally is a charming, confident, articulate girl who does not understand fractions very well. For her, fractions seem to be comprised of a disconnected set of procedures for which she has few conceptual anchors. What might have led to her developing these misconceptions?

It is possible that Ally's mathematics learning experiences may have focused on a set of procedures to be memorized rather than a set of concepts to be understood. So what might we do next to help her understand these concepts?

A key element of all instruction is to make sure that students understand the concept. Students need to visualize concepts and relationships. This usually is best done with some sort of manipulative material, asking students to solve problems and examine the reasonableness of their solutions. The table below lists several common misunderstandings and what a teacher can do to help children with these misunderstandings.

IF students think that ...	THEN have students . . .
all whole numbers are greater than *all fractions* (including improper fractions) (e.g., $1 > \frac{4}{3}$ because 1 is a whole number and $\frac{4}{3}$ is a fraction)	*model* each number with a manipulative material and compare them again. Encourage students to generalize that fractions don't just exist between 0 and 1 but exist between all integers.
fractions with a smaller difference between the denominator and numerator, such as $\frac{1}{2}$, are closer to 1 than fractions with a larger difference, such as $\frac{4}{6}$	*model* selected non-examples, such as $\frac{1}{2}$ and $\frac{4}{6}$, with a manipulative material and compare them again. Encourage students to generalize that the difference between the denominator and numerator doesn't always indicate closeness to 1.
the fraction with the bigger denominator is the bigger fraction (e.g., $\frac{1}{6} > \frac{1}{3}$ because $6 > 3$)	*model* each fraction with a manipulative material and compare them again. Emphasize the inverse relationship between the denominator and the size of each piece: in other words, the more pieces into which a whole is cut, the smaller the pieces are.

If you were Ally's teacher, what might a follow-up lesson on comparing fractions include? Ally's teacher might decide to focus on helping students understand what fractions mean, the relationship between the size of the denominator and the size of the fraction pieces, and benchmark fractions.

Next, take a moment to view the clip "IMAP—Developing Operation Sense for Fractions" on MyEducationLab, which shows a second-grade girl finding the sum of $\frac{3}{4} + \frac{1}{2}$. Until this point, Felisha had not been formally taught how to add fractions, but she had participated in many rich experiences focusing on partitioning a whole, naming fractions, and learning about equivalence.

How did Felisha solve the problem $\frac{3}{4} + \frac{1}{2}$? Based on what you saw in the video clip, what does Felisha understand about fractions? Felisha knows how to draw a picture to represent fractions and the sum of fractions, she can partition the whole into equal-sized pieces, and she is able to use fraction names and symbols. She is able to draw on her understanding of fractions to solve a new type of problem and to provide a clear explanation for her solution.

Now think about what we've learned about Ally's and Felisha's understandings. How does Ally's understanding of fractions compare to Felisha's? Felisha seems to have a rich conceptual understanding of fractions and is able to apply it with meaning to new situations. In contrast, Ally seems to view fractions as a set of isolated procedures to apply without making sense of them. These video clips provide examples of the complexity of working with fractions and the importance of helping children develop a rich understanding of fraction concepts.

PEARSON myeducationlab The Power of Classroom Practice Go to the Assignments and Activities section of Topic 8: "Fraction Concepts and Computation" in the MyEducationLab for your course and complete the activity "IMAP—Developing Operation Sense for Fractions." Compare Felisha's understanding with Ally's."

What Are Fractions?

The fractions studied in elementary school are rational numbers that can be written as $\frac{a}{b}$ where a and b are integers with b not equal to zero. The term *fraction* is derived from a Latin word meaning "to break." Fractions are numbers representing objects that have been "broken" into parts.

When thinking of fractions as "parts of a whole," the fractions are sometimes thought of as objects rather than as numbers. For example, one-fifth of a pizza is a certain-sized piece of pizza, not necessarily a number that answers the question *"How much?"* The idea of fractional parts representing numbers emerges over time. Having children respond to the question *"How much?"* or *"What is the share?"* helps focus their thinking on fractions as numbers.

What Do Children Know About Fractions?

What do we know of the fraction understanding of children in the United States? The 2003 National Assessment of Educational Progress (NAEP) noted that while students' understanding of basic fraction concepts continues to improve, we still have a long way to go before we can say that students understand everything they need to about fractions. Students seem to view fractions almost exclusively as equal-sized parts of a whole. The problem is that this understanding is so dominant that many students are unable to focus on other situations or interpretations of fractions, or to think flexibly about fractions as quantities. For example, 83% of the fourth-graders tested were able to correctly identify which picture below showed $\frac{3}{4}$ (see Figure 10.1), but only 19% were able to correctly name and shade fractions equivalent to $\frac{1}{2}$. This could be because many students think about $\frac{1}{2}$ in only one way: as a whole that's been cut into two equal-sized pieces rather than as a quantity that may have

FIGURE 10-1 Which Shows 3/4 of the Picture Shaded?

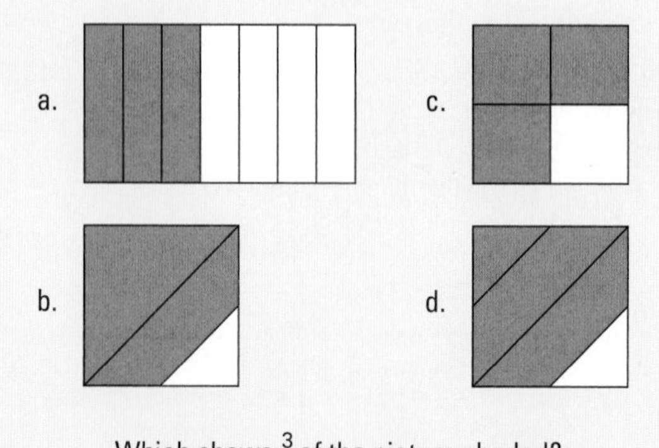
a.
b.
c.
d.
Which shows $\frac{3}{4}$ of the picture shaded?

NCTM NUMBER AND OPERATIONS STANDARDS AND EXPECTATIONS ADDRESSED IN THIS CHAPTER

Instructional programs from Pre-K–12 should enable all students to—	In Prekindergarten through grade 2 all students should—(NCTM, 2000, p. 78)	In grades 3–5 all students should— (NCTM, 2000, p. 148)	In grades 6–8 all students should— (NCTM, 2000, p. 214)
• understand numbers, ways of representing numbers, relationships among numbers, and number systems.	• understand and represent commonly used fractions, such as $\frac{1}{4}$, $\frac{1}{3}$, and $\frac{1}{2}$.	• develop understanding of fractions as parts of unit wholes, as parts of a collection, as locations on number lines, and as divisions of whole numbers. • use models, benchmarks, and equivalent forms to judge the size of fractions. • recognize and generate equivalent forms of commonly used fractions, decimals, and percents.	• work flexibly with fractions, decimals, and percents to solve problems. • compare and order fractions, decimals, and percents efficiently and find their approximate locations on a number line.

been broken into many pieces, such as 2 out of 4 or 50 out of 100. Figure 10.2 shows one student's thinking about fractions.

FIGURE 10-2 One Student's Thinking about Fractions

The shaded part of each strip below shows a fraction.

a.

This fraction strip shows $\frac{3}{6}$.

b.

What fraction does this fraction strip show? $\frac{2}{1}$

c.

What fraction does this fraction strip show? $\frac{10}{5}$

What do the fractions shown in a, b, and c have in common?

a. show $\frac{6}{3}$

b. show $\frac{2}{1}$

c. show $\frac{10}{5}$

Shade in the fraction strips below to show two different fractions that are equivalent to the ones shown in a, b, and c.

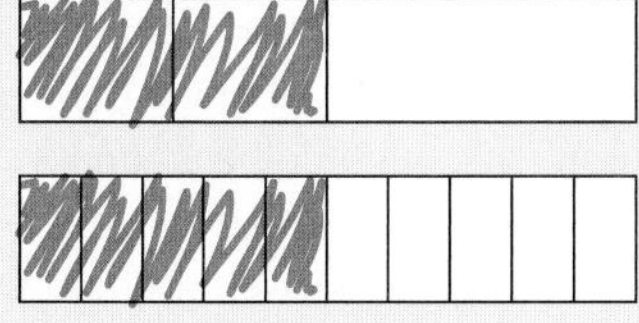

Eighth-graders performed a little better but had difficulty comparing fractions and using fractions in measurement. For example, only 46% of the eighth-graders tested were able to correctly arrange fractions in order from least to greatest, while 73% were able to correctly shade $\frac{1}{3}$ of a rectangle cut into 6 equal parts. Findings such as this point to the importance of teachers' helping children truly make sense of fraction concepts.

Hiebert and Behr (1988) recommended that increased attention be devoted to developing the meaning of fraction symbols, developing concepts such as order and equivalence that are important in fostering a sense of the relative size of fractions, and helping children connect their intuitive understandings and strategies to more general, formal methods.

According to Bezuk and Bieck (1993), "Instruction [is crucial] to strengthen students' understandings before progressing to operations on fractions, rather than assuming that students already understand these topics" (p. 119).

Cramer and her colleagues (1997) summarized four principles to help children understand fractions:

1. Children learn best through active involvement with a variety of concrete models;
2. Most children need extended experiences with manipulative materials in order to develop mental images of fractions in order to reason and think conceptually about fractions;
3. Children benefit from opportunities to talk about their fraction understandings with each other and with their teacher; and
4. Learning experiences should begin with helping children develop conceptual knowledge of fractions before moving to more formal work with symbols and computation.

Mack (1990) noted that children often possess informal, real-world knowledge about fractions that they are able to use to understand fraction symbols and procedures. You should help children connect their real-world experiences with fractions to classroom work with fractions to strengthen children's understanding.

What Should Children Understand about Fractions?

Children must understand several aspects about fraction concepts and relationships before beginning fraction computation. The prerequisite topics include understanding fraction concepts, comparing fractions and developing number sense about fractions, and recognizing equivalence. These topics are discussed in detail in this chapter.

We also will discuss how to utilize strategies for reaching all learners throughout the chapter. As discussed in Chapter 2, these strategies help all students, including those who are English language learners (ELLs), be successful in learning fraction concepts. These strategies include making real-world connections, using manipulative materials and pictures, using advanced organizers, previewing and reviewing concepts, and using math word walls.

Developing Fraction Concepts and Number Sense

Understanding Sharing Situations

Understanding fraction concepts builds on familiarity with situations involving sharing. Children use what they already understand to build their understandings of new concepts. And we know that children are experts in fair shares! Ask any elementary-school-aged child, and they'll be able to tell you if something has been shared fairly or not.

Consider the following problem. Take a minute and solve this problem. Then think about how a child might solve this problem.

> 4 children want to share 3 candy bars equally. How much can each child have?

How might a child solve this problem? One way (see the sketch below) is to start by cutting the first 2 candy bars in half, which produces 1 piece ($\frac{1}{2}$ of a candy bar) for each child. Then the remaining candy bar is cut into 4 equal parts, creating 1 more piece ($\frac{1}{4}$ of a candy bar) for each child. So each child gets two pieces (shown as shaded below): 1 bigger piece and 1 smaller piece. The next step is to figure out how much of a candy bar that is. Each child gets $\frac{1}{2}$ and $\frac{1}{4}$, which is $\frac{3}{4}$ of a candy bar altogether.

Another way to solve this problem (see the sketch below) is to start by cutting each candy bar into 4 equal pieces. Each child would get 1 piece from each candy bar, which is $\frac{3}{4}$ of a candy bar altogether.

Sharing problems help children connect their everyday experiences with fractions (Empson, 1999). Sharing problems involve a group of people sharing a certain quantity of something, such as candy bars in the previous problem. Commonly shared items include objects often shaped as rectangles, such as candy bars, brownies, and sandwiches, along with objects often shaped as circles, such as cookies, cakes, and pizzas.

Teachers can make sharing problems easier or more difficult by changing the number of children and the number of items being shared. Consider the following problems. Which would be more difficult, and why? Would it make a difference if the problems involved sharing cookies instead of candy bars?

Problem 1 *4 children want to share 3 candy bars equally. How much does each child get?*

Problem 2 *3 children want to share 2 candy bars equally. How much can each child have?*

Problem 3 *2 children want to share 5 candy bars equally. How much can each child have?*

Let's discuss each problem. Problem 2 is a little harder than Problem 1, since it involves splitting a whole into 3 parts, which is a little harder than splitting into halves or fourths. Problem 3 is different because each child ends up with more than one candy bar, which could make it a little harder for some children. In terms of sharing cookies instead of candy bars, think about representing fractions by using circles instead of rectangles.

Sharing problems lay an important foundation for understanding fraction concepts (Empson, 1995). As children describe their solution processes for sharing problems, help them connect mathematical language and symbols with the sharing they've done. For example, sharing solutions for Problem 1 above could be an opportunity to introduce (or reinforce) the notion that when a whole has been cut into four equal parts, those parts are called "fourths."

NCTM Principles and Standards Link 10-1

Content Strand: Number and Operations

Students' understanding and ability to reason will grow as they represent fractions and decimals with physical materials and on number lines and as they learn to generate equivalent representations of fractions and decimals. (NCTM, 2000, p. 33)

Number Sense with Fractions

Number sense with fractions develops over a long period of time; therefore, elementary and middle school teachers need to focus on this topic. A first goal is for children to develop conceptual understanding of fractions as numbers. Then there are various abilities that children must acquire to work effectively with fractions:

- The ability to represent fractions using words, models, diagrams, and symbols and make connections among various representations;
- The ability to give other names for fractions and justify the procedures used to generate the equivalent forms; and
- The ability to describe the relative magnitude of fractions by comparing them to common benchmarks, giving simple estimates, ordering a set of fractions, and finding a number between two fractions.

Guidelines for developing these abilities together with conceptual understanding are included in this chapter.

Assessing fraction number sense. When assessing fraction number sense, teachers can ask children to model fractions concretely, pictorially, and symbolically. At times, teachers may present a task in one mode and have children respond in another mode. Vance (1990) suggests the following tasks for assessing fraction number sense:

Task 1 *Represent six-tenths with the fraction circles. Can you show six-tenths on a number line?*

Task 2 *Can you read this number? (Show $\frac{2}{5}$ on a card.) Can you draw a picture to show what it means? Explain what the 2 and the 5 mean.*

Task 3 *If the following diagram, shows $\frac{3}{5}$ of a set; draw the whole set.*

Could another set be used? Explain.

Task 4 *If this length is four-tenths of a unit long, draw a length that's one whole unit long.* __________

If this part is three-tenths of a unit, draw the whole unit. __________

FIGURE 10-3 Examples of Children's Stories about One-Half

One Half

One day I went to the "Dollar Store" and I bought 14 scratch 'n' sniff stickers. The next day I went to my friend's house and we traded stickers. We traded and I gave her 7 stickers, or half of the stickers.

P.S. Half means you have two equal parts and you take one away. Then you have half.

Jack, Grade 3

Half

My mommy got a pizza for me and my brother. My mommy cut it in eight pieces.

I had 2 pieces and my brother 2 pieces of pizza. All together, we ate half the pizza.

Beth, Grade 3

Task 5 *Can you give this fraction another name?*

$\frac{3}{5}$

Another name?

Writing is a powerful way to assess children's understandings (NCTM, 1989). Teachers are encouraged to ask children to write about the mathematics they are doing. For example, children's responses to a simple direction such as "Write about what you did" or "Write about what you learned" can reveal much about a child's fraction understandings. Two examples of children's responses to the invitation to write a story about one-half or one-third are presented in Figure 10-3.

Developing the meaning of "half." Children usually come to school knowing the term *half* because they have used it in their sharing experiences. However, this does not mean that they know the fractional term *half* in its precise meaning: that is, half is one of two equal parts. Three activities to help develop the concept of half are described next. The first involves sets rather than a region model. It is included here because of its focus on half.

1. **Sharing for Two**
   - Set the context by relating a story such as "Jane and Jill are sisters, and they often have things to share.

They each should get half of the things they're sharing."

- Ask the children to tell how the sisters will share each of the following:

  6 pieces of gum
  10 baseball cards
  12 dimes
  8 barrettes

- Encourage the children to talk about the situation. Listen for expressions like "They shared the gum, and they each got the same amount. So they each got half the gum."

2. Cutting in Half

- Obtain a knife and two oranges, two apples, two soft cookies, or two other objects suitable for cutting.
- Explain that you are going to cut each orange into two parts.
- Cut one orange into two parts, as equal as possible, then ask, "How have I cut this orange? What can you say about the pieces?"
- Cut the other orange into two obviously unequal parts, and then ask, "How have I cut this orange? What can you say about the pieces?"
- Encourage the children to verbalize. Some expressions could include the following:

  This orange is cut in two parts that are the same size. The parts are equal.

  The orange is cut in half. Each piece is one-half the orange. The other orange is not cut in half because the pieces are not the same size. The pieces are not equal.

In the preceding verbalization, note the dual expressions "same size" and "equal." For some time, both should be used to develop and consolidate the meaning of the term *equal.*

3. Partitioning a Square in Half

- You will need a large colored square cut from heavy paper, art foam, or other suitable material and several narrow strips of white poster board to demonstrate "cutting" lines. The strips should be at least as long as the diagonal of the square.
- Set the context by asking the children to pretend that one day their mother baked a small square cake for them to share with a friend.
- Ask the children to explore the possibilities of "cutting the cake" in two parts that are the same amount. The white strips are to be used to show cuts on the cake.
- Ask the children to indicate or record the cuts they think produce parts that show the same amount. The recording can be done in one of two ways: Provide children with squares drawn on a piece of paper and have them draw the cutting line, or provide a square for the children to trace on paper and then have them mark the partitioning line.

NCTM Principles and Standards Link 10-2

Process Strand: Problem Solving

Beyond understanding whole numbers, young children can be encouraged to understand and represent commonly used fractions in context, such as $\frac{1}{2}$ of a cookie or $\frac{1}{8}$ of a pizza, and to see fractions as part of a unit whole or of a collection. Teachers should help students develop an understanding of fractions as division of numbers. (NCTM, 2000, p. 33)

For the purpose of a class discussion, the teacher could draw a series of squares on a transparency. Children, in turn, can show one way to cut the cake in two parts that are the same amount. Discuss each type of cut. Ask questions such as "Does this cut show two parts that are the same amount?" "How can you tell?" and "How much cake will each of you get?"

The teacher can explain the meaning of *half* as follows and then have the children verbalize the various expressions.

> Cutting in half means that we show two parts that are the same amount. The parts are the same size. When a figure has been cut in half, each part is half the shape, a half, or one-half.

The last expression should be encouraged because it helps name other fractions such as two-halves, three-halves, and so on.

myeducationlab The Power of Classroom Practice — To explore your own understanding of partitioning, go to Chapter 10 in the Book-Specific Resources section in the MyEducationLab for your course. Select the Activities section and complete the activity "Partitioning Figures in Half."

Activity 10-1 can be used to assess a child's mental development level as well as to help children develop the concept of "half." Some children in grades 5 and 6 are unable to reason that if the figures are the same size (congruent) and the parts within each are the same size, then all the parts are the same amount or have the same area. The activity should be used after children have had experiences in partitioning squares, rectangles, triangles, and pentagons.

ACTIVITY 10-1 Determining Whether Parts Are the Same Size

Materials

Pairs of partitioned figures as shown

Procedure

1. A child is shown the partitioned figures in pairs as in the diagram.
2. Look at these two figures. Are parts (a) and (b) the same size? [or, Do parts (a) and (b) show the same amount?] Explain how you know.

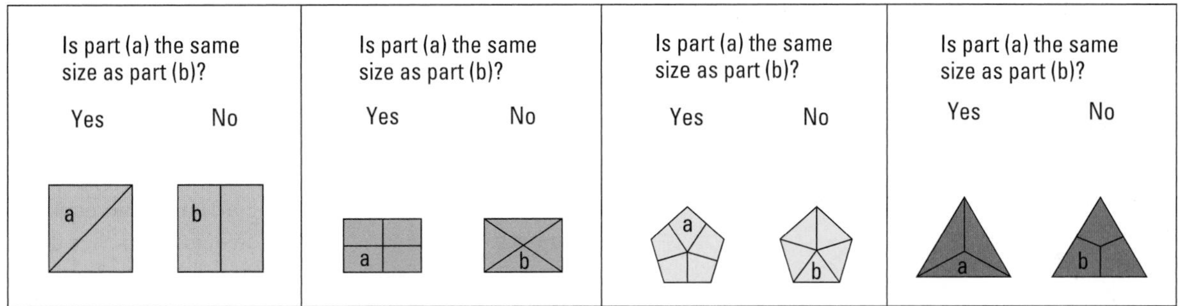

Different Interpretations of Fractions

Fractions can be interpreted in several ways. Kieren (1980) identifies four meanings: part-whole, quotient, ratio, and multiplicative operator. The part-whole interpretation is the one emphasized in elementary mathematics programs, though the other interpretations are often included as well.

Part-whole interpretations. The part-whole meaning of fractions comprises different units. It can be:

- A region (an object to be shared or an area to be divided);
- A set of objects; or
- A unit of linear measure.

Teaching considerations about each type are presented in the following subsections.

Region model. There is substantial agreement that the *region model* of fractions should be learned before the model of "parts of a set" (Hollis, 1984; Payne, 1984; Skypek, 1984). Traditionally, regular geometric regions have been considered to be good fraction models because any unit fraction can be shown fairly easily. Children should have opportunities to experiment with partitioning (or cutting) different figures or regions rather than having to work solely with prepartitioned figures. Without the personal experience of partitioning figures into equal parts, children are unable to use the model in problem-solving activities (Kieren, Nelson, & Smith, 1985; Pothier & Sawada, 1990).

Equality of parts. Children often are satisfied that parts "look the same size" when modeling fractions. For example, children often incorrectly say that a regular pentagon or a heart shape partitioned by a horizontal "half cut" is being shared equally (see Figure 10-4). Therefore, in early fraction work, children should be required to cut shapes into parts that are congruent, that is, the same size and shape.

At a later time, children will come to see that noncongruent parts of regions can be equal. For example, consider a set of tangrams, illustrated in Figure 10-5. Notice

FIGURE 10-4 Which Figures Show One-Half?

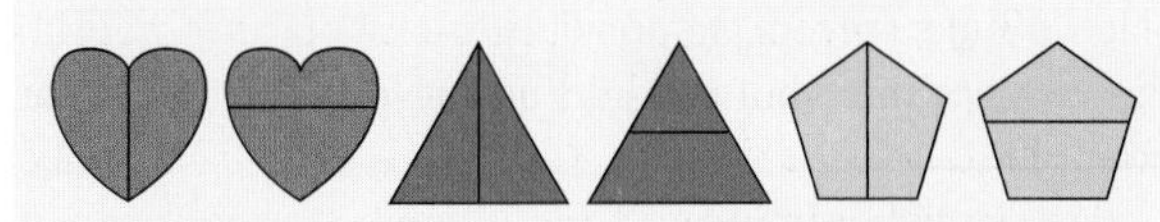

FIGURE 10-5 Parts of a Tangram Representing Fractions

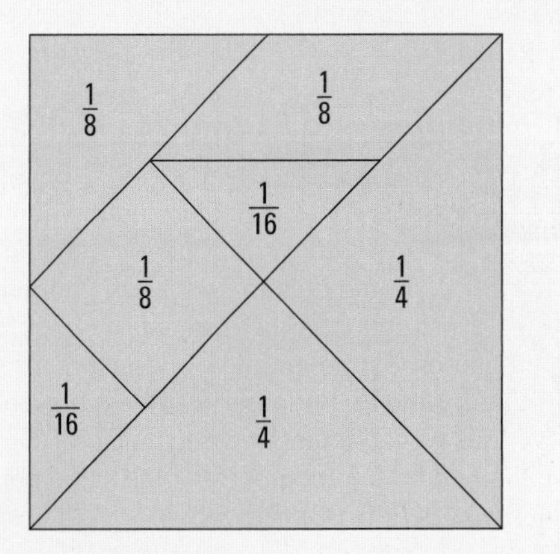

FIGURE 10-6 Children's Explanations of Why Parts Are Equal

Children's Explanations of Parts

Barry (7 years)

"All the same size. Not the same shape."

Ryan (7 years)

"*This part* looks smaller but it's just the same size because like I split it in half this way and I split it in half this way."

Joshua (7 years) "I think I could do four!" He partitions the triangle. "It looks bigger but it isn't bigger . . . Cause it's thinner here and thicker here."

that there are three different tangram shapes that represent one-eighth of the whole tangram square. These three shapes are not congruent, but they each cover one-eighth of the area of the whole tangram square, so they each are one-eighth of the tangram. This example provides another opportunity to discuss with children that *fractions do not have to be congruent to be the same part of the whole.*

Figure 10-6 shows children's explanations about why the parts they created are equal. In each case, think about a follow-up question you could ask each child to encourage them to think more deeply about their answer.

Pothier and Sawada (1990) recommend that you give children opportunities to practice partitioning physical objects into equal-sized parts rather than just drawing lines on the outlines of shapes. You can ask children to place coffee stirrers or popsicle sticks on an object to show where the whole should be cut to make thirds, for example.

Parts drawn on cut-out figures can be tested to see if they are congruent by folding the figure or by cutting out each part and then laying the parts on top of each other. Older children can measure the angles and sides of the parts produced. Activity 10-2 provides children with an

NCTM Principles and Standards Link 10-3

Content Strand: Number and Operations

Representing numbers with various physical materials should be a major part of mathematics instruction in the elementary school grades. By the middle grades, students should understand that numbers can be represented in various ways, so that they see that $\frac{1}{4}$, 25%, and 0.25 are all different names for the same number. (NCTM, 2000, p. 33)

NCTM Principles and Standards Link 10-4

Content Strand: Number and Operations

In addition to work with whole numbers, young students should also have some experience with simple fractions through connections to everyday situations and meaningful problems, starting with the common fractions expressed in the language they bring to the classroom, such as "half." At this level, it is more important for students to recognize when things are divided into equal parts than to focus on fraction notation. (NCTM, 2000, p. 82)

opportunity to explore cutting a figure into equal parts and naming the parts. The following two teacher-directed activities focus on developing the concept of equality of parts in fractions:

ACTIVITY 10-2 Given a Part, Draw the Whole

Materials

Figures drawn on paper

Procedure

1. If this is one-fifth of a chocolate bar, what size is the whole bar?

2. This is three-fourths of a cake. Draw the whole cake.

3. This is three-eighths of a cheese block. Draw the whole block.

1. **Developing the Concept of Equality of Parts in Fractions**
   - Materials: Figures drawn on paper to represent giant cookies: a heart, an equilateral triangle, and a regular pentagon.
   - Provide children with at least two heart-shaped cookies and direct them to show how a cookie could be shared equally between two friends.

- Focusing on a vertical cut, ask, "How can you prove each person gets the same amount?" or "How can you prove the pieces are equal?" Suggest that children fold one part over the other to see whether the parts are equal.
- Ask, "Can you cut the cookie a different way so that each person gets the same amount?"
- Focusing on a horizontal cut, ask, "Would each person get the same amount now?" Have children cut the shape on the fold line and superimpose the two parts.
- Ask, "How are you sure the parts are equal? Why?"
- Say, "When we're sure the parts are equal, we can say that each part is one-half of the cookie."
- Repeat the procedures with a triangle, a pentagon, and other figures.

2. **Equality of Parts: One-Fourth**
   - Materials: A square, a triangle, a parallelogram, a pentagon, a heart, and other figures.
   - Say: "Let's try two cuts on different figures to find out whether they produce equal parts."
   - In each case, ask, "Can the parts be called one-fourth of the figure? Why or why not?"

The following story could be used to assess children's understanding of equality in fractions:

A boy named Don told me that a heart-shaped cake cut into four parts like this [demonstrate a vertical and a horizontal halving line] makes parts equal because "this line is in the middle of this one." What would you say to Don?

Children's responses can show if they are focusing on how the whole was cut or on the size of the parts produced when deciding if the parts are equal.

A teacher who plans partitioning activities for children will learn which fractional parts are easy and which are difficult for children to create on a circle, square, or other regular geometric figure. Children should be allowed to discover for themselves, for example, how to show thirds and fifths on a circle or fifths on a pentagon. In time, children should be able to partition a region to model unit fractions with even and odd denominators, but note that odd denominators, such as thirds, fifths, and sevenths, are more difficult for children to show.

Children should have lots of experiences in partitioning figures, at different times during the year and at different grade levels, because further partitioning experiences will help children discover more relationships. The following questions could be the focus of class discussions:

- On what figures is it easy to make thirds? fourths? fifths? sixths? eighths? tenths? Why?
- What partitioning techniques work best on a particular figure? Why?

FIGURE 10-7 Partitioning Techniques

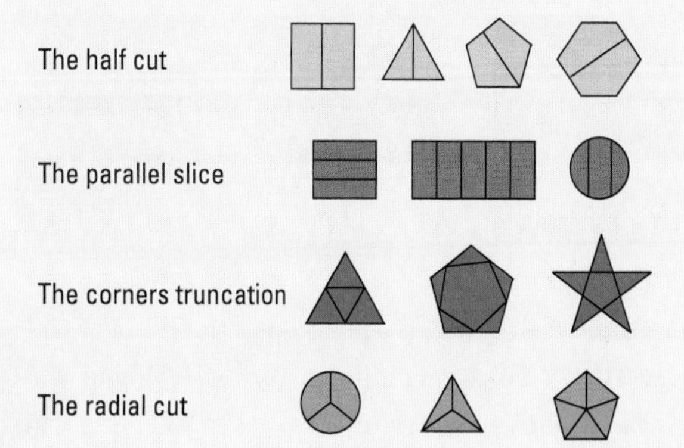

Successful partitioning of regions requires capabilities such as the following:

- An awareness of some geometric properties of figures, such as numbers of sides and vertices, the diagonals, midpoints of sides, and the center point of the figure.
- Knowledge of possible operations on figures, for example, how to divide sides into equal segments, how to construct points in the interior of a figure, and how to create differently shaped parts within a given figure.
- Partitioning techniques such as the half cut using different orientations, the parallel slice, the corners truncation, and the radial cut, as shown in Figure 10-7.

These capabilities emerge slowly over time and provide children with one model for fractional numbers.

One excellent model for representing fractions is fraction circles. Sets of fraction circles can be made economically from paper. Draw circles on white paper and then duplicate each different denominator onto different colors of paper, which children can cut out (see Blackline Masters 7, 8, and 9 in Appendix B). Laminating the paper before cutting will help retain the shape of the pieces and extend their usefulness. Fraction circles also are available commercially as sets of plastic circles partitioned into different numbers of equal-sized pieces.

Fraction circles are the model that perhaps is most familiar to children, but this is a difficult model for children to construct on their own. Using pre-made sets provides children with a convenient, easy-to-understand model for fractions.

The commercial set of Fraction Factory pieces is another example of the region model. The set is made of colored plastic rectangular pieces representing a whole and its fractional parts (halves, thirds, fourths, fifths, sixths, eighths, tenths, and twelfths), as shown in Figure 10-8. Exploratory activities can be planned for children using the materials as in Activity 10-3.

FIGURE 10-8 Fraction Factory Pieces

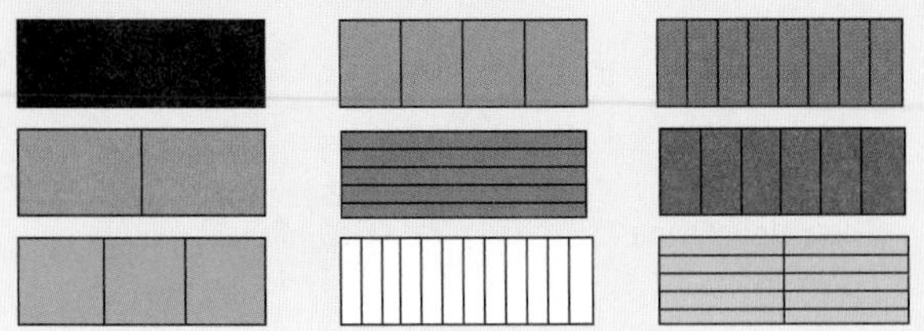

> **ACTIVITY 10-3** Fractional Parts of a Whole
>
> *Manipulative Strategies*
>
> **Materials**
>
> Fraction Factory pieces
>
> **Procedure**
>
> 1. Find how many
>   - thirds are in a whole
>   - fifths are in a whole
>   - tenths are in a whole
>   - twelfths are in a whole
> 2. Do you notice a pattern?
> 3. Write a statement about what you have found.

Part-of-a-set model. The part-of-a-set model for fractions is often more difficult for children. Its difficulty is based on identifying the unit (or "whole") as more than one object, and on using fractions to correctly name the result. For example, children can easily share 20 candies among four friends but when asked *what part* of the candies each one gets, children often incorrectly respond "five," rather than "one-fourth of the candies." Help children recognize that different questions require different answers: The question *how many?* warrants a whole-number answer (5), while the questions *how much?* and *what part?* have fraction number answers (one-fourth or $\frac{1}{4}$).

When working with sets, children often find it easier to find, for example, one-tenth of a set of 10 than to find one-fifth of 10 objects. Students appear to think of "fifth" as "five." Thus, when finding one-fifth of 10, they partition the set in two groups of five rather than in five groups of two. The concept to emphasize is that, for example, when talking about fifths, the whole is partitioned into five parts. The number of objects in each fifth depends on the size of the set (see Figure 10-9). Activities 10-4 to 10-6 should be helpful in developing this important idea.

For Activity 10-4, children should draw pictures of what they have done and write statements such as:

Twelve buttons are one-half of 24 buttons.

One-fourth of 24 buttons is 6.

Children might respond to Activity 10-5 with a construction and statements such as:

Here are 12 discs.

I can make four groups of three.

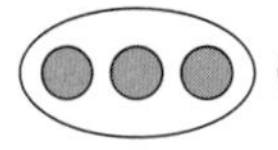 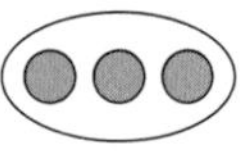 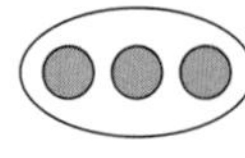 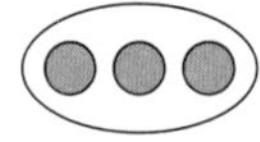

So three is one-fourth of 12.

Activity 10-6 also focuses on the set interpretation, providing more practice finding the whole set based on the size of a part.

> **ACTIVITY 10-4** Finding a Fractional part of a Set: Concrete
>
> 
>
> *Realia Strategies*
>
> **Materials**
>
> A set of 24 buttons for each child and 8 small plates or "mats"
>
> **Procedure**
>
> Place buttons on the plates to show:
>
> 1. One-half of 24 (use 2 plates).
> 2. One-fourth of 24 (use 4 plates).
> 3. One-sixth of 24 (use 6 plates).
> 4. One-eighth of 24 (use 8 plates).

> **ACTIVITY 10-5** Naming the Fractions
>
> **Materials**
>
> A set of 20 discs or other small objects
>
> **Procedure**
>
> Use the discs (or other objects) to answer the following:
>
> 1. What part of 12 is 3?
> 2. What part of 6 is 2?
> 3. What part of 20 is 4?
> 4. What part of 20 is 5?

> **ACTIVITY 10-6** Draw the Whole Set
>
> **Procedure**
>
> Draw pictures to help you answer the following questions.
>
> 1. Kevin has a collection of model airplanes. Three-tenths of his collection is three airplanes. How many airplanes does Kevin have in his collection?
> 2. Sanai enjoys taking pictures. She has taken 9 pictures, which is one-fourth of the pictures she can

FIGURE 10-9 Examples of Parts of Sets

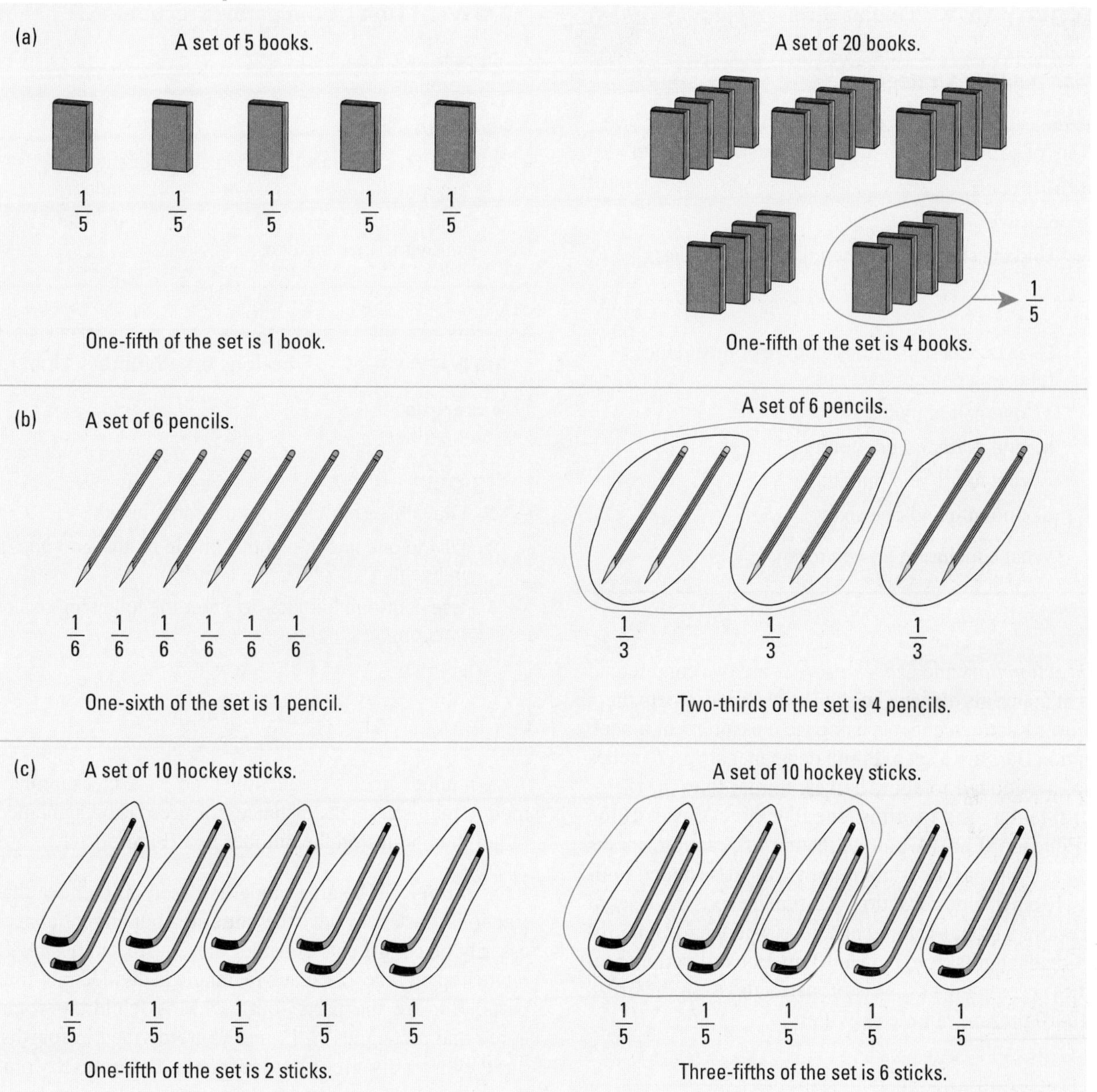
(a)
A set of 5 books.
1/5 1/5 1/5 1/5 1/5
One-fifth of the set is 1 book.
A set of 20 books.
1/5
One-fifth of the set is 4 books.
(b)
A set of 6 pencils.
1/6 1/6 1/6 1/6 1/6 1/6
One-sixth of the set is 1 pencil.
A set of 6 pencils.
1/3 1/3 1/3
Two-thirds of the set is 4 pencils.
(c)
A set of 10 hockey sticks.
1/5 1/5 1/5 1/5 1/5
One-fifth of the set is 2 sticks.
A set of 10 hockey sticks.
1/5 1/5 1/5 1/5 1/5
Three-fifths of the set is 6 sticks.

take with that roll of film. How many pictures can Sanai take with that roll of film?

3. Tanya has a paper route. Having delivered 12 papers means that she has one-third of the papers left to deliver. How many papers does Tanya deliver each day?

Measurement model. The measurement model can be shown using tape, ribbon, or other appropriate material. The key factor here is to choose a material that is long and narrow to emphasize *length* rather than *area*. Children can be asked, for example, to find fractional parts of a given strip of paper. Number lines are another example of the measurement model for fractions.

Folding is one way to find fractional parts of strips of paper. Activity 10-7 could be used for this purpose. One conclusion children should come to as a result of doing this activity is that when comparing two unit fractions, the one with the smaller denominator is the larger fraction.

ACTIVITY 10-7 Folding Strips to Find Fractional Parts

Manipulative Strategies

Materials

A set of paper strips about 30 inches long for each child

Procedure

1. Fold the strips to find the following fractions:

$$\frac{1}{2}, \frac{1}{4}, \frac{1}{3}, \frac{1}{5}, \frac{1}{6}, \frac{1}{8}, \frac{1}{10}$$

2. Use your set of fractions strips to compare the following pairs of fractions:
   a. one-half of fractions
   b. one-third and one-fourth
   c. one-fourth and one-fifth
   d. one-fifth and one-sixth

   What conclusion do you reach?

Fraction Bars and *Cuisenaire rods* are two commercial sets of materials that can be used by children to help them discover fraction concepts using the measurement model. Fraction Bars are a set of laminated paper strips, 6 inches long, partitioned to show halves, thirds, fourths, fifths, sixths, tenths, and twelfths (see Blackline Master 10 on MyEducationLab). A unique feature of Fraction Bars is that each bar has a certain number of parts shaded to illustrate a particular fraction. Cuisenaire rods are a set of three-dimensional colored plastic or wooden rods of proportional lengths from 1 cm to 10 cm. Books describing activities accompany both sets of materials. Activities 10-8 to 10-10 present sample activities.

myeducationlab The Power of Classroom Practice — Go to Chapter 10 in the Book-Specific Resources section in the MyEducationLab for your course and select Blackline Masters to obtain "Blackline Master 10."

ACTIVITY 10-8 Comparing Fractions—A

Materials

Fraction bars

Procedure

Use Fraction Bars to compare the following:

a. 1 part out of 3 and 1 part out of 4
b. 5 parts out of 6 and 3 parts out of 4
c. 1 part out of 2 and 5 parts out of 12

ACTIVITY 10-9 Comparing Fractions—B

Materials

Fraction Bars

Procedure

1. Find Fraction Bars that have a greater shaded amount than a blue bar with 3 parts shaded.
2. Find Fraction Bars that have less shading than a red bar with 1 part shaded.

ACTIVITY 10-10 Fractions on a Number Line

Materials

Number lines

Procedure

1. Draw three number lines the same length.
2. Divide one line in eighths, one in tenths, and one in twelfths.
3. Use your number lines to order the following sets of fractions:

$\frac{1}{3}\ \frac{5}{8}\ \frac{3}{5}$ $\frac{9}{12}\ \frac{6}{10}\ \frac{5}{8}$

$\frac{4}{8}\ \frac{3}{10}\ \frac{5}{12}$ $\frac{7}{8}\ \frac{11}{12}\ \frac{9}{10}$

A number line is frequently used as a measurement model. In this case, the distance from zero is being named rather than points on the number line (Figure 10-10).

Area model. The area model is based on the idea that fractional parts may have the same area but might not necessarily be congruent. Consider the four rectangles, A–D on the top of page 221. Each rectangle is divided into four parts. But are the parts fourths? Most children would agree that rectangles A, B, and C are divided in fourths, but they may disagree about rectangle D, because two of the parts are shaped differently than the other two parts.

How might children determine whether the four parts in rectangle D are the same size? One way is to cut one of the triangular pieces and rearrange it to form a small rectangle—which will be exactly the same size and shape as the two small rectangular pieces.

FIGURE 10-10 Measurement Model

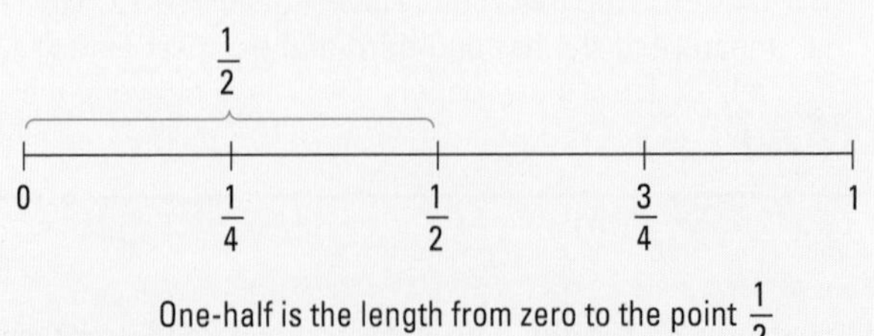

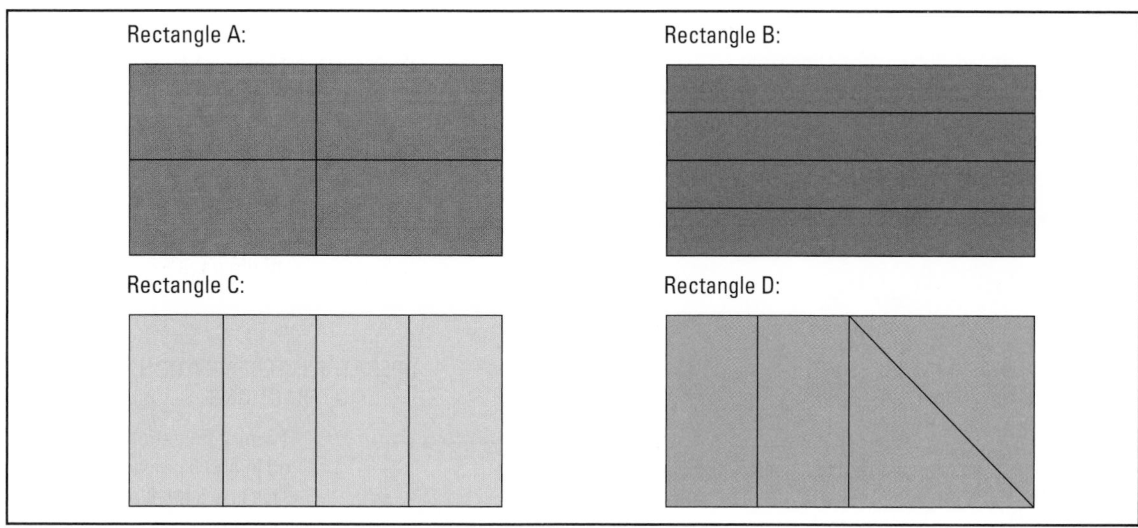

Other examples of shapes that have been cut into fractional parts using the area model are shown below. How might you verify that each part has the same area as other parts within the whole?

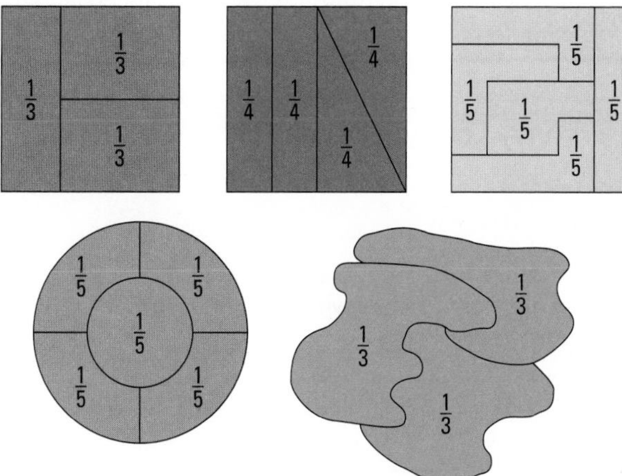

Geoboards can be used to represent the area model. A geoboard is a square that has several pegs, usually a 5-by-5 arrangement, on which rubber bands can be stretched to outline shapes. Children can be asked to show how a geoboard can be split into fractional parts, such as halves, fourths, or eighths. Figure 10-11 shows several ways in which a geoboard could be split into halves. Note that some of the halves are congruent, but others aren't. It is important for children to understand that shapes that are not congruent can still cover the same fractional part of a whole.

Other interpretations of fractions. In addition to the part-whole interpretation of fractions, described in the preceding pages, there are three other interpretations of fractions: ratio, quotient, and multiplicative operator (see Figure 10-12).

Ratio interpretation of fractions. The ratio interpretation of fractions is based on the idea that a fraction can represent a ratio between two quantities. For example, if a set of marbles contains 10 red and 14 blue marbles, the ratio of red to blue marbles in that set can be represented by the fraction $\frac{5}{7}$. Note that the denominator of this fraction, 7, has a different meaning than in the part-whole

FIGURE 10-11 Various Ways to Use Geoboards to Represent Halves

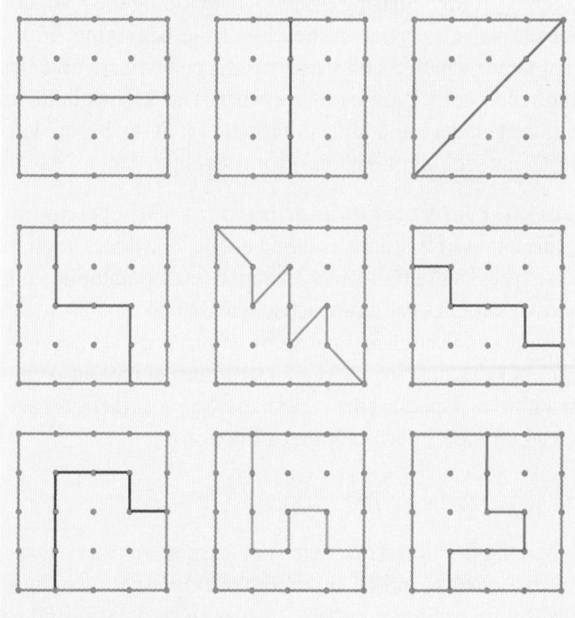

FIGURE 10-12 Various Interpretations of Fractions

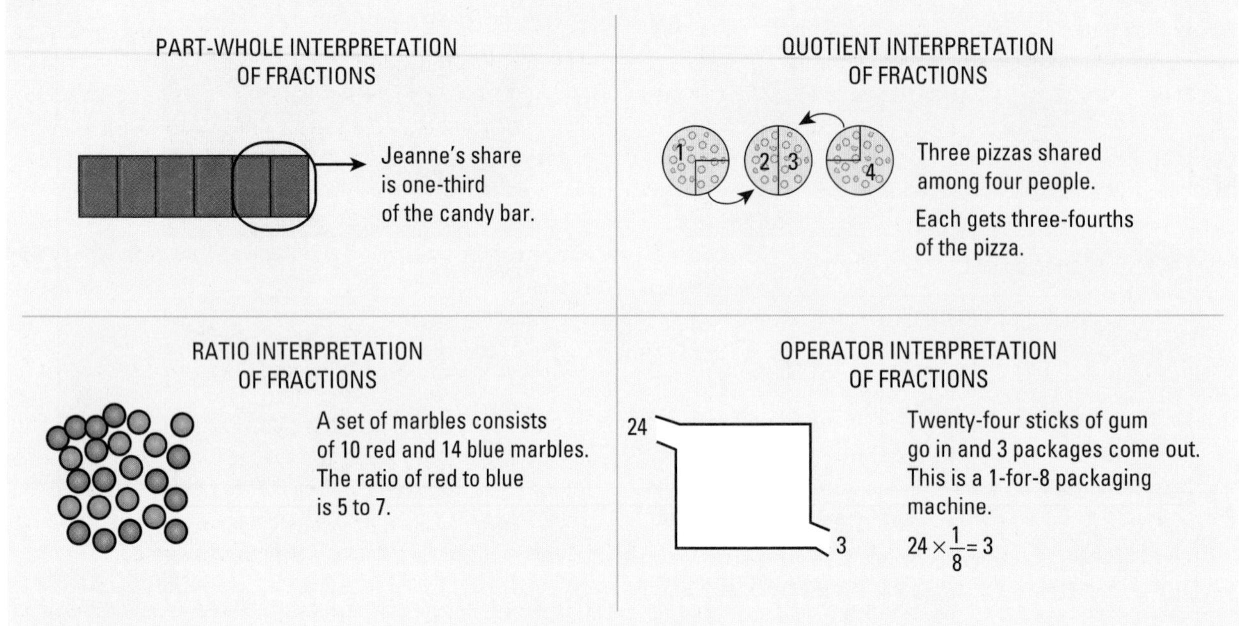

interpretation of fractions. In the ratio interpretation, the 5 and 7 represent different quantities; in this case, the number of red and blue marbles. In the part-whole interpretation, the denominator represents the total number of elements (or parts) in the whole. This difference is sometimes confusing to children and makes this interpretation more difficult than the part-whole interpretation.

Quotient interpretation of fractions. The quotient interpretation of fractions is based on the idea that a fraction can express a division or sharing. For example, if three pizzas are shared by four people, each person gets $\frac{3}{4}$ of a pizza. In this interpretation, $\frac{3}{4}$ expresses 3 wholes split into 4 equal groups. Sharing problems, including the problem Felisha solved earlier in the clip at the beginning of the chapter, in which 5 children shared 2 cookies, involve the quotient interpretation of fractions. The key to helping children understand this interpretation is to begin with problems set in familiar, real-world settings.

Operator interpretation of fractions. The operator interpretation of fractions is based on the idea that a fraction can express a multiplicative operation (either multiplication or division). For example, a machine that takes in 24 sticks of gum and produces 3 packs of gum represents a $\frac{24}{3}$ or $\frac{8}{1}$ operator, because every 8 sticks of gum come out of the machine as 1 pack. This is perhaps the most difficult and least common interpretation of fractions.

Fraction Names

When the fraction names are first learned, such as halves, thirds, fourths, and so on, children might confuse these terms with ordinal numbers, such as second, third, and so on. Thus, comparisons between, for example, *second* and *half, third* and *thirds, fourth* and *fourths,* should be made to help clarify the differences. An activity similar to Activity 10-11 may be helpful in developing understanding of fraction terms.

ACTIVITY 10-11 Meaning of Number Terms

Materials

Paper and pencil

Procedure

Draw a picture to show what each of the following terms means to you:

two	second	half
five	fifth	fifths

In early fraction work, the fraction words should be used without the symbols. Children can record findings such as "one-sixth of the pie has been eaten" or "one-half and one-fourth is the same as three-fourths." This manner of recording makes children focus on "what objects are being considered" and not merely on "how many." In time, recording work with fractions can be abbreviated to "1 half + 1 fourth = 3 fourths." Formal symbolization should be required only when children demonstrate an understanding of fractions through problem-solving activities.

It is important not to assume that children who use fractional terms properly in some context have an understanding of fractions. Children who use fraction terms such as *half* and *quarter* frequently use them in a narrow sense and sometimes erroneously. "Split the cookie in half in three pieces" and "Break it in half in four pieces" are common statements made by young children. You should provide many opportunities for children to use familiar fractional terms to determine what meaning each child affixes to them. For example, a child may use the term *half* when referring to an action as in "halve it" or "cut it in half," not to name a part. Another child may use the term *half* to name parts when a whole is divided in two, three, or more parts. Frequently, the parts need not be the same size to be labeled "half." This knowledge is important before moving on to further work with fractions.

Fraction symbolism. Fraction symbols should be introduced only when children understand the meaning of the terms *one-half, one-third, one-fourth,* and so on, and when children can use fractions in problem situations involving regions and parts of a set and in measurement. Fraction symbols should be written with a horizontal bar, although a slanted bar often is used on keyboards and calculators.

There is no reason children should learn the terms *numerator* and *denominator* when fraction symbols are introduced. Referring to the "top number" and "bottom number" in a fraction symbol would be understandable to children. The more formal terminology can be taught later, after children understand the meanings of the top number and bottom number in a fraction.

Help children connect each number in the fraction symbol with the fraction language that children have been using by developing a chart such as the one shown here. For example, have children count fraction circles. As they count, write the fraction words such as "one-sixth" on the board, as shown:

one-sixth	1 sixth	$\frac{1}{6}$
two-sixths	2 sixths	$\frac{2}{6}$
three-sixths	3 sixths	$\frac{3}{6}$
four-sixths	4 sixths	$\frac{4}{6}$
five-sixths	5 sixths	$\frac{5}{6}$
six-sixths	6 sixths	$\frac{6}{6}$

Ask the children, "What is a short form we have been using when writing fractions?" Then write the third column on the board. Finally, write the last column, explaining that there is a still shorter form in which to write fractions.

The teacher should facilitate discussion by matching the "two" and both "2"s in the same row and asking what each represents. Repeat with the "sixths" and "6." Ask, "Why was the term *sixth* repeated when you counted? Why were the counting numbers used?"

For children who understand fraction parts, the following explanation of the fraction symbol should be adequate:

In fractions, the top number counts the parts and the bottom number tells what sized parts are being counted.

To consolidate this idea, have children count eighths and record the fractions in pictorial, written, and symbolic forms. Then you can encourage children to use any of the fraction forms whenever they are recording their work. In time, they can use the fraction symbols alone.

Different units. The meaning of fractions is developed by considering different units. Units generally are represented by continuous quantities, such as regions, and discrete quantities, such as a set of distinct objects. A unit also can be:

- Continuous but divisible (e.g., a cake cut into squares to be shared among three siblings),
- A discrete set with divisible elements (e.g., six cookies to be shared among four children), or
- A discrete set with separate subsets (e.g., 5 boxes of candy, 12 candies per box, to be shared among 4 people).

For certain problems, a unit may also consist of part of a whole or more than one whole. These are not simple concepts for young children. See Figure 10-13.

Examining Children's Reasoning: Meaning of the Unit

How do children come to understand the meaning of the unit? The clip "IMAP—Models for Understanding Operations on Fractions" on MyEducationLab shows Felisha two years later as a fourth grader solving the following problem:

Five girls share 2 cookies and they want to do it evenly because they love peanut butter cookies. How much cookie does each girl get?

PEARSON myeducationlab The Power of Classroom Practice Go to the Assignments and Activities section of Topic 8: "Fraction Concepts and Computation" in the MyEducationLab for your course and complete the activity "Models for Understanding Operations on Fractions" to see how one fourth grader solves problems.

FIGURE 10-13 Using Different Units to Model Fractions

(a) A continuous quantity.

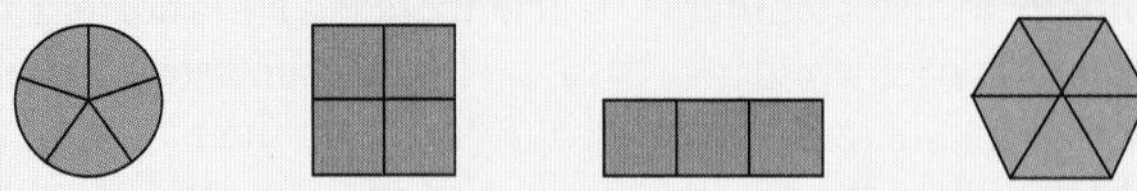

These regions are considered continuous quantities. The parts are measured rather than counted.

(b) Sets of discrete objects as the unit.

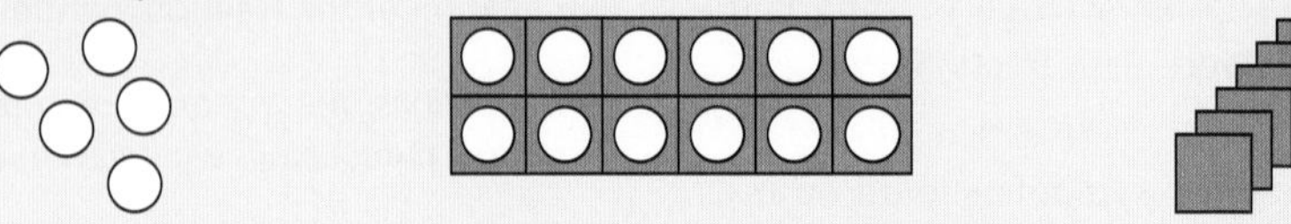

These are sets of discrete objects; that is, one can count the objects in each set.

(c) The unit is a continuous quantity that has been divided.

A Hershey bar cut up. Gerry's share is these 4 pieces, or one-third of the bar.

(d) The unit is a discrete set with the elements divisible.

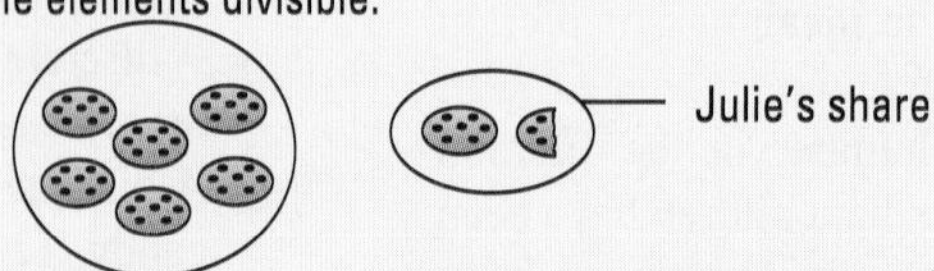

Four children share 6 cookies. What is each child's share? Julie's share is one and one-half cookies.

(e) The unit is a discrete set with divisible subsets.

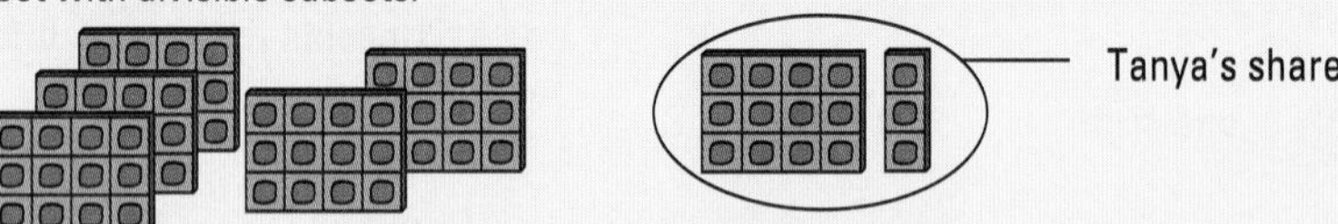

A set of 5 boxes of candy with 12 candies per box, to be shared among 4 friends. How much does each person get? Tanya's share is one and one-fourth boxes of candies.

(f) Part of a whole as a unit.

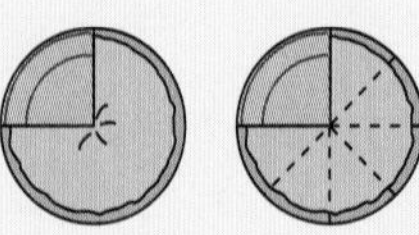

What portion is one-half of the remaining pie? Three-fourths of the pie is the unit. One-half of three-fourths is three-eighths.

(g) The unit is more than a whole.

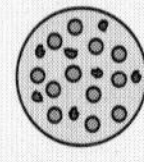
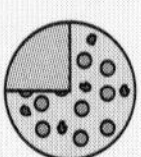
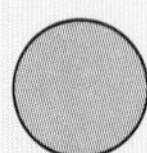

The shaded parts show how much pizza Paul has eaten. Paul has eaten one and one-fourth mini pizzas.

Felisha draws a picture to help her solve the problem and concludes, "Each person would get one-fifth of each cookie or two-tenths with the cookies added together."

How do you think Felisha was thinking about this problem? What did she mean by saying "one-fifth of each cookie or two-tenths with the cookies added together?"

Notice that the interviewer follows up by asking a sometimes overlooked question: "Of what?" He asked Felisha, "When you say that each gets two-tenths, *what* is that two-tenths *of*?" Felisha states that it's two-tenths of both cookies, not of one cookie.

This solution highlights a fine point in understanding fractions: the meaning of the unit. It's important to always keep in mind that fractions refer to part of something. The answer should not just be a fraction, but should have an "of what" phrase added to the end of that statement.

In this problem, Felisha draws a picture to show that each girl will get $\frac{1}{5}$ of the first cookie and $\frac{1}{5}$ of the second cookie, which could be considered as $\frac{2}{10}$ of some other quantity. It's not clear, however, if Felisha understands that each child gets $\frac{2}{5}$ of one cookie.

You can help students understand that the whole can be made up of more than one unit by carefully choosing problems to be solved, making sure that the answer does not always ask for what part it is of one whole but sometimes asks what part it is of a larger whole, such as two cookies.

Developing Comparison and Ordering of Fractions

Another important fraction topic is comparison and ordering. This refers to a child's ability to judge the relative size of two or more fractions and to arrange two or more fractions in order based on their size.

Comparing and Ordering Fractions

Students need opportunities to *compare* and *order* fractions. Fractions should be compared by representing them concretely and pictorially before using an algorithm (Figure 10-14).

Experiences in comparing fractions at the concrete and pictorial levels will help children develop an intuitive sense of the numeric value of fractions, proceeding to more formal symbolic work after understanding is developed (see Activities 10-12 and 10-13).

ACTIVITY 10-12 Comparing Fractions

Procedure

1. Which is greater: $\frac{4}{5}$ or $\frac{2}{3}$?
2. How do you know?
3. Use materials or draw a picture to show that you are right.

FIGURE 10-14 Comparing Fractions

Which is the largest fraction:
2 fourths, 4 tenths, or 4 sixths?

$\frac{2}{4}$ $\frac{4}{10}$ $\frac{4}{6}$

4 sixths is the largest.

Order the fractions from smallest to largest:
1 half, 2 thirds, 5 sixths, 3 fourths, 5 eighths.

$\frac{1}{2}$ $\frac{5}{8}$ $\frac{2}{3}$ $\frac{3}{4}$ $\frac{5}{6}$

ACTIVITY 10-13 Ordering Fractions

Procedure

1. Order the fractions from smallest to largest.

   $\frac{1}{3}$ $\frac{3}{8}$ $\frac{5}{16}$ $\frac{1}{2}$ $\frac{5}{12}$

2. Write how you know.

A child's work for Activity 10-12 might look like this:

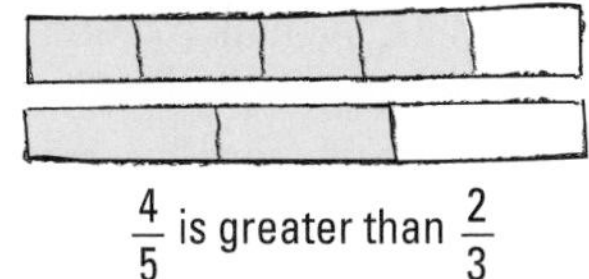

Children could be asked to compare a set of fractions with the same denominator, with the same numerator, and with different numerators and denominators to help them develop fraction number sense (see the following examples). Then, they could model the fractions to verify their work as pictured in Figure 10-15.

Note the importance of helping children understand the value of using benchmarks, such as $\frac{1}{2}$, in comparing fractions.

FIGURE 10-15 Comparing Fractions

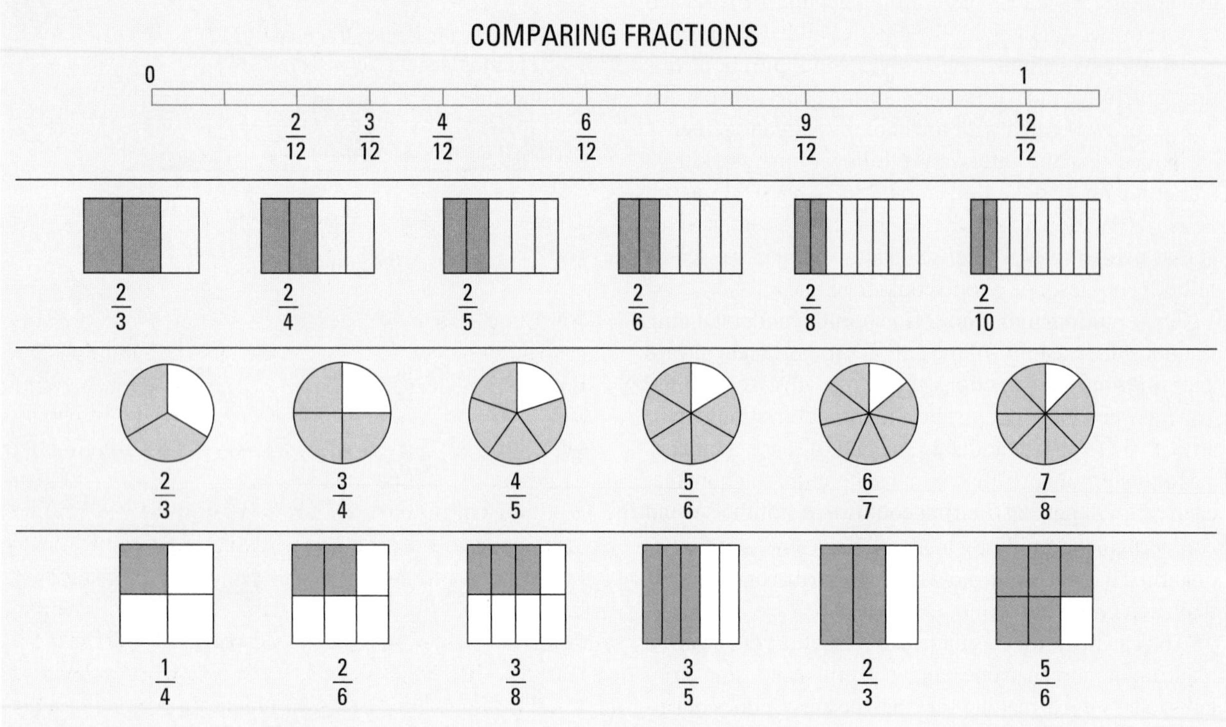

Examples:

Set A $\frac{3}{12}, \frac{6}{12}, \frac{2}{12}, \frac{9}{12}, \frac{12}{12}, \frac{4}{12}$

Set B $\frac{2}{7}, \frac{2}{3}, \frac{2}{9}, \frac{2}{5}, \frac{2}{10}, \frac{2}{15}$

Set C $\frac{2}{3}, \frac{3}{4}, \frac{4}{5}, \frac{5}{6}, \frac{6}{7}, \frac{7}{8}$

Set D $\frac{5}{6}, \frac{3}{8}, \frac{2}{3}, \frac{1}{4}, \frac{2}{6}, \frac{3}{5}$

Ortiz (2006) describes the "Roll Out Fractions" game to help children develop an understanding of fraction size. In this game, students use multiple representations, including manipulative materials, such as fraction tiles, pictures of objects cut into fractional parts, and symbols, such as a fraction chart, to compare the fractions they create by rolling dice.

Activities 10-14 to 10-15 also help children develop a sense of fraction size.

ACTIVITY 10-14 Variations on a Theme

Procedure

1. Write fractions that get closer and closer to 1, staying above 1.
2. Write fractions that get closer to 1 by alternating above and below 1.

ACTIVITY 10-15 Getting Close to $\frac{3}{4}$

Given set A = $\{\frac{1}{2}, \frac{1}{3}, \frac{1}{4}, \frac{1}{5}, \frac{1}{6}, \frac{1}{7}, \cdots\}$, get close (and closer) to $\frac{3}{4}$ using three numbers from the set and the operation of addition.

For variation in Activity 10-15, more than one operation can be used or four or more numbers can be used from the given set.

When comparing fractions at the symbolic level, the use of equivalent fractions is powerful. Children can find common denominators for the given fractions and then compare the numerators.

Using a calculator to compare fractions. The Math Explorer calculator can help children compare and order fractions. Using a calculator helps encourage children to look for patterns, so that eventually they can reason out most comparisons without using a calculator.

Relative Size of Fractions

In learning the relative size of fractions, children should first compare fractions concretely and pictorially. Comparisons are made relative to certain benchmark numbers such as one, one-half, and zero. Activities 10-16 through 10-19 provide examples.

ACTIVITY 10-16 Relative Size of Fractions (Pictorial: Region)

Procedure

About what size is the shaded part in each figure?

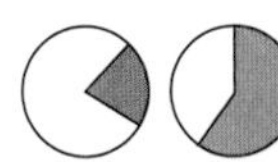
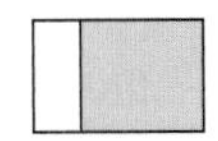
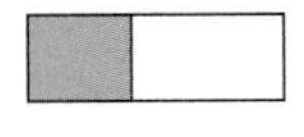
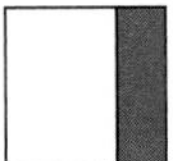

ACTIVITY 10-17 What Makes Almost One? (Concrete: Region)

Manipulative Strategies

Procedure

1. Use fraction pie pieces to help you find two different fractions that make almost one.
2. Can you find another pair of fractions that make almost one?

ACTIVITY 10-18 Fractions That Add up to Almost One (Symbolic)

Procedure

1. Use the numbers 1, 2, 3, 4, 5, 6, 8, and 10 to make two fractions that add up to almost one.

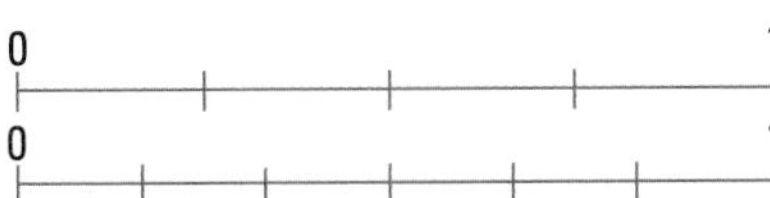

Example:
Three-fourths and one-sixth make almost one.

2. Can you make other fraction pairs that add up to almost one?

ACTIVITY 10-19 Fractions That Are about Zero, One-Half, or One

Procedure

Which of these fractions are close to zero, one-half, or one?

$\frac{12}{20}$	$\frac{1}{50}$	$\frac{2}{10}$	$\frac{8}{9}$	$\frac{3}{5}$
$\frac{6}{7}$	$\frac{1}{25}$	$\frac{15}{32}$	$\frac{4}{14}$	$\frac{6}{15}$
$\frac{99}{100}$	$\frac{15}{16}$	$\frac{4}{9}$	$\frac{2}{100}$	$\frac{11}{23}$

NCTM Principles and Standards Link 10-5

Content Strand: Number and Operations

In grades 3 through 5, students can learn to compare fractions to familiar benchmarks such as $\frac{1}{2}$. (NCTM, 2000, p. 52)

Improper Fractions and Mixed Numbers

An interpretation of fractions as numbers less than one probably led to a distinction between such fractions and those representing numbers greater than one. The terms *proper fraction* and *improper fraction* are used to distinguish between fractions less than one and greater than or equal to one, as described in Figure 10-16.

It is usually more difficult for young children to represent improper fractions concretely or diagrammatically than it is to represent proper fractions. For example, in Figure 10-17 children often label the shaded portion $\frac{4}{6}$ rather than $\frac{4}{3}$, but $\frac{4}{3}$ is correct, since $\frac{4}{3}$ of 1 whole is shaded. As in earlier examples, this shows the importance of asking children to identify the unit or the whole by asking "$\frac{4}{6}$ (or $\frac{4}{3}$) of *what*?"

Any fraction that is greater than one can be written as an improper fraction or as a *mixed number.* A mixed number is a way of expressing a number greater than one as a whole number and a fraction. Addition is implied in a mixed number as shown here, even though the addition symbol is not written:

Example: $3\frac{2}{5} \rightarrow 3 + \frac{2}{5}$

The process of changing an improper fraction to a mixed number can be demonstrated as follows:

Example: Change $\frac{18}{5}$ to a mixed number.

Recall: $1 = \frac{5}{5}$

Think: $18 = 5 + 5 + 5 + 3$

Therefore, $\frac{18}{5}$ can be written as $\frac{5}{5} + \frac{5}{5} + \frac{5}{5} + \frac{3}{5}$,

FIGURE 10-16 Types of Fractions

PROPER FRACTIONS

$\frac{1}{2}, \frac{2}{3}, \frac{4}{5}, \ldots$

For every $\frac{a}{b}$, $a < b$

IMPROPER FRACTIONS

$\frac{3}{2}, \frac{4}{3}, \frac{5}{4}, \frac{5}{5}, \ldots$

For every $\frac{a}{b}$, $a > b$ or $a = b$

FIGURE 10-17 Representing Fractions Greater Than One

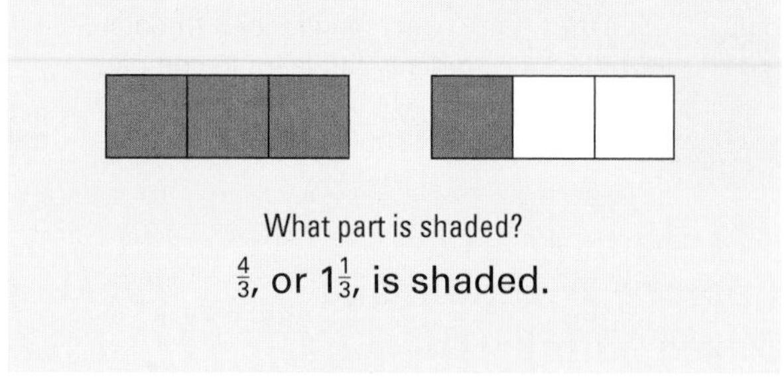

What part is shaded?

$\frac{4}{3}$, or $1\frac{1}{3}$, is shaded.

$$\text{which } = 1 + 1 + 1 + \frac{3}{5}$$
$$= 3 + \frac{3}{5} \text{ or } 3\frac{3}{5}$$

Introduce this problem by asking children, "How many wholes are in $\frac{18}{5}$, and how many fifths are left?" Children can use manipulatives or draw pictures to solve this problem, and then look for patterns to generalize a procedure that works and makes sense to them. In working through this process several times, children may see that what is essentially being done is dividing 18 by 5 to obtain the quotient 3, with 3 left over, so the answer is $3\frac{3}{5}$. This analysis also connects with the *quotient* interpretation of fractions, that is, $\frac{18}{5}$ is the same as 18 divided by 5.

Using the Math Explorer calculator. Converting improper fractions to mixed numbers can be performed on the Math Explorer calculator by using the [Ab/c] key.

Example: Change $\frac{8}{5}$ to a mixed number
Enter 8 [/] 5 [Ab/c] Display 1 u 3/5
(The u separates the whole number from a fraction.)

Understanding Equivalent Fractions

Another important fraction topic is *equivalent fractions*, a concept that refers to the notion that different fractions can represent the same amount. For example, $\frac{1}{2}$ and $\frac{2}{4}$ are different fractions that represent the same amount; however, to many children these are two completely different fractions that have no relation to each other. Many children incorrectly believe that $\frac{2}{4}$ must be greater than $\frac{1}{2}$, because the numbers are larger. Indeed, understanding equivalent fractions is another important prerequisite to fraction computation and helps children evaluate the reasonableness of answers.

Dealing with Equivalent Fractions

When dealing with fractions, the notion that every number can be expressed in several ways is critical. Just as whole numbers may be represented in several equivalent forms, for example, 32 is also 20 + 12 or 10 + 22 or 30 + 2, fractions can also be represented in several equivalent ways. When assigning different names for a specified fraction, we say that we are writing *equivalent fractions.*

Children should understand unit fractions and composite fractions and be able to compare fractions before they are introduced to equivalent fractions. For example, children should be able to readily compare fractions such as $\frac{1}{4}$ and $\frac{1}{6}$, and $\frac{7}{10}$ and $\frac{5}{10}$, and $\frac{2}{4}$ and $\frac{2}{8}$.

Bezuk and Bieck (1993) recommend that you discuss the meaning of the word *equivalent* ("equal value") and also discuss how equivalent fractions are both alike and different. They also recommend that you help children generalize the symbolic algorithm for finding equivalent fractions from their experiences with manipulatives.

Although the idea of equivalent fractions can be introduced early to children, mastery of the concept should not be expected until upper elementary grades or later (Driscoll, 1984).

Children can engage in activities with fraction circles, Fraction Factory pieces, or Fraction Bars to discover for themselves that fractions such as one-half and two-fourths name the same amount. They can fold paper strips or rectangles to discover equivalent fractions. Several activities that are designed to help children understand equivalent fractions are presented in this section (see Activities 10-20 and 10-21).

ACTIVITY 10-20 Equivalent Fractions

Procedure

1. What part of the bar is red?

2. Divide each part of the bar in half. What part of the bar is red now? Write an equivalent fraction.
3. Divide each part of these bars in half. Write equivalent fractions for the parts.

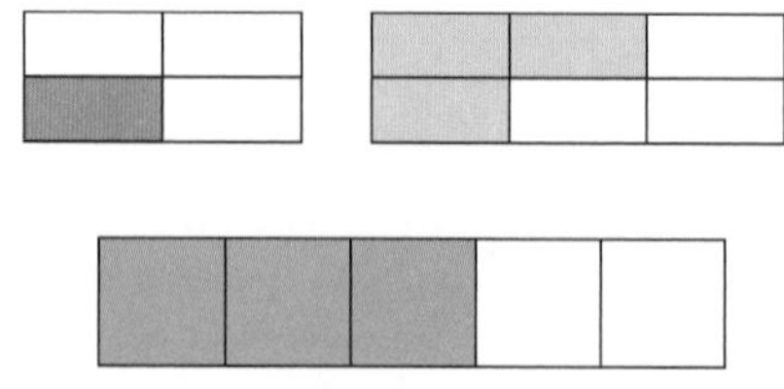

NCTM Principles and Standards Link 10-6

Content Strand: Number and Operations

Through a variety of activities, [children] should understand that a fraction such as $\frac{1}{2}$ is equivalent to $\frac{5}{10}$ and that it has a decimal representation (0.5). (NCTM, 2000, p. 149)

ACTIVITY 10-21 Writing Equivalent Fractions

Visual Scaffolding

Materials

A sheet of paper on which three same-sized rectangles have been drawn

Procedure

1. Draw thirds on the first rectangle.
2. Draw sixths on the second rectangle.
3. Draw twelfths on the third rectangle.
4. Write equality statements about what you observe in your figures.

Example:

2 thirds = 4 sixths.

1. **Equivalent Fractions**
   - Provide each child with narrow strips of paper.
   - Ask children to fold one strip of paper into two equal pieces. Have them identify the fractional parts and label the midpoint as $\frac{1}{2}$ and the end point as $\frac{2}{2}$.
   - Note that the $\frac{1}{2}$ is the distance from the beginning point to the center and the $\frac{2}{2}$ is the distance from the beginning point to the end.
   - Have children fold a second strip of paper in fourths, open it up, and name the four parts on the fold-lines and the end points as $\frac{1}{4}$, $\frac{2}{4}$, $\frac{3}{4}$, and $\frac{4}{4}$.
   - Direct children to fold a third strip of paper in eighths and label each part produced in eighths. The strips should be labeled as in the following diagram:

$\frac{0}{2}$	$\frac{1}{2}$	$\frac{2}{2}$

$\frac{0}{4}$	$\frac{1}{4}$	$\frac{2}{4}$	$\frac{3}{4}$	$\frac{4}{4}$

$\frac{0}{8}$	$\frac{1}{8}$	$\frac{2}{8}$	$\frac{3}{8}$	$\frac{4}{8}$	$\frac{5}{8}$	$\frac{6}{8}$	$\frac{7}{8}$	$\frac{8}{8}$

   - Ask children to find equal lengths on the strips that have been labeled differently. The idea that fractional lengths can be named differently or that fractions can have more than one name should be highlighted in the discussion. Equality statements could be written on the board.

     Examples: $\frac{1}{2}$ and $\frac{2}{4}$ are the same length.
     $\frac{2}{2}$, $\frac{4}{4}$, and $\frac{8}{8}$ all indicate the same length.
2. **Finding Equivalent Fractions**
   - Provide Fraction Factory pieces for each group of children.
   - Direct children to select the black rectangle.
   - Ask them to use other pieces to cover half of the black rectangle in at least two different ways.
   - Have them cover other fractional parts of the rectangle in at least two different ways.
   - Have children write equality statements about what they have done.
   - Have children read aloud what they have written.
   - Display the statements on a bulletin board under the caption "Fractions Have More Than One Name."
3. **Equivalent Fractions**
   - Provide a set of buttons in two colors for each child.
   - Have children arrange 12 buttons, 6 of each color, in a two-row array.

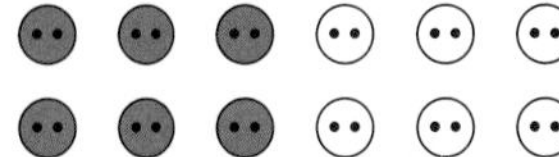

   - Ask: "What part of the buttons are white?" (one-half)
   - Ask: "Can you group the buttons another way so that you can give a different fraction name to the group of white buttons?"
   - Have children repeat the last step.

   Possible solutions include the following:

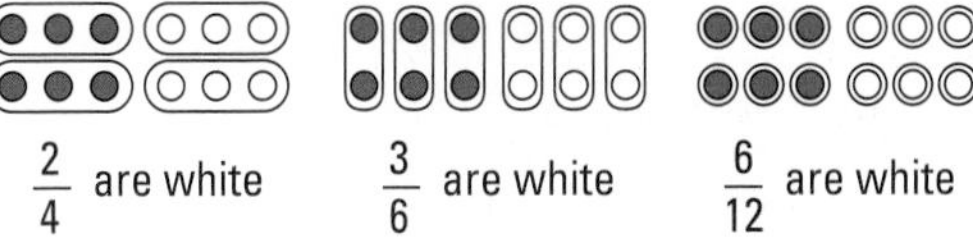

   - Provide children with 24 buttons, 12 of each color. Ask the students to find equivalent fractions for one-half; for two-thirds.
   - Given an appropriate number of buttons, the process can be repeated for any unit or composite fraction.

 Go to the Assignments and Activities section of Topic 8: "Fraction Concepts and Computation" in the MyEducationLab for your course and view the clip "A Lesson on Fractions" to see a class work on fraction equivalents.

Renaming and Simplifying Fractions

The idea that each fraction number can be represented in different numeric form is an important one for children to learn (Example: $\frac{1}{2} = \frac{2}{4} = \frac{3}{6} = \ldots$).

Some children may detect the pattern and articulate a rule for easily *renaming a fraction* (writing equivalent fractions), such as multiplying each part of the fraction numeral by the same number. What may not be readily evident to children is that the multiplicative identity element, one, is being used in a different form, that is, as $\frac{2}{2}$, $\frac{3}{3}$, $\frac{4}{4}$, and so on. Middle school children should understand the following reasoning:

Any number that multiplies 1 or is multiplied by 1 equals 1.

Examples: $6 \times 1 = 6$ $\qquad \frac{1}{2} \times 1 = \frac{1}{2}$

$1 \times 45 = 45$ $\qquad 1 \times \frac{2}{5} = \frac{2}{5}$

Represent "1" as $\frac{2}{2}, \frac{3}{3}, \frac{4}{4}$, and so on

If $\frac{1}{2} \times 1 = \frac{1}{2}$ $\qquad$ If $\frac{1}{2} \times 1 = \frac{1}{2}$

and $\frac{1}{2} \times \frac{2}{2} = \frac{2}{4}$ $\qquad$ and $\frac{1}{2} \times \frac{3}{3} = \frac{3}{6}$

then $\frac{1}{2} = \frac{2}{4}$ $\qquad$ then $\frac{1}{2} = \frac{3}{6}$

Being able to easily rename fractions is a very important skill when comparing fractions and as a preparation for computation. The following activity helps children understand the concept of renaming.

1. **Renaming Fractions** (adapted from Jensen & O'Neil, 1982)
   - For this activity, each group of children will need egg cartons separated into 2, 4, 6, 8, and 12 "cups" and small objects to represent eggs.
   - Have the children choose a 4-cup tray and place 2 eggs in it. Ask: "What part of the tray is filled?" (elicit $\frac{1}{2}, \frac{2}{4}$).
   - Continue in this manner, using in turn, a 6-, an 8-, and a 12-cup tray. Each time, have children indicate in several ways what part of the tray is filled (12-cup tray, 6 eggs: $\frac{1}{2}, \frac{2}{4}, \frac{3}{6}, \frac{6}{12}$).
   - Have children record their work on paper.
   - Ask: "What conclusions do you reach about the fractions you have written?"

Simplifying fractions is the process of renaming a fraction through division. The fraction is divided by the multiplicative identity element represented in fraction form. The choice of representation for the identity element depends on the fraction being simplified, that is, a divisor common to each term of the fraction numeral must be used.

Examples:

$\frac{4}{6} \div 1 = \frac{4}{6}$ $\qquad \frac{5}{15} \div 1 = \frac{5}{15}$

$\frac{4}{6} \div \frac{2}{2} = \frac{(4 \div 2)}{(6 \div 2)} = \frac{2}{3}$ $\qquad \frac{5}{15} \div \frac{5}{5} = \frac{(5 \div 5)}{(15 \div 5)} = \frac{1}{3}$

The algorithmic work of renaming fractions should be accompanied for some time by concrete (Figure 10-18) or pictorial (Figure 10-19) representations of the process.

Renaming and simplifying fractions using a calculator. After children understand the process of renaming and simplifying fractions, they can be allowed to use a calculator with that capability to assist them in problem solving. In renaming fractions with the Math Explorer calculator, the procedure is as follows:

Example: Write an equivalent fraction for $\frac{3}{8}$.

Enter 3 [/] 8 [×] 2 [/] 2 [=] Display: $\frac{6}{16}$

The fact that the multiplicative identity is employed (1 written as $\frac{2}{2}$ in this case) in renaming fractions will be emphasized when using a calculator. A child who merely multiplies a fraction by a whole number factor will note that the denominator has not changed.

Example: Simplifying a fraction can be performed in two ways:

Enter 2 [/] 16 [×] 2 [=] Display: $\frac{4}{16}$

1. The calculator can choose the common factor, or
2. The child can do so.

Example: Simplify $\frac{4}{24}$

Enter 4 [/] 24 [Simp]

FIGURE 10-18 Concrete Representations of Renaming Fractions

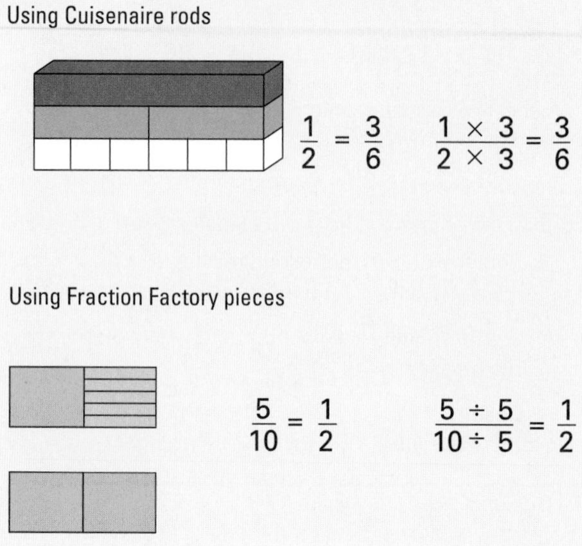

Using Cuisenaire rods
$\frac{1}{2} = \frac{3}{6}$
$\frac{1 \times 3}{2 \times 3} = \frac{3}{6}$
Using Fraction Factory pieces
$\frac{5}{10} = \frac{1}{2}$
$\frac{5 \div 5}{10 \div 5} = \frac{1}{2}$

FIGURE 10-19 Pictorial Representations of Renaming Fractions

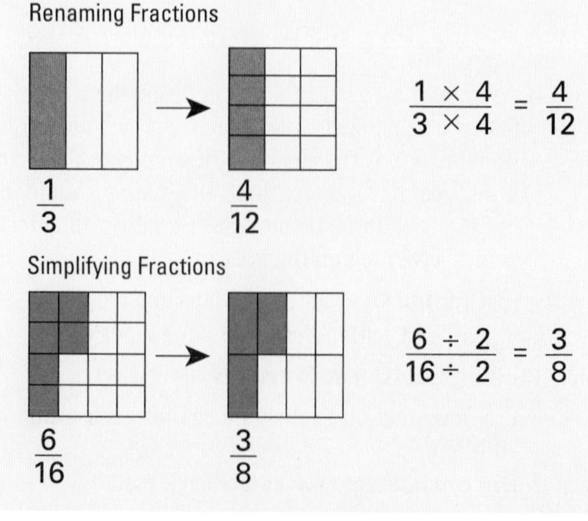

Literature Link 10-1

Fraction Concepts

Matthews, Louise. (1995). ***Gator Pie.*** Littleton, MA: Sundance.
Murphy, Stuart J. (1986). ***Give Me Half!*** New York: HarperCollins.

Children begin school with basic understandings of many mathematics concepts. Fraction terms like *half* referring to "half of a cookie" or *quarter after* to "quarter after five" when telling time may already be a part of their informal mathematical knowledge. In the story ***Gator Pie,*** two alligators, Alvin and Alice, find a delicious-looking pie near the swamp. They plan to share the pie equally in two halves, but other alligators come along, and they are forced to think about cutting the pie into thirds, fourths, and eventually hundredths. In the end, Alvin comes up with a clever solution.

- On several pages of the book, fractions are written in words and pictorial models of a circular region are shown. Practice writing the words and the numerals and drawing various pictures as models for some common fractions.
- Use paper plates as circular region models of the pie in the story. Attempt to do what Alice did and cut the pie into 100 equal pieces by drawing lines on the paper plates to indicate the slices.
- Investigate "halves" using other region models such as squares, rectangles, triangles, and pentagons cut from construction paper. Fold each shape to create two equal halves.
- Introduce concepts and terms such as *partitioning* and *congruence* by investigating construction paper cutouts of different shapes. Use a ruler to measure and cut these region models into thirds, fourths, fifths, sixths, and so on. By cutting the pieces of construction paper apart, children can place each piece on top of others to compare to be sure all pieces are the same shape and size.
- Use manipulatives such as fraction circles (or fraction pies) to identify common fractions in a circular region model. Introduce children to representations of fractions in numbers, words, pictorial models, and concrete models.
- Books such as ***Give Me Half!*** help children to understand beginning concepts of "half." Examine a paper cutout of a half-circle, a half-square, and half of a group of 6 counters (3 counters). Discuss why all of these representations are called "half" when it is empirically obvious that they do not look the same. Talk about what "half" means so that children have the opportunity to abstract this concept through various representations.

Source: Dr. Patricia Moyer-Packenham, Utah State University.

The calculator displays [Simp] N/D → n/d in the left corner, indicating that the fraction can be simplified. The two ways to proceed to simplify the fraction are:

1. Calculator chooses the common factor

   Enter = to get $\frac{2}{12}$.

   The calculator reduces the fraction to the next simpler term. If N/D → n/d still is displayed, that means that the fraction can be simplified further. Pressing the [Simp] and the [=] keys again simplifies the fraction to the next simpler term.

   To find out which factor the calculator used, enter the [x⤾y] key and the factor will be displayed.

   Enter the [x⤾y] key again to display the simpler fraction.

2. Child chooses the common factor:

   Enter 2 (a common factor of 4 and 24).

   Enter [=] to obtain $\frac{2}{12}$.

   To reduce the fraction further, press 2 (a common factor of 2 and 12) and [=] to obtain the simplest fraction $\frac{1}{16}$. If a number is entered that is not a common factor of the two fraction terms, the calculator will simply display the fraction again.

Example: $\frac{4}{24}$ Enter [Simp] 5 [=] Display is $\frac{4}{24}$.

Conclusion

Fractions are an important part of the mathematics curriculum. Understanding fraction concepts, comparison, ordering, number sense, and equivalence lays the foundation for later work with fraction computation and prepares children for using mathematics in their everyday lives.

CHAPTER

10

Sample Lesson

A Lesson on Comparing Fractions

Grade level: Third

Materials:

- At least one fraction manipulative, such as fraction circles
- Index cards with one fraction written on each card. Sample sets of fractions (clip each set together):
  - Set A: $\frac{3}{5}$, $\frac{2}{5}$, $\frac{4}{5}$
  - Set B: $\frac{1}{2}$, $\frac{1}{4}$, $\frac{1}{8}$
  - Set C: $\frac{2}{5}$, $\frac{2}{9}$, $\frac{2}{3}$
  - Set D: $\frac{1}{2}$, $\frac{3}{4}$, 1, $1\frac{2}{3}$, $\frac{7}{4}$
  - Set E: $\frac{99}{100}$, $\frac{6}{7}$, $\frac{15}{16}$
- A string tied across the front of the classroom (the tray on the chalkboard may be used instead of the string). If using the string, fold each card so that it will hang on the string, or use binder clips to attach cards to the string.

Lesson objective: Students will use models and benchmark fractions to correctly compare and order fractions. Then they will explain their reasoning.

Standards link: Students solve problems that involve comparing and ordering fractions by using models, benchmark fractions, or common numerators or denominators. (NCTM (2006) *Curriculum Focal Points*, grade 3)

Launch: Display index card Set A. Ask students how to arrange them from smallest to largest, with the smallest on the left. Have students share their answers and place their cards on the string in the correct order. Then ask students to explain how they decided on the size of each fraction. Desired response is that all the fractions in Set A have the same denomination, so they have the same-sized pieces, and the different numerators tell us that each fraction has a different number of pieces that are the same size.

Explore: Arrange students in groups of 3 to 4 students. Give each group one of each of the remaining sets of cards. Have each group arrange Set B in order and explain their reasoning to each other. Then have a whole-class discussion about ordering Set B. Continue for Sets C, D, and E.

Summarize: Have students individually order another set of fractions, such as $\frac{1}{2}$, $\frac{3}{8}$, and $\frac{6}{7}$, and explain their reasoning in their math journals.

FOLLOW-UP

Complete the following questions.

1. What would be the advantages of using fraction circles in this lesson? Are there any disadvantages? What other manipulatives might work well? What would be the advantages and/or disadvantages of each manipulative?
2. Comment on each set of fractions. For example, what math understandings related to comparing fractions does each set address? What would you want students to generalize about each set of numbers? Which sets might be hardest for students, and why? Create two additional sets of fractions and describe the math understandings each set would help students develop.
3. What might the *next* lesson focus on, and why?

IN PRACTICE

Complete the following activities to include in your professional portfolio.

1. Administer the *Chapter 10 Preassessment* to one or two intermediate-grade students to assess their understanding of fraction concepts, comparison, and equivalence. Analyze and describe their understanding of these topics. What concepts do they appear to understand well? Do they have any misunderstandings or limited understandings? What factors might have contributed to these understandings?
2. Based on the students' performance on the preassessment, what would your next lesson with their class focus on? What would the objective of that lesson be? Describe an activity or problems that you would include in this lesson, and explain why you would include them. Explain how these next steps follow from your analysis of student understanding.

PEARSON myeducationlab The Power of Classroom Practice Now go to Topic 8: "Fraction Concepts and Computation" in the MyEducationLab (www.myeducationlab.com) for your course, where you can:

- Find learning outcomes for "Fraction Concepts and Computation" along with the national standards that connect to these outcomes.
- Apply and practice your understanding of the core teaching skills identified in the chapter with a Building Teaching Skills and Dispositions learning unit.
- Complete Assignments and Activities that can help you understand the chapter content more deeply.
- Complete *enVision MATH* Sample Curricula assignments that allow you to examine and work with chapters from *enVision MATH*, a K-6 mathematics program.
- Check your comprehension on the content covered in the chapter by going to the Study Plan in the Book-Specific Resources for your text. Here you will be able to take a chapter quiz, receive feedback on your answers, and then access Review, Practice, and Enrichment activities to enhance your understanding of chapter content.
- Go to the Book-Specific Resources for Chapter 10 to explore mathematical reasoning related to chapter content in the Activities section.

LINKS TO THE INTERNET

ProTeacher: Fractions and Decimals

http://www.proteacher.com/100014.shtml
Contains lesson plans on fractions and decimals.

Who Wants Pizza?

http://math.rice.edu/~lanius/fractions/index.html
Contains many lessons on fractions and lists of other resources.

Fresh-Baked Fractions

http://www.funbrain.com/fract/
Contains games on finding equivalent fractions.

RESOURCES FOR TEACHERS

Children's Literature

Adler, David (1997). *Fraction Fun*. New York: Holiday House

Greenberg, Dan (1996). *Fun and Fabulous Fraction Stories*. New York: Scholastic.

Leedy, Loreen (1996). *Fraction Action*. New York: Holiday House.

McMillan, Bruce (1992). *Eating Fractions*. New York: Scholastic.

Murphy, Stuart J. (1996). *Give Me Half!* New York: HarperCollins.

Palotta, Jerry (1999). *Hershey's fractions*. New York: Cartwheel.

Palotta, Jerry (2003). *Apple Fractions*. New York: Cartwheel.

Tierney, Cornelia (2004). *Different Shapes, Equal Pieces: Fractions and Area*. New York: Scott Foresman.

Tierney, Cornelia & Mary Berle-Carman (1998). *Fair Shares: Fractions*. New York: Scott Foresman.

Books on Fractions

Brodie, J. (1995). *Constructing Ideas about Fractions, Grades 3–6*. Mountain View, CA: Creative.

Cramer, K., Behr, M., Post, T., & Lesh, R. (1997). *Rational Number Project: Fraction Lessons for the Middle Grades, Level 1*. Dubuque, IA: Kendall/Hunt.

Cramer, K., Behr, M., Post, T., & Lesh, R. (1997). *Rational Number Project: Fraction Lessons for the Middle Grades, Level 2*. Dubuque, IA: Kendall/Hunt.

Empson, Susan B. (1995, October). Using sharing situations to help children learn fractions. *Teaching Children Mathematics*. 2(2): 110–114. Reston, VA: NCTM.

Empson, Susan B. (1999). Equal sharing and shared meaning: The development of fraction concepts in a first-grade classroom. *Cognition and Instruction*, 17(3): 283–342. New York: Routledge.

National Council of Teachers of Mathematics (2006). *Curriculum Focal Points for Prekindergarten through Grade 8 Mathematics*. Reston, VA: Author.

Ortiz, Enrique (2006). Roll out fractions game: Comparing fractions. *Teaching Children Mathematics*, 13(1): 56–62. Reston, VA: NCTM.

CHAPTER 11

Developing Fraction Computation

NCTM CONNECTING WITH THE STANDARDS

The National Council of Teachers of Mathematics (NCTM) Principles and Standards emphasizes the importance of helping children deepen their understanding of fractions to include making sense of operations on fractions, noting that "teachers need to be attentive to conceptual obstacles that many students encounter as they make the transition from operations with whole numbers" (NCTM, 2000, p. 217). The NCTM document goes on to note that "The study of rational numbers in the middle grades should build on students' prior knowledge of whole-number concepts and skills and their encounters with fractions, decimals, and percents in lower grades and in everyday life" (NCTM, 2000, p. 212).

The NCTM (2006) *Curriculum Focal Points* mentions developing an understanding of and fluency with operations on fractions in both grade 5, for addition and subtraction of fractions, and in grade 6, for multiplication and division of fractions. They state that students in grade 5 should:

- apply their understandings of fractions and fraction models to represent the addition and subtraction of fractions with unlike denominators as equivalent calculations with like denominators;
- develop fluency with standard procedures for adding and subtracting fractions and decimals;
- make reasonable estimates of fraction and decimal sums and differences; and
- add and subtract fractions and decimals to solve problems, including problems involving measurement (NCTM, 2006, p. 17).

In addition, the *Curriculum Focal Points* states that students in grade 6 should:

- use the meanings of fractions, multiplication and division, and the inverse relationship between multiplication and division to make sense of procedures for multiplying and dividing fractions and explain why they work;
- use common procedures to multiply and divide fractions and decimals efficiently and accurately; and

Developing Your Math Teaching Skills

When you have finished studying this chapter, you should be able to do the following:

- Explain the prerequisites for operations on fractions.
- Discuss what it means to help children develop operation sense.
- Describe the meaning of each operation on fractions and give an example of a real-world situation that exemplifies each operation on fractions.
- List and discuss models that help children understand operations on fractions.

NCTM Principles and Standards Link 11-1

Content Strand: Number and Operations

As students acquire conceptual grounding related to rational numbers, they should begin to solve problems using strategies they develop or adapt from their whole-number work. At these grades, the emphasis should not be on developing general procedures to solve all decimal and fraction problems. Rather, students should generate solutions that are based on number sense and properties of the operations and that use a variety of models or representations. (NCTM, 2000, p. 154)

NCTM Principles and Standards Link 11-2

Content Strand: Number and Operations

The development of rational-number concepts is a major goal for grades 3–5, which should lead to informal methods for calculating with fractions. For example, a problem such as $\frac{1}{4} + \frac{1}{2}$ should be solved mentally with ease because students can picture $\frac{1}{2}$ and $\frac{1}{4}$ or can use decomposition strategies, such as $\frac{1}{4} + \frac{1}{2} = \frac{1}{4} + (\frac{1}{4} + \frac{1}{4})$. . . . By grades 6–8, students should become fluent in computing with rational numbers in fraction and decimal form. (NCTM, 2000, p. 35)

- multiply and divide fractions and decimals to solve problems, including multistep problems and problems involving measurement (NCTM, 2006, p. 18).

Teachers need to understand how to help children develop a conceptual understanding of fraction computation and to use fraction operations to solve problems. As with many other mathematics topics, traditionally there has been a rush to introduce abstract symbols before children understand the underlying concepts. This chapter discusses how to help children develop a strong understanding of fraction computation.

Throughout the chapter we will discuss how to utilize strategies for reaching all learners. As discussed in Chapter 2, these strategies help all students, including those who are English language learners, be successful in learning fraction computation. These strategies include making real-world connections, using manipulative materials and pictures, using advanced organizers, previewing and reviewing concepts, and using math word walls.

ASSESSING MATHEMATICS UNDERSTANDING

In order to become familiar with the mathematics concepts and procedures discussed in this chapter, take a few minutes and complete the following *Chapter 11 Preassessment.* Answer each question on your own. Then think about the possible misunderstandings some elementary-school children might have about each topic. If you are able, administer this assessment to a child, and analyze his or her understanding of these topics.

1. Choose the best estimate for the sum of $\frac{9}{10} + \frac{6}{7}$ and explain your thinking:

a. 1 **b.** 2 **c.** 15
d. 17 **e.** none of these

Solve the following problems and explain how you solved them. You might want to draw a picture to solve or to explain your solution.

2. $\frac{3}{4} + \frac{1}{2} =$

3. $4 - \frac{1}{8} =$

4. If you had 4 pizzas, and you ate $\frac{1}{8}$ of one pizza, how much pizza would be left?

5. $\frac{1}{2} \times \frac{1}{3} =$

6. $1 \div \frac{1}{3} =$

7. $1\frac{1}{2} \div \frac{1}{3} =$

All of these problems involve adding, subtracting, multiplying, or dividing fractions. What was your general reaction to solving the problems? Were you able to estimate the result to each problem, or to decide if your answer was reasonable? What in general do you think a teacher's goals should be regarding fraction computation?

myeducationlab — The Power of Classroom Practice

Go to the Video Examples section of Topic 8: "Fraction Concepts and Computation" in the MyEducationLab for your course and view the Annenberg clip "Fraction Tracks."

Examining Classroom Practice

Hilory Paster's fifth graders often play a game in which children draw fraction cards from a deck and move markers on their game boards' "Fraction Tracks." Each game board (p. 236) has seven tracks, one each marked in halves, thirds, fourths, fifths, sixths, eighths, and tenths. The object of the game is to move one marker on each track from 0 to 1 by moving them the distance specified on the card drawn. Children are encouraged to rename the fraction drawn as a sum of equivalent fractions, allowing them to advance on more than one track at a time.

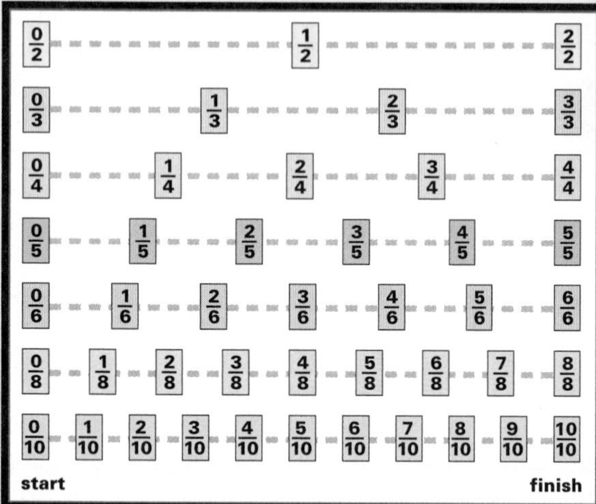

Today the class begins the game by drawing the card labeled "$\frac{8}{10}$." They could move the marker on the tenths track from 0 to $\frac{8}{10}$, but Ms. Paster asks the class if there is a way to move a piece on another track. A girl suggests moving the marker on the fifths track to $\frac{4}{5}$, because $\frac{4}{5}$ is equivalent to $\frac{8}{10}$.

Then Ms. Paster asks if there is a way to move *two pieces* a distance equal to $\frac{8}{10}$. Another girl suggests moving one marker to $\frac{4}{10}$, since it is halfway to $\frac{8}{10}$, and moving another marker to $\frac{4}{5}$. After some discussion, the girl changes the second number to $\frac{2}{5}$, and summarizes by saying "Since $\frac{2}{5}$ plus $\frac{4}{10}$ equals $\frac{8}{10}$, that would be another way to get to $\frac{8}{10}$."

Prior to playing this game, Ms. Paster's class spent a lot of time developing an understanding of fraction equivalence. They matched fractions with pictures of equivalent fractions and constructed a number line with many equivalent fractions positioned on the number line. They kept a classroom list of equivalent fractions that they knew, adding to it and referring to it as needed.

When children are playing the game with a partner, Ms. Paster asks them to write down two or three possible moves for each fraction drawn and then decide which move to use. The goal of the game is for the team to move all seven of its markers all the way across the board to 1.

For example, when $\frac{4}{10}$ was drawn, one pair of children considered using three different options: $\frac{4}{10}$, or $\frac{2}{10} + \frac{1}{5}$, or $\frac{2}{5}$. Another group, trying to move $\frac{8}{8}$, noted that $\frac{8}{8}$ could be split into $\frac{6}{8}$ plus $\frac{2}{8}$, or $\frac{6}{8}$ plus $\frac{1}{4}$.

One child decided to use fraction pieces to help him and his partner figure out how to break down the fraction $\frac{7}{8}$. Using the pieces, they saw that $\frac{7}{8}$ could be split into $\frac{2}{4}$ and $\frac{3}{8}$. These children went on to use the fraction pieces to rename $\frac{9}{10}$ as $\frac{1}{2}$ plus $\frac{4}{10}$ or $\frac{3}{6}$ plus $\frac{4}{10}$.

Toward the end of the class session, Ms. Paster gathers the class to discuss the strategies they used to solve the problems. During this discussion, Ms. Paster sometimes asks children to rephrase another child's strategy. This encourages children to listen carefully to each other and also provides Ms. Paster with a way to assess children's understanding.

Analyzing Assessment Results

Analyze each problem in the *Chapter 11 Preassessment*. How did you (and/or the student you administered the assessment to) solve each of the following problems?

1. Choose the best estimate for the sum of $\frac{9}{10} + \frac{6}{7}$:

a. 1 **b.** 2 **c.** 15 **d.** 17 **e.** none of these

Comments: Look at choices (a) through (d). What might a child who chose any of these items understand about addition of fractions? A child choosing choice (a) might be thinking that "any time you add fractions, your answer is a fraction, so about 1." Another possibility for picking choice (a) is a common error that children make when adding fractions: to add the numerators, then add the denominators. In this case, that would give us $\frac{15}{17}$, which is close to 1 (and is incorrect!). Choice (b) is correct; a child choosing choice (b) might be thinking that "$\frac{9}{10}$ is almost 1 and $\frac{6}{7}$ is almost 1, and 1 plus 1 is 2." A child choosing choice (c) might have just added the numerators: $9 + 6 = 15$. A child choosing choice (d) might have just added the denominators: $10 + 7 = 17$. Each of these errors made when selecting choices (a), (c), or (d) are very common. What do these errors tell us about those students' understanding of addition of fractions?

2. $\frac{3}{4} + \frac{1}{2} =$

Comments: How did you (and/or your student) solve this problem? Did you draw a picture, or did you work with the symbols alone? Think back to the clip "IMAP—Developing Operation Sense for Fractions" on MyEducationLab that you viewed in Chapter 10.

It showed Felisha, a second-grade girl, finding the sum of $\frac{3}{4} + \frac{1}{2}$. You might want to view that video clip again. Felisha drew a picture to represent fractions and the sum of fractions and was able to correctly use fraction names and symbols to identify the sum. How does that compare with what you (and your student) did?

3. $4 - \frac{1}{8} =$

4. If you had 4 pizzas, and you ate $\frac{1}{8}$ of one pizza, how much pizza would be left?

Comments: How are problems 3 and 4 alike and different? They are both the same problem, posed in different ways. Problem 3 is posed symbolically, while Problem 4 is posed as a word problem in a real-world setting. Was one problem easier to solve than the other? If so, why? Did you solve each problem in the same way, or in different ways? For many students, Problem 4 is easier because the real-world setting helps them estimate the answer: Since you are starting with 4 pizzas and eat less than 1 pizza, you will have more than 3 pizzas left, so the answer will be greater than 3.

5. $\frac{1}{2} \times \frac{1}{3} =$

Comments: How did you (and/or your student) solve this problem? Sometimes students feel that multiplication of fractions is the easiest operation since "you just need to multiply straight across"; in other words, you just multiply the numerators and the denominators. But many students have more difficulty deciding if their answers are reasonable. How could you explain why the correct answer, $\frac{1}{6}$, makes sense?

6. $1 \div \frac{1}{3} =$

7. $1\frac{1}{2} \div \frac{1}{3} =$

Comments: How did you (and/or your student) solve problems 6 and 7? Did you use the "invert and multiply" algorithm? Did you draw pictures to help you solve the problems? Were you (and your student) able to decide if the answers you got were reasonable? Students often have difficulty with dividing fractions. If they've learned the "invert and multiply" algorithm, sometimes they have trouble remembering how to use it—for example, remembering, which fraction gets "flipped"? Perhaps even more importantly, students have particular difficulty in deciding if their solutions are correct. Students often think that the answer to a division problem has to be smaller than the number they started with, but in division of fractions, this pattern is not always true. We will discuss these problems in more detail later in the chapter, and view a video clip of a sixth grade student solving these problems.

Take a minute and reflect on this assessment. What aspects of fraction computation are particularly difficult for you and/or for the student you assessed? What do you want to learn more about in order to teach these concepts effectively?

Common Student Misunderstandings about Fraction Computation:

- "Operations on fractions work just like whole numbers" or "Just pretend they're whole numbers." This misunderstanding leads students to what is perhaps the most common error when adding fractions: adding the numerators and then adding the denominators.
- Lack of understanding of the meaning of operations.
- Lack of the ability to estimate the solution to a fraction computation problem.

Are there any other misunderstandings that children may have about operations with fractions? It's important to assess what children understand, and are still working on understanding, in order to plan instruction that meets their needs.

Building on Assessment Results

Now that we've analyzed your assessment results, let's think about what can be done to help strengthen children's understandings and minimize (and hopefully eradicate) their misunderstandings and misconceptions. What might have led students to develop these misconceptions? It is possible that students' mathematics learning experiences may have focused on a set of procedures to be memorized rather than a set of concepts to be understood. So what might we do next to help students understand these concepts?

A key element of all instruction is to make sure that students understand the concept. In the case of fraction computation, students need to understand both what fractions mean and what operations mean. They need to be able to visualize concepts and relationships. This usually is best done with some sort of manipulative material, asking students to solve meaningful problems and examine the reasonableness of their solutions. The table on page 238 lists several common misunderstandings and what a teacher can do to help children with these misunderstandings.

IF students think that . . .	THEN have students . . .
to add fractions, add the numerators and the denominators, and to subtract fractions, subtract the numerators and the denominators	*pose* a problem in a familiar, real-world situation, and *model* the problem with a manipulative material. Encourage students to *estimate* what would be a reasonable solution for the problem.
multiplication of fractions doesn't make sense, but it's easy to do: just multiply the numerators and multiply the denominators	make sure that students *understand* the area interpretation of whole number multiplication. *Model* the problem with a manipulative material. Encourage students to *estimate* what would be a reasonable solution for the problem.
division of fractions doesn't make sense, but just "flip" the second number and multiply	make sure that students *understand* the measurement interpretation of whole number division. *Model* the problem with a manipulative material. Encourage students to *estimate* what would be a reasonable solution for the problem.

What Do Children Know about Fractions?

What do we know of the fraction understanding of children in the United States? The 2003 National Assessment of Educational Progress (NAEP) noted that while students' performance on one-step fraction computation problems has shown improvement since 1996, they continue to "struggle with their understanding of rational numbers" (Kastberg and Norton, 2007). For example, only 27% of the fourth-graders and 55% of the eighth-graders tested were able to correctly solve a multiple-choice word problem involving multiplication of fractions (see below).

> *Jim has $\frac{3}{4}$ of a yard of string that he wishes to divide into pieces, each $\frac{1}{8}$ of a yard long. How many pieces will he have?*

Only 53% of the fourth-graders tested were able to correctly solve the problem $\frac{4}{6} - \frac{1}{6}$ presented as a multiple-choice problem. Findings such as this point to the importance of teachers' helping children truly make sense of fraction computation.

Historically, fraction computation is the mathematics topic with which most adults have had the least success and the most unhappy memories. The traditional curricular emphasis on mastering algorithms for adding, subtracting, multiplying, and dividing fractions without first developing understanding leads to this frustration and lack of achievement.

One reason for the difficulty many children have with fraction computation is that children often are expected to compute with fraction symbols before they have developed a good understanding of fractions and related concepts. The temptation to have children progress quickly to working symbolically with fraction computation may arise from the thinking that because the children already know how to add, subtract, multiply, and divide whole numbers, it follows that they are ready to use these operations to compute with fractions.

Often this is not the case. Most children have great difficulty linking what they already know about operations on whole numbers with operations on fractions. You need to help children make these connections by carefully designing instruction to link the concepts. If these connections are not made, children will not be able to predict what a reasonable answer might be or make sense of the process, forcing them to memorize meaningless procedures. Too often, the result is frustration and lack of learning.

Some suggest that operations on fractions should be relegated to calculators, maintaining that calculators have eliminated the need for any instruction on fraction computation. It is true that the availability and power of calculators certainly reduces the level of paper-and-pencil mastery of fraction computation that children must achieve. But the availability of technology also increases the importance of children's developing *operation* sense, which refers to an understanding of the meaning of operations, as well as the need for the ability to determine the reasonableness of solutions.

Teachers must carefully consider what children need to know about fraction computation. There are *four goals of instruction* regarding fraction computation:

1. Children need to recognize situations that involve operations on fractions.
2. Children need to find the answer to fraction computation problems by using models.
3. Children need to estimate the answer and understand the reasonableness of results to fraction computation problems.
4. Children need to find an exact answer to fraction computation problems.

Notice that finding an exact answer is only one goal of instruction. The other three goals are equally important and will help children be successful in finding exact answers.

NCTM NUMBER AND OPERATIONS STANDARDS AND EXPECTATIONS ADDRESSED IN THIS CHAPTER		
Instructional programs from Pre-K–12 should enable all students to—	**In grades 3–5 all students should—** (NCTM, 2000, p. 148)	**In grades 6–8 all students should—** (NCTM, 2000, p. 214)
• understand numbers, ways of representing numbers, relationships among numbers, and number systems. • understand meanings of operations and how they relate to one another. • compute fluently and make reasonable estimates.	• develop and use strategies to estimate computations involving fractions and decimals in situations relevant to students' experience. • use visual models, benchmarks, and equivalent forms to add and subtract commonly used fractions and decimals. • select appropriate methods and tools for computing with whole numbers from among mental computation, estimation, calculators, and paper and pencil according to the context and nature of the computation and use the selected method or tools.	• work flexibly with fractions, decimals, and percents to solve problems. • understand the meaning and effects of arithmetic operations with fractions, decimals, and integers. • use the associative and commutative properties of addition and multiplication and the distributive property of multiplication over addition to simplify computations with integers, fractions, and decimals. • select appropriate methods and tools for computing with fractions and decimals from among mental computation, estimation, calculators or computers, and paper and pencil, depending on the situation, and apply the selected methods. • develop and analyze algorithms for computing with fractions, decimals, and integers and develop fluency in their use. • develop and use strategies to estimate the results of rational-number computations and judge the reasonableness of the results.

Prerequisites for Fraction Computation

What must children understand *before* beginning work on fraction computation? There are two prerequisites for fraction computation.

1. Understanding of fraction concepts, comparison, and equivalence; and
2. Understanding of the meaning of operations on whole numbers.

Attempts to teach children to perform fraction computation prior to their attainment of these prerequisites will result in frustration for both the child and the teacher. Children will be forced to mindlessly memorize procedures rather than understand what they are doing and why. Instead of rushing toward algorithms, teachers should spend time helping children master the prerequisites, which will enable the children to perform fraction computation with a greater degree of understanding and success.

Introducing Computation

Developmental Activities

As children work through introductory fraction activities, they progress from thinking of fractions as "parts of things" to operating with them as numbers, each with a precise location on the number line.

Throughout developmental activities, children should have opportunities to construct concrete representations of fraction quantities and, from the representations, to record their findings on paper. Using concrete models to assist in problem solving should be looked on as the norm in elementary classrooms. Therefore, appropriate manipulative materials should be available to children for as long as they find them helpful.

Although regular figures such as triangles, rectangles, pentagons, hexagons, octagons, and decagons are good models for illustrating fractional parts, the circular shape is more versatile because any unit fraction can easily be represented (Figure 11-1). Also, the circles can be used to model fraction computation.

FIGURE 11-1 Using a Circle to Represent Fractions

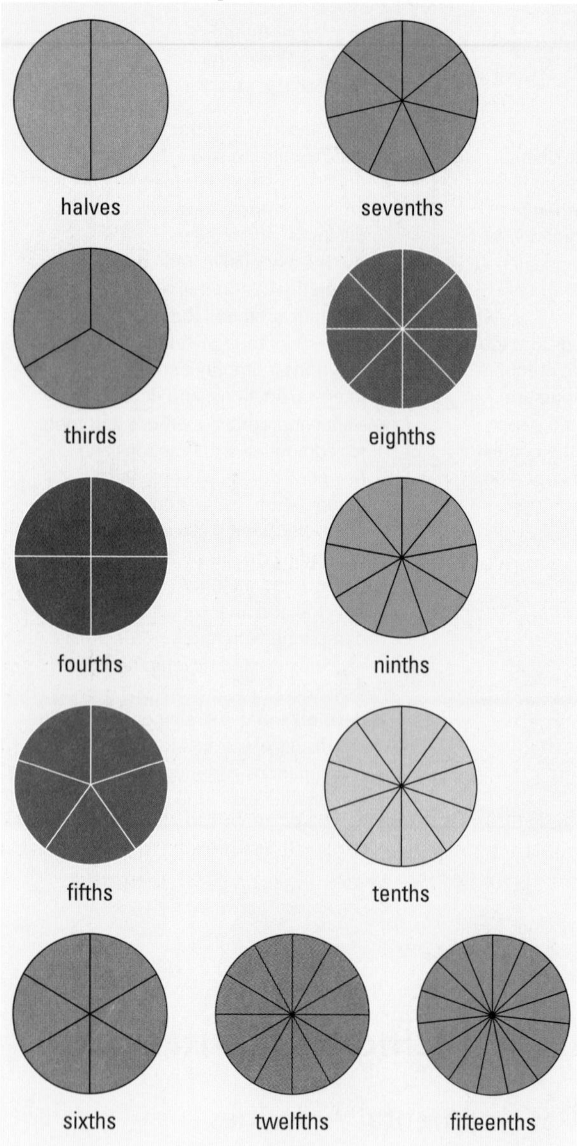

Your introductory computational activities should allow the children to work with fractions in different contexts because a narrow view of what fractions are (e.g., fractions are parts of a whole) is thought to be a reason for the generally unsatisfactory performance in fraction work (Hope & Owens, 1987). The part-whole, measurement, and part-of-a-set interpretations should be embodied in different problem-solving situations. In time, the quotient, operator (multiplicative aspect), and ratio interpretations will also be explored (Kieren, 1976).

You need to allow adequate time for the algorithmic computation processes to emerge from children's active explorations with concrete and pictorial representations.

Learning About Algorithms

The complexity of the algorithms for computing with whole numbers can be said to depend on the numbers used in the computation. For example, in subtraction, children find it difficult to subtract numbers with zeros, such as 4002 – 307. In multiplication, it is easier to find the product with a one-digit multiplier than with a two-digit multiplier; in division, single-digit divisors are easier than two-digit divisors when working through the long division algorithm, and zeros in the quotient add to the complexity. Because of these difficulties for children, the algorithms for computing with whole numbers generally are developed in stages over several grade levels.

The algorithms for computing with fractions are simple when compared with whole-number computation algorithms. Because of the simplicity of these algorithmic rules, children may readily learn them so that they can compute with fractions. However, when procedures are not understood, some children become confused about which rule to use in a particular computation situation. They do not recall which fraction to invert or when common denominators are needed.

The goal is to have children learn to compute with fractions in a meaningful way. Therefore, children's first computations with fractions should be with concrete and pictorial models.

Connecting Operations on Whole Numbers with Operations on Fractions

There are several different interpretations of operations on whole numbers, as discussed in Chapter 7. Several of those interpretations work well for helping children understand operations on fractions, but a few are a bit confusing. Figure 11-2 shows examples of word problems using whole numbers and word problems using fractions for many of the different interpretations of the operations. These interpretations are discussed in more detail throughout this chapter. The key factor in helping children make sense of operations on fractions is to help them connect their existing understanding of whole-number operations to operations on fractions.

Properties

Learning to compute with fractions at the middle school level will include "testing" whether fractions possess the same properties as whole numbers. Through explorations, children will conclude that the commutative and associative properties hold for addition and multiplication; that multiplication is distributive over addition; and that the closure property holds true for addition, multiplication, and division. The new property

FIGURE 11-2 Word Problems for Fractions

Addition

Tom ate $\frac{1}{2}$ of an apple pie yesterday and $\frac{1}{4}$ of an apple pie today. How much pie did Tom eat altogether? (Join)

Number sentence: $\frac{1}{2} + \frac{1}{4} =$ ____

Subtraction

Alberto has $\frac{3}{4}$ of a chocolate chip cookie and Juana has $\frac{1}{4}$ of a cookie. How much more does Alberto have? (Comparison)

Number sentence: $\frac{3}{4} - \frac{1}{4} =$ ____

Alberto has $\frac{3}{4}$ of a chocolate chip cookie. He ate $\frac{1}{4}$ of a whole cookie. How much cookie does Alberto have left? (Separate)

Number sentence: $\frac{3}{4} - \frac{1}{4} =$ ____

Multiplication

There is $\frac{2}{3}$ of a chocolate pie in the refrigerator. Peter ate $\frac{1}{2}$ of it. What part of the whole pie did Peter eat? (Area and Array)

Number sentence: $\frac{1}{2} \times \frac{2}{3} =$ ____

Shawntrice had 4 bags of cookies, with $\frac{1}{2}$ of a cookie in each bag. How many cookies did Shawntrice have? (Repeated addition)

Number sentence: $4 \times \frac{1}{2} =$ ____

Division

Steve has 4 cups of sugar. He needs $\frac{2}{3}$ of a cup of sugar to make one batch of his favorite cookies. How many batches of cookies can Steve make? (Measurement/repeated subtraction)

Number sentence: $4 \div \frac{2}{3} =$ ____

Steve has 4 cups of sugar. That is enough to bake $\frac{2}{3}$ of a batch of his favorite cookies. How much sugar will he need to make 1 batch of cookies? (Partitive/fair sharing*)

Number sentence: $4 \div \frac{2}{3} =$ ____

*Notice that partitive division/fair sharing is NOT very easy to understand with fractions!

from whole-number computation is the closure property for division; that is, any fractional number can be divided by any fractional number except zero to obtain a quotient within the system.

Addition and Subtraction of Fractions

The concepts of addition and subtraction of fractions are the same as for addition and subtraction of whole numbers. The same addition and subtraction problem types discussed in Chapter 7 apply to addition and subtraction of fractions. As with whole numbers, fraction addition problems are most often expressed as Join problems, while subtraction problems are most often posed as Separate or Comparison problems.

NCTM Principles and Standards Link 11-4

Content Strand: Number and Operations

Through teacher-orchestrated discussions of problems in context, students can develop useful methods to compute with fractions, decimals, percents, and integers in ways that make sense. Students' understanding of computation can be enhanced by developing their own methods and sharing them with one another, explaining why their methods work and are reasonable to use, and then comparing their methods with the algorithms traditionally taught in school. (NCTM, 2000, p. 219)

Developing Addition of Fractions

Children in grades 3 and 4 enjoy finding addition sentences when working with concrete materials such as Fraction Bars, Fraction Factory pieces, and fraction circles (Figure 11-3). After constructing a number of "simple" examples, they can progress to find more complicated ones, such as fractions with unlike denominators and some with more than two addends.

The addition sentences provided by the children could be classified as "easy" ones and "complicated" or "tricky" ones. Picking up on a child's example involving unlike denominators, you could ask, "How did you figure that out? Could you write those fractions a different way?"

Example: $\frac{1}{4} + \frac{2}{3} = \frac{11}{12}$

Possible thinking:

I found that 1 fourth is the same as 3 twelfths and that 2 thirds is the same as 8 twelfths. So we can write

1 fourth → *3 twelfths*
+2 thirds → *8 twelfths*
11 twelfths or $\frac{3}{12} + \frac{8}{12} = \frac{11}{12}$

Several of the activities in this chapter have children construct addition sentences using Fraction Bars (Activities 11-1 and 11-2). The activities could be repeated to advantage using a different set of materials such as fraction pies, fraction squares, or a set of objects. Other addition problems could be embedded in familiar contexts such as parts of a dozen eggs (12 as lowest common denominator [LCD]), parts of a day (24 as LCD), or parts of an hour or minute (60 as LCD). (Activity 11-3)

Following several sessions of constructing addition number sentences, children could collect and organize different addition statements on a chart or bulletin board. The display could be the focus of a class discussion, with the intention of having children verbalize how they know the sentences are true.

FIGURE 11-3 Modeling Addition of Fractions

Part of a Whole

Fraction Bars

Fraction Factory Pieces

Fraction Circles

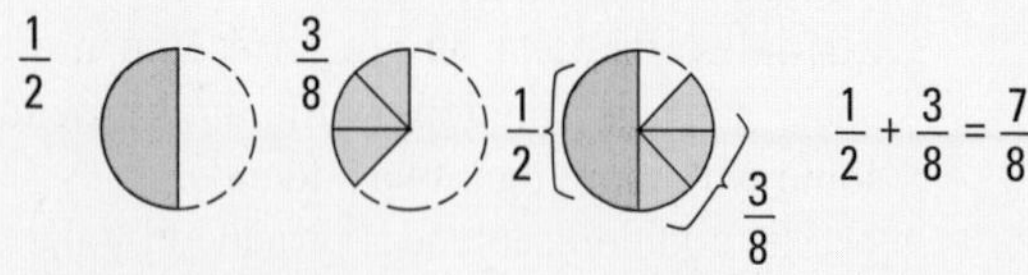

Fraction Rods

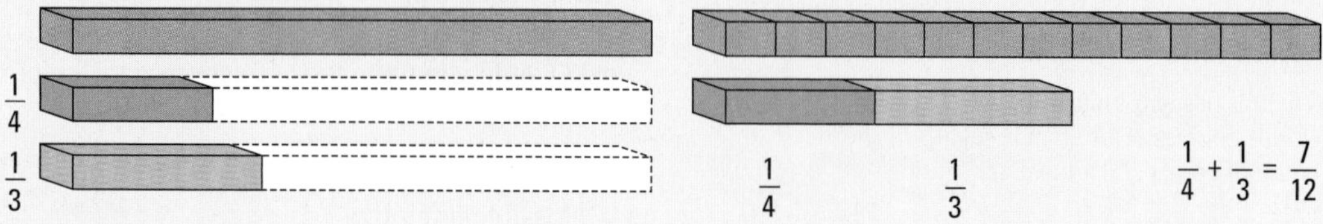

Part of a Set

How much is $\frac{1}{3} + \frac{3}{4}$?

Thirds and fourths can be modeled with a set of 12.

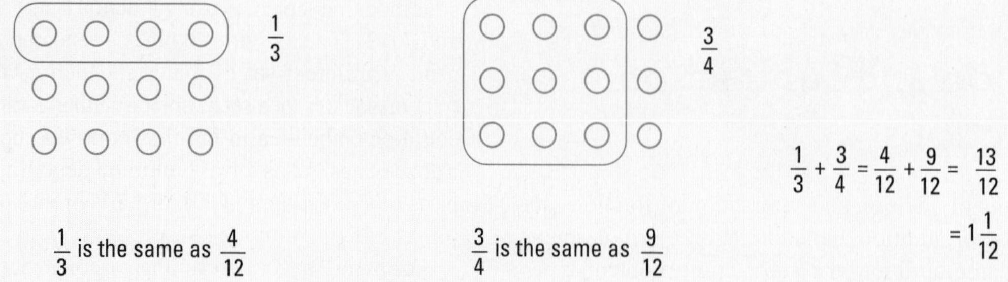

$\frac{1}{3}$
$\frac{3}{4}$
$\frac{1}{3} + \frac{3}{4} = \frac{4}{12} + \frac{9}{12} = \frac{13}{12}$
$= 1\frac{1}{12}$
$\frac{1}{3}$ is the same as $\frac{4}{12}$
$\frac{3}{4}$ is the same as $\frac{9}{12}$

ACTIVITY 11-1 Finding a Sum of 1

Materials
Fraction Bars

Procedure

1. Use the Fraction Bars to help you find two fractions that equal 1.
2. How many different pairs of fraction addends can you find to equal 1?

ACTIVITY 11-2 Finding a Sum of 1 with More Than Two Addends

Manipulative Strategies

Materials
Fraction Bars

Procedure
Use the Fraction Bars to help you write addition sentences that add up to 1 using more than two fraction addends.

Example: 1 fourth + 1 third + 1 sixth + 3 twelfths is the same as 1 bar (or equals 1).

ACTIVITY 11-3 Adding Fractions

Procedure

1. Use fraction families (equivalent fractions) to add $\frac{3}{4} + \frac{1}{5}$.
2. Do some other addition problems.

Possible solution:

3 fourths → 15 twentieths
1 fifth → 4 twentieths
19 twentieths or $\frac{19}{20}$

myeducationlab The Power of Classroom Practice To explore your own understanding of Addition of Fractions, go to Chapter 11 in the Book-Specific Resources section in the MyEducationLab for your course and complete the various activities.

Addition algorithms. Addition of fractions should not be difficult for children if they have a solid understanding of fraction concepts; that is, if children can talk and write about fraction numbers, compare and estimate fractional quantities, and readily verify their work with concrete or pictorial representations.

Adding unlike fractions. Computing unlike fractions should evoke an automatic move to rewrite the fractions with same-sized denominators before proceeding with addition. The special characteristic of equivalent fractions enables one to add any set of fractions by first rewriting each fraction so that all fractions in the expression have same-sized denominators before proceeding with addition.

Children should be encouraged to formulate computation rules. Children's procedural descriptions might be like the following:

Examples:

$\frac{1}{5} + \frac{3}{5} =$ ____ *I'm adding fifths, so I find how many fifths in all.*

$\frac{2}{3} + \frac{1}{2} =$ ____ *I have 2 thirds and 1 half, so I change the fractions so they are the same-sized parts, then I add the number of parts in each group.*

Children's natural inclination to merely add the numerators and the denominators can be minimized by having children verbalize and explain the meaning of fractions in the problems.

Examples:

$\frac{3}{10}$ means 3 parts, each 1 tenth in size.

$\frac{3}{10}$ = *1 tenth + 1 tenth + 1 tenth, or 3 × 1 tenth*

$\frac{3}{10} = \frac{1}{10} + \frac{1}{10} + \frac{1}{10}$, or $3 \times \frac{1}{10}$

Addition: 3 tenths
+ 5 tenths
8 tenths

Therefore, $\frac{3}{10} + \frac{5}{10} = \frac{8}{10}$ *(NOT* $\frac{8}{20}$*).*

Finding common denominators. Adding unlike fractions involves finding a common denominator of the fractions being added. There are several ways to find common denominators of two or more fractions.

1. The common denominator of two fractions can be found using Fraction Bars (see Figure 11-4).

$$\frac{1}{4} + \frac{2}{3} = ?$$

$$\frac{1}{4} + \frac{2}{3} = \frac{3}{12} + \frac{8}{12} = \frac{11}{12}$$

2. At the symbolic level, common denominators can be found by first listing successive multiples of the given denominators and then identifying a common multiple. Usually, one selects the lowest common multiple (LCM) so that the sum will be in simplest form.

Example:

$$\frac{1}{4} + \frac{2}{3}$$

The multiples of 4 are 4, 8, 12, 16, . . .
The multiples of 3 are 3, 6, 9, 12, . . .

FIGURE 11-4 Using Fraction Bars to Find the Common Denominator

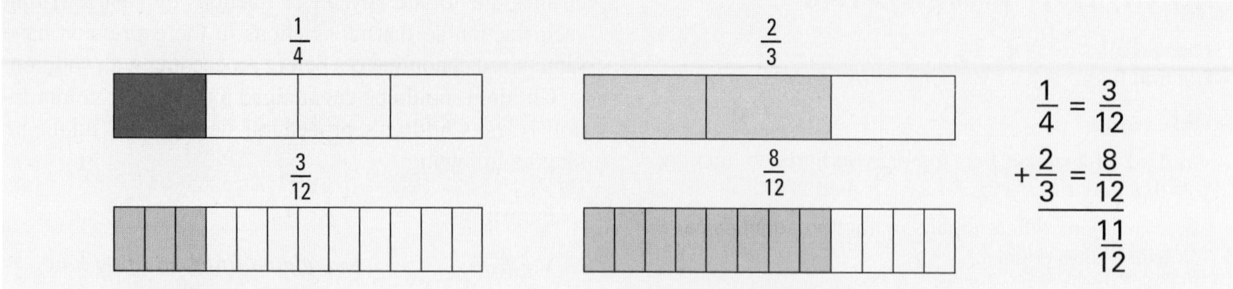

Twelve is the least common multiple of 4 and 3, and therefore is the lowest common denominator for renaming the fractions $\frac{1}{4}$ and $\frac{2}{3}$.

Therefore, $\frac{1}{4} + \frac{2}{3} = \frac{3}{12} + \frac{8}{12} = \frac{11}{12}$.

3. Common denominators can be found by listing equivalent fractions until a common denominator is found.

Example:

$$\frac{1}{4} + \frac{2}{3}$$

$$\frac{1}{4} \rightarrow \frac{1}{4}, \frac{2}{8}, \frac{3}{12}, \frac{4}{16}, \frac{5}{20}, \ldots$$

$$\frac{2}{3} \rightarrow \frac{2}{3}, \frac{4}{6}, \frac{6}{9}, \frac{8}{12}, \frac{10}{15}, \ldots$$

The fractions $\frac{3}{12}$ and $\frac{8}{12}$ have a common denominator, so $\frac{1}{4} + \frac{2}{3} = \frac{3}{12} + \frac{8}{12} = \frac{11}{12}$.

4. The lowest common denominator of two or more fractions can also be identified by factoring each denominator as a product of prime numbers, and then finding the product of the set of unique prime factors.

Example:

$$\frac{1}{4} + \frac{1}{6}$$

Denominators	Prime Factorization
4	2×2
6	2×3

The product of the unique prime factors is $2 \times 2 \times 3$; that is, one can find the prime factorization of 4 in the set and the prime factorization of 6 in the set.

Product: $2 \times 2 \times 3 = 12$

$2 \times 2 \times 3$

prime factors of 4 prime factors of 6

Children should be allowed to use the method they prefer to find a common denominator of a set of fractions.

When working with Fraction Bars or other materials, children may record addition sentences as follows:

Examples:

$$\frac{1}{2} + \frac{1}{4} = \left(\frac{1}{4} + \frac{1}{4}\right) + \frac{1}{4} = \frac{3}{4}$$

$$\frac{1}{6} + \frac{1}{2} = \frac{1}{6} + \frac{3}{6} = \frac{4}{6} \text{ or}$$

$$= \frac{1}{6} + \left(\frac{1}{6} + \frac{1}{6} + \frac{1}{6}\right) = \frac{4}{6}$$

Developing an addition algorithm. Algorithms for adding unlike fractions require finding a common denominator for the fractions being added. One of the methods described in the preceding section can be used to find a common denominator.

Example:

$$\frac{3}{4} + \frac{5}{6}$$

The multiples of 4 are 4, 8, 12, 16, ...

The multiples of 6 are 6, 12, 18, ...

Twelve is the least common multiple of 4 and 6, and therefore is the lowest common denominator for renaming the fractions $\frac{3}{4}$ and $\frac{5}{6}$.

$\frac{3}{4} = \frac{?}{12}$ Because 4 was multiplied by 3 to get 12, the numerator 3 must also be multiplied by 3 to find the number of twelfths equal to $\frac{3}{4}$.

$\frac{5}{6} = \frac{?}{12}$ Similarly, 5 must be multiplied by 2 to obtain the number of twelfths equal to $\frac{5}{6}$.

$\frac{3}{4} + \frac{5}{6} = \frac{9}{12} + \frac{10}{12} = \frac{19}{12}$ or $1\frac{7}{12}$

In algorithmic form, this process can be represented as each fraction being multiplied by one, which is using the multiplication property of one, described in Chapter 8.

$$\frac{3}{3} = 1 \quad \frac{2}{2} = 1$$

$$\frac{3}{4} + \frac{5}{6} = \frac{3 \times 3}{4 \times 3} + \frac{5 \times 2}{6 \times 2} = \frac{9}{12} + \frac{10}{12} = \frac{19}{12}$$

When adding fractions, it is necessary to find a common denominator, but it is *not* necessary to find the *lowest* common denominator. The problem may be a little shorter and seem a little simpler if the lowest common denominator is used, but any common denominator could be used. In the last example above, we saw that 12 is the lowest common denominator of 4 and 6. But there are other common denominators that could be used, such as 24 or 36. Let's solve the preceding example problem again, but this time we use the common denominator of 24.

Example:

$$\frac{3}{4} + \frac{5}{6}$$

A common denominator is 24, so I want to write $\frac{3}{4}$ and $\frac{5}{6}$ as $\frac{?}{24}$.

$\frac{3}{4} = \frac{?}{24}$ I'll multiply the denominator (4) by 6 to get 24, so I have to also multiply the numerator by 6, to find the number of twenty-fourths equal to $\frac{3}{4}$.

$\frac{5}{6} = \frac{?}{24}$ Similarly, since I have to multiply the denominator by 4 to get 24, I'll also multiply the numerator by 4, to find the number of twenty-fourths equal to $\frac{5}{6}$.

$$\frac{3}{4} + \frac{5}{6} = \frac{18}{24} + \frac{20}{24} = \frac{38}{24} = \frac{19}{12} = 1\frac{7}{12}$$

Notice that we got the same answer as when we used the lowest common denominator of 12 in the previous example. The only difference was that we had to work with slightly bigger numbers, which may sometimes lead to more mistakes. It is important to note that we got the correct answer even without using the lowest common denominator.

Addition of mixed numbers. Addition of mixed numbers is similar to adding whole numbers, but just a little more complicated because mixed numbers also have a fractional part.

Example:

$$\begin{aligned} 76 &= 7 \text{ tens} + 6 \text{ ones} \\ +\ 61 &= 6 \text{ tens} + 1 \text{ one} \\ &= 13 \text{ tens} + 7 \text{ ones or } 137 \end{aligned}$$

Example:

$$\begin{aligned} 3\tfrac{1}{5} &= 3 + \tfrac{1}{5} \\ +\ 2\tfrac{2}{5} &= 2 + \tfrac{2}{5} \\ & \quad 5 + \tfrac{3}{5} \text{ or } 5\tfrac{3}{5} \end{aligned}$$

Just as some whole-number addition problems require regrouping, so do some fraction addition problems.

Example:

$$\begin{aligned} 47 &= 40 + 7 \\ +\ 25 &= 20 + 5 \\ 72 \quad & \; 60 + 12 = 60 + 10 + 2 = 72 \end{aligned}$$

Example:

$$\begin{aligned} 3\tfrac{1}{5} &= 3 + \tfrac{8}{40} \\ +\ 1\tfrac{7}{8} &= 1 + \tfrac{35}{40} \\ & \quad 4 + \tfrac{43}{40} \\ &= 4 + \tfrac{43}{40} \\ &= 4 + \tfrac{40}{40} + \tfrac{3}{40} \\ &= 4 + 1 + \tfrac{3}{40} \\ &= 5\tfrac{3}{40} \end{aligned}$$

Developing Subtraction of Fractions

The procedures for developing subtraction of fractions are similar to those for addition. So it would seem that children who can add fractions would be equally successful with subtracting fractions. However, children usually make more errors in subtracting fractions involving renaming than in whole-number subtraction with renaming. Also, somewhat surprisingly, subtraction seems to be the most difficult of the four basic operations with fractions.

Early subtraction activities. First subtraction activities should have children writing subtraction statements based on their work with manipulative materials. You could ask children to write fraction subtraction stories (Activity 11–4) to demonstrate understanding of fractions and the subtraction operation.

ACTIVITY 11-4 **Subtraction Fraction Stories**

Realia Strategies

Procedure

1. Write a story about three friends who ate part of a cake that had been cut into eight equal pieces. Use fraction circle pieces to help you think of sharing the cake, then draw a picture of the cake before

any pieces had been eaten and after the friends had had their share.

2. Write a fraction story about someone who decides to donate some books from a set of 36 books. Tell what part of the set of books is given away and what part is left.

After children have had experiences in writing subtraction sentences from their work with concrete materials, they can be asked to solve specific subtraction problems. Activities 11-5 and 11-6 have children modeling subtraction sentences to find the missing addend. Each activity should be followed with a class discussion.

ACTIVITY 11-5 Subtracting Fractions (Concrete)

Manipulative Strategies

Materials

Fraction circle pieces

Procedure

Use fraction circle pieces to find

$\frac{5}{8} - \frac{1}{4} = ?$ $\frac{3}{4} - \frac{1}{2} = ?$

Solve other examples.

ACTIVITY 11-6 Finding the Missing Addend (Concrete)

Materials

Fraction Bars

Procedure

Use Fraction Bars to find the missing number.

$\frac{3}{4} - \_\_\_ = \frac{5}{8}$ $\frac{4}{5} - \_\_\_ = \frac{7}{15}$

Solve other examples.

myeducationlab The Power of Classroom Practice To explore your own understanding of subtracting fractions, go to Chapter 11 in the Book-Specific Resources section in the MyEducationLab for your course. Select the Activities section and complete the activity "Subtracting Fractions."

Renaming fractions. The process of writing equivalent fractions is sometimes called *renaming fractions*. In fraction subtraction, another renaming process is introduced that is similar to renaming in whole-number subtraction. For example, when subtracting 28 from 175, the 7 tens and 5 ones are renamed as 6 tens and 15 ones before the subtraction is carried out. Similarly, renaming is required in some fraction subtractions.

Example:

$$5\frac{3}{8} - 2\frac{7}{8}$$

Although $2\frac{7}{8}$ is less than $5\frac{3}{8}$, is less than $5\frac{3}{8}$, the fraction part of $2\frac{7}{8}$ is greater than the fraction part of $5\frac{3}{8}$, so we need to regroup. In other words, we don't have enough eighths to take away $\frac{7}{8}$, so we need to get some more by trading in one of the wholes for $\frac{8}{8}$, which gives us $\frac{8}{8} + \frac{3}{8}$ *or* $\frac{11}{8}$. Now we can subtract $\frac{7}{8}$ from that, giving us $\frac{4}{8}$. This process is shown below:

$$\begin{array}{lll} 5\frac{3}{8} & = 4 + \frac{8}{8} + \frac{3}{8} & = 4\frac{11}{8} \\ \underline{-\ 2\frac{7}{8}} & & = 2\frac{7}{8} \\ & & 2\frac{4}{8} = 2\frac{1}{2} \end{array}$$

Take care that children do not erroneously show this renaming as changing $5\frac{3}{8}$ as $4\frac{13}{8}$. This is a common error children make. But why would they make this error?

When regrouping in whole-number subtraction, it is a "ten" that is added to the ones column; in fraction subtraction, it is a "one" that is added to the fraction part of the addend. The "one" is expressed with the same denominator as the fraction addend. In the example above, the "one" was expressed as $\frac{8}{8}$, and added to the $\frac{3}{8}$ we started with, so that we could then subtract $\frac{7}{8}$ from $\frac{11}{8}$ to get the answer.

As throughout this book, the key to helping children be successful with addition and subtraction of fractions is to help them make sense of what they're doing, not by forcing them to memorize procedures that may be meaningless to them.

Multiplication and Division of Fractions

General Considerations

In helping children understand the operations of multiplication and division with fractions, as for addition and subtraction of fractions, help them connect these new ideas to their understanding of the operations with whole numbers. For example, multiplication can be interpreted as repeated addition, whereas division can be presented as repeated subtraction. Also, the equal groups and array interpretations of multiplication and division will be particularly useful for operations on fractions, as will measurement division. We will further explore this later.

Two common misunderstandings related to multiplication and division of fractions are that "multiplication makes bigger" and "division makes smaller," as was discussed with whole numbers in Chapter 7. This means that many children expect the product to be greater than both factors in multiplication of fractions problems, as it is in

Literature Link 11-1

Fraction Computation

Adler, David. (1996). ***Fraction Fun.*** New York: Holiday House.
Leedy, Loreen. (1994). ***Fraction Action.*** New York: Holiday House.

Understanding fractions is difficult for children because children are often introduced to symbols and operations without a strong conceptual foundation. Children need many opportunities to construct meaning in the context of concrete and pictorial models and allow abstract ideas to emerge from these experiences. Key ideas in learning about factors, such as partitioning and equivalence, can be found in books like such as ***Fraction Fun*** and ***Fraction Action.*** The authors show various representations of common fractions, both region and set models, fair sharing, fractions and money, and pictorial ways to represent fractions using paper plates, graph paper, and other models.

- Identify real-world models of fractions such as sharing a pizza, using a recipe, or dividing candy equally. Using realistic problem-solving contexts in which children try to make sense out of a fraction problem prior to learning the mathematical procedures helps children to abstract fraction ideas.
- Draw pictorial models to solve fraction problems and try to determine a reasonable answer prior to using formal operations.
- Use pattern blocks to name fractions, find equivalent fractions, and add and subtract fractions. The fraction amounts that can be identified with the blocks are dependent on determining what represents "one whole."
- Draw halves, fourths, and eighths on paper plates and compare these circular region models. Use scissors to cut a radius in each paper along one of the fraction lines. Combine two plates to add and subtract fractions. (For example, to add $\frac{1}{4}$ and $\frac{4}{8}$, combine the fourths plate with the eighths plate.)
- Use geoboards to show various ways to make "one-half" or "one-third" using the area model of fractions. The parts must be the same size (or area) but they do not have to be the same shape.
- Use a set of 24 two-color counters. Break the group of counters into halves, thirds, fourths, sixths, and eighths by grouping the counters and flipping the correct number. Challenge children to flip the counters to show $\frac{3}{8}$ in red or $\frac{2}{3}$ in yellow. Children need many experiences working with set models of fractions to abstract this concept.
- Other books, such as ***The Hershey's Milk Chocolate Fraction Book*** (Pallotta, 1999), use a manipulative (a Hershey bar) to explore parts of a whole, equivalent fractions, simple addition of fractions, lowest terms, subtraction, and improper fractions. Use a real candy bar or a construction paper copy to model operations in the book and explore further operations with "twelfths."

Source: Dr. Patricia Moyer-Packenham, Utah State University.

multiplication of whole numbers. Similarly, children expect the quotient to be smaller than the numbers being divided in division of fractions problems, as it is in division of whole numbers. For example, many children expect that $6 \div \frac{1}{2}$ is 3, because they expect the answer to a division problem to be smaller than the numbers in the problem. But this generalization is true only for whole-number division. According to Bezuk and Bieck (1993), a goal of instruction should be "to enable students to determine the reasonableness of the results of operations on fractions" (p. 131). Your instruction must help children recognize that the generalizations they made for operations on whole numbers *do not hold true* for operations on fractions, and it must help them make sense of answers to fraction computation problems.

Because the algorithms for multiplying and dividing fractions are fairly easy to use, it is tempting for teachers to try to save instructional time and just teach children the algorithms. For multiplication, the informal rule is "multiply the top numbers and then the bottom numbers" and for division it is "change the sign and invert the second fraction." Even though these rules seem simple to use, unfortunately they do not enable children to make sense of what they are doing. Children who learn to compute with fractions using these rules often have no idea whether their results are correct or not, and they often have to wait years before the mystery of fraction computation is revealed and understanding emerges.

Instead of taking what seems to be the easy way out, teachers can invest in their children by helping them develop a rich understanding of these two important operations, as described in the following section.

Developing Multiplication of Fractions

As for operations with whole numbers, begin instruction on fraction multiplication with word problems set in familiar situations, as was shown in Figure 11-2. To help children solve these real-world problems, you should have a variety of concrete materials available for their use.

After children have solved the problem, ask them to draw a diagram or to write some kind of symbolic record of the solution process. This could be a description using words, mathematical symbols, or a combination of both. Examples of diagrams and possible solution records are presented in the activities and problems that follow.

There are several different types of fraction multiplication problems:

- Multiplying a fraction by a whole number;
- Multiplying a whole number by a fraction;
- Multiplying a fraction by a fraction; and
- Multiplying mixed numbers.

Each type is discussed below.

Multiplying a fraction by a whole number. Probably the easiest multiplication situation for children to interpret is to multiply a fraction by a whole number. This type of problem can be related to whole-number multiplication.

> **Example:** Tom wanted to bake 5 batches of cookies. He needs $\frac{3}{4}$ of a cup of sugar for each batch. How much sugar does he need to make 5 batches of cookies? (Equal Groups problem)
>
> $5 \times \frac{3}{4}$ means 5 group of 3 fourths, or 15 fourths.

So Tom needs $3\frac{3}{4}$ cups of sugar

$$\text{Algorithm: } 5 \times \frac{3}{4} = \frac{5 \times 3}{4} = \frac{15}{4} \text{ or } 3\frac{3}{4}$$

Activity 11-7 and Problem 1 will help children understand why the value of the product ends up less than the whole-number factor (5 in the example above) and the fraction factor ($\frac{3}{4}$, in the example above). When the whole number is 1, the product equals the fraction factor.

ACTIVITY 11-7 Multiplication: Times as Much

Manipulative Strategies

Materials

Fraction circles to represent pizzas

Procedure

1. Take one-third of a pizza.
2. Now take twice as much pizza. How much is 2 times $\frac{1}{3}$?
3. Make your share 3 times as large as two-thirds. How much pizza is this? How much is 3 times $\frac{2}{3}$?
4. How much pizza is a share 4 times as large as two-thirds?
5. Write multiplication sentences for your findings.

A possible solution to Activity 11-7 is shown in Figure 11-5.

Problem 1 is a simple problem that can be solved in several ways. Four possible solutions are presented.

PROBLEM 1

The remaining Ritz crackers in a box were all broken and Carl's mother gave him 7 half crackers. How many crackers did Carl get?

Possible solution strategies:

1. A child could use real crackers or paper circles cut in half, and then assemble them to make whole crackers/circles. The product could then be easily determined.
2. A child could reason:

   Two halves make one. With 7 halves, Carl has 3 whole crackers with an extra half. So, Carl's mother gave him the same amount as 3 and $\frac{1}{2}$ crackers.

FIGURE 11-5 A Solution to Activity 11-7

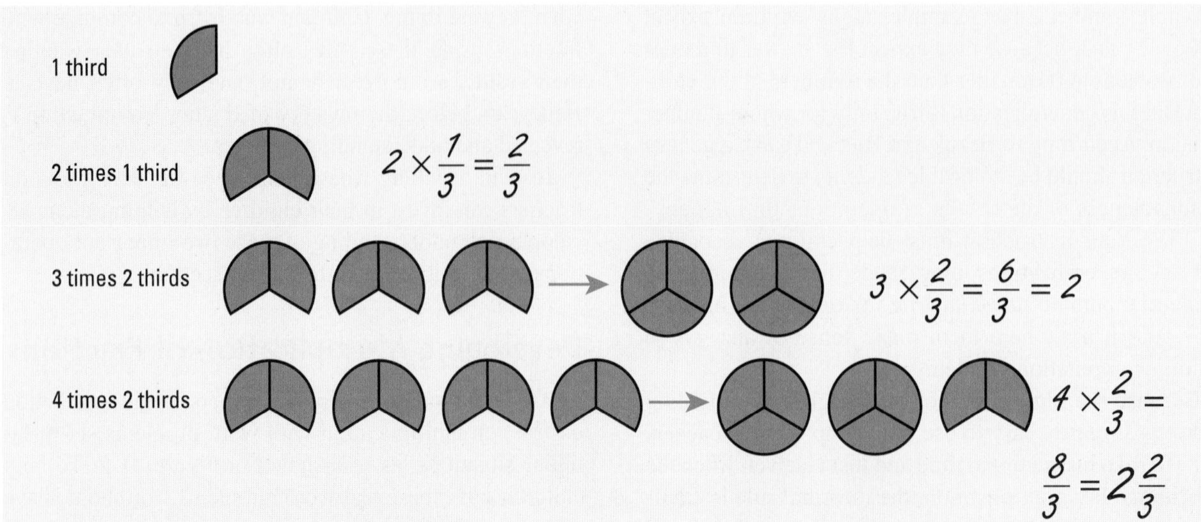

NCTM Principles and Standards Link 11-5

Content Strand: Number and Operations

Students should also develop and adapt procedures for mental calculation and computational estimation with fractions, decimals, and integers. . . . Because these methods often require flexibility in moving from one representation to another, they are useful in deepening students' understanding of rational numbers and helping them think flexibly about these numbers. (NCTM, 2000, p. 220)

3. Repeated addition can be used to find the answer.
   $\frac{1}{2} + \frac{1}{2} + \frac{1}{2} + \frac{1}{2} + \frac{1}{2} + \frac{1}{2} + \frac{1}{2} = \frac{7}{2}$ or $3\frac{1}{2}$
   $1 + 1 + 1 + \frac{1}{2} = 3\frac{1}{2}$
4. Number sentence: $7 \times \frac{1}{2} = 3\frac{1}{2}$

Multiplying a whole number by a fraction. Problems such as these are more difficult than the first type discussed in this section because the equal-groups interpretation does not make sense in this case. In Problem 1, we were able to make 7 groups of $\frac{1}{2}$. But consider Problem 2.

PROBLEM 2

Kim has a collection of 15 books. One-third of them are science fiction. How many books are science fiction?

Notice that we don't have 15 groups of $\frac{1}{3}$ here, so we can't add $\frac{1}{3}$ fifteen times to get the answer.

But we can set up an array. We could use 15 tiles or counters to represent the 15 books, and we can arrange the tiles in one row of 15 or in three rows of 5. Because we want to find $\frac{1}{3}$ of the 15 books (or tiles), it will be helpful to arrange them into 3 rows of five, as below:

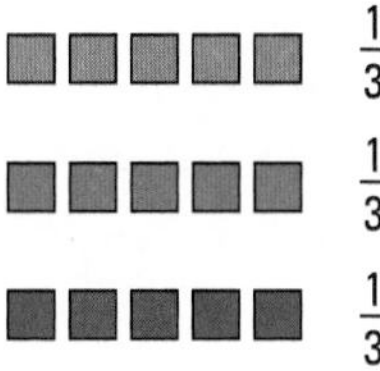

We see that there are 3 rows, which represent the three thirds in the whole set.

So one-third of 15 is 1 row, or 5 books.

So Kim has 5 science fiction books.

Number sentence: $\frac{1}{3} \times 15 = 5$

After solving a number of similar problems, children should come to realize that taking a fractional part of something implies multiplication. Thus, "$\frac{1}{2}$ of 8" means 8 multiplied by $\frac{1}{2}$ or 4. The statements "$\frac{1}{2}$ times 8" and "$\frac{1}{2}$ of 8" are both appropriate for the expression $\frac{1}{2} \times 8$. In situations in which the multiplier (in the previous example, $\frac{1}{2}$) is not a whole number, the multiplication symbol is usually read as "of" rather than "times."

Problem 3 provides more practice with multiplying a whole number by a fraction.

PROBLEM 3

Monique had 8 candies and she ate $\frac{3}{4}$ of them during recess. How many candies did she eat?

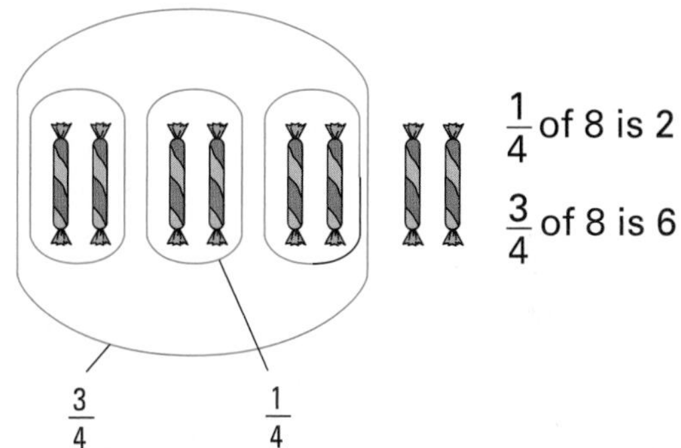

SOLUTION PROCESS

Because $\frac{1}{4}$ of 8 candies is 2 candies, and Monique ate $\frac{3}{4}$ of the candies, that means Monique ate 6 candies.

Number sentence: $\frac{3}{4} \times 8 = 6$

Multiplying a fraction by a fraction. When multiplying two proper fractions, the product is smaller than either factor. This result may not match the children's expectations for multiplication. So be sure to provide realistic problem situations so that children can develop good estimates of the solutions and come to understand that fraction multiplication works this way.

Building an array is a useful strategy to help solve a problem when both factors are fractions. Consider the situations in Problems 4 and 5.

PROBLEM 4

How much is $\frac{1}{2}$ of $\frac{1}{3}$ of a candy bar?

POSSIBLE SOLUTION PROCESS

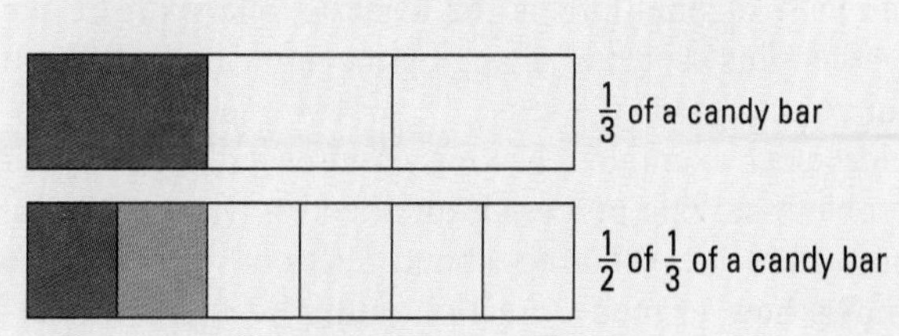

So one-half of one-third is one-sixth.

Number sentence: $\frac{1}{2} \times \frac{1}{3} = \frac{1}{6}$

FIGURE 11-6 Fraction Multiplication

$\frac{1}{5} \times \frac{1}{2}$ Draw two congruent rectangles and show each fraction.

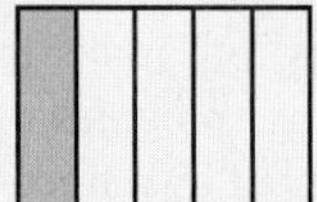

Then draw a third rectangle congruent to the others and shade $\frac{1}{5}$ and $\frac{1}{2}$ of the rectangle as shown below.

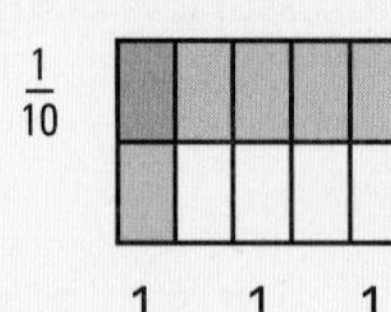

$\frac{1}{5} \times \frac{1}{2} = \frac{1}{10}$

The part where the shading intersects shows $\frac{1}{5}$ of $\frac{1}{2}$.

$\frac{1}{5}$ of $\frac{1}{2}$ is $\frac{1}{10}$.

$\frac{1}{2} \times \frac{3}{4}$ Draw two congruent rectangles. Show $\frac{1}{2}$ on one rectangle and $\frac{3}{4}$ on the other rectangle as shown.

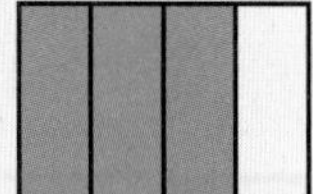

Draw another rectangle, congruent to the others and show eighths as pictured.

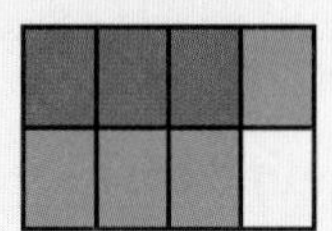

Shade in $\frac{1}{2}$ of the rectangle, then $\frac{3}{4}$.

The part where the shading intersects shows $\frac{1}{2}$ of $\frac{3}{4}$.

$\frac{1}{2} \times \frac{3}{4} = \frac{3}{8}$

The twice-shaded part is $\frac{3}{8}$ of the figure.

Multiplying two fractions involves taking a *part of a part*. One aspect that students often have difficulty with is deciding how to name the result, and to what unit it refers. For example, in the previous problem $\frac{1}{2} \times \frac{1}{3} = \frac{1}{6}$, we are finding $\frac{1}{2}$ (part) of $\frac{1}{3}$ (another part). The answer, $\frac{1}{6}$, refers to one-sixth of one whole. In other words, one-half of one-third is the same as one-sixth of one whole. This aspect of changing the unit can be difficult for children to make sense of, so it is important to provide clear examples. Having children talk about their problem-solving process is an effective way to find out how they are thinking about fractions. Figure 11-6 shows how to model fraction multiplication with rectangles.

PROBLEM 5

What part of a dozen is $\frac{1}{4}$ of $\frac{2}{3}$ of a dozen eggs?

POSSIBLE SOLUTION PROCESS

Two-thirds of a dozen eggs is 8 eggs.

One-fourth of 8 eggs is 2 eggs.

Therefore, one-fourth of two-thirds is two-twelfths.

Number sentence: $\frac{1}{4} \times \frac{2}{3} = \frac{2}{12}$

TABLE 11-1 Analyzing the Number Sentences in Problems 1 through 5

Problem Number	Number Sentence	Writing Number Sentences in Fraction Form
1	$7 \times \frac{1}{2} = \frac{7}{2}$	$\frac{7}{1} \times \frac{1}{2} = \frac{7}{2}$
2	$\frac{1}{3} \times 15 = 5$	$\frac{1}{3} \times \frac{15}{1} = 5$
3	$\frac{3}{4} \times 8 = 6$	$\frac{3}{4} \times \frac{8}{1} = 6$
4	$\frac{1}{2} \times \frac{1}{3} = \frac{1}{6}$	$\frac{1}{2} \times \frac{1}{3} = \frac{1}{6}$
5	$\frac{1}{4} \times \frac{2}{3} = \frac{2}{12}$	$\frac{1}{4} \times \frac{2}{3} = \frac{2}{12}$

Notice the importance of a diagram (or concrete materials) in the preceding problems. After solving each problem with a diagram, children have confidence in the accuracy of the answer. Have children write a number sentence that represents what they did with the diagram. Next, rewrite each number sentence so that all whole numbers are written in fraction form, for example, writing 7 and $\frac{7}{1}$. Then carefully examine the number sentences for patterns and try to come up with a generalization or rule that works for all of these problems. Table 11-1 contains all the number sentences from Problems 1 through 5. Is there a rule or pattern that would give us the correct answer in each of these problems?

Children will often notice that the answers can be obtained by multiplying the numerators and multiplying the denominators. Children may wonder if this only works in these five problems—so now have them solve several more problems, adding to Table 11-1. They will find that this pattern holds for all problems involving multiplication of fractions. And because they noticed this pattern on their own, this generalization will stick with them much better than a rule they were asked to memorize but did not understand.

As children solve problems, some of their "rules" could be written on the board or on an overhead transparency to provide the focus for a class dialogue. Reflecting on their problem-solving processes and discussing them with classmates can lead to insights about related procedures and to a refinement of the procedures. This will lead children to develop an algorithm for multiplying fractions that will be meaningful to them.

Multiplying mixed numbers. To help children make sense of multiplying mixed numbers, relate it to multiplying whole numbers, particularly two-digit numbers. In the following two examples, notice how the distributive property is helpful in solving these problems.

Example 1: Find the product of 23×45.

Make an array that is 23 by 45:

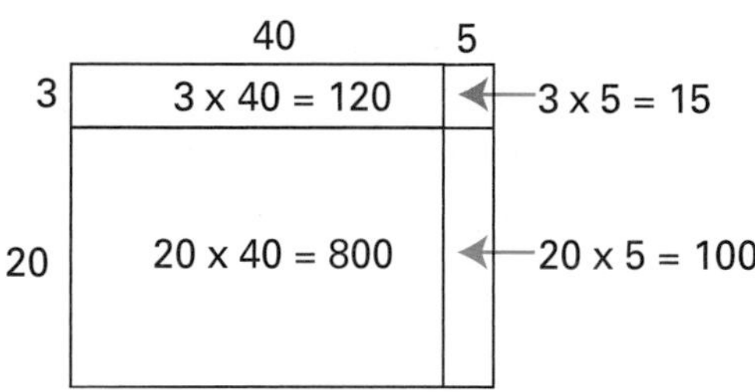

Notice in the array the partial products are 800, 100, 120, and 15. Adding them together gives 1,035.

$$\begin{aligned} 23 \times 45 &= (20 + 3) \times (40 + 5) \\ &= (20 \times 40) + (20 \times 5) + (3 \times 40) + (3 \times 5) \\ &= 800 + 100 + 120 + 15 \\ &= 1{,}035 \end{aligned}$$

Example 2: Find the product of $3\frac{2}{5} \times 4\frac{1}{3}$.

Make an array that is $3\frac{2}{5} \times 4\frac{1}{3}$:

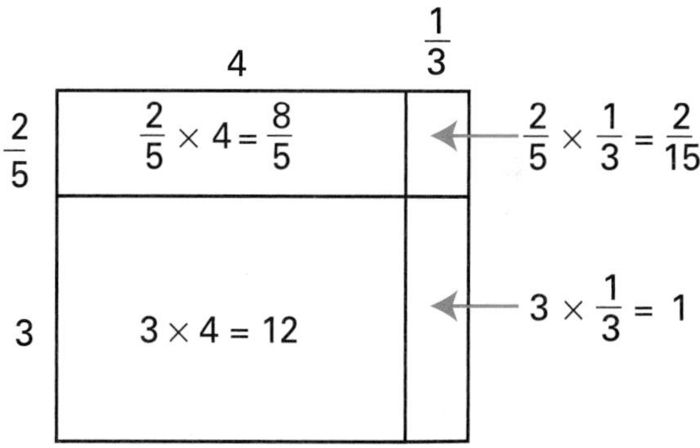

Notice in the array the partial products are 12, 1, $\frac{8}{5}$, and $\frac{2}{15}$, which is equal to $14\frac{11}{15}$.

$$\begin{aligned} 3\tfrac{2}{5} \times 4\tfrac{1}{3} &= (3 + \tfrac{2}{5}) \times (4 + \tfrac{1}{3}) \\ &= (3 \times 4) + (3 \times \tfrac{1}{3}) + (\tfrac{2}{5} \times 4) + (\tfrac{2}{5} \times \tfrac{1}{3}) \\ &= 12 + \tfrac{3}{3} + \tfrac{8}{5} + \tfrac{2}{15} \\ &= 12 + 1 + 1\tfrac{3}{5} + \tfrac{2}{15} \\ &= 14 + \tfrac{9}{15} + \tfrac{2}{15} \\ &= 14\tfrac{11}{15} \end{aligned}$$

Another way to approach multiplication of mixed numbers is to change each mixed number to an improper fraction and then multiply the two fractions, as shown in Example 3.

Example 3: Find the product of $3\frac{2}{5} \times 4\frac{1}{3}$.

Understanding that $3 = \frac{15}{5}$, and $4 = \frac{12}{3}$, the child might write:

$$\begin{aligned} 3\tfrac{2}{5} \times 4\tfrac{1}{3} &= (\tfrac{15}{5} + \tfrac{2}{5}) \times (\tfrac{3}{12} + \tfrac{1}{3}) \\ &= \tfrac{17}{5} \times \tfrac{13}{3} \\ &= \tfrac{221}{15} \\ &= 14\tfrac{11}{15} \end{aligned}$$

Other considerations.

Simplifying fractions. When children begin to work symbolically with fraction multiplication, they often are encouraged to simplify the factors before starting to multiply. Simplifying should be thought of as a process of renaming or exchange and not cancellation (Example 1). Thinking of simplifying as cancellation can lead to errors in computation. For example, if children are told to "cancel like factors" as in Example 2 below, they may go on to incorrectly cancel common digits as in Example 3.

Example 1:

$$\frac{2}{6} \times \frac{3}{8} =$$

Thinking process:

Rename $\frac{2}{6}$ as $\frac{1}{3}$, then simplify

$$\frac{2}{6} \times \frac{3}{8} = \frac{1}{3} \times \frac{3}{8} = \frac{3}{3 \times 8} = \frac{3}{24} = \frac{1}{8}$$

or

$$\frac{2}{6} \times \frac{3}{8} = \frac{2 \times 3}{6 \times 8} = \frac{6}{6 \times 8} = \frac{6}{48} = \frac{1}{8}$$

Example 2:

$$\frac{2}{6} \times \frac{3}{8} =$$

$$\frac{2}{6} \times \frac{3}{8} = \frac{\cancel{2}}{\cancel{2} \times \cancel{3}} \times \frac{\cancel{3}}{2 \times 4} = \frac{1}{8}$$

Example 3: (Incorrect procedure)

$$\frac{2\cancel{3}}{\cancel{3}5} = \frac{2}{5}$$

Unfortunately, in a few cases it seems that canceling does work, where the like digits can be cancelled and the resulting fraction will be a correct simplification. Examples: $\frac{16}{64}$ and $\frac{1}{4}$. This just happens to be a coincidence in this example; canceling digits is an incorrect procedure that should not be taught or reinforced. If children feel that canceling digits sometimes works, invite them to conduct an investigation to find other fractions for which this procedure holds true. They will find that canceling digits works for only a *very small* number of cases. Therefore, the procedure should be thought to be generally incorrect.

Reciprocals. As do whole numbers, fractions have a reciprocal or multiplicative inverse (except a fraction with a numerator of 0). Recall that the reciprocal of a whole number is 1 over that number:

Number: 3 Reciprocal: $\frac{1}{3}$

The product of a number and its reciprocal is always one. So for the example above, notice that the product of 3 and $\frac{1}{3}$ is indeed one.

What about for fractions? Here's an example:

Number: $\frac{2}{3}$ Reciprocal: ?

If we make a guess that the reciprocal of $\frac{2}{3}$ is $\frac{3}{2}$, we can check it by seeing if the product is one.

$$\frac{2}{3} \times \frac{3}{2} = \frac{6}{6} = 1$$

So $\frac{3}{2}$ is the reciprocal or $\frac{2}{3}$, and vice versa. This procedure is helpful in understanding the fraction division algorithm.

Developing Division of Fractions

As discussed in Chapter 7, there are two types of division problems: Partitive and Measurement. These two types of division problems also are possible in fraction division. Before introducing fraction division, spend some time making sure children are familiar with both types of whole-number division problems. This will help children make sense of fraction division problems and enable them to focus on the process of division with fractions.

Before we talk about division of fractions, let's review partitive and measurement division with whole numbers. Consider the problem 6 ÷ 2. Take a minute and write two story problems for this number sentence, one Partitive division problem and one Measurement division problem.

Here are two problems for 6 ÷ 2. What problem type is each one?

Problem A: Steve had 6 apples. He decided to eat the same number of apples every day for 2 days. How many apples did he eat each day?

Problem B: Steve had 6 apples. He decided to eat 2 apples every day. How many days could he eat apples?

What's the difference between these two problems? Both problems are about Steve's eating 6 apples. The key is the meaning of the number 2 in each problem, which is the divisor. What does the 2 mean in each problem? In Problem A, the 2 tells us how many equal groups are being made. This is a *Partitive division* problem, and the 2 tells us the number of groups (or parts) that are being made. In Problem B, the 2 tells us the size of the equal groups that are being made. This is a *Measurement division* problem, and the 2 tells us the size (or measure) of the groups that are being made.

Now let's change this problem to a fraction division problem: $6 \div \frac{1}{2}$. And let's try to rewrite Problems A and B to make them fit this number sentence.

Problem C: Steve had 6 apples. He decided to eat the same number of apples every day for $\frac{1}{2}$ of a day. How many apples did he eat each day? (Notice that this problem doesn't make a lot of sense!)

Problem D: Steve had 6 apples. He decided to eat $\frac{1}{2}$ an apple every day. How many days could he eat apples?

What do you notice about Problems C and D? Problem C doesn't make much sense, but Problem D does, and the answer is 12 days. We could rewrite Problem C in an attempt to make it make more sense: What if Steve said that the 6 apples were enough for $\frac{1}{2}$ a day; how many apples would he need for 1 whole day? But it's still awkward and somewhat contrived. But notice that Problem D makes sense and is easy to solve.

What type of division problem is Problem D? It's a Measurement division problem. Problem C is a Partitive division problem. It is important to note here that Measurement division seems to be the interpretation that makes the most sense for division of fractions. This also has important implications for teaching whole-number division: It is important that children have experiences solving Measurement division problems with whole numbers so that they then are familiar with these problems and can make sense of Measurement division problems with fractions.

Examining Children's Reasoning: Division of Fractions

How do children think about division of fractions? View the clip "IMAP—Meaning of Division on Fractions" on MyEducationLab. In this clip, Elliot is a sixth-grader who understands $a \div b$ as "How many b's are in one a?" He is able to solve $1 \div \frac{1}{3}$, and he explains his solution by saying that "one-third goes into one three times because there are three pieces in one whole." When asked to do so by the interviewer, Elliot draws a diagram to represent that expression, showing a rectangle cut into thirds, with one-third shaded, and then showing the one-third connecting with another rectangle cut into thirds three times.

PEARSON **myeducationlab** The Power of Classroom Practice Go to the Assignments and Activities section of Topic 8: "Fraction Concepts and Computation" in the MyEducationLab for your course and complete the activity "IMAP—Meaning of Division on Fractions" to see how one student uses mathematic reasoning.

Next Elliot is asked to solve $1\frac{1}{2} \div \frac{1}{3}$. He thoughtfully builds on his solution to $1 \div \frac{1}{3}$ when he reasons that there must be another $\frac{1}{3}$ in $\frac{1}{2}$, saying that "one-third goes into one-half one time with one-sixth left over," so the answer is $4\frac{1}{6}$.

How did Elliot decide that the part left over was $\frac{1}{6}$ and the answer was $4\frac{1}{6}$? You may need to watch the last 20 seconds of the video clip again. Here's what Elliot says: "Two-sixths equals one-third and three-sixths equals one-half, so I take away two-sixths because I'm taking away one-third out of the one-half and I have one-sixth left."

Whew! Can you figure out what Elliot did? Did he get the correct answer? Remember, Elliot is thinking about this problem as "How many thirds are in $1\frac{1}{2}$." He knows there are 3 thirds in one whole, so next he focuses on how many thirds are in one-half. He sees that he can find one more third in the one-half, so the answer is now 4, but he also sees that he has some left over and tries to label it. The question is one of how to label the leftovers. Elliot realizes that when he takes away $\frac{1}{3}$ from the $\frac{1}{2}$ he has $\frac{1}{6}$ left, since $\frac{1}{2} - \frac{1}{3} = \frac{1}{6}$.

But is this the correct answer? How should we quantify the leftovers in this sort of problem? Remember, we want to know how many thirds are in $1\frac{1}{2}$. Elliot is correct that there are 4 thirds with some left over. The leftover is $\frac{1}{6}$ of a whole—but how much of $\frac{1}{3}$ is that? Because we want to know how many thirds are in $1\frac{1}{2}$, we need to express the leftovers in terms of what part of $\frac{1}{3}$ they are, rather than what part of one whole they are. This is where Elliot makes a mistake. The leftover amount, $\frac{1}{6}$, is half of $\frac{1}{3}$, so the answer is $4\frac{1}{2}$, meaning that there are $4\frac{1}{2}$ thirds in $1\frac{1}{2}$.

This video clip shows a sixth-grader who knows a lot about division of fractions and who still makes an error. It shows the complexity of the problem as well as the importance of understanding the unit. In other words, whenever we use fractions, we must pay particular attention to what we're referring to. Usually a fraction is referring to part of a whole, but in this problem, the fraction answer is referring to what part of one-third we have. As we have emphasized throughout this book, the key factor is helping children make sense of the mathematics they are doing.

Considering Different Cases of Division of Fractions

Division problems involving fraction divisors and whole-number dividends are easiest and should be presented first. Both even and uneven division should be modeled. Example problems with fraction and whole-number divisors are presented below. Problems 6 and 7 are examples of Measurement division problems; problem 8 is a Partitive division problem.

Whole number divided by a fraction: Even division

PROBLEM 6

Randy has 6 sticks of gum. He wants to give each of his friends $\frac{1}{2}$ of a stick of gum. How many friends will get gum? *(Measurement division)*

POSSIBLE SOLUTION PROCESS

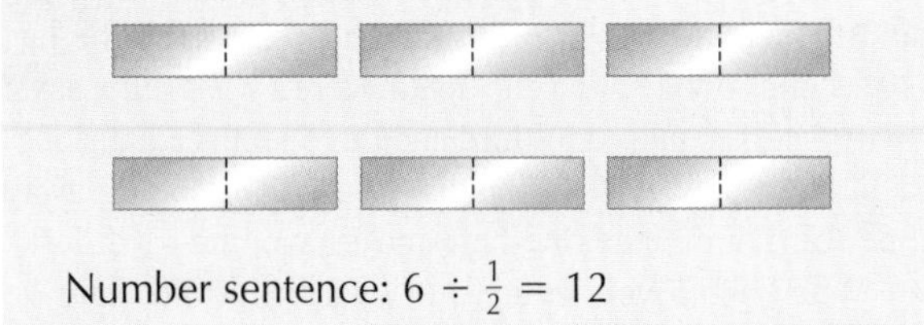

Number sentence: $6 \div \frac{1}{2} = 12$

Whole number divided by a fraction: Uneven division

PROBLEM 7

Jane is responsible for wrapping small packages for the local fall fair. She is cutting a roll of ribbon into $\frac{3}{4}$-yard lengths to make bows for the packages. How many pieces of ribbon $\frac{3}{4}$-yard long will she get from 5 yards of ribbon? *(Measurement division)*

POSSIBLE SOLUTION PROCESS

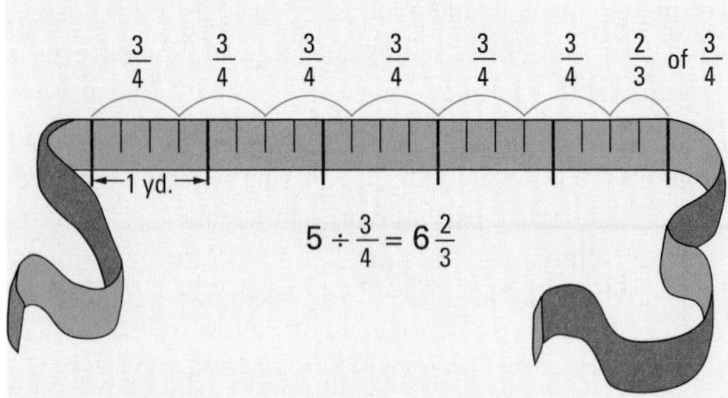

Jane will get 6 pieces of ribbon $\frac{3}{4}$-yard long. She will have $\frac{2}{3}$ of another piece leftover.

Number sentence: $5 \div \frac{3}{4} = 6\frac{2}{3}$

Fraction divisor and whole-number dividend

PROBLEM 8

For her birthday, Molly received a box of chocolates with 32 chocolates in it. After her family had some, Molly calculated that $\frac{3}{4}$ of the chocolates remained. One day, she shared the remaining chocolates equally among herself and five friends. What part of the box of chocolates did each friend receive? *(Partitive division)*

POSSIBLE SOLUTION PROCESS

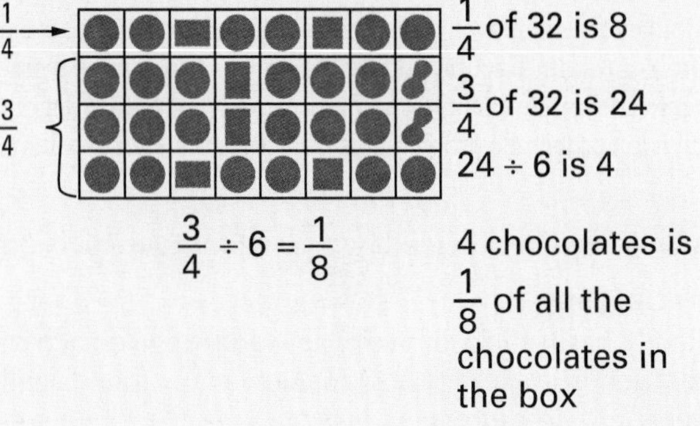

Each friend received $\frac{1}{8}$ of the chocolates, or 4 chocolates ($\frac{1}{8} = \frac{4}{32}$).

Number sentence: $\frac{3}{4} \div 6 = \frac{1}{8}$

Fraction divisor and dividend. When children are able to concretely represent problems with a whole-number divisor or dividend, they can be asked to solve problems that have fraction divisors and dividends. Quotients may be whole numbers or fractions. Problem 9 is an example with a whole number quotient.

PROBLEM 9

Max has $\frac{1}{2}$ quart of lemonade. He wants to pour $\frac{1}{6}$ quart each into small glasses. How many servings of lemonade will Max have?

POSSIBLE SOLUTION PROCESS

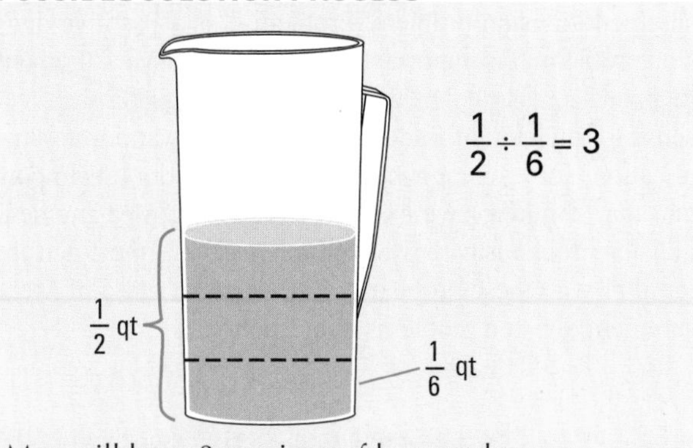

Max will have 3 servings of lemonade.

Number sentence: $\frac{1}{2} \div \frac{1}{6} = 3$

Mixed-number dividend

PROBLEM 10

Mrs. Hanson bought $2\frac{1}{2}$ yards of magnetic tape to use in displaying a set of geometric figures on the classroom metallic board. She wants to cut each yard into 12 equal pieces, that is, each piece is to be $\frac{1}{12}$-yard long. How many pieces $\frac{1}{12}$-yard long can Mrs. Hanson get?

POSSIBLE SOLUTION STRATEGY

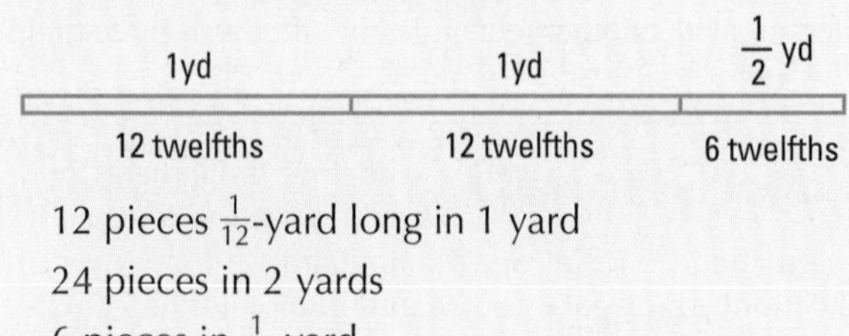

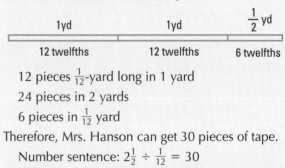

12 pieces $\frac{1}{12}$-yard long in 1 yard
24 pieces in 2 yards
6 pieces in $\frac{1}{12}$ yard

Therefore, Mrs. Hanson can get 30 pieces of tape.

Number sentence: $2\frac{1}{2} \div \frac{1}{12} = 30$

Problems with fractions for both divisor and dividend are more difficult to represent pictorially, and children may need extra support when working on these problems. Figure 11-7 shows example problems solved with a rectangular model.

FIGURE 11-7 Modeling Division of Fractions with a Rectangular Model

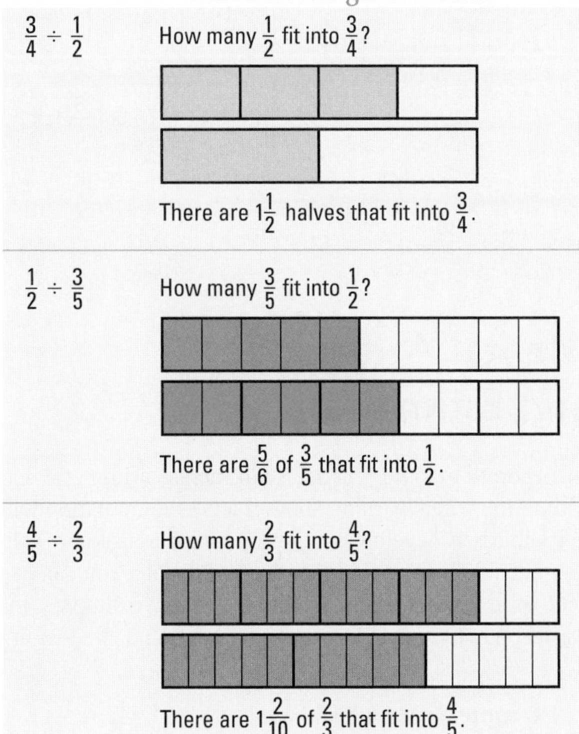

$\frac{3}{4} \div \frac{1}{2}$
How many $\frac{1}{2}$ fit into $\frac{3}{4}$?
There are $1\frac{1}{2}$ halves that fit into $\frac{3}{4}$.
$\frac{1}{2} \div \frac{3}{5}$
How many $\frac{3}{5}$ fit into $\frac{1}{2}$?
There are $\frac{5}{6}$ of $\frac{3}{5}$ that fit into $\frac{1}{2}$.
$\frac{4}{5} \div \frac{2}{3}$
How many $\frac{2}{3}$ fit into $\frac{4}{5}$?
There are $1\frac{2}{10}$ of $\frac{2}{3}$ that fit into $\frac{4}{5}$.

Developing a symbolic division algorithm. The previous section showed how several different types of problems can be solved with concrete materials or pictures. As children solve division problems, encourage them to record their work in number sentences and to organize these number sentences into a table, as in Table 11-2. Then at appropriate times, use class discussions to draw children's attention to patterns or relationships in their solution procedures. Continue posing problems and adding number sentences to this table. Encourage children to verbalize and discuss the patterns they observe in the table. This process is very powerful because children are using data they believe in, that they produced, to make generalizations.

The following activities illustrate this strategy.

1. Provide each pair of children with a fraction division question similar to $6 \div \frac{1}{2}$ to solve by drawing a diagram. Have pairs of children check each other's work.

   Examples:

   $6 \div \frac{1}{2} = \quad 5 \div \frac{1}{2} = \quad 3 \div \frac{1}{3} =$

   $6 \div \frac{1}{5} = \quad 4 \div \frac{1}{3} = \quad 5 \div \frac{1}{4} =$

   - When all pairs of children have solved the problems, write their number sentences on the board.
   - Invite children to examine the number sentences and write about their observations.
   - Ask children to share their observations. For example, they may notice that the whole number (dividend) and the denominator of the divisor are multiplied to get the result.
   - Ask children to write a multiplication equation for each division equation.

2. Follow the procedures above but use a different set of questions.

   Examples:

   $5 \div \frac{3}{4} = \frac{20}{3}$ or $6\frac{2}{3}$ $\quad 3 \div \frac{2}{3} = \frac{9}{2} \quad 4 \div \frac{2}{3} = \frac{12}{2}$

   Question: How can you get a result of $6\frac{2}{3}$ from the problem $5 \div \frac{3}{4}$? See Figure 11-8. Observation: Multiply the dividend (5) and the denominator of the divisor (4), then divide this number by the numerator of the divisor (3).

   The rule may be verbalized: Change the problem to a multiplication problem and invert the divisor, and then multiply the two numbers.

   Number sentence: $5 \div \frac{3}{4} = 5 \times \frac{4}{3} = \frac{20}{3}$ or $6\frac{2}{3}$

   Children can then test whether this procedure works whenever fractions are divided.

Throughout the development of computation algorithms, teachers should keep in mind that the aim in fraction computation is conceptual understanding of the operations and not memorization of algorithmic procedures. The fractions used in problems should be those that can be visualized concretely or pictorially and are likely to be encountered in everyday situations (NCTM, 1989).

TABLE 11-2 Analyzing the Number Sentences in Problems 6 through 10

Problem Number	Number Sentence	Writing Number Sentences in Fraction Form	Writing Number Sentences as Multiplication Problems
6	$6 \div \frac{1}{2} = 12$	$\frac{6}{1} \div \frac{1}{2} = 12$	$\frac{6}{1} \times \frac{2}{1} = 12$
7	$5 \div \frac{3}{4} = 6\frac{2}{3}$	$\frac{5}{1} \div \frac{3}{4} = \frac{20}{3}$	$\frac{5}{1} \times \frac{4}{3} = \frac{20}{3}$
8	$\frac{3}{4} \div 6 = \frac{1}{8}$	$\frac{3}{4} \div \frac{6}{1} = \frac{1}{8}$	$\frac{3}{4} \times \frac{1}{6} = \frac{1}{8}$
9	$\frac{1}{2} \div \frac{1}{6} = 3$	$\frac{1}{2} \div \frac{1}{6} = 3$	$\frac{1}{2} \times \frac{6}{1} = 3$
10	$2\frac{1}{2} \div \frac{1}{12} = 30$	$\frac{5}{2} \div \frac{1}{12} = 30$	$\frac{5}{2} \times \frac{12}{1} = 30$

FIGURE 11-8 Using a Model to Solve a Division of Fractions Problem

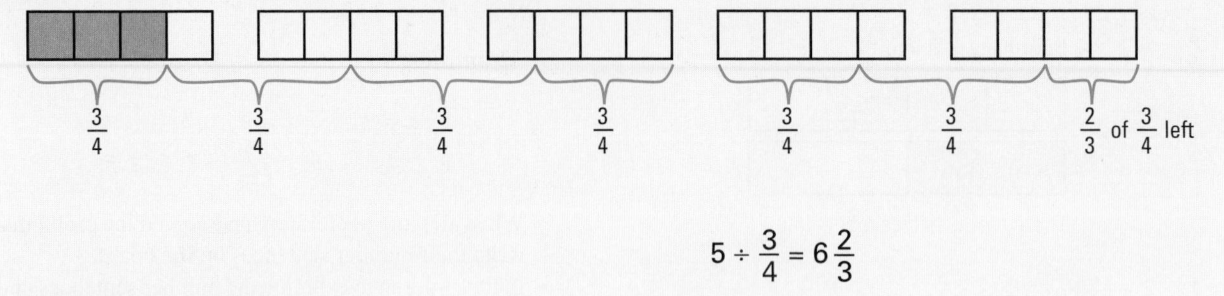

Computing Fractions with a Calculator

Calculators that display fractions, such as the Texas Instruments Math Explorer, can be useful in helping children understand and observe patterns in fraction computation. The use of a calculator frees children's thinking so that they can focus on looking for patterns. Make sure that children understand fraction operations and can estimate answers before proceeding to use calculators.

Examples:

- Find $\frac{1}{2}$ of these fractions: $\frac{2}{3}, \frac{4}{5}, \frac{5}{6}, \ldots$
- Find $\frac{1}{3}$ of these fractions: $\frac{2}{5}, \frac{2}{6}, \frac{2}{7}, \frac{2}{8}, \ldots$
- Divide these fractions by 2: $\frac{1}{2}, \frac{1}{3}, \frac{1}{4}, \frac{1}{5}, \ldots$
- Divide these fractions by 2: $\frac{2}{8}, \frac{3}{8}, \frac{4}{8}, \frac{5}{8}, \ldots$

Ask children to compare answers to finding $\frac{1}{2}$ of a number with dividing that number by 2.

Children can be invited to draw diagrams or model the problems they solve with a calculator. When using the Math Explorer to add and subtract fractions, the calculator displays the answer with the lowest common denominator.

Example:

2 [/] 3 [+] 5 [/] 8 = Display: 31/24

To convert the improper fraction $\frac{31}{24}$ to a mixed number, follow the procedure:

31/24 [Ab/c] = Display: 1 u 7/24 (1 unit and 7/24)

In multiplying fractions, the calculator displays the product of the numerators and that of the denominators. In division, the calculator uses the invert and multiply rule. To simplify the answers in multiplication and division, the function [Simp] is used.

Example:

	Display		Display
5 [/] 8 [×] 2 [/] 3 =	10/24	[Simp]	5/12
4 [/] 7 [+] 2 [/] 3 =	12/14	[Simp]	6/7

Mental Arithmetic and Estimation

Incorporating some practice with mental arithmetic and estimation when learning about fraction computation will help children develop fraction operation sense and help them decide if their solutions are reasonable. You can use sets of exercises such as the following examples for warm-up activities or brief practice sessions.

Example 1: Mental arithmetic

Problem	Possible Thinking Processes
$5\frac{3}{4} + 3\frac{1}{2}$	$\rightarrow$ 8, 9, $9\frac{1}{4}$
$7 - 2\frac{1}{3}$	$\rightarrow$ 5, $4\frac{2}{3}$
$\frac{1}{7} \times 280$	$\rightarrow \frac{280}{7} = 40$
$8 \div \frac{1}{3}$	$\rightarrow 8 \times 3 = 24$

Example 2: Estimation

Problem	Possible Thinking Processes
$\frac{3}{5} + \frac{9}{10} + \frac{1}{23}$	$\rightarrow \frac{1}{2} + 1 + 0 \rightarrow 1\frac{1}{2}$
$6\frac{1}{8} - 2\frac{4}{7}$	$\rightarrow$ 4, $3\frac{1}{2}$
$1\frac{1}{2} \times 5\frac{6}{7}$	$\rightarrow 1\frac{1}{2} \times 6 \rightarrow 6 + 3 = 9$
$6\frac{1}{5} \div \frac{1}{2}$	$\rightarrow 6 \div \frac{1}{2} \rightarrow 12.$
$\frac{2}{3} \div \frac{7}{8}$	$\rightarrow$ divisor is close to 1, quotient is greater than $\frac{2}{3}$ but less than 1

Conclusion

In this chapter, important ideas about helping children understand computation with fractions have been presented. Remember to make extensive use of concrete materials to model fraction computation and to help children connect their understanding of operations on whole numbers with operations on fractions.

CHAPTER

11

Sample Lesson

A Lesson on Estimating Fraction Sums and Differences

Grade level: Fifth

Materials: At least one fraction manipulative, such as fraction circles

Lesson objective: Students use models to make reasonable estimates of the solutions of fraction addition problems.

Standards link: Students make reasonable estimates of fraction sums. (NCTM *Curriculum Focal Points,* grade 5).

Launch: Display a fraction addition problem, such as $\frac{9}{10} + \frac{7}{8}$. Ask students, "What would be a good estimate of the sum of $\frac{9}{10}$ and $\frac{7}{8}$?" Review the meaning of *estimate,* which is an approximate answer. Solicit recommendations about how to determine an estimate, including using a fraction manipulative, such as fraction circles. Then model the students' recommendations. For example, use fraction circles to model the sum. Discuss what students notice, for example, that each fraction is close to 1, so their sum is close to 2.

Then discuss the term *reasonable.* Ask students what a reasonable estimate would be. Regarding the problem $\frac{9}{10} + \frac{7}{8}$, is 2 a reasonable answer? What would be an *unreasonable* estimate for that sum? Unreasonable estimates would include larger numbers, such as 5 and above, and smaller numbers, such as $\frac{1}{2}$.

Next pose a problem with one fraction close to 1 and the other fraction close to 0, for example, $\frac{5}{6} + \frac{1}{8}$. Ask students to find a reasonable estimate of this sum and explain their process.

Explore: In pairs, have students find reasonable estimates for several problems involving the sum of two or three fractions. In creating the problems, make sure to select a variety of fractions, including the following types: (1) close to 1, (2) close to 0, (3) close to $\frac{1}{2}$. Ask students to estimate the sum and explain how they found that sum. Remind students that they may use fraction manipulatives to assist them.

Summarize: Coming together as a whole class, select pairs of students to come to the front of the room and explain their estimates for a problem. Focus on their explanations of how they found their estimates, and how they determined that their estimates were reasonable.

FOLLOW-UP

Complete the following questions.

1. Consider any cautions regarding selecting the fractions to use in this lesson. How might you select the fractions? In what order? Why?
2. Consider difficulties students might have with this concept and this lesson. What modification could you make to avoid or minimize these issues? What modifications could you make for students with special needs?
3. What might the *next* lesson focus on, and why?

IN PRACTICE

Complete the following activities to include in your professional portfolio. Some may be completed online at MyEducationLab in the Book Specific Resources Section:

1. For each operation on fractions, write a word problem and draw a picture showing how to solve the problem using a model.
2. How can a teacher help children understand fraction computation?
3. What does it mean for a person to have *operation sense*?
4. Visit a fifth- or sixth-grade classroom. Informally interview several children about their understanding of fraction operations. Write a summary of their understandings and list ideas about instructional activities you might plan to enhance their understanding.
5. Write a lesson to introduce a fraction operation of your choice. Pay particular attention to the real-world situations and models used in the lesson.

myeducationlab — The Power of Classroom Practice. Now go to Topic 8: "Fraction Concepts and Computation" in the MyEducationLab (www.myeducationlab.com) for your course, where you can:

- Find learning outcomes for "Fraction Concepts and Computation" along with the national standards that connect to these outcomes.
- Apply and practice your understanding of the core teaching skills identified in the chapter with a Building Teaching Skills and Dispositions learning unit.
- Complete Assignments and Activities that can help you understand the chapter content more deeply.
- Complete *enVision MATH* Sample Curricula assignments that allow you to examine and work with chapters from *enVision MATH*, a K-6 mathematics program.
- Check your comprehension on the content covered in the chapter by going to the Study Plan in the Book-Specific Resources for your text. Here you will be able to take a chapter quiz, receive feedback on your answers, and then access Review, Practice, and Enrichment activities to enhance your understanding of chapter content.
- Go to Chapter 11 of the Book-Specific Resources for your text to explore mathematical reasoning related to chapter content in the Activities section.

LINKS TO THE INTERNET

Ask Dr. Math (Fractions and Decimals)

http://www.mathforum.org/library/drmath/sets/elem_fractions.html

Contains a list of interesting questions about fractions and decimals and Dr. Math's answers.

Hungry for Math

http://library.thinkquest.org/J002328F

Contains information on fractions, including great diagrams and pictures.

RESOURCES FOR TEACHERS

Children's Literature

Daniel, Becky (1990). *Hooray for Fraction Facts!* Carthage, IL: Good Apple.

Greenberg, Dan (1996). *Fun and Fabulous Fraction Stories*. New York: Scholastic.

McMillan, Bruce (1992). *Eating Fractions*. New York: Scholastic.

Murphy, Stuart J. (1996). *Give Me Half.* New York: HarperCollins.

Nelson, Joanne (1990). *Half and Half.* New York: Modern Curriculum Press.

Palotta, Jerry (1999). *Hershey's Fractions*. New York: Cartwheel.

Palotta, Jerry (2003). *Apple Fractions*. New York: Cartwheel.

Tierney, Cornelia (2004). *Different Shapes, Equal Pieces: Fractions and Area*. New York: Scott Foresman.

Tierney, Cornelia and Mary Berle-Carman (1998). *Fair Shares: Fractions*. New York: Scott Foresman.

CHAPTER 12

Developing Decimal Concepts and Computation

NCTM CONNECTING WITH THE STANDARDS

The National Council of Teachers of Mathematics (NCTM) Principles and Standards emphasizes the importance of children developing conceptual understanding of decimals, including "what they are, how they are represented, and how they are related to whole numbers" (NCTM, 2000, p. 151). The NCTM document goes on to note that the "foundation of students" work with decimal numbers must be an understanding of whole numbers and place value; . . . they should also understand decimals as fractions whose denominators are powers of 10. The absence of a solid conceptual foundation can greatly hinder students" (NCTM, 2000, p. 215).

The NCTM (2006) *Curriculum Focal Points* mentions developing understanding of decimal concepts and computation in grades four through seven. They state that fourth-grade students should develop "an understanding of decimals, including the connections between fractions and decimals" (NCTM, 2006, p. 16). They further recommend that fourth-graders should:

- understand decimal notation as an extension of the base-ten system of writing whole numbers that is useful for representing more numbers, including numbers between 0 and 1, between 1 and 2, and so on;
- relate their understanding of fractions to reading and writing decimals that are greater than or less than 1, identifying equivalent decimals, comparing and ordering decimals, and estimating decimal or fractional amounts in problem solving; and
- connect equivalent fractions and decimals by comparing models to symbols and locating equivalent symbols on the number line (NCTM, 2006, p. 16).

Similarly, they state that fifth-grade students should develop "an understanding of and fluency with addition and subtraction of fractions and decimals" (NCTM, 2006, p. 17). In addition, they recommend that fifth-graders should:

- apply their understandings of decimal models, place value, and properties to add and subtract decimals;

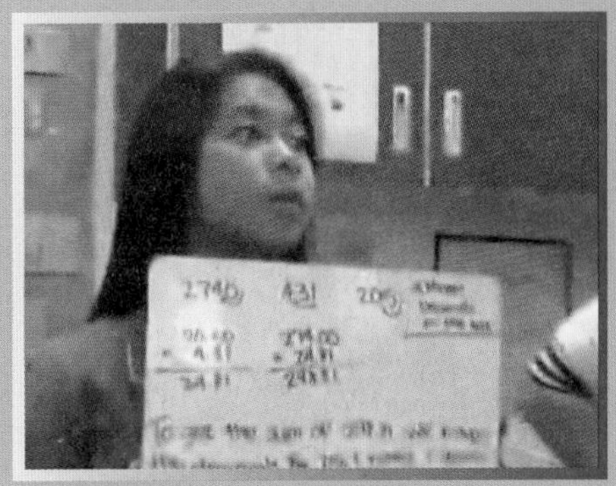

Developing Your Math Teaching Skills

When you have finished studying this chapter, you should be able to do the following:

- Show how to use models to help children understand decimals and operations on decimals.
- Describe how decimals are related to whole numbers and fractions.
- Explain the meaning of each operation on decimals. Give a real-world situation that exemplifies each operation on decimals.

- develop fluency with standard procedures for adding and subtracting fractions and decimals;
- make reasonable estimates of fraction and decimal sums and differences; and
- add and subtract fractions and decimals to solve problems, including problems involving measurement (NCTM, 2006, p. 17).

In sixth grade, students should develop "an understanding of and fluency with multiplication and division of fractions and decimals" (NCTM, 2006, p. 17). Sixth graders should:

- use the relationship between decimals and fractions, as well as the relationship between finite decimals and whole numbers (i.e., a finite decimal multiplied by an appropriate power of 10 is a whole number), to understand and explain the procedures for multiplying and dividing decimals;
- use common procedures to multiply and divide fractions and decimals efficiently and accurately;
- multiply and divide fractions and decimals to solve problems, including multistep problems and problems involving measurement; and
- extend their work in grade 5 with division of whole numbers to give mixed number and decimal solutions to division problems with whole numbers (NCTM, 2006, p. 17).

Finally, seventh-grade students should "use division to express any fraction as a decimal, including fractions that they must represent with infinite decimals. They find this method useful when working with proportions, especially those involving percents" (NCTM, 2006, p. 19).

ASSESSING MATHEMATICS UNDERSTANDING

In order to become familiar with the mathematics concepts and procedures discussed in this chapter, take a few minutes and complete the following Chapter 12 Preassessment. Answer each question on your own. Then think about the possible misunderstandings or difficulties some elementary-school children might have when solving each problem. If you are able, administer this assessment to a child, and analyze his or her understanding of these topics.

Solve each problem. Think about how you get your answer.*

1. Circle the larger number in each pair below. If the numbers are equal, place an equal sign (=) between the numbers.

a. .73 .8 **b.** .6 .16 **c.** .59 .2

d. .30 .3 **e.** 1.2 .85 **f.** 4.7 4.70

Choose one problem from above and explain your thinking.

2. 3.69 + 1.5 **3.** 4 − .7

4. 1.3 × .4 **5.** 1.3 ÷ .4

Examining Classroom Practice

Vanessa is an average fifth-grade child who has had considerable instruction on decimals, and Andrew is a third-grader who has not had any instruction on decimals. To see how Vanessa and Andrew think about adding and comparing decimals, view the clip "IMAP—Decimal Assessments" on MyEducationLab. In this clip the children solve the addition problem and compare the pairs of numbers listed below.

> PEARSON **myeducationlab** The Power of Classroom Practice Go to the Assignments and Activities section of Topic 9: "Decimal Concepts and Computation" in the MyEducationLab for your course. Complete the activity "IMAP—Decimal Assessments" to see how two students solve problems. Pay particular attention to the children's reasoning.

$$\begin{array}{r}3.69\\+1.51\\\hline\end{array}$$

.73	.8
.6	.16
.30	.3
.59	.2
.25	.4
.2	.35
1.8	.18

First let's examine how they solve the addition problem. Both children get the correct answer. Do you think they understand the problem? How are they thinking about adding decimals? What language do they use to describe their solution process? Notice that neither child uses any decimal language when solving the problem. They seem to solve the problem as if it is a whole-number addition problem,

*Adapted from R. Philipp and C. P. Cabral (2005), IMAP: Integrating Mathematics and Pedagogy to Illustrate Children's Reasoning.

placing a decimal point in the answer just below its location in the two addends.

What about the comparison problems? Except for the last problem, both children consistently get the wrong answers. What strategy are they using? They seem to be ignoring the decimal points and thinking of each number as a whole number. For example, when comparing .2 and .35, Vanessa states, "Two is a little and thirty-five is a lot." This error is very common. Children frequently try to apply rules that work for whole numbers when solving decimal problems.

On the basis of what you observed in this clip, what do you think Vanessa and Andrew understand about decimals? What would you conclude that they do not understand? If you were Vanessa's or Andrew's teacher, what are some things you would consider doing next to help them understand decimal numbers? And perhaps the most important question is, what does it mean to truly understand decimals?

Analyzing Assessment Results

Now let's look at the results from the Pre-Assessment. All of these problems involve comparing, adding, subtracting, multiplying, or dividing decimals. What was your general reaction to solving the problems? Did they all seem to be equally difficult, or were some problems easier for you to think about? Did you draw pictures or use a manipulative material to help you make sense of the problem? What aspects of problems do you think make them easier or harder for children to solve? What in general do you think a teacher's goals should be regarding developing understanding of decimals? If you had a chance to give the *Chapter 12 Preassessment* to a child, take a few minutes and analyze the results. How did the child solve these problems? How did the child think about these problems?

Analyze each problem. How did you (and/or the student you administered the assessment to) solve each of the following problems? Look at problem 1 first.

1. Circle the larger number in each pair below. If the numbers are equal, place an equal sign (=) between the numbers.

a. .73 .8 **b.** .6 .16 **c.** .59 .2

d. .30 .3 **e.** 1.2 .85 **f.** 4.7 4.70

Comments: How are these problems alike, and how are they different? Which were more difficult, or were they equally difficult? Did you use counters or draw a picture, or solve it in another way? How did Vanessa and Andrew solve these problems? What misunderstandings did they have, and what aspects did they understand?

2. $\begin{array}{r} 3.69 \\ +1.51 \\ \hline \end{array}$

3. $4 - .7$

4. $1.3 \times .4$

5. $1.3 \div .4$

Comments: These problems are typical operations problems. If you asked a child to solve these problems, did he or she draw pictures to help them solve them? Did the child seem to understand the concepts, or was the child just using rules without understanding? Many children do not understand decimals conceptually, and try to apply rules that work with operations on whole numbers. This often means that children are unable to judge the reasonableness of their answers.

Take a minute and reflect on this assessment. Were some problems easier than others? What factors made them easier? What do you want to learn more about in order to help children understand decimal concepts and operations?

Common Student Misunderstandings About Decimal Concepts and Operations:

- Decimals are just like whole numbers—everything you do with whole numbers works with decimals.
- The more digits to the right of the decimal point, the bigger the number is (for example, many children think that 0.3 is less than 0.30).
- Decimals are completely different from fractions.

Are there any other misunderstandings that children may have about whole number operations? It's important to assess what children understand and are still working on understanding, in order to plan instruction that meets their needs.

Building on Assessment Results

Think about what can be done help strengthen children's understandings and minimize (and hopefully eradicate) their misunderstandings and misconceptions.

Sometimes teaching about decimals focuses on memorizing procedures and ignores the concepts on which the operations are based. While we want students to be able to compute with decimals, they also need to be able to estimate what the answer should be. This will enable them to make sense of problem situations. So what might we do next to help students understand decimal concepts and operations?

A key element of all instruction is to make sure that students understand the concept. Students need to visualize concepts and relationships. This usually is best done with some sort of manipulative material, asking students to solve problems set in familiar, meaningful situations and to examine the reasonableness of their solutions.

In order to understand operations on decimals, students need to understand what decimals mean and also understand what the operations mean. The table below lists several common misunderstandings and what a teacher can do to help children overcome these misunderstandings.

Understanding Decimals

What do we know about U.S. children's understanding of decimal concepts and computation? The Seventh National Assessment of Educational Progress (NAEP) noted that most fourth-, eighth-, and twelfth-graders tested had fairly weak understanding of these topics. Only about one-third of the fourth-graders tested were able to correctly round decimal numbers to the nearest whole number (Wearne & Kouba, 2000). The 2003 NAEP showed that the performance of eighth-grade students had not changed substantially, while fourth-graders' ability to add, subtract, and divide decimals improved slightly (Kastberg & Norton, 2007). There clearly is room to improve.

Research on children's learning of decimals consistently shows a lack of understanding of the concepts related to decimals, which leads to difficulty in determining the reasonableness of answers. The Third International Mathematics and Science Study (TIMSS) (Mullis et al., 1997) showed that U.S. students' performance on questions involving decimals was lower than that on questions involving fractions (Glasgow et al., 2000). Hiebert and Wearne (1986) found that children often lack "a link between their conceptual knowledge (of decimals) and a notion that written answers should be reasonable" (p. 220).

Owens and Super (1993) also commented on children's difficulties with understanding decimals. "Because decimal fractions look similar to the familiar whole numbers, it seems reasonable to predict that children . . . might understand them without much difficulty. However, appearance is deceiving. The research on learning decimal fractions agrees on one point: There is a lack of conceptual understanding" (p. 137).

IF students think that . . .	THEN have students . . .
decimals are just like whole numbers—everything you do with whole numbers works with decimals	*model* a problem, such as 3.69 + 1.51, with a manipulative material and relate that to the procedure, and discuss how the procedure is the same as and different from the same operation with whole numbers (for example, when adding 369 + 151).
the more digits to the right of the decimal point, the bigger the number is	*model* two decimals, such as 0.3 and 0.30, with a manipulative material, and compare them.
decimals are completely different from fractions	*model* a fraction and its decimal equivalent, such as 1/2 and 0.5, with a manipulative material, and discuss how they are alike and how they are different.
calculating with decimals involves just memorizing procedures	*discuss* with students any difficulties they have when calculating with decimals, and discuss how they can use estimation to help them decide if their answers make sense.

Instructional Strategies for Teaching Decimals

Two different approaches can be used to help children learn decimals: (1) building on place-value knowledge and (2) building on fraction knowledge.

Although it is tempting to assume—or hope—that children will easily connect what they know about place value to decimals, the place-value approach can result in fairly low-level performance and a lack of understanding, particularly if concepts are taught procedurally. This approach encourages children to build on their knowledge of place value, for example, by "lining up" the places when adding and subtracting decimals. But this method has limitations, especially regarding multiplication and division of decimals, in which children do not need to "line up" the decimal points. Instruction that merely focuses on "moving the

NCTM NUMBER AND OPERATIONS STANDARDS AND EXPECTATIONS ADDRESSED IN THIS CHAPTER

Instructional programs from Pre-K–12 should enable all students to—	In grades 3–5 all students should— (NCTM, 2000, p. 148)	In grades 6–8 all students should— (NCTM, 2000, p. 214)
• understand numbers, ways of representing numbers, relationships among numbers, and number systems.	• understand the place-value structure of the base-ten number system and be able to represent and compare whole numbers and decimals. • recognize and generate equivalent forms of commonly used fractions, decimals, and percents.	• work flexibly with fractions, decimals, and percents to solve problems. • compare and order fractions, decimals, and percents efficiently and find their approximate locations on a number line.
• understand meanings of operations and how they relate to one another.		• understand the meaning and effects of arithmetic operations with fractions, decimals, and integers. • use the associative and commutative properties of addition and multiplication and the distributive property of multiplication over addition to simplify computations with integers, fractions, and decimals.
• compute fluently and make reasonable estimates.	• develop and use strategies to estimate computations involving fractions and decimals in situations relevant to students' experience. • use visual models, benchmarks, and equivalent forms to add and subtract commonly used fractions and decimals. • select appropriate methods and tools for computing with whole numbers from among mental computation, estimation, calculators, and paper and pencil according to the context and nature of the computation and use the selected method or tools.	• select appropriate methods and tools for computing with fractions and decimals from among mental computation, estimation, calculators or computers, and paper and pencil, depending on the situation, and apply the selected methods. • develop and analyze algorithms for computing with fractions, decimals, and integers and develop fluency in their use. • develop and use strategies to estimate the results of rational-number computations and judge the reasonableness of the results.

decimal point" is difficult for children to make sense of, resulting in a lack of ability to estimate and determine the reasonableness of solutions.

The second approach to helping children learn decimals is to connect understanding of decimals with children's existing fraction understanding. This approach helps children develop conceptual knowledge of decimals as well as an understanding of the meaning of operations on decimals. For example, when multiplying 0.3×0.7, why will there be two decimal places in the answer? The traditional procedural response to this is "because you count the number of decimal places in both factors." But why is this true? Because 0.3 can be written as $\frac{3}{10}$ and 0.7 can be written as $\frac{7}{10}$, and $\frac{3}{10} \times \frac{7}{10}$ means we're finding 3 tenths of 7 tenths, which is $\frac{21}{100}$, which can be written as 0.21 (which has two decimal places). This sort of connection must be made if children are to understand procedures, which too often are quickly forgotten, rather than merely memorize them.

$$0.3 \times 0.7 = \_\_\_\_\_\_$$

$$0.3 = \frac{3}{10}$$

$$0.7 = \frac{7}{10}$$

$$\frac{3}{10} \times \frac{7}{10} = \frac{21}{100} = 0.21$$

$$\text{So } 0.3 \times 0.7 = 0.21$$

This chapter presents an integrated approach to instruction on decimals, connecting place-value understanding and fraction understanding to help children develop a strong foundation in decimal concepts and operations.

Instructional Considerations

Connections to Familiar Concepts

In introducing decimals to children, it is important to connect decimals with familiar concepts. Decimals are closely related to *whole numbers* in that the characteristics of whole-number numeration apply to decimals. Also, the computation algorithms are basically the same for whole numbers and decimals. However, to understand decimals quantitatively, one must develop *fractional number* concepts. Ordinarily, fraction concepts are developed before decimals are introduced; in this sequence, students draw on their knowledge of fractions. For example, the decimal number 0.2 can also be expressed as the fraction $\frac{2}{10}$.

Whole-number connection. Learning to read and interpret whole numbers involves learning the characteristics of our number system. These characteristics were discussed in Chapter 6. It may be helpful to review the characteristics when children begin to work with decimals. Then, investigations to find out whether the characteristics also describe decimal numbers can be part of the development of decimal number concepts.

Place value. An understanding of the place-value system for whole numbers is a prerequisite for reading and interpreting decimals. When learning whole-number place value, children group numbers in 10 and multiples of 10. They learn that for whole numbers, the value of a place is *ten times* the value of the place to its immediate right. Another way to state this relationship is to say that the value of a place in a numeral is *one-tenth* the value of the place to its immediate left. This latter relationship is important in interpreting decimal numbers. The value of the place to the right of the tens is one-tenth of 10, or 1; the value of the place to the right of the ones is one-tenth of 1 or one-tenth. Kieren (1984) cautions that acting out fractional regrouping may not be easy for children. He states that "we should not assume that the grouping–ungrouping action that allows one to go from ones to tens to hundreds will also allow one to go from ones to tenths to hundredths; dividing up is simply different from ungrouping" (p. 3). Allow children time to explore such regroupings concretely.

Whole numbers. Compare the value of each 1 in the numeral 115. What is the relationship of the leftmost 1 and the 1 on its right? Modeling the number 115 with bundled sticks and singles shows that the value of the leftmost 1 is 10 times the value of the 1 on its right.

The middle digit, or the 1 to the immediate left of the 5, can be represented by one bundle of 10 sticks. It has the value of 10. To show the value of the leftmost 1, group

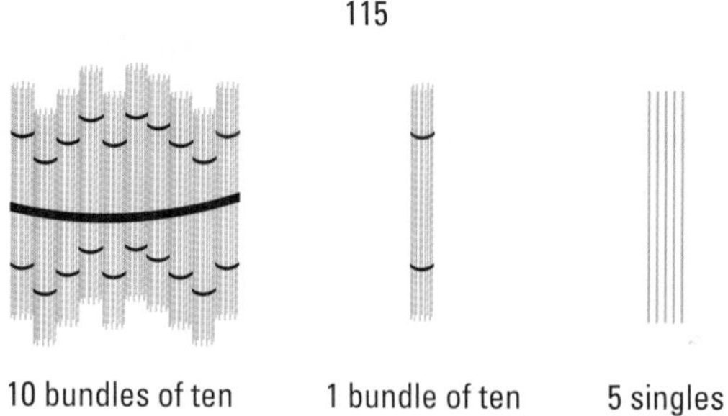

together 10 groups of 10 sticks. Its value is hundred, or 10 times 10. Its value is *10 times* the value of the 1 on its right.

One can also ask, what is the relationship of the 1 on the immediate left of the 5 to the leftmost 1? Modeling the numbers shows that the 1 next to the 5 is *one-tenth* the value of the 1 on its left.

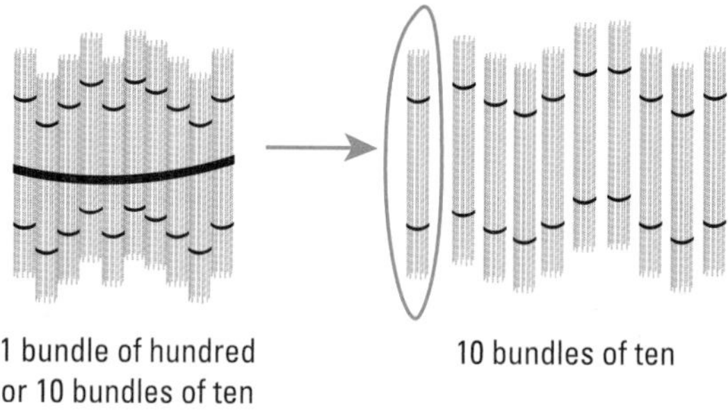

The leftmost 1 has the value of hundred. To show the value of the 1 on its right, take a large bundle (10 groups of ten) and separate it into 10 bundles of ten. One small bundle (a group of 10 sticks) shows the value of the 1 to the left of the 5. Its value is *one-tenth* the value of the leftmost 1.

Children who understand and can verbalize the "ten times" and the "one-tenth" relationships between adjacent digits in whole numbers are ready to interpret decimal numeration.

Decimal numbers. Consider 21.1 as an example. The 1 before the decimal point has the value of 1. It can be represented with a square.

The value of the 1 on the right of the decimal point can be represented by dividing a square (1) in 10 parts.

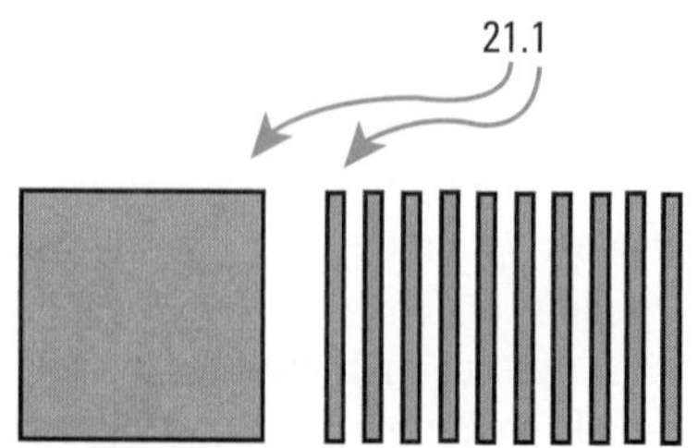

FIGURE 12-1 Place-Value Chart Showing Decimal Places

Thousands	Hundreds	Tens	Ones	Tenths	Hundredths	Thousandths
2	3	6	4.	1	2	7

The value of the 1 on the right of the decimal point is *one-tenth* the value of the 1 to the left of the decimal point. This maintains the place-value relationship established above.

As a second example, consider the number 2.11. Using a square to represent 1 unit (as above), the process of subdividing can be extended a step further to demonstrate the value of the rightmost 1 in the number 2.11.

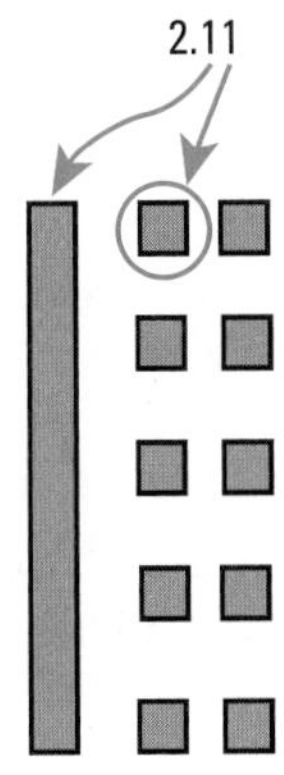

The rightmost 1 has a value of *one-hundredth.* It is one-tenth the value of the 1 on its left. One-hundredth is one-tenth of one-tenth.

The familiar whole-number place-value chart can be extended to include decimal places as in Figure 12-1. Notice that the chart is symmetric about the ones place rather than about the decimal point.

Middle school children may appreciate the patterns inherent in the symbolic representation of place values as in Figure 12-2.

The following two exercises will help children develop the meaning of decimal numbers by connecting them to whole numbers.

1. Begin by asking children to respond to the following questions:
    - How many hundreds in 66,600? (six hundred sixty-six)
    - How many tens in 6,660? (six hundred sixty-six)
    - How many ones in 666? (six hundred sixty-six)

    Next, continue the pattern using decimals.
    - How many tenths in 66.6? (six hundred sixty-six)
    - How many hundredths in 6.66? (six hundred sixty-six)
    - How many thousandths in 0.666? (six hundred sixty-six)

2. Have children read and write numbers in the following manner:
    - 444,000 four hundred forty-four thousands
    - 44,400 four hundred forty-four hundreds
    - 4,440 four hundred forty-four tens
    - 444 four hundred forty-four ones

    Then, continue the pattern using decimals.
    - 44.4 four hundred forty-four tenths
    - 4.44 four hundred forty-four hundredths
    - 0.444 four hundred forty-four thousandths

Reading numbers as described in the second exercise helps to reinforce the fact that no matter where the decimal point is, each digit is 10 times as much as the digit on its right and one-tenth of the digit on its left.

You should also point out to students the different reading sequences:

- *Whole numbers reading sequence:* thousands, hundreds, tens, ones
- *Decimal reading sequence:* tenths, hundredths, thousandths

Additive quality. To develop the idea that decimals, like whole numbers, are additive, have children first show different ways to write specified whole numbers, then decimal numbers. For example:

Whole numbers

45 = 40 + 5

643 = 600 + 40 + 3

or 6 hundreds + 4 tens + 3 ones

FIGURE 12-2 Symbolic Representation of Place Values

10^3	10^2	10^1	10^0	10^{-1}	10^{-2}	10^{-3}
1000	100	10	1	$\frac{1}{10}$	$\frac{1}{100}$	$\frac{1}{1000}$
7	8	2	3	5	4	5

Decimal numbers

$0.45 = 0.4 + 0.05$
or 4 tenths + 5 hundredths
$= 0.40 + 0.05$
or 40 hundredths + 5 hundredths

$6.43 = 6 + 0.4 + 0.03$
or 6 + 4 tenths + 3 hundredths

Multiplicative quality. The multiplicative aspect of decimal numbers can be highlighted when children learn to write decimals in expanded notation. For example:

$$452.69 = (4 \times 100) + (5 \times 10) + (2 \times 1) + (6 \times 0.1) + (9 \times 0.01)$$
$$= (4 \times 100) + (5 \times 10) + (2 \times 1) + (6 \times \tfrac{1}{10}) + (9 \times \tfrac{1}{100})$$

Connection to fractions. Pause a moment and order the following fractions from least to greatest:

$$\frac{5}{100} \quad \frac{5}{1000} \quad \frac{51}{100} \quad \frac{5}{1000} \quad \frac{150}{1000}$$

How does this task compare with ordering decimals? Many children find ordering fractions when the denominators are powers of 10 easier than ordering decimals. Why is this so? One reason may be that it is easier to visualize the size of a fraction such as $\frac{51}{100}$ (51 parts of 100 parts) than it is to concretize "point five one" (0.51).

The common practice of reading decimals by naming the digits rather than expressing them properly as decimal fractions makes it more difficult to think about decimals as fractional numbers. The number 0.51 should be read as "fifty-one hundredths" rather than "point five one," to emphasize its meaning and value. This will be discussed in the next section.

Another factor that can contribute to children's difficulty in determining the value of a decimal number is the lack of concrete and semiconcrete experiences that children have when working with decimal numbers. In the past, some mathematics programs have not encouraged extensive modeling of either decimals or fractions. Quite often, decimals were modeled with concrete materials less often than were fractions. But children need lots of practice to make sense of decimals, and modeling with concrete materials is a great way to support the development of this understanding.

Children who understand fractions prior to studying decimals are better able to make connections between the two systems of representing rational numbers.

Example:

$8.45 = 8$ and $0.4 + 0.05$
or 8 and 0.45
or 8 and $\frac{4}{10} + \frac{5}{100}$
or 8 and $\frac{45}{100} = 8\frac{45}{100}$

Reading and Writing Decimals

In elementary classrooms, one frequently hears children reading decimals with a "point," such as "two point six" for the number 2.6. Recall that in the video clip at the beginning of this chapter, Andrew and Vanessa read 1.8 as "one point eight." Some teachers accept this (some textbooks recommend it!) and children go on to say things like "three point four plus five point two equals seven point six." On the lips of adults, statements like these do not upset us. However, if children use such expressions when learning the meaning of decimal numbers, it is possible they may not readily develop understanding of the quantitative value of decimal numbers. The practice is similar to reading whole numbers by naming the digits that form a number as, for example, reading 647 as "six four seven." The expression "six hundred forty-seven" conveys some understanding of the value of each digit in the numeral. The same is true when reading decimals. Children should be required to state the quantitative value of digits when they read a decimal numeral.

Examples: 4.5 Read as "four and five-tenths."
0.35 Read as "zero and thirty-five hundredths" or "thirty-five hundredths."

Decimal point. In fraction form, it is easy to distinguish between the whole number and the fraction part (e.g., $4\frac{5}{10}$). With decimal numeration, the denominator is not visible; therefore, a sign is needed to denote when a fraction part of a number is indicated. The sign is the decimal point and is read "and" when reading decimal numbers. As stated in Chapter 6, it is not proper to use "and" when reading whole numbers.

Example: 100, 101, 102, . . .

Not correct:

"one hundred, one hundred *and* one, one hundred *and* two, . . ."

Correct:

"one hundred, one hundred one, one hundred two, . . ."

Decimal names. Take care to pronounce the decimal terms distinctly (possibly slightly exaggerating the *th* and *ths* endings) so that children will be able to discriminate between them and whole-number terminology.

Example: ten and tenth; tens and tenths
hundred and hundredth; hundreds and hundredths
thousand and thousandths, . . .

In early work with decimals, it is recommended that decimal numerals be written on the board or on a chart for reference (a teacher can point to the parts) when communicating decimal numbers orally. This will aid children in matching the *th* and *ths* endings with the numeric place values and in distinguishing them from whole-number place-value terms.

Decimal notation. Decimal notation has changed over the years and even today it is not uniform throughout the world. In the United States, a point is used and it is placed immediately after (to the right of) the ones digit; people in some European countries use a comma in the same position.

Example:

ENGLISH	FRENCH
0.05	0,05
245.63	245,63

This symbolization transfers to monetary values.

Example:

\$ 4.95	4,95\$
\$56.08	56,08\$
\$ 0.05	0,05\$

When reading a number, the decimal point is read as "and."

Example: 6.5 or 6,5
Read as: six *and* five-tenths

Example: \$1.49 or 1,49\$
Read as: one dollar *and* forty-nine cents

If children read decimals properly, writing decimals will be a simple exercise. Reading decimals properly also enhances children's ability to readily identify denominators, which enables them to think of decimals as fractional numbers.

Children may more easily visualize a fraction in concrete terms than a decimal. For example, it is easier to visualize $\frac{3}{4}$ of a cookie than 0.75 of a cookie. Thinking about decimals as fractions, rather than manipulating digits, helps to develop decimal number sense. Teaching ideas for developing decimal number sense through concrete and semiconcrete models are provided in the next section of this chapter.

The following activities provide practice in reading and writing decimal numbers:

1. Reading and Writing Decimals
   - Provide a calculator for each child and a calculator for use on an overhead projector.
   - Dictate the decimal number *seven and fifty-five hundredths.*
   - Ask children to enter the number in their calculators.
   - Then display the number on an overhead projector calculator (or on a transparency if a calculator is not available) for the children to self-check.
   - Repeat the procedure with other numbers:

     three and four-hundredths
     sixty and sixteen-thousandths
     two hundred three and five-hundredths

2. Reading Decimal Numbers
   - Display a decimal numeral on an overhead projector calculator or write it on the board.

   Example: 4.65
   - Ask a child to read the number.
   - Repeat with other numerals:

     40.08 0.095 0.002 306.36 500.05

3. Writing Decimal Numbers
   - Write several decimal numerals on the board.

   Examples:

     0.405 60.05 300.003

   - Have children write the numbers in words.

Developing Decimal Number Sense

It is important to devote time to developing the meaning of decimal numbers through concrete and semiconcrete models. Several examples are described here together with suggestions for activities.

Base-Ten Blocks

Children will have used base-ten blocks when learning to interpret whole numbers and their operations. These materials also can be used to represent decimal numbers provided children are able to understand that different blocks can be selected to represent the unit.

A "tens" block as the unit. A first activity could be to select a tens block (called a *rod* or a *long*) to represent the unit. Questions such as the following can be asked:

- If this piece represents (or is worth) one, what is the value of this piece (small cube)?
- What is the value of 2 of these small cubes? 3 small cubes? . . . 10 small cubes?

Change the questioning to:

- If this piece (a rod) is one, show me one-tenth; three-tenths; nine-tenths.

A "hundreds" block as the unit. Take a "hundreds" block (called a "square" or a "flat"). Say:

- Now let's say that this square block is one or one whole. Can you find a block that is one-tenth of this square block?

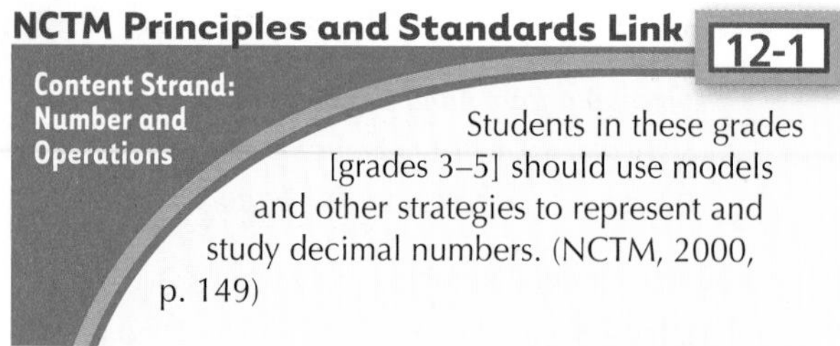

NCTM Principles and Standards Link 12-1

Content Strand: Number and Operations

Students in these grades [grades 3–5] should use models and other strategies to represent and study decimal numbers. (NCTM, 2000, p. 149)

- Can you show two-tenths of this square block with the blocks? three-tenths? . . . ten-tenths?

Change the questioning to:

- I have five rods (tens) here. What part of the square are they?
- I have one small cube in my hand. Can you tell what part of the square this small cube is? Why do you call it that?

A "thousands" block (large cube) as the unit. Encourage children to write relational statements about the various blocks when a thousands block is designated as the unit. They can be challenged to write as many different relationships as they can. Two other activities with base-ten blocks follow:

1. A Square as the Unit
   - Designate a square as the unit.
   - Write the numeral 2.5 on the board (or display it on an overhead projector calculator or transparency).
   - Have children model the number with the blocks. Children can check each other's work.
   - Ask a child to tell what number has been modeled.
   - Repeat with other numerals such as:

     1.6 0.2 0.12 0.06 0.56

2. Choose a Unit
   - Tell children to select a block as the unit and then to represent a number with the blocks. Have them record what they have done.

   Possible sample work:

   I chose the square as one. I made the number 2.25. This is how I made the number.

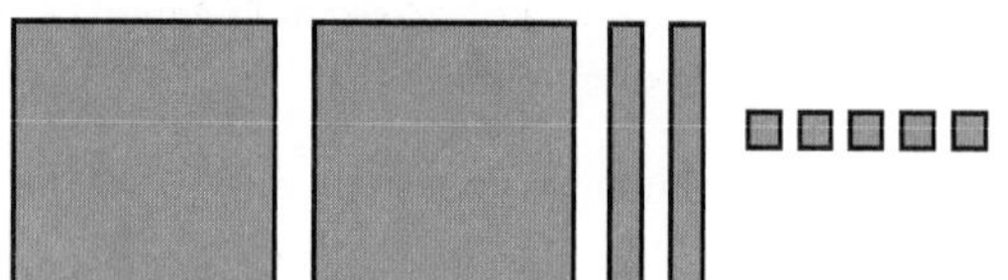

I chose the large cube as one. I made the number 0.036. This is how I made the number.

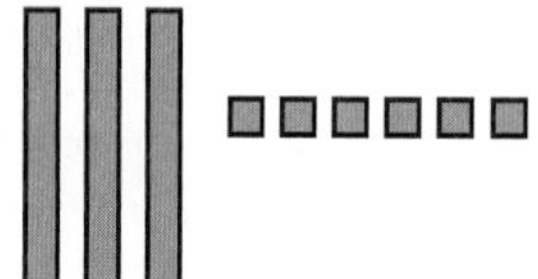

Examining Children's Reasoning

To see two children using base-ten blocks to model decimals, view the clip "IMAP—Decimal Work with Base-Ten Blocks" on MyEducationLab. In this clip, two average fifth-graders, Megan and Donna, attempt to model 1.8 with base-ten blocks in two different ways. First they use the unit cubes, using one cube to represent 1 and eight cubes to represent 0.8. Then the interviewer suggests the girls use a long to represent 1, and both girls then use one long to represent 1, eight longs to represent 0.8, and a cube to represent the decimal point. Unfortunately, both of these representations are incorrect. Their representations did not distinguish between the value of the ones and the value of the tenths, using the same block to represent both ones and tenths.

> PEARSON **myeducationlab** The Power of Classroom Practice Go to the Assignments and Activities section of Topic 9: "Decimal Concepts and Computation" in the MyEducationLab for your course and complete the activity "IMAP—Decimal Work with Base-Ten Blocks" to watch how two students use base-ten blocks.

On the basis of what you observed in this clip, what do you think Megan and Donna understand about modeling decimals, and what are they confused about? How would you have hoped that they would have used base-ten blocks to represent 1.8? Megan and Donna seem confused about the meaning of decimals. They seem to be viewing the number 1.8 as 1 of something and 8 more of the same thing. They could have either used 1 long and 8 cubes, or one flat and 8 longs, to correctly represent 1.8.

Decimal Squares

The commercial Decimal Squares kit consists of colored paper squares 1 dm^2 or 1 sq. dm partitioned in tenths (red), hundredths (green), and thousandths (yellow). The 10 tenths squares are shaded to represent 0.1, 0.2, . . ., 1.0. The hundredths and thousandths squares are shaded to represent multiples of 5 and 10 fractional parts. Children can use the squares to compare decimal fractions (Activity 12-1) and for simple addition and subtraction. Teachers can construct a similar model using decimal grids (see Blackline Masters 11 through 15 on MyEducationLab), which can be used to represent one whole, tenths, hundredths, and thousandths.

> PEARSON **myeducationlab** The Power of Classroom Practice Go to Chapter 12 in the Book-Specific Resources section in the MyEducationLab for your course and select Blackline Masters to access Blackline Masters 11–15.

ACTIVITY 12-1 Comparing Decimal Fractions: Tenths and Hundredths

Materials
A set of Decimal Squares (red and green) for each child

Procedure

1. Select a red square. Now find a green square with the same amount shaded. Write a statement about the two amounts.

   Example: Eight-tenths and eighty-hundredths are the same amount.

2. Find other pairs of decimal squares that show the same amount shaded and write a statement about the pairs of decimal fractions.

Graph-Paper Grids

Graph paper marked in 10-cm squares or grids is useful for showing different decimal fractions. The paper can be centimeter or millimeter graph paper (see Blackline Master 16 on MyEducationLab). Children can be asked to shade parts of the squares to show different decimal fractions, to compare decimal fractions, or to show addition and subtraction of decimal fractions.

1. Modeling Decimal Fractions Pictorially (Hundredths)
   - Provide children with several pieces of centimeter graph paper marked in 10-cm squares.
   - Direct children to show decimal fractions on the graph-paper squares by coloring or shading.

   Examples: 0.4, 0.45, 0.5, 0.05, 0.25

2. Modeling Decimal Fractions Pictorially (Thousandths)
   - Provide children with millimeter graph paper marked in 10-cm squares.
   - Direct children to show decimal fractions on the graph paper by coloring or shading.

   Examples: 0.35, 0.08, 0.075, 0.009, 0.016

Working with millimeter graph paper will communicate to children how relatively small the third place value in a decimal fraction really is. Another way to get children to realize the relative sizes of decimal fraction place values is to have them partition a centimeter hundreds square in thousandths and then in ten-thousandths. Procedures for this exercise are described below.

1. Provide children with a 10-cm square piece of centimeter graph paper.
2. Direct them to shade in the amount of 0.57142 by first shading in 5 tenths, next 7 hundredths, then 1 thousandth, then 4 ten-thousandths, and finally 2 hundred-thousandths. Children will soon realize that it is difficult to designate the area for ten-thousandths.
3. **Discussion:** What did you learn from this exercise?

Number Line

A number line is a good model to demonstrate the density property of decimals. Provide children with number lines drawn on paper and have them write several numbers between 0 and the given number. For example:

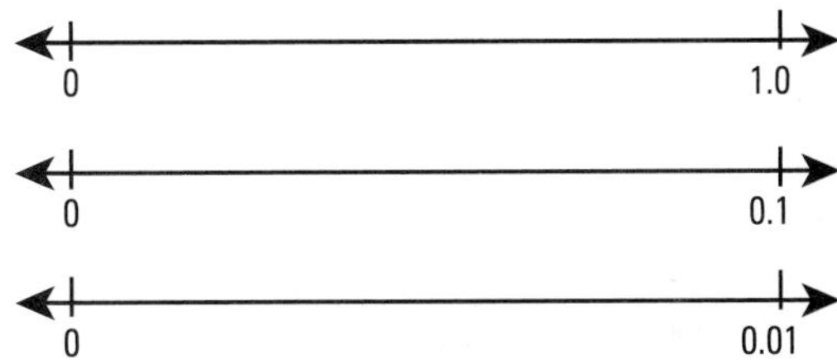

The kind of exercise can help children realize that it is always possible to name decimal numbers between any two given numbers.

A number line also can be used to write decimal numbers in specified increments such as 0.1, 0.5, or 0.01. This type of activity helps children count from one place value to another larger one, for instance, from hundredths to tenths. This is not a trivial task for children because of the strong influence of whole numbers. With whole numbers, when counting up, one goes from tens to hundreds; with decimals, one goes from hundredths to tenths.

Give children appropriate number lines drawn on paper. Ask them to:

- Begin with 0.8, count by tenths.
- Begin with 7.5, count by 5 tenths.
- Begin with 0.56, count by tenths.

Two examples of children's counting errors are

12.08, 12.09, <u>13.00</u>

20.97, 20.98, 20.99, <u>30.00</u>

NCTM Principles and Standards Link 12-2

Content Strand: Number and Operations

Students can develop a deep understanding of rational numbers through experiences with a variety of models, such as fraction strips, number lines, 10 × 10 grids, area models, and objects. These models offer students concrete representations of abstract ideas and support students' meaningful use of representations and their flexible movement among them to solve problems. (NCTM, 2000, p. 215)

NCTM Principles and Standards Link 12-3

Content Strand: Number and Operations

At the heart of flexibility in working with rational numbers is a solid understanding of different representations for fractions, decimals, and percents. In grades 3–5, students should have learned to generate and recognize equivalent forms of fractions, decimals, and percents, at least in some simple cases. In the middle grades, students should build on and extend this experience to become facile in using fractions, decimals, and percents meaningfully. (NCTM, 2000, p. 215)

Activity 12-2 contains an additional number line activity.

ACTIVITY 12-2 Labeling Points on a Number Line

Visual Scaffolding

Write numbers for A, B, and C on each line.

0.96 0.97 0.98 A B C

1.06 1.07 1.08 A B C

0.096 0.097 0.098 A B C

Money

Some teachers use coins to model decimals. Recording amounts in dollars and cents does involve decimal fractions, but care must be taken that children see the connection between the coins and the fractional part of a decimal number. For example, children do not readily relate \$2.25 to 2 dollars and 25 hundredths of a dollar or a dime to one-tenth of a dollar. If money is used as a model for decimals, children need to think of dimes and pennies as fractional parts of a dollar.

Examples: 5 pennies = 5 hundredths of a dollar
3 dimes = 3 tenths of a dollar

Provide children with pennies, dimes, and a dollar coin (play money is fine). Ask them to first display the following sets of coins and then to write the decimal number that they represent.

- 1 dollar, 4 dimes (1.40 or 1.4)
- 3 dimes, 5 pennies (0.35)
- 15 pennies (0.15)
- 2 dimes, 12 pennies (0.32)

It is not uncommon to find in commercial advertisements an incorrect use of decimal notation when recording costs. For example, the price of an item may be indicated as .25¢. The assumption is that .25¢ means the same as \$0.25 when in fact it means 25 hundredths of a cent, that is, less than one cent! Activity 12-3 can help children practice recording money properly.

ACTIVITY 12-3 Recording Prices

Realia Strategies

Sara and her brother Bill have set up a lemonade stand at the beach. They want to make a sign to indicate the price of large, medium, and small glasses of lemonade. What are two ways Sara and Bill can show the prices?

Large glass: ninety-five cents
Medium glass: seventy-five cents
Small glass: fifty cents

The expected answers to Activity 12-3 would be \$0.95 or 95¢, \$0.75 or 75¢, and \$0.50 or 50¢.

Other Materials for Modeling Decimals

Most base-ten models can be used to represent decimal numbers. For example, children may like to work with place-value charts or a vertical abacus. If such materials are used, the ones place should be indicated in some manner on the materials (Figure 12-3).

Equivalent Decimals

Usually, more attention is given to equivalent fractions than to equivalent decimals in mathematics programs. Equivalent fractions are necessary for fraction computation, whereas one can work through decimal computations without thinking of equivalent decimals. Nonetheless, equivalent decimals help children understand decimal computation.

If the process of naming equivalent decimals is connected to that of writing equivalent fractions, there is nothing new to learn. The fact that each decimal fraction can be written differently will not be surprising to children.

Example: $\frac{4}{10} = \frac{40}{100} = \frac{400}{1000}$

The fraction $\frac{4}{10}$ was multiplied by "one" in the form of $\frac{10}{10}$ and $\frac{100}{100}$. In a decimal numeral, the process is the same although the denominator is not visible.

FIGURE 12-3 Base-Ten Models Used to Represent Decimal Numbers

Hundreds	Tens	Ones	Tenths	Hundredths
	3	1	4	5

31.45

Place Value Chart

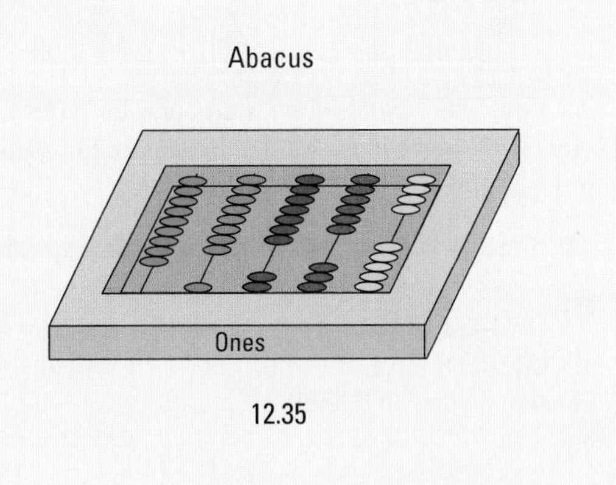

FIGURE 12-4 Using Base-Ten Blocks to Compare Decimals

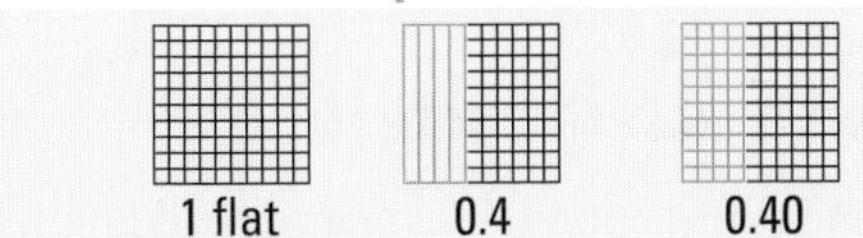

Example: 0.4 = 0.40 = 0.400

These numerals are read as 4 tenths, 40 hundredths, and 400 thousandths. This is similar to the equivalent fractions above.

A concrete "proof" of the equivalency could be demonstrated by using base-ten blocks and comparing, for example, 4 tenths (4 rods) and 40 hundredths (40 ones) on a square unit (a hundreds flat) (Figure 12-4). As with many other concepts, it is important to help children understand the meaning rather than just learn rules, such as "adding a zero to the end of the number."

Children who have had experiences in modeling decimal fractions and in recording amounts in different ways (e.g., 5 tenths or 50 hundredths, 0.5 or 0.50) should develop a sense of the size of decimal numbers. In particular, they should be able to compare tenths and hundredths and to rename one decimal fraction to an equivalent form. They will have a mental referent for the process. The generalization that adding zeros to decimal fractions produces numbers of equivalent value is not difficult to conceptualize.

Ordering and Comparing Decimals

Children who have developed decimal number sense will be able to order decimals. Children who do not understand decimals sometimes use erroneous thinking strategies when ordering decimals. Think back to the incorrect reasoning used by Vanessa and Andrew in the clip "IMAP—Decimal Assessments" on MyEducationLab. What misunderstanding did they have?

One line of thinking is that "longer is greater"; for example, 0.65 is less than 0.0345 because "65" is shorter than "345." Another false method of comparison is that "shorter is greater"; for example, 0.3 is greater than 0.41 because tenths are greater than hundredths (Vance, 1986b). It is wise for a teacher to ask children to explain how they got their solutions in order to learn their thinking processes.

Children can be taught to compare decimals by focusing, in turn, on each place-value position beginning from the left and moving to the right until a comparison can be made. This is similar to the process of comparing whole numbers.

Examples:

1. 1.52 and 1.48

   Comparison: Ones place—same digit; tenths place—5 tenths and 4 tenths. Therefore, 1.52 > 1.48.

2. 0.0156 and 0.85

   Comparison: 0 tenths and 8 tenths or 1 hundredth and 85 hundredths. Therefore, 0.0156 < 0.85.

3. 0.314 and 0.28

   Comparison: 31 hundredths and 28 hundredths. Therefore, 0.314 > 0.28.

Another method used to order decimals is to write equivalent decimal fractions.

Example: Order the following decimals from least to greatest.

1.06 0.36 0.06 0.0306 0.0063

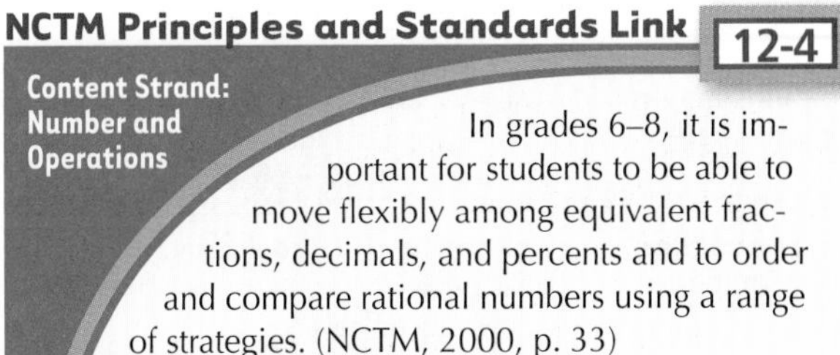
NCTM Principles and Standards Link 12-4

Content Strand: Number and Operations

In grades 6–8, it is important for students to be able to move flexibly among equivalent fractions, decimals, and percents and to order and compare rational numbers using a range of strategies. (NCTM, 2000, p. 33)

Changing all the numbers to the same-sized decimal fraction, one obtains:

1.0600 0.3600 0.0600 0.0306 0.0063

It is now easy to list the numbers in order of size. Activity 12-4 provides practice in constructing and ordering decimals.

> myeducationlab The Power of Classroom Practice — Go to Chapter 12 in the Book-Specific Resources section in the MyEduationLab for your course to complete additional activities on decimals.

Computation

Understanding computation with decimals requires an understanding of place value, decimal concepts, and computation of fractions. Investing time in developing that understanding before beginning decimal computation will pay off in enhanced understanding and increased achievement for children.

Children who have developed an understanding of decimal concepts and place value will have no difficulty adding and subtracting decimals. For multiplication and division, teachers may want to review the operations with 10 and multiples of 10 as a factor. The ability to mentally multiply and divide by 10, 100, etc., greatly facilitates the operations of multiplication and division, particularly in determining the reasonableness of an answer.

ACTIVITY 12-4 Constructing and Ordering Decimals

Materials

Four small cards for each child with the numerals 0, 1, 2, and a decimal point written on the cards

Procedure

1. Use the cards to show as many different decimal numbers as you can.

   Examples: 0.12 1.02

   (Discuss with the class whether numerals such as 012. or .120 are allowed.)

2. Record each number as you make it.
3. When you are sure you cannot make any more numbers, order all your numbers from least to greatest.

Children who have a sense of the quantitative value of decimal numbers can be expected to compute with greater accuracy than when computation is done by applying meaningless rules.

Addition and Subtraction

Addition and subtraction of decimals should be related to addition and subtraction of whole numbers and of fractions. As discussed in Chapters 7 and 11, solving word problems set in familiar, real-world situations helps children understand operations and judge the reasonableness of answers. An easy-to-understand interpretation of addition is the Join interpretation, in which two quantities are combined. The Separate and Comparison interpretations of subtraction, in which two quantities are separated or compared, also are easy to understand.

Addition and subtraction of decimals should be introduced by posing problems based on Join and Separate situations involving quantities measured in decimal units, such as lengths of ribbon, pounds of food, and amounts of money. Figure 12-5 contains sample word problems for addition and subtraction of decimals and compares them with similar problems involving fractions. Notice the similarities between the problem contexts.

FIGURE 12-5 Sample Word Problems for Addition and Subtraction of Fractions and Decimals

	Word Problem with Fractions	Number Sentence	Word Problem with Decimals	Number Sentence
Addition (Join)	Tom ate $\frac{1}{2}$ of an apple pie yesterday and $\frac{1}{4}$ of an apple pie today. How much pie did Tom eat altogether?	$\frac{1}{2} + \frac{1}{4}$ = ____	Tom ate 0.25 pound of turkey and 0.10 pound of cheese. How much food did Tom eat altogether?	0.25 + 0.10 = ____
Subtraction (Separate)	Alberto has $\frac{3}{4}$ of a cookie. He ate $\frac{1}{4}$ of a whole cookie. How much cookie does Alberto have left?	$\frac{3}{4} - \frac{1}{4}$ = ____	Maria had 0.37 meter of ribbon. She used 0.25 meter to make a bow. How much ribbon does Maria have left?	0.37 − 0.25 = ____
Subtraction (Comparison)	Alberto has $\frac{3}{4}$ of a cookie and Juana has $\frac{1}{4}$ of a cookie. How much more does Alberto have?	$\frac{3}{4} - \frac{1}{4}$ = ____	Maria has 0.37 meter of red ribbon and 0.25 meter of blue ribbon. How much more red ribbon does she have than blue ribbon?	0.37 − 0.25 = ____

Examining Children's Reasoning

How do children think about addition and subtraction of decimals? Go to MyEducationLab to view the clip "IMAP—Addition and Subtraction of Decimals." In this clip, you see Brooke, a fifth-grade girl, making sense of subtraction of decimals when asked to solve $4 - 0.7$. She seems to understand tenths. While working the problem, she talks aloud, making her reasoning easy to follow.

> PEARSON myeducationlab The Power of Classroom Practice Go to the Assignments and Activities section of Topic 9: "Decimal Concepts and Computations" in the MyEducationLab for your course and complete the activity "IMAP—Addition and Subtraction of Decimals." Notice how Brooke is able to clearly demonstrate her understanding of fractions and decimals.

Brooke sees relationships among various representations. Her spoken language, use of pictures, and use of symbolic fraction and decimal representations are nicely related for her, providing her with more powerful means for thinking about decimals.

More about addition and subtraction. Addition problems can also be represented on 10-cm graph paper squares. Children can shade in a set of addends and subsequently "read" the number shaded.

The children have measured the mass of some paperback storybooks in the classroom. The four books that Therese and Monica weighed had a mass of 0.25 kg, 0.3 kg, 0.17 kg, and 0.09 kg. What is the mass of the four books? Show the shadings on graph paper.

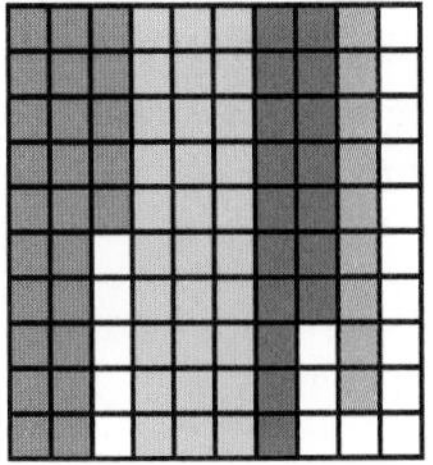

OR

0.25
0.3
0.17
0.09

The mass of the books is 0.81 kg.

If children are required to add several sets of numbers by shading the amounts, they probably will find that it helps to shade in the tenths first, then to add the hundredths and shade them in as tenths plus hundredths, as in the right-hand grid above. For example, for the numbers listed above, a child would first shade in 1, 2, and 3 tenths to make 6 tenths; next, the child would shade in 2 tenths plus 1 hundredth for a total of 0.81 shaded. This procedure causes one to think of the value of each digit and should help children learn how to properly write ragged decimals in vertical columns.

When adding ragged decimals (decimals that have a different number of decimal places so that their right sides don't "line up"), encourage children to write equivalent decimal fractions by adding zeros as required.

Example: *Given:* $0.4 + 0.078 + 0.1056 + 0.23$

Rewrite as: $0.4000 + 0.0780 + 0.1056 + 0.2300$

This method can be thought of as adding the numerators of same-sized decimal fractions.

In subtraction, it is also helpful to rename the decimal fractions to same-sized fractions with the same number of decimal places by adding zeros. This assists in using the standard algorithm.

Two alpine skiers finished a race with the following time scores: 13.5 seconds and 12.96 seconds. What is the time difference of their scores?

SOLUTION PROCESS

Given: $13.5 - 12.97$

Rewrite as: $13.50 - 12.97$

Addition and subtraction questions with mixed decimals can be modeled using base-ten blocks. A concrete demonstration of regrouping is easily carried out with these materials (Figure 12-6).

Other concrete and semiconcrete materials used to add and subtract whole numbers can be used to add and subtract decimals provided there is a way of showing place values smaller than the ones place.

Regrouping in addition and subtraction can also be carried out with dollar and dime coins. However, these are visually nonproportional materials, as discussed in Chapter 6, and therefore should not be the first materials used.

> PEARSON myeducationlab The Power of Classroom Practice Go to the Assignments and Activities section of Topic 9: "Decimal Concepts and Computation" in the MyEducationLab for your course and complete the activity "Decimal Points."

Multiplication

As with addition and subtraction, multiplication and division of decimals should be related to those operations on whole numbers and on fractions. The interpretations of multiplication and division of decimals that are easiest to

FIGURE 12-6 Adding Mixed Decimals with Base-Ten Blocks

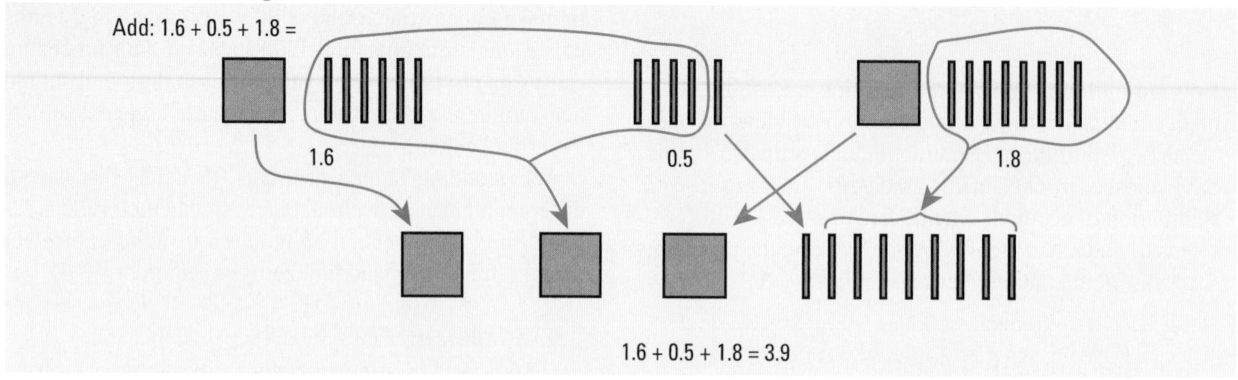

FIGURE 12-7 Sample Word Problems for Multiplication and Division of Fractions and Decimals

	Word Problem with Fractions	Number Sentence	Word Problem with Decimals	Number Sentence
Multiplication (Equal Groups)	Shawntrice had 4 bags of cookies, with $\frac{1}{2}$ of a cookie in each bag. How many cookies did Shawntrice have?	$4 \times \frac{1}{2} =$ ______	Shawntrice had 4 bags of sliced cheese, with 0.75 pound of cheese in each bag. How much cheese did Shawntrice have?	$4 \times 0.75 =$ ______
Multiplication (Area and Array)	There is $\frac{2}{3}$ of a chocolate pie in the refrigerator. Peter ate $\frac{1}{2}$ of it. What part of the whole pie did Peter eat?	$\frac{1}{2} \times \frac{2}{3} =$ ______	Peter has a garden that is 2.5 meters long and 1.5 meters wide. What is the area of Peter's garden?	$2.5 \times 1.5 =$ ______
Division (Measurement—Repeated Subtraction)	Steve has 4 cups of sugar. He needs $\frac{2}{3}$ of a cup of sugar to make one batch of his favorite cookies. How many batches of cookies can Steve make?	$4 \div \frac{2}{3} =$ ______	Steve has $4.00. He wants to buy several candy bars that cost $0.65 each. How many candy bars can Steve buy?	$4.00 \div 0.65 =$ ______

understand are Equal Groups, Area and Array multiplication, and Measurement division (repeated subtraction). Recall that Equal Groups problems involve making a certain number of groups that are the same size, whereas Area and Array problems involve finding the area of a rectangular region. Measurement division, also known as repeated subtraction, involves measuring out groups of a certain size from a whole. Figure 12-7 contains sample word problems for multiplication and division of decimals and compares them with similar problems involving fractions. Notice the similarities between the problem contexts.

Multiplication of decimals should be introduced with simple problems involving tenths and then gradually progressing to smaller decimal fractions.

The following is a suggested sequence for multiplication of decimals:

1. *Tenths by a whole number* — 4×0.2, 3×0.4
2. *Hundredths by a whole number* — 3×0.05
3. *Tenths by tenths* — 0.4×0.6
4. *Hundredths by tenths* — 0.3×0.04, 0.4×0.15
5. *Hundredths by hundredths* — 0.05×0.09, 0.04×0.56, 0.12×0.23

Multiplication problems such as the first two types above can be represented concretely with base-ten blocks using a square (hundreds block) as the unit.

Example: $4 \times 0.2 = 0.8$

Read: 4 times two-tenths = eight-tenths

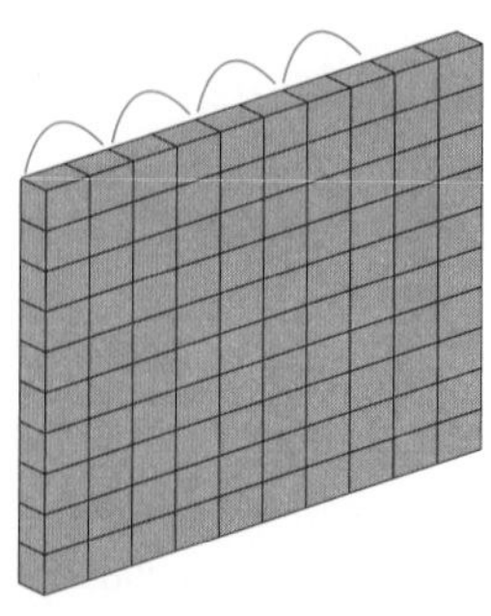

Example: $3 \times 0.4 = 1.2$

Read: 3 times four-tenths = twelve-tenths

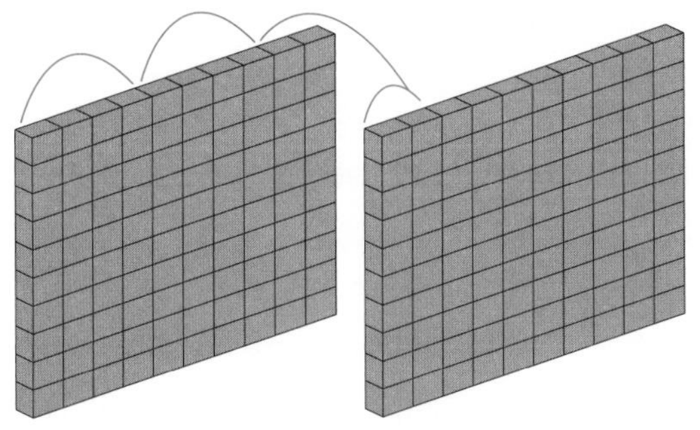

Similarly, hundredths multiplied by a whole number can be represented with base-ten blocks.

Example: $5 \times 0.05 = 0.25$

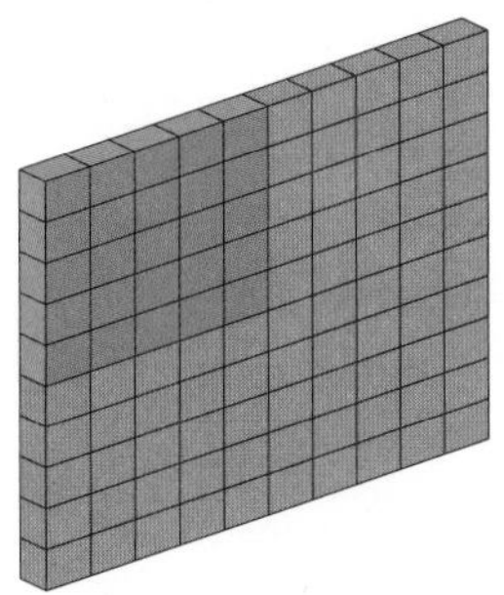

Read: 5 times five-hundredths = 25 hundredths

Multiplication of a decimal number by a whole number can also be pictured on a number line as in Figure 12-8.

When multiplying tenths by tenths, it is helpful to interpret the question as, for example, four-tenths of three-tenths. A teacher-guided lesson to help children understand this concept could be as follows:

1. Designate a square (hundreds block) as the unit.
2. Ask the children to show three-tenths in two ways using the blocks.

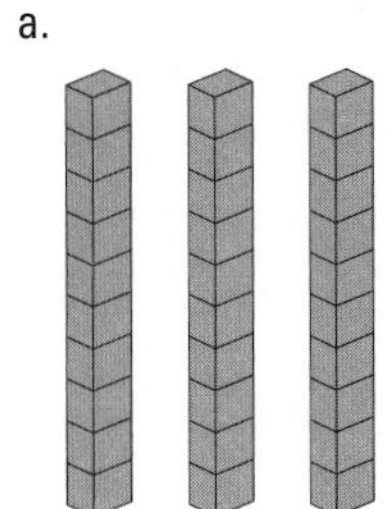

b.

3. Ask, "Which arrangement allows us to remove four-tenths of three-tenths?" (Arrangement b, showing thirty-hundredths, should be chosen.)
4. Ask the children to identify four-tenths of three-tenths.
5. Ask, "How can we state what number this is?" (twelve-hundredths)

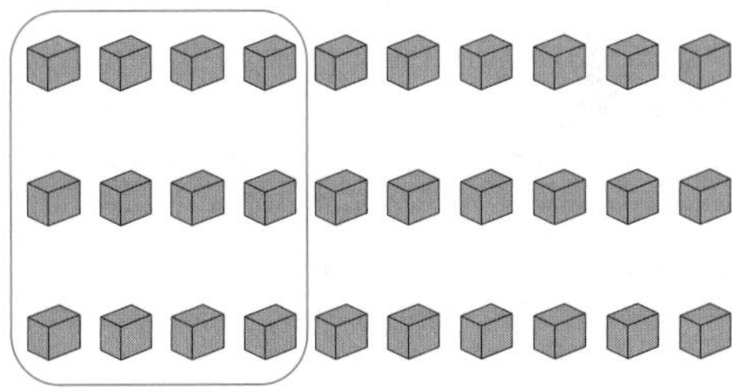

The process can be shown pictorially on a 10-cm square piece of graph paper (Figure 12-9).

A commercial set of Decimal Squares made of colored acetate is available for use on an overhead projector. To use Decimal Squares for multiplication, overlay two squares as in shading grid paper. The region where the shaded parts overlap represents the product (Figure 12-10).

FIGURE 12-9 A Pictorial Representation of Multiplication

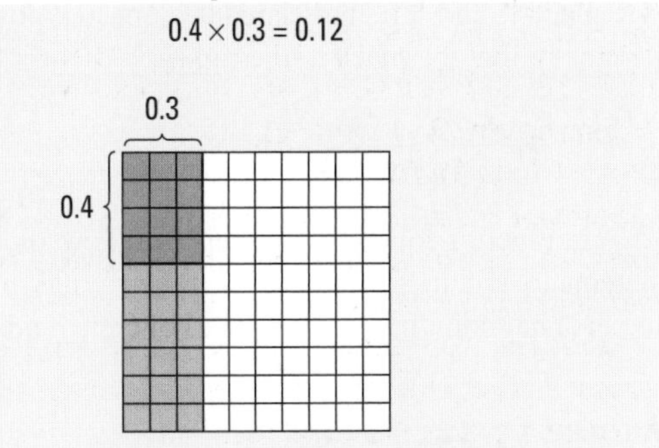

FIGURE 12-8 Multiplying Decimals

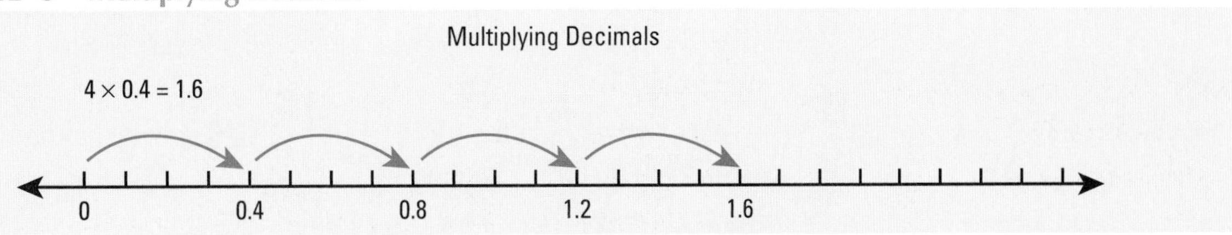

FIGURE 12-10 Use of Decimal Squares for Multiplication

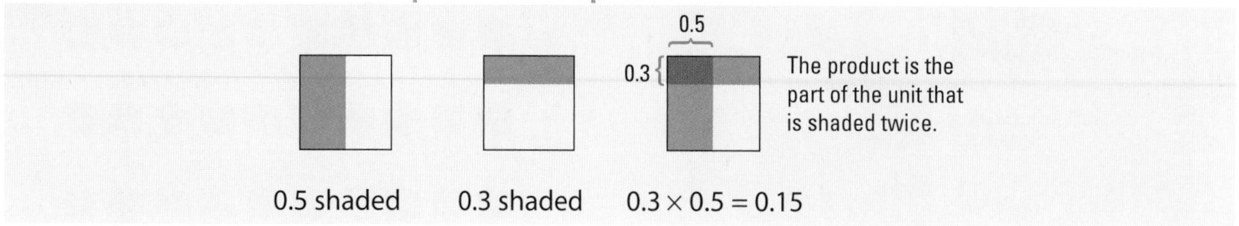

FIGURE 12-11 Multiplying with Powers of 10

$10 \times 0.3 = 3$	$100 \times 1.85 = 185$
$100 \times 0.6 = 60$	$400 \times 0.28 = 112$

Rule: Move the decimal point the same number of places to the right of its original position as there are zeros in the multiple-of-10 multiplier.

Multiplying decimals by powers and multiples of 10 is an important skill to develop. Progressing from concrete representations to paper-and-pencil work to mental calculations, children should develop a rule for the placement of the decimal point in products when multiplying by a power of 10 (Figure 12-11).

A place-value chart can be used to justify the rule for multiplying by 10 (by 100, and by 1,000).

Example:

HUNDREDS	TENS	ONES	TENTHS	HUNDREDTHS
		3	2	5
	3	2	5	
3	2	5		

Because the value of each position is 10 times that of the position to its right, multiplying by 10 "moves" each digit one place to the left. This is equivalent to "moving" the decimal point one place to the right.

Example: $3.25 \times 10 = 32.5$
$32.5 \times 10 = 325$

A number of concrete experiences followed by written statements will help children generalize a rule for placing the decimal point in products. The concrete modeling can proceed systematically to help children notice patterns that will help them develop rules (Figure 12-12). The following are examples of lists that children can write as they multiply decimals concretely or pictorially.

4 × 1 tenth = 4 tenths	$4 \times 0.1 = 0.4$
4 × 2 tenths = 8 tenths	$4 \times 0.2 = 0.8$
4 × 3 tenths = 12 tenths	$4 \times 0.3 = 1.2$
4 × 4 tenths = 16 tenths	$4 \times 0.4 = 1.6$
4 × 5 tenths = 20 tenths	$4 \times 0.5 = 2.0$
4 tenths × 1 tenth = 4 hundredths	$0.4 \times 0.1 = 0.04$
4 tenths × 2 tenths = 8 hundredths	$0.4 \times 0.2 = 0.08$
4 tenths × 3 tenths = 12 hundredths	$0.4 \times 0.3 = 0.12$
4 tenths × 4 tenths = 16 hundredths	$0.4 \times 0.4 = 0.16$
4 tenths × 5 tenths = 20 hundredths	$0.4 \times 0.5 = 0.20$

Patterns can be generated with a calculator when studying multiplication with decimals. The following are examples:

ENTER:	DISPLAY:
5 × 0.1 =	0.5
0.5 × 0.1 =	0.05
0.05 × 0.1 =	0.005
0.005 × 0.1 =	0.0005

If the calculator has a multiplicative constant, one needs only to press the equals sign after the first multiplication to generate the products listed above.

Example: 5 × 0.1 = = = =

FIGURE 12-12 Looking for Patterns in the Number of Decimal Places When Multiplying Decimals

Problem	Decimal Places: *First Factor*	Decimal Places: *Second Factor*	Product	Decimal Places in Product
3 × 0.2	0	1	0.6	1
3.1 × 4.71	1	2	14.601	3
0.3 × 5.2	1	1	1.56	2
0.25 × 0.11	2	2	0.0275	4

Children could use a calculator to complete a table as in Figure 12-12, and then look for a pattern to help them articulate a rule for placing the decimal point in products.

Carefully select the numbers used in such an exercise because for some numbers it appears that the rule does not work.

Example: $0.24 \times 39.5 = ?$

According to the rule, there should be three decimal places in the product. However, a calculator may show the answer as 9.48. Why is this? In this case, the calculator drops final zeros after a decimal point. Children need to be aware of how their calculator displays numbers.

Division

Children who know a division algorithm for whole numbers should be able to divide with decimals. Instruction on division of decimals should begin with problems with whole number divisors.

Example: $5\overline{)25.75}$

Begin by estimating the quotient; $25.75 \div 5$ should be a little more than 5. Then model the problem with base-ten blocks. Separating the blocks into 5 equal groups results in 5.15 in each group.

Then look at the symbols and think about what process would give us the answer we know is correct from our work with the blocks: 5.15. Notice that the same process that works for whole-number division will work in this case.

Then proceed to division with decimal number divisors, which is a little more complicated. It could be introduced with a problem and dialogue similar to that presented in Figure 12-13.

Problems involving decimal fraction divisors in the hundredths and mixed decimal numbers should be presented to children to discuss and solve. The goal is for children to be able to make the following generalization: Multiplying both the divisor and the dividend by the same multiple of 10 does not affect the answer. The connection to equivalent decimals should be made as well (also to equivalent fractions, if appropriate at the time).

Example: $0.62\overline{)744}$ is like $\frac{744}{0.62}$

Writing equivalent fractions, we have

$$\frac{744}{0.62} = \frac{7440}{6.2} = \frac{74400}{62}$$

Decimal form: $0.62\overline{)744} \quad 6.2\overline{)7440} \quad 62\overline{)74400}$

Although a decimal division problem is usually rewritten so that the divisor is a whole number, some children may wish to change both divisor and dividend to whole numbers before dividing.

Example: $0.36\overline{)2.695}$

$$\frac{2.695 \times 1000}{0.36 \times 1000} \rightarrow \frac{2695}{360} \rightarrow 360\overline{)2695}$$

Decimal form: $0.36 \times 1000 = 360$

$2.695 \times 1000 = 2695$

Therefore, $0.36\overline{)2.695} \rightarrow 360\overline{)2695}$

If children use the expression "move the decimal point *n* places to the right in the two numbers" when dividing decimals, you should question them to find out whether they understand why that "works."

FIGURE 12-13 Helping a Child Make Sense of Decimal Division Through Solving a Word Problem and Asking Questions

Problem: Sheilagh has bought 12 m of ribbon to make bows to decorate flower pots. It takes 0.8 m of ribbon to make one bow. Sheilagh wants to figure out how many bows can be made with the length of ribbon she has.

Sheilagh first writes the problem question as

$$0.8\overline{)12}$$

Then she thinks: There are 10 tenths in 1 m.

Therefore 12 m = 120 tenths.

Using this knowledge, she rewrites the question as 120 tenths divided by 8 tenths.

$$8\overline{)120}$$

Sheilagh then divides and finds that 12 m of ribbon can make 15 bows.

Questions to ask:

- What do you think of Sheilagh's work?
- Why is it proper to change the division question as Sheilagh did?
- Could Sheilagh have written a different division question and still have arrived at the answer?

Some children make errors in division situations that require zeros in the dividend. A good way to have children represent such division questions is to use money. Children can use play money (coins and bills) to solve division problems by sharing amounts of money among different-sized groups of people. The situation of winning a lottery can provide a context for dividing up large amounts. By working through a problem such as \$7,387.20 to be shared among 24 people using "play" money, children will see why it is necessary to include a 0 in the dividend.

Estimating with Decimals

In their daily lives, children probably will estimate with decimals more frequently than they will calculate exact answers. It is therefore important that they learn estimation skills.

What are some of the techniques that help children estimate with decimal numbers? First of all, children must be able to read and write multidigit decimal numbers and understand place value of decimal fractions. They must also be able to order and compare decimals, and they must be able to round decimals (Vance, 1986a).

Children should have practice rounding decimal numbers. Two strategies to use are using the leading digit and using the rounded leading digit in a number.

Examples:

	Number	Rounded
Leading digit	365.75	300
	0.0463	0.04
Rounded leading digit	365.75	400
	0.0463	0.05

Estimates for sums and differences of decimal numbers can be obtained by using either the leading-digit or the rounded-leading-digit strategy. Children should recognize which strategies will give estimates that are more than or less than the actual numbers. This knowledge will enable them to decide when to use each strategy. Have them consider situations such as the following and decide which strategy they would use.

- You want to be certain that you have enough cash to pay for groceries.
- You know the amount the family pays for electricity per month, and you want an estimate of the yearly cost.
- You have measurements to the nearest meter of the distance run by an athlete in a certain time during practice sessions. You want an approximation of the average distance the athlete runs in that time span.

In multiplication questions, the leading-digit strategy can produce significantly lower estimates than the actual product.

Example: 485×0.23

Leading digit	$400 \times 0.2 \rightarrow 80$
Rounding	$500 \times 0.2 \rightarrow 100$
Actual	$485 \times 0.23 \rightarrow 111.55$

It appears that the rounded-digit strategy gives an estimate that is closer to the actual product than the leading-digit strategy. When rounding digits, one can round both factors up or round one factor up and the other factor down.

Example:

$783 \times 0.26 \rightarrow 800 \times 0.3 \rightarrow 240$

or $\rightarrow 800 \times 0.2 \rightarrow 160$

or $\rightarrow 700 \times 0.3 \rightarrow 210$

actual $\rightarrow 203.64$

In this case, the closest estimate is 210.

In division, when estimating quotients, it is a common practice to round both numbers in the same direction—either both up or both down.

Example:

$0.28\overline{)675.94} \rightarrow 0.3\overline{)700} \rightarrow 2333.30$

or $0.2\overline{)600} \rightarrow 3000.0$

actual $\rightarrow 2414.07$

In this case, the best estimate is the first one. If you used compatible numbers (evenly divisible), the division question would become $0.3\overline{)690}$, to arrive at an estimate of 2300.

Writing Fractions as Decimals

Understanding decimals in relationship to fractions helps children develop number sense for decimals. Focus on systematically understanding the decimal forms of different fractions in a systematic way to discover patterns and relationships.

Examples:

1. $\frac{3}{10} = 0.3 \quad \frac{3}{100} = 0.03 \quad \frac{3}{1000} = 0.003$

$\frac{45}{10} = 4.5 \quad \frac{45}{100} = 0.45 \quad \frac{45}{1000} = 0.045$

2. Change the denominator to a power of ten:

$$\frac{2}{5} = \frac{4}{10} = 0.4$$

$$\frac{3}{20} = \frac{15}{100} = 0.15$$

$$\frac{1}{8} = \frac{125}{1000} = 0.125$$

3. Divide

$$\frac{3}{8} = 8\overline{)3}$$

Using the Math Explorer Calculator The Math Explorer calculator has the function [F⤺D] to change fractions to decimals or decimals to fractions in one step.

Example:

To change $\frac{1}{3}$ to a decimal, enter:

1/3 [F⤺D]

Display: 0.3333333

Some fraction sequences that children could write as decimals are presented in Activity 12-5. After they complete the activity, have children examine the sets of decimals for patterns. Discuss these patterns as a class.

When changing decimals to fractions, the Math Explorer calculator works only with terminating decimals (see next section).

Terminating and Repeating Decimals

When changing fractions to decimals by dividing, children will notice that some divide evenly, and others do not. In the case of even division, the decimals produced are said to be *terminating decimals.* In uneven division, the decimals produced are called *repeating decimals.* In a repeating decimal, the group of digits that repeats is known as the *repetend.* The repetend is indicated by a bar over the repeating digits.

Example:

$\frac{2}{3}$	0.666666 . . .	$0.\overline{6}$
$\frac{1}{12}$	0.0833333 . . .	$0.08\overline{3}$
$\frac{1}{7}$	0.142857142857 . . .	$0.\overline{142857}$

ACTIVITY 12-5 Converting Fractions to Decimals

Materials
Calculator

Procedure
Use a calculator to change several of the following fraction sequences to decimals. Look for patterns.

Write the decimals:

1. $\frac{1}{2}, \frac{1}{3}, \frac{1}{4}, \frac{1}{5}, \frac{1}{6}, \frac{1}{7}, \frac{1}{8}, \frac{1}{9}.$
2. $\frac{1}{3}, \frac{2}{3}, \frac{1}{4}, \frac{2}{4}, \frac{3}{4}, \frac{1}{5}, \frac{2}{5}, \frac{3}{5}, \frac{4}{5}.$
3. All the proper fractions with 7 as denominator.
4. $\frac{1}{13}, \frac{1}{17}, \frac{1}{19}, \frac{1}{23}, \frac{1}{29}, \frac{1}{37}.$
5. $\frac{1}{9}, \frac{2}{9}, \frac{3}{9}, \frac{4}{9}, \frac{5}{9}, \frac{6}{9}, \frac{7}{9}, \frac{8}{9}.$
6. $\frac{1}{11}, \frac{2}{11}, \frac{3}{11}, \frac{4}{11}, \frac{5}{11}, \ldots$

Conclusion

This chapter has described how to help children develop a conceptual understanding of decimals. The main goal of instruction is to develop an understanding of decimals in order to use them intelligently and effectively. Children should come to view decimals as an extension of place-value numeration and as an application of fractions. Activities in this chapter help children develop a good sense of decimals so that together with fractions, children are able to use these rational numbers to solve problems.

CHAPTER

12

Sample Lesson

A Lesson on Comparing Decimals

Grade level: Fourth

Materials: At least one decimal manipulative, such as base-ten blocks

Lesson objective: Students will use models to compare and order decimals.

Standards link: Students relate their understanding of fractions to comparing and ordering decimals. (NCTM *Curriculum Focal Points*, grade 4).

Launch: Write two decimal numbers, such as 0.73 and 0.8, on the board. Ask students, "which number is larger, and how do you know?" Ask students to think about it and write their answers and reasoning in their math journals.

Next, solicit recommendations about how to compare these two numbers, including using base-ten blocks to model each number. Discuss how to use base-ten blocks to represent decimal numbers. For example, if a flat represents one whole, a long represents one tenth and a small cube represents one hundredth.

Ask two students to come to the front of the room. Have each student represent one of the numbers with base-ten blocks. Display the blocks on the overhead projector or document camera. Then ask the class, "who has more and how do you know?" Discuss ways to determine which is more. In the example of 0.73 and 0.8, 0.8 is more because it has 8 tenths while 0.73 has 7 tenths and 3 hundredths. Discuss this result with students. Was it what they expected? Common error: Some students may have thought that 0.73 is more, because $73 > 8$. This common misunderstanding uses whole number reasoning to incorrectly compare two decimals less than one.

Explore: In pairs, have students compare each pair of numbers below and explain their thinking.

a. 0.6 0.16
b. 0.59 0.2
c. 0.30 0.3
d. 1.2 0.85
e. 4.7 4.70

Summarize: Coming together as a whole class, select pairs of students to come to the front of the room and explain how they compared one pair of numbers. Focus on their explanations of how they determined which number was larger and why.

FOLLOW-UP

Complete the following questions.

1. Consider any cautions regarding using base-ten blocks in this lesson. What other manipulatives might work well? Why? What would be the advantages and/or disadvantages of each manipulative?
2. Consider difficulties students might have with this concept and this lesson. What modification could you make to avoid or minimize these issues? What modifications could you make for students with special needs?
3. What might the *next* lesson focus on, and why?

IN PRACTICE

Complete the following activities to include in your professional portfolio.

1. Write a lesson to help children understand a decimal concept of your choice.
2. Write a lesson to introduce decimal computation (for an operation of your choice) by linking this topic to fraction computation.
3. Visit an intermediate-grade classroom and informally interview several children to assess their understanding of decimal concepts and computation. Write a short paper describing their understanding and discuss what you would do next if you were their classroom teacher.

PEARSON myeducationlab The Power of Classroom Practice Now go to Topic 9: "Decimal Concepts and Computation" in the MyEducationLab (www.myeducationlab.com) for your course, where you can:

- Find learning outcomes for "Decimal Concepts and Computation" along with the national standards that connect to these outcomes.
- Apply and practice your understanding of the core teaching skills identified in the chapter with a Building Teaching Skills and Dispositions learning unit.
- Complete Assignments and Activities that can help you understand the chapter content more deeply.
- Complete *enVision MATH* Sample Curricula assignments that allow you to examine and work with chapters from *enVision MATH*, a K-6 mathematics program.
- Check your comprehension on the content covered in the chapter by going to the Study Plan in the Book-Specific Resources for you text. Here you will be able to take a chapter quiz, receive feedback on your answers, and then access Review, Prectice, and Enrichment activities to enhance your understanding of chapter content.
- Go to the Book-Specific Resources for Chapter 12 to explore mathematical reasoning related to chapter content in the Activities section.

LINKS TO THE INTERNET

CyberChase

http://pbskids.org/cyberchase/games.html

Contains links to games and activities involving decimals. "Railroad Repair" is a fun game to practice adding decimals.

Decimal Games

www.gamequarium.com/decimals.html

Contains links to games and activities involving decimals. "Builder Ted" is a fun game using ordering decimals.

RESOURCES FOR TEACHERS

Children's Literature

Gifford, Scott (2003). *Piece = Part = Portion.* Berkeley, CA: Ten Speed Press.

Wells, Robert E. (1995). *What's Smaller Than a Pygmy Shrew?* Morton Grove, IL: Albert Whitman & Company.

Wilkinson, Elizabeth (1989). *Making Cents: Every Kid's Guide to Money.* London: Little Brown.

Books on Decimals

Bennett, A. (1982). *Decimal Squares: Step-by-Step Teacher's Guide.* Fort Collins, CO: Scott Resources.

Creative Publications. (1991). *Decimal factory.* Mountain View, CA.

Creative Publications. (1994). *Beyond Activities Project, Mathematics Replacement Curriculum: Getting to the Point! Investigating Decimals.* Mountain View, CA.

Glasgow, R., Ragan, G., Fields, W. M., Reys, R., & Wasman, D., (2000, October). The decimal dilemma. *Teaching Children Mathematics*, 7 (2), 89–93.

Kastberg, S. E., & Norton III A., (2007). Building a system of rational numbers. In Peter Kloosterman & Frank K. Lester, Jr. (Eds.), *Results and interpretations of the 2003 mathematics assessment of the National Assessment of Educational Progress*. Reston, VA: National Council of Teachers of Mathematics.

Mullis, I. V. S., Martin, M. O., Beaton, A. E., Gonzalez, E. J., Kelly, D. L., & Smith, T. A., (1997). *Mathematics achievement in the primary school years: IEA's Third International Mathematics and Science Study*. Chestnut Hill, MA: International Association for the Evaluation of Educational Achievement (IEA).

National Council of Teachers of Mathematics (2006). *Curriculum Focal Points for Prekindergarten through Grade 8 Mathematics*. Reston, VA: Author.

CHAPTER

13

Understanding Ratio, Proportion, and Percent

NCTM CONNECTING WITH THE STANDARDS

The National Council of Teachers of Mathematics (NCTM) Principles and Standards emphasizes the importance of children developing an understanding of proportionality, noting that it "connects many of the mathematics topics studied in grades 6–8" (NCTM, 2000, p. 216). The NCTM document goes on to note, "Facility with proportionality involves much more than setting two ratios equal and solving for a missing term. It involves recognizing quantities that are related proportionally and using numbers, tables, graphs, and equations to think about the quantities and their relationship" (NCTM, 2000, p. 216).

The NCTM (2006) *Curriculum Focal Points* mentions developing understanding of the meaning of ratio, proportions, and percents in two different grade levels. These concepts play an important role in seventh grade. The *Focal Points* state that seventh-grade students should:

- extend their work with ratios to develop an understanding of proportionality that they apply to solve single and multistep problems in numerous contexts;
- use ratio and proportionality to solve a wide variety of percent problems, including problems involving discounts, interest, taxes, tips, and percent increase or decrease;
- solve problems about similar objects (including figures) by using scale factors that relate corresponding lengths of the objects or by using the fact that relationships of lengths within an object are preserved in similar objects;
- graph proportional relationships and identify the unit rate as the slope of the related line; and
- distinguish proportional relationships ($y/x = k$, or $y = kx$) from other relationships, including inverse proportionality ($xy = k$, or $y = k/x$) (NCTM, 2006, p. 19).

Similarly, they state that eighth-grade students should "recognize a proportion ($y/x = k$, or $y = kx$) as a special case of a linear equation of the form $y = mx + b$, understanding that the constant of proportionality (k) is the slope and the resulting graph is a line through the origin" (NCTM, 2006, p. 20).

Developing Your Math Teaching Skills

When you have finished studying this chapter, you should be able to do the following:

- Find how ratios, rates, unit rates, proportions, and percents differ from one another.
- Notice real-world settings in which ratio, rate, unit rate, proportion, and percent are used.
- Recognize models that can be used to help children understand percents.

ASSESSING MATHEMATICS UNDERSTANDING

In order to become familiar with the mathematics concepts and procedures discussed in this chapter, take a few minutes and complete the following *Chapter 13 Preassessment.* Answer each question on your own. Then think about the possible misunderstandings or difficulties some elementary- and middle-school children might have when solving each problem. If you are able, administer this assessment to a child, and analyze his or her understanding of these topics.

Solve each problem. Think about how you get your answer.

1. Pizza Palace is having a special on medium pizzas, selling 2 pizzas for $8. Steve wants to buy 6 pizzas for a party. How much money will Steve spend on pizza?
2. Two candy bars cost $1. How much will 5 candy bars cost?
3. The map scale is 1 inch: 1,000 miles. If our destination is 3.5 inches away on the map, how many miles is that?
4. The speed limit is 65 miles per hour. How far will I travel if I drive the speed limit for 3 hours?
5. For each of the following, fill in the blank to make the number sentence true.

   a. 1/2 = __/6 **b.** 2/3 = 6/__
6. Basketball shoes are on sale at 20% off. How much will a pair of $80 shoes cost on sale?

Examining Classroom Practice

Ms. Cramer poses the following problem to her seventh-grade class:

> *Pizza Palace is having a special on medium pizzas, selling 2 pizzas for $8. Steve wants to buy 6 pizzas for a party. How much money will Steve spend on pizza?*

The children solve the problem by working in small groups, discussing the problem and possible solution strategies with their partners. Ms. Cramer circulates around the classroom, asking clarifying questions as the children work on the problem. After all the children have solved the problem, Ms. Cramer reconvenes the class as a whole group.

She begins by asking children to share their solution strategies and answers. Jeremy is the first to share his work:

> *2 pizzas cost $8, so 1 pizza costs $4. Then 6 pizzas cost $24, since 6 times $4 is $24.*

Jennifer solves the problem in another way:

> *2 pizzas cost $8, and Steve needed 6 pizzas, so he needs to buy 3 orders of 2 pizzas, and 3 times $8 per order is $24.*

Karen solves the problem in a third way:

> *I set up two fractions:*
>
> $\frac{2}{8} = \frac{6}{n}$
>
> *And solved for n.*
>
> $2n = 48$
>
> *So* $n = 24$

Think about the ways these three children solve this problem. Notice that Jeremy uses the cost for 1 pizza, which is known as the *unit rate,* to find the cost for 6 pizzas. Jennifer looks at the problem from a different perspective, focusing on comparing the number Steve needed to buy with the number offered in one order. She noted that Steve needed *three times as many* pizzas as are in one order. Karen solves the problem a third way, using the *cross multiplication* procedure often taught in textbooks. What do children need to understand about ratios and proportions to be able to use each method?

Analyzing Assessment Results

Now look at the results from the preassessment. All of these problems involve ratios, proportions, or percents. What was your general reaction to solving the problems? Did they all seem to be equally difficult, or were some problems easier for you to think about? Did using counters or drawing pictures help make sense of the problem? What aspects of problems do you think make them easier for children to solve? What in general do you think a teacher's goals should be regarding developing meaning of these concepts? If you had a chance to give the *Chapter 13 Preassessment* to a child, take a few minutes and analyze the results. How did the child solve these problems? How did the child think about these problems?

Analyze each problem. How did you (and/or the student you administered the assessment to) solve each of the following problems? Let's look at problem 1 first.

1. Pizza Palace is having a special on medium pizzas, selling 2 pizzas for $8. Steve wants to buy 6 pizzas for a party. How much money will Steve spend on pizza?

Comments: This problem can be solved in at least two ways. One way is to find the cost for 1 pizza ($4), and then multiply by 6 to get the total cost, $24. Another way is to notice that Steve is buying 3 groups of 2 pizzas for $8, so his cost would be 3 x $8 or $24. Both ways work fine in this case. The first method always works, though it will sometimes take longer than the second method. The second method works particularly well when the quantities are multiples; for example, his desired amount of 6 pizzas is 3 times the quantity (2 pizzas) stated in the price. Which way did you solve the problem?

2. Two candy bars cost $1. How much will 5 candy bars cost?

3. The map scale is 1 inch: 1,000 miles. If our destination is 3.5 inches away on the map, how many miles is that?

4. The speed limit is 65 miles per hour. How far will I travel if I drive the speed limit for 3 hours?

Comments: These problems are similar to the first problem. All involve presenting one rate and asking to complete another rate. Can you identify the rates in each problem? How can estimation help you solve these problems?

5. For each of the following, fill in the blank to make the number sentence true.

   a. $\frac{1}{2}$ = __/6　　　**b.** $\frac{2}{3}$ = 6/__

Comments: These problems are typical proportion problems. What method(s) did you use to solve the problems? How do these problems compare with Problems 1–4? All of these problems are proportional reasoning problems, but Problem 5 is presented symbolically rather than as a word problem. Were any of the problems easier than others to solve? Why?

6. Basketball shoes are on sale at 20% off. How much will a pair of $80 shoes cost on sale?

Comments: This is a typical percent problem. How did you solve it? What are some common student errors? Students sometimes will find the amount of discount or savings, which is $16 in this problem, and stop there, forgetting that the problem asked for the sale price.

Take a minute and reflect on this assessment. Were some problems easier than others? What factors made them easier? What do you want to learn more about in order to help children understand these concepts?

Common Student Misunderstandings About Ratio Proportion, and Percents

- Lack of understanding of and familiarity with different problem situations.
- Using procedures without thinking about the reasonableness of answers.
- Ending the solution process without answering the question stated in the problem.

Are there any other misunderstandings that children may have about ratio, proportion, and percents? It's important to assess what children understand, and are still working on understanding, in order to plan instruction that meets their needs.

Building on Assessment Results

Think about what we can do to help strengthen children's understandings and minimize (and hopefully eradicate) their misunderstandings and misconceptions.

Sometimes teaching about ratio, proportion, and percents focuses on memorizing rules and procedures and producing answers quickly. While we want students to learn rules and procedures, they also need to understand the concepts. This will enable them to make sense of problem situations and decide if their answers make sense. So what might we do next to help students understand these concepts?

The first step is to help students understand the problem situation and relationships. This usually is best done by posing problems set in familiar, meaningful situations and by asking students to examine the reasonableness of their solutions. The table below lists several common misunderstandings and what a teacher can do to help children with these misunderstandings.

Being able to make sense of problem situations such as the pizza problem at the start of this chapter requires that children have many experiences making sense of similar situations. Notice that the children in this class approach the problem in many different ways, making sense of the situation, with each getting the correct answer.

Children's experience in working with rational numbers helps develop their understanding of and ability to reason proportionally. Ratio, proportion, and percent are important topics in the mathematics program of the middle-school grades. Meaningful instruction builds on and extends children's understanding of fractions and decimals and emphasizes problem solving and applications in real-world situations. This chapter discusses how to help children understand the concepts of ratio, proportion, and percent.

IF students think that . . .	THEN have students . . .
solving problems means just pulling out the numbers and doing something to them	*model* the problem with a manipulative material, and *ask* if their answers make sense.
there is only one way to solve these problems	*share* their solution strategies, modeling other methods as needed.
solving problems means doing one operation and then stopping	*focus* on whether they are answering the question asked in the problem.

Ratio and Rate

A *ratio* is a comparison of two numbers or quantities. Real-world examples involving the ratio concept include the following:

Two candy bars cost 97¢.

The map scale is 1 inch: 1,000 miles.

The speed limit is 65 miles per hour.

Sales tax is 7%.

As you can see from the examples above, the ratio concept arises in many familiar situations and in several different mathematical contexts. When the measuring units describing two quantities being compared are different, the ratio is called a *rate.* Many everyday examples involve speed (Lisa ran 100 m in 12 sec) or price (12 ears of corn cost $2.50). When the second term is 1, the rate is referred to as the *unit rate.* For example, typing 40 words per minute and earning $5.50 per hour are unit rates.

In the early grades, children learn about comparison subtraction situations. In intermediate grades, ratio is introduced as another way of comparing two quantities. For example, given 6 balls and 3 bats, we could say that there are 3 more balls than bats, but we also note that there are twice as many balls as bats or that there are 2 balls for every bat. The idea of ratio involves *multiplicative* rather than additive comparisons.

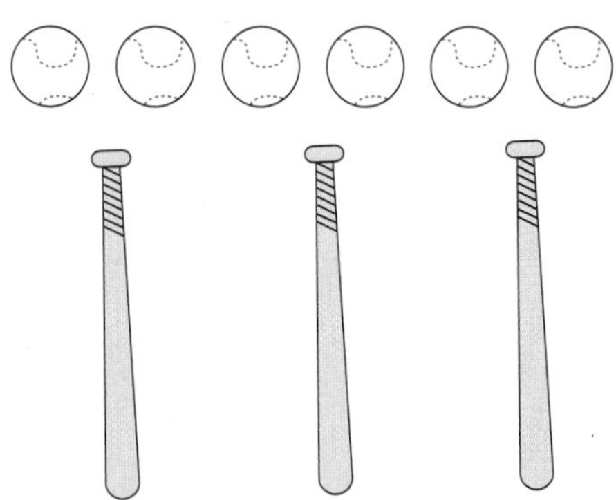

There has been a disappointingly low level of understanding about ratio and proportion among children in the United States (Cramer, Post, & Currier, 1993; Hoffer & Hoffer, 1992). The seventh National Assessment of Educational Progress (NAEP) also noted a low level of success by eighth- and twelfth-graders (Wearne & Kouba, 2000) on proportional reasoning problems. For example, only 12% of the eighth-graders tested were able to use proportions or rates to solve a problem, and only 1% of them were able to compare amounts using proportions and justify their answers. These results indicate that we need to place more emphasis on understanding and reasonableness when teaching children about ratio and proportion.

PEARSON myeducationlab The Power of Classroom Practice Go to the Assignments and Activities section of Topic 10: "Ratio, Proportion, and Percent" in the MyEducationLab for your course and complete the activity "Rate and Ratio." How does the teacher introduce the concepts of rate and ratio?

Language and Notation

To introduce the language and notation of ratio and proportion, a teacher might refer to a picture or a sketch of 3 pelicans and 2 frogs such as the one shown on page 286. The children are told that the *ratio* of pelicans to frogs in this picture is 3 to 2 and that this can be written 3:2 or $\frac{3}{2}$. They can then be asked to state and write the ratio of frogs to pelicans (2:3) and the ratio of pelicans to animals (3:5). Note that this last ratio is a *part-to-whole comparison,* whereas the other two are *part-to-part comparisons.* The two numbers in a ratio are referred to as the *first term* and the *second term.*

Ratio and Rational Number

Number and ratio are different concepts, but the word *rational* and the use of the fraction symbol for a ratio suggest that there are overlapping elements. Because a fraction

represents a part-to-whole relationship, fractions are types of ratios. In the previous example, the ratio of pelicans to animals is 3 to 5 and three-fifths of the animals are pelicans. The two ideas are essentially the same and both are represented by the symbol $\frac{3}{5}$. However, 2 frogs to 3 pelicans is a part-to-part comparison and, in this situation, the ratio 2 to 3 is quite different from the fraction $\frac{2}{3}$. This sort of comparison is usually more difficult for children to understand, probably because they have much more experience with part-whole relationships. Also notice that although the ratios 2 to 3 and 3 to 2 can both be used to express the relationship between the numbers of pelicans and frogs in this example, the fractions $\frac{2}{3}$ and $\frac{3}{2}$ name different rational numbers.

Children should also understand that combining ratios is not the same as adding fractions. For example, suppose there are 2 boys and 3 girls in one group and 3 boys and 4 girls in another group. If the two groups joined, the ratio of boys to girls would be 5 to 7. However, the sum of the numbers $\frac{2}{3}$ and $\frac{3}{4}$ is definitely not $\frac{5}{7}$! Similarly, the ratio of boys to children could be expressed as $\frac{5}{12}$, but it would be incorrect to write $\frac{2}{5} + \frac{3}{7} = \frac{5}{12}$. Arithmetic operations such as addition are performed on numbers, not on ratios.

Proportion

Aaron reasons:

If three oranges cost sixty cents, then six oranges would cost one dollar twenty cents, and one orange would cost twenty cents.

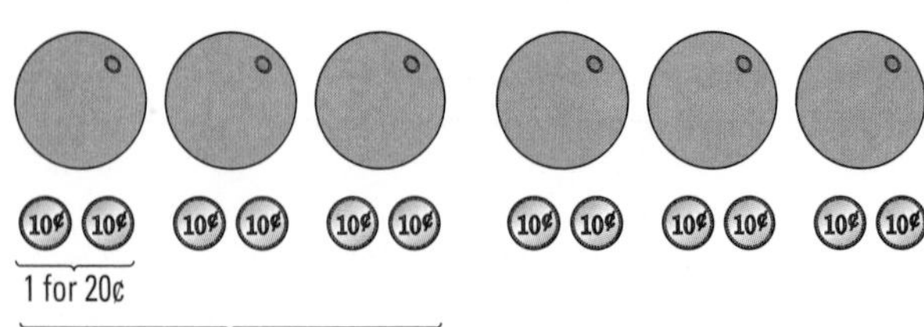

A *proportion* is a statement that two ratios are equal. Finding unit rates and making scale drawings are examples of proportion problems.

> myeducationlab — The Power of Classroom Practice. Go to the Assignments and Activities section of Topic 10: "Ratio, Proportion, and Percent" in the MyEducationLab for your course. Complete the activity "Proportion" to see how a teacher explains proportion.

Proportional Reasoning

The ability to understand ratios is one aspect of *proportional reasoning,* which is considered to be an indicator of a shift from concrete to formal operational levels of thought. Proportional reasoning involves both qualitative and quantitative thinking and concerns prediction and multiple comparisons (Lesh, Post, & Behr, 1989).

Ratio is a difficult concept because it involves a relationship between two quantities. At first, children tend to focus on only one of the parts of a ratio. Quintero (1987) found that many 9-year-olds predicted that 6 tablespoons of white sugar mixed with 8 tablespoons of brown sugar would be lighter in color than 3 tablespoons of white sugar mixed with 4 tablespoons of brown sugar, because 6 is larger than 3.

Considerable research has been conducted to investigate children's thinking as they solve proportion problems. A version of one widely used task, "Mr. Short and Mr. Tall" (Karplus, Karplus, & Wollman, 1974), is described in Figure 13-1. On items such as this, many children use an incorrect addition strategy, focusing on the difference between the numbers rather than on their ratio. Because Mr. Tall is 2 buttons taller than Mr. Short, students who use an additive strategy think that Mr. Tall will be 8 paper clips high, because $6 + 2 = 8$. Even children who have been taught ratio and proportion will sometimes use this method, particularly if the ratio involved is not a simple one such as 1:2.

On easy proportion questions, some children will consistently use repeated addition rather than multiplication. Consider the following problem:

Snakes are fed according to their length. If the 5-inch-long snake is fed 2 cubes of food, how many cubes of food should the 10-inch and 15-inch snakes be fed?

FIGURE 13-1 Using Ratios to Find the Height of Mr. Tall and Mr. Short

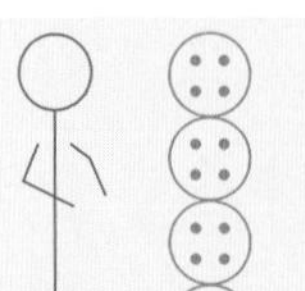

Mr. Short (shown) is 4 buttons high.
Mr. Tall (not shown) is 6 buttons high.
Use paper clips to measure Mr. Short (6).
How many paper clips high will Mr. Tall be?

NCTM NUMBER AND OPERATIONS STANDARDS AND EXPECTATIONS ADDRESSED IN THIS CHAPTER		
Instructional programs from Pre-K–12 should enable all students to—	**In grades 3–5 all students should—** (NCTM, 2000, p. 148)	**In grades 6–8 all students should—** (NCTM, 2000, p. 214)
• understand numbers, ways of representing numbers, relationships among numbers, and number systems. • compute fluently and make reasonable estimates.	• recognize and generate equivalent forms of commonly used fractions, decimals, and percents.	• work flexibly with fractions, decimals, and percents to solve problems. • compare and order fractions, decimals, and percents efficiently and find their approximate locations on a number line. • develop meaning for percents greater than 100 and less than 1. • understand and use ratios and proportions to represent quantitative relationships. • develop, analyze, and explain methods for solving problems involving proportions, such as scaling and finding equivalent ratios.

NCTM Principles and Standards Link 13-1

Content Strand: Number and Operations

As different ways to think about proportions are considered and discussed, teachers should help students recognize when and how various ways of reasoning about proportions might be appropriate to solve problems. (NCTM, 2000, p. 220)

A common solution is to add 2 cubes of food for the 10-inch snake and 2 more for the 15-inch snake, rather than multiplying 2 times 2 and 3 times 2 (Hart, 1989). Children who use addition rather than multiplication often have difficulty solving proportions involving more complex relationships. Children may begin solving problems such as this by adding, but encourage them to use multiplication, which will be more useful in more complicated problems.

Equal Ratios

Beginning experiences for equal ratios include activities involving number patterns and repeated addition. For example, children in the early grades could be asked to make a table showing the relationship between the number of horses and the number of legs. The children might use toy animals to make sketches in solving the problem.

number of horses	1	2	3	4	5
number of legs	4	8	12	–	–

It is important that older children see the multiplicative relationship in the number pairs. They should be able to use multiplication directly to determine how many legs 9 horses have and to use division directly to figure out the number of horses that have a total of 28 legs. Ask questions such as "If a video costs four dollars to rent, how much would it cost to rent seven videos?" and "If three movie tickets cost fifteen dollars, how much would one ticket cost?"

As children examine the horses and legs table on this page, they should note that if 1 horse has 4 legs, then 2 horses have 8 legs, and so on. The teacher states that the ratios 1 to 4 and 2 to 8 are *equal* and writes:

$$1{:}4 = 2{:}8 \text{ or } \frac{1}{4} = \frac{2}{8}$$

Encourage children to discover and describe the procedure for generating equal ratios: Multiply both terms by the same number. They should also explore what happens when the same number is added to both terms and conclude that the resulting ratios are usually not equal. For example:

$$\frac{1}{4} \neq \frac{(1+2)}{(4+2)}$$

Children will likely see the connection with the rule for writing equivalent fractions. The use of the same notation for ratios and fractions could be discussed in this context. One can find a ratio in lower terms by dividing both terms by the same number. Many children will notice the connection to the procedure for simplifying fractions. This idea is used in finding a unit rate, as in the following problem.

Brian types 100 words in 4 minutes. How many words is that per minute?

Because $\frac{100}{4} = \frac{25}{1}$, *the unit rate is 25 words per minute.*

In Activity 13-1, children write equal ratios suggested by a diagram.

ACTIVITY 13-1 Marble Ratios

Manipulative Strategies

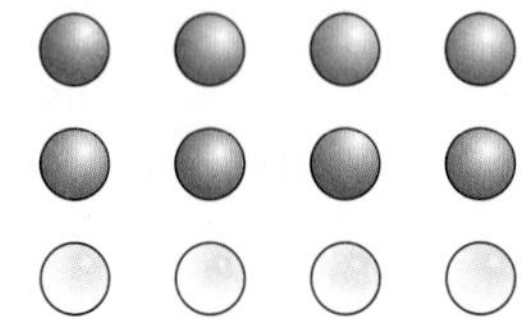

- What is the ratio of blue marbles to white marbles in the picture? Can you write the ratio in more than one way?
- Now write the ratio of blue marbles to all marbles in as many ways as you can.

Introductory questions that require children to find a missing term in a pair of equal ratios should involve only whole-number multiplication, as in the following problem:

If the ratio of children to adults is 17 to 2 and there are 6 adults, how many children are there?

If we let n *represent the number of children,* $\frac{17}{2} = \frac{n}{6}$.

Because $6 = 2 \times 3$, $n = 17 \times 3 = 51$. *There are 51 children.*

Comparing Ratios

Which mixture will be lighter in color: 3 parts white sugar to 5 parts brown sugar or 2 parts white sugar to 3 parts brown sugar? Questions such as this can be used to encourage children to rename the two ratios so that they have the same second term. So to compare $\frac{3}{5}$ and $\frac{2}{3}$, we might look at $\frac{9}{15}$ and $\frac{10}{15}$. We conclude that the ratio of white to brown sugar is greater in the second mixture because $\frac{10}{15}$ is greater than $\frac{9}{15}$. The second mixture will be slightly lighter in color, although this might be difficult to notice with the naked eye.

This is, of course, the same procedure as that learned for comparing two fractions. A common second term, or denominator is a common multiple of the two second terms, or denominators. In some cases, it is easiest to use the least common multiple. For example, to compare $\frac{3}{4}$ and $\frac{5}{8}$, we would likely consider $\frac{6}{8}$ and $\frac{5}{8}$, and for $\frac{3}{4}$ and $\frac{5}{6}$ we might write $\frac{9}{12}$ and $\frac{10}{12}$. However, children should appreciate that any common multiple of the two second terms will work and that a particularly easy one to find is the product of the two numbers. So $\frac{3}{4}$ and $\frac{5}{6}$ could also be compared as $\frac{18}{24}$ and $\frac{20}{24}$, where 24 is the product of 4 and 6.

In a basketball game Amy made 3 of 5 free throws and Diane made 4 of 7 attempts. Which performance was better?

We write equal ratios with 5×7 *as the second term.*

$$\frac{3}{5} \quad \frac{4}{7}$$

$$\frac{3 \times 7}{5 \times 7} \quad \frac{5 \times 4}{5 \times 7}$$

$$\frac{21}{35} \quad \frac{20}{35}$$

Amy's shooting was slightly better than Diane's.

Number sense reasoning, which is similar to that used in comparing fractions, can also be used to compare ratios. For example, the relations $\frac{4}{7} > \frac{4}{9}$, $\frac{5}{6} < \frac{6}{7}$, and $\frac{3}{5} > \frac{4}{9}$ are true whether the symbols apply to fractions or to ratios. Although these relations can be verified by computing equal ratios, children should be challenged to use quantitative explanations. A child might think about the preceding relations as follows: 4 hits out of 7 times at bat is better than 4 hits out of 9; if I have made 5 of 6 free throws during a game and make my next one, I will be 6 for 7; 3 out of 5 is more than half, whereas 4 out of 9 is less than half.

Cross Products

Given several pairs of equal ratios such as $\frac{3}{6} = \frac{5}{10}$, children can be challenged to find a relationship among the four terms. They should be able to discover that the *cross products* of equal fractions are equal: $3 \times 10 = 6 \times 5$.

Children should also be able to explain why this relationship holds. Comparing $\frac{3}{6}$ and $\frac{5}{10}$ by finding equal ratios with 60 as the second term, we multiply both terms of the first ratio by 10 and both terms of the second ratio by 6, giving 3×10 and 6×5, respectively, as the first terms. So computing cross products provides a simple test for determining whether two ratios (or fractions) are equal. We can tell, for example, that $\frac{2}{3}$ is not equal to $\frac{3}{4}$ because 2×4 is not equal to 3×3.

Also, if three of the four terms in a proportion are given, the fourth can be found by using the cross-product relationship. This method is particularly useful when the ratio between two fractions is not a whole number.

If 3 pounds of apples cost \$4.00, how many pounds could you get for \$6.00?

$\frac{3}{4} = \frac{n}{6}$

$4 \times n = 3 \times 6 = 18$; $n = 18 \div 4 = 4.5$.

You would get 4.5 pounds.

NCTM Principles and Standards Link 13-2

Content Strand: Number and Operations

Instruction in solving proportions should include methods that have a strong intuitive basis. The so-called cross-multiplication method can be developed meaningfully if it arises naturally in students' work, but it can also have unfortunate side effects when students do not adequately understand when the method is appropriate to use. Other approaches to solving proportions are often more intuitive and also quite powerful. (NCTM, 2000, p. 220)

Notice that instead of considering the pounds-to-dollar ratios, we could have written the proportion $\frac{3}{n} = \frac{4}{6}$, which relates the pound-to-pound ratio and the dollar-to-dollar ratio. Two other proportions that model this situation and lead to the same computations are created by interchanging the first and second terms: $\frac{4}{3} = \frac{6}{n}$ and $\frac{n}{3} = \frac{6}{4}$.

A more direct way to solve the first proportion above is to reason that because 6 is 1.5 times 4, $n = 3 \times 1.5 = 4.5$. But in most real-life situations the numbers are large or "messy" and the cross-product method, along with using a calculator to perform the multiplication and division, is the most efficient procedure. In the previous example, the apples would more likely be priced at 3 pounds for \$3.95 rather than \$4.00.

Most of the proportion problems in the intermediate grades should be able to be solved without using cross products. Although the cross-product algorithm is a powerful tool, children should appreciate that many problems can be solved in more than one way and be encouraged to look for alternative solutions. See Activity 13-2 and the soup problem that follows.

ACTIVITY 13-2 Travel On

Solve the following problem in at least two different ways:

A car travels 212 km in 4 hours. At this rate of speed, how far would it travel in 7 hours?

> *A recipe for soup for 8 people calls for 6 onions. How many onions should be used to make enough soup for 12 people?*
>
> $\frac{8}{6} = \frac{12}{n}$
>
> *Then* $8n = 6 \times 12 = 72$, *so* $n = 9$
>
> *Therefore, 9 onions are needed.*

There are several things that a class can discuss after examining this solution. First, the proportion $\frac{8}{6} = \frac{12}{n}$ can be solved without using cross products. One solution method is to notice that $\frac{8}{6} = \frac{4}{3}$ and consider $\frac{4}{3} = \frac{12}{n}$. Because $12 = 4 \times 3$, $n = 3 \times 3$ or 9. Second, we could have also considered the ratios, 8 people to 12 people and 6 onions to n onions, and written the proportion $\frac{8}{12} = \frac{6}{n}$. Two other proportions describing the same situation are $\frac{6}{8} = \frac{n}{12}$ and $\frac{12}{8} = \frac{n}{6}$. In all three cases, the numerical ratio can be simplified. Finally, we could reason that because there are 4 more people and 4 is half of 8, you would make a recipe and a half. Therefore, you would need 6 plus 3 onions.

Scale Drawings

Reading maps and floor plans, enlarging or reducing pictures, and finding corresponding dimensions of similar geometric figures all involve the idea of a *scale.* A scale drawing is a smaller or larger representation of an object. The scale is the ratio of a dimension in the drawing to the corresponding dimension of the actual object. Three sample problems and solutions follow.

> *Below is a scale drawing of a bee. Find the bee's actual length.*

Scale $\frac{3}{1}$

The length of the bee in the scale drawing is about 48 mm. Therefore the bee's length is one-third of 48 mm, which is about 16 mm. The related proportion is $\frac{3}{1} = \frac{48}{n}$.

> *The scale on a city street map reads "1 in. = 3 miles."*
>
> *1:3*
>
> *Find the distance between two schools 7 inches apart on the map.*

Seven inches represents 7×3 miles $= 21$ miles. So the schools are about 21 miles apart. The related proportion is $\frac{1}{3} = \frac{7}{n}$.

> *In the following diagram, the second triangle is an enlargement of the first. Find the scale ratio of the enlargement and compute the length of the longest side of the larger triangle.*

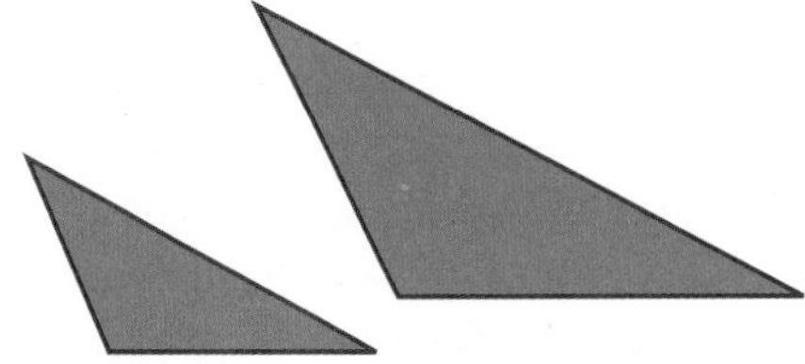

Using a ruler, we find that the bases of the triangles measure 2 cm and 3 cm. So the scale ratio for the enlargement is 3:2 (or 150%). Measuring the longest side of the smaller triangle, we find that its length is 3 cm. We can find the length of the corresponding side (the longest side) of the enlarged triangle using a proportion, and then compare the answer with the measured length.

$\frac{2}{3} = \frac{3}{n}$

The length is 4.5 cm.

Comparison Shopping

Deciding which size of package is the best buy is another type of problem involving ratios that can be solved in several ways. Consider the following example about finding the best buy for bread at a local supermarket.

> *A 16-ounce loaf of bread costs \$1.99, and a 24-ounce loaf costs \$2.49. Which loaf of bread is the better buy?*

The unit price is the cost of 1 ounce of bread. The unit price of the smaller loaf is $\frac{\$1.99}{16} = \$0.12$ per ounce, and the unit price of the larger loaf is $\frac{\$2.49}{24} = \$0.10$ per ounce. Because the larger loaf has a lower unit price, it is the better buy.

This solution involves complex calculations that would usually be done using a calculator. A shopper in a store might use mental arithmetic to solve this problem as follows: The 16-ounce loaf is 1 pound and the 24-ounce loaf is $1\frac{1}{2}$ pounds. One-and-a-half of the smaller loaves would cost \$1.99 plus half of \$1.99, which is about \$2 + \$1 = \$3. The larger loaf costs only \$2.49, which is less than \$3, so the larger loaf is the better buy. See Activity 13-3 for a similar activity.

The class should discuss why the largest size package does not always have the lowest unit price and also why the lowest unit price might not always represent the "best buy."

ACTIVITY 13-3 Buying Potatoes

Realia Strategies

A 10-lb. bag of potatoes costs \$1.49, and a 25-lb. bag costs \$2.99.

- Determine which is the better buy in at least two different ways.
- Discuss your conclusion.

Percent

Percents are used in many everyday situations. Unfortunately, they are also often used incorrectly. For example, a store advertises prices reduced by 100%, rather than 50%; an interest rate of .13% is offered, rather than 13%; and a newspaper reports murders up by 200%, which is correct, but a little misleading, since they went from 1 to 3. As with ratio and proportion, we need to devote increased emphasis to understanding and reasonableness when teaching about percents.

Meaning and Notation

The term *percent* means "parts per hundred." Notice that the second part of the word, *cent,* is connected with 100: There are 100 cents in a dollar and 100 years in a century. A *percent* is a part-to-whole ratio that has 100 as its second term. For example, you could teach students that seven percent means seven parts per hundred, which is written 7:100, or $\frac{7}{100}$. Then introduce the notation 7%, noting the connection between the percent symbol and the numeral 100—the percent symbol has 2 zeros and a slash that can be thought of as indicating "per 100."

7 per hundred

7 percent

7:100

7%

A 7% tax on a \$100 item is \$7. The \$100 is referred to as the *base,* 7% is the *rate,* and \$7 is the *percentage.* Because percents are part-to-whole ratios, they can also be thought of as fractions with denominators of 100. Expressed as common or decimal fractions, percents can be treated as numbers and used in arithmetic computations.

Number Sense

Introductory activities should help children develop visual images and develop a quantitative feel for numbers expressed as percents. At the concrete level, use base-ten blocks, with the flat representing 100 percent, and place small cubes on the flat to represent various percents. For example, 7 small cubes placed on the flat would show 7%. At the pictorial level, children can shade squares on a 10-by-10 grid to represent various percents (Figure 13-2 and Blackline Master 12).

Place special emphasis on developing understanding of the benchmarks of 1%, 50%, and 100%. Other important benchmarks are 10% and 25%. Children naturally come to associate these ratios with their corresponding common fractions. Percents less than 1 (such as $\frac{1}{2}$%) and percents greater than 100 (such as 150%) can also be represented using the grid model (Figure 13-3).

The following activities, which use an unmarked rectangle, can help children develop estimation skills with percents.

1. Shade about 50%, 10%, 75%, 2%, 97%, 35% of each rectangle.

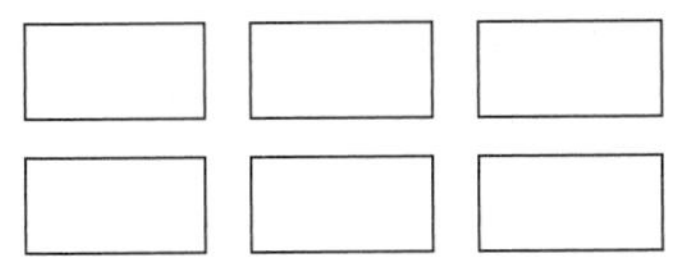

2. About what percent has been shaded in each rectangle?

Fraction and Decimal Equivalents

A key idea in mathematics is that numbers can be represented in many ways. A rational number can be expressed as a fraction, a decimal, or a percent. As children show percents on a 10-by-10 grid and reflect on the language they use to describe their representations, the fraction and decimal names for the numbers will become apparent. For example, because 9% means 9 out of 100, it is nine-hundredths, which is written $\frac{9}{100}$ in fraction notation and 0.09 in decimal notation.

9% nine-hundredths 0.09

Further, $150\% = \frac{150}{100} = 1.5 = \frac{3}{2} = 1\frac{1}{2}$

Decimals as percents. Writing a decimal as a percent involves finding an equivalent decimal in hundredths. For example,

three-tenths = thirty-hundredths = thirty percent
0.3 = 0.30 = 30%

Generalizing from examples such as 17 hundredths = 17 percent (0.17 = 17%), children find that to change a decimal to a percent, one multiplies by 100, which means "moving" the decimal point two places to the right. So 0.135 = 13.5% and 9.1 = 910%. To express a percent as a decimal, the opposite rule is employed: Divide by 100. So 6.9% = 0.069.

Fractions as percents. Children can be challenged to apply their understanding to find ways of writing a fraction as a percent. A basic method is to find an equivalent fraction having a denominator of 100. For example,

$$\frac{2}{5} = \frac{40}{100} = 40\%$$

Another method is to first write the fraction in decimal form and then multiply this number by 100. Children may decide to find the decimal equivalent by first dividing the numerator by the denominator and then multiplying by 100: 2 ÷ 5 = 0.4 = 40%. Multiplying the numerator by 100 before dividing by the denominator would give the same answer: 200 ÷ 5 = 40, which means 40%.

$$\begin{array}{r} 0.4 \\ 5\overline{)2.0} \\ \underline{2.0} \\ 0 \end{array} \qquad \begin{array}{r} 40 \\ 5\overline{)200} \\ \underline{20} \\ 00 \end{array}$$

FIGURE 13-2 Using a 10-by-10 Grid to Represent Percents

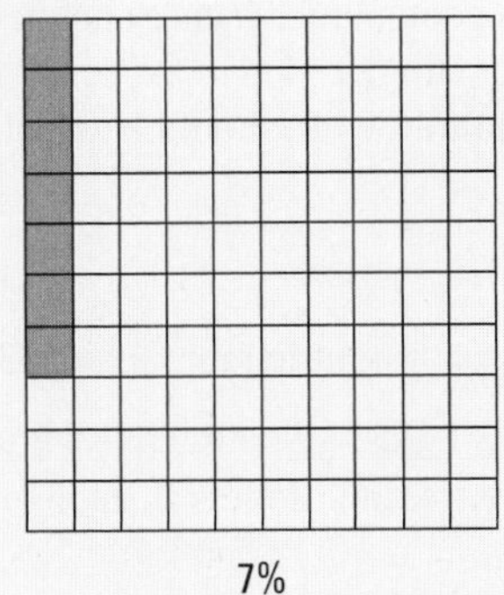

7%

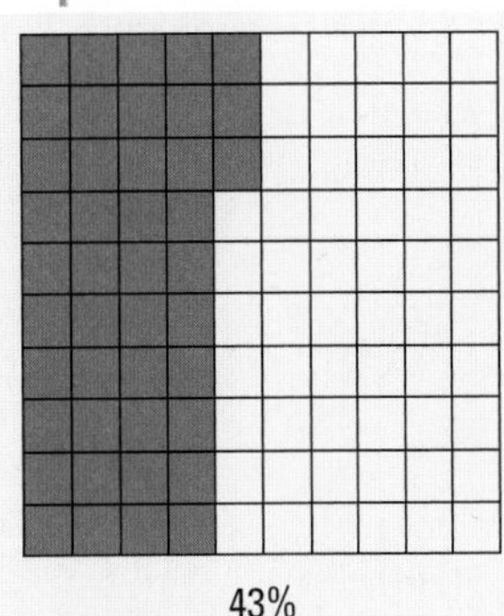

43%

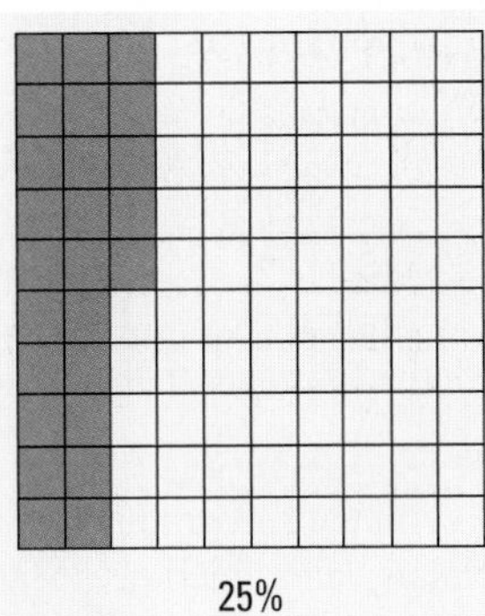

25%

FIGURE 13-3 Using 10-by-10 Grids to Represent Percents Less Than 1% and Greater Than 100%

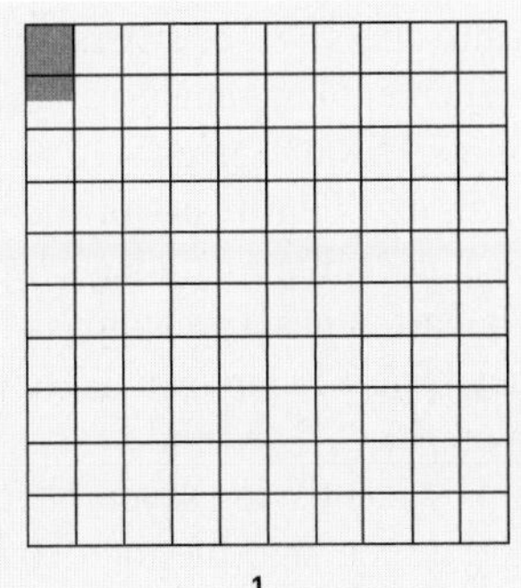

$1\frac{1}{2}$ %

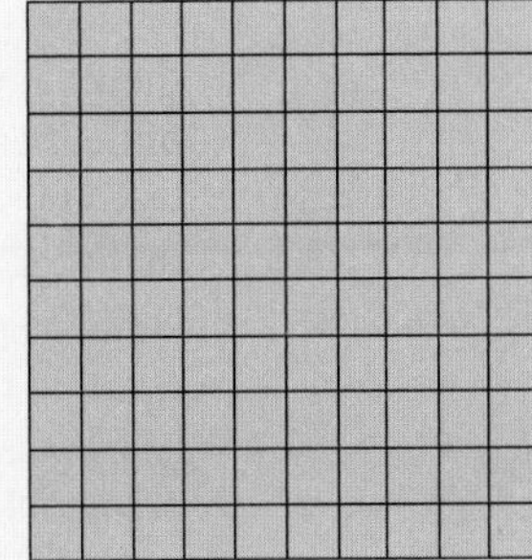

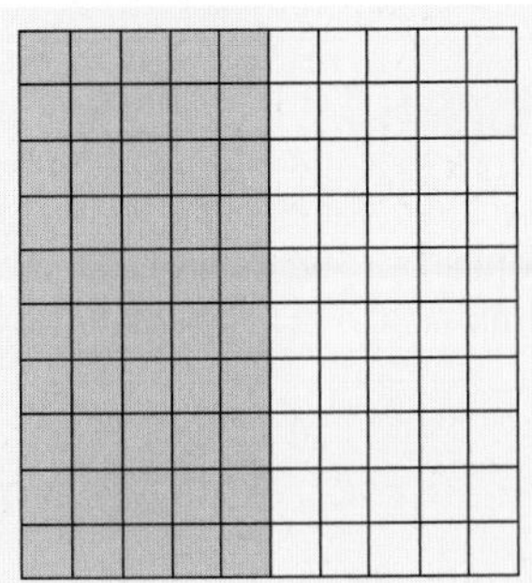

150%

In most cases the computation would be carried out with the aid of a calculator. To express $\frac{3}{8}$ as a percent, press 3 ÷ 8 = and mentally multiply the answer 0.375 by 100. Alternatively, pressing 300 ÷ 8 = gives 37.5. Children can later be shown that on most simple calculators, pressing 3 ÷ 8% gives 37.5 directly.

Some fractions have repeating decimal representations. When children try to shade $\frac{1}{3}$ of 100 squares, they find they shade 33 whole squares and a third of one square. So $\frac{1}{3} = 33\frac{1}{3}\%$. Rounding to the nearest whole number, we say that $\frac{1}{3}$ is about 33%. Calculators should be used to help find approximate percent equivalents for fractions with repeating decimal representations. For example,

$$\frac{5}{12} = 0.410666\ldots, \text{ which a child might round to } 42\%$$

Percents as fractions. Expressing a percent as a fraction with a denominator of 100 can be done by using the definition of percent: for example, $67\% = \frac{67}{100}$. In some cases, the resulting fraction can be written in simpler form:

$$8\% = \frac{8}{100} = \frac{2}{25}$$

$$87.5\% = \frac{87.5}{100} = \frac{875}{1{,}000} = \frac{7}{8}$$

The Math Explorer calculator (Texas Instruments) is programmed to carry out these computations.

KEYSTROKES	DISPLAY
87.5%	0.875
F⊃D	$\frac{875}{1000}$
Simp =	$\frac{175}{200}$
Simp =	$\frac{35}{40}$
Simp =	$\frac{7}{8}$

Several computer programs deal with equivalent percents, decimals, and fractions. Math Rummy (Brown, 1973), for example, provides practice in recognizing fraction, decimal, and percent names of common numbers.

> PEARSON myeducationlab The Power of Classroom Practice — To explore your own understanding of percents, go to the Chapter 13 in the Book-Specific Resources section in the MyEducationLab for your course. Select the Activities section and complete the activity "Math Rummy."

Finding the Percent of a Number

Computing sales tax, discount, commission, and interest are examples of everyday situations involving finding a percent of a number. To help children understand that the operation involved is multiplication, a problem such as the following might be presented:

In our class of 28 children, 50% went skiing during winter break. How many of our class members went skiing?

Children know that 50% is one-half and that one-half of 28 can be expressed by $\frac{1}{2} \times 28$. The general procedure then is to express the percent in either fraction or decimal form and multiply by the other given number.

Early examples should involve percents that have simple fraction or decimal equivalents (such as 50%, 25%, 10%, 200%), together with numbers chosen so that the computation can be carried out using mental arithmetic procedures for multiplying a whole number by a unit fraction or power of 10.

$$\begin{aligned}
50\% \text{ of } 28 &= \tfrac{1}{2} \times 28 = 14\\
25\% \text{ of } 80 &= \tfrac{1}{4} \times 80 = 20\\
10\% \text{ of } 70 &= \tfrac{1}{10} \times 70 = 7\\
100\% \text{ of } 63 &= 1 \times 63 = 63\\
200\% \text{ of } 45 &= 2 \times 45 = 90\\
30\% \text{ of } 80 &= 0.3 \times 80 = 24\\
10\% \text{ of } 235 &= 0.1 \times 235 = 23.5\\
1\% \text{ of } 469 &= 0.01 \times 469 = 4.69
\end{aligned}$$

Because most real-life computations will be carried out using a calculator, it is important for children to be able to estimate answers and judge the reasonableness of results. This requires good number sense and the ability to do mental arithmetic with rounded or "special" numbers. Examples such as the following should be discussed and practiced.

49% of 85	about $\frac{1}{2}$ of 84
102% of 543	a little more than 543
31% of 68	about $\frac{1}{3}$ of 69 or 0.3×70
9.5% of 752	a little less than 75

To estimate a 6% sales tax on a purchase of \$135.97, the shopper might think: 10% is about \$14; 6% would be a bit more than half or about \$8. With a calculator: $135.97 \times 0.06 = 8.1582$; the tax is \$8.16. Later, children learn that they can use the percent key rather than the decimal form of the percent: $135.97 \times 6\%$ gives 8.1582 directly.

Shopping is an excellent real-world context for practicing percents. For example, students working in pairs could be given department store catalogs (and calculators) and told that they have \$400 to spend. They could assume a 20% discount on prices listed and 6% sales tax. The children could begin by identifying several items they wanted to buy. They could then find the total cost, compute the discount and the sale price, and finally compute the tax and find the total cost. After comparing this figure with

$400, they could add or delete items and repeat the process. The problem then may become finding the maximum list price that would lead to a final cost of not more than $400 after the discount and tax were considered. Several interesting alternative procedures and hypotheses can be generated and evaluated by the various groups as they work toward a solution.

1. Could you simply subtract 14% (20% – 6%) from the list price to get the final cost price? (No)
2. Do you get the same final answer if you first add the tax and then subtract the discount (on the list plus the tax), rather than doing it the other way? (Surprisingly, yes.)
3. Can you compute the sale price in one step? (Yes, multiply by 0.8.)
4. Given the sale price, can you compute the final cost in one step? (Yes, multiply by 1.06.)

Given the last two results, some groups wrote the following equation:

$$\text{Final cost} = \text{list price} \times 0.8 \times 1.06 = \text{list price} \times .848$$

They were then able to compute the maximum list price directly:

$$\$400 \div 0.848 = \$471.70$$

Several children came close to this figure by repeatedly using the guess-and-check method.

Finding the Percent One Number Is of Another

The Owls soccer team won 13 of 20 games played last season.

What percent of its games did the team win?

Finding what percent one number is of another involves expressing the corresponding fraction as a percent. So $\frac{13}{20} = \frac{65}{100} = 65\%$. As previously discussed, this can be done on a calculator by dividing 13 by 20 and (mentally) multiplying by 100, by dividing 1,300 by 20, or by pressing 13 ÷ 20%. Before children are shown this last calculator procedure, they need to have many experiences computing easy examples and estimating answers to more difficult questions. Consider the following sample questions and solutions:

$\frac{3}{5} = \frac{60}{100} = 65\%$

$\frac{4}{7}$ is just over half, so it is just over 50%.

$\frac{23}{70}$ is about $\frac{1}{3}$, so it is about 33%.

$\frac{8}{9}$ is almost 1, so it is a little less than 100%.

$\frac{3}{478}$ is small—under 1%.

Other Procedures for Solving Percent Problems

The previous two sections described instructional strategies for finding the percentage and the rate. For both types of problems, the solutions follow directly from the meaning of percent. Three other approaches to solving percent problems are now considered: the proportion method, the equation method, and the unitary analysis method.

The proportion method. The statement 30% of 70 = 21 can be written as a proportion:

$$\frac{30}{100} = \frac{21}{70}$$

So if we are given two of the three numbers 30, 21, and 70, we can compute the third using cross products. To find 30% of 70, we let n represent the percentage and solve the proportion $\frac{30}{100} = \frac{n}{70}$. To find what percent 21 is of 70, we let n represent the rate and solve the proportion $\frac{n}{100} = \frac{21}{70}$.

Although this can be a meaningful and very powerful method, it should not be introduced until children have learned to find a percent of a number and what percent one number is of another, as previously discussed. Writing a proportion is an excellent way of solving problems in which the base is to be found.

Of the sixth-grade children in a school, 21 usually walk to school. This represents 30% of the sixth-grade children.

How many sixth graders are there?

$\frac{30}{100} = \frac{21}{n}$

$30n = 2,100$

$n = 70$

There are 70 sixth graders.

To help children see the structure of a proportion problem and estimate the answer, students can complete a comparison scale. The steps for the previous example are shown in Figure 13-4. From the two scales it seems reasonable that because 30 is just less than a third of 100, n should be a bit more than 3 times 21.

The equation method. The statement 30% of 70 = 21 can be represented by the equation 30% × 70 = 21. So if we have two of these three numbers, the third can be found by solving the equation. To find what percent 21 is of 70, we solve for the variable n in the equation $n \times 70 = 21$. Because $n = 0.3$, the rate is 30%.

If the base is unknown, we solve for n in the equation $0.3 \times n = 21$. Neither this method nor rules such as "to find the base divide the number by the percent" should be

FIGURE 13-4 A Comparison Scale to Help Children Solve Percent Problems

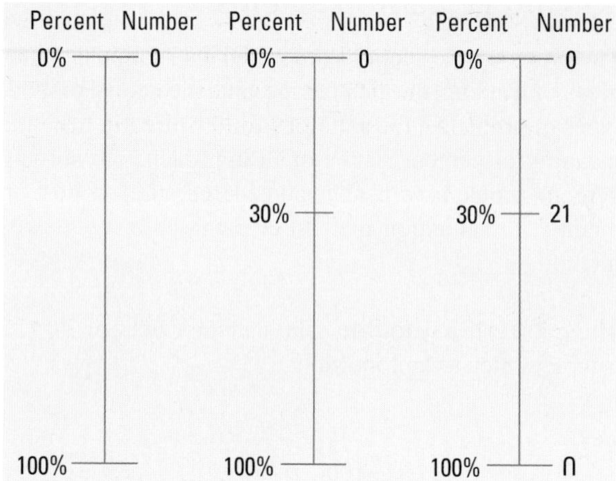

Source: "Another look at the teaching of percent," by A. M. Dewar, 1984, *Arithmetic Teacher, 31*(71), p. 49.

formally taught to elementary school children. These learners should, however, be encouraged to use their understanding of percent and the guess-and-check strategy to find answers to questions such as the following:

> *50% of __________ = 32*
>
> *6 is 10% of __________*
>
> *78 is 120% of some number. What do you know about the number?*

The unitary analysis method. The unitary analysis or unit method was once popular in schools in the United States. It is presented here because it illustrates logical reasoning and mental computation strategies. Examples for each of the three types of percent problems follow:

Find 5% of 700.

1% of 700 is 7.

Therefore, 5% of 700 is 5 × 7 = 35.

What percent is 2 of 5?

5 is 100% of the total.

So 1 is 20% of the total. (100% ÷ 5)

And 2 is 2 × 20% = 40% of the total.

60 is 20% of what number?

20% of the number is 60.

So 1% of the number is 3. (60 ÷ 20)

And 100% of the number is 300.

The numbers in these examples are easy to work with. In many problems, however, the intermediate steps involve cumbersome fractions or decimals. For this reason, this method generally is not taught formally today.

Assessment and Instruction

Assessing Proportional Reasoning

In addition to missing-value problems (such as the "Mr. Short and Mr. Tall" task shown earlier in Figure 13-1) and comparison problems (such as predicting the relative strength of orange juice given different mixtures of concentrate and water), qualitative prediction or comparison situations such as the following can be used to assess proportional reasoning:

> *If today Eric ran fewer laps in more time than he did yesterday, was his speed faster, slower, the same, or can't you say for sure?*
>
> *If Lisa ran more laps than Craig, and she ran for less time, who was the faster runner—Lisa, Craig, they ran the same speed, or can't you say for sure?*

As for other concepts, the key factor to observe when determining children's understanding of ratio and proportion is their ability to model the problem situation, use solution strategies, successfully solve the problem, and judge the reasonableness of their solution.

Everyday-Life Problem Settings

Newspaper and magazine articles, as well as radio and television reports, are continuing sources of up-to-date information on topics of interest to young people, such as sports, entertainment, and environmental concerns. Such data can be used in concept and skill development activities related to ratio and percent. For example, children could write various part-to-part and part-to-whole ratios based on the number of medals won by a country at a recent Olympic Games: e.g., Winter—2 gold, 3 silver, and 2 bronze; Summer—6 gold, 5 silver, and 7 bronze.

Children who collect sports cards or follow professional teams might be asked to explain what certain statistics mean and how they are computed:

- a hitter's batting average of .317
- a pitcher's earned run average of 2.85
- a hockey team's power-play percentage of 21%
- a quarterback's passing percentage of 62%
- a player's 3-point shooting percentage of 46%

Encourage children to keep various statistics on games in a sport in which they participate or serve as spectators. Class members could then generate and solve problems or class projects based on data from these printed sources.

Another source of information is data collected in surveys conducted by children. For example, the number of people who prefer certain soft drinks, watch certain TV shows, or recycle paper can be reported and compared in ratio or percent form. Activities such as these have obvious connections to topics and concepts in the data analysis strand, which focuses on collecting, representing, and interpreting quantitative information (see Chapter 16).

Conclusion

As with other mathematics concepts, children develop understanding of the concepts of ratio, proportion, and percent best when instruction emphasizes reasoning, number sense, and understanding. Children should rely on conceptual understanding rather than mechanical rules when solving problems, and they should know that problems can be solved in many different ways. Mental computation and estimation skills need to be developed for these topics. Calculators should be used for complex computations.

CHAPTER

Sample Lesson

A Lesson on Understanding Proportions

Grade level: Seventh

Lesson objective: Students will use reasoning to solve proportion problems.

Standards link: Students extend their work with ratios to develop an understanding of proportionality that they apply to solve single and multistep problems in numerous contexts (NCTM *Curriculum Focal Points*, grade 7).

Launch: Display the following problem:

Pizza Palace is having a special on medium pizzas, selling 2 pizzas for $8. Steve wants to buy 6 pizzas for a party. How much money will Steve spend on pizza?

Ask students, "How could we figure out how much money Steve will spend on pizza?" Solicit recommendations about how to determine this, including making a table showing the cost of various numbers of pizza, using a drawing or diagram, or determining the price for one pizza, known as the *unit price*. Explain to students that their task is to work with a partner to solve two problems from the following list in **at least two ways** and to explain each method. (Note: decide if you'd like the students to choose two problems from the list, or if you'd rather choose the problems for the class.) Students should prepare a written explanation of how they solved the problem.

1. Pizza Palace is having a special on medium pizzas, selling 2 pizzas for $8. Steve wants to buy 6 pizzas for a party. How much money will Steve spend on pizza?
2. Two candy bars cost $1. How much will 5 candy bars cost?
3. The map scale is 1 inch: 1,000 miles. If our destination is 3.5 inches away on the map, how many miles is that?
4. The speed limit is 65 miles per hour. How far will I travel if I drive the speed limit for 3 hours?

Explore: In pairs, have students solve two problems in **at least two ways**, explain each method, and prepare a written explanation of their method.

Summarize: Coming together as a whole class, select pairs of students to come to the front of the room and explain how they solved a problem. Focus on their explanations on the method they used to solve the problem. Highlight the different types of solution strategies they used, including equal ratios and unit rates.

FOLLOW-UP

Complete the following questions.

1. How might you change the problems in this lesson to make them easier? To make them harder? Describe other ways you might modify the problem or the task to make it more accessible to students.
2. What might the next lesson focus on, and why?

IN PRACTICE

Complete the following activities to include in your professional portfolio.

1. Visit an intermediate-grade or middle school classroom and informally interview several children. Have them solve and describe their solution methods for a few ratio, proportion, and percent problems. Write a short description of their solution strategies and their understandings of these kinds of problems. If you were their teacher, what would you plan for their next lessons about these topics?
2. Write a lesson plan to help children understand the meaning of ratio and proportion by linking these concepts to their everyday lives.
3. Write a lesson plan to help children understand and use unit rates to solve proportion problems.
4. Write a lesson plan to help children understand percents by using a model.

myeducationlab The Power of Classroom Practice Now go to Topic 10: "Ratio, Proportion, and Percent" in the MyEducationLab (www.myeducationlab.com) for your course, where you can:

- Find learning outcomes for "Ratio, Proportion, and Percent" along with the national standards that connect to these outcomes.
- Apply and practice your understanding of the core teaching skills identified in the chapter with a Building Teaching Skills and Dispositions learning unit.
- Complete Assignments and Activities that can help you understand the chapter content more deeply.
- Complete the *enVision MATH* Sample Curricula assignments that allow you to examine and work with chapters from *enVision MATH*, a K-6 mathematics program.
- Check your comprehension of the content covered in the chapter by going to the Study Plan in the Book-Specific Resources for your text. Here you will be able to take a chapter quiz, receive feedback on your answers, and then access Review, Practice, and Enrichment activities to enhance your understanding of chapter content.
- Go to the Book-Specific Resources for Chapter 13 to explore mathematical reasoning related to chapter content in the Activities section.

LINKS TO THE INTERNET

Fibonacci Numbers and the Golden Section

http://www.mcs.surrey.ac.uk/Personal/R.Knott/Fibonacci/fib.html

Contains information about Fibonacci numbers and the Golden Section (or ratio), including how they appear in nature and how to calculate them.

Vitruvian Man: Ideal Proportions

http://mathforum.org/alejandre/frisbie/math/student.leonardo.html

Contains information about da Vinci's Vitruvian Man and explores the ratio of a person's arm span to his height.

RESOURCES FOR TEACHERS

Children's Literature

Briggs, Raymond (1997). *Jim and the Beanstalk*. New York: Putnam Juvenile.

Farmer, J. (1999). *Bananas*. Watertown, MA: Charlesbridge Publishing.

Orwell, G. (2003). *Animal Farm*. New York: Plume.

Schwartz, David L. (1999). *If You Hopped Like a Frog*. New York: Scholastic.

Smith, David J. (2002). *If the World Were a Village: A Book About the World's People*. Toronto: Kids Can Press, Ltd.

Taylor, Mildred D. (2004). *Roll of Thunder, Hear My Cry*. New York: Puffin.

Wells, Robert (1997). *What's Faster Than a Speeding Cheetah?* Morton Grove, IL: Albert Whitman & Company.

Reference Books

Cramer, K., Post, T., & Currier, S. (1993). Learning and Teaching Ratio and Proportion: Research implications. In D. Owens (Ed.), *Research Ideas for the Classroom* (pp. 159–178). New York: Macmillan.

Curcio, F. R., & Bezuk, N. S. (1994). *Understanding Rational Numbers and Proportions: Curriculum and Evaluation Standards for School Mathematics Addenda Series, Grades 5–8*. Reston, VA: National Council of Teachers of Mathematics.

National Council of Teachers of Mathematics (2006). *Curriculum Focal Points for Prekindergarten through Grade 8 Mathematics*. Reston, VA: Author.

CHAPTER

14

Developing Geometric Thinking and Spatial Sense

With Contributions from Dr. Sally Robison

NCTM CONNECTING WITH THE STANDARDS

The National Council of Teachers of Mathematics (NCTM) Principles and Standards emphasizes the importance of children being actively involved in learning geometry, stating that "As students sort, build, draw, model, trace, measure, and construct, their capacity to visualize geometric relationships will develop. At the same time they are learning to reason and to make, test, and justify conjectures about these relationships" (NCTM, 2000, p. 164). The NCTM document goes on to note that, because some children are better with geometric and spatial concepts than with number, it is important for teachers to provide opportunities for children to experience these concepts in addition to topics in the number strand. "Building on these strengths fosters enthusiasm for mathematics and provides a context in which to develop number and other mathematics concepts" (NCTM, 2000, p. 96).

The NCTM (2006) *Curriculum Focal Points* includes geometric concepts from prekindergarten through eighth grade. The *Focal Points* state that students at the grades listed should:

- find shapes in their environments and describe them in their own words (prekindergarten, p. 11);
- identify, name, and describe a variety of shapes, such as squares, triangles, circles, rectangles, (regular) hexagons, and (isosceles) trapezoids presented in a variety of ways (e.g., with different sizes or orientations), as well as such three-dimensional shapes as spheres, cubes, and cylinders (kindergarten, p. 12);
- compose and decompose plane and solid figures (e.g., by putting two congruent isosceles triangles together to make a rhombus), thus building an understanding of part-whole relationships as well as the properties of the original and composite shapes (grade 1, p. 13);
- by composing and decomposing two-dimensional shapes (intentionally substituting arrangements of smaller shapes for larger shapes or substituting larger shapes for many smaller shapes), they use geometric knowledge and spatial reasoning to develop

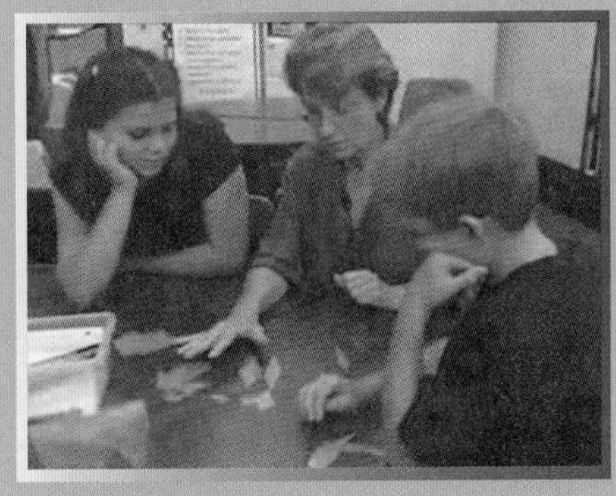

Developing Your Math Teaching Skills

When you have finished studying this chapter, you should be able to do the following:

- Describe the van Hiele levels of geometric thought that are often observed in elementary school children.
- Discuss how you could help children develop spatial sense.
- Describe activities you could use to encourage children to investigate, describe, and recognize geometric shapes and properties of geometric shapes.

foundations for understanding area, fractions, and proportions (grade 2, p. 14);

- describe, analyze, compare, and classify two-dimensional shapes by their sides and angles and connect these attributes to definitions of shapes (grade 3, p. 15);
- build on their earlier work with symmetry and congruence in grade 3 to encompass transformations, including those that produce line and rotational symmetry (grade 4, p. 16);
- relate two-dimensional shapes to three-dimensional shapes and analyze properties of polyhedral solids, describing them by the number of edges, faces, or vertices as well as the types of faces (grade 5, p. 17);
- select appropriate two- and three-dimensional shapes to model real-world situations and solve a variety of problems (including multi-step problems) involving surface areas, areas and circumferences of circles, and volumes of prisms and cylinders (grade 7, p. 19);
- apply this reasoning about similar triangles to solve a variety of problems, including those that ask them to find heights and distances (grade 8, p. 20) (NCTM, 2006).

The Curriculum Focal Points for geometry emphasize the importance of developing spatial reasoning and understanding of relationships between shapes and parts of shapes.

ASSESSING MATHEMATICS UNDERSTANDING

In order to become familiar with the mathematics concepts discussed in this chapter, take a few minutes and complete the following *Chapter 14 Preassessment.* Complete the assessment on your own. Then think about the possible misunderstandings or difficulties some elementary-school children might have when completing this assessment. If you are able, administer this assessment to a child, and analyze their understanding of these topics.

Which of the shapes below are triangles? Explain why each shape is or is not a triangle.

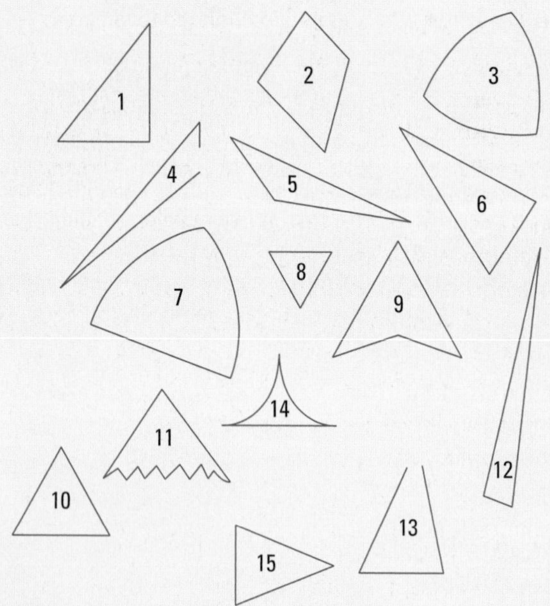

Examining Classroom Practice

In "Shapes from Squares," Marco Ramirez begins a geometry lesson for his bilingual second and third graders with the children sitting together on the rug in front of the classroom. Each child has a square of construction paper, which they fold by following Mr. Ramirez's instructions. He carefully models each of his verbal instructions by folding his square as he gives an instruction. Mr. Ramirez repeats the instructions in Spanish to ensure that all the children understand the instructions.

> PEARSON **myeducationlab** The Power of Classroom Practice — Go to the Video Examples section of Topic 11: "Geometric Thinking and Spatial Sense" in the MyEducationLab for your course to view the Annenberg clip "Shapes from Squares."

After all children successfully fold their square, their task is to make as many different shapes as they can, but they can fold their squares only on a prefolded crease. Working in small groups, the children record the different shapes they create. As the children are solving the problem, Mr. Ramirez circulates throughout the classroom, asking clarifying questions to encourage children to communicate mathematically and justify their reasoning.

Sam and Jordi, two boys in Mr. Ramirez's class, discuss how to name the five- and six-sided figures they create. Their interaction with Mr. Ramirez is presented below:

> **Mr. Ramirez:** You guys had an idea that you were talking about earlier. What were you calling the shapes?

Jordi: A five-a-gon.

Mr. Ramirez: Why did you call it a five-a-gon?

Jordi & Sam: Because it had 5 sides.

Mr. Ramirez: Because it had 5 sides. What did you call this one? (*pointing to a hexagon*)

Sam: A six-a-gon.

Jordi: A hex-a-gon.

Mr. Ramirez: A six-a-gon. Or a what? A hexagon? Why did you call it a hexagon?

Sam: Because it has 6 sides.

Jordi: Hex and six rhyme.

Mr. Ramirez: Do you know another shape that you can tell me that has 6 sides to it? (*pause*) Which one do we call a hexagon when we're working with pattern blocks? (*pause*) What shapes do we have with our pattern blocks?

Sam: The green one is the square, no, the triangle.

Mr. Ramirez: The triangle, okay. And then what's that yellow one?

Chris: The hexagon.

Mr. Ramirez: The hexagon, that's the one. And how many sides does that one have? (6) And how about this one? (6) Six. Hmm.

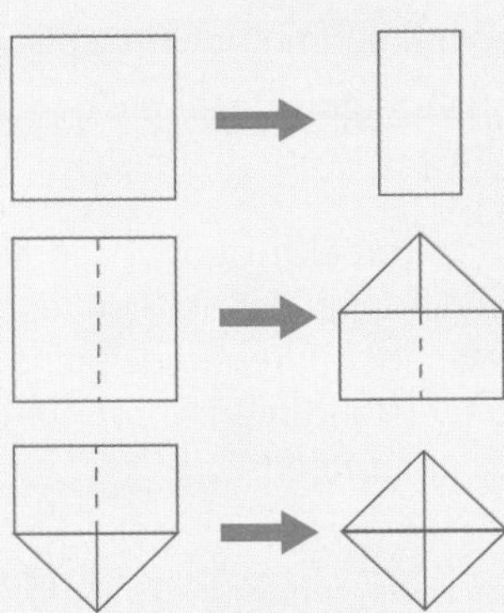

The Final Product:
The Shape for Folding

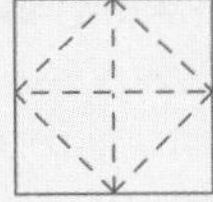

How does Mr. Ramirez help Sam and Jordi communicate mathematically? What strategies does he use?

After the lesson, Mr. Ramirez brings the children together again in a large group to discuss the shapes they created, having individual children share their thinking with the group so that children can learn from each other. He calls individual children to the board to present the shapes they made, choosing children who had basic shapes first, then building on those shapes to make sense of the more difficult shapes. In this discussion, Mr. Ramirez emphasizes mathematical language, including the names of the shapes and the number of sides.

Mr. Ramirez also uses the whole-group summary portion of the lesson to assess what individual children have done and to allow children time to think more about how other children think about the problem. From this discussion, children may decide to adapt their strategies based on what they learned by listening to how other children solved the problem.

Analyzing Assessment Result

Now let's look at the results from the preassessment. This assessment focuses on identifying triangles. What was your general reaction to this assessment? Were any of the shapes harder to determine than others? What aspects of shapes do you think make them easier for children to identify? What in general do you think a teacher's goals should be regarding developing understanding of geometry? If you had a chance to give the *Chapter 14 Preassessment* to a child, take a few minutes and analyze the results. How did the child think about these shapes?

Analyze each shape. How did you (and the student you administered the assessment to) think about each shape? Look at shapes in a few groups. Let's start with shapes 8, 10, and 15.

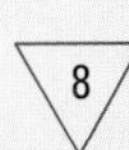

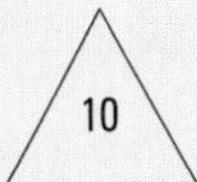

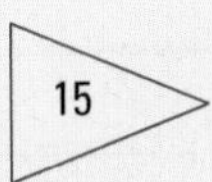

Comments: These shapes are usually the easiest for students to recognize as triangles, particularly number 10, which is an equilateral triangle "pointing up." Sometimes students will be somewhat confused about numbers 8 and 15 because of their orientation.

Next consider shapes 1 and 6.

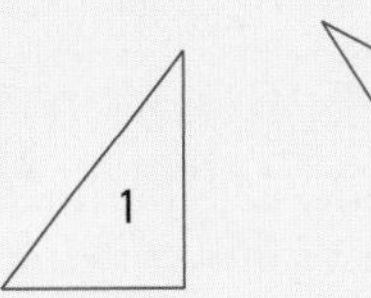

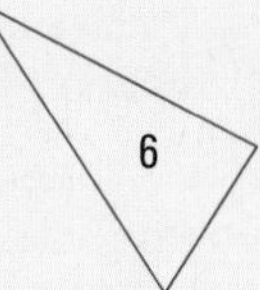

Comments: These shapes are usually fairly easy for students to recognize as triangles. But since these are both right triangles, sometimes students will think that they are not triangles, saying something such as, "Triangles can't have a square corner."

Now look at shapes 3, 7, 11, and 14.

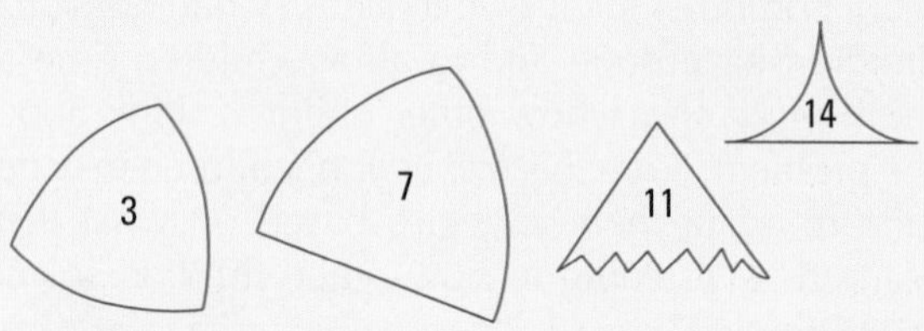

Comments: These shapes all have something different about their sides. Three of these shapes, numbers 3, 4, and 14, have curved sides, while number 11 has zig-zag sides. But sometimes students will assume that someone made a mistake in drawing these shapes and will drawing lines to "correct" the sides.

Next let's consider shapes 5 and 12.

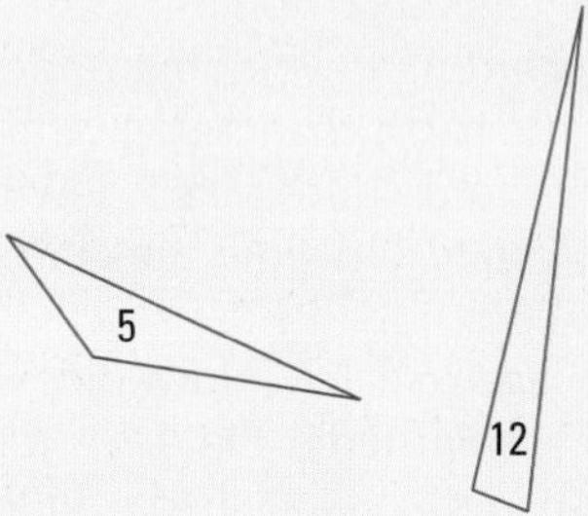

Comments: These shapes are sometimes difficult for students since the length of their sides and the size of their angles are less common. Both shapes are obtuse triangles since one of their angles is an obtuse angle. But some students will believe that these shapes are not triangles, commenting that "the angle is too big," "their sides are too long," or "they're too skinny."

Now look at shapes 4 and 13.

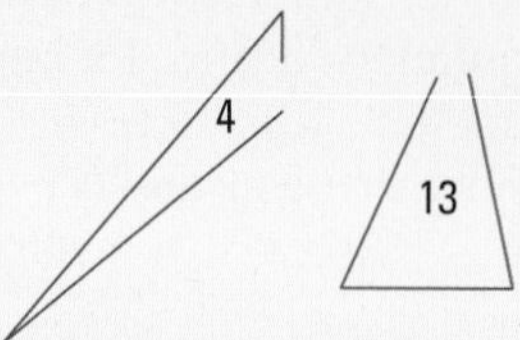

Comments: These shapes are sometimes confusing for students. They often think that there was just a problem with the copy and will draw a line to close the side of each shape. As drawn, these shapes are not triangles, since they are open rather than closed figures.

Last, consider shapes 2 and 9.

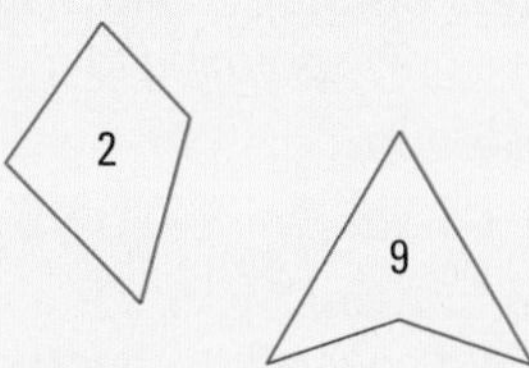

Comments: As drawn, these shapes are both quadrilaterals, since they have 4 sides. Number 2 is usually fairly easy for students to identify as not being a triangle, but as they often do for other shapes, students will frequently try to "fix" shape number 9, drawing a line to "straighten" the base of that shape.

Take a minute to reflect on this assessment. Were some shapes easier for you to think about than others? What factors made them easier or harder? What do you want to learn more about in order to help children understand about geometry?

Common Student Misunderstandings about Geometry:

- Lack of awareness of, understanding of, and experience with geometric concepts.
- Difficulty distinguishing between relevant and irrelevant aspects of a shape.

Are there any other misunderstandings that children may have about geometry concepts? It's important to assess what children understand and are still working on understanding, in order to plan instruction that meets their needs.

Building on Assessment Results

Think about what can be done to help strengthen children's understandings and minimize (and hopefully eradicate) their misunderstandings and misconceptions.

Sometimes teaching about geometry focuses on memorizing definitions and a limited set of shapes. While we want students to accomplish those things, we also want them to understand geometric concepts more broadly, which will enable them to use these concepts more flexibly. So what might we do next to help students understand geometry?

A key element of all instruction is to make sure that students understand the concept. Students need to visualize concepts and relationships. This usually is best done with some sort of model, enabling students to examine different aspects of a concept. The table below lists several common misunderstandings and what a teacher can do to help children with these misunderstandings.

Think back to Mr. Ramirez's lesson. How does he involve his children in actively learning about geometric concepts? What modes of representation does he incorporate into this lesson? The ideas presented in this chapter are about "getting to know" objects in the world so that eventually such objects can be measured and quantified. Working with concrete objects leads to intuitive discoveries of geometric properties and relationships. As you read this chapter, pay particular attention to ways in which you can get children actively involved in learning about geometry, rather than merely memorizing the names and properties of shapes.

IF students think that . . .	THEN have students . . .
shapes have to be oriented in certain directions (for example, a triangle must "sit on its bottom")	*examine* a variety of shapes with different orientations and in different contexts, and *discuss* critical elements of each shape.
shapes have a limited range of variations, such as the limits on the length of sides and the size of angles	*examine* a variety of shapes with a range of variations, and *discuss* critical and irrelevant elements of each shape.

Development of Geometric Thinking

Why Teach Geometry?

Children typically enjoy the topics found in a geometry unit because they can relate so much of what they explore to the real world. Learning about geometric properties and shapes helps them make sense of their environment as they become more capable of describing their world. As a result, they find the subject naturally interesting and, therefore, are more motivated to learn.

Geometry is a foundational subject to many other areas of mathematics, such as algebraic thinking involving patterns and problem-solving activities involving area and perimeter of geometric shapes. As children work on geometric topics through the use of models and hands-on activities, they discover examples and nonexamples of geometric figures; grow in spatial abilities; learn to apply geometric concepts, terminology, and formulas; and gain in what NCTM refers to as mathematical power: problem solving, communication, reasoning, representing, and connections.

The geometry component of the mathematics program at the elementary level includes, in part, the study of two-dimensional and three-dimensional shapes and objects. As their understanding develops, children are able to recognize different shapes and figures, name and describe them, deduce their properties, and eventually express relationships both within and between shapes and figures. The study of geometry also is about developing spatial sense—the ability to build and manipulate mental representations of two- and three-dimensional objects and perceive them accurately from different perspectives (NCTM, 2000).

What do we know of the geometry understanding of children in the United States? The 2003 National Assessment of Educational Progress (NAEP) noted that improvement is needed in students' understanding of geometry. According to Blume, Galindo, and Walcott (2007), "the significant decline in performance for some items, coupled with the general level of performance being less than what is desired, suggests that much work remains to be done to improve students' learning of measurement and geometry" (p. 137).

Students had higher levels of success on items involving frequently encountered geometric figures, such as right angles, triangles, squares, rectangles, cubes, and cylinders, but were less successful on items involving less familiar geometric objects and concepts such as rays, parallelograms, Pythagorean theorem, and scalene, isosceles, and equilateral triangles. Students did fairly well on geometric transformations, such as reflections, but results were mixed on items involving spatial visualization and geometric reasoning. Findings such as these point to the need for improvement in students' understanding of geometry,

NCTM Principles and Standards Link 14-1

Content Strand: Geometry

Geometry offers students an aspect of mathematical thinking that is different from, but connected to, the world of numbers. . . . Some students' capabilities with geometric and spatial concepts exceed their numerical skills. Building on these strengths fosters enthusiasm for mathematics and provides a context in which to develop number and other mathematical concepts. (NCTM, 2000, p. 97)

and the importance of teachers' helping children make sense of geometric concepts.

The van Hiele Levels of Geometric Thought

The work of two Dutch educators, Dina van Hiele-Geldof and Pierre van Hiele (pronounced "van HEEley"), has influenced the teaching of geometry. The van Hieles were concerned about the difficulties their students were having with geometry (Geddes & Fortunato, 1993), so they conducted research aimed at understanding children's levels of geometric thinking to determine the kinds of instruction that could best help children. The van Hieles (1959/1985) observed five levels of geometric thinking, listed in Table 14-1. Each level describes how children think about geometric concepts.

Visualization level. Children at the visualization level think about shapes in terms of what they resemble. For example, a child at this level might describe a triangle as a "mountain." The child, however, might not recognize the same triangle after it is rotated 180°, saying, "It's not a triangle because it doesn't look like a triangle. A triangle can't stand upside down." Children at this level are able to sort shapes into groups that look alike based on their perceptions. They can sort, identify, match, and describe objects in a limited capacity. They need examples and nonexamples of the geometric shapes to help them formulate their perceptions of the shapes. Children should be encouraged to construct and draw shapes as well as practice in putting shapes together to form figures they recognize followed by practice in taking them apart.

Analysis level. Children at the analysis level think in terms of properties. They understand that all shapes in a group such as parallelograms have the same properties, and they can describe those properties. For example, they are able to describe a parallelogram as having four sides, with opposite sides parallel, with opposite sides congruent, and with opposite angles congruent. However, they don't see any relationships between any of the properties. Because they don't realize that some properties imply others, children's thinking at this level will list every property of a shape that they can think of. Children should be encouraged to solve problems involving geometric shapes, to use models that help them explore the properties of shapes, and to classify figures based on certain properties, such as all shapes that have right angles.

TABLE 14-1 van Hiele Levels of Geometric Thinking

Level	Description
0—Visualization	Children recognize shapes by their global, holistic appearance.
1—Analysis	Children observe the component parts of figures (e.g., a parallelogram has opposite sides that are parallel) but are unable to explain the relationships between properties within a shape or among shapes.
2—Informal deduction	Children deduce properties of figures and express interrelationships both within and between figures.
3—Formal deduction	Children create formal deductive proofs.
4—Rigor	Children rigorously compare different axiomatic systems.

PEARSON myeducationlab The Power of Classroom Practice Go to the Assignments and Activities section of Topic 11: "Geometric Thinking and Spatial Sense" in the MyEducationLab for your course and complete the activity "Geometry Lesson" to see how one teacher uses stations to introduce geometry concepts.

Informal deduction level. Children at the informal deduction level not only think about properties of shapes but are also able to notice relationships within and between figures. It is at this level of thinking that children are first able to understand inclusion relationships, using words such as *all, some,* and *none;* for example, "All dogs are animals, but not all (only some) animals are dogs." Or, to give a mathematical example, "All squares are rectangles, but not all rectangles are squares." Converse statements involving if–then conditions, such as "If this shape is a rectangle, then it has four right angles" versus the converse, "If this shape has four right angles, then it is a rectangle," should be explored for validity.

It is also at this level that children are first able to formulate meaningful definitions. Definitions acquired prior to this level will generally be memorized without real understanding. Children working at this level should make property lists of shapes, discuss necessary and sufficient conditions required to make a shape, use descriptive language leading to meaningful definitions, and learn to identify a class of shapes based on certain properties. At this level, children are also able to make and follow informal deductive arguments. Making and testing hypotheses about the shapes, such as "Do the diagonals of all parallelograms bisect each other?" will lead to generalizations and counterexamples.

Formal deduction level. Children at the formal deduction level think about relationships between properties of shapes and also understand relationships between axioms, definitions, theorems, corollaries, and postulates. They understand how to construct a formal proof, understand why proof is needed, and learn to argue meaningfully. For successful completion, the typical high school geometry course requires geometric understanding at the formal deduction level.

NCTM NCTM GEOMETRY STANDARDS AND EXPECTATIONS ADDRESSED IN THIS CHAPTER

Instructional programs from Pre-K–12 should enable all students to	In Prekindergarten through grade 2 all students should (NCTM, 2000, p. 96)	In grades 3–5 all students should— (NCTM, 2000, p. 164)	In grades 6–8 all students should— (NCTM, 2000, p. 232)
• analyze characteristics and properties of two- and three-dimensional geometric shapes and develop mathematical arguments about geometric relationships. • specify locations and describe spatial relationships using coordinate geometry and other representational systems. • apply transformations and use symmetry to analyze mathematical situations. • use visualization, spatial reasoning, and geometric modeling to solve problems.	• create mental images of geometric shapes using spatial visualization. • recognize and represent shapes from different perspectives. • relate ideas in geometry to ideas in number and measurement. • recognize geometric shapes and structures in the environment and specify their location. • describe, name, and interpret relative positions in space and apply ideas about relative position. • describe, name, and interpret direction and distance in navigating space and apply ideas about direction and distance. • find and name locations with simple relationships such as "near to" and in coordinate systems such as maps. • recognize and apply slides, flips, and turns. • recognize and create shapes that have symmetry. • create mental images of geometric shapes using spatial memory and spatial visualization. • recognize and represent shapes from different perspectives.	• investigate, describe, and reason about the results of subdividing, combining, and transforming shapes. • explore congruence and similarity. • make and test conjectures about geometric properties and develop logical arguments to justify conclusions. • describe location and movement using common language and geometric vocabulary. • make and use coordinate systems to specify locations and to describe paths. • find the distance between points along horizontal and vertical lines of a coordinate system. • predict and describe the results of sliding, flipping, and turning two-dimensional shapes. • describe a motion or a series of motions that will show that two shapes are congruent. • identify and describe line and rotational symmetry in two- and three-dimensional shapes and designs. • build and draw geometric objects. • create and describe mental images of objects, patterns, and paths. • identify and build a three-dimensional object from two-dimensional representations of that object.	• precisely describe, classify, and understand relationships among types of two- and three-dimensional objects (e.g., angles, triangles, quadrilaterals, cylinders, cones) using their defining properties. • understand relationships among the angles, side lengths, perimeters, areas, and volumes of similar objects. • create and critique inductive and deductive arguments concerning geometric ideas and relationships, such as congruence, similarity, and the Pythagorean relationship. • use coordinate geometry to represent and examine the properties of geometric shapes. • use coordinate geometry to examine special geometric shapes, such as regular polygons or those with pairs of parallel or perpendicular sides. • describe sizes, positions, and orientations of shapes under informal transformations such as flips, turns, slides, and scaling. • examine the congruence, similarity, and line or rotational symmetry of objects using transformations. • draw geometric objects with specified properties, such as side lengths or angle measures. • use two-dimensional representations of three-dimensional objects to visualize and solve problems such as those involving surface area and volume.

(*continued*)

NCTM NCTM GEOMETRY STANDARDS AND EXPECTATIONS ADDRESSED IN THIS CHAPTER (*Continued*)

Instructional programs from Pre-K–12 should enable all students to	In Prekindergarten through grade 2 all students should (NCTM, 2000, p. 96)	In grades 3–5 all students should— (NCTM, 2000, p. 164)	In grades 6–8 all students should— (NCTM, 2000, p. 232)
	• relate ideas in geometry to ideas in number and measurement. • recognize geometric shapes and structures in the environment and specify their locations.	• identify and build a two-dimensional representation of a three-dimensional object. • use geometric models to solve problems in other areas of mathematics, such as number and measurement. • recognize geometric ideas and relationships and apply them to other disciplines and to problems that arise in the classroom or in everyday life.	• use visual tools such as networks to represent and solve problems. • use geometric models to represent and explain numerical and algebraic relationships. • recognize and apply geometric ideas and relationships in areas outside the mathematics classroom, such as art, science, and everyday life.

Rigor level. Children at the rigor level can think in terms of abstract mathematical systems. They can work with a variety of axiomatic systems that do not require the need for parallel lines to remain parallel when examining the infinite case. Advanced college mathematics majors and mathematicians are at this level.

In the 1990s, Clements and Battista (1992) hypothesized that a level exists that is below visualization, called *prerecognition.* Children operating at this level would not be able to distinguish a three-sided figure from a four-sided figure. Observing a child performing the task of putting a puzzle together at this level, the observer will notice the child does not recognize the need for a certain shape or the correct orientation of the correct shape.

Connecting van Hiele levels to elementary school children. Most children at the elementary level are at the visualization or analysis level; some middle school children are at the informal deduction level; and those who successfully complete a typical high school geometry course generally reach the formal deduction level. The NAEP noted that "most of the students at all three grade levels (fourth, eighth, and twelfth) appeared to be performing at the 'holistic' level [visualization] of the van Hiele levels of geometric thought" (Strutchens & Blume, 1997, p. 166). It is desirable to have a child at the informal deduction level or above by the end of middle school.

For convenience, each of the activities in this chapter has been cross-referenced with the appropriate van Hiele level(s) of geometric thinking. When a range is given, it is because the level is dependent on which questions in the activity are being presented and the complexity of the figure being made.

Comments on the Levels of Thought

The following additional points about the van Hiele levels must be considered:

- The levels are not age dependent, but are related more to the experiences children have had.
- The levels are sequential; that is, children must pass through the levels in sequence as their understanding increases. (The only exception is highly gifted children, who appear to skip levels because of their highly developed logical reasoning ability.)
- To move from one level to the next, children need to have many experiences in which they are actively involved in exploring and communicating about their observations of shapes, properties, and relationships.
- For learning to take place, language must match the child's level of understanding. If the language used in instruction is above the child's level of thinking, the child may only be able to learn procedures and memorize relationships without truly understanding geometry.
- It is difficult for two people who are at different levels to communicate effectively. For example, a person at the informal deduction level who says "square" thinks about the fact that a square has four congruent sides and four congruent angles and will know the properties of a square, such as having opposite sides that are parallel and diagonals that are perpendicular bisectors, meaning the diagonals are perpendicular and bisect each other. A person at the visualization level may think of a compact disc case, because that is what a square looks like to that person. A teacher must realize that the meaning of many terms is different to the child than it is to the teacher, so the teacher must adjust communication accordingly yet precisely.

Thus, it is important for teachers to assess the van Hiele levels of thinking of the children in their classes and use this information to plan instruction on geometry and spatial sense that is appropriate and relevant to the children's level of thinking.

Other Instructional Notes

Developing the Language

The formal language of geometry develops over time. According to Lindquist and Clements (2001, March), "Vocabulary is important but is not the purpose of studying geometry" (p. 409). The use of informal terms and expressions should be accepted in the elementary grades. For example, both teacher and children can use such terms as *corners, square corners, flips,* and *slides;* these terms eventually will be replaced with *vertices, right angles, reflections,* and *translations,* respectively. When children talk about what they are doing, their descriptions will become more precise and correct.

Method of Instruction

There is strong agreement among educators that geometry learning for elementary school children should be informal, involving explorations, discovery, guessing, and problem solving. Children must participate in many geometric experiences before they are able to formulate precise descriptive statements using formal terminology and symbols. Indeed, a child may progress through more than one grade level before being able to intelligently use both symbols and precise terminology to communicate an idea or relationship.

Although the study of geometry is to be informal in elementary school, experiences should not be haphazard and totally unstructured. Teachers should systematically develop a sequence of activities so that some direction and progress become evident to the children and children's thinking progresses through the van Hiele levels.

To make good decisions about the type of activities suitable for children, a teacher must try to discern their geometric thinking level. Engaging children in open-ended geometry explorations is one way to accomplish this. The following chart shows examples of open-ended tasks.

van Hiele Level	Sample Task
0	Look at a wooden block. Use sticks and marshmallows to make a skeleton model of the shape.
1	Draw as many different four-sided figures as you can. Write about how they are different and how they are the same.
2	Explain how many different ways you can connect six square tiles with at least one side attached.

NCTM Principles and Standards Link 14-2

Content Strand: Geometry

The geometric and spatial knowledge children bring to school should be expanded by explorations, investigations, and discussions of shapes and structures in the classroom. Students should use their notions of geometric ideas to become more proficient in describing, representing, and navigating their environment. (NCTM, 2000, p. 97)

Open-ended tasks such as these allow all children to engage in a common activity. Although their output from these tasks will differ, children will have had a common experience that could successfully be followed by a class discussion. Such sharing enables some children to see relationships that, left to themselves, they might have missed.

As children engage in discovery-oriented activities, you can, as you mingle with the children, ask questions such as "What do you notice?" "How would you describe this?" and "Can you make a different shape?" Responses can provide insight into the children's level of geometric thinking.

Connecting with the World

Geometry provides children with an opportunity to connect mathematics to their world. Teachers should choose activities that involve the recognition and classification of shapes and figures and operations on objects that are familiar to children. A collection of boxes and other containers that the children bring to school can be the focus of discussions about different shapes and figures. Likewise, a "geometry walk" on a city street or on a nature trail can serve to connect geometry work to the environment.

Geometric ideas such as patterns, symmetry, and similarity can be explored in the school environment or neighborhood by examining both living and nonliving things. Upper-elementary and middle school children can, for example, explore packaging possibilities for different products in response to environmental concerns or the architectural design of the local school.

Learning about Topology

A child's view of the world is first *topological*; that is, the child sees objects as changeable, depending on perspective or position (Piaget, Inhelder, & Szeminska, 1960). Gradually, the view changes to recognize that objects do not change when they are moved.

Topology is the study of the properties of figures that stay the same even under distortions, except tearing or

FIGURE 14-1 Helping Children Identify Things That Change

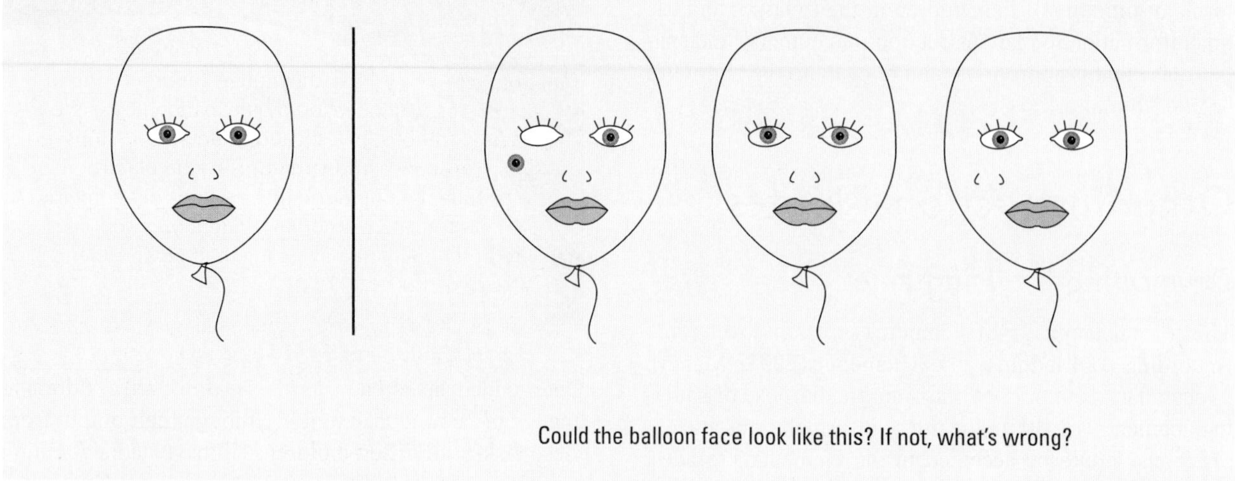

Could the balloon face look like this? If not, what's wrong?

Source: Pictures are adapted from E. Robinson, 1975, "Geometry" as described in Joseph N. Payne (Ed.), *Mathematics Learning in Early Childhood. Yearbook.* Reston, VA: National Council of Teachers of Mathematics.

cutting. By stretching and reforming, something like a doughnut can be transformed into a coffee cup. Aspects of topology should be included in elementary school geometry programs.

Place and Order

The concepts of *place, order, between, inside,* and *outside* can also be studied using real objects or pictures. For example, a teacher could set up classroom furniture or equipment, or group children in such a way that the children could respond to questions in the following manner: "Tom is sitting *on* the rug," "Annette is *behind* the chair," "The geoboards are *inside* the cupboard," or "The box of cubes is *under* the table." Suitable large pictures can replace real objects for similar activities. Children can be taken outside and asked to describe what they notice. Statements showing order such as the following should be encouraged: "The fir tree is *after* the maple tree," "The white house is *between* the brick house and the store," and "We walk *through* the door before we enter the building."

Things That Change and Things That Do Not Change

Using a balloon with markings on it, Robinson (1975) asked children to indicate which features changed and which did not as the balloon was being inflated. For example, a round balloon with facial features drawn on it can serve to model the following properties that do not change when the balloon is inflated:

- Something *inside* something (the eyes in the face);
- Something *not* closed (nose drawn this way);
- Something involving *order* (the nose above the mouth);
- Something *intersecting* (eyelashes with the eyes); and
- Something *connected* and something *not connected* (any of the features on the face). (p. 213)

Things that could change when the balloon is being inflated would be that one eye might be larger than the other or the mouth could become nonsymmetrical.

After working with real balloons, Robinson (1975) suggests showing children pictures of balloons with faces drawn on them properly and improperly and asking them to tell which picture the balloon could look like (Figure 14-1). Repeat this activity with other characters or shapes drawn on a balloon or piece of stretchy material. Children can experiment with pieces of material that have figures drawn on them to find out how they can transform the figures by stretching the material.

Mazes and Networks

Children enjoy working with mazes, and upper-elementary schoolchildren can work with networks, which are lines connecting two or more points. A study of networks involves deciding if a network can be traversed, referred to as a *traversable network,* meaning that it can be traced in one continuous motion without retracing over a line. This activity leads to an exploration of Euler circuits and Hamiltonian circuits. Try to discover which types of networks can be traversed by experimenting with figures that have

- All even vertices (two or four lines meeting at a point).
- All odd vertices (three or five lines meeting at a point).
- Only two odd vertices, others are even.
- More than two odd vertices.

Figure 14-2 shows examples of networks.

FIGURE 14-2 Examples of Networks

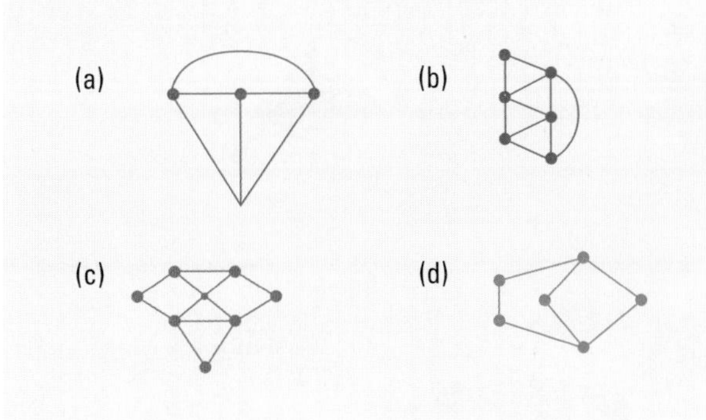

Distortion of Figures

In the preceding section, activities about distortion of figures were presented using the example of inflating a balloon or stretching fabric. Besides stretching, distortions can be achieved by twisting, bending, and shrinking. Experimenting with Möbius strips is one type of activity that involves figure distortion by twisting (see Activity 14-1).

 Go to the Assignments and Activities section of Topic 11: "Geometric Thinking and Spatial Sense" in the MyEducationLab for your course and complete the activity "Geometer's Sketchpad." Note the kind of technology the teacher uses to support learning of geometry.

ACTIVITY 14-1 Explorations with Möbius Strips (van Hiele Levels 1–2)

Materials

Use strips of narrow adding machine tape approximately 1 m in length. Mark each end of the strip with a large dot on the same side.

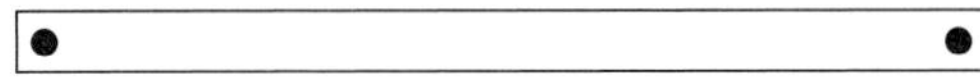

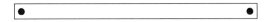

Procedure

1. Take one strip, twist it once, then glue the ends together (the dots should touch each other).
   - Cut the strip in half following the lengthwide direction. Describe the results.

   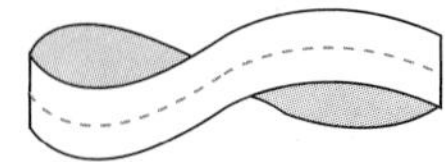

   - Use another strip and locate a line that is about one-third of the way across the strip. Cut along this line until you reach the "end." Describe what happened.

   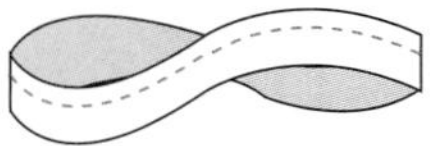

   - What would happen if you wanted to make one side of a strip one color and the other side another color? Try this and describe what you found.
2. Make Möbius strips with two twists and conduct cutting and coloring experiments.

Learning about Euclidean Geometry

Three-Dimensional Shapes

Along with topology activities, children can begin the study of rigid shapes or ideas related to Euclidean geometry. Children in kindergarten and grade 1 should be involved in manipulating different three-dimensional shapes to find out similarities and differences. Koester (2003) describes how students can actively explore three-dimensional shapes using everyday materials. When children explore such shapes, they should be asked to describe them: Some shapes can roll, some have flat faces, and some have pointed corners. The sophistication of the responses will depend on the children's geometric knowledge. Possible descriptions of faces are:

- Some faces are round, some have pointed corners.
- Some faces are squares, some are triangles.
- Some faces have four sides, some have three sides.

Children learn to recognize two-dimensional figures and name them (van Hiele level 0) well before they are able to articulate their properties (van Hiele level 1). Middle school children should be able to classify three-dimensional shapes and two-dimensional figures by explaining some relationships between properties within a shape or figure and among shapes or figures (van Hiele level 2).

Polyhedra. Polyhedra are three-dimensional shapes with *faces* consisting of polygons, that is, plane figures (two-dimensional) with three, four, five, or more straight sides. In a polyhedron, the lines where the sides of two polygons meet are the *edges* of the shape, and the points where edges meet are the *vertices* of the polyhedron (*vertex* is the singular form of the plural *vertices*).

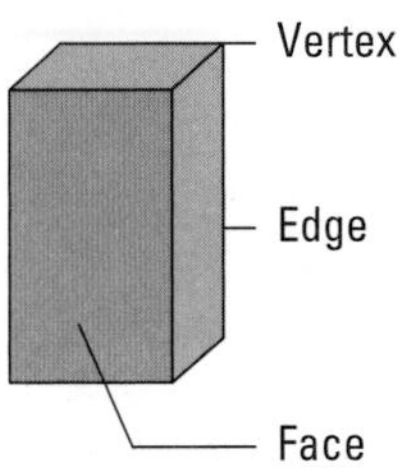

FIGURE 14-3 Platonic Solids

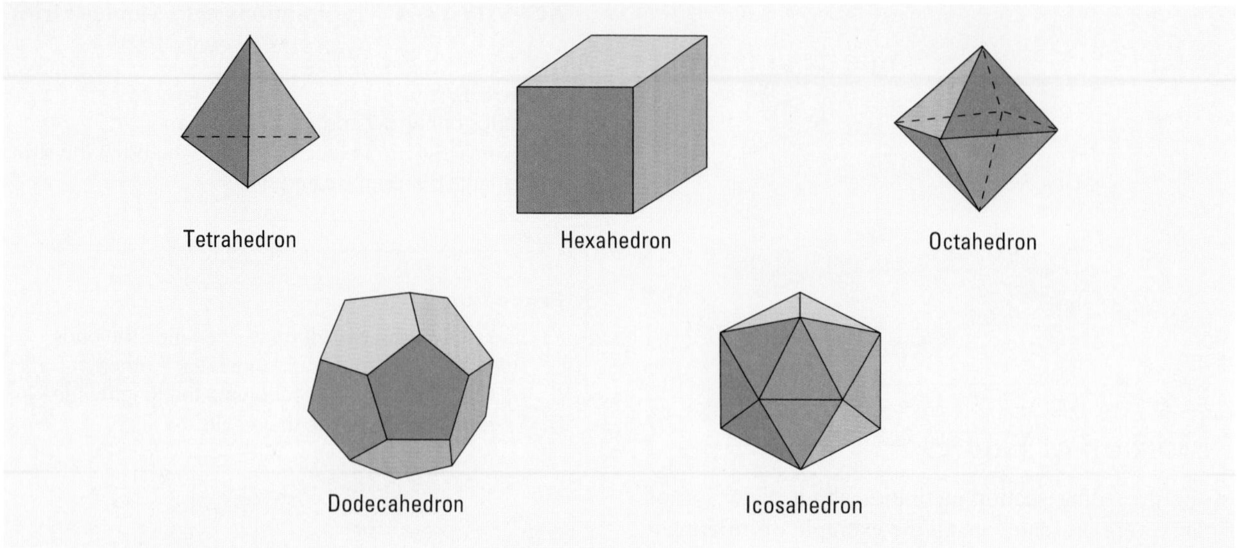

Regular polyhedra. *Regular polygons* are plane figures with sides that are all the same length and angles of equal measure, such as an equilateral triangle or a square. A *regular polyhedron* is one whose faces consist of the same kind of regular congruent polygons (e.g., all squares or all equilateral triangles) with the same number of edges meeting at each vertex of the figure (Billstein, Libeskind, & Lott, 1990). It is possible to construct only five regular polyhedra:

Shape	Type and Number of Faces
Tetrahedron	4 equilateral triangles
Octahedron	8 equilateral triangles
Icosahedron	20 equilateral triangles
Hexahedron	6 squares
Dodecahedron	12 regular pentagons

The study of polyhedra is thought to have begun with Pythagoras (582–500 B.C.). Historians believe that Pythagoras probably brought his knowledge of the cube, the tetrahedron, and the octahedron from Egypt, but the icosahedron and the dodecahedron seem to have been developed in his own society of Greece. The study of the five regular polyhedra was passed on to the school of Plato, a Greek philosopher (427–347 B.C.), and subsequently these polyhedra became known as the *Platonic solids* (Figure 14-3).

Semiregular polyhedra. Another set of polyhedra, known as the *Archimedean solids,* are semiregular shapes composed of more than one kind of regular polygon. There are 13 semiregular solids, all of which are ascribed to Archimedes (287–212 B.C.), who wrote about the entire set. Semiregular solids are shown in Figure 14-4.

Truncated and stellated polyhedra. The study of polyhedra did not end with the discovery of the solids. In the middle ages, the systematic study of solids by the astronomer Johannes Kepler (1571–1630) led him to create other solids through a process called *stellating.* This process consists of building onto solids to form different solids. For example, attaching a tetrahedron to each face of an octahedron produces a solid known as the stella octangula or the eight-pointed star (see Figure 14-5). It also is possible to modify solids by cutting off sections in a systematic way. This process is known as *truncating* and also can lead to the formation of new solids. Figure 14-5 also shows examples of a truncated cube and a stellated

FIGURE 14-4 Semiregular Solids

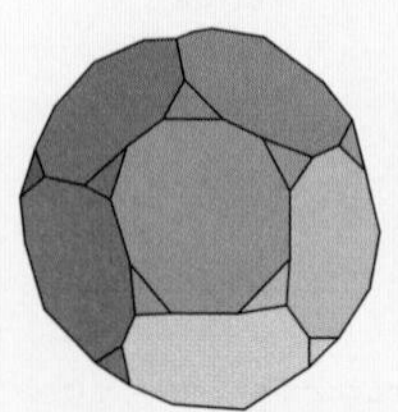
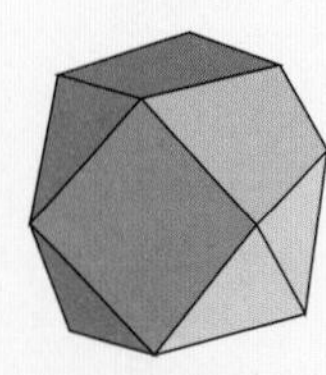
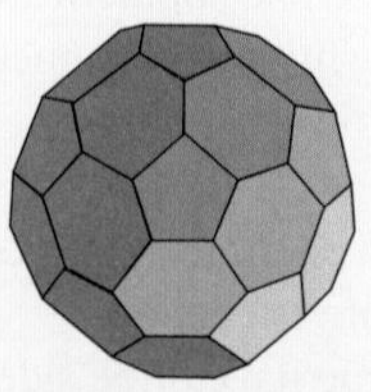
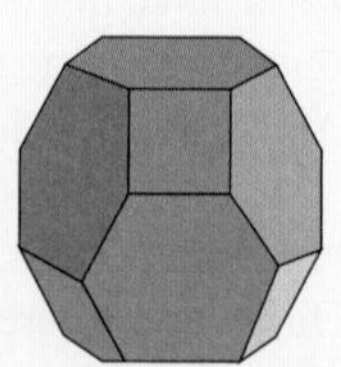

FIGURE 14-5 Truncated and Stellated Polyhedra

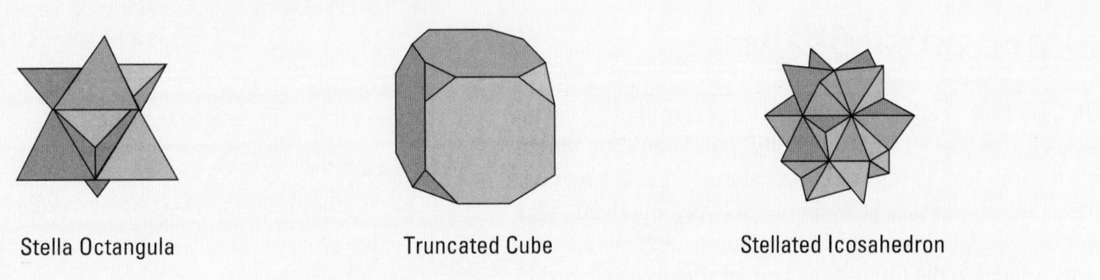

icosahedron. Stellating and truncating solids are interesting enrichment activities for upper-elementary and middle school children, who can model them with clay, Play-Doh, or commercially available polydron forms.

Other three-dimensional shapes. Other three-dimensional shapes also are included in the elementary and middle school mathematics curriculum. These shapes include prisms, pyramids, cylinders, and cones, which are described below and shown in Figure 14-6.

A *prism* is a polyhedron with two congruent, parallel bases that are polygons, and with all remaining faces being parallelograms. A cube is a special type of prism, with squares for all its faces.

A *pyramid* is a polyhedron whose base is a polygon and all the rest of the faces are triangles that meet at a common point called the *vertex*. A pyramid is regular if the base is a regular polygon and the other faces are congruent isosceles triangles. Special types of pyramids include *square pyramids,* with a square base, and *triangular pyramids,* with a triangular base.

A *cylinder* is a surface generated by a family of all lines parallel to a given line and passing through a curve in a plane. Special types of cylinders include *circular cylinders,* whose bases are circles, and *right circular cylinders,* whose axes are perpendicular to the bases. Other cylinders can have bases that are ellipses.

A *cone* is a surface generated by a family of all lines through a given point and passing through a curve in a plane. The base of a cone can be a circle or an ellipse.

FIGURE 14-6 Other Types of Three-Dimensional Shapes

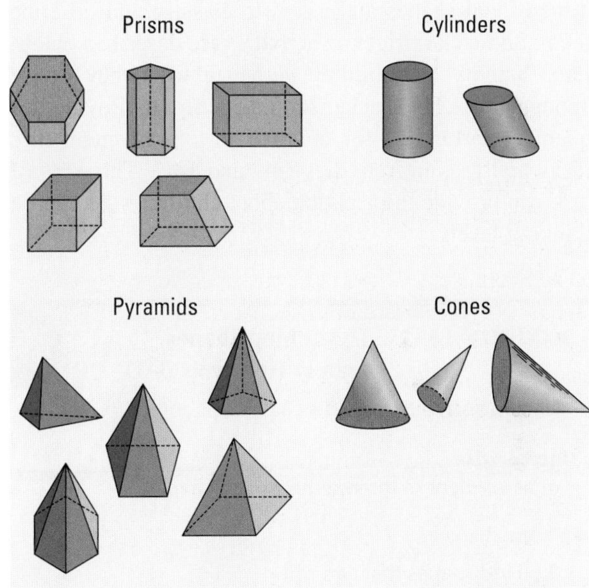

Discovering Euler's rule. A special relationship, known as Euler's rule, exists among the number of faces (F), vertices (V), and edges (E) of polyhedra. The relationship is such that given the value of two of the three variables (F, V, and E), one can calculate the value of the third variable. Examine some models and complete a table similar to the one in Table 14-2, then look for a pattern in the data.

TABLE 14-2 **Discovering Euler's Rule: Examining Relationships Between Faces, Vertices, and Edges**

Polyhedron	Faces	Vertices	Edges
Tetrahedron			
Cube			
Octahedron			
Triangular prism			
Square pyramid			

What relationship do you notice among the shapes?

Learning about Three-Dimensional Shapes

The previous section was loaded with terminology—but it was not meant to imply that children should be taught this information as if it were a vocabulary test. Remember that children learn best by being actively involved. This section discusses ways to help children understand concepts related to the three-dimensional shapes described in the previous section.

Comparing Polyhedra

Children can be given a collection of various three-dimensional shapes and asked to classify and describe them. Some classification activities are described below. Each activity has children verbalize what they notice about shapes. The teacher should attempt to provide frequent opportunities for children to express geometric ideas orally, as in Activities 14-2 and 14-3. This kind of task can provide information about children's geometric thinking levels.

ACTIVITY 14-2 Describing Shapes (van Hiele Levels 0–1)

Manipulative Strategies

Materials

An assortment of three-dimensional shapes

Procedure

1. Find shapes that can roll.
2. Find shapes that cannot roll.
3. How are the shapes different? How are they the same?

ACTIVITY 14-3 Classifying Shapes (van Hiele Levels 1–2)

Materials

A set of three-dimensional shapes

Procedure

1. Put the shapes in two different groups.
2. Tell why the shapes in each group belong together.

Constructing Three-Dimensional Shapes

Children should be actively involved in constructing three-dimensional shapes. Polyhedra can be constructed using various mediums such as clay and stiff paper (see Activity 14-4). Children can construct *skeleton* or *edge models* of polygons and polyhedra using different materials. These can include:

- Toothpicks and miniature marshmallows or small gumdrops
- Struts made of rolled paper and taped together
- Straws and pipe cleaners or some thin cord (crochet cotton, twine, or elastic thread) (see Figure 14-7).

A *net* is a flat version of a three-dimensional shape that, when folded along the connecting edges of the faces of the solid, forms a shape where all faces are connected edge to edge with no faces overlapping or leaving open gaps. Wiest (2005) noted that students "lack much-needed skill in spatially oriented tasks" (p. 142), and recommended using nets as a way to help students develop their spatial reasoning ability. As children construct polyhedra from nets they have drawn (Activity 14-5), they will learn that the beauty of the finished product is proportional to the care taken in accurately measuring, drawing, and cutting the nets.

FIGURE 14-7 Constructing Models of Polyhedra and Polygons

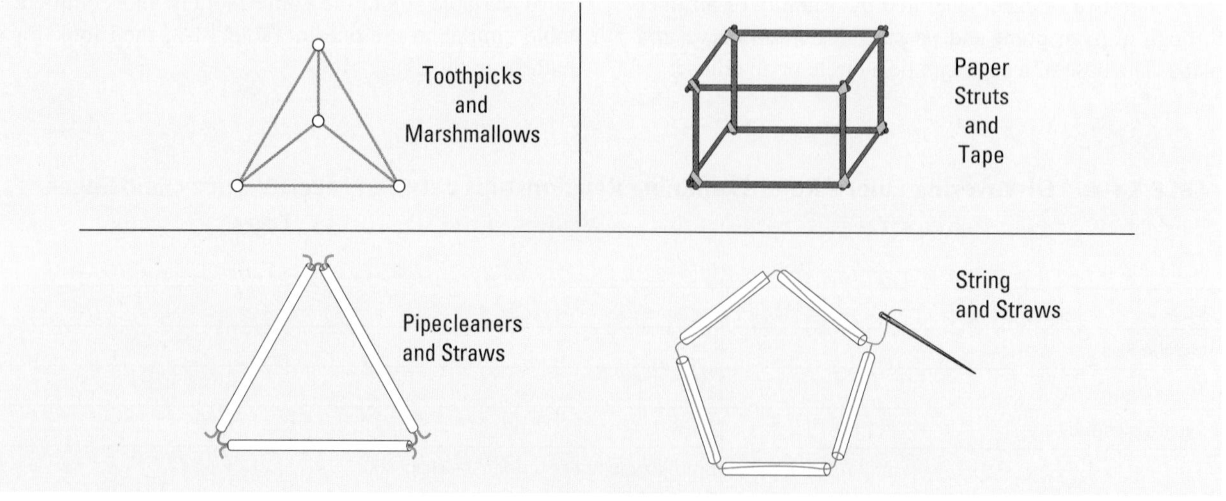

ACTIVITY 14-4 Constructing Three-Dimensional Shapes with Clay (van Hiele Levels 0–1)

Materials

A set of three-dimensional shapes
clay

Procedure

1. Select a three-dimensional shape.
2. Construct a similar shape using clay.

ACTIVITY 14-5 Constructing Polyhedra from Nets (van Hiele Levels 1–2)

Materials

Nets of shapes drawn on paper

Procedure

1. Cut out nets of shapes (see Figure 14-8).
2. By folding and taping, construct models of polyhedra.
3. As an alternative, draw 1-cm tabs around some edges of the nets and then construct models of polyhedra by cutting and pasting.

NCTM Principles and Standards Link 4-3

Content Strand: Geometry

Beginning in the early years of schooling, students should develop visualization skills through hands-on experiences with a variety of geometric objects and through the use of technology that allows them to turn, shrink, and deform two- and three-dimensional objects. Later, they should become comfortable analyzing and drawing perspective views, counting component parts, and describing attributes that cannot be seen but can be inferred. Students need to learn to physically and mentally change the position, orientation, and size of objects in systematic ways as they develop their understandings of congruence, similarity, and transformations. (NCTM, 2000, p. 42)

A set of polygons with tabs made from stiff paper (Figure 14-8) enables children to engage in investigative work regarding the composition of polyhedra. If available, the commercial set of Polydrons provides excellent pieces for explorations in polyhedra. Children can experiment with regular and nonregular polygons and try to construct shapes.

FIGURE 14-8 Nets of Polyhedra

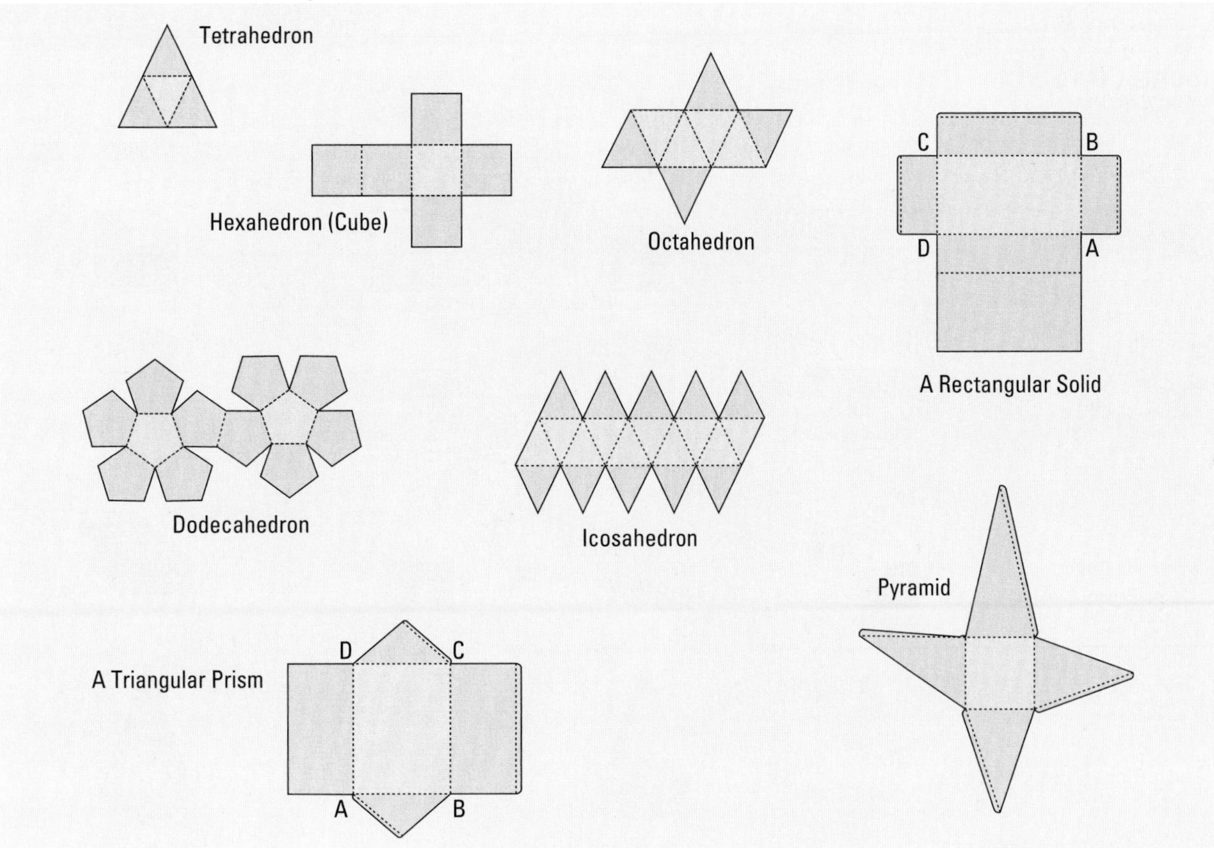

FIGURE 14-9 Materials for Constructing Polyhedra

1. Cut out regular triangles.
2. Draw an 8-mm tab on each side.
3. Punch a hole near each vertex and clip off the point. Fold each tab outward.
4. Use elastic bands to construct 3–D shapes.
5. Cut out squares and other kinds of polygons. Follow steps 2 through 4.

Constructions should be followed by descriptions and comparisons and by discussions about successful and unsuccessful construction attempts. Activities 14-8 through 14-12 are sample investigations children can be asked to do using the materials described in Figure 14-9.

ACTIVITY 14-6 Constructing Semiregular Polyhedra (van Hiele Levels 1–2)

Materials

Squares and equilateral triangles with tabs, elastics

Procedure

1. Can you construct a three-dimensional shape using equilateral triangles and squares with the same side length? Describe your shape.*
2. Compare your shape with an icosahedron. What are the similarities? What are the differences?

*Children could be provided with a picture of the semiregular shape that they are to construct.

Polyhedra can also be constructed with modeling clay. The stroke of a knife through a clay model serves to exemplify a plane passing through at given angles. In this manner, truncated figures can be formed to display different sections of solids. Predicting and testing the face of the slice made in the solid will encourage an improvement in mental imagery, which leads to an improvement in spatial sense. Children can experiment with different cuts on a solid as shown in Figure 14-10. A dissection activity is presented in Activity 14-7.

Exploring the faces of a polydron can be accomplished in several ways: casting the shadow of the shape on the wall with a flashlight or overhead projector, pressing the solid into moldable material, making jackets out of centimeter paper to fit the solid, or using finger paint and pressing the solid into the paint. Commercially available clear geometric solids that allow the entry of water into the center of the solid enable children to examine the slice of a plane without actually slicing the solid.

FIGURE 14-10 Different Cuts on Solids

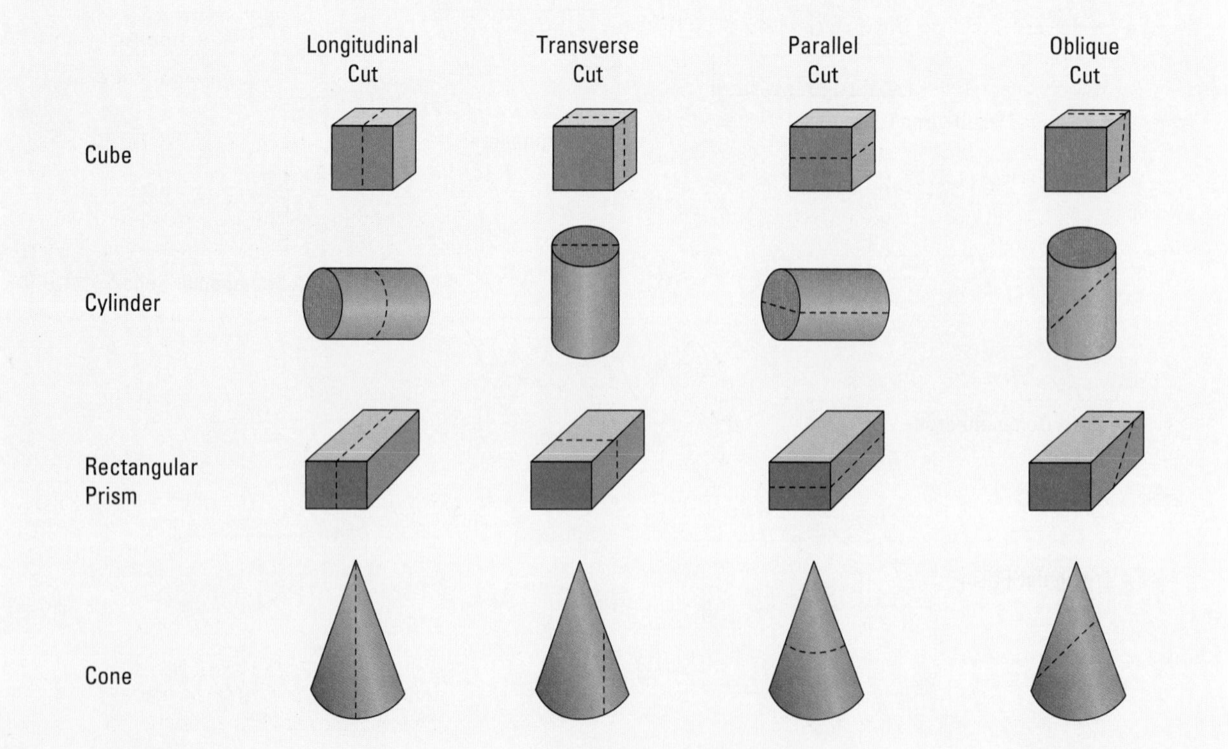

FIGURE 14-11 Examples of Geometric Curves

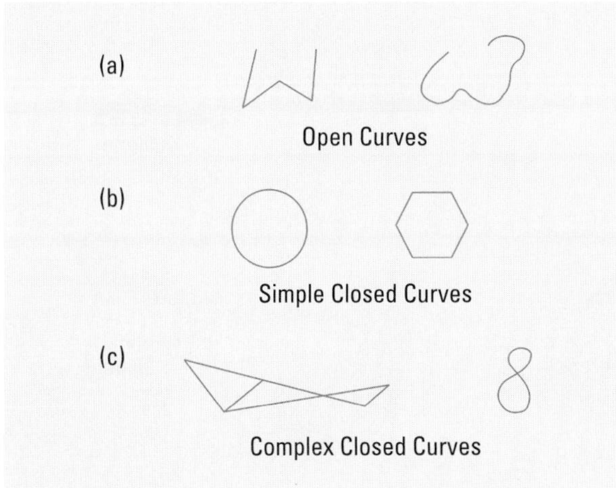

ACTIVITY 14-7 Dissection of a Cube (van Hiele Levels 1–3)

Materials

Modeling clay

Knife

Procedure

1. What various polygons do you get when a plane cuts through a cube? Experiment to find out.

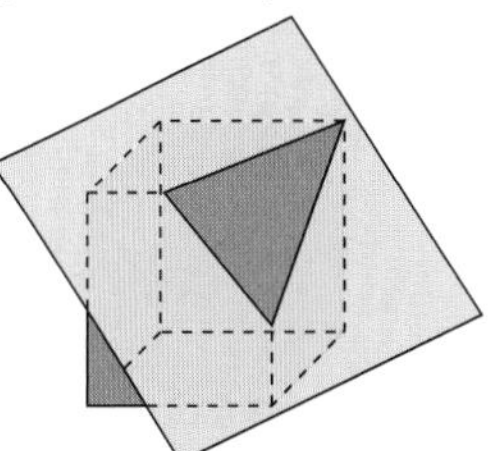

2. Make predictions for the answers to the following questions. Then, using a clay model of a cube and a knife, verify your predictions. Record both your predictions and your final answers.

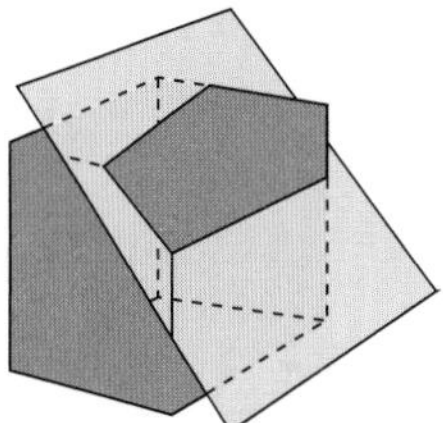

- Are all cross sections of a cube bounded by quadrilaterals?
- What kinds of polygonal regions could be cross sections of a cube?
- Find as many types of cross sections as you can.
- What is the least number of edges that a cross section can have?
- What is the greatest number of edges that a cross section can have?

3. Make predictions about the cross sections of a rectangular solid, a cone, and a right cylinder. Verify your predictions in the same manner as for the cube.

Learning about Two-Dimensional Figures

Polygons

Polygons can be described as two-dimensional figures with straight-line segments. Polygons are examples of *simple, closed geometric curves* composed of straight-line segments. A geometric curve in a plane may be straight or curved. Therefore, parallelograms and circles are both simple closed curves. They are simple curves because no lines in the figure cross each other; only one region is formed. Examples of open and closed curves and simple and complex curves are shown in Figure 14-11. The line segments of a polygon are sides, and each point where two line segments meet is a *vertex*. A *diagonal* of a polygon is formed by drawing a line segment that connects two non-adjacent vertices (see Figure 14-12).

Polygons can be *convex* or *concave.* A convex polygon is one whose interior angles are all less than 180°; that is, any two points in a figure can be connected by a line segment that will be completely within the figure and all diagonals will remain inside the figure. A nonconvex polygonal region is called a concave polygon (see Figure 14-12).

FIGURE 14-12 Convex and Concave Polygons

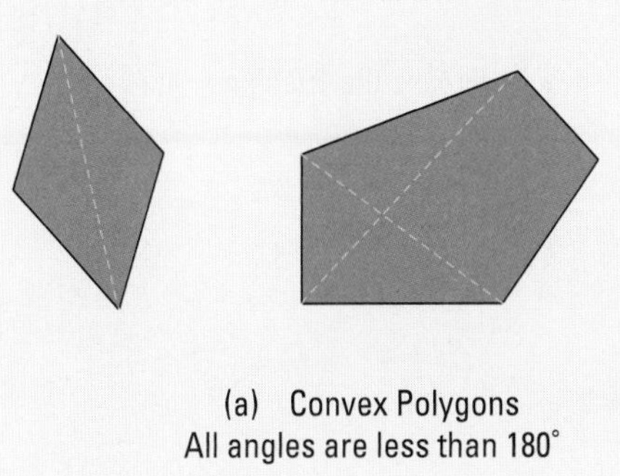

(a) Convex Polygons
All angles are less than 180°

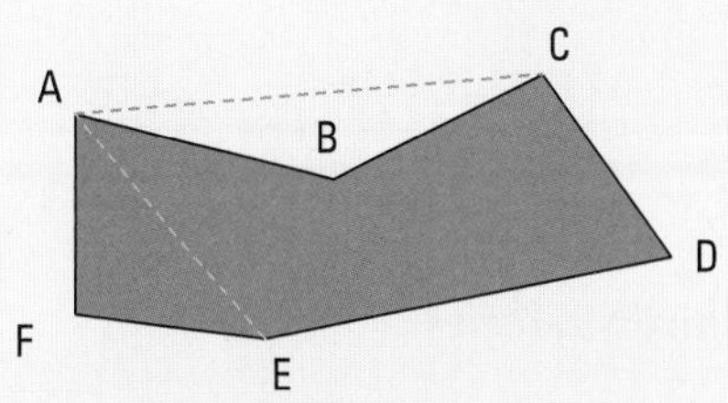

(b) Concave Polygons
Segment AC is outside the figure.
Interior angle ABC is greater than 180°

FIGURE 14-13 Classifying Triangles by Angles and Sides

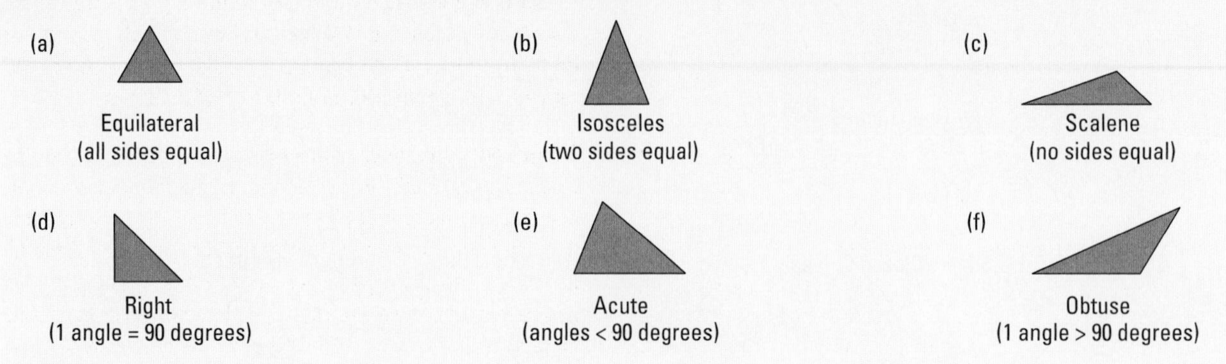

Convex polygons are named according to the number of sides:

Number of Sides	Name of Polygon
3	triangle
4	quadrilateral
5	pentagon
6	hexagon
7	heptagon
8	octagon
9	nonagon
10	decagon

Triangles. *Triangles* are classified according to their sides, angle measures, or both. Figure 14-13 shows a classification of triangles according to angles and sides.

Children's experiences with triangles should be with different sizes in different orientations. A geoboard is a good tool for explorations with such plane figures. Constructions on a geoboard can be recorded on dot paper. Activity 14-8 has children explore different triangles. As a related activity, provide children with a set of plane figures, as in Figure 14-14, and ask them to find the triangles. Follow this with a class discussion by asking, "In what ways are some alike? Different?"

ACTIVITY 14-8 Constructing Triangles (van Hiele Levels 1–2)

Manipulative Strategies

Materials

Geoboards

Rubber bands

Dot paper

Procedure

1. Make different triangles on a geoboard.
2. Draw a picture of the triangles you made on dot paper.

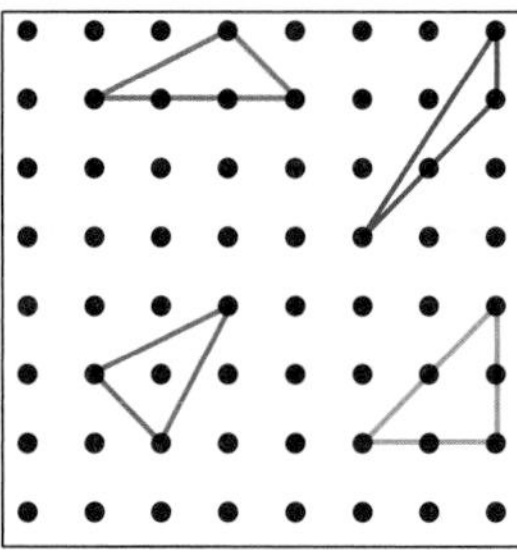

3. Is there one type of triangle that you cannot make on the geoboard? Why?

Quadrilaterals. Like triangles, quadrilaterals are classified according to their sides, angle measures, or both. A quadrilateral refers to any simple closed figure consisting of four straight lines.

A *trapezoid* is usually defined as a quadrilateral with at least one pair of parallel sides. Sometimes this definition is modified slightly to "exactly one pair of parallel sides." You should be aware of which definition is used in your textbook and in any state content standards and use that definition consistently.

FIGURE 14-14 A Set of Plane Figures

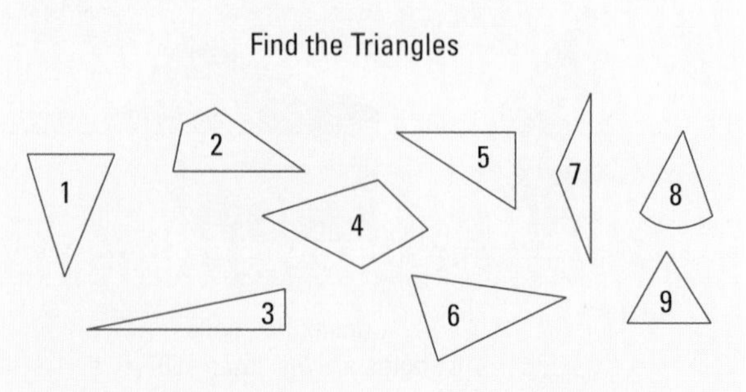

FIGURE 14-15 Classifying Quadrilaterals

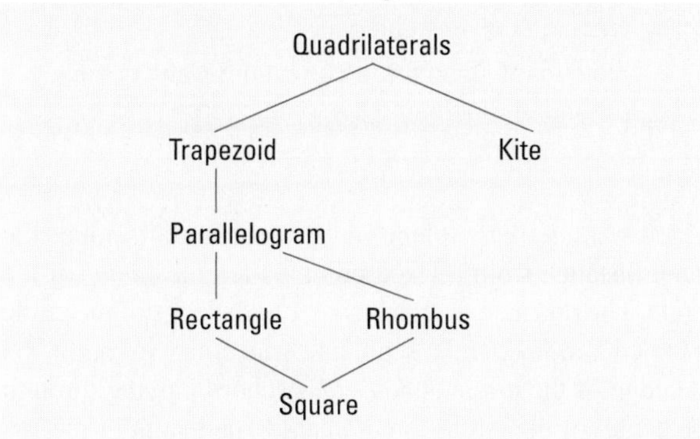

A *parallelogram* is a polygon with two pairs of parallel sides. A *rectangle* fulfills that requirement, and therefore is a parallelogram, but it is a special parallelogram that has all right angles. A *rhombus* also has parallel opposite sides and is also a special parallelogram because it has equal sides. A *square* also is a parallelogram. Because a square has four right angles, it is a rectangle; and it has equal sides, so it is also a rhombus. A *kite* is a quadrilateral with two pairs of adjacent sides that have equal lengths.

Children will recognize properties of shapes according to their geometric thinking level. For example, primary-grade children may articulate only the number of sides and corners; upper-elementary grade children may note that sides are equal or parallel and that angles are right or equal; middle school children will be able to provide formal descriptions and classify figures in "families," such as the family of parallelograms (see Figure 14-15). Concise definitions of quadrilaterals are included in Figure 14-16.

FIGURE 14-16 Definitions of Quadrilaterals

Parallelogram: A quadrilateral with two pairs of parallel sides.

Rectangle: A parallelogram with 90-degree angles.

Square: A rectangle with equal sides.

Rhombus: A parallelogram with all sides equal.

Trapezoid: A quadrilateral with at least one pair of parallel sides.

Isosceles Trapezoid: A trapezoid with two nonparallel sides equal.

Kite: A quadrilateral with two pairs of adjacent sides equal.

In preparation for an oral activity, display a set of different polygons. Ask the children to choose a figure and examine it, then ask, "What can you say about the figure?" Activities 14-9 through 14-12 suggest some explorations with polygons, including quadrilaterals.

Diagonals. Creating a table of shapes in which the sides increase by one each time and finding the number of diagonals in each figure is another aspect of the study of polygons that leads to a numerical pattern and a possible algebraic generalization. A *diagonal* is a line segment joining any two nonadjacent vertices of a figure, with the line segment completely in the interior of the figure (Henderson & Collier, 1973). For example, in the following diagram, the line segment FD is a diagonal, whereas the line segment AC is not.

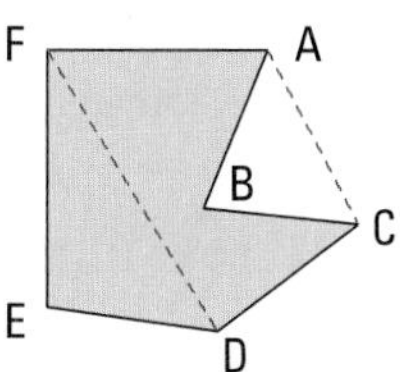

ACTIVITY 14-9 Rectangles (van Hiele Levels 1–2)

Materials

Polygons as shown below.

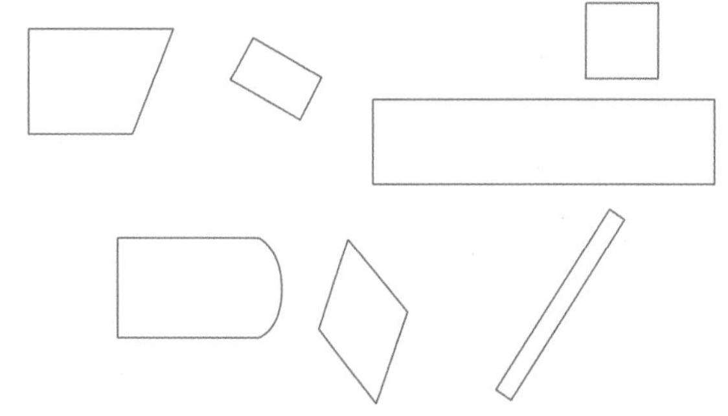

Procedure

1. Which of the figures are rectangles?
2. Tell why you think the nonrectangles are not rectangles.

ACTIVITY 14-10 Describing and Comparing Polygons (van Hiele Level 2)

Materials

A set of polygons

Procedure

1. Select a polygon. Write about the figure, mentioning as many characteristics as you can.
2. Choose another polygon and write about how it is different from and how it is similar to the first one.

3. Now examine the whole set of polygons. Make a list of all the different characteristics you notice as you examine the polygons. Which polygons have one or more characteristics in common?

Procedure

1. Examine the 12 figures.
2. How many figures can you name? Can you give more than one name for some figures?

ACTIVITY 14-11 How Many Squares Can You Find? (van Hiele Levels 0–2)

Materials

Geoboards
Rubber bands
Dot paper
Pencils

Procedure

1. Make different squares on a geoboard.
2. Sketch each of the squares you make on the dot paper. Some possible squares are shown below:

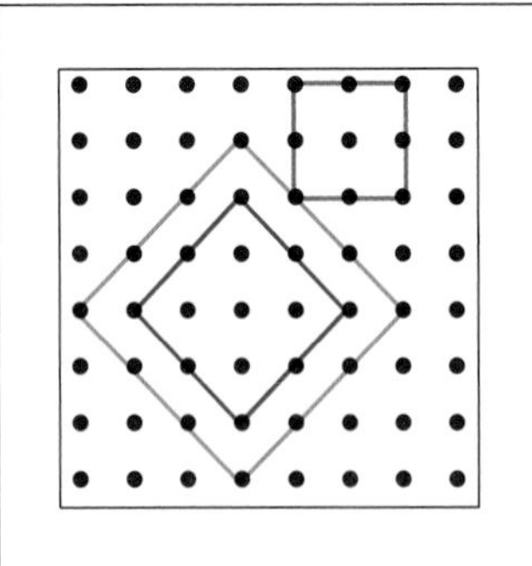

3. How many squares did you find? How do you know you have found all the squares possible? *Extension*: How many different rectangles can you make on a geoboard?

ACTIVITY 14-12 Naming Figures (van Hiele Levels 0–1)

Materials

The 12 figures shown below

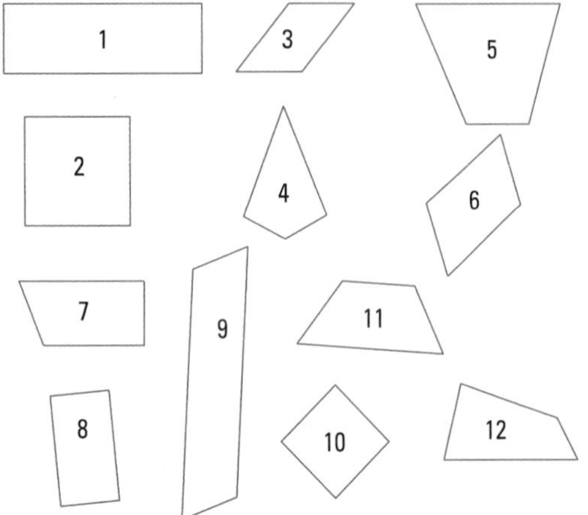

Circles. A *circle* is a plane figure that has all its points the same distance from a fixed point, called the *center* of the circle. The distance from the center to the edge of the circle is called a *radius,* and a segment connecting two points on the edge of the circle is a *chord.* A chord passing through the center of the circle is a *diameter.* The length of the circle (distance around) is the *circumference*. A segment of the circle is called an *arc.*

Learning about Symmetry, Congruence, and Similarity

Symmetry

The idea of *symmetry* can first be introduced to children with examples from nature, art, and pictures of familiar objects. Moyer (2001) recommends using symmetry and patterns as a starting point for integrating culture into mathematics lessons. Symmetrical figures possess the quality that when the figure is bisected into two congruent parts, every point on one side of the bisection line (referred to as the line of symmetry) will have a reflective point on the other side of the bisection line. Folding is a means of testing for line symmetry. For example, by folding, one will find out that a square has four lines of symmetry, a rectangle has two lines of symmetry, whereas some other parallelograms have none. Exploring all parallelograms provides excellent examples and nonexamples of lines of symmetry. Figures can be classified according to the number of lines of symmetry in each. For polygons, lines of symmetry can be of three types: a line connecting two vertices, a line connecting a vertex to a midpoint of a side, and a line connecting the midpoints of two sides.

ACTIVITY 14-13 Symmetrical Patterns on Graph Paper (van Hiele Levels 2–3)

Materials

Graph paper

Procedure

1. Draw 3-by-3 squares on graph paper. Shade three of the small squares so that the figure created has one line of symmetry. Two examples are shown here.

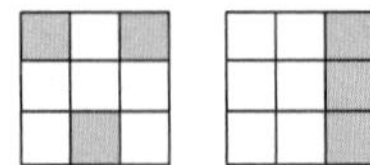

Literature Link 14-1

Geometry

Dodds, Dayle Ann. (1994). ***The Shape of Things.*** Cambridge, MA: Candlewick Press.

Children's spatial abilities often exceed their numeric skills. Therefore, it is important to give children many opportunities to explore both two- and three-dimensional shapes using concrete materials. ***The Shape of Things*** introduces young children to common shapes and shows where such shapes can be seen in the world around them.

- Draw or create a picture using only the shapes in the story. Using each of the shapes cut from colored construction paper, draw each shape into a picture using the correct name of the shape on the page. Combine the pages to create a shapes book for each child.
- Find pictures in magazines that show shapes in nature, in architecture, and other places. Design a shapes book with the pictures.
- Identify both two- and three-dimensional shapes hidden in a shoebox by using Attribute blocks or wooden solids. Record the features of each shape that are identified by touch.
- Explore three-dimensional geometry by using cutouts of various two-dimensional shapes and taping them together to see what three-dimensional shapes can be constructed from them. This helps children to connect the two-dimensional attributes with a three-dimensional shape and to visualize three-dimensional solids.
- Using large chart paper, write the name of a two- or three-dimensional shape, such as "parallelogram" or "cylinder," at the top of each piece of paper. Under the name of the shape use precise mathematical language to write as many descriptive words as possible to distinguish the attributes of this shape from other shapes. As shapes are added to the display, check to be sure that each shape has its own characteristics that make it distinct from other shapes.
- In ***The Greedy Triangle*** (Burns, 1994), children learn correct mathematical terminology for identifying polygons by the number of sides. Children can use toothpicks and minimarshmallows to create a triangle, then a quadrilateral, then a pentagon, and so on, modeling the shape changes the triangle makes in the story.
- Other books that introduce children to basic concepts about two-dimensional shapes include ***Shapes, Shapes, Shapes*** (Hoban, 1996), ***Bear in a Square*** (Blackstone, 1998), and ***Brown Rabbit's Shape Book*** (Baker, 1994).

Source: Dr. Patricia Moyer-Packenham, Utah State University.

2. How many different patterns with one line of symmetry can you make by shading in three small squares?
3. Can you make patterns with two lines of symmetry?
4. Shade in four small squares and make figures with one line of symmetry; with two lines of symmetry.
5. Can you make figures with more than two lines of symmetry?
6. Compare your work with your classmates. (Adapted from Eperson, 1982)

A Mira is a good instrument to test for lines of symmetry in a figure. A Mira is a piece of colored Plexiglas that allows one to view the reflection of a figure through the glass rather than on it, as with a mirror. The process of paper folding, known as origami, offers ample opportunities to improve spatial sense as children bend and fold square sheets of paper to make many three-dimensional shapes and objects.

Children can be asked to create symmetrical designs using pattern blocks, construct some symmetrical figures on a geoboard, or draw some on graph paper. Activities 14-22 and 14-23 are about creating symmetrical figures using pattern blocks and graph paper.

The following nine numbered activities have children examine familiar objects (leaves, windows), pictures of familiar objects (magazine pictures), and geometric figures for symmetry. Children are asked to construct symmetrical pictures and figures. In all of these activities, it is important to listen to children as they describe what they are doing and what they observe.

1. **Symmetry**
   - Provide children with a set of leaves to examine.
   - Have them discuss what they observe. Listen for observations about "sameness" within a shape ("I think this side is the same as this side because ...").
2. **Symmetry**
   - Provide children with a set of pictures from magazines, some symmetrical, others not.
   - Have children examine the pictures, looking for some that are the same on two sides of a central line, and describe what they notice.

3. **Symmetry**
   - Provide a set of pictures of homes or windows.
   - Have children examine the pictures to find windows that are symmetrical.
   - Have them tell why they think some windows are not symmetrical.
   - Have them verify the shapes that are symmetrical with a Mira.
4. **Line Symmetry**
   - Have children construct symmetrical figures on a geoboard.
   - Have them tell how they know the figures are symmetrical by identifying the line or lines of symmetry.
5. **Line Symmetry**
   - Have children draw on paper different figures that have line symmetry.
   - Have them cut out the figures and test for symmetry by folding.
   - Be sure to examine the diagonal cuts of parallelograms and rectangles to serve as nonexamples of line symmetry.
6. **Line Symmetry**
   - Draw symmetrical shapes on patty paper (such as the paper hamburgers are wrapped in; also available commercially) or some type of transparent paper.
   - Have students fold the paper along a line of symmetry to see that one side of the shape can be placed directly on top of the other shape.
7. **Line Symmetry**
   - Provide children with a set of different polygons drawn on paper.
   - Have them examine the figures for lines of symmetry and tell where each line of symmetry is.
   - Listen to find out how children describe each line of symmetry in a figure.
8. **Line Symmetry**
   - Have children draw on paper figures with only one line of symmetry.
   - Ask, "Can you draw figures with two lines of symmetry? Can you draw one with three lines of symmetry? With more than three lines of symmetry?"
9. **Drawing Triangles and Quadrilaterals**
   - Have children draw or construct triangles on a geoboard with exactly one line of symmetry, with more than one line of symmetry, and one with no lines of symmetry.
   - Repeat the above steps with quadrilaterals.

Upper-elementary grade and middle school children can study three-dimensional shapes for planes of symmetry. A three-dimensional shape has *plane symmetry* if a plane passing through the figure bisects it such that every point of the figure on one side of the plane has a reflection image on the other side of the plane. Activity 14-24 explores planes of symmetry.

FIGURE 14-17 Rotational Symmetry of a Square

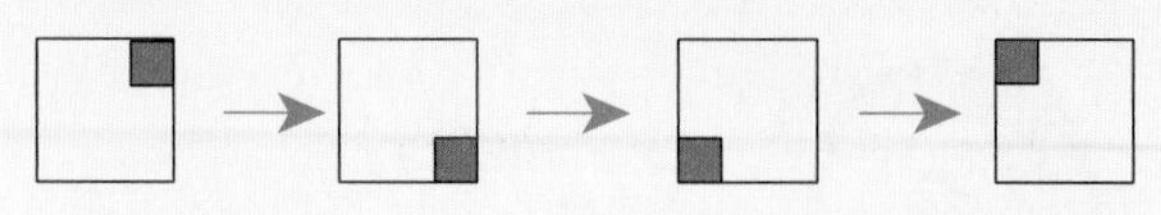

Some three- and two-dimensional shapes and figures have *rotational symmetry.* A shape is said to have rotational symmetry if, when rotated about a point for an amount less than 360°, the rotated shape matches the original shape. For example, a square has 90°, 180°, and 270° rotational symmetry (Figure 14-17). Children can be asked to examine shapes and figures for rotational symmetry. For example, in explorations with figures, they will find that some figures have rotational symmetry but not line symmetry (e.g., a parallelogram), some have line symmetry but not rotational symmetry (e.g., an isosceles triangle), and regular polygons have both line and rotational symmetry, whereas some figures have neither. Letters of the alphabet, numbers, or commercially made pentomino shapes are excellent tools for exploring rotational symmetry.

Congruence and Similarity

Congruent figures are those that have the same size and shape; that is, all corresponding angles and the length of corresponding sides are equal. Superimposing figures is one way to test for congruency. Another is by measuring sides and angles to identify that each shape has corresponding parts.

ACTIVITY 14-14 Planes of Symmetry (van Hiele Levels 2–3)

Materials
A cube

Procedure
Consider a cube.

1. How many horizontal planes of symmetry does a cube have?

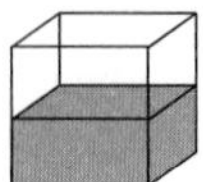

2. How many vertical planes of symmetry does a cube have?
3. How many planes of symmetry pass through each pair of opposite edges?

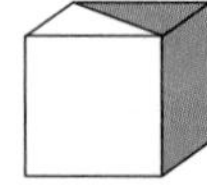

4. How many planes of symmetry can you find for a cube? Consider other solids.
5. Does the tetrahedron have the same number of planes of symmetry as the cube?
6. Does an octahedron, an icosahedron, or a dodecahedron have planes of symmetry?
7. Record your findings on a chart. Compare your findings with those of some classmates.

Similar figures have the same shape but not necessarily the same size. If two figures are congruent, they are also similar. Similar polygons have equal angles and proportional sides. Examples of similar figures can be obtained by enlarging or reducing a picture on a photocopying machine. Similar shapes possess the quality that when creating a ratio of two sides of one shape, the same ratio will exist in the similar figure. Or when selecting a side of one shape and its corresponding side on another shape, the same ratio will exist when comparing a different side on the first shape to the corresponding side on the other shape. This ratio can represent the scale value of the second object to the first object. For example, a ratio of 1:2 indicates that each dimension of the second figure is twice as big as the first shape's dimensions. Each dimension has been increased, but children should explore what effect this will have on the area of the shape. Congruent and similar figures can be constructed on a geoboard, patty paper, and graph paper.

Congruent Figures

Similar Figures

Learning about Transformational Geometry

Rigid Transformations

The idea that objects can be moved from one position to another without changing shape and size is a fundamental part of the study of transformation geometry. Movements of an object where the object itself is not distorted or changed in any way are called *rigid transformations.* Rigid transformations can be contrasted with topological transformations (e.g., stretching), in which the shape and size of objects change.

Transformation geometry (also called motion geometry) can be introduced by discussing different movements observed in nature and in the environment, such as a falling leaf, an airplane taking off, a boat moving on a river, or a door being opened.

Elementary schoolchildren study three fundamental types of rigid transformations: translations, reflections, and rotations. Children usually name these motions *slides, flips,* and *turns,* respectively. A *translation* is a movement along a straight line. It has direction and distance. The direction can be horizontal, vertical, or oblique. A *reflection* is the movement of a figure about a line outside the figure, on a side of the figure, or intersecting with a vertex. A *rotation* is the movement of a figure around a point. The turning point may be inside the figure, on the figure, or outside the figure (see Figure 14-18).

Materials used in the following 12 transformation geometry activities include a Mira, paper cutouts, patty paper, figure templates, tracing paper, Attribute blocks, pattern blocks, and a geoboard.

1. **Constructing Reflections**
   - Provide children with a set of Attribute blocks.
   - Have them construct a figure such as a house or animal.
   - Have them construct a horizontal and vertical reflection of the figure.
2. **Transformations on a Geoboard**
   - Ask children to make a figure on a geoboard.
   - Show a slide of the figure; a flip; a turn.
3. **Drawing Reflection Images**
   - Provide children with a Mira and some figures printed on a page.
   - Have them draw reflection images about given lines.
4. **Modeling Transformations**
   - Using several paper cutouts of nonsymmetrical figures (e.g., boats, birds), have children explore different motions on their desks. For example, have them demonstrate different slides (horizontal, vertical, oblique).
   - Have children record their work.
5. **Constructing Reflections**
   - Provide children with an irregular figure or a shape made from pattern blocks.
   - Have them draw the figure.
   - Then have them draw the figure showing a horizontal reflection; a vertical reflection; an oblique reflection across a diagonal.
   - Use Miras to verify their answers or use a hinged mirror where part of the shape is placed at the vertex of the hinged mirror. The image they drew should match the shape they see in the mirror.

FIGURE 14-18 Translations, Reflections, and Rotations

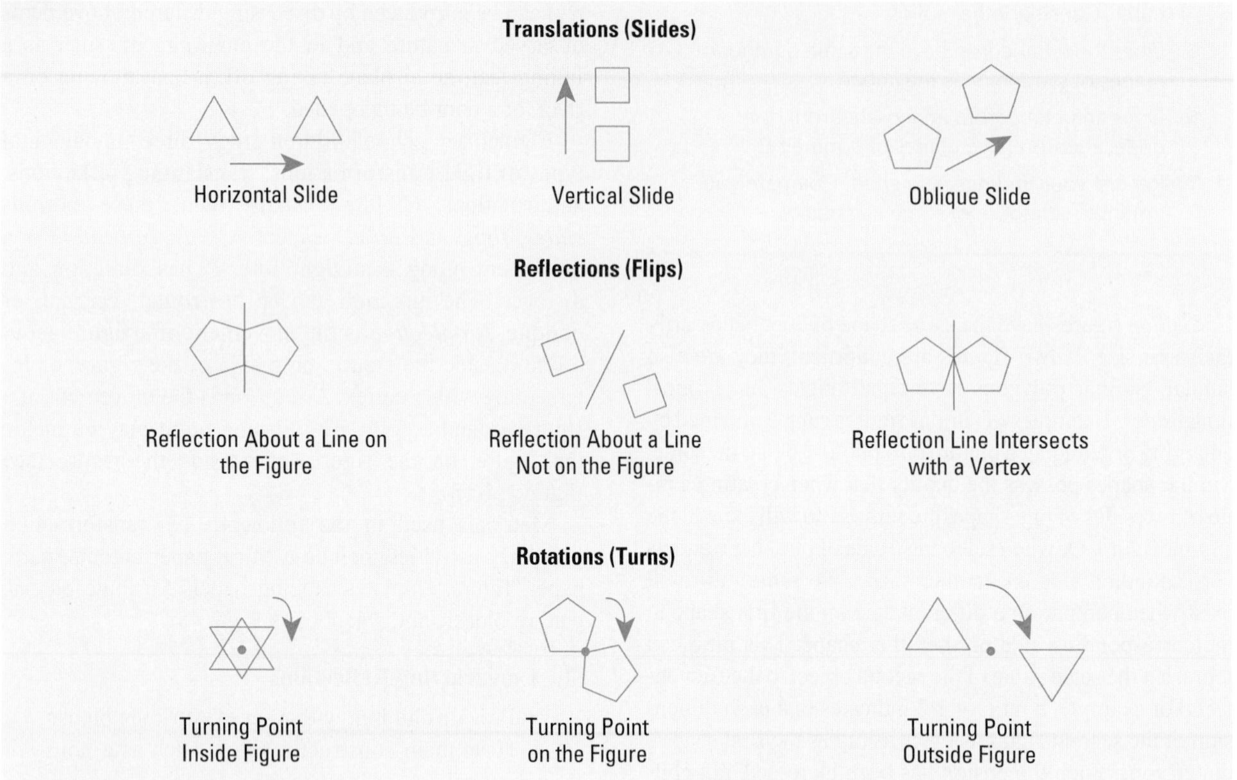

6. **Making a Transformation**
   - Have children make a shape on paper.
   - Have them trace the shape on patty paper or some type of transparent paper.
   - Have them flip over the transparent version from left to right.
   - Children should compare the two shapes to see that when they are placed adjacent to each other, a line of symmetry exists between the two shapes.
   - Orient the two on top of each other again and explore a slide, a rotation, and an oblique flip.
7. **Making Reflective Inkblots**
   - Take a piece of paper and place paint on one half of the paper.
   - Have children fold the paper onto the wet paint.
   - Open the paper and examine the reflective image that appears.
8. **Constructing Rotations**
   - Provide children with a paper cutout of a nonsymmetrical figure such as an animal.
   - Have children explore with different rotations on their desks. In time, children should be able to demonstrate a rotation about a point on a figure, a rotation about a point outside a figure, and a rotation about a point inside a figure.
9. **Constructing Rotations**
   - Provide children with a template of a small nonsymmetrical figure.
   - Have them trace the figure and then draw a half turn; a quarter turn clockwise; a quarter turn counterclockwise; combinations of rotations.
10. **Constructing Rotations**
    - Direct children to make a figure using pattern blocks.
    - Have them make one that is a quarter turn of the first figure; a half turn; a three-quarter turn.
11. **Constructing a Pattern Showing Transformations**
    - Provide each child with a 4-by-4 square grid (with each small square measuring approximately 5 cm) and a cutout of a small figure.
    - Ask children to trace the figure in each square following a pattern of rigid motions (for example, horizontal reflections and vertical half turns).
12. **Constructing a Pattern Showing Transformations**
    - Provide each child with a figure to use as a template (or use tracing paper or patty paper).
    - Invite children to create borders for a bulletin board by using translations, reflections, and rotations of a figure.

At the middle school level, children can conduct explorations with combinations of motions. Explorations to pursue include the following:

1. Draw any Figure A and then make two successive translations to produce Figures B and C. Compare Figures A and C. Is the result of a single translation

FIGURE 14-19 Different Types of Tessellations

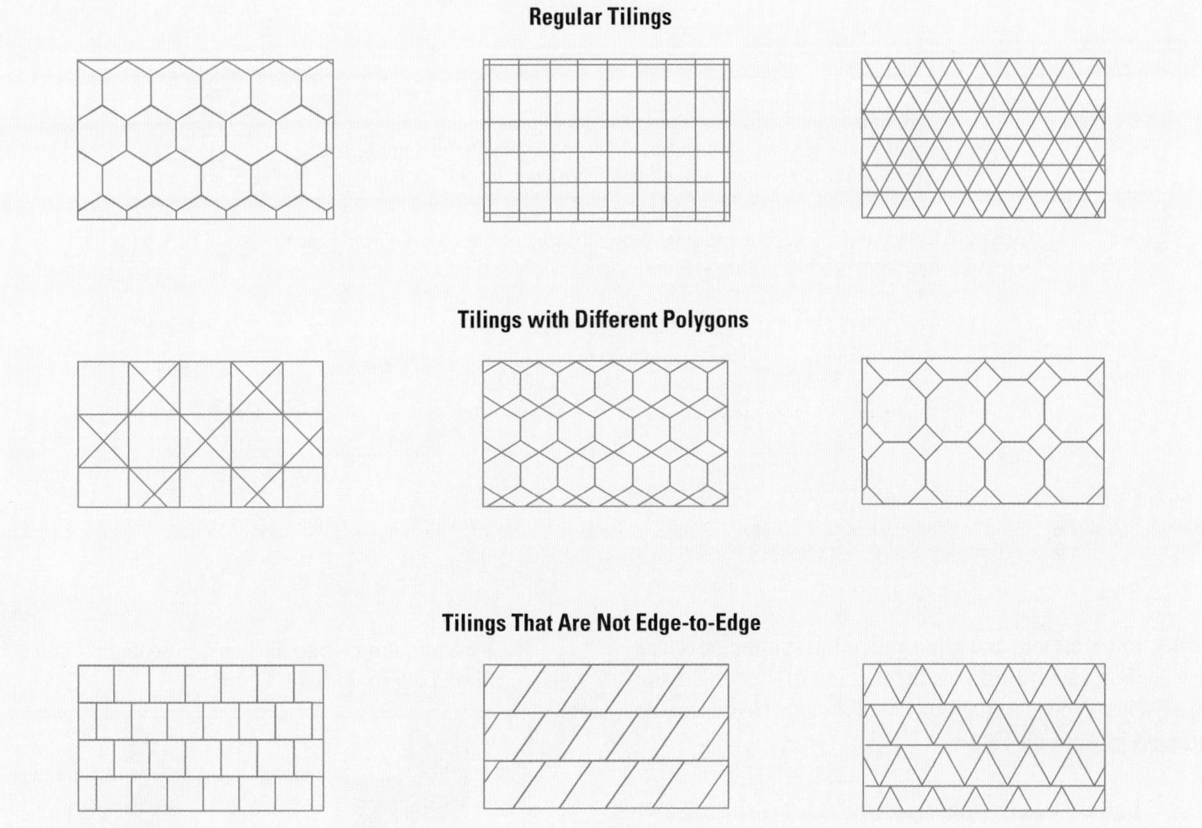

different from the result of two successive translations? Why?

2. Draw any Figure A and then make two successive flips to produce Figures B and C. Compare Figures A and C. Are the results the same as for translations? Why not?
3. Compare the results of other successive motions:
   - A slide followed by a flip and a flip followed by a slide.
   - A turn followed by a flip and a flip followed by a turn.
   - Other combinations including oblique flips and their reverse.

Write about your findings.

Learning about Tessellations

When thinking about *tessellations,* what generally comes to mind is a flat region being covered with repetitions of the same figure without any overlapping. A floor covered with square tiles is an example of a tessellation. Young children can be given a number of different types of regular figures and invited to explore which figures can cover a region (Activity 14-15). This is best explained by placing a large dot on the paper and having children take a vertex of the shape and place it on the dot. Follow with more vertices of the additional shapes being placed on the dot until no gaps or overlaps occur, if possible.

Eventually, children will not need to place just the vertices on the dot. They will discover that triangles, convex quadrilaterals, and regular hexagons will tessellate by themselves, as will varied kinds of irregular shapes (Figure 14-19). Children can be challenged to explore why some figures tessellate and why others do not as they explore the concept of angles. This exploration could begin with triangles by asking the question: "Will all types of triangles tessellate?" Next, explore the questions "Why do all rectangles tessellate?" and "Will all convex quadrilaterals tessellate?" can be explored.

Other polygons and combinations of figures, including the use of hinged mirrors to see the tessellation about a point, can be used for further investigations. By modifying tessellating polygons a certain way, children can make Escher-type designs that will also tessellate. Explorations in Escher-type tessellations offer children opportunities to extend their understanding of symmetries, such as translation,

FIGURE 14-20 Constructing Escher-Type Tessellations

Step 1. Select a polygon; for example, a square.

Step 2. Select a transformation, for example, a rotation. Label the vertices and sides of the square. Rotating the square four times around vertex C produces the diagram at the right. One can see that 2 and 3 fit together. If the four-square pattern was translated horizontally and vertically, it would show that sides 1 and 4 fit together.

Step 3. Modify the square. The example shows that the piece removed from side 1 has been attached to side 4. Sides 2 and 3 could similarly be modified. The modified square has the same area as the original square, and it will tessellate in the same manner as did the original square.

Step 4. Invite children to use their ingenuity to make cuts on a square to produce a tessellation. An example follows.

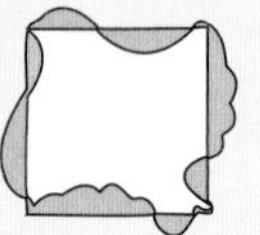

Source: "Transformational geometry and the artwork of M.C. Escher," by S. Haak, 1976, *Mathematics Teacher, 69*(B), p. 650. Copyright 1976 by the National Council of Teachers of Mathematics, Reston, VA. Used with permission.

reflection, rotation, and glide-reflection symmetry (Haak, 1976). Figure 14-20 shows the process of creating a simple Escher-type tessellation. Tessellation activities are described in Activity 14-16.

ACTIVITY 14-15 Tiling a Floor (van Hiele Levels 1–2)

Realia Strategies

Materials

Several equilateral triangles, squares, and regular pentagons, hexagons, and octagons with sides of equal length

Procedure

1. Pretend that the shapes are ceramic tiles. What kind of shape could you use to tile a bathroom floor using only one kind of shape?
2. Could you tile a floor using two different shapes?
3. Draw pictures of different tiled floors.

ACTIVITY 14-16 Tessellations (van Hiele Levels 1–2)

Materials

Graph paper

Procedure

1. Draw an outline of a figure that will tessellate on the graph paper.
2. Color or shade in the figure.
3. By alternating white and color, create an interesting tiling pattern with the figure.

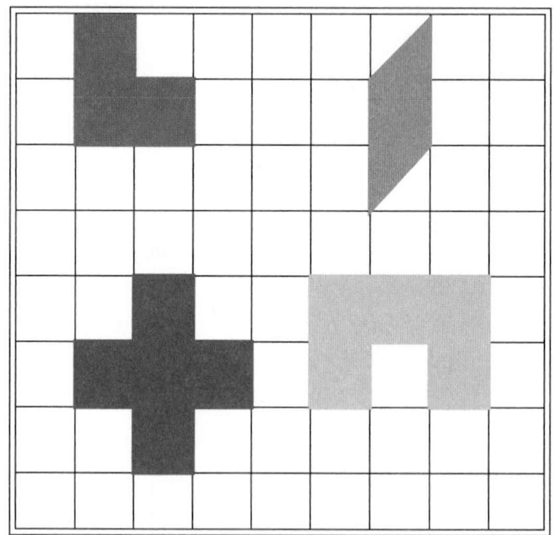

myeducationlab The Power of Classroom Practice — To explore your own understanding of Geometry concepts, go to Chapter 14 in the Book-Specific Resources section in the MyEducationLab for your course. Select the Activities section and complete any of the various activities in this topic.

Learning about Fractals

Fractals are complex yet simplistic in design. A fractal is generated by a repetitive process in which an alteration is made to each stage of the fractal design. Many rotations,

FIGURE 14-21 Fractals

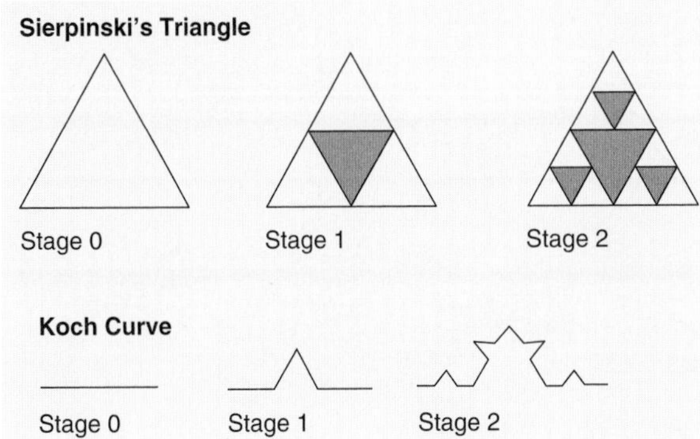

NCTM Principles and Standards Link 14-4

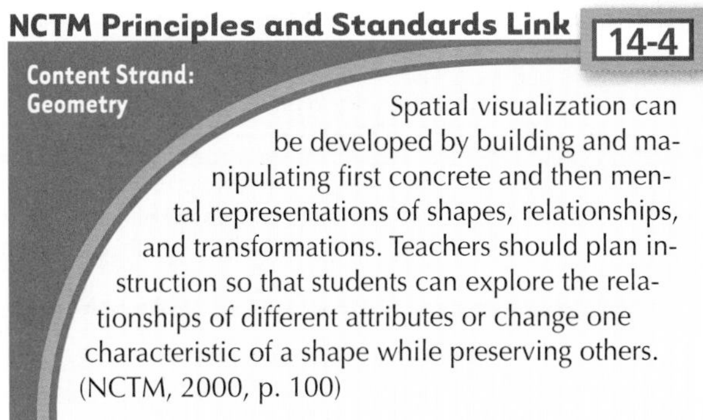

Content Strand: Geometry

Spatial visualization can be developed by building and manipulating first concrete and then mental representations of shapes, relationships, and transformations. Teachers should plan instruction so that students can explore the relationships of different attributes or change one characteristic of a shape while preserving others. (NCTM, 2000, p. 100)

reflections, and slides are made, as well as a change in reduction of the stage before and a replication of the previous stage to make the next stage. An interesting observation about fractals is that a certain portion of a fractal takes on the shape and image of the original fractal, only in a miniaturized form.

Making a Fractal

Fractals can be made by starting with a simple geometric shape. For instance, the Sierpinski triangle begins with a simple equilateral triangle (Stage 0) and then, by connecting the midpoints of each side, a smaller equilateral triangle one-fourth the size of the original will be formed in the center (see Figure 14-21). This triangle is removed, and three congruent triangles (at the top, left, and right) remain (Stage 1). The area of this new shape is three-fourths that of the original shape. This process is repeated for each of the smaller triangles to make the next stage, and so on. Other fractal drawings, such as the Koch curve (see Figure 14-21), are generated by reducing, replicating, translating, and rebuilding the previous stage to form the next stage.

Developing Spatial Sense

Spatial sense involves both visualization and orientation factors (Owens, 1990). *Visualization* is the ability to mentally picture how objects appear under some rigid motion or other transformation. *Orientation* includes the ability to note positions of objects and to maintain an accurate perception of the objects under different orientations. Research shows that the two types of ability do not always reside within the same individual and that, generally, boys score higher than girls on tests of spatial abilities (Owens, 1990).

Activities to Develop Spatial Sense

Beginning at the primary level, geometry activities should aim to develop children's spatial abilities. Many of the activities described in this chapter can contribute to the development of visual perception. Activities involving tangrams and polyominoes, as well as the process of describing figures and dissecting figures, help to develop spatial sense.

Tangram Puzzles

A *tangram* is a seven-piece puzzle consisting of five triangles (2 large, 1 medium, and 2 small), one square, and one parallelogram cut from a square. These parts can be arranged to create different shapes, such as a rectangle, a large triangle, a boat, or a building (see Figure 14-22). In *Grandfather Tang's Story* (Tompert, 1990) (see Literature Link 14-2), the tangram pieces are used to create many animals. Children can be asked to compare the tangram pieces. Following are some possible comparisons:

- Compare the small triangle to the two larger triangles.
- Compare the small triangle to the parallelogram and then to the square.
- Compare the square to the largest triangle.

Such comparisons can use fraction language, such as "The square is one-half the size of a large triangle" or "A small triangle is one-fourth the size of a large triangle." Making the square worth one whole and deciding on the fractional value of each piece can encourage discussions of one-fourth, one-eighth, and one-sixteenth.

A common activity uses the pieces to construct or "cover" different figures, as shown in Figure 14-22. Other activities can involve children in constructing geometric figures with some or all of the pieces, as in the following examples:

- Use two tangram pieces to make a square. Can you make a square with two other pieces? With four pieces? With all seven pieces?
- Can you make a parallelogram with two pieces? With three pieces?
- How many different trapezoids can you make?
- Can you make a rectangle? A pentagon? A hexagon? A large triangle?

Children can be asked to keep a record of the different geometric figures they constructed and the number of tangram pieces they used.

FIGURE 14-22 Creating Figures with Tangrams

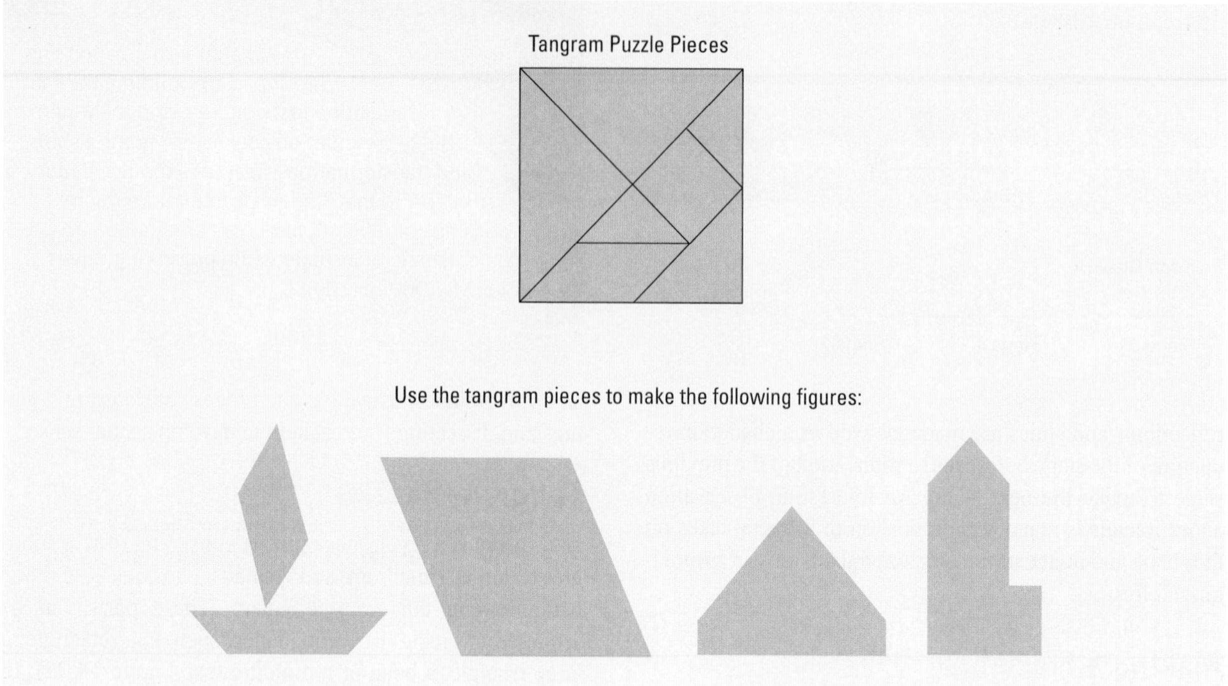

Tangram Puzzle Pieces
Use the tangram pieces to make the following figures:

Literature Link 14-2

Geometric Designs: Patterns, Symmetry, and Tessellations

Friedman, Aileen. (1994). *A Cloak for the Dreamer.* New York: Scholastic.

Although children may lack the vocabulary and conceptual understanding necessary to express geometric relationships in formal terms, teachers can develop their repertoire by providing meaningful investigations that begin at the very basic level and move to more complex analytical activity. ***A Cloak for the Dreamer*** describes a tailor and his sons who sew together pieces of cloth to create beautiful cloaks. The geometric designs throughout the text can be used to begin a variety of mathematical investigations.

- The pictures in the text show children a variety of geometric designs that tessellate. Model these geometric patterns using commercially made blocks (such as pattern blocks, tangrams, Attribute blocks) or construction paper cutouts of different shapes.
- Recognize examples of tessellating patterns that have elements that repeat, highlighting that there are no gaps or spaces between the shapes. Pattern blocks can be used to create *tessellations* and patterns that have *symmetry.* These mathematical terms and their properties should be discussed as they emerge naturally from children's investigations.
- Analyze and represent geometric designs found in different cultures. Tessellating and repeating patterns are found in Islamic culture, where designs decorate mosques and palaces; in Navajo culture, where they appear on blankets; and in the pueblo homes of the Hopi people. Use pattern blocks to re-create these tiling patterns.
- Investigate the rotational symmetry found in Native American intricate basket designs. Create a design that demonstrates rotational symmetry using a computer drawing program.
- Other books that explore geometric shapes and patterns and are representative of designs found in various cultures include ***The Sultan's Snakes*** (Turpin, 1990) and ***Grandfather Tang's Story*** (Tompert, 1990). Geometric designs can be explored using concrete materials such as tangrams, children's drawings, or computer programs such as Geometer's *Sketchpad* and *Tessellmania.*

Source: Dr. Patricia Moyer-Packenham, Utah State University.

FIGURE 14-23 Pentominoes

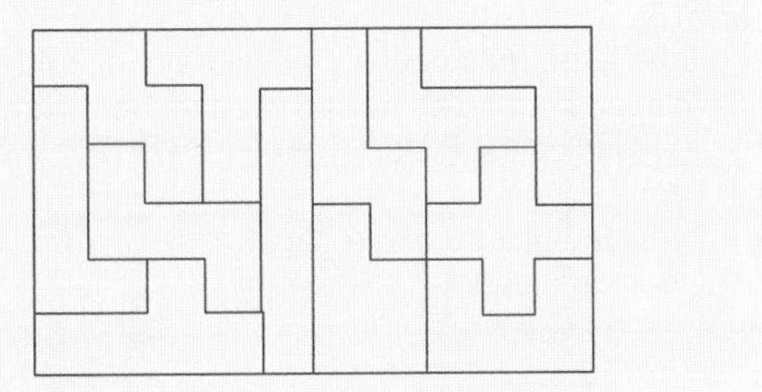

FIGURE 14-24 How Many Triangles Do You See in This Figure?

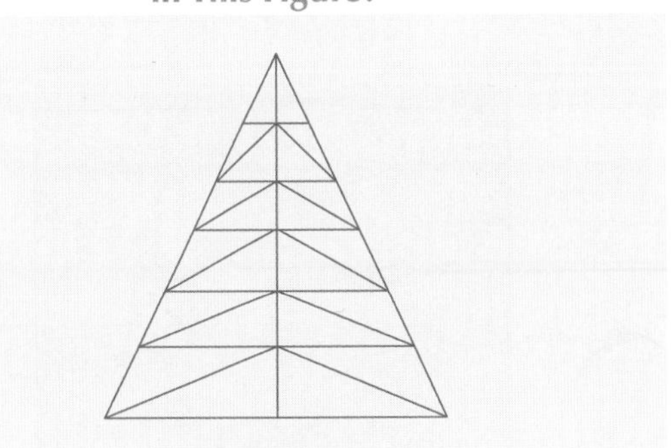

Polyominoes

Polyominoes are arrangements of different numbers of squares: A triomino is constructed with three squares, a tetromino has four squares, a pentomino has five squares, a hexomino has six squares, etc. Combining color tiles or squares edge to edge and recognizing that a reflection or rotation of the shape does not create a new shape, children can discover the shapes for themselves. Figure 14-23 shows the 12 pentomino shapes. In Activity 14-17, children create figures using triominoes. The study can be extended to tetrominoes through, for example, the Four-Stamp problem.

Four-Stamp Problem

Stamps are sometimes printed in sheets of 100 stamps (10 rows of 10 stamps). How many different four-stamp arrangements could you buy?

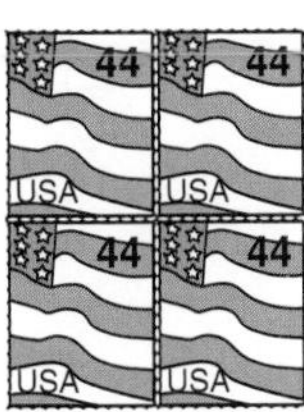

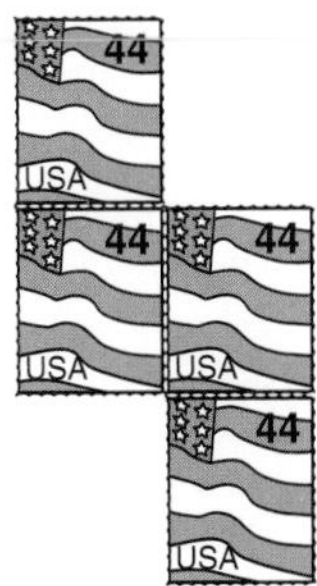

Describing Figures

An activity that encourages children to verbalize what they visualize is to have them describe a figure through feeling. Using a feely bag and placing a pentomino shape inside the bag, have children reach in and describe the shape to the class. Or group the children into pairs and provide each pair with an irregular figure cut from poster board. One child holds the figure under the desk cover (neither child has seen the figure) and, through feeling it, describes the figure to a partner, who attempts to draw the figure. The roles of describing and drawing can be interchanged. The exercise can be simple or complex depending on the figure. This activity often does not produce a correctly drawn-to-scale or size-oriented replica and emphasizes the need for communication in mathematical drawings.

Another activity is to have a figure drawn on a card and to ask one child to describe the figure to a partner, who draws the figure as she or he visualizes what has been described (Sgroi, 1990). Another type of visualization is to provide children with a complex figure and ask them to find different figures within it (see Figures 14-24 and 14-25). Another more complex visualization is to provide the children with a three-dimensional object

ACTIVITY 14-17 Triominoes (van Hiele Levels 1–3)

Materials

A set of small ceramic or paper square tiles

Procedure

1. Try to visualize which of the figures below can be made from two triominoes. Test your responses.
2. Use your triominoes to make figures that can be covered with three triominoes. Draw the outline of the figures on graph paper.
3. Draw the outline of some 9 square-unit figures on graph paper that cannot be covered with three triominoes. Ask a classmate to "solve your puzzles."*

*Adapted from Eperson, 1983.

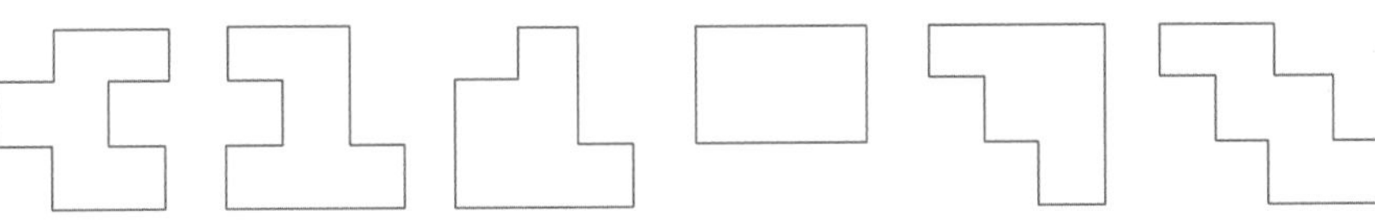

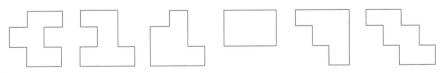

FIGURE 14-25 How Many Different-Sized Squares Do You See in This Figure?

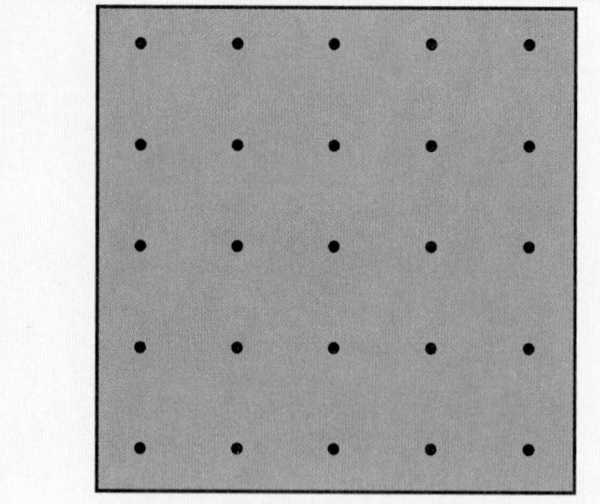

FIGURE 14-27 Visualizing Paper Unfolded

Take large rectangular pieces of paper, fold each one, and cut holes as indicated in the diagrams.
------ indicates a fold.

Draw the picture of the paper as it would look when unfolded.

1. 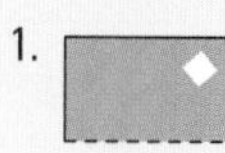

2. 

3. 

4. 

made up of interlocking cubes or multilink cubes and to have them draw on graph paper the side view, the front view, and the top view. Then, reverse the task by giving them a drawing of a shape's side, front, and top view and have them construct the object.

Figures 14-26 and 14-27 show two kinds of activities that help develop visualization skills and orientation abilities. Figure 14-26 can lead to interesting numeric patterns as the cube begins to increase in size. A generalization of the *n*th size cube can challenge many middle school children.

FIGURE 14-26 Visualizing Cubes

1. Let us say that a 1-by-1-by-1 cube has "order 1." Suppose that you were to dip such a cube into a can of paint. How many sides of the cube would be covered with paint?

2. Now imagine a 2-by-2-by-2 cube or a cube of order 2. Again, suppose you dip the cube into a can of paint and after the paint has dried, you sawed along each of the lines of its faces to obtain eight smaller cubes.
How many of the small cubes have six sides painted?
How many of the small cubes have five sides painted?
Four sides painted? Three sides? Two sides?
One side? No side?

3. BIG DIP! Now consider a cube of order three.
Once again, you follow the procedure of dipping and sawing. Can you answer the questions in part 2 for a cube of order 3?

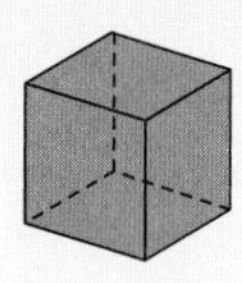

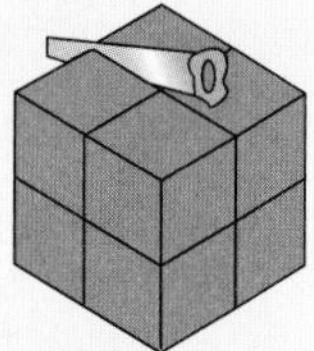

Dissection Motion Operations

Spatial sense can be developed through dissection motion operations on figures. A *dissection motion operation* (DMO) is the operation of partitioning and then dissecting a figure for the purpose of rearranging the pieces (Rahim & Sawada, 1986). DMO has not commonly been a part of geometry programs, although children use such motions spontaneously when partitioning figures to attain equal-sized parts (Pothier & Sawada, 1990). Activity 14-18 is an example of a dissection activity.

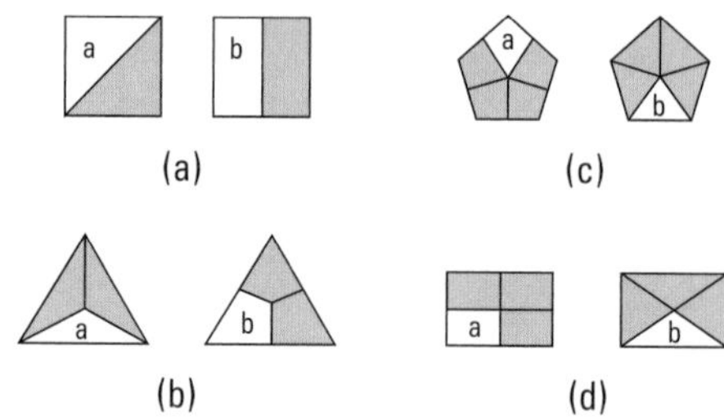

ACTIVITY 14-18 Dissecting Figures (van Hiele Levels 1–2)

Manipulative Strategies

Materials

Several paper rectangles (the same size) for each child

Procedure

1. Select one rectangle.
2. Cut it into two pieces so that the pieces can be put together again to make a large triangle.
3. Cut other rectangles into two pieces to make the following:
   - A parallelogram
   - A rhombus

- A right-angled triangle
- A trapezoid
- Other figures

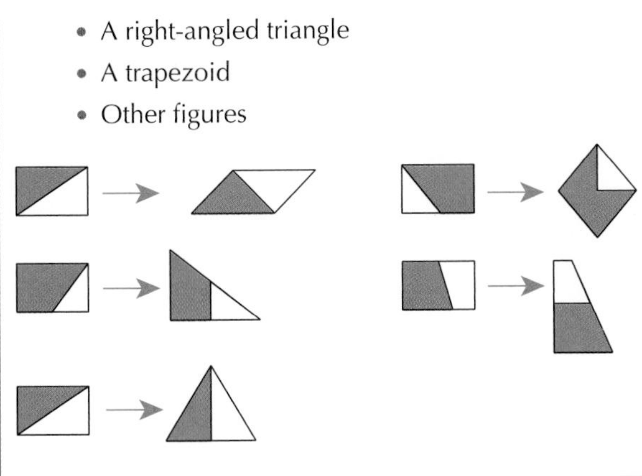

Learning about Coordinate Geometry

Upper-elementary school children are introduced to notions of coordinate geometry. A first introduction could be with real-life situations such as finding a seat in a theater or sports arena or a car in a parking lot. Rows and columns could be labeled with letters and numbers (e.g., Row F, Seat 8) and later changed to numbers only (e.g., Row 6, Column 8). The ordered pair notation (6,8) can be presented by drawing graphs.

ACTIVITY 14-19 Naming Points on a Grid (van Hiele Levels 1–2)

Materials

A grid with points labeled as in the figure

Procedure

Name the points labeled A, B, C, D, and E.

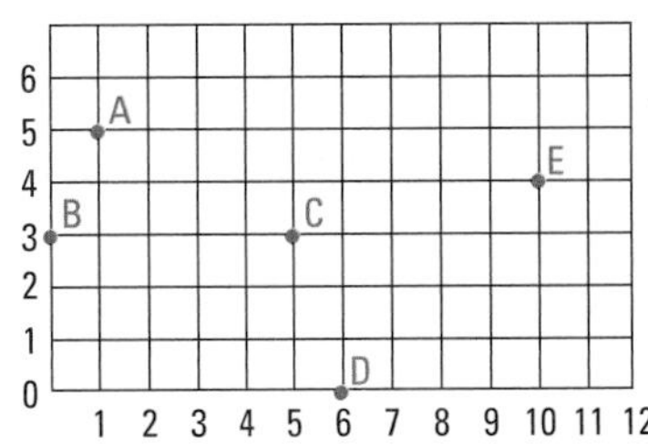

Children may connect locating points on a coordinate grid with the popular game *Battleship*. Activities for children can consist of drawing figures on a coordinate grid by plotting points from sets of given ordered pairs or by identifying points on a grid figure (Activity 14-19). Geoboards and pegboards are good materials for coordinate geometry activities.

Conclusion

This chapter discussed introductory aspects of different geometric concepts. Elementary school children should be introduced to ideas of each type in an informal manner. As children's geometric thinking progresses, the topics should be discussed in a progressively more formal manner. The development of spatial abilities should be a focus of geometry activities at all grade levels. Pay particular attention toward helping children progress on the van Hiele levels of geometric thought.

CHAPTER 14

Sample Lesson

A Lesson on Solid Geometry

Grade level: Fifth

Materials: Collection of polyhedra, including cubes, rectangular prisms, pyramids.

Lesson objective: Students will analyze and describe polygons.

Standards link: Students relate two-dimensional shapes to three-dimensional shapes and analyze properties of polyhedral solids, describing them by the number of edges, faces, or vertices as well as the types of faces (NCTM *Curriculum Focal Points*, grade five).

Launch: Display a cube. Ask students, "What makes up a cube? How should we name and describe the parts of a cube?" Solicit recommendations about how to describe this. Clarify the name of and point to the important parts: *faces*, *edges*, and *vertices* (note that this is the plural of *vertex*). Discuss what shape each of those parts are: *Faces* of a cube are squares, *edges* are line segments, and *vertices* are points. Display a rectangular prism and a pyramid and ask students, "What are the parts of these other shapes?"

Explore: In pairs, have students repeat this process with other polyhedra, including at least a rectangular prism and a pyramid: (1) select and examine a polygon, (2) list its parts, and (3) list the shapes of each part.

Summarize: Coming together as a whole class, select one pair of students to come to the front of the room and explain their findings. Make a class list of the parts of each polygon, and discuss these findings, focusing on similarities and differences.

FOLLOW-UP

Complete the following questions.

1. Why were these polygons used in the lesson? What other polygons might be used? What about other solid objects, such as cylinders and spheres? What would be the advantages and/or disadvantages of each type of solid object?
2. Consider difficulties students might have with this concept and this lesson. What modification could you make to avoid or minimize these issues? What modifications could you make for students with special needs?
3. What might the *next* lesson focus on, and why?

IN PRACTICE

Complete the following activities to include in your professional portfolio.

1. Examine a textbook's section on geometry and describe it in relation to the van Hiele levels.
2. Write a lesson plan to introduce a geometry concept of your choice to children at van Hiele level 0. Then write a lesson to introduce a related topic to children at van Hiele level 1.
3. Write a lesson plan to help children develop spatial sense.

myeducationlab The Power of Classroom Practice Now go to Topic #11: "Geometric Thinking and Spatial Sense" in the MyEducationLab (www.myeducationlab.com) for your course, where you can:

- Find learning outcomes for "Geometric Thinking and Spatial Sense" along with the national standards that connect to these outcomes.
- Apply and practice your understanding of the core teaching skills identified in the chapter with a Building Teaching Skills and Dispositions learning unit.
- Complete Assignments and Activities that can help you understand the chapter content more deeply.
- Complete *enVision MATH* Sample Curricula assignments that allow you to examine and work with chapters from *enVision MATH*, a K-6 mathematics program.
- Check your comprehension on the content covered in the chapter by going to the Study Plan in the Book-Specific Resources for your text. Here you will be able to take a chapter quiz, receive feedback on your answers, and then access Review, Practice, and Enrichment activities to enhance your understanding of chapter content.
- Go to the Book-Specific Resources Chapter 14 to explore mathematical reasoning related to chapter content in the Activities section.

LINKS TO THE INTERNET

Math Forum: Regular Tessellations

http://mathforum.org/pubs/boxer/student.tess.html

Contains information about tessellations, including what they are and how to create them.

Totally Tessellated

http://library.thinkquest.org/16661/

Contains information about tessellations, including historical information, information about mosaics, and about M. C. Escher.

Geoboards in the Classroom

http://www.mathforum.org/trscavo/geoboards/

Contains a unit on exploring the length and area of two-dimensional geometric figures using geoboards.

Tangrams

http://www.mathforum.org/trscavo/tangrams.html

Contains a unit on using tangrams to find the area of polygons without employing formulas.

RESOURCES FOR TEACHERS

Books on Geometry

Creative Publications. (1994). *Beyond Activities Project: Mathematics replacement curriculum: Polyhedraville.* Mountain View, CA: Author.

Del Grande, J. (1993). *Geometry and Spatial Sense: Curriculum evaluation standards for school mathematics addenda series, grades K–6.* Reston, VA: National Council of Teachers of Mathematics.

Geddes, D. (1992). *Geometry in the Middle Grades: Curriculum evaluation standards for school mathematics addenda series, grades 5–8.* Reston, VA: National Council of Teachers of Mathematics.

Picciotto, H. (1984). *Pentomino Activities, Lessons, and Puzzles.* Sunnyvale, CA: Creative Publications.

Rectanus, C. (1994). *Math By All Means: Geometry Grade 2.* Sausalito, CA: Math Solutions Publications.

Rectanus, C. (1994). *Math By All Means: Geometry Grade 3.* Sausalito, CA: Math Solutions Publications.

Seymour, D., & Britton, J. (1989). *Introduction to Tessellations.* Palo Alto, CA: Dale Seymour Publications.

Tremaine, J. (1997). *Step by Step Origami.* Surrey, UK: Combe Books.

Walker, K., Reak, C., & Stewart, K. (1995). *20 Thinking Questions for Geoboards, Grades 3–6.* Mountain View, CA: Creative Publications.

Walker, K., Reak, C., & Stewart, K. (1995). *20 Thinking Questions for Geoboards, Grades 6–8.* Mountain View, CA: Creative Publications.

Winter, M., Lappan, G., Phillips, E., & Fitzgerald, W. (1986). *Middle Grades Mathematics Project: Spatial visualization.* Menlo Park, CA: Addison-Wesley.

Children's Literature

Dotlich, Rebecca Kai (1999). *What Is a Square?* New York: HarperFestival.

Ehlert, L. (1989). *Color Zoo*. New York: J.B. Lippincott.

Emberley, Ed (2006). *Ed Emberley's Picture Pie: A Circle Drawing Book.* New York: LB Kids.

Emberley, Ed (2001). *The Wing on a Flea: A Book about Shapes.* New York: Little, Brown Young Readers.

Ernst, Lisa Campbell (1992). *Sam Johnson and the Blue Ribbon Quilt*. New York: HarperTrophy.

Greene, Rhonda Gowler (2001). *When a Line Bends . . . a Shape Begins.* Boston: Houghton Mifflin.

Grifalconi, Ann (1989). *The Village of Round and Square Houses.* London: Macmillan Children's Books.

Hewitt, S. (1996). *Taking Off with Shapes*. Austin, TX: Raintree Steck-Vaughn.

Pilegard, Virginia Walton (2000). *The Warlord's Puzzle.* Gretna, LA: Pelican Publishing Company.

Pinkney, J. (1985). *The Patchwork Quilt*. New York: Dial Books for Young Readers.

Pluckrose, H. (1995). *Math Counts: Shapes*. Chicago: Children's Press.

Rau, Dana Meachen (2005). *A Star in My Orange: Looking for Nature's Shapes*. Minneapolis: First Avenue Editions.

Ringgold, F. (1991). *Tar Beach*. New York: Scholastic.

Sachar, Louis (2003). *Holes.* New York: Yearling.

Whitford, A. (1991). *Eight Hands Round.* New York: HarperCollins Juvenile.

CHAPTER

15

Developing Measurement Concepts and Skills

NCTM CONNECTING WITH THE STANDARDS

The National Council of Teachers of Mathematics Principles and Standards emphasizes the importance of helping children connect the topic of measurement to their everyday lives, stating that "Measurement is a process that students . . . use every day as they explore questions related to their school or home environment" (NCTM, 2000, p. 170). The NCTM document goes on to note that "measurement . . . bridges two main areas of school mathematics—geometry and number. Measurement activities can simultaneously teach important everyday skills, strengthen students' knowledge of other important topics in mathematics, and develop measurement concepts and processes that will be formalized and expanded in later years" (NCTM, 2000, p. 102).

Grade level	Curriculum Focal Points Related to Measurement
Prekindergarten	Children compare objects based on quantity and length.
Kindergarten	Children compare and order objects based on length or weight.
Grade 1	Children measure objects by laying a unit end to end and then counting the units.
Grade 2	Children understand linear measure and the need for using standard units of measure.
Grade 3	Children understand linear measure and fractional parts of linear units, and develop an understanding of and solve problems involving perimeter.
Grade 4	Children develop an understanding of and solve problems involving area.
Grade 5	Children develop an understanding of and solve problems involving volume and surface area.
Grade 6	Children extend their understanding of and solve problems involving area and volume.
Grade 7	Children develop an understanding of and solve problems involving surface area and volume of three-dimensional shapes.
Grade 8	Children develop an understanding of and solve problems involving distance and angles, to learn properties of particular configurations of lines and about similar triangles to solve a variety of problems, and to explain why the Pythagorean theorem is valid and use the Pythagorean theorem to find distances between points and analyze polygons and polyhedra.

Developing Your Math Teaching Skills

When you have finished studying this chapter, you should be able to do the following:

- Describe the difference between standard and nonstandard units of measure, and give an example of each.
- Give some examples of situations in which measurement is needed. Choose at least one example for each attribute: length, area, volume, capacity, mass, time, temperature, and angle.

The NCTM (2006) *Curriculum Focal Points* mentions measurement in all grade levels from prekindergarten through grade eight. The table on page 331 lists these recommendations for each grade.

ASSESSING MATHEMATICS UNDERSTANDING

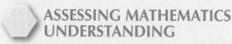

In order to become familiar with the mathematics concepts and procedures discussed in this chapter, take a few minutes and complete the following *Chapter 15 Preassessment.* Answer each question on your own. Then think about the possible misunderstandings or difficulties some elementary-school children might have when solving each problem. If you are able, administer this assessment to a child, and analyze his or her understanding of these topics.

Solve each problem. Think about how you get your answer.

1. Which of the units of measure listed below would be the best to use to measure the length of a school building?

   a. millimeters **b.** centimeters

   c. meters **d.** kilometers

2. If the area of the shaded triangle below is 4 square inches, what is the area of the entire square? Show how you solved the problem.

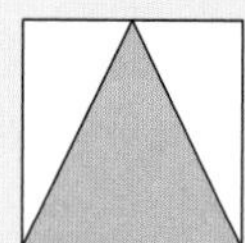

   a. 2 square inches
   b. 4 square inches
   c. 8 square inches
   d. 16 square inches

3.

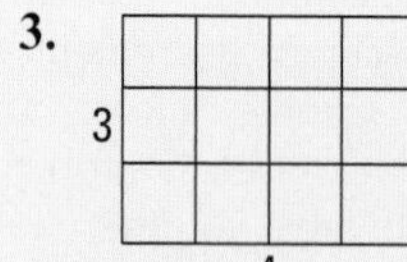

   Which rectangle below has the same perimeter (distance around) as the rectangle above, and why?

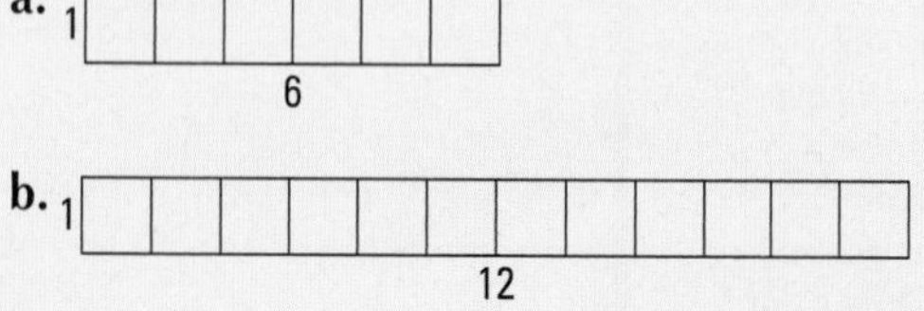

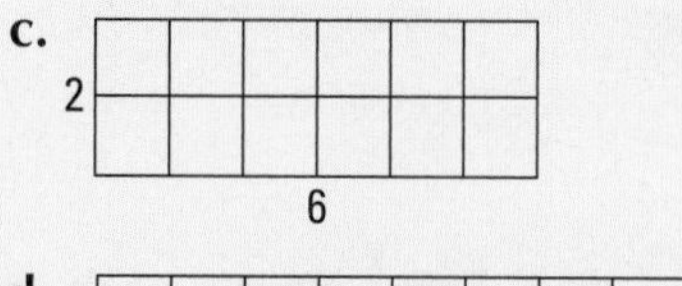

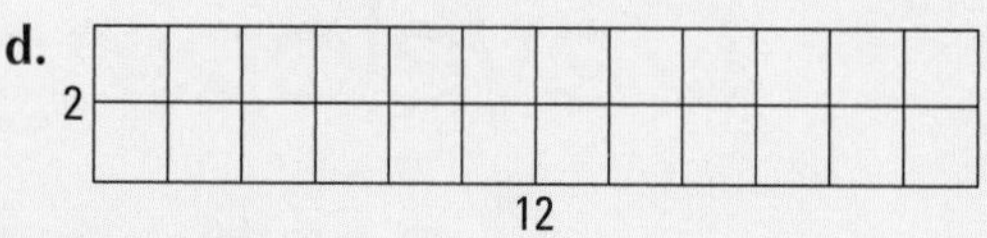

4. A stop sign has 8 sides of equal length. Ryan knows that the length of each side is 10 inches.

   a. Explain how Ryan can find the perimeter of the sign.

   b. What is the perimeter of the sign?

5. Mark's room is 12 feet wide and 15 feet long. Mark wants to cover the floor with carpet.

   a. How many square feet of carpet does he need?

   b. The carpet costs $2.60 per square foot. How much will the carpet cost?

Examining Classroom Practice

Sharon Moore begins a measurement lesson for her fifth-graders by reading *Spaghetti and Meatballs for All!* (Burns, 1997). In this story, Mr. and Mrs. Comfort are hosting a dinner for 32 guests, including family members and neighbors. Mr. and Mrs. Comfort rented eight square tables and 32 chairs that they arrange as shown below, with four chairs at each table. In this diagram, the squares represent the tables and the line segments show where the guests can sit.

As guests arrive, they rearrange the furniture in many different ways so they can sit together. Ms. Moore displays the book while reading so that the children can see the illustrations that show the different ways the guests arranged the tables and chairs.

After finishing the book, the class discusses the story. Ms. Moore attaches squares of paper to the blackboard to represent the tables, starting with the original arrangement with eight separate tables.

A key issue is what happens when tables are pushed together. Ms. Moore asks, "Couldn't they just push the tables together like this (see right)? Since they're still using eight tables, wouldn't that mean that 32 people could still sit there?"

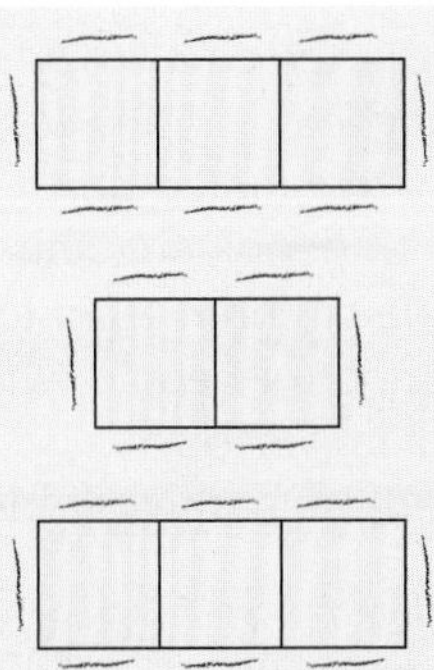

Tammy said, "No, because you lose seats when tables touch. Nobody can sit in the middle then. Only 22 people can sit there now."

To make sure all the children understand this point, Ms. Moore uses the overhead projector and square tiles to show what happens with four tables.

Ms. Moore starts with four separate tables, an arrangement that seats 16 people. The class suggests other ways to arrange the four tables. For each different arrangement, they record the number of people who could sit there and the number of tables used (see chart below).

Arrangement	Number of Seats	Number of Tables
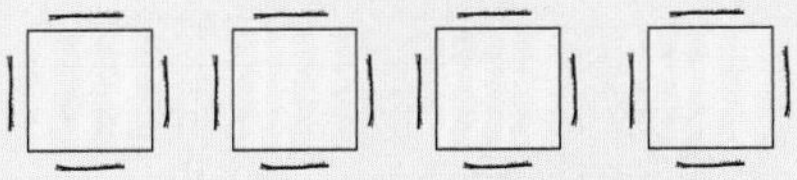	*16*	*4*
	12	*4*
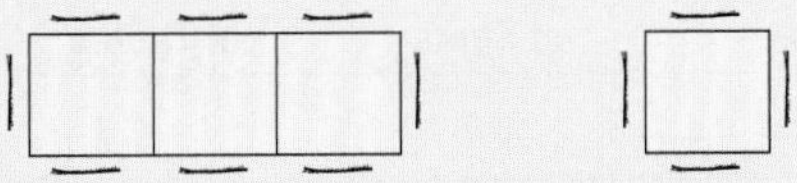	*12*	*4*
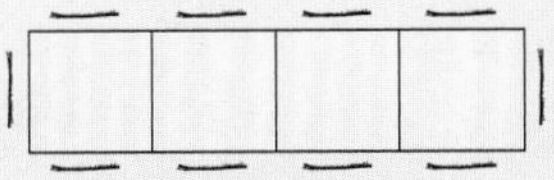	*10*	*4*
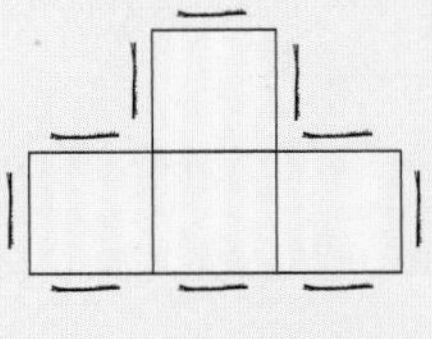	*10*	*4*
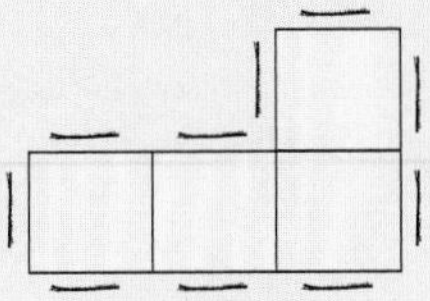	*10*	*4*
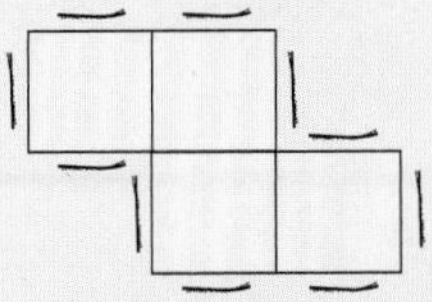	*10*	*4*
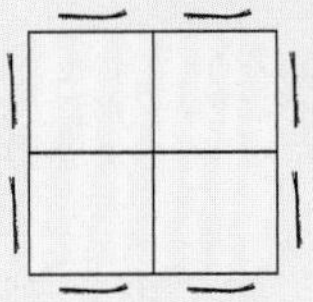	*8*	*4*

Ms. Moore asks the children what they notice in the different arrangements. They comment that more people fit when the tables don't touch, and the smallest number of people are able to sit when lots of sides touch. The children seem to understand the effect on the number of people who can be seated when the sides of tables touch.

Ms. Moore poses another problem to the class:

How many different rectangular arrangements can Mr. and Mrs. Comfort make that will seat exactly 16 people?

Children work with a partner to solve the problem. Some use square tiles to represent the tables while others draw squares on a sheet of paper. After children solve the problem, Ms. Moore calls the class together to share their findings. She asks for volunteers to come to the overhead and use the tiles to show and discuss one arrangement they found. As children share their solutions, they make a large class chart that includes a sketch of the table arrangement, the number of seats, and the number of tables used (see chart below).

Once again, Ms. Moore asks the children what they notice in this chart. The children notice that they found four different rectangular arrangements that would seat 16 people, and each arrangement used a different number of tables but seated the same number of people.

Ms. Moore asks the children to think about how they figured out how many people could sit at an arrangement. Several children said they just counted, and some of them drew lines to help them keep track as they counted.

Mike said, "I saw a short-cut. I realized that I could count one long side and one short side and just double it." Ms. Moore asks if anyone else found a short-cut. Karen said, "I counted the long side and added it to itself. Then I counted the short side and added it to itself. Then I added them all together."

Ms. Moore suggested that the children continue to be on the lookout for patterns that might help them save some time, and to think about why those patterns work.

Analyzing Assessment Results

Now look at the assessment results. What was your general reaction to these problems? Did they all seem to be equally difficult, or were some problems easier for you to think about? What aspects of

Arrangement	Number of Seats	Number of Tables
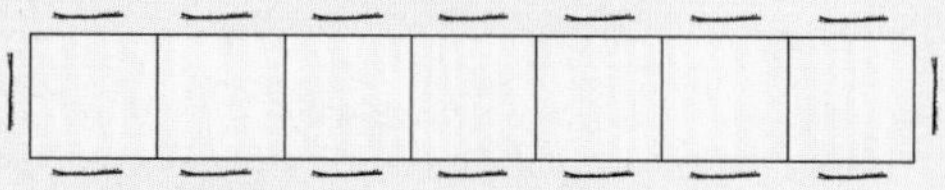 1 × 7 tables	16	7
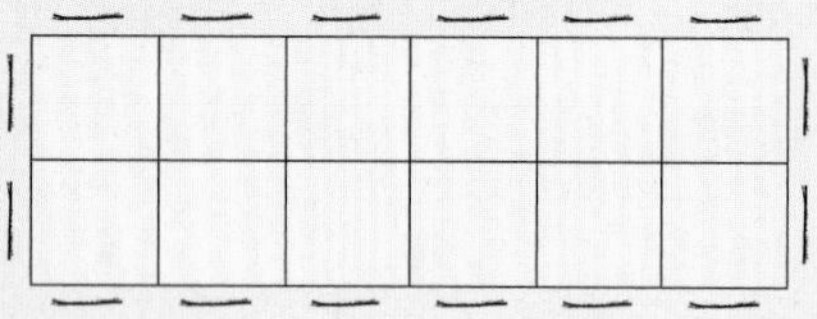 2 × 6 tables	16	12
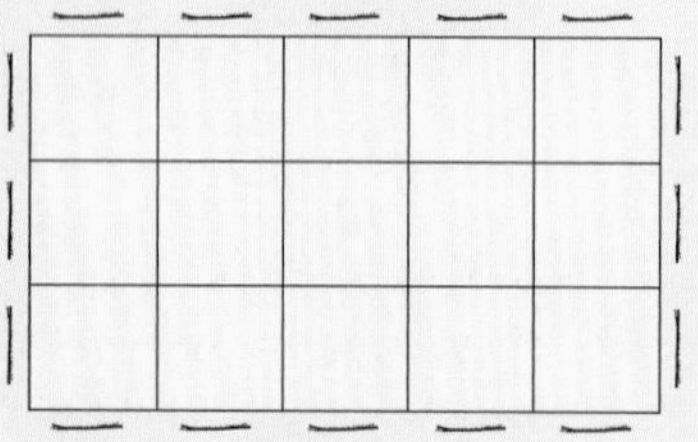 3 × 5 tables	16	15
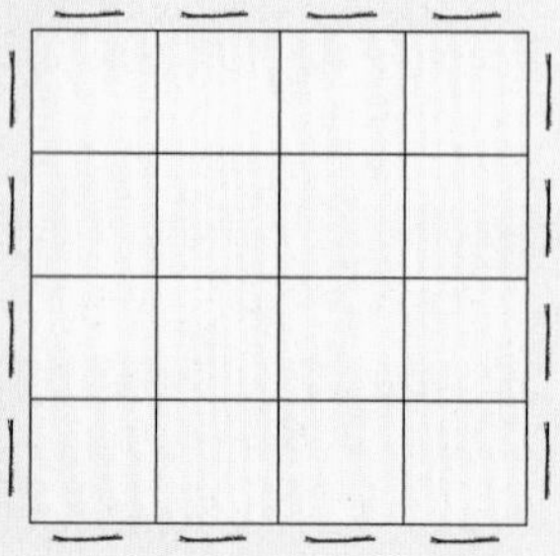 4 × 4 tables	16	16

problems do you think make them easier to solve? What in general do you think a teacher's goals should be regarding developing understanding of measurement? If you had a chance to give the *Chapter 15 Preassessment* to a child, take a few minutes and analyze the results. How did the child solve these problems?

Analyze each problem. How did you (and/or the student you administered the assessment to) solve each of the following problems? Let's look at problem 1 first.

1. Which of the units of measure listed below would be the best to use to measure the length of a school building?

a. millimeters **b.** centimeters

c. meters **d.** kilometers

Comments: This problem asks the learner to think about what unit is most appropriate to use when measuring a building. Millimeters and centimeters would be too small to use to measure a building, while kilometers would be too large.

2. If the area of the shaded triangle below is 4 square inches, what is the area of the entire square?

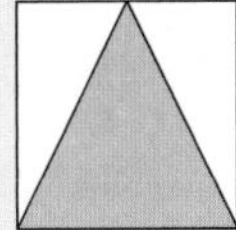

a. 2 square inches

b. 4 square inches

c. 8 square inches

d. 16 square inches

Comments: To solve this problem, think about the relationship between the triangle and the square. The triangle is half the size of the square, so if the area of the triangle is 4 square inches, the area of the square is twice as much, or 8 square inches. There's no need to use a formula to figure the problem out; you need only to consider the relationship between the triangle and the square. Unfortunately, many learners rely on using formulas for all measurement tasks.

3.

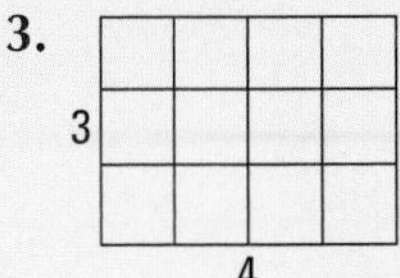

Which rectangle below has the same perimeter (distance around) as the rectangle above?

a.

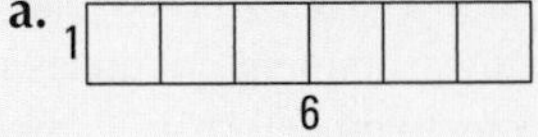

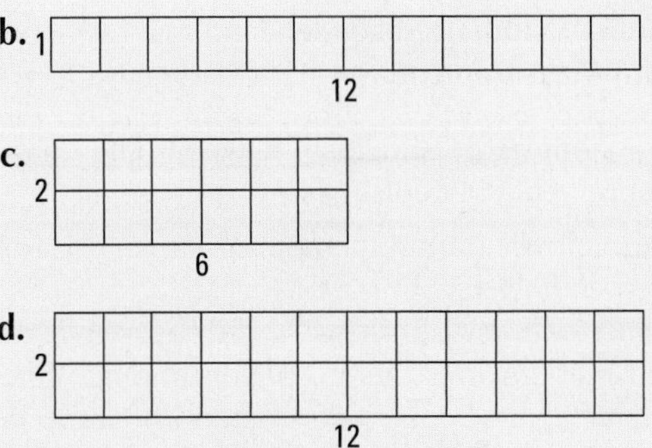

Comments: This problem can be solved by finding the perimeter either by using a formula or just by counting the distance around the outside of each figure. The perimeter of the given rectangle is 14 units, found by adding 3 + 4 + 3 + 4 or by using the formula for perimeter of a rectangle: $2 \times 3 + 2 \times 4 = 14$. Then find out which of the four given shapes has a perimeter of 14 units. The correct answer is (a). A common incorrect answer is (b); this shape has the same area as the given shape, but their perimeters are different.

4. A stop sign has 8 sides of equal length. Ryan knows that the length of each side is 10 inches.

a. Explain how Ryan can find the perimeter of the sign.

b. What is the perimeter of the sign?

Comments: Ryan could find the perimeter by multiplying 8 times 10, so the perimeter is 80 units. Most learners don't know a formula for finding the perimeter of an octagon, but it's easy to find the perimeter if they understand that perimeter means the distance around the shape.

5. Mark's room is 12 feet wide and 15 feet long. Mark wants to cover the floor with carpet and put baseboard around the room. How many square feet of carpet does he need? How many feet of baseboard does he need?

Comments: This problem combines two math concepts: area and perimeter. We need to find the area of the floor for the amount of carpet, and the perimeter for the amount of baseboard. It may be helpful to make a sketch of the room before beginning the calculations.

Take a minute and reflect on this assessment. Were some problems easier than others? What factors made them easier? What do you understand about the concepts of area and perimeter? What do you want to learn more about in order to help children understand these and other concepts of measurement?

Common Student Misunderstandings about Measurement:

- Inability to distinguish between different measurement concepts.
- Confusion about the appropriate units of measurement.

Are there any other misunderstandings that children may have about measurement? It's important to assess what children understand, and are still working on understanding, in order to plan instruction that meets their needs.

Building on Assessment Results

Think about what we can do to help strengthen children's understandings and minimize (and hopefully eradicate) their misunderstandings and misconceptions.

Sometimes teaching about measurement focuses on memorizing formulas and producing answers quickly. While we want students to be able to determine measurements quickly, we also want them to understand and make sense of measurement, which will enable them to decide if their solutions are reasonable. So what might we do next to help students understand measurement?

A key element of all instruction is to make sure that students understand the concept. Students need to visualize concepts and relationships. This usually is best done with some sort of manipulative material or model, asking students to solve problems set in familiar, meaningful situations and to examine the reasonableness of their solutions. The table below lists several common misunderstandings and what a teacher can do to help children correct these misunderstandings.

Think back to Ms. Moore's lesson. What measurement concepts does the lesson include? In this lesson, the number of tables represents the area of the arrangement, while the number of people who can be seated represents the perimeter. This lesson provides a conceptual introduction to the concepts of areas and perimeter. Notice that Ms. Moore encouraged the children to look for patterns, and two children, Mike and Karen, found "short-cuts" that can later be developed into a pattern or rule for finding the perimeter of a rectangle. With a rich conceptual foundation, the process of finding perimeter will make more sense to children.

IF students . . .	THEN have students . . .
think that measurement means just pulling out the numbers and putting them into a formula	*model* the problem with a manipulative material and/or *draw* a sketch of the problem situation to make sense of it.
think that area and perimeter are the same	*model* the problem with a manipulative material and/or *draw* a sketch of the problem situation to make sense of it.
think that the only way to find area is L × W	*model* the problem with squares and count the number of squares inside the shape.
think that the only way to find perimeter is 2L + 2W	*model* the problem with squares and count the distance around outside of the shape.
are confused by what units to use to measure length, area, and volume	*show* students a linear inch, and square inch, and a cubic inch and discuss what sorts of measurement each unit could be used for.

Measurement Concepts and Instructional Sequence

Teaching about Measurement

Measurement can be one of the most interesting and useful topics in the elementary curriculum. Children and adults use measurement ideas in their everyday lives, and questions involving measurement can be identified in virtually every subject taught during the school day. Learning the concepts and processes associated with measurement requires active participation in a wide variety of physical and mental situations; instruction naturally lends itself to a problem-solving approach. As children study measurement, they apply concepts from number and geometry and thus have opportunities to gain new insights and discover new connections within and between these mathematical topics (Lindquist, 1989).

Children's Understanding of Measurement

What do we know of the measurement understanding of children in the United States? The 2003 National Assessment of Educational Progress (NAEP) noted that while students' understanding of measurement continues to improve, we still have a long way to go before we can say that

NCTM MEASUREMENT STANDARDS AND EXPECTATIONS ADDRESSED IN THIS CHAPTER

Instructional programs from pre-K–12 should enable all students to	In prekindergarten through grade 2 all students should— (NCTM, 2000, p. 102)	In grades 3–5 all students should— (NCTM, 2000, p. 170)	In grades 6–8 all students should— (NCTM, 2000, p. 240)
• understand measurable attributes of objects and the units, systems, and processes of measurement. • apply appropriate techniques, tools, and formulas to determine measurements.	• recognize the attributes of length, volume, weight, area, and time. • compare and order objects according to these attributes. • understand how to measure using nonstandard and standard units. • select an appropriate unit and tool for the attribute being measured. • measure with multiple copies of units of the same size, such as paper clips laid end to end. • use repetition of a single unit to measure something larger than the unit, for instance, measuring the length of a room with a single meter stick. • use tools to measure. • develop common referents for measures to make comparisons and estimates.	• understand such attributes as length, area, weight, volume, and size of angle and select the appropriate type of unit for measuring each attribute. • understand the need for measuring with standard units and become familiar with standard units in the customary and metric systems. • carry out simple unit conversions, such as from centimeters to meters, within a system of measurement. • understand that measurements are approximations and how differences in units affect precision. • explore what happens to measurements of a two-dimensional shape such as its perimeter and area when the shape is changed in some way. • develop strategies for estimating the perimeters, areas, and volumes of irregular shapes. • select and apply appropriate standard units and tools to measure length, area, volume, weight, time, temperature, and the size of angles. • select and use benchmarks to estimate measurements. • develop, understand, and use formulas to find the area of rectangles and related triangles and parallelograms. • develop strategies to determine the surface areas and volumes of rectangular solids.	• develop an understanding of large numbers and recognize and appropriately use exponential, scientific, and calculator notation. • understand both metric and customary systems of measurement. • understand relationships among units and convert from one unit to another within the same system. • understand, select, and use units of appropriate size and type to measure angles, perimeter, area, surface area, and volume. • select and apply techniques and tools to accurately find length, area, volume, and angle measures to appropriate levels of precision. • develop and use formulas to determine the circumference of circles and the area of triangles, parallelograms, trapezoids, and circles and develop strategies to find the area of more complex shapes. • develop strategies to determine the surface area and volume of selected prisms, pyramids, and cylinders. • solve problems involving scale factors, using ratio and proportion. • solve simple problems involving rates and derived measurements for such attributes as velocity and density.

students understand everything they need to about measurement. Fourth-grade students had difficulty in "applying appropriate measurement techniques, tools, and formulas to determine measurements" (Blume, Gallindo, and Walcott, 2007, p. 96), while eighth-graders did better on these topics. Findings such as these point to the importance of teachers' helping children truly make sense of measurement.

This chapter consists of two major sections. This first section discusses measurement concepts and processes along with a recommended instructional sequence. The second section presents teaching strategies and learning activities for each of the following elementary and middle school measurement topics: length, area, volume, capacity, mass, time, temperature, and angle.

> PEARSON myeducationlab The Power of Classroom Practice Go to the Assignments and Activities section of Topic 12: "Measurement Concepts and Skills" in the MyEducationLab for your course. Complete the activity "Concepts of Measurements" to see how one teacher introduces the concept of *measurement.*

What Is Measurement?

Although counting involves discrete objects, measuring involves continuous properties. A *measurable attribute* of an object or event, such as mass or time, is a characteristic that can be quantified by comparing it to a *unit*. The *process* of measuring is the same for each attribute: An appropriate unit is chosen and the object or event being measured is compared to the unit. The result of measuring is a number and a unit, such as 27 kg or 9.8 seconds.

To illustrate, if you had a large box to measure, you would first have to decide which attribute of the box you were interested in and then select a unit that possesses that same attribute. If you wanted to know how long the box was, possible choices for the unit could include your hand span, a paper clip, or the centimeter. Depending on the unit chosen, the length of a given box might be 3 hand spans, 20 paper clips, or 62 cm. If you wanted to know how heavy the box was, you could use a balance scale to compare it with a unit of mass such as a book or the pound. To measure how much the box holds, you could find how many smaller boxes of a particular size would fit into it or measure its length, width, and height in *centimeters* and compute the volume in *cubic centimeters* using the formula $V = lwh$.

NCTM Principles and Standards Link 15-1

Content Strand: Measurement

The study of measurement is important in the mathematics curriculum from prekindergarten through high school because of the practicality and pervasiveness of measurement in so many aspects of everyday life. The study of measurement also offers an opportunity for learning and applying other mathematics, including number operations, geometric ideas, statistical concepts, and notions of function. It highlights connections within mathematics and between mathematics and areas outside of mathematics, such as social studies, science, art, and physical education. (NCTM, 2000, p. 44)

Instructional Sequence

Although the meanings, units, instruments, and formulas associated with the various attributes are different, the process, concepts, and instructional sequence for each measurement topic are basically the same (Inskeep, 1976). First, the meaning of the attribute is developed through activities involving perception and direct comparison. Second, children begin to measure, using arbitrary or nonstandard units. Third, they measure and estimate, using standard units. Related experiences involve learning to use instruments and read scales and developing formulas to determine measurements. The following paragraphs present key concepts and principles for teaching measurement in each of these phases.

Perception and direct comparison. This first stage is sometimes referred to as *premeasurement* because it does not require a unit nor assigning a number to the object being measured. Activities such as those that follow in this chapter allow children to experience the properties of the attribute and to use sight and touch to compare and order objects with respect to those properties. The focus is on the development of conceptual understanding.

The use of appropriate *language* in direct comparison tasks is critical to allow the children to relate the concept to their experience and to distinguish among the various attributes. Deciding which of two objects is "bigger" depends on the meaning of the term *big.* Children also appreciate the need for different words to describe different attributes. For determining length, the child can be asked which of two sticks is *longer*. The problem can be solved by placing the sticks side by side. For determining capacity, the child can be asked to determine which of two cups

NCTM Principles and Standards Link 15-2

Content Strand: Measurement

A measurable attribute is a characteristic of an object that can be quantified. Line segments have length, plane regions have area, and physical objects have mass. As students progress through the curriculum from preschool through high school, the set of attributes they can measure should expand. (NCTM, 2000, p. 44)

holds more. Pouring from one cup into the other allows the child to answer without knowing how much either cup holds. Similarly, questions such as the following can be used to introduce mass, area, and temperature, respectively: Which book is *heavier*? Which paper *covers more surface*? Which liquid is *hotter*?

Building on what we discussed in Chapter 2 about Piaget's work in helping teachers understand children's thinking, we can use classical Piagetian *conservation* tasks at this stage to provide insight into the child's thinking (Steffe & Hirstein, 1976). To test for conservation of length, the child is asked to find a stick as long as a given stick and to show this by placing the sticks side by side. One stick is then moved forward and the child is asked whether that stick is now longer than, shorter than, or as long as the other stick. Children who do not conserve length believe that the length of an object changes when it is moved.

You should not attempt to "correct" nonconservers and should not conclude that such children are not "ready" to learn basic measurement ideas and skills (Hiebert, 1984). Maturation and experience—particularly in settings in which children discuss their work with each other and the teacher—are factors that contribute to cognitive development, and, over time, children become conservers. Both nonconservers and conservers can benefit from comparison and other early measurement activities. Conservation tasks can also be presented as problems to be solved by the class or by small groups of children. It is through experiences such as these that children construct and modify their views of reality. Children can discuss conflicting answers and different reasons for them. Children who conserve generally give one of three arguments to explain why the quantity still is the same after a transformation: (1) reversibility—"you can move it back the way it was"; (2) identity—"you didn't add any or take any away"; and (3) compensation—"this one sticks out more here but this one sticks out more here" (Cathcart, 1971).

Seriation tasks involve ordering three or more objects according to a particular attribute. For example, children might be given six containers and asked to order them by capacity. Although this requires a series of direct comparisons, other properties are also involved. Children use *transitivity* when they reason as follows: "I found that the bottle holds more than the jar and the jar holds more than the can, so I know that the bottle holds more than the can without actually pouring."

Nonstandard units. At this stage the question is "How big?" rather than "Which is bigger?" and invites the further question: "Compared to what?" When children see a need for a referent, they are encouraged to choose a variety of units with which to measure the object. The first criterion for selecting an *appropriate* unit is that it has the same attribute as that to be measured. Thus, a long thin object such as a pencil would be a good unit for measuring length but it would not be a very good unit for measuring area or angles. Another consideration is the size of the unit relative to the object to be measured. The unit should usually be smaller than the object but large enough so that the counting can be completed in a reasonable time, and the resulting number has a reasonable magnitude. One would not want to measure the thickness of a page with an eraser or the length of a classroom with a paper clip.

An important concept is that physical measurement of continuous quantities is always *approximate* (Kastner, 1989). Children are exposed to this reality when they measure the length of a pen in paper clips and find that a whole-number multiple of this unit does not exactly match the object's length. In the drawing shown next, the length of the pen is closer to 5 paper clips than to 6; we can say that the pen is about 5 paper clips long, the pen is a bit more than 5 paper clips long, or to the nearest paper clip the length of the pen is 5. Similarly, children might find that the capacity of a large juice can is about 10 paper cups, and that the mass of an eraser is a bit more than 5 pieces of chalk.

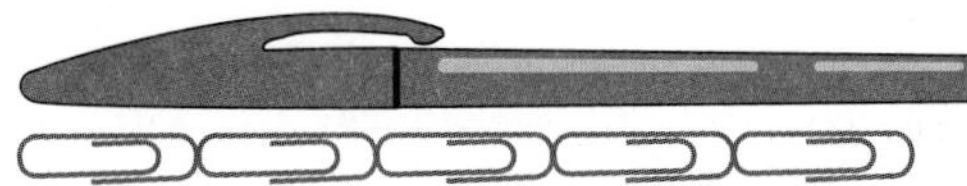

As children gain experience working with nonstandard units, they should be encouraged to *estimate* their answers before they measure. In particular, they should be challenged to predict the effect of using a larger or smaller unit: Will the number obtained be larger or smaller? Examining the results of measuring an object using several different units leads children to discover the inverse relationship between the size of the unit and the number of units required to match the object. Learners should be encouraged to verbalize this concept in their own words. A child might say, "If the unit is shorter, it will take more of them to be as long."

The idea of *subdividing* a unit so that the number of units more closely matches the object introduces the concept of *precision* in relation to the approximate nature of measurement. Dividing the unit into smaller parts results in a more precise answer. The length of the pen below is about 5 of the larger units and 10 of the smaller units.

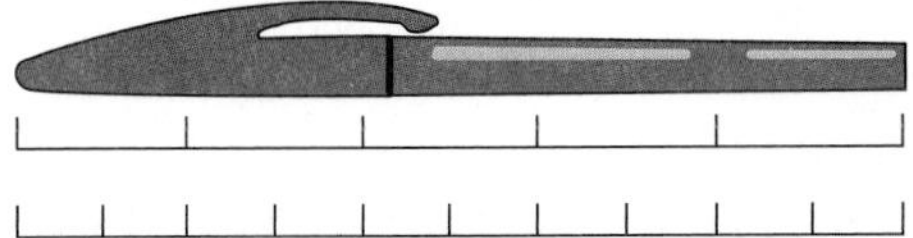

When two children accurately use the same unit to measure a particular object, both should get the same number. However, if they use different units, two different answers can be correct. It is helpful to discuss this idea when using body parts as arbitrary units. An example is measuring the width of the room in shoe lengths. Thus, another characteristic of a good unit is that others can easily replicate and understand it. It is interesting to discuss historical measures such as the cubit (the distance from the elbow to the tip of the middle finger) in this connection.

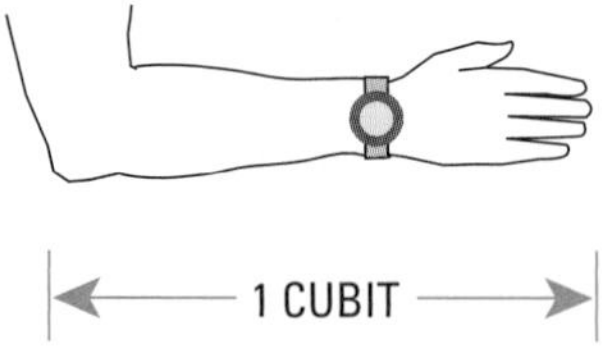

Standard units. Even though the children all get the same answers using arbitrary classroom units and know what these units mean, they can appreciate the problems associated with trying to communicate such measures outside their class or school. They might discuss telling their parents about a rock with a mass of 23 blocks or trying to buy a board 13 textbooks long. But children will come to see that it is difficult to communicate measurements done with nonstandard units to other people. So something else is needed.

That something is standard units. *Standard units* are units that have been agreed on and accepted by a group of people. In the United States, two systems of standard units are used: the customary system and the metric system. Table 15-1 lists common units of measure in each system to measure different attributes.

The customary system may seem to be easier to most adults, because it is widely used in the United States. But this system has difficult equivalences: For example, there are 5,280 feet in a mile and there are 16 ounces in a pound. The equivalences in the metric system are much easier to learn because the metric system is based on powers of 10. For example, there are 1,000 millimeters in a meter and 1,000 milliliters in a liter. In the metric system, there are three prefixes for smaller units: *milli-* (one-thousandth), *centi-* (one-hundredth), and *deci-* (one-tenth). Likewise, there are three prefixes for larger units: *kilo-* (one thousand), *hecto-* (one hundred), and *deka-* (ten). So a child can use these prefixes to help understand the following:

There are	1,000 millimeters in 1 meter
	100 centimeters in 1 meter
	10 decimeters in 1 meter
And that	1 dekameter is equal to 10 meters
	1 hectometer is equal to 100 meters
	1 kilometer is equal to 1,000 meters

These same equivalences are true for all different units of measure—including meters, grams, and liters—and, hence, make the metric system easy to use.

It is important that children learn to use both systems of measurement. Note, however, that you should *not* spend important instructional time converting measurements from one system to the other. Instead, instruction should focus on developing understanding of and skill in measuring using both systems of units. Table 15-2 lists a common scope and sequence for teaching measurement.

Knowledge of the units appropriate for a given task and the ability to decide when and how to *estimate* are components of "measurement sense" (Shaw & Cliatt, 1989).

TABLE 15-1 Common Standard Units of Measure

Attribute Being Measured	Customary System	Metric System
Length	inch foot yard mile	millimeter centimeter meter kilometer
Area	square inch square foot square yard acre	square centimeter square meter hectare
Volume	cubic inch cubic foot cubic yard	cubic centimeter cubic meter
Capacity	fluid ounce cup quart gallon	milliliter liter
Weight	ounce pound ton	gram kilogram metric ton
Temperature	degrees Fahrenheit	degrees Celsius
Time	second minute hour day week month year	
Angles	degrees radians	degrees radians

NCTM Principles and Standards Link 15-3

Content Strand: Measurement

Estimating is another measurement technique that should be developed throughout the school years. Estimation activities in prekindergarten through grade 2 should focus on helping children better understand the process of measuring and the role of the size of the unit. Elementary school and middle-grades students should have many opportunities to estimate measures by comparing them against some benchmark. (NCTM, 2000, p. 46)

TABLE 15-2 Scope and Sequence Chart for Teaching Measurement

Grade Level	K	1	2	3	4	5	6
Length	direct comparison, nonstandard units, cm, in. ruler	m, ft	dm, yd	mm, km, mi perimeter rectangle			prefixes circle
Area		direct comparison, nonstandard units	cm^2, $in.^2$	m^2, ft^2, yd^2 rectangle	km^2, parallelogram, circle	mm^2	hectare surface area
Volume			direct comparison, nonstandard units	cm^3, $in.^3$	m^3, ft^3, yd^3	rectangular prism	$dm^3 = L$ $cm^3 = mL$ $m^3 = kL$
Capacity	direct comparison, nonstandard units	L, C	mL	graduated beaker	pt, qt, gal	kL	
Mass	direct comparison, balance	nonstandard units	kg	g	t	mg	g – mL kg – L t – kL
Time	sequencing events, direct comparison, nonstandard units, calendar	minute, hour, second, digital clock	dial clock	date notation	A.M., P.M. 24-hr clock	time zones	
Temperature	weather	temperature, direct comparison	°C, °F thermometer		Celsius referents		
Angles					right, obtuse, acute, straight	degree protractor	interior angles in triangle

Thus, a child would identify the kilometer or mile, as opposed to the meter or centimeter or yard or foot, as the most appropriate unit for describing distances between two cities and would want to know only the approximate distance in order to estimate how long it would take to drive that far. Strategies used by good estimators include *referents* (using a known quantity such as your own height to estimate another person's height), *chunking* (estimating the area of a room by first breaking it into several workable parts), and *unitizing* (estimating the volume of a pitcher by mentally dividing it into smaller, equal parts such as glassfuls of 250 mL each) (Lindquist, 1987). Children should have referents for common metric units. For instance, an average adult male's mass is about 80 kg, a quart of milk is about a liter, a dime is about 1 mm thick, room temperature is about 70°F.

Relationships among metric units can often be discovered directly. For example, it takes 10 cm to make a train 1 dm long. To successfully convert from one unit to another, the child needs to know the meaning of the prefixes, be able to multiply and divide by powers of 10, and understand that the larger unit will be associated with the smaller number. Generally, conversion questions should occur in the context of realistic problem-solving situations rather than as sets of contrived exercises.

Instruments. In the elementary grades, children learn to use the following measuring instruments: ruler (length), pan balance (mass), graduated beaker (capacity), protractor (angles), thermometer (temperature), and clock (time). Although these instruments are based on standard units, children should invent and construct their own instruments to simplify various tasks at earlier stages. For example, a balance is used to find which of two objects is heavier, a paper clip chain ruler is used to measure length in these arbitrary units, and a clear bottle is calibrated to show the water heights for whole numbers of paper cup units. Such devices help children see the connection between the attribute and the standard instrument. Careful teaching, demonstration, and appropriate classroom activities are required to ensure that children use measuring instruments correctly and with understanding.

Formulas. According to Bright and Hoeffner (1993), "Formulas should be a product of exploration and discovery" (p. 81). The authors recommend that children have hands-on experiences with measuring, "with emphasis more on understanding the underlying concepts than on applying formulas" (p. 82).

In the intermediate grades, children learn and apply *formulas* for finding the perimeter, area, and volume of simple two- and three-dimensional figures. Children can often discover these relationships on their own. For example, children who have been finding the distance around a number of different polygons by measuring the individual sides notice that when a rectangle is involved, only two sides need to be measured; the perimeter can be found by doubling the sum of the length and the width or by adding twice the length and twice the width. Developing formulas in this way is meaningful and makes it possible for children to solve problems when rules are forgotten. Formulas for the area of a rectangle, parallelogram, and triangle and for the surface area and volume of a rectangular prism can similarly be discovered by children. The relationship between the circumference and the diameter of a circle (pi) can be explored by children at various grade levels. Primary-grade children can use string to compare the distances around and across disks of varying sizes; intermediate-grade children can measure these distances in millimeters and find their ratio using a calculator.

Problem solving and applications. There are a number of interesting problems in which relationships between two attributes can be investigated. For example, children can make many different rectangles having a fixed perimeter and find the area of each. Activities of this nature are appropriate at various grade levels since formulas and relationships do not depend on particular units. Practical real-life problems might include finding the cost of painting or carpeting a room. Cooking, carpentry, and outdoor education are other settings in which measurement skills can be learned and applied.

Summary of Teaching Sequence

The first part of this chapter described the measurement process and an instructional sequence for the important concepts and skills. The early emphasis is on developing understanding and vocabulary through activities involving visual perception, direct comparison, and measuring with arbitrary units. Later, children learn to estimate and measure with appropriate metric units, use measurement instruments, and discover formulas and relationships. Finally, teachers should use an active learning, problem-solving approach at all levels.

The remainder of the chapter describes sample teaching strategies and learning activities for the three stages of the instructional sequence for each of the attributes. You can adapt questions and activities for use in whole-class, small-group, and individual learning settings.

Teaching Strategies and Learning Activities

Length

In studying linear measure, we refer to the *length* of an object and to the *distance* between two objects. We also talk about the *height* of a building, the *width* of a hall, and the *thickness* of a piece of paper. Related vocabulary includes the terms *long* and *short, near* and *far, tall* and *short, narrow* and *wide,* and *thick* and *thin. Perimeter* is the total distance around a closed figure.

Research on children's knowledge of measuring has identified several difficulties (Wilson & Rowland, 1993). To assess children's understanding of the inverse relationship between the size of the unit and the number of units used, first- and second-graders were shown two identical strips. When one strip was covered with small units and the other with larger units, children said that the strip covered by the smaller units was longer because there were more units. In another study, third-grade students were told the number of sheets of paper used by two different people to measure the height of a door. More than half of the children claimed that the person who had used the most sheets had the longest sheets. On a task involving measuring with a ruler in an unfamiliar situation, most third-grade children and half of the seventh-grade children could not give the length of a line segment when it was placed on a pictured ruler such that the end of the ruler was not aligned with the end of the segment.

Length: Perception and direct comparison. Battista (2006) commented on the various ways the word *longer* is used in everyday life, noting that *longer* can refer to length or time. He noted that students can reason in two different ways about length: *nonmeasurement* reasoning and *measurement* reasoning. *Nonmeasurement reasoning* does not use numbers, but rather uses visual judgments, direct comparison. For example, a student might decide that one pencil is longer than another by putting them side-by-side and comparing their lengths. *Measurement reasoning* involves "finding the number of unit lengths that fit end to end along an object, with no gaps or overlaps" (Battista, 2006, p. 141). Teachers should help students develop both types of reasoning about length.

Beginning activities focus on language and concept development (Jensen & O'Neil, 1981). The following are sample questions and directions you might use with a group of children who have been given a set of rods or cardboard strips cut into different lengths.

1. Find a strip that is long (short). Find another strip that is longer (shorter) than this strip. Can you tell by looking? How do you place the strips to determine this? Find another strip as long as your strip. Show how you know these two strips have the same length.

Literature Link 15-1

Developing Measurement Concepts

Adler, David. (1999). ***How Tall, How Short, How Faraway.*** New York: Holiday House.
Hightower, Susan. (1997). ***Twelve Snails to One Lizard.*** New York: Simon & Schuster.
Lasky, Kathryn. (1994). ***The Librarian Who Measured the Earth.*** New York: Little, Brown and Company.
Lionni, Leo. (1960). ***Inch by Inch.*** New York: Astor-Honor.
Maestro, Betsy. (1999). ***The Story of Clocks and Calendars: Marking a Millennium.*** New York: Lothrop, Lee & Shepard Books.
Neuschwander, Cindy. (1997). ***Sir Cumference and the First Round Table.*** Watertown, MA: Charlesbridge Publishing.
Neuschwander, Cindy. (1999). ***Sir Cumference and the Dragon of Pi.*** Watertown, MA: Charlesbridge Publishing.
Older, Jules. (2000). ***Telling Time.*** Watertown, MA: Charlesbridge Publishing.

Measurement is a common and practical mathematics skill used in science and in everyday life. Children need experiences in measuring attributes of objects using both standard and nonstandard units. ***Twelve Snails to One Lizard*** is the story of mischievous Bubba the Bullfrog, who uses nonstandard units (like snails, lizards, and a boa constrictor) to help Milo Beaver build a dam. The humorous illustrations demonstrate for children the importance of using standard units of measure.

- Challenge children to develop their own nonstandard units of length measure. For example, what unit would children use to measure the length of their thumbs, a desk, their classroom, the hallway, or a football field?
- Collect groups of objects that measure 1 inch, 1 centimeter, 1 foot, 1 yard, or 1 meter in length so that students begin to recognize when an object is approximately 1 centimeter or 1 foot. Use these objects as length referents for estimating the lengths of other objects in the classroom.
- Children can read the book ***Inch by Inch*** and use commercially made inch worms or inch tiles to measure various objects in the classroom. After exploring nonstandard measuring units, they will gradually discover the need for more standard units of length.
- ***How Tall, How Short, How Faraway*** also explores length measurement.
- ***The Story of Clocks and Calendars: Marking a Millennium*** shows the evolution of time measurement exploring a variety of clocks and calendars. Children can investigate different time zones using maps and globes. They can create an eight-panel storyboard to show the time and what students in different time zones might be doing when it is noon in New York. ***Telling Time*** teaches children about minutes, hours, days, weeks, years, decades, and how to tell time.
- There are several books for older children that investigate the measurement of circles. ***The Librarian Who Measured the Earth*** is the story of Eratosthenes and his quest to find a way to measure the circumference of the earth. Children can use the library or the Internet to explore other contributions Eratosthenes made to mathematics, history, and geography. ***Sir Cumference and the First Round Table*** introduces students to the vocabulary of circle measurement (circumference, diameter, and radius) and ***Sir Cumference and the Dragon of Pi*** reveals how the diameter and circumference measures of circles arrive at pi (π).

2. Now choose any strip and sort the other strips into three groups: longer, shorter, and the same length. Choose any five strips and put them in order from longest to shortest.

Many young children do not understand that the length of an object is the distance between the two end points. They focus on only one aspect of the situation and consider only the position of the end point. The test for conservation of length was described earlier in this chapter. After the child has stated whether the moved stick is longer, shorter, or the same length as the other stick, you can ask the child to "explain how you know."

The idea of the length of a curved path can be investigated with string. The child is asked to cut two pieces the same length. You then bend one of them and ask if it is still the same length.

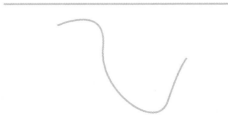

As a further activity, children can sort and order pieces of string of different lengths.

Activities and questions such as the following are useful for introducing related vocabulary and further exploring basic concepts.

- Name something in the room that is *near* you (*far* from you). Find something that is *nearer* (*farther*). Is it farther from you to the door or from the door to you?
- Name someone who is *tall* (*short*). Who is taller, Marie or Peter? How do you know? Find a child who is *taller than, shorter than,* and *as tall as* Pam.
- We can see that Paul and Kim have the same *height.* (Have Paul stand on a chair.) Are Paul and Kim still the same height? Can you tell by looking? How do you know?
- Form a group of three or four children. Who is the tallest, and who is the shortest? Show how you know. With their backs against the chalkboard, have the children in the group stand side by side in a line from tallest to shortest. Have another classmate mark the height of each member of the group on the chalkboard.
- Tell or write a story about the members of your family using the words *tall, taller, tallest, short, shorter, shortest.*
- If Jim is taller than Kate, and Kate is taller than Don, is Jim shorter or taller than Don? Can you tell without seeing them together?

To introduce the idea that objects have more than one linear dimension and that children need additional vocabulary to describe them, show the children a pencil and a shorter, thicker crayon and ask them which they think is *bigger.* The children might say that the pencil is longer but that the crayon is *thicker* or *fatter* or *wider.* Then assemble a collection of pencils, felt pens, markers, and crayons and ask the children to sort them and to order them according to size. Next, you can challenge the children to sort the objects in another way.

Length: Nonstandard units. As a transition to the idea of using a unit, the children can compare two lengths or distances where direct comparison is not possible. *Indirect comparison* involves comparing representations of the objects (Hiebert, 1984). Sample problems and possible solution strategies are as follows:

- Which is longer—the distance around your wrist or the length of an eraser? (String might be used.)
- Which is higher—the doorknob or the top of the filing cabinet? Because we cannot move the door or the filing cabinet, how can we find out? (The children might stand by the doorknob and use masking tape to mark a point on their bodies, then walk to the filing cabinet and compare its height with the tape mark.)
- Could we move the teacher's desk through the door without first tipping the desk on its side? (Provide an unmarked stick about a meter in length.)

To introduce the idea of measuring with a unit, students can find how many paper clips it would take to make a train *as long as* their pencils. Tell the class that they are *measuring the length* of their pencils in paper clips. Then point out that a whole number of paper clips will not exactly match a pencil length but that the number that most closely fits is to be reported. You should demonstrate the correct procedure for measuring with this unit and also show common errors and invite the children to tell what is wrong in each case.

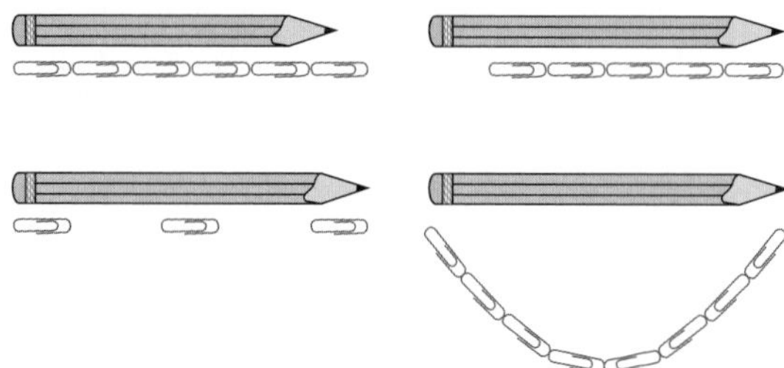

At first, you should provide the children with enough paper clips to measure the selected objects. Later, children may move a single paper clip along the object. This procedure is called *iteration of the unit.* After children have had some practice, they are encouraged to estimate before they measure. Children can record their work on a chart such as the following.

OBJECT	ESTIMATE	MEASURE
pencil	9 paper clips	6 paper clips
eraser	________	________
book	________	________
________	________	________

Another beneficial exercise is to invite children to use paper clips to make straight paths the same length as broken or curved paths. In one setting for this task, children are shown a "road" that has curves or bends and are instructed to use short rods to make a straight road that would be just as far to walk on.

You then explain that the paper clip is a *unit* for measuring length and ask the children to suggest other objects that could be used as units. The children then use several different units to measure the length of a page in their notebooks and record their findings on a chart as follows:

UNIT	ESTIMATE	MEASURE
chalk	5	4
eraser	9	7
pencil	________	________
________	________	________

During and after this activity, you should ask questions such as the following to focus attention on the role of the unit: Why did you get different answers for the length of the page? If you were told that the length of a page was 4, would you know how long the page was?

What else would you need to know? Did you need more units for measuring the page when you used a long unit or a short unit? Why?

Other questions relate to the choice of an appropriate unit. Do you think an eraser would be a good unit for measuring the length of our classroom? Why or why not? Is a new pencil a good unit for measuring the length of a piece of chalk? Why or why not?

Body parts can also be used as nonstandard units of length. For example, children can use their *span* (the distance between the thumb and little finger on an outstretched hand) to measure the length of their desks. To increase their understanding, the children should discuss the reason different children get different answers when they use this unit.

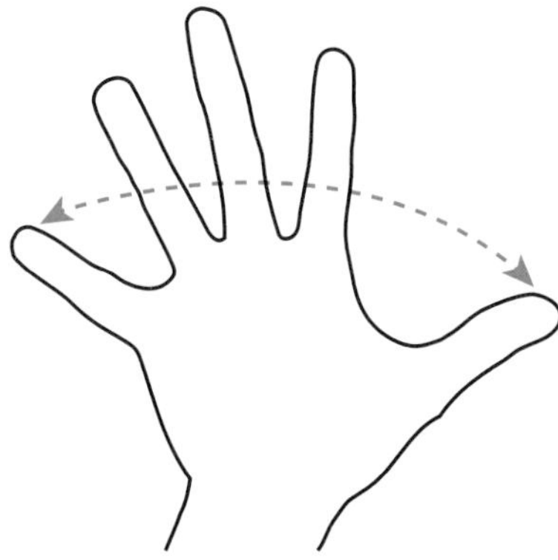

To introduce the idea of a *ruler,* have children make a paper clip chain. Then ask, "How do you think you can use your chain to measure the length of your pencil?" The children could also connect about 10 interlocking cubes together and use this device to measure the lengths of various objects in cubes. They could discuss whether it is easier or harder to measure by using individual cubes or the cube stick.

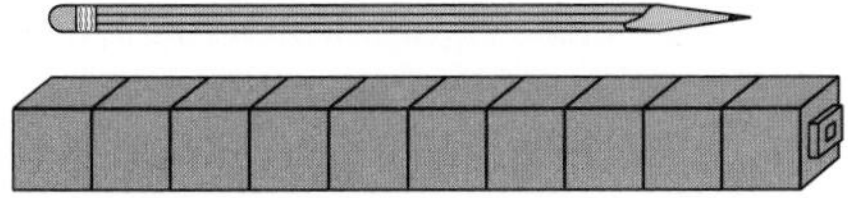

Children can use squared paper (Activity 15-1) and geoboards (Activity 15-2) to explore interesting and worthwhile problems involving the lengths of broken line segments and distances around polygons.

Length: Standard units. Children who have measured lengths by using a variety of units can appreciate the need for a unit that can be understood and communicated beyond the classroom. The book *How Big Is a Foot?* by Rolf Myller (1990) makes this point in a delightful way. The king in the story orders an apprentice to make him a bed 6 feet long and 3 feet wide. The apprentice uses his own foot to measure the bed, with predictable results.

The centimeter is usually the first standard unit taught to children. It is presented as a unit of length known throughout the world. Children become familiar with the size of the centimeter by using the small cubes from the base-ten blocks or interlocking centimeter cubes (called *centicubes*) to measure objects. They should note that one of their fingernails is about a centimeter in length. They are told that the *symbol* for centimeter is cm and that five centimeters is written 5 cm. They then practice measuring and estimating length using this unit, recording their findings on a chart such as the following:

OBJECT	ESTIMATE	MEASURE
pencil	12 cm	14 cm
eraser	________cm	________cm
your span	________cm	________cm
________	________	________

ACTIVITY 15-1 Exploring Distances on Squared Paper

Materials

Squared paper

Procedure

1. Copy Figures A and B on a piece of squared paper.

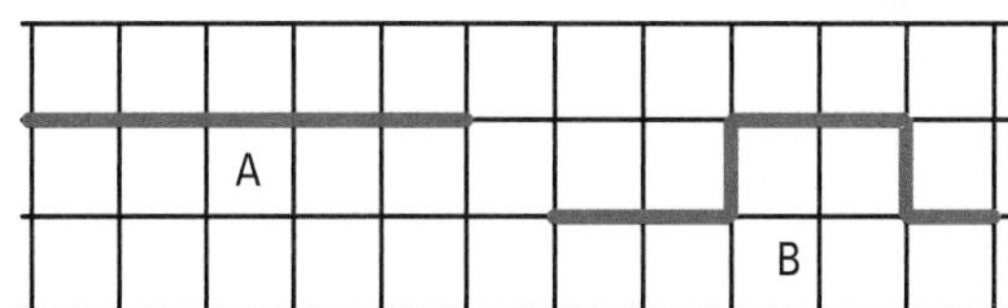

2. If the unit is the distance between two lines, the total length of Figure A is 5 units. Figure B has a length of 7 units.
   - By tracing over grid lines, draw some other figures and find their lengths.
   - How many different figures can you draw that have a total length of 10 units?
3. Figure C is closed. The distance around it is 16 units.
   - Draw some other closed figures by following grid lines and find the distance around each of them.
   - How many different closed figures can you draw that have a distance around of 12 units?

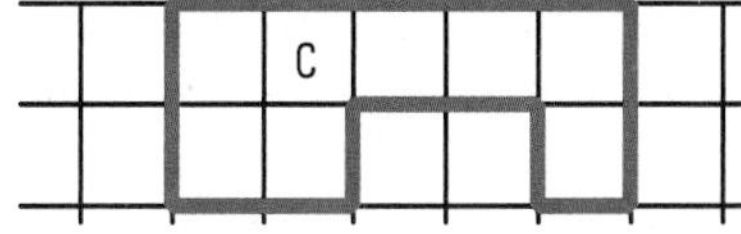

ACTIVITY 15-2 Perimeters on a Geoboard

Manipulative Strategies

Materials

Geoboard or dot paper

Procedure

The distance around a closed figure is called its *perimeter*. How many different figures that have a perimeter of 10 units can you make on a 5 × 5 geoboard?

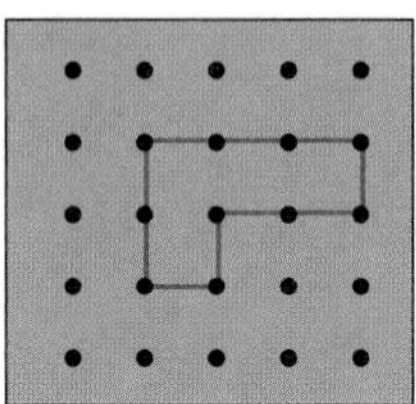

Before demonstrating the standard ruler, invite children to use the ten rod from the base-ten materials or a connected centicube stick to find lengths in centimeters (Thompson & Van de Walle, 1985). The first ruler they use should have centimeter markings without numbers along one edge so they see that the unit on the ruler is represented by the space, not the mark. Children then learn to measure using the other edge that has numbers under the markings. The teacher needs to demonstrate the correct procedure for using this tool, emphasizing the importance of placing the zero mark at the beginning of the object. Children should also realize that a ruler with the front end broken off still can be used to find the length of an object (by subtraction or counting units between the end points).

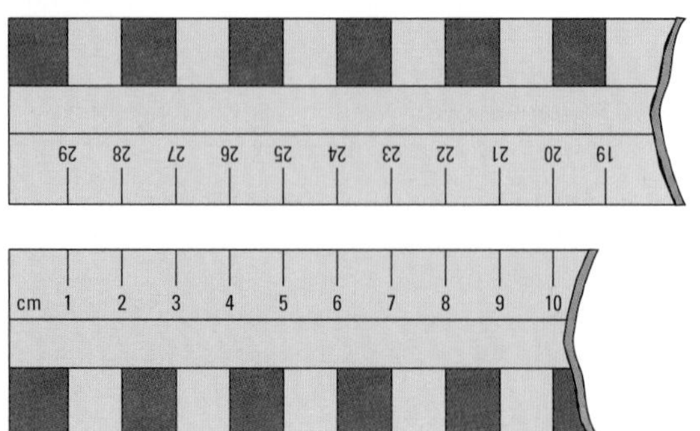

As a practice activity, children can work in pairs. One child draws a line segment on a piece of paper. The partner estimates its length in centimeters and then measures it using a ruler. The children then switch jobs. They might also try this with broken-line or curved paths. Similar activities can be done using inches.

The *meter* is introduced as a standard unit for measuring longer distances, such as the length of the classroom. Activities such as the following help children gain an appreciation for the size of this unit and relate it to the centimeter:

- Use an unmarked meter stick to find a point on your body that is 1 meter from the floor. Put the meter stick on the floor. How many of your steps make a meter? Find objects in the classroom that are about 1 meter in length or have a height of about 1 meter. How many meters long (wide) do you think the classroom is? Measure and compare the actual length with your estimate.
- Use a trundle wheel to measure the length of the hall, the distance around the gym, and so on. Estimate before you measure.
- How many centimeters does it take to make a meter? Estimate first, then look at the side of the meter stick marked in centimeters to find out. If an object is 2 m long, how many centimeters is that?

Similar activities can be done for feet, inches, and yards, using a ruler with customary units.

To measure in *decimeters* children can use the 10-cm Cuisenaire rod, the "long" from the base-ten materials, or a 10 centicube stick. The meter stick pictured in Figure 15-1 is marked to show the relationships among the meter, decimeter, and centimeter. The meaning of the prefixes *centi* and *deci* can be discussed in this connection.

In relation to the concept of precision, children can measure the length of the chalkboard to the nearest meter, decimeter, and centimeter. They can discuss which unit is most appropriate in this case and which of the three results is the most precise.

The *millimeter* is introduced as a unit to measure very small things, such as insects. Two sample activities involving this unit are:

- Use a ruler marked in centimeters and millimeters to measure, to the nearest millimeter, the length of several objects or line segments drawn on paper.
- Make a stack of 10 dimes. Measure the height of the stack. What is the approximate thickness of one dime?

FIGURE 15-1 Sample Meter Stick

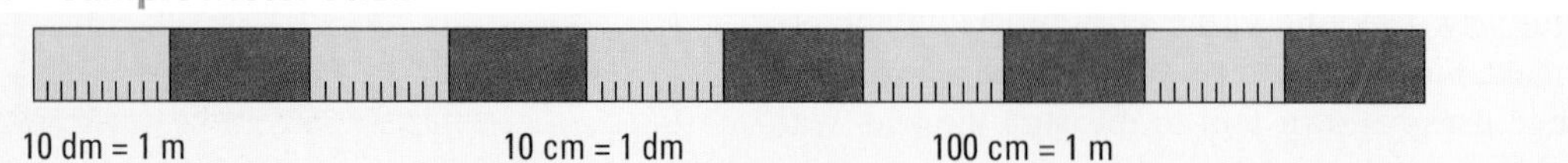

Sample questions and activities relating to the *kilometer* are as follows:

- What place would be about 1 kilometer (km) from your home (the school)? How long does it take you to walk (jog, run) a kilometer? Identify places that are about 2 km (10 km) apart.
- Use a road map or atlas to find the distances between your town or city and other cities you have visited or would like to visit. How far is it from Los Angeles to New York? From Chicago to Seattle? What is the distance around the earth? How far is it to the moon?

In Activities 15-3 and 15-4, children measure in metric units to collect data to develop formulas or discover relationships.

myeducationlab The Power of Classroom Practice Go to the Assignments and Activities section of Topic 12: "Measurement Concepts and Skills" in the MyEducationLab for your course and complete the activity "A Measurement Lesson" to see how students learn to measure perimeter.

Area

Area is the amount of surface enclosed by a curve in the plane. We consider area when we hang wallpaper, carpet a floor, or wrap a present. Although any plane region that tessellates can be used as a unit for measuring area, the standard unit is the measure of a square having an edge with a length of one unit. Children should learn about measuring area by covering figures with square tiles and by drawing figures on squared paper before being taught to use formulas. Units of area are derived from corresponding linear units.

Area: Perception and direct comparison. To introduce the notion of area, you might show the class two rectangular pieces of cardboard, one measuring about 30 cm by 3 cm and the other 20 cm by 10 cm, and ask the question, "Which is bigger?" Even though the first piece is longer, children will generally say that the other looks bigger in the sense that it *covers more surface.* They might also argue that the two areas could be compared directly if the long strip were cut into two pieces.

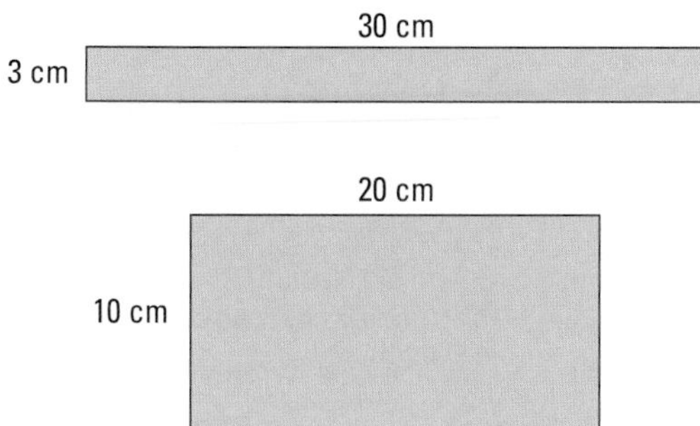

As a follow-up activity, children working in small groups can compare the areas of pairs of rectangles having the following dimensions: 10 cm by 6 cm and 8 cm by 8 cm; 6 cm by 8 cm and 12 cm by 4 cm.

ACTIVITY 15-3 Perimeter of a Rectangle

Materials

Ruler, meter stick

Procedure

1. Find and record the *perimeter* (distance around) of your textbook, the door, a window, the top of the filing cabinet. Use appropriate units.
2. How many different sides did you need to measure to find the perimeter of these things? Write a sentence telling how to find the perimeter of a rectangle.

ACTIVITY 15-4 Circumference of a Circle

Materials

Circular objects

Tape measure

Calculator

Procedure

1. Using a tape measure marked in millimeters, measure the *diameter* (distance across) and the *circumference* (distance around) of several circular objects. Enter these numbers in the chart and use a calculator to compute the ratios.

Circumference (C)	*Diameter (d)*	$C \div d$
270 mm	85 mm	3.18
______	______	______
______	______	______

2. Can you state a relationship between the diameter and the circumference of a circle?

To test for conservation of area, two squares of the same size are shown. The teacher cuts one square along a diagonal and rearranges the two pieces to form a triangle or parallelogram. Then the teacher asks the students whether the two shapes have the same area and to explain their answers.

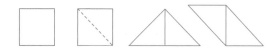

Area: Nonstandard units. To introduce the idea of a unit of area, the teacher can ask the class how many pieces of construction paper would be required to cover the

FIGURE 15-2 Using Small Squares to Introduce the Concept of Area

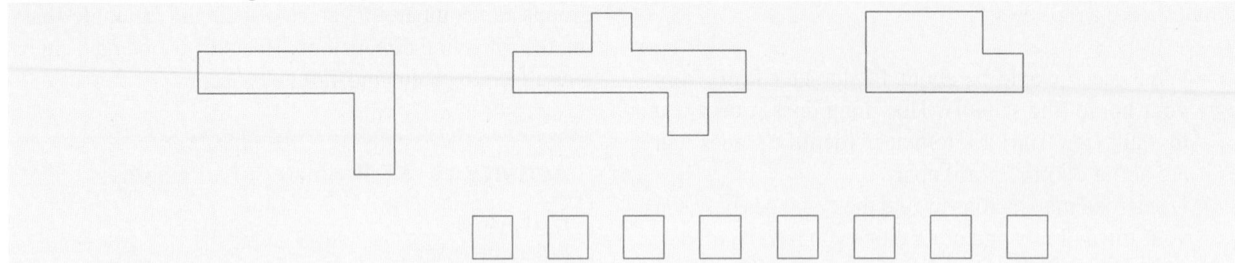

bulletin board. At their seats, they could use small file cards to cover a page or the surface of their desks. Children could also find out how many of their hands it takes to cover their desks and then compare and discuss their results.

In another activity, children can be given small squares (Figure 15-2) and asked if they can use them to find which two of three specially constructed figures cover the same amount of surface. The number of squares covering each figure is the area measure of the figure with respect to that unit.

Given pattern blocks such as the six shapes shown next, children can be asked to find how many copies of each shape are required to cover a card measuring about 10 cm by 13 cm.

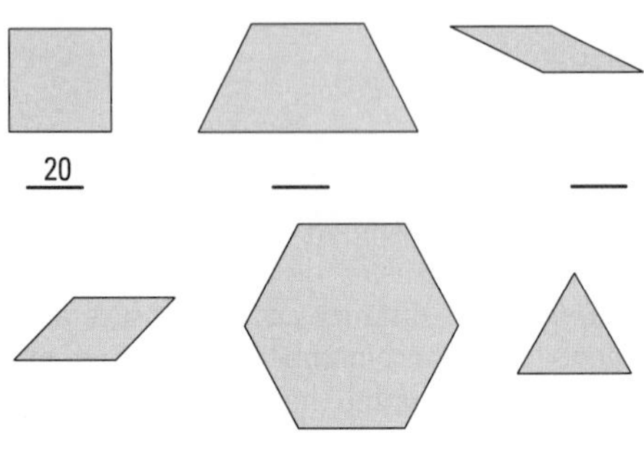

Asking children to use objects such as toothpicks and circular counters to cover a surface can lead to a discussion about the desirable characteristics of a unit of area. Key ideas are that the unit should possess the attribute of covering and that it should cover without overlapping; the figure tessellates the plane. Children should also use three different sizes of squares to measure a particular surface and note the relationship between the number of units needed and the size of the unit.

Several geoboard tasks involving area are shown in Activity 15-5. Activity 15-6 leads children to discover the formula for the area of a rectangle; other excellent activities with squared paper are described by Shaw (1983). See Blackline Masters 17 and 18 on MyEducationLab for a geoboard template and geoboard recording paper.

 Go to Chapter 15 in the Book-Specific Resources section in the MyEducationLab for your course and select Blackline Masters to obtain "Blackline Masters 17 and 18."

Area: Standard units. The basic units of area are the *square meter, the square inch,* and the *square foot.* To give children a feel for the square meter, outline a square 1 m by 1 m on the chalkboard or on the floor (with masking tape). Children need to know that the symbol m^2 is read "square meter" and not "meter squared." The class could determine the number of square meters of carpet needed to cover the classroom floor and the area of the gym floor in square meters. Similar activities can be done for square inches and square feet.

Children can become familiar with the *square centimeter* (cm^2) by using centimeter graph paper (Horak & Horak, 1982). One task is to find the approximate area of their hands by tracing around them on graph paper and counting squares. Children also can be asked to outline polygons enclosing specified numbers of square centimeters. For example, enclose a region with an area of 43 cm^2. Do this in several different ways. (See Blackline Master 16 in Appendix B for centimeter graph paper.)

ACTIVITY 15-5 Geoboard Areas

Materials

Geoboard

Procedure

1. Copy the figure below on your geoboard. The unit is the square region formed as shown. The area of the figure is 7 units.

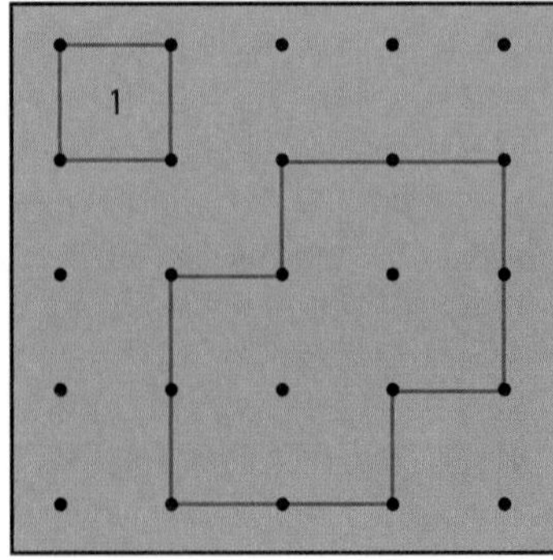

2. On your geoboard, enclose figures with areas of 3, 6, and 11 units.
3. On your geoboard, how many different figures can you make having an area of 5 units?
4. Find the perimeter of each figure in step 3.

Literature Link 15-2

Perimeter and Area of Polygons

Burns, Marilyn. (1997). ***Spaghetti and Meatballs for All!*** New York: Scholastic.

Being able to connect conceptual understanding to the processes for determining perimeter and area is crucial for children, who often have great difficulty explaining or illustrating these two ideas. When formulas for determining perimeter and area of common polygons are presented, children become easily confused because the procedures for finding the area and perimeter of squares and rectangles are quite similar. In ***Spaghetti and Meatballs for All!***, Mrs. Comfort is planning a family reunion and designs a seating chart with square tables based on these ideas of perimeter and area. As the tables in the story are arranged and rearranged, children make some discoveries about these concepts.

- Model the arrangement and rearrangement of the tables in the story using blocks or color tiles. Note that shapes with the same area can have different perimeters (or combined perimeters).
- Design different table arrangements using 1-in. square tiles. As children create their own table arrangements, they can measure these perimeters and areas using various tools and methods.
- Create a class chart of the perimeters and areas of the different table arrangements created by the class. Compare arrangements with the same areas and different perimeters and recognize patterns in the measurements.
- Create and record the perimeters and areas of various table arrangements using geoboards and dot paper.
- Explore different kinds of quadrilaterals such as a square, rhombus, rectangle, parallelogram, and trapezoid. Write descriptions that show the distinct characteristics of each shape.

Source: Dr. Patricia Moyer-Packenham, Utah State University.

ACTIVITY 15-6 Areas of Rectangles

Materials
Squared paper

Procedure

1. Draw several different rectangles on squared paper.
2. For each rectangle find the length and width in linear units and the area in square units.

Length	*Width*	*Area*
3	2	6
______	______	______
______	______	______

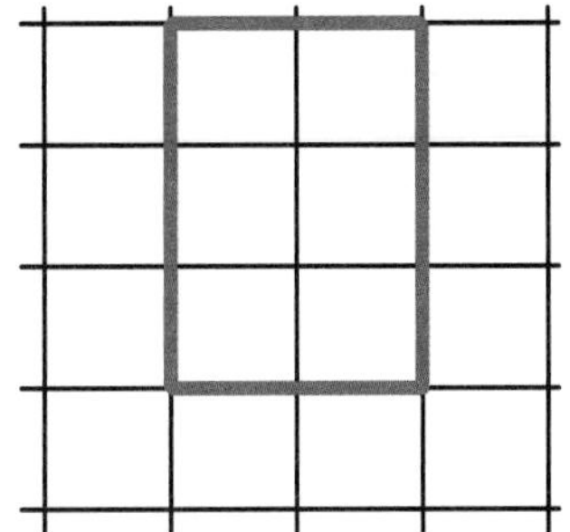

3. State a rule for finding the area of a rectangle given its length and width.

The faces of the small cube of the base-ten materials have sides 1 cm in length, and thus each face has an area of 1 cm^2. The 10-by-10 flat is a *square decimeter.* By comparing these two blocks, children can find that 1 dm^2 = 100 cm^2. They should also be able to determine that 1 m^2 = 10,000 cm^2 by considering 100 rows of 100 square centimeters in a square meter. From Activity 15-6, children found that the area of a rectangle is the product of its *length* and *width.*

Children can use geoboards to investigate triangular areas. Children see that a right triangle can be enclosed in a rectangle and because the two resulting triangles are congruent, the area of the original triangle is half that of the rectangle. A triangle without a right angle can also be enclosed in a rectangle, as illustrated next, and its area found by subtracting the areas of the right triangles formed from the area of the rectangle.

In general, two copies of any triangle form a parallelogram, as shown in the following diagram. Children can reason that since the triangle and the parallelogram have the same base and height, the area of a triangle can be computed by finding half the product of its base and height.

ACTIVITY 15-7 Parallelogram Areas

- How are the parallelograms the same?
- How are they different?
- Find the area of each.

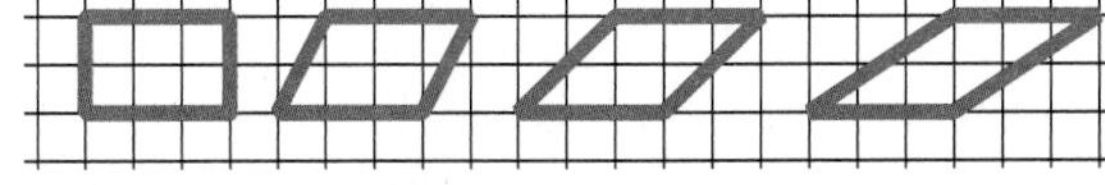

ACTIVITY 15-8 Geoboard Triangles

Materials

Geoboard

Procedure

1. Find the areas of these geoboard triangles by enclosing them in rectangles and subtracting the areas of the right triangles formed.

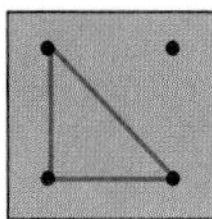

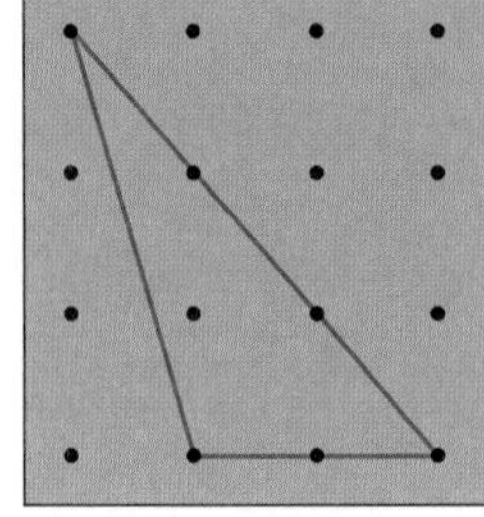

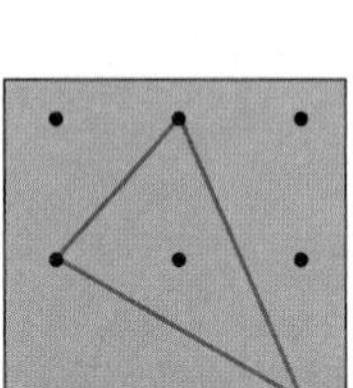

2. On a 25-nail geoboard it is possible to make 8 different triangles that have an area of 1. How many can you find?

ACTIVITY 15-9 Covering a Box

Materials

Shoebox (or similar box)
Paper
Scissors

Procedure

1. Cut pieces of paper to match each of the faces of the box. Use them to completely cover the box.
2. How many pieces of paper did you cut? How many different sizes were there?
3. Find the dimensions of each rectangular piece of paper in centimeters and compute the areas.
4. The *surface area* of a box is the sum of the areas of its faces. Find the surface area of the box in square centimeters.
5. State a rule for finding the surface area of a box given its length, width, and height.

Activities 15-7 through 15-9 are problems and investigations relating to the areas of rectangles, parallelograms, and triangles. The surface area of a rectangular solid is introduced in Activity 15-9.

To help children see that the formula for the area of a circle, $A = \pi r^2$, is sensible, show them the following diagram in which a circle of radius r is inscribed in a square of side $2r$:

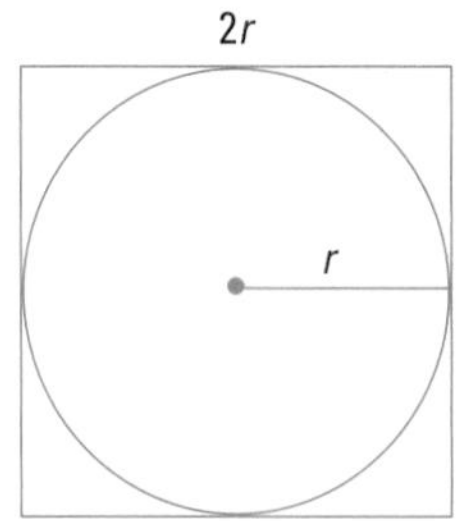

The area of the square is $4r^2$. It appears that the area of the circle is about three-fourths of the area of the square, or about $3r^2$. Children can also draw circles on squared paper and find their approximate areas by counting squares. They will find that the ratio of the area to the square of the radius is a bit more than three. This ratio is known as pi(π), which is approximately 3.1416.

myeducationlab The Power of Classroom Practice To explore your own understanding of measurement, go to Chapter 15 in the Book-Specific Resources section in the MyEducationLab for your course. Select the Activities section and complete the various activities.

Volume

Volume is a measure of the amount of space inside a closed three-dimensional region, or the amount of space occupied by a three-dimensional object. *Interior volume* refers to the amount of space confined within the boundaries of a container such as a box. The unit is the measure of a cube having an edge with a length of one unit. Concept development activities include building solids with cubes and filling boxes with cubes (Hart, 1984). Units for volume are derived from linear units.

Volume: Perception and direct comparison. To introduce the concept of cubic volume, you might hold up two solid rectangular prisms and ask which is "bigger." Although linear dimensions and surface areas of these three-dimensional objects could be compared, the discussion should lead to the question of which one *occupies more space.* Two empty boxes, one of which fits within the other, are then shown and compared directly for *volume.* You and your students can generate a list of everyday examples of objects that have a large volume or a small volume, but in most cases direct comparison cannot be carried out, and beginning instructional activities involve the use of nonstandard units.

To determine whether a child conserves volume, you can use wooden cubes to build a solid shape, such as a $2 \times 3 \times 2$ prism. Explain that you are making a house with blocks and that each block is a room. Instruct the child to copy the house and to confirm that the two structures have the same number of rooms. You then rearrange the 12 blocks to form a prism with different dimensions, such as $6 \times 2 \times 1$, and ask the child if this house has more, fewer, or the same number of rooms as the child's house. The child is asked to justify her or his explanation.

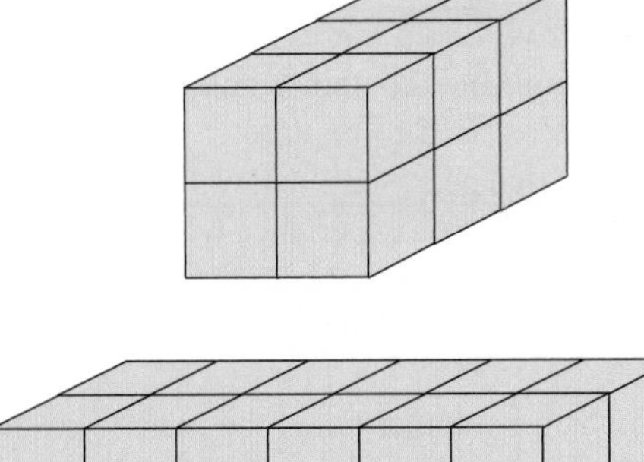

Volume: Nonstandard units. Common (2.5-cm cube) wooden or plastic blocks can be used as a unit of volume in many concept development activities. For one task, you can construct open boxes that can be filled by the cubes arranged in the following ways: $3 \times 3 \times 3$, $4 \times 3 \times 2$, and $5 \times 5 \times 1$. The children first predict which of the boxes will hold the most cubes and then carry out the measurement.

Children can also use the blocks to make solid shapes with a given volume (such as 7 or 13) and to make as many different rectangular solids as possible using a fixed number of blocks (12, for example). Activity 15-10 is designed to lead children to discover the formula for the volume of a rectangular prism. In Activity 15-11 children investigate the surface areas of rectangular solids with a constant volume.

You should discuss with children the problem associated with using spherical-shaped objects, such as marbles or Ping-Pong balls, as units of volume. Using different-sized cubes (such as sugar cubes and interlocking cubes) to measure the volume of a box provides a setting for reviewing the relationship between the unit size and the number of units needed.

ACTIVITY 15-10 Volume of a Rectangular Solid

Manipulative Strategies

Materials

At least 25 wooden or plastic cubes

Procedure

1. Use cubes to build the rectangular solid pictured here. Its length is 4, its width is 2, and its height is 2.

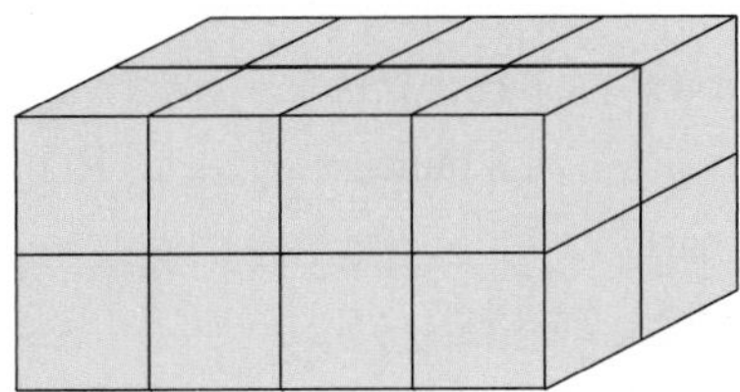

2. Find its volume by counting the number of blocks used to build the solid.
3. Build other rectangular solids with different dimensions.
4. Record their lengths, widths, heights, and volumes.

Length	*Width*	*Height*	*Volume*
4	2	2	16
5	1	3	______
______	______	______	______

5. Can you state a rule for finding the volume of a box given its length, width, and height?

ACTIVITY 15-11 Surface Area of a Rectangular Solid

Materials

24 wooden or plastic cubes

Procedure

1. Arrange 24 cubes to form a rectangular solid 4 blocks long, 2 blocks wide, and 3 blocks high.

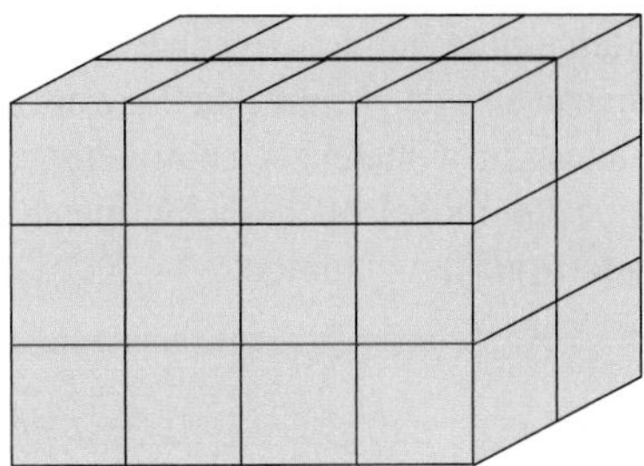

2. Find the prism's surface area—the total number of squares (the size of a face of a unit cube) needed to cover all faces of the prism.
3. Using all 24 cubes each time, make as many other different solid rectangular prisms as you can.
4. Record your findings.

Length	*Width*	*Height*	*Surface Area*
4	3	2	52
12	2	1	______
______	______	______	______

5. These prisms all have the same volume. Which has the greatest/least surface area?
6. Suppose you wanted to build an apartment building containing 24 rooms of equal size. How would you arrange the 24 rooms? Consider factors such as cost, view, heating, availability of land, need for elevators.

Volume: Standard units. A model for a *cubic meter* can be constructed using 12 meter-length sticks. After you introduce the symbol for cubic meters (m^3), you might ask the class to calculate the approximate volume of the classroom using its length, width, and height in meters. A similar activity can be done for yd^3 and ft^3.

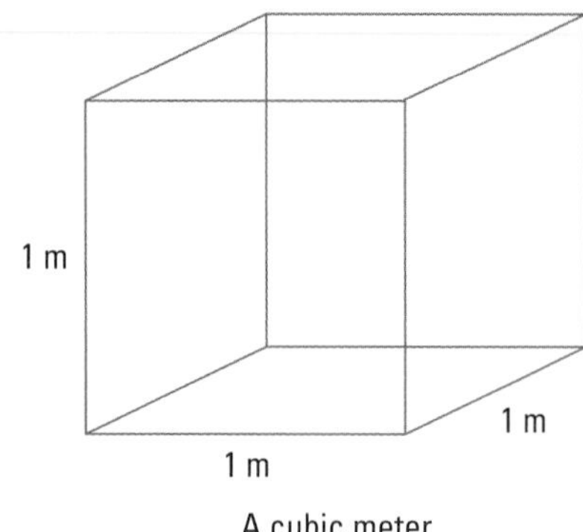

A cubic meter

The cubic centimeter (cm^3) is modeled by the small cube of the base-ten materials and by the centicube block. Children should use these blocks to build solids having volumes of given numbers of cubic centimeters. They should also use a ruler to measure the length, width, and height of a box to the nearest centimeter and compute the approximate volume in cubic centimeters.

The large cube of the base-ten materials provides a model for a *cubic decimeter* (dm^3). Comparing the small cube to the large cube, children find that $1\ dm^3 = 1{,}000\ cm^3$.

Children can also determine that there are a million cubic centimeters in a meter. A centimeter cube can be placed inside the model of the cubic meter to help students visualize this large number.

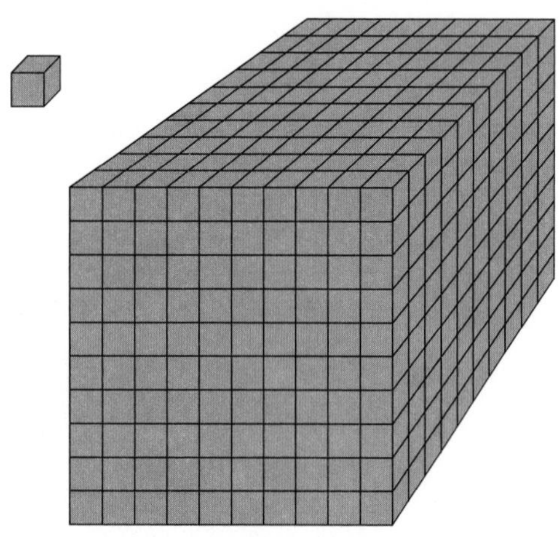

$1\ dm^3 = 1000\ cm^3$

Capacity

Whereas volume is the amount of space occupied by an object, the term *capacity* is often used to refer to the amount of space that can be filled. Capacity is usually used in connection with liquid measure. In the elementary curriculum, children learn about capacity in kindergarten and grade 1; cubic volume is first encountered in grade 3 or 4.

Capacity: Perception and direct comparison. To introduce the attribute of capacity, children can be shown two containers and asked which one *holds more.* If one container fits into the other, the children can see that the large container will hold more. If not, the question is answered by filling one container and pouring it into the other. Substances used to explore capacity in the classroom include dried peas, sand, and water. Children require a great deal of hands-on experience with a variety of cans, bottles, paper cups, and other containers of different sizes and shapes. The following instructions might be given:

1. Find which container holds the most/least. Estimate first, and then check by pouring.
2. Can you find two different containers that hold about the same amount?
3. Order the containers according to how much they hold.

To check for conservation, show the students two identical glasses sitting side by side. Pour water into one of the glasses, and ask a child to fill the other glass so that it contains the same amount. The child pours water into the glass until the water level is the same in the two glasses. You then pour the water from the first glass into a tall narrow container and ask if it contains more water, less water, or the same amount of water as the child's glass. You then ask the child to explain or justify her or his answer.

Capacity: Nonstandard units. To describe *how much* a container holds, the children find how many times a smaller container must be filled to hold the same amount as the larger container. Again, children should be encouraged to estimate before they measure and to record their results as they find the capacities of a variety of containers using a nonstandard unit. Children will find that the container will not be filled exactly by a whole number of units. They are instructed to measure to the nearest unit, but answers such as cups are not uncommon.

Container	Estimate	Measure
mug	8 ounces	10 ounces
yogurt carton	________	________
________	________	________

Next, children can use units of different sizes to measure an object such as a cottage cheese container. They should predict what will happen when a smaller unit is used and explain why more of these units will be needed to fill the container.

UNIT	ESTIMATE	MEASURE
paper cup	4	5
ladle	______	______
______	______	______

A body unit for capacity is the "handful." Several different children can be asked to find how many handfuls of corn it takes to fill a margarine tub. Children can compare results and discuss the problems associated with using handfuls as a unit of measurement.

Children can make their own *calibrated beaker* by adhering a strip of masking tape to the length of a tall, clear glass and marking with a felt pen the water level for 1, 2, 3, and 4 smaller containers. They can then use this device to find the approximate capacities of various containers with respect to the given unit.

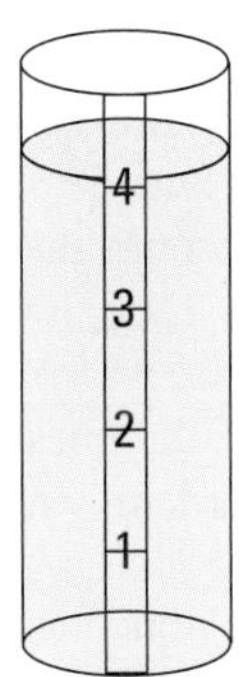

Capacity: Standard units. You can instruct children about measuring capacity in standard units by first telling them that a standard unit for measuring how much a container holds is a *liter* and that its symbol is L. Then you can show the children several different-shaped liter containers and give them the opportunity to verify that the containers have the same capacity. An early activity with this unit is to sort a variety of containers using the categories "more than a liter," "about a liter," and "less than a liter." Familiar containers such as a 1-L water bottle should be displayed and referred to in connection with this unit. Similar activities can be done using quarts and gallons.

The *milliliter* (mL) is a very small unit, and children usually first experience it by measuring with a set of uncalibrated beakers of sizes 500 mL, 250 mL, 100 mL, and 50 mL. Spoon sets including sizes 1 mL, 2 mL, 5 mL, 15 mL, and 25 mL can also be used to measure smaller amounts. Children can then learn to use graduated 1000-mL beakers marked in 100-mL or 50-mL intervals to measure capacity. They note that reading the scale is similar to using a ruler to measure length.

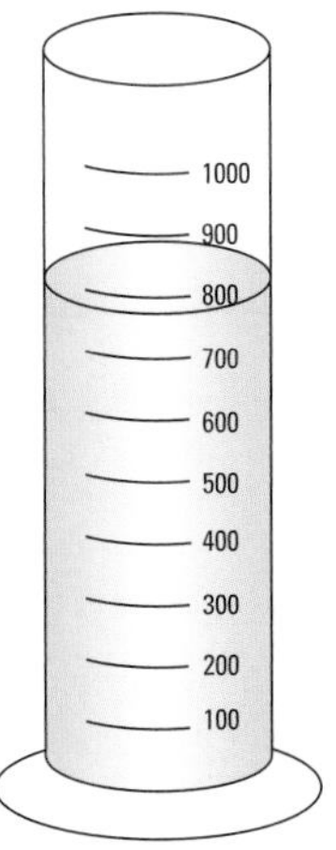

Mass

Mass is a measure of the amount of matter in an object, whereas *weight* is the force of gravity acting on that mass. When astronauts orbit the earth in the space shuttle, their weight is less than it is on earth, but their mass does not change. To compare two masses or to quantify mass, children first use a *two-pan balance.* Because this apparatus does not directly show what mass means, the concept is a difficult one for children to grasp. Whereas the pound is a unit of weight in the customary system of measurement, the *kilogram* is a metric unit for mass. Compression scales and spring balances are calibrated to measure mass in standard units.

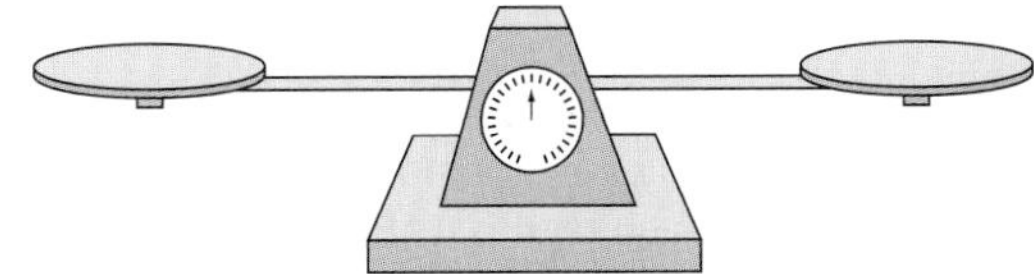

Mass: Perception and direct comparison. To test for conservation of matter, you can use clay to make two balls that the children judge to have the same amount of clay. The teacher then rolls one ball into a sausage shape and asks the children whether it has more clay, less clay, or the same amount of clay as the other ball. The teacher then asks the children to elaborate on their answers.

To introduce the concept of mass, you might hold a brick in one hand and a basketball in the other and ask, "Which is bigger?" From their experience, children will likely know that although the ball has a larger volume, the brick is *heavier.* You then ask the class to name some things that are *heavy* and *light.* These ideas are further developed as the children hold objects and feel the pull of gravity. In most cases, the masses of two objects cannot be compared by sight; they must be held to determine which is heavier. Activity 15-12 describes a task for partners.

The pan balance is helpful for making more accurate comparisons. Children should discuss why the side with the heavier object is lower. In Activity 15-13, children first estimate which of two objects is heavier, then check using a pan balance.

ACTIVITY 15-12 Which Is Heavier?

Materials
Various objects

Procedure

1. Choose two objects.
2. Decide which is heavier first by looking, then by holding one object in each hand.
3. See if your partner makes the same decision.
4. Do this for other pairs of objects.
5. Record what you do and find.

Heavier	*Lighter*	*Partner Agrees*
book	ball	yes
scissors	stapler	no
________	________	________

ACTIVITY 15-13 Using a Pan Balance to Compare

Materials
Pan balance
Various objects

Procedure

1. Use the pan balance to compare pairs of objects. Estimate first. Then record which is heavier.

Objects	*Estimate*	*Balance*
book and ball	book heavier	book heavier
scissors and tape	same	scissors heavier
________	________	________

2. Arrange the objects in order from lightest to heaviest.
3. Are big things always heavier than small things? Why or why not?

Mass: Nonstandard units. Objects that can be used as nonstandard units of mass include common wooden or plastic blocks, interlocking cubes, paper clips, and bolts or nuts. The children might be asked to estimate how many wooden blocks are *as heavy as* a glue stick and to use the pan balance to measure. If five blocks are required, you explain that the *mass* of the glue stick is about five blocks. You should then repeat the procedure with several other objects.

OBJECT	ESTIMATE	MEASURE
glue stick	7 blocks	5 blocks
eraser	________	________
________	________	________

To explore the relationship between the size of the unit and the number of units required to measure an object, the mass of a particular object, such as a glue stick, is then found by using several different units.

UNIT	ESTIMATE	MEASURE
wooden cube	7	5
interlocking cube	12	15
bottle cap	________	________

Mass: Standard units. The *kilogram* (kg) is introduced as a standard unit for measuring mass. Sample activities include the following:

- Hold a kilogram mass. Use clay to make a ball with a mass of 1 kg. Check using a pan balance. Make another shape using this same clay. Is its mass still 1 kg? How do you know?
- Find things in the room that have a mass of about 1 kg, greater than 1 kg, and less than 1 kg. How many notebooks does it take to make a mass of 1 kg?
- At home use your bathroom scale to find your mass in kilograms. Ask your family members to do the same.

Similar activities can be done using pounds.

The *gram* (g) is one-thousandth of a kilogram. The centicube is designed to have a mass of 1 gram. Children can use individual gram units to compare masses of objects, such as the small cube from the base-ten materials and a paper clip, and to find the mass of various objects in grams.

OBJECT	ESTIMATE	MEASURE
nickel	10 g	5 g
eraser	________	________
pen	________	________
________	________	________

Children can also use a set of standard masses (1 kg, 500 g, 200 g, 100 g, 50 g, 20 g, 10 g) to find the masses of various objects to the nearest 10 g.

OBJECT	ESTIMATE	MEASURE
glue bottle	200 g	250 g
stapler	________	________
________	________	________

At home, children should look for products that are packaged or sold by mass and report these to the class (e.g., a sack of sugar, a cake mix, a box of cereal, a candy bar, a bag of apples).

Children learn relationships between metric units of volume and mass when they find that the mass of a liter (cubic decimeter) of water is close to a kilogram. It follows that a milliliter (cubic centimeter) of water has a mass of 1 gram. Furthermore, because a cubic meter is 1,000 cubic decimeters, the mass of water required to fill a tub of length, width, and height 1 m is 1000 kg, which is a *tonne* (t). Because an average football player has a mass of about 100 kg, it would take about 10 football players to make a tonne.

Time

We use *time* to specify *when* an event occurred or will occur and also to describe *how long* an event lasted. Can you identify both aspects of time in the following sentence?

> *In 2000, Maurice Greene set a new Olympic record of 9.87 seconds in the 100-m dash.*

Judging the passage of time is not an easy task for children, and adults remark that "time flies when you're having fun." Learners should have many concept development experiences related to the *sequencing* of events and the *duration* of time periods before they are taught the complex process of *telling time* by reading a clock (Horak & Horak, 1983).

Time: Perception and direct comparison. Questions such as the following help children develop concepts and vocabulary related to the sequencing of events:

- When you get dressed, which do you put on *first*—your shoes or your socks? When you get ready for bed do you brush your teeth *after* you put on your pajamas or *before* you put on your pajamas? What is the *last* thing you do before you go to bed?
- Name some things we do in class *before* lunch and some things we do *after* lunch.
- List in order five things you do *after* you wake up on Saturday mornings.

Early comparison tasks rely on memory. You might describe two events and ask the child which takes longer, or more time, to complete. Examples are eating breakfast or walking to school, watching a cartoon or playing a soccer game. The class might also make a list of activities done during a school day (such as music, sharing time, and recess) and vote on which takes the least amount of time and which takes the most amount of time. A related task is to list several events in order according to how much time each takes.

To check for conservation of time, you can place two toy animals side by side on a table. You then tell the children that the animals are going for a walk and to say when to start and when to stop. When the children say "go," you hop the animals along the table so that they remain side by side. At "stop," you ask the children if the animals started and stopped at the same time. The procedure is then repeated but with one animal taking longer hops so that when they stop, it will be farther ahead. You then ask the children if the animals started and stopped at the same time.

Although we cannot see time, it is sometimes possible to observe which of two events takes longer. To carry out direct comparisons of time, the two events must start simultaneously. Children are familiar with the idea that in a race the two runners must start at the same time. Comparing two different activities can help children focus on the concept of time duration rather than on "who won." For example, one child jumps up and down 10 times while another stacks seven blocks. The class observes which event took more time to complete.

Time: Nonstandard units. To establish the need for a unit for measuring time, the children should compare the times of two events that cannot be carried out concurrently; for example, the children may be asked how they might find out whether it takes Samantha longer to print her name neatly or tie the laces on her shoes. The problem then becomes one of determining how to measure *how long* an event takes.

Any repeated, regular action can serve as a nonstandard unit. One procedure is to have one child tap a pencil on a table according to a steady beat while another counts the taps. The number of taps required by other children to perform various tasks is then recorded. Later, children experiment with increasing and decreasing the rate of tapping and discuss the relationship between this variable and the number of taps associated with a given event.

Children could make a *pendulum* as an instrument for measuring time by attaching a metal nut to a piece of string. Working in pairs, one partner counts the number of times the string swings back and forth while the other performs a task.

TASK	ESTIMATE	MEASURE
saying the alphabet	6 swings	5 swings
joining 10 cubes	________	________
________	________	________

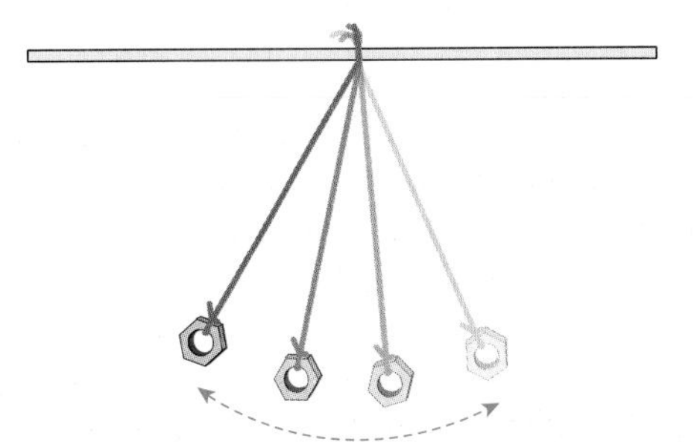

FIGURE 15-3 An Example of a Daily Timeline

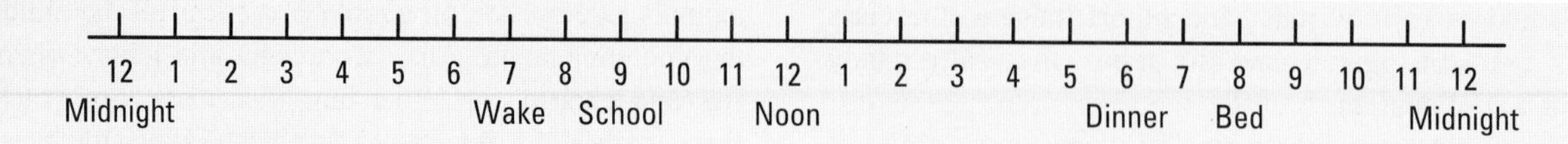

A *metronome* is also useful for measuring time. One person performs a task while others count the "ticks." The class can observe and discuss the effect of adjusting the device to tick at different speeds. The children might also use a *sand timer* to find how many times they can perform various actions, such as jumping up and down, before the sand runs out.

Time: Standard units. To introduce the *second* (s), you should set the metronome so that its ticks are 1 second apart. If a metronome is not available, a pendulum of length 25 cm may be used. Children count in time with the metronome or the swing of the pendulum so that they are saying one number per second. They then measure the time required to do various tasks in seconds.

The following activities acquaint the children with the *minute* (min):

- Put your heads on your desks and close your eyes. I will tell you when a minute has passed. Now I will read to you for 1 minute. Next we will jump up and down for 1 minute. Did the length of these minutes seem the same to you? What are some things you can do that take about a minute? Less than a minute? More than a minute? Now close your eyes again and raise your hand when you think 1 minute has passed.
- Make a minute book. On each page describe something you can do in a minute or how many times you can do some activity in a minute. For example, how many sit-ups can you do in a minute? How many times can you bounce a ball?

If there is a dial clock in the classroom with a second hand, you can relate the minute to the time it takes this hand to make a complete revolution. The class might also discuss the fact that this is equivalent to 60 seconds. Longer periods of time can then be referred to: Recess is 15 minutes long; a music class lasts for 40 minutes.

The *hour* (hr) can be related to the child's experience as follows: Lunch break is 1 hour; we go to school for 3 hours in the morning; movies last about 2 hours; you should get about 10 hours of sleep each night. Children are familiar with the concept of a *day* and the ideas of *yesterday* and *tomorrow.* They might be asked to make a list showing how many of the 24 hours in a day they spend on the following activities: sleeping, eating, going to school, playing, doing chores, and watching television.

The *week, month,* and *year* are studied in connection with the *calendar.* In problems such as the following, children use equivalencies among these units.

- How many years have you lived? How many months?
- Can you give your age in weeks? Days? Hours? Minutes? Seconds? You may want to use a calculator.

Telling time. We now turn our attention from questions related to measuring *how long* an event took to questions about describing *when* an event occurred or is scheduled to occur. Children should be familiar with the dates of special events such as their birthday. The idea of *telling time* is motivated by the need to specify when events occur during the day. The related question is "What time is it?" To introduce this concept, you might draw an hour timeline on the board starting and ending at midnight (Figure 15-3). A dialogue such as the following might be used:

> *At 1 o'clock in the morning, most people are asleep. You probably wake up at about 7 o'clock. School starts at 9 o'clock and ends in the morning at 12 o'clock, which is also called noon. An hour later it is 1 o'clock in the afternoon. School lets out at 3 o'clock. You might have dinner at 6 o'clock and go to bed at 8 o'clock. 12 o'clock at night is also called midnight.*
>
> *We write 4 o'clock like this: 4:00. Between 1 o'clock and 2 o'clock we indicate the number of minutes past the hour. If it is 23 minutes past 1 o'clock, we write the time like this: 1:23. Four minutes past 1 o'clock is written 1:04, and one minute before 2 o'clock is 1:59. Times such as 1:23 are also read, "one twenty-three."*
>
> *Digital clocks show the time of day in this way. If a digital clock shows 5:40, what would it show 1 hr later? 7 hr later? 8 hr later? 10 min later? 20 min later?*

To introduce the *dial clock,* you could draw a horizontal 12-hour timeline and then discuss and draw how this looks when it is rearranged to form a circle with the number 12 at the top. You then show a demonstration clock and ask questions such as the following: Which number is at the top (bottom)? Which number comes before 8? After 3? Before 12? After 12? The hour hand and the minute hand are identified and the positions of these hands for 5 o'clock, 8 o'clock, and 12 o'clock are shown. Children note how these clock times are the same and how they are different and then use individual demonstration clocks to practice showing times on the hour.

To teach children to tell time between hours, teachers should use a clock with a minute scale as well as an hour scale (Thompson & Van de Walle, 1981). Prerequisite skills include counting by fives and reading a number line scale with numbers provided only for the multiples of five. Children first learn to place the minute hand for times such as 20 or 50 minutes past the hour and later for 23 or 57 minutes past the hour. They should realize that at 5:40 the hour hand will be between 5 and 6, but precise placement is not important at this stage. Later they will relate the fraction of the circle traversed by the minute hand to the fractional part of the distance between two numbers moved by the hour hand. The ideas of "half past" and "quarter past" the hour and "before the hour" are taught after children can express all clock times "after the hour."

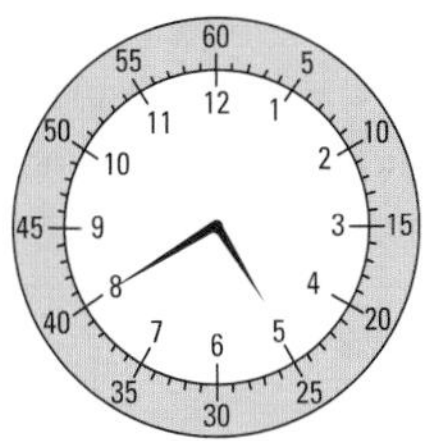

Other time topics usually found in the later elementary curriculum include A.M. and P.M. and the 24-hour clock.

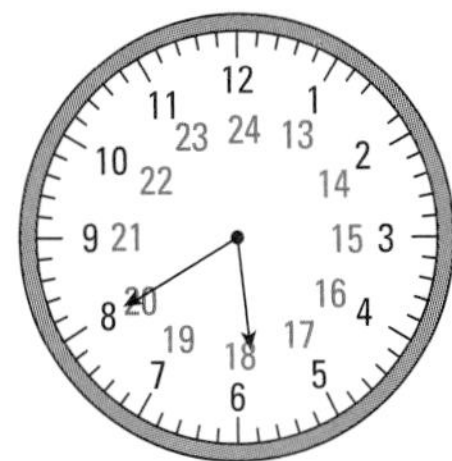

Temperature

Temperature is a measure of how hot or cold an object is. A reading of a *thermometer,* the instrument used to measure temperature, does not reflect the quality of heat or temperature, and this can cause difficulties for some children. The *Celsius scale* is commonly used for recording temperature in the metric system.

Temperature: Perception and direct comparison. Although temperature is not visible, large differences can be sensed by feel, and we notice even relatively small changes in room temperatures. Questions using the expressions "hot and cold" and "warm and cool" are used in concept development activities.

- Is it *hotter* in summer or in winter? Is it *cooler* on a sunny day or on a cloudy day? Is it *warmer* inside our classroom or outside today?
- How do you dress when you go outside on a *cold* day? Name something you drink when it is *cold/hot* outside. We use the word *temperature* when we talk about how hot or cold something is.

You can collect and display pictures clearly indicating heat. The class could discuss how these pictures might be ordered using the idea of hot and cold. For a hands-on activity, you could prepare several containers with water of varying temperatures: hot and cold tap water, water at room temperature, and water from a refrigerator. The children feel the water in each container and order them from warmest to coldest.

The class can discuss what happens to water when it gets very hot and very cold and how you can tell when some objects are very hot (for example, coals in a barbecue grill or an element of an electric stove).

Temperature: Standard units. No activities for measuring temperature using nonstandard units are suggested. Children will be familiar with hearing temperatures reported in *degrees Fahrenheit.* You can state that the temperature in the room is about 70°F. The class should also discuss temperature readings on hot and cold days, the meaning of 32°F, and temperatures below zero.

Introduce the *thermometer* as an instrument for measuring temperature. To make a demonstration thermometer, join a piece of white ribbon and a piece of red ribbon and fit the ends through horizontal slits in a piece of cardboard. Mark a scale on the cardboard and slide the ribbon up and down to indicate the temperature rising and falling. The height of the red section indicates the temperature. The teacher should demonstrate how to read the scale, first at 10- or 5-degree intervals and then to the nearest degree.

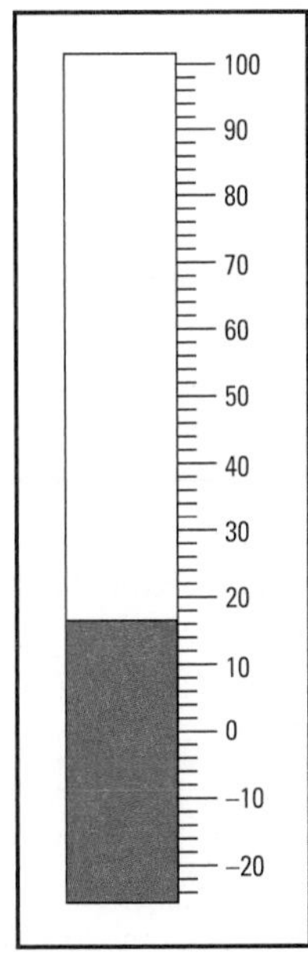

The teacher can explain that in a real thermometer the liquid in the tube expands as the temperature increases and the level rises. Children can then use a thermometer to find the temperature of water under several conditions to the nearest degree Fahrenheit.

	ESTIMATE	MEASURE
water left sitting	20 °C	18 °C
hot tap water	________	________
cold tap water	________	________
ice water	________	________

Two useful benchmarks are the temperature at which water boils (212 °F) and normal body temperature (about 98.6 °F). As an ongoing activity, children can record and graph the outside temperature (or the high and low temperatures) for a month. As a telecommunications project, students could share these data with schools in different parts of the world.

Angle

As a geometric figure, an *angle* is the union of two rays that have the same end point. When we measure an angle, we assign a number to the *spread* between the two arms, or rays. Angular measure can also be thought of in terms of the *amount of turning* about a point, which is used in defining the degree. For children to use a *protractor* correctly and understand what is being measured, they first require experiences in comparing angles directly and in using arbitrary units of angular measure.

Angle: Perception and direct comparison. Developing the concept of angle as a "turn" is particularly appropriate in the early elementary years (Wilson & Adams, 1992). Children can explore turning their bodies to make half, full, and quarter turns and use their arms to represent clock hands. They can also examine and discuss angles made by a swinging door.

To introduce the notion of the size of an angle, the teacher might open a pair of scissors and direct children's attention to the *angle* formed by the two blades. The teacher asks the students whether they think this angle is "big" or "small" and how a bigger or smaller angle might be formed. The key idea is that the size of an angle has to do with the *spread* between the two blades, not their length. To make this point, compare angles formed by two pairs of scissors of different sizes, paying special attention to examples in which the angle formed by the larger scissors is smaller than the angle formed by the scissors with shorter blades.

Drawing representations of angles on a chalkboard or paper makes use of the static view of angles. To develop basic concepts, the teacher might use an overhead projector to display two angles, as shown next, and ask the class members which angle they think is bigger and how they might check their estimates.

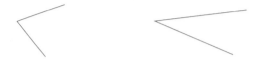

Again, children find that they must focus on the relationship between the arms and not their length. Mention that geometrically, the arms of an angle are rays and thus extend indefinitely. To compare the two angles, one first makes a tracing of one of them and directly compares the tracing with the other angle. When the vertices and one of the arms are matched, the other arm of the smaller angle lies in the interior of the larger angle.

Next, give the children tracing paper and a sheet containing angles of various measures in a number of different positions, with instructions to order the angles according to size. Two of these angles should have the same measure.

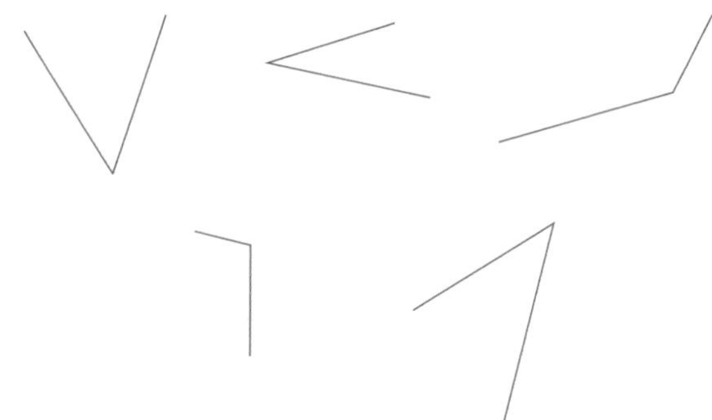

Angle: Nonstandard units. The teacher can draw an angle on the chalkboard and ask the children how they might determine "how big" the angle is. One strategy that is often suggested is to use a ruler to measure the distance between the arms. It should be recognized that children can use this procedure to compare and quantify angular measure, provided that they take the measurement at a fixed distance from the vertex along the arm(s).

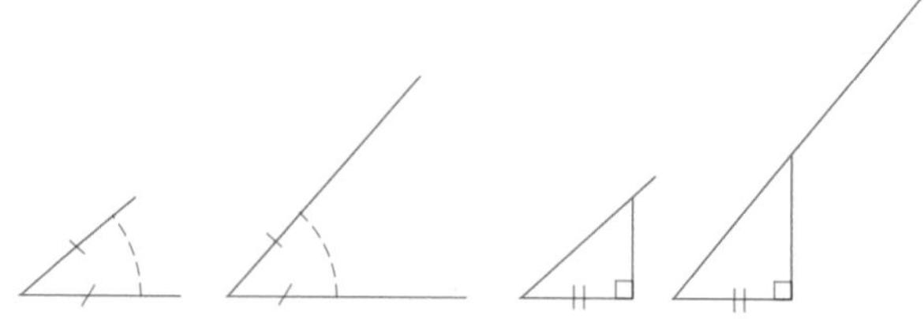

When children are reminded that an important characteristic of a unit is that it has the same attribute as that to be measured, they should realize that a small angle can be used as a unit. The question then is how many copies of this small angle fit inside the angle to be measured. A wedge cut from cardboard is useful as a unit to measure an angle drawn on a chalkboard.

Children should predict and verify the result of using a smaller unit angle to measure the angle in question. As an activity, children could prepare several copies of cardboard wedges representing angles of three different sizes. They would then draw an angle on paper and measure it using the three different units. You should remind children to estimate before measuring and to measure to the nearest unit.

Children can create an instrument for measuring angles by partitioning a paper half-circle into equal sectors by folding. You can then challenge them to use this "protractor" to find the measures of angles of various cardboard wedges.

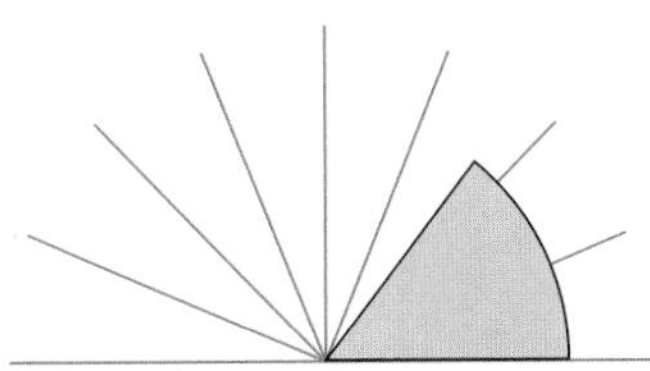

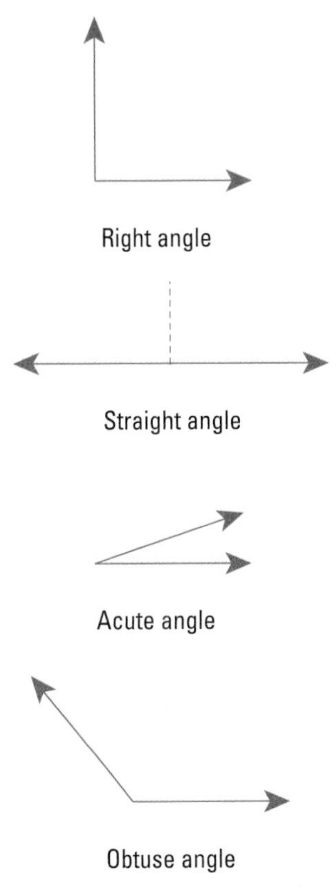

Angle: Standard units. Before children learn about the degree as a standard unit of angular measure, they can use the familiar *right angle* as a referent. This special angle can first be introduced in relation to body turns. Some children reason that because a quarter turn right is called a right angle, a quarter turn left is called a "left" angle. Later, children should be shown how to fold a piece of paper twice to produce a right angle. They then use this "right angle tester" to identify right angles on familiar objects at their desk and in the room and to classify other angles as greater than or less than a right angle. To illustrate a *straight angle,* two right angles can be placed together. Tell the children that an *acute angle* has a measure that is less than a right angle and an *obtuse angle* has a measure greater than a right angle but less than a straight angle.

Children explore angle measurements for triangles and quadrilaterals in Activity 15-14.

The *degree* can be defined as the amount of turning (or the size of unit angle) such that the measure of a quarter turn (or right angle) is 90°. It follows that the measure of a half turn (or straight angle) is 180° and the measure of a full turn is 360°.

At this point, you can ask the class to estimate the measures of various acute and obtuse angles drawn on the board. (You should draw angles of approximately 45°, 60°, 135°, and 170°.) You then demonstrate how to use a *protractor* to measure angles in degrees, emphasizing the correct placement of the baseline and the vertex. Children can practice using a protractor to measure angles and construct angles with given measures. Working in pairs, one child draws an angle, and the other estimates and then measures it. Next, the children reverse roles. Later, children learn to measure and construct angles greater than 180°.

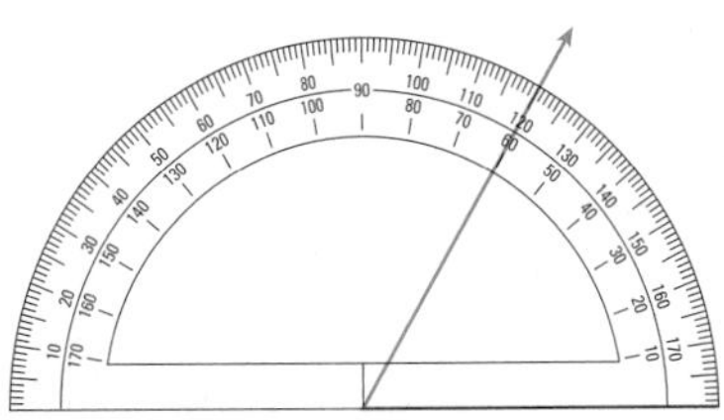

ACTIVITY 15-14 Triangle Angles

Visual Scaffolding

Materials

Light cardboard

Scissors

Procedure

1. Cut a triangle out of cardboard.
2. Cut off each of the corners as shown and place the three angles together. What kind of angle is formed?

3. Repeat with a different-shaped triangle. Did you get the same result?

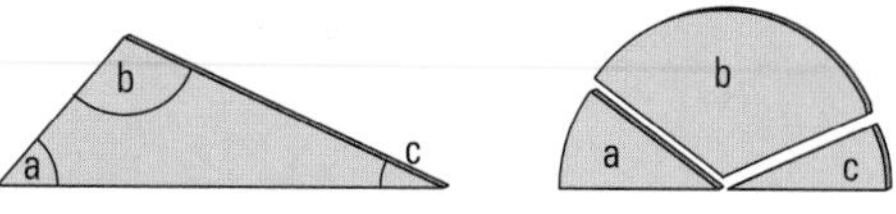

4. Cut a cardboard quadrilateral.
5. Cut off the four corners and place the four angles together. What did you find?

Conclusion

When we measure, we assign a number to a physical property of an object or to an event by comparing it with a unit. Beginning instruction in measurement stresses language development and involves activities that give meaning to the attribute. Observation and physical materials are used to make direct and indirect comparisons. Measuring should be carried out first with nonstandard units, then with standard units. Children need to be able to identify appropriate units for given situations and estimate and use instruments or formulas to measure with those units. As they learn measurement concepts and skills, learners are actively involved in solving problems.

Measurement is a practical, useful skill. Children should appreciate the role it plays in their everyday lives and in modern society. Measurement ideas should be identified, applied, and reinforced in other school subjects, including science, social studies, physical education, art, and music. Children should enjoy measuring and have confidence in their ability to use their knowledge and skills to solve problems in the real world.

myeducationlab The Power of Classroom Practice — Go to the Assignments and Activities section of Topic 12: "Measurement Concepts and Skills" in the MyEducationLab for your course. Complete the activity "Recording Data" to see how students approach *measurement.*

Sample Lesson

A Lesson on Understanding Perimeter

Grade level: Third grade

Materials: Squares, such as tiles or squares of paper.

Lesson objective: Students will use squares to find the perimeter of rectangles, and will analyze the process of finding the perimeter.

Standards link: Students form an understanding of perimeter as a measurable attribute and select appropriate units, strategies, and tools to solve problems involving perimeter (NCTM *Curriculum Focal Points,* grade three).

Launch: Display a rectangle constructed of square tiles, for example, one with 2 rows and 3 tiles in each row. Explain that this represents a garden that's 2 feet wide and 3 feet long, and that we want to put a fence around the garden to keep out the rabbits. Ask students, "How much fencing should we buy?" Solicit recommendations about how to determine this.

Explore: Choose another rectangle, such as one from the collection below. In pairs, have students find the amount of fencing needed to enclose that rectangle. Have them make a drawing of their rectangles and show how they found the solution. Encourage them to find a second way to find the solution.

a.

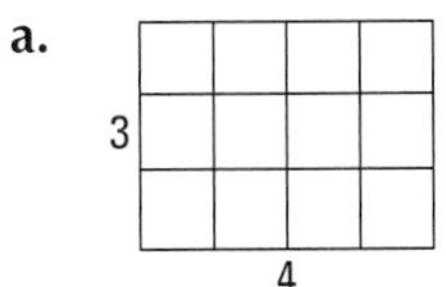

b.

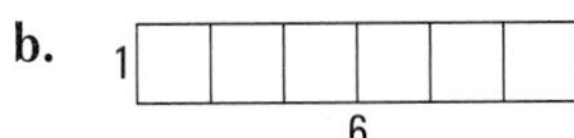

c.

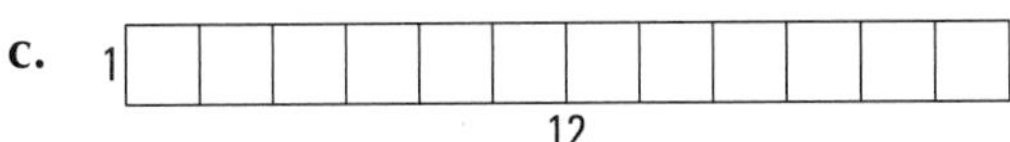

d.

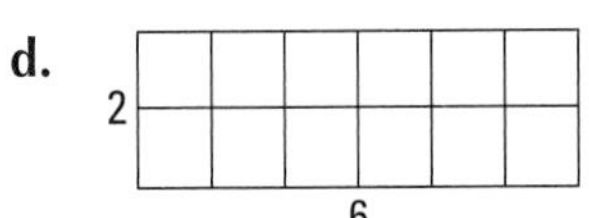

e.

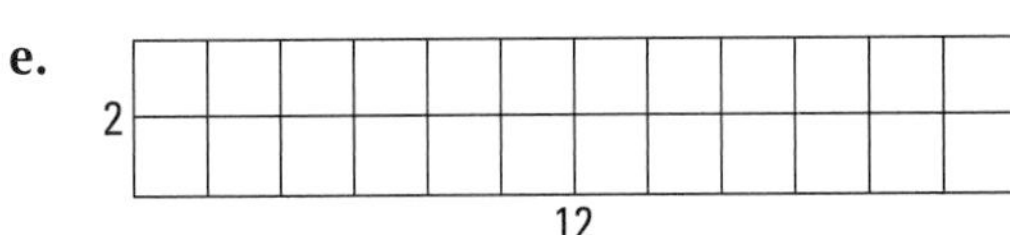

Summarize: Coming together as a whole class, select one pair of students to come to the front of the room and explain how they found the distance around the rectangle. Ask for another pair who solved the problem in a different way to share their solution. Explain that the distance around a rectangle is referred to as its perimeter. Ask if there's a way to find the perimeter of a rectangle without constructing it with squares or drawing a picture. Hopefully students will notice that the perimeter includes the length plus the width plus the length plus the width, which can be expressed as follows:

$$P = l + w + l + w$$

This also could be written as follows:

$$P = l + l + w + w \quad \text{and} \quad P = 2 \times l + 2 \times w$$

FOLLOW-UP

Complete the following questions.

1. Consider any cautions regarding selecting the shapes to use in this lesson. Would other shapes work well? Might you want to avoid using certain shapes or certain sized shapes? Why? What would be the advantages and/or disadvantages of each shape?
2. Consider difficulties students might have with this concept and this lesson. What modification could you make to avoid or minimize these issues? What modifications could you make for students with special needs?
3. What might the *next* lesson focus on, and why?

IN PRACTICE

Complete the following activities to include in your professional portfolio.

1. Visit a middle school classroom, and informally interview several children to assess their understanding of area and perimeter. What were their understandings and misconceptions about these concepts?
2. Examine a textbook's section on measurement. Discuss it in relation to the content of this chapter. How is actual measurement provided for in the textbook activities?
3. Write a lesson plan to introduce nonstandard measurement of an attribute of your choice (length, area, volume, capacity, mass, time, temperature, or angle).
4. Write a lesson plan to introduce standard measurement of an attribute of your choice (length, area, volume, capacity, mass, time, temperature, or angle).

LINKS TO THE INTERNET

Measurement Lessons

http://www.geocities.com/smilecdg/measuremtles.html

Contains many lessons on measurement.

Shape Surveyor

http://www.funbrain.com/poly/index.html

Contains a game on finding area and perimeter.

myeducationlab The Power of Classroom Practice Now go to Topic 12: "Measurement Concepts and Skills" in the MyEducationLab (www.myeducationlab.com) for your course, where you can:

- Find learning outcomes for "Measurement Concepts and Skills" along with the national standards that connect to these outcomes.
- Apply and practice your understanding of the core teaching skills identified in the chapter with a Building Teaching Skills and Dispositions learning unit.
- Complete Assignments and Activities that can help you understand the chapter content more deeply.
- Complete *enVision MATH* Sample Curricula assignments that allow you to examine and work with chapters from *enVision MATH,* a K-6 mathematics program.
- Check your comprehension on the content covered in the chapter by going to the Study Plan in the Book-Specific Resources for your text. Here you will be able to take a chapter quiz, receive feedback on your answers, and then access Review, Practice, and Enrichment activities to enhance your understanding of chapter content.
- Go to the Book-Specific Resources for Chapter 15 to explore mathematical reasoning related to the course content in the Activities section.

RESOURCES FOR TEACHERS

Children's Literature

Adams, B. J. (1992). *The Go-around Dollar*. New York: Simon & Schuster.

Anderson, L. (1998). *Tick-Tock*. New York: R&S Books.

Axelrod, A. (1994). *Pigs Will Be Pigs*. New York: Simon & Schuster Childrens.

Briggs, Raymond (1997). *Jim and the Beanstalk*. New York: Putnam Juvenile.

Brisson, Pat (1995). *Benny's Pennies*. New York: Dragonfly Books.

Dale, E. (1998). *How Long?* London: Orchard Books.

Florian, Douglas (2000). *A Pig Is Big*. New York: Greenwillow.

Jenkins, Steve (1996). *Big and Little*. Boston: Houghton Mifflin.

Jenkins, Steve (1997). *Biggest, Strongest, Fastest*. Boston: Houghton Mifflin.

Jenkins, Steve (2004). *Hottest, Coldest, Highest, Deepest*. Boston: Houghton Mifflin.

Leedy, Loreen (2000). *Measuring Penny*. New York: Henry Holt and Company.

McMillan, B. (1989). *Time to . . .* . New York: Scholastic.

Myller, Rolf (1992). *How Big Is a Foot?* New York: Dell Publishing Company.

National Council of Teachers of Mathematics (2006). *Curriculum Focal Points for Prekindergarten through Grade 8 Mathematics*. Reston, VA: Author.

Nolan, Helen (2002). *How Much, How Many, How Far, How Heavy, How Long, How Tall Is 1000?* Tonawanda, New York: Kids Can Press Ltd.

Olney, R., & Olney, P. (1984). *How Long? To Go, to Grow, to Know*. New York: William Morrow.

Pluckrose, H. (1995). *Math Counts: Length*. Chicago: Children's Press.

Schwartz, David M. (1985). *How Much Is a Million?* New York: HarperCollins.

Thornhill, Jan (2005). *Before & After: A Book of Nature Timescapes*. Toronto: Maple Tree Press.

Viorst, Judith (1978). *Alexander, Who Used to Be Rich Last Sunday*. New York: Atheneum.

Wells, Robert E. (1996). *How Do You Lift a Lion?* Morton Grove, IL: Albert Whitman & Company.

Wells, Robert E. (1993). *Is a Blue Whale the Biggest Thing There Is?* Morton Grove, IL: Albert Whitman & Company.

Wells, Robert E. (1995). *What's Faster Than a Speeding Cheetah?* Morton Grove, IL: Albert Whitman & Company.

Wells, Robert E. (2004). *What's Older Than a Giant Tortoise?* Morton Grove, IL: Albert Whitman & Company.

Wells, Robert E. (1997). *What's Smaller Than a Pygmy Shrew?* Morton Grove, IL: Albert Whitman & Company.

Books on Measurement

Geddes, D. (1994). *Measurement in the Middle Grades: Curriculum evaluation standards for school mathematics addenda series, grade 5–8*. Reston, VA: National Council of Teachers of Mathematics.

Rectanus, C. (1997). *Math By All Means: Area and perimeter, grades 5–6*. Sausalito, CA: Math Solutions.

Shroyer, J., & Fitzgerald, W. (1986). *Middle Grades Mathematics Project: Mouse and elephant: Measuring growth*. Menlo Park, CA: Addison-Wesley.

CHAPTER

16

Collecting, Organizing, and Interpreting Data

NCTM CONNECTING WITH THE STANDARDS

The National Council of Teachers of Mathematics (NCTM) Principles and Standards emphasizes the importance of having children collect and analyze data, stating that "through their data investigations, young students should develop the idea that data, charts, and graphs give information. When data are displayed in an organized manner, class discussions should focus on what the graph or other representation conveys and whether the data help answer the specific questions that were posed" (NCTM, 2000, p. 112). The NCTM document goes on note that "as students learn to describe the similarities and differences between data sets, they will have an opportunity to develop clear descriptions of the data and to formulate conclusions and arguments based on the data" (NCTM, 2000, p. 177).

The NCTM (2006) *Curriculum Focal Points* mentions developing understanding of data analysis in prekindergarten through grade eight. They state that prekindergarten students should:

- learn the foundations of data analysis by using objects' attributes that they have identified in relation to geometry and measurement (e.g., size, quantity, orientation, number of sides or vertices, color) for various purposes, such as describing, sorting, or comparing (NCTM, 2006, p. 11).

Kindergarten students should:

- sort objects and use one or more attributes to solve problems (NCTM, 2006, p. 12).

First-grade students should:

- strengthen their sense of number by solving problems involving measurements and data (NCTM, 2006, p. 13).

In third grade:

- Addition, subtraction, multiplication, and division of whole numbers come into play as students construct and analyze frequency tables, bar graphs, picture graphs, and line plots and use them to solve problems (NCTM, 2006, p. 15).

Developing Your Math Teaching Skills

When you have finished studying this chapter, you should be able to do the following:

- Describe the stages of graphing experiences that children should encounter, and give an example of each stage.
- Discuss the different types of graphs used for organizing and interpreting data, and give an example of each type.
- Explain the three measures of central tendency, and how teachers can help children to better understand each of these measures.
- Describe how to use technology to help in collecting, organizing, and interpreting data.

Fourth-grade students should:

- continue to use tools from grade 3, solving problems by making frequency tables, bar graphs, picture graphs, and line plots. They apply their understanding of place value to develop and use stem-and-leaf plots (NCTM, 2006, p. 16).

Fifth-grade students should:

- apply their understanding of whole numbers, fractions, and decimals as they construct and analyze double-bar and line graphs and use ordered pairs on coordinate grids (NCTM, 2006, p. 17).

Seventh-grade students should:

- use proportions to make estimates relating to a population on the basis of a sample. They apply percentages to make and interpret histograms and circle graphs. Students understand that when all outcomes of an experiment are equally likely, the theoretical probability of an event is the fraction of outcomes in which the event occurs. Students use theoretical probability and proportions to make approximate predictions (NCTM, 2006, p. 19).

Eighth-grade students should:

- use descriptive statistics, including mean, median, and range, to summarize and compare data sets, and they organize and display data to pose and answer questions. They compare the information provided by the mean and the median and investigate the different effects that changes in data values have on these measures of center. They understand that a measure of center alone does not thoroughly describe a data set because very different data sets can share the same measure of center. Students select the mean or the median as the appropriate measure of center for a given purpose (NCTM, 2006, p. 20).

ASSESSING MATHEMATICS UNDERSTANDING

In order to become familiar with the mathematics concepts and procedures discussed in this chapter, take a few minutes and complete the *Chapter 16 Preassessment.* Answer each question on your own. Then think about the possible misunderstandings or difficulties some elementary-school children might have when solving each problem. If you are able, administer this assessment to a child, and analyze their understanding of these topics.

Solve each problem. Think about how you get your answer.

1. What is the median of the numbers listed below?

4, 8, 3, 2, 5, 8, 12

a. 4 **b.** 5 **c.** 6
d. 7 **e.** 8

2. The table below shows the scores of a group of 11 students on a history test. What is the average (mean) score of the group to the nearest whole number?

Score	Number of Students
90	1
80	3
70	4
60	0
50	3

3. The graph below represents Marisa's riding speed throughout her 80-minute bicycle trip. Use the information in the graph to describe what could have happened on the trip, including her speed throughout the trip.

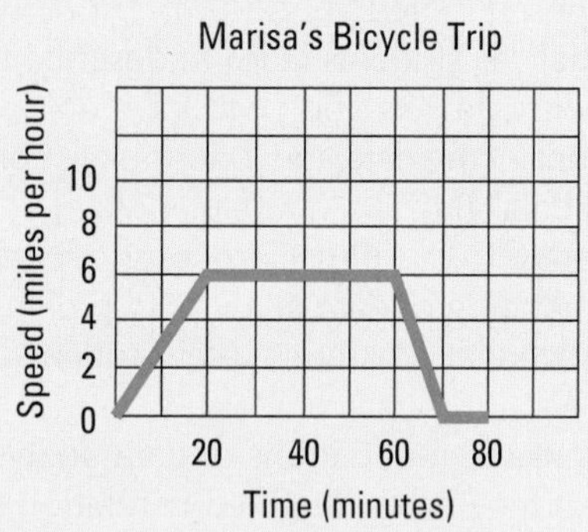

During the first 20 minutes, Marisa__________

From 20 minutes to 60 minutes, she__________

From 60 minutes to 80 minutes, she__________

4. The balls in the picture below are placed in a box and a child picks one without looking. What is the probability that the ball picked will be the one with dots?

a. 1 out of 4 **b.** 1 out of 3
c. 1 out of 2 **d.** 3 out of 4

5. There is only one red marble in each of the bags shown below. Without looking, you are to pick a marble out of one of the bags. Which bag would give you the greatest chance of picking the red marble?

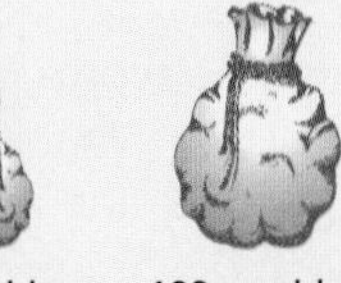
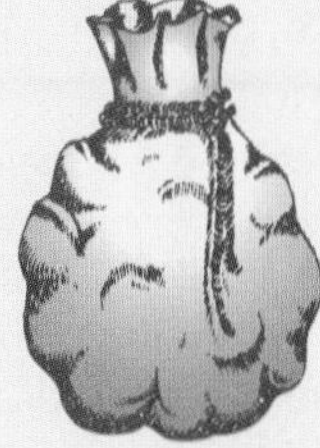

10 marbles 100 marbles 1000 marbles

a. Bag with 10 marbles

b. Bag with 100 marbles

c. Bag with 1000 marbles

d. It makes no difference

6. A box contains 3 chips numbered 1 through 3. One chip will be taken at random from the box and then put back into the box. Then a second chip will be taken from the box.

In the list provided below, list all possible pairs of chips.

Number on First Chip	Number on Second Chip

Source: U.S. Department of Education, Institute of Education Sciences, National Center for Education Statistics, National Assessment of Educational Progress (NAEP), 2003 Mathematics Assessment.

Examining Classroom Practice

Gail Moriarty's fourth graders are exploring data by investigating the number of raisins in a box (Russell & Corwin, 1989). Ms. Moriarty begins the lesson by giving a small box of raisins to each child. She holds up one box and asks the children how many raisins they think are in that box. She records their estimates on the blackboard.

Then she asks the children to open their boxes and look at the top layer of raisins. She asks if anyone wants to revise their initial estimate and, if so, why. Mirasol said she wanted to change her estimate. She thought there would be 100 raisins in the box, but since there were only 5 raisins in the top layer, she thinks there are about 50 in the box.

Then Ms. Moriarty asks the children if they think there will be the same number of raisins in every box. Some of the children think there will be the same number, because all the boxes are the same size. Jeremy disagrees, saying, "Some of the raisins might be bigger than others and some might be squished. I think there will be more in some boxes and less in others."

Ms. Moriarty instructs the children to open their boxes and count the number of raisins inside. As the children finish, they raise their hands, reporting the number of raisins in each box, and Ms. Moriarty records the numbers in a list on the blackboard. This produces a long list of numbers, since there are 30 children in the class.

Ms. Moriarty asks the children what they might do to organize these data. Several children make suggestions, including making a table and making a graph. Ms. Moriarty has the children work in groups to organize the data using whatever method they choose. She also asks each group to write three sentences about what they notice about the data after they organize them.

After the children finish their work, Ms. Moriarty reassembles the class to share their methods. One group shows a table with tally marks that they created, which is shown below.

Number of Raisins	Number of Boxes
29	/
30	
31	𝍸
32	///
33	////
34	𝍸 /
35	𝍸 /
36	//
37	///
38	
39	/
40	
41	
42	/

Another group shows a line plot they made, using an X to represent each box of raisins.

					X								
					X	X							
		X		X	X	X							
		X	X	X	X	X		X					
		X	X	X	X	X	X	X					
X		X	X	X	X	X	X	X		X			X
29	30	31	32	33	34	35	36	37	38	39	40	41	42

Number of Boxes Containing Different Numbers of Raisins

Ms. Moriarty displays the chart and the line plot on the blackboard for everyone to see. She asks, "What can we say about the data we collected?" She writes the children's statements on the blackboard. Here are a few of them:

- The smallest number of raisins in a box is 29.
- The largest number of raisins in a box is 42.
- More boxes have 34 raisins than any other number.
- No boxes have 30, 38, 40, or 41 raisins.

Then she asks, "Are there any things in these data that surprise you?" Heather comments, "I didn't think there could be 42 raisins in a box! That's a lot!" Ms. Moriarty asks, "Whose box was that?" Patrick raises his hand, saying "I counted them twice, and there really were 42!"

Ms. Moriarty asks the class to speculate why Patrick's box has several more raisins than other boxes. Children comment that it may have smaller raisins, or that they may be packed in more tightly, or that the machine may have made a mistake, and Patrick's box might weigh more than it should.

Ms. Moriarty tells the children that mathematicians have a name for a piece of data that's far away from the rest—it's called an *outlier*. So 42 is an outlier in the class's raisin data.

Then Ms. Moriarty asks the children, "What if we opened another box of raisins? How many raisins do you think would be in it, and why?" Most children think that there would be 34 raisins because that is the most common number in the boxes the class opened. Ms. Moriarty asks, "Will there definitely be 34?" Jeremy responds, "There will probably be 34, but there might be a few more or less than 34 if there are lots of big raisins or small raisins in the box."

Ms. Moriarty asks, "What if someone asked you, 'How many raisins are in a box?' What would you say?" Susan said, "There will be about 35, but it could be more or less, depending on the size of the raisins."

Analyzing Assessment Results

Now let's look at the pre-assessment results. What was your general reaction to solving the problems? Did they all seem to be equally difficult, or were some problems easier for you to think about? What aspects of problems do you think make them easier for children to solve? What in general do you think a teacher's goals should be regarding developing meaning of data analysis and probability?

Analyze each problem. How did you (and/or the student you administered the assessment to) solve each of the following problems? Let's look at problems 1 and 2 first.

1. What is the median of the numbers listed below?

4, 8, 3, 2, 5, 8, 12

a. 4 **b.** 5 **c.** 6
d. 7 **e.** 8

2. The table below shows the scores of a group of 11 students on a history test. What is the average (mean) score of the group to the nearest whole number?

Score	Number of Students
90	1
80	3
70	4
60	0
50	3

Comments: These problems focus on two common but often confused topics in data analysis: median and mean, or average. In order to answer these correctly, students need to understand that *median* means the number "in the middle." To solve Problem 2, students need to understand how to use the fact that different numbers of students got the same scores, which means they need to find the weighted average. Was one problem easier for you? The eighth-graders tested on the 2003 NAEP found Problem 1 to be much easier, with 57% answering Problem 1 correctly but only 19% answering Problem 2 correctly.

3. The graph below represents Marisa's riding speed throughout her 80-minute bicycle trip. Use the information in the graph to describe what could have happened on the trip, including her speed throughout the trip.

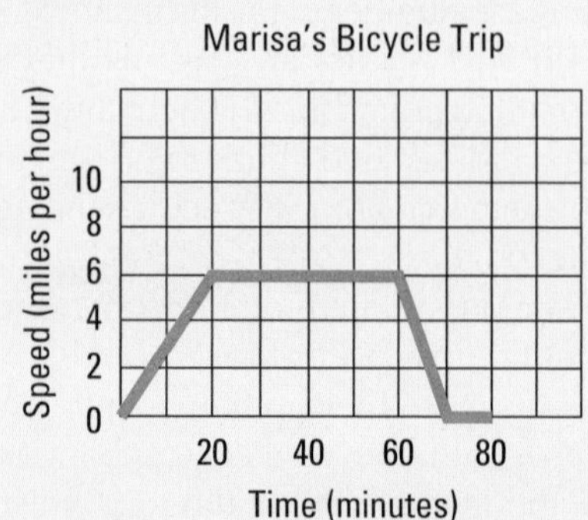

During the first 20 minutes, Marisa __________

From 20 minutes to 60 minutes, she __________

From 60 minutes to 80 minutes, she __________

Comments: This problem involves interpreting the meaning of a graph. This involves combining what's happening on the two axes. Sometimes students will think that the graph that's sloping upward means that the bike rider was climbing a hill, which is not correct in this graph. This problem was very difficult for the eighth-graders tested on the 2003 NAEP, with only 8% of answering this problem correctly.

4. The balls in the picture below are placed in a box and a child picks one without looking. What is the probability that the ball picked will be the one with dots?

a. 1 out of 4 **b.** 1 out of 3
c. 1 out of 2 **d.** 3 out of 4

5. There is only one red marble in each of the bags shown below. Without looking, you are to pick a marble out of one of the bags. Which bag would give you the greatest chance of picking the red marble?

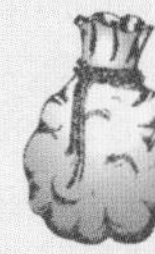
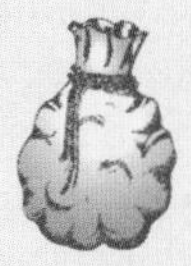

10 marbles 100 marbles 1000 marbles

a. Bag with 10 marbles
b. Bag with 100 marbles
c. Bag with 1000 marbles
d. It makes no difference

Comments: These problems deal with basic aspects of probability, including that the probability of an event is the number of desired outcomes out of the number of total possible outcomes. These problems are fairly easy for students; in the 2003 NAEP, 65% of the fourth-graders tested answered these problems correctly.

6. A box contains 3 chips numbered 1 through 3. One chip will be taken at random from the box and then put back into the box. Then a second chip will be taken from the box.

In the list provided below, list all possible pairs of chips.

Number on First Chip	Number on Second Chip

Comments: This problem focuses on organizing data and listing possibilities. If you asked students to solve this, did they use a strategy for making sure they listed all possibilities, or did they list pairs at random? This problem was a bit harder for students, with 45% of the eighth-graders tested answering this problem correctly on the 2003 NAEP.

Take a minute to reflect on this assessment. Were some problems easier than others? What factors made them easier? What do you want to learn more about in order to help children understand data analysis and probability?

Common Student Misunderstandings about Data Analysis and Probability:

- Confusion about the meanings of the concepts.
- Lack of familiarity with the terminology.
- Lack of familiarity with different problem situations.

Are there any other misunderstandings that children may have about data analysis and probability? It's important to assess what children understand, and are still working on understanding, in order to plan instruction that meets their needs.

Building on Assessment Results

Think about what can be done to help strengthen children's understandings and minimize (and hopefully eradicate) their misunderstandings and misconceptions.

Sometimes teaching about data analysis and probability focuses on memorizing formulas and producing answers quickly. While we want students to know how to find various data measures, we also want them to understand the concepts behind these measures, which will enable them to make sense of problem situations. So what might we do next to help students understand the concepts of data analysis and probability?

A key element of all instruction is to make sure that students understand the concepts. Students need to visualize concepts and relationships. This usually is best done by asking students to solve problems set in familiar, meaningful situations and to examine the reasonableness of their solutions. The table below lists several common misunderstandings and what a teacher can do to help children resolve these misunderstandings.

Think back to Ms. Moriarty's lesson. How did she involve her children in collecting and organizing data? How did she support children in constructing graphs, analyzing the data, and making generalizations and conclusions based on the data? The ideas in this chapter focus on helping children learn how to collect, organize, and interpret data.

In this chapter, we will describe data collection techniques, examine methods for organizing and displaying data, and discuss ways of interpreting data to make predictions—all with the intent of designing mathematics instruction to help children use and interpret data in decision making.

IF students think that . . .	THEN have students . . .
using statistics and probability is something that they'll never do outside of math class,	*find* familiar, real-world situations in which statistics and probability are useful.
the terminology used in statistics and probability problems is meaningless,	*help* them understand the meaning of the terms; for example, *median* is "in the middle," just like the median on a highway.

Collecting and Organizing Data

Data are all around us. Indeed, sometimes there is so much data that we can become overwhelmed. Children, too, are bombarded with all kinds of data that they would like to understand. *How? What? When? Where? Who?* and *Why?* are real-life questions that often require the collection, organization, and interpretation of data if they are to be answered. Principles and Standards Link 16-1 notes the importance of students collecting data.

What Do Children Know about Data Analysis and Probability?

What do we know of children's understanding of data analysis and probability? The 2003 National Assessment of Educational Progress (NAEP) noted that students' ability to calculate the mean and median of a set of data has improved since the last assessment, and their ability to create graphs and tables was strong. But students continue to have difficulty in interpreting information in tables and graphs (Tarr & Shaughnessy, 2007), such as Problem 3 in this chapter's preassessment. Similarly, students are fairly successful in finding simple probabilities but have difficulties in finding more complicated probabilities and in applying probability concepts. Findings such as these point to the importance of teachers' helping children truly make sense of data and probability concepts. Teaching about data analysis must be more than just creating and reading graphs; instruction must help children to understand, interpret, and apply reasoning in studying data.

NCTM Principles and Standards Link 16-1

Content Strand: Data Analysis and Probability

The Data Analysis and Probability Standard recommends that students formulate questions that can be answered using data and addresses what is involved in gathering and using the data wisely. Students should learn how to collect data, organize their own or others' data, and display the data in graphs and charts that will be useful in answering their questions. (NCTM, 2000, p. 48).

There must be a reason for collecting data. Children need to have some question they want to answer—a question they agreed on after a brainstorming session, perhaps, or a question that arises from a class discussion in some other subject area or from someone's recent experience. A provocative question by the teacher may also give rise to the need to collect data; for example, "Do more children have dogs than cats for pets?" or "I think vanilla is the favorite ice cream flavor of children in this class. Do you agree?" These questions arouse interest. Children want to find out—even if only to prove that the teacher's supposition is wrong.

Scenarios such as those just described suggest that we are involved with an investigation or research project rather than a short in-class activity. The first two steps in a research model appropriate for elementary school mathematics proposed by Bohan, Irby, and Vogel (1995) involve choosing a question to answer or problem to solve. The complete model consists of seven steps:

1. **Step 1:** Brainstorm for questions that children would like answered.
2. **Step 2:** Choose one of the questions or problems.

NCTM DATA ANALYSIS AND PROBABILITY STANDARDS AND EXPECTATIONS ADDRESSED IN THIS CHAPTER

Instructional programs from pre-K–12 should enable all students to—	In prekindergarten through grade 2 all students should— (NCTM, 2000, p. 108)	In grades 3–5 all students should— (NCTM, 2000, p. 176)	In grades 6–8 all students should— (NCTM, 2000, p. 248)
• formulate questions that can be addressed with data and collect, organize, and display relevant data to answer them. • select and use appropriate statistical methods to analyze data. • develop and evaluate inferences and predictions that are based on data. • understand and apply basic concepts of probability.	• pose questions and gather data about themselves and their surroundings. • sort and classify objects according to their attributes and organize data about the objects. • represent data using concrete objects, pictures, and graphs. • describe parts of the data and the set of data as a whole to determine what the data show. • discuss events related to students' experiences as likely or unlikely.	• design investigations to address a question and consider how data-collection methods affect the nature of the data set. • collect data using observations, surveys, and experiments. • represent data using tables and graphs such as line plots, bar graphs, and line graphs. • recognize the differences in representing categorical and numerical data. • describe the shape and important features of a set of data and compare related data sets, with an emphasis on how the data are distributed. • use measures of center, focusing on the median, and understand what each does and does not indicate about the data set. • compare different representations of the same data and evaluate how well each representation shows important aspects of the data. • propose and justify conclusions and predictions that are based on data and design studies to further investigate the conclusions or predictions. • describe events as likely or unlikely and discuss the degree of likelihood using such words as *certain, equally likely,* and *impossible.*	• formulate questions, design studies, and collect data about a characteristic shared by two populations or different characteristics within one population. • select, create, and use appropriate graphical representations of data, including histograms, box plots, and scatterplots. • find, use, and interpret measures of center and spread, including mean and interquartile range. • discuss and understand the correspondence between data sets and their graphical representations, especially histograms, stem-and-leaf plots, box plots, and scatterplots. • use observations about differences between two or more samples to make conjectures about the populations from which the samples were taken. • make conjectures about possible relationships between two characteristics of a sample on the basis of scatterplots of the data and approximate lines of fit. • use conjectures to formulate new questions and plan new studies to answer them. • understand and use appropriate terminology to describe complementary and mutually exclusive events.

(*continued*)

NCTM DATA ANALYSIS AND PROBABILITY STANDARDS AND EXPECTATIONS ADDRESSED IN THIS CHAPTER (*Continued*)

Instructional programs from pre-k–12 should enable all students to—	In prekindergarten through grade 2 all students should— (NCTM, 2000, p. 108)	In grades 3–5 all students should— (NCTM, 2000, p. 176)	In grades 6–8 all students should— (NCTM, 2000, p. 248)
		• predict the probability of outcomes of simple experiments and test the predictions. • understand that the measure of the likelihood of an event can be represented by a number from 0 to 1.	• use proportionality and a basic understanding of probability to make and test conjectures about the results of experiments and simulations. • compute probabilities for simple compound events, using such methods as organized lists, tree diagrams, and area models.

3. **Step 3:** Predict what the outcome will be.
4. **Step 4:** Develop a plan to test the predicted outcome.
5. **Step 5:** Carry out the plan.
6. **Step 6:** Analyze the data. Is the hypothesis supported?
7. **Step 7:** Look back. Answer the question. Should the information be shared? With whom? How could it be shared?

It is very important that children collect their own data (Russell & Friel, 1989). This contributes ownership, interest, and reality to their experience. A class survey is one of the most obvious and easy ways of getting information with which all children can identify. The following section presents a number of ideas for surveys, including exploring children's favorites—one of the most fruitful sources of data (Young, 1991). Children can make surveys on favorite pets, fruits, ice cream flavors, colors, and so on and then graph the data. For some topics, children can extend the survey to include other classes or the whole school. For example, older children can take surveys of traffic outside the school, the types of clothing worn by people who enter a nearby mall, or the amount of sugar or fiber in several brands of cereal.

Candy-coated chocolate candies in various colors also can be used by children as firsthand data (Brosnan, 1996; Browning, Channell, & Meyer, 1994). The children can predict the number of each color of candy to be found in one box, then count and graph for themselves.

Food is popular in data activities. In addition, children's literature can provide a rich source of ideas for data management projects (Litton, 1995). Bankard and Fennell (1991) and Brahier and Speer (1995) also provide some projects that would involve gathering data firsthand, then organizing and displaying them in graphical form.

The Internet and e-mail can be interesting ways to collect data. Comparing data collected and shared by children from different countries can lead to some valuable learning in mathematics and beyond.

Tallies are a useful technique for recording data. You can demonstrate this technique to the whole class by taking a survey of children's favorite fast food, weekend activity, or similar topic. Demonstrate making a tally for each child's preference as in Figure 16-1.

Young children should also have opportunities to discover that the way data are organized varies with the kinds of questions one wants to ask. Figure 16-2 shows three ways in which data from a survey of class members' favorite fruit could be organized. Figure 16-2(a) would be the best display if you wanted to know Nathan's favorite fruit. On the other hand, if you were interested in the number of people who prefer oranges

FIGURE 16-1 Example of a Tally Sheet for Recording Data

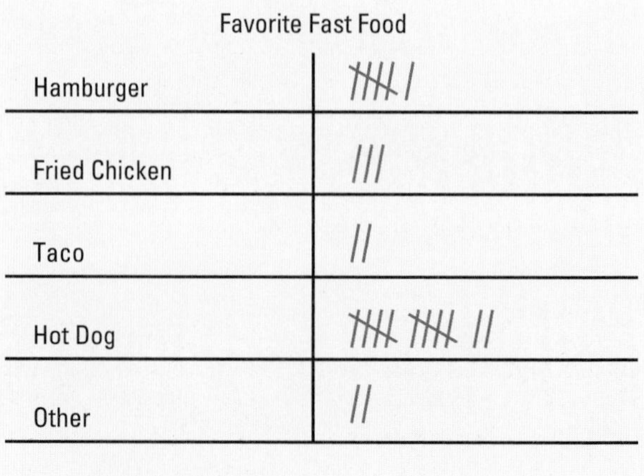

Favorite Fast Food

Hamburger	~~||||~~ |
Fried Chicken	|||
Taco	||
Hot Dog	~~||||~~ ~~||||~~ ||
Other	||

FIGURE 16-2 Three Ways to Organize Survey Data

Fruit Survey	
Name	**Fruit**
Wendy	Apples
Seyi	Oranges
Nathan	Bananas
Mavis	Oranges
John	Apples
	Grapes

(a)

Fruit Survey	
Fruit	**Choices**
Oranges	✓ ✓ ✓ ✓ ✓ ✓ ✓ ✓
Apples	✓ ✓ ✓ ✓ ✓ ✓
Bananas	✓ ✓ ✓
Grapes	✓

(b)

Fruit Survey	
Fruit	**Frequency**
Oranges	12
Apples	6
Bananas	3
Grapes	1

(c)

or were determining the most popular fruit in the class, you would consult the display in either Figure 16-2(b) or 16-2(c).

Graphing Data

Graphs present data in a concise and pictorial form. Graphing, while a legitimate mathematics education topic in its own right, is also an integrative component of the math program, because graphs can be used when developing other mathematical topics. Graphs, for instance, can be used to create computational exercises for showing the number of prisms as opposed to pyramids children can find in the classroom, the various temperatures outside the classroom at noon over a period of a week, and many other relationships. An understanding of ratios, proportions, percents, fractions, and other topics is often needed to construct or interpret more advanced graphs.

Graphing is also integrative in the sense that it brings together mathematics and other curriculum subjects such as science, physical education, and social studies. So, from a teaching standpoint, graphing should be thought of not as a strand to be covered in a 4-week unit but as something to be done throughout the school year.

Children may be introduced to graphing as early as the first grade. Skills associated with graphing include constructing graphs, reading information from graphs, and interpreting the information by discussing or writing about it. Principles and Standards Link 16-2 discusses the importance of students organizing data.

Early Experiences

Most graphic representations at the primary level will be some form of bar graph. Some introduction to coordinate graphing is often done in the primary grades. At this level, children's graphing experiences generally progress through four overlapping stages: *concrete*, *concrete-pictorial*, *pictorial-abstract*, and *abstract*.

Concrete stage. Children's early graphing experiences should involve constructing graphs with concrete materials. Each object, such as a block, should represent only one thing, and children should compare only two events or things.

There are numerous dichotomous (either–or) events that young children enjoy graphing. Some of them include:

- Eyeglasses—no eyeglasses
- Walked to school—rode to school
- Left-handed—right-handed

When modeling graphs concretely, children like to be the objects. A beginning prompt might be "I wonder if more children walked to school than rode to school this morning." Children could form two straight lines, with those who walked standing in one line and those who rode in the other. Depending on the ratio in the class, children may or may not

NCTM Principles and Standards Link 16-2

Content Strand: Data Analysis and Probability

A fundamental idea in prekindergarten through grade 2 is that data can be organized or ordered and that this "picture" of the data provides information about the phenomenon or question. In grades 3–5, students should develop skill in representing their data, often using bar graphs, tables, or line plots. They should learn what different numbers, symbols, and points mean. Recognizing that some numbers represent the values of the data and others represent the frequency with which those values occur is a big step. Students in grades 6–8 should begin to compare the effectiveness of various types of displays in organizing the data for further analysis or in presenting the data clearly to an audience. (NCTM, 2000, p. 48).

be able to notice a difference in the length of the lines. If children formed two lines based on whether they print with their right hand or left hand, the lines would most likely be very different in length. In these examples, the line is similar to a bar in a bar graph, so you may want to discuss the following aspects of graphing with the children:

- The beginning of the lines should be along the same line (axis).
- Distance between children in line should be uniform.

Although children like to "act out" the graph, there are some disadvantages to this approach. The most significant is that children have difficulty noticing which line is longer because they are part of a line. They often need to "get out of line" to check, which can create problems with the line as it was initially formed. Other disadvantages include the possible lack of uniformity in spacing and the possibility of the lines not starting at the same imaginary axis.

Experiences such as the one described in Activity 16-1 avoid such difficulties. This activity is probably best done in a group of about one-half the class; otherwise, the stacks of blocks used in the activity may become too high and topple before all the blocks are placed. The two groups can compare their graphs afterward.

An activity that might serve as a transition to the next level would be to have children draw a picture of themselves on an index card. A query to the children might be "Would you like to be younger or older than you are?" Each child could then post his or her picture in the appropriate section of a bulletin board chart the teacher has created (see Figure 16-3).

Because the pictures will be somewhat randomly placed on the board, it may not be easy to see whether there is a difference. Children could count to decide, or they might be asked to organize the cards on each side of the board into an array.

FIGURE 16-3 Example of a Pictorial Way to Represent Data

I Would Like to Be:

Younger	Older

ACTIVITY 16-1 Concrete Graph (Light Versus Dark Hair)

Manipulative Strategies

Materials

- Two sheets of paper on which the words *Light hair* and *Dark hair* have been printed (or a light and dark sheet of colored construction paper).
- Selection of light- and dark-colored blocks that can easily be stacked.

Procedure

1. Each child should
   - Select a block that he or she thinks most resembles his or her hair color.
   - Place the block on the stack on the appropriate sheet, as shown in the figure.
2. Talk about what the graph tells you.
3. Talk about things the graph does not tell you. (The teacher may need to ask a leading question, such as "Does this graph tell us how many children are absent today?")

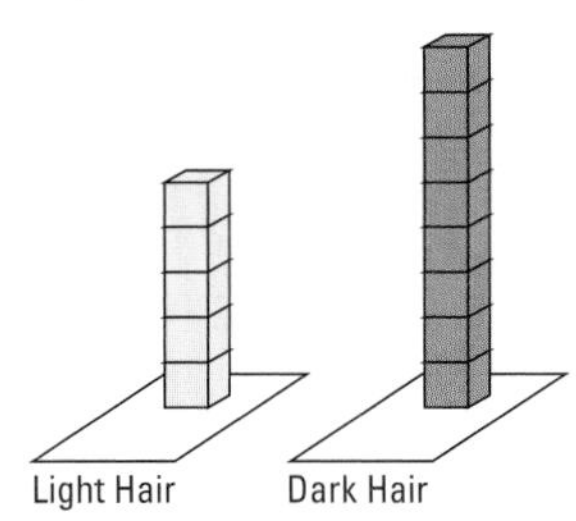

This activity can help the teacher learn more about individual children. For example, you could follow a question such as "Do more children prefer to be younger, or do more prefer to be older?" with "Why would you like to be older (younger)?"

Concrete-pictorial stage. In this stage, children use pictorial representations of objects in addition to concrete materials. They may compare more than two events but still maintain the one-to-one correspondence between object or picture and what is being graphed.

The last example in the previous section was a transition to this level. To make it a true stage 2 activity, change the bulletin board chart to include three boxes, as in Figure 16-4.

Children like to talk about birthdays. They could make a block graph of birthday months. Normally, a comparison of 12 things is too much for primary-grade children, but birthdays may be an exception because of children's familiarity with and interest in them. Also, such an activity helps children learn the months of the year. Figure 16-5 shows one form that this graph might take. If you had photocopies of the children's photos, each child could tack his

FIGURE 16-4 A Stage 2 Example of a Concrete-Pictorial Way to Collect Data

I Would Like to Be:

Younger	Same Age	Older

or her picture above the appropriate month to make a bulletin board graph.

Children's favorites is an excellent setting for a variety of stage 2 graphing activities; favorite flavor of ice cream is one possibility. An introductory comment could be "I think most children in the class like chocolate ice cream the best." A bulletin board display like the one in Figure 16-6 could be prepared as well as several cutouts of each of the anticipated flavors. Ask the children to take one of the paper cones representing their favorite flavor and pin it above the appropriate model.

A primary-grade teacher can capitalize on the variety of characteristics of buttons to develop stage 2 graphing experiences. For example, children in cooperative learning groups could each take a handful of buttons, put their selections together, and create a graph as shown in Figure 16-7. Some possible comparisons include

- Number of holes: 0, 2, 4
- Flat versus raised
- Material: plastic, metal, wood
- Shapes: round, square, other
- Texture: smooth, rough, fabric-covered, other

FIGURE 16-6 Bulletin Board Display on Which to Graph Favorite Ice Cream

FIGURE 16-7 An Example of a Concrete Button Graph

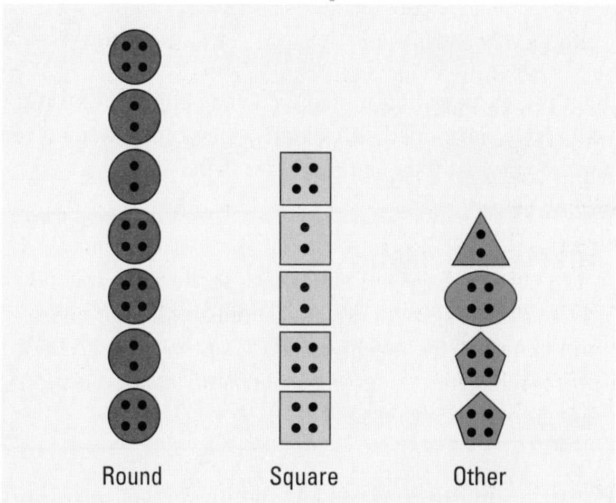

Encourage the children to "interpret" the graph by asking one or two leading questions, such as "What does the graph tell you?" or "What can you learn from the graph?" Children might also discuss how this graph could help

FIGURE 16-5 An Example of a Concrete Birthday Graph

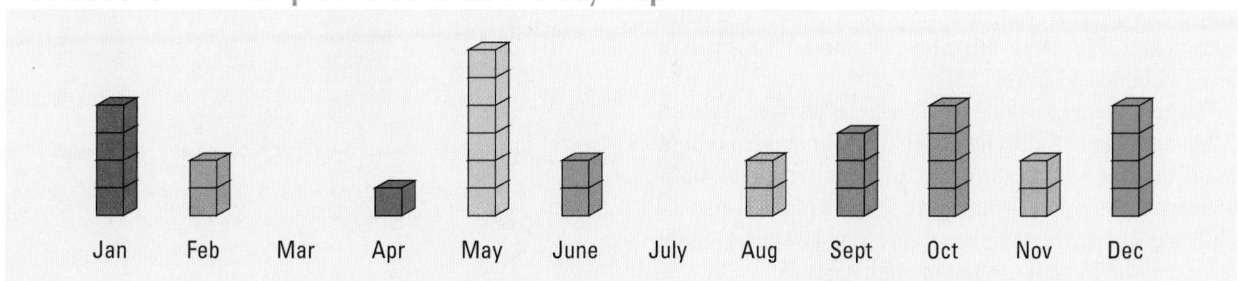

FIGURE 16-8 Stage 3 Pictorial-Abstract Graph

Favorite Fruit

(a)

Favorite Fruit

(b)

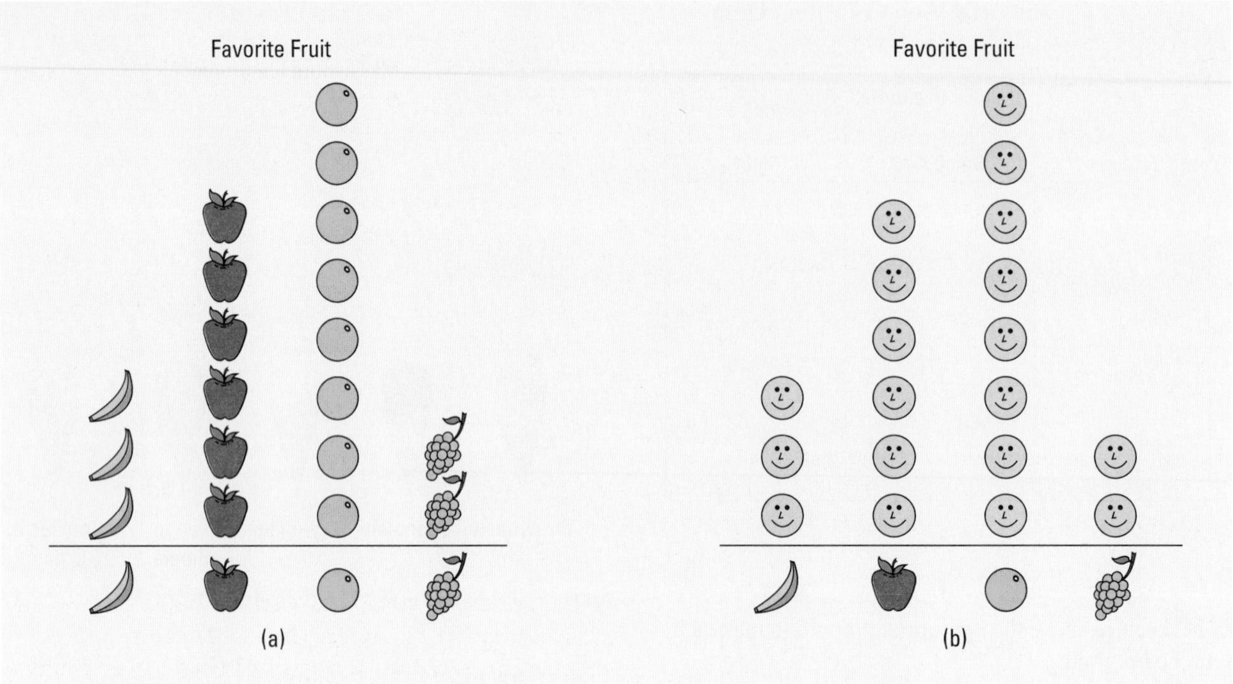

them if they were button makers. Once children's writing skills have developed sufficiently, they could write a report about what they learned.

> **myeducationlab** The Power of Classroom Practice Go to the Assignments and Activities section of Topic 13: "Data Analysis" in the MyEducationLab for your course and complete the activity "Early Graphing" to see how one teacher introduces her students to data collection and graphing concepts.

Pictorial-abstract stage. At the third level, *pictorial-abstract*, primary children continue to make bar graphs with pictures, but they also make a transition to the abstract by using gummed stickers, colored cards, etc., to form the graph.

Any of the topics used in the previous two levels could be used at stage 3. Children could pin objects or pictures of objects on the bulletin board or on paper as before. Then they could construct the same graph by putting gummed stickers on a chart. In Figure 16-8(a), the children pinned pictures of their favorite fruits on a bulletin board chart. Figure 16-8(b) shows the same information using gummed stickers.

To help them transition to the next level, have children fill in one square for each tally on their survey. This could easily be done with the favorite fruit activity. Provide children with a template as in Figure 16-9 (without the shading) and challenge them to figure out how they could represent the same information on this graph.

FIGURE 16-9 Stage 3 Pictorial-Abstract Graph Using Colored Boxes

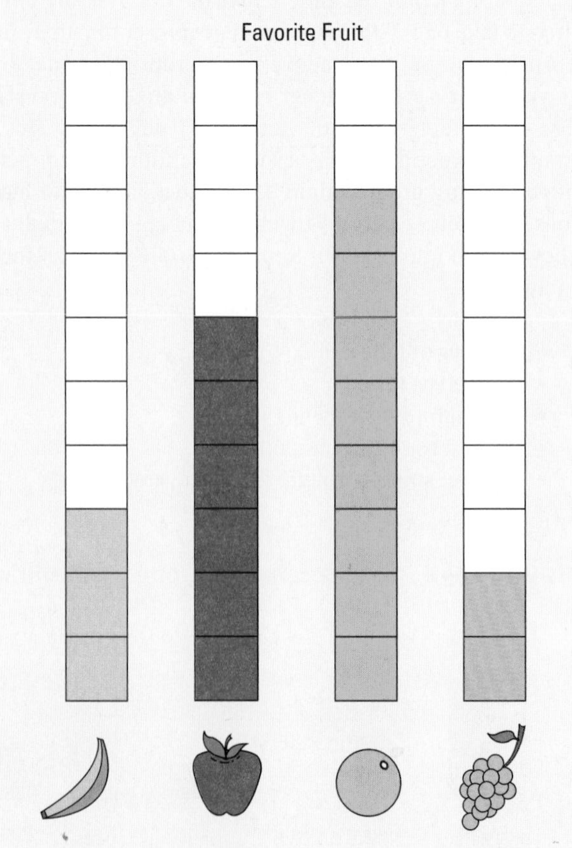

FIGURE 16-10 Stage 3 or 4 Pictograph Showing Number of Brothers and Sisters

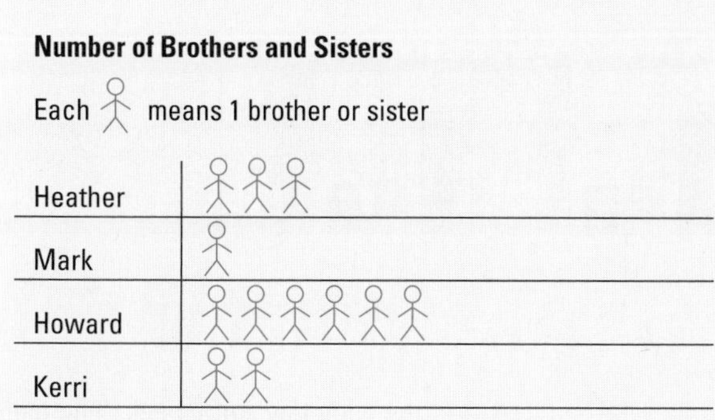

Pictographs. Although most pictographs are a stage 4 (abstract) activity, they can be introduced at stage 3 in a setting in which the one-to-one correspondence is convenient. For example, children could be given the graph in Figure 16-10 and asked to read, interpret, and discuss it through questions such as the following:

- How many brothers and sisters does Heather have?
- Who has the most brothers and sisters?
- Does Kerri have more brothers and sisters than Heather?
- What else does the graph tell you?

To create a simple one-to-one pictograph, children could be given a template as shown in Figure 16-11. They would tally the number of library books in their desk, print their name in one of the rows, then draw one square for each book they found. Some may have no books, in which case they would print only their name. Children could follow this by writing a short paragraph about the graph.

Abstract stage. If children have had adequate experiences in stages 1 to 3, their transition to abstract representation will be relatively smooth. At this stage, one-to-one correspondence of objects to events is replaced with a one-to-many correspondence. This normally requires a scale

FIGURE 16-11 Stage 3 Pictograph Showing Number of Library Books in

Library Books in Desks

Each ☐ means 1 book

Name	

FIGURE 16-12 Sample Bar Graphs (Abstract Stage)

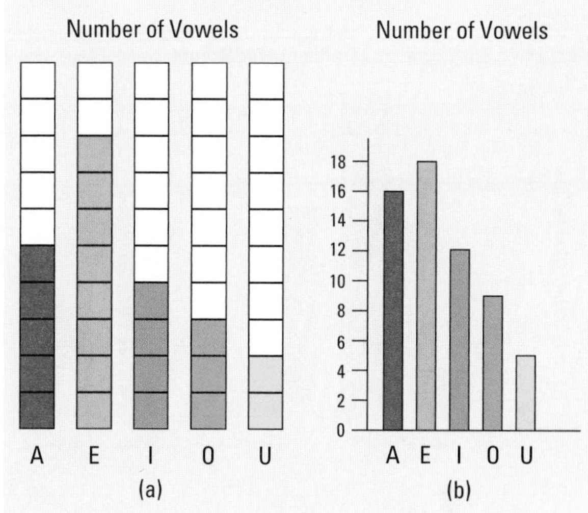

for one of the axes. Rectangular bars replace the colored squares and line graphs can be introduced.

Again, many of the topics graphed earlier could be used at this level. It is not the topic but rather the way the data are presented that determines the level. Consider the query, "I wonder which vowel occurs most often in writing." At stage 3, children might select a sentence from their readers or library books, tally the occurrence of each vowel, and then color squares, one square for each occurrence, as in Figure 16-12(a).

At stage 4 (abstract level), children could choose a paragraph and tally the occurrence of vowels as before. A paragraph may provide more vowels than they wish to handle on their graph using one square for each occurrence. A scale of 1 square representing 2 occurrences may be convenient. Later the squares can be replaced with rectangular bars. The graph shown in Figure 16-12(b) may result.

The one-to-many relationship leads naturally into pictographs in which the object may represent 2, 5, 10, or some other convenient number of things. Figure 16-13 shows a pictograph of the number of soda can tabs a few children

FIGURE 16-13 Sample Pictograph (Abstract Stage)

Soda Can Tabs Collected

Each = 10 tabs

Wendy

Bill

Carlo

Heather

Joy

FIGURE 16-14 Sample Bar Graph (Abstract Stage)

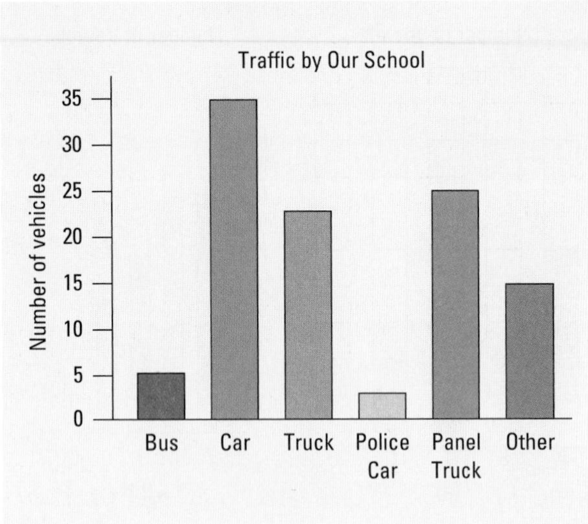

brought to school as part of a class project investigating how much room 1,000 soda can tabs would take up.

Another activity that would involve stage 4 graphing could be instigated with the query "What kind of vehicle passes by our school most often?" This is best done on a day when a parent volunteer or teacher assistant is available to help. One or two small groups could go out with the parent or aide for a 20- or 30-minute period to collect the data by keeping a tally of the different kinds of vehicles that pass by.

Afterward, children could color a rectangular bar, as shown in Figure 16-14, rather than preexisting squares. A good interpretation activity could involve writing a letter to the principal describing the traffic activity and perhaps making some safety recommendations.

Line graphs are another way to represent information at stage 4. For example, children could record the outside

FIGURE 16-15 Comparison of Bar Graphs and Line Graphs (Abstract Stage)

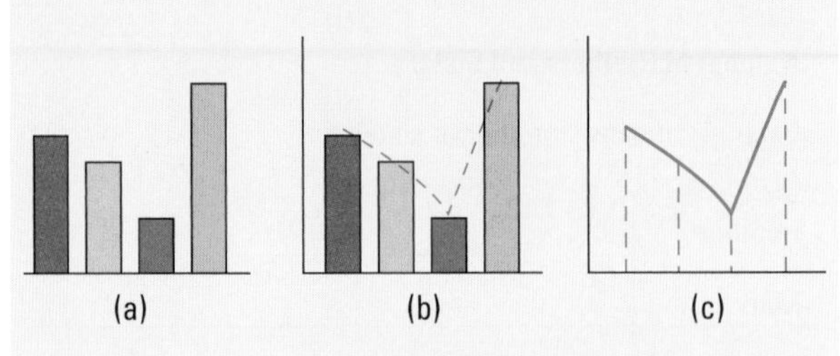

temperature at a given time each day for a week. The data could be graphed using a bar graph as shown in Figure 16-15(a). Discuss how each data point can be joined with a line, as shown in Figure 16-15(b). Line graphs are not so mysterious for young children if they understand this difference: that in a bar graph, data points determine the height of a rectangle (the bar) from the axis, whereas in a line graph the same data points are simply joined with a line. Figures 16-15(b) and 16-15(c) show this distinction.

Another important distinction between line and bar graphs that children need to understand is that bars represent a category or event, whereas line graphs represent continuous data, such as temperature. Both axes on a smooth line graph involve a continuous scale. In the case of a broken line graph, one scale may not be numeric but is at least ordered, as in the case of the months of the year (see Figure 16-16).

A good reading/interpretation activity is to give children a line graph with a title and the nature of the units for each axis and ask them to describe orally or in writing what is happening. This will also reinforce the continuous nature of the data. Activity 16-2 is an example of this type of exercise.

FIGURE 16-16 Another Line Graph (Abstract Stage)

	Jan	Feb	Mar	Apr	May	June	July	Aug	Sept	Oct	Nov	Dec
Maximum	2	16	22	48	56	62	78	80	62	56	40	20
Minimum	– 18	0	10	18	40	44	56	46	38	24	16	– 6

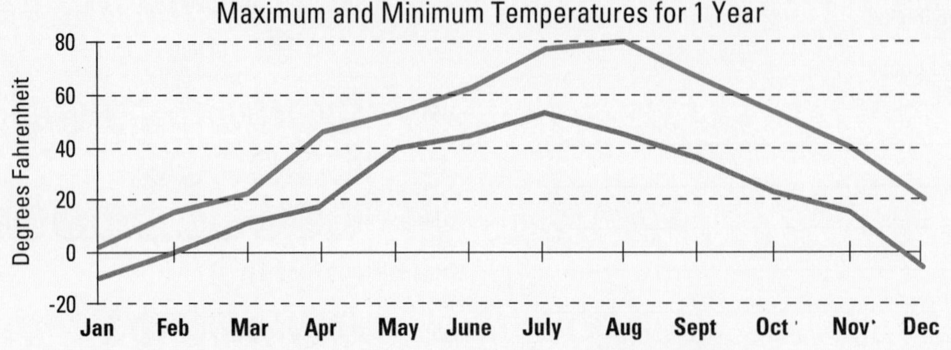

ACTIVITY 16-2 Gas Stop

Materials

Graph (below)

Filling a Gas Tank

Level of Gasoline in Tank

A B C D E F G H I

Time

Procedure

This graph shows the level of gasoline in the tank of a car as it is being filled. Write as interesting a story as you can about this. Include what happened at points (Time) A, B, C, D, E, F, G, H, and I.

Once this basic understanding is developed, upper-elementary and middle school children are ready for more advanced line graphs. Upper-elementary and middle school children can use a multiple-line graph to compare two or more things. For example, a group of children could obtain the maximum and minimum temperatures for each month of the year from the local weather office. They would plot two line graphs on the same chart, one showing the maximum, the other the minimum temperature each month, and orally report their observations and conclusions to the class or prepare a written report. Upper-elementary or middle children who have had some experience with a computer spreadsheet may volunteer to enter the data and have the computer produce the graph. Figure 16-16 shows a line graph and the spreadsheet from which it was generated.

Coordinate Graphing

Coordinate graphing is usually introduced at about the grade 3 level. Smith (1986) found that "third graders are able to understand the concepts and master the skills required" (p. 11). He recommends that coordinate graphing be presented "as an integrated unit rather than in a piecemeal fashion" (p. 11). Superimposing a grid on a "community" and using coordinates to locate buildings on a map might be an example of an integration of a social studies unit with mathematical skills.

To introduce coordinate graphs, Smith (1986) suggests beginning with the geoboard. Children can decide how to label each nail or peg on a 5-by-5 square geoboard. They might begin by simply labeling them A through Y, as shown in Figure 16-17(a). With some guidance, they can be led to name just the rows and columns, as in Figure 16-17(b). The need for the 0 coordinates can be shown by presenting a grid similar to that of Figure 16-17(c) on the overhead projector. Place a small object such as a small plastic animal (it is all right that children will see only the outline) at a particular location and ask the children to tell you where the animal is hiding. After a few repetitions, place the animal on one of the points on one of the axes, say (0, 3), and ask where the animal is hiding. Children could now suggest labels for the points on each of the axes.

Using the geoboard or dot paper, children can do activities such as copying shapes from coordinate descriptions and playing simple versions of tic-tac-toe and Battleship (Smith, 1986).

Start by using the language of the child. A teacher might project a simple grid, as in Figure 16-18, and ask the children to describe how to find the lost puppy if they are standing at the origin (0, 0). Children will probably use statements such as "go over 3 and up 2." Beginning activities use terms such as *over, across,* and *up.* Once children understand the concept, it is relatively easy to

FIGURE 16-17 Connecting Geoboards to Coordinate Graphing

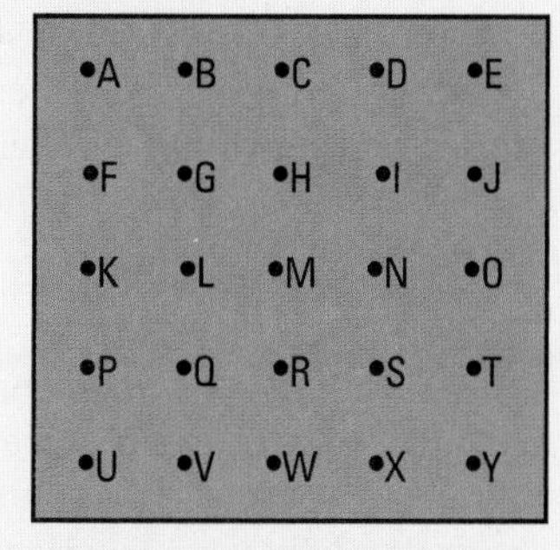

(a) Coordinates named A–Y

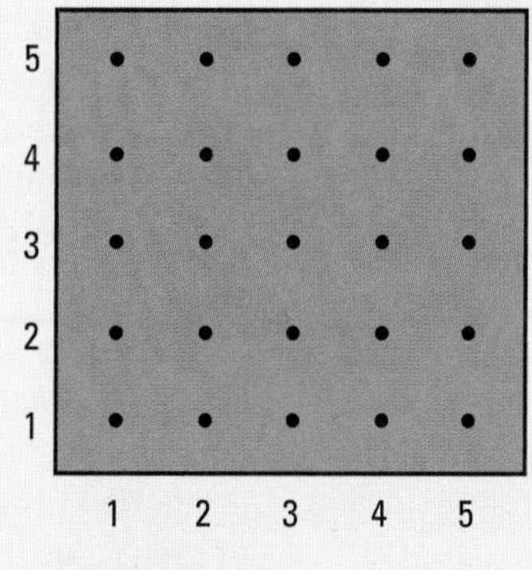

(b) Coordinates named by rows and columns

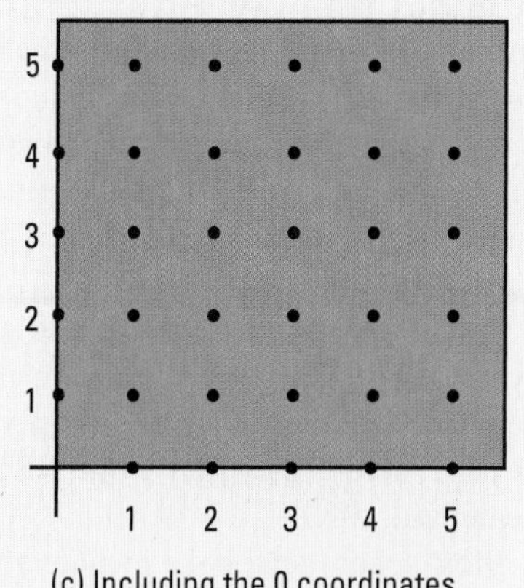

(c) Including the 0 coordinates

FIGURE 16-18 Coordinate Graphing Practice Grid

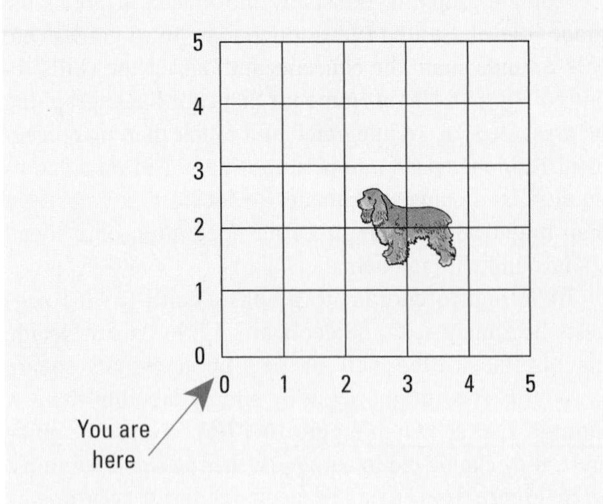

introduce notation such as (→3, ↑ 2) and then the standard notation (3, 2). Once children reach this stage of understanding, they can apply their understanding to some more practical or integrative activities, as in Figure 16-19 (Smith, 1986).

Next, the grid can be expanded to include 10 or more coordinate points on each axis. Give children coordinates, and ask them to plot and connect the coordinates to discover a design, as in Figure 16-20. Extend this by having children create a design, record and give only the ordered coordinates to a friend, and ask the friend to draw the design.

Circle or Pie Graphs

Circle or pie graphs appear frequently in newspapers, brochures, and many business documents. A circle graph clearly shows how a whole is broken into parts. Sources of revenue or a breakdown of expenditures is usually shown with a circle or pie graph. Temperatures are appropriate for a line graph but not normally for circle graphs. Likewise, a circle graph clearly shows the amount of time that a child devotes to various activities during the day. A line graph of such data would not be as easy to understand. Although bar graphs could show this information, the relationship among the activities and of each activity to the whole is more clearly seen in a circle graph.

Reading and constructing circle graphs is usually delayed until grade 6 or later because children need to have an understanding of fractions, percents, and angular measure before they can work with circle graphs in a meaningful way.

Most school textbooks include a family budget as an example of a circle graph. In this case, the circle represents the total budget, and each sector represents a budget category as a percent of the total budget. The family whose budget is represented in Figure 16-21 spent 25% of its budget for food, 18% for clothing, and so on.

Constructing a circle graph. The following six steps are helpful in guiding children through constructing a circle graph:

1. Collect the data and calculate the total.
2. Calculate the fractional part each data piece is of the total.
3. Express each fraction as a percent. This is not mandatory, although many circle graphs include the percent as part of the labeling process.
4. Calculate the number of degrees out of 360° that each fractional part represents.
5. Draw the graph, using the degrees from step 4 to determine the size of each sector.
6. Label the graph and each sector.

Class surveys can provide data for constructing circle graphs. Children might survey the class (or a sample of the school population) to determine favorite sport, ice cream flavor, TV show, month or season of the year, etc. Rather than draw bars as they did earlier, children would determine the fraction of children who responded in each category, calculate the corresponding angle, and construct the circle graph. Statistics from government documents and newspaper articles also provide suitable graphing data that are of interest to children. Again, children need to talk or write about what the graph tells them and, perhaps, what it does not tell.

Histograms, Line Plots, and Stem-and-Leaf Plots

Histograms, line plots, and *stem-and-leaf plots* are different forms of graphs often used to represent characteristics of a set of scores. They are often discussed and used in the context of statistical topics. We include them here because of their graphical nature. Another type of graph, called *box-and-whisker plots,* is discussed later in this chapter. These forms of representation are often introduced in the later middle grades.

Histograms and line plots. The histogram is a graphical representation of the frequency with which scores occur. To construct a histogram, separate the data into categories (usually equal intervals), tally the occurrence of each value in the appropriate category, and then plot the total count in each category.

Suppose a group of children found last year's monthly precipitation in inches in their city to be 25, 19, 23, 35,

FIGURE 16-19 Applying Coordinate Graphing to Map Reading

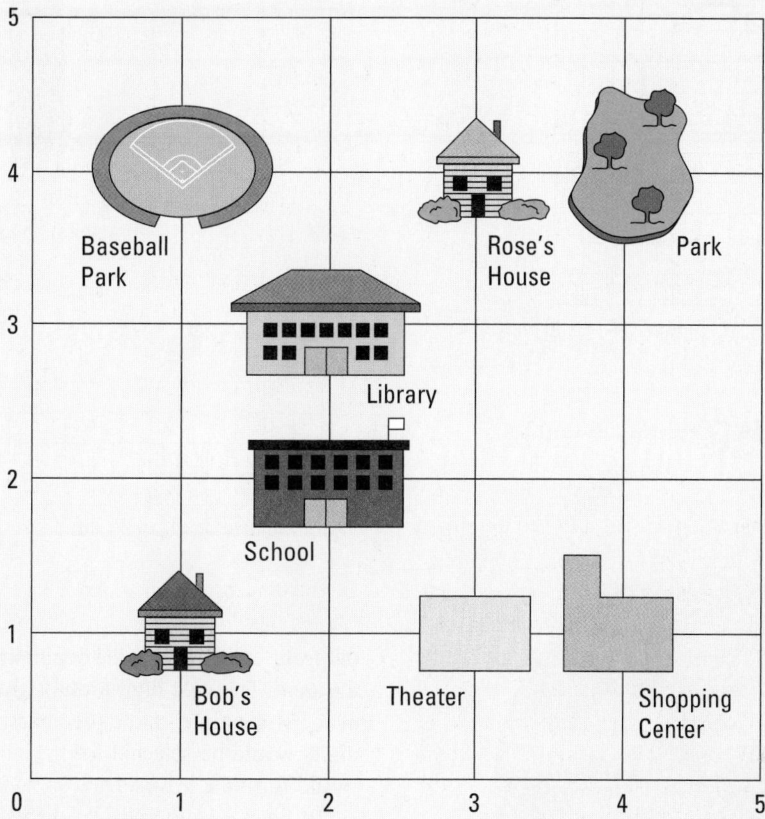

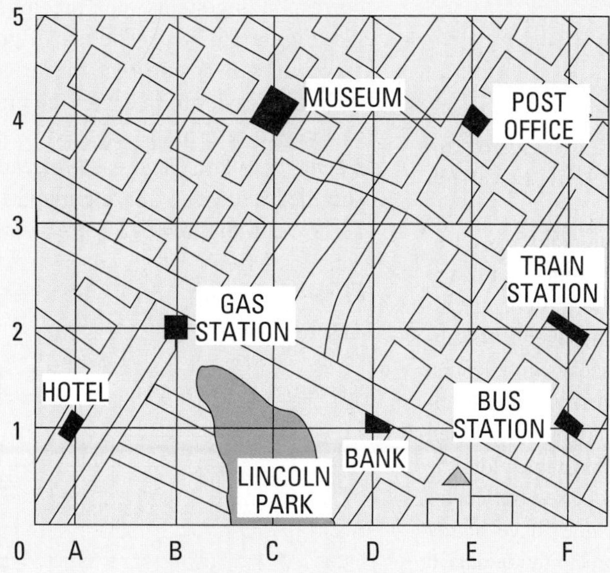

Source: "Let's do it: Coordinate geometry for third graders," by R. F. Smith, 1986, *Arithmetic Teacher, 33*(8), 6–11. Used with permission.

FIGURE 16-20 Using Coordinate Graphing to Make a Design

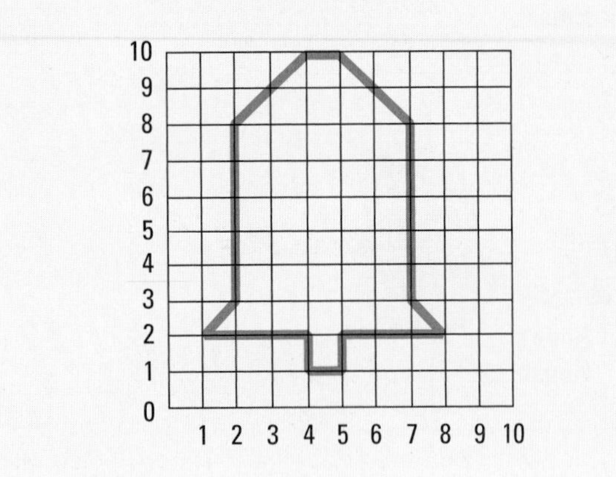

FIGURE 16-21 Circle Graph of a Sample Family Budget

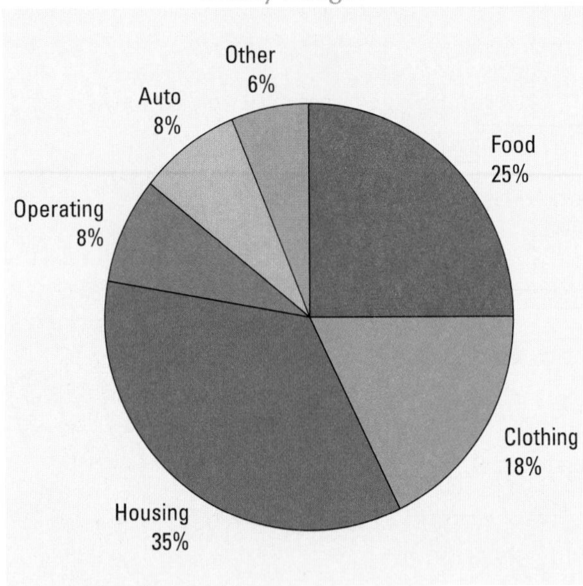

22, 19, 15, 24, 42, 29, 13, 9. Figure 16-22 is a histogram of these data using intervals: 0–9, 10–19, 20–29, 30–39, 40–49.

Line plots have replaced histograms in many cases. Recall that Ms. Moriarty's class constructed a line plot of the raisin data, as discussed at the beginning of this chapter. To construct a line plot, draw a number line and label it with appropriate values. For each data value, place a symbol, such as an X, above the corresponding point on the scale. If appropriate, the data may be rounded to make plotting easier. Figure 16-23 shows the precipitation data on a line plot. The grid format used in Figure 16-23 is not required but makes plotting easier, especially when some values have higher frequencies than those occurring in the precipitation data.

Stem-and-leaf plots. In the early 1990s, the *stem-and-leaf plot* was introduced into the middle grades curriculum. To construct a stem-and-leaf plot, select a certain number

FIGURE 16-22 Histogram of Precipitation

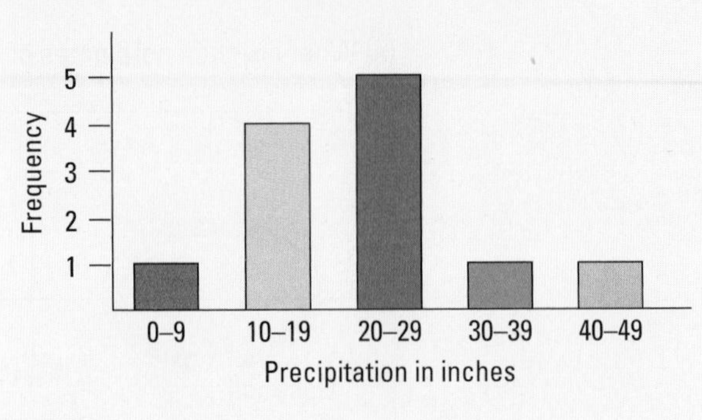

FIGURE 16-23 Line Plot of Precipitation

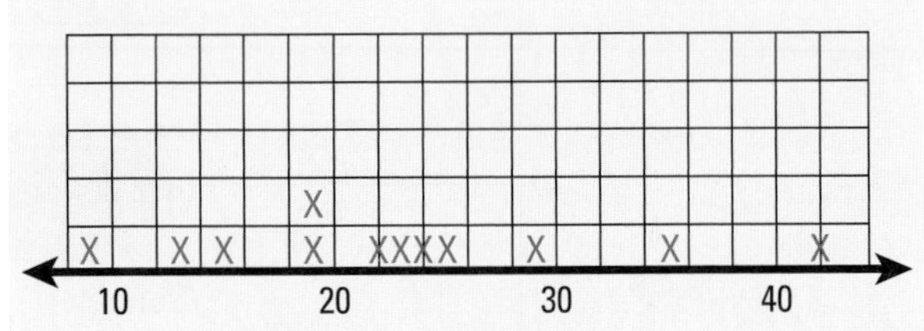

of "front-end" digits at the beginning of each value to form the *stem.* The next digit to the right of the stem forms the *leaf.* For example, in the precipitation data above, the tens digits would be selected for the stems and the ones digits would form the leaves.

To form a stem-and-leaf display, first place the stems in either ascending or descending order, as shown in Figure 16-24(a). Next, draw a vertical line to the right of the stems. Now place the leaves (units digits) to the right of the vertical line but on the same horizontal line as their corresponding stems. The precipitation data would look like Figure 16-24(b). The use of grid paper is not necessary but will ensure that the leaves are evenly spaced, making it easier to interpret the graph. Note the addition of a key to inform the reader of what the data values represent. For clarity and ease of reading, it is also wise to sort the leaves. The final stem-and-leaf display in this case is shown in Figure 16-24(c).

FIGURE 16-24 Stem-and-Leaf Plot of Precipitation

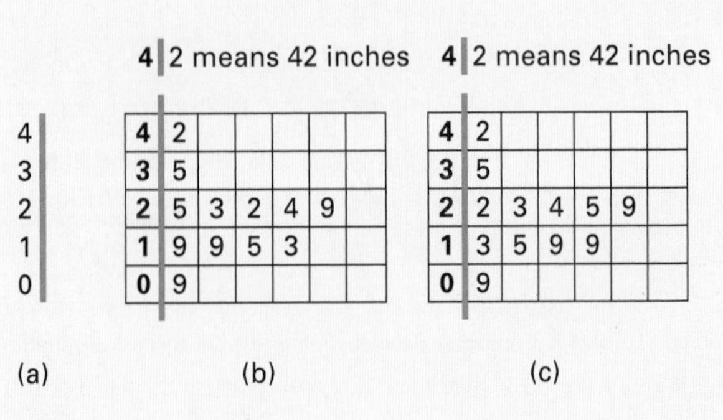

FIGURE 16-25 Sample Stem-and-Leaf Plot

Stem	Leaves
95	4
86	
•	8 9 9
•	6 6 6 6 6 7 7 7
•	4 4 5 5 5 5
•	2 3
85	

85 | 3 means 853 cm

Source: Adapted from *Curriculum and evaluation standards for school mathematics* (p. 117), by NCTM, 1989, Reston, VA: Author.

Note that these stem-and-leaf plots look a bit like a histogram. However, in a stem-and-leaf display, all the data values are retained and can be identified, the categories are not arbitrary, construction is easier, the data can be easily ordered, and other descriptive statistics can be calculated from the display.

Applications. Measurement activities provide an excellent setting for collecting data that could be displayed in a stem-and-leaf plot. An example from the Curriculum Standards (NCTM, 1989, p. 117) suggests that children use a meter tape to measure the length of a room to the nearest centimeter. Each child's measure could be recorded on the chalkboard and then pairs of children could construct a stem-and-leaf plot for the data. Figure 16-25 illustrates a possible stem-and-leaf display resulting from this activity. Notice how the one extreme value is handled. Note also how the remainder of the data clusters between 85 and 86. These values still serve as stems, but the leaves between them are partitioned into pairs (0 and 1, 2 and 3, etc.) marked in this example, with a bullet (•).

Children could also measure their heights or masses and prepare a stem-and-leaf display of the class data (Bankard & Fennell, 1991). This may be an ideal setting in which to develop a stem-and-leaf plot comparing two groups. Suppose the height measurements (in centimeters) turned out to be:

Girls: 154, 136, 138, 113, 122, 145, 131, 136, 124, 132, 146, 135, 147, 157, 142

Boys: 117, 136, 148, 154, 146, 129, 124, 131, 124, 120, 134, 134, 127

Figure 16-26 is a stem-and-leaf display comparing these two sets of data.

Children enjoy collecting data over a reasonable period of time. (If the time frame is too long, they lose interest.) For example, they might determine the temperature at a particular time each day for 2 weeks. Daily precipitation,

FIGURE 16-26 Stem-and-Leaf Plot Comparing Girls' and Boys' Heights

GIRLS		BOYS
4 7	15	4
2 5 6 7	14	6 8
1 2 5 6 6 8	13	1 4 4 6
2 4	12	0 4 4 7 9
3	11	7

15|4 means 154 centimeters

maximum temperatures, value of a particular stock, and other things could provide data that could be displayed by a stem-and-leaf plot.

For each stem-and-leaf plot, encourage children to make observations about and discuss, orally or in the form of a written paragraph, features such as:

- How wide a range there is in the data values;
- The smallest value—the largest value;

FIGURE 16-27 Two Graphs of the Same Data Made by Using *ClarisWorks*

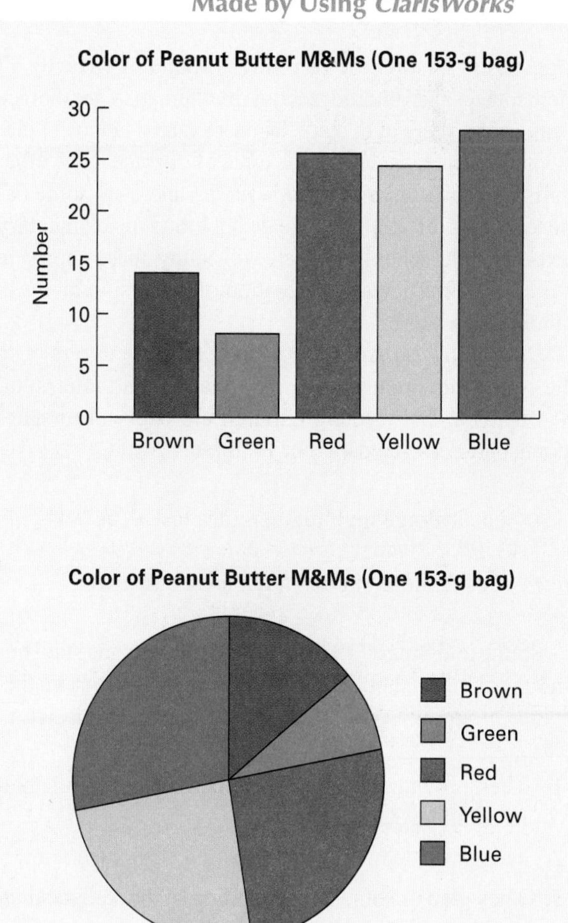

- How concentrated the values are;
- The symmetry of the distribution;
- Gaps in the data;
- Extreme values; and
- What was learned from the plot.

Computer-Generated Graphs

A number of easy-to-use commercial graphing programs are available for elementary and middle school children. *Lemonade for Sale* (Sunburst), *Graphers* (Sunburst), and *GraphPower* (Ventura Educational Systems) are three software packages that younger children can use to produce a variety of types of graphs. *Table Top* (Sunburst) is more suitable for middle school children.

Most integrated productivity packages such as *MicrosoftWorks* (Microsoft) and *ClarisWorks* (Claris Corporation) also have graphing capabilities. Figure 16-27 shows two graphs of the same data produced by *ClarisWorks.*

Refer to suppliers' catalogs for information on the newest versions of these and other software packages.

Interpreting Data: Statistics

Statistics is a topic that currently is found in virtually all elementary and middle school mathematics textbooks. Only a few years ago, statistics were rarely taught in elementary school, except for the topic of *average.* Now other statistics topics such as *median mode,* and even some basic concepts of *dispersion* can be found in elementary texts. Middle school children will study these topics in more depth, particularly the notion of dispersion or variation in data.

Descriptive statistics is a general term used to refer to the collection, organization, presentation, and interpretation of data. Even young children are exposed to statements that *describe* data. For example:

- "The average high temperature last week was only 13°F."
- "Most children in this room are 11 years old."

Shulte and Smart (1981) identify five reasons statistics and probability should be included in the school mathematics program:

1. They provide meaningful applications of mathematics at all levels.
2. They provide methods for dealing with uncertainty.
3. They give us some understanding of the statistical arguments, good and bad, with which we are continually bombarded.

FIGURE 16-28 Sample Distribution Table

Distribution of Team Scores		
Score	Tally	Frequency
0–4		
5–9		
10–14		
15–19		
20		

4. They help consumers distinguish sound use of statistical procedures from unsound or deceptive uses.
5. They are inherently interesting, exciting, and motivating topics for most children. (p. ix)

Frequency

The notion of how often something occurs is inherent in many of the graphing activities that involve collecting data and discussing the relative frequency of different events, as discussed earlier in this chapter. For example, oranges were more frequently mentioned as a favorite fruit than grapes; *e* occurred more frequently than any of the other vowels in a piece of writing; 5 buses, 35 cars, 22 trucks, 3 police cars, 25 panel trucks, and 15 other vehicles passed the school in one-half hour.

Older children can make more elaborate frequency distributions. If each member of a team tossed counters at a target with possible scores ranging from 0 to 20, the team might prepare a distribution table like the one shown in Figure 16-28. A histogram could then be drawn for their data. Some children may prefer to tally each score and show the frequency through a stem-and-leaf display.

Central Tendency

Measures of *central tendency* describe what is "typical" or "average" in a set of data. At the elementary and middle school levels, three types or measures of central tendency are normally considered: mode, median, and arithmetical average (mean).

Mode. The concept of the *mode,* but not the term, is introduced informally early in a child's school experience, when a child examines a graph and reports:

- "September has the most birthdays."
- "Most members of the class like chocolate ice cream the best."
- "The vowel that occurs most often is *e.*"

The *mode* is the most frequently occurring value in a set of data. Sometimes one or two values in a data set can

FIGURE 16-29 Frequency Table

Size	Tally	Count
7	/	1
6	////	4
5	//	2
4	//	2
3	/	1

distort the "typical" value described by the mean. In these cases, the mode is sometimes the preferred measure of central tendency. For example, a shoe manufacturer is more interested in the most frequently sold shoe size than the mean size of shoes.

The mode is usually easily determined from a frequency distribution. For example, 10 children in a classroom reported the following shoe sizes: 6, 5, 4, 6, 7, 4, 6, 3, 5, 6. The mode is not easy to see in this list, but once a frequency table (Figure 16-29) is prepared, the mode—6—is apparent. Line plots and stem-and-leaf plots also provide good visual representations of the mode.

Median. A second measure of central tendency, the *median,* often is not introduced until the middle grades. Computational procedures should be left until the middle grades, but the concept of the median should be introduced to elementary school children because they "need many experiences with data sets and the median before they can understand how the mean represents the data" (Russell & Mokros, 1996, p. 362).

The *median* is the middle number in a set of numbers. Some children may have seen the highway sign "DO NOT CROSS MEDIAN." Here the term is used to refer to the section between two parts of the highway, that is, the middle position. Reference to the use of the term outside of mathematics may help children understand the concept.

The concept of the median can also be easily modeled. Suppose that in one learning group, five children record their ages on index cards:

11	10	13	12	10

To find the median age, the children order the cards from youngest to oldest, or vice versa.

10	10	11	12	13

The children might discover the need for sorted data by first working with unsorted data. They will soon recognize that with unsorted data the middle card could have any number on it.

Children now simultaneously remove a card from each end and continue this process until there is only one card left. This card is the midpoint or middle value, because the cards were ordered.

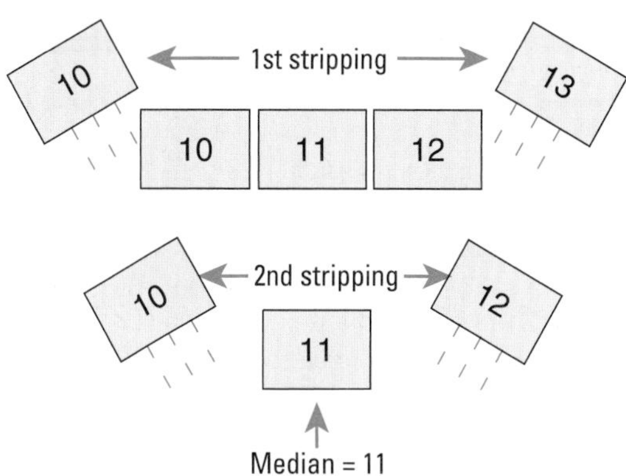

What happens if there is an even number of children in the group? Again the children order the cards and remove the first and last as before. This time, however, there will be two cards left in the middle, which provides children with an excellent opportunity to discuss what the median is in this situation.

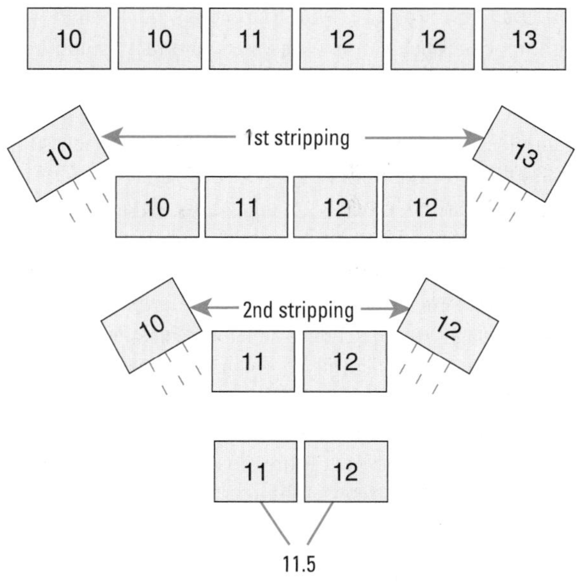

Median = mean of 11 and 12
or 11.5

These experiences with manipulatives help children understand that the median is the midpoint of a set of values. If the number of values is odd, the median is the middle number; if the number of values is even, the median is the mean of the *two* middle values.

Mean. The *mean* is the most commonly used measure of central tendency. It is what most people speak of simply as the *average*. It is found by dividing the sum of a set of numbers by the number of numbers in the set. This is a rule that is easily forgotten by children unless they have

FIGURE 16-30 A Concrete Method for Finding the Mean

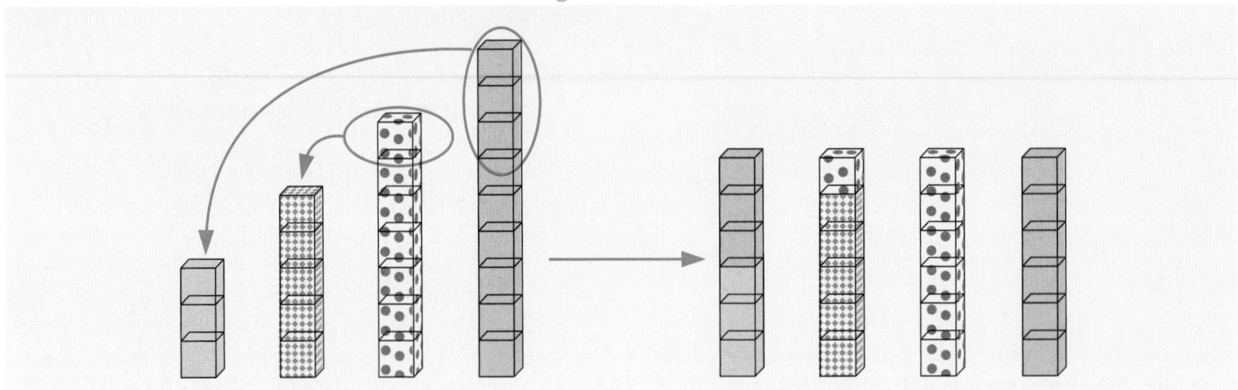

some understanding of the concept. A good introduction might be to have children engage in a discussion about "being average" (Paull, 1990). What does it mean? Is being average desirable? Is anyone average?

An understanding of the mean can be developed through concrete and visual manipulation (Rubenstein, 1989). Begin with two numbers. Using interlocking cubes, ask the children to build a tower with four blocks and another with eight blocks. They can now discuss what they would have to do to make both towers the same height, using only the blocks they have used to construct the towers. After several examples with two numbers, children can apply their strategy to three or four numbers, say, 3, 5, 7, and 9. Figure 16-30 illustrates the process of concretely determining the mean of these numbers. Later, children can attempt to apply the process and discuss a situation in which the cubes cannot be evenly shared. Allow the children to use their own language, but the end result should be an understanding that the mean is simply one number that describes or characterizes all the numbers in the data set.

Once the children understand the concept, provide them with an activity that more closely matches the computational algorithm. A problem such as the following would serve that purpose:

> *While trick-or-treating on Halloween, Peter collected 4 chocolate bars, Seamus collected 8, Patrick got 3, and Kyle placed 5 in his sack. What is the average number of bars collected by the 4 children?*
>
> *HINT: To find the average, put all 4 collections together and share them equally.*

The process could be simulated with pictures or counters (Figure 16-31). First find the sum (put everybody's bars into one pile), and then separate the total pile into four equal piles (the number of people to share). Finally, count to see how many bars each person received. This process parallels the computational algorithm. To help children discover the "add-'em-up and then divide" rule, Zawojewski (1988) suggests giving children:

> . . . a bundle of eight pencils of varying lengths and ask them to cut a straw to the length that they would estimate as the average length of all the pencils. After the estimates are in, lay the pencils end-to-end and cut a strip of adding machine tape the same length. This action illustrates the "add-em-up" step. Then fold the strip into eight equal parts to illustrate the division step. (p. 26)

Russell and Mokros (1996) use "construction" problems (given a statistic, children construct the data) to help children understand the concepts of central tendency. One type of problem involves an "unpacking" task to construct the data given the mean. The authors use an example in which the mean family size is 4. Assuming there were 8 families, a line plot could be constructed by placing eight stick-on notes above the 4 on the line. At an early level, children could "unpack" the data by taking one stick-on note from the set and placing it above the 3. To balance

FIGURE 16-31 Another Way to Find the Mean Concretely

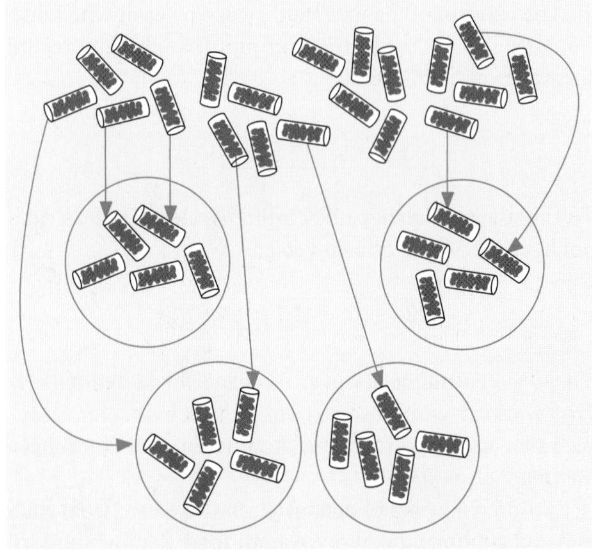

FIGURE 16-32 "Unpacking" to Construct a Data Set from the Mean

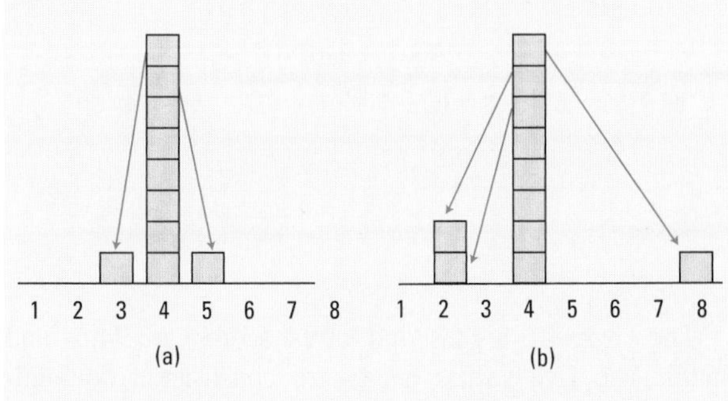

this, the next one would go above the 5, and so on, as in Figure 16-32(a).

After a series of symmetrical balancing as above, children might be asked what would happen if one family had 8 members. One stick-on note could be moved above the 8 on the line, but it does not make sense to balance this with a note above 0. Russell and Mokros (1996) maintain in their work that "students have always come up with the idea of moving two different stick-on notes down a total of 4 units so as to balance the upward move of 4" (p. 363). This is shown in Figure 16-32(b).

Integrating activities. Problems such as the following will stimulate small-group discussion resulting in increased understanding of the mean, median, and mode. They will also stimulate discussion about the relationships among the measures.

a. Seven girls are at a slumber party. Their shoe sizes range from 5 to 9 (with half-sizes included). If the median shoe size for the girls is 7, what are some possible combinations of shoe sizes for the girls?

b. The mean of five brothers' ages is 4, and the mode is 3. What are some possible ages for the five brothers? (Zawojewski, 1988, p. 26)

See Loewen (1991) for some other integrating activities based on a card game.

Variation

Children are often interested in learning about the longest and shortest jump distances achieved at the school field day, the tallest and shortest heights in class, or the highest and lowest grades given on an examination. These children are asking about the *range,* or the difference between the greatest and least number in a set of numbers. The *range* is a simple measure of the spread or dispersion of scores. The range of shoe sizes in Figure 16-29 is 7 – 3, or 4. In addition to central tendency, spread or variation is another way to describe or characterize data.

The range, like the mean, is often not a good characterization of the data, however, because it is directly affected by extreme scores. For example, consider these two sets of data:

SET 1: 3, 3, 13, 13 *Mean = 8; range = 10*

SET 2: 3, 8, 8, 13 *Mean = 8; range = 10*

Although the mean and range are the same for each set, the dispersion or scatter of scores is quite different. The first set has scores clustering around the extremes, while the second set has scores more uniformly distributed about the mean. The histograms, line plots, and stem-and-leaf plots discussed earlier in this chapter provide more useful representations of the variation in scores. Another representation, the box-and-whisker plot, is discussed next.

Box-and-whisker plots. In the NCTM Curriculum Standards for grades 5 to 8, box-and-whisker plots are mentioned as appropriate activities for these grades in both Standard 10 (Statistics) and Standard 13 (Measurement). A box-and-whisker plot includes the median and charts data in a way that adds information about the spread of scores not directly available from a stem-and-leaf display. To construct a simple (sometimes referred to as a *skeletal*) box-and-whisker plot, five values are required: *median, upper quartile, lower quartile, upper extreme,* and *lower extreme.* These terms will be explained in the following paragraphs as they are used. Note that the median is the middle quartile.

The median, quartiles, and extremes can be readily obtained by sorting the data in ascending order and adding a *depth* column beside the sorted data. The depth simply indicates how far a particular value is from the high or low end of the set of values. The lowest and highest value each have a depth of 1, the next highest and next lowest a 2, and so on. The life expectancy at birth for males in 15 selected countries is shown in Table 16-1, with the depth of each

TABLE 16-1 Life Expectancy at Birth for Males

Depth	Life Expectancy
1	74.54
2	73.62
3	72.75
4	72.70
5	72.52
6	72.09
7	71.50
8	71.45
7	71.34
6	71.00
5	70.41
4	70.41
3	69.69
2	67.04
1	65.09

Source: Canada Yearbook 1990 (pp. 3–18), Statistics Canada, 1989. Ottawa, ON: Author, Publications Division.

value listed to the left of the data. When the number of data values is odd, the median is the "deepest" value. The eighth value from both the top and the bottom is 71.45.

The *upper* and *lower quartiles* are roughly the medians of the two halves of the data determined by the median. The quartiles can therefore be found by repeating the depth-finding process using the median as the starting point and going both directions. The following simplified examples may clarify the process.

Example 1

Data	Median	Depth for Upper Quartile	Lower Quartile
63	1	1	
60	2	2	
59	3	← 59.5 2	
55	← 4	1	1
48	3		2
46	2		← 47 2
45	1		1

Example 2

Data	Median	Depth for Upper Quartile	Lower Quartile
63	1	1	
60	2	← 60 2	
59	← 3	1	
55	3		1
48	2		← 48 2
46	1		1

Example 3

Data	Median	Depth for Upper Quartile	Lower Quartile
63	1	1	
60	2	← 60 2	
59	← 3	1	1
55	2		← 55 2
48	1		2

Using the life-expectancy data from Table 16-1, the median has a depth of 8. The greatest depth for the upper quartile would be 4, corresponding to both 72.70 and 72.52. The upper quartile would then be the average of these, or 72.61 years. What is the value of the lower quartile?

FIGURE 16-33 Box-and-Whisker Plot of Life Expectancy

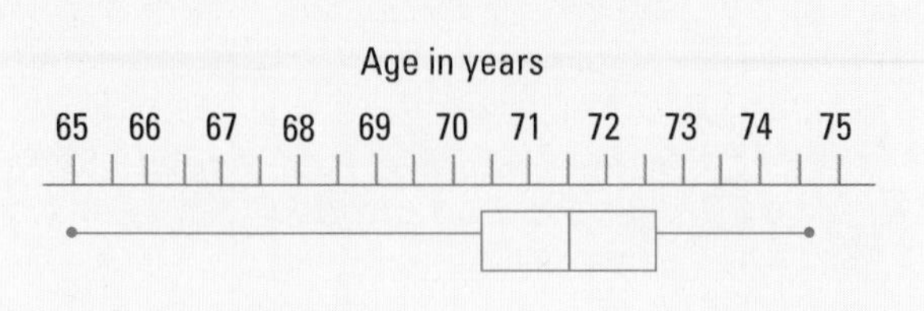

The *extremes* (highest and lowest scores) are 74.54 and 65.09. The five values needed to construct a box-and-whisker plot (Figure 16-33) are now available. Begin by drawing a number line horizontally or vertically that encompasses both extremes and as many other reference points as desired. On the side of the line opposite the reference points construct a *box* (rectangle) with one pair of opposite sides perpendicular to the number line at the points corresponding to the quartiles, as illustrated in Figure 16-33. Draw another line through the box parallel to the quartiles at the point on the number line corresponding to the median. Now draw a *whisker* (line) parallel to the number line from the midpoint of the side corresponding to the lower quartile to a point corresponding to the lowest value in the data set. Similarly, draw a whisker from the upper quartile to the point corresponding to the greatest data value.

Two or more box-and-whisker plots could be superimposed on the same reference line. Box charts for the heights of boys and girls (data from Figure 16-26) could be placed side by side, as shown in Figure 16-34.

Children and box-and-whisker plots. Box-and-whisker plots are relatively new in school curricula. For this reason, the preceding explanation was more extensive and formal than is necessary for children in the middle grades. To find

FIGURE 16-34 Box-and-Whisker Plot of Girls' and Boys' Heights

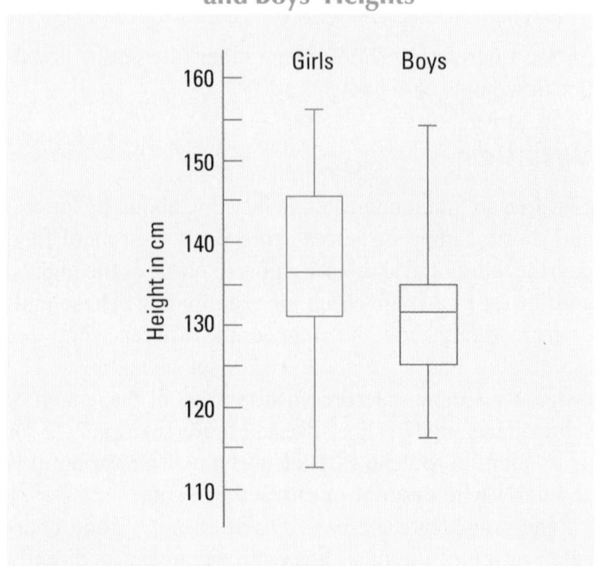

the median, children already know that they need to work with sorted data. Rather than use a depth column, they could simply count up from the bottom or down from the top to the middle value or middle pair of values. For the upper quartile, they could count down from the top to the score that represented one-quarter of the scores. Similarly, they could count one-quarter of the scores from the bottom to find the lower quartile. They could then draw the box-and-whisker plot.

Even more important than the precision of the construction is the interpretation or discussion that takes place as a result of the data. Children can write a paragraph or two stating their observations. It is helpful to draw attention to such features as the extremes, the range, and the range within which most of the scores fall (the box contains the middle 50%). Children also can discuss such questions as "What does a long box tell you?" and "What does a short box with long whiskers mean?"

We have provided some data for illustrative purposes. It is important, however, that children draw box-and-whisker plots for data they collect themselves. Activity 16-3, adapted from Brosnan (1996), provides one idea for doing this.

ACTIVITY 16-3 Count the Raisins

Materials

14-g box of raisins for each child

1-cm grid paper

Procedure

- Don't open the box. Each person writes down an estimate of how many raisins he or she thinks is in the box. (The teacher records all the estimates from each group on the board.)
- Count the number of raisins in each box. (Again, the teacher records the actual count for each box on the board.)
- Construct a back-to-back stem-and-leaf plot. One side will show the estimates, the other side the actual counts.
- Construct a box-and-whisker plot for both the estimates and the counts. Use one number line to show both box plots.
- Answer these questions:
  1. Which actual count occurred most often? Which plot tells you this?
  2. What is the lowest count? The highest count? What is the range?
  3. What is the lowest estimate? The highest estimate? What is the range?
  4. How can you find the medians from your plots?
  5. What can you say about the estimates compared to the actual counts?

Interpreting Data: Probability

"I think it will snow today."

"If I throw this rock in the pool it will sink."

"I hope I roll a 6."

Young children often make these sorts of statements in their lives outside school. But in most cases, children don't realize that these statements express probabilities. Children benefit from experiences in school that help them connect everyday activities with mathematics concepts such as probability.

Probability activities enhance children's problem-solving skills because these activities engage children in collecting and organizing data to determine the probability of an event. Probability activities can also be used to reinforce other concepts and skills. Also, activities in probability can be fun, adding motivation, excitement, and variety to the mathematics program. "Classroom activities involving probability should be active, involve physical materials, and furnish opportunities for questioning, problem solving, and discussion" (Fennell, 1990, p. 18). And according to Bright and Hoeffner (1993), "Students need to be exposed to problems for which intuitions alone are insufficient for finding solutions" (p. 87).

Overview

Probability is the area of mathematics that analyzes the chance of something occurring. The probability that a given *event* will occur is the ratio of the number of *favorable* or *desirable outcomes* to the total number of *possible outcomes*. This is often written in the form:

$$P(\text{event}) = \frac{\text{Number of Desired Favorable Outcomes}}{\text{Number of Total Possible Outcomes}}$$

For example, if you flip a coin, the probability of its landing with heads up is $\frac{1}{2}$, because there is one desired outcome (landing heads) and two possible outcomes (heads, tails). This provides another setting in which children can use some of the ratio and percent ideas (Chapter 13) they have learned.

Go to the Assignments and Activities section of Topic 13: "Data Analysis" in the MyEducationLab for your course and complete the activity "Probability Lesson: Flipping a Coin" to see how students develop prediction skills.

In an experiment, events must be *random,* and each event or outcome must have the same likelihood of occurring on each trial. To illustrate, each time you roll a die, each of the six outcomes is equally likely, and the probability of the die landing with a 2 on top is the same for each trial. On the other hand, if you drew a card from a deck of ordinary playing cards, replaced it at the bottom of the deck and drew again, the probability of drawing the same card would not be the same the second time. The deck would need to be thoroughly shuffled after each draw to ensure randomness.

This does not mean that all possible outcomes have the same probability. For example, if a Styrofoam cup is tossed into the air and allowed to land on the table, the probability of its landing on its side is greater than its landing on either its top or bottom, but the likelihood of its landing on its side does not change from toss to toss. Based on studies in the United States and England, it is evident that many children do not have a good understanding of randomness (Dessart, 1995).

Rolling a die or flipping a coin are examples of *sample spaces* with *equally likely* outcomes because each of the six faces of the die (or two sides of the coin) has the same chance of turning up. Tossing a Styrofoam cup involves a sample space with outcomes that are *not equally likely.* Experiments such as these involve events that are *independent.* The fact that a 2 turned up last time has no bearing on what will come up on the next roll of a die. The probability of getting a 2 is always $\frac{1}{6}$ regardless of how many times 2 came up previously. This is sometimes a difficult concept for adults to understand, let alone children.

Dependent events are events in which the probability of a second outcome is different based on what happened earlier, in the first outcome. For example, if a bag contains eight yellow and four red marbles, the initial probability of drawing a red marble at random is $\frac{4}{12}$, or $\frac{1}{3}$. If, after each draw, the marble is replaced and the bag is shaken, the probability of drawing a red marble on subsequent draws remains at $\frac{1}{3}$, since these events are independent. If, however, the marble is not replaced, the probability on subsequent draws changes. If a red marble was drawn on the first trial, the probability of a red on the second draw would now be $\frac{3}{11}$ since there are now 11 marbles in the bag, 3 of which are red. If a yellow marble was drawn on the first trial, the probability of a red on the second draw would now be $\frac{4}{11}$.

In some situations the number of favorable outcomes is equal to the number of possible outcomes. In this case, the event is said to be *certain* and has a probability of 1. If there are no favorable outcomes, the event has a probability of 0 and is said to be *impossible.*

General Teaching Considerations

Early experiences. You can introduce some informal, nonnumeric probability activities to young children to help them think about concepts such as *certain, impossible, equally likely, more likely,* and *less likely.* Terms such as these may or may not be used explicitly. *Prediction* and *experimentation* are important components of many of the activities in the early years. Principles and Standards Link 16-3 discusses how probability can be introduced to young children.

What do young children understand about probability? Children seem to have intuitive understandings of chance, in particular, that some events are less likely to occur than others. Teachers can build on and extend these understandings to help children develop a strong concept of probability. Frykholm (2001) suggests that teachers can recognize children's intuitions and develop them as they explore situations involving probability and make predictions. Teachers can help children "recognize what 'should' happen when an event takes place and be able to explain unlikely outcomes as products of chance" (Frykholm, 2001, p. 117).

There are several "big ideas" about probability that we'd like children to understand (Tarr, 2002). (1) Probability is a measure of the likelihood of future events; (2) a sample space is a the set of all possible outcomes and their associated probabilities of occurring; (3) probability helps predict outcomes of simple experiments; and (4) students can make estimates of probability by using data from experiments. Tarr also notes that probability connects nicely with several other mathematics topics, including rational numbers, data analysis, area, and coordinate geometry.

Build on the natural language of the children to help them think in probability terms. For example, a child may come bounding in one morning and say, "It's going to rain today." Many times you will accept this statement, but on occasion you might respond, "Are you *certain* it is going to rain today, or do you think it *might* rain today?"

The following four activities are samples of experiences children in the late primary grades might find interesting and which would help develop intuitive understanding as a foundation for later work.

1. **What's in the Bag?**
   - Without the children's knowledge, place 3 blue blocks in a bag.
   - Tell the children that you have some blocks in the bag and that you are going to draw one out, note the color, and then replace it in the bag.

NCTM Principles and Standards Link 16-3

Content Strand: Data Analysis and Probability

In prekindergarten through grade 2, the treatment of probability ideas should be informal. Teachers should build on children's developing vocabulary to introduce and highlight probability notions, for example, "We'll *probably* have recess this afternoon," or "It's *unlikely* to rain today." Young children can begin building an understanding of chance and randomness by doing experiments with concrete objects, such as choosing colored chips from a bag. (NCTM, 2000, p. 51)

FIGURE 16-35 Recording Sheet for "One of Each" Activity

Draw number	1	2	3	4	5	6	7	8	9	10
Color										

- Ask the children to keep a record of the color drawn.
- Draw and replace two or three times, then ask the children to make a prediction about the color of the block you will draw next time. Record their guesses.
- Draw two or three more times. Ask again for a prediction for the color of the next block.
- Ask "Can anyone guess what is in the bag?" and "What are the chances that I will draw a red block?"

2. **One of Each**
   - Place 1 red and 1 blue block in a bag, shake, and draw 1 block out.
   - Give the children a recording sheet like the one shown in Figure 16-35. Ask them to color the square under "1" the color of the first block drawn.
   - Return the block to the bag, shake the bag and draw another block without looking, and have the children color each square as you go along.
   - Do this a total of 10 times.
   - Ask "How many red blocks were drawn?" and "How many blue blocks were drawn?"
3. **Guess the Color**
   - Use the setting from the previous activity, but this time have the children record their guesses of the outcome before a block is drawn (see Figure 16-36).
   - Have the children shade in the first square opposite "Guess" with either blue or red before the draw. After the draw they should color the square opposite "Color drawn" with the color of the block drawn.
   - After 10 draws, have the children complete the totals below the chart.

     Total guessed: _______ *red and* _______ *blue.*
     Total drawn: _______ *red and* _______ *blue.*

FIGURE 16-36 Recording Sheet for "Guess the Color" Activity

Draw number	1	2	3	4	5	6	7	8	9	10
Guess										
Color drawn										

4. **Sort the Statements**
   - Give the children a set of cards with probability statements on them or have the children make up their own statements. For example:

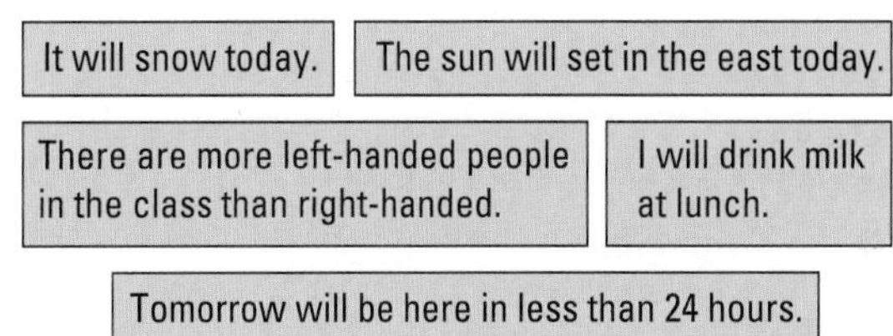

   - Prepare containers so that the children can sort the statements into groups.

   - Have the children compare their groupings and discuss any differences.

Upper-elementary experiences. In the upper-elementary grades children will begin to use some of the conventional probability terms and can start to assign probability values to some events. The emphasis still is on experimental probability as opposed to *theoretical* probability, although theoretical values can be assigned to some simple events such as flipping a coin or shaking a die. Some simple *simulations* can be done at this level. Children could also be exposed to examples of *fair* and *unfair* experiments or games. Here, and at higher grade levels, considerable integration of graphing and statistics with probability can take place. Principles and Standards Link 16-4 summarizes what upper-elementary students should learn about probability.

Children often demonstrate biases when dealing with familiar materials such as coins or dice. Biases did not seem apparent when using thumb tacks, Styrofoam cups, or other materials with which students may be less familiar. It might be wise, then, to start a more formal development of basic probability concepts in the upper-elementary grades with relatively unfamiliar objects. Activity 16-4 provides one example. Before starting this activity, a number of washers (or equivalent) will need to have a small piece of masking tape placed on one side.

NCTM Principles and Standards Link 16-4

Content Strand: Data Analysis and Probability

In grades 3–5 students can consider ideas of chance through experiments—using coins, dice, or spinners—with known theoretical outcomes or through designating familiar events as impossible, unlikely, likely, or certain. Middle-grades students should learn and use appropriate terminology and should be able to compute probabilities for simple compound events, such as the number of expected occurrences of two heads when two coins are tossed 100 times. (NCTM, 2000, p. 50)

ACTIVITY 16-4 Flip a Washer

Realia Strategies

Materials

Washers with masking tape on one side

Procedure

- Predict how many times the washer will land tape side up in 10 tosses.
- Toss a washer 10 times, and keep a record of how it lands.
- Compare your results with your prediction.
- Repeat the experiment several times, and calculate a total for each outcome.
- Compare your results with those of another group, and discuss similarities and differences.

Children who are ready to begin quantifying the probability of an outcome could complete a recording sheet, as shown in Figure 16-37. (Tossing a single die is essentially the same experiment, except that the sample space now contains six possible outcomes rather than two. However, each outcome still is equally likely.)

Experiments in which different outcomes have different chances of occurring add another element of interest for children. Figure 16-38 illustrates the three possible outcomes—each with a different probability—when a Styrofoam cup is tossed. Children should toss the cup a large number of times to feel confident that they have a reasonable estimation of the actual probability.

FIGURE 16-37 Recording Sheet for Activity 16-5

	After 10 Tosses		After 40 Tosses	
Outcome	Number	Fraction	Number	Fraction
Tape up		$\frac{\quad}{10}$		$\frac{\quad}{40}$
Tape down		$\frac{\quad}{10}$		$\frac{\quad}{40}$

FIGURE 16-38 Possible Outcomes When Tossing a Styrofoam Cup

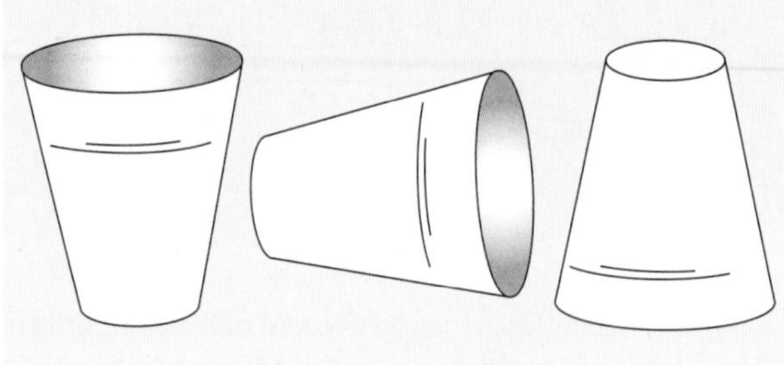

Challenge children to think about factors that could affect the probability of a particular event's occurring. Would the probabilities be different if the cup landed on a piece of plush carpet? Would the size of the cup change the probabilities? These challenges could serve as the basis for a long-term project for one or two groups of children.

Tossing a thumbtack is another popular activity using unfamiliar probability materials with outcomes not equally likely. There are only two possible outcomes if children toss the tack on the floor or a desk. Here is a case in which tossing the tack on a plush carpet might not only change the probabilities associated with each outcome but also add a third possible outcome to the sample space, namely, the point going down into the carpet. Of course, please keep safety considerations in mind when having students toss thumbtacks, and make sure to review behavior expectations prior to beginning the activity.

Drawing Numbered Balls

- Write the numeral 5 on one Ping-Pong ball (or card), 6 on two balls, 7 on four balls, 8 on two balls, and 9 on one ball.
- Place all 10 balls in a bag. Tell the children that you have 10 balls in the bag but give no other information.
- Have one child record the outcomes on the chalkboard or overhead projector as another child draws the balls from the bag.
- After 3 or 4 draws, solicit predictions as to what the 10 balls are.
- After approximately 20 draws, ask the recorder to organize the data on the chalkboard.
- Then tell the children that each ball had a 5, 6, 7, 8, or 9 on it.
- Divide the children into groups to discuss and write a new prediction.
- Have one child count the number of times each number was drawn and announce this to the class so that children can compare the count with their predictions.

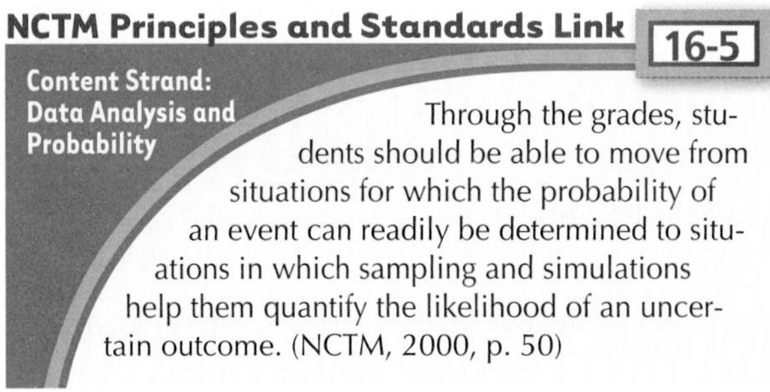
NCTM Principles and Standards Link 16-5

Content Strand: Data Analysis and Probability

Through the grades, students should be able to move from situations for which the probability of an event can readily be determined to situations in which sampling and simulations help them quantify the likelihood of an uncertain outcome. (NCTM, 2000, p. 50)

You can include probability discussions in some of the graphing and statistics activities suggested previously. For example, one activity suggested earlier in this chapter involved selecting a paragraph, recording the number of vowels, and then graphing these data. Children could also use the data to calculate statistics such as the mean, median, and mode; to draw a stem-and-leaf display; and to make a box-and-whisker plot. Some probability questions could then be explored. For example, suppose you were blindfolded and randomly placed the tip of your pencil anywhere on a page from a book. Suppose also that your pencil pointed to a word. Based on your data,

- What would be a "good" guess for the length of the word?
- What would be some "poor" guesses?
- What is the probability that the word has one letter? Three letters? Eight letters?

Survey activities could also be expanded to include some probability questions. For example, children might take a survey of the class to determine how many children are left handed. What is the probability that the next child to walk through the door is left handed? Use the data from your room to guess how many children in the room next door are left handed. Survey that class to find out. Use these data to predict how many children in the school are left handed. Bankard and Fennell (1991) suggest a similar activity based on hair color.

Simulations are another popular probability activity. Simulating an experiment is known as the *Monte Carlo* method. Consider the following scenario:

> *A certain cookie manufacturer designs a set of six different hockey cards. One card is randomly inserted into each bag of cookies. On the average, how many bags of cookies would you have to buy to get at least one of each card?*
>
> *(Assume that equal numbers of each card are printed and distributed.)*

Challenge children to think of ways to simulate this problem. One suggestion is to place the numerals 1 through 6 on six different cards. Then have the children shuffle the cards, place them in a bag, draw one out, record the number, and replace the card, continuing the process until one of each of the six numbers is drawn. Have the children note how many draws were made to get one of each card, repeat this complete process a number of times, and then calculate the mean to get a better estimate of the answer to the problem. Most problems can be simulated in a variety of ways. A regular die could also be used for this problem, because there are six different and equally likely outcomes.

Children in the upper-elementary grades can also explore the concept of a *fair* game. For example, you might take a few minutes one day to suggest to your children that you will play a game with them. Shake a die; if it shows a number greater than 4 they win, otherwise you win. Each game consists of 10 shakes. Keep a tally on the chalkboard for each game, and note the winner beside each set. It likely won't take long for someone to object to this game because "it's not fair!"

Middle grades experiences. More emphasis is placed in middle school on determining theoretical values, although the experimental aspect should not be neglected. More advanced work can be done with simulating events and with some of the other ideas developed earlier. Principles and Standards Link 16-5 discusses a progression of probability experiences.

An activity commonly done at this level is to have children shake and roll a pair of dice and record the sum. Activity 16-5 provides a good opportunity for children to compare experimental with theoretical probability.

A related but more complicated activity involves tossing two Styrofoam cups. The three possible outcomes for one cup (top, bottom, side) are not equally likely and their theoretical probability cannot readily be determined. Furthermore, the probability will vary with the size of cup, type of landing surface, etc. Encourage the children to toss the two cups many times to gain some assurance that their experimental probability is reasonable. If the children worked in pairs and each pair tossed the cups 50 times and then pooled their results, they would have at least 500 tosses. Each group could complete a chart like the one shown here:

Cup 1	Side	Top	Bottom
Side	___/50	___/50	___/50
Top	___/50	___/50	___/50
Bottom	___/50	___/50	___/50

Cup 2

ACTIVITY 16-5 Dice Sum

Manipulative Strategies

Materials

Dice (different colors)

Procedure

1. Shake and roll a pair of dice 36 times. Find the sum of each roll. Tally and record each sum in the first chart below. Write the probability for each outcome based on your experiment.
2. Now compare your results with the *theoretical* probability. Analyze how many possible ways there are for each sum to occur by completing the chart at right.

Red die						
6						
5						
4						
3		𝍸				
2						
1	//					
	1	2	3	4	5	6

White die

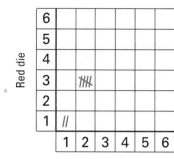

4. Compare the *experimental* with the *theoretical* results by drawing a bar graph with the bars for each type of result adjacent and in a different color.

Outcome	2	3	4	5	6	7	8	9	10	11	12
Frequency											
Experimental Probability	$\frac{}{36}$	$\frac{}{36}$	$\frac{}{36}$	$\frac{}{36}$	$\frac{}{36}$	$\frac{}{36}$	$\frac{}{36}$	$\frac{}{36}$	$\frac{}{36}$	$\frac{}{36}$	$\frac{}{36}$

Outcome	2	3	4	5	6	7	8	9	10	11	12
Frequency											
Theoretical Probability	$\frac{}{36}$	$\frac{}{36}$	$\frac{}{36}$	$\frac{}{36}$	$\frac{}{36}$	$\frac{}{36}$	$\frac{}{36}$	$\frac{}{36}$	$\frac{}{36}$	$\frac{}{36}$	$\frac{}{36}$

3. Count the frequency of each sum, and record it in the first line of the chart immediately above. Write the theoretical probability in the last line.
5. Write a paragraph describing similarities and differences.

An approach that helps children understand dependent events involves giving children a problem that they can simulate and then having them develop and discuss a tree diagram of the problem. For example, prepare two identical boxes, one containing one hockey card and two baseball cards, the other containing one of each. Label the bottom of the first box A and the bottom of the second box B; place a label on the bottom of each box so that the label is not visible when a box is selected. In groups of three, one child shuffles the boxes, one keeps a record, and the other randomly chooses a box, randomly chooses a card from that box, and then checks the label so the recorder can keep a proper record. Each group member should perform each role 10 times; then the group should discuss their results. One expected observation is that if Box B is chosen, the chance of getting a hockey card is better than if Box A is chosen. After children have discussed this problem, develop a tree diagram for the problem (Figure 16-39).

Trial	Box A		Box B	
	H	B	H	B
1		✓		
2			✓	
3		✓		
4				✓

More advanced *simulation* activities are appropriate for the middle grades. Consider the following problem:

Ten hunters are hunting together. All 10 are perfect shots; that is, they never miss. Ten Canadian geese fly up at the same time. The 10 hunters stand at the same time, randomly choose a goose, and simultaneously shoot. On the average, how many geese would survive?

In the earlier simulation, shaking a die or drawing a card from a set of six worked well. Although the cards would work here as well, challenge children to think of other ways to simulate this problem. Children may suggest that 10 children each should write the number of the goose he or she chooses (0 to 9 or 1 to 10) on a piece of paper. Then they could record all numbers chosen and determine which numbers were not chosen by any of the group.

This may also be a good time for children to explore a table of random numbers. Give children a table of random numbers and challenge them to use it to solve the hunters and geese problem. The partial table in Figure 16-40 suggests that you begin at any random position and record the next 10 digits either horizontally or vertically. Digits from 0 to 9 not included in the list would represent the geese that survived. Repeat the experiment several

FIGURE 16-39 Tree Diagram for Hockey and Baseball Card Problem

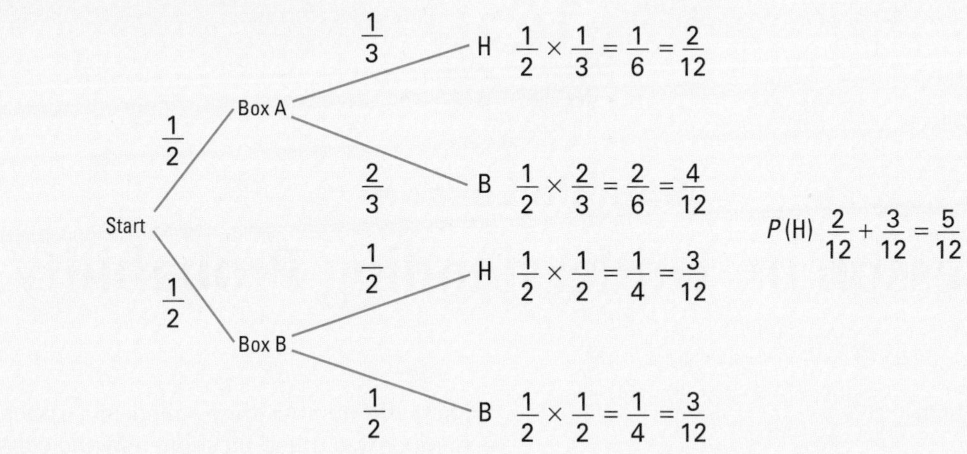

FIGURE 16-40 Partial Table of Random Numbers

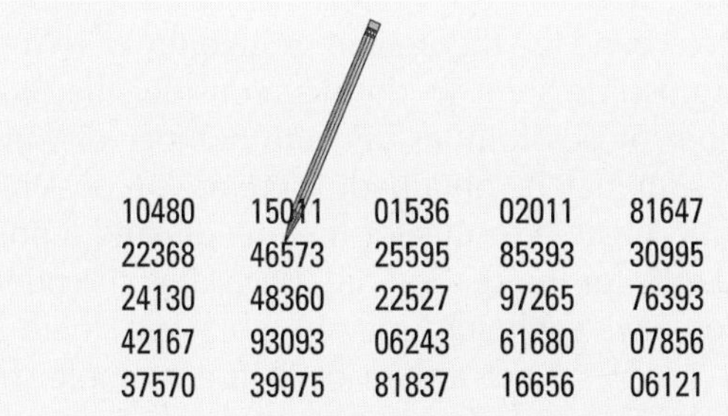

10480	15011	01536	02011	81647
22368	46573	25595	85393	30995
24130	48360	22527	97265	76393
42167	93093	06243	61680	07856
37570	39975	81837	16656	06121

Beginning from the point of the pencil, 10 random numbers reading horizontally are: 5, 7, 3, 2, 5, 5, 9, 5, 8, 5. Digits not included are: 0, 1, 4, 6. For this trial, 4 geese survived.

times to answer the question "On the *average,* how many geese would survive?"

> **myeducationlab** To explore your own understanding of percents, go to chapter 16 in the Book-Specific Resources section in the MyEducationLab for your course. Select the Activities section and complete the activity "Fair Games."

Technology and Data

Analyzing data can involve a significant amount of computation. This work may, at times, be used to reinforce paper-and-pencil computation. However, because the emphasis should not be on computation but on obtaining, understanding, and using the calculated results, consider having children do most of the computation on a calculator or computer.

The graphing software mentioned earlier in this chapter can be used to graph collected data. The visual display often makes it easier to interpret the data. In most cases, computers construct graphs from data entered into a spreadsheet. A spreadsheet is also a useful medium for understanding measures of central tendency and other statistics. Most spreadsheets have built-in functions for mean, median, mode, maximum, and minimum, as well as procedures for sorting data. Given a set of data, children could be encouraged to change one or more values, predict what effect the change will have on one or more of the measures of central tendency, and then observe the change or changes. This kind of exploration could help children understand the key ideas before they learn computational procedures (Wilson & Krapfl, 1995).

> **myeducationlab** Go to the Assignments and Activities section of Topic 13: "Data Analysis" in the MyEducationLab for your course and complete the activity "Laptops for Data in 5th Grade." Note what the teachers have to say about using laptops as part of instruction.

Conclusion

In today's technological age, the collection, organization, and interpretation of data are important to almost everyone of almost every age. Children need to have experiences with data analysis to help them deal with the large amount of information that is available to them.

Initially, children can collect data themselves through surveys or other means to answer questions they have identified. Later, they can gather information from secondary sources such as encyclopedias, newspapers, and the Internet.

Similarly, the first approach to probability needs to be experimental. Children can conduct experiments to determine the probability of particular events occurring. This active approach will make these topics interesting and enjoyable and it will also enable children to develop conceptual understanding that will serve them well in their everyday lives and careers.

CHAPTER

16

Sample Lesson

A Lesson on Understanding Probability

Grade level: Seventh

Materials: One pair of dice for each pair of students

Lesson objective: Students will use dice to examine, calculate, and understand experimental and theoretical probability.

Standards link: Students use theoretical probability and proportions to make approximate predictions (NCTM *Curriculum Focal Points*, grade 7).

Launch: Display a pair of dice and ask students, "If I rolled these two dice, what number is most likely to come up?" What numbers are possible when rolling two dice? Since we're rolling two die, each numbered 1 through 6, the range of possible sums is 2 through 12. Is each sum equally likely? Optional: make a class chart of students' predictions for the most likely sum of two dice.

Solicit recommendations about how to determine the most likely sum, including conducting an experiment and making a chart of possible rolls. Explain that students will be rolling two dice 50 times and recording the sum of the dice. Discuss possible ways of recording the data, such as a chart showing the possible sums from 2 through 12, along with space to tally each roll.

Explore: Have students individually make a prediction for the most likely sum. Then in pairs, have each student take turns rolling the dice a total of 50 times and recording the sum of the dice. Which number came up most often?

Summarize: As students complete their 50 rolls, have one student from each group come to the front of the room and record on a large class tally chart the number they rolled most often. What number was rolled most often by the class? What numbers were close? What numbers were rarely rolled? Discuss possible reasons for this distribution of sums.

Determine the theoretical probability of rolling each possible sum. To do this, consider the total number of possibilities and the number of ways each sum may be obtained. There are 36 possible rolls: 6 possible results for the first die and 6 possible rolls for the second die. Regarding the number of ways each sum may be obtained, there is only 1 way to get a sum of 2, for example: by rolling a 1 and a 1. In contrast, there are 5 ways to roll a sum of 8: 2 and 6, 3 and 5, 4 and 4, 5 and 3, 6 and 2.

Calculate the theoretical probability of rolling each possible sum. For example, the probability of rolling an 8 (P(8)) is 5/36, meaning 5 possibilities out of 36 total possibilities. Have each group find the experimental probability from their 50 rolls. For example, the experimental probability of rolling an 8 can be found by counting the number of times they rolled an 8 out of the total number of rolls, which was 50.

Reflect on the findings from the class experiment. How well did your findings match the theoretical probability?

FOLLOW-UP

Complete the following questions.

1. Consider difficulties students might have with this concept and this lesson. What modification could you make to avoid or minimize these issues? What modifications could you make for students with special needs?
2. What might the *next* lesson focus on, and why?

IN PRACTICE

Complete the following activities to include in your professional portfolio.

1. Visit a middle school classroom and informally interview several children to assess their understanding of data analysis, statistics, and probability. What are their understandings and misconceptions?
2. Imagine that you are a classroom teacher, and a parent of one of the children in your class is concerned that you are devoting too much instructional time to data analysis, statistics, and probability. How would you respond?
3. Write a series of lesson plans to introduce the three measures of central tendency.

 Now go to Topic 13: "Data Analysis" in the MyEducationLab (www.myeducationlab.com) for your course, where you can:

- Find learning outcomes for "Data Analysis" along with the national standards that connect to these outcomes.
- Apply and practice your understanding of the core teaching skills identified in the chapter with a Building Teaching Skills and Dispositions learning unit.
- Complete Assignments and Activities that can help you understand the chapter content more deeply.
- Complete *enVision MATH* Sample Curricula assignments that allow you to examine and work with chapters from *enVision MATH,* a K-6 mathematics program.
- Check your comprehension of the content covered in the chapter by going to the Study Plan in the Book-Specific Resources for your text. Here you will be able to take a chapter quiz, receive feedback on your answers, and then access Review, Practice, and Enrichment activities to enhance your understanding of chapter content.
- Go to Chapter 16 of the Book-Specific Resources for your text to explore mathematical reasoning related to chapter content in the Activities section.

LINKS TO THE INTERNET

Exploring Data

http://www.mathforum.org/workshops/usi/dataproject/

Contains lesson plans for collecting, analyzing, and displaying data, links to statistics software on the Internet, and suggested discussion questions.

Math Goodies: Probability

http://www.mathgoodies.com/lessons/toc_vol6.html

Contains many lessons on probability.

RESOURCES FOR TEACHERS

Books on Data and Probability

Burns, M. (1995). *Math by All Means: Probability, Grades 3–4.* Sausalito, CA: Math Solutions Publications.

Lindquist, M. M. (1992). *Making Sense of Data: Curriculum Evaluation Standards for School Mathematics Addenda Series, Grades K–6.* Reston, VA: National Council of Teachers of Mathematics.

Zawojewski, J. S. (1991). *Dealing with Data and Chance: Curriculum Evaluation Standards for School Mathematics Addenda Series, Grades 5–8.* Reston, VA: National Council of Teachers of Mathematics.

Children's Literature

Ash, Russell (1999). *Factastic Book of 1,001 Lists.* New York: DK Children.

Geringer, L. (1987). *A Three Hat Day.* New York: Harper Trophy.

Juster, Norton (2000). *The Phantom Tollbooth.* New York: Random House Books for Young Readers.

Meddaugh, Susan (1998). *Martha Blah Blah.* Boston: Houghton Mifflin/Walter Lorraine Books.

Van Allsburg, Chris (1981). *Jumanji.* Boston: Houghton Mifflin.

CHAPTER

17

Developing Algebraic Thinking

NCTM CONNECTING WITH THE STANDARDS

The National Council of Teachers of Mathematics (NCTM) Principles and Standards emphasizes the importance of helping children investigate and analyze patterns, stating that "students should investigate numerical and geometric patterns and express them mathematically in words or symbols. They should analyze the structure of the pattern and how it grows or changes, organize this information systematically, and use their analysis to develop generalizations about the mathematical relationships in the pattern" (NCTM, 2000, p. 159). The NCTM document goes on to note that "systematic experience with patterns can build up to an understanding of the idea of function (Smith, 2000), and experience with numbers and their properties lays a foundation for later work with symbols and algebraic expressions" (NCTM, 2000, p. 37).

The NCTM (2006) *Curriculum Focal Points* mentions developing understanding of algebraic concepts from prekindergarten through grade eight. They state that students in prekindergarten, kindergarten, and first grade should develop understanding of sequential and growing patterns and properties of numbers, such as odd and even numbers and multiples and factors.

Starting in grade three, students examine functional relations and use rules to describe a sequence of numbers. In fifth grade, students "use patterns, models, and relationships as contexts for writing and solving simple equations and inequalities; create graphs of simple equations; and develop an understanding of the order of operations" (NCTM, 2006, p. 17). In grades six through eight, students write equations and expressions; use commutative, associative, and distributive properties; and solve linear equations.

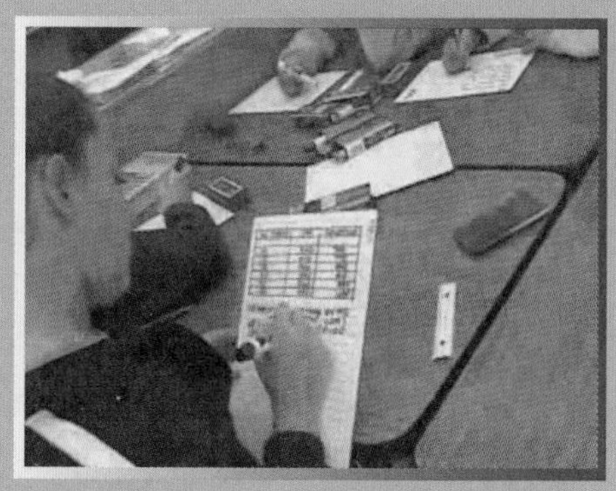

Developing Your Math Teaching Skills

When you have finished studying this chapter, you should be able to do the following:

- Describe models to help children understand operations on integers, and give an example of how to use a model for each operation.
- Discuss how work with patterns helps children think algebraically.
- Discuss what children should understand about variables.

ASSESSING MATHEMATICS UNDERSTANDING

In order to become familiar with the mathematics concepts and procedures discussed in this chapter, take a few minutes to complete the following *Chapter 17 Preassessment.* Answer each question on your own. Then think about the possible misunderstandings or difficulties

some elementary school children might have when solving each problem. If you are able, administer this assessment to a child, and analyze his or her understanding of these topics.

Are these number sentences true or false?

1. $5 + 4 = 9$
2. $7 = 3 + 4$
3. $8 = 8$
4. $6 + 5 = 6 + 5$
5. $7 + 4 = 14 - 3$
6. $7 + 4 = 11 - 2$
7. What number can you put in the box to make this a true number sentence?

   $8 + 4 = \square + 5$

   Explain your thinking.

Examining Classroom Practice

Steve Klass's sixth-graders are exploring patterns by solving the "Tiling a Patio" problem from the NCTM *Navigations* series (Cuevas & Yeatts, 2001):

> *Alfredo Gomez is designing square patios. Each patio has a square garden area in the center. Alfredo uses brown tiles to represent the soil of the garden. Around each garden, he designs a border of white tiles. The figures above show the three smallest square patios that he can design with brown tiles for the garden and white tiles for the border. How many tiles will be in the next largest patio? (p. 18)*

Mr. Klass began the lesson by introducing the problem and displaying the three smallest patios on the overhead projector, using transparent color tiles to represent the soil and the border. He asked the children to describe the three patios.

Gail said, "They all have a brown square in the middle." Mike said, "I agree, and I see a pattern in the number of brown tiles in the middle—it goes one, four, nine."

Mr. Klass asked the children to work with a partner. They should use tiles to build the three smallest patios on their tables and then think about the next patio. He said, "After you've built the first three patios, think about the patterns that you see in them and predict what Patio 4 would look like. Think about how you can organize the data and patterns you observe to help you predict Patio 4."

After building the three patios with tiles, children talked with their partners about what they saw and how to proceed. Many of the groups built Patio 4 with tiles, while others made a sketch. Several groups decided to make a table showing the data.

Mr. Klass called the class back together to discuss their findings. Together they created a class chart containing the data for the first three patios.

Patio Number	Number of Brown Tiles	Number of White Tiles	Total Number of Tiles
1	1	8	9
2	4	12	16
3	9	16	25

The class discussed the patterns they observed in the patios and in the table. Roberto noticed that Gail's and Mike's comments that the brown tiles were squares were correct, and predicted that there would be 16 brown tiles in the middle of Patio 4, since $4 \times 4 = 16$.

Linda noticed that the total number of tiles were square numbers, and predicted that the total number of tiles for Patio 4 would be 36, since 36 is the next perfect square after 25. Tammy agreed, but said she figured it out in a different way: Because all the patios had to be squares, and because Patio 3 was a

Patio 1

Patio 2

Patio 3

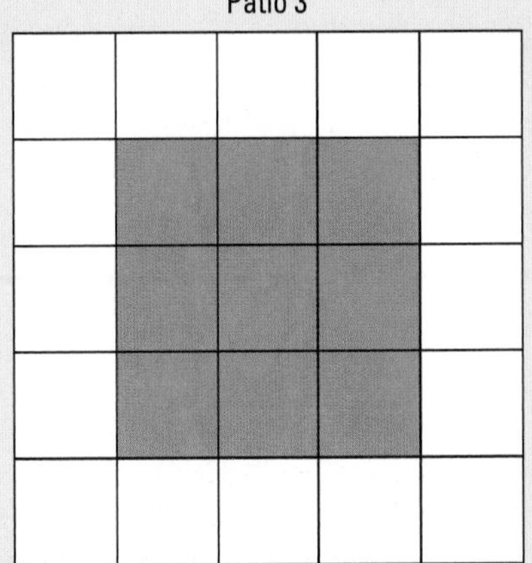

5-by-5 square, Patio 4 had to be a 6-by-6 square, which would take 36 total tiles. The class agreed that each patio and the brown tiles in the middle were all squares.

Then Mr. Klass asked the children about the number of white tiles: "Did anyone see any patterns in the number of white tiles?" Andre said, "They go eight, twelve, sixteen, so the next one will be twenty, four more than sixteen." Mr. Klass asked, "Why do they go up by four?" After some discussion, Jim noticed that when he made Patio 3, he had to add one white tile to each side of those he used for Patio 2. He demonstrated, first counting the white tiles on Patio 2, starting at the top left corner and counting down the side, "one, two, three, one, two, three, one, two, three, one, two, three. That's four groups of three so it's twelve. But on Patio 3, it's one, two, three, four; one, two, three, four; one, two, three, four; one, two, three, four, so that's sixteen."

Mr. Klass asked, "Why did you count in four groups instead of just counting all the tiles?" Jim replied, "Because the square has four sides, so I tried to see what was happening with each side."

Mr. Klass asked, "So what about Patio 4?" Jim said, "it would be one, two, three, four, five, 4 times, so that's twenty." Other children agreed that there would be twenty white tiles in Patio 4. The class added a row for Patio 4 to their class chart.

Patio Number	Number of Brown Tiles	Number of White Tiles	Total Number of Tiles
1	1	8	9
2	4	12	16
3	9	16	25
4	16	20	36

Next Mr. Klass asked, "What if one of Mr. Gomez's clients wanted a huge patio, say Patio 100? How many tiles would be needed for that patio? Can we find a rule that Mr. Gomez could use to find the number of tiles he'd need to build any sized patio? Try to write a sentence or an equation to help Mr. Gomez. Once you write a sentence or a rule, you might want to check to see if it works with the patios we've already built."

The children went back to working with their partners to solve this new problem. After lots of discussion within each group, the class reconvened to share their thinking. Mr. Klass recorded their equations in the class table as children shared them.

Mr. Klass began the discussion by asking children to share their rules for finding the number of brown tiles. Melissa said, "That was pretty easy. It's just the patio number times itself. So for Patio 5, we'd need five times five or twenty-five brown tiles." Mr. Klass asked if she was able to write an equation for this rule; Melissa wrote "$brown = p \times p$." Mr. Klass asked if anyone else wrote an equation for the number of brown tiles. Mike said, "I wrote $b = p^2$." The class discussed these two equations and decided that both were correct and that Mr. Gomez would need 100^2 or 10,000 brown tiles for Patio 100.

Next, Mr. Klass asked children to share their rules for finding the total number of tiles. Linda said, "That was pretty easy, too. We saw that they were all squares so I just needed to figure out what number squared gave me the total number of tiles. The patio number squared was too small, so I tried other numbers and noticed that it was two more than the patio number squared. My equation was $total = (p + 2)^2$. So for Patio 100, Mr. Gomez would need 102^2 or 10,404 total tiles."

Mr. Klass then asked children to share their rules for finding the number of white tiles. Gail started, saying "I used Jim's pattern. He found the number of white tiles by looking at it as four groups,

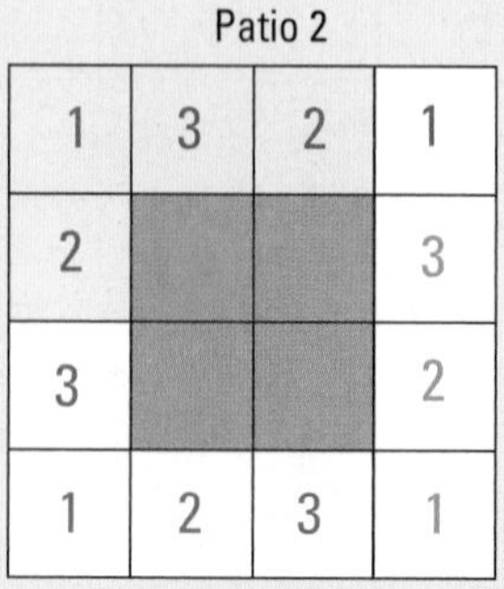

Patio 2

1	3	2	1
2			3
3			2
1	2	3	1

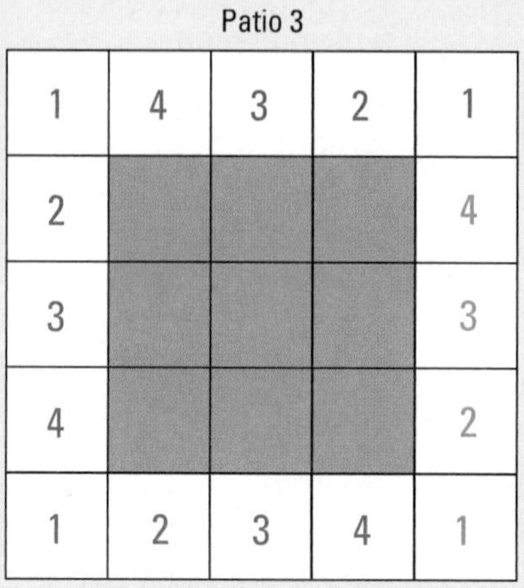

Patio 3

1	4	3	2	1
2				4
3				3
4				2
1	2	3	4	1

so that's four times something. So I tried four times the patio number, but that was too small. Then I noticed that four times one more than the patio number gave me the right answer. So my equation was *white* = $4(p + 1)$. For Patio 100, Mr. Gomez needs 4×101 white tiles, which is 404."

Patio Number	Number of Brown Tiles	Number of White Tiles	Total Number of Tiles
1	1	8	9
2	4	12	16
3	9	16	25
4	16	20	36
100	10,000	404	10,404
p	p^2	$4(p + 1)$	$(p + 2)^2$

Analyzing Assessment Results

All of these problems involve adding or subtracting. What was your general reaction to solving the problems? Did they all seem to be equally difficult, or were some problems easier for you to think about? Do you think any of the problems would be harder for elementary-school children to solve? What aspects of problems do you think make them harder for children to solve?

Analyze each problem. How did you (and/or the student you administered the assessment to) solve each of the problems?

1. $5 + 4 = 9$

2. $7 = 3 + 4$

3. $8 = 8$

4. $6 + 5 = 6 + 5$

Comments: Were these problems equally difficult? Problem 1 is usually the easiest of all of these problems; it's presented in the most common form for addition problems, with two addends (5 and 4) on the left side, and the sum, 9, on the right side. Notice that problem 2 is switched, with the sum, 7, on the left side and the two addends (3 and 4) on the right side. This arrangement is used less often, and children are less familiar with it. Many children will say that the number sentence in Problem 2 is false because "it's written wrong." Problems 3 and 4 also are presented in different forms. Problem 3 doesn't include an operation sign, so most students think that it's false. Problem 4 has two operations signs, one on each side of the equals sign, and this is often unfamiliar to students.

5. $7 + 4 = 14 - 3$

6. $7 + 4 = 11 - 2$

Comments: These problems each have two operations signs, as in Problem 4. But these problems are more difficult, since the numbers on the left side of the equals sign are not identical to those on the right side, as in Problem 4. Students often have a hard time with problems such as this, since they believe that the answer needs to follow the equals sign.

7. What number can you put in the box to make this a true number sentence?

$8 + 4 = \square + 5$

Comments: Once again, we have a problem that seems to be quite easy. But most elementary school students believe that 12 should be in the box, since $8 + 4 = 12$. These students sometimes will add another equals sign at the end of the number sentence, and add a 17, as below:

$8 + 4 = 12 + 5 = 17$

Take a minute and reflect on this assessment. Were some problems easier than others? What factors made them easier? What do you want to learn more about in order to help children understand these concepts?

Common Student Misunderstandings about Algebra:

- Inability to make sense of concepts.
- Lack of understanding of the meaning of the equals sign.

Are there any other misunderstandings that children may have about algebra concepts? It is important to assess what children understand and are still working on understanding, in order to plan instruction that meets their needs.

Building on Assessment Results

Think about what can be done to help strengthen children's understandings and minimize (and hopefully eradicate) their misunderstandings and misconceptions. What might we do to help students understand algebra concepts?

A key element of all instruction is to make sure that students understand the concept. Students need to visualize concepts and relationships. This usually is best done with some sort of manipulative material, asking students to solve problems set in familiar, meaningful situations and to examine the reasonableness of their solutions. The table below lists several common misunderstandings and what a teacher can do to help children with these misunderstandings.

Think back to Mr. Klass's lesson. How did he involve his children in actively searching for patterns? How did he support children in constructing, analyzing, and generalizing patterns? The ideas in this chapter focus on helping children understand algebraic concepts and think algebraically.

IF students think that . . .	THEN have students . . .
all number sentences need to have two numbers on the left of the equals sign and the answer on the right	*model* the problem with a manipulative material to determine if the quantities on each side of the equals sign are equivalent.
they can string a series of numbers and operation signs together with several equals signs (such as $8 + 4 = 12 + 5 = 17$)	*ask* them to find the value of what they started with ($8 + 4 = 12$) and decide if that's equal to the last quantity (17).

What Is Algebra?

Algebra, as defined by *Random House Word Menu* (Glazier, 1998), is a "theory and practice of arithmetic operations that uses symbols, especially letters, to represent unknown variables in equations" (p. 143). Algebraic reasoning requires representing, generalizing, and formalizing patterns and regularities found in all aspects of mathematics. In algebra, these patterns are generalized through the use of symbolic notation with variables. Equations and formulas are developed to represent the relationships that occur from the patterns. The study of relationships that develop from these meaningful contexts leads to the study of functions.

Algebra is a language of relationships and patterns of symbols and is an abstract system with its own rules, operations, and definitions (Usiskin, 1992, p. 27). Algebra is best learned in context and is more easily understood if pre-algebraic topics are a part of the mathematics curriculum throughout children's early and intermediate school years. Thus, mathematics in the middle grades can bridge the transition between the concretely based elementary mathematics curriculum and the more abstract, symbolic secondary curriculum.

What do we know of U.S. children's understanding of algebra? In the Third International Mathematics and Science Study (Peak, 1996), eighth-grade students scored close to the international average in algebraic patterns, relations, expressions, and equations. Compared with the top-scoring countries such as Singapore, Japan, Hong Kong, and Korea, the U.S. eighth-graders performed at the seventh-grade level. Nonalgebra class textbooks focused more on arithmetic skills than on algebra, geometry, and measurement, and what little algebra was included was found to be at a low level of knowledge and skills (Silver, 1998). The 2003 Mathematics Assessment of the National Assessment of Educational Progress (NAEP) showed improved performance in algebra, though performance gaps continue to exist between racial and ethnic groups (Chazan et al., 2007). We can continue to do a better job helping children understand the many algebraic concepts and connecting that understanding with the processes and skills that help make algebra accessible to more children by laying a foundation for algebraic thinking in earlier years.

Algebra is often defined as generalized arithmetic and is identified as a gateway to higher mathematical development. Kaput (1998) comments that it is difficult to identify an area of mathematics that does not require some degree of algebraic reasoning. Nasser and Carifio (1995) believe that algebraic reasoning is the entry-level skill in most sciences as well as for business, industry, and technical jobs. Yet, eight percent of 17-year-olds reported that their highest mathematics course taken in high school was below the level of algebra. However, the inclusion of algebra as one of the five content standards in the *Principles and Standards for School Mathematics* (NCTM, 2000) indicates the seriousness of the effort to engage teachers in seeing the need for providing children the opportunity to learn to reason algebraically.

The foundation of algebra begins with a strong understanding of arithmetic. Teachers can help students see algebra as a generalized form of arithmetic and be able to make algebraic generalizations without necessarily using algebraic notation (Kieran, 2007). Bay-Williams (2001) notes that algebraic experiences in elementary school lay the foundation for a more formalized study of algebra in middle and high school.

According to House (2001), in order to think algebraically, children must be able to do the following:

- Understand patterns, relations, and functions;
- Represent and analyze mathematical situations and structures using algebraic symbols;

NCTM ALGEBRA STANDARDS AND EXPECTATIONS ADDRESSED IN THIS CHAPTER

Instructional programs from pre-K–12 should enable all students to—	In prekindergarten through grade 2 all students should— (NCTM, 2000, p. 90)	In grades 3–5 all students should— (NCTM, 2000, p. 158)	In grades 6–8 all students should— (NCTM, 2000, p. 222)
• understand patterns, relations, and functions. • represent and analyze mathematical situations and structures using algebraic symbols. • use mathematical models to represent and understand quantitative relationships. • analyze change in various concepts.	• sort, classify, and order objects by size, number, and other properties. • recognize, describe, and extend patterns such as sequences of sounds and shapes or simple numeric patterns and translate from one representation to another. • analyze how both repeating and growing patterns are generated. • illustrate general principles and properties of operations, such as commutativity, using specific numbers. • use concrete, pictorial, and verbal representations to develop an understanding of invented and conventional symbolic notations. • model situations that involve the addition and subtraction of whole numbers, using objects, pictures, and symbols. • describe qualitative change, such as a student's growing taller. • describe quantitative change, such as a student's growing two inches in one year.	• describe, extend, and make generalizations about geometric and numeric patterns. • represent and analyze patterns and functions, using words, tables, and graphs. • identify such properties as commutativity, associativity, and distributivity and use them to compute with whole numbers. • represent the idea of a variable as an unknown quantity using a letter or a symbol. • express mathematical relationships using equations. • model problem situations with objects and use representations such as graphs, tables, and equations to draw conclusions. • investigate how a change in one variable relates to a change in a second variable. • identify and describe situations with constant or varying rates of change and compare them.	• represent, analyze, and generalize a variety of patterns with tables, graphs, words, and when possible, symbolic rules. • relate and compare different forms of representation for a relationship. • identify functions as linear or nonlinear and contrast their properties from tables, graphs, or equations. • develop an initial conceptual understanding of different uses of variables. • explore relationships between symbolic expressions and graphs of lines, paying particular attention to the meaning of intercept and slope. • use symbolic algebra to represent situations and to solve problems, especially those that involve linear relationships. • recognize and generate equivalent forms for simple algebraic expressions and solve linear equations. • model and solve contextualized problems using various representations, such as graphs, tables, and equations. • use graphs to analyze the nature of changes in quantities in linear relationships.

- Use mathematical models to represent and understand quantitative relationships; and
- Analyze change in various contexts. (p. 2)

The goal of this chapter is to show how the whole-number system can be extended and how concepts related to integers, patterns and relationships, variables, expressions, functions, and graphing can be developed so that children learn how to use the powerful language of algebra and develop algebraic thinking. When algebraic thinking is developed in a meaningful way, children can learn to utilize that thinking as a useful tool for solving many real-world problems.

Integers

The study of integers provides children with an opportunity to extend the whole-number system. Integers provide a way for us to express numbers as positive and negative. Even though models for negative numbers may be less intuitive to children than models for fractions and decimals that they may have previously learned, children generally find learning about the system of integers to be easier than working with the positive rational numbers. The notation for negative numbers is less complex than that for rational numbers, and typically only one- or two-digit numbers are used in examples and problems. Furthermore, the rules for operating on integers are easier to learn and apply than the corresponding algorithms with fractions. The challenge for teachers is to assist children in understanding *why* as well as *how* these rules work. The following sections describe an instructional approach that connects computational procedures to number properties and patterns and to the meaning of operations, using integers in the context of real-world applications.

Introducing Integers

Many situations in everyday life require numbers that deal with direction as well as magnitude. Children know, for example, that a temperature of 5° Fahrenheit below zero is referred to as "five below" and written −5°F. Young children encounter negative numbers when they use calculators to find answers for expressions such as 2 − 5 or continue to "count down" past zero and see −1, −2, −3, and so on, appear in the display.

The concept of a negative number is used when a person spends more money than he or she earns and when a football team loses more yards than it gains. Other real-world examples include profit and loss, credits and debits, above and below sea level, winning and losing points, golf scores above and below par, and positive and negative electrical charges.

NCTM Principles and Standards Link 17-1

Content Strand: Algebra

Much of the symbolic and structural emphasis in algebra can build on students' extensive experiences with number. Algebra is also closely linked to geometry and to data analysis. The ideas included in the Algebra Standard constitute a major component of the school mathematics curriculum and help to unify it. Algebraic competence is important in adult life, both on the job and as preparation for postsecondary education. All students should learn algebra. (NCTM, 2000, p. 37)

NCTM Principles and Standards Link 17-2

Content Strand: Algebra

In lower grades, students may have connected negative integers in appropriate ways to informal knowledge derived from everyday experiences, such as below-zero winter temperatures or lost yards on football plays. In the middle grades, students should extend these initial understandings of integers. Positive and negative integers should be seen as useful for noting relative changes or values. Students can also appreciate the utility of negative integers when they work with equations whose solutions require them, such as $2x + 7 = 1$. (NCTM, 2000, p. 217)

Teachers can introduce negative numbers as *opposites* of counting numbers. To make the distinction between the sign of the number and the operation of subtraction, the *opposite* of 3 is written −3 and is read *negative 3* rather than *minus 3*. The counting numbers, their opposites, and zero form the set of integers: . . . −3, −2, −1, 0, 1, 2, 3, . . . Teachers can now refer to the counting numbers as the *positive integers*; the number 3 is sometimes called *positive 3* and written +3. The integer 0 is neither positive nor negative. Integers are sometimes referred to as *signed* or *directed* numbers.

A number line can help children visualize integers. Even in the early grades, it is important to introduce an integer number line so children begin to have a sense of the relationships among numbers. To construct the integer number line, first mark a point to represent 0 and measure equal segments to the right to identify the positive points 1, 2, 3, . . . and equal segments measured to the left to determine the negative points −1, −2, −3, ...

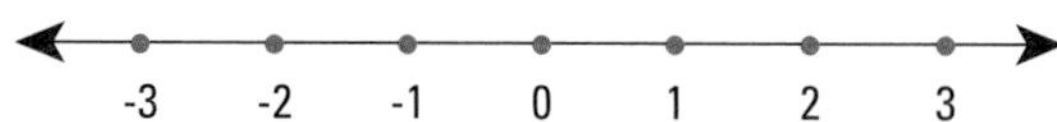

You can provide children with a real-world context for integers by using the idea of the negative direction as heading west and the positive direction as heading east, with the student's home at position zero (see Figure 17-1). If children walk five blocks east to the local school and seven blocks west to the library, they will be at the position −2 or rather 2 blocks west of home. Figure 17-1 shows several similar scenarios that will help children see that negative number operations are easy to visualize. Another possibility is to place a number line on the classroom floor. Designate a middle location that can be labeled 0 and designate one side with positive values and the other with negative values; include + or − signs at the end of the respective sides. Have one student stand on the 0 and move 5 spaces in the positive direction, and have another student begin at 0 and move 5 spaces in the negative direction. Ask children to identify who is farther

FIGURE 17-1 Real-World Integer Models

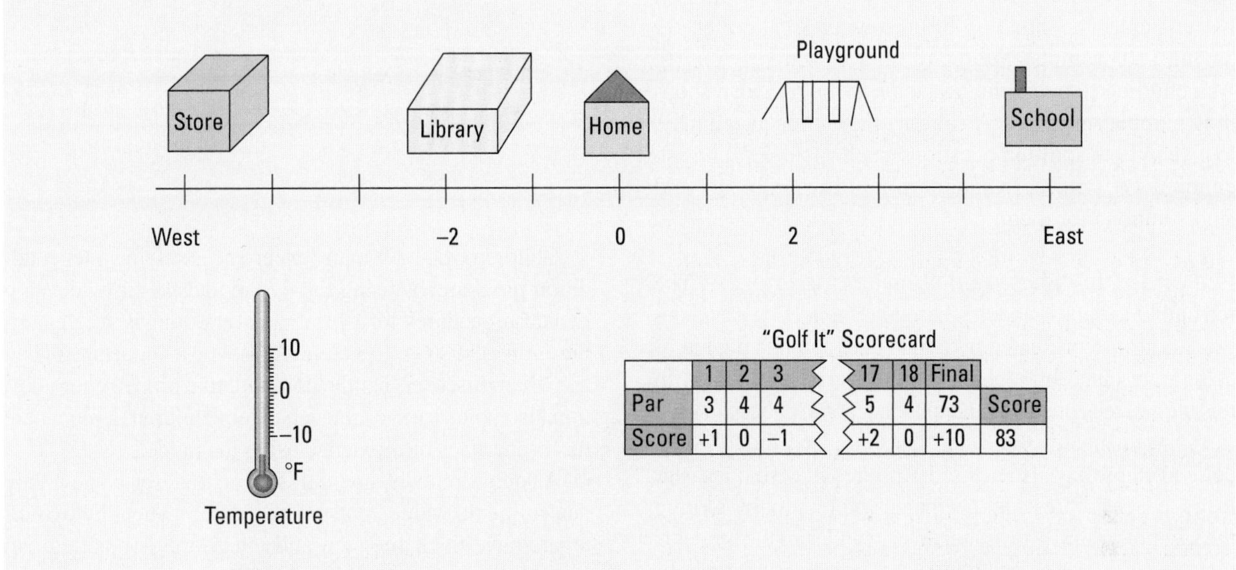

from 0. Children can then model $5 - 7$ and $-3 + 4$ on the number line.

Opposites, such as 3 and -3, are equal distances from zero on the number line. Integers may also be thought of as directed distances on the number line rather than points. As such, integers may be represented by arrows that indicate both length and direction. Thus, -3 can be represented as an arrow 3 units in length and pointing left. Note that the arrow can be moved along the line to positions other than the 0 to -3 segment. Using this type of explanation and the previous example involving the number line on the floor, children can come to understand the idea that the absolute value of a number is the distance to the point from 0. For instance, $|3|=|-3|=3$, and $|2-5|=|-3|=3$. In addition, the use of arrow notation will be useful when working with the operations on integers in the following sections.

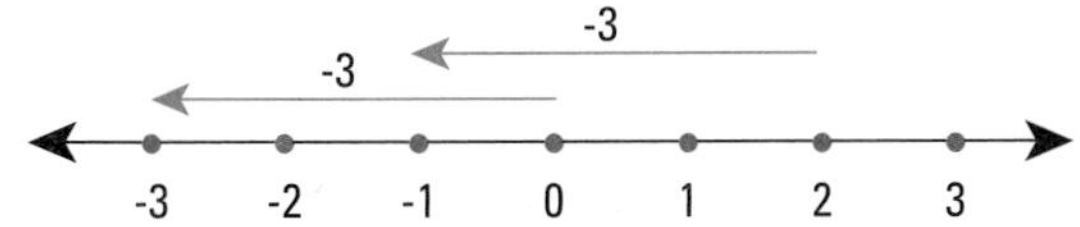

Ordering Integers

The number line is a particularly useful model for ordering integers. For the whole numbers, the greater of two numbers is situated to the right of the preceding number on the number line; this is also true for the negative integers. Children need to use words and symbols to indicate order relations between particular pairs of integers, such as $-3 < 2$ and $4 > -5$. Encourage children to look for these patterns in words or in writing. Children might note, for example, that any negative number is less than zero and is also less than any positive number.

The fact $-7 < -4$ may at first seem confusing; however, a basic explanation that -7 is farther to the left on the number line, making it smaller than -4, should rapidly clear up any confusion. Thinking in terms of temperature, teachers may ask questions such as "Is it colder at $-7\,°C$ than it is at $-4\,°C$"; or, considering depth, "Is 700 m below sea level deeper than 400 m below sea level?" Extensive practice in ordering negative and positive integers, identifying the direction from zero, and labeling points on the number line will familiarize children with a basic knowledge of integers.

Before engaging children in operations on integers, have them consider real-life situations that require the process of ordering negative and positive integers. Ask children to draw models to represent their ideas. The following are some examples:

- What happens if the temperature falls 16 degrees at night, but rises 20 degrees during the day? If the temperature started off at 60 degrees, what is the ending temperature?
- You are in an elevator that moved up 6 flights and then down 9 flights. If you are now on the seventh floor, on which floor did you start?

Providing real-world settings will motivate children to explore and understand the concept of integers.

Adding Integers

Of all the operations on integers, addition is the easiest for children to understand. Two approaches suggested for developing integer addition include the red and blue cubes model and the number line. Before providing any direct instruction, however, give children opportunities to draw on their previous knowledge to construct solutions to addition problems. The teacher might begin with real-world situations involving earning and spending money. For example, the situation of borrowing \$7 and then repaying \$10 prompts children to find the sum of −7 + 10. Ask children to solve the problems and write corresponding number sentences. An alternative approach would be to give integer addition questions, such as 5 + −7, and ask children to write corresponding real-life problems and find solutions for them.

Red and blue cubes model for adding integers. The red and blue cubes model is based on the idea that one degree of heat, represented by a red cube, and one degree of cold, represented by a blue cube, neutralize each other. In this model, red (positive) and blue (negative) cubes are used to represent positive and negative numbers, though two-colored chips may also be used. Children may find it easier if the teacher represents the charges pictorially by writing the symbols + and − on cubes. The key idea in the model is that a positive and a negative "cancel" each other; symbolically, 1 + −1 = 0. This has been depicted as "Zero, my Hero" in some classrooms and in the short film *Multiplication Rock.* By combining required numbers of red (+) and blue (−) cubes, children easily find answers for different types of addition questions (see Figure 17-2). Note that in the figure, 5 + −2 can also be viewed as the solution to a comparison subtraction problem for whole numbers: How many more red cubes than blue cubes? Pay special attention to finding solutions that equal zero, such as −1 + 1, 2 + −2, etc. This fact will be important in helping children understand the concept of subtracting integers where the minuend (first number) is smaller than the subtrahend (second number), such as 3 − 6. One child wrote the following in her journal after a lesson on adding integers:

> *The interesting thing was how you would add a negative and a posetive [sic] you ended up with a lower number than you started with so it would be like subtracting. (Vance, 1995, p. 14)*

Number line model for adding integers. To use the number line to add two numbers, begin at the point represented by the first addend and move the distance and direction (positive–right, negative–left) indicated by the second addend. Thus, for 2 + −5, start at 2 and move five spaces to the left (negative direction). Children will find that although the number line solution for −5 + 2, where they begin at −5 and move right (positive direction) two spaces, looks different from the previous explanation for 2 + −5, the final result is the same, as shown in Figure 17-3.

FIGURE 17-2 Using Cubes to Add Integers

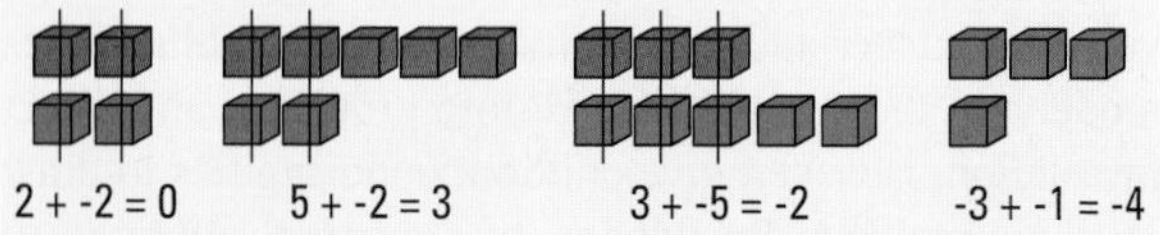

FIGURE 17-3 Using the Number Line to Add

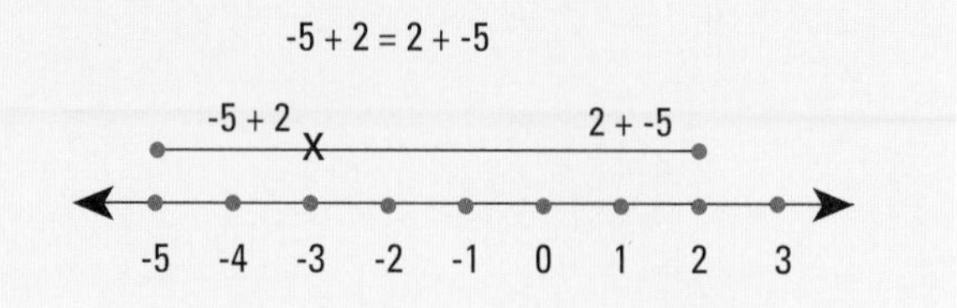

Children who have many experiences solving integer addition problems by using the two models begin to develop mental procedures for getting answers quickly (see examples in Figure 17-4). As children use these models, you can help them discover that the commutative property for addition also holds true for integers. Help children demonstrate this property as they practice using the models.

Ask children who are at this stage to describe how they determine the value and sign of the sum when the two integers have the same sign and when one is positive and one is negative. Some children will begin to generalize the procedure in ways that include the following:

- *When the signs are the same,* add the numbers and maintain the sign.
- *When the signs are different,* subtract the smaller number from the larger number and use the sign of the larger number.

Subtracting Integers

The general rule that states "to subtract an integer, add its opposite" is fairly easy to remember and apply. In fact, because subtraction can always be changed to an addition problem, the previous discussion applies.

However, rather than simply telling children this procedural rule, which offers very little conceptual development about subtraction, you should take time to provide opportunities for children to engage in problem-solving and sense-making experiences involving subtracting integers. These experiences will help them understand the concept behind the rule. For example, ask children to think about the temperature's being −3° and dropping another 6°, resulting in an expression of −3 − 6, and a final temperature of −9°. Children can work in small groups to make up integer subtraction problems involving number sentences, such as 3 − 5 = □ and 3 − −2 = □, and decide on answers and explanations for their problems. Procedures for developing subtraction by using patterns, the number line, and electric charges are discussed in the following paragraphs.

Number pattern approach for subtracting integers. Teachers can ask children to continue patterns such as the following and discuss possible rules suggested by the results.

FIGURE 17-4 Using the Number Line and Red and Blue Cubes Models to Add Integers

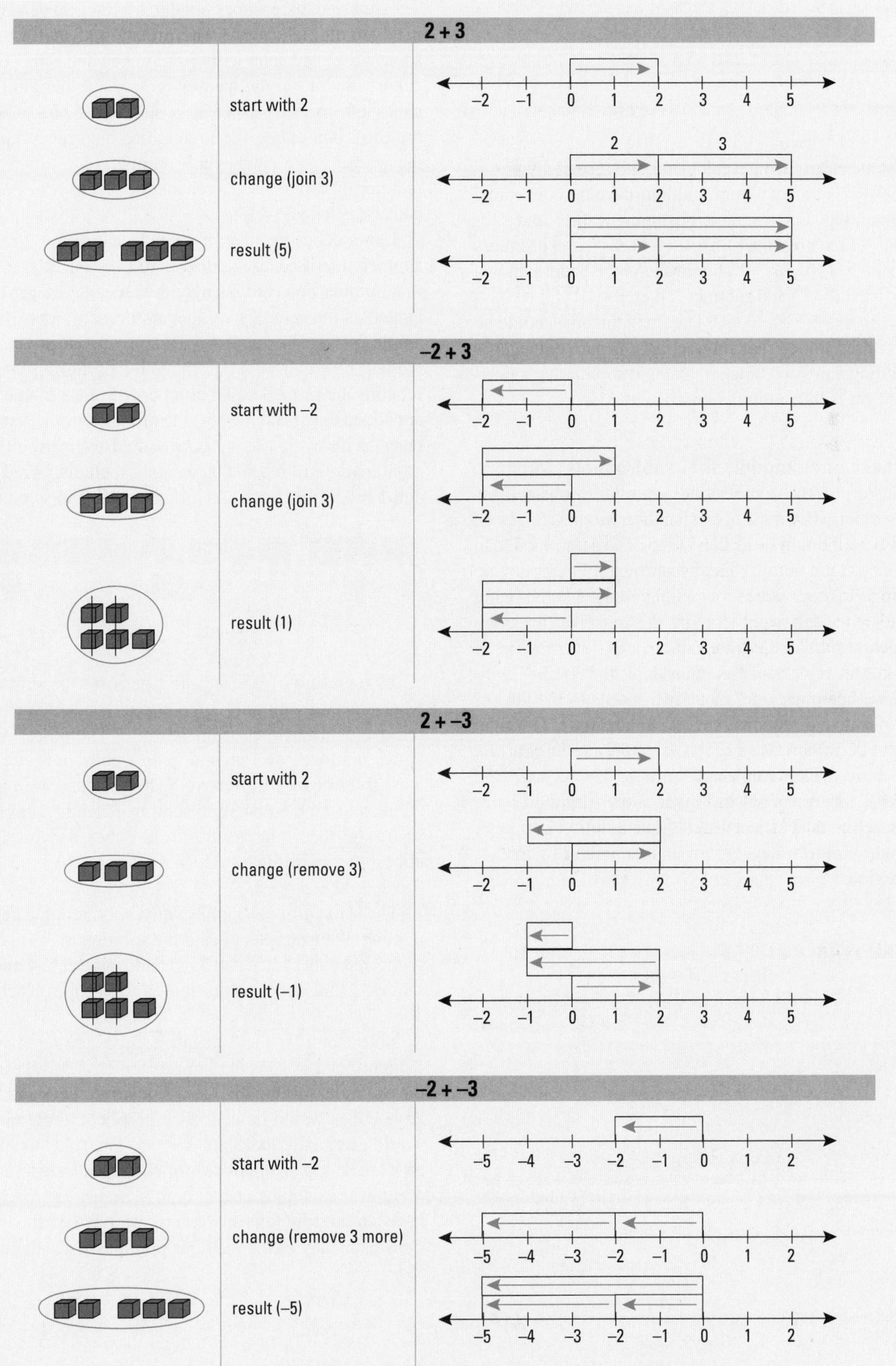

$3 - 1 = 2$	$3 - 2 = 1$
$3 - 2 = 1$	$3 - 1 = 2$
$3 - 3 = 0$	$3 - 0 = 3$
$3 - 4 = \square$	$3 - -1 = \square$
$3 - \square = \square$	$3 - \square = \square$

In some cases, using a calculator and repeatedly pressing the [=] sign may help children develop conceptual understanding. For instance, beginning with 3 and subtracting 1, then pressing [=], [=], [=], [=], [=] produces results of 2, 1, 0, −1, −2 and develops the pattern shown above. Next try −3 and subtract 1; then [=], [=], [=], [=] will result in −4, −5, −6, −7. The final outcome should be that children notice that subtracting a negative integer is like adding a positive integer, and that subtracting a positive integer is like adding a negative integer.

Number line model for subtracting integers. Subtraction on the number line is similar to missing addend addition. If we think of fact families, we know $5 - 2 = \square$ can also be thought of as $2 + \square = 5$. The solution, 3, can be found on the number line by starting at 2 and moving right to 5. In other words, beginning on the 2 and moving 3 spaces to the right (or in the positive direction 3 spaces) results in the final value, 5.

Similarly, $3 - 5 = \square$ is equivalent to $5 + \square = 3$. To solve, we begin at 5 and move two spaces to the left (or in the negative direction 2 spaces) to land on 3. The final answer reflects the *number* of spaces moved and the *direction* of the move. This example and those for $3 - -2 = \square$, and $-1 - 3 = \square$ are shown in Figure 17-5. Although it requires a bit of practice, this "think addition" strategy will help children develop an understanding of integer subtraction.

FIGURE 17-5 Using the Number Line to Subtract Integers

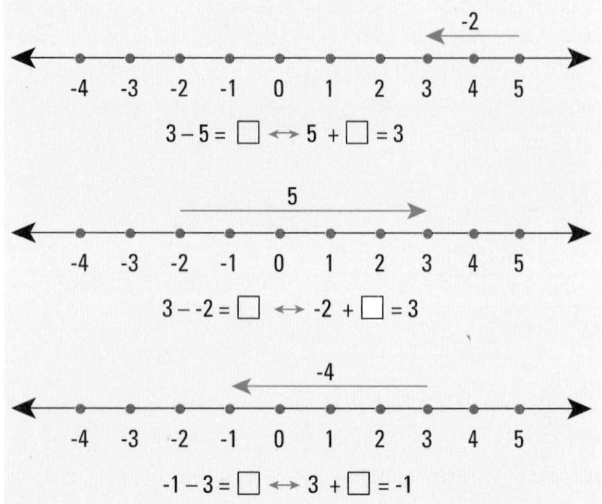

Red and blue cubes model for subtracting integers. The red and blue cubes model of integers lends itself nicely to the "take away" interpretation of subtraction. To solve $5 - 2$, we start with 5 red cubes and remove 2 red cubes; obviously, the answer is 3, since there are 3 red cubes left. To solve $-5 - -2$, we start with 5 blue cubes and remove 2 blue cubes; the 3 remaining blue cubes represent the answer, −3. As with whole numbers, addition from the fact family can be used to check the result: $-5 - -2 = -3$ because $-2 + -3 = -5$.

Using cubes to solve problems such as $3 - 5$ requires another step. Because adding zero ($1 + -1$, $2 + -2$, etc.) to a number does not change its value, an integer can be named as the sum of two integers in many ways. For example, $3 = 3 + (1 + -1) = 3 + (2 + -2)$, and so on. In the red and blue cubes model, the value of a group of cubes remains the same if equal numbers of red and blue cubes are added to (or taken from) the pile. It follows that an integer, such as 3, can be represented by many different combinations of red and blue cubes, including 4 red cubes and 1 blue cube, 5 red and 2 blue cubes, and so on.

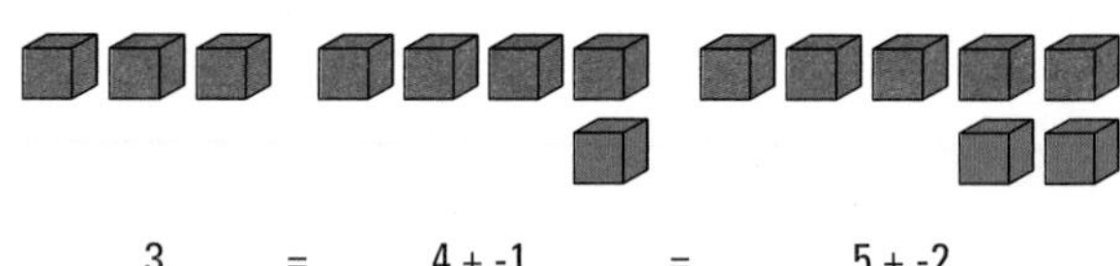

To represent $3 - 5$, we can't perform the subtraction when starting with only 3 red cubes, because we need to remove 5 blue cubes from the pile. Therefore, we add equal numbers of red and blue cubes until we have enough red cubes to remove 5. In this case, we can add 2 cubes of each color (representing +2 and −2 for a total of 0) and then remove the 5 red cubes, leaving 2 blue cubes; the answer is −2. Thus, $3 - 5 = 3 + (2 + -2) - 5 = 3 + 2 + -2 - 5 = -2$.

The same process applies when subtracting a negative number. For example, to find the solution to $3 - -2$, start with 3 red cubes, then add 2 red and 2 blue cubes, and then remove 2 blue cubes, which leaves 5 red cubes. Therefore, $3 - -2 = 5$.

Note that after the 3 negative cubes are removed, the diagram for $2 - -3$ is the same as for $2 + 3$. If we examine the example, solving for $3 - 5$, 5 positive cubes and 5 negative cubes would be added to the pile and the diagram would eventually look like $3 + -5$. The rule "to subtract an integer, add its opposite" follows from an examination of several examples of this type. Another approach is to have children find the answers to two related sets of questions using any of the methods previously developed.

Compare	$5 - 2$	to	$5 + -2$
Compare	$3 - -4$	to	$3 + 4$
Compare	$-2 - 5$	to	$-2 + -5$
Compare	$-6 - -2$	to	$-6 + 2$

FIGURE 17-6 Using the Number Line to Subtract Integers

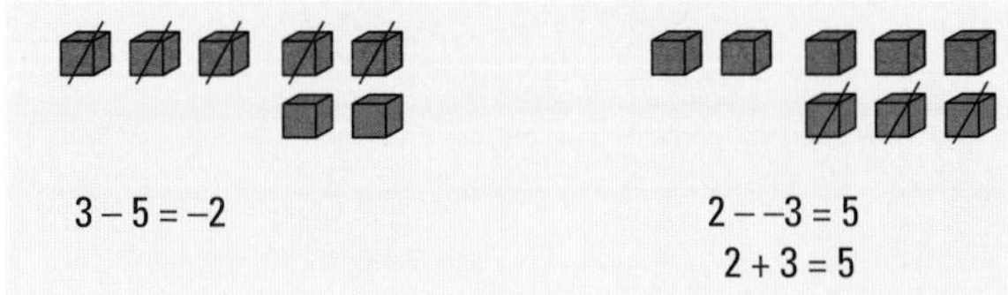

The class then can examine the two groups of problems and discuss how the problems are the *same* (first number and answer) and how they are *different* (the first set of problems is made up of subtraction sentences, whereas the other set consists of addition sentences; the second numbers in corresponding sentences are opposites). Once again, the repeat feature of the calculator will help generalize the rule for subtracting integers. Teachers might then ask children to verbalize a shortcut procedure for subtracting an integer. The result "to subtract an integer, add its opposite" could then be compared with the rule "to add a negative, subtract its positive value" (Figure 17-6).

Additional number line and red and blue cubes models for subtraction are provided in Figure 17-7.

Multiplying Integers

The rules for multiplying integers are straightforward; "the product of two positive or two negative integers is positive," and "the product of a positive and a negative integer is negative." But, as for other operations, it is important that children also understand the meaning of multiplication of integers. When the first factor is positive, children can apply the interpretation of multiplication as repeated addition to find the product. For example, 3 times −2 is the same as three groups of negative 2:

$$3 \times -2 = 3 \text{ groups of } -2 = -2 + -2 + -2 = -6$$

As is true for addition and subtraction, both the red and blue cubes model and the number line model work to explain multiplying of integers.

Red and blue cubes model for multiplying integers. One way to model integer multiplication is the red and blue cubes model, which begins with an empty circle from which cubes will be removed or added. In multiplying integers, the first factor will be either positive or negative. When the first factor is negative, children will think about removing cubes, and when the first factor is positive, children will think about adding cubes. The value of the first factor indicates the number of groups of cubes that are to be added or removed. For example, a first factor of −2 means to remove two groups of cubes, and a first factor of +3 means to add 3 groups of cubes.

The sign of the second factor indicates the size and color of the groups of cubes to be removed or added. If the second factor is negative, groups of blue cubes of that size should be removed or added, and if the second factor is positive, groups of red cubes of that size should be removed or added. Consider the problem −2 × 3. The first factor of −2 means to remove two groups of cubes, whereas the second factor of 3 means to remove groups of 3 red cubes, so −2 × 3 means to remove two groups of 3 red cubes. To do this, we must once again consider the concept of inserting zero; in this case 6 zero pairs of red cubes and blue cubes must be inserted. Now it is possible to remove 2 groups of 3 red cubes, which results in 6 blue cubes, or −6 (see Figure 17-8). Subsequent explanations will explain the other situations, such as −2 × −3 meaning to remove two groups of 3 blue cubes, and 2 × −4 meaning to add two groups of 4 blue cubes.

Number line model for multiplying integers. Another way to model multiplication of integers is to use the number line model, which starts at zero on a number line and moves the number of "jumps" in the indicated direction.

The first factor indicates the number of jumps and the direction of the jumps, with a negative factor meaning to jump to the left and a positive factor meaning to jump to the right. The second factor indicates the length of each jump. For example, consider the problem −2 × 3. The first factor of −2 means to make two jumps to the left. The second factor of 3 means that each jump will be three units long. The jumps will end at −6, which is the answer.

The problems get a little more complicated when the second factor is negative. For example, consider the problem −2 × −3. The first factor of −2 means to make two jumps to the left. The second factor −3 means that each jump will be three units long *in the opposite direction* or, in other words, two jumps that are each three units long *to the right.* The jumps will end at 6, which is the answer, and is the same result as 2 × 3 (see Figure 17-8).

Products such as a negative number times a positive number (e.g., −3 × 2) or a negative number times a negative number (e.g., −3 × −2) do not lend themselves easily to physical models of repeated addition. One approach to understanding these situations involves extending whole-number properties and patterns. If 3 × −2 = −6, then −2 × 3 should also be −6 because of the commutative property. A pattern leading to this conclusion, and also for a negative number times a negative number (e.g., −3 × −2 = 6), follows:

$2 \times 3 = 6$	$-3 \times 2 = -6$
$1 \times 3 = 3$	$-3 \times 1 = -3$
$0 \times 3 = 0$	$-3 \times 0 = 0$
$-1 \times 3 = \square$	$-3 \times -1 = \square$
$-2 \times 3 = \square$	$-3 \times -2 = \square$

Dividing Integers

Making sense of division of integers involves considering the fact families and the inverse relationship between division and multiplication. Children recall that the

FIGURE 17-7 Using the Number Line and Red and Blue Cubes Models to Subtract Integers

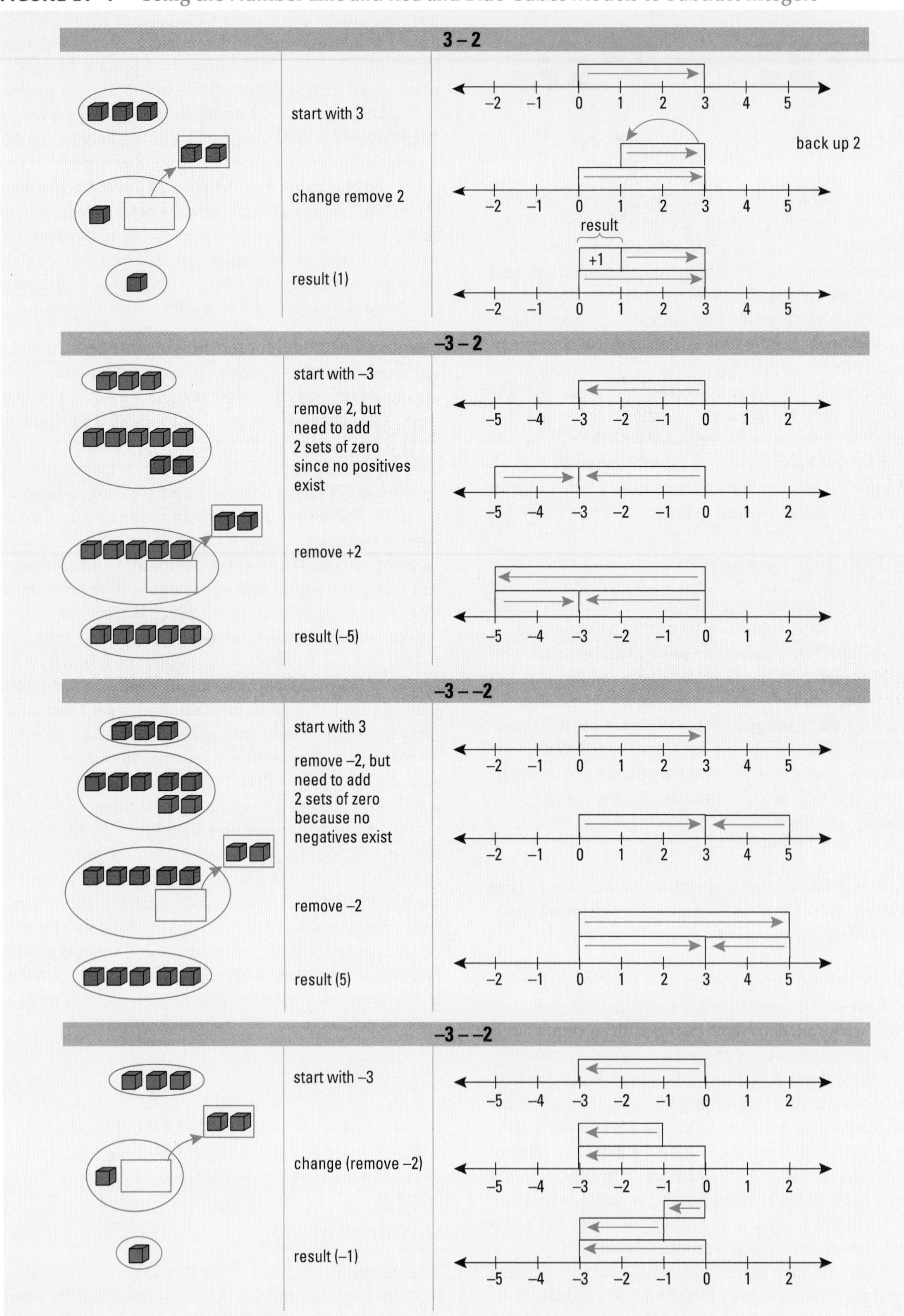

FIGURE 17-8 Using the Number Line and Red and Blue Cubes Models to Multiply Integers

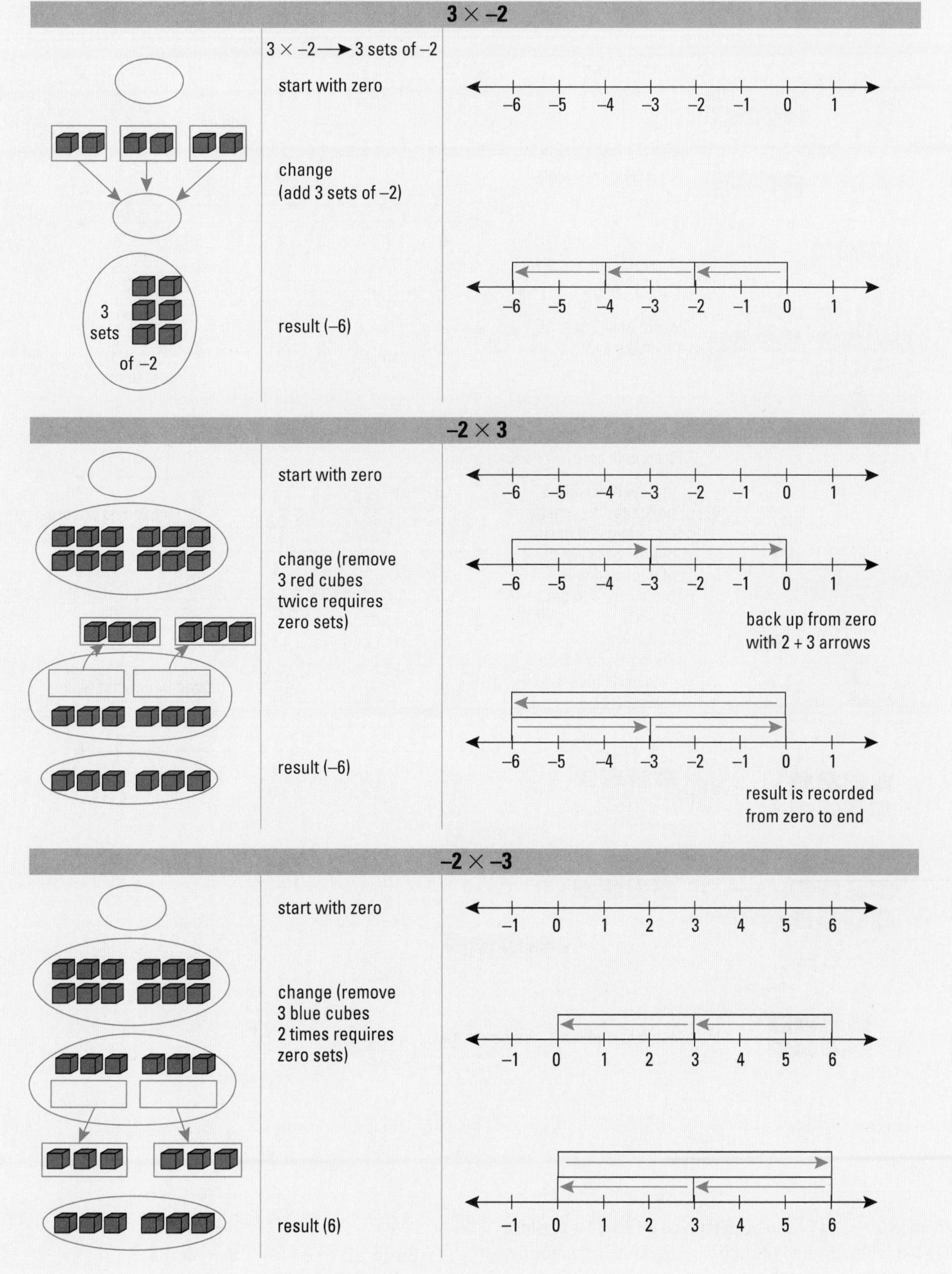

FIGURE 17-9 Using the Number Line and Red and Blue Cubes Models to Divide Integers

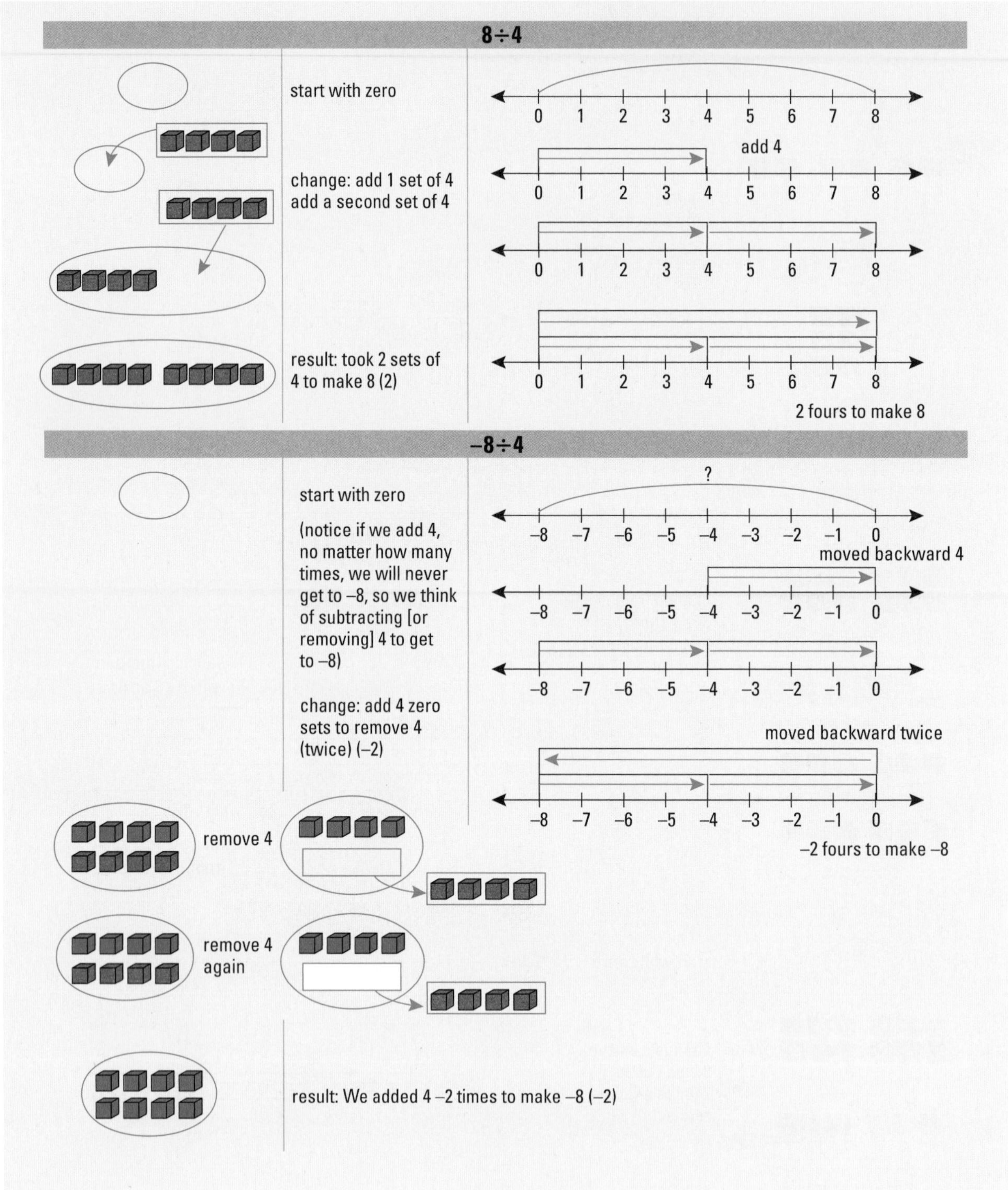

sentence $6 \div 2 = \square$ can be expressed as $2 \times \square = 6$. Since division is the inverse of multiplication, the rules for determining the sign of the answer to a division of integers problem are the same as for multiplying integers. The problems below show three examples relating multiplication of integers to division:

Since $2 \times -3 = -6$	that means	$-6 \div 2 = -3$
Since $-2 \times -3 = 6$	that means	$6 \div -2 = -3$
Since $-2 \times 3 = -6$	that means	$-6 \div -2 = 3$

Red and blue cubes model for dividing integers. This model extends the meaning of division of whole numbers.

FIGURE 17-9 Continued

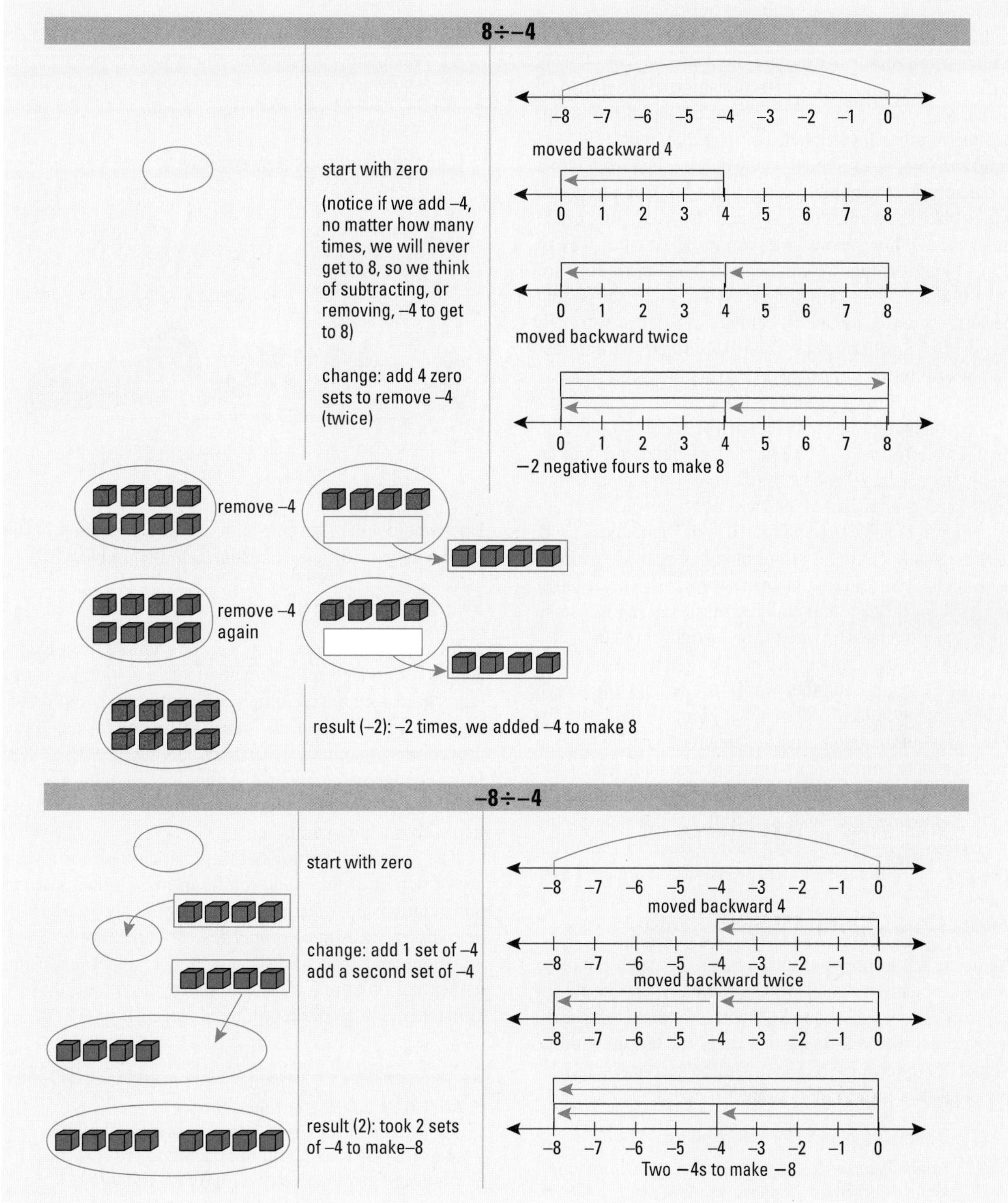

Once again, division is simply viewed as repeated subtraction. Recall that 12 divided by 3 can have two possible meanings: partitive and measurement. In partitive division, we think "Three sets of what size make 12?" In measurement division, we ask "How many sets of 3 are in 12?" Generally, the second approach is used with integer division.

Figure 17-9 shows concrete examples for division of integers, using the red and blue cubes model and the number line model. The examples $8 \div 4$, $-8 \div 4$, $8 \div -4$, and $-8 \div -4$ are illustrated using both models. These models match the procedures for multiplying integers and make more sense when we consider fact families.

Number line model for dividing integers. Although this model can seem a bit confusing at first, the model will come to make more sense with practice. Always begin with a whole-number example, for instance 8 ÷ 4. This will reacquaint children with the meaning of division, particularly the measurement interpretation, and show how to use the number line model. For example, with 8 ÷ 4, a child can look at a segment on the number line from 0 to 8 and determine the number of four-unit-long segments into which this eight-unit-long segment can be split; or, in other words, how many fours are in 8? Another way to think about it is that we can begin at 0 and move forward from 0 in four-unit-long jumps two times to reach 8. And because we moved to the right to get to 8, the answer will be positive. Similarly, for −8 ÷ −4, children again start at 0 once and move toward −8 in two segments or "jumps" each −4 units long; thus, −8 ÷ −4 = 2.

The following two examples are a bit more complicated. First, let's look at −8 ÷ 4. Once again, children begin on the number line at 0 and attempt to move in jumps of four units long as many times as necessary to reach −8. However, they are unable to jump from 0 to the right to reach −8. It will actually require 2 jumps moving backward (or left) to reach the −8, resulting in an answer of −2. The negative comes from the fact that children must back up (or move left), rather than go forward (or move right) from 0.

For 8 ÷ −4, children begin at 0 and try to move in jumps of −4 units (in other words, to the left) to reach 8. Once again, children will find that jumps to the left from 0 will not get them to 8. Instead, they will need to change directions (or move to the right) in two jumps that are 4 units long to reach the 8. The process of changing direction (moving right instead of left, as indicated by the negative sign of −4) will result in a negative answer, in this case, −2. Additional examples are shown in Figure 17-9.

Assessing Operations on Integers

As discussed in previous chapters, assessment should be consistent with the goals of instruction. A test should include questions that require the children to relate integers to everyday life and to justify rules for the operations. Some test questions (Q) and sample responses (R) by sixth- and seventh-graders follow:

Q: Write and solve a story problem for −5 + 13.

R: Adrian Peterson lost 5 yards on his first run from scrimmage and gained 13 yards on his second run. How many yards did he gain in both runs? −5 + 13 = 8. He gained 8 yards.

Q: Write a question to make a problem using the following information. "At noon, the temperature was 8 °F. At midnight, the temperature was −5°F." Solve the problem.

R: How many degrees did the temperature fall? (A diagram of a thermometer was drawn.) 8 − −5 = 13. The temperature fell 13 °.

Q: Write a story problem for 3 × −4. Solve using a number line.

R: Stephen had 3 library cards. If he owed $4.00 on each, how much does he owe? (A number line showing 3 jumps of 4 starting at 0 and moving to the left to −12 was drawn.) 3 × −4 = −12. He owed $12.00.

Q: Write and solve a story problem for −8 ÷ 2. Show how you would check that your answer is correct.

How would you assess the skill and understanding of the child who gave the above response to the problem?

Practice Settings

As discussed in the previous sections, children should be able to use models and mathematical reasoning to justify the rules for adding, subtracting, multiplying, and dividing integers. Children also need to be able to use these procedures automatically when solving problems and learning algebraic concepts. Activities 17-1 and 17-2 are examples of problem-solving activities that provide practice with integer operations.

The remaining sections of this chapter describe a variety of activities that allow children to examine patterns and relationships, evaluate expressions, apply order of operations, illustrate properties of operations, solve equations and inequalities, and explore functions using contextual situations, tables, graphs, and symbols that are aimed at helping children think algebraically.

ACTIVITY 17-1 Integer Target

Use the first three listed integers together with two operations to make a number sentence having the fourth integer as the answer (target). The three numbers can appear in any order in the sentence.

Example:	7	−2	−5	−6
Solution:	(7 − −5) ÷ −2 = −6			
1. −9	4	3		−23
2. −8	2	−7		3
3. 6	−9	6		0
4. −7	1	12		−2

ACTIVITY 17-2 Two-Color Game

Materials

10 two-color counters (chips with a different color on each side)

Procedure

Use 10 chips that are two sided—one color on one side and, another color on the other side. Designate that one color will represent a negative number and the other a positive number. Put the chips in a cup. Students will shake up the chips and pour them out on the table. They will count the number for each color to determine the two numbers. For example, two reds and 5 whites will mean $-2 + 5$. Students will add the two numbers for their score for that turn. After 10 turns, students should add their scores for each turn. The student with the highest total score at the end of 10 turns is the winner.

Alternatives

a. Select another operation (–, ×, ÷) for the game.
b. Use two spinners or two dice instead of the chips.
c. Scoop out two colors of beans for students to add.
d. Use more than 10 chips.
e. Make a game board like that shown below.

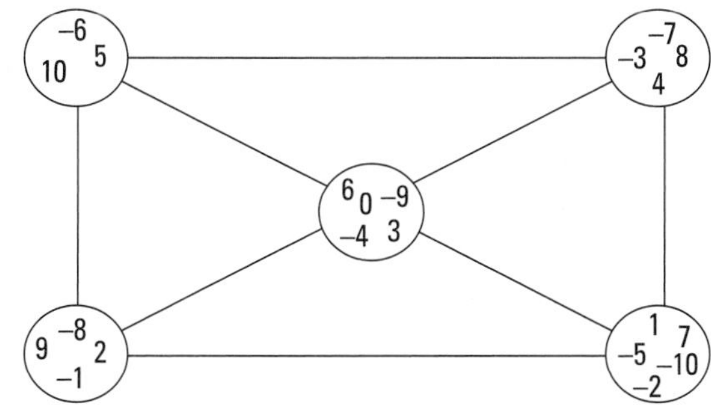

Move from one corner across to the opposite corner.

Patterns

Algebra can be defined as the study of patterns, which form the foundation for the logical connections in all of mathematics. Through the study of patterns, children can learn to see relationships and make connections, generalizations, and predictions about the world around them. According to NCTM's *Principles and Standards for School Mathematics,* studying patterns leads to generalizations about relationships and to the development of supporting logical arguments, which is an important aspect of algebraic thinking. To help children think algebraically, encourage them to analyze existing patterns, extend the patterns they see, recognize when a similar pattern has occurred, and generate patterns of their own.

Through experiences with the world, young children explore patterns. You can build on children's interest in patterns by providing experiences in the classroom in which children sort, describe, compare, predict, and create patterns. At higher levels, children look for relationships in concrete materials, tables, charts, and graphs; describe these patterns in numbers, symbols, words, and graphs; and make predictions.

Children's first experiences with patterns should focus on repeating patterns, with children participating in handclap exercises, listening to the rhythmic beat of music, looking at pattern-shape cards, and examining natural patterns found in nature. No matter what the medium, exposure to a wide variety of patterns is invaluable in the understanding of patterns and the relationship of the component parts that form them.

Another way to help children make sense of the patterns in their mathematics worlds is through the hundreds chart. For example, have groups of children color in all the numbers that have a 4 or 8 or 6. Display the patterns for the entire class, and discuss what children observe. Give children a number, for example, 37, and ask what number would be above (27), below (47), to the right (38), or to the left (36) in the hundreds chart. Ask children to describe the patterns they notice.

PEARSON **myeducationlab** The Power of Classroom Practice Go to the Assignments and Activities section of Topic 14: "Algebraic Thinking" in the MyEducationLab for your course and complete the activity "Pre-Algebra Strategies." Note what the video clip says about introducing Algebraic concepts at an early age.

Repeating Patterns

As children are involved in experiences with patterns, encourage them to describe the patterns they see or hear in a variety of ways. One way to describe patterns is by classifying the *core,* which includes two complete repetitions of the repeating pattern segment, or, in other words, the shortest string of elements that repeats in a pattern. A core pattern might be a boy–girl–boy–girl arrangement, or square–circle–square–circle arrangement. We refer to this type of pattern as an *AB pattern.*

Experiences with patterns using manipulatives—e.g., pattern blocks, attribute blocks, Unifix cubes, and other

FIGURE 17-10 Examples of Repeating Patterns

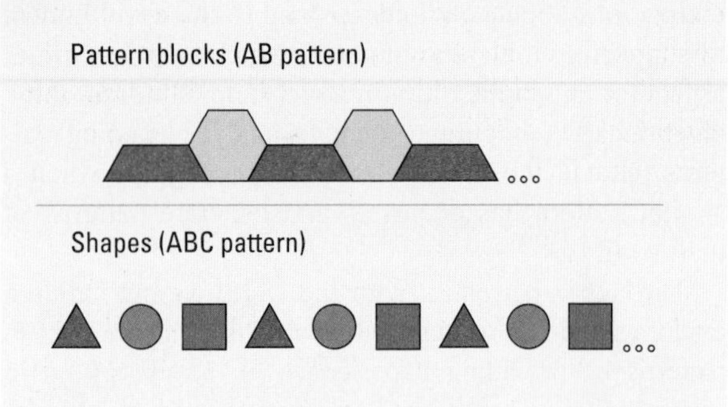

FIGURE 17-11 T-Table for Growing Patterns

N Number of People	E Number of Eyes
1	2
2	4
3	6
4	

assorted shapes such as those found in Figure 17-10—support children's ideas of order in their world. Many experiences with patterns are crucial to the development of algebraic concepts in young learners. See Activity 17-3 for one example. It is helpful for children to name patterns in a variety of ways, such as ABAB; 1, 2, 1, 2; or red, green, red, green. When these patterns are described orally and written in words or symbols, children start making sense of the concept of the pattern. As children become more confident with simple patterns, encourage them to make more complicated patterns such as ABBCC or ABBA, using a variety of symbols, numbers, or manipulatives. Challenge children to generate their own patterns using a variety of materials and to look for patterns that are similar, or ask them to explain patterns using letters in the alphabet.

ACTIVITY 17-3 Match the Patterns

Realia Strategies

Procedure

1. The teacher demonstrates creating ABC patterns, first using learning links then using color tiles.
2. Provide groups of children with various materials, such as colored beads and string, interlocking links or cubes, attribute shapes, bags of buttons, etc.
3. Ask children to generate various patterns using the above materials and have them discuss what materials their groups used to represent the pattern.

Growing Patterns

Repeating patterns lead into *growing patterns,* which are patterns that grow or change. At first, children need lots of exposure to different growing patterns until they begin to see how patterns continue. Next comes identifying the "rule" for the pattern. Once children are able to verbalize the rule, they can use symbolic notation to represent the changes. Graphs are another component. They help visual learners see the relationships. The pattern (usually listed in a T-table, which is a two-column data table such as that shown in Figure 17-11), the rule, the symbolic notation, and the graph form a link of understanding for algebraic relationships that become more complex in the middle grades.

Once children have fully explored an assortment of progressively more complicated experiences and exposure to natural and musical patterns, manipulatives (e.g., pattern blocks, color tiles, Cuisenaire rods) and abstract representations (e.g., using letters or numbers), they will be ready to begin understanding growing patterns. Introducing children to growing patterns should begin early and extend into the study of sequences (which are basically growing patterns) and their related functions at upper-level mathematics. Using real-world objects or pictures helps children make connections with what they already understand. Typically, children begin displaying growing patterns by recording a pattern in a T-table. The first experience with this could be a class lesson comparing the number of people with their number of eyes, as in Figure 17-11. Another example is illustrated in Activity 17-4, "The Growing Worm."

ACTIVITY 17-4 The Growing Worm

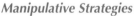

Manipulative Strategies

Materials

Pattern blocks

Procedure

1. Using an overhead projector, display three pattern blocks (as in the following diagram) to represent the worm. Tell the class that this is a worm, and this worm eats a lot and grows a lot every day.

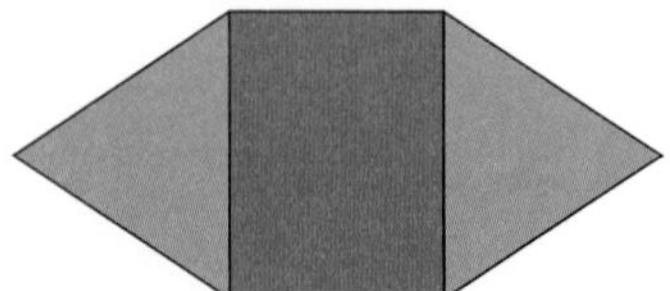

2. Ask students how many blocks were used for the first day. Make a T-table to record the days and number of blocks used.
3. On Day 2 the worm gets larger, and now is made up of four pattern blocks, as in the diagram here. Record these data in the T-table.

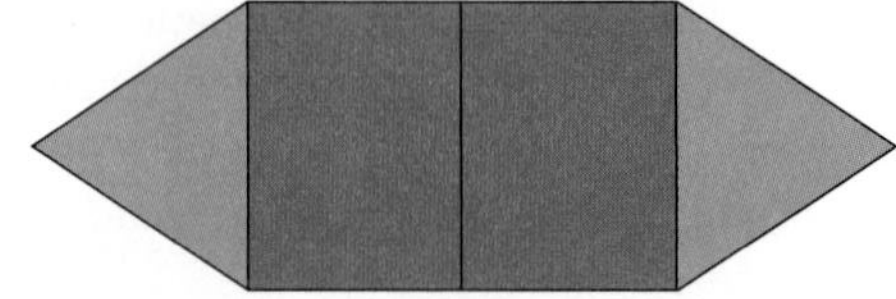

4. The worm's body gets one square longer every day. Model how the worm grows by adding one square in the body and record the data in the T-table.
5. Have the children use pattern blocks to continue to build the figures and draw them on a recording sheet, recording the numbers in the T-table each time.
6. As a class, discuss the pattern and move toward discovering the "rule" and recording the rule in symbolic equation.

Once children have about three entries in the T-table, ask them to predict what the next result will be. Questioning such as this helps children to begin to examine the way the T-table works. When children are able to make some accurate predictions, ask them to explain their thinking. See if they can predict what would happen for the 10th case. The aim is to have children see a pattern that they can generalize into a rule. As children become more experienced with verbalizing a rule, you can show them how the rule can be written using symbolic notation with letters from the T-table and numbers. Figure 17-12 shows a sample of a child's work on this problem.

FIGURE 17-12 Example of Child's Work on "The Growing Worm" Problem

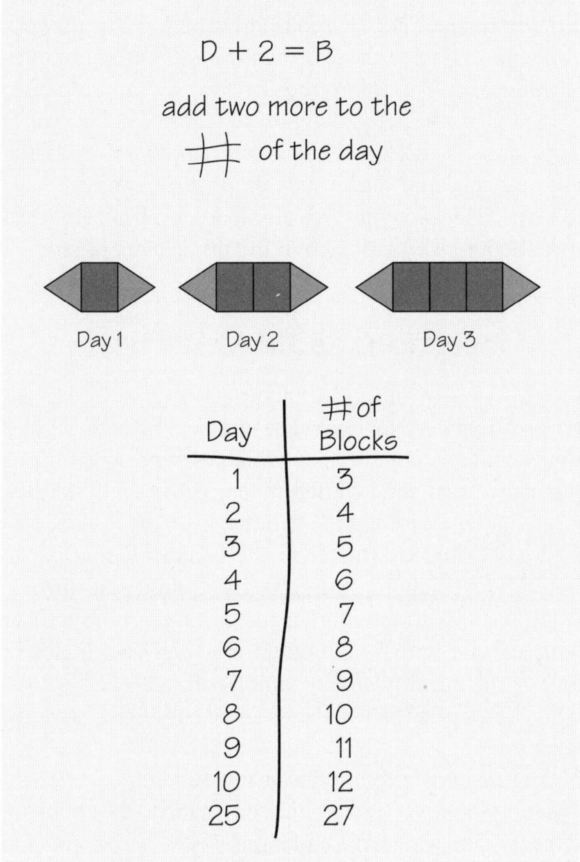

Sometimes children in lower grades have difficulties writing letters—capital letters are acceptable in these problems. As children advance through the grades, it is preferable for children to use lowercase letters to represent patterns in order to better prepare them for more formal algebraic learning.

Relationships

Encourage children to describe and analyze the relationship that exists among objects or numbers. As they become proficient in recording patterns in T-tables and discovering the rules for growth, children are ready for more complicated patterns and are ready to display the rule in graph form to "see" the relationship. For example, consider using toothpicks to make triangles. If the triangles are separate from one another, three toothpicks are needed for each triangle and the pattern rule is *toothpicks* = 3 × □. Suppose, however, that triangles can share a common side. Looking at the illustration shown next, children predict that 21 toothpicks are needed to make 10 triangles. The rule can be expressed as *toothpicks* = 2 × □ + 1.

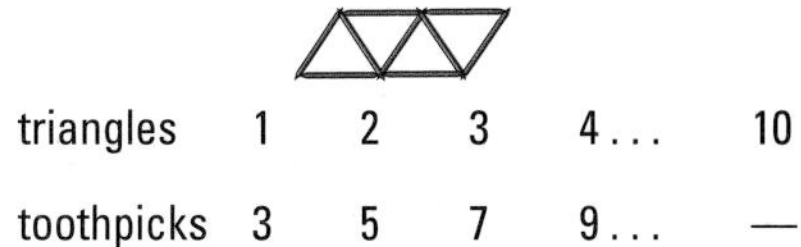

triangles	1	2	3	4...	10
toothpicks	3	5	7	9...	—

By representing this pattern as a graph, children have another way to understand the relationship between toothpicks and triangles in this problem. The idea that the pattern continues is more evident in the visual form and helps to confirm the relationship. Enabling children to see the connections among the data, the rule, and the graph also lays the groundwork for understanding functions.

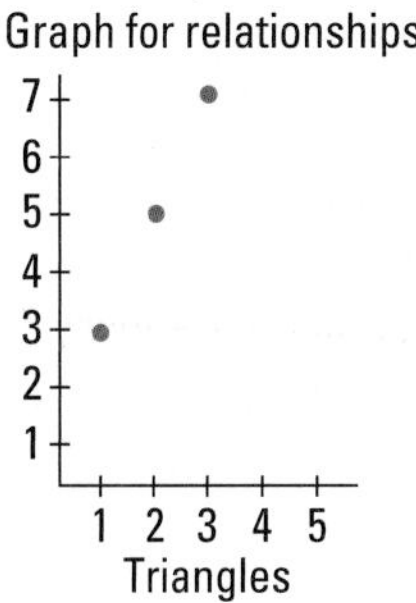

Variables

According to Peck and Jencks (1988), "Algebra can and should arise as a by-product of making arithmetic sensible" (p. 85). Children can represent mathematical situations and properties first with objects and numbers and later with symbols, including variables, which are letters that represent quantities that may or may not vary or change.

Mathematicians often think of a *variable* as a symbol for an element from a specified replacement set (Usiskin, 1988). A variable provides children with a new language they can use to generalize patterns and complex situations.

According to Kieran and Chalouh (1993), instruction should focus on the exploration of key algebraic ideas in which children "(a) think about the numerical relations of a situation, (b) discuss them explicitly in simple everyday language, and (c) eventually learn to represent them with letters or other nonmisleading notation" (pp. 181–182).

Meanings of a Variable

Variables are letters that represent quantities that may or may not vary, or change. Quantities that do not vary are often referred to as *unknowns* or *missing elements* when they are used in number sentences. In primary grades, children encounter the notion of a variable, or unknown quantity, when they solve missing addend problems and when they use words to generalize patterns. Consider the following examples:

$4 + \square = 9$	$\square + 7 = 15$	$12 + 7 = \square$
$14 - \square = 5$	$3 \times \square = 12$	$25 \div \square = 5$

In the example $4 + \square = 9$, the square represents the unknown, or missing addend, 5. In the example $3 \times \square = 12$, the square represents the unknown, or missing factor, 4.

In later experiences, children can begin to work with variables that change. Earlier experiences with repeating and growing patterns and generalizing to a stated rule and symbolic notation form the foundation for more complex ideas. It continues to be important to link concepts with real-world situations. Experiencing and recording the pattern helps consolidate understanding of the pattern. After practicing and generalizing many patterns, recording the rule can easily be shifted to the more standard (x, y) notation.

Letters may be used to represent numbers in different mathematical contexts and, consequently, variables take on several different meanings. A symbol or variable may represent one or more numbers, called values of the variable. The term *variable* also can imply a symbol that may have two or more values in a particular situation. Variables can be used as follows:

1. In equations as a specific unknown number.

   Example: $3 + x = 7$

2. To state properties or to generalize a pattern.

   Example: $a + 0 = a$, or $ab = ba$

3. To describe functions or sequences of quantities that are joint variations.

   Example:

in:	n	7	4	12
out:	$3n - 1$	20	11	35

   Example: 2, 5, 8, . . . , $3n - 1$

4. In formulas to express relationships.

   Example: $C = \pi d$

In the first case, the variable x is used as a placeholder for a specific unknown. The task is to solve for x, that is, to find a single number to substitute for x that will make the sentence true. In the other cases, the variable represents a range of values. In the second case, for example, the statements are true for all numbers. In the third case, the expression $3n - 1$ defines a function: for any number n that is input, the output number is found by applying the relationship "multiply n by 3 and subtract 1." A variable can also be used to describe a sequence; successive terms are found by replacing the variable with the numbers 1, 2, 3, and so on. In the fourth case, the formula expresses the relationship between the diameter and the circumference of a circle; the circumference varies as the diameter changes and, given one of the quantities, the other can be determined. This also describes a function relationship of independent and dependent values.

You should provide middle school children with many experiences with different variable situations so they can build their own understanding of the different uses of a variable. Interestingly, Willoughby (1997) and Sulzer (1998) found that fourth graders who were exposed to variable notation could use the notation "$x + 5$" versus simply saying "add 5."

After working with many examples involving one variable or one unknown, children may begin to work with two variables or two unknowns. For example, in working with Cuisenaire rods previously, children have learned that 2 red equal 1 purple ($2R = P$). They have also learned that 1 nickel equals 5 cents ($n = 5c$). Later, children can note that 5 nickels plus 3 pennies equals 28 cents. This slow progression lends itself nicely to an introduction to equations and the procedures of solving equations.

Misconceptions about Variables

Several types of misunderstandings are associated with the use of letters to represent numbers (Booth, 1988). Some children believe that variables represent objects rather than numbers. Children sometimes think that the particular letter used as the variable in an expression corresponds to the first letter in the quantity being represented. For example, in one study a child said that $8y$ would have to mean eight yachts or yams or some other word starting with y, and could not represent apples or dogs or any quantity *not* beginning with the letter y. Writing "5 times n" as $5n$ also leads some children to write 56 when $n = 6$.

Wagner (1981) found that many children believe that changing the letter in an equation changes the problem. Subjects were shown the equations $7 \times W + 22 = 109$ and

$7 \times N + 22 = 109$ and asked whether W or N would have a larger value. Some children said that they couldn't tell without solving the equation, whereas others believed that the order of the letters alphabetically must correspond to the order of the size of the numbers, so W would be larger because it comes after N in the alphabet.

Many children have difficulty accepting algebraic expressions, particularly those containing addition or subtraction symbols, as answers to problems. Typical computational error finds children rewriting $3 + 4b$ as $7b$ and $2x + 3y$ as $5xy$. A basic misunderstanding of the meaning of a variable is quite noticeable. The conventions of writing the product of variables creates the fact that $4ab$ means $4 \times a \times b$ and 4×5 is not equal to 45. We often express the commutative property as $ab = ba$, but notice that 35 is not equal to 53.

Translation errors sometimes occur when children write comparison relationships with variables. For instance, when children are asked to translate the relationship "twice as many feet as noses," the typical response is to write "$2 \times$ feet = noses." However, a closer examination indicates that "feet = $2 \times$ noses" would be more accurate.

> PEARSON **myeducationlab** The Power of Classroom Practice — To explore your own understanding of variables, go to Chapter 17 in the Book-Specific Resources section in the MyEducationLab for your course. Select the Activities section and complete the activities "Ways to Make 10" and "Detective Work."

Understanding Equality and Expressions

Many adults may have memories of solving equations in an algebra course. But before children can learn how to solve equations, a strong foundation based on understanding the notion of equality must be established.

Understanding Equality

In a recent study (Falkner, Levi, & Carpenter, 1999), a group of 145 sixth-graders was asked to identify the number that should go in the box in the equation below:

$$8 + 4 = \square + 5$$

All of the children thought that either 12 or 17 should go in the box. What do these responses indicate about these children's understanding of equality and the equals sign, and what can teachers do to help them develop richer understandings?

According to Falkner et al. (1999), elementary school children often think that the equals sign means to "carry out the calculation that precedes it and that the number after the equals sign is the answer to the calculation. [They] generally do not see the equals sign as a symbol that expresses the relationship 'is the same as'" (p. 233).

It is important for children to understand that equality is a relationship that states that two mathematical expressions have the same value. This understanding not only helps children solve algebraic equations, such as $4x + 7 = 20$, but also helps younger children understand relationships expressed as number sentences, such as $8 + 9 = 8 + 8 + 1$, which is a useful thinking strategy in learning basic facts.

In the early grades, children can be introduced to the concept of equality through the idea of balance. Using a pan balance, children can explore how to maintain balance by adding or subtracting the same weight on each side of the balance, noting that replacing objects with other objects having the same weight will not make the pans go out of balance. Activity 17-5 challenges children to reason and examine patterns.

Understanding Expressions

An expression is different from an equation. An *expression* is a symbolic statement and can be either an arithmetic expression, such as $2 + 3$, or an algebraic expression, such as $2x + 3$. Expressions may be constants (e.g., 3, 4, −2), variables (e.g., m, x, w), operations (e.g., addition, subtraction), and grouping symbols (e.g., parentheses). An *equation* includes an equals sign and states the equality of two expressions. Equations that contain only numbers, such as $2 + 3 = 5$, are known as *number sentences.*

ACTIVITY 17-5 Balancing Act

Manipulative Strategies

Materials

Copy of Pan Balance Worksheet for each group (see below)

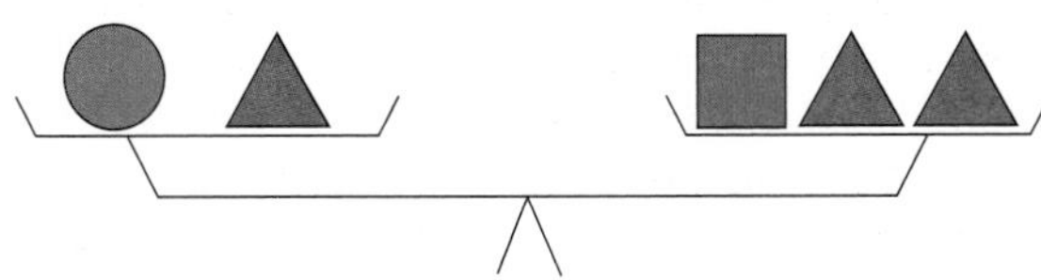

20 counters for each group

Procedure

1. Explain the rules:

   Find the value of each shape, given the following assumptions:
   - The pans must balance.
   - The same shapes have the same value.
   - No shape has a value of zero.

2. Ask how many counters will be on each side of the scale if there are 20 counters altogether.

3. Have children examine the pan balance and determine values for the shapes.
4. Have children explain how they got their answers.
5. Enter the values in a chart as below:

Pan Balance Chart

●	▲	■
9	1	8
8	2	6
7	3	4
6	4	2

6. Discuss the patterns in the table. (This activity can be used with many other even numbers of counters.)

Children first encounter expressions and number sentences when they study addition. For instance, the number sentence expressing that two birds are joined by three other birds can be written in a number expression as $2 + 3$ or as a number sentence $2 + 3 = 5$. For example, if the *expression* $2 + 3$ tells how many birds there are now, when we write the *number sentence* $2 + 3 = 5$, we are saying that 5 is another name for the total number of birds. The *equals* sign means that $2 + 3$ and 5 are different names for the same number. Show children that this relation can also be written as $5 = 2 + 3$, and provide them with experiences writing number sentences such as $2 + 3 = 3 + 2$ and $2 + 3 = 4 + 1$. Asking children to examine families of basic facts that have the same sum or product or to write expressions in order to name a particular number in many different ways allows these concepts to be discussed and reinforced. This process will also improve number-sense abilities for operations.

An important point here is that an arithmetic expression such as $2 + 3$ can be an answer as well as an instruction to add. Children with this understanding will later be better able to accept algebraic expressions such as $3 + a$ and $x + y$ as correct and meaningful final representations. The ideas that the addition symbol can show the result of an operation as well as the action of addition, and that the equals sign can indicate an equivalence relation as well as represent a signal to give the answer, are essential to algebraic understanding (Booth, 1988).

Throughout the elementary years, children have many opportunities to interpret, write, and evaluate arithmetic expressions by replacing the unknown values with a known quantity. As each of the four operations is introduced, children have experiences connecting physical actions and real-world situations with mathematical expressions. Learning the basic facts and computational algorithms involves finding single numbers to rename expressions. It is important to note that textbook and teacher-made exercises requiring children to "add," "find the product," or "complete" may or may not include the equals sign. Regardless of the format, the goal is for children to learn the various ways to interpret expressions in order to find the "answer."

$$\begin{array}{r} 4 \\ +\ 9 \\ \hline \end{array} \qquad 5 \times 8 = \square \qquad 63 \div 7$$

Simplifying Algebraic Expressions

Other skills learned in beginning algebra involve simplifying and expanding expressions. Children learn that a *term* can be either a number, a variable, or a product or quotient that includes one or more variables. Terms are separated by addition or subtraction operation symbols to create algebraic expressions. Thus, in the expression, $7x - 3xy + y - 8 + 2x$, there are five terms, with some common terms. In this example, $7x$, $3xy$, y, and 8 are *unlike terms*, whereas $7x$ and $2x$ are *like terms* because they contain the same variable, x. Like terms can be combined to simplify an expression. Thus, $7x + 2x$ can be written as $9x$, but the terms in $7x + y$ and $9x + 8$ cannot be combined.

Moving from numeric expressions to algebraic expressions is accompanied by the introduction of new notations for multiplication and division. The symbol $\times$ is no longer used to indicate multiplication; "3 times a" is written $3a$, "3 times the sum of a and b" is written $3(a + b)$, and "3 times 4" is written $3(4)$ or $3 \cdot 4$. As noted earlier, this notation can be a source of confusion for children. For division, the $\div$ symbol is most commonly used to denote "a divided by b." Children first make this connection when they study fractions and decimals. For example, they see that both $6 \div 3$ and $\frac{6}{3}$ are 2, and they find that the fraction $\frac{3}{5}$ can be expressed as a decimal by performing $3 \div 5$. Thus, the fraction bar can be either a number or an instruction to divide. The expression $(a + b) \div 3$ is written without parentheses as $\frac{a + b}{3}$.

The concept of an algebraic expression can be developed with materials such as straws, base-ten blocks, and Algebra Tiles. For instance, cutting straws of equal length to represent an unknown value, say, x, and using straws of another length to represent units, children can model expressions such as $x + 2$, and $2x + 4$ using the materials. In using base-ten blocks, the unit can remain units, whereas the rods become x values. These devices allow children to visualize the expression and leads them to understand why $3x$ is not the same as $3 + x$ and why $2(x + 3)$ is not the same as $2x + 3$. Various models for representing expressions are provided in Figure 17-13. Algebra Tiles are described in more detail later in this chapter.

Children may use straws to represent the following relationship. Have the children model the sides of a triangle with straws given the following conditions: The length of the second side of the triangle is three times the first side, whereas the third side is twice the length of the first side.

FIGURE 17-13 Concrete Models Representing Expressions

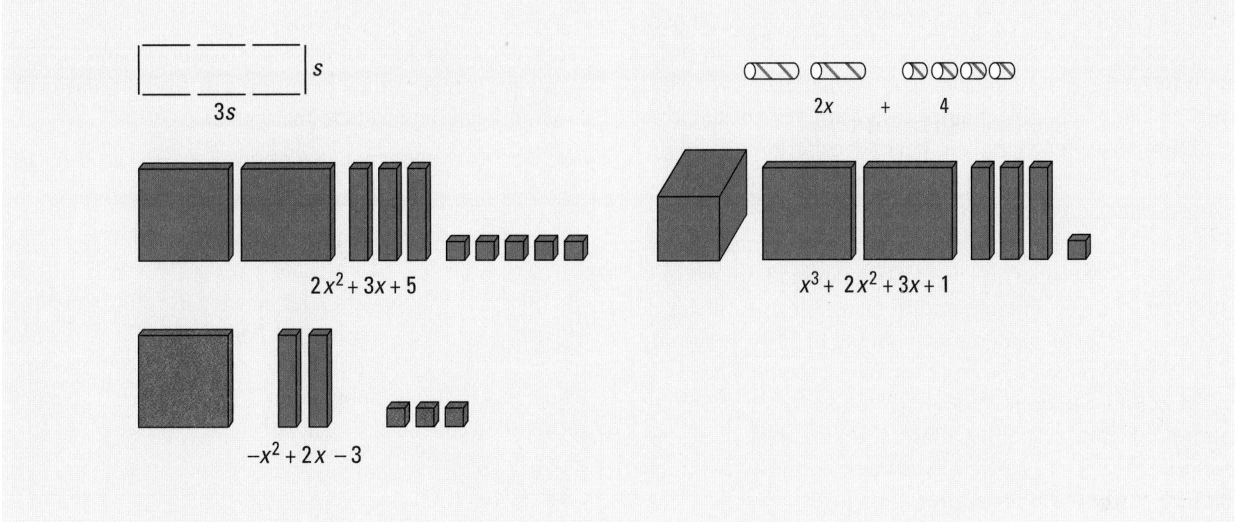

The same approach can be used to model a rectangle such that the length is three times the width. Students can make many possible designs and keep a table of the results. You could also specify a perimeter, say, 40 units, and ask children to use patterns and relationships to find the length and width.

Children can learn to write and interpret expressions involving variables. The phrase "4 more than a number" can be written $p + 4$; the letter p is a placeholder for a number. To evaluate the expression, a specific number is substituted for the variable p and the resulting number expression is evaluated. For $p = 2$ the value of the expression is 6, for $p = 5$ the value is 9, and so on. Carefully translating phrases into algebraic expressions as well as analyzing expressions for contextual setting will prove beneficial in the formation of algebraic thinking. Wrap-around games, bingo-type games, and expression domino games like those described in Activity 17-6 can be used to help children connect the symbolic nature of an expression with the contextual expression.

Understanding Algebraic Properties

Children learned about arithmetic properties as they worked with number sentences, as discussed in Chapter 8. As children learn about algebra, they need to understand the similarity between arithmetic and algebraic properties.

In the early grades, children apply the *commutative* and *associative* properties of addition and multiplication but do not need to know these formal terms. In the intermediate years, the terms can be introduced and the properties described using variables, as in Table 17-1.

ACTIVITY 17-6 Express Yourself

Find the expression for each of the following:

a. 25 more than an integer
b. $4 less than the cost
c. Twice the width
d. Half the distance around
e. Three more than twice the value

Write a situation for each of the following:

a. $4x$
b. $3 + m$
c. $12 - w$
d. $4n + 2$
e. $\frac{d}{7}$

TABLE 17-1 Examples of Properties in Arithmetic and Algebra

Property	Arithmetic Example	Algebraic Example
Commutative property of addition	$2 + 3 = 3 + 2$	$a + b = b + a$
Commutative property of multiplication	$2 \times 3 = 3 \times 2$	$ab = ba$
Associative property of addition	$(2 + 3) + 4 = 2 + (3 + 4)$	$(a + b) + c = a + (b + c)$
Associative property of multiplication	$(2 \times 3) \times 4 = 2 \times (3 \times 4)$	$(ab)c = a(bc)$
Distributive property of multiplication over addition	$2(3 + 4) = 2 \times 3 + 2 \times 4$	$a(b + c) = ab + ac$
Addition property of 0	$2 + 0 = 2$	$a + 0 = a$
Multiplication property of 1	$2 \times 1 = 2$	$a \cdot 1 = a$

It is important for teachers to help children see the connections between the arithmetic properties they already understand and the algebraic statements of those same properties. One way to do this is to encourage children to express in their own words what each property means, and then give numerical examples to support each property. Teachers can then help children use their understanding of variables to represent these properties with variables, as in the third column of Table 17-1. The key idea is that the statements are true for all numbers. Although the properties are first examined for whole numbers, they are later found to also hold for integers, rational numbers, and real numbers. In this situation, variables are being used to generalize patterns. The goal is for children to come to appreciate the power and simplicity of this symbolic representation of the ideas. Activities 17-7 and 17-8 provide an opportunity for children to verify these properties.

ACTIVITY 17-7 Modeling the Properties

Procedure

Use color tiles, counters, graphing paper, or another manipulative to show the following true statements:

1. $3 + 5 = 5 + 3$
2. $4 \times 7 = 7 \times 4$
3. $4 \times (2 + 7) = 4 \times 9$

ACTIVITY 17-8 Combining Like Terms with Models

Manipulative Strategies

Procedure

Use base-ten blocks or Algebra Tiles to simplify the following problems:

1. $(x + 5) + (x - 3)$
2. $(x^2 - 3x + 3) + (x^2 + 5x - 4)$
3. $(x^2 + 2x + 7) - (x^2 - 2)$
4. $(2x + 3)(x - 3)$
5. $(x^2 + x + -7) / (x + 4)$

Understanding the Order of Operations

Evaluate the expression $2 + 3 \times 4$. Is the correct answer 20 (found by adding 2 plus 3 and then multiplying by 4) or is it 14 (found by multiplying 3 times 4 and then adding 2)? Because two answers are possible in cases such as this, a hierarchy for performing operations, called the *order of operations*, was developed. The following order of operations should be used when evaluating an expression containing more than one operation:

1. Operations in parentheses. If multiple parentheses exist, perform the operations left to right and working from the inside to the outside.
2. Perform exponent calculations.
3. Perform multiplication and division from left to right.
4. Perform addition and subtraction from left to right.

A common abbreviation for these steps is the expression "*P*lease *E*xcuse *M*y *D*ear *A*unt *S*ally" (PEMDAS), which corresponds to "*P*arentheses, *E*xponents, *M*ultiplication, *D*ivision, *A*ddition, *S*ubtraction." The following example shows the sequence of evaluating the expression $3 \times 5 - (12 + 8) \div 4 + 2^2$:

$$\begin{aligned} &= 3 \times 5 - (12 + 8) \div 4 + 2^2 \\ &= 3 \times 5 - 20 \div 4 + 2^2 \\ &= 3 \times 5 - 20 \div 4 + 4 \\ &= 15 - 20 \div 4 + 4 \\ &= 15 - 5 + 4 \\ &= 10 + 4 \\ &= 14 \end{aligned}$$

In evaluating expressions such as $3n + 6$ and $7 - [(\frac{n}{2}) - 3]$, the order of operation rules must be applied. When $n = 10$, the values for the above expressions are 36 and 5, respectively.

Writing the steps for solving the expression one stage at a time may seem cumbersome at first, but taking shortcuts at the beginning can result in inaccurate answers, especially when additional operations of multiplication and division are included later. Writing each stage of the solution process will allow for more accurate solutions and an easier process for checking answers.

Several software programs that provide practice with order of operations are available. In the strategy game *How the West Was One + Two × Three* (Sunburst), players create equations using three randomly generated numbers with two different operations of their choice to produce answers in order to move a stagecoach or locomotive along a trail. For example, possible answers using the numbers 6, 2, and 5 include $6 \div 2 + 5 = 8$, $(6 - 5) \times 2 = 2$, and $6 - 5 \times 2 = -4$.

The commercial game *Krypto* (Creative Publications) for two to eight players is based on the same idea. The game includes a deck of 52 cards numbered as follows: three each 1 through 10, two each 11 through 17, and one each 18 through 25. Five cards are dealt to each player and a common objective card for all players is turned up. The first player to use his or her 5 numbers, together with any combination of the operations, to match the objective card number wins the hand.

The commercial game *24* (Suntex International) has children compete to see who can find an arrangement of four given numbers to reach the designated value of 24 by incorporating the order of operations conventions. Given the numbers 5, 5, 2, and 1, a possible solution would include $5 \times 5 - 2 + 1$.

Several problem-solving activities requiring the use of grouping symbols to alter the order of operations are suggested by Sanfiorenzo (1991):

1. Use grouping symbols to make a sentence true.
   Example: $11 - 5 \times 2 + 3 = 30$
   Solution: $(11 - 5) \times (2 + 3) = 30$
2. Use grouping symbols to produce multiple values for an expression.
   Example: $4 + 8 \div 4 - 2$
   Solution: $(4 + 8) \div (4 - 2) = 6$
   $(4 + 8) \div 4 - 2 = 1$
3. Find operations and use grouping symbols to make a sentence true.
   Example: $5 \square 4 \square 2 = 2$
   Solution: $(5 - 4) \times 2 = 2$

Activities 17-9 and 17-10 will help children better understand order of operations.

ACTIVITY 17-9 Calculator Explorations

Procedure

Perform the operations as they occur left to right on paper first and then explore the order of operations for the following problems using a calculator.

1. $12 - 3 + 5$
2. $24 + 3 \times 2$
3. $-3 - 8 - 1$
4. $3 + \frac{5}{2}$
5. $24 - 4^2$

ACTIVITY 17-10 Arithmetic Rabbits

Procedure

1. Draw a rabbit—4 squares, 2 ears, and 1 tail.
2. Write any four numbers in the four squares.
3. Add across and down and write the sums. Add diagonally and write the sums in the ears.
4. Add the two "across" sums. Write this number in the tail. Add the two "down" sums. Add the two "diagonal" sums. What do you notice?
   - Do this using your own four numbers. Is the final sum always the same? Why?
   - Try this with multiplication instead of addition.
   - Now try it using subtraction.

Understanding Algebraic Equations

An algebraic equation is formed when two or more algebraic expressions containing at least one variable are joined by an equal sign, such as $4x + 7 = 19$. To help children develop understanding of equations, provide tables of real-world data that require children to extend and generalize the pattern, and help children understand how to use algebraic equations to represent these patterns.

Early Equations Development

Nibbelink (1990) outlined an instructional sequence for teaching equations that provides a gradual transition from arithmetic to algebra. In the early stages (up to the middle of grade 2), he recommends working with basic facts in vertical, rather than horizontal, format because young children can more easily discriminate up from down than right from left. Many children read $\square - 5 = 3$ as $3 = 5 - \square$ and write 2 in the blank, yet this type of reversed reading rarely occurs when problems are written in vertical form. Nibbelink recommends the following gradual steps:

Step 1: Hidden and missing numbers. Story lines and special characters are used at this stage. For example, a cat wearing a large mitten covers a number with its paw, and a gerbil eats a hole in the paper where a number was written (Figure 17-14).

Step 2: Replaced numbers. The character at this stage (which can begin about the middle of grade 3) is a thief who steals numbers and leaves, as a mark, the letter of his or her first name at the scene of the crime. The idea is that the letter marks the spot and the task is to replace that letter with the number that will make the sentence true (Figure 17-15). In this context, it is reasonable that a given letter can replace different numbers in different problems, and that in a given problem any one letter will always represent the same number. This provides a beginning for the understanding of variables.

Step 3: Number aliases (unknowns). The idea in this stage (beginning in the middle of grade 4) is that

FIGURE 17-14 Examples of Using Story Lines to Understand Hidden and Missing Numbers

Hidden Number	Missing Number
2	(hole)
+ (paw)	− 3
7	5

FIGURE 17-15 An Example of Using a Fun Context to Understand Replaced Numbers

Replaced Numbers

23 +B 29	4 × H = 28 T − 3 = 18

numbers use aliases that are letters of the alphabet. Note that different numbers can use the same alias in different problems and that a given number can choose different pseudonyms from problem to problem. The task in $P + 8 = 13$ is to find which number is using the name P in this instance. Thus, the letter is a name for a number. Solving equations is likened to detective work aimed at finding the true (number) identity of the letter. Children do not see a variable as only one number any longer, but rather as an unknown with many possibilities yet only one known value for the specific scenario.

Step 4: Variables over specified domains. The formal concept of a variable is studied in algebra courses.

In the early grades, children find missing or unknown numbers in open number sentences by using their knowledge of basic facts or by applying the guess-and-check strategy. For example, if $m - 6 = 8$, then $m = 14$ because $14 - 6 = 8$. If they had first selected, say, 16, from a guess-and-check method, they would plug the value in to find that the expression $16 - 6$ is 10, which is high for the value of 8 and, therefore, in need of adjustment. In the intermediate years, children begin to learn procedures to solve equations that rely on inverse relationships, noting, for example, that because addition and subtraction are *inverse* operations (see Chapter 7), subtraction will undo addition and vice versa.

Kieran (1988) found two different perspectives on solving equations among children in beginning algebra (in grade 7). One group used the guess-and-check approach by substituting different numbers for the letter until they found one that made the sentence true. Another group used inverses of the operations and transposed terms to the other side to solve for the variable. Kieran recommended that elementary school experiences with placeholders should emphasize the substitution method, because this method lends greater meaning to the idea that the letter is really a number in its own right within the equation.

NCTM Principles and Standards Link 17-4

Content Strand: Algebra

Most middle-grade students will need considerable experience with linear equations before they will be comfortable and fluent in transforming or solving them. (NCTM, 2000, p. 226)

Modeling Algebraic Equations

As discussed in the previous section on equality, the notion of balance as a metaphor for an equation is powerful. Provide children with experiences using pan balance scales to help them recognize that any operation performed on one side of an equation must be balanced with the same operation on the other side. Balance scales help children understand that removing or adding something to one pan of the balance scale will offset the balance unless the same procedure is performed to the other pan.

Several models for balancing and solving equations, such as Hands-on Algebra, pan balances, base-ten blocks, and Algebra Tiles, are commercially available. Each model offers an interesting method of representing equations, balancing operational activities, and solving for unknown quantities. Figure 17-16 shows how an equation is represented with each model. Each model offers a method of "seeing" the equation and recognizing the significance of the equal sign, the need for balancing the equations as the solution is explored, and the concept of a unique solution to an equation, independent of the variable used.

Figure 17-17 shows a method of using colored chips (white for positive numbers, black for negative numbers) and some device to represent the unknown for the equation $x + 5 = 2x - 3$. This example moved slowly to remove an x and add a 3 to both sides to find the solution of 8. After finding the unknown value of the variable, this method also allows children to replace the unknowns to verify their answers.

The next step is to reconnect with the order of operations procedures discussed previously. Children may need to combine like terms in order to find solutions. *Like terms* refers to a single term (a *monomial* term) whose variables, as well as the powers of each variable, correspond. For example, $3x$ and $2x$, $5x^2$ and $7x^2$ can be combined with methods discussed previously, as shown in Figure 17-18.

Algebra Tiles, or base-ten blocks in two to four colors, can be used to model equations in one or two variables (see Figure 17-18). These devices allow the introduction of a *trinomial* (three-term) polynomial, in which the highest power of one variable is 2 or less.

Binomial linear expressions, which are two-term polynomials with a highest power of 1, such as $(2x + 1)$ or $(3x - 7)$, can be used to demonstrate multiplication in an array, much like that used with base-ten blocks earlier (Figure 17-19). The result is called a *quadratic expression*,

FIGURE 17-16 Concrete Models for $2x + 5 = 17 - 4$

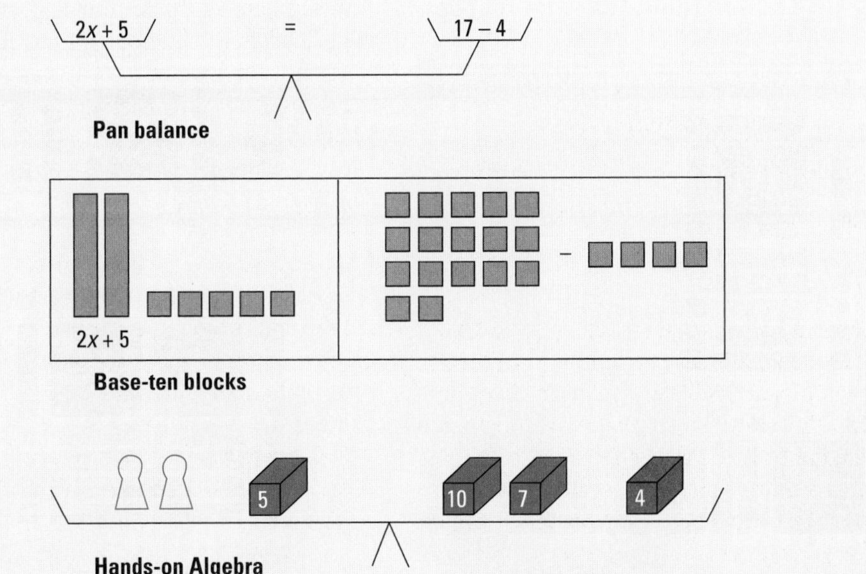

which involves x to the second power, also known as "x squared." Although the process involves variables, take particular care when showing children how this process matches whole-number multiplication (see Figure 17-19). The reverse process is used with quadratics to demonstrate division, often referred to as finding factors of the quadratic. Most algebra classes teach the process of using FOIL (*F*irst, *O*utside, *I*nside, *L*ast) to multiply two binomial expressions together, as in the following example:

$$(2x + 3)\ (x + 1) = 2x^2 + 5x + 3$$

*F*irst terms $(2x)\ (x)$, *O*utside terms $(2x)\ (1)$, *I*nside terms $(3)\ (x)$, *L*ast terms $(3)\ (1)$.

FIGURE 17-17 Model for Solving $x + 5 = 2x - 3$

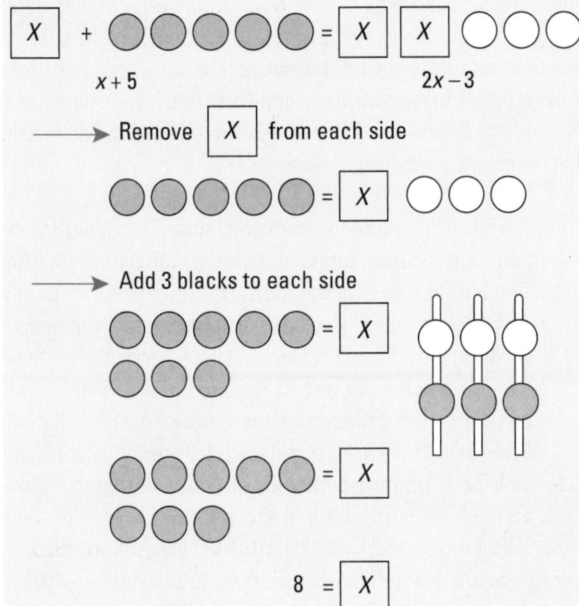

Using the reverse thinking can help children find factors of a quadratic. For instance, when looking for factors of $2x^2 - 7x - 4$, children should first multiply 2 and 4 together. Next, they look for all the factors of 8 that when added are equal to -7, such as $(1, -8)$, $(-1, 8)$, $(2, -4)$, $(-2, 4)$. Now, split the $-7x$ into x and $-8x$. Rewrite the equation as four terms $(2x^2 - 8x + 1x - 4)$ and group the first two and the last two within parentheses $(2x^2 - 8) + (x - 4)$. Last,

FIGURE 17-18 Using Algebra Tiles to Model Algebraic Expressions and Equations

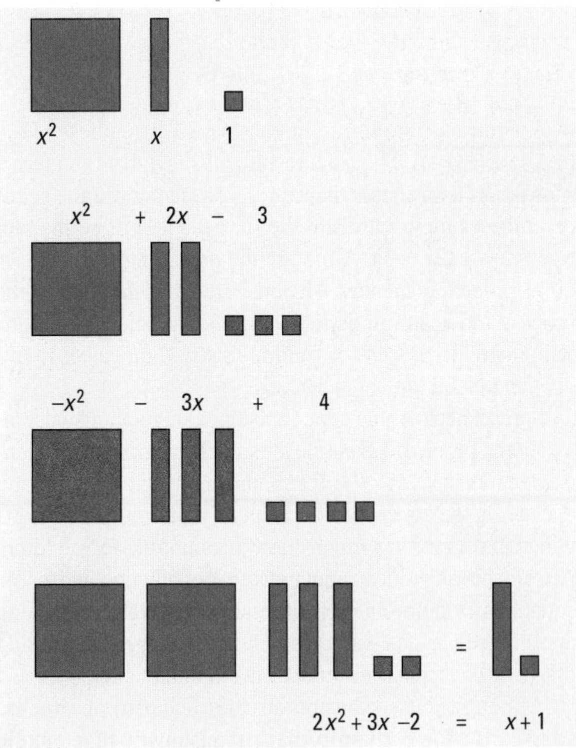

FIGURE 17-19 Using Algebra Tiles to Model Multiplication and Division of Algebraic Expressions

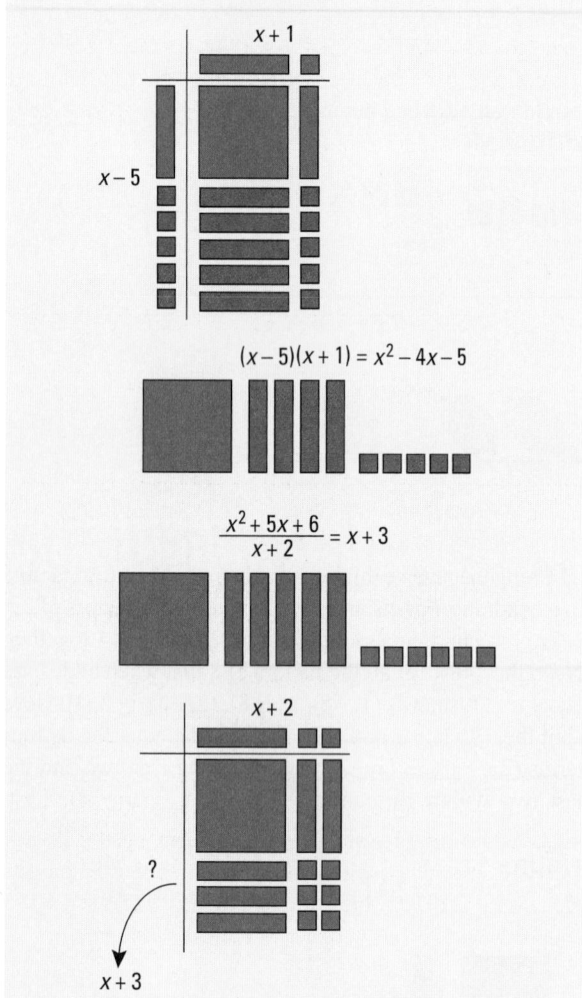

FIGURE 17-20 Using Algebra Tiles to Factor Algebraic Expressions

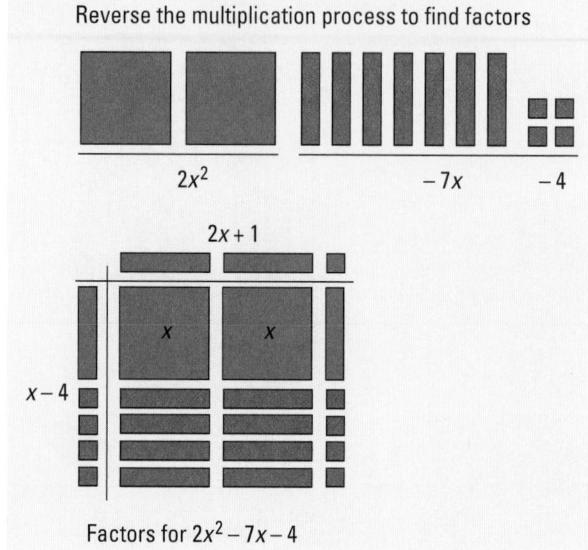

factor out any like terms in each set of parentheses [$2 \times (x-4) + (x-4)$]. The final result will show that both terms possess a factor that is the same. Now, factor out the set of parentheses they share and the final result will be the factors $(x - 4)(2x + 1)$. Although the preceding technique is quite procedural, using Algebra Tiles to demonstrate the process and examining the graphs of quadratic expressions will make the process of finding factors a bit easier to understand (see Figure 17-20).

Spreadsheets or the table function on a graphing calculator should be used to examine the values and graphs of the linear equations: x, $2x$, $x + 1$. Examining many linear graphs and discussing the concept of the slope of a line and y intercepts will make graphing much more meaningful for children. After exploring linear equations, try quadratics and cubic equations to help children generalize the typical graphing appearance of lines, parabolas, and cubic curves. Exploring graphing concepts is discussed later in this chapter.

Although these concepts usually occur in an algebra course, provide early informal lessons involving concrete models that illustrate the differences between a constant (or number), a binomial, or a trinomial of power two (quadratic). Teaching lessons about the combining of like terms, performing simple operations, and solving equations will prove easier than expected and will lead to a better understanding of variables, expressions, equations, and functions.

Real-World Settings for Algebraic Equations

There are many real-world settings for problems using algebraic equations. Problems involving proportional reasoning, such as finding values of similar figures, identifying unit prices, and map/scale diagrams, can lead nicely into realistic algebraic equations with one variable. Although more than one approach can be used to solve a proportion, the traditional approach using a cross product will create an algebraic equation. The following are examples of real-world settings for which children can use algebraic equations to solve:

- A scale drawing of my backyard shows the length to be two more centimeters than twice the size of the width. The length was exactly 8 cm. If the scale factor of my diagram implies that every centimeter represents 3 yards, find the dimensions of my yard. Will I have enough fencing if I have 150 yards of material?
- Two out of 3 children drink 1 pint of milk at lunch each day. If the cafeteria sold 480 pints of milk today, how many people drank milk at lunch? How many people did not drink milk?
- Two ladders differ in length by 5 m. When the ladders are placed end to end, the total length is 70 m. What is the length of each ladder?

- A pet store always stocks 3 cats to every 2 dogs. All together there are 75 pets. How many of each pet does the store have in stock?
- I have 43 cents in my pocket. What are the possible coins in my pocket?
- I have a recipe that serves 6 people. How many times should I make the recipe to serve 132 people?

Activity 17-11 will help children better understand algebraic equations.

ACTIVITY 17-11 What's My Value?

Materials
Algebra Tiles

Procedure
Use Algebra Tiles to simplify the following expressions

a. $4(x + 3) + 2\ (x - 1)$

b. $(3x^2 + 2x - 6) + (2x^2 - 4x + 5)$

c. $-3x - 7 - (-5x + 6)$

d. $(2x^2 - 4x - 5) - (x^2 - 4x + 7)$

Evaluate each expression when $x = 1$, when $x = 0$, and when $x = -1$.

 Go to the Assignments and Activities section of Topic 14: "Algebraic Thinking" in the MyEducationLab for your course and complete the activity "Real World Application" to see how one teacher helps her students use mathematic reasoning.

Solving Inequalities

An *equation* is a statement that two expressions are equal. An *inequality* is a statement that one expression is greater than (or less than) the other. In the early grades, children learn to use the symbols < and > to write sentences expressing relationships between unequal numbers (for example, $2 < 5$ and $3 + 4 > 6$). Children need to practice using these symbols because they often confuse the signs or do not associate the terms "greater than" and "less than" with the proper symbols. When integers are introduced, children often need more practice to see that $-4 > -8$. As with equations, the notion of balance applies to inequalities. However, with inequalities, the pan balance will show the two sides to be *out* of balance, with one pan higher than the other.

Solving an inequality containing a variable involves finding all possible values from the replacement set that will make the sentence true. For example, if the replacement set is the set of whole numbers, then the solution set for $x + 1 < 4$ consists of the numbers 0, 1, and 2. If the replacement set for this inequality is the integers, then the solution set consists of all integers less than 3—an infinite set. The solution in the set of rational numbers is expressed symbolically as $x < 3$, where x represents a rational number. Another method is to use the concept of infinity and parentheses, i.e., $(-\infty\ 3)$. The solution sets should be found and can be expressed symbolically on a number line as is done in the following examples:

$4x + 2 < 14$ leads to $x < 3$ or $(-\infty, 3)$

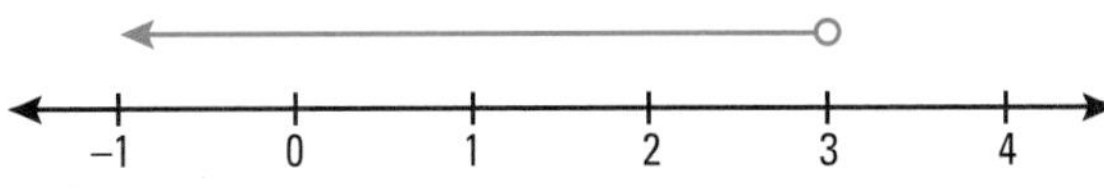

$4x - 8 > 2(x - 4)$ leads to $x \geq 0$ or $(0, +\infty)$

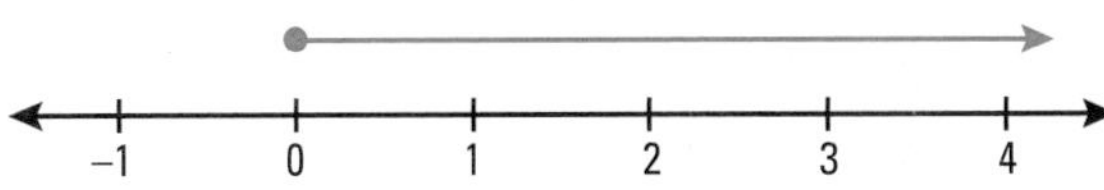

First, take special care to explain when the end point is and is not included in the solution set (for example, is the solution $x > 3$ or $x > 3$?) and what it means to go to infinity. Next, show how to represent a combined solution set such as $x < -1$ and $x > 4$. All operational methods for solving equations and the order of operations apply to inequalities, with the exception of one specific situation. If the inequality requires the multiplication or division of a negative number, the result is that the sign flips the opposite way. This can be explained to children by comparing and contrasting the tables of data and the graphs for congruent inequalities such as $-x > 4$ and $x < -4$.

Functions

The concept of function is one of the fundamental ideas in mathematics. In the school curriculum, a function is viewed both as a concept—the study of regularity—and as a process—analyzing relationships (Howden, 1989). "Joint variation is at the heart of understanding patterns and functions. As children grow in their ability to derive meaning for variables in contexts, they encounter variables that are changing in relation to each other" (Lappan, 1998, p. 57). This section discusses how teachers can help children understand functions.

What Is a Function?

When the value of one quantity (*dependent* variable) depends on or varies with the value of another (*independent* variable), we say that the first quantity is a *function* of the second quantity. For example, the height of a burning candle is a function of time: The longer the time it burns, the shorter the candle becomes.

NCTM Principles and Standards Link 17-5

Content Strand: Algebra

The study of patterns and relationships in the middle grades should focus on patterns that relate to linear functions, which arise when there is a constant rate of change. Students should solve problems in which they use tables, graphs, words, and symbolic expressions to represent and examine functions and patterns of change. (NCTM, 2000, p. 223)

In general, a *function* is a rule of correspondence connecting the elements of one set (the *domain* of the function) with the elements of another set (the *range* of the function) such that each member of the domain corresponds to a unique member of the range. For example, the perimeter of a square is determined by the length of its sides. For each value of a side, there is one and only one corresponding value for the perimeter. The domain and the range of this function are the non-negative real numbers. In this case, the rule of correspondence can be expressed algebraically as an equation, $P = 4s$. It can also be represented as an arrow diagram, a table, and a graph (Figure 17-21). Using formal functional language and notation, we say that the perimeter of a square is a function of the length of its side and write $f(s) = 4s$.

Many equations written in two variables can be considered functions, if one variable depends on the input of the other variable. Another way of defining a rule of correspondence is to give all possible pairings of elements in a table or arrow diagram, as in Figure 17-22(a). This diagram is called a *mapping* of the relationship. The relation defined by the arrow diagram in Figure 17-22(b) is not a function because the element 3 in the domain corresponds

FIGURE 17-22 Different Mappings

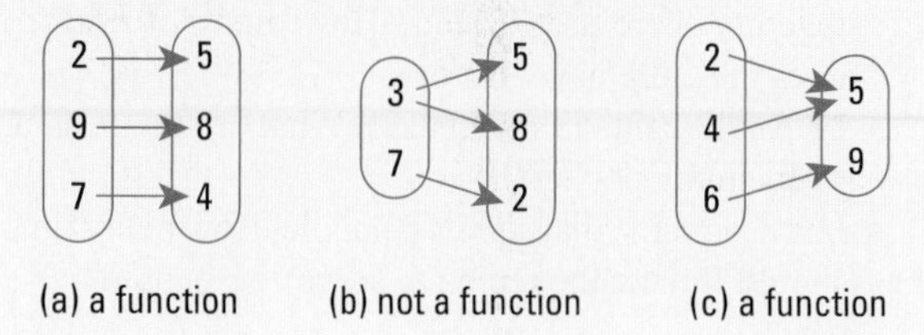

(a) a function (b) not a function (c) a function

to two different elements, 5 and 8, in the range. The relation represented in Figure 17-22(c) is a function even though two different elements in the domain are paired with the same element in the range. The key attribute of a function is that each first element corresponds to only one other element.

Developing Function Concepts

There are at least five different ways to represent a function. Each way communicates the same functional relationship. It is important to provide children with as many different ways of viewing a function as possible so that they can meaningfully interpret situations. The representations include the following: contextual setting, table representations, language expressions, graphical representations, and symbolic representations.

First and foremost, a function should begin with a contextual setting, preferably a real-world setting, to provide a meaningful experience with the function. Such settings help children understand the function.

Second, children can collect data and create a table. This is particularly important when the independent variable is ascending. With the help of a calculator and a few basic statistical options, data can be graphed to look for a pattern, and an equation can be generalized. Starting with the data allows for a connection with the contextual

FIGURE 17-21 Expressing Function Rules as an Arrow Diagram, Table, and a Graph

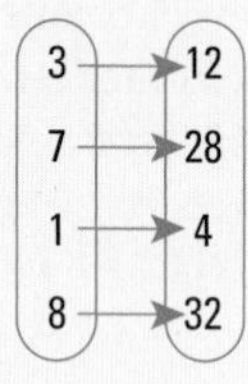

side s	perimeter $4s$
5	20
2	8
6	24
4	16

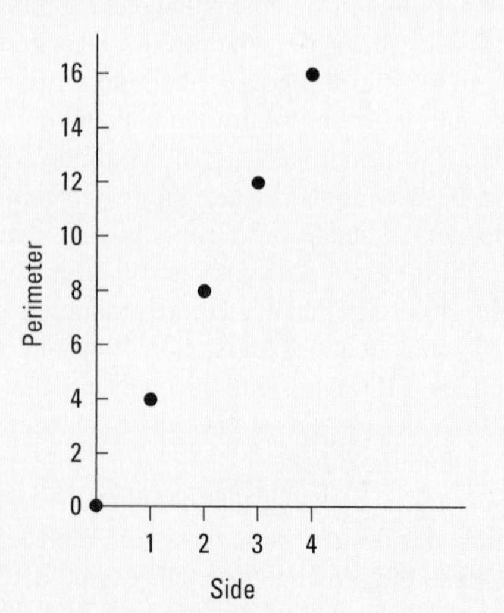

problem. Using a calculator and the Computer-Based Lab (CBL™) probes to capture real data, such as the distance from a location or the temperature of an item, allows children to establish a pattern and make a generalization from the graph of the data. This technique will help children determine if each element is paired with a unique functional value.

Third, language expression helps children describe the relationship in a meaningful and useful manner. The expression should be generated by describing, either in writing or in spoken words, the effects of one variable on the other and the relationship between the variables. This verbalization will provide a bridge to the other representations and provide an understanding of the function.

Fourth, graphical representation is the most commonly used mode of representing a function. A graph provides a visual representation of the function and can often help children understand the meaning of a situation. Children can interpret the relationship between the variables by analyzing the graphs as linear or nonlinear, increasing or decreasing, continuous or discontinuous. Analyzing graphs provides a close connection to the process of finding the equation. However, warning children that extrapolating the data to extend indefinitely may not make sense for the problem provided. Limitations may exist that are not being addressed through the extended graph or the data may not provide a clear functional relationship. For instance, if a teacher provides children with a list of student ID numbers and corresponding mathematics and science grades, they will see that a pattern does not necessarily emerge in all cases.

Fifth, converting the functional relationship into an equation results in a more abstract form than any of the previously mentioned representations. This method utilizes the symbolism often found in the mathematics curriculum. The general form assists in making calculations for any part of the function. The equation can be entered into a calculator to produce the table of data and the graph. This method allows us to explore the graph without the tedious job of plotting points.

The following problems can be used to practice using each representation of a function:

1. Suppose we need to convert the temperature reported to us in Fahrenheit into Celsius. The function $C(f) = \frac{5}{9}(F - 32)$ provides the converted value. Have children make a table of data for an assortment of temperatures. Encourage them to graph the ordered pairs (32, 0) and (212, 100). Connect the two points. Explore the connections between the table of data and the line they just created. Have children describe in their own words the reverse relationship for finding a temperature in Fahrenheit if the temperature is given in Celsius.
2. Imagine you are the vendor at a newspaper stand. *The New York Times* costs $1 per copy and the local paper costs 50 cents per copy. If you sell an average of 50 copies of each paper per day, find your weekly income based on this daily average. Make a chart showing the cumulative income for the week and plot the data. Generalize the formula to find your cumulative income for any given day.
3. Explore all the possible rectangles that can be formed with a piece of string 24 inches long—the area will vary in each. If you begin with the thinnest rectangle formed by integers, its dimensions will be 1×11 inches. List all possible integer dimensions in a table of data. Identify the shape that will produce the maximum area. Graph length and width and notice the functional relationship. Write a relationship that gives the area of the shape as the dimensions vary. In your own words, explain what occurs to the area as the length and width vary.
4. Ask children "Are you a square?" Have children measure the height and arm span of several classmates. Have them generate a table, plot the points, and generalize a pattern. Children can verbalize the relationship, then look for other kinds of patterns that match this function. A student who is a short rectangle will have a height less than the arm span, a tall rectangle will have a height greater than the arm span, and a square's values will be equal.
5. Assign each group of children a different Cuisenaire rod. Have them calculate and tabulate the volume and surface area of their rod. Next, have them place another rod side by side, with the longest sides together. Have children calculate the volume and surface area again. Collect the data and graph the sequence number to the volume, the sequence number to the surface area, and the volume to the surface area. Ask children to explain in their own words what relationships they noticed as they added a rod each time. Can they generalize this solution for each case? Examine the rods and the relationships in tabular, graphical, verbal form and as an equation of the other groups' findings.

NCTM Principles and Standards Link 17-6

Content Strand: Algebra

It is essential that [students] become comfortable in relating symbolic expressions containing variables to verbal, tabular, and graphical representations of numerical and quantitative relationships. Students should develop an initial understanding of several different meanings and uses of variables through representing quantities in a variety of problem situations. (NCTM, 2000, p. 223)

Regardless of which representation is used, it is important to realize that each representation describes the relationship of the function. In fact, having children generate all five representations will provide a more diverse

FIGURE 17-23 Example of Children's Use of a Table to Show Number Patterns

children	1	2	3	4	10
eyes	2	4	6	8	—

approach and provide different access routes for children with different learning styles.

Functional Patterns

In the primary grades, children's experiences with the concept of function focus on number patterns and mathematical relationships. For example, children could explore the problem of finding the total number of eyes in a small group or in the class (Howden, 1989). They might do this by first counting, drawing pictures, or using chips or blocks to model the process and then making a table to record their findings (Figure 17-23).

In the discussion, encourage children to use words to describe the patterns and generalize the result. The children might relate the "eyes" pattern to skip counting, counting by twos, or adding two each time. The idea of a functional relationship is encountered in predicting (without continuing the pattern) the total number of eyes in a group of 10 children. When explaining their answers, children might say that the number of eyes is equal to the number of people added to itself or doubled (multiplied by 2).

Writing the pattern rule in a generalized form as $\square + \square$, or $\square \times 2$, introduces the use of a variable as a placeholder for any number. In this example, the number of eyes is dependent on the number of children involved or f(*children*) = 2 × *children*. Similar problems involve finding the relationship between tricycles and the number of wheels or hands and the number of fingers. Children might also be asked to find real-world examples of relationships that match given rules, such as $\square \times 10$.

Next, encourage the development of a functional relationship where one value is obviously dependent on another value by asking children to answer real-world questions that have a functional relationship. For instance, ask children "How many toothpicks are needed to make 10 triangles?" If the triangles are separate from one another, three toothpicks are needed for each triangle and the pattern rule is $3 \times \square$. Suppose, however, that triangles can share a common side. Looking at the illustration on p. 415 in the right column, we predict that 21 toothpicks are needed to make 10 triangles. The rule can be expressed as $2 \times \square + 1$.

Try asking children the following questions:

- How many snap cubes can you connect together in relationship to the time given?
- How long will it take you to pass a ball around to 100 children?
- How far will a plastic car travel if the height of the ramp varies?
- How long will it take you to walk up a flight of stairs?
- What is the relationship between the time it takes you to get lunch and your position in line?
- How long do you spend on the bus given the distance the bus travels?
- How many Ping-Pong balls would be needed to fill a room?

Function Machines and Tables

A popular way of introducing functions in the elementary grades is through *function machines.* The idea is that something is fed into the machine (the "input") and operated on by a rule, and the resulting output comes out of the machine. Children's first exposure to a function machine should be with manipulatives at pre-K–2. For example, the rule may be that a shape drops in and the shape is shrunk down into one-__________th its size, or a given shape is dropped in and a shape with one more side comes out. Next, move into a number function machine. The rule "multiply by 3 and add 1" might first be described in words. Children can drop in several sequential numbers to see the effects of the function machine on their value. The task is to find for given "input" numbers the associated "output" numbers and record these numbers in a table, as in Figure 17-24(a). Children can graph the values on a Cartesian graph to visualize the pattern. Later, this function would be represented using an algebraic expression: $3 \times \square + 1$ or $3n + 1$.

A related activity is "Guess My Rule," in which the objective is to determine the rule used to produce a given set of values. Include special functions such as the constant shown in Figure 17-24(b). The rule might be verbalized as "the answer is always 3," or "double the first number and add the second to get the third number." These explanations

FIGURE 17-24 Function Machine and Related Tables

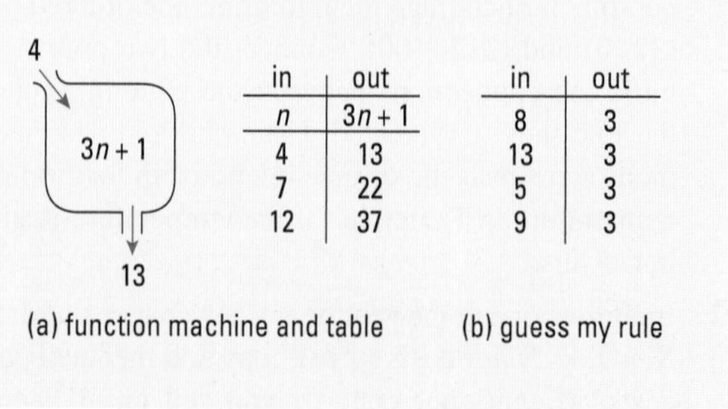

4
3n + 1
13
in | out
n | 3n + 1
4 | 13
7 | 22
12 | 37
in | out
8 | 3
13 | 3
5 | 3
9 | 3

(a) function machine and table (b) guess my rule

can then be expressed as a function and tested for the values provided to derive a set of values that fit the rule.

Sequences

A number *sequence* is an ordered set of numbers such that there is a *first term,* a *second term,* a *third term,* and so on. The arrangement proceeds from left to right, with each term separated by a comma. If the "in" values in a function table are 1, 2, 3, and so on, the corresponding "out" values constitute a sequence. Thus, a sequence is a function in which the "in" values are indicated by the position of the term (first–1, second–2, third–3, and so on).

Some sequences can be described algebraically by finding a pattern that relates the number of the term to the term itself. The pattern rule is called the general, or *n*th, term of the sequence. For example, the *n*th term of the sequence of positive even numbers 2, 4, 6, . . . is $2n$, which means that every even number is the product of 2 and a counting number and that a given term of the sequence is found by replacing n in the general term by the term number. Thus, the 10th term is $2(10) = 20$.

Other elementary sequences and their *n*th terms are as follows:

Name	Sequence	*n*th Term
Counting numbers	$1, 2, 3, \ldots, n$	$f(n) = 2n$
Odd numbers	$1, 3, 5, \ldots, 2n - 1$	$f(n) = 2n - 1$
Multiples of 5	$5, 10, 15, \ldots, 5n$	$f(n) = 5n$
Skip counting	$4, 10, 16, \ldots, 6n - 2$	$f(n) = 6n - 2$
Square numbers	$1, 4, 9, \ldots, n^2$	$f(n) = n^2$
Triangular numbers	$1, 3, 6, \ldots, (n^2 + n)$	$f(n) = (n^2 + n)$

Given the first few terms of a sequence, children must find the rule for that pattern, write the next few terms, generalize the pattern to determine a term not found and, where possible, give the *n*th term.

The Fibonacci numbers are an interesting sequence, as follows:

$$0, 1, 1, 2, 3, \ldots, f(n - 1) + f(n)$$

Notice that each new value in the sequence is the sum of the previous two values. Explorations of the Fibonacci numbers can include generalizing the approximation for the golden ratio, 1.618. . . . By looking at the ratio of $\frac{f(n)}{f(n-1)}$, the value will eventually approach the golden ratio.

Functions on the Calculator

Most inexpensive calculators have built-in constant features that permit the user to evaluate expressions such as $n + 3$, $n - 3$, $3n$, and $n \div 3$ for different values of the variable by entering a number and pressing [=]. For example, the function $3n$ is established by keying 3 [×]. Successively pressing 5 [=], 8 [=], 12 [=] produces 15, 24, 36 in the display. To establish the function $n - 3$, press [−] 3 [=]. This calculator feature might be explored in conjunction with function machines to illustrate the idea of a machine operating on the input of sequential numbers according to a given rule to produce output numbers. Programmable calculators can handle more complex expressions.

Graphing calculators and CBL probes capture real data and generate a scatter plot of the data. Good exploratory questions can be asked to generate more interesting functional relationships. For instance, ask children to create a linear descending line, an increasing line, a parabola, a horizontal line, and a vertical line using a motion detector. They will find this challenging, perhaps even impossible. Using probes and calculators allows one to look for patterns and to generalize many realistic formulas resulting from the graph of the data.

Data that do not lend themselves well to analysis can often be entered into the calculator to identify the line of best fit. When collecting real data, the pattern is not always as obviously linear, or quadratic, as one might anticipate. The graphing calculator's statistical options allow for a formula or function relationship to emerge.

> PEARSON myeducationlab The Power of Classroom Practice Go to the Assignments and Activities section of Topic 14: "Algebraic Thinking" in the MyEducationLab for your course and complete the activity "Linear Equations and Graphing Calculators" to see how one teacher helps her students use mathematic reasoning.

Graphing Functions

In geometry, children learn to plot ordered pairs of numbers on a coordinate system. A function can be represented graphically by thinking of the "in" and "out" elements in a table of values as the horizontal and vertical coordinates, respectively, and plotting the points. The transition to naming the axes x and y is accomplished by expressing the rule as an equation in x and y and using these variables as column headings in a table of values. Consider $y = 4x - 3$.

x	$y = 4x - 3$
1	1
2	5
3	7
4	?

Children's first experiences with graphing functions often involve familiar formulas such as $P = 4s$, which relates the length of a side of a square and its perimeter (Figure 17-25). Children can observe that the points lie on a line. Later, the points may be connected and extended. Encourage children to find how the relation "increasing the side by 1 increases the perimeter by 4" is shown in the graph and how it directly relates to identifying the slope of a line of the

FIGURE 17-25 Graphing Perimeter and Area of a Square and Volume of a Cube

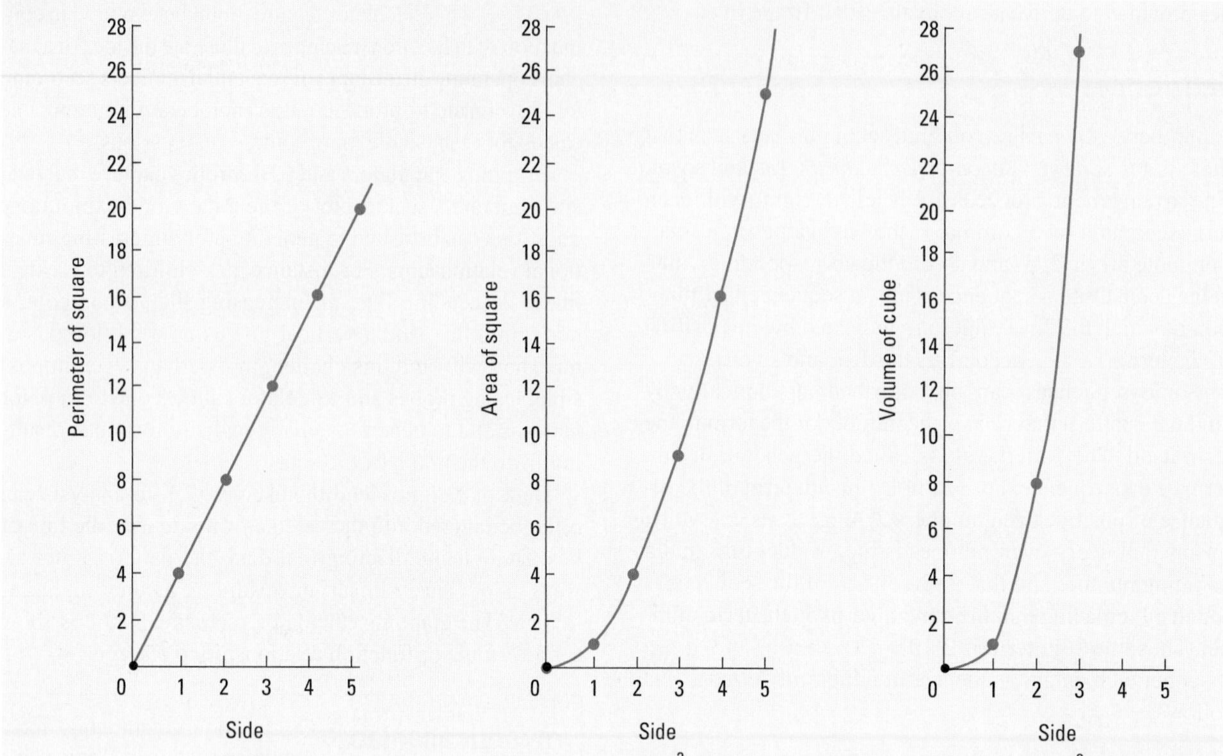

given form $y = mx + b$. Encourage children to examine two points and to calculate the rise versus the run. This value is called the *slope* and in the previous example will prove to be 4. The next interesting values result when the graph crosses the axes, in particular the y-axis. Using the calculator to graph and adjust the m and b values will help children make generalizations about the role of the constants m and b. This is a particularly important development with which many children learning algebra struggle.

Graphs representing the formulas for the area of a square ($A = s^2$) and the volume of a cube ($V = s^3$) can also be constructed. Children will find that these are not straight-line graphs. A discussion of the family of graphs for lines, quadratics, and cubic equations will be more meaningful when the graphs are available. The calculator can be used to explore many families of graphs and simple shifts in constants to see the effects of those shifts.

Formulas

Children's first encounters with algebraic expressions usually involve *formulas* that contain more than one variable. For example, children discover that the perimeter of a rectangle can be found by adding twice the length and twice the width or by adding the length and width and doubling the result. After expressing this relationship in words, they write it using symbols: $P = 2l + 2w$, or $P = 2(l + w)$. The perimeters of different rectangles are then determined by substituting the values of their dimensions in the formula. Next, children quickly learn to cover up a shape with square color tiles; however, teachers do not always make it clear to children that this means finding the area of the rectangle. The dimensions become an integral part in the formula development of $A = lw$. Other well-known formulas include $V = lwh$ (volume of a rectangular prism), $A = \pi r^2$ (area of a circle), and $i = prt$ (simple interest).

Activities 17-12 and 17-13 will help children to better understand formulas.

ACTIVITY 17-12 Function Machine

Procedure

Find the values returned from each of the function machines for the following input:

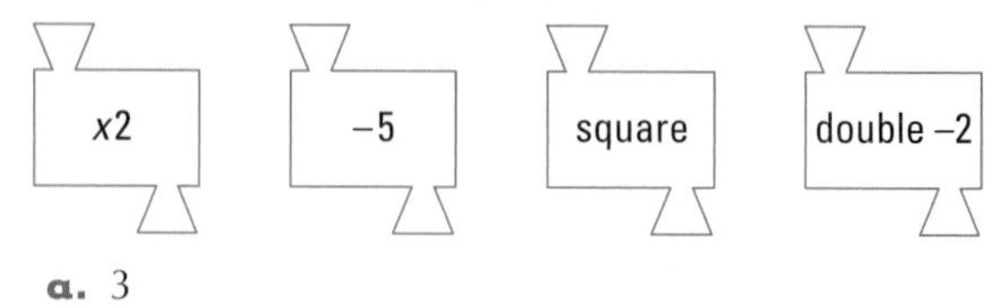

a. 3

b. −1

c. 5

d. $x + 1$

FIGURE 17-26 Graphs Showing Relationships between Height and Arm Span and Wrist and Neck Sizes

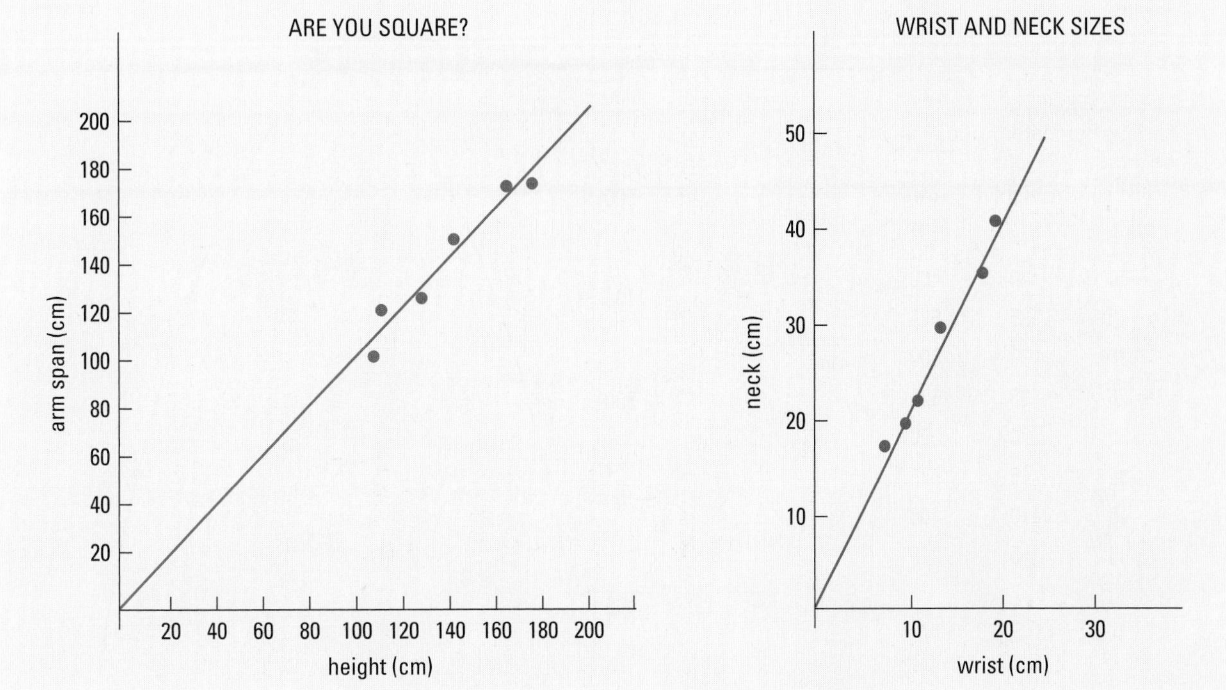

ACTIVITY 17-13 Analyze It!

Calculate sample data values in the functional relationships below. Determine which is the dependent event and which is the independent event.

- The speed of a toy car compared with the height of the ramp it runs down
- The time it takes to pass a book along a line compared with the number of people in the line
- The time it takes for the last person in line to go through the lunch line compared with the number of people in line
- The time spent traveling in an airplane compared with the distance traveled
- The time it takes an ice cube to melt compared with the temperature exerted on the ice cube

---

Instruction and Assessment Activities

In addition to drawing graphs for formulas, children can take measurements or collect data for two related variables and plot the information on a graph. Problems of this nature include finding the relationship between height and arm span and between the distances around the wrist and neck (Figure 17-26). If appropriate graphing software is available, some children may wish to construct these graphs on a computer.

Problems involving relationships between measurement concepts such as perimeter and area or volume and surface area provide further opportunities for children to generate data, organize them in a table, and construct a graph (Phillips, 1991). For example, if you had 100 m of fencing to enclose a rectangular garden plot, what dimensions would you choose? To investigate this problem, children might systematically list selected integer values for the base and height and compute the areas of corresponding rectangles. They could then draw a graph showing the relationship between the base and the area of these rectangles (Figure 17-27). This table and graph reveal that the rectangle with the greatest area is actually a square with sides measuring 25 m. Long, narrow rectangles have small areas. In answering the original question of this example, children can identify other factors that might be considered in choosing the shape of the plot.

Many of the activities to help children understand functions require them to describe patterns in words, extend patterns visually, represent relationships using tables and graphs, make predictions based on relationships, and generalize functional relationship. All of these components support the development of algebraic thinking.

FIGURE 17-27 Relationship between the Base and Area of Rectangles

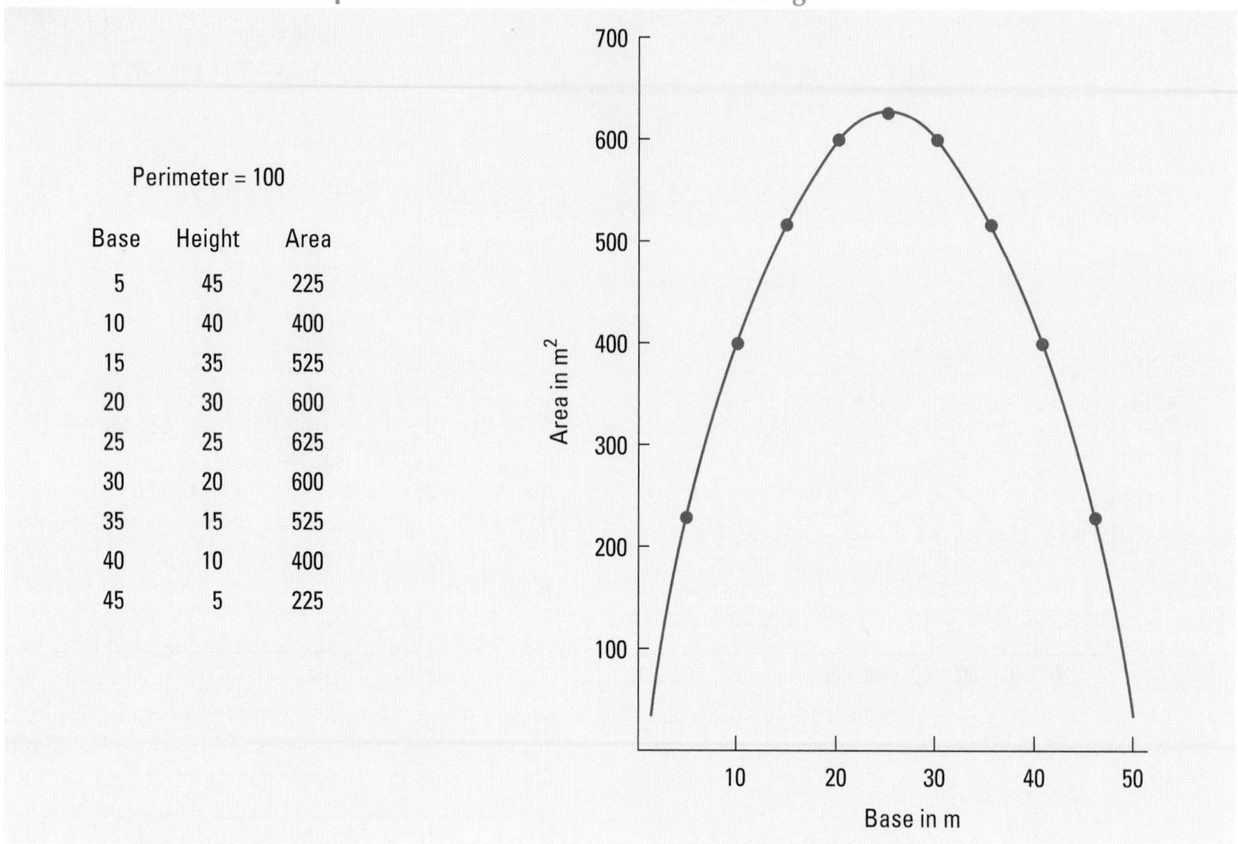

Perimeter = 100

Base	Height	Area
5	45	225
10	40	400
15	35	525
20	30	600
25	25	625
30	20	600
35	15	525
40	10	400
45	5	225

Conclusion

The development of algebraic thinking in the mathematics curriculum begins in the early grades and occurs as a gradual building from informal to formal concepts (Schultz, 1991). Key ideas that run through the grades include patterns, relationships, variables, exponents, expressions, properties, equations, inequalities, functions, and graphing. The transition from arithmetic to algebra provides many opportunities for children to engage in problem solving and to make connections. Experiences such as those described in this chapter will help children understand mathematics through sense-making activities as they study algebraic thinking during the primary years through to algebra in the middle school and high school years.

CHAPTER

17

Sample Lesson

A Lesson on Equality

Grade level: Second

Materials: At least one type of counters, such as Unifix cubes.

Lesson objective: Students will use objects to correctly represent and compare whole numbers.

Standards link: Students use number patterns to extend their knowledge of properties of numbers and operations (NCTM *Curriculum Focal Points,* grade 2).

Launch: Display the open number sentence below and ask, "What number can you put in the box to make this a true number sentence?"

$$8 + 4 = \square + 5$$

Solicit answers. Common answers include 12, 17, and 7. Discuss ways to determine the correct answer, such as using counters.

Present students with a collection of several problems such as the following. Their task is to determine if each problem is true or false and explain why.

1. $6 + 5 = 6 + 5$
2. $7 + 4 = 14 - 3$
3. $7 + 4 = 11 - 2$

Explore: In pairs, have students consider the preceding problems, deciding the correct solution for the first problem, and deciding which of the last three problems are true or false. For each problem, students should draw a picture or write about their reasoning.

Summarize: Coming together as a whole class, select one pair of students to come to the front of the room and explain their thinking on each problem. Focus on their explanations of how they decided if they were equal. The key concept here is that both sides of an equation are like a balance scale; each side needs to be equal to the other side.

FOLLOW-UP

Complete the following questions.

1. Consider difficulties students might have with this concept and this lesson. What modification could you make to avoid or minimize these issues? What modifications could you make for students with special needs?
2. What might the *next* lesson focus on, and why?

IN PRACTICE

Complete the following activities to include in your professional portfolio.

1. Visit a middle school classroom and informally interview several children to assess their understanding of variables and integers. Ask the children questions such as the following:
   - What does the expression $3b$ mean?
   - What is n if $n - 4 = 9$? $2n = n$? $2n = 1$?
   - Which is greater, $2n$ or $n + 2$? Explain.
2. Write a lesson plan that would encourage children to develop a geometric pattern and connect it to a table of data that would generalize the nth term.
3. Examine a mathematics textbook's section on operations on integers. Describe the models used in the textbook to represent operations on integers.
4. Using a model and an operation of your choice, write a lesson plan to introduce an operation with integers to middle school children.
5. Write a lesson plan using a real-world situation to introduce the concept of variables to middle school children.
6. Using a model of your choice, write a lesson plan to introduce a method for solving an equation.

LINKS TO THE INTERNET

Math Forum: Algebra

http://mathforum.org/algebra/k12.algebra.html

Contains many lists of algebra resources available on the Internet.

Project Interactivate

http://www.shodor.org/interactivate/activities/#fun

Contains many activities on functions and algebraic concepts such as linear functions, plotting, graphs on the coordinate plane, function machines, and reading graphs.

RESOURCES FOR TEACHERS

Books on Algebraic Thinking

Charles, L. H. (1990). *Algebra Thinking: First Experiences.* Sunnyvale, CA: Creative Publications.

Picciotto, H. (1990). *The Algebra Lab: Middle School.* Sunnyvale, CA: Creative Publications.

Children's Literature

Anno, M. (1995). *Anno's Magic Seeds*. New York: Philomel.

Appelt, Kathi. (1999). *Bats on Parade.* New York: Morrow Junior Books.

Boynton, Sandra. (1995). *Horns to Toes and in Between.* New York: Simon & Schuster.

Chwast, Seymour. (1993). *The 12 Circus Rings.* San Diego: Harcourt Brace & Co.

Clement, Rod. (1991). *Counting on Frank.* Milwaukee: Gareth Stevens Publishing.

Day, Nancy Raines. (2003). *Double Those Wheels.* New York: Dutton Children's Books.

Dodds, Dayle Anne. (1999). *The Great Divide.* Cambridge, MA: Candlewick.

Glass, Julie. (2000). *Counting Sheep.* New York: RandomHouse.

Hong, Lily Toy. (1993). *Two of Everything.* Morton Grove, IL: Albert Whitman & Co.

Hutchins, Pat. (1986). *The Doorbell Rang.* New York: Mulberry Books.

Pinczes, Elinor. (1993). *One Hundred Hungry Ants.* Boston: Houghton Mifflin.

Schwartz, D. (1998). *How Much Is a Million?* New York: Mulberry.

Scieszka, J. & Smith, L. (1995). *Math Curse.* New York: Viking.

References

American Association for the Advancement of Science. (1989). *Science for all Americans: A Project 2061 report on literacy goals in science, mathematics, and technology.* Washington, DC: Author.

Anghileri, J., & Johnson, D. C. (1992). Arithmetic operations on whole numbers: Multiplication and division. In T. R. Post (Ed.), *Teaching mathematics in grades K–8: Research-based methods* (pp. 157–200). Boston: Allyn & Bacon.

Artzt, A. L., & Newman, C. M. (1990a). Implementing the standards: Cooperative learning. *Mathematics Teacher, 83*(6), 448–452.

Artzt, A. L., & Newman, C. M. (1990b). *How to use cooperative learning in the mathematics class.* Reston, VA: National Council of Teachers of Mathematics.

Ashlock, R. B. (2009). *Error patterns in computation: Using error patterns to help each student learn* (10th ed.). Upper Saddle River, NJ: Merrill/Prentice Hall.

Ashlock, R. B., Johnson, M. L., Wilson, J. W., & Jones, W. L. (1983). *Guiding each child's learning of mathematics: A diagnostic approach to instruction.* Columbus, OH: Merrill.

Baker, A., & Baker, J. (1990). *Mathematics in process.* Portsmouth, NH: Heinemann Educational Books.

Bankard, D., & Fennell, F. (1991). Ideas. *Arithmetic Teacher, 39*(1), 26–33.

Baratta-Lorton, M. (1987). *Mathematics their way.* Palo Alto, CA: Addison-Wesley.

Barchas, S. E. (1975). *I was walking down the road.* New York: Scholastic.

Baroody A. J. and Benson, A. (2001, November). Early number instruction. *Teaching Children Mathematics*, 154–158.

Baroody, A. J. (1984). Children's difficulties in subtraction: Some causes and questions. *Journal for Research in Mathematics Education, 15*, 203–213.

Battista, Michael T. (2006, October). Understanding the development of students' thinking about length. *Teaching Children Mathematics, 13*(3), 140–146.

Bay-Williams, Jennifer M. (2001, December). What is algebra in elementary school? *Teaching children mathematics*, *8*(4), 196–200.

Behr, M. J., Lesh, R., Post, T. R., & Silver, E. A. (1983). Rational number concepts. In R. Lesh & M. Landau (Eds.), *Acquisition of mathematics concepts and processes* (pp. 91–126). New York: Academic Press.

Bezuk, N. S., & Bieck, M. (1993). Current research on rational numbers and common fractions: Summary and implications for teachers. In D. T. Owens (Ed.), *Research ideas for the classroom: Middle grades mathematics* (pp. 118–136). New York: Macmillan.

Bezuk, N. S., Whitehurst-Payne, S., & Aydelotte, J. (2000). Successful collaborations with parents to promote equity in mathematics. In W. G. Secada (Ed.), *Changing the faces of mathematics* (pp. 143–148). Reston, VA: National Council of Teachers of Mathematics.

Bidwell, J. K. (1991). Readers' dialogue: Susan's personal algorithm. *Arithmetic Teacher, 39*(3), 1.

Billstein, R., Libeskind, S., & Lott, J. W. (1990). *A problem-solving approach to mathematics for elementary school teachers* (4th ed.). New York: Cummings.

Blume, G. W., & Heckman, D. S. (2000). Algebra and functions. In E. A. Silver & P. A. Kenney (Eds.), *Results from the Seventh Mathematics Assessment of the National Assessment of Educational Progress* (pp. 269–300). Reston, VA: National Council of Teachers of Mathematics.

Blume, Glendon W., Enrique Galindo, & Crystal Walcott (2007). Performance in measurement and geometry. In Peter Kloosterman & Frank K. Lester, Jr. (Eds.), *2003 Mathematics Assessment of the National Assessment of Educational Progress*. Reston, VA: National Council of Teachers of Mathematics.

Bohan, H. J., & Shawaker, P. B. (1994). Using manipulatives effectively: A drive down rounding road. *Arithmetic Teacher, 41*(5), 246–248.

Bohan, H., Irby, B., & Vogel, D. (1995). Problem solving: Dealing with data in the elementary school. *Teaching Children Mathematics, 1*(5), 256–260.

Booth, L. R. (1988). Children's difficulties in beginning algebra. In A. F. Coxford (Ed.), *The ideas of algebra, K–12*(pp. 20–32). Reston, VA: National Council of Teachers of Mathematics.

Brahier, D. J., & Speer, W. R. (1995). Investigations: Nuts about mathematics. *Teaching Children Mathematics, 2*(4), 228–232.

Bright, G. W., & Hoeffner, K. (1993). Measurement, probability, statistics, and graphing. In D. T. Owens (Ed.), *Research ideas for the classroom: Middle grades mathematics* (pp. 78–98). New York: Macmillan.

Bright, G. W., Harvey, J. G., & Wheeler, M. M. (1981). Fair games, unfair games. In A. P. Shulte & J. R. Smart (Eds.), *Teaching statistics and probability* (pp. 49–59). Reston, VA: National Council of Teachers of Mathematics.

Brosnan, P. A. (1996). Implementing data analysis in a sixth-grade classroom. *Mathematics Teaching in the Middle School, 1*(8), 622–628.

Brown, C. R. (1973). Math rummy. *Arithmetic Teacher, 20*(1), 44–45.

Brownell, W. A. (1947). An experiment on "borrowing" in third grade arithmetic. *Journal of Educational Research, 41*(3), 161–171.

Brownell, W. A., & Moser, H. E. (1949). Meaningful vs. mechanical learning: A study in grade 3 subtraction. *Duke University Studies in Education, 8*, 1–207.

Browning, C. A., Channell, D. E., & Meyer, R. A. (1994). Preparing teachers to present techniques of exploratory data analysis. *Mathematics Teaching in the Middle School, 1*(2), 166–172.

Burbank, I. K. (1987). Probability without formulas and equations. *Delta-K, 26*(2), 32–39.

Burns, M. (1991). Introducing division through problem-solving experiences. *Arithmetic Teacher, 38*(8), 14–18.

Burns, M. (1998). *Math: Facing an American phobia*. Sausalito, CA: Math Solutions Publications.

Buschman, Larry (2002, October). Becoming a problem solver. *Teaching Children Mathematics, 9*(2), 98–103.

Buschman, Larry (2003, May). Children who enjoy problem solving. *Teaching Children Mathematics, 9*(9), 539–544.

California Mathematics Council. (1996). *Constructive assessment in mathematics*. San Diego: Author.

Cappo, M., & Osterman, G. (1991). Teach students to communicate mathematically. *The Computing Teacher (How Learning & Leading with Technology), 18*(5), 34–39.

Carpenter, T. P., & Moser, J. M. (1982). The development of addition and subtraction problem-solving skills. In T. P. Carpenter, J. M. Moser, & T. A. Romberg (Eds.), *Addition and subtraction: A cognitive perspective* (pp. 9–24). Hillsdale, NJ: Erlbaum.

Carpenter, T. P., Corbitt, M. K., Kepner, H. S. Jr., Lindquist, M. M., & Reys, R. E. (1981). *Results from the Second Mathematics Assessment of the National Assessment of Educational Progress*. Reston, VA: National Council of Teachers of Mathematics.

Carpenter, T. P., Fennema, E., Franke, M. L., Levi, L., & Empson, S. (1999). *Children's mathematics: Cognitively guided instruction*. Portsmouth, NH: Heinemann.

Casey, M. Beth, Ronald L. Nuttall, & Elizabeth Pezaris (2001). Spatial-mechanical reasoning skills versus mathematics self-confidence as mediators of gender differences on mathematics subtests using cross-national gender-based items. *Journal for Research in Mathematics Education, 32*(1), 28–57.

Cathcart, W. G. (1971). The relationship between primary students' rationalization of conservation and their mathematical achievement. *Child Development, 42*, 755–765.

Cathcart, W. G. (1990). Implementation of an Apple Center for Innovation and year 1 results. In L. Pereira-Mendoza & M. Quigley (Eds.), *Canadian Mathematics Education Study Group: Proceedings 1989 Annual Meeting* (pp. 87–98). St. Johns, Newfoundland: Memorial University of Newfoundland.

Cathcart, W. G. (1991). Achievement in a computer-rich environment. In S. Gayle (Ed.), *Proceedings: NECC 91*(pp. 188–194). Eugene, OR: International Society for Technology in Education.

Chang, L. (1985). Multiple methods of teaching the addition and subtraction of integers. *Arithmetic Teacher, 33*(4), 14–19.

Charles, R. I., & Lester, F. K., Jr. (1982). *Teaching problem solving: What, why, & how*. Palo Alto, CA: Seymour.

Chazan, Daniel, Aisling M. Leavy, Geoffrey Birky, Kathleen M. Clark, H. Michael Lueke, Wanda McCoy, & Farhaana Nyamekye (2007). What NAEP can (and can't) tell us about performance in algebra. In Peter Kloosterman & Frank K. Lester, Jr. (Eds.), *2003 Mathematics Assessment of the National Assessment of Educational Progress*. Reston, VA: National Council of Teachers of Mathematics, pp. 169–190.

Clements, D. H., & Battista, M. T. (1992). Geometry and spatial reasoning. In D. A. Grouws (Ed.), *Handbook of research on mathematics teaching and learning* (pp. 420–464). New York: Macmillan.

Clements, D. H., & McMillen, S. (1996). Rethinking "concrete" manipulatives. *Teaching Children Mathematics, 2*(5), 270–275.

Cochran, B. S., Barson, A., & Davis, R. B. (1970, March). Child-created mathematics. *Arithmetic Teacher, 17*, 211–215.

Collison, J. (1992). Using performance assessment to determine mathematical dispositions. *Arithmetic Teacher, 39*, 40–47.

Confrey, J. (1990). What constructivism implies for teaching. In R. B. Davis, C. A. Maher, & N. Noddings (Eds.), *Constructivist views on the teaching and learning of mathematics. (Journal for Research in Mathematics Education,* Monograph No. 4, pp. 107–122). Reston, VA: National Council of Teachers of Mathematics.

Cramer, K., Post, T., & Currier, S. (1993). Learning and teaching ratio and proportion: Research implications. In D. T. Owens (Ed.), *Research ideas for the classroom: Middle grades mathematics* (pp. 159–178). New York: Macmillan.

Crowley, M. (1987). The van Hiele model of the development of geometric thought. In M. M. Lindquist & A. P. Shulte (Eds.), *Learning and teaching geometry, K–12*. Reston, VA: National Council of Teachers of Mathematics.

Crowley, M. L. (1993). Student mathematics portfolio: More than a display case. *Mathematics Teacher, 86*, 544–547.

Cuevas, G. J. & Yeatts, K. (2001). *Navigating through algebra in Grades 3–5*. Reston, VA: National Council of Teachers of Mathematics.

Cuoco, A. A. (2001). *The roles of representation in school mathematics*. Reston, VA: National Council of Teachers of Mathematics.

Davidson, N. (1990a). Small-group cooperative learning in mathematics. In T. J. Cooney & C. R. Hirsch (Eds.), *Teaching and learning mathematics in the 1990s* (1990 NCTM Yearbook, pp. 52–61). Reston, VA: National Council of Teachers of Mathematics.

Davidson, N. (1990b). Cooperative learning in mathematics: A handbook for teachers. Reading, MA: Addison-Wesley.

Dessart, D. J. (1995). Randomness: A connection to reality. In P. A. House & A. F. Coxford (Eds.), *Connecting mathematics across the curriculum* (1995 Yearbook, pp. 177–181). Reston, VA: National Council of Teachers of Mathematics.

Dewar, A. M. (1984). Another look at the teaching of percent. *Arithmetic Teacher, 31*, 48–49.

Driscoll, M. (1984). What research says. *Arithmetic Teacher, 31*(6), 34–35, 46.

Eperson, D. B. (1982a). Puzzles, pastimes, problems. *Mathematics in School, 11*(1), 15.

Eperson, D. B. (1982b). Puzzles, pastimes, problems. *Mathematics in School, 11*(2), 10.

Eperson, D. B. (1983). Puzzles, pastimes, problems. *Mathematics in School, 12*(2), 20–21.

Evans, C. S. (1984, December). Writing to learn in math. *Language Arts, 61*(8), 828–835.

Falkner, K. P., Levi, L., & Carpenter, T. P. (1999, December). Children's understanding of equality: A foundation for algebra. *Teaching Children Mathematics*, 232–236.

Fennell, F. (1990). Implementing the standards: Probability. *Arithmetic Teacher, 38*(4), 18–22.

Fennell, F., & Ammon, R. (1985). Writing techniques for problem solvers. *Arithmetic Teacher, 33*(1), 24–25.

Fennema, E., Carpenter, T. P., Levi, L., Franke, M. L., & Empson, S. (1997). *Cognitively guided instruction: Professional development in primary mathematics*. Madison: Wisconsin Center for Education Research.

Ford, M. I. (1990). The writing process: A strategy for problem solvers. *Arithmetic Teacher, 38*(3), 35–38.

Frykholm, Jeffrey A. (2001, October). Eenie, meenie, minie, moe . . . Building on intuitive notions of chance. *Teaching children mathematics*, *8*(2), 112–118.

Garrison, Leslie, Gregorio A. Ponce, and Olga M. Amaral (2007, August). Ninety percent of the game is half mental. *Teaching Children Mathematics*, *14*(1), 12–17.

Geddes, D., & Fortunato, I. (1993). Geometry: Research and classroom activities. In D. T. Owens (Ed.), *Research ideas for the classroom: Middle grades mathematics* (pp. 199–222). New York: Macmillan.

Gelman, R., & Gallistel, C. R. (1978). *The child's understanding of number*. Cambridge, MA: Harvard University Press.

Ginsburg, H. P., & Baron, J. (1993). Cognition: Young children's construction of mathematics. In R. J. Jensen (Ed.), *Research ideas for the classroom: Early childhood mathematics* (pp. 3–21). New York: Macmillan.

Glasgow, Robert, Gay Ragan, Wanda M. Fields, Robert Reys, and Deanna Wasman (2000, October). The decimal dilemma. *Teaching Children Mathematics*, *7*(2), 89–93.

Glazier, S. (1998). *Random House Webster's word menu*. New York: Random House Reference.

Glennon, V. J. (1963). Some perspectives in education. *In Enrichment mathematics for the grades* (27th Yearbook). Washington, DC: National Council of Teachers of Mathematics.

Goldin, G. A. (1990). Epistemology, constructivism, and discovery learning in mathematics. In R. B. Davis, C. A. Maher, & N. Noddings (Eds.), *Constructivist views on the teaching and learning of mathematics (Journal for Research in Mathematics Education,* Monograph No. 4, pp. 31–47). Reston, VA: National Council of Teachers of Mathematics.

Good, T. L., Reys, B. J., Grouws, D. A., & Mulryan, C. M. (1989/90). Using work-groups in mathematics instruction. *Educational Leadership, 47*(4), 56–62.

Grady, M. B. (1978). A manipulative aid for adding and subtracting integers. *Arithmetic Teacher, 26*(3), 40.

Greer, B. (1992). Multiplication and division as models of situations. In D. A. Grouws (Ed.), *Handbook of research on mathematics teaching and learning* (pp. 276–299). New York: Macmillan.

Haak, S. (1976). Transformational geometry and the artwork of M. C. Escher. *Mathematics Teacher, 69*(8), 647–652.

Hamic, E. J. (1986). Student's creative computations: My way or your way. *Arithmetic Teacher, 34*(1), 39–41.

Harel, G., & Behr, M. (1991). Ed's strategy for solving division problems. *Arithmetic Teacher, 39*(3), 38–40.

Hart, K. (1984). Which comes first: Length, area, or volume? *Arithmetic Teacher, 31*(9), 16–18, 26–27.

Hart, K. (1989). Ratio and proportion. In J. Hiebert & M. Behr (Eds.), *Number concepts and operations in the middle grades* (pp. 198–219). Reston, VA: National Council of Teachers of Mathematics.

Hart, L. C., Schultz, K., Najee-Ullah, D., & Nash, L. (1992). The role of reflection in teaching. *Arithmetic Teacher, 40*(1), 40–42.

Hembree, R., & March, H. (1993). Problem solving in early childhood: Building foundations. In R. J. Jensen (Ed.), *Research ideas for the classroom: Early childhood mathematics*. Reston. VA: National Council of Teachers of Mathematics.

Henderson, G. L., & Collier, C. P. (1973). Geometric activities for later childhood education. *Arithmetic Teacher, 20*(10), 444–453.

Herrell, Adrienne, and Jordan, Michael (2008). *Fifty Strategies for Teaching English Language Learners* (3rd ed.). Upper Saddle River, NJ: Pearson Education, Inc.

Hiebert, J. (1984). Why do some children have trouble learning measurement concepts? *Arithmetic Teacher, 31*(7), 19–24.

Hiebert, J. (1990). The role of routine procedures in the development of mathematical competence. In T. J. Cooney & C. R. Hirsch (Eds.), *Teaching and learning mathematics in the 1990s* (1990 Yearbook, pp. 31–40). Reston, VA: National Council of Teachers of Mathematics.

Hiebert, J., & Behr, M. J. (1988). Capturing the major themes. In J. Hiebert & M. J. Behr (Eds.), *Number concepts and operations in the middle grades* (pp. 1–18). Hillsdale, NJ: Erlbaum.

Hiebert, J., & Wearne, D. (1986). Procedures over concepts: The acquisition of decimal number knowledge. In J. Hiebert (Ed.), *Conceptual and procedural knowledge: The case of mathematics* (pp. 199–223). Hillsdale, NJ: Erlbaum.

Hoban, T. (1996). *Shapes, shapes, shapes*. New York: Mulberry. (Grades K–3)

Hoffer, A. R., & Hoffer, S. A. K. (1992). Ratios and proportional thinking. In T. R. Post (Ed.), *Teaching mathematics in grades K–8: Research-based methods* (pp. 303–330). Boston: Allyn & Bacon.

Hoffman, M. (1990). *Nancy no-size*. London: Little Mannoth.

Hofstetter, E. B., & Sgroi, L. A. (1996). Data with snap, crackle, and pop. Mathematics *Teaching in the Middle School, 1*(9), 760–764.

Hollis, L. Y. (1984). Teaching rational numbers: Primary grades. *Arithmetic Teacher, 31*(6), 36–39.

Holmes, E. E. (1990). Motivation: An essential component of mathematics instruction. In T. J. Cooney & C. R. Hirsch (Eds.), *Teaching and learning mathematics in the 1990s* (1990 Yearbook, pp. 101–107). Reston, VA: National Council of Teachers of Mathematics.

Hope, J. A., & Owens, D. T. (1987). An analysis of the difficulty of learning fractions. *Focus on Learning Problems in Mathematics, 9*(Fall), 25–40.

Horak, V. M., & Horak, W. J. (1982). Making measurement meaningful. *Arithmetic Teacher, 30*(3), 18–23.

Horak, V. M., & Horak, W. J. (1983). Teaching time with slit clocks. *Arithmetic Teacher, 30*(5), 8–12.

House, P. A. (2001). Navigating through algebra. Four volumes: Navigating through algebra in prekindergarten–grade 2, grades 3–5, grades 6–8, and grades 9–12. Reston, VA: National Council of Teachers of Mathematics.

Howden, H. (1989). Patterns, relationships, and functions. *Arithmetic Teacher, 37*(3), 18–24.

Hughes, M. (1986). *Children and number: Difficulties in learning mathematics*. Oxford: Basil Blackwell.

Inskeep, J. E. (1976). Teaching measurement to children. In D. Nelson (Ed.), *Measurement in school mathematics* (pp. 60–86). Reston, VA: National Council of Teachers of Mathematics.

Isaacs, A. C., & Carroll, W. M. (1999, May). Strategies for basic-facts instruction. *Teaching Children Mathematics, 5*, 508–515.

Jensen, R., & O'Neil, D. R. (1981). Meaningful linear measurement. *Arithmetic Teacher, 29*(1), 6–12.

Jensen, R., & O'Neil, D. R. (1982). That's eggzactly right. *Arithmetic Teacher, 29*(7), 8–13.

Kamii, C. (1990). Constructivism and beginning arithmetic (K–2). In T. J. Cooney & C. R. Hirsch (Eds.). *Teaching and learning mathematics in the 1990s* (1990 Yearbook, pp. 22–30). Reston, VA: National Council of Teachers of Mathematics.

Kamii, C., & Joseph, L. (1988). Teaching place value and double-column addition. *Arithmetic Teacher, 35*(6), 48–52.

Kaput, J. J. (1998). Transforming algebra from an engine of inequity to an engine of mathematical power by "algebrafying" the K–12 curriculum. In *The nature and role of algebra in the K–14 curriculum: Proceedings of a national symposium* (pp. 25–26). Washington, DC: National Academy Press.

Karplus, E. F., Karplus, R., & Wollman, W. (1974). Ratio: The influence of cognitive style. *School Science and Mathematics, 74*(6), 476–482.

Kastberg, Signe E., & Anderson Norton III (2007). Building a system of rational numbers. In Peter Kloosterman & Frank K. Lester, Jr. (Eds.), *Results and interpretations of the 2003 mathematics assessment of the National Assessment of Educational Progress*. Reston, VA: National Council of Teachers of Mathematics.

Kastner, B. (1989). Number sense: The role of measurement applications. *Arithmetic Teacher, 36*(6), 40–46.

Kennedy, L. M., & Tipps, S. (1999). *Guiding children's learning of mathematics* (9th ed.). Belmont, CA: Wadsworth.

Kieran, C. (1988). Two different approaches among algebra learners. In A. F. Coxford (Ed.), *The ideas of algebra, K–12* (pp. 91–96). Reston, VA: National Council of Teachers of Mathematics.

Kieran, C., & Chalouh, L. (1993). Prealgebra: The transition from arithmetic to algebra. In D. T. Owens (Ed.), *Research ideas for the classroom: Middle grades mathematics* (pp. 179–198). New York: Macmillan.

Kieran, Carolyn (2007). What do we know about the teaching and learning of algebra in the elementary grades? National Council of Teachers of Mathematics *Research Brief*. Reston, VA: National Council of Teachers of Mathematics.

Kieren, T. (1976). On the mathematical, cognitive, and instructional foundations of rational numbers. In R. E. Lesh (Ed.), *Number and measurement: Paper from a research workshop*. Columbus, OH: ERIC/SMEAC.

Kieren, T. (1984). Helping children understand rational numbers. *Arithmetic Teacher, 31*(6), 3.

Kieren, T. E. (1980). The rational number construct: Its elements and mechanisms. In T. E. Kieren (Ed.), *Recent research on number learning*. Columbus, OH: ERIC/SMEAC.

Kieren, T. E., Nelson, D., & Smith, G. (1985, April). Graphical algorithms in partitioning tasks. *Journal of Mathematical Behavior, 4*, 25–36.

Kloosterman, Peter, & Frank K. Lester, Jr. (Eds.), (2007). *Results and interpretations of the 2003 mathematics assessment of the National Assessment of Educational Progress*. Reston, VA: National Council of Teachers of Mathematics.

Koester, Beverly A. (2003, April). Prisms and pyramids: Constructing three-dimensional models to build understanding. *Teaching Children Mathematics, 9*(8): 436–442.

Kouba, V. L., & Franklin, K. (1993). Multiplication and division: Sense making and meaning. In R. J. Jensen (Ed.), *Research ideas for the classroom: Early childhood mathematics* (pp. 103–126). New York: Macmillan.

Kouba, V. L., & Wearne, D. (2000). Whole number properties and operations. In E. A. Silver & P. A. Kenney (Eds.), *Results from the Seventh Mathematics Assessment of the National Assessment of Educational Progress* (pp. 141–161). Reston: VA: National Council of Teachers of Mathematics.

Kroll, D. L., & Miller, T. (1993). Insights from research on mathematical problem solving in the middle grades. In D. T. Owens (Ed.), *Research ideas for the classroom: Middle grades mathematics* (pp. 58–77). New York: Macmillan.

Labinowicz, E. (1980). *The Piaget primer: Thinking, learning, teaching*. Palo Alto, CA: Addison-Wesley.

Labinowicz, E. (1985). *Learning from children: New beginnings for teaching numerical thinking*. Palo Alto, CA: Addison-Wesley.

Lambdin, D. V., & Walker, V. L. (1994). Planning for classroom portfolio assessment. *Arithmetic Teacher, 41*, 318–324.

Lapointe, A. E., Mead, N. A., & Phillips, G. W. (1989). *A world of differences: An international assessment of mathematics and science* (Report No. 19-CAEP-01). Princeton, NJ: Educational Testing Service.

Lappan, G. (1998). Capturing patterns and functions: Variables and joint variation. In *The nature and role of algebra in the K–14 curriculum: Proceedings of a national symposium* (pp. 57–60). Washington, DC: National Academy Press.

Lee, K. S. (1991). Left-to-right computations and estimation. *School Science and Mathematics, 91*(5), 199–201.

Lesh, R., Post, T., & Behr, M. (1989). Proportional reasoning. In J. Hiebert & M. Behr (Eds.), *Number concepts and operations in the middle grades* (pp. 93–118). Reston, VA: National Council of Teachers of Mathematics.

Lesser, C. (1999). *Spots: Counting creatures from sky to sea*. San Diego: Harcourt Brace & Co.

Lindquist, M. M. (1987). Estimation and mental computation: Measurement. *Arithmetic Teacher, 34*(5), 16–17.

Lindquist, M. M. (1989). The measurement standards. *Arithmetic Teacher, 37*(2), 22–26.

Lindquist, Mary M. & Douglas H. Clements (2001, March). Geometry must be vital. *Teaching Children Mathematics, 7*(7): 409–415.

Litton, N. (1995). Graphing from A to Z. *Teaching Children Mathematics, 2*(4), 220–223.

Loewen, A. C. (1991, March). M and M and Ms: An alternative context for teaching mean, median, and mode. *Delta-K, 29*, 36–40.

Lovin, L., Kyger, M., & Allsopp, D. (2004, October). *Differentiation for special needs learners. Teaching Children Mathematics, 11*(3), 158–167.

Mack, N. K. (1990). Learning fractions with understanding. *Journal for Research in Mathematics Education, 21*(1), 16–32.

Madell, R. (1985). Children's natural processes. *Arithmetic Teacher, 32*(7), 20–22.

Marchand, L. C., Bye, M. P., Harrison, B., & Schroeder, T. L. (1985). *Assessing cognitive levels in the classroom.* Edmonton, Alberta: Alberta Education. (ERIC Document Reproduction Service No. ED 266 033)

Martin, W. G., & Strutchens, M. E. (2000). Geometry and measurement. In E. A. Silver & P. A. Kenney (Eds.), *Results from the Seventh Mathematics Assessment of the National Assessment of Educational Progress* (pp. 193–234). Reston, VA: National Council of Teachers of Mathematics.

Martinez, J., & Martinez, N. (1996). *Math without fear.* Needham Heights, MA: Allyn & Bacon.

Mathematical Sciences Education Board and National Research Council. (1989). *Everybody counts: A report to the nation on the future of mathematics education*. Washington, DC: National Academy Press.

Mathematical Sciences Education Board and National Research Council. (1990). *Reshaping school mathematics: A philosophy and framework for curriculum*. Washington, DC: National Academy Press.

McGraw, Rebecca, and Sarah Theule Lubienski (2007). Findings related to gender: Acheivement, student affect, and learning experiences. In Peter Kloosterman & Frank K. Lester, Jr. (Eds.), *Results and interpretations of the 2003 mathematics assessment of the National Assessment of Educational Progress*. Reston, VA: National Council of Teachers of Mathematics, pp. 261–287.

McIntosh, M. E. (1991). No time for writing in your class? *Mathematics Teacher, 84*(6), 423–433.

McKenzie, W. S. (1990). Meaning: The common element in both reading and mathematics. *Ontario Mathematics Gazette, 28*(3), 8–13.

Meyer, L. (2000). Barriers to meaningful instruction for English learners. *Theory into Practice, 34*(2), 228–236.

Moser, J. M. (1992). Arithmetic operations on whole numbers: Addition and subtraction. In T. R. Post (Ed.), *Teaching mathematics in grades K–8: Research-based methods* (pp. 123–155). Boston: Allyn & Bacon.

Moses, B., Bjork, E., & Goldenberg, E. P. (1990). Beyond problem solving: Problem posing. In T. J. Cooney (Ed.), *Teaching and learning mathematics in the 1990s* (1990 Yearbook, pp. 82–91). Reston, VA: National Council of Teachers of Mathematics.

Moyer, Patricia S. (2001, November). Patterns and symmetry: Reflections of culture. *Teaching Children Mathematics, 8*(3): 140–144.

Mullis, Ina V. S., Michael O. Martin, Albert E. Beaton, Eugenio J. Gonzalez, Dana L. Kelly, and Teresa A. Smith (1997). *Mathematics achievement in the primary school years: IEA's Third International Mathematics and Science Study*. Chestnut Hill, MA: International Association for the Evaluation of Educational Achievement (IEA).

Nasser, R., & Carifio, J. (1995). Algebra word problems: A review of the theoretical models and related research literature. Paper presented at the Annual Meeting of the American Research Association, April 5–6, 1994.

National Council of Teachers of Mathematics. (1980). *Curriculum and evaluation standards for school mathematics*. Reston, VA: Author.

National Council of Teachers of Mathematics. (1989). *Curriculum and evaluation standards for school mathematics*. Reston, VA: Author.

National Council of Teachers of Mathematics. (1991). *Professional standards for teaching mathematics*. Reston, VA: Author.

National Council of Teachers of Mathematics. (1991, February). *Position statement on calculators and the education of youth.* Reston, VA: National Council of Teachers of Mathematics.

National Council of Teachers of Mathematics. (1995). *Assessment standards for school mathematics*. Reston, VA: Author.

National Council of Teachers of Mathematics. (2000). *Principles and Standards for School Mathematics*. Reston, VA: Author.

National Council of Teachers of Mathematics (2006). *Curriculum Focal Points for Prekindergarten Through Grade 8 Mathematics*. Reston, VA: Author.

Neufeld, K. A. (1991). Computational pizzazz: Teach your students to create puzzles for their peers—Magic cross-out. *Ontario Mathematics Gazette, 30*(2), 23–24.

Nibbelink, W. H. (1990). Teaching equations. *Arithmetic Teacher, 38*(3), 48–51.

Oppenhiem, J., & Reid, B. (1986). *Have you seen birds?* Richmond Hill, Ontario: Scholastic-TAB.

Owens, D. T. (1990). Research into practice: Spatial abilities. *Arithmetic Teacher, 37*(6), 48–51.

Owens, D. T., & Super, D. B. (1993). Teaching and learning decimal fractions. In D. T. Owens (Ed.), *Research ideas for the classroom: Middle grades mathematics* (pp. 137–158). New York: Macmillan.

Pa, N. A. N. (1986). Meaning in arithmetic from four different perspectives. *For the Learning of Mathematics, 6*(1), 11–16.

Page, A. (1994). Helping children understand subtraction. *Teaching Children Mathematics, 1*(3), 140–143.

Pandey, T. (1991). *A sampler of mathematics assessment*. Sacramento: California Department of Education.

Parker, J. (1988). *I love spiders*. New York: Scholastic.

Paull, S. (1990). Not just an average unit. *Arithmetic Teacher, 38*(4), 54–58.

Payne, J. N. (1984). Curricular issues: Teaching rational numbers. *Arithmetic Teacher, 31*(6), 14–17.

Payne, J. N. (1988). Research into practice: Place value for tens and ones. *Arithmetic Teacher, 35*(6), 64–66.

Peak, L. (1996). Pursuing excellence: *A study of U.S. eighth-grade mathematics and science teaching, learning, curriculum, and achievement in international context*. Washington, DC: U.S. Government Printing Office.

Peck, D. M., & Jencks, S. M. (1981, March). Share and cover. *Arithmetic Teacher, 28*(7), 38–41.

Peck, D. M., & Jencks, S. M. (1988). Reality, arithmetic, and algebra. *Journal of Mathematical Behavior, 7*(1), 85–91.

Philipp, R. A. (1996). Multicultural mathematics and alternative algorithms: Using knowledge from many cultures. *Teaching Children Mathematics, 3*(3), 128–135.

Phillips, E. (1991). Patterns and functions: Curriculum and evaluation standards for school mathematics addenda series, grades 5–8. Reston, VA: National Council of Teachers of Mathematics.

Piaget, J. (1965). *The child's conception of number*. New York: Norton.

Piaget, J., Inhelder, B., & Szeminska, A. (1960). *The child's conception of geometry*. New York: Basic Books.

Plisko, Val W. (December 14, 2004). The release of the 2003 Trends in International Mathematics and Science Study (TIMSS). http://nces.ed.gov/whatsnew/commissioner/remarks2004/12_14_2004.asp

Polya, G. (1949). On solving mathematical problems in high school. Reprinted in S. Krulik & R. E. Reys (Eds.), *Problem solving in school mathematics* (1980 Yearbook, pp. 1–2). Reston, VA: National Council of Teachers of Mathematics.

Polya, G. (1957). How to solve it (2nd ed.). New York: Doubleday.

Pothier, Y. (1992). Writing to communicate mathematics. In D. Sawada (Ed.), *Communication in the mathematics classroom*. Edmonton, Alberta: Mathematics Council of the Alberta Teachers' Association.

Pothier, Y. M., & Sawada, D. (1990). Partitioning: An approach to fractions. *Arithmetic Teacher, 38*(4), 12–16.

Pothier, Y., & Sawada, D. (1990). Students value time and a patient teacher. *Mathematics in School, 19*(3), 38–39.

Quintero, A. H. (1987). Helping children understand ratios. *Arithmetic Teacher, 34*(9), 17–21.

Rahim, M. H., & Sawada, D. (1986). Revitalizing school geometry through dissection-motion operations. *School Science and Mathematics, 86*(3), 235–246.

Rathmell, E. C. (1978). Using thinking strategies to teach the basic facts. In M. N. Suydam & R. E. Reys (Eds.), *Developing computational skills* (1978 Yearbook, pp. 13–38). Reston, VA: National Council of Teachers of Mathematics.

Reuille-Irons, R., & Irons, C. J. (1989). Language experiences: A base for problem solving. In P. R. Trafton & A. P. Shulte (Eds.), *New directions for elementary school mathematics* (1989 NCTM Yearbook, pp. 85–98). Reston, VA: National Council of Teachers of Mathematics.

Reys, B. J. (1985). Mental computation. *Arithmetic Teacher, 32*(3), 43–46.

Reys, B. J. (1986). Teaching computational estimation: Concepts and strategies. In H. L. Schoen & M. J. Zweng (Eds.), *Estimation and mental computation* (1986 Yearbook, pp. 31–44). Reston, VA: National Council of Teachers of Mathematics.

Reys, B. J., & Reys, R. E. (1986). One point of view: Mental computation and computational estimation: Their time has come. *Arithmetic Teacher, 33*(7), 4–5.

Reys, B. J., & Reys, R. E. (1990). Estimation: Directions from the standards. *Arithmetic Teacher, 37*(7), 22–25.

Reys, R. E., Suydam, M. N., & Lindquist, M. M. (1984). *Helping children learn mathematics*. Upper Saddle River, NJ: Prentice Hall.

Riedesel, C. A. (1990). *Teaching elementary school mathematics* (5th ed.). Upper Saddle River, NJ: Prentice Hall.

Rigelman, Nicole R. (2007, February). Fostering mathematical thinking and problem solving: The teacher's role. *Teaching Children Mathematics, 13*(6), 308–314.

Robinson, G. E. (1975). Geometry. In J. N. Payne (Ed.), *Mathematics learning in early childhood*. Reston, VA: National Council of Teachers of Mathematics.

Ross, R., & Kurtz, R. (1993, January). Making manipulatives work: A strategy for success. *Arithmetic Teacher, 40*(5), 254–257.

Ross, S. (1986). *The development of children's place-value concepts in grades 2 through 5*. Paper presented at the American Education Research Association, San Francisco.

Ross, S. (1989). Parts, wholes, and place value: A developmental view. *Arithmetic Teacher, 36*(6), 47–51.

Rubenstein, R. N. (1989). Building statistical concepts through visualization and verbalization. *Ontario Mathematics Gazette, 28*(2), 10–15.

Russell, S. J., & Friel, S. N. (1989). Collecting and analyzing real data in the elementary school classroom. In P. R. Trafton & A. P. Shulte (Eds.), *New directions for elementary school mathematics* (1989 Yearbook, pp. 134–148). Reston, VA: National Council of Teachers of Mathematics.

Russell, S. J., & Mokros, J. (1996). What do children understand about average? *Teaching Children Mathematics, 2*(6), 360–364.

Russell, S., & Corwin, R. (1989). *Used numbers: The shape of the data*. Palo Alto, CA: Dale Seymour Publications.

Sanfiorenzo, N. R. (1991). Evaluating expressions: A problem-solving approach. *Arithmetic Teacher, 38*(7), 34–38.

Sawada, D. (1985). Mathematical symbols: Insight through invention. *Arithmetic Teacher, 32*(6), 20–22.

Schultz, J. E. (1991). Teaching informal algebra. *Arithmetic Teacher, 37*(3), 34–37.

Serfoza, M. (1988). *Who said red*? New York: Scholastic.

Sgroi, R. J. (1990). Communicating about spatial relationships. *Arithmetic Teacher, 37*(6), 21–24.

Shaw, J. M. (1983). Exploring perimeter and area using centimeter squared paper. *Arithmetic Teacher, 31*(4), 4–11.

Shaw, J. M., & Cliatt, J. P. (1989). Developing measurement sense. In P. R. Trafton (Ed.), *New directions for elementary school mathematics* (pp. 149–155). Reston, VA: National Council of Teachers of Mathematics.

Shulte, A. P., & Smart, J. R. (Eds.). (1981). *Teaching statistics and probability*. Reston, VA: National Council of Teachers of Mathematics.

Silver, E. (1998). *Improving mathematics in middle school: Lessons from TIMSS and related research*. Washington, DC: U.S. Department of Education, Office of Educational Research and Improvements.

Skemp, R. (1989). *Structured activities for primary mathematics* (Vol. 1). London: Routledge.

Skypek, D. H. B. (1984). Special characteristics of rational numbers. *Arithmetic Teacher, 31*(6), 10–12.

Smith, M. S. (2000). Balancing old and new: An experienced middle school teacher's learning in the context of mathematics instructional reform. *Elementary School Journal, 100*(4), 351–375.

Smith, R. F. (1973). Diagnosis of pupil performance in place-value tasks. *Arithmetic Teacher, 20*(5), 403–408.

Smith, R. F. (1986). Let's do it: Coordinate geometry for third graders. *Arithmetic Teacher, 33*(8), 6–11.

Sowder, J. T. (1990). Mental computation and number sense. *Arithmetic Teacher, 37*(7), 18–20.

Sowder, L. (1988). Children's solutions of story problems. *Journal of Mathematical Behavior, 7*(3), 227–238.

Stanic, G. M. A., & McKillip, W. D. (1989). Developmental algorithms have a place in elementary school mathematics instruction. *Arithmetic Teacher, 36*(5), 14–16.

Steffe, L. P., & Hirstein, J. J. (1976). Children's thinking in measurement situations. In D. Nelson (Ed.), *Measurement in school mathematics* (pp. 35–39). Reston, VA: National Council of Teachers of Mathematics.

Stenmark, J. K. (Ed.). (1991). *Mathematics assessment: Myths, models, good questions, and practical suggestions*. Reston, VA: National Council of Teachers of Mathematics.

Stigler, J. W. (1988). Research into practice: The use of verbal explanation in Japanese and American classrooms. *Arithmetic Teacher, 36*(2), 27–29.

Stigler, J. W., Fuson, K. C., Ham, M., & Kim, M. S. (1986). An analysis of addition and subtraction word problems in American and Soviet elementary mathematics textbooks. *Cognition and Instruction, 3*, 153–171.

Stinson, K. (1982). *Red is best*. Toronto, Ontario: Annick.

Strutchens, M. E., & Blume, G. W. (1997). What do students know about geometry? In P. A. Kenney & E. A. Silver (Eds.), *Results from the Sixth Mathematics Assessment of the National Assessment of Educational Progress* (pp. 165–193). Reston, VA: National Council of Teachers of Mathematics.

Sulzer, J. S. (1998). The function box and fourth graders: Squares, cubes, and circles. *Teaching Children Mathematics, 4*, 442–447.

Suydam, M. (1984). Research reports: Problem solving. *Arithmetic Teacher, 31*(9), 36.

Tarr, James E. & Shaughnessy, J. Michael (2007). Student performance in data analysis, statistics, and probability. In Peter Kloosterman & Frank K. Lester, Jr. (Eds.), *2003 Mathematics Assessment of the National Assessment of Educational Progress*. Reston, VA: National Council of Teachers of Mathematics, pp. 139–168.

Tarr, James E. (2002, April). Providing opportunities to learn about probability concepts. *Teaching Children Mathematics, 8*(8), 482–487.

Thompson, C. S., & van de Walle, J. (1981, April). A single-handed approach to telling time. *Arithmetic Teacher, 28*, 4–9.

Thompson, C. S., & van de Walle, J. (1985). Learning about rulers and measuring. *Arithmetic Teacher, 32*(8), 8–12.

Thornton, C. A. (1978). Emphasizing thinking strategies in basic fact instruction. *Journal for Research in Mathematics Education, 9*, 214–277.

Thornton, C. A. (1990). Strategies for the basic facts. In J. N. Payne (Ed.), *Mathematics for the Young Child* (pp. 133–151). Reston, VA: National Council of Teachers of Mathematics.

Trafton, P. R., & Zawojewski, J. S. (1990). Meaning of operations. *Arithmetic Teacher, 38*(3), 18–22.

Travers, K. J., & McKnight, C. C. (1984). *International Association for the Evaluation of Educational Achievement—Second study of mathematics—The international mathematics curriculum*. Urbana-Champaign, IL: International Coordinating Center.

Usiskin, Z. (1988). Conceptions of school algebra and uses of variables. In A. F. Coxford (Ed.), *The ideas of algebra, K–12* (pp. 8–19). Reston, VA: National Council of Teachers of Mathematics.

Usiskin, Z. (1992). Where does algebra begin? Where does algebra end? *In Algebra for the twenty-first century: Proceedings of the August 1992 Conference* (pp. 27–28). Reston, VA: National Council of Teachers of Mathematics.

Usiskin, Z. (1998). Paper-and-pencil algorithms in a calculator-and-computer age. In L. J. Morrow (Ed.), *The teaching and learning of algorithms in school mathematics* (1998 yearbook, pp. 7–20). Reston, VA: National Council of Teachers of Mathematics.

Van de Walle, J. A. (1994). *Elementary school mathematics: Teaching developmentally* (2nd ed.). White Plains, NY: Longman.

Van de Walle, J. A. (2004). *Elementary and middle school mathematics: Teaching developmentally* (5th ed.). Boston: Pearson Education.

Van Hiele, Pierre M. (1959/1985). The child's thought and geometry. In David Fuys, Dorothy Geddes, and Rosamond Tischler (Eds.), *English Translation of Selected Writings of Dina van Hiele-Geldof and Pierre M. van Hiele*, pp. 243–252. Brooklyn, NY: Brooklyn College, School of Education. ERIC Document Reproduction Service No. 289,697.

Vance, J. (1986a). Ordering decimals and fractions: A diagnostic study. *Focus on Learning Problems in Mathematics, 8*(2), 51–59.

Vance, J. (1986b). Estimating decimal products: An instructional sequence. In H. L. Schoen (Ed.), *Estimation and mental computation* (1986 Yearbook, pp. 127–134). Reston VA: National Council of Teachers of Mathematics.

Vance, J. (1990, August). Rational number sense: Development and assessment, *Delta-K, 13*(2), 23–27.

Vance, J. H. (1982). Individualizing instruction through multi-level problem-solving activities. *The Canadian Mathematics Teacher*, pp. 3–9.

Vance, J. H. (1995). Developing and assessing understanding of integer operations. *Delta-K, 32*(3), 10–14.

Wagner, S. (1981). Conservation of equation and function under transformation of variable. *Journal for Research in Mathematics Education, 12*(2), 107–118.

Walsh, E. S. (1991). *Mouse count*. Orlando: Voyager. (Grades K–2)

Watson, J. M. (1991). Models to show the impossibility of division by zero. *School Science and Mathematics, 9*(8), 373–376.

Wearne, D. & Kouba, V. L. (2000). Rational numbers. In E. A. Silver & P. A. Kenney (Eds.), *Results from the Seventh Mathematics Assessment of the National Assessment of Educational Progress* (pp. 163–191). Reston, VA: National Council of Teachers of Mathematics.

Weill, B. F. (1978). Mrs. Weill's hill: A successful subtraction method for use with the learning-disabled child. *Arithmetic Teacher, 26*(2), 34–35.

Wiest, Lynda R. (2005, October). Investigation students' thinking about nets. *Mathematics Teaching in the Middle School, 11*(3): 140–143.

Wilkinson, J. D., & Nelson, O. (1966). Probability and statistics: Trial teaching in sixth grade. *Arithmetic Teacher, 13*(2), 100–106.

Willoughby, S. S. (1997). Functions from kindergarten through sixth grade. *Teaching Children Mathematics, 3*, 314–318.

Wilson, M. R., & Krapfl, C. M. (1995). Exploring mean, median, and mode with a spreadsheet. *Mathematics Teaching in the Middle School, 1*(6), 490–495.

Wilson, P. S., & Adams, V. M. (1992). A dynamic way to teach angle and angle measure. *Arithmetic Teacher, 39*(5), 6–13.

Wilson, P. S., & Rowland, R. E. (1993). Teaching measurement. In R. J. Jensen (Ed.), *Research ideas for the classroom: Early childhood mathematics* (pp. 171–194). New York: Macmillan.

Young, J. L. (1984). Uncovering the algorithms. *Arithmetic Teacher, 32*(3), 20.

Young, S. L. (1991). Ideas. *Arithmetic Teacher, 38*(8), 26–33.

Zawojewski, J. S. (1988). Teaching statistics: Mean, median, and mode. *Arithmetic Teacher, 35*(7), 25–26.

Zawojewski, J. S., & Shaughnessy, J. M. (2000). Data and chance. In E. A. Silver & P. A. Kenney (Eds.), *Results from the Seventh Mathematics Assessment of the National Assessment of Educational Progress* (pp. 235–268). Reston, VA: National Council of Teachers of Mathematics.

Index